HORARY ASTROLOGY

Your

Ultimate Horary Textbook

with

124 Example Cases

Ema Kurent

HORARY ASTROLOGY

First published in 2019 by Stella, Ema Kurent s.p., Cesta Ceneta Štuparja 120,
1231 Ljubljana, Slovenia

Cover design by **Miha Murn**, Atelje Art Murn International
Book interior layout by Premedia, **Andrej Juvan**, s.p.
The charts with the accompanying pages created by **Solar Fire**, Astrolabe Inc.

Contacts:
www.emakurent.com
www.astroakademija.si
ema.kurent@gmail.com

CIP - Kataložni zapis o publikaciji
Narodna in univerzitetna knjižnica, Ljubljana

133.52

KURENT, Ema
    Horary Astrology : Your Ultimate Horary Textbook with 124 Example Cases / Ema Kurent. - Ljubljana : Stella, Ema Kurent, 2019

Izv. stv. nasl.: Horarna astrologija

ISBN 978-961-94637-0-3

298756608

Disclaimer: The techniques described in this book have been utilized successfully by the author. There is no guarantee of future success. No liability is assumed by the author for unsuccessful answers arrived at through the use of methods described in this volume.

CONTENTS

FOREWORD 9

THEORY

PRELIMINARY CONSIDERATIONS 13
   HOW TO BEGIN 13
   TIME AND PLACE OF THE QUESTION 24
   THE MAKING OF A HORARY CHART 27
   THE HORARY SCRIPT...29
ZODIACAL SIGNS IN HORARYASTROLOGY 31
   ZODIAC 31
      THE BIRTH OF THE ZODIAC 31
      THE YEARLY RHYTHM...35
      POLARITY...35
      ELEMENTS 36
      QUADRUPLICITIES 38
      OTHER TRADITIONAL SIGN CLASSIFICATIONS 40
   THE TWELVE SIGNS 41
      ARIES ♈...42
      TAURUS ♉ 42
      GEMINI ♊ 43
      CANCER ♋ 43
      LEO ♌...44
      VIRGO ♍ 44
      LIBRA ♎ 45
      SCORPIO ♏..45
      SAGITTARIUS ♐ 46
      CAPRICORN ♑ 46
      AQUARIUS ♒ 47
      PISCES ♓ 48
HOUSES IN HORARY ASTROLOGY 49
   GENERAL PROPERTIES OF THE TWELVE HOUSES...............................50
   ASCENDANT AND THE TWELVE HOUSES 56
      HOUSE ASSIGNMENT 63
      OTHER HOUSE CONSIDERATIONS 65
      DERIVED HOUSES 67
PLANETS IN HORARY ASTROLOGY 70
   BASIC CLASSIFICATIONS OF PLANETS 70
      THE MOON ☽ 77
      THE SUN ☉..80
      MERCURY ☿ 81
      VENUS ♀ 82
      MARS ♂ 83
      JUPITER ♃ 84
      SATURN ♄...85

TRANSSATURNIANS 86
  URANUS ♅ 87
  NEPTUNE ♆ 88
  PLUTO ♇ (♇) 88
PLANETARY DIGNITY..89
  ESSENTIAL DIGNITY 89
    DOMICILE 90
    DETRIMENT (ESSENTIAL DEBILITY) 91
    EXALTATION 92
    FALL (ESSENTIAL DEBILITY)...93
    TRIPLICITY 93
    TERM 94
    FACE..95
    MONOMOIRIA 95
    DISPOSITION, RECEPTION AND MUTUAL RECEPTION 96
    PEREGRINE (ESSENTIAL DEBILITY) 98
    ALMUTEN 98
    HOW TO CALCULATE ESSENTIAL DIGNITIES 99
  ACCIDENTAL DIGNITY 100
    HOUSE PLACEMENT 101
    DIRECT VS. RETROGRADE MOTION 101
    RETROGRADE AND STATIONARY PLANETS IN HORARY ASTROLOGY.....................102
    VELOCITY...104
    PLANETS IN RELATION TO THE SUN 104
    EXACT ASPECTS WITH BENEFICS AND MALEFICS 106
    CONJUNCTIONS WITH FIXED STARS.................................106
  DIFFERENCES BETWEEN ESSENTIAL AND ACCIDENTAL DIGNITY................106
  HOW TO EXAMINE PLANETARY DIGNITY 107

LOOKING FOR THE ANSWER...111
  STRICTURES AND CAUTIONS 111
  PLANETARY HOURS...117
  THE OUTCOME..122
    ASPECTS...122
    MUTUAL RECEPTION 127
    TRANSLATION OF LIGHT 127
    COLLECTION OF LIGHT...128
    FRUSTRATION 129
    PROHIBITION 130
    REFRANATION 130
    BESIEGEMENT 131
  TIMING..132

ADDITIONAL TECHNIQUES...136
  MOON'S NODES 136
  ECLIPSES...138
  FIXED STARS 140
  ARABIC PARTS 147
  ANTISCIA...149
  DECLINATION 151

PRACTICE

LOVE AND MARRIAGE 154

    1/1: Will my ex-wife return to me? 158
    1/2: Is she staying with me? 160
    1/3: Are we staying together? 162
    1/4: Is this the end of our relationship? 164
    1/5: Will we go steady? 166
    1/6: How long is this relationship going to last? 168
    1/7: Should I stay or should I go? 170
    1/8: When will I find a boyfriend? 172
    1/9: How will our relationship develop? 174
    1/10: Why is my husband jealous? 176
    1/11: Will she decide for me or for him? 178
    1/12: Will we be together again, and when? 180

PREGNANCY 182

    2/1: Am I pregnant? 186
    2/2: Am I pregnant? 188
    2/3: Are we staying together if I decide to abort? 190
    2/4: Am I pregnant? 192
    2/5: Am I pregnant now? 194
    2/6: Am I pregnant? 196
    2/7: Is my girlfriend pregnant? 198
    2/8: Will my sister ever have children? 200

EMPLOYMENT AND CAREER 202

    3/1: Will I get this job? 204
    3/2: Should I take this job? 206
    3/3: Will I get this job? 208
    3/4: Potato chips, candies, both, or none? 210
    3/5: Will I succeed in organizing a course at Obala? 212
    3/6: Will the book series get translated? 214
    3/7: Will I get the promised job despite the sick leave? 216
    3/8: Should I retire? 218
    3/9: Is this a good business opportunity? 220
    3/10: Will the planned workshop take place? 222
    3/11: Will the K Club project bring me success? 224
    3/12: Will Rosalie qualify for the national championship? 226

REAL ESTATE 228

    4/1: Will I sell the house? 232
    4/2: Can I rent this surgery? 234
    4/3: Should we buy this house? 236
    4/4: Should I let my apartment to this woman? 238
    4/5: Should I rent my flat to this man? 240
    4/6: Will we sell the house? When? 242
    4/7: Should I sell the apartment to this buyer? 244
    4/8: Should we buy this house? 246
    4/9: When will we move? 248
    4/10: When will we move to our apartment? 250

4/11: When will I sell my apartment? Should I lower the price? 252
4/12: Will I be able to rent these premises? 254

FINANCE 256
5/1: Should I invest in gold or in Chinese stocks? 260
5/2: Am I going to win this Sunday's lottery? 262
5/3: Should I ask for a bank loan, or try to get it from my father? 264
5/4: Will the bank give us the loan? 266

MISSING ARTICLES 268
6/1: Where are my daughter's slippers? 278
6/2: Where are the application forms? 280
6/3: Where are my daughter's sandals? 282
6/4: Where are my husband's keys? 284
6/5: Where are my keys? 286
6/6: Where IS my wallet? 288
6/7: Where is my husband's jacket? Will he get it back? 290
6/8: Where are my sneakers? 292
6/9: Where IS my purse? 294
6/10: Where IS my watch? 296
6/11: Where is Masha's pencil case? 298
6/12: Where is the missing book? 300
6/13: Where is the missing remote key? 302
6/14: Where is my daughter's purse? Will she get it back? 304
6/15: My friend's car got stolen, will he get it back? 306
6/16: Will I get back the stolen purse? 308
6/17: Where is my missing gaus? 310

MISSING PEOPLE AND PETS 314
7/1: Where is Peter? Is he alive and well? 316
7/2: Where is my daughter? 318
7/3: Where is my father? Is he hurt, will they find him? 320
7/4: Where is Toni R.? Will he return home safely? 322
7/5: What HAS happened to Kt Boehrer? 324
7/6: Where is the missing R.H.? Will he return safely? 326
7/7: Where is the missing Natasha? Is she alive? 328
7/8: What happened to Maddie? Will they find her? 330
7/9: Where is Tomaž Humar? Will they find him alive? 332
7/10: When will Gigi return? 334
7/11: Will the missing kitten be back? 336
7/12: Will our kitten be back? 338
7/13: Where is my dog? Will we find him? 340

PHYSICAL WELL-BEING 344
8/1: How will my husband's surgery go? Will he recover? 352
8/2: Am I sick? What will the laboratory tests show? 354
8/3: Will my husband's uncle get well? 356
8/4: Is Masha going to be OK? 358
8/5: Has Ruby got granuloma? 360
8/6: Will Adam fall ill with scarlet fever? 362
8/7: Will my cousin's husband get well again? 364

8/8: Has Steven really got cancer?..366

8/9: Will my father get well and be able to walk again?......................................368

8/10: Will Sonia get well?..370

LEGAL QUESTIONS...372

9/1: Will PK be found guilty of murdering his wife?...376

9/2: Will John appeal against the court ruling?...378

9/3: Will John succeed with his court appeal?...380

9/4: Will my husband get convicted?...382

TRAVEL...384

10/1: Will Ruby receive her passport in time?...386

10/2: Will P and V travel to Greece this summer?..388

10/3: Will I be able to join the excursion to Ireland?..390

10/4: Will we visit Sarajevo for the New Year holidays?.....................................392

10/5: Will we compete at the European Championship?......................................394

10/6: Will I travel to India to Rajeev's marriage?...396

10/7: Will I go to the ISAR conference in LA?...398

10/8: Will my husband go to Hungary?...400

SERVICES..402

11/1: Should we demand a re-laying of parquet flooring?...................................404

11/2: Can this carpenter do his job well and will he build the roof?..................406

11/3: Will my designer get his work done by Monday?.......................................408

11/4: Will Tony construct our fireplace?..410

11/5: When will the workers arrive?...412

11/6: Whom should I hire, Arif or Stephen?...414

MISCELLANEOUS CASES...416

12/1: Will Milan Kučan be re-elected?..416

12/2: Will my parents-in-law watch our kids today?...418

12/3: Will I have my B-day party in the Gromka club? 420

12/4: Is my dancing partner quitting the agreement?..422

12/5: Who has been harassing me over the phone ?...424

12/6: Will Chris come to me before the meeting?..426

12/7: When will my husband be released from prison?..428

12/8: Will I buy a minivan this year?..430

12/9: Will Olimpija Hertz become national champs this year?...........................432

12/10: What will be the result of the market inspection?....................................434

12/11: Will I throw a party next Saturday?..436

12/12: When will my daughter be back from hospital?..438

12/13: Are we getting any snow this winter? 440

12/14: Will I buy the dog?...442

12/15: Will the UAC committee change the schedule? 444

12/16: Will we get a medal? 446

12/17: When will this book be finished?..448

CONSULTATION CHARTS..451

TABLES
    TEMPERATURE, MOISTURE AND TEMPERAMENTS OF THE PLANETS 71
    PLANETARY QUALITIES RELATIVE TO THE SUN 71
    THE SUN'S SEASONAL QUALITIES 72
    TRIPLICITY RULERS 93
    LILLY'S TABLE TO EXAMINE PLANETARY DIGNITY 108
    TABLE TO EXAMINE PLANETARY SECT 108
    TABLES OF PLANETARY HOURS 119
    TABLE OF AFFINITY BETWEEN SIGNS AND PLANETARY HOUR RULERS 120
    BASIC CLASSIFICATIONS OF PLANETS 121
    TABLE OF ORBS AND HALF-ORBS 123
    TABLE OF TIMING 134
    UNIVERSAL PARTS 147
    PARTS, RELATED TO INDIVIDUAL HOUSES 148
    PLANETS, SIGNS AND ASPECTS 454
    SIGNS AND THEIR RULING PLANETS 454
    ALMUTENS: DAY 455
    ALMUTENS: NIGHT 456
    MONOMOIRIA 457
    TABLE OF ESSENTIAL DIGNITIES OF PLANETS 458

INDEX 459

FOREWORD

Dear reader,

This book is the result of my 25 years' study of horary astrology. It was originally written (and published) in my native, Slovenian language. A little press conference was held at the occasion of its »birth« in November 2015, just before I flew off to Cape Town to speak at the Astrology Restored conference which was organised by my friend Ana Carrapichano. I took a copy with me but felt sorry because it was written in a language foreign to the participants of that fabulous conference which was dedicated to the restoration of the ancient art. I then decided that all my future astrology books would be written in English, from the start. My native language, after all, is spoken by less than 2.5 milllion people.

In the practice part of the book, there are some charts that were created already in the early 1990-s during my studies at the Qualifying Horary Practitioner's Course under the tutelage of my mentor (and the course founder) Olivia Barclay. At the time of enrolling the course, I had already studied astrology for several years and was officially a D.F.Astrol.S., meaning that I held the diploma of the English Faculty of Astrological Studies, the then best European source of astrological education. But because the prevailing trend at that time was psychological astrology which (in my opinion) lacked the precision and profound understanding of how astrology really "works", it was only with the study of horary astrology that many ancient secrets of this field of knowledge were disclosed to me. I came to understand the key role of the Moon in astrology, the importance of precise evaluation of planetary strengths and, above all, the remarkable predictive power of those old, traditional astrological techniques.

As my studies progressed, I started to incorporate the horary technique into my "armoury" of predictive tools, until it gradually became indispensable. Although I had been employing secondary progressions, transits, solar returns, solar arcs etc., in my daily client work, it was only with the horary technique that I was able to arrive at some clear, concrete and precise answers which my clients expected from me. I soon started to teach horary in my Slovenian school and I contributed an article now and then to the two periodicals which were dedicated to horary and traditional astrology, The Traditional Astrologer (published in UK by Deborah Houlding) and The Horary Practitioner (published in US by JustUs & Associates).

By the time of starting to write the Slovenian version of this book – which was in about 2008 – I had a large collection of horary charts which accompanied my teaching manual, and a long list of comments and observations which I had been assembling during my practice. The book took long years to complete, the reasons being manifold: as a busy mother, wife, consultant, teacher, publisher and researcher into ever new vistas of astrology, only bits of time could be dedicated to writing, but the main reason for my slowness was the fact that I wanted to write a book that would be much more than a mere collection of horary charts, based on the dry and age-old rules that students can find in any other horary astrology book. I wanted to give the readers the results of my long-time practice and ample experience, a collection of tips on how to make the best use of the ancient horary rules, adapted to new discoveries in astrology and enriched by some new techniques that had never been used in horary before – like locational astrology and eclipses which I have come to employ in horary astrology in a different way that some of my predecessors did. I first presented these two techniques in a lecture given at the ISAR conference in Arizona in September 2014.

In the theoretical part of the book, an effort has been made to explain the foundations on which rest the ancient rules. Many pages are dedicated to the source of every horary chart – the »birth« of the question. Some philosophical debate could not be avoided – like is there destiny, or do we have "free will"?

Hopefully, this book will not only teach beginners but inspire experienced horary practitioners towards a new, fresh understanding of our art. The ultimate aim of this book is, though, to bring the reader to a better understanding of not only the horary art, but of astrology *per se*. Understanding the ancient foundations of astrology serves to deepen the knowledge of natal astrology, for the start. I am convinced that natal charts can only be properly understood by traditional delineative techniques that are at the core of the horary art. Only such approach enables us to truly understand the birth chart potential, both in terms of energy and psychological make-up which together contribute to the shaping of our destiny. (They are, after all, inextricably linked.) In my horary classes, I always encourage the students to try reading a birth chart as a "horary case" - the question being, of course: *Who am I, what is my path in life, what is my destiny?* Students are always fascinated by the answers!

Although I have done my best to make this book an autonomous source of knowledge, there are, of course, several other books that I reccommend for additional reading. I particularly recommend old authors such as William Lilly, Guido Bonatti, Mashallah, Al Biruni and Abraham Ibn Ezra. The late Olivia Barclay, Ivy Goldstein-Jacobson, Barbara Watters, Sylvia de Long and Derek Appleby are those semi-contemporary authors whose books have inspired and taught me, and there are quality contemporary writers who have done much towards the restoration of horary astrology, the most prominent being Deborah Houlding, Anthony Louis, Lee Lehman, John Frawley and Barbara Dunn. Read as much as you can, but never forget the saying that became the title of the famous book by my first ever astrology teacher, the late Croatian astrologer Mile Dupor: Believe nothing, check everything! In other words – take nothing for granted, test every rule, check and recheck. Honestly, this is the only way you will learn, not only horary astrology but any other astrology. True knowledge, like true love, don't come easily.

My sincere thanks goes to several people who helped in the process of creating the English edition of this book: to the late Jillian Norris of Tasmania who made the initial English language proof-reading of the first chapters in the practice part; to Alex Trenoweth who re-read the book for the language slips and, most of all, to my dear student and friend Andrew Khabaza of London UK who whole-heartedly dedicated himself to a thorough re-checking of the material for all kinds of language mistakes and other slips, and who also made some useful editorial suggestions. A big thank you goes to my both Slovenian artists, Miha Murn for the beautiful book cover and to Andrej Juvan who created the interior layout of the English edition. Last but not least I want to thank all my astrology friends and supporters, mostly members of my Facebook group Horary Astrology Group who knew my pain in the process of the creation of the book and never stopped nagging me with their WHEN is your book coming out, say, really…? Thank you, my dears, every word you wrote was a much-needed flame which warmed my heart and set my fingers in motion.

Ljubljana, 27 January 2019

E. Knunt

THEORY

PRELIMINARY CONSIDERATIONS

HOW TO BEGIN

QUESTIONS AND ANSWERS

 orary astrology is an ancient divinatory art of seeking answers to concrete questions. Its practitioners, called "horary astrologers", cast "horary charts" which are like any other astrological charts, but these are based on the precise time and location of a question. Astrologers then seek answers to these questions in accordance with the rules of horary astrology.

We proceed from the premise that a horary chart reflects the "quality of time". While such definition can actually be applied to all astrological charts, a horary chart reflects the state of the querent's (questioner's) mind at the time when the question is "born", as well as the accuracy of the situation which his conscious mind has not (yet) been able to recognize. In other words, once the question is formed in our mind, the answer we are seeking, at some level already exists. It is shown by indications in a horary chart which an able astrologer knows how to recognize and "decipher".

Every horary chart is a kind of a "time map", offering insight into present, past and future events, related to the question. The chart cast for the time of the question provides clues to the future development of the situation in question. The answer provided by "the heavens" (that is, by our divinatory skills) helps us overcome uncertainty and receive guidelines as per the subject matter of the question. By horary astrology we answer questions by asking for a **yes or no, who, when, where, why, how, how much** and similar.

While the horary technique can be used autonomously – and is presented in this book as such – I often combine it with other astrological techniques. When clients ask about a partnership, job, travel, study, money, health and so on, I want to confirm indications in horary charts with indications in natal charts as well as in time-oriented charts (transits, progressions, eclipses and similar), and, depending on the nature of the question, I sometimes also use synastry, locational and medical astrology. A skillful combining of different approaches and techniques is certainly the most reliable way to obtain reliable answers. It is, however, true that there are questions that can only be answered by means of horary astrology.

TYPES OF QUESTIONS

Questions can apply to practically all spheres of life (health, work, property, relationships, travel, study and similar) and to all people: ourselves, our relatives, partners, friends, colleagues… And even to people whom we don't personally know and are not specifically related to us. We can also pose questions about our friends' partners, our husbands' lost phones, our nephews' jobs, colleagues' health problems, children's school successes, siblings' journeys… Horary can help us find missing things, animals and people. Questions can also apply to the unfoldment of a political situation or even to completely abstract matters. We can ask anything, in fact, although we may not receive an answer to just every question. *Which numbers will win the lottery this week? What is the exact amount of my director's last salary? What is the name of my future husband?* These are but a few examples of questions that horary charts are just not able to deal with!

QUESTIONS SHOULD BE CONCRETE AND CLEARLY FORMULATED

Questions to be answered by horary astrology can apply to a variety of people and situations. If a question makes sense it will be "fit to be judged" (a term to be discussed later in the book). It is, however, advisable to only ask questions concerning current affairs and concrete life situations. The main purpose of horary astrology is to reveal the unfoldment of current trends and processes which are already in course or are just about to begin. Horary astrology is not used for questions which are too general, like *Will I be happy in life? What will my future be like? Will I succeed in my profession? Will I ever get rich?* At least not nowadays, in spite of the fact that astrologers of the past used it also for such purposes. Centuries ago when birth times were not yet recorded, horary was the only (or at least the most popular) astrological method of personal prediction. In the book **CHRISTIAN ASTROLOGY** by William Lilly, the famous English renaissance astrologer, as well as in the works of his contemporaries and predecessors, there are many cases showing that astrologers of the past applied the horary technique to many a question which nowadays would rather be dealt with by other (natal and predictive) methods.

In principle, I encourage all kinds of questions, although we should be aware that we would have to wait for years to get answers to questions like the ones mentioned above; in fact we probably wouldn't get them at all as they are too general and allow for subjective interpretation which excludes precision. *Will I be happy in life?* Life is long, and happiness a relative and hard to define concept! I also see little point in answering questions like *What would be my ideal vocation?* with the horary method. Natal charts offer much more reliable information in this respect.

Questions like *Is my financial situation going to improve soon?* are risky too. Any answer to such a question, be it affirmative or negative, is open to the querent's subjective interpretation. (The querent is the person asking the question.) Let's say the astrologer would say yes, your financial situation will improve soon. The querent would indeed receive some extra money the next day, but as he'd immediately spend it he would tell the astrologer that as his financial situation did not improve, the astrologer was wrong! And who'd be to blame? The astrologer, of course, because he didn't prompt the querent to formulate an unambiguous question. *Will I receive the last two salaries my employer has been owing me, and if so, when?* Now, this is a sensible question, providing for a completely unequivocal answer.

We should avoid questions, formulated in such a way that they don't allow for a concrete answer. *Is my husband likely to find a job soon?* Now, what is "soon" for the querent? A horary chart cast for such a question could, of course, show "perfection of the matter" (promise of a positive answer), and such charts usually also offer time indications as per the desired outcome. However, if the chart indications were negative, the client would probably be very disappointed if the answer was just "no". The fact is, though, that in cases when no perfection is to be found in a chart, the astrologer simply cannot say anything but "no"! An exact or concrete answer would only be possible if the client asked *Will my husband get the job he is applying for?* That's completely different: a concrete job, a concrete answer!

If someone asks *Will I (ever) sell my house, get a job, pass the driving licence test...?* we have to tell them that we may not receive a concrete answer due to the long-term character of their question. (Except, of course, as explained in the previous paragraph, in cases when a horary chart cast for such a question clearly indicates "perfection of the matter" together with the timing of the anticipated event.)

Every question must therefore be formulated in such a way that the astrologer (and querent!) clearly understand its meaning. When asked to formulate a question, people will often say something like *I am interested in love...* OK, but this is not a question! A question is a sentence ending with a question mark. (As a horary astrologer you will have to keep telling this to your clients.)

So let us repeat: **A question is a sentence ending with a question mark.** Hearing this, clients often frown a bit and start thinking and brooding. It's really surprising how hard it is for some people to formulate a clear and understandable question. But how can we find a clear answer without a clear question?!

Now let's say that you ask a client to pose a concrete question, and she says: *OK, I'd like to know if my fitness coach fancies me?* This question seems more concrete, yet it doesn't facilitate a "right" answer, because, to be honest, this is not what she she truly wants to know. Let us assume that her question is clear in the sense of only wanting to know whether he finds her attractive in a romantic or sexual way, and the chart says yes. You can be 100% sure that her immediate next question will be whether anything would happen between them – would they become a couple, will he ask her out and the like. (In fact she may pose this question even if you tell her he doesn't fancy her at all!) Isn't it better, therefore, to encourage the client to form a clear question right from the start? Bear in mind, also, that the chart might reveal that the coach doesn't really fancy her, and yet something sexual would happen between them. (*He doesn't like you yet you will obviously make every effort to have an affair with him, that'll happen and you'll regret it later.*)

Just recently, an astrology student posted a question on my horary forum. The question was: *Is it my soul purpose to live and work in Jamaica?* Ouch. Tricky! Whenever somebody speaks of their "soul purpose" or veils their true interest in some other "cloudy" form, you can be sure they actually don't know what they're asking, or that they don't want to reveal their true question to you. (This often happens in times of retrograde Mercury.) Such charts usually show any of the several "strictures and warnings" (explained later in the book), so that the astrologer is warned and prompted to make additional inquiries before attempting the answer. As it turned out, that student actually had a complicated situation of having to decide whether to wait for a job offer in Jamaica, or risk money by buying a plane ticket for Jamaica just because she wanted badly to visit the country again - which would affect her finances badly if she didn't get a job there. It became clear that her question had actually nothing to do with her "soul purpose", was unclear and undefined, and such was the chart for the question – with a void-of-course Moon and an ascendant on the cusp of a sign.

The querent should be encouraged to disclose all the circumstances and reasons that have led to the question and could be useful to the astrologer. Suppressing information, insincerity or even naive attempts to "check" on the astrologer with deliberate concealment of vital facts have a negative impact on the quality of the astrologer's work. On the other hand, the astrologer has to make every effort to help the querent formulate the question and to get to the essence of the question in case of uncertainty. In case of a relevant or sensible question the horary chart will be easy to interpret; if not, it will surely show any of the several "strictures and warnings", discussed at length in one of the following chapters.

JUST DIVINATION OR ALSO COUNSELLING?

Can horary charts help us make right (good, propitious) decisions? Let me start by an observation that a good many horary questions ask for advice nowadays – many more than decades and centuries ago when horary method was in the process of development. The current, prevailing life philosophy is different from that in the past because, unlike our ancestors, people nowadays strongly believe in the power of free will. While contemporary horary astrologers do not hesitate to answer questions seeking advice and help with decision-making (quite to the contrary – they cherish them, as they demand much less of expertize in prediction), horary questions in the past were quite different. Querents were simply (and mainly) interested in what would happen in the future.

Years of practice have led me to believe that all horary (as well as other predictive) charts show our "fate", which also includes the nature of our decisions. Let me explain. If someone asks an astrologer for advice - what to do in a certain situation and how to decide - the astrologer can find, even in a horary chart, the arguments for and against such and such course of action. He can certainly advise the client as per what he should do, but since a horary chart indicates the future development of events, related to the question, it also discloses the nature of the querent's future decision, regardless of the astrologer's advice, or suggest that the planned action will not be carried out despite his decision. It seems therefore that in the moment of the question "the sky" already "knows" all about the querent's future actions (or absence of them) and how his destiny would turn out! An astrologer can advise the querent but the horary chart often shows whether the latter will (be able to) follow his advice or not.

Basically, we are dealing with a deep philosophical question, concerning the nature of our reality. Does fate (destiny, predetermination) exist or not? Every astrologer must confess that the findings of astrology – including horary and other branches – make us question the sanctity and even the existence of free will. It is true, though, that most contemporary (and many past) astrologers recognize free will, yet we can't ignore the fact that **astrology can only prove predetermination. It cannot prove free will.**

Destiny, alas, is a much feared concept, suggesting our inability to freely decide about ourselves and our lives. Are people in general willing to accept the notion that we are supposed to yield to some higher force which decides on the course of our lives? No, they aren't. Regardless of whether they believe in astrology or not, they are generally unwilling to believe in such force, perceiving themselves as beings who create their lives in accordance with their own wishes and "free will". They are perfectly sure of that although practically every moment of their lives proves them wrong. We keep making wrong decisions, doing irrational things, making stupid mistakes, regretting things, wishing to have decided differently. Why didn't we, if we have "free will"?!

Thousands of astrologers perfectly happily conduct their business by telling their clients that they can freely decide about their lives. They tell them that "the stars incline, but do not compel".

But the truth is that all our thoughts, words and actions – speaking in terms of ourselves only, although this truth extends to nature, weather, politics and other mundane events – are in every moment correlated to the then energy state, determined by the cosmic (natural) rhythms. These very rhythms are studied by astrology, which has since time immemorial been a field of knowledge dealing with fate, not with free will. If astrology was based on the premise that our lives are controlled by "higher forces" (i.e. cosmic order, constantly revealed in everything that comes into being), it would never have started to develop in the first place. Last but not least, if we truly had the power of choosing our own destiny and astrology was but a tool for creating a better and happier life, astrologers would no doubt be the first to profit by this knowledge, leading happier and more successful lives than other people. We know, alas, that this is not true.

Am I saying that we don't have free will? Astrological practice inclines me to think that the belief in **free will is probably the greatest and most persistent illusion of humanity**. Yet on the other hand we can't deny the fact that we cannot even imagine our existence without believing in the possibility of "free" choices and "free" decision making. This is also our self-perception, although, seen from a higher perspective, it's just an illusion. One way or the other, the question of free will is basically a deep philosophical question that each of us has to deal with on our own. As such, however, it has nothing to do with astrology.

The philosophical purpose of this book is not to persuade you, the reader, to start believing in "fate". **The philosophical purpose of this book is to make you familiar with the methods that will help you find your own truth about the nature of our reality**. We all have the right to our own philosophy of life, including the right to our own "philosophy of astrology". Believers and non-believers, determinists and advocates of free will, everyone can learn and practice horary astrology.

I had to write all this to clarify my attitude towards horary astrology, as well as to astrology in general, because it differs from that of many practitioners. Among my horary cases there are quite a number of those asking for advice. With each question of this kind I'm trying to get into the skin of the querent who believes in the power of his own "free" decision making, in accordance with the code of ethics. I can't force my beliefs upon anyone; after all, those who don't practise astrology, can't even understand them. But think: can I really prove that any of my clients followed my advice? No, I can't do that. I never know if they would have decided the way they did, had I not advised them so. That is exactly why I keep saying that "free will" can't be proved. It can't be proved because we only live in one (perceptible) reality. If there were two parallel worlds and we could simultaneously take one decision in one world and another decision in another world, only then could we prove the existence of free will.

Destiny (or fate), on the other hand, can be proved with every correct answer to questions, posed either by our clients or by ourselves. However, I have to say that these are not questions relating to the possibility of choice, but rather questions relating to predetermination. Concretely, if a client asks *When will my husband get a job?* and the astrologer correctly answers that this would happen in 4 months and a half, this is a proof of destiny at work and at the same time also a proof of credibility of horary astrology. (Mind you, there are many even better cases in this book, which altogether exclude the possibility of any suggestion.)

You might wonder, what if someone asks *Where are my lost keys?* and the astrologer helps him find the keys by pointing out the direction of the sky and the position of the object? Is the astrologer in such cases not an active agent of the object's find - a helper, an adviser? That's what we would wish, of course, and it is also true in a way, with a horary chart and astrologer's interpretation serving as a light, illuminating dark corners, so to speak. However, things get complicated by the fact that horary charts relating to lost objects also indicate whether the missing thing would be found or not. They often show *when* it would be found and sometimes even *who* the founder would be! The more skilled the astrologer is, the more such information he gets from the chart. For example, an astrologer can describe the place where the missing thing is located, but the million dollar question is whether he can truly affect the course of search and the time of finding. After all, it is not even in his power to make the querent understand his answer correctly. The latter may misunderstand him or may not even try to find the missing item, as at a certain moment it may not be important enough anymore to be worth the effort. Astrologer might find, for example, that the object has been mislaid and no one would ever locate it, which obviously contradicts the established belief that a horary astrologer is the one who's capable of helping his client find the missing thing. In fact he can only help him if that be the will of the "sky" ("God")!

But let us say that the querent listened to the astrologer and found a missing thing. Can it be proven that the querent would not have found the lost object had he not consulted the astrologer? No, of course not. Although we *can* believe that an astrologer can actually help the querent in such cases, we have, unfortunately, seen all too many horary charts concerning missing objects which were not correctly interpreted in time - even if, looking back, the object's location and timing of the find were accurately described in the horary chart. Obviously, these were the charts when "fate" decided that the astrologer could not help the querent.

As for counselling and advising, we should know that horary astrology imposes an even greater responsibility on the astrologer than "simple" prediction - although prediction is actually more difficult from the professional point of view.

Let's say that a client asks *Should I join my friend who is planning a trip to Guatemala in May this year?* This is a very concrete question or, rather, a request for advice. We can surely give the advice (based on the "cosmic" state of the planet signifying her potential journey), but because every horary chart by its very definition reveals the future of the question, the chart may easily indicate that the person will simply never set off for this journey. So – why advise her?

Similarly, a chart may show that this journey is meant for her, yet it may also point out dangers ahead. Should we advise her against going? This would only be right and ethical, however, as already mentioned, predetermination excludes the possibility of counselling. It is of course possible, theoretically, that the client would decide to follow the given advice, but what would happen if her friend - having set on the journey alone - reported on having had a marvellous time in Guatemala? The querent would probably regret listening to the astrologer; what's more, she would blame him/her for having deprived her of a beautiful experience. And how would that make the astrologer feel? Isn't it fairer, in such cases, to admit our real perception of the matter? And wouldn't that be the only sensible thing to do, after all?

Ideally, we would see a nice journey ahead and judge that it is to be recommended and that she is "destined" to go. We would therefore advise her to go, but - alas – she would also have gone contrary to our advice as that was the course of events, predicted by the horary chart!

Let's have a look at another example. A while ago a member of my Facebook Horary Astrology Group posed the following question: *Should I accept the job in the South?* This was a concrete job that the querent had been offered. Some members answered in the positive, the others in the negative. I decided to not participate in the discussion as the chart clearly showed that she would accept the offer and had probably already done so, in fact. An imminent start of work was indicated, so why even bother to advise?

After she had been working in the South for a while, I asked her how she would comment on the answers she had received. Is she happy with the job? Is she sorry to have accepted it? She said the job was fine, except that she was lonely and bored down there. It was not a dream job, but at least it was kind of satisfactory, she said. She concluded that those who were in favour of the job, were "right". Like, they gave the correct answer. I wondered how she knew that theirs were the correct answers? How can she tell what would have happened had she listened to those advising against the job? Maybe she would have been given a new, better offer in a few days! I say "maybe", because we can't know! The question referred to that concrete job only. (And the chart, in this case, really suggested a "mediocre" job.)

I hope that it's obvious that the accuracy or adequacy of such answers is highly dubious. A correct answer simply can't be given in such cases! It can still be helpful, but what if the woman in the above case would initially be happy with her job, but started to hate it at some later time. In other words, the advice that she should take the job may be seen as correct today while it may be seen as wrong tomorrow!

Before attempting to answer horary questions asking for advice, we should understand the delicacy of giving advice. As axplained in the above paragraphs, astrology and free will are not the best of friends, but if querents ask you to advise them what to do and how to decide, try to step into their shoes, examine the horary chart and give them a sensible answer. If you advise them to act in the way you consider best and the chart clearly indicates they are simply not meant to follow your advice, that is what you should tell them. If you deem such sincerity exaggerated, no problem, you can always come up with a perfectly decent "excuse": your advice was right except that they didn't listen and didn't try hard enough. (That's a common astrologers' excuse for providing a bad service, if you ask me, but considering a high regard for free will on the part of their clients, it usually works.)

You should be aware, though, that one can only try as hard as one is meant to at any given moment. This is the "fate" I am talking about. Belief in free will is a perfect dungheap for the bacilli of guilt! You'd therefore be perfectly justified to tell your clients that fate excludes free will, except that this would mean you'd soon be out of work. Clients ask for advice (and that's even an ever-growing trend today!), so try not to deprive them of the joy of getting it.

AN AUTONOMOUS TECHNIQUE?

There are questions that ask for a combination of several astrological techniques. *Is this man a suitable partner for me?* A horary chart, cast for such a question, would ideally be combined by synastry (a set of astrological techniques dealing with inter-relatedness of two or more natal charts) so as to define the spheres of compatibility versus incompatibility. However, if a client asks whether he would enter into a relationship with a certain person, horary method is clearly the most applicable or even the only one facilitating the answer. Nevertheless, synastry is useful for providing extra information on compatibility and mutual attraction of the two potential partners, as well as on their chances to enjoy a quality, long-term and happy relationship.

Clients nowadays know that their astrologers can help them decide on propitious times for different activities. That's why they often come up with questions like *What is the best time for such-and-such activity (change of residence, journey, filing an application, etc.)?* Such questions are NOT to be answered by horary astrology! They are to be dealt with by electional astrology and by various predictive techniques instead. The question *When are we moving?* however, IS a horary question! I hope you understand the difference. Horary astrology answers concrete questions, pointing to their resolution, especially in relation to processes that are already in course. (In the latter case it would certainly be easier to ascertain the time of the move if the move had already been planned and the activities related to it were in course.)

As already mentioned in the introductory passages of this chapter, I frequently combine horary with other techniques. Not because I'd believe that horary method can't be used independently, but because I want to lessen the chance of mistakes. If a question relates to a job, partnership, journey, health, outcome of a legal dispute and similar, and if I have birth data of the querent and the quesited (that is, of the person asking the question and of the one/s asked about), along with other necessary data (like the date of the planned journey, for example), I always check the querent's situation by means of forecasting techniques such as transits, progressions, eclipses and similar, which can confirm or negate indications in the horary chart. After all, when you're a practising astrologer, getting paid for your work, you can't afford to make mistakes!

SHOULD QUESTIONS BE REALLY VERBALLY EXPRESSED?

My students often ask if it's possible that a querent does not verbalize his question, but only formulates it in his mind, while the astrologer writes down the time of this unspoken question and then casts a horary chart. The logical question is: if the querent refuses to disclose the question, how can he expect a sensible answer? Some people may be shy and reserved, but even if they don't speak their minds in the beginning phase, they will have to open up to the astrologer sooner or later. But still: is this even possible? I believe it is, but only if the astrologer is experienced enough to work out the question from the querent's significators, or if he/she is sufficiently familiar with the querent to anticipate the problem. However, we can't rely on this and such guesswork is really meaningless. It is true, though, that placements of significators in houses often clearly indicate the sphere of querent's interest and their momentary state, but I really do not recommend such guesswork, especially to beginners. There's also an educational side of astrological counselling to this: laymen (querents, clients) could get the wrong impression that the astrologer should somehow intuitively guess their problem - which is far from the truth, of course. **Querents should trust their astrologers with everything they know so as to learn what they don't know**. After all, this is the very reason why they turned to the astrologer!

But what do we do when someone approaches us with a question when they don't know that we're astrologers? Can horary astrology help in such cases? A while ago a horary forum member wrote that a friend called her, wondering if she might have seen his late mother's purse, which was supposed to be somewhere in the living room. She frequently stayed there so he assumed she could have been of help with the search. The girl noted the time of his question and the chart accurately described the querent (friend) as well as the situation. This is logical and this case shows that horary charts can be cast even in cases when people, seeking an answer, are not in the "formal" role of querents.

Let me illustrate this with another, albeit a slightly different case. A while ago my daughter told me that she'd lost her wallet. She did not directly ask me if I can find the wallet by horary, naturally assuming that I would make a horary chart for the question anyway. Indeed I made it for the moment she informed me about her loss, and in this case too the procedure was the same as above – I cast the chart as if she had inquired me directly as an astrologer.

CAN A HORARY QUESTION BE ONLY ASKED ONCE?

According to many horary astrologers whose writings I have come accross, each question can only be asked once. All the subsequent charts, cast for the same question, are supposed to be inaccurate or "invalid". Why ask twice at all, when you have asked once, you may wonder, but the problem is more relevant than it seems. When in critical life periods and situations, one and the same question often keeps popping up. *Does he love me?* This question can baffle a worried woman's mind every sleepless night and you as her astrologer might end up with dozens of horaries, asking one and the same question. I agree that the "best" horary chart is usually the one created for the time the question first came up, but the same question *can* be asked again – provided it descibes the situation as well as the first one. This is possible and my practice has often confirmed the validity of such approach, but it is nevertheless recommended to insist on the first, original chart.

We also have cases when the situation changes in some respect between the first and the second question on the same topic, so that the second question is slightly modified. Similarly if two (or even several) different people inquire after the same thing. In such cases a horary with the same subject matter, asked by another person, can offer additional information and that chart can serve to confirm the first one. *Will the faculty grant my application for the study abroad? Will my daughter's application for the study abroad be approved by her faculty? The faculty's decision will be known tomorrow – what will be the result, will my sister's application be granted?* Three questions, posed at different times by three different persons, relating to the same matter; all the three are relevant, and if asked sincerely, the "sky" will give the same answer to all of them!

MUST THE QUESTION BE REALLY THOUGHT OUT WELL?

Although it is not "forbidden" to ask for "heavenly help" at any phase of our search for an answer, I suggest that you ask a horary question only after you've realized that there's no other way to find it.

Suppose you've lost your panties. (OK, you have plenty, but tonight you just really want to wear those pink lacy ones.) It would be a little weird to jump at your computer and cast a horary immediately after realizing that they're not at their usual place (in the underwear drawer, for example). You'd be likelier to search all the places where you think they could be, and cast a horary only after at least a 5 minutes' search. This would most probably save your time - especially if you are a beginner, meaning that the process of studying all your horary books' lost items sections might take you at least two hours. In that time you'd probably have searched every inch of your apartment! (But you could do that, of course, if you wanted to test your horary knowledge and had enough time to play with the interesting, albeit time-consuming task.)

On the other hand, I don't agree with the opinion that the question should mature in us for at least 24 hours before being expressed. (This belief, based on the writings of *Guido Bonatti*, an Italian astronomer and astrologer of the 13th century, is the occasional hot topic on horary discussion forums.) Astrologers of old seem to have believed that the "sky" would only synchronise with our consciousness after a long period of contemplation ("praying to the Lord God"), as if not being able to give us the answer any sooner. But the reality of horary practice shows that a very important question can pop up in our minds in a split second - just when the time is right for it to be "born"! A question can linger in our subconscious minds for hours or days and manifest itself in that very moment when the "sky" is perfectly set up for the answer. It follows that what is really important and relevant is **the intensity of our consciousness, not the length of contemplation**.

CAN WE ASK TRIVIAL QUESTIONS?

Some horary astrologers believe that we should not ask trivial (commonplace, ordinary, banal) questions. Such are supposed to be the teachings of old astrologers, and we know of at least one who explicitly stated it: William Lilly. But as much as I value and respect this master teacher, I have to disagree.

Let's get to the core of this issue and ask ourselves what is the criterion that divides the trivial from the non-trivial (deep, significant, serious) questions. Does such a criterion exist? An objective one certainly doesn't. *Will Billy call me tonight?* Is that a trivial or a seriuos question? It depends! While it may seem trivial to you and me, it might be deadly important to the querent, a woman in love. *Should I buy a lottery ticket today?* A rather banal question, don't you think? But who has the right to decide what's trivial, except for the querent? How do we know what degree of importance any question holds for the one who asks it?

The fact is that people rarely ask questions that we could deem - according to the general criteria - really deep, profound and important. We're usually interested in trivia, because life is composed of a series of relatively unimportant, fleeting feelings and events. *Where are my pink lacy panties?* You've searched and not found them in your room – go cast a horary! Why should that be "forbidden"? You might discover you've left them at your lovers' place, and this would save you an hour's search.

More importantly, experience has taught me that **the "sky" simply doesn't distinguish between trivial and non-trivial questions**. It only distinguishes between those that can and those that can't be answered.

Driven by the desire to learn more and to test the validity of their technique, passionate horary astrologers of all ages have set themselves a myriad of trivial questions. We would learn our art at a much slower pace if we waited patiently until a really deep question arose in our minds. *Will at least one red car drive by in the course of the next half an hour?* This question is, we probably agree, distinctly trivial, but why would it be forbidden? Looking for answers to such questions does not harm anyone - and may also not benefit anyone, true, except the budding astrologer to whom they can serve as a fun way of learning. (We do have a planet and a house in the horary chart for a car, as well as a planet for red colour, so we definitely can look for an answer - and also find one!)

Finally, the horary chart itself may show whether the question is really trivial (from the standpoint of the querent, NOT the astrologer!) or not. During the long centuries of its evolution horary astrology has developed techniques which enable the astrologer to discard truly banal, unimportant and unanswerable questions. (See STRICTURES AND CAUTIONS on p. 111) So why not accept any "trivial" question, and go where the chart leads us?

CAN WE ASK "THIRD-PARTY" QUESTIONS?

Of course we can! A high percentage of horary questions refer to "third parties" - that is, to people other than the querent. They can be related to the querent in a number of ways (relatives, friends, coworkers...), or they can be those with whom the querent has no specific relationship. We can ask questions about people that we know from the media or have heard about from friends. There is simply no astro-logic to the belief that our horaries can only "work" with the issues with which we are personally or emotionally involved. A horary chart will prove to be equally valid if it refers to the fate of a missing person about whom we've read in an online article (and we basically don't care whether they'll be found or not, as we're not emotionally attached to them - except, of course, for the natural compassion which we feel for fellow human beings), as if it's asking about the chances of one's own sick child's recovery. This might seem strange, but experience shows that it's true.

CAN ASTROLOGERS ANSWER THEIR OWN QUESTIONS?

Some astrologers are of the opinion that horary astrologers should not (or shouldn't be able to) answer their own questions; instead, they should forward their own questions to other astrologers who should be more able to deal with them. The main setback, they say, is the astrologer's lack of objectivity.

I disagree. Horary astrology, like any other branch of astrology, is a discipline practiced according to a set of rules. If we follow these rules and if the question is "fit to be judged" (that is, if there're no strictures and warnings alleviating us from attempting the answer), we can't be any more wrong with our own questions as with other people's questions. Our judgment can of course suffer from lack of objectivity, but that's no less possible when dealing with our clients' questions, especially when we want to please them. (Which happens often, especially to beginners who don't want to disappoint their clients and therefore overlook or misinterpret crucial indications, with the result of obtaining a wrong answer.) I think that answering our own questions is often even easier, especially when trying to locate a mislaid object because we know our home environment much better than we know the apartments of our clients who call us on the phone or write us by email. We are also much less likely to fool ourselves with wrong interpretations of intricate and complicated questions. We don't need to go through the often tedious process of asking a number of questions to our clients when trying to better understand their situation or circumstances which have led them to ask their questions.

Guido Bonatti wrote that an astrologer can forward his question to another astrologer who wants to help him, so that he asks the question again, as if it would be his own. (See chapter TIME AND PLACE OF THE QUESTION on p. 24 for particulars.) A little complicated but not impossible; I often do this for my friends when charts cast for their own questions don't give me clear indications. But in such questions, the querent is me, of course, not them!

Another reason is supposed to be the (alleged) fact that the right (proper) time for a horary chart is that time when the astrologer receives the question from the querent. This, they say, is the "magic moment", giving "birth" to a horary chart. But how can that "magic moment" ever happen if the astrologer doesn't receive the question from another person? Because, in every horary chart, H1 (the 1st house) represents the querent and H7 (the 7th house) the astrologer, and their interaction is supposed to be necessary for a chart to be "valid".

Again, I disagree. My firm belief is that the right time of the question is that moment when the question arises in the mind of the querent – either that of our clients or our own. Anyone who has ever felt a need for a question to be answered, knows that such moments are very clear and distinct, and no less "magic" than those when the question is received by another person. We astrologers are even in an advantage because we usually know when the question pops up in our minds, while our clients, not so versed in horary practice, are often hesitant and unsure of when exactly the question "found" them. H7 may indeed rule the astrologer, but only when he's not the querent. (More in chapter TIME AND PLACE OF THE QUESTION on p. 24).

THE TIME RANGE OF HORARY CHARTS

Students sometimes ask what is the time range or "validity" of horary charts. In other words, how long do horary charts "last"? The answer is simple – **a chart is valid for as long as it takes for the subject matter of the question to complete**. This may take from a few minutes up to several years. Many examples in the practice part of this book didn't reach a conclusion until several years after the question was asked, which proves that horary charts are not limited by any time boundaries except for those set by the outcome of the case.

DON'T CONFUSE HORARY ASTROLOGY WITH OTHER TECHNIQUES!

I have noticed that many astrologers and astrology students mix horary, elective and event charts. They treat them as equal, although they differ in contents, interpretive purposes and interpretive techniques. Know that by horary astrology we answer specific questions, by elective astrology we choose the best or most propitious times for certain activities while by event charts we aim to understand the planetary "workings" behind important events (like signing a contract, meeting of an important person, marriages, accidents, earthquakes and the like), either to improve our understanding of the universal laws or to predict the future unfoldment of those events.

ETHICAL CONSIDERATIONS

Some astrologers argue that it is not ethical to deal with questions concerning other people's affairs. *Will my daughter and her boyfriend reconcile, or does their latest dispute mean that their relationship is over?* That's entirely their business, they might say; we should not pry into affairs in which we're not personally involved. But on the other hand, we are only humans and the affairs of those close to us are often even more important to us than our own. It's only natural, therefore, that such questions often come up and that we end up casting horaries for them, whether we think it ethical or not. It's the astrologer's responsibility to decide whether to accept such question from a client or not. Personally, I don't impose my ethical beliefs upon my clients, nor upon my students. I practice and teach astrology, not ethics. Still, if I think that a question is "inapropriate", I'll tell them, and I'll warn them that it's their responsibility to decide what they'll do with the information they get from me. (This said, I must add that I have yet to come upon a question that would seem truly unethical. *I've just robbed a bank, will they get me?* Not happened yet!)

When faced with ethically contentious questions, I suggest you to follow the general rule: **Never do to others what you don't want to be done to yourself!** If you don't want your mother asking astrologers whether you'll stay with your husband or get divorced, you might feel a need to decline the answer to a querent who approaches you with such a question. But before doing that, I suggest that you ask them about their motives. If it's only curiousity, you might decide to refuse to answer, but if your answer is vital to the querent because an important decision depends on it, regarding the safety or financial wellbeing of their family, you'd probably realize that the querent really needs help, and therefore accept the question.

Personally, I only do forecasts for clients' adult children when their motives are really selfless, when they are worried and when I feel that my answer will help them, either to better understand their children or to assist them in their own plans and ambitions. *My adult son is sick and is considering seeking treatment abroad. Would that help him?* Such a question makes sense, at least from the querent's (mother's) perspective - but then again, it won't be helpful if she asks without her son's consent or if the astrologer's answer can't affect his decision. (You asked an astrologer? Come on, mum, don't be stupid!)

But I wouldn't hesitate if the question was: *My adult son is sick and is considering seeking treatment abroad. Will he go or not?* There's nothing unethical in such types of questions, especially because the questions asking for prediction, not advice, are (in my opinion, as explained elsewhere) truly reasonable and answerable horary questions.

Clearly, the most ethical stance is to accept questions only when our answers are potentially informative and helpful. Unfortunately, in practice it's virtually impossible to know that in advance! In the above case where the question asked for advice, our answer might not be helpful despite our true wish to the contrary. Let's say that our judgement would be negative. We could say to the mother, based on the horary chart's indications, that the planned treatment in a foreign country would not be helpful to her son, or would be even harmful. What would she do, in case her son wouldn't listen? To worry is all she could do, although we did the best we could – as astrologers. There's a thin line between being helpful and being unhelpful, so we must decide – do we want to be astrologers or "counsellors"? If you think that's a simple question, think again.

Do you think you can be both? Let's look at the problem from another perspective. Let's say that the querent asks about himself, and our answer is negative in the sense that we break bad news. That can happen – even often. My firm stance is that every querent should take it as their responsibility to accept the answer – whatever it is. But, alas, many people are not mature enough for that!

I remember a case when my longtime friend phoned to ask whether her boyfriend who recently left her, would get back to her. I cast a horary and the chart revealed that this was not going to happen. I saw that he was with another girl and that their relationship was serious and was going to last. What's more, I even hinted (because the chart was so clear and eloquent) that she'd soon get pregnant. I was really sorry to had to tell her this, because I knew how difficult the situation was for her; she suffered greatly because she truly loved him. I told her that she was always welcome to call me, so that we could chat, go for a drink or whatever. She thanked me – and never called back. She didn't answer my calls or the messages I sent her. When after a couple of years we incidentally met, she told me how my answer had hurt her. *I only expected consolation*, she said. *I was not ready for the answer.* I could quite understand her but think what would happen if I denied what I saw, if I told her that everything would come up roses and so on? You know, things like counsellors say, like don't give up, he might come back, just think positive? If not sooner, after several years when it would finally transpire that my answer was incorrect, she'd have a legitimate reason to tell people how an incompetent astrologer I am because my answer was totally wrong!

Finally, there's the question – did my answer really harm her, or might it have helped her anyway, in spite of her rejection? Like grounding her a bit, so that her suffering would end sooner? There's no knowing but that would be the ultimate benefit of my reading– if she was mature enough, of course, to understand that we should accept our fate. The sooner we do that, the better for us.

The lesson of the above story is obvious: We should always warn our querents that by recieving the answer they are also accepting the responsibility to deal with it – whatever it might be.

You might be faced with a question: *Has my husband ever had a lover?* Once I even received a question *Did my late husband ever have a lover?* Instead of answering such obviously disputable questions, I try to make these women aware of the futility of their enquiries. If a woman doubts her lover's loyalty, she'll doubt him even if we say no, he's never had a lover, but if we say yes, this information will hardly help her. Why dig into something that might have happened a long time ago? We can't change our past, let alone the past of someone else, but we can change our attitude towards it.

A part of every astrologer's ethics is also to inform the client about our "imperfection". I find it strange how often astrologers like to underline their answers by reassurances such as *I'm certain of that, I'm 100%, I'm confident…* I always say: The chart shows this and that; indications are such and such, therefore it's likely that this and that will happen. "Likely" is what we should say even if we're 99% sure of the answer – because, after all, there's always a possibility, even if a slight one, that we could be wrong. Not because we'd be incompetent but because our art is very difficult and because answering people's questions is such a tricky business due to sheer unpredictability of human nature. Our clients should always bear in mind that astrology is a most difficult divinatory skill because we astrologers have to realign our rules with every new case we deal with. While it's true that horary rules are very clear and precise, it's also true that every chart factor works differently in combination with every other factor, so that no combination of factors ever works in exactly the same way. What's more, our rules have to be continuously adapted to every new situation that arises, and why not recognize that, and value the sheer complexity and intricacy of our art? **We'll do more for the recognition of our art if we educate our clients about its fallibility rather than spoil its (and our!) reputation by giving wrong answers which we present as "perfectly true" and "definitely correct".**

TIME AND PLACE OF THE QUESTION

he time of the question is that moment when we feel a strong need to get an answer to a question. It's very important that we write the question down – word for word, since many mistakes in interpretation are due to the fact that questions are not clearly expressed. If the querent is someone else than ourselves, it's even more important that the question is formulated as clearly as possible. This way we avoid misunderstandings – as has been explained in the first chapter of this book.

Next we write down the **date and exact time** of the question. If we are our own astrologers, we'll obviously do that as we know how important this is – except, of course, if we have no watch at hand or if our question is such a burning one that we can't figure when it was that we first thought of it. The time also presents no dilemma if astrologer and the querent talk face to face, on the phone or through other means of direct electronic communication.

The problem of the right time of the question can occur if the question was posed in a letter, either conventional or electronic. Most modern horary astrologers believe that a horary chart should be cast for the moment when the astrologer reads (or hears) and understands the question. Thus a link between the querent and astrologer is established and this is supposed to be the "magical moment" when the question really comes to life and is ready to be "divined".

Now, think. An urgent question pops up in the mind of the querent and he feels a strong desire to get the answer, so he rings up his astrologer. But, alas, the astrologer does not answer, so he leaves a message on the answering machine, or sends him an IM, email or similar. There're many ways to leave a message nowadays. But when is his astrologer going to read his question? Well, it depends on the time he'll spend in the toilet! (Utterly banal, yes, but also utterly serious.) If the astrologer hears (or reads) and understands the question within a few minutes or even within half an hour after the message was sent, the ascendant of the chart created for the question will be close to that at the time of asking, but if half an hour or more elapse, it will probably already be in the next sign and indications in the horary chart will be significantly different from those at the time of asking. So, which time is more correct?

Not only logic, but my long-standing practice and research have convinced me that **the true time of a horary question is the time when the question is "born" in the mind of the querent** - felt, brought to consciousness, expressed, written down. The question "belongs" to the querent, not to the astrologer! The "heavens" have an answer ready for any question "born" at any time and place, regardless of astrologers who cast charts. What's more, those answers are ready regardless of any conscious realization of any person that they can be arrived at by means of horary astrology. Remember that **astrologers didn't invent the rules of cosmos, they're just decoding them.**

But ever since the possibility of divination was discovered, we have querents and astrologers. A person feeling a need for an answer can put his question forward to an astrologer or try to find the answer himself (if he's an astrologer), or, not knowing that questions can be answered by horary astrology, try to find other means of getting the answer, or else – simply drop the question and wait until the situation resolves by itself.

Guido Bonatti, a famous Italian astronomer and astrologer of the 13th century, instructs the astrologer to cast the chart "*as soon as he can, accurately, immediately, without any delay or any length of interval, once the words leave the mouth of the one asking about the matter*" **(LIBER ASTRONOMIAE, *Treatise 6 – Questions, Chapter 2*).** The original time of the question was even so "sacred" to him that in Chapter 2 of the same treatise, dealing with the dilemma of an astrologer's asking "for himself", he writes: "*Indeed, after the other person were to understand his question, he would be able to look for himself, and answer his own question, or he may give his own question to another (whether in writing or not) – naturally to such a person who is concerned about his matter. And he may offer it on his own behalf after he has posed it, when he wishes.*" He continues by saying that "he" (the second, third or fourth astrologer) may even wait for a certain sign and make that be the ascendant of the question, but note how important it was to him that the original question was **asked again by the new astrologer**, empathizing with the querent, so as to really get the "right" moment for casting the chart. He didn't simply cast it for the time he received the question! (I'm stressing this because I've read an article by a famous contemporary astrologer who, unfortunately, misinterpreted Bonatti's writings in this part, and the rest of astrologers, sadly, followed suit.)

In his famous book **CHRISTIAN ASTROLOGY** (*Of The Time of receiving Any Question*) William Lilly states: "*Without doubt the true houre of receiving any question is then, when the Querent propounds his desire unto the Astrologer, even that very moment of time, in my opinion, is to be accepted.*" He continues by saying that if he receives a question in a letter, he casts the chart for the moment when he breaks it open and perceives the intention of the querent. Such proceeding directly contradicts his statement of "the Querent propounding his desire unto the Astrologer", but he obviously saw this to be the only option, so he went with it – and even found it successful. "*This way and manner have I practiced, and found successe answerable,*" he writes. Unfortunately, he doesn't say which example charts in his book were created for the times when he received the questions in person and which ones for the times when he received them in a letter. It's likely, though, that he received a vast majority of questions in person, as postal services were just being introduced in England in his days, so there's no logic in believing that this was his daily practice.

But the fact is that his system of taking the time of "receiving and understanding the question" was strictly followed and adhered to by most modern horary astrologers who have learned their discipline from his books. Olivia Barclay, my personal tutor at *The Qualifying Horary Practitioner's Course*, was among them, so it's understandable that in the beginning of my studies I followed suit. I changed my approach only after realizing that it (mainly) gave false results. I found – as I hope to prove to the reader by several examples in the practice part of this book – that best results are given by charts cast for the exact times when the questions are truly "propounded" (thought of, put forward, expressed).

And yet - can we deny the correctness of any approach, given the evidence that it works? Of course not. Correct answers to the questions by themselves justify the techniques and approaches of the astrologer. But how many are there, really? In none of the several horary books that I have read do astrologers state in what manner they had received the questions! Many claim that they use the above mentioned approach successfully, but I'm leaving it to them to prove their point, as I am proving mine.

Still, let's assume that they're right. What would be the logical premise behind that? The only one seems to be the one set forth by Guido Bonatti – a question indirectly received can only be answered by an astrologer who feels an affinity with it. Only such attitude could, logically speaking, result in an astrologer opening the letter (whether conventional or electronic) at a time that would be synchronized with the nature and the aim of the question.

But why torture ourselves by such tedious and doubtful proceedings in cases when the time of the question is known? Lilly obviously used this approach only when there was no other way to get to the original time of the question. But, hey, it's a whole new world today! An extremely large majority of people don't use "snail mail" for personal correspondence any more. They use phones and electronic mail which precisely record the time of all communications.

But let us dig deeper. Nowadays, astrology students often post questions on astrology forums, asking professionals and more experienced colleagues for help. If it was true that the "right" time of a question is when the astrologer reads and understands it, then all forum members who wanted to help would have to cast their own charts which would, of course, vary substanially, not just because they'd read them at various times but also because they live all around the world, in locations belonging to various time zones. "*Hi there, my American friend, I'm back from holiday and I see that a week ago you asked this question, I've just read and understood it, I'm in Paris, it's ten to two p.m. and this is the chart I have cast for your question …*" Just think of the confusion if, say, 25 different charts were produced by 25 different astrologers! But such confusion actually does exist and this is one of the reasons why horary astrology nowadays tends to regress instead of progress.

It's obvious, therefore, that to get the right chart, reflecting the true nature of the question and offering clear, unambiguous grounds for delineation, querents should always provide the exact data (time and place) for their question.

The problem, however, can occur when the querent is a layman and doesn't know the rules of horary astrology, so that he poses a question without providing the time when the question arose in his mind. But there' s solution to that too, at least in modern times. As already mentioned, nowadays we usually receive questions via phone or electronic communicaton (emails, IM-s, forums, chatrooms etc.). Those media nearly always record the time of receiving bits of communications. As for emails – we usually receive them only a second after they've been sent to us (except those which pass through several servers as is sometimes the case), but if after a couple of days the information dissapears from the main email window, it's easy to retrieve it: open the mail, go to "More" and click "Show original" - there're the date and the exact time of sending, but note that the recorded time is the clock time at the location from which the mail had been sent, so don't forget to adjust the information. It should be easy to ask the querent about his whereabouts at the time when he posed the question.

It's true, of course, that the time of sending the letter might not be the same time that the quetsion popped up in the mind of the querent – although this usually is the case. If not, we just have to educate our clients that they should note down the exact time of any question, as this is the only way to assure the relevance of a horary chart. (It's a tedious job, but it's worth the trouble.)

Astrologers who still receive questions from clients by classic mail, will probably not be able to produce meaningful and relevant horary charts, except if they proceed as described in the above paragraphs, so that - guided by a strong desire to help – they cast their own charts for any moment that they find "propitious", or trust that the "sky" led them to open the letter at the time when it "offered assistance".

I used to solve this problem so that I asked the clients who posed questions in classical letters, to note down the exact time and place of their questions. If they didn't, I told them that due to lack of information I can't answer their question, or I turned to other predictive techniques.

As for the place of question – **we always use the coordinates of the querent's location**, which in turn asks to also use their times and time zones, of course. In other words, create the chart as if at the time of asking you were in the querent's mind and body.

THE MAKING OF A HORARY CHART

USE CORRECT TIME ZONES

 owadays it's very easy to create technically correct charts, as a large majority of astrological software use a dependable atlas, although there are still some programs which ask you to choose (enter) the time zone manually. Note that some countries use summer times. Be aware of those and make use of various internet sources for the correct time zones.

HOUSE SYSTEM

For the purpose of horary astrology I've always used the Regiomontanus house system. Some astrologers prefer other house systems but my own research has led me to believe that this system – used also by William Lilly and his conteporaries – gives the best results. It is still being used by a large majority of horary astrologers, especially by those who follow tradition. (Which is the best way, anyway.)

Recently, during the 2010s, some horary astrologers have come to prefer the "whole sign" house system - the most ancient of house systems which gives a sign to every house, beginning with the ascending sign. This system is extremely simple and is actually not a house system at all, as it equals signs with houses. It doesn't even consider the ascendant as the starting point of the mundane circle, but it starts counting the houses by the first degree of the ascending sign. This "house system" was used by ancient astrologers but throughout long centuries our art has evolved, and I wonder why contemporary astrologers who use it, have decided to take such a significant step back? Our predecessors have developed and refined the art of horary astrology immensely since those ancient times. They have handed us over a plethora of extremely effective, useful, functional rules regarding the use of houses, based on the mundane dissection of the zodiacal circle, so why ignore them? What's more, those dozens of books that we contemporary horary astrologers have learnt from, have all been written in the tradition of Regiomontanus or (rarely) any other sophisticated house system, whereas the "whole sign house system" has only (or mainly) been defended on theoretical, not on practical grounds. And what is theory without practice? I think I can confidently leave the answer to you. My own belief is that that those horary trachers who nowadays propund the whole sign house system, have just never learnt horary astrology in any depth.

There are 124 example cases in the Practice part of this book. At least two charts prove a distinct advantage of Regiomontanus system over the Placidean one. In both cases the Placidean system gave house cusps in different signs than the Regiomontanus system, resulting in wrong answers that I gave because I was inattentive to the house system that I used. (When creating charts, I swap between both systems regulary because I use the Placidean system for natal astrology.)

House cusps are extremely important in horary astrology, as their signs give rulers and significators. Ignoring or miscalculating them can result in serious mistakes. Needless to say, the discrepancy between the Regiomontanus and whole sign cusps is even much greater than that between the Regiomontanus and Placidean ones.

SIGNS IN THE SOUTHERN HEMISPHERE

All charts presented in the Practice part of this book are cast for the northern hemisphere locations. I have a hypothesis that zodiacal signs in the southern hemisphere should be reversed – in horary as well as in natal and other astrology that uses signs as the background of planetary paths. This is because the qualities / characteristics of signs are largely dependent on the qualities of the seasons. Consider my reasoning in the chapter on the zodiacal signs and think whether reversing of signs in the southern hemisphere wouldn't be only logical. Testing this hypothesis by horary is the soundest method possible, because wishful thinking has no place in our art. In horary astrology, we seek exact answers. We don't evaluate charts for personal characteristics and are therefore subject to less flaws and inadequacies as when interpreting natal charts. By reversing the signs we get wholly different charts resulting in wholly different answers. My research so far has confirmed my belief that the signs should be reversed in the southern hemisphere. Sign rulers, on the other hand, should stay. Aries, for example, should be Libra in the southern hemisphere charts, and ruled by Venus. Cancer should be Capricorn, ruled by Saturn. And so on.

SIDEREAL SIGNS?

Sidereal signs have no place in the western astrological tradition. They are currently 25 degrees off tropical sign cusps, meaning that the so-called "cardinal signs" do not begin with the "cardines" (the Sun's four turning points), have no links to the seasons and are therefore completely irrational. The whole of western astrological and horary tradition has been built upon tropical signs and should be understood and practiced as such. In a way, my objection to sidereal signs is similar to my objection of using the zodiacal circle, created in the northern hemisphere, in the southern hemisphere. Remember that zodiac is not about the starry firmament but about the time and its quality, as created by the path of the Sun.

THE HORARY SCRIPT

A horary chart can be compared to a stage play or a movie. A stage play develops according to the scenario written by the playwright, while the horary "script" unfolds in real life. When someone asks a question, he's like a curious observer interested in how the story on the "stage of life" will unfold.

Who is the script writer in our horary world? We can call him God or "cosmic order", while the script as such is what we call "destiny" or "fate". Just as the joy of art encourages us to go to the theater, the awareness of the power of destiny and the universal order encourages us to ask questions about the future.

The person who asks the question is called **the querent**, while the subject matter of the question (the person, object or a situation inquired after) is called **the quesited**. If an astrologer asks the question himself, he himself is the querent, of course, but querents are often other people – astrologer's clients, friends, relatives and so on.

After having cast a horary chart, we must decide on the "actors" who play the major and minor roles. In theatre and film, we have leading roles, supporting roles and bit roles. Same here! All these people are always signified by **planets** which in horary art we call **significators**. (Note: when speaking of planets, we also refer to the Sun and the Moon - for purely practical reasons, of course, although we know that they are not planets, because the Sun is the star of our solar system while the Moon is the Earth's satellite.)

We should know, though, that planets don't always signify (rule) people; they can also refer to animals, objects, concepts, developments and situations – whatever it is that we're asking about. Significators can thus stand for *John, Mary, colleague, wife, father, son, job, apartment, travel, illness, exam, phone, cat* and so on.

For an ever better understanding, we can relate the horary "script" to grammar. Remember – in horary grammar, **significators** (planets) are always **nouns**.

But how do we know *which planet in our horary chart stands for John and which for Mary? Which for Romeo and which for Juliet? Which for Thomas and which for his job? Which for Charlotte and which for the apartment she's buying? Which for the father and which for his illness? Which for Peter and which for his missing phone?*

To be able to understand what follows, complete beginners in astrology would first have to study the next chapters dealing with the basic building blocks of general astrology, but for those who know the basics, it should be easy.

Planets "rule" or "control" **signs**. Each sign has its own planetary ruler (some even two - an old and a new one, the traditional and the modern one), and this is the planet which has its "domicile" in that sign. (Individual degrees and parts of signs also have additional rulers which we call **almutens**, but more on this later.) **Houses** (12 segments of the sky obtained by dividing the celestial sphere along the horizontal and vertical axes) represent the spheres of life into which individual people, things and concepts "belong". For example, the querent "belongs" to the first house (H1), his property to the second house (H2), his brothers, sisters, neighbours and vehicles to the third house (H3), his father and real estate to the fourth house (H4), and so on. The planet which is the **sign ruler** of the sign at the cusp (beginning) of a certain house, also rules this house together with people (things, concepts) which belong to (or "fall into") it. After having studied the chapters on houses and planets, you will have a solid understanding of how to find significators of people and things you will be asking about.

The next step is to study **the state (condition) of significators**. *How does Juliet feel about her relationship with Romeo? Is she happy or not? Is John in love with Mary? Are Mary's feelings for John strong or weak? Is the job that Thomas is applying for, a promising one? Should Charlotte buy the apartment she's watching, is it worth her money? Is father strong enough to overcome the disease? Is Peter's phone misplaced somewhere in the house, is it in his office, buried under the mud or hidden in the thief's pocket?*

We can get answers to all such questions by evaluating **planetary dignities** (essential and accidental), their **house positions** and the **links between planets, signs and houses**. The next chapters will teach you how to get through the labyrinth of meanings that hide the key to answering various aspects of our questions.

In the horary grammar, **houses** are basically **nouns** (like planets), but they can also be **adverbs**, answering questions starting with *where, how, when, to what extent* etc., whereas **signs** are usually **adjectives** and **adverbs**. Signs usually help us find answers to questions starting with *what kind* and *how*, because they **modify the character of**

the planets. Signs can also show various kinds of environments, things, people, parts of the body, directions of the sky and even countries, so they are sometimes nouns, too, but their primary role is that of adjectives because they modify and describe nouns.

Finally, we want to know *whether Romeo and Juliet will get married? Will John and Mary stay together or not? Will Thomas get the job? Will the father's condition worsen, or is he on the healing course? Will Charlotte buy the apartment? And, finally, will Peter find his phone?*

The answers to such questions are usually found with the help of future **aspects** and other planetary movements which show what will happen to the "protagonists" of our "drama". Aspects are therefore like **verbs**.

We also have **personal pronouns** - *my, yours, his* ... They're usually described by the relations between houses, as well as by dispositions, and then there're **exclamation marks** (planets in exact conjunctions with the angles, for example, and other distinct chart features), **question marks** (strictures and warnings), and so on. The following chapters will teach you all the "grammar" you need to know in order to get to the final punctuation mark (the **full stop** or the answer) of course, but at this stage, it's most important for you to **distinguish between the functions of signs, houses, planets and aspects**.

The next chapters will help you become familiar with the building blocks of horary astrology and you will find that this special field of astrology is subject to exact rules of interpretation. But know that when you'll start applying those rules to practice, you will probably find that delineation is not as simple as you might have thought. You willl find that there are realatively few "ideal" (clean, clear, easy) horary charts. In most of them, you'll find contradictory indications. Students are often easily discouraged when they find that one chart indication points to one direction and the other to a different one. In order to avoid mistakes and disappointment, you'll need to carefully study all the example cases in the second part of the book. Those will teach you how to properly combine all the intricate rules and give priority to those which are clearer, stronger and more eloquent. When faced with a dilemma, remember that **horary astrology is not a game of chess**. "The sky" cannot place planets and angles into the "best" positions that facilitate an easy answer at any moment when a particular question arises in our (or others') minds. Certain placements will necessarily give rise to contradicting conclusions, but that's what we must reckon with. Know that the greatest challenge of horary astrology is how to skillfully apply the plethora of rules and techniques to the requirements of each individual chart. Our task is often similar to that of a physician who must choose between several different cures, and decide on the best one on the basis of a combination of factors, knowing "intuitively" (based on the years of experience) which one will provide the most effective care to the patient.

Practice makes mastery, but it is time now to deal with the individual elements of horary grammar that will enable you to make clear, understandable sentences, and enjoy your horary "dramas".

ZODIACAL SIGNS IN HORARY ASTROLOGY

ZODIAC

THE BIRTH OF THE ZODIAC

arly "stargazers" (they could also be called ancient astronomers / astrologers, since both fields of research were once inextricably linked) studied the skies for purely practical reasons. In order to organize their daily lives, our ancestors had to create a calendar that told them when the seasons would change, and when they could expect droughts, rains, floods and other weather changes. The paths of the "moving stars" (the Sun, the Moon and the visible planets) and the positions of seemingly immovable stars were dutifully traced through millenia, and the space behind them was divided into segments. Both the number and the size of those segments differed from continent to continent and from country to country, as each part of the world developed its own, unique astronomy. The Sumerians and later Babylonians or the Chaldeans (the beginners of our, western astrology) who lived in the territory of today's Iraq between 2000 and 500 BC, grouped the stars in all visible firmament into 17 (or 18 - due to scarcity of sources, opinions are divided) uneven segments or "constellations". The formation of constellations focused primarily on the areas that were occupied by the "moving stars" (the Sun, the Moon and the planets of our solar system). The basis for the classification of constellations and later of the zodiac, invented by the Babylonians, was, as with other cosmological traditions, the ecliptic - the apparent annual path of the Sun around the Earth. The number of the ecliptic constellations decreased over time; only 13 remained, of which 12 are "zodiacal" - meaning that they bear the same names as the 12-fold division of ecliptic which we term "zodiac". But throughout the ages, with the advance of astronomy, the number of "off-the-ecliptic" constellations gradually inceased. In his book **MATHEMATICA SYNTAXIS** (later **ALMAGEST**), the famous Greek astronomer/astrologer Ptolemy from the 2nd century AD, lists 48 constellations, including no less than 1022 stars. In later centuries, new constellations were added, and today there are 88. The constellations visible from the southern hemisphere were formed and named last, of course, as our ancestors in the northern hemisphere could not see them.

But the historians say that Babylonians, the founders of western astrology, whose records on the collections of stars were found on a pair of clay tablets (called MUL.APIN, likely compiled around 1000 BC), decided to divide all constellations (uneven groups of stars) into 12 equal parts – nowadays known as zodiacal signs. This supposedly happened in the early part of the first millennium BC. Why 12? Why did they leave out Ophiuchus, for example, which was then already categorized as a constellation? Or any other constellation that lies in the background of the Sun? The answer is simple – they needed 12 signs for timing purposes, because the natural yearly cycle is composed of 12 lunations. Their reasons were the same as ours - we "need" exactly 12 months to make up a year! We have 12 sinodic lunar months in a year (a synodic month being the time that elapses from one New Moon to another - 29.5 days) whereas the number of sidereal lunar months (one Moon's orbit around the Earth – 27 days) is between 12 and 13, and this is probably the reason why the number of all zodiacal constellations was initially reduced to 13, not to 12.

Anyway, I hope you now understand that the 12 zodiacal constellations have practically nothing to do with the stars, but only with the natural Sun/Earth/Moon cycles. Some 2000 years ago, astronomers/astrologers started to differentiate between constellations and signs, understanding that the first were a spatial while the latter were a time category. Alas, they still share the same names, and it's important that we understand the origin of their names. So, how were the names of the constellations/signs chosen? The ignorant think that the ancient "stargazers" actually looked at the stars and star groups, and saw in them the shapes of animate and inanimate objects after which they were named (for example leo, the scales, scorpio, etc.). But such thinking is wrong, of course. If we didn't know the constellations' names today, we'd have to stare into them, even with all our modern telescopic equipment, until our eyes fell out - and we still wouldn't recognize the crab, goat, a pair of fish and so on.

The truth is that the names of the constellations themselves should tell us that their origins are to be sought on Earth, not in the sky! The only star that has anything to do with the constellations' names is our Sun. These names are a living proof that the ancient astrologers chose them in accordance with the particular developments in nature in every month that they chose to associate with a particular animal or object. For each month when the Sun passed through a certain section of the sky, they sought out the name of an animal (or object) that they deemed the most appropriate - from the point of view of life on earth, not of the figures in the sky! I will describe these periods and corresponding descriptions very briefly and simply because I want to make you familiar with the ancient "symbolism" based on the observation of natural, astronomical cycles. The naming and fixing of the signs' borders (cusps) was carried out in several phases, by a process that is practically impossible to summarize in a few sentences. We should know, though, that the Babylonians began to use the zodiac as a time belt, divided into 12 equal parts, between the 7th and 5th centuries BC, although the beginnings (zero degrees) of the four "cardinal" signs (Aries, Cancer, Libra, Capricorn) were back then not yet equated with the beginnings of the four seasons, as they are today – and as they already were in the first centuries AD, that is in the period when the signs' characteristics began to be ascertained and categorized. (Can "siderealists" read this again, please?)

The earliest part of spring when the weather warms up and days start getting longer than nights, when the seeds germinate, the buds sprout and leaves start to grow, was in the eyes of our earliest (known) astrologers associated with a ram - an animal that's always embodied courage, boldness, self-initiative and independence. And so they decided that the section of the sky that the Sun traversed during that time should be called The Ram/**Aries**, and they named the group of stars behind that section of the ecliptic by the same name. (Sumerians, predecessors to Babylonians, named it "Field Dweller" or "The Agrarian Worker", which also alludes to the fact that work on the fields - plowing, sowing and planting - began at that time of the year.). **The second part of the spring**, when the plants get stronger by "hungrily" drawing nourishment from the soil, was called The Bull/**Taurus** - after the vigorous, powerful, sturdy animal which almost incessantly feeds on grass and also symbolizes fertility. The symbolism is appropriate also because the Sun at that time persistently rises over the equator, lengthening the days slowly but surely, as if letting the world know that it is here to stay! **The third part of the spring** is when the Sun approaches (and reaches) the highest point above the equator (summer solstice), from where it begins to slowly descend to reach the same declination as it had during the rising period. This "duality" might be the reason why that part of the sky was called The Twins/**Gemini**, although the "official" explanation is that the constellation was so named because of the two big stars Castor and Polux which shone brightly behind the Sun's path at that time, and which they called "the celestial twins" due to their close proximity to each other. But let us remember that around 1000 BC, the Sun reached the summer solstice at around the middle of The Twins (Gemini) - the fact which perfectly validates the name of the sign. The **first summer sign** The Crab/**Cancer** followed - a logical name for the time when the Sun begins to descend from the highest northern declinations (today exactly from the day of the summer solstice, the longest day of the year). We know that crabs move backwards! Then came The Lion/**Leo** – describing the time of the year when the nature is at its fullest and most opulent. Leo is the symbol of excellence, power, pride and authority, just like the **middle part of the summer** when trees are full of delicious fruits and nature smells of "wealth". Next comes the third and **last summer sign**, **Virgo**, in the ancient Babylonian scriptures called "furrow". Of course, the end of the summer calls for harvesting of the crop! The Virgin which holds a wheat ear in her hands is, for this part of the year, definitely a very eloquent symbol.

On the autumn equinox or **beginning of autumn**, day and night are equal in length - just like perfectly balanced scales. By this day, the Sun had made half of its yearly cycle since the spring equinox, so The Scales/**Libra** is a very appropriate name for this "constellation" - but by now we already know that we are speaking of the natural yearly cycle and not of the starry firmament, right? (Again, let us remember that at the autumnal equinox, the sign behind Libra was Virgo about 3000 years ago, but as already said, the signs have become exactly aligned with the beginnings of the astronomical seasons gradually.) Next came **Scorpio** – a dangerous, poisonous animal which in extreme danger is likely to commit suicide. It symbolically corresponds to **mid-autumn** when cold, "poisonous" winds start blowing, leaves are falling off and nature is "dying". Scorpio is inimical to life! Then came **Sagittarius**, originally a "centaur", called also "defender" and "soldier". Just like Gemini which lies opposite to it in the time circle, it's a double-bodied sign, with its animal back part looking towards Capricorn and its human fore part looking towards Scorpio. (Which is just an unfortunate picturing, if you ask me – the creature should be turned around so that the fore part, with the arrow, would look at Capricorn.) In the course of Sagittarius, the Sun reaches solstice again (the winter one this time), the lowest point in the sky, from whence it starts to rise again, to repeat the course, albeit in the opposite direction. Sagittarius therefore is a double-bodied sign for a reason! The creature obviously is a fighter and a traveller. During its first part, there was still some (wild and windy) way to go until the longest night, while during its second part, the new, upward cycle began, comparable to a setting off on a long, "inspirational" journey. Back then, **Capricorn** which is the **first winter sign**, started soon after the winter solstice when night is at its longest and day at its shortest, but from then on, with the ascent of the Sun towards the equator, each day would be longer than the night. The mountain goat (Capricorn) is the animal that can climb highest; this symbolism corresponds to the Sun which from now on has the task to climb all the way to the equator and from there to its highest northern declination (Tropic of Cancer) again. (Note that this animal was once also portrayed as a "goat-fish" - an animal with a goat's head and a fish tail, probably because this period was rainy.) The Water-Bearer/**Aquarius** corresponds to mid-winter which used to experience the strongest rainfall in the ancient Mesopotamian and Mediterranean climates, and the symbolism - a young man pouring water from a large vessel down on Earth, is indeed very clear. When the Sun traverses the segment of the sky called The Fish/**Pisces**, winter is already taking leave but the earth is soaked with water which enables the dormant seeds to swell and prepare for the coming spring. This sign is double-bodied, too: one fish looks back towards the winter while the other looks forward towards the spring. The equator (today zero degree of the next sign, Aries, back then the point behind Pisces) is an important dividing line.

The zodiacal circle is therefore a time category, just like our calendar, but it is a natural, cosmically defined time. **Signs are projected onto the space, but they would exist even if there was not a single star in the sky!** (Except for our Sun, of course, which is the star of our solar system and the actual reason for the existence of zodiac.) Although zodiac is defined as a belt of the sky, extending about 8-9 degrees north and south of the ecliptic (in order to embrace the planets which move above and below the ecliptic - with the exception of Pluto which reaches greater celestial latitudes, but Pluto was not known at the time when zodiac was formed), it is primarily a time circle. A year is basically divided into four segments (seasons) with each of the four furtherly divided into three so that it forms 12 equal parts, called zodiacal signs. As already said, this is consistent with the twelve lunations or twelve months in the course of a year.

The "purely natural" astrological months begin with New Moons which are among the most important astronomical/astrological markers. The soli-lunar cycle was extremely important for the development of all astronomy and astrology. In Chinese cosmology, for example, the astrological year always begins with the first New Moon in Aquarius. There is also the opinion that the Babylonians defined their original constellations by the Moon and not by the Sun, since they could not observe distant stars during the day. But with the progress of time, the zodiacal circle was formed by the more predictable and steady movement of the Sun. This is how our current "tropical" sign borders were established.

The study of lunar declination has prompted me to consider the possibility that the constellations/signs were first named on the basis of the lunar and not the solar motion. The Moon' path was more easily observable than the Sun's in those ancient times, and the illuminated sky at the Full Moon made it easier to group the stars. Each month, the Moon rises from its lowest to its highest declination (declination being the measurement north and south of the celestial equator). It reaches its highest declination when traversing Gemini and then starts to decline like the backwards-moving crab (Cancer), while at the time of its lowest declination it crosses from Sagittarius to Capricorn, from where it has to travel a long way to reach the top (summer solstice) again - like a mountain goat.

The "zodiacal year" doesn't begin on January 1, like the calendrical year, of course. It actually doesn't start anywhere, since it's a circle having no beginning and no end. But the four Sun's turning points - 2 solstices and 2 equinoxes - are important boundaries, and the astrological (zodiacal) year is often considered to begin with Aries which starts at the spring equinox on (or about) March 21.

As already said, when the Chaldean zodiac was invented, the four "cardinal" signs (Aries, Cancer, Libra and Capricorn) did not yet start on the Sun's turning points. Around 1700 BC, zero Aries (spring equinox) was approximately in the middle of the constellation (or the "then" sign) Aries. Later on, zero Aries drew nearer to the equinoctial point until this was finally defined as the beginning of the sign in the Ptolemaic era when constellations and signs were roughly covering the same space and the Greek astrologers aligned the beginnings of the four cardinal signs with the Sun's turning points. This definition of zodiacal signs was postulated by Ptolemy in his Tetrabiblos, written in the 2nd century AD. At that time astronomy was already developed to the degree that the precession of the equinoxes was a known and accepted fact.

So, what is precession? The Earth does not rotate only around its axis, but the axis itself revolves slowly so that it makes a whole circle in 26 thousand years. (Think of a peg-top, that'll give you the idea.) The consequence of this slow circular movement of the Earth's axis is that the equinoctial points (the points at which the Sun crosses the celestial equator and are the basis for the measurement of the natural year) slowly move backwards through the "fixed" firmament, with that motion being opposite to the motion of the Sun along the ecliptic. As the equinoctial points move backwards, the stars (measured in the ecliptic system) move forward, by 51 seconds of arc per year which is 1 degree in 72 years. This is called the **precession of the equinoxes** or the backward shift of the equinoctial points. The logical consequence is that the entire constellations slowly move forward, by about 30 degrees in 2000 years. This is the reason why constellations are not aligned with the signs – nor are they supposed to be and they were never supposed to be. They were (approximately) aligned when zodiac came into existence, but astrologers started to recognize and formulate the qualities and innate natures of zodiacal signs after the 4 cardinal signs' cusps had been aligned with the 4 turning points of the Sun. Before that time, signs were a 12-fold division of space and time, serving orientation purposes only/mainly. All astrology, related to sign meanings, was developed later.

Precession was discovered by the ancient Greek astronomer Hiparchus in the 2nd century BC. Ptolemy who lived in the 2nd century AD, of course knew all about it, but because he could distinguish between constellations and zodiacal signs, he defined zodiac as "tropical" - pertaining to the ecliptic (Sun's path). There is another kind of zodiac, called "sidereal"; this developed within the Vedic astrological tradition (jyotish) and remains bound to constellations. It is therefore immovable - unlike ours, which, due to the precession of the equinoxions, is a movable one. In other words, while our zodiac begins with the spring equinox, the sidereal zodiac starts at a point which is distanced from the equinox by the length of "ayanamsa" which is currently approximately 24° so that each of the 360 degrees of our zodiac is 24° ahead of each degree in the sidereal zodiac. (When, say, the Sun in our zodiac is at 27° Aries, it is at 3° Aries in the sidereal zodiac.)

We should be aware that Indian astrology has developed separately from ours and that sidereal zodiac has nothing to do with the classical tropical zodiac that has evolved entirely apart from the "constellational signs" ever since the ancient Greeks, Persians and other nations who bulit upon Babylonian astrology. **Our zodiac is, again, a time circle that would exist without a single star in the sky – except for the Sun which defines it.**

Initially, astrologers deduced the basic "qualities" of individual signs from the quality of the seasons and their constituent parts (individual months), as described in chapter THE YEARLY RHYTHM (see p. 35). Later on, that simple body of knowledge was developed and built upon by the Babylonian planetary exaltations and sign triplicities, whereas Greeks added sign rulers, elements and qualities. The psychology of zodiacal signs did not fully develop until the 19th and 20th centuries; during the development of horary astrology the psyschology was still in its beginnings, yet it was already sufficiently thorough and clear to form an important element of judgment.

What about constellations and stars? Is there a link between them and zodiacal signs? As already said, the ancient astronomers/astrologers diligently recorded the positions of individual stars and placed them into the "head, heart, neck, left shoulder, right knee, tail" etc. of certain constellations. But this was done after the constellations/signs had been named, in accordance with the above mentioned criteria (Sun's path, seasonal activities etc.). The stars were grouped into meaningful forms (and their parts) for purely practical reasons, just so that the ancient "stargazers" could orientate themselves in time and space. Because in those ancient times perception of reality was probably quite different from today's, it's even possible that they thought that gods arranged the stars so that they could recognize in them the forms of animals and objects, but this was most probably done after they had named them, and certainly did not affect their astrological insights which were arrived at by observation. As for the influence of individual stars, they were also inferred from the events in nature at the time when one or the other star was rising, setting or culminating – in the same way as they recognized the mode of action of the "moving stars", that is, the visible planets of our solar system. Western astrologers make use of several fixed stars, but independently of zodiacal signs.

Zodiacal signs play a less important role in horary astrology than in modern, psychologically-oriented natal astrology, but the understanding of how the ascendant, the Sun, the Moon and the planets express themselves in different signs, is essential to the understanding and interpretation of a horary chart. More on that in chapter ESSENTIAL DIGNITY (see p. 89). Let us now briefly look at the factors that are the basis for determining the qualities and characteristics of each individual sign.

THE YEARLY RHYTHM

As zodiacal signs are the 12-fold division of the Sun's path, the yearly rhythm is the basic measure for their characterisation. It refers to the seasonal changes which the Sun creates by its apparent path around the Earth. Each season vibrates with different energies seen as cyclical changes in nature (as its awakening in spring, fullness in summer, disintegration in autumn and stillness in winter), while in our inner worlds those are cyclical changes of our energy levels. Ancient astrologers first classified signs according to the average levels of heat and moisture which dominated individual seasons. Basically, warmth and moisture create and mainatin life while coldness and dryness inhibit it.

Spring is warm and moist.
Summer is hot and dry.
Autumn is cold and dry.
Winter is cold and moist.

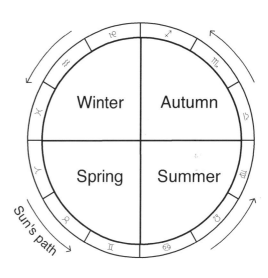

Each quarter encompasses three zodiacal signs: **spring** Aries, Taurus and Gemini, **summer** Cancer, Leo and Virgo, **autumn** Libra, Scorpio and Sagittarius, **winter** Capricorn, Aquarius and Pisces.

It should be noted that our astrology was developed in the northern hemisphere and that zodiacal signs have been qualified within the northern hemisphere climatic conditions, dependent on the specific regional Earth/ecliptic relationship. Food for thought for the southern astrologers!

POLARITY

In this category, signs are divided into positive (+) and negative (-). They follow each other in a rhythmic sequence, so that each second sign is positive or negative: Aries is positive, Taurus is negative, Gemini is positive, Cancer is negative, Leo is positive, and so on.

Positive signs are Aries, Gemini, Leo, Libra, Sagittarius and Aquarius.
Negative signs are Taurus, Cancer, Virgo, Scorpio, Capricorn and Pisces.

Those are two different modes of expressing primal energy or establishing a relationship with the outside world. The positive signs are extroverted - energy is directed outwards (active principle) while the negative signs are introverted – energy is directed inwards (passive principle). Ancient astrologers called positive signs **male** or **day** signs and the negative ones **female** or **night** signs. In this context, Chinese cosmology speaks of **yang** (male, expressive) and **yin** (female, impressive) energies.

Physics teaches the concepts of electric and magnetic polarity. Applied to the polarity of the astrological signs, we can speak of **electric** (positive) and **magnetic** (negative) signs. In the body, positive signs correspond to breathing-out while negative signs correspond to breathing-in.

Positive signs find it easier to emit energy than to receive it. They tend to be more active, outspoken, expressive, lively and quick while the **negative signs** find it easier to receive energy and are therefore more passive, thoughtful, re-active, quiet and reserved.

The concept of positivity and negativity should not be confused with the concepts of activity and inactivity, because negative signs can be very active, but they operate more on the principle of "reaction", so that they respond to external stimuli, while positive signs operate more on the principle of "action", so that they themselves generate those stimuli.

Significators (planets representing people and things in horary charts) in positive signs tend to have more of a "masculine" nature- they are active, lively, brave, direct, outspoken and the like, while significators in negative signs tend to be more "feminine" - they are re-active, calm, gentle, intuitive, shy, discreet and mysterious.

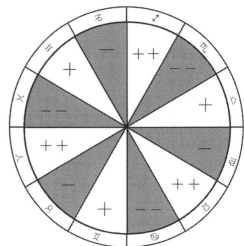

In the category of **elements,** fire signs are more positive (extroverted) than air signs, while water signs are more negative (introverted) than earth signs:

fire:	+ +
air:	+
earth:	–
water:	– –

ELEMENTS

The ancient philosophical concept of elements perceived the whole creation as consisting of the **four basic elements**: **fire, earth, air** and **water**. This classification corresponds to the modern scientific thesis of the four states of matter observable in everyday life: **plasma** (fire), **gas** (air), **solid** (earth) and **liquid** (water). The four elements include everything that complex organisms need for living: fire is the light and heat that keep us warm, air is the oxygen that we breathe, the earth is the food that we eat and water is just water or the liquids that we drink.

The theory of elements is an essential part of nearly all world cosmologies. The Chinese and Japanese knew five elements, those being earth, water, fire, wood (or tree) and metal. Classical Greek writers (Aristotle, for example) also spoke of the fifth element, called **ether**, which was supposed to be giving life to all the other elements and was therefore perceived as the "quintessence" of all creation. Medieval alchemists named it *aqua vitae* – "water of life" or "life force", which acted as a medium transmitting life from the heavens. Ether later disappeared from mainstream astrology.

The famous ancient Greek physician Hippocrates, known as the father of modern medicine, developed the theory of four internal "humors" which were directly related to the elements and were supposed to regulate our health. The first was **choleric (fire)**, the second **sanguine (air),** the third **melancholic (earth)** and the fourth **phlegmatic (water)**. Each humor was evaluated according to the degree of heat and humidity that it produced: choleric was hot and dry, sanguine warm and moist, melancholic cold and dry and phlegmatic cold and moist. Each element had its planetary ruler and its "seat" in the human body: choleric in the gallbladder, sanguine in the liver, melancholic in the spleen and phlegmatic in the lungs. Heart, however, was the seat of ether. The individual's contents of bodily humors determined his temperament, as well as his health. In a healthy organism, *aqua vitae* flowed freely through the body, while in the sick it was necessary to establish the lost balance by help of herbs which regulated the levels of individual physical "juices".

Choleric, sanguine, melancholic and phlegmatic psychological types are nowadays on the secondary schools curricula. Also well known is the thesis of the famous Swiss psychologist of the modern era, Carl Jung, who distinguished between four functions of consciousness by which men experience reality: thinking (air), sensation (earth), feeling (water) and intuition (fire).

In natal astrology, the predominance of this or that element in the birth chart (assessed by the occupancy of signs by planets and angles) offers important information regarding the temperament of the individual, which is crucial for the understanding our character, needs, health and so on.

In horary astrology, the understanding of the elements is important because it helps us assess the mode of action of people, ruled by planets which occupy certain elements, as well as to understand why the individual elements (and signs) are related to certain locations, characters and similar.

FIRE (Aries, Leo, Sagittarius)

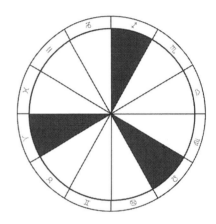

FIRE stands for the universal radiation of vital energy. It is the light and heat that animates all of creation. It aims upwards, into the heights and into the future. Symbolically, Aries is the first fire sign, simbolyzing the spark which ignites the fire, or the primal red flame that burns strongest. Leo is the second fire sign represented by the wide yellow flame that burns brightest and reaches a bit further into the space, whereas Sagittarius as the third fire sign is the high blue flame which shoots highests and lasts longest, although it is the least hot of all.

In the category of temperaments, fire is **choleric** (++), its nature is **hot and dry**.

EARTH (Taurus, Virgo, Capricorn)

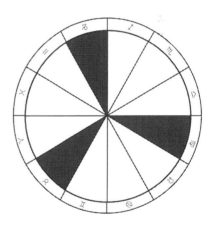

EARTH stands for everything concrete, tangible, solid, stable, realistic, practical, material and immediately useful. It aims towards the creation of the material world and maintenance of that which already exists. Symbolically, Taurus as the first earth sign stands for fertile soil, Virgo as the second earth sign is fine sand while Capricorn as the third earth sign is symbolized by stones and solid, immovable rocks.

In the category of temperaments, earth is **melancholic** (-), its nature is **cold and dry**.

AIR (Gemini, Libra, Aquarius)

AIR is the invisible which comes into contact with all that is visible. It constantly moves around, it is light and unrestrained. It stands for freedom, movement and communication. Philosophically, air is the world of archetypal ideas - cosmic energy, translated into patterns of thinking. Thus it represents the abstract side of life, encompassing our thoughts and minds. If, symbolically, air is an idea, then Gemini as the first air sign brings it to light, Libra as the second air sign considers its pros and cons, while Aquarius, third air sign it, passes it on to the crowds.

In the category of temperaments, air is **sanguine** (+), its nature is **warm and moist.**

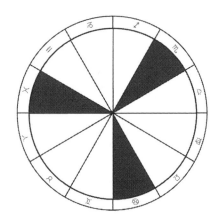

WATER (Cancer, Scorpio, Pisces)

Water stands for depth, attachment, emotion, instinct, intuition, psychic sensitivity and subconscious. It aims downwards, towards the past and to the primordial source. Cancer as the first water sign is symbolically the clear, bubbling creek, Scorpio as the second water sign is the powerful, rushing river while Pisces as the third water sign is the deep, vast sea.

In the category of temperaments, water stands for **phlegmatic** (--), its nature it is **cold and moist.**

As we'll see in the chapter ESSENTIAL DIGNITY, (see p. 89) the elements were once called **triplicities**. Each **triplicity** (fire, air, earth and water) had two or even three planetary rulers - one for the day charts (those which were cast for the day, with the Sun above the horizon) and another for the night charts (those which were cast for the night, with the Sun below the horizon), while each triplicity had a common third ruler. This classification is still in use today.

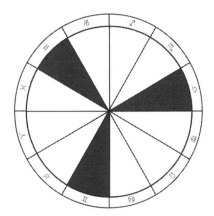

> **Fire sign**s are enthusiastic, dynamic and courageous. The key is WILL (intention).
> **Air signs** are intellectual, light-hearted and connective. The key is MIND (reflection).
> **Earth signs** are practical, stable and well-organized. The key is MATTER (realization).
> **Water signs** are sensitive, caring and protective. The key is FEELING (sensation).

QUADRUPLICITIES

Each of the three signs belonging to a particular element is manifested through a different *mode* (hence another name of this classification - **modalities**): the first is **cardinal**, the second **fixed** and the third **mutable**. Modes, like elements, also follow each other in a rhythmic sequence: every fourth sign is cardinal, fixed or mutable. The twelve primary energy patterns, called zodiacal signs, are therefore the combination of the four elements and three modes.

CARDINAL SIGNS (Aries, Cancer, Libra, Capricorn)

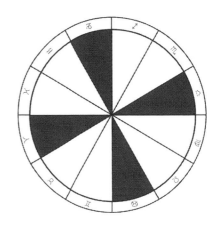

Those four signs look very different at first glance, as each belongs to a different element; besides, two are positive and two negative. But let's remember that those signs are the ones which introduce each of the four seasons, as they begin with both equinoxes and solsticies. They start a new cycle in nature which astrologically correlates with new beginnings. The energy of the cardinal signs can be compared to the centrifugal force which is moving away from the center. These are the most enterprising, courageous and ambitious signs. In horary charts, they can also show proximity and/or speed. **Significator** in a cardinal sign is ready to act!

FIXED SIGNS (Taurus, Leo, Scorpio, Aquarius)

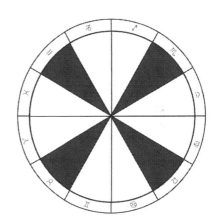

Fixed signs are those which follow the cardinal ones and are central in every season: Taurus follows Aries, Leo follows Cancer, Scorpio follows Libra and Aquarius follows Capricorn. Their mode of action can be described by centripetal (as opposed to centrifugal) force which causes movement toward the center. Generally speaking, fixed signs consolidate that which cardinal signs create. They tend to be very focused - whether on an idea, project, person or thing. **Significator** in a fixed sign shows a person who is strong, steady, hardworking, firm and loyal, but can also be unreasonably stubborn, rebellious or "immovable". Fixed signs represent the longest time. In case of a missing object, its significator in a fixed sign can show that the object is stuck somewhere and/or that it'll take long before it'll be found.

MUTABLE SIGNS (Gemini, Virgo, Sagittarius, Pisces)

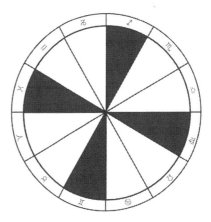

Mutable signs are those that follow fixed signs and complete seasons. Gemini follows Taurus, Virgo follows Leo, Sagittarius follows Scorpio and Pisces follows Aquarius. Their mode of action can be described by a spiral – a curve which revolves around a center so that it's constantly zooming in and out. The word "mutability" in this context means flexibility and the accompanying need for freedom and room for maneuver. **Significator** in a mutable sign can describe a person who is flexible, adaptable, considerate and accommodating, but also weak, indecisive, unstable, unreliable and the like. In horary astrology, these signs represent recurring situations, while from the timing perspective they show medium-length time units.

(See also OTHER TRADITIONAL SIGN CLASSIFICATIONS: DOUBLE-BODIED SIGNS on p. 40.)

OTHER TRADITIONAL SIGN CLASSIFICATIONS

Tradition divides the signs into some other subcategories. I will name just the most important ones, because the others don't have much user value:

- **animal**: Aries, Taurus, Leo, Capricorn, the second half of Sagittarius;
- **human**: Gemini, Virgo, Libra, Aquarius;
- **fertile**: Cancer, Scorpio, Pisces;
- **barren**: Gemini, Leo, Virgo;
- **double-bodied**: Gemini, Sagittarius, Pisces, Virgo.

Animal signs are those which bear the names of the the four-footed animals. They tend to be instinctive, passionate, rebellious, disobedient and "untameable". They are hot-headed and led by passion more than by reason, so they can be difficult to deal with. They also tend to be physically robust, strong and forceful. **Significator** in an animal sign can indicate a person who has such a character (or plays such a role in the horary chart), or a missing thing that is in the vicinity of an animal.

Human are all the three air signs plus Virgo. **Significator** in any of these signs can show a smart, reasonable, friendly and civilized person, or a missing object which is in the vicinity of people.

Fertile are all the three water signs. This classification plays an important role in questions related to pregnancy and fertility. They are also called "mute", as s**ignificator** in any of them can describe a person as taciturn, quiet and secretive. In other types of questions, fertile signs can show multitude.

Barren signs also play a role in questions related to pregnancy. Obviously they tend to show a lower fertility or infertility, or they can contribute to a negative result if the question relates to the possibility of pregnancy.

Double-bodied are those signs whose symbols contain two bodies: Gemini as a (human) couple, Pisces as a pair of fish that swim in the opposite directions, Sagittarius as a centaur (half man, half horse) while Virgo is often depicted as a young woman with wings (half woman, half angel). These signs represent duality, repetition, dispersion, disunity, versatility, complexity and the like. That all of them are also "mutable" (see QUADRUPLICITIES on p. 38), is no coincidece, of course, since they occupy those time segments (signs) when nature is completing one cycle and is preparing for the next, and therefore contain elements of both. The **significator** of a person in a double-bodied sign indicates that he/she could be faced with a "double" or even "triple" situation – that they have two or even three relationships, jobs, important plans and the like. A significator of a missing thing in a double-bodied sign can mean that the item is no longer in one piece or that the querent will not find it but will receive its duplicate (or a substitute). Ascendant in a double-bodied sign often shows that there are two (or more) people involved in the situation which is the subject matter of the question.

Experience has shown me that various forms of duality are most often expressed by Gemini and Pisces (that is, either by the ascendant or a significator in those signs). It is interesting that these are the only two signs (among four) which are depicted as being truly double because they are composed of two equal parts. Pisces shows even greater multiplicity. I wonder whether the reason for such a variety and flexibility, observable in this sign, is due to the combination of two factors, the first being the fact that the Moon moves very quickly in declination while traversing this sign, thereby covering a large space (up to about 5 degrees), and the second that it's at the same time a "fertile" water sign, also suggestive of "more numbers".

Zodiacal signs are also divided into those of short and long ascension. The first are Gemini, Taurus, Aries, Pisces, Aquarius and Capricorn while the second are Sagittarius, Scorpio, Libra, Virgo, Leo and Cancer. Due to the tilt of the ecliptic (23.5 degrees) which causes declination, the signs of short ascension need less time to rise above the horizon as the signs of long ascension. The average rising time of a sign is 2 hours, but at the geographical latitude of 45 degrees, Aries and Pisces, the central signs of short ascension, rise in only about 45 minutes, while Virgo and Libra, the central signs of long ascension, have a much longer rising period - about 2 hours and 45 minutes. All of this refers to the northern hemisphere, while it's the other way around in the southern hemisphere.

THE TWELVE SIGNS

lthough signs basically act as "adjectives", helping us to better understand **how** the planets act while occupying them, tradition also attributes them some very tangible things - parts of the body, locations, particular types of people, countries and the like. They're listed below, under individual headings. I have only omitted countries, as practice has not convinced me of their practical value. (I use the more modern locational astrology instead.)

Under **ESSENTIAL DIGNITY**, the stronger dignities (domicile and exaltation) are listed first, second come triplicities which are followed by weaker dignities. Under **ESSENTIAL DEBILITY** you will sometimes find a planet that also has a dignity in that sign. This should not confuse you; dignities and debilities sometimes indeed coincide, as we'll learn in chapter ESSENTIAL DIGNITY (see p. 89) where you'll learn how to precisely calculate the strengths and weaknesses (dignities and debilities) of all planets in all signs and parts of signs.

I want to stress that the descriptions in the sections **MODE OF ACTION** do not relate to the characters of people born under those signs, and not even to the characters of people which they rule in horary charts. Any person's significator tells us how he feels and acts **in a specific situation, described by the horary chart**; it does not say anything (or at least not much) about that person's general character, temperament and the like. You can have a very pessimistic and melancholic person, described by the horary ascendant in Sagittarius. Why? Well because his question was *Will my lottery ticket win tonight?*! Although mostly depressed, he happened to ask this particular question in a state of high-spirited optimism. When you'll learn to calculate the strengths and weaknesses of the planets (their essential and accidental dignity), you will also find that the level of the querents' significators' strength reflects the degree of their capacity to influence the development of a particular situation, or the degree of their power to succeed, reach their goal and similar.

PHYSICAL APPEARANCE should also be read with a grain of salt. The significator of the querent, the quesited or some other person in this or that sign is supposed to describe certain physical characteristics of those people, typical of the sign. This could have an outstanding practical value, of course - if only it was reliable. William Lilly assessed people's physical appearances by the signs holding their radix or derived ascendants, by the planets which occupied those signs and by the planets which ruled those signs or parts of the signs. So far so good, but such procedure is extremely questionable, if you ask me. The same querent will ask several questions but his significator will, obviously, always be placed somewhere else. In the course of our lives, our bodies and even personalities can change a bit, of course, but think that the very same person can ask two different questions within a few hours span, and during that time the ascendant and all the factors associated with it, will completely change. The logic linking the horary ascendant with one's physical appearance therefore simply doesn't hold water.

My own experience confirms this approach only to a certain extent - usually involving "third parties" or unknown people whom a horary chart indicates. By knowing the specifics of signs (and their ruling planets) holding their significators, those people can often be at least partially described.

Similarly with **PEOPLE**. As you know by now, people are ruled by planets, not signs, therefore their social functions (occupation, social status and the like) are usually described by their ruling planets, not by signs. (Fortunately, signs have similar characteristics to their ruling planets.) More importantly – if someone's significator is in (say) Gemini, he **can** indeed be a journalist, writer or a postman, but it's likelier that the sign describes him as being currently involved in a situation akin to the sign's meaning (he might be asking about an article, a sale or an email message, is in a dual situation, is of two minds, and the like). Only in certain cases can we use those associations literally – like in questions asking for someone's occupation.

Classification **IN THE BODY** is more useful because it can help identify a disease, for example, or the cause of the querent's or quesited's physical stress, and similar. **LOCATIONS** and **DIRECTIONS** obviously have a lot of practical value in questions related to missing persons, animals and things.

OBJECTS AND CONCEPTS and COLORS are helpful in a variety of questions. *What car should I buy, the black one or the red one?* We could also be deciding between a sports and and elegant type, a big and a small or between a new and an old one, and so on. The cusp of H3, indicating cars, or the car's significator in Aries, for example, would show a red sports car or a newer one while Capricorn would tend towards a dark (black) one, a traditional brand or an older car. I must add, though, that horary authors (old and modern) are not uniform as per colors, so don't be surprised if you find different color associations in other horary literature. Mine are based on Lilly and tradition.

ARIES ♈

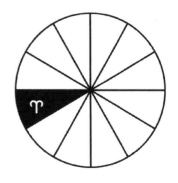

GENERAL PROPERTIES: spring, positive, masculine, fire, day, cardinal, choleric, animal sign
ESSENTIAL DIGNITY: Mars (domicile); Sun (exaltation and day triplicity); Jupiter (night triplicity)
ESSENTIAL DEBILITY: Venus (detriment); Saturn (fall)
IN THE BODY: head
MODE OF ACTION: quick, instincitve, go-ahead, direct, self-motivated, brave, daring, independent; restless, impatient, aggressive, violent
PHYSICAL APPEARANCE: slim, athletic build; medium height, broad shoulders, strong bones and limbs, elongated or triangular face, long neck, bold gaze, brisk walk
PEOPLE: travelers, explorers, fighters, pioneers, leaders, shepherds, hunters, soldiers, butchers, blacksmiths, ironworkers, railroad workers, criminals
LOCATIONS: uninhabited, secluded and unexplored areas; burnt-down places; hide-outs; drained, untreated, sandy or irrigated fields, as well as newly plowed earth, ready for sowing; roof, ceiling, garage, boiler room, workshop facilities; garages; animal pens and stables; tents and similar temporary accommodation; sports grounds
OBJECTS AND CONCEPTS: paneling, plaster and stucco; furnace, stoves, fireplaces, radiators; knives and other sharp objects; weapons; broken things; objects and tools, made of iron or iron compounds; sharp spices (pepper, mustard etc.)
COLOR: red
DIRECTION: E (east)

TAURUS ♉

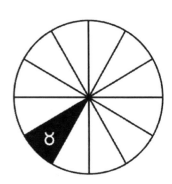

GENERAL PROPERTIES: spring, negative, feminine, earth, night, fixed, melancholic, animal sign
ESSENTIAL DIGNITY: Venus (domicile and day triplicity); Moon (exaltation and night triplicity)
ESSENTIAL DEBILITY: Mars (detriment)
IN THE BODY: neck, throat, lips, tongue; tasting, chewing
MODE OF ACTION: sensual, loving, patient, calm, persistent, relaxed, stable, quiet; slow, clumsy, stubborn, selfish, materialistic
PHYSICAL APPEARANCE: strong body; broad forehead; big face and eyes; broad, powerful shoulders; sensuous, fleshy lips; shovel-like hands
PEOPLE: farmers, ranchers, shepherds, bankers, money lenders, architects, singers, sculptors, fashion artists, landscape designers
LOCATIONS: rural areas; meadows, pastures, grain fields, gardens and other cultivated areas; shrubs; stables; cellars, granaries, warehouses; banks; ground floor, low areas (close to the ground)
OBJECTS AND CONCEPTS: money, cash, property; purses, briefcases, handbags, safes, decorative items, cosmetics; arts and crafts; anything safely stored
COLORS: sandy shades (brown, beige, terracota), green
DIRECTION: SSE (south by east)

GEMINI ♊

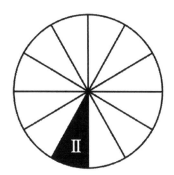

GENERAL PROPERTIES: spring, positive, masculine, air, day, mutable, sanguine, human, double-bodied sign

ESSENTIAL DIGNITY: Mercury (domicile and night triplicity), Saturn (day triplicity)

ESSENTIAL DEBILITY: Jupiter (detriment)

IN THE BODY: hands, fingers, the nervous system; breathing (inhaling)

MODE OF ACTION: eloquent, clever, imaginative, lively, skillful, flexible, curious, freedom-loving; childish, capricious, unstable, of two minds, superficial, nervous

PHYSICAL APPEARANCE: medium-tall to tall, slender, upright body; long arms; dark hair, sharp eyes, quick and restless walking, quick reflexes

PEOPLE: pupils, students, salesmen, traders, brokers, journalists, writers, translators, postmen, drivers; mime artists, comedians; thieves, crooks, hypocrites

LOCATIONS: hilly, barren, dry, windy landscape; places where people learn or play (schools, libraries, study rooms, playgrounds, casinos); corridors, windows, staircases, bookcases; in a house, the upper floors and the upper parts of furniture

OBJECTS AND CONCEPTS: messages, mails, letters, documents, papers, books, magazines; writing implements; various small items; phones, computers; bikes, cars and buses; keys; fun games

COLOR: pastel yellow and brighter colorful shades

DIRECTION: WWS (west by south)

CANCER ♋

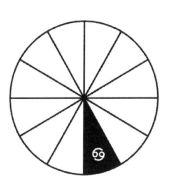

GENERAL PROPERTIES: summer, negative, feminine, water, night, cardinal, phlegmatic, fruitful, mute sign

ESSENTIAL DIGNITY: Moon (domicile), Jupiter (exaltation), Venus (day triplicity)

ESSENTIAL DEBILITY: Saturn (detriment), Mars (fall)

IN THE BODY: stomach, breasts, womb; feeding

MODE OF ACTION: instinctive, sensitive, emotional, sympathetic, careful, protective, patronizing, patriotic, dedicated; shy, introverted, anxious, hypersensitive

PHYSICAL APPEARANCE: small stature; the upper body stronger than the lower; round face; pale, whitish complexion; dark brown hair; small eyes

PEOPLE: mothers, babies, pregnant women; caretakers, cooks, waiters; school teachers, pediatricians, gynecologists, nurses, gardeners, housekeepers, landowners

LOCATIONS: springs, streams, thermal water locations; fertile soil close to water sources; areas, overgrown with reeds or rushes; restaurants and bars; vegetable gardens; in the house: kitchen, bathroom, dining room, laundry, plumbing

OBJECTS AND CONCEPTS: all kinds of food and beverages, especially water and milk; homes, apartments

COLOR: white, silver, green

DIRECTION: N (north)

LEO ♌

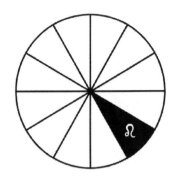

GENERAL PROPERTIES: summer, positive, masculine, fire, day, fixed, choleric, animal, barren sign

ESSENTIAL DIGNITY: Sun (domicile), Jupiter (night triplicity)

ESSENTIAL DEBILITY: Saturn (detriment)

IN THE BODY: heart, spine; blood circulation

MODE OF ACTION: proud, sincere, honest, affectionate, courageous, creative, generous, optimistic, self-confident; authoritative, domineering, selfish, arrogant, dogmatic, commanding, wasteful

PHYSICAL APPEARANCE: large, strong, sporty body; a relatively high stature; broad shoulders, narrow waist; bright, curly hair; healthy complexion; big round head; large, slightly bulging eyes

PEOPLE: kings, queens, princes, princesses; stage artists, producers, directors, managers, workers in the entertainment industry, hosts, restaurant owners; goldsmiths; treasurers, presidents; brokers; speculators

LOCATIONS: recreational areas such as parks, gyms and playgrounds; zoos; high, solitary, inaccessible, rocky areas, as well as forests and fisheries; theatrical and other stages; galleries, museums and other exhibition areas; palaces, castles, hotels; auction houses; boiler rooms, chimneys, fireplaces, radiators and stoves; children's room, living room, playroom

OBJECTS AND CONCEPTS: objects made of gold; jewelry, works of art; lights and heaters; toys, hobby equipment

COLORS: gold, bright yellow, orange

DIRECTION: EEN (east by north)

VIRGO ♍

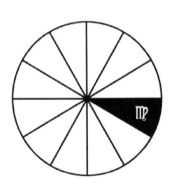

GENERAL PROPERTIES: summer, negative, feminine, earth, night, mutable, melancholic, barren, human sign

ESSENTIAL DIGNITY: Mercury (domicile and exaltation), Venus (day triplicity), Moon (night triplicity)

ESSENTIAL DEBILITY: Jupiter (detriment), Venus (fall)

IN THE BODY: small intestine, spleen, stomach; metabolism and digestion

MODE OF ACTION: thorough, thoughtful, analytical, careful, hard-working, modest, dutiful, helpful, hesitant, orderly, reliable; melancholic, pessimistic, anxious, fretful, critical

PHYSICAL APPEARANCE: slender and proportionate stature, slightly shorter limbs; darker hair and skin; thin lips, high forehead, high-pitched voice, quick and agile movements

PEOPLE: service workers; farmers; accountants, secretaries, office workers; officials; veterinarians, nutritionists, natural healers, pharmacists; nurses; sales people; technicians and technologists

LOCATIONS: gardens, fields, wheat fields; food shops, markets, fast-food corners; offices, bureaus; tool repair workshops; premises where food is stored (storage rooms, kitchen cabinets), utility rooms, drawers, shelves; kennels

OBJECTS AND CONCEPTS: various work tools, aids and precision instruments; small pets; medicinal herbs

COLOR: discreet "natural" shades; brown, gray, black

DIRECTION: SSW (south by west)

LIBRA ♎

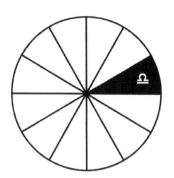

GENERAL PROPERTIES: autumnal, positive, masculine, air, day, cardinal, sanguine, human sign

ESSENTIAL DIGNITY: Venus (domicile), Saturn (exaltation and day triplicity), Mercury (night triplicity)

ESSENTIAL DEBILITY: Mars (detriment), Sun (fall)

IN THE BODY: lower back, kidneys, bladder

MODE OF ACTION: balanced, thoughtful, just, considerate, peaceful, sensible, tactical, social, elegant, engaging, aesthetic; indecisive, vain, lazy

PHYSICAL APPEARANCE: well-shaped, slender body; round or oval, handsome face; fair and curly hair; friendly smile

PEOPLE: artists, designers, decorators, fashion models, hairdressers, cosmeticians, make-up artists; lawyers; legal advisers, marriage counsellors

LOCATIONS: hilly areas with lots of fresh and clean air; forested, hilly or sandy landscape; beautiful town houses; luxury apartments; art galleries; beauty salons; flower gardens; bedrooms, porches, bright rooms on the upper floors; attics; top shelves of cabinets

OBJECTS AND CONCEPTS: jewelry, fashionable clothes; fragrances, cosmetics, decorative items; copper and copper products; partnership contracts, alliances, peace negotiations

COLORS: pastel shades of green, brown and blue

DIRECTION: W (west)

SCORPIO ♏

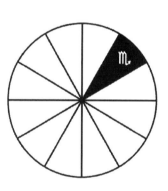

GENERAL PROPERTIES: autumnal, negative, feminine, water, night, fixed, phlegmatic, mute, fruitful, animal sign

ESSENTIAL DIGNITY: Mars (domicile and night triplicity), Venus (day triplicity), Moon (night triplicity)

ESSENTIAL DEBILITY: Venus (detriment), Moon (fall)

IN THE BODY: colon; reproductive organs; secretion

MODE OF ACTION: focused, intense, dedicated, loyal, magnetic, passionate, mysterious, persistent, calm; jealous, hateful, revengeful

PHYSICAL APPEARANCE: strong, muscular, hairy body; broad, angular face; dark complexion; dark, thick hair; short neck

PEOPLE: surgeons, detectives, insurance agents; gynecologists, therapists; butchers, soldiers; prostitutes; pimps, gangsters, mourners

LOCATIONS: marshy areas; flood regions; mines; places flooded with insects; rivers, as well as standing or stagnant water reservoirs (lakes and ponds); garbage dump (bins, garbage containers, dumpsters, skips); cemeteries, tombs; shafts, caves, abysses; toilets, drains, sewerage; secret passageways and other hidden places and hideouts

OBJECTS AND CONCEPTS: critical situations; operations, death; minerals and hidden treasures; weapons, martial arts; taxes; inheritance; debts; criminal gangs and organized crime; prostitution, sexual diseases

COLOR: black, dark red

DIRECTION: NNW (north by west)

SAGITTARIUS ♐

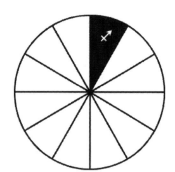

GENERAL PROPERTIES: autumnal, positive, masculine, fire, day, mutable, choleric, double-bodied, (partly) animal sign

ESSENTIAL DIGNITY: Jupiter (domicile), Sun (day triplicity)

ESSENTIAL DEBILITY: Mercury (detriment)

IN THE BODY: hips, thighs; breathing (exhaling)

MODE OF ACTION: honest, sincere, enthusiastic, optimistic, freedom-loving, eloquent, confident, dynamic, quick; reckless, impatient, insensitive, superficial

PHYSICAL APPEARANCE: large, proportionate, strong body; long, but full face; healthy complexion

PEOPLE: lawyers; scholars, philosophers; professors, teachers; diplomats; priests; global travelers; foreign correspondents; spokespeople, TV and radio announcers; publishers; researchers; foreign trade workers

LOCATIONS: hilly areas, usually forested; mountain tops; horse stables, riding trails; playgrounds, sports parks, hunting grounds; large, spacious buildings and richly decorated rooms; university buildings, churches, cathedrals; law firms; larger rooms on the upper floors and rooms with wooden floors or objects; ceilings and areas close to sources of heat; religious corners

THINGS AND CONCEPTS: objects made of zinc (brass); religious items; foreign countries, long journeys; foreign trade; horse riding, horse racing, hunting, safari, climbing, tennis, archery; printing, publications, mass media; higher education; law, ethics, morality

COLOR: blue, purple, sea green

DIRECTION: EES (east by south)

CAPRICORN ♑

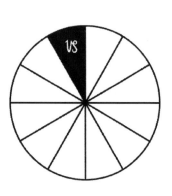

GENERAL PROPERTIES: winter, negative, feminine, earth, night, cardinal, melancholic, animal sign

ESSENTIAL DIGNITY: Saturn (domicile), Mars (exaltation), Venus (day triplicity), Moon (night triplicity)

ESSENTIAL DEBILITY: Moon (detriment), Jupiter (fall)

IN THE BODY: knees, bones, teeth, skin

MODE OF ACTION: realistic, pragmatic, disciplined, composed, practical, efficient, authoritarian, well-organized, ambitious, patient; pessimistic, reactionary, cold, selfish

PHYSICAL APPEARANCE: low stature; longish face with pronounced cheekbones; dark hair; narrow chest

PEOPLE: managers, directors, presidents, governors, judges, real estate brokers; police officers, customs officers, collectors; dermatologists, dentists, dental technicians, osteopaths, rheumatologists; construction workers, engineers, locksmiths, masons, railway workers; old and sick people

LOCATIONS: rocky mountains, secluded areas; mines and quarries; tanneries; borderlands; courts, police stations; offices; government and commercial buildings; cemeteries; storage places for agricultural tools; shoe and other leather products' stores and factories; abandoned and poorly maintained areas; shanty towns and poor districts; in a house: spaces close to the ground, basements and other dark places with low ceilings; lumber rooms and all the uncomfortable, dark or unfurnished rooms

OBJECTS AND CONCEPTS: stones and stone products; articles made of lead compounds; locks, grilles, chains; railway tracks; everything that restricts and cramps; the state apparatus, laws, legislation, official institutions; companies and business associations in general

COLOR: black, grey

DIRECTION: S (south)

AQUARIUS ≈

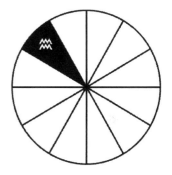

GENERAL PROPERTIES: winter, positive, masucline, day, air, fixed, sanguine, human sign

ESSENTIAL DIGNITY: Saturn (domicile and day triplicity), Mercury (night triplicity)

ESSENTIAL DEBILITY: Sun (detriment)

IN THE BODY: ankles; bloodstream

MODE OF ACTION: independent, impartial, inventive, original, eccentric, connecting, social, altruistic, reformatory; dogmatic, idiosyncratic, rebellious, inflexible

PHYSICAL APPEARANCE: strong and medium-sized, squarish body; long face; sandy hair; clean complexion

PEOPLE: elected representatives (delegates); astronomers; astronauts, astrologers, physicists; sociologists; technicians; political speakers; revolutionaries, eccentric reformers

LOCATIONS: hilly, windy landscapes; mountain peaks; classrooms, lecture rooms and halls; club rooms; modern accommodation; locations close to electrical, aeronautical, transport and communication devices (TVs, phones, computers); windows, balconies, verandas; fans; upper rooms and upper parts of rooms

OBJECTS AND CONCEPTS: electricity, electronics, computer science; winds, storms, lightning; aviation, aeronautics; bellfries; ballooning, paragliding, gliding, surfing, windsurfing; modern science; radioactivity; trade unions; human rights; street demonstrations; revolution, progress

COLOR: sky blue

DIRECTION: WWN (west by north)

PISCES ♓

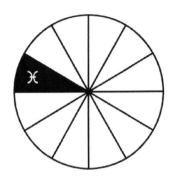

GENERAL PROPERTIES: winter, negative, feminine, water, night, mutable, phlegmatic, double-bodied, mute, fruitful sign

ESSENTIAL DIGNITY: Jupiter (domicile), Venus (exaltation and day triplicity), Mars (night triplicity)

ESSENTIAL DEBILITY: Mercury (detriment and fall)

IN THE BODY: feet; the lymphatic system; psyche

MODE OF ACTION: sensible, intuitive, gentle, trusting, responsive, flexible, compassionate, imaginative, inspiring, mysterious; weak, gullible, elusive, frail

PHYSICAL APPEARANCE: low stature; big face, pale complexion; tendency towards bloating and crooked posture

PEOPLE: fishermen, sailors, divers; refugees, migrants, immigrants, deportees; martyrs; monks and nuns; health professionals, nurses and other medical staff; psychoanalysts, psychologists, psychiatrists; chemists; drug addicts, alcoholics, neurotics; orphans, illegitimate children; psychics; fraudsters

LOCATIONS: sea; ponds; marshy, lowland areas; standing water, flooded areas; swimming pools, spa-s; hospitals, clinics, shelters, asylums, monasteries; prisons and other institutions of closed type; in a house: bathrooms and cold, damp rooms on the ground floor or basement

OBJECTS AND CONCEPTS: mist, fog; gas, alcoholic beverages; chemicals, medicines and other pharmaceutical products; cleaning liquids; chemistry, pharmacy; kitsch; discarded and decrepit objects; drugs; photography, film; ballet; occultism, spirituality; helplessness, weakness, uncertainty, disappointment; ghosts, phantoms; dreams, the subconscious; mysticism; martyrdom

COLOR: sea green

DIRECTION: NNW (north by west)

HOUSES IN HORARY ASTROLOGY

In horary astrology, as distinguished from natal astrology, houses are more important than signs. Horary astrology doesn't deal with our life potential, but with finding answers to specific questions from everyday life. It deals not with the querent himself as much as it deals with everything that encompasses the reality of his question. It copes with a variety of people, situations, objects etc. which have come to momentarily occupy the querent's mind and the chart in question. Whereas zodiacal signs mainly show particular "modes" or ways in which the planetary energies express themselves, houses stand for very concrete things – like a job, a partner, an apartment, an illness, a phone, an exam, travel, a pet and the like. Theoretically, every living and nonliving thing belongs to one of the twelve houses, but in practice, ascribing individual people and other issues to the "proper" houses can often be challenging. What's most important is to understand the essential nature or meaning of each house, as this greatly helps us find the proper houses for things and concepts about which we are in two minds.

It's true, on the other hand, that students sometimes overestimate the importance of houses. Some cases can be solved by an almost complete disregard for the houses! Such cases are not so numerous, true, but when in doubt, it's always good to depend on other means of finding an answer - like planetary dignities, aspects, natural rulerships and the like. Beginners especially are too fixed on finding the "right" house; they should know that this is one of the most challenging aspects of our discipline, and not let be put off if they find it too difficult.

As for the choice of house system, I have explained my reasons for using the Regiomontanus system in the chapter THE MAKING OF A HORARY CHART (see p. 27).

Know that the houses follow each other and that their meanings sometimes overlap. It's very important to see what the chart is trying to say to you. You can have, for example, a planet in a sign which is occupied by the cusp of the next house. It can be quite distanced from it, but just because it's in that same sign, it can have at least some bearing upon the next house. I say that such a planet is "in the sign of the next house" and I see this as an indication that the planet in that house influences the matters of the next house. Several examples in the Practice part of the book will teach you the validity and usefulness of this approach.

GENERAL PROPERTIES OF THE TWELVE HOUSES

hroughout the history of astrology, astrologers classified houses according to several criteria, so that their functions and meanings could be more easily understood. But although the houses are twelve, as many as there are signs, and although there are certain similarities between houses and signs, houses should not be confused with signs! Some astrologers argue that H1 can be equated with Aries, H2 with Taurus, H3 with Gemini and so on. In spite of the fact that some parallels that can be drawn between the two categories, their assimilation leads to misunderstandings and hence to erroneous interpretations – in horary as well as in natal astrology. Let's not forget that signs are a twelve-fold division of the ecliptic and as such refer to the yearly cycle, whereas houses are a twelve-fold division of the horizon and as such refer to the daily cycle. What's more, the cusps of the signs are always the same while the cusps of the houses change constantly, depending on the time and location of a chart. It follows then that we must learn to distinguish between the natures of signs and houses, and know how to skillfully combine both.

THE DAY AND NIGHT HALVES OF THE CHART

Horizontal axis (ascendant/descendent) divides the chart into upper and lower halves. The area **above the horizon (houses 7, 8, 9, 10, 11 and 12)** is **southern** and this is the **day** half of the chart, as the Sun is always above the horizon in this region. The area below the horizon **(houses 1, 2, 3, 4, 5 and 6)** is **northern** and this half of the chart is the **night** one – because, obviously, the Sun doesn't shine there.

Vertical axis (MC/IC) divides the chart into the left and right halves. The area to the left of the vertical axis **(houses 3, 2, 1, 12, 11 and 10)** is **eastern** while the area to the right of the vertical axis **(houses 4, 5, 6, 7, 8 and 9)** is **western**.

The four main dividing lines of the horizontal system of measurement show directions:

ascendant = east
descendant = west
MC = south
IC = north

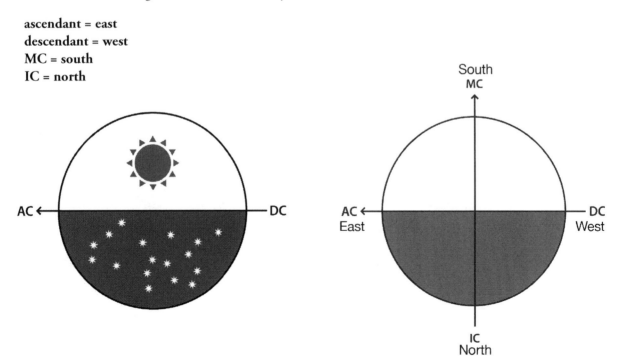

The distinction between the day and night halves of the chart was very important in the ancient astrological tradition. As we'll learn in the chapter PLANETARY SECT (see p. 73), astrologers of the past were well aware of the fact that the "heavenly lights" (the Sun and the Moon) and planets "acted" differently depending on their placement above or below the horizon. From this perspective, there's also a difference between the planets on the eastern and western sides of the chart, but that distribution played a less important role.

The preponderance of planets on one side of the horizontal axis (that is, below or above the horizon) is in itself a relatively unimportant horary consideration. What is important, however, is the placement (distribution) of the significators, and that of the Sun and the Moon. Tradition teaches that in charts asking about missing objects, people and animals, for example, both "lights" above the horizon increase the possibility of the find while their placement below the horizon reduces it. (We should be aware, though, that the Moon should be given major consideration in night charts and the Sun in day charts.)

When considering the eastern and western sides of the chart, we must be careful not to confuse this concept with the eastern and western placements of the planets **in relation to the Sun**. This is a different criterion, and it plays a much more important role in horary (and natal) astrology - except in cases when we're looking for locations and directions. I'm stressing this because students are often confused when it comes to the eastern and western planetary placements. This criterion, as said, usually refers to the planetary relationships to the Sun, not to their positions in the "mundane" zodiac.

QUADRANTS

By dividing the chart into the northern, southern, eastern and western halves, we get the four quadrants (quarter-sections of a circle).

The first quadrant extends from the ascendant to MC and includes houses 12, 11 and 10. This quadrant is eastern, of spring, masculine and sanguine. It corresponds to childhood.

The second quadrant extends from MC to the descendant and includes houses 9, 8 and 7. This quadrant is southern, of summer, feminine and choleric. It corresponds to youth.

The third quadrant extends from the descendant to IC and includes houses 6, 5 and 4. This is the western quadrant, of autumn, masculine and melancholic. It corresponds to mature years.

The fourth quadrant extends from IC to the ascendant and includes houses 3, 2 and 1. This quadrant is northerly, of winter, feminine and phlegmatic. It corresponds to old age.

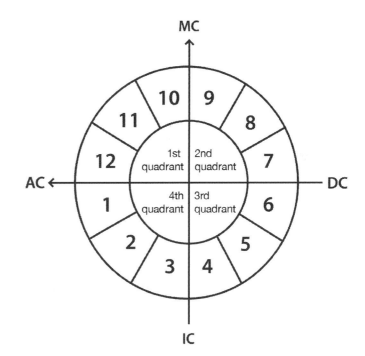

Comparing the quadrants with the seasonal quarters, we can see that their characteristics do not overlap. The *spring* (sanguine) signs are **Aries, Taurus and Gemini,** the *summer* (choleric) signs are **Cancer, Leo and Virgo,** the *autumnal* (melancholic) signs are **Libra, Scorpio and Sagittarius,** and the *winter* (phlegmatic) signs are **Capricorn, Aquarius and Pisces**.

The differences in meaning are logical, as the houses are based on the Earth's rotation around its axis, whereas the signs are conditioned by the rotation of the Earth around the Sun (or vice versa, by geocentric measure). We therefore have two different frames of reference, and although there're some parallels between them, the Sun's role and quality which is the basis for the spatial energy evaluation, substantially differs in both systems. **The daily (geocentric) rotation of the Sun actually produces exactly opposite qualities to the yearly one.** Let us see, why.

The first quadrant (houses 12, 11, and 10) is the one which has just risen above the horizon, so its energy is seen as "young", fresh, light, spontaneous and creative. At sunrise, the Sun is exactly on the ascendant and at noon exactly on the MC, so this quadrant can be seen to describe the nature of time between sunrise and noon. Then we are at our freshest, potentially most hardworking and creative, and because the Sun, when in this quadrant, is gaining momentum, this quadrant has always been seen as masculine. **The second quadrant** (houses 9, 8 and 7) corresponds to the afternoon. The Sun, when in this quarter, looses strength, but the accumulated light and energy are strong, so this is a time when life becomes more enjoyable and leisurely, with people more ready to connect with each other. As such, this quadrant is related to youth and summer, but is feminine (receptive) in nature. **The third quadrant** starts with the sunset and lies beneath the earth. It covers the period from sunset to midnight and corresponds to autumn and maturity. The melancholy, associated with it, relates to calmness, introversion and rest that we're seeking in those hours, but because the night is then gaining momentum, this quarter is (like the opposite one) masculine in nature. **The fourth quadrant** is the one which has waited the longest to be "born"; the Sun is exactly on the IC at midnight, so this quadrant encompasses the time between midnight and sunrise. It's the time of maximum calmness, associated with old age and winter, while (towards the end of this phase) it also represents the restored power of the body and spirit which are most strongly expressed in the first house - in the "self", the point of awakening and self-awareness.

Although quadrants are deeply meaningful and offer a rich interpretive potential, they have through the ages become increasingly less important, giving way to other interpretive schemes. The reasons for this are manifold. One is undoubtedly that each quadrant is composed of three houses which have entirely different meanings, and it's easier to categorize the subject matters of questions according to the houses than to the quadrants. Moreover, the natures of some houses do not directly coincide with the general natures of the quadrants in which they are situated. Houses require a complex understanding, as specific meanings are attributed to them on the basis of several different criteria.

ANGULAR, SUCCEDENT AND CADENT HOUSES

Each quadrant contains three houses. The first house of each quadrant is called **angular** because it's receiving and "angle" (ascendant, descendant, MC or IC) then coming into existence. They are followed by the **succedent** houses, and the last come the **cadent** (from lat. *cadens* – falling) which are so called because they fall back from the angles.

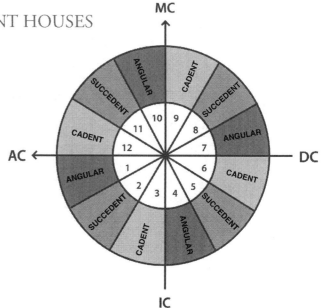

Angular houses: 1, 4, 7, 10
Succedent houses: 2, 5, 8, 11
Cadent houses: 3, 6, 9, 12

Planets are most strongly expressed in angular houses, moderately strongly in succedent houses and weakly in cadent houses. The level of their strength diminishes by their distance from the departing angles, and increases by their closeness to the approaching angles.

In order to understand the various levels of planetary "potency" in relation to the angles, we must understand that angles are the four fundamental astronomical points, determined by the interaction of the Earth and the ecliptic. As such, they are strong energy points acting as some kind of "antennas" through which the cosmic energy channels onto the Earth. Planets which are at the same (or nearly the same) degree as any of these points, are expressed much more powerfully than those in other areas, and their effect is felt more strongly in the mundane sphere. The further they are from the angles, the lesser their influence. Astrologers usually allow for their maximum intensity up to around 5 degrees on each side of an angle (knowing that the exact degree of the angle is by far the most potent), but the intensity is reduced much more gradually in the direction in which the heavens move. (In the geocentric system of measurements, of course, with an observer on Earth perceiving the sky as moving around him, not vice versa.). As the Earth rotates to the west, the sky slips backwards, with the angular points moving forward. Planets which are placed in angular houses are seen to be moving towards those angular points and are therefore more powerful than those in cadent houses which are moving away from them.

I have noticed that astrologers generally pay too little attention to the angles and are not aware of their extreme importance - in horary as well as in other fields of astrology. In practice, proper understanding of the angular, succedent and cadent houses helps us in a variety of ways.

Significators in angular houses are strong; they express themselves openly and easily and show the quickest action and results. When significators stand for people, they are shown to be powerful, influential, they have a decisive say in a matter inquired after, or they can easily reach the goal to which they aspire. (But know that this is not the only criterion!) In timing, the angular houses suggest the shortest time while location-wise, they show closeness and the minimum distance (to the object of the search). If the significator is a benefic and/or an essentially dignified planet, its inherent quality is expressed to the best interests of the querent (or the subject matter of the question), but if it is a malefic and/or an essentially weak planet, its strength works accordingly - as a powerful negative energy that can bring loss or defeat to the querent or the quesited. (More on this in chapter PLANETS IN HORARY ASTROLOGY on p. 70) **The strongest angular houses are H1 and H10.**

Significators in succedent houses are less powerful. Everything mentioned above is a bit impaired here. From the timing perspective, the "completion of the matter" (the outcome or the attainment of an objective) tends to be achieved a little later while a lost item can be more distant. On the other hand, due to their central position in a quadrant, these houses show reliability and endurance, so the significators in them are not unwelcome. This is particularly true of H11 and H5 which are the most "fortunate" of the twelve houses while H8 belongs to the most unfortunate ones, so perseverance here can be expressed as a deep, continuous crisis, or even as a fatal loss.

The succedent houses also show possessions and other material resources of people (or institutions) ruled by the angular houses which precede them.

Significators in cadent houses have the least power to openly and visibly express themselves and can be even helpless, as these are the "falling" houses - the areas of greatest distance from the approaching angles. They can show people who are not in a position to achieve their goals. They might need to wait (too) long for that to happen, or the goal can be denied to them. If the significator of a lost (missing) person or thing is in a cadent house, this may indicate that the quesited is far away, maybe even lost.

Planets in cadent houses are not necessarily undesirable - much depends on the content of the question. Houses H12 and H6 are the weakest of all, as they follow the horizontal axis which is considered the stronger of the two.

THE HOUSES AS TEMPLES OF THE PLANETS

The old astrologers attributed to each of the seven visible heavenly bodies (the Sun, the Moon, Mercury, Venus, Mars, Jupiter and Saturn) their natural "homes" - astrological houses which were due to their natural characteristics the most akin to the individual planetary natures. Marcus Manilius (1st cent. AD), the famous ancient Roman poet and astrologer, author of **Astronomica**, called them **temples**. Planets are supposed to show their best qualities when in their own temples; they "enjoy" themselves there, they said, and therefore old authors also called them "planetary joys".

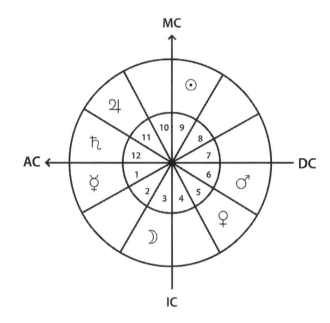

The temples are:

The Sun: H9
The Moon: H3
Mercury: H1
Venus: H5
Mars: H6
Jupiter: H11
Saturn: H12

These definitions should not be confused with the house **rulerships** which are much more useful and effective in practice! (Each house is ruled by the planet which rules the sign on its cusp.) While we should be aware that planets have their natural "homes" in certain houses, we must know that through the history of the development of horary (and other) astrology, a considerably more vital role has been attributed to the rulership of the planets over signs as to their "joys" in houses. In other words, signs have rulers which are assumed by the houses projected onto them, while the planetary "temples" have preserved only a symbolical, in practical astrology a much less significant role.

Planetary temples, however, help us better understand the natures of the houses. **Mercury**'s temple is H1, and this house represents the consciousness, thoughts, the head and bodily communication with the ouside world. **The Sun**'s temple is H9 which in the traditional astrology is related to "God" or the divine consciousness which comes to the Earth from afar. (Whence the traditional association of this house with divination which stands for the revelation of God's plans.) There is no coincidence, of course, that H9 is linked to the ascendant and H1 by a trigonal aspect which reflects coherence, harmony and creativity! **The Moon** belongs to H3 which is opposite to that of the Sun and stands for movement and communication - consistent with the nature of the Moon, by far the fastest celestial body. **Venus** delights in H5, which is (as H9) also in trine with H1 and as such represents all the basic joys of human race - love, sexuality (and its product - children), entertainment, hobbies, dance, sports and all other things which give us pleasure. H11, on the other side of the circle, is the temple of **Jupiter**. H11 is the house of early morning, bringing all the joys of a young, promising day. It is associated with heart desires and their fulfillment, and it seems quite logical that this is the joy of Jupiter, the biggest and most benevolent among the planets. (Let us add that Manilius gave this house to Venus, but later astrologers digressed.) The remote, cold **Saturn** delights in the "hidden" H12. You may think that it would be more appropriate if it had its temple in any of the nocturnal houses, but tradition places it among the diurnal planets, so it reigns here, in the section of the earliest part of the daily light, like a silent, invisible ruler, controlling everything that is about to come. Saturn is the traditional "lord of time", so in this house it symbolically stands for "karma" and "destiny". But Saturn is also related to H4 (the end, the grave); Manilius attributed it to this temple – which is, "accidentally", in trine from it. **Mars** reigns in H6 which is the house of physical toil, servants, soldiers, effort, war, disease and small animals. And where would this hot, dry and destructive planet feel better? In the ancient Anglo-Saxon astrological tradition Mars stood for the entire animal world.

FORTUNATE AND UNFORTUNATE HOUSES

Traditional astrology is very clear and straightforward with regard to the benevolence of the houses: some houses are very fortunate, the others a bit less so, some are neutral and some are unfortunate. This classification helps us define the circumstances which affect the querent and the quesited, and are directly related to the planetary temples, presented in the previous section. Both benefics "delight" in the two of the most fortunate houses while the malefic have their joys in the two of the most unfortunate ones.

It is desirable that significators in a horary chart asking for the chances of success or the attainment of an objective, are placed in fortunate houses, as these indicate good, encouraging and helpful (fortunate) circumstances while significators in unfortunate houses show the opposite.

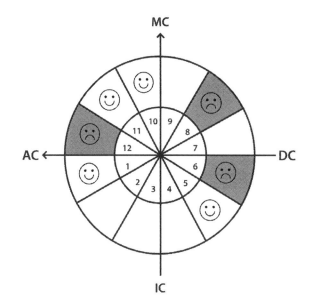

Most fortunate houses: 11, 5, 10, 1
Moderately fortunate houses: 9, 3
Neutral houses: 4, 7, 2
Unfortunate houses: 12, 6, 8

ASCENDANT AND THE TWELVE HOUSES

 n this chapter, you will find all the essential meanings of the ascendant and the twelve houses, together with the general guidelines for placing the "quesited" (subject matter) in the proper house/s. In my accompanying book *Horary Astrology: Practice,* general theory is supported by further rules pertaining to specific horary topics. The meanings of the houses given below should therefore serve only as basic guidelines.

As for the colors associated with each house, we should be careful: they are not unquestionable facts but only tendencies. Because certain colors are also associated with planets and signs, there's a complexity resulting in almost impossible choices in practice. Fortunately, we don't need colors that often. They can help us ascertain the whereabouts of a missing thing, or serve as a confirmation of known facts – when looking for the proofs of the "radicality" of a chart, for example. Personally, I rarely make use of colors in horary charts, mainly for the reasons already stated (high level of risk due to the complexity of criteria), as well as because opinions vary considerably as per which colors stand for which sign, planet or house.

Similarly, I rarely make use of the associations of body parts with individual houses, because my practice has not confirmed their validity. I encourage the reader to conduct further research, of course, but I have found that physical attributes of zodiacal signs are much more reliable.

The information on the directions, associated with individual houses, is much more useful, especially when searching for missing things, people and animals.

THE FIRST HOUSE (H1)

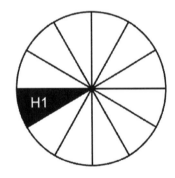

H1 starts with the the *ascendant* (AC, east). **The ascendant** is **the most important point** in any horary chart and - together with its ruler and eventual planets in H1 - it usually **"rules" (represents) the person asking the question.** We call this person **the querent**. If an astrologer asks the question himself, he himself is the querent, shown by H1, but if it's somebody else that asks, the ascendant represents them.

If the querent asks about a personal matter, the ascendant, together with its dispositor (the ruler of the sign in which it is located, or the almuten of its degree) **always** shows him in his current situation, describing the issues surrounding and conditioning his question, and often also points to the circumstances related to the subject matter of his question. In questions relating to health, H1 describes his current vitality.

Some astrologers believe that the ascendant describes the querent's appearance or physical body. William Lilly claimed that on the basis of the ascending degree he even identified the querent's birthmarks or scars. But such analysis demands extreme caution. As mentioned elsewhere, one and the same querent can ask countless questions, with the ascendant continuously changing signs and degrees, but his physical body will always be the same – except for minor changes, such as weight loss or gain, for example. It's true that the ascendant in natal charts always describes physical appearance, body and temperament of the native, but horary charts are different; here - in my belief and experience - the ascendant describes only the querent's "energy" which he carries at the time of the question, not his actual body and physical appearance.

The ascending sign often reflects the nature of the question. Charts relating to love, for example, often have ascendant in Libra, the sign of romantic love and relationships; questions about work and career are common when Capricorn rises; travel "loves" Sagittarius; trading Gemini; cars, sports and technical issues Aries; crisis situations Scorpio; property and real-estate affairs Cancer and Capricorn; financial issues Taurus; creative projects Leo; and so on.

The ascendant does NOT represent the querent when his question is distinctly impersonal, like when he asks of people, things and situations which don't directly involve him. *Who's going to win the next election?* Nothing to do with you - unless you ask as a presidential candidate, of course!

In charts related to mundane affairs (political, national, weather and similar questions), the ascendant with H1 rules the **nation** (people). *Is life going to change for us Slovenians under the new government?* As a nation, we're all in H1!

It's the same if the question refers to two or more people who form a **unity** (like a married couple, passengers in a vehicle, pupils in a class, members of a political party and similar). *Are I and my husband taking that trip?* H1 in this case stands for the querent AND her husband, not just for herself. In her consciousness, they form a whole, because the question assumes that they travel both - or none of them. However, if she asks *Am I going on this trip alone or will my husband accompany me?*, that's a different situation; in this case, she is ruled by H1 and her husband by H7. Nevertheless, in the first of the two cases, we can use H7 as the querent's partner, but only if we're looking for additional information related exclusively to the situation of the partner, which could affect the outcome of the case. Let's say that we received a negative answer and the "frustrator" (the planet preventing the positive outcome) was the H7 ruler; we can safely conclude that they're not taking the trip because the husband will not want or not be able to go. Additional insight could reveal that the frustrating planet was in aspect with the H12 (the derived H6) ruler, so the reason might be his sudden disease; if it was linked to the H4 (the derived H10) ruler, his career obligations might prevent him from going, and so on. (In case you don't understand the recent statements, see DERIVED HOUSES on p. 67)

The ascendant can also rule **the quesited, when they're unrelated to us**. Such people can sometimes – but rarely - be also ruled by the descendant. If we don't know them personally or if we feel at least a little sympathy to them or if we have no reason to treat them as our opponents – in all such cases, those people are ruled by the ascendant and H1. Good examples are horary charts of missing people whom we don't know personally and we learn of their disappearance in media.

The planet ruling the ascendant is called the **querent's** (or **quesited's** – in cases of impersonal questions) **significator** or **ruler** and is of key importance in delineation. (As we'll learn later, any zodiacal degree can have more rulers, therefore the querent – or the quesited – can sometimes be ruled by two or even three planets). When the querent asks about himself, his ruler's placement in a particular house often shows the object of his interest. (If it's H5, for example, this can be a child or pregnancy, if H10, it's a job or career question, if H9, it can be related to his studies or travels, and similar.)

If there is a planet in H1, this planet is the querent's **cosignificator** – an additional, but less important significator. If there are more planets in H1, theoretically they can all play the role of cosignificators, but in practice it's much better to rely on the planet that is closest to the ascendant. This can also be a planet which is conjunct the ascendant from H12 – if within a 5 degree orb, and especially if in the same sign as the ascendant. Although one planet can rule several people and things in any horary question, planets in H1 are usually not cosignificators of the querent if they play the role of the quesited's rulers.

But let us get back to the ascendant as such. I have noticed that in practice, astrologers usually give the ruler of the ascendant a crucially important role, but the ascendant itself (that is, the degree where it is located) is often ignored. The reason probably lies in the fact that planets seem more tangible and concrete; not only do they have bodies, but they each have their innate qualities and natures whereas a point is just a point and its nature can be judged only according to the sign where it is located. **But from the energy point of view the ascendant is very important; it represents the "moment of birth", therefore its (eventual) aspects with planets should always be carefully analysed. These aspects can significantly affect the outcome!**

At the very beginning of the development of horary astrology, the ascendant represented just nearly everything, pertaining to the question. Houses were developed much later. The then astrologers answered questions only by the ascendant and the planet ruling it. This fact alone should tell us the ascendant with H1 is of crucial importance in virtually every horary chart. When asking about other people's affairs, astrologers often err by relying too heavily on the derived houses, with the ascendant being neglected or even ignored, because they think that once they have the derived chart, the ascendant is no longer important. Wrong! All the angles should be considered as vital, because they are the astronomical pivots, "drawing" the energy from space. Don't underestimate them! There's no such concept as "derived angles". They don't exist.

Students often ask: if the ascendant is **in late degrees** (up to the last three), is it still regarded as being in that sign, or should we consider it as being in the next sign – considering that the largest part of H1 in such cases is in the next sign? The answer is YES, go by that sign and the ruling planet. Still, we must be aware that such an ascendant usually indicates some kind of transition, change, adjustment. The situation is changing, the querent will soon turn his attention elsewhere and his significator will soon be another planet – but as for the time being, that's what it is! Such placement can sometimes indicate that the querent is losing hope or despairing over his situation. Much depends on the context of the question. If the querent asks about the completion of something, this may indicate that yes, the matter will soon be over. Is he going to travel? Yes. Look also at the nature of the signs involved. *In one recent case, a student asked if she'd get another opportunity to write an exam, as due to weather conditions she couldn't leave the house to take it in the regular term. The ascendant was in the last degree of Taurus, changing to Gemini. The answer was yes, she received the next term the next day – Gemini is the sign of learning, papers, school. Thus, the chart vividly described the imminent change of conditions, acting in her favor.* Let the chart guide you, always!

The ascendant **in early degrees** (0, 1, 2) usually indicates the opposite: the querent is at the beginning of something, the question relates to some novelty, or a long time will pass before he reaches his goal.

Old astrologers used to reject charts with the ascendant in the first or the last three degrees of signs. They said that such charts were "unfit to be judged". (See STRICTURES AND CAUTIONS, on p. 111.) Part of the reason for doing so is probably attributable to the fact that in the past, the exact time was not so self-evident as it is today. Only a few centuries ago, time was only displayed on church towers' clocks, and astrologers could probably never be quite sure whether the fast-moving points really were where they thought them to be. An error was particularly easily made when the ascendant was passing through the signs of quick ascension (from Sagittarius to Cancer) which rise faster than the others.

For many astrologers who abide by tradition, however, the dilemma still exists. You will hear them saying that the ascendant in the last degrees of a sign indicates that it is "too late for the question", or, if it's in the first degrees, that the question is "premature". I never reject such charts! I'm convinced that any chart holds a clue to that dilemma – just look at it and think WHY would it be "too late" or "too early"? It might be so, true, but my point is that such ascendant's placement should not deter us from trying to find a meaningful answer in the chart. As said, those degrees usually show some kind of transition, and this information by itself should serve us to find the answer we're seeking.

OLD NAMES: Vita (life, *Firmicus Maternus*), Stilbon (Greek name for Mercury which "presides" in H1, *Marcus Manilius*); Horoscope (hour watcher, *Ptolemy* and other Greek astrologers).

DIRECTION: E (east)

BODY PARTS: head

COLORS: white, grey

THE SECOND HOUSE (H2)

H2 stands for the preservation and survival of the body, represented by H1. It is succedent and neutral (as per its benevolence), although some authors consider it moderately fortunate.

As the house of substance, it rules the querent's personal belongings, earnings, movable assets, profit (or loss, depending on the ruler's condition in the chart); all products pertaining to daily care and sustenance (food, clothing, makeup etc.); lost, misplaced or stolen articles (other than those which due to their specific functions belong to other houses); all such goods that he wants or intends to buy (in questions relating to shopping and purchases); money lent; in legal disputes witnesses who support the querent.

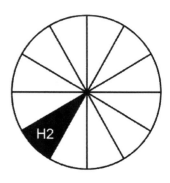

OLD NAMES: Porta Inferna (Gate of Hell, *Firmicus;* Gate of Hades, *Ptolemy*). Other ancient astrologers gave it similarly scary names (Portal of Pluto, Abode of Typhon). At first sight, such descriptions don't agree with the contents of the house (food, possessions, money), but all these things are necessary for the survival of the body, therefore lack of good energy in H2 means scarcity of resources which can lead to the matters of the opposite house - H8 of crisis and death.

DIRECTION: ENE (east-northeast)
BODY PARTS: throat and neck
COLOR: green

THE THIRD HOUSE (H3)

H3 stands for our thinking, learning and direct (personal) communicating, and for the people and things, associated with it. It is cadent and moderately fortunate, the temple (joy) of the Moon.

It rules the querent's siblings (brothers, sisters and cousins); phone calls, messages, articles and other pieces of writing that he authors; neighbors, neighborhood; short trips, courses, seminars, interviews; transportation means (cars, bicycles, motorcycles and similar). This house also generally rules all kinds of news, messages, letters, documents, magazines, newspapers and other periodicals; phones, fax machines, computers and other means of communication; primary schools; transportation means; postal services.

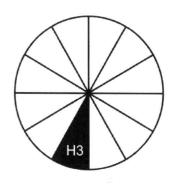

OLD NAMES: Dea (Goddess, *Manilius*), Fratres (brothers, *Firmicus*)
DIRECTION: NNE (north-northeast)
BODY PARTS: shoulders, arms, hands, fingers
COLORS: red, yellow, orange, light brown

THE FOURTH HOUSE (H4)

H4 begins with IC (*Imum Coeli*, the "base of heaven"). It follows H3 and is one of the four cardinal (initial, basic) houses. It stands for our foundations (roots, ancestry, home, family) and for our ends (burial, grave). It's like the deepest source from where it all comes and to where it all returns.

It rules the querent's real estate, houses, apartments, gardens, fields, family legacy (immovable only), and father. It also rules all kinds of real estate that he's renting or buying (offices and other workplaces). From the mundane perspective, it rules all buildings, cities, one's natal country, regions and provinces; also fields, gardens, orchards, construction lots, mines, graves, cemeteries. In a house, it relates particularly to the central part (the living room, for example). In charts of missing articles, if they've been mislaid in a house, H4 helps describe the location and surroundings of their whereabouts.

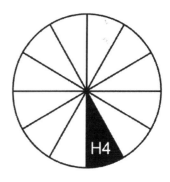

As this is the lowest angular house, starting with the degree of the anticulmination of the Sun, it is also called "terminal" (final) and is therefore supposed to indicate the "end of the matter" in all questions. In practice, this principle is not particularly useful, as the outcome of any question is much more clearly indicated by other factors, but it is true that if this house is strongly emphasized in a chart, this may indicate that the matter is coming to an end or that it's in the final stage of a process.

OLD NAMES: Daemonium (evil spirit, *Ptolemy*); Parentes (parents, *Firmicus*)
DIRECTION: N (north)
BODY PARTS: breasts, lungs
COLOR: red

THE FIFTH HOUSE (H5)

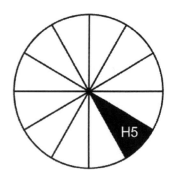

H5 stands for our personal creativity and all the things that give us pleasure and make us happy. It is cadent and very fortunate, the joy of Venus.

It rules the querent's children, pregnancy, luck, speculation, gambling, shares (as a short-term or speculative form of investment), entertainment, parties, hobbies, creative undertakings and other free-time activities (sports, dancing, mountaineering and similar), and holidays. It generally rules all kinds of cultural and artistic events (concerts, festivals and such), gambling, stock exchange, bets, gifts, pubs, restaurants, dance and sports halls, discotheques, cinemas, theaters and other entertainment centers, kindergartens; sports, athletes and sporting events; holiday arrangements. In mundane charts, it rules ambassadors.

OLD NAMES: Bona Fortuna (good fortune, *Firmicus*), Filii (children, *Firmicus*);
DIRECTION: NNW (north-northwest)
BODY PARTS: upper back, stomach, belly, heart, liver, hips
COLORS: black, white, beige, honey

THE SIXTH HOUSE (H6)

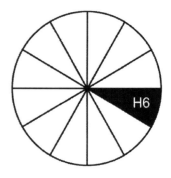

H6 is the last of the six houses of the lower (night) half of the chart. It corresponds to the time immediately following sunset, bringing the dark, and stands for the necessity of "cleaning up" after ourselves and of clean(s)ing our bodies so as to prepare them for the long night which follows the evening. It stands for daily toil, routine work and services, and for weakness of the body (disease). It is cadent and the traditional "joy" of Mars.

It rules the querent's illnesses, employees, "servants" (various kinds of services and service workers he employs, like plumbers, carpenters, masons, nannies, nurses, au-pairs, hairdressers, agents, mediators and the like), coworkers, work surroundings, various tools and aids (machines, instruments and other tools he uses for work, except for means of communication which belong to H3), pets, tenants and the father's brothers and sisters (aunts and uncles) . In mundane charts, it rules the social and public services (including the army and the police), farmers and working class.

OLD NAMES: Laboris (hard work, toil, *Manilius*); also Mala Fortuna (bad luck)
DIRECTION: WNW (west-northwest)
BODY PARTS: the lower part of the stomach, intestines
COLOR: black

THE SEVENTH HOUSE (H7)

H7 begins with the west angle, descendant (DC, the west point). This house lies opposite of H1 which it complements and at the same time opposes. It basically stands for people who complete us (our partners) or oppose us (enemies, competitors). As it directly faces H1 which shows our immediate environment, it also describes the places we are visiting or moving to.

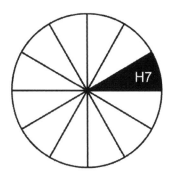

In horary charts, it stands for the querent's love or business partner/s (either current, former or potential), husband or wife, marriage, separation, contract; buyer of his movable or immovable property; any person with whom he negotiates something or deals with him face-to-face or in regard to his personal affairs; doctor, therapist, counselor, astrologer; "open enemy", opponent, rival, competitor, thief; relocation; travel destination. This house also generally rules fugitives and any known or unknown persons who don't belong to any other house (except missing people). In legal disputes charts, it shows the opposing party (prosecutor or the accused).

For Manilius, this was the "house of death", as the Sun (life force, vitality) sets here, but ever since Ptolemy, death belongs to H8.

In horary astrology, H7 is very important also because it stands for the querent's astrologer – except, of course, when the querent is his own astrologer, when he's ruled by H1. H7 can show whether the astrologer would be able to help the querent by giving a correct and helpful answer.

OLD NAMES: Occident (west, *Ptolemy*)
DIRECTION: W (west)
BODY PARTS: kidneys, small intestine, bladder, lower back
COLOR: black

THE EIGHT HOUSE (H8)

H8 lies across H2. It is succedent and very unfortunate. While H2 shows acquisition, H8 shows loss. In this house, our material possessions (H2) are directly challenged and trasformed. As the second of the seventh it also stands for our partners' resources and possessions, as well as for finances and other material goods which are jointly owned or inherited.

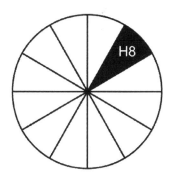

It rules crises, operations, loss, death; the querent's will and inheritance; his insurance, taxes, credit, debt, banks and bank affairs. This house also generally stands for emotional crisis and fears, while in legal disputes it represents the witnesses who assist the opponent.

OLD NAMES: Mors (death, *Firmicus*)
DIRECTION: WSW (west-southwest)
BODY PARTS: buttocks, groin, colon, genitals
COLORS: black and very dark colors

THE NINTH HOUSE (H9)

H9 opposes H3 and basically rules distance: foreign lands, travel abroad and international affairs, as well as spiritual and mental expansion. It also rules international communication. It is cadent and moderately fortunate, the traditional "temple of God" (the Sun).

In horary charts, it rules the querent's foreign affairs, travel, college, studies, legal affairs, lawyers, visions and prophetic dreams. It generally also stands for religion, divination, research, print, books (especially those with philosophical, religious, divinatory or mystical contents). In mundane charts, it represents the ministries, rites, clergy, religious groups (sects), travelers, foreigners, publishers, professors, lawyers and researchers.

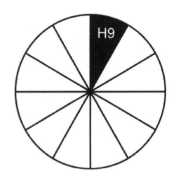

OLD NAMES: Deus (God, *Manilius*); Peregrinatio (travel, *Firmicus*)
DIRECTION: SSW (south-southwest)
BODY PARTS: hips and thighs
COLORS: green, white

THE TENTH HOUSE (H10)

H10 begins with the southern angle, the Midheaven (MC, Medium Coeli, the middle of the sky) and is generally considered to be the second strongest and vitally important house in any chart. Planets culminate in it, so they represent people who have power, authority and fame. Our own "fame" is also there, but also our "destiny" –in a very general sense.

In horary charts, H10 rules the querent's job, career, profession, company, business projects; status, honor, reputation; mother; employer, superior and other authorities. It stands for presidents and other authority figures, and for companies. In charts related to commerce and real estate, it shows the sales price of the article (property); in lawsuits, the judge; in mundane charts, the government, the king (queen), the Prime Minister, civil service and the supreme court - in short, all the institutions with the role of authority and leadership.

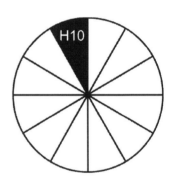

OLD NAMES: Fortuna (fortune, *Manilius*), Honores (honor, *Firmicus*)
DIRECTION: S (south)
BODY PART: knees
COLORS: red, white

THE ELEVENTH HOUSE (H11)

H11 is the most fortunate of all houses. This is the "temple" of Jupiter, the largest and the most benevolent among the planets. Symbolically it stands for the attainment of our heart's desires, and astrologers of old called it "the house of the good spirit". It is succedent and masculine.

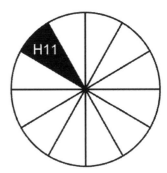

In horary charts, it shows the querent's friends, patrons, benefactors; organizations, associations, groups, clubs, political parties; heart desires; adopted children. In mundane charts this house stands for the parliament while in charts related to legal disputes, jury.

OLD NAMES: Fortuna Felix (the great fortune, *Manilius*), Bonus Daemon (good spirit, *Ptolemy*)
DIRECTION: SSE (south-southeast)
BODY PART: ankles
COLORS: yellow, saffron

THE TWELFTH HOUSE (H12)

H12 is cadent and very unfortunate - the "joy" of Saturn. Here, the spirit is strong but the body is weak, as if the house was still overpowered by the dark forces of night which immediately preceded it.

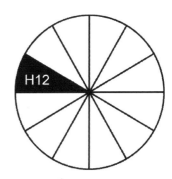

In horary charts, this house stands for hospitals, prisons, monasteries and other isolated, secluded institutions; secrets, secret enemies, traitors, spies; monks and nuns; prisoners; large animals (cattle, horses and the like); isolation, secrecy; exile, disappearance; refugees; scandals; loss; remote places; dreams. (Let me add that dreams in traditional horary astrology fall in H9, but I think they also have a place in H12. If you get a question about the meaning of someone's dreams, check both houses and go with the one that better describes the dream. Know that H9 is particularly assigned to prophetic, not every-day, casual dreams.)

OLD NAMES: Malus Daemon (evil spirit, *Ptolemy*), Laboris, the Portal of Toil (*Manilius*)
DIRECTION: ESE (east-southeast)
BODY PART: feet
COLOR: green

HOUSE ASSIGNMENT

As soon as we've cast a chart, we need to decide which houses are involved, and assign significators of the querent and the quesited to them. Every person, every object and even some concepts fit into any of the twelve houses. So, we need to identify them, so as to avoid confusion when searching for the answer. It's very important to have properly understood the question, because this is the only way to find the right houses that are related to the question and hold the key to the answer.

The truth is that finding the "right" significators (which usually depend on the houses), is a frequent "headache" of horary astrologers - not only beginners, but also skilled practitioners. Not only that it's sometimes really difficult to decide on this or that house; astrologers are often so overwhelmed by the importance of houses that they overlook obvious answers that charts sometimes offer even without considering the houses. True, houses ARE very important, but not always.

Although in principle we know which matters belong to which house – as the basic assignments are ancient, pretty well-defined and well-tested – we're often faced with difficult decisions in practice. Dilemmas and discord occur even on very basic topics, like jobs, for example. Some astrologers claim that ordinary, commonplace jobs belong to H6 whereas H10 should rule only career-oriented jobs. But tradition teaches (and my own practice confirms that), that any kind of job is ruled by H10. The only exception is when we deal with a "job within a job" situation, that is when a new job enquired after is more of a work environment change than really a new job, and/ or that which takes place within the same company.

In this book you'll read that cars belong to H3 but in some others you'll find that cars are ruled by H2 or even H1. Cars and other vehicles are among the most controversial issues of modern horary astrology. Clearly, in ancient times they didn't exist, and, unfortunately, neither Lilly nor any of his contemporaries left us a horary case involving, say, a carriage. Lilly only published an example of a ship, lost at sea, but he placed it in H1. This is logical, considering the question didn't only refer to the ship but also to its crew and passengers, and the querent was interested in the fate of ALL of them. Thinking of that, what other choice did Lilly have? Normally, though, all transportation and the means of it belong to H3.

Many astrologers claim that all personal belongings are ruled by H2, but practice shows that various papers and documents are "found" in H3, books in H9 and work tools in H6.

Based on my long-time experience, I have quite definitive views about house allocations. In the Practice part of the book you will find several examples, confirming the validity of some of my not-so-mainstream house assignments. I'm stressing this because some authors only give opinions and theoretical rules, without concrete examples, but what is theory without practice?

When assigning significators to the houses, ask yourself: What is the basic function of the "quesited" (the subject of the question)? *Will I succeed in organizing an astrology course in Obala?* This is one of my example cases discussed in the practice book. Where do courses belong, a beginner would wonder, and upon a short contemplation, probably choose H3, the house of learning. Wrong! What does the course mean to me, the querent? I'm an astrology teacher, so the course is a business project, of course, ruled by H10! The essence of my question was whether I'd be able to carry out a business (professional) project. Whether this is a course or something else, is of secondary importance. All businesses are in H10, and that is where the course belongs, although in such cases as the one at hand we'll probably find links between H10 and H3 (learning, study courses) or H11 (groups of people), and possibly even with H9, the house of "higher learning". (Those links actually exist in that chart.)

Let's take another example. The querent says: *I love Lucas. What does he feel for me?* Lucas is the querent's coworker, so he should be ruled by H6? No! Lucas is indeed her coworker, but the context of the question does not refer to some professional task they're dealing with, so it doesn't really matter whether Lucas is her co-worker, neighbour, friend or her friend's cousin. She's interested in him as a potential partner, lover, or anything in that sense. And this specific "sense" belongs to H7, which is also why Lucas in this particular question would be ruled by H7. It is likely, though, that such a chart would show some connection/s between H1 (the querent) and/or H7 (the quesited) with H6 (co-workers).

But although it's very important to find the right house or houses, ruling the quesited, we shouldn't give up when in doubt and unable to decide what belongs where. The answer can often be found in some other way; for example, by means of natural significators or/and lunar aspects. I have noticed that horary students and practitioners are often so absorbed in the search of the proper houses that they completely neglect natural significators, which often give valuable clues.

Some things (or people) can be ruled by a combination of two (or even three) houses (and planets). *Which house rules a faculty mentor?*, a student once asked. Basically, mentors are professors, so they're ruled by H9, but since there's a one-to-one relationship involved, we must consider H7 too, while the natural significator of mentors is Jupiter. All the three factors should be equally considered and examined.

We must also remember that many questions can be pared down to the angular houses, and to the aspects with the angles, as they (together with lunar aspects) hold the most information as per the immediate future. Most important, though, is the awareness of the essence of the question and the function of the significators that "seek" their proper houses – once we know that, the decision should be easy!

OTHER HOUSE CONSIDERATIONS

HOUSE SIZES AND HOUSE CUSPS

As we have learnt, houses are mundane sections of the zodiac circle and are of various sizes (as opposed to signs). Their individual sizes depend on the house system we use, and on the geographical coordinates of the location of the chart. Each house starts in one of the twelve zodiacal signs, and the initial degree of every house is called a **house cusp**. The sign on the cusp is most important because the whole house is "ruled" by the planet ruling that sign. This planet is called the **ruler of the house** (or **house ruler**) and is always the **significator** of people or things that we are asking about.

If, for example, the cusp of H5 is in Aries, we say that H5 is ruled by Mars (the ruler of Aries). If the cusp of H2 is in Virgo, H2 is ruled by Mercury (the ruler of Virgo). If the cusp of H1 (ascendant) is in Leo, the ruler of H1 (ascendant) is the Sun (the ruler of Leo), and so on.

I can hear you ask: but what if the cusp of a house is very close to the next sign, like in the last degree of a sign? It's true that such cases are somewhat delicate due to the relatively fast rotation of the Earth around its axis, which causes a quick succession of cuspal degrees through the zodiac - especially in the so-called "signs of short ascension" (from Capricorn to Gemini). In such cases it's reasonable to consider a "co-ruler" - the planet ruling the next sign. Still, similarly to the ascendant in one of the last degrees of a sign, we must be aware of the fact that if the cusp is about to slip into the next sign, also the matters of the house in question could be in the process of change, or that process could soon begin.

PLANETS IN CONJUNCTION WITH HOUSE CUSPS

Technically speaking, each house reaches from its cusp to the cusp of the next house, but the most sensitive are the early degrees of a house. Planets find their strongest expression in those degrees. If there's a planet situated here, it has a very strong influence on the matter/s signified by that house – the closer to the cusp, the more powerful. What's more - ever since Ptolemy, we know that **a planet which is up to 5 degrees from the cusp of the next house, has a strong bearing on that (next) house**, while its influence in the house where it's technically located, is negligible. We say that such a planet is in conjunction with the cusp of the next house, therefore its impact on that house is even stronger as it would be if it was in any of the subsequent degrees of that house (in the middle or towards the end of it). This planet strongly defines the meaning of the house, especially if its' an angular one - H1, H10, H7 or H4.

This might seem strange, as planets in those degrees are actually leaving the houses which they so strongly define. But, on the other hand, they were in those houses at the time when we were (consciously or subconsciously) contemplating our question, and are therefore strongly influencing it! On the other hand, if viewing the houses as fixed and planets as moving, such planets are actually on the verge of entering into those next houses – except if retrograde, of course.

This is particularly true when **the planet is in the same sign as the cusp of the house** - the kind of situation described in the first two cases (see CASE 1 and CASE 2).

EXAMPLE 1: *Cusp of H5 is at 16° Pisces. 12° of that sign is occupied by Mars. That planet is technically in H4, but practically in H5, therefore we take it as a H5 planet.*

EXAMPLE 2: *Cusp of H9 is at 5° Cancer, Mercury is at 3° Cancer and technically in H8, but we say that Mercury belongs to H9 and not to H8.*

EXAMPLE 3: *Cusp of H2 is at 2° Sagittarius, Jupiter at 28° Scorpio and therefore technically in H1, but practically, Jupiter strongly influences H2.*

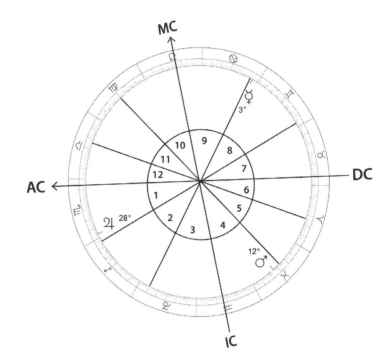

In the last case, the situation is a bit different. Jupiter indeed influences H2, but as it is located **in the sign of H1**, it also bears influence on H1 and therefore connects both houses.

In practice, the interpretive rules should be always carefully adapted to situations at hand. It's important to figure out how to combine the two houses, or why a planet came to be conjuncting a cusp – because, as already mentioned, there might be some transition or change involved. Such situations require more experience, but we must always let the chart guide us. Instead of letting difficult charts discourage us, let us allow them give us additional information. Houses, after all, pass one into another contextually, not just spatially. The planet which is in the phase of transition from one to the next house, may indicate a person who actually passes from one situation (or place) to another. It really depends on the question. If, in **CASE 1**, the question was *Is my son coming back home soon?* the answer would be obvious: yes, he is. And if Mars was retrograde, even more so!

INTERCEPTED SIGNS

As we know, a house is a section of zodiac, starting at some degree of the zodiac and ending at another - which is also the cusp of the next house. This next cusp can be in the same sign as the cusp of the previous house, it can be in the next sign or even in the sign following the next one. In the latter case we are talking about "intercepted signs". Such signs are almost as important as the signs bearing house cusps, and we assign them an additional significator – the planet ruling the intercepted sign.

EXAMPLE: *Cusp of H5 is in Libra and cusp of H6 in Sagittarius, so that the whole of Scorpio is in H5. We say that Scorpio is an "intercepted sign" in H5. The main ruler of H5 is therefore Venus (the ruler of Libra) and the additional ruler (or co-ruler) is Mars, the ruler of the intercepted Scorpio. We have the same situation at the opposite side of the chart, of course, where Taurus is the intercepted sign of H11.*

Intercepted signs often show "hidden" or unknown facts related to the things or people ruled by the house in question. They suggest that the matter is probably more complex as it seems. The querent can be completely unaware of those hidden facts, but sometimes he knows them and hides them from the astrologer. Sometimes it is "a question within a question" situation, or another situation develops after the first one is resolved. Sometimes, this sign (along with its ruler) represents a person, unknown to the querent (or to the astrologer) who is important for the understanding of the situation at hand. Such houses certainly require a more detailed insight, more questioning on the part of astrologer, and a deeper contemplation.

In missing articles charts, an intercepted sign in the house ruling it can indicate that the missing article is hiding within another object (it's in a box, for example).

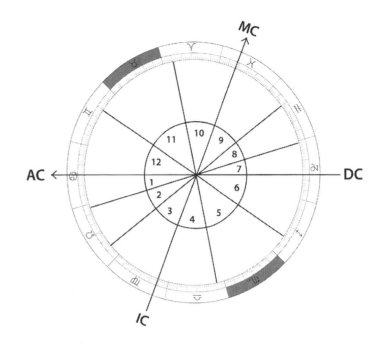

EMPLACEMENT

Emplacement is a situation where the significator of the querent is in the house of the quesited, or vice versa. *Am I going on this trip?* If the ruler of H1 is in H9 or the ruler of H9 is in H1, this is a case of emplacement. Emplacement is considered when looking for answers to the yes/no types of questions. It shows a strong tendency towards completion (yes), but it does not in itself grant a positive answer. (More on the various ways of completion in chapter THE OUTCOME on p. 122)

Emplacement is slightly stronger if the significator of the quesited is in H1. This is like the thing (or person) that we want to attract is "gravitating" towards us. But we will get it only if that's confirmed by other indications.

Emplacement is not always to be desired, though. If, for example, the H6 ruler is in H1, this can show that the illness is "within" the querent. Not so nice, eh?!

I should add that emplacement is fairly common, but it usually only points to the sphere of interest of the querent. This is of course very astro-logical! Questions related to business projects, for example, often occur when the ascendant ruler (significator of the querent) is in H10, a question regarding your pet may pop up when your ruler is in H6, money matters will "find" ascendant rulers in H2, and so on. (The Moon behaves similarly, so she too can be found in any of the relevant houses.)

DERIVED HOUSES

Besides their "direct" or primary meaning, houses also have "indirect", secondary meanings – depending on the new order of houses, created when a question involves the issues of the quesited. When serving such purpose, we call them "derived" houses.

Let me explain. A chart cast for the time and place of the question is called a **radix** (primary, original) **chart**. Houses in this chart refer to the querent or indicate his situation. If, for example, he's asking about his partner, the partner is ruled by H7, if about his child, the child is ruled by H5, and so on. But very often we ask about other people's affairs. *Where is my sister's wallet? Is my daughter happy with her current partner? Is our cat ill, or just having a bad day?* In such cases, we number the houses beginning with the one which stands for the quesited. The cusp of the house, ruling the quesited, is the **derived ascendant** (of that person or animal) and the houses numbered from it are the **derived houses**. The same process is (although rarely) applied to questions related to objects and concepts, such as profession, real estate, travel and the like.

If, for example, a man asks about matters relating to his wife, descendant (cusp of H7) becomes the derived ascendant for the wife; radix H8 becomes the derived H2 (ruling wife's property), radix H9 the derived H3 (ruling, for example, the wife's sister or her car), radix H10 the derived H4 (ruling the wife's father etc.), and so on, right up to the radix H6 which is the derived H12.

We label the derived houses as follows: 2/7 (second from seventh), 3/5 (third from fifth), 12/6 (twelfth from sixth), and so on, with the last of the two numbers standing for the quesited and the first standing for the affairs related to them.

Where is my sister's wallet? The cusp of H3 (sister) is the derived ascendant for the sister and H4 is the derived H2, ruling her missing wallet, as this house is the second from the third (2/3). *Is my daughter happy with her current partner?* Radix H5 stands for my daughter while radix H11 is her partner, as it is the derived seventh from fifth (7/5). *Is our cat ill, or just having a bad day?* The cat is ruled by H6 and her (potential) illness by H11 (6/6).

But the derived houses can get more complicated. *Is my son's girlfriend going to successfully implement her business project abroad?* The son is ruled by H5, his girlfriend by H11 (7/5), her business project by H8 (10/11) and the foreign land she's planning to succeed in, by H7 (9/11). (Although we could, for simplicity's sake, skip the last one.)

My father's coworker is seriously ill, is he going to get well again? Which house stands for the disease of the querent's father's coworker? The father is H4, his coworker is H9 (6/4) and his illness is H2 (6/9 or 6/6/4). *When will my great-grandchild be born?* H5 is the daughter (or son), grandchild is H9 (5/5) and the great-grandchild is H1 (5/5/5).

But know: the radix chart can never be simply ignored! The angles (ascendant, descendant, MC and IC) are astronomically the most sensitive and astrologically the most powerful points, and angularity does not get "transferred" to the new set of houses. In other words, **planets can only be angular in the original, not in the derived chart**. In one of the above cases, for example, H8 ruled the son's girlfriend's business project. Although this house is the derived H10 (10/11), it can't be treated as angular! If we'd calculate the strength of a planet placed there, for example, that planet would still be treated as being in H8 (weak). But if the ruler of that house was placed in the radix H10, that would add to its strength.

Because the angles basically "dissect" the chart into four quadrants, also the houses, associated with them, always retain their original meaning - even when we're looking for the answer by means of the derived houses. *Will my father-in-law's operation go well?* Father-in-law is my husband's father, ruled by the radix H10, while his operation is ruled by radix H5 (8/10). But the radix H8 remains the "house of operations", so we need to check that too. This naturally leads to a dilemma: which house is more important - the radix or the derived one? In principle, derived houses are usually more important, but experienced astrologers skillfully combine both sets of houses, and in case of doubt, they seek the final answer by help of additional factors (lunar aspects, natural significators and the like).

Students often ask: what houses rule grandmothers, grandfathers and other distant relatives? In principle, we are considering the original parentage. Specifically, if the grandmother is the father's mother, she's ruled by H1 (10/4), but if she's the maternal grandmother, she's shown by H7 (10/10). Following the same principle we might also look for the rulers of our great-grandfathers and great-grandmothers, but in practice, we often place such people in H4, the house standing for our ancestry in a general sense. The logic of the original kinship is also used in the assignment of significators for aunts and uncles, while cousins are traditionally placed in H3 – whatever their parentage.

I should add, of course, that the derived houses are even more of a "headache" for a diligent student who is sometimes just too keen to find the "definitely right" derived house for this or that thing, person or concept. What house rules a letter sent from abroad? H11, because it's the third from the ninth? No! A letter is a letter, and as such it belongs to H3, although we'd have to check H9 too as it's the house of distant communication. But generally all letters go into H3, no matter from whom or where they come from.

DERIVED HOUSES - EXAMPLES

THE FIRST HOUSE: friend's neighbor (3/11), death or surgery of a pet (8/6), child's travel or studies (9/5), wife's or husband's business partner (7/7), great-grandchild (5/9 or 5/5/5), father's job (10/4), parental grandmother (10/4).

THE SECOND HOUSE: partner's debt (8/7), husband's operation (8/7), child's occupation (10/5), grandson's disease (6/9) friend's apartment (4/11), father's political party (11/4).

THE THIRD HOUSE: our friends' kid (5/11), our children's friends (11/5), mum's disease (6/10), friend's travel (9/11), the opponent party's lawyer in a legal dispute (9/7).

THE FOURTH HOUSE: brother's possessions (2/3), wife's success (10/7), friend's disease (6/11), the boss's wife (7/10), the child's secret (12/5), the missing article of the child's friend (2/11/5)

THE FIFTH HOUSE: father's money (2/4), the value of the property (2/4) friend's wife (7/11), disease of the mother's sister (6/12 or 6/3/10), sister's car (3/3), brother's mail (3/3) , company's debt (8/10)

THE SIXTH HOUSE: children's toys (2/5), mother's voyage (9/10), brother's land (4/3) partner's secret enemy (12/7) friend's operation (8/11)

THE SEVENTH HOUSE: paternal ancestors (4/4), great-grandmother's apartment (4/4), nephew (3/7), child's trip (3/5), friend's lawyer (9/11), sister's pregnancy (5/3), mother's boss (10/10)

THE EIGHT HOUSE: business partner's funds (2/7), child's apartment (4/5), cousin's disease (6/3), friend's mother (10/11), neighbors' cat (6/3)

THE NINTH HOUSE: brother-in-law (3/7), sister's husband (7/3), grandchild (5/5), father's coworker (6/4), mum's secret (12/10), husband's car (3/7), friend's mother's purse (2/10/11)

THE TENTH HOUSE: father-in-law (4/7), child's illness (6/5), neighbor's operation (8/3), sister's debt (8/3); partner's real estate (2/9), wife's boss (10/7)

THE ELEVENTH HOUSE: company's funds (2/10), partner's children (5/7), coworker's opponent (7/6), employer's earnings (2/10), mother's coat (2/10), daughter-in-law (7/5), neighbors' lawyer (9/3)

THE TWELFTH HOUSE: maternal aunt (3/10), husband's hairdresser (6/7), daughter-in-law's possessions (2/11 or 2/7/5), sister's job (10/3), mother's neighbor (3/10), child's bank account (8/5), friend's money (2/11)

PLANETS IN HORARY ASTROLOGY

BASIC CLASSIFICATIONS OF PLANETS

he Sun, the Moon and the planets (for practical reasons, all these bodies are often be called planets in the book, although the Sun, as we know, is the star of our solar system and the Moon is the Earth's satellite) are the main characters in our "horary script" and therefore the most important elements of any horary chart. They embody the querents, the people and sometimes also objects and concepts that are the subjects of questions. The Moon has an even more important role, as in horary charts it doesn't only stand for people, but it also "rules" the course of events, and, most importantly, plays a vital role in timing.

For horary astrologers, it's very important to know how to evaluate the nature of the planets and their mode of action. We must understand when and why a planet shows a winner or a loser, a hero or a "fool". We must carefully consider the condition of each planet that represents someone or something, so that we can decide how it would affect the outcome of the question.

Through the ages, several classifications were formed, defining the natures, qualities, characters and strengths of the planets. Obviously, they only involved planets that are visible to the naked eye, as only those could be studied by ancient astrologers. Planets which have been discovered only in the last few centuries (Uranus, Neptune and Pluto) are not included in these classifications, although they also have each their own characteristics and are of much help to the contemporary horary astrologer.

TEMPERATURE, MOISTURE AND TEMPERAMENT

Ancient astrologers first studied the movements of the planets with a view to predict seasons and weather. This is how astrology began to develop - as a natural, empirical science. By a precise and consistent observation they gradually came to realize that the Moon, the Sun and the planets make the weather. They carefully observed changes in atmosphere which took place primarily at syzygys (new and full moons) and at times of conjunctions and oppositions of planets with the "heavenly lights". These celestial events told them when the weather would be getting dry, warm, moist or cold.

Temperaments were developed later. As mentioned in the chapter on the signs, the theory of the four bodily humors was developed by the ancient Greek physician Hippocrates (based on an earlier thesis on the four elements attributed to Empedocles), and later astrologers upgraded it into the system of temperaments. Those were reflected through the zodiacal signs and planets, and in both categories the combination of hot and moist was **sanguine**, of hot and dry **choleric**, of cold and dry **melancholic** and of cold and moist, **phlegmatic**.

The Sun is generally warm and dry, but it changes its characteristics depending on the season. While traversing the first half of the zodiac (from Aries to Virgo - spring and summer), it's warmer but in its course through the other half (from Libra to Pisces - autumn and winter) it's colder. From the perspective of humidity, the winter and spring seasons tend to be moist while summer and autumn tend to be dry.

The Moon is generally cold and moist, but it changes its properties and temperament according to its varying distances from the Sun (see table on p. 72).

Planets had been evaluated in a similar manner. The ancient "stargazers" found that Venus moisturises the atmosphere while Mars dries it, and that Jupiter warms it up and Saturn cools it down. These classifications are general, as the characteristics of the planets are slightly modified depending on the **time of day**: at night, planets "produce" more coldness and moisture while in daytime they contribute to heat and dryness. They are further modified by their position **above or below the horizon**: planets above the horizon are warmer and drier, those below the horizon colder and wetter. Besides, they change their qualities according to their relation to the Sun: eastern planets (those rising before the Sun, up to about 120 ° in the case of Mars, Jupiter or Saturn) tend to be warm and dry while western planets (those setting after the Sun, again up to about 120 ° in case of Mars, Jupiter and Saturn) tend to be cold and moist.

TEMPERATURE, MOISTURE AND TEMPERAMENTS OF THE PLANETS

PLANET	TEMPERATURE AND MOISTURE	TEMPERAMENT
MOON	cold and moist (but changeable according to its distance from the Sun)	phlegmatic
SUN	hot and dry	choleric
MERCURY	cold and dry (but changeable - warm and moist when eastern, cold and dry when western)	melancholic, sanguine (eastern) or melancholic (westerxn)
VENUS	moderately warm and moist, changeable	sanguine (eastern) or phlegmatic (western)
MARS	hot and very dry	choleric
JUPITER	very warm and moist	sanguine
SATURN	very cold and dry	melancholic

PLANETARY QUALITIES RELATIVE TO THE SUN

SATURN	eastern	cold and a little moist (phlegmatic)
	western	cold and dry (melancholic)
JUPITER	eastern	hot and moist (sanguine)
	western	warm and moist (sanguine)
MARS	eastern	hot and dry (choleric)
	western	hot and dry (choleric)
VENUS	eastern	warm and moist (sanguine)
	western	coldish and moist (phlegmatic)
MERCURY	eastern	warm and moist (sanguine)
	western	cold and dry (melancholic)

THE MOON	from new moon to first quarter (waxing)	warm and moist (sanguine)
	from first quarter to full moon (waxing)	hot and dry (choleric)
	from full moon to last quarter (waning)	cold and dry (melancholic)
	from last quarter to new moon (waning)	cold and moist (phlegmatic)

THE SUN'S SEASONAL QUALITIES

Sun in Aries, Taurus and Gemini (spring)	warm and moist (sanguine)
Sun in Cancer, Leo and Virgo (summer)	warm and dry (choleric)
Sun in Libra, Scorpio and Sagittarius (autumn)	cold and dry (melancholic)
Sun in Capricorn, Aquarius and Pisces (winter)	cold and moist (phlegmatic)

Long centuries had passed between those weather observations and the realization that we people are also part of the nature and that we have our own internal "weather" which expresses itself in the form of character and temperament. These observations have been gradually incorporated into the astrological "canon" (set of rules) and firmly established in the astrological theory and practice.

Below are some of the main characteristics of each of the four temperaments:

SANGUINE TEMPERAMENT (warm and moist; spring and air signs)
CHARACTER: cheerful, playful, lively, youthful, sociable, extroverted, optimistic, trusting, sincere, honest, loving, warm, peaceful, liberal, confident, superficial, flirtatious, changeable
ASSOCIATED PLANETS: Jupiter; Mecury and Venus as morning stars (eastern); Moon in the 1st phase

CHOLERIC TEMPERAMENT (hot and dry, summer and fire signs)
CHARACTER: intense, strong, passionate, bold, aggressive, competitive, optimistic, demanding, forceful, hasty, impatient, rebellious, headstrong, persuasive, with leadership potential
ASSOCIATED PLANETS: Sun; Mars; Moon in the 2nd phase

MELANCHOLIC TEMPERAMENT (cold and dry, autumn and earth signs)
CHARACTER: cautious, careful, thoughtful, methodical, analytical, focused, critical, austere, slow, steady, distrustful, suspicious, tenacious, tough, ambitious, solitary
ASSOCIATED PLANETS: Saturn, especially when western; Mercury as evening star (western); Moon in the 3rd phase

PHLEGMATIC TEMPERAMENT (cold and moist, winter and water signs)
CHARACTER: sensitive, reflective, introverted, submissive, detached, reserved, loyal, faithful, compassionate, obliging, dependent, indecisive, fearful, distrustful, slow, weak-willed
ASSOCIATED PLANETS: Saturn when eastern; Venus as evening star (western); Moon in the 4th phase

PLANETARY SECT

As mentioned in the previous chapter, the ancient astrologers found that planets had varying qualities and strength levels depending on whether they were above or below the horizon. This classification is called **planetary sect**. We distinguish between **diurnal** and **nocturnal** sects.

Planets belonging to the **diurnal sect** are **Sun, Jupiter and Saturn**, whereas those belonging to the **nocturnal sect** are **Moon, Venus and Mars**. The Sun and the Moon as the "lights" of the day or night come first or are the so-called "sect leaders" while the other two planets have the role of their followers. **Mercury** varies according to its relative position to the Sun: it is a diurnal planet (belonging to the diurnal sect) when a morning star (that is, when rising before the Sun) and a nocturnal planet (belonging to the nocturnal sect) as an evening star (when setting after the Sun). In day charts (those with the Sun above the horizon) astrologers gave more importance to the planets of the diurnal sect while in the night ones (with the Sun below the horizon) to the planets of the nocturnal sect.

Planets of the diurnal sect (the Sun, Jupiter, Saturn) are stronger in:
- day charts;
- positive (diurnal) signs;
- day charts above the horizon, in night charts below the horizon.

Planets of the nocturnal sect (the Moon, Venus, Mars) are stronger in:
- night charts;
- negative (nocturnal) signs;
- night charts above the horizon, in day charts below the horizon.

If a planet fulfills all of the three conditions, listed above, this is a powerful feature called *hayz* (completely in its sect), but if it fulfills none, it is said to be *ex conditione* (completely outside its sect).

In traditional horary astrology, the use of planetary sect is close to non-existent. It seems that this classification simply slipped the attention of the renaissance and later horary authors. William Lilly actually does mention them, but apparently he never used them in practice, except to a certain degree in medical horaries where he gave more importance to the Sun in diurnal charts and to the Moon in nocturnal ones, but only in terms of understanding these bodies as "givers of life". In all other respects, sect was not employed.

I believe that planetary sect deserves to be added to the horary astrologer's arsenal of techniques, but it certainly needs more research. I have been including it to my horary practice only in the later years, therefore sect is rarely mentioned in the example cases, many of which originate from earlier years. Students are nevertheless encouraged to study them and see how they fit in and what additional information they provide.

PLANETARY GENDER

Is the thief male or female? Planetary classification according to gender can provide the answer, but that's not its only purpose. Planetary gender can also help us determine the planetary mode of action. Generally, the female planets describe people (of both genders) as more gentle, calm, quiet, sensitive and reserved, while the male planets show them to be more active, courageous, strong, daring, dynamic, and similar:

The Moon and Venus are **female**.
The Sun, Mars, Jupiter and Saturn are **male**.
Mercury is **neutral** (genderless), but tends toward masculinity when east of the Sun and toward femininity when west of the Sun.

Although tradition ascribes a specific gender to each planet, we must know that in horary charts, men can be ruled by female planets and vice versa. If a man, for example, asks what kind of wife he would get, and the descendant was in Aries, the woman would be ruled by Mars, of course, or possibly by the Sun (if almuten ruler), although these are male planets. But she'd be described as "bold, competitive, unruly" and similar, that is, possessing the traditional "male" qualities.

Planets also assume **female natures** when they're **western** (in relation to the Sun) and when they occupy **female signs** and **female quadrants** (2 and 4).

Planets also assume **male natures** when they're **eastern** (in relation to the Sun) and when they occupy **male signs** and **male quadrants** (1 and 3).

Please bear in mind that the Moon, unlike the planets, is considered eastern (and therefore "male") when waxing (from the conjunction to the opposition of the Sun) and western (and therefore "female") when waning (from the opposition to the conjunction of the Sun).

Getting back to the above example: a woman described by Mars (or the Sun) would tend to have even more of the traditionally "male" character, if Mars was eastern, in a male quadrant and/or in a male sign, whereas she'd show some more femininity (grace, subservience, tenderness and the like) if Mars was western, in a female quadrant and/or in a female sign.

PLANETARY AGE

In this section we're not discussing the ages of planets as such, of course, but the (relative) age of people (and objects), described by their significators in horary charts. *Is my next partner going to be younger or older from me? About what age is the thief who stole my bike? Is our new boss going to be an older man, of middle age or young? Should I buy an older car, or rather go for a new one?* These and similar questions require our knowledge of planetary "ages".

Planetary age is usually examined when questions refer to unknown people (and objects). Several criteria are taken into account: **the intrinsic age of individual planets, lunar phases, eastern and western placements** (as related to the Sun) and the planetary **placements in quadrants and signs**.

Old age: Saturn
Late middle age: Jupiter
Early middle age: Mars, Sun
Youth: Venus
Adolescence: Mercury
Childhood: Mercury, the Moon

Lunar phases indicate the following ages: **the first quarter** (from 0° to 90° ahead of the Sun) a young person (a child or an adolescent), **the last quarter** (from 270° to 360° ahead of the Sun) an old person, the **full Moon** stage (around the Moon's opposition to the Sun) shows them to be of middle age, while the intermediate stages suggest intermediate ages, of course. The further the Moon is from the Sun (in the direction of its waxing), the older the person. (Note: this is not a 100% reliable rule, but only a trend!)

Eastern and western placements: significators as eastern planets (rising before the Sun) reveal younger people, western (setting after the Sun) older.

What about **quadrants**? Significators in the first quadrant (houses 12, 11 and 10) show childhood or youth, in the second quadrant (houses 9, 8 and 7) young to middle age, in the third quadrant (house 6, 5 and 4) maturity and in the fourth quadrant (houses 3, 2 and 1) old age.

People's age can sometimes be also inferred from the planets' occupying the early, middle or late sign degrees. Planets in earlier degrees are "younger" while those in later degrees are "older".

In practice, all indications must be carefully combined. If only one criterion is fulfilled, the indication may not be reliable, but if we have, for example, Saturn in the final degrees of a sign, in the fourth quadrant and west of the Sun, it's almost certain that is stands for an older person (or thing). In contrast to that, Mercury as a morning star, in an early degree of a sign and in the first quadrant would show a younger person or a new, modern or trendy item.

We should be aware, of course, that those are not clear-cut, definite rules. They are just tendencies that need to be carefully mixed with the known facts and the rest of the chart ingredients.

BENEFICS AND MALEFICS

The natural **benefics** are Jupiter and Venus, **malefics** are Saturn and Mars.

Benefic (from Lat. *bene*, well) means that a planet has good, positive, beneficent energies while malefic (from lat. *male*, badly) means the opposite: a planet has bad, destructive energies.

Venus and Jupiter are benefics because they are warm and moist. As such, they contribute to fertility, growth, comfort, love, happiness, friendship, peace, success and so on. Mars is extremely hot and dry, therefore destructive to life. It causes haste, violence, aggression, fights, accidents, inflammation and the like. Saturn is also life-averse because it's cold and dry. It causes restrictions, delays, hostility, disease, obstructions and failures.

However, this is only a general definition and in doesn't imply that Jupiter and Venus always bring good and that Saturn and Mars always do bad. Benefics can become "accidental malefics" - and vice versa, malefics can under certain conditions act as benefics! Much depends on the placement of planets in signs, houses and aspects, which will be discussed in the following sections. In the chapter ESSENTIAL DIGNITY (see p. 89) we'll learn that the power of benefics can be significantly impaired when they are in their signs of detriment and fall, whereas malefics can act very beneficially if in their domicile and exaltation signs. Besides, benefics are particularly good (beneficial) in harmonious aspects and in their domicile signs while malefics are particularly bad (harmful, destructive) in disharmonious aspects and in their detriments and falls. Benefics can become "accidental malefics" when ruling unfortunate houses, while malefics can become "accidental benefics" when ruling fortunate houses (or being placed therein). On the other hand, benefics can only exceptionally be as harmful as malefics, as they are a natural source of good.

The Moon, the Sun and Mercury are somehow neutral, but they take on the nature of whichever planet they're in aspect with. This is particularly true of Mercury, while the Sun is mostly beneficial – except when acting detrimentally upon planets which come too close to it, as then they become "combust". (More in chapter ACCIDENTAL DIGNITY on p. 100)

PLANETS AS SIGNIFICATORS

In horary charts, planets are called **significators** when they "signify" or "rule" someone or something - people, objects, parts of the body, professions, diseases and similar. We often use the word **ruler** in this context, as it's easier on the tongue.

Planets can be:
- **main significators**
- **cosignificators**
- **natural significators**

Main significators (and partly cosignificators) are detemined by the signs on the cusps of the houses, standing for the querent or the quesited, whereas natural significators are planets whose natural, inherent qualities best describe them.

MAIN SIGNIFICATORS

In the majority of cases, the main significator is the planet ruling the degree of the cusp of the house of the quesited (or of the ascendant, for the querent). This is usually the **sign ruler** (that is, the planet which has its domicile in that sign), but it can also be the **almuten ruler** - the planet having most dignity in the degree of the house cusp. Almuten is often the same planet as the sign ruler, but sometimes it's a different one (see ALMUTENS on p. 98).

I have noticed that contemporary horary astrologers, even those with a traditional bend, rarely use almutens as main significators. Most often, they don't use them at all. But in my experience, they're well worth considering. If the almuten describes the querent or the quesited better than the sign ruler, take it as the main significator, but if not, stay with the sign ruler.

Will I get the job that I've applied for? If the H10 cusp, ruling the job, is 12° Virgo, Mercury can be the only main significator of the job - as the sign ruler and as the almuten ruler (both in day and night charts). If, instead, the cusp of H10 was 25° Libra and it was a night chart, the only main significator of the job would be Venus as the sign ruler and as the night almuten ruler of that degree, but if it was a day chart, almuten rulers would be Saturn and Venus, as they both have most dignity in 25°Libra in daytime charts.

Sometimes, the main significator can also be **a planet that occupies the house of the querent or the quesited**. Mostly, such a planet is given priority because it's on the cusp of a house, and as such has a strong bearing upon the matters of the house, but sometimes because it is also the natural significator of the quesited (like Saturn or Mercury for lost keys, Venus for a necklace, Sun for the husband, Jupiter for a purse, and similar).

COSIGNIFICATORS

Cosignificators (or **corulers**) are planets which act as additional rulers of the querent or the quesited. A cosignificator can be:

- the Moon;
- a planet in the house ruling the querent or the quesited. (Can be more than one planet, with the most important being the one closest to the cusp, or the one which also acts as the natural significator.);
- the natural significator (see below);
- the ruler of the intercepted sign.

NATURAL SIGNIFICATORS

Natural significators are planets which co-rule certain people and things due to their inherent natures. *If jewelry, this is Venus, if a letter or keys, it's Mercury, if an operation or competition, it's Mars, if a divorce, Uranus, and so on.*

In the following chapters on the planets, you'll find comprehensive lists of natural significators, whereas in the second part of the book (Practice), the most common natural significators for specific types of questions are listed.

If the natural significator supports the main one, this can be very helpful. Suppose that a question refers to an operation, and the cusp of H8 (operations) is in Aries, ruled by Mars, and Mars is also located in that house. Mars, as the natural ruler of operations, thus becomes the singular most important significator of the operation. More often, though, you'll find natural significators somewhere else in the chart. Venus, for example, is always important in charts of love and relationships, and we should check her even if it doesn't have any relation to H1 and H7 which are always the main houses to be considered in this respect. Venus doesn't only rule women but it's an age-old ruler of "marriage".

Nowadays, it's especially important to consider transsaturnians as natural rulers, too, as we have learnt of their immense value in astrology through other forecasting techniques (progressions, transits), so why not apply them to horary? Although I as a "modern traditionalist" keep the classical planets as sign rulers, I'm far from ignoring transsaturnians in the many roles they play in the modern world (computers, phones, mass-media, TV, commercials, drugs, refugees, bombs, psychotherapy, etc.)

THE MOON ☽

BASIC QUALITIES: basically cold and moist (phlegmatic), but varying according to phase, sign and the planet which it aspects
ESSENTIAL DIGNITY: Cancer (domicile), Taurus (exaltation), earth triplicity by night
ESSENTIAL DEBILITY: Capricorn (detriment), Scorpio (fall)
SECT: nocturnal
GENDER: female
DAY: Monday
COLORS: white, silvery, greenish
TASTE: salty
EMOTIONS: various – depending on the aspected planets

The Moon is by far **the most important body** in horary astrology. We consider it in every chart, as it's always the cosignificator of the main characters in the horary "drama" – either of the querent or of the people or things of which he asks. The aspects which it makes with the planets describe **the course of action** and indicate the outcome of the situation which is the subject matter of the question.

Why is the Moon so important? Simply because it is, due to the proximity to Earth, the largest and the fastest celestial body. Its daily motion is between 12 and 15 degrees. In its course, the Moon constantly moves from one body to another and thus connects them and transfers their energy. The Moon "creates" change and helps planets to express themselves. We could say that she "enlivens" the planetary energies and brings them down to the Earth and into our lives. (This is poetical speech, of course, as we don't know how the celestial "mechanics" really works – we only know that it does!)

The Moon is **the leading light of the nocturnal sect**. It's at its strongest when above horizon at night. It's gaining momentum when in the waxing phase (between new and full moon phase) and is somewhat more powerful in the negative (nocturnal) signs, especially in earth signs in night charts since it's the night ruler of the earth triplicity.

I must stress that the Moon is not always the cosignificator of the querent! **It corules the querent when the question relates to his/her personal affairs.** This is often the case when the querent is emotionally involved in the situation, since the Moon, from a psychological point of view, is "the queen" of our inner worlds, impulses, instincts, desires, emotions, wishes and fears. However, the Moon also corules the querent when he's not driven by powerful emotions, but only has a (relatively) slight interest in the development of his/her situation (like, when searching for a missing book). The crucial criterion is the querent's **attention**! While it is true that the more emotionally involved the querent is, the more bearing the Moon has on his own role in the resolution of the question, it is even truer that the Moon always rules **the core subject of the question**. *Is my friend Tania going to accept my proposal?* The Moon is my coruler. *Is my friend Tania going to find her lost purse?* In this case, the Moon is not my coruler.

As the last of the above two examples suggests, when our questions relate to people and things that we're not emotionally involved with (in that particular situation), but are only interested in the unfolding of a situation in which we participate as observers, then the Moon doesn't rule us, but the quesited. Again: what's crucial here is the attention! *When is my daughter getting a leave from the hospital? When will the tenants leave my premises? Where are my keys? Will my husband's business project succeed?* In these cases, the Moon corules the daughter, the tenants, the key and my husband's business project. It doesn't rule me!

It's true, on the other hand, that it's often difficult to rigorously define the level of our emotional involvement. In the first of the above cases, if we are interested in the daughter's coming back from the hospital, we are certainly emotionally involved, at least to a certain degree. We might be a bit worried. But the attention is on the daughter and HER situation! It's not upon us to decide, we're only interested in the fate of something that exists outside of ourselves. Similarly, if we ask about the whereabouts of our keys. We might not be able to arrive at the office in time if we don't find them soon, but our attention is on the keys. And if we want to know when our tenants would leave, we're also emotionally involved; we might want them to move as soon as possible, or we might want them to stay as long as possible. We might want our husband's business project to succeed, or we might want it to falter. But in spite of that, the key criteria or our **focus** in these questions exists outside ourselves, and the Moon goes along.

The ultimate key to understanding the role of the Moon is to realize that the Moon stands for the **cosmic consciousness**, pervading our reality and often being expressed at the level of our **gut feelings.** The Moon comes before our rational minds. It's what brings the all-pervading cosmic (natural) laws to the highest levels of our subconscious perception. That's why it leads us to formulate a question at exactly the moment when our subconscious mind corresponds to the reality of a specific situation – which holds the key to its future unfolding.

Although, in psychological astrology, the Moon "rules" emotions, in horary astrology it doesn't relate to any specific emotion. We can say that it stands for **all emotions**, but the nature of these emotions is always determined (defined) by the planets which it comes to aspect, as well as by its house and sign position.

In defining the role of the Moon in a horary chart we must be truly flexible, as it can simultaneously rule several people or things. It can be a cosignificator of the querent or of the quesited; it can stand for the matters of the house with its cusp in Cancer, and it ALWAYS shows the course of events or the development of situations. It often has the major say in the final outcome of the question. As such, it requires our special attention.

The **house** which the Moon occupies in a horary chart often indicates the subject of the question or the area of the development or change. Where the Moon is, there is the querent's interest, either conscious (expressed by his thoughts), or subconscius and therefore indicating the hidden essence of the question. (Note: this applies to both the radical and the derived houses!)

The **aspects** which the Moon had recently completed and from which it's separating, show the past events related to the question while the aspects which she's in the process of forming, reveal future developments.

In the majority of horary charts, the Moon plays **crucial role** in **timing**. The number of degrees separating it from an aspect with a planet (or a point – an angle, node or even a house cusp) correspond to the number of hours, days, weeks, months or years that have passed since an important past event, related to the question, or – more importantly - are going to pass until the resolution of the question. (More on this in the chapter TIMING on p. 132)

As people's significator, the Moon describes them as soft, gentle, feminine, peaceful, indecisive, shy, changeable and versatile, but they can also be oversensitive, inert, cowardly, irresponsible, lazy or prone to drunkenness. (According to tradition, but nowadays addicts of all kinds are ascribed to Neptune.) They have pale complexions, round faces, dark hair and (possibly) wrinkled skin.

I must stress, though, that the Moon's qualities are substantially modified by its sign, phase and aspects. A waxing Moon in a male sign and an angular house will certainly show someone more courageous and strong from someone signified by a waning Moon in a female sign. Besides, we must not forget that the Moon (as well as the planets) describes "characters" only as far as the context of the question goes! If the Moon rules someone who is by nature far from gentle, shy and peaceful, this can mean that in the particular situation which is the subject of the horary chart, he is strongly emotionally engaged, oversensitive, driven by security needs, interested in home or family matters, and similar.

Astronomically, there are two longitudinal positions of the Moon: the first is the usual one, measured from the center of the Earth (same as the Sun, planets and stars), while the other takes into account **parallax** (or geocentric parallax) - an apparent angular offset of the Moon when viewed from the Earth's surface. Planets also have parallaxes but they're extremely small, while the Moon's average deviation from the "official" celestial longitude due to parallax is one degree – this being the mean value between zero and two degrees, as is the maximum parallax between the two points which are on opposite sides of the Earth. Parallax is only observable when the Moon is in the east (close to the ascendant) or west (close to the descendant); when the Moon is close to MC or IC, its parallax is zero. Due to parallax, the Moon is always a little lowered in the chart, which actually means that in longitude, when in the east, it's in a later degree, and when in the west, it's in an earlier degree.

Does this make sense and is it applicable to horary astrology? Our ancestors did not use parallax, and modern astrologers don't normally use it, either. I have yet to come upon a horary chart delineated by the use of parallax, and yet, horary astrology is certainly the best method to prove its validity, because with the Moon, the one or two degrees difference translates into a one or two time units difference – which can be significant. In practice, I have found that the actual timing sometimes deviates from the predicted one by one or two units of time – the fact which could be explained by parallax. Alas, it's not that simple. As we'll see in the chapter on timing, that difference can also be ascribed to the varying daily motions of the Moon (a fast Moon shortens the time while a slow one prolongs it), and also to different definitions of the month which sometimes cause delay in longer time periods (see the following paragraph). Therefore it's actually very difficult to decide what causes the occasional deviation. The dilemma of which position of the Moon to use, whether the one with parallax or the one without it, therefore (for the time being) remains.

We should also be aware that the synodic, sidereal and calendar months vary in length. Astrologically "correct", of course, are only the synodic and the sidereal month. A sidereal month (one lunar roration around the Earth) lasts 27.3 days and as such it is a little shorter from the synodic one (the time elapsing between two consecutive lunar conjunctions with the Sun) which takes an average of 29.5 days, while the calendar month, as we know, is even a little longer. Ignoring those differences can result in timing mistakes – especially in cases when longer time periods are observed. My own research shows that the most reliable is thy synodic month. (See also TIMING on p. 132.)

The Moon is the natural significator of:
- silver, pearls, crystal, glass, mirrors, eyeglasses
- bodily fluids, the left eye, bladder, breast, stomach, mucous membrane, female organs, menstruation, pregnancy, fetus
- mothers, wives, girls, daughters and other females; pregnancy; babies
- home, family, kitchen, bathroom
- missing people, animals and objects
- nations (in mundane charts)
- animals that live in water
- plants with thick, soft and succulent leaves; cucumbers, pumpkins, cabbage, mushrooms
- streams, rivers, ponds, pools and other water sources

THE SUN ☉

BASIC QUALITIES*: hot and dry, choleric; benefic (except in conjunctions)
ESSENTIAL DIGNITY*: Leo (domicile), Aries (exaltation), fire triplicity by day
ESSENTIAL DEBILITY*: Aquarius (detriment), Libra (fall)
SECT: diurnal
GENDER: male
DAY*: Sunday
COLORS*: yellow, golden, orange
TASTE*: sweet & sour, aromatic, slightly bitter and sharp
EMOTIONS: happiness, pride

The Sun is the star of our solar system, so it's synchronized with the light, heat, day, activity and the creative principle. It generally rules all the male population, like the Moon rules the females.

It's the leading body of the diurnal sect, hence it's stronger in diurnal charts (that is, when above the horizon), as well as in the positive (masculine, day) signs. The strongest is in Leo, its domicile sign, and in Aries, its exaltation sign – in both especially during the day, as it is the fire triplicity ruler in diurnal charts.

Generally speaking, the Sun is a benefic, but not unconditionally. Like the king on the chessboard, which can't be closely approached by any other figure, the Moon and the planets are endangered when coming too close to it; when this happens, the Sun "blinds" them and takes away their powers of constructive action. Planets at a distance of up to 17° from the Sun are "under the Sun's beams" (sunlit, partially weakened) and up to 8° from the Sun are "combust" (burnt, significantly weakened), but when within 17' of the Sun (in the heart of the Sun, "cazimi"), they are supposed to suddenly become very strong. (More on this in chapter PLANETARY DIGNITIY on p. 89)

As significator in horary charts, the Sun stands for honest, healthy, proud, powerful, noble, trustful, dependable and generous people who may speak little but do much, but an afflicted (badly placed) Sun would describe them as vain, bossy, arrogant, domineering, extravagant and selfish. (But remember: these characteristics only apply to people as behaving in the context of the question, and the Sun, like any other body, can be considerably modified by its sign, house and aspects.)

The typical physical appearance of the person, represented by the Sun: medium to tall stature, healthy complexion, high forehead, lighter (often curly) hair, large bright eyes, confident appearance.

The ascendant is often placed in Leo, the sign of the Sun, when people ask of their creative projects and other personal aspirations, or (if afflicted) when their ego has been hurt.

The Sun is the natural significator of:
- gold and rubies
- basic vitality, heart, bloodstream, brain, the right eye
- father, husband; directors, presidents and other authority figures; financiers, stockbrokers, goldsmiths
- red and yellow plants with a pleasant smell, which strengthen the heart and eyes
- big and impressive buildings, such as theaters and palaces

MERCURY ☿

BASIC QUALITIES: cold and dry (melancholic), but changeable according to phase: a bit warmer and moister as eastern (morning), but colder and drier as western (evening) planet
ESSENTIAL DIGNITY: Gemini (day domicile), Virgo (night domicile, exaltation), air triplicity by night
ESSENTIAL DEBILITY: Sagittarius (detriment), Pisces (detriment and fall)
SECT: changeable (diurnal as morning star, nocturnal as evening star)
GENDER: neutral
DAY: Wednesday
COLORS: blue, grey
TASTE: -
EMOTION: -

Mercury, by itself, is neither a benefic nor a malefic, neither male nor female: it's a neutral planet which assumes the nature of the planet with which it forms the nearest aspect. It is the fastest planet, as its daily motion can be as much as two degrees and a half. It's often combust or under the Sun's beams, because its maximum distance from the Sun is 28°. (This might be the reason why some of the ancient astrologers considered a planet to be combust or under the Sun's beams only if it was in the same sign as the Sun. Without this condition, Mercury would be under the Sun's beams in most charts! Today, opinions vary on this matter, but mine is that sign boundaries should be disregarded, and that "under the Sun's beams" should be regarded a really minor debility – at least as fas as Mercury goes.

Retrograde Mercury in horary charts shows that the querent may be concealing an important fact, necessary for the astrologer's divination, or that he's uncertain, or is about to change his mind.

As significator, Mercury stands for clever, curious, lively, eloquent, educated, sophisticated and well-informed people who might be teachers, agents, merchants or intellectuals. When afflicted, it can show a liar, a fraudster or a foolish, irresponsible, immature, uneducated or even a mentally unstable person. But know that these are only possibilities and that planets show people's characters only as far as the context of the question goes! A badly placed Mercury doesn't necessarily mean that the person it stands for, is just generally uneducated or a liar, but it can mean that in this particular instance, he's hiding the truth or is ignorant of important facts.

No specific emotion is attributed to Mercury. We could say that it represents indifference (emotional non-involvement), but we must always check for additional indications in its sign and aspects. If it's, say, connected with Mars, he might be angry, if with Venus, he's happy or in love, and the like.

Mercurian people (those under the influence of this planet) are tall and slim, with a high forehead and long arms and fingers. Their eyes are usually brown.

Ascendant in a Mercury-ruled signs (Virgo or Gemini) often points to matters related to learning, communicating, commuting, writing, traveling and similar.

Mercury is the natural significator of:
- mercury; multicolored stones
- head, tongue, hands, shoulders, nerves; breathing; brain diseases, headaches, stuttering, dry cough, loss of memory, nervousness
- words, letters, messages (verbal or written), notes, books, newspapers, libraries, contracts and all the other documents, publications; short routes; means of transport (cars, bikes, motorbikes, buses); keys
- deception, falsehood or perjury
- traders, brokers, postmen, drivers, operators, office workers, administrators, accountants, printers, moderators, writers, scientists, inventors and various other intellectual workers; children and young people; thieves and fraudsters
- multicolored plants that grow on sandy, dry soil; various grasses
- schools, shops, markets, bookshops, libraries, post offices, offices.

VENUS ♀

BASIC QUALITIES: moderately warm and moist, sanguine; benefic, "lesser fortune"
ESSENTIAL DIGNITY: Taurus (night domicile), Libra (day domicile), Pisces (exaltation), water and earth triplictiy ruler by day
ESSENTIAL DEBILITY: Scorpio (detriment), Aries (detriment), Virgo (fall)
SECT: nocturnal
GENDER: female
DAY: Friday
COLORS: white and all pastel and light colors, especially green
TASTE: sweet
EMOTIONS: romantic love, joy, erotic feelings

Venus is the brightest planet visible to the naked eye. It's a benefic, once called "lesser fortune" (while the "greater fortune" was Jupiter). Where there is Venus, there are love, joy, peace and happiness. As a warm and moist planet it brings nice weather and stirs positive emotions in humans.

As significator, it represents agreeable, peaceful, likeable, happy, fun-loving, charming, seductive, attractive, romantic, musical, and/or otherwise artistically talented people, but if afflicted, it shows them to be lazy, idle, self-indulgent, narcissistic, wasteful, morally depraved or sinful.

In the eastern position (as morning star) and in the positive (diurnal) signs it expresses more "masculinity" - is more outspoken, sexy, courageous, creative and lustful, while in the western position (as evening star) and in the negative (nocturnal) signs it expresses itself more consistently with its natural characteristics of femininity, grace and kindness.

As for their characters, Venus-ruled people must be judged on the same principle as other planets in horary charts: they should be understood in the context of the question. Generally, Venus shows people to be sociable, friendly, artistic and such, but if this planet stands for a man who is by nature far from "venusian", this might describe him as (currently) being in love, or the question might concern his financial situation, for example, or it can show him to have a positive attitude towards the problem he's involved in, or is seeking a peaceful resolution of a strife, or is simply lucky (all things considered, of course). Venus could also stand for a man (or a woman) who in the context of the question acts as an object of romantic expectations.

"Venusians" are physically attractive, have full lips, seductive looks, a well-rounded physique and (sometimes) dimples in their cheeks. Again, don't expect all the people ruled by Venus in horary charts to have those looks! But if Venus stands for an unknown person, it's possible that he/she will have the looks, ascribed to this planet.

If the ascendant of a horary chart is in Taurus or Libra – Venus' ruled signs – the querent may be interested in love, fashion, relationships, contracts and art (mostly Libra), or in financial matters, food, personal belongings, a purchase and similar (mostly Taurus).

Venus is the natural significator of:
- copper; lapis lazuli, coral, alabaster, carnelian, blue sapphire
- kidneys, lower back, neck, throat, thyroid
- love, happiness, weddings, parties, dance, celebrations
- decorative items, fashion accessories, cosmetics; money, jewelry, safes, artwork
- young women, lovers, artists, singers, models, dressmakers, florists, confectioners, fashion designers, hairdressers, milliners, jewelers
- sweet fruits, especially apples, pears and apricots; roses, lilies, lily of the valley
- gardens, orchards, parks, flowerbeds, fountains, art galleries; in the house: bedrooms, beds, wardrobes, pillows, paintings and other works of art and decorative items

MARS ♂

BASIC QUALITIES: hot and dry, choleric; malefic, the "lesser misfortune"
ESSENTIAL DIGNITY: Aries (day domicile), Scorpio (night domicile), Capricorn (exaltation), water triplicity by night
ESSENTIAL DEBILITY: Libra (detriment), Taurus (detriment), Cancer (fall)
SECT: nocturnal
GENDER: male
DAY: Tuesday
COLOR: red
TASTE: sharp, burning, spicy
EMOTIONS: anger, passion

Mars is a hot, violent, destructive planet – a malefic which was due to its reddish appearance and destructive qualities once called a "lesser infortune". It causes hot, dry and harsh weather, resulting in droughts and fires. It's particularly "militant" when eastern (rising before the Sun) and above horizon in day charts, while it shows its more desirable qualities of courage, vigor, boldness and self-initiative in night charts, especially when above horizon and in one of its own signs (Scorpio, Aries and Capricorn) or triplicity.

As significator of people, it shows them to be brave, strong, active, energetic, fearless and enterprising, but when afflicted, they can be angry, violent, headstrong, hasty, bossy, aggressive, destructive, traitorous and dangerous – to self and others. In certain cases, an afflicted Mars can also warn of the dire (dangerous) circumstances for the querent or quesited.

Martian people are muscular and lean, but with strong bones; they sometimes have reddish complexion and fair or reddish hair, and sharp, poignant eyes.

As is the case with the other planets, Mars in a horary chart can stand for people who are not at all "martian" by nature. It can stand for a woman who is by nature quiet and inoffensive, but in the concrete situation, described by the horary chart, she may be angry or forced to fight to achieve her objective, so she temporarily assumes a "Martian" role. But if Mars describes an unknown person, it's more likely that their physical appearance and manners will fit the nature and character of Mars; this person could therefore have a strong, muscular physique, he'd be bold and headstrong, engaged in sports and the like. As a significator, it can also stand for someone with whom we're connected through tensions and conflicts - or sexual passion.

Mars as a significator of the project which we plan and ask about, can mean that we'll have to fight or compete with someone to achieve our goal, and it can even warn us that the matter could be dangerous for us. As with other planets, additional indications are provided by Mars' sign and house placement and by its dispositors, receptions and aspects.

Ascendant in Aries or Scorpio – Mars' ruled signs – suggests that the querent's question may relate to a new project, sports, cars or machines (Aries), or that he's experiencing a crisis (Scorpio).

Mars is the natural significator of:
- iron and steel
- muscles, blood (red blood cells), the male sexual organs, the left ear; fever, inflammation, cuts, scars, high blood pressure; operations
- metal and sharp objects; engines, cars, trains, industry, machinery; weapons
- anger, fights, fires, war; blood; crime
- athletes, soldiers, captains, adventurers, engineers, car mechanics, blacksmiths, plumbers, hunters, butchers, surgeons, firefighters
- thorny plants and those that grow from dry, hot soil; nettle, radish, horseradish, thistle and other prickly plants

JUPITER ♃

BASIC QUALITIES: very warm and moist, sanguine; benefic, the "greater fortune"
ESSENTIAL DIGNITY: Sagittarius (day domicile), Pisces (night domicile), Cancer (exaltation), fire triplicity by day
ESSENTIAL DEBILITY: Gemini (detriment), Virgo (detriment), Capricorn (fall)
SECT: diurnal
GENDER: male
DAY: Thursday
COLOR: blue
TASTE: sweet, rich, juicy
EMOTIONS: hope, confidence, joyful expectation, enthusiasm

Jupiter is a benefic, the "greater fortune" which serves to enlarge, increase and multiply. It brings success, honors and rewards. It causes nice weather, but in combination with malefics it can contribute to storms and winds. It's the biggest planet of our solar system, and modern scientists have recognized its links with the cycles of sunspots and solar storms. Astrophysics has discovered that these cycles are closely synchronized with synodic conjunctions and oppositions of Jupiter and Saturn, the two largest planets of our solar system.

People ruled by Jupiter in horary charts have high morals, are kind-hearted, optimistic, honest, successful, generous, noble, magnanimous and philosophically or religiously inclined; they can be rich and powerful, but also (if Jupiter is afflicted) conceited, wasteful or immoral. They love nature, traveling and educational activities.

Their stature is high and strong, with powerful thighs and long legs. They can have a bulging stomach and big, sometimes uneven teeth. Their faces are oval and eyes are large, revealing a honest, trustworthy and optimistic spirit.

In horary astrology, all of these qualities must be understood in the context of each question, of course! Jupiter as a significator of any person adds to their integrity, honesty and goodness, although much, of course, depends on the specific conditioning of the planet by sign, house and aspects. As a significator of the quesited, it can also show somebody from whom much is expected or who is associated with our ambitious plans, hopes and desires. (This also applies to situations, plans, projects and the like.) But whether the person or thing that is ruled by Jupiter, will meet our expectations, of course depends on the actual conditioning of the planet in a horary chart.

When the ascendant is in any of Jupiter's signs, the querent is often interested in travel, education or legal affairs (Sagittarius), or in spiritual matters (Pisces).

Jupiter is the natural significator of:
- zinc and brass; amethyst, topaz, emeralds; marble
- forests, wood and wood products
- liver, lungs, hips, thighs
- lawyers, attorneys, judges, counselors, priests, philosophers, teachers, professors, publishers, members of the parliament; angels
- money, wealth; gambling, stock market; publishing, marketing, advertising
- fertility
- big but tame animals, especially horses
- courts, universities, large halls, churches; foreign destinations
- linden trees, figs, mulberries; aromatic plants

SATURN ♄

BASIC QUALITIES: cold and dry, melancholic; malefic, the "greater misfortune"
ESSENTIAL DIGNITY: Capricorn (night domicile), Aquarius (day domicile), Libra (exaltation), air triplicity by day
ESSENTIAL DEBILITY: Cancer (detriment), Leo (detriment), Aries (fall)
SECT: diurnal
GENDER: male
DAY: Saturday
COLORS: gray, black
TASTE: sour, bitter
EMOTIONS: sadness, worry, fear, depression, anxiety

Saturn is the last planet, visible to the naked eye. As such, it has always been associated with everything that is distant, final and ultimate. In modern times, some of its functions have been "relegated" to Pluto, but in the traditional astrological symbolism, and also experientially, such definitions still apply. This mighty "planet of time" has been associated with illness, old age and death, but also with wisdom, erudition and maturity. It represents obstacles, restrictions, restraints and frustration, but also the safety and reliability of all that is old, established and proven.

In nature, it brings cold weather and low air pressure, and causes decay.

As significator is stands for serious, strict, reliable, careful, demanding, thoughtful, solitary, diligent, detached, industrious, studious, patient, persistent, secretive and uncompromising people who progress slowly and surely. If badly placed, such people can be selfish, cold, suspicious, hateful, evil, envious, harsh, grim, gloomy, stubborn, or dissatisfied, unhappy, sad, pessimistic, depressed, sick, lonely and similar. Such can also be the "fate" of people ruled by an afflicted Saturn in a horary chart, whereas a dignified Saturn could suggest that they'll get by their ambition by diligent work or through a slow and steady progress.

"Saturnians" are of medium height and tend to be thin; they have pale complexion, prominent bones (especially the cheeks) and dark hair and eyes.

Again, as with the other planets, all this does not mean that the querent (or the quesited) ruled by Saturn in a horary chart, should have such physique and character! A person who's lively, bold and optimistic by nature, can be ruled by Saturn when worrying about their health or when depressed due to a disappointing love affair. Saturn can also stand for someone coming back into our lives from the past - especially, of course, if retrograde. If the querent asks a question at the time when the ascendant in any of Saturn's signs (Capricorn and Aquarius especially), he may be interested in official affairs, career, long-term goals, real-estate and the like, or, if asking about other matters, he may be driven by a calculated ambition – or by worry, fear and sadness.

Saturn is the natural significator of:
- lead, coal, diamonds and other stones, especially of black and gray colors
- teeth, bones, skin, right ear; diseases in general, especially colds, rheumatism, deafness, anxiety, depression, nightmares, hypothermia, suffocation and falls from height
- job, business projects, career ambitions
- managers, government and civil service employees, inspectors, planners, controllers, historians, archaeologists, museum stuff; manual workers, stonemasons, bricklayers, engineers, builders, plumbers; service workers who deal with metal, stones or heavy machinery; farmers, miners, cavers; administrators; puritans, monks; old, sick and diseased people
- heavy and hard objects
- real-estate property, land, building plots, fields; mines, caves; factories, warehouses; in the house: doors, walls, cellars, cold and rundown rooms
- rocks, deserts, caves, tunnels, ruins, cemeteries, graves and all the dark, abandoned and dirty places

TRANSSATURNIANS

TRANSSATURNIANS AS SIGN RULERS AND SIGNIFICATORS

hould we use transsaturnians (Uranus, Neptune and Pluto) in horary astrology, or not? That's a frequent question and the issue is one of the most controversial among the contemporary horary community. The "transsaturnians" - so called because they orbit outside of Saturn - were discovered only in the last few centuries, and as such have not been incorporated into the traditional astrology practice. As horary is such an ancient discipline, most horary astrologers don't allow for their sign rulership which has been infiltrated into the modern natal astrology, whereby Uranus rules Aquarius, Neptune Pisces and Pluto Scorpio. That would be unacceptable, they say, considering the ancient, traditional sign rulership system is extremely sophisticated and wonderful in its simplicity and logic. It this system, both the Sun and the Moon, our "heavenly lights", rule one sign each while all the planets rule two, one as the day and the other as the night rulers. (See ESSENTIAL DIGNITY on p. 89). To ruin this system by replacing the old rulers with the new ones would interfere with the very foundations of our art which has been carefully built over the millennia.

The mainstream traditional horary astrology, therefore, denies those planets the role of sign rulers – and, consequently, the role of house rulers and significators.

But, think, astrology is evolving, just like all fields of knowledge are. I certainly give priority to traditional rulers, but I don't completely exclude the modern planets in this role. While I never give them main rulerships, I do consider them in their co-rulership function. Experience has showed that modern rulers often provide additional indications and that they can sometimes (but only sometimes) even replace the traditional ones. This goes for those charts where any of those planets is strongly emphasized – for example, by conjuncting AC, DC, MC, IC, lunar nodes, the Sun or the Moon, or when there's a stellium (three or more planets) in a sign which they're supposed to rule in modern astrology. Sometimes, even their placement in an angular house (1, 4, 10, 7) suffices. I've also noticed that they can co-rule the querent in cases of the horary chart's ascendant being in Aquarius, Pisces or Scorpio for those querents who have those planets strong in their natal charts – according to the above criteria.

In spite of that, traditional rulers can never be completely ruled out and negated! The late American astrologer Sylvia de Long wrote a book with 101 cases of horary charts (**THE ART OF HORARY ASTROLOGY IN PRACTICE**, AFA, 1980), in which she strictly used Uranus, Neptune and Pluto as rulers of Aquarius, Pisces and Scorpio respectively. On the first sight, her interpretive logic makes sense, but a careful study of all those charts revealed that the same answer – or even a clearer and more adequate one – would be received if she used only the traditional sign rulers.

Traditional rulers are usually more reliable when a horary question concerns the ordinary, usual, everyday people, situations and articles. However, when it comes to issues relating to politics, society, science and modern trends (in culture, art and the like), or to people who in horary charts play such a role (political leaders, scientists, researchers, visual artists, musicians etc.), the use of modern significators (in addition to the traditional ones, which almost always retain their main rulership) often makes sense and is therefore, of course, useful and desirable.

It is also reasonable to use transsaturnians as cosignificators when they occupy a house (in particular its cusp) which stands for the subject of the question.

TRANSSATURNIANS AS NATURAL SIGNIFICATORS

The hard-core traditionalists completely exclude the trassaturnians on the grounds that if horary astrology could have been developed and used effectively in ancient times, when astrologers weren't aware of their existence, it could do so today as well. Alas, the world of today is not the world of yesterday. Today, we have electricity, phones, computers, internet, photography, psychology, films, electronic music, pharmaceuticals, petroleum industry, atomic bombs… We live in an age when many things and concepts clearly meet the characteristics of transsaturnians, so it certainly makes sense to use them as natural significators, as well as those forces (energies) which influence the development of situations associated with the above (and other similar) things and concepts. Their usefulness has been time and again proven by various other astrological techniques (natal and forecasting), so it would be really foolish to ignore them in horary. From this perspective, insisting on the "holy seven" visible celestial bodies seems not only reactionary, but also harmful – to the development of our art as such.

In some horary charts, transsaturnians (even when not in the role of significators) exert the kind of energy which could be described as *force majeure* – a "higher force" over which the querent has no control. They can point to major social, political and economic changes which have a decisive impact on the achievement of the querent's goal, or they can only indicate specific kinds of "energy" which, one way or another (depending on the nature of the planet) affect the outcome of the question. **With Uranus, this can be an abrupt and unexpected end (of a relationship, an establishment, a process etc.) or a sudden insight or discovery, leading to a constructive change; with Neptune, this can be a "fatal" mistake, delusion or deception, or "miraculous" help; with Pluto, it's regeneration, revitalization or transformation, or a fatal obstruction.** (In all cases, the actual expression depends on the aspects and other conditioning).

By themselves, transsaturnians are neither benefics nor malefics. Much depends on the aspects they receive from the other planets, but in a very general sense, they exhibit more "malevolence" when acting on everyday, firmly established principles and well-known objects, whereas they exert a more benevolent influence when acting on some modern, new-age, specialized objects, ideas, principles and similar. Besides, they often exert a negative influence when in conjunctions, as they represent those "distant", unexplored, out-of-ordinary and therefore overpowering things (people, objects, processes) which can "derail" us or compel us to find new, creative ways of dealing with them.

Lunar aspect with the transsaturnians are certainly not to be ignored. Know, though, that the closer to an angle at least one of the planets (that is, either the Moon or a transsaturnian) is, the more probable the event associated with the aspect (see below). Same goes for the aspects of the significators (and cosignificators) with those planets.

URANUS ♅ ♂

Uranus is the **natural significator** of lightning, thunderstorms, earthquakes; electricity, electronics, computers and other modern communications (telephone, radio, TV); airplanes, airports, space travel; revolutions, reforms; astrology; trade unions; explosions; shocks; heart attacks, strokes; separation, divorce.

Uranus is synchronized with all sudden and unexpected events or "twists of fate" that conflict what was planned or anticipated. Its energy, when negatively expressed, has the power to suddenly "disconnect" us from other people or things, with the consequence of our position becoming radically changed. The positive expression (harmonious aspects) has, on the contrary, the power to suddenly and unexpectedly improve our situation for the better. It can feel as if a light has been turned on, suddenly illuminating the dark corners and giving as a solution that we had been seeking.

People ruled by Uranus in horary charts are unconventional, nonconformist, innovative, unique, unpredictable, obstinate, independent and freedom-loving. They can be geniuses or freaks. Uranus also rules progressive politicians, reformers, computer scientists, engineers, audio and video technicians and inventors.

As **significator of the quesited**, Uranus can stand for someone who meets the above criteria, or someone who will act unpredictably, will do contrary to what's expected, or someone to whom something along those lines could happen (depending on the context of the question).

COLORS: "electric" blue, sky blue

EMOTIONS: stress, shock; excitement

NEPTUNE ♆

Neptune is the **natural significator** of the sea, fish, fishing, ship, sea voyages; chemicals, medicines and other pharmaceuticals; monasteries, hospitals, asylums, refugee camps; alcohol, drugs, poisons; gases; lies, deceit, scandals, fallacies; dreams, visions, hallucinations; photography, film, TV image; poets, dancers, musicians, painters, illusionists; commercials, mass media marketing, propaganda; high ideals; illusion, fantasy; charities; religion, spirituality; slavery; physical weakness.

People, ruled by Neptune, can be of an ethereal, frail appearance, or they can be weak, helpless, disappointed or disappointing. Neptune stands for visionaries, humanitarians and artists (especially dancers, painters and musicians), but also for cheaters, alcoholics, drug addicts, religious fanatics and the like.

Neptune blurs the boundaries of physical reality and represents an expansion which is even greater than that of Jupiter, but most often not supported by logic, reality and facts. It can bring temporary good, but such as is not grounded in actual possibilities, so that the end result is usually disappointment. In disharmonious aspects, Neptune causes people to be misled, although it allows for feelings of oblivion, bliss and euphoria (as under the influence of alcohol or drugs).

As **significator of people**, Neptune stands for those who might disappoint us by being unreliable, elusive, mysterious, untruthful and the like, but it can also show someone who is extremely kind-hearted, compassionate and self-sacrificing. Much depends on the aspects and additional factors in the chart. If the Moon as cosignificator of the querent applies to it by a conjunction or a dynamic aspect, this is a warning that the querent will soon find himself on "slippery" grounds and will be misled, cheated or disappointed. In harmonious aspects, however, Neptune can bring help of an unusual kind – as if a "guardian angel" came to his rescue.

COLOR: sea green

EMOTIONS: compassion; euphoria, disappointment, helplessness, despair, confusion

PLUTO ♇ (♇)

Pluto is the **natural significator** of crisis, death and transformation; "fatal" (unconquerable) obstructions; *force majeure*; buried wealth, joint funds, financial embezzlement; abysses, caves; insects (especially those transmitting disease), rats, lizards and vultures; corpses; rape; tyrants, dictators, anarchists, terrorists, moneylenders, criminals, murderers, robbers; detectives, secret intelligence service; underground and secret organizations (secret police); (atomic) bombs; genetic research; geriatrics; hypnosis; depth psychology and psychotherapy; regeneration and re-incarnation.

"Plutonians" can have dark and menacing looks, and a piercing, threatening or hypnotic gaze. As **significator of people**, Pluto can stand for those who go through some kind of crisis (physical, emotional, psychological, financial and similar); they may be vindictive and dangerous, or even contemplate a murder or a suicide, but it can also stand for people who go through some kind of major transformation that they experience as positive. Additional indications are provided by aspects and other chart factors.

The Moon, when applying to Pluto by a harmonious aspect, suggests some kind or renewal, restoration or re-vitalization. In missed items charts, this aspect often indicates a re-possession (of that which was lost or mislaid), whereas in other kind of charts, it suggests that the querent could regain his former strength, influence, power and similar. In medical horaries, it points toward recuperation. In disharmonious aspects, there's often a "fatal" obstruction which can completely shut off the querent from his goal, plan or ambition.

COLOR: black

EMOTIONS: rage, panic, revengefulness, disgust

PLANETARY DIGNITY

lanetary dignity deals with assessing strengths and weaknesses of the planets, and as such it plays an extremely important role in all traditional astrology. In previous centuries, it went without saying that astrologers mathematically calculated planetary dignities – in natal as well as in horary charts - so as to evaluate which planets were strong and which were weak. In natal astrology, this helped them evaluate their clients' good or bad fortune in certain spheres of life. If, for example, planets associated with finances were very strong (dignified) in someone's chart, they judged that he would earn lots of money and be financially successful, but if they were weak (had little dignity), he might have had to beg for his daily bread.

Such evaluation has almost completely disappeared from modern, psychologically oriented astrology, mainly because this tends to shun from all notions of predestination. But I'm convinced that today, as ever, a quality natal chart reading should include the evaluation of planetary dignity (strength). I can't even imagine doing natal astrology and skipping that all-important step!

In horary astrology, we calculate planetary dignity to evaluate the degree of power (or powerlessness) of significators, standing for people, things and concepts. This can be extremely helpful when searching for answers. If the querent, say, is wondering whether he'd succeed in a certain undertaking, the strength of his significator significantly raises the possibility of a positive answer, and vice versa. Same with animals, projects, objects, plans, etc. *Is my kitten going to get well?* If its significator is strong, it'll recover from the disease, if very weak, it could succumb to it. *Is my new job going to meet my expectations?* If the job's significator is very dignified, it certainly will, if not, I might regret that I accepted the offer. And so on.

In some cases, significators' strengths are all we need for the answer: in lawsuit cases, for example, if the plaintiff's significator is significantly stronger than that of the defendant, he'll most probably win – and vice versa. The same goes for all kinds of duels and competitions - whenever we're interested in who has better chances for a win.

There are two types of planetary dignity: **essential** and **accidental**. They differ both in method of calculation and in function. Usually we calculate both, and use the one (or primarily the one) which in the context of the question provides more information. More on this in chapter DIFFERENCES BETWEEN ESSENTIAL AND ACCIDENTAL DIGNITY on p. 106), but first let us look at what each of them means and how they're calculated.

ESSENTIAL DIGNITY

Essential dignity is based on planetary placements in signs or in fractions of signs. In the order of importance (strength), essential dignities are:
- **domicile**
- **exaltation**
- **triplicity**
- **term**
- **face**
- **monomoiria**

A special kind of essential dignity is **mutual reception**, which can include all of the above dignities. The planet with the most dignity in a certain degree is called **almuten**, while the planet which in a certain degree has no dignity at all, is called **peregrine**. The two main dignities (domicile and exaltation) also have their counter-placements which are called **essential debilities**. In calculating planetary strengths, peregrine planets are also perceived as being essentially debilitated.

DOMICILE

Planets received their **domiciles** in ancient Greece. GREEK HOROSCOPES, a book by O. Neugebauer and H. B. Van Hoesen (American Philosophical Society, 1987), reveals that this happened in the first century BC. As such, planetary domiciles have a later origin than planetary exaltations which were created in the Mesopotamian period.

Planetary domicile is, to put it simply, that sign in which the planet feels most "at home". In the past, those signs were even called planetary "houses"; although that word later became established as marking the 12-fold divisions of the sky in the horizontal system of measurement, it originally referred to the 12 signs. Anyway - astrologers of old believed that each planet "feels best" in a certain sign (or a couple of signs), therefore they assigned them their individual "domiciles".

Planets and their domicile signs share similar characteristics, therefore they express themselves in their domiciles more strongly and more in line with their inherent qualities, as in any other sign. Where do we (normally) feel more safe and comfortable – in our own house or in a friend's house? The answer is obvious, I think, and the same goes for planets. People, shown by planets in their domiciles, are capable, confident and strong, and they have much going on for them in the process of achieving their goals. (See also DIFFERENCES BETWEEN ESSENTIAL AND ACCIDENTAL DIGNITY on p. 106.)

We say that planets **rule** their individual domicile signs.

In his *Tetrabiblos,* the famous Greek astrologer Ptolemy gave a clear explanation for the specific arrangements of planetary domiciles. Since in the northern hemisphere, where our astrology developed, the Sun is at its most powerful when in Cancer and Leo, both lights received their domiciles in these signs: the **Sun** in the day (masculine) sign Leo and the **Moon** in the night (feminine) sign Cancer. The Sun and the Moon, of course, are a couple, so their domiciles must be together! The five visible planets were then arranged in relation to their natural distances from the Sun; each received its day domicile in a positive (masculine) and its night domicile in a negative (feminine) sign. Only the Sun and the Moon received one domicile each, due to their distinctly masculine (the Sun) and feminine (the Moon) natures.

The closest planet to the Sun is **Mercury**, which has its day domicile in the positive Gemini and its night domicile is in the negative Virgo. (You will notice that 0° Leo, the boundary between Leo and Cancer, is at a 30° distance from the cusps of both of Mercruy's domicile signs, and 30° is, incidentally, about as much as the maximum elongation of Mercury, which never departs from the Sun by more than 28°).

Next comes **Venus**, the "goddess" of love and beauty: its day domicile is in the positive Libra and its night domicile in the negative Taurus. Venus was once called "the lesser fortune", which is nicely reflected by the fact that the boundary between Leo and Cancer is in a harmonious sextile (60° aspect) to the cusps of Libra and Taurus. Since Venus can never depart from the Sun by more than 48°, this allocation also pretty much maintains their natural (maximum) distances.

Venus is followed by **Mars**, the planet of passion, aggression and war: its day domicile is in the positive Aries and its night domicile in the negative Scorpio. The destructive Mars was once called "the lesser misfortune", so it's no coincidence that the cusps of Aries and Scorpio are in a tense, disruptive square aspect (90°) to 0° Leo.

Jupiter, "the greater fortune", has its day domicile in the positive Sagittarius and its night domicile in the negative Pisces. In accordance with the most fortunate effects attributed to this magnanimous planet, the cusps of Sagittarius and Pisces are connected to 0° Leo by the most harmonious aspect of trine (120°).

Saturn is the most distant planet from the Sun and therefore also the slowest. Its characteristics are in a stark contrast to those of the two "givers of life", as the Sun and the Moon were also called. This traditional planet of cold, darkness and death, which was once called "the greater misfortune", has its day domicile in the positive Aquarius and its night domicile in the negative Capricorn. The boundary between the two is exactly opposite to the boundary between Cancer and Leo; we say that they're in opposition (180 °) which is considered to be the most unfortunate aspect (!). (Exclamation mark because you'll read in many modern astrological textbooks that a square is stronger and more destructive aspect than opposition. This doesn't agree with the traditional teachings – although there are some variations depending on which planets are involved, especially as regards disharmonious aspects of the Moon with Mars and Saturn.)

Many Greek astrologers believed that the male planets (Saturn, Jupiter and Mars) express themselves more strongly when in their day domiciles, while Venus, the female planet, was supposed to be better placed in her night domicile. According to them, Saturn is therefore stronger (more dignified) in Aquarius as in Capricorn, Jupiter is stronger in Sagittarius as in Pisces, Mars is stronger in Aries as in Scorpio, and Venus is stronger in Taurus as in Libra. Mercury, which since antiquity has been seen as a genderless planet, was stronger in Virgo, because in this sign it retains its natural distance from the Sun.

In practice, it has been agreed that when calculating planetary strengths by domicile, planets get the same number of points regardless of their day/night placements, but when those dignities are combined with triplicity and sect, Saturn is indeed stronger in Aquarius in day charts, Jupiter in Sagittarius in day charts and Venus in Taurus in night charts, while Mars is stronger in Scorpio in night charts. Mars is the only masculine planet which is stronger in its night domicile than in its day domicile, as it belongs to the night sect.

DETRIMENT (ESSENTIAL DEBILITY)

The sign which lies opposite to a planet's domicile is called that planet's **detriment**. In that sign, the planet is at its weakest; it finds it difficult to express its inherent qualities, as it experiences the "vibrations" of that sign as foreign and uncomfortable. The querent or the quesited, ruled by a detrimented planet, can be seriously thwarted in his ambition and unable to achieve his goal.

In his book CHOICE ASTROLOGICAL APHORISMS (Merlini Anglici Ephemeris, 1676), William Lilly wrote that the planet in its detriment is "*like a person cast out of all his estate without hopes of recovery*". Past astrologers found that those who in their birth charts have many planets in detriment or fall (see FALL, p. 93), cannot rise in life, are unlucky, ineffective or of poor health.

In horary astrology, if a significator is in detriment, this can show a weak, unpromising, unsuccessful, endangered, damaged or otherwise restricted state of that which the planet represents, be it a person, animal, object or concept. In questions asking for the quality of an object (like a planned purchase of a particular car, construction lot and similar) or desirability of a project (partnership, job, travel and the like), their significator in detriment inclines towards a negative answer. Significators of missing articles in detriment may indicate that they are damaged. On the other hand, if a detrimented planet rules a disease, this is not "weak", but can be destructive and dangerous!

Know that while benefics and neutral planets (the Sun, the Moon, Venus, Mercury and Jupiter) in detriment usually only show weakness, incompetence, ineffectiveness and similar, malefics (Mars and Saturn) in detriment can express their "frustration" in damaging and destructive ways – either as active agents or the recipients of such energy. In other words, they can stand for aggressors or for the victims of aggression. The key to understanding is that planets can't express themselves in healthy ways when detrimented, and this can have a variety of expressions.

A detrimented **Mars**, for example, is like a dog on a chain. Since he's been denied freedom of movement, he becomes overly aggressive in defending his personal space - come too close and he'll bite! This also tells us: if a planet applies to a conjunction with a detrimented Mars, it's in danger – except if it's stronger than Mars, of course! Generally speaking, Jupiter and Saturn - plus transsaturnians - are stronger than Mars, especially when dignified. On the other hand, the dog's master (planet ruling the Mars' sign) is in control of the dog on a chain, and in relation to him, the dog is definitely weaker. But I should add that since Mars' dispositor, when in detriment, is always the benevolent Venus, this also teaches us that we can only conquer hate with love and aggression with non-violence.

Like all planets, Mars is detrimented in two signs: Taurus and Libra. I have noticed that it responds more fiercly to frustration when in **Taurus** (it's an animal sign, after all), and in a more placid way when in **Libra**. Here it's like a dog that has lost much of his animal qualities because he's become just a house pet – spoilt, castrated, a "toy". Such a dog will wave its tail to a burglar, instead of barking. As for people, Mars in detriment can stand for a charming lover who is married and incapable of meeting the expectations of his mistress, and as such he can be seen as unfair, treacherous and similar.

Saturn in detriment is, on the contrary, a silent and hidden enemy. Its slow motion tells us that when detrimented, it suggests long-lasting difficulties, so in many charts ruled by a detrimented Saturn, the querent will be in an unenviable position. Saturns' detriments are Leo and Cancer. In **Leo,** this planet definitely has more power. As significator of people, it can stand for those in command who are unable to perform their roles well, perhaps due to unhealthy ambition, greed, selfishness, noncooperation and the like - which sooner or later leads them to fall from office —that is, express the function of a detrimented planet. But as Saturn is a planet of time, this would normally not happen soon, and while in power, Saturn so placed can do much harm. (Note that the querent, ruled by it, can also be the recipient of such energies!) Saturn in **Cancer** is harmful for other reasons. We could compare it to a scientist who had lost his job and is forced to stay at home and cook, feed the kids and clean up while his wife is at work. The poor man wanted to do scientific research! His inner nature resists household chores, he's unhappy and messes things up instead of helping his family.

But there's another side to the coin. Planets in detriment **don't always act negatively**. I have noticed that they sometimes stand for people who are literally "away from home" - like living in a foreign country, or being of a foreign origin. For in the same way as planets in their domicile signs stand for that which is our own (possessions, home, apartments), planets in detriment stand for that which is foreign or alien. So, in questions relating to foreign countries, foreigners and travel, a planet in detriment can stand for just that - a foreign country, a foreign nationality of the querent or quesited, or for someone who is about to travel abroad – or is returning from there. Depending on the context of the question, it can also show "our" people in foreign countries (travelers) or on foreign grounds – like a misplaced article in an unusual place where it certainly doesn't belong, or out of the house, for example. Always think in terms "home / away from home".

EXALTATION

Exaltation originates in Mesopotamian astrology and as such precedes planetary domiciles. There are several speculations as for the reasons for planetary exaltations, none totally convincing.

Each planet is "exalted" in a certain degree of a certain sign, meaning that in that degree it "shines" most brightly (not literally, of course). The concept was later transferred to the whole of signs.

In the hierarchy of dignities, exaltation is second in order. A planet in its exaltation stands for **dignity, honor** and **excellence**, but most authors agree that it doesn't offer the same degree of freedom and self-confidence as domicile. Some ancient astrologers believed that planetary domiciles should be used mainly for "ordinary mortals" while exaltations were more fitting in charts cast for the nobility (kings, rulers). In today's astrological practice, exalted planets are seen as very strong, although slightly less than in their domiciles.

The exaltation signs and degrees are:

Sun: Aries 19°
Moon: Taurus 3°
Mercury: Virgo 15°
Venus: Pisces 27°
Mars: Capricorn 28°
Jupiter: Cancer 15°
Saturn: Libra 21°

Exaltations have also been attributed to the lunar nodes, although this criterion is rarely used in practice:

Moon's north node: Gemini 3°
Moon's south node: Sagittarius 3°

As already said, exaltations in practice refer to the wholes of signs, not only the the specified degrees. This means that the Sun is exalted in the whole of Aries, not only at 19° Aries, the Moon is exalted in the whole of Taurus, not only at 3°, and so on.

FALL (ESSENTIAL DEBILITY)

In the signs, opposite to their exaltations, planets are in their **fall**. Symbolically - and experientially – this shows a fall from "height" or from a certain position. Planets in their falls are impeded, especially in terms of influence, prestige and power of the person or project that they represent. With Mars and Saturn, the fall works similarly to detriment: they can express their frustration by acting harmfully or detrimentally (to the querent or the quesited). But Mars has its fall in Cancer, where it also has some dignity as it rules the water triplicity by night, so that a "fallen" Mars has a somewhat better reputation than a "fallen" Saturn, whose expression in Aries, the sign of its fall, is very destructive due to the diametrically opposite natures of the planet and sign.

TRIPLICITY

In ancient Greek astrology, **triplicity** was an extremely important category. It is based on the division of zodiacal signs into three groups of four. All the signs of one group (triplicity) are in mutual trines (at distances of 120°). The four triplicities are: **fire** (Aries, Leo, Sagittarius), **earth** (Taurus, Virgo, Capricorn), **air** (Gemini, Libra, Aquarius) and **water** (Cancer, Scorpio, Pisces). Today, triplicities are also called **elements**. The distribution of signs into elements plays an important role in modern astrology, albeit with a single – but important - difference: triplicitiy **rulers** have completely disappeared from modern practice! They vary depending on whether it's a day or a night chart. (Remember: day charts are those in which the Sun is above horizon, in houses 7 to 12, and night charts are those in which the Sun is below the horizon, in houses 1 to 6.)

TRIPLICITY RULERS

FIRE TRIPLICITY	day ruler Sun
	night ruler Jupiter
EARTH TRIPLICITY	day ruler Venus
	night ruler Moon
AIR TRIPLICITY	day ruler Saturn
	night ruler Mercury
WATER TRIPLICITY	day ruler Venus
	night ruler Mars

Each triplicity also has a **common ruler**: fire triplicity Saturn, earth triplicity Mars, air triplicity Jupiter and water triplicity the Moon.

Triplicity is the only dignity which has preserved the distinction between daytime (diurnal) and night-time (nocturnal) charts. As such, it is closely associated with the sect of the planets.

William Lilly who took over the triplicity rulers of Ptolemy (*the author of* **TETRABIBLOS**), used Mars as the day and night ruler of the water triplicity. This rulership scheme is still used by most horary astrologers today, but I have decided to go back to the original Hellenistic scheme where the water triplicity is ruled by Venus in daytime charts. I've done so because I have always found it strange that one of the triplicities should have the same day and night ruler; besides, it seems logical that the water triplicity which is so intimately related to love and fertility, should be ruled by at least one feminine planet. This system also agrees more with planetary sect, as the nocturnal sect is composed of the Moon, Venus and Mars, which in the triplicity scheme in turn rule over all nocturnal (water and earth) signs.

In natal astrology, ancient Greek astrologers carefully studied the triplicity rulers' placements. They considered all three (day, night and common) rulers. In day charts, they considered the Sun sign, in night charts, the Moon sign. The triplicity rulers of the Sun or the Moon sign's were the primary factors of their divination. If, for example, someone was born at night and the Moon was in Aquarius, which belongs to the air triplicity, they first studied Mercury (the night ruler of air triplicity), then Saturn (the day ruler of air triplicity) and then also Jupiter (common ruler of air triplicity). If it was a day birth and the Sun was, say, in Virgo, they first studied Venus (day ruler of earth triplicity), then the Moon (night ruler of earth triplicity) and then Mars (common ruler of earth triplicity).

In horary astrology, a planet in its triplicity is moderately dignified. It's quite strong, but not as strong as in its domicile or exaltation. Lilly says that a planet in its triplicity shows *"a man who is moderately endowed with goods of this world"*, while the Hebrew astrologer Ibn Ezra compared such a planet with *"a man in the house of his relatives"*. (Which is, of course, not so good as being in your own house, but still better as being in a stranger's house.)

TERM

Terms (or *bounds,* from lat. *termini,* meaning boundaries) are an ancient division of each sign into five unequal parts. Each term is ruled by one of the seven planets - the Sun and the Moon being exempt from the scheme. A planet in its term is slightly dignified, meaning it has some power, but not much.

The origins of terms are shrouded in mystery. Lilly used them to describe the querent's (or quesited's) physical appearance: a planet in a Saturn's term suggested that the person had "saturnian" looks (was skinny, dark, with high cheekbones), for example.

Terms have already been used by the ancient Egyptians and Mesopotamians, but their systems were different. It seems that Hellenistic astrologers (with rare exceptions) used the Egyptian system, with the exception of Ptolemy's contemporary Vettius Valens who used a significantly different system, as it included the Sun and the Moon, and what's more, his system had two variations which he alternated between diurnal and nocturnal charts. Ptolemy used a system which he is supposed to have found in an old book and is a combination of Egyptian and Mesopotamian systems. This was taken over by medieval and renaissance astrologers. There were apparently even more systems, so it's no wonder that today, this is one of the most controversial subjects of traditional (horary) astrology.

> Lately, the old Egyptian (and Hellenistic) system has been gaining grounds, and because I find it the most logical of all, I have started using it too. All dignities in the Practice part of this book (example charts) are calculated according to this system.

In all systems of terms, the sum of all the degrees that are ruled by a particular planet, is the so-called "greater" number of their years: Saturn's years are 57, Mars's 66, Mercury's 76, Jupiter's 79, Venus' 82 (total 360). Old astrologers also knew the "mean" and "least" numbers of planetary years, which were used for predictive purposes, but not in horary astrology.

As regards the distribution of terms, systems vary, but there's a general pattern to be observed. The sequence of the ruling planets depends on the level of power or strength that each planet has in a certain sign, and this was judged according to several criteria, including planetary domicile, exaltation, triplicity and sect. The first criterion was obviously the benevolence of the planet: the first term of a particular sign was given to the planet which according to the hierarchy of "merits" best reflected the nature of that sign, while the last two were normally given to the malefics Mars and Saturn. But the combination of criteria yields a unique sequence: the malefic Saturn rules the first term of Libra, as this is the sign of its exaltation and day triplicity, while also having some power in it as a planet of the diurnal sect in a diurnal sign. Similarly, the malefic Mars takes first term in two of the three water signs, this being Scorpio (Mars' domicile, night triplicity ruler and a planet of the nocturnal sect in a nocturnal sign) and Cancer (night triplicity ruler and and also a planet of the nocturnal sect in a nocturnal sign), while in Pisces the first term was given to Venus, as it is the sign of its exaltation and the day triplicity, and because it is a night sign with Venus belonging to the nocturnal sect.

A close observation reveals, however, that no system is completely consistent. I have decided to follow the Hellenistic system (see **TABLE OF ESSENTIAL DIGNITIES OF PLANETS** on p. 458), although I'm not completely convinced of its merit, but since terms are not a major dignity and - according to my research - the outcome of any horary chart is not dependent on terms, that doesn't really matter.

As already said, planets in their terms have a little power. Ibn Ezra compared such a planet to *"a man sitting in his chair"*. We could also compare it to a man living in a rented house. He lives in foreign premises but has a temporary right to use them and is surrounded by some of his personal belongings.

FACE

Faces stem from the ancient Egyptian calendar, in which a year was divided into 36 periods of 10 days, and each was ruled by one of the nine bodies: the seven planets, the Sun and the Moon. Accordingly, every sign was divided into three equal parts of ten degrees - the first, second and third face or **decan**, as this dignity is also called.

Faces were very important in Egyptian, but also in Roman astrology. The Roman astrologer Firmicus Maternus from the 4th century even wrote that the planet in its face is as strong as in its own sign (domicile)! At that time, it was considered that the ruler of the face, rising at birth, indicated whether the person would have a good or a bad life. The name "faces" was given to them because they were originally depicted with animal and human faces.

But the importance of faces gradually diminished. Lilly said that a planet in its face can be compared to *"a man struggling to maintain his position"*.

There are two systems of faces. In the Egyptian system, which was also used by other ancient and medieval astrologers, the face rulers were arranged in the order of their relative speeds, as seen from Earth. Such order was called Chaldean. It starts with 0°Aries and continues until the end of the zodiacal circle. The first face of Aries is ruled by Mars, the second by the Sun, the third by Venus; the first face of in Taurus is ruled by Mercury, the second my the Moon, the third by Saturn; the first face of Gemini is ruled by Jupiter, the second by Mars, the third by the Sun, and so on. (See **TABLE OF ESSENTIAL DIGNITIES OF PLANETS** on p. 458.)

The Egyptian system is firmly rooted in horary astrology and is used as a minor essential dignity, but in general astrology, there's another system which is called "rulership by triplicity". The name is misleading, though, as each decan of a sign in this system is ruled by one of the sign rulers of the same triplicity (in order of signs), and not by the classical triplicity rulers. The sequence is: Aries – Mars, Sun, Jupiter; Taurus - Venus, Mercury, Saturn; Gemini – Mercury, Venus, Saturn; Cancer – Moon, Mars, Jupiter, and so on.

MONOMOIRIA

This dignity (from Greek *mono moiria*, "one degree") is virtually unknown today. I'm including it here because I think that it's a little gem that has fallen out of the treasure box of our ancestor's techniques, and deserves to be re-evaluated.

Monomoiria was the subject of the essay that I wrote as part of the final examination at Olivia Barclay's **QUALIFYING HORARY COURSE**. I had chosen it because I've been always interested in dignities, and I found that monomoiria was only mentioned in some very old texts. Lilly and his contemporaries never used it. The entire essay is published on my website *www.emakurent.com* (see Articles section).

Monomoiria stands for the planetary rulership of each individual zodiacal degree. We start with the first (zero, 0°) degree, which is ruled by the ruler of the whole sign, and continue in the Chaldean order to the end of the sign. Remember, the Chaldean order is: Saturn, Jupiter, Mars, Sun, Venus, Mercury, Moon. (See **TABLE OF MONOMOIRIA** on p. 457.)

There is another, more complicated system, in which the first degree of any sign is ruled by the triplicity ruler (different for day and night charts), and the others follow by the same Chaldean order.

A detailed study of monomoiria has led me to believe that they're quite important and that they seem to have been neglected unjustly. Any planet in the degree, ruled by a particular planet, assumes the nature of the planet, and when planets are in "their" degrees, they are more powerful and are expressed more coherently with their inherent natures.

In horary practice, I have noticed that the degree ruler of the ascendant (or the Moon) is very often that planet which is closely associated with the question, whether as natural or as accidental significator. If, for example, the chart relates to an illness, those planets can be Saturn, Mars or the H6 ruler; if it's about career, it's the H10 ruler; if it's about a study course or an exam, it can be Mercury or the H3 ruler; if the question is about money, success, happiness, partying and the like, this could be Venus, Sun, Jupiter or rulers of adequate houses (5, 10 or 11), and so on.

I'm far from saying that we can't find the answer to a horary question without the use of monomoiria. But although they're not the decisive influence as per the outcome of the question, they can certainly give us helpful additional indications. They can be very suggestive and revealing when the astrologer is trying to find out the querent's real intention. But students – especially beginners - should apply them carefully, so as to prevent the confusion which can arise with their improper and superficial use.

You will see that I often mention monomoiria in the practice part of the book, as I want to encourage you to start observing them and adding them to your technique.

DISPOSITION, RECEPTION AND MUTUAL RECEPTION

Disposition is actually just another word for rulership. We have dispositions by all planetary placements in signs or fractions of signs - by sign, triplicity, term, face and degree (monomoiria), but in practice we mostly use the disposition by sign. The planet ruling the sign (or a fraction of the sign) where a planet is placed, is called that planet's **dispositor**. If a planet is in its own dignity, it doesn't have a dispositor by that dignity, of course, as it's the same planet.

If Mercury is in Capricorn, its dispositor is Saturn (ruler of Capricorn). If Venus is in Cancer, its dispositor is the Moon (the ruler of Cancer). If Mars is in Aries, it doesn' have a dispositor by sign, as Aries is its domicile sign.

Reception is directly related to disposition. When a planet is not in its own sign (or in any other dignity), we say that the ruler of that sign (or of any other dignity) **receives** it - either in its domicile sign, exaltation sign, triplicity, term, face or degree. We mostly speak of **reception by domicile**, although **receptions by exaltation and triplicity** are also quite common, whereas the receptions by term and face are used less frequently. They gain more importance, though, when receiving each other (**mutual reception**). The planet which receives another planet is its dispositor, of course!

If Venus is in Cancer, the Moon (the ruler of Cancer and Venus' dispositor by domicile) receives it in its domicile, and Jupiter receives it in its exaltation. If Jupiter is in Aries, Mars (the ruler of Aries and Mars' dispositor by domicile) receives it in his domicile, and the Sun receives it in its exaltation.

What's the use of reception? Old authors teach that a planet in the dignity of another planet is **subordinate** to that planet which acts as its **host**. We could also say that such planet is **in the power** of another (its host). This is logical, of course. We don't have the same amount of freedom in a stranger's apartment as we do in our own. Our well-being, in such cases, depends on our host. We might enjoy the stay, or we might regret that we ever stepped through that door. What's more, our host can enjoy our company – or can't wait for the moment we'll say goodbye. In any case, we are not at home there and are therefore restricted or limited, as regards our freedom of expression. Besides, the nature of our host's home is important to our well-being. It can be comfortable, pleasant, clean and hospitable, but it can also be dirty, ugly and unfriendly (with an empty refrigerator and wine cellar, for example).

There're all kinds of scenarios as per the relationship between the guest and the host (that is, between the planet occupying a certain sign and its dispositor), and skillful blending allows for a wealth of interpretive possibilities.

But how do we know, from a horary chart, what type of relationship we're dealing with? The first step to understanding is – ask the querent! Much depends on the context of the question, but from the technical point of view, the dignity of a planet is very important. If the planet is in its detriment, the guest will probably not feel good, even if his host will go beyond his means to please him! (Exceptions are, to a certain extent, relationship charts related to romantic love, when our fortune is entirely in the hands of the beloved. This can make us feel fantastic - at least for as long as we have hope. In practice, significators of people in love are often in their detriments – for precisely the said reason.)

The well-being of the person (or thing) ruled by a planet in another planet's dignity, also depends on other planets occupying that sign. If Saturn is in the same sign, for example, the host's home may be cold and unwelcoming, but with Jupiter in that sign, it would be comfortable, warm and have a fridge full of goodies.

Of crucial importance is also the state of its dispositor (the host). If the latter is placed in the sign where the significator of the guest is essentially debilitated (in its detriment or fall), the guest may have entered the house against his host's will, or the host may not trust him, or the host is not capable of helping his guest, or their cooperation may prove detrimental to the host, and similar (depending on the nature of the question and on the situation). But if the host is in a sign where the guest has dignities, the host respects, admires or even loves the guest (depending on the context), and goes out of his way to please him. In such cases, the connection between the two planets (people, things) is particularly strong, and we call it **mutual reception**.

There is a popular opinion that the planet, placed in another's dignity, "loves" its dispositor. Such understanding is erroneous. We could indeed speak of an impersonal kind of love, the kind that exists between a piece of iron and a magnet - except of course in cases of love, where such situation would literally reflect strong feelings. But as explained above, the relationships between the two planets can be manifold, depending on their specific conditioning. Love it can be, but it can also be hate or indifference. The guest may have come to visit (speaking metaphorically) simply because the host's home was on his way, or even because his intention was to steal!

Reception is a situation where there's a relationship/correlation between two planets, based on their essential dignities, whereby the planet situated in another's dignity ("the guest") is subordinated to its dispositor ("the host").

Suppose that someone asks: *I hate my wife, is she moving out, and when?* A look at the chart reveals that his significator is in the sign ruled by his wife's significator (in H7 questions, that would be its detriment, of course), meaning that the wife "receives" him in her domicile. Hey, this could literally mean that the apartment belongs to the wife, reducing the prospects of her moving out. It would definitely not show that he loves her! But what if the apartment belonged to him? In this case, we should check the wife's significator, to see what her intentions are, but in any case such a situation would show that he's quite powerless, dependent on her decision. If, however, the querent was single and his question was: *Is my girlfriend moving in with me?*, the same planetary situation could mean that he's going to move in with her and not vice versa.

As so much depends on the context of the question, as well as on other chart's factors (aspects, lunar applications etc.), it's always very important that the question is well understood and that reception is combined with other techniques.

The already mentioned **mutual reception (MR)** has a special place among receptions. This is a situation when **two planets are in each other's dignities**. They can be mutually received by any kind of dignity, but the most commonly used are MRs by domicile and exaltation. Only these two forms of mutual reception are included among essential dignities' point calculation.

Examples of MR by domicile are: *Venus in Gemini and Mercury in Taurus, Saturn in Scorpio and Mars in Capricorn, Moon in Leo and Sun in Cancer.*

Examples of MR by exaltation are: *Moon in Libra and Saturn in Taurus, Venus in Capricorn and Mars in Pisces, Sun in Taurus and Moon in Aries.*

A pair of planets can also be in a "mixed mutual reception", whereby they are mutually received by a mixture of various dignities - domicile and exaltation being the most common (and strongest). Examples of mixed MR by domicile and exaltation are: *Sun in Cancer and Moon in Aries, Jupiter in Taurus and Venus in Cancer, Venus in Aries and Mars in Pisces.* (In the last case, though, care is needed in interpretation, since Venus is in detriment in Aries and therefore weak, so its capability of helping Mars is reduced. Same for other similar combinations.) Mixed mutual receptions, involving lesser dignities, are weaker and much less used in practice, although they sometimes give interesting and useful additional insights.

Mutual receptions (especially by domicile and exaltation) strengthen the planets which are in turn seen as being dignified. **They help each other, support one another, cooperate and work for mutual benefit.**

In practice, mutual receptions are used in a variety of ways, but they always show some kind of a **link**. They can relate to friendship, love, business association, and similar. The stronger the reception, the stronger the bond! *How will I get along with the new boss?* If our significators are in a strong mutual reception (by domicile, exaltation or mixed MR), the answer tends to be "superbly", but if MR is weak or non-existent, we might not have the best of relationship and will gradually loose interest in each other. *Who stole my ring? Is it someone I know?* If there's a weak MR between our significators (by face and term, for example), I've probably already met the thief before or I know him by sight. If the MR involves triplicity, I might be meeting this person on a daily basis (he could be my colleague, client or acquaintance), but if MR is by main dignities (domicile and/or exaltation), the thief might even be a friend or a relative!

Mutual reception can help us "decipher" other life situations. Planets in MR can show two people or things that have **swapped places**. MR also often occurs when we have **a choice**. *Should I take this job?* If the significator of the job is in a strong MR with another planet, this can mean that the querent will soon be offered another job which will give him the possibility of a choice, but it can also reveal that such a possibility already exists (at the time of asking the question).

According to some astrologers, planets in MR can exchange places in our minds. In doing so, the planets should, according to one theory, also exchange their degrees, not only signs, while another theory proposes that they should retain their original degrees. Personally, I have found merit in the theory that planets also exchange degrees, not only signs.

Modern astrological literature mentions MR by essential debilities (like *Venus in Cancer, the detriment of Saturn, and Saturn in Scorpio, the detriment of Venus*). I can't agree, as such pair of planets are basically unconnected. By default, mutual reception means "receiving one another", but to be able to receive one another, planets must have respective mutual dignities. In other words, you can't exchange something that you don't have!

PEREGRINE (ESSENTIAL DEBILITY)

If a planet has no essential dignity (that is, if it is neither in its domicile, exaltation, triplicity, term or face), nor can it exchange with another planet into such position, it is said to be **peregrine** (from lat. *peregrinare* – to wander, roam, travel or go abroad), meaning something like being an alien, or homeless. In a horary chart, such a planet can literary stand for a stranger, perhaps even for such a one having no personal documents (if afflicted), or for someone without property, reputation, knowledge, honor, influence, and the like. Articles ruled by peregrine planets can be unattractive, useless, broken, worthless, or have no owner. When it comes to the significator of a job, this can be dull, routine, with no possibility of promotion, or even dishonorable. In charts of theft, a peregrine planet often shows the thief, especially if related to H7 or H2.

In practice, we can safely assume a planet to be peregrine even if it is a mutual reception with another planet by a minor dignity (term or face).

I have noticed that some astrologers use the word peregrine for a planet which is void-of-course or unaspected, so that it seems to be without a direction or somehow "lost". (See also ACCIDENTAL DIGNITY on p. 100.)

ALMUTEN

Almuten is the planet that has most dignities in a certain degree of a sign. Almutens can replace sign rulers in their roles of the main significators, therefore they are very important! In practice, astrologers often ignore them, as they are more difficult to ascertain than sign rulers, but I have found that it's worth the trouble. The addition of almutens increases the number of significators, of course, which can complicate the interpretation, but with skillful use, it rather enriches it and makes it easier.

Almutens vary according to day/night, as they partly depend on triplicity rulers, so we have two tables of almutens: the day and the night one. Each degree can have one, two or even three almutens. Depending on the system of rulerships the astrologer uses, almutens can vary. I use Hellenistic terms and triplicities, therefore my tables are a bit different from those you'll find in other sources. Monomoiria are not included, though for no other reason but to not confuse the reader with completely new tables. (See **ALMUTENS: DAY** and **ALMUTENS: NIGHT** on p. 455 and 456.)

Almuten is often the same planet as the sign ruler. **Remember that in Virgo, Scorpio and Sagittarius almuten rulers of all degrees are the same as sign rulers.** Besides, Venus is almuten of all degrees in Taurus in day charts, whereas at night, this is the Moon, which in the first seven degrees shares the rulership with Venus. The Sun is almuten of all degrees of Leo in day charts, while in night charts, it shares the rulership of the first five degrees with Jupiter, and so on.

As every zodiacal degree has its almuten, we can, of course, check almutens of the ascendant and other angles, and of planets and house cusps, in all our horary charts.

Let's see some examples. *A house with the cusp at 5° Taurus would normally be ruled by Venus, the sign ruler. If it's a day chart, Venus is also the almuten ruler of that house, since it has the maximum number of points in that degree (10) by day, but if it's a night chart, almuten rulers are Moon and Venus, since they both have the maximum number of points (7) in that degree by night.*

Ascendant is 19° Cancer, a night chart. Cancer is ruled by the Moon, but at night, almuten of that degree is Jupiter, having more dignities in that degree by night than the Moon. If it was a day chart, the Moon and Jupiter would share the almuten rulership of ascendant, as they are equally strong there.

Almutens of the 21° of Capricorn in day charts are Saturn and Venus, but in night charts, this is only Saturn.

But now to the main question. Which planet is to be taken as significator (of the querent or quesited) - the sign ruler or the almuten ruler(s)? The answer is simple: consider them ALL, but give priority to that planet which better describes them – and the role they perform in the question, of course.

Let's take an example. The almuten of all degrees in Libra, ruled by Venus, is often Saturn, whereas the almuten of all degrees in Aries, ruled by Mars, is often the Sun. If the axis 1/7 was in this pair of signs in the degrees ruled by the almutens Saturn and the Sun, and the question related to love, I'd give priority to Venus and Mars, but if the question related to business cooperation or signing of a contract, I'd choose Saturn and the Sun.

A valid criterion is also the additional role assumed by any of the potential significators. If the ascending sign ruler, say, has another important role in the question, we might decide for the almuten, and vice versa. *Suppose that the same planet rules H1 and H10, and the question relates to career. If this planet is also the almuten of H1 while H10 has a different almuten ruler, we'd take the sign ruler as ruling H1 but H10 would be ruled by the almuten. (This logic can't work with Virgo and Gemini, obviously, as Mercury is the sign and almuten ruler of all degrees in both signs, day and night.)*

Our decision can also be based on natural significators. If, for example, in the process of deciding about a significator for a lawyer we must choose between Venus and Jupiter, we'd probably be wiser to opt for Jupiter.

> I have noticed that students and practitioners of horary astrology often neglect almutens. They're usually aware of their existence, but they don't use them in practice. This is a big mistake, because **almutens often have a decisive influence on the outcome of the question**. Many examples in the Practice part of this book should convince you of that.

HOW TO CALCULATE ESSENTIAL DIGNITIES

William Lilly created a scoring system which gives planets a varying number of points according to the hierarchy of their dignities:

- domicile: 5 points
- mutual reception by domicile: 5 points
- exaltation: 4 points
- mutual reception by exaltation: 4 points
- triplicity: 3 points
- term: 2 points
- face: 1 point

Planets in their domiciles get five points irrespective of their day and night domiciles, whereas with planets in triplicity we distinguish between daytime and night-time charts.

Essentially debilitated planets are weak and receive minus points:
- in detriment: - 5 points
- in fall: - 4 points
- peregrine: - 5 points

In practice, you'll find that some of the dignities are mutually exclusive. Virgo, for example, is the fall of Venus (minus 4 points) but it's also its day triplicity (3 points), so Venus in Virgo in a day chart is left with minus 1 point. Simple math, right?

We can choose our own scoring system. We can, for example, choose to score mutual receptions of weaker dignities (triplicity / triplicity, term / term and face / face), or mixed mutual receptions of these dignities (such as triplicity / face, triplicity / term, term / face, etc.), or mixed mutual receptions of the main dignities (domicile and exaltation) with weaker dignities. Scoring all the possible receptions is obviously tiring, but today, modern astrological software can do that for us. I use **Solar Fire** which allows for choosing our own settings and for the creating of a scoring system according to our choice.

Planets in the second part of the book (Practice) are scored according to a combination of the Hellenistic and Egyption systems.

We can also score **planetary sect.**

Plus points are given to:
- diurnal planets in diurnal charts / nocturnal planets in nocturnal charts: 1 point
- diurnal planets in diurnal signs / nocturnal planets in nocturnal signs: 1 point
- diurnal planets above horizon in diurnal charts / nocturnal planets above horizon in nocturnal charts: 1 point

Minus points are given to:
- diurnal planets in nocturnal charts / nocturnal planets in diurnal charts: - 1 point
- diurnal planets in nocturnal signs / nocturnal planets in diurnal signs: - 1 point
- diurnal planets below horizon in diurnal charts / nocturnal planets below horizon in nocturnal charts: - 1 point

ACCIDENTAL DIGNITY

Accidental dignity of the planets is calculated according to their specific placement in the chart, based on their:
- house placement
- direct vs. retrograde motion
- velocity
- relation to the Sun (eastern, western or combust)
- aspects with other planets
- conjunctions with fixed stars

HOUSE PLACEMENT

Planets are accidentally **strongest** in angular houses (1, 10, 7, 4), of **moderate strength** in succedent houses (2, 5, 8, 11), and **weak** in cadent houses (3, 6, 9, 12). They exert their maximum power when close to the angles, and minimum power when furthest from the angles, but not when still in conjunction with the preceding angles. (See ANGULAR, SUCCEDENT AND CADENT HOUSES on p. 52.)

We should be aware, though, that the power we speak of is related to the tangible, perceptible, operable qualities of the planets. Planets in cadent houses can be very strong, but in a "hidden" way. Whatever their qualities (beneficient or maleficient), they can't be openly expressed, they can't be seen, they can't be heard, they can't be touched. They just "sit" there, waiting for their time to come. That's why tradition speaks of malefics in the "unfortunate" H6, H8 and H12 as very dangerous – they can show a hidden enemy or a critical illness inside the body.

In practice, further differentiation depends on whether the planet is a benefice or a malefic, whether it is essentially strong or weak, and the like. For example, Jupiter in H12 in Sagittarius, Pisces or Cancer (Jupiter's domicile and exaltation signs) has the same number of (negative) points as Saturn in H12 in Cancer, Leo or Aries (Saturn's detriment and fall signs), but such an accidentally debilitated Jupiter would be much less hurtful than Saturn. Its goodness would simply be poorly expressed or unexpressed while Saturn's malevolence would be hidden and the querent would be unaware of it – and we know that hidden enemies are often more dangerous than the open ones.

As we know by now, houses are also divided into **fortunate** and **unfortunate**. The fortunate houses are 11, 5, 10 and 1, moderately fortunate are 9 and 3 and unfortunate are 12, 6 and 8, while the others are more or less neutral. As would be expected, planets in fortunate houses are generally more dignified than those in unfortunate houses.

TABLE TO EXAMINE PLANETARY DIGNITY (see p. 108), created by the famous English Renaissance horary astrologer William Lilly (author of **CHRISTIAN ASTROLOGY**) and still used today, shows that Lilly assigned the most accidental dignity ("fortitude") to planets in H1 and H10 and the least to planets in H12.

In interpretation, we must be aware of the fact that planets have the most impact on the matters described by the house they occupy, in the first degrees of those houses, and the least towards their end. As mentioned in the chapter on houses, in practice it even applies that the last degrees (up to 5) of any house are charged with the energies of the next house. *If, for instance, the cusp of H9 is at 12° Cancer and Venus at 8° Cancer, Venus is technically in H8 but practically in H9. When calculating planetary dignities, Venus should therefore be considered as a H9 planet!*

DIRECT VS. RETROGRADE MOTION

As seen from Earth, planets usually travel "directly", in order of signs, but every now and then they seem to stop and then start moving backwards. This apparent reversal of direction in their orbits is called **retrograde motion**. It's due to the fact that planets (including the Earth) revolve around the Sun from west to east, while the Earth rotates around its axis in the opposite direction, from east to west. When planets are farthest away from the Earth, the Earth "overtakes" them, thus creating an optical illusion which results in the apparent retrogradation of the planets.

The frequency and duration of individual planets' retrograde phases varies depending on their distances from Earth. Retrograde phases of those planets nearer to Earth are more frequent and shorter, while the more distant planets have less frequent and longer retrograde phases.

Before their retrograde phases, the planets' speed slows down, until they apparently cease to move. This phase is called **first station**. Then (after one to several days, depending on their distances from the Earth) they start to move backwards and after a period of such retrograde motion they stop again at their **second station**, after which they start moving directly again.

All planets have retrograde phases, but the Sun and the Moon are always direct. Retrograde motion of the planets is marked with the letter R.

Mercury is retrograde approximately every 4 months for 3 weeks, Venus every 18 months for 6 weeks, Mars every two years for 10 weeks, Jupiter every 13 months for 4 months, Saturn every year for 5 months, while Uranus, Neptune and Pluto are retrograde for about half a year, each year. Outer planets (including Mars) are retrograde at the times of their oppositions with the Sun, being exactly opposite to the Sun right in the middle of their retrograde paths. Mercury turns retrograde when ahead of the Sun by approximately 15°- 23°, and moves backwards for about

3 weeks until it reaches approximately the same number of degrees behind the Sun. Venus turns retrograde about every year and a half when ahead of the Sun by approximately 30°, and moves backwards for about 6 weeks until it reaches approximately 30° degrees behind the Sun.

Astrologers have discovered long ago that retrograde planets express themselves differently than direct. Metaphorically speaking, the direct motion of a planet can be compared to a man courageously stepping forward and constantly discovering new sights, whereas retrograde motion is more like a man walking back along the path he'd already taken, and looking again at the things he'd already seen.

People with many retrograde planets in their natal charts tend to do a lot of exploring and observing, are more introverted, subjective and sensitive. Life unfolds at a slower pace for them than for the others; they often fear the future, dig into the past and doubt their own selves. In youth, they easily get disheartened as it seems that life doesn't offer them opportunities for advancement, but in later years, they profit by being more mature, wiser and stronger from their peers – as a result of their slower process of "growing up". Modern psychological astrologers often emphasize the spiritual dimensions of retrograde planets. This seems logical and justified, but as for the outward, external expression of retrograde energies, those are invariably reduced and weakened.

RETROGRADE AND STATIONARY PLANETS IN HORARY ASTROLOGY

As above, so below. **Retrograde** planets in horary charts often point to someone or something who/that is returning, retreating, re-connecting, correcting or repeating something, and similar. But that's just one side of the coin. In calculating accidental dignities, retrograde planets get minus points, for the obvious reason that they can't act constructively and creatively - except when re-doing something. They often point to something (or someone) weak, uncertain, depleted, sickly and similar - depending on the context of the question.

The horary ascendant ruled by a retrograde significator is a warning. The querent may not have disclosed all the facts needed to understand the question. He may hide something (deliberately or not) or has no power to move forward (with his plans and wishes, or physically), or wants (plans) to return (to a place, person or situation), or feels helpless, and the like.

All questions asked in times of retrograde Mercury should be approached carefully. The querents (even when not ruled by Mercury) at such times are often insincere (sometimes unintentionally, though), they come up with the wrong facts or they formulate questions in such a way that the astrologer doesn't understand them properly. The reasons can be manifold: sometimes the querent doesn't know how to communicate his question to the astrologer, or tries to manipulate him by not telling the (whole) truth, or is afraid of the answer and too scared to tell the truth, or doesn't know all the facts – and insists on his own truth in spite of the astrologer trying to convince him to the contrary. My worst horary experiences are those with the charts, asked at times of retrograde Mercury, and I have observed a similar mess with the charts posted at such times in various horary forums.

Other most common manifestations of retrograde significators in horary charts are:
- If the question refers to a missing (lost, mislaid) person, animal or article, their retrograde significator shows that they'll be found or will return. (A very reliable rule!)
- In relationship horaries, if the querent wants to know if he's staying together with his partner, a retrograde significator of the quesited can mean that he/she is leaving – or might have already done so. However, if the querent asks whether his ex is coming back, the answer is yes, this is obviously going to happen, as retrogradation indicates a return. But if the two are separating (divorcing), a retrograde significator of one of them can show him/her changing his/her mind.
- If the question relates to the viability/desirability of a project or a plan (business or private), a retrograde significator of the querent or the quesited suggests that it would be better to cancel (the plan or project).
- In career and employment horaries, retrograde ruler of H10 (or the planet occupying that house) can mean that the querent is returning to the previous position or would find employment in a company where he once used to work. If the querent asks whether he'd be able to keep his current job, a retrograde significator of the job usually indicates to the contrary.

- If the retrograde planet stands for someone who had promised something, this can mean that he/she would not be able to fulfill the promise, either because they'd change their minds or because they'd be prevented from doing it, or due to any other reason.
- If the querent is buying something, the retrograde ruler of H2 (or a retrograde planet in that house) can point to his insufficient means, or the purchase will not come through due to some other reason.
- A retrograde significator of the property we're buying can mean that we'd regret the deal later or not be able to keep it long. It can also show that we'd change our minds even before the deal comes through.
- A retrograde significator of a missing article sometimes indicates that we'll find it by chance, or when least expected.

Keeping in mind the core meanings of retrogradation, we should easily relate them to any retrograde significator, but we must carefully combine the information with other indications in the horary chart. In any chart – horary, natal or any other – everything is connected with everything else!

In assessing planetary strengths, retrograde planets are weak, but this weakness must be understood in the context of the question. If, for example, a retrograde significator indicates a desirable come-back or a finding of something gone missing, the "weakness" of such planets relates to their inability (or the inability of that what they stand for) to move away from us. It's not about "good" or "bad". Weakness can be good. Strength can be bad. Astrology calls for objective evaluations, not subjective opinions.

Planets are **stationary** when in their first or second station, that is, just before turning retrograde (first station) or turning direct (second station). This process takes from one to several days, depending on the planetary distances from Earth. Planets are then at their slowest (see VELOCITY on p. 104), as if losing power and determination. People, ruled by such planets, are uncertain and hesitant, as if not knowing what to do next. Sometimes, stationary planets also show people who have little power to act or influence a situation.

The first station is much more critical than the second, when the planet is regaining its power and getting ready to move on. A planet in its second station is like a man who after a long sickness starts feeling better, and is ready to get out of his bed.

In his book **BEGINNING OF WISDOM**, Abraham Ibn Ezra, the 12th century Hebrew astrologer, writes: *"The star, which is about to assume a retrograde motion, is like a man bewildered and trembling at the misfortunes which will befall him. The star in its second station is like a man who expects good luck."* (Generalizations 91 and 93) And: *"The planet, which is in its first station, is like a man who does not know what he will do, and its result is bad; if it is in its second station, it is like a man who expects something and whose hope will not be in vain."* (Generalization 33)

VELOCITY

Planetary **velocity** is an almost completely neglected criterion in modern astrology - even in modern horary astrology - but in assessing planetary strengths it plays quite an important role.

A planet is said to be **fast** when its daily motion is greater than the average, and **slow**, when it's lesser than the average. Planets are slowest when at their "stations" (see DIRECT VS. RETROGRADE MOTION on p. 101).

Average daily motions of the planets are:
- Sun   0°59'
- Moon   13°11'
- Mercury   1°23'
- Venus   1°12'
- Mars   0°31'
- Jupiter   0°05'
- Saturn   0°02'
- Uranus   0'42"
- Neptune   0'24"
- Pluto   0'14"

Most astrology software calculates daily motions of the planets, but if you want to calculate it by hand, check the ephemeris and find the difference between the previous and the next midnight (or noon) position of the planet. If Mars' daily motion is, for example, 43', that's above average, meaning that Mars on that day was fast, but if it made only 12' (below average), it was slow.

Planetary velocity reflects the "speed" of that which the planets stand for; it can literally point to quickness of slowness – of a person, project, animal… *Is my husband going to be late today?* If his significator is slow – probably; if fast – no, he can't wait to throw his arms around you!

If the Moon, as the major horary "timer", is fast in the chart, the matter can be accomplished a bit earlier (or faster), if slow, a bit later (or slowlier). But mind you, I really mean "a bit"! Velocity is not such an all-important factor and we must use it cautiously – especially in combination with other timing measures. (See TIMING on p.132.) Ideally, our software would remind us whether a planet (the Moon) is speeding up or slowing down.

If a direct planet is very slow in the chart, this should remind you of its approaching first station - an important consideration, so don't forget to check the ephemeris for its future movement!

We should also be aware that retrograde planets, although moving backwards, can be quick in motion (fast). Once they gain velocity (after having turned retrograde), they can fasten things (processes), or suggest something (or someone) who is returning speedily.

Ibn Ezra wrote (Generalizations 94 and 95): *"The star, which is delayed in its course, corresponds to a man exhausted and lacking strength to go on. The star accelerated in its course is like a young man running."*

PLANETS IN RELATION TO THE SUN

Depending on their positions in relation to the Sun, planets can be **eastern** (*matutine*, "morning stars"), **western** (*vespertine*, "evening stars"), **combust, under the Sun's beams** and **cazimi**. In old astrological texts, the words "morning" and "evening" were usually used with reference to Venus and Mercury, as they can be nicely observed in their morning rising or evening setting.

Eastern planets rise before the Sun while the evening ones set after the Sun. In the astrological chart, the eastern planets are those which, in the order of signs, are before the Sun, while the western ones follow it.

The only exception is the Moon which is said to be east of the Sun in its waxing phase and west of the Sun in its waning phase. In the chart, the Moon is in its waxing phase after the Sun while in its waning phase it's before the Sun.

Basically, the criterion for their eastern and western classifications was their **visibility**. Planets lose their morning or evening "tags" when they come so close to the Sun as to not be visible any more. Usually, they become invisible when in conjunction with the Sun for up to about 8° when they're said to be **combust** (from Latin *combustus* meaning burnt-up). This distance is normally used as the criteria for combustion, although Venus - as *Al Biruni* teaches – is not combust when in conjunction with the Sun at high latitude. (Venus can reach as much as 8° of latitude – more than any other visible planet.) Lilly wrote that for combustion to be valid, the planet must be in the same sign as the Sun, but this has been refuted by later researchers, as the concept of combustion was clearly related to planetary visibility, not to sign boundaries. Generally, it was believed that when planets become invisible, the Sun "burns them up", meaning that it withdraws their power. In practice, combustion is more critical when applying (approaching, intensifying) than when separating (that is, when the planet is already leaving the conjunction with the Sun).

When planets are in the stage of lesser visibility, which is approximately from 8° to 17° distance of the Sun, they're said to be **under the Sun's beams.** At this stage, they're within the solar aura, dimmed and less clear and visible, which is in practice treated as a weak combustion.

But planets are said to suddenly get very powerful when **cazimi** ("in the heart of the Sun"). Lilly and other ancient authors limit the orb of cazimi to 17' (minutes), although in much of the contemporary literature, you'll find the orb for cazimi as being one degree. At this stage, they say, planets light up in all their power, and cazimi planets are therefore considered to be accidentaly strongly dignified.

Why do I say that "they say"? The fact is that my own practice has not convinced me of the validity of cazimi. I leave it to you to come to your own conclusions, but the writings of Guido Bonatti, the famous Italian mathematician, astronomer and astrologer from the 13th century, make it clear that **for a planet to be cazimi, it doesn't need to be within a 17' orb of conjunction with the Sun by longitude only, but also by latitude** (measurement north and south of the ecliptic)! This happens very rarely, but it would pay to take his condition into consideration when evaluating planets for cazimi.

Some say that Mars can't be combust because it's hotter than the Sun, but my own findings don't support this. Having researched the ancient sources for the origin of this belief, I have come to the conclusion that some contemporary researcher has misunderstood an old text.

Combustion is a serious accidental debility. Depending on the context of the question, it can show people who are helpless, hindered, ignorant (uninformed, unaware of the facts), threatened, frightened, "blind", caught up in ill conditions, and the like. They may not have the power of independent decision-making, they are forced to hide (or to hide something), or are under severe pressure. If such a planet stands for a lost article, this can be severely damaged or is invisible because it is covered with something or hiding under (or within) another object. If it's food, it may be rotten. If the question relates to vitality, it can mean that the querent's health deteriorates. Caution should be applied to the applying vs. separating phases (worsening/improvement). Know that in horary, combustion is to be treated differently than in natal astrology, although parallels can be drawn.

Note: if a combust (or under the Sun's beams) planet applies to the Sun, or vice versa, "completion of the matter" is still indicated, in spite of the hypothetical "endangered" state of the combust planet. *Suppose that the Sun is the significator of the querent and Jupiter stands for a missing article. The Sun applies to the conjunction of Jupiter within a 8° orb, so that, technically speaking, Jupiter is combust. But because the Sun will soon reach Jupiter, this is one of the classic means of completion - the querent is going to be reconnected with the missing article. (But it's possible, of course, that due to the planet's combustion, the article is well hidden, possibly damaged or otherwise endangered.)*

Examination of accidental dignity involves the differentiation between the eastern and western placements. Don't confuse this with the eastern and western placements with reference to house division, where the planets to the left side of the chart (in houses 10, 11, 12, 1, 2 and 3) are said to be eastern while those to the right side of the chart (in houses 4, 5, 6, 7, 8 and 9) are said to be western.

Know also that when the outer planets are elongated from the Sun by more than 120°, they become **retrograde** and **don't count as being eastern or western** any more. At least they shouldn't be, according to ancients, but modern opinions vary on this matter.

EXACT ASPECTS WITH BENEFICS AND MALEFICS

Planets in **exact** (within 1° orb) **conjunctions** or **harmonious aspects** (sextile and trine) **with benefics** are considered to be very fortunate, while those in **exact disharmonious aspects** (square and opposition) **with malefics** are very unfortunate. This is logical because benefics enrich planets and harmonious aspects help them achieve (express) maximum good, while malefics endow them with undesirable qualities and suppress them, both in conjunctions and in disharmonious aspects.

It would seem logical that planets should be allocated plus points also for exact harmonious aspects with the Sun (no conjunctions, of course), but Lilly's system to examine planetary fortitudes doesn't take them into consideration. We can add them in our minds - no system is perfect!

CONJUNCTIONS WITH FIXED STARS

This criteria is similar to that of exact aspects of significators with the planets, except that here, **only conjunction** is to be considered. The orb can be more than 1° - depending on the star's size and power. Conjunctions with bright, beneficial stars "elevate" planets while conjunctions with dim, harmful stars "hurt" them, as fixed stars are supposed to be stronger than planets. (More on this in chapter FIXED STARS on p. 140.)

DIFFERENCES BETWEEN ESSENTIAL AND ACCIDENTAL DIGNITY

Essentialy dignified planets stand for inner strength, ability, talent, quality, respectability, durability, erudition, and the like. People, animals, articles or concepts, ruled by essentially dignified planets, have a (relatively) high value and deserve our respect, trust, attention, praise and similar.

If, for example, such a planet rules a service worker, he'd be well qualified for the job, would be experienced, reliable and trustworthy. *Should I trust this carpenter? Will he do his job well?* An essentially dignified significator would give a YES, a debilitated one a NO. An article, signified by such a planet, would be high-quality, valuable, well preserved, undamaged, and the like. *My phone got soaked in water, is it totally destroyed or can it be repaired?* If its significator has much essential dignity, it can probably be repaired. *Should I buy this garden furniture?* An essentially debilitated significator of the furniture could mean that it's made of bad materials or is of poor quality. *Should I accept this job offer?* An essentially dignified significator of the job would mean that it's worthwhile as it would fulfill the querent's ambition.

If the question refers to a missing animal, its essential dignity could mean that it's a pedigreed dog, having a great value for the owner, but it can also mean that the animal is safe and not injured.

Essential dignity must always be understood in the context of the question. *Will my son get a role in that movie?* An essentially debilitated significator of the son does not necessarily mean that he's a bad actor, but it does mean that he might not be selected because the judges would find him unsuitable for that particular role. *Will I get this job?* An essentially debilitated significator of the querent can mean that he doesn't have the necessary qualifications, but it can also mean that he'd not fit certain requirements of the employer, even if he's able and basically well qualified.

Where are my keys? My significator is essentially debilitated. Does that mean that I'm a stupid, incompetent person? Well, to say the truth, the horary chart won't show that, but in the context of the question it could be me who was to blame, as I could have inadvertently left the keys in an unsafe place.

Accidentally dignified planets also indicate planetary strengths, but of a different kind. An accidentally dignified planet is like someone who is in the right place at the right time. As significator of the querent, applying for a career position, such a planet would show that the applicant has very good chances to succeed, but more through luck than due to competence (knowledge, education). Maybe he'll get it through "connections" (his uncle is the business owner, for example), or he may be the only candidate, or he'll get lucky due to some other reason.

If the significator of a missing article has much accidental dignity, it's more likely that we'll get it back, as if it would be accidentally debilitated. (But be careful with the criterion of retrogradation, because this indicates return, although adding to accidental debility!)

Is my daughter going to pass the exam? Suppose that the significator of the daughter has small essential dignitiy but a strong accidental one; this might indicate that the daughter had not studied hard enough and is unprepared (essential debility), but on Day D her professor is going to be in a good mood and will let her pass the exam. In other words, she'll be lucky (accidental dignity)!

Since the criteria for the examination of accidental dignity are more complex than the criteria for assessing the essential dignity, we must be able to distinguish between the various forms of accidental dignity and debility. I have already mentioned retrograde motion, but attention should also be paid to the **differences in meaning** between, for example, house dignity and planetary velocity, as they show two quite different things. It is therefore important to be aware of **why** a certain planet is accidentally weak or strong.

Essential and accidental dignity of the planets should be skillfully combined in every chart, and the indications we thereby get should be carefully applied to other factors (aspects, applications, separations, dispositions and similar).

HOW TO EXAMINE PLANETARY DIGNITY

Lilly's **TABLE TO EXAMINE PLANETARY DIGNITY** on p. 108 will help you calculate planetary dignities and debilities. Although a number of computer programs calculates essential dignities (and debilities), I suggest you start by doing it by hand, as this will gradually lead you through the process of evaluating the planets for their strengths and weaknesses. To my knowledge, at the time of this writing no program calculates accidental dignities yet.

I suggest you first calculate both sets of dignities separately and then get the final score.

As for the **accidental dignities of the Sun and the Moon**, calculation can be a bit confusing as they are always direct, and the Sun, of course, can never be combust, under its own beams or cazimi. So – do we give them plus points for those dignities? My own way of dealing with this dilemma is to always give them 5 points for direct motion, and I give the Sun the additional 5 points for not being combust or under its own beams. If handled differently, the Sun – which, besides, never gets any points for being either eastern or western - would very often end up with much fewer points than the planets, which would be neither fair not reasonable. After all, it's the star of our system, which is a power in itself!

Another controversial issue are the **eastern vs. western** placements. Do we also score them when combust (invisible), and do we score the outer planets (from Mars onwards) when they're retrograde (more than 120° elongated from the Sun), or not? Based on ancient teachings, I think that such planets should be exempt from scoring for these criteria, in spite of them being (theoretically) eastern or western.

Also, be careful with **velocity**. At the time of this writing, the program that I use (*Solar Fire*) doesn't give the velocity values to retrograde planets. In other words, when a planet is retrograde, it's simply stated as retrograde, not "fast" or "slow". But this distinction should be made, in my opinion, so until the problem is resolved, I advise you to calculate those values by hand.

To get more accurate results for planetary strenghts, I suggest including sect (see PLANETARY SECT on p. 73 and the calculation table below).

LILLY'S TABLE TO EXAMINE PLANETARY DIGNITY

ESSENTIAL DIGNITY	POINTS	ESSENTIAL DEBILITY	POINTS
domicile	5	detriment	- 5
MR by domicile	5	fall	- 4
exaltation	4	peregrine (no dignity)	- 5
MR by exaltation	4		
triplicity	3		
term	2		
face	1		

ACCIDENTAL DIGNITY	POINTS	ACCIDENTAL DEBILITY	POINTS
in H1 or H10	5	in H12	- 5
in H7, H4 or H11	4	in H8 or H6	- 4
in H2 or H5	3	retrograde	- 5
in H9	2	slow	- 2
in H3	1	♂ ♃ ♄ western	- 2
direct	4	☿ ♀ eastern	- 2
fast	2	☽ waning	- 2
♂ ♃ ♄ eastern	2	combust	- 5
☿ ♀ western	2	under the Sun's beams	- 4
☽ waxing	2	♂ ♄ or ♂ (orb 1°)	- 5
not combust or under the Sun's beams	5	besieged by ♄ and ♂	- 5
cazimi	5	♂ ☋ (orb 1°)	- 4
♂ ♃ or ♀ (orb 1°)	5	☍ ♄ or ♂ (orb 1°)	- 4
♂ ☊ (orb 1°)	5	□ ♄ or ♂ (orb 1°)	- 3
△ ♀ or ♃ (orb 1°)	4	♂ Algol (orb 1°)	- 5
✶ ♀ or ♃ (orb 1°)	3		
♂ Regulus (orb 1°)	6		
♂ Spica (orb 1°)	5		

TABLE TO EXAMINE PLANETARY SECT

SECT PLUS POINTS		SECT MINUS POINTS	
planet in chart (D in D, N in N)	1	planet in chart (D in N, N in D)	-1
horizon (harmony)	1	horizon (disharmony)	-1
planet in sign (D in D, N in N)	1	planet in sign (D in N, N in D)	-1

EXAMPLE 1

9/1 - *Will P.K. be found guilty of murdering his wife?* - We want to examine the dignities and debilities of Mars and Venus, significators of the plaintiffs (Mars) and the defendant (Venus), as this will help us decide on the winner.

We will also calculate the power of the Moon which in the chart stands for the jury.

For calculation purposes, we need Lilly's **TABLE TO EXAMINE PLANETARY DIGNITY** (p. 108) and **TABLE OF ESSENTIAL DIGNITIES OF PLANETS** (p. 458), whereas for the calculation of accidental dignities we use the tables attached to each chart.

MARS

Essential dignity: A look into the table of essential dignities of the planets tells us that Mars has no essential dignity, but because it's in mutual reception (MR) with the Sun by domicile (it's in the domicile of the Sun while the Sun is in the domicile of Mars) it gets **5 points**.

Accidental dignity: in H10 (+ 5), direct (+ 4), not combust or under the Sun's beams (+ 4), in exact trine with Jupiter (+ 4), slow (- 2), western (- 2). Total score for accidental dignity: **13 points**

Total score: 5 + 13 = 17 points

Sect: a nocturnal planet in a night chart (+1), a nocturnal planet above the horizon in a night chart (+1), a nocturnal planet in a day sign (-1).

Total score incl. sect: 17 + 1 = 18 points

VENUS

Essential dignity: Venus is exalted: **4 points**.

Accidental dignity: in H5 (+ 3), direct (+ 4), fast (+ 2), not combust or under the Sun's beams (+ 5), eastern (+ 2), in exact conjunction with Saturn (- 5). Total score for accidental dignity: **7 points**.

Total score: 4 + 7 = 11 points

Sect: a nocturnal planet in a night chart (+1), a nocturnal planet below the horizon in a night chart (-1), a nocturnal planet in a night sign (+1).

Total score incl. sect: 11 + 1 = 12 points

Result: Mars has more total dignity scores, therefore the plaintiffs have more power.

MOON

Essential dignity: Moon is in its triplicity: **3 points**.

Accidental dignity: in H11 (+ 4), direct (+ 4), fast (+ 2), not combust or under the Sun's beams (+ 5), eastern (+ 2). Total score for accidental dignity: **17 points**.

Total score: 3 + 17 = 20 points

Sect: a nocturnal planet in a night chart (+1), a nocturnal planet above the horizon in a night chart (+ 1), a nocturnal planet in a night sign (+1).

Total score incl. sect: 20 + 3 = 23 points

Result: The Moon is extremely dignified, which in the context of the question means that the decision of the jury will be of paramount importance.

EXAMPLE 2

12/1- *Is President Kučan going to be reelected?* - We want to calculate the dignities of Mercury and Jupiter, the significators of the president and his contestants. (Mercury rules H10 for the president and Jupiter H4 for the contestants). This will help us decide if President Kučan is able to overcome the opposing candidates running for presidency.

MERCURY
Essential dignity: Mercury is peregrine: - **5 points**
Accidental dignity: in H10 (+ 5), direct (+ 4), fast (+ 2), eastern (- 2), under the Sun's beams (- 4). Total score for accidental dignity: **6 points**
Total score: - 5 + 6 = 1 point
Sect: a diurnal planet in a day chart (+1), a diurnal planet above the horizon in a day chart (+ 1), a diurnal planet in a day sign (+ 1). Total score: **3 points**
Total score incl. sect: 1 + 3 = 4 points

JUPITER
Essential dignity: Jupiter is peregrine: - **5 points**
Accidental dignity: in H3 (+ 1), not combust or under the Sun's beams (+ 5), retrograde (- 5), slow (-2). Total score: - **1 point**.
Total score: - 5 - 1 = - 6 points
Sect: a diurnal planet in a day chart (+ 1), a diurnal planet below the horizon in a day chart (- 1), a diurnal planet in a day sign (+ 1). Total score: **1 point**
Total score incl. sect: - 6 + 1 = - 5 points

Result: Both planets have the same minus scores for essential dignity, but Mercury is much stronger by accidental dignity and sect, therefore it's obvious that President Kučan's position is stronger and that he'd be reelected. (As he indeed was.)

LOOKING FOR THE ANSWER

STRICTURES AND CAUTIONS

radition teaches that not every horary chart is valid or suitable for interpretation. The ancient astrologers believed that we should check every chart for the possible "strictures" and "cautions". In case of the existence of any of them, the chart should be read with utmost care or it should even be discarded. In other words, if a chart shows a stricture, we should tell our clients to go home and hope for more luck next time! Cautions are less severe; while a stricture is supposed to give an invalid chart, completely inappropriate for delineation, a caution is just a caution, asking us to be careful with the chart, and suggesting that it might be better to refrain from judgment.

Some say that strictures and cautions were developed because in old times astrologers could be severely punished for giving a wrong answer. Times have changed (hopefully), but, more importantly, modern times call for reevaluation of those criteria simply because experience has shown that some of them are unnecessary. Instead of unquestioningly discarding those charts, we should ask ourselves what they really mean and what they're trying to convey.

Often, strictures and cautions alert us to something which could potentially destroy our capacity to give the proper answer, but they can mean a variety of other things. William Lilly, for instance, found that charts gave him a stricture or a caution when the querent wanted to try him, like "show me how good an astrologer you are", without feeling a real and sincere need for an answer.

In practice, it's often difficult to decide how severe those "warnings" are. While many can be completely discarded, the others are to be taken seriously – and treated accordingly. In the majority of cases, however, some kind of answer is possible. What's more, an able astrologer can transform many of those weaknesses into strengths, by understanding what they really mean, and use them as aids instead of as obstacles.

ASCENDANT IN THE FIRST OR THE LAST THREE DEGRESS OF SIGNS (0°, 1°, 2°, 27°, 28° AND 29°)

A couple of paragraphs have been dedicated to the ascendant in those degrees in chapter ASCENDANT AND THE TWELVE HOUSES on p. 56. Lilly writes that when the ascendant is in the first three degrees of a sign, "*you may not adventure judgment*", except if "*the querent was very young, or if the complexion, moles and scars of his body agreed with the sign ascending*". Similarly with late degrees, except if the querent was an older person ("*of age*"). This caution was to be observed especially when the ascendant was in the signs of short ascension (from Capricorn to Gemini). Later astrologers spoke of the question being asked "too early" (the first degrees) or "too late" (the last degrees).

Late degrees sometimes indicate that the querent is in a hopeless situation which he has no power to influence. The question can be meaningless, the matter might have already been resolved (unknown to the querent), so that the answer or advice is futile. In such cases, it's indeed "too late". (*Should I apply for this job?* Too late, the position's already taken.) Sometimes this is an indication that the querent will change his mind (as per the planned course of action, for example). Often, however, a late ascendant shows only that the querent is finalizing or completing something, or moving somewhere, or that his situation is changing. In this case, look at the nature of the following sign! This, together with its ruler, will indicate the nature of the imminent change. If the question refers to the possibility of a planned change, a late ascendant might not be a caution, but simply an indication of a positive answer. If someone is asking about a job he had recently started, the late ascendant might indicate that he'd not keep the job long.

My late tutor Oliva Barclay wrote: *"I find a late degree can indicate despair."* (See **HORARY ASTROLOGY REDISCOVERED**, Whitford Press, 1990, p. 124.)

Ascendant in the **early degrees** of a sign, by contrast, often indicates that querents are starting something new. They might be asking about something that's in the initial stage (a business project or a love affair with a prospective new lover whom they recently met, for example). They might have relocated recently and are asking about something related to their new surroundings, or their question involves something that they have never done before. They might feel insecure and such an ascendant might indicate that it'll take some time before they'll get used to the new situation.

All these instances should tell you that the early and late degrees are not necessarily a caution – far from that! They can provide valuable additional information, so make use of them.

SATURN IN H7 OR IN H1

H1 usually stands for the querent while H7 for the astrologer (unless we're our own astrologers, of course, in which case we're obviously ruled by H1). Saturn (especially if retrograde, combust, essentially debilitated or peregrine) in H7 is a caution that the astrologer may get the answer wrong. The closer it is to the cusp of H7, the worse his judgment. (Like all planets, if it's in the sign of H8 or much distanced from the descendant, its restrictive influence is less severe.) If the querent is his own astrologer, this rule applies to Saturn in H1, but since Saturn in H1 acts directly on H7 and as H1 stands for the querent and to a certain extent for the question itself, this is also not a desirable placement.

Saturn in H1 sometimes indicates that querents are very upset and deeply concerned about their situation, have a negative attitude or are somehow aware of the "fatally" unfavorable conditions. Care should be taken that our answers do not deepen their trauma. Sometimes, the querent is guilt-ridden. *I remember when an elderly lady asked whether she should catch up with her studies which she had left behind years ago. She said that she only needs a year to get a degree. Saturn was exactly on the ascendant of the horary chart, warning me of two things: firstly, she was worried, self-conscious and guilt-ridden, and secondly, Saturn was like a red light, indicating an obstruction. Other indications spoke against her ever finishing her studies, but because of Saturn I didn't answer with a direct NO. Instead, I tried to give her hope and told her that she should try, but even if she doesn't succeed, she shouldn't take it that seriously. It's not a life-and-death situation!*

In the above example, however, the case would be "closed" even without any additional indications. My practice has shown that **any chart with Saturn in a tight (up to 1 degree) orb with any angle, not only the ascendant, is like a red light showing a "fatal" obstruction. Such questions, to put it simply, have no future. The case is closed, period.** Only in rare cases, when Saturn is strongly dignified (in Aquarius, Capricorn, Libra or in any of the signs of its own triplicity, and at the same time not retrograde or combust etc.), and in harmonious aspects with the significators, can it show a positive result.

It should be noted that Saturn has a similar expression when in an exact **square with the angles**. But it's important to consider a **1 degree orb** only.

We often get this caution when people ask the same question again and again, in the hope of finally getting the answer that they want. In such cases, it's like Saturn was saying: Now, stop. You've asked too many times, the answer was NO, so what it is that you don't understand?

Sometimes, such Saturn placement asks for a re-check. *Recently, a colleague from Sweden sent me the data for a horary chart that she had cast for her son's question. She was unsure how to interpret it, so she asked me for help. But she wrote in a hurry and stated the date as 17th instead of 27th. My chart, cast for the 17th, had a (retrograde) Saturn in an exact conjunction with IC. In accordance with my findings, I replied that, sorry, this question has no future. She wrote back that, ooops, she made a mistake! It transpired that, indeed, that chart had no future – because it was a wrong chart!*

This example teaches how important it is to deal with such situations seriously.

Saturn's exact square with the horizontal axis (AC / DC) may point to a difficult communication between the querent and the astrologer, or to the astrologer's inability to arrive at a meaningful (or any) conclusion. In partnership questions, such placement of Saturn suggests a serious hindrance: the partnership (a deal, agreement, cooperation) is not going to happen.

Saturn in H7 is NOT a warning when the question relates to partnerships and other H7 issues. In such cases, Saturn in H7 is simply the cosignificator (or main significator) of people (or things), ruled by this house.

I have noticed that charts with Saturn in H7 (and sometimes in H1), posted in my facebook group Horary Astrology Group, have a poor feedback; members are unwilling to participate (comment), or the discussion develops along undesirable routes (complaints, conflicts and disputes, resulting in somebody's being offended or even signing out of the group), so that, in the final run, there's the impression that it would be better if the discussion had never started.

Let us recap: Saturn is H7 – especially debilitated or conjunct DC, can be a caution. You, as the astrologer, should treat such questions carefully.

VOID-OF-COURSE MOON

Void-of-couse (VOC) Moon is one of the hottest discussion topics among contemporary horary community, for a simple reason: astrologers can't seem to agree what it actually means.

For many years, I relied on the definition given by Olivia Barclay, my horary teacher, who followed in the tradition of William Lilly: *"Once the Moon has left the sign it is in, matters are beyond the scope of the question asked. If it makes no aspect between its present position and the end of the sign it is in, it is called void of course, and nothing can be done; the matter is not achieved."* (**HORARY ASTROLOGY REDISCOVERED**, p. 48).

Only the so-called Ptolemaic aspects (conjunction, opposition, square, sextile and trine) and traditional planets (up to Saturn) plus the Arabic part called part of fortune were to be considered. But a detailed research of Lilly's charts, carried out by some contemporary astrologers (notably the English astrologer Sue Ward), revealed that Lilly actually didn't consider the Moon to be VOC when within an orb of an aspect which was to perfect when the Moon would already be in the next sign. Ward's research actually showed that his true criterion for a VOC Moon were not sign boundaries, but orbs!

The ancient Greeks considered the Moon to be VOC when not perfecting a (Ptolemaic) aspect within the next 30 degrees. No mention of sign boundaries! In keeping with their tradition, contemporary astrologers seem to agree that the Moon can be VOC even when in the beginning of a sign, provided she's not within an orb of a Ptolemaic aspect with another planet.

But what about the planets? Do we consider transsaturnians (Uranus, Neptune and Pluto), or not? This is where astrologers' opinions differ. My research has shown that **the Moon is NOT VOC when in an orb of an aspect with any planet, including transsaturnians, but only when those transsaturnians are natural or accidental significators (if and when we consider them as the co-rulers of the respective signs), and/or they're conjunct an angle within a three degrees orb.** When transsaturnians don't meet any of these criteria, I disregard them and consider the Moon to be VOC even if within an orb of aspect with any of them.

But what is the meaning of a VOC Moon? Is it a stricture, a caution or none of that? Generally speaking, such Moon is "directionless"; it doesn't "go" anywhere, it wanders aimlessly, it has no goal. Therefore, the situation will "stay as it is", or it is very difficult to say how it will develop, or it won't develop according to plan, and the judgment is risky. But it's very important that the astrologer understands the question. If it involves a decision between YES and NO, the answer is usually NO. *Should I travel to America?* No. *Am I going to lose my job?* No. Always bear in mind that a VOC Moon's doesn't show any change – no matter how the question is formulated – and judge accordingly. *Am I keeping this job?* Yes. *Will I have to stay at home tonight?* Yes.

But Lilly teaches that in Cancer, Taurus, Sagittarius and Pisces, *"sometimes she performs"*. Obviously, the first two signs are the Moon's major dignities, while Sagittarius and Pisces are ruled by the great benefic Jupiter, so the Moon is stronger in those signs, and even when VOC, she might "do some good". In such cases, the answer is not necessarily "NO, nothing will come out of it". It can be a (tentative) yes. *In a recent case, the querent asked if her mother would get back the money she lent to a friend years ago. The Moon was VOC in Cancer in H4, while the Sun, ruling her derived H8, was in the strong H10, conjunct MC by 5 degrees. The mother received some money (1/5th) 5 days after the question.* Here, the Moon's essential and accidental strength and angularity of another significator gave a (partly) positive answer.

When asking for advice, a VOC Moon usually means that there's nothing we can do - or will do - about the situation; we're stuck, we have no power to change things, or the question might have come too late because a change has been underway of which we've been unaware. The question has no future.

But when asking about a missing article, person or animal, a VOC Moon usually means that they'd be found. Likewise, when we're worried that some misfortune would come upon us. *Will the river overflow this season?* The answer is no, no worries.

You can, however, forget about the VOC Moon cautions in cases **when the main significators give a clear answer**. *Will Donna and I get married?* If the rulers of H1 and H7 apply to a conjunction or a harmonious aspect, the answer is yes, even if the Moon is VOC.

In practice, the Moon is often VOC when a question is not really meaningful. *Am I going to move to Australia?* If the querent has never really thought about moving to Australia, but is asking just for fun, because the thought has suddenly crossed his mind, this could be shown by a VOC Moon. On the other hand, if someone keeps asking the same question again and again, unwilling to accept the first answer, the chart can also show a VOC Moon. In such cases, the Moon is a caution, asking the astrologer to stop answering.

My own practice has confirmed that the Moon is not to be considered VOC when within an orb of aspect with another planet, irrespective of sign boundaries. However, in cases when the Moon is within an orb of an aspect which it won't perfect while in its present sign, **we should make note of the Moon's sign change as this usually points to a change in circumstances which will at least partially affect the outcome**. The number of degrees that separate the Moon from the next sign, correspond to the number of time units elapsing until the change.

At least two notable astrologers from the past, Ivy Goldstein-Jacobson and Olivia Barclay, believed that the Moon is not VOC when in aspect to Fortuna (part of fortune). Barclay refers to the electional chart for the coronation of Queen Elizabeth I, cast by the famous English astrologer of the 16th century, John Dee. *"He would not have elected so important an event with the Moon VOC"*, says she (HAR, p. 155), but that was an unfortunate slip, as she had calculated the Moon position and the angles wrongly. (I don't blame her, this could have happened to anyone – remember that decades ago we calculated all chart placements by hand!) In her chart, the Moon has just passed a sextile with Jupiter, whereas in the true chart, the aspect is an applying one – and what's more, there's another lunar aspect, a square to Venus. What Barclay probably wanted to say is that he'd not choose a time when the Moon wouldn't apply to a harmonious aspect, and in the coronation chart, there is such an aspect to Fortuna.

But let's face it: Fortuna is just one of the many parts (lots) that can be calculated by planets and angles; if we accept this point as playing a role in the VOC Moon definition, we'd have to accept at least some of the others too. What's more, we should take into account the angles, as they're such important energy points in any chart. Or midpoints – why not?! But it seems that the creators of horary astrology defined the VOC Moon with reference to the planets only, so I suggest we stay with that. There's one exception I'm inclined to allow for, though, and these are the Moon's nodes. They are extremely important astronomical points and their influence in horary charts is indisputable (see THE MOON'S NODES on p. 136). If the Moon is within an orb of an aspect to the nodes, the action is not over; some further development in the situation is definitely indicated.

Based on the writings of the already mentioned American astrologer Ivy Goldstein Jacobson, some astrologers believe that the Moon is not VOC when in a parallel with a planet (or Fortuna). Declinations are certainly valuable tools (see DECLINATION on p. 151), but they're based on a different system of measurement. I think that astrologers would first have to come to an agreement of the allowed orbs (which are certainly smaller than those in longitude!) before venturing to redefine the VOC Moon definition. Having said that, I'm convinced that declinations deserve to be integrated into the horary astrologers' toolkits.

I think, of course, that we have to refute the Goldstein Jacobson's belief that the Moon is not VOC when in parallel to Fortuna. She pleaded her case by two charts from her practice, published in her book **HORARY ASTROLOGY SIMPLIFIED**, but the Japanese astrologer H. Shuseh Kokubu, QHP, noted that, in both cases, the Moon was in one of the signs where the Moon is supposed to "somehow perform" (Cancer and Pisces); besides, those were not horary, but electional charts. (See http://www.qhdc.org/parallel.htm)

What about the traditionally less important aspects? As you can see in the Practice part of this book, I do check them, as those aspects certainly help to better understand a chart, but they are to be disregarded in the VOC Moon definition.

Let me add that already in the Middle Ages, the VOC definition has been expanded to the planets. Modern astrologers often speak of **VOC planets** – meaning those planets that are not in orb of aspect with another planet.

> The Moon is void-of-course when not within an orb of an applying Ptolemaic aspect with a planet. Transsaturnians are to be considered only when acting as natural or accidental significators and/or when they are in an up to 3-degree orb of conjunction with any of the angles. If they don't meet those criteria, the Moon is considered to be VOC even if applying to them.
>
> If the Moon, prior to the completion of an aspect, enters a new sign, expect a change that will have a bearing on the result, but will not prohibit the completion of the matter.

THE MOON IN *VIA COMBUSTA*

The zodiacal belt between 15° Libra and 15° Scorpio is called *via combusta* (Lat. for "the burning way"). The Moon in *via combusta* is supposed to bring unpredictable developments and sudden, sometimes radical reversals, therefore the charts with the Moon in those degrees were considered unsafe for judgment. Barclay advised to "*discard these charts*".

Frankly, I find this caution/stricture irrelevant. Some say that it originates in those ancient times when numerous malefic fixed stars occupied the region, which is highly improbable, as malefic stars are distributed quite evenly all over the zodiac; and, due to precession, this impediment would be immaterial today, anyway. Al-Biruni gives a more plausible explanation for the alleged malice of this zodiacal section, saying that Libra and Scorpio are not congenial to the Sun and Moon, each of them being the fall of one of the luminaries. Besides, both malefics, Saturn and Mars, are dignified there (Saturn in Libra and Mars in Scorpio), with the adjacent parts of both signs being occupied by terms of the malefic Mars.

This certainly seems a more plausible cause for caution, but still not convincing in the sense that charts with the Moon in *via combusta* should not be read.

SIGNIFICATOR OF THE QUERENT COMBUST

This is a caution, warning the astrologer that the querent is secretive and may be concealing an important fact necessary for the astrologer's proper understanding of the question. He could be worried, frightened, desperate, seriously ill, in some kind of danger or incapable of action. In horaries relating to disease, an applying combustion is worrying because it indicates a worsening of the patient's condition. A combust significator of the querent is therefore a caution, asking the astrologer to treat the querent carefully. (More in ACCIDENTAL DIGNITY on p. 100.)

THE H7 PLANET/S AFFLICTED

Similarly as with Saturn in H7, an afflicted (by aspect or being essentially debilitated, retrograde, combust and such) ruler or occupant of H7 is a caution that the astrologer could err, or that the querent would not listen to his advice – even if it was sensible. One way or the other, the astrologer ruled by an unfortunate H7 is supposed to be unable to help the querent.

Caution should be taken, however, when the question relates to a H7 matter (partnership, litigation, house move and similar). In such cases, H7 primarily rules something (or somebody) else, not the astrologer.

Don't you think that all of this fits in nicely with my theory of "fate"? When "the sky" refuses to cooperate, all of the astrologer's wisdom and erudition is in vain!

DISHARMONIOUS PLANETARY HOUR RULER

If the planetary hour ruler is disharmonious with the ascendening sign, the chances of getting a true (and/or a favorable) answer are lessened. As this is an important and complex subject, I'm dealing with it in a separate chapter, PLANETARY HOURS on p. 117.

RETROGRADE MERCURY

When Mercury, the planet of communication, is retrograde, astrologers should be careful because clients then tend to get secretive. They sometimes fail to provide the relevant information, they forget something crucially important, they deliberately withhold some fact (for whatever reason), or they suddenly don't need the answer any more after they had received it. **This is particularly true when retrograde Mercury is the ascendant ruler or planetary hour ruler, and when it closely aspects the Moon.**

It's advisable to re-check such questions and encourage the querent to formulate the question as clearly as possible. But this is only a caution. Such charts certainly can be read – especially when they're related to the past or to a missing something or someone. It always pays to find what retrograde Mercury really is trying to hide (or reveal), and judge accordingly. Retrograde planets have specific interpretative potential - let's use it!

See also RETROGRADE AND STATIONARY PLANETS IN HORARY ASTROLOGY on p. 182.

PLANETARY HOURS

The system of planetary hours played an important role in ancient and medieval astrology. It almost completely disappeared from modern (psychological) astrological practice, and if it wasn't for traditional and horary astrology, it probably wouldn't have survived.

But although planetary hours are more important to astrologers than planetary days, the last are better known to the general public. Even those who are not astrologically educated know that the ancient astrological tradition gave each day of the week its planetary ruler - a planet which "governed" or "ruled" it. Sunday is (obviously) ruled by the Sun and Monday by the Moon, Tuesday by Mars, Wednesday by Mercury, Thursday by Jupiter, Friday by Venus and Saturday by Saturn. In most Romanic and Germanic languages, the names of the week have roots, belonging to individual "gods" or planets which ruled them. In Italian, stemming from the Latin, Monday is *lunedi* (Moon = *Luna*), Tuesday is *martedi* (Mars = *Marte*), Wednesday is *mercoledi* (Mercury = *Mercurio*), Thursday is *giovedi* (Jupiter = *Giove*) Friday is *venerdi* (Venus = *Venere*) Saturday is *sabato* (Saturn = *Saturno*) and Sunday is *domenica* (from Lat. *dominus* – Lord, God - meaning "Lord's day", obviously related to the Sun).

The 7-day week, based on the 4-fold division of the monthly lunar cycle into four quarters, was introduced by astrologers in the early Hellenistic era and was later adopted by the Roman and other European empires. But how did the planetary day rulership get established?

To be able to understand this, we must know that planetary day rulers depend on planetary hour rulers. Planetary hour rulers form the basis of the system and they determine the planetary day rulers. But planetary hours are different from the usual 60-minutes forming one clock-hour! The ancient Egyptians started the tradition of dividing the 24 hours of each day into 12 day and 12 night hours, but those hours were not all of the same length; their length was dependent on the length of the day or night at a given period. Planetary hours are exactly 60 minutes long only at the time of both equinoxes, while the daytime hours are longer in summer, when nights are shorter, and vice versa in winter, of course.

The length of each planetary daytime hour is obtained by dividing the time from sunrise to sunset by 12, while the length of each planetary night-time hour is obtained by dividing the time from sunset to sunrise, again by 12. Thus we get 24 planetary hours for each (whole) day, those being of various lengths, depending on the duration of each day and night.

The hours then received their "rulers". Whatever planet received the rulership of the first daytime hour, became the planetary day ruler. The planetary hour rulers then followed in the Chaldean order of rulership: Saturn, Jupiter, Mars, Sun, Venus, Mercury, Moon, Saturn, Jupiter, Mars, and so on, right through the whole 168 hours of the week when the numbering begins again with the first daytime hour of the next 7-day period. The Chaldean order is never interrupted; it runs in a never-ending sequence, getting back to the same day ruler every 8th day.

As already said, the natural or "astrological" day begins at sunrise, the night at sunset. If we want to know, for example, which planet rules the 3rd planetary hour of Sunday, we'd start with the Sun, ruling the first hour; next comes Venus, ruling the second hour, and then Mercury, ruling the third hour. (See **TABLES OF PLANETARY HOURS** on p. 119). When examining the tables, note that planetary days begin at sunrise, and nights at sunset. *If a chart, for example, is cast for early Sunday morning, before sunrise, we'll find the planetary hour ruler in the column for Saturday night (NIGHT - Saturday), not in the column for Sunday night, as the whole night between late Saturday and early Sunday hours belongs to the "Saturday night"!*

Today, almost every astrological software can calculate planetary hour rulers for any location on Earth, but they can also be given a rough estimate by a quick look at the position of the Sun in a chart, cast in the Placidean system. In that system, which is based on time division, each house represents two planetary hours. The first hour begins when the Sun rises above the ascendant. The area between AS (cusp of H1) and cusp of H12 are the first two hours, the area between the cusps of H12 and H11 are the next two hours, and so on. MC stands for the noon, descendant for sunset, IC for midnight. The dividing line between two planetary hours is exactly in the middle of each house. If it's a diurnal chart (with the Sun above the horizon), we count the hours from AC backwards through MC towards

DC, but if it's a nocturnal one (with the Sun below the horizon), they're counted from DC through IC towards AC. In order to determine the current planetary hour, all we have to look at is the position of the Sun: if it's in the first half of H8, it's the 10th day hour; if in the second half of H11, it's the 3rd day hour; if in the first half of H4, it's the 6th night hour, and so on. Then we check the planetary hour ruler in the tables on p.

But, getting back to the basics, when did the counting start? Shouldn't that be all-important? All calendars are man-made (even if following natural cycles), so shouldn't there be some astro-logic behind the old wise men's decision for naming a certain day Sunday, or Monday, or whatever day? Wouldn't the whole system be too far-fetched to be taken seriously, if there was no such logic behind it? I'm inclined to say yes. Unfortunately, the origins of planetary hours are shrouded in mystery, but the system is congruent and reliable, therefore I think that we just have to trust that their "first day of the first week" was instigated by some fact that our minds have not yet been able to grasp.

The use of planetary hour rulers in horary astrology

Old authors teach that a horary chart is **radical** or "fit to be judged", if its ascending sign is in harmony with the planetary hour ruler.

The harmony of affinity of individual signs with the planetary hour rulers are laid down in the **TABLE OF AFFINITY BETWEEN SIGNS AND PLANETARY HOUR RULERS** (see p. 120), but in general, the planetary hour is harmonious, when:
- it rules the ascending sign;
- it rules the ascending sign's triplicity;
- it's of the same nature as the ascending sign or its ruler.

Tradition teaches that only those horary charts that show such harmony, should be interpreted, and all the others discarded. Such strictness is certainly unnecessary, but it is nevertheless true that **the disharmony of the ascending sign with the planetary hour ruler is a warning**. We should approach such charts more carefully than the others, having in mind that one of the following features may apply:

> A harmonious planetary hour adds to the possibility of an affirmative answer (all things considered, of course), while a disharmonious one points to the contrary and tends towards a negative answer. (Again - this being just a tendency, not a rule!) Might this be the reason why the old astrologers advised to discard such charts? A disharmonious hour ruler doesn't mean that the answer is not to be received from the chart, but it advises that the querent might not like it! It might be something they don't want to hear, and we'd be better off if we don't give such an answer. By all means, such charts should be treated with caution, especially when it comes to sensitive questions.

A common feature of a disharmonious hour ruler is also that the chart is technically "readable" - that is, an answer can be given - but the astrologer might be unable to find the correct or useful answer. Many of those charts that are left unanswered until the result is known, fall into this category.

I never discard charts with a disharmonious planetary hour ruler, but I have noticed that charts with a harmonious planetary hour ruler actually work better. In most cases when my answer really helped the querent, the ascending sign agreed with the planetary hour ruler.

I have noticed that the planetary hour ruler (whether harmonious or not) is often **a planet playing an important role in the chart. It often shows someone ovr something which contributes key information needed for the answer**. This planet can be the same as the significator of the querent or quesited, it can be their natural significator, but often it's a planet which is not directly linked to the question. This convinced me to always take note of the planetary hour ruler, and consider it an important factor in the interpretation of the chart.v

TABLES OF PLANETARY HOURS

DAY (from sunrise to sunset)

SUNDAY	MONDAY	TUESDAY	WEDNESDAY	THURSDAY	FRIDAY	SATURDAY
Sun	Moon	Mars	Mercury	Jupiter	Venus	Saturn
Venus	Saturn	Sun	Moon	Mars	Mercury	Jupiter
Mercury	Jupiter	Venus	Saturn	Sun	Moon	Mars
Moon	Mars	Mercury	Jupiter	Venus	Saturn	Sun
Saturn	Sun	Moon	Mars	Mercury	Jupiter	Venus
Jupiter	Venus	Saturn	Sun	Moon	Mars	Mercury
Mars	Mercury	Jupiter	Venus	Saturn	Sun	Moon
Sun	Moon	Mars	Mercury	Jupiter	Venus	Saturn
Venus	Saturn	Sun	Moon	Mars	Mercury	Jupiter
Mercury	Jupiter	Venus	Saturn	Sun	Moon	Mars
Moon	Mars	Mercury	Jupiter	Venus	Saturn	Sun
Saturn	Sun	Moon	Mars	Mercury	Jupiter	Venus

NIGHT (form sunset to sunrise)

SUNDAY	MONDAY	TUESDAY	WEDNESDAY	THURSDAY	FRIDAY	SATURDAY
Jupiter	Venus	Saturn	Sun	Moon	Mars	Mercury
Mars	Mercury	Jupiter	Venus	Saturn	Sun	Moon
Sun	Moon	Mars	Mercury	Jupiter	Venus	Saturn
Venus	Saturn	Sun	Moon	Mars	Mercury	Jupiter
Mercury	Jupiter	Venus	Saturn	Sun	Moon	Mars
Moon	Mars	Mercury	Jupiter	Venus	Saturn	Sun
Saturn	Sun	Moon	Mars	Mercury	Jupiter	Venus
Jupiter	Venus	Saturn	Sun	Moon	Mars	Mercury
Mars	Mercury	Jupiter	Venus	Saturn	Sun	Moon
Sun	Moon	Mars	Mercury	Jupiter	Venus	Saturn
Venus	Saturn	Sun	Moon	Mars	Mercury	Jupiter
Mercury	Jupiter	Venus	Saturn	Sun	Moon	Mars

TABLE OF AFFINITY BETWEEN SIGNS AND PLANETARY HOUR RULERS

ARIES	**Sun**	same nature (hot & dry) and triplicity ruler by D
	Mars	sign ruler
	Jupiter	triplicity ruler by N
TAURUS	**Mercury**	same nature (cold & dry)
	Venus	sign ruler
	Saturn	same nature (cold & dry)
	Moon	triplicity ruler by N
GEMINI	**Mercury**	sign ruler and triplicity ruler by N
	Jupiter	same nature (hot & moist)
	Saturn	triplicity ruler by D
CANCER	**Moon**	sign ruler and and triplicity ruler by N
	Venus	same nature (cold & moist) and triplicity ruler by D
	Mars	triplicity ruler by N
LEO	**Sun**	sign ruler and triplicity ruler by D
	Mars	same nature (hot & dry)
	Jupiter	triplicity ruler by N
VIRGO	**Mercury**	sign ruler
	Saturn	same nature (cold & dry)
	Moon	triplicity ruler by N
	Venus	triplicity ruler by D
LIBRA	**Venus**	sign ruler
	Jupiter	same nature (hot and moist)
	Saturn	triplicity ruler by D
	Mercury	triplicity ruler by N
SCORPIO	**Mars**	sign ruler and triplicity ruler by N
	Moon	same nature (cold & moist)
	Venus	same nature (cold & moist) and triplicity ruler by D
SAGITTARIUS	**Jupiter**	sign ruler
	Sun	same nature (hot & dry)
	Mars	same nature (hot & dry)
CAPRICORN	**Saturn**	sign ruler
	Venus	triplicity ruler by D
	Mercury	same nature (cold & dry)
AQUARIUS	**Saturn**	sign ruler and triplicity ruler by D
	Mercury	triplicity ruler by N
	Jupiter	same nature (hot & moist)
PISCES	**Jupiter**	sign ruler
	Mars	triplicity ruler by N
	Venus	same nature (cold & moist) and triplicity ruler by D
	Moon	same nature (cold & moist)

HOT AND DRY are all masculine (positive, diurnal) signs: Aries, Gemini, Leo, Libra, Sagittarius and Aquarius.

COLD AND MOIST are all feminine (negative, nocturnal) signs: Taurus, Cancer, Virgo, Scorpio, Capricorn, Pisces.

BASIC CLASSIFICATIONS OF PLANETS

PLANET	BENEFIC MALEFIC	GENDER	TEMPERA-TURE	MOISTURE	SECT	TEMPERA-MENT
SUN	-	male	hot	dry	diurnal	choleric
MOON	-	female	cold	moist	nocturnal	phlegmatic
MERCURY	-	-	cold	dry	-	-
VENUS	benefic	female	warm	moist	nocturnal	phlegmatic
MARS	malefic	male	very hot	dry	nocturnal	choleric
JUPITER	benefic	male	warm	moist	diurnal	sanguine
SATURN	malefic	male	cold	dry	diurnal	melancholic

THE OUTCOME

ll horary charts are cast with a view to get the answer, and the largest number of horaries basically ask about a YES or a NO. *Is something going to happen, take place, be found, get accomplished?* The rules indicating either a positive or a negative outcome are well defined and should be strictly followed. No chart is black-and-white, of course, and to get a correct answer, we must often combine a variety of techniques, but the planetary inter-relationships are most important.

While the affirmative answer can also be received by some other indications (such as planetary strengths), the most reliable indications for a YES are:
- an applying conjunction or a harmonious aspect of the significators
- translation of light
- collection of light
- mutual reception by domicile

A negative answer is usually indicated by:
- an applying disharmonious aspect of the significators
- prohibitionv
- refranation
- frustration
- besiegement

In certain exceptional cases, the affirmative can also be indicated by a disharmonious aspect of the significators (see ASPECTS, p. 122).

ASPECTS

An aspect is a certain angular distance between a pair of planets or between a planet and a point. We say that two planets are **in aspect** or that **one planet aspects the other**. Although the word **aspect** means zero deviation from the angular distance that defines it, the planets interact with each other already before and after the exactness, that is, when these angular distances deviate from exactness by certain numbers of degrees (depending on the nature of the aspect and planets involved). This deviation from exactness is called **orb**, and we say that two planets are "within an orb of aspect". It's important to know that **without a completed** (totally exact) **aspect there's no action** (change, event, outcome). In order, therefore, for something to happen, the aspect must actually get accomplished.

APPLICATION VS. SEPARATION

In traditional horary astrology, only the major or so-called "Ptolemaic" aspects are considered when considering the outcome. These are **conjunction, opposition, square, trine** and **sextile**. Other aspects (mainly inconjunction, semi-sextile, semisquare and sesquisquare) can provide additional insights, but a positive or a negative outcome is indicated by the main aspects only. **Parallel** and **contraparallel** (aspects in declination) are worth noting, but they belong to a different coordinate system (see DECLINATION on p. 151)

Crucial to the understanding of the action shown by an aspect is the distinction between the **application** and **separation**. The action is always done by the faster of the two planets. A planets is **applying to an aspect** when the faster planet approaches the slower one (bodily or by an aspect), so that it's in lesser degrees of a sign (except if retrograde), while a planet is **separating from an aspect** when the faster planet is leaving the aspect with the slower planet, so that it's in later degrees (except if retrograde).

According to their average speeds, the planetary order (from fastest to slowest) is: Moon, Mercury, Venus, Sun, Mars, Jupiter, Saturn, Uranus, Neptune, Pluto. (See VELOCITY on p. 104). We therefore say that the Moon aspects the Sun, Mars aspects Jupiter, Venus aspects Uranus, and so on. But "average" means just that, so we have to be careful when planets are faster or slower than their average daily motion (which can be quite often). Mercury is often slower than the Sun, and Saturn can be quicker than Jupiter, or even than Venus and Mars when they're stationing. To avoid mistakes, we always need to check the ephemeris, or make use of the handy tables that our software provides.

The distinction between the applying and separating aspects is extremely important in horary astrology. The separating aspects show what has already happened while the applying aspects show what is "in the making" or going to happen in the future.

Since we're usually interested in future developments, we pay more attention to the applying aspects, but the separating ones can also be revealing as they show what has brought the situation to the current stage.

With the applications, however, we need to check the ephemeris to see if a certain aspect will indeed take place, as there're a number of possible impediments which can prevent either an aspect as such or a smooth, uninterrupted formation of the aspect. (See FRUSTRATION, PROHIBITION, REFRANATION on p. 129-130.)

As already said, an aspect is only the situation where two bodies (or points) are distanced by an exact angle, but in practice we often use the word "aspect" also for their applying and separating stages. For the purpose of knowing when the planetary energies are within reach of each other, we use **orbs**. An orb is like an aura surrounding the planet. It shows the range of its "radiation". If two planets are within each other's orbs, we know that something's going on between the people or things they represent. Orbs vary depending on the bodies' (observable) sizes. (See **TABLE OF ORBS AND HALF-ORBS** on p. .) The most important are the applications and separations of the Moon, and the Moon also has the second-largest orb. To understand the past developments, we can check all the aspects that the Moon has completed in the sign it presently occupies, and for the future, all those she's going to make. I must stress, though, that this is usually unnecessary. **To get the answer, the first applying aspect usually suffices - especially if it's to a significator. If it's not, we can look further, but we should be careful not to exceed the orbs.**

It matters a great deal whether the aspect is almost exact (within a 1° orb) or very loose. The tighter the orb, the stronger the bond (or action). *If, for example, a pair of planets standing for a couple of friends, are in a sextile within a 2° orb, this shows a stronger bond than if the sextile has a 5° orb.*

To get the valid orb for each aspect, we must add together both bodies' half-orbs. *If, for example, the Sun and Jupiter are 16°30´ apart, they're still within orbs, but if they're 17° apart, they're outside orbs and don't have any influence upon each other.*

Half-orbs are also called **moieties** whereas an aspect within a 1 degree orb is called a **partile** (or **partill**) aspect. Originally, though, an aspect was only considered partile if also both degrees were the same.

TABLE OF ORBS AND HALF-ORBS

PLANET	ORB	HALF-ORB
SUN	17	8° 30´
MOON	12° 30´	6° 15´
JUPITER	12°	6°
SATURN	10°	5
VENUS	8°	4°
MARS	7° 30´	3° 45´
MERCURY	7°	3° 30´

ASPECTS IN HORARY ASTROLOGY

CONJUNCTION, TRINE AND SEXTILE are harmonious aspects and signify a meeting (coming together) of two people (concepts, things), the completion of a situation or the desirability of action which is the subject of the question. If two significators apply to a harmonious aspect, the answer is positive (affirmative). In questions of yes/no type the answer is YES, but only in cases such as: *Will I get the job for which I have applied?* Answer: Yes. *Should I buy this car?* Answer: Yes. *Will my ex get back to me?* Answer: Yes.

Now consider these questions: *Are we going to divorce? Is my business partner quitting the agreement? Is my opponent going to sue me?* The answer to any of these question is NO, because the harmonious application of both significators (in this case, the rulers of H1 and H7) means that the two parties will find their way back to each other, will find an agreement, will not stop cooperating. Remember that **the phrasing of a question is not important** – what counts are the contents! *Is my wallet lost?* The same logic applies here. If the rulers of H1 and H2 (the significators of the querent and his wallet) are applying to a harmonious aspect, the answer is NO, the wallet is not lost, only misplaced, and the querent will get it back.

Note, though, that for a positive outcome, the aspect between significators must be **immediate** (without an interference like FRUSTRATION, REFRANATION and PROHIBITION, see p. 129-130).

Know also that although we are here considering one of the most dependable horary interpretative rules, not every harmonious aspect gives a positive answer. I have seen cases when two significators (or the Moon and a significator or co-significator) applied harmoniously to each other but the result was negative. But in all of these cases, the planets were either essentially or accidentally very weak. This teaches us that harmonious aspects will only bring positive results when the planets involved are not seriously "damaged" – which is when they are in detriment or fall, in any of the weak or infortunate houses (or ruling them), retrograde, combust, extremely slow, involved in a disharmonious aspect with a malefic, or (an important consideration) without any reception. The more the planet/s are damaged or weakened, the stronger the possibility of their aspect not bringing about the desired result. For example, if you have a harmonious aspect between two significators which are both in detriment and at least one of them is in H12, H6, H8 or (possibly) in H3 or H9 (which are cadent and therefore less expressive), etc., the trine or sextile between them will not "work".

OPPOSITIONS AND SQUARES usually stand for **disagreement or separation of two people (objects), a failure (of a plan, desire, course of action) or undesirability of a planned action**. The procedure is the same as above. *Are my wife and I staying together?* The answer is NO, but if the question is *Are we going to get divorced?* the answer is YES. We must know that an opposition in horary astrology is a more difficult aspect than a square, because it's a so-called separation aspect, while a square often presents obstacles that must be overcome before reaching the goal. Still, a square most often gives a negative answer, except under exceptional circumstances which are listed below.

If significators apply to an opposition or a square, but are in a strong mutual reception and at least one of them is also in an angular or a fortunate house (1, 7, 4, 10, 5, 11 and sometimes 3 and 9), or if translation of light or collection of light is involved, the situation can still be completed, but usually with difficulty, or only a partially satisfactory result is acheived (see MUTUAL RECEPTION, TRANSLATION OF LIGHT and COLLECTION OF LIGHT on p. 127-128). Alternatively, the querent may regret to have decided on a certain course of action, although this action was possible and perhaps even indicated (predicted) by any of the "auxiliary" configurations mentioned above. Rarely, the "perfection of matter" can also happen if such significators are essentially very strong or if at least one receives the other in its domicile or exaltation sign, but, as already mentioned, strong houses must be involved. Unfortunate and weak houses take away planetary power to act. Beware, though: if at least one of the significators involved in an opposition or a square is a malefic (Mars or Saturn), the matter most probably won't get perfected, even if translation of light is involved. Planets conjunct angles (or being placed in angular houses) make matters worse in such cases.

It is to be understood, of course, that in seeking the answer, only aspects made by significators (and co-significators - the Moon and planets located in a certain house) are to be considered. Planets not related to the question are disregarded. Such planets can give additional information or describe the circumstances related to the question, but they don't partake in the main "story".

When there are no aspects between the main significators, look for any aspects between the Moon and the main significators and co-significators. They are equally important and dependable as the aspects between the main significators – especially aspects made by the Moon.

Aspects often give a very clear (yes or no) answer, but sometimes, things are more complicated and call for a more careful approach. Planetary house placements, their essential and accidental dignities and house rulerships must be considered before attempting the answer.

The outcome is most reliable if the aspect perfects when the planets are still in the same signs as at the time of the question. If the aspect perfects when one (or both) of the planets is in the next (or previous, in case of retrogradation) sign, we must be careful (see REFRANATION on p. 130).

When considering applications and separations, note the special status of **retrograde** planets. If one planet is retrograde and applying towards a direct one, they are actually applying towards each other. This reflects a strong "wish" of them to come together (harmonious) or to get apart (disharmonious), and from the timing perspective, the situation usually develops a bit more quickly as it otherwise would. But if both planets are retrograde, the action is delayed.

> For a matter to "get perfected", planets must **apply to an aspect, not separate** from one! Application is like coming together, separation is like getting away (from each other). Suppose that the significators of a husband and his wife are applying to an opposition. *Are they going to get divorced?* Yes, they are, because their significators indicate that kind of future activity. But if both planets would already be separating from an opposition, we can assume that the worst is behind them and that, following some serious disputes they have recently had, they would get reconciled.

When considering the workings of aspects, it's important to evaluate the essential and accidental dignities of the planets, as well as their dispositions, receptions and mutual receptions.

If at least one planet receives the other, the aspect is stronger as it would be without a reception.

Any "help" provided by a fortified planets enhances the aspect, either a positive or a negative one. A disharmonious aspect of the Moon with a malefic, say, will not work so negatively if the malefic receives the Moon in any of its dignities (or vice versa) or if the malefic is essentially dignified. Such a situation (that is, with a positively expressed malefic) may indicate that the querent (or quesited) faces a difficult challenge, obstacle or problem that must be resolved before the goal can be reached. Otherwise (no reception, an essentially weak or otherwise afflicted malefic) the energy of the planets is too weak to sustain the stress produced by the disharmonious aspect.

In the Practice part of this book, there is an example where the Moon (in H8) closely applies to a square of Mars. The Moon is in Aries, Mars is in Capricorn. Mars is exalted and receives the Moon in its domicile, whereas the Moon receives Mars in its triplicity. This aspect indicated an immediate operation, but because both bodies were dignified and mutually received, the square proved beneficial to the patient, as the operation was successful and helped him recover.

> Planets applying to an aspect should be carefully examined to see whether the aspect will actually perfect or not. When close to their stationary points, planets are much slower than their average. (Example: *Jupiter applies to an aspect with Saturn, which is usually slower than Jupiter, but at the time of the question, Jupiter is slowing down while Saturn is speeding up, so the seemingly applying aspect will never perfect.*)

ASPECTS OF SIGNIFICATORS WITH OTHER PLANETS

When a significator is in an aspectual relationship with a planet or planets which are not directly related to the querent or quesited, a number of interpretations are possible. For example:

- In love and other relationship / partnership questions, such a planet can stand for another person with whom the querent / quesited is involved beside the querent;
- In missing people, animals or articles charts, their significators' aspects with malefics can point to their difficult circumstances, whereas benefics in such places can show helpful circumstances, or indicate people who serve as their rescuers, and similar;
- In health questions, applying aspects of significators of sick people to malefics can point to the deterioration of their health, or progression of disease.
- A benefic in a harmonious aspect with the significator of the querent can indicate a person who will help the querent achieve their goal (get a job, for example).

And so on. It's important to know that every aspect of the significator with any planet means something. What exactly, is shown both by the nature of the planet as such and from its house and sign position, house rulership/s and so on. *If this planet is, for example, Jupiter, this will likely be a fortunate influence, but not if it's severely debilitated (essentially weak, ruling an unfortunate house, retrograde and similar). See also which houses have their cusps in Sagittarius and Pisces (Jupiter's signs) to get additional information as per the manner, quality and source of influence.*

EXACT CONJUNCTIONS OF PLANETS WITH THE ANGLES

If a planet is exactly (within a one degree orb) conjunct any of the angles of the chart, it is expressed very strongly and we have to take it into account even if not acting as a significator. This planet can contribute key information needed for the answer. We should note the innate nature of the planet (its natural rulership), as well as its essential dignity. A retrograde planet sometimes means a repetition or a return (of something or someone).

In this context, the planets generally mean:
- **The Sun:** happiness, success, a decisive influence of an important man
- **The Moon:** the querent is led by strong instincts and emotions; security needs, home and family play a key role; a change is in the making
- **Mercury:** news, message
- **Venus:** love, peace and happiness; the key role of a young woman
- **Mars:** a dispute is looming; the case is "hot"
- **Jupiter:** luck or an influential person will play an important role, acting to the benefit of the querent; financial gains, profit
- **Saturn:** the question is prompted by fear; case is closed, obstacles are too great
- **Uranus:** an "exotic" or unusual question; an imminent change or shock
- **Neptune:** the querent is being misled; dissapointment; an "unfortunate" error
- **Pluto:** a "fatal" obstruction; the question might be prompted by manipulative motives

To a lesser degree, planets in exact aspects to angles also have a similar bearing on the outcome. Note the difference between harmonious and disharmonius aspects, and the house/s involved (house position and rulerships).

MUTUAL RECEPTION

Mutual reception (MR) has already been discussed in the chapter DISPOSITION, RECEPTION AND MUTUAL RECEPTION (see p. 96). Let me add that MR of significators can sometimes have the meaning similar to a harmonious applying aspect, but the influence is weaker; it may contribute to a positive outcome, but of a temporary nature or not promising permanent results. When in doubt, we should turn to the Moon and its aspects for additional indications.

The strongest MR is the one by domicile. Any MR is also stronger when the involved planets (or at least one of them) are in angular houses (1, 4, 7 and 10); of middle strength when in succedent houses (2, 5, 8 and 11); and weakest when in cadent houses (3, 6, 9 and 12).

Mutual reception often means that the querent has a choice: he can decide on the one or the other option. This situation often comes up in questions referring to the desirability of a certain job, partner, real estate and similar. Sometimes, MR suggests that an item has been moved from one place to another, or that there was an exchange of some kind, or that two people (or things) have swapped places. Context is of crucial importance here. If, for example, you're looking for a missing item, it could have been removed from the original place and you'd be likely to find it in an unexpected place.

There is a variation of mutual reception, **mutual reception by house**. For example, if the ruler of H4 is in H1 while the ruler of H1 is in H4, the two planets are in mutual reception by house. Although such MR is quite common and nearly as important as MR by sign, astrologers rarely make use of it. It often indicates a close relationship or cooperation, exhibited by people or objects ruled by both significators.

TRANSLATION OF LIGHT

An affirmative answer or the completion of the matter can also be shown by **translation of light**. This is a situation where two significators are not in aspect, but are joined together by the third planet, faster than both, which separates from an aspect with the one significator and applies to an aspect with the other significator. Thus the quicker planet "transmits" or "translates" the influence of one planet to another, whereby their energies become connected. The "translator" is usually the Moon, on account of its quick motion. As is the case with the aspects, translation is stronger (more effective) when at least one of the involved planets receives the other (by domicile, exaltation, triplicity, term or face), and strongest when they're in mutual reception. (The most effective being MR by domicile.)

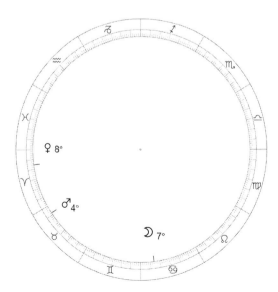

EXAMPLE: *Mars at 4° Taurus, the Moon at 7° Cancer, Venus at 8° Aries. Significators are Mars and Venus. The planets are not in aspect, but are being re-connected by the Moon which is separating from the sextile of Mars and applying to a square with Venus. Translation of light is quite powerful here, as Mars is in the exaltation of the Moon while the Moon is in Mars' night triplicity, while also being strong in its own sign. If this was a day chart, the Moon would be in Venus' triplicity. You will also notice that Venus and Mars are in MR by domicile, making an affirmative answer an even greater possibility.*

Depending on the nature of the question, the translating planet can stand for someone who's in a position to make two people meet (come to an agreement, begin an association, etc.) or help bring the matter to conclusion. If the translator in not the Moon (which always shows the general course of events) but a planet, see whom this planet represents in the chart.

If, for example, it rules the querent's H11, a friend could help him; if it rules H3, it could be his sister, neighbor or classmate; if it rules H7, it would be his spouse, and the like. The translating planet doesn't necessarily represent a person; it can also stand for situations and concepts like someone's job, a trip abroad, a party, a sports event or any situation that can be involved in the two party's meeting, or in helping to bring the matter to a successful end.

A pair of planets can be involved in translation of light even if they're in aspect. In such cases, a positive outcome is certain, even if the aspect which connects them is disharmonious (a square or an opposition). Under normal circumstances, such an aspect would lead to a negative answer (to the disassociation or separation of people or things that are the subject of the question), but the translation of light connects them so as to enable the "completion". (Be careful, however, with Mars and Saturn – see below.)

> When evaluating the effects of translation of light, be careful: if the Moon (or a planet) translates light between malefics (Mars and Saturn), especially when they're poorly placed (essentially and/or accidentally weak) and afflicted by being in disharmonious aspects with other planets, the action is not desirable or the completion of the matter will be unfavorable for the querent. Note also that translation of light between malefics won't work if the translating Moon applies to any of them by a disharmonious aspect. But if it happens that the matter would get accomplished, the querent would regret it. Exceptions are those cases where the completion of the matter is absolutely desirable (such as a planned pregnancy).

A special type or "subspecies" of translation of light is when the translating planet is lower in degrees than both the significators. This can give a positive outcome but it's not the classical translation of light, and it doesn't work when the planets which the "translator" in about to connect, are themselves in a disharmonious aspect. In such cases, the translation works more in the sense of negating a positive outcome.

EXAMPLE: *Jupiter at 5° Virgo, Venus at 9° Virgo, the Moon at 3° Taurus. The Moon will first trine Jupiter and then translate its light to Venus (by its next aspect, a trine).*

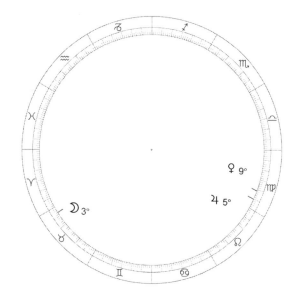

COLLECTION OF LIGHT

Collection of light is another way of completion. This is a situation where a pair of significators are not applying to an aspect but both are applying to an aspect with the third planet, slower from them both, which thus connects them so that their energies are joined together. We say that it "collects their lights". In question of yes/no nature, the suggested answer is yes. The result can be achieved with the help of a third party or by means of whatever the collecting planet represents. But, like in translation of light, we must be careful: if the collecting planet is a malefic and/or badly placed, collection can make matters worse. The result can still be achieved but it might be better if it wasn't! As with aspects, collection of light is stronger if the collecting planet receives the faster planets in their dignities (especially by domicile or exaltation), or vice versa.

EXAMPLE 1: *Jupiter at 15° Libra, Mars at 16° Pisces, Neptune at 18° Capricorn. Jupiter and Mars are significators. They're not in aspect, but both apply to an aspect with Neptune (Mars by a sextile, Jupiter by a square) which thus collects their lights. Collection is strong in this case, as Neptune receives Mars in its (modern) domicile and Mars receives Neptune in its exaltation, while Jupiter receives Mars in its domicile.*

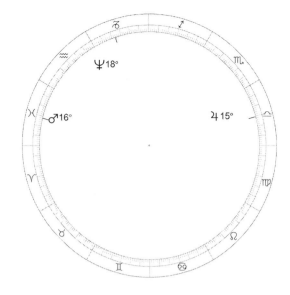

EXAMPLE 2: *Venus at 15° Leo, Mercury at 20° Libra, Saturn at 23° Libra. Significators are Venus and Mercury. Mercury separates from sextile with Venus, but both apply to Saturn (Mercury by conjunction, Venus by sextile), which thus collects their lights. Although Saturn is a malefic, its influence in this case can›t be detrimental, as Libra is the sign of its exaltation and day triplicity, while Venus, although in Saturn's detriment, receives it in its domicile, which is another helpful indication.*

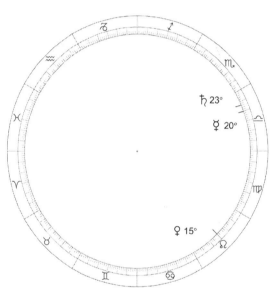

FRUSTRATION

Frustration is when a pair of significators are applying to an aspect, but before the aspect is completed, one of them connects with another planet (by conjunction or any other aspect). It should be easy to imagine how the significators that have thus been prevented from meeting, become "frustrated": the action cannot be completed, somebody or something is going to intervene and redirect the course of events. The potential "yes" thus becomes a "no".

> In practice, care is needed because a configuration can technically be a case of frustration while practically it is not. True frustration is usually marked by an opposition or a square of a significator (or the Moon) with a malefic, whereas harmonic aspects can act as a subspecies of translation of light, thus achieving the opposite result, that is, supporting and not inhibiting the desired (planned, anticipated) result.

EXAMPLE 1: *Mars at 24° Aquarius, Venus at 20° Sagittarius, Saturn at 21° Gemini. Significators are Mars and Venus. Venus applies to sextile Mars, but before the aspect is made, Venus completes an opposition with Saturn which thus inhibits (frustrates, denies) the significators' meeting.*

EXAMPLE 2: *Mars at 24° Aquarius, Venus at 20° Sagittarius, Jupiter at 25° Aquarius. Significators are Mars and Venus. Venus applies to sextile Mars, but Mars reaches Jupiter before the aspect with Venus is completed, thus "escaping" it.*

Example 2 is technically a case of frustration, but Jupiter as a benefic (especially if also essentially and accidentally dignified) can stand for some kind of facilitator - a benefactor who contributes to the meeting of two people ruled by Venus and Mars. They'd meet anyway, as they're applying to an aspect, but Jupiter could play out as a friend who throws a party which both are attending, thus facilitating their meeting. On the other hand, Jupiter could "steal" Mars from Venus! Context is crucial here, and students are advised to carefully consider the situation before attempting the answer. The real-life circumstances should be skillfully applied to the interplay of the involved planets and aspects, not forgetting house rulerships and other chart factors.

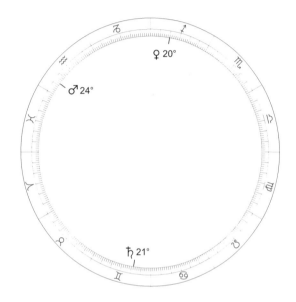
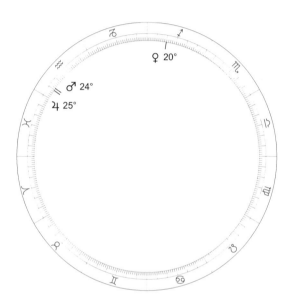

PROHIBITION

Prohibition is similar to frustration. A pair of significators are applying to an aspect, but the formation of the aspect is prevented by a third, faster planet which makes an aspect with one of the significators before the first one takes place. Completion of the matter, suggested by the anticipated aspect between significators, is thus disabled.

EXAMPLE: *The Sun at 5° Aries, Mars at 9° Gemini, Mercury at 2° Aries. The Sun and Mars are significators. The Sun applies to sextile Mars, but Mercury reaches the Sun before the completion of that aspect, and thus "prohibits" their meeting.*

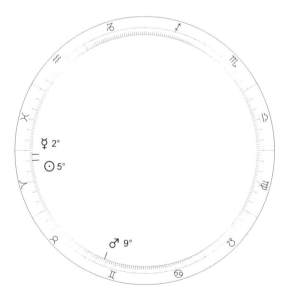

REFRANATION

Refranation is a situation when a pair of significators are applying to an aspect, but before the aspect is made, one of the significators changes signs or direction (from direct to retrograde, or vice versa). The anticipated result is thus hindered. In order to ascertain whether, in a particular case, refranation would indeed take place, we must check the future movement of the planets in the ephemeris.

EXAMPLE 1: *Jupiter at 27° Taurus, Saturn at 29° Aquarius. Jupiter applies to square Saturn, but before the aspect is made, Saturn slips into Pisces. The aspect will (all things considered) therefore complete in the next pair of signs, thus affecting the outcome.*

EXAMPLE 2: *Venus at 16 Gemini, Mars at 19 Leo. Venus applies to sextile Mars, but before the aspect is made, Venus turns retrograde, thus "refraining" from the action suggested by the anticipated aspect.*

In case of refranation taking place due to a sign change, we must be careful, though. We should comply with the same definition as for the void-of-course Moon, which means that the Moon (or a planet) is not "void" (inoperative) when the planets are already in orb of an aspect. The result can still be achieved, but there will probably be a change in circumstances which will affect the outcome. The nature of the change is shown by the new sign and its dispositor.

BESIEGEMENT

Although this is an important condition, it is nevertheless the most unreliable way of "non-completion". It might be more appropriate to qualify it as a special situation in a horary chart which serves as a kind of warning, but in itself does not give a negative answer to the question.

According to tradition, the planet is *besieged* when it is situated between Mars and Saturn, the two traditional malefics. In other words, to be qualified as besieged, a planet must separate from a conjunction with the one malefic and apply to a conjunction with the other malefic. Besiegement in the original sense of the word implies that all the three planets are in the same sign, but modern horary astrologers have somehow adapted this rule, so that today a planet is considered to be besieged even if the three planets are not in the same sign. It is important, however, that there's no other planet in between. Yet other astrologers consider a planet to be besieged when it separates from a conjunction, opposition or square with one malefic and applies to a conjunction, opposition or square with another malefic. Such a situation is damaging, by all means, but it is not, strictly speaking, besiegement in the traditional sense of the word. In modern horary astrology, one malefic (or even both of them) can be replaced by Pluto, Uranus or Neptune – the planets which often act destructively when in conjunction, and usually so when in opposition or square.

Besiegement suggests that the querent or quesited, ruled by the besieged planet, is in a difficult situation which prevents him/her/it from acting in a positive, constructive way. It often shows danger. Symbolically, it is a kind of "imprisonment", implying that someone (something) can't avoid or escape dangerous or even life-threatening circumstances. What's more, things are obviously going from bad to worse. In charts of missing people and animals their besieged significator usually indicates that they are in dire circumstances - unable to move, in the hands of their adversaries, badly hurt or dead.

My research has shown that besiegement only works when the besieged planet does not make a harmonious aspect with the Moon or another planet before completing a conjunction (or a disharmonious aspect) with the second malefic. The intervention of such an aspect "saves" the besieged planet from the impending danger. This can also be the case if the malefic to which the besieged planet applies, is essentially strong (in its domicile or exaltation), or if it is the significator (ruler) of the quesited. In the latter case, such an application rather suggests the accomplishment of the matter i.e. the achievement of the objective/goal.

In modern astrological literature you may come upon the notion of besiegement by two benefics (Venus and Jupiter). The situation here is to the contrary, of course – the "besieged" planet stands for extreme luck, with the querent's/quesited's circumstances being most fortunate.

TIMING

The querent often wonders **when** something would happen. *When will I get a job? When do we move? When will I start a new relationship?* All these questions refer explicitly to the **time** when something would take place, but horary charts often suggest timing even without our asking for it. They show time units which have passed since an event, related to the chart, or time units that will elapse before the resoultion of the question (or some specific aspect of the question).

Timing is certainly a touchstone of an astrologer's skill. Being able to predict the exact time which will elapse until the resolution of the question, is more difficult than to find out whether something will get accomplished (be found, be done, be achieved etc.). It's true that some charts are very clear and easy in this respect, and that there are others which demand a whole lot more of expertise on the astrologer's part. Revising our charts usually shows where we have made a mistake. Even skilled astrologers are sometimes dumbfounded when they learn of the result and find that the time was actually suggested by the chart, only they didn't succeed in getting it right. I believe that all horary charts show timing, in any of the several possible ways - provided the chart shows completion, of course.

By checking these charts in retrospect, we learn a lot. I have discovered fabulous new vistas of timing by studying charts which on the first sight did not disclose proper timing. But it pays to be persistent. I don't give up easily when trying to "decode" a chart from the timing perspective. There always comes that flash of insight when I say "bingo"!

My practice has convinced me of the value of the **angles** in calculating the timing. This is not a common approach, although it's no less astro-logical than any other. Angles are extremely sensitive points. Not only AC, DC, MC and IC, but also vertex and antivertex. Many times has the timing been ascertained by the distance of the Moon or a significator from an angle. Some astrologers disapprove on theoretical grounds, saying that we can't mix the two reference circles (the horizontal and ecliptic). But that's nonsense, of course, as we're doing that constantly – what are planetary transits to the natal angles, for example, if not a mixing of the two systems?

The most reliable indicator of time is the Moon. Its separating aspects show the past while its applying aspects show the future. The number of degrees that separate it from an aspect with a significator or an angle, show the number of time units (minutes, hours, days, weeks, months or years) that have elapsed since a past event or that will elapse until the predicted event.

Remember: when considering the **distance of the Moon or the planets from the angular (cardinal) points**, we don't use applications and separations. We only measure distances, regardless of whether the angles apply to those bodies or separate from them. Practice has shown that what really counts is the number of degrees that separate the points from the Moon/planet. In other words, although the angles move the fastest (as they are based on the rotation of the Earth on its axis), for the purpose of horary timing we view them them "fixed", so that we only consider the degrees that they occupy at the time of the question. As for the aspects, by far the most reliable here is conjunction, but sometimes the number of time units is also shown by any other Ptolemaic aspect.

EXAMPLE 1: *MC at 3° Leo, the Moon or significator at 5° Leo – the resolution is due in 2 time units.*

EXAMPLE 2: *MC at 3° Leo, the Moon or significator at 1° Leo – the resoultion is due in 2 time units.*

Time units are sometimes (although rarely) also indicated by **interplanetary aspects**, but here we usually consider the further actual planetary movement, not the symbolic one, as with the Moon. This means that we must check the ephemeris to see when both significators will actually complete the aspect, and then convert the number of days (or hours, or days and hours) that will elapse until the completion of the aspect, into the most probable time units (days, weeks, months.)

Timing can also be done by means of **transits**. Sometimes the matter is resolved when one of the significators reaches any of the four cardinal points of the horary chart, or any aspect with another significator (as it is in the chart). In other words, we can perceive a horary chart as some kind of "natal" chart, and observe transits to it.

In those charts where the Moon is at one of the last degrees of a sign, we can get the proper timing (that is, the time elapsing until the resolution of the question or until some change of circumstances) by the number of degrees that **separate it from the following sign**.

Sometimes, however, the time can be shown even by the number of degrees that separate the significator from the cusp of the next house! In *Christian Astrology*, William Lilly cites the example when a soldier's significator was located 2° from the cusp of his H9: the soldier went abroad in 2 months. In **HORARY ASTROLOGY REDISCOVERED**, Olivia Barclay demonstrates an example of a sick cat; its H8 ruler was 1.5 degrees distant from the cusp of H6 – the cat's ascendant – and the cat died in a day and a half! It is mostly due to such cases that many modern horary astrologers still use the Regiomontanus' house system, which was in use during the medieval and Renaissance astrology when horary astrology blossomed.

After having calculated the number of degrees separating the Moon from the significator (or from an aspect with it), from an angle or from the following sign, we need to decide for the most appropriate time unit. **TABLE OF TIMING** (see p. 134) shows which are the most logical (likely) time units, depending on the placement of the Moon (and planets) in signs and houses. In choosing them we must, however, use common sense. If, for example, you think it logical that something should get accomplished within hours (or in the same day), then it will most likely be hours, although the table points to days or weeks. *The meeting starts in ten minutes, when is Mike coming?* Suppose that Mike's significator is 4 degrees from an angle, in a fixed sign and in a cadent house. Will Mike arrive in 4 months? No! Minutes are the most logical time unit in this case – except if Mike had an accident and would come out of the hospital in 4 months (or weeks, or days)!

On the other hand, logic can fool us. We expect, for example, that a certain matter would be completed in three days (as this would be the most logical time unit, under the circumstances), but then it happens in three weeks - which the chart might have indicated, but we didn't want to "see"! *There's an interesting example of this among my relocation charts. The querent asked when would her family move to the flat that they had been renovating. Initially, I told her that they'd move in 3.5 months, as this was most in line with the* **TABLE OF TIMING**, *but she insisted that it's impossible, they should be moving in 3.5 weeks, according to the contract. "3.5 months is totally out of the question," she said. As it turned out, the timing that the chart showed was correct – they moved in 3.5 months.*

It follows, then, that logical thinking and consideration of real life circumstances can sometimes be helpful, but sometimes deceptive. What's more, sometimes it's clearly impossible to decide what a "short" or a "long" time unit should be. *One of my real-estate charts, for example, clearly showed "action" in 5 very short time units, as the Moon was in a cardinal sign and an angular house, applying to a significator in a fixed sign and an angular house. I told the querent that she'd find a better buyer from the existing one (she asked about the desirability of accepting an offer from a potential buyer of her flat) in five days, but he actually arrived in five hours!*

For a final touch, it's always good to check the **Moon's speed**. If the Moon is quick (that is, if its daily motion is greater than the average of 13°11'), the matter can be accomplished a little earlier, if slow, a little later. (But only a little! We can add a day or two to 15 days, for example.) The same applies to the slowness of motion - time is slightly prolonged here.

From this perspective, we can also check **planetary speeds**. The faster planets represent faster or quicker people / events / processes, the slower the slower ones. Both the actual daily motion of the planets and their relative speeds need to be considered. If a significator moves slowly (at the time of the question) or is one of the slower-moving planets, that which it rules in the chart will also be slow or long-lasting, if quickly (or is a quick planet) vice-versa.

If the Moon (or a planet) applies to a **retrograde planet**, the matter can be completed a little sooner, because in such cases the two bodies apply to one another, suggesting a hastening of the matter.

Time can also be defined more broadly, considering the Moon's or significator's sign modality: **cardinal signs suggest short, fixed long and mutable medium duration**. Asking about the duration of a disease, for example, its significator in a cardinal sign would show a short and passing disease, in a fixed sign a long-lasting one and in a movable sign something in-between, or a chronic, recurring disease.

The same goes for the houses: **angular houses stand for (relatively) short, succedent for medium and the cadent for long-lasting (processes, events etc.).**

Ascendant in a cardinal sign (Aries especially) suggests that the matter will be resolved quickly / soon; in a fixed sign, it will take long before the goal is reached, while mutable signs show middle lengths of time or recurring, repetitive situations / processes.

TABLE OF TIMING

THE MOON (OR A PLANET) IN	TIME UNIT
cardinal sign and angular house	the shortest (hours or days)
cardinal sign and succedent house	of middle length (days or weeks)
cardinal sign and cadent house	the longest (weeks or months)
movable sign and angular house	the shortest (days or weeks)
movable sign and succedent house	of middle length (weeks or months)
movable sign and cadent house	the longest (months or years)
fixed sign and angular house	the shortest (weeks or months)
fixed sign and succedent house	of middle length (months or years)
fixed sign and cadent house	the longest (indefinable)

Let's consider the **TABLE OF TIMING**. As you can see, it refers to the Moon or "a planet" (significator). So – which of them is more important? In case of a conjunction, there's no dilemma (usually), but if the Moon and the planet are connected through an aspect, we deal with a combination of signs and houses. Always **give preference to the Moon**, but know that the sign and house of the planet to which it applies, have some influence. *If the Moon, for example, is in an angular house and a cardinal sign, and the planet to which it applies is also in an angular house and a cardinal sign, it's likelier that the time unit will be the shortest possible, as if the planet was in a fixed or mutable sign and in a succedent or a cadent house.*

Alas, it's not easy! The following example will show you just how complicated it can get. *In the Practice part of this book you will find a chart where the Moon is in a fixed sign and a cadent house, applying to square Mars which is also in a fixed sign and a cadent house. The number of degrees that separates them from an exact aspect, showed the number of **weeks** that passed until the predicted event. So far so good, but the Moon also applies to trine Mercury placed in a cardinal sign and a succedent house. In this case, the number of degrees that separates them from the exact aspect, coincided with the number of **days** that passed until another event, indicated by this aspect! The cardinal signature of Mercury affected timing by making the "Mercury event" correspond with a shorter time unit.*

What do such examples teach us?

If the Moon in a horary chart applies to more than one planet, with both (or all of them) being related to the subject matter of the question, time units for each development are chosen in accordance with the sign/house placement of those planets.

Complicated? Yes! But don't worry, practice makes perfect!

Horary astrology is wonderful in its ability to predict time. But to get there, we sometimes have to dig really deep. Tradition teaches, for example, that for timing purposes, only those lunar aspects are to be considered which are already within orb. But the truth is that its scope extends far beyond! Consider the question *When will my husband be released from prison?* (see p. 428). The Moon in this chart needs 32.5 degrees to Venus, the significator of the husband – and exactly that number of weeks passed until his release!

Lately, I have been discovering the benefits of timing by the **lunar declination**. I have discovered that the time (till the predicted event) can be indicated by the number of degrees that separate the Moon from a parallel or contraparallel with the significator, or by the number of days (and hours) that will pass until such an aspect. Timing can also be done by counting the number of days that will elapse until the next lunar turning point (maximum northern or southern declination degree). Time units can vary here too, same as in the longitudinal system of measurement, with the criterion being the Moon's sign and house position. (See example on p. 312.)

Timing could also be affected by the Moon's **parallax**. (See THE MOON, p. 79.)

There's another consideration which horary students often overlook – obviously because no horary astrology literature has mentioned it yet. (At least to my knowledge.) Namely, when dealing with months, we must bear in mind that there are **different definitions of a month**. **Synodic, sidereal** and **calendar** month vary in length. Astrologically relevant are only the synodic and sidereal month. Sidereal month (one lunar revolution around the Earth with respect to the background stars) lasts 27.3 days and is as such a little shorter from the synodic month (the time between two consecutive conjunctions of the Moon and the Sun), which takes an average of 29.5 days, while the calendar month is still a little longer (30 or 31 days). Sidereal month might seem like a credible time unit, but my practice has shown that the most reliable is the **synodic** month. Although it's just a little bit shorter than the calendar month, a discrepancy arises when dealing with a larger number of months. In 15 months, for example, we'd get a mistake of approximately 10 days if using the calendar instead of the synodic month. Several examples in the second part of the book prove the importance of this consideration.

ADDITIONAL TECHNIQUES

MOON'S NODES

Moon's nodes (or lunar nodes) are not planets, but they are nevertheless extremely important. They are astronomical points which have been used since times immemorial in all branches of astrology, including horary.

What are they – astronomically? Planets that apparently orbit the Earth, are not all on the same plane. The zodiac with planets, mapped onto a circle, is an optical illusion! In reality, the Moon and the planets are sometimes above and sometimes below the Sun's line (ecliptic). Distances north and south of the Sun are called **celestial latitudes** - as opposed to their placements measured eastwards from 0° Aries which are called celestial longitudes. With the exception of Pluto, which presently goes as far as 17.5 degrees N or S, the Moon and the planets deviate from the ecliptic for up to about 8°. The Moon has a very regular motion, reaching (in the course of a month) 5° N and (half a month later) 5° S.

Lunar nodes are the two points in the lunar orbit where the Moon, in the course of its rotating around the Earth, crosses the ecliptic (the Sun's path). The **north or ascending node** is the point where it crosses it from south to north, whereas the **south or descending node** is the point where it crosses it from north to south. Both points are always exactly opposite each other. They move in a zigzag motion - a little forwards and some more backwards, so that, on average, they are retrograding. The full circle takes 19 years.

Planets also have nodes, but they are not in mutual oppositions and have, to my knowledge, never been mentioned in horary literature. (Which doesn't mean that they shouldn't be! That's one area of astrology which still calls for research.)

When the Moon comes into a conjunction or an opposition with the Sun when crossing one of its nodes, the Sun, the Moon and Earth are in the same line, causing eclipses (see ECLIPSES on p. 138).

In Indian astrology, the so called "nodal line" is depicted by a dragon with its head at the northern and its tail at the southern node. The head is called **rahu**, the tail **ketu**. A rich mythology has evolved out of the fact that rahu and ketu "cause" eclipses. The heavenly dragon occasionally "devours" the Sun and the Moon, givers of life, resulting in the belief that both celestial points have a negative character: Rahu became associated with the greater malefic Saturn and Ketu with the lesser malefic Mars. Both are harmful to life.

In our, western astrology, a different concept of the nodes has evolved. While the names of the two nodes refer to the "heavenly dragon" in both traditions (*Caput Draconis* for the north node and *Cauda Draconis* for the south node), traditional western astrology associates the **north node** with **Jupiter** and the **south node** with **Saturn**. Why? To my knowledge, no ancient or modern astrologer has ever explained the reasons for this, although it's actually very simple. The Moon, from the moment when it reaches the ecliptic going north, begins to **rise** (ascend, go upwards) above it, and this – similarly to its rising phase in declination, when it pushes up from equator towards the northern maxima - corresponds to **growth** and **expansion** (of the likes of Jupiter), while after crossing the ecliptic from north to south it begins to **fall**, and this stage of its celestial journey corresponds to **decline, weakening** and **reduction** (of the likes of Saturn).

Intermediate stages are to be considered, too: the Moon is at its **highest** celestial latitude (northern maxima) when in **the rising square** to the north node, and at its **lowest** when in the **falling square** (southern maxima). If, in a horary chart, the Moon is in any of the two aspects with the nodes, we should pay attention, as they point to crucial stages of development (turning points) in the subject matter of the horary chart.

William Lilly describes the **north node** as **masculine and benevolent**, of the nature of Jupiter and Venus. He says that its conjunction with benefics improves and refines them, while its conjunction with malefics lessens their malice. The **south node**, on the contrary, is **feminine** and **malevolent**; its conjunctions with malefics were supposed to double or triple their malice (destructive power). He found that conjunctions of significators with the south node can seriously harm the matter, cause complications or even insurmountable difficulties, thus denying a positive outcome even if other indications promise success.

His understanding of the nodes differs slightly from that of Guido Bonatti who also speaks of the north node as "good" and of the south node as "bad", while stressing that the main function of the **north node** is to **increase** and that of the **south node** is to **decrease**. According to him, the benevolence of benefics in conjunction with the south node is therefore lessened, but the malice of malefics is also lessened, whereas the conjunction of benefics with the north node increases their benevolence while the malefics in such an aspect retain their malice. *"The head becomes a benefic with benefics and malefic with malefics; the tail becomes malefic with benefics and benefic with malefics"*, says Bonatti in his **BOOK OF ASTRONOMY** (The Cazimi Press, 2007, translated by Benjamin N. Dykes).

As for the houses, according to the old teachings and to my own research, **the house occupied by the north node** is "good", there are advantages and benefits, progress and development. By contrast, in the field of life, indicated by **the house of the south node**, there are problems, obstacles and frustration. **The house of the north node points to the sphere of growth (success) while the house of the south node points to the sphere of decline and downfall.**

In her book **HORARY ASTROLOGY AND THE JUDGMENT OF EVENTS**, American astrologer Barbara H. Watters wrote that a planet that is on the same degree as the lunar nodes (in any sign, the only criterion is the degree) is subject to "fatality": *"In horary astrology, any planet falling in the exact degree of the Nodes, regardless of what sign it is in, is a fateful testimony."* (p. 96). She continues to say that if malefics form inconjuncts with the lights and ascendant and if malefics are simultaneously in the degrees of the nodes, this pattern can even indicate the death of someone vital to the question. On the other hand, benefics in the degrees of the nodes can bring sudden fortune – but even here possibly through someone else's misfortune.

I have noticed that the significator (or the Moon) in the applying square to the nodes predicts a separation or an ending (of the matter asked about). The situation is more difficult when the significator (or the Moon) is separating from the south node and applying to the north node, since at that time it is in the southern latitude, that is, at a stage when planets have less power of constructive action. (See picture below right: that would be the case if the Moon was, say, at 5 Cancer – applying to square the nodes while in the falling stage, but the situation would be less severe if it was at 5 Capricorn – the rising stage.) Such configurations can significantly alter the outcome and should not be ignored!

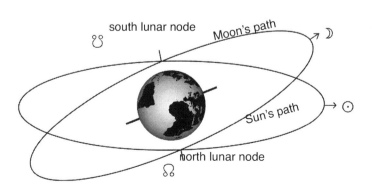

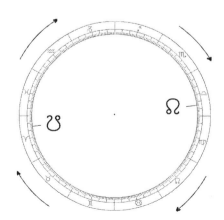

In my horary class, we recently discussed a chart, contributed by one of the students. The question was whether an international company where the querent was employed, would close their office in Slovenia. This would result in a job loss for the querent – which actually happened. Venus, the almuten of MC, in Pisces, was in a close applying square (within a 3.5 degrees orb) with the nodal axis. Mars, H6 ruler (office, work environment) applied to an opposition with retrograde Saturn, placed in H6, which suggested an imminent closing of the office, but the job loss for the querent (and her colleagues - the nodes stand for groups of people, where applicable) was most clearly indicated by the square of Venus, ruling her job, to the nodal axis.

ECLIPSES

clipses are my favorite forecasting technique. I first learnt of them in the horary astrology correspondence course back in 1993, when my tutor Olivia Barclay presented them as a vital part of the ancient astrologers' legacy. For homework, we had to study an important mundane event (I have chosen an earthquake in Guatemala) from the accompanying eclipses' viewpoint, but we didn't include them in our horary charts. Today, I can't imagine my mundane and personal predictive work without them, and because they have become such an important tool in practically all my astrology, I have started to research their role in horary charts. After several years of research I must say that they have proven extremely valuable.

Basically, there are two kinds of eclipses. **solar and lunar**. They are important celestial events which can occur only at new and full moons, when the Moon is on one of its nodes (see MOON'S NODES on p. 136). If the Moon is then in conjunction with the Sun (new moon), a **solar eclipse** occurs, but if it's in opposition with the Sun (full moon), it's a **lunar eclipse**. The lunation points are very rarely in exact conjunctions and oppositions with the nodes, and the level of proximity (orb) determines what kind of eclipse it is - a partial or a total one. The tighter the orb, the stronger (darker) the eclipse. On average, we have 2 solar and 3 lunar eclipses per year. Some are total, the others are partial. Total eclipses are much more powerful than partial.

2000 years ago, Ptolemy knew that eclipses are very important for the prediction of "mundane" (of the world, affecting the weather, politics etc.) events. He knew that every eclipse chart remains "active" (alive, producing effects) for several months and even years ahead, as if the energy at those important moments of time would somehow get "imprinted" into time and space and have an impact on all the consequent celestial (and, consequently, earthly) events. As we know now, eclipses also work backwards in time – they can be felt several months (solar) or weeks (lunar) before they actually take place!

So, how do we use eclipses in horary astrology? Barbara H. Watters noted that if a question is raised on the day of an eclipse, the querent's efforts aimed at achieving a certain goal would become void due to *force majeure*. I can attest to this. I have noticed that if someone asks of success (of a project, plan) shortly (up to a couple of days), before an eclipse, there is considerable chance that the answer is negative. This is logical, of course; one of the lights will soon experience a darkening which implies collapse, failure and destruction. Consequently, the querent's chances of success are severely damaged.

My study of eclipses in horary astrology has revealed some other interesting facets. Horary charts asking for missing persons or animals that were later found dead or were never found at all, and those asking for missing property which was never found (lost, stolen, ruined etc.), were very often closely related to one of the accompanying eclipses. Usually, this was the closest total eclipse, either solar or lunar. In these charts, the significator of the missing person (animal, lost property), or the Moon, MC or ascendant were in a tight conjunction or a disharmonious aspect to the eclipse degree – or to the accompanying node.

Pay attention to horary charts where one of the angular points (AC, DC, MC, IC, Vx or Avx), the Moon or the significator (of the querent or quesited) is tightly conjunct (up to 1° orb) the nearest eclipse degree! This usually indicates some kind of fatality or destruction.

In the Practice part of this book, eclipses are mentioned on several occasions, notably in the chapters on missing people and animals. Just recently, the validity of this approach has been confirmed by an interesting example. *In my facebook group Horary Astrology Group, someone posted a chart* **What happened to the missing kitten? Is it still alive and will it be back?** *The querent feared that the kitten was murdered by strayed dogs, as her neighbors suggested. Ascendant was at 27° Pisces, Moon at 29.5° Virgo, both in an exact opposition to the preceding total solar eclipse. The Moon plays an especially important role in charts of missing animals, therefore I judged that the kitten was indeed murdered - which was confirmed, as one of the neighbors later told her that she actually saw it happen.*

Due to the unquestionable importance of eclipses, I have attached the table of the nearest eclipses to all the charts in the Practice part of this book. I am convinced that in future, eclipses will play a much more important role in horary as they do today.

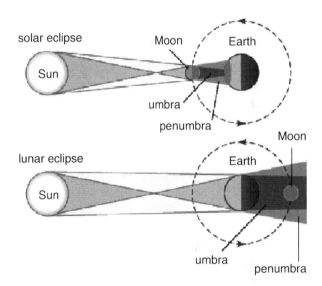

FIXED STARS

ORIGIN

strologers of old have always attributed great importance to fixed stars. Although we could simply call them "stars", the full name has been preserved for two reasons: the first is that we have one star in our solar system (this being our Sun, of course), and the other is that the ancients spoke of two kinds of stars: "movable" and "fixed". The first were the planets (of our solar system) while the second were those other celestial bodies which lie at such great distances that they appear to be practically motionless.

Constellations into which individual stars were grouped, were initially associated with weather conditions that prevailed during a certain period of the year. *Aquarius, Argo, Capricorn, Whale, Crater, Delfin, Eridanus, Hydra* and *Pisces* - all the so-called "water constellations" - are situated in the area of the sky through which the Sun travelled during the rainy season in Mesopotamia and Egypt. Many individual stars received their characteristics after the kind of weather they "brought" when rising or setting. In those ancient times, Sirius (the Dogstar) was seen in its evening rising in early January and in its evening setting in early May, which the Roman poet/astrologer Manilius from the 1st century, described as follows: *"No star comes on mankind more violently or causes more trouble when it departs. Now it rises shivering with cold, now it leaves a radiant world open to the heat of the Sun."* (See **ASTRONOMICA**, Harvard University Press, 1977.)

Ptolemy, too, diligently observed the risings and settings of stars and wrote down the effects they had on the weather (See **THE PHASES OF THE FIXED STARS** by Claudius Ptolemy, Project Hindsight, The Golden Hind Press, 1993), but in his **TREATISE ON THE BRIGHT FIXED STARS** (published by Project Hindsight in 1993) an unknown Greek author (referred to as Anonymous of 379) from the 4th century, already speaks of the effects the fixed stars have on human destiny.

While the constellations and individual stars have been used to forecast the weather since times immemorial, astrologers often wonder whether their astrological connotations came from observing their effects, or by way of myth. As already mentioned in the chapter on zodiacal signs, and as can be inferred from the writings of those early astrologers, it must have been observation.

Most of the stars' individual characteristics reflect the general characters of the constellations in which they are situated. In ancient times, the stars were skillfully grouped into human or animal forms, and placed in a constellation's *head, heart, neck, left shoulder, right knee, tail* and similar. The stars in the Ram's *horn*, Perseus *arm with a sword*, Scorpio's *sting* or Sagittarius' *bow* were considered violent and unfortunate while those in the *wings* of Virgo, the *belt* of Andromeda, the *head* of Cygnus or the *bosom* of Cassiopeia were thought (observed) to have mild and beneficial natures.

Shiny, clear and bright stars have acquired the meaning of luck, power, benevolence and success, while the dark stars, stellar nebulae and undefined groups of stars have become associated with weakness, disease, violence, blindness, and similar. It would seem that their characteristics were ascertained mainly on the basis of their appearance, but I guess it's the same kind of synchronicity that is observable with, for example, the size of Jupiter and its characteristics of greatness and expansion, or with the reddish shine of Mars and its connotations of war and aggression, or with the rings of Saturn and its relatedness to restrictions and limitations, and so on.

Old authors have always emphasized the need to consider, in astrological readings, not only the zodiac signs and the moving stars (planets), but also their eventual combinations with the fixed stars. Whenever a planet was in conjunction with a star of a similar nature, its characteristics were strengthened, but if it was conjunct a star with an opposite nature, its impact was lessened or even completely altered.

As regards the aspects, only conjunctions and sometimes (in the case of major stars) oppositions are usually being considered. The orb is about 1°; only with very big, bright stars it extends to up to 5°.

In ancient Greece they knew 48 constellations, but today there are 88. They are divided into:

• zodiacal
• northern
• southern

Stars close to the ecliptic (up to approximately 8° N or S) were found to act more strongly and more directly than those with higher and lower celestial latitudes. A good example is the case of Spica and Arcturus: in celestial longitude there is only a 20 minutes difference between them while in latitude they are as much as 32 degrees apart. Both are 1st magnitude stars but Arcturus belongs to the constellation Bootes and is close to 31 degrees north of ecliptic while Spica is the brightest star of the constellation Virgo and lies within 2 degrees of ecliptic (to the south), so Spica is considered to act more strongly than Arcturus.

It is also believed that stars at northern latitudes exert a stronger influence on the northern hemisphere while those with southern latitudes on the southern hemisphere.

THE USE OF FIXED STARS IN HORARY ASTROLOGY

Fixed stars are generally more often used in mundane and natal than in horary astrology. In horary, we tend to only use them with questions concerning nations, their leaders and other mundane and political affairs. Some astrologers also take them into account in everyday, ordinary questions, but I have yet to see a horary chart resolved by means of a fixed star only. They only act as "aids". As you can see in the Practice part of this book, I refer to them only when they closely conjunct significators, but even that seldom, as I don't pay much attention to them. I'm including this section to encourage students to do better than me, because I think that stars might have a potential that has not yet been fully explored.

Below are some of the more important stars. More comprehensive star lists and descriptions can be found at various other sources (like V.E. Robson's FIXED STARS, Reinhold Ebertin's FIXED STARS AND THEIR INTERPRETATION, and there is a comprehensive online source at *www.constellationofwords.com*).

The stars' zodiacal positions (in brackets) are for the year 2000. Although we call them "fixed", the stars actually do move (geocentrically speaking), albeit extremely slowly. Due to precession (the shifting of the equinoxes), they slowly move forward. Their average annual motion is 50.25 "(50 seconds of celestial longitude), or 1° in 72 years. If we want to know the accurate position of a star for any given year, we have to add or deduct the multiple of 50" corresponding to the number of years before or after 2000. (For 2018, for example: 18 x 50.25" = 904" = 0°15'.)

Next (in brackets) comes **magnitude** (**mag** = magnitude, size). The smaller the number, the greater the magnitude or the stronger, the more powerful the star. The strongest are the 1st magnitude stars. The letter V which occasionally replaces a number, refers to variable stars that substantially change their sizes.

In the next place, there's reference to a **planet** (or two) whose nature comes closest to the nature of a particular star. For example, the stars of Saturn's and Mars' nature are destructive while those of Venus' and Jupiter's nature are good, mild and generally positive. Combinations give us the combined influence of the two planets.

When reading the interpretations, know that the descriptions - which I have taken from the above mentioned sources - are archaic. There's no deep psychology here, but merely an indication of the observed effects, expressed in a rather direct language. Descriptions refer to both the temperamental properties and the "destiny" they bring to the natives under their influence, and from these descriptions, their meanings in horary charts should be inferred.

It is really important that we do not give the fixed stars more say than to the Sun, the Moon and the planets! This could easily mislead us into giving wrong answers. The fixed stars should serve only as additional indications, not capable of significantly modifying or altering the answer given by other, more significant and important chart factors.

STARS IN ARIES

DIFDA (2°35′, mag 2, Saturn), a yellow star in the tail of the Whale. It is destructive; it brings obstacles, difficulties, losses and enforced changes. May elicit a tendency to laziness, idleness and self-destructive behaviour, but also gives wisdom, discernment, willingness to help and an ability to command.

ALGENIB (9°09′, mag 2, Mars/Mercury), a white star situated at the tip of the wing of Pegasus. It gives ambition, pride, self-love, enthusiasm and a sharp and penetrating intellect, but also a quick temper. Danger of accidents and violence. Difficulties can arise due to ill-health and poor judgment.

ALPHERATZ (14°18′, mag 2, Venus), a double star, white and purple, in the hair of Andromeda. It gives a keen intellect, independence, honors, recognition, wealth and preferment from others.

BATEN KAITOS (21°57′, mag 3, Saturn), a greenish-yellow star in the body of the Whale. Associated with compulsory changes, emigration, falls, accidents, violent changes and shipwrecks.

ALPHERG (26°49′, mag 3, Jupiter/Saturn), a double star near the tail of the Northern Fish. Brings success through perseverance and diligence.

STARS IN TAURUS

MIRAH (0°24′, mag 2, Venus), a yellow star in the girdle of Andromeda. It gives creative inspiration, friendship, happiness, harmony, forgiveness, a love of home and good fortune in marriage.

MIRA (1°31′, mag 2, Saturn), named also Stella Mira, "a wonderful star" in the Whale's neck. Due to its exceptional variability, it gives rise to frequent life changes. It gives one idleness, but also an emotional and amiable nature, and an ability to command.

SHERATAN (3°58′, mag 2, Mars/Saturn), a pearly white star in the left horn of the Ram. Its influence is violent and disruptive. It causes impulsiveness, bodily injuries and destruction in war or by fire.

HAMAL (7°40′, mag 2, Mars/Saturn), a yellow star in the head of the Ram. It's associated with danger, violence, cruelty and crime.

SCHEDIR (7°47′, mag 2, Saturn/Venus), a pale pink star on the breast of Cassiopeia. It is "demonic" and gives vanity, boastfulness and exaggerated pride, but also personal attraction.

MENKAR (14°19′, mag 2, Saturn), a bright orange star in the jaw of the Whale. It causes disease, bad luck, injury from beasts, legal problems and loss of fortune.

BOTEIN (20°51′, mag 4, Venus), a weak star in the flank of the Ram. Mild and good-natured, supposed to help the finding of treasures and retaining of captives.

ALGOL (26°10′, mag 2, Saturn/Mars), A white binary and variable star, situated in the hand of Perseus, also known as Medusa's head. Traditionally the most evil star associated with extreme violence, dangers and misfortune. Gives a dogged and cruel nature. Can cause death through hanging or decapitation.

STARS IN GEMINI

ALCYONE (0°00′, mag 2, Moon/Mars), a greenish yellow star, the brightest of Pleiades, on the shoulder of the Bull. It has an unfortunate reputation due to its association with blindness and accidents to the face, although it also gives ambition and eminence.

ALDEBARAN (9°47′, mag 1, Mars/Jupiter), a reddish star in the right eye of the Bull, one of the four royal stars in Persia (around 3000 BC). It is very powerful and gives intelligence, courage, power, wealth and success due to exceptional energy, ambition and hard work, but it can also cause problems and legal disputes due to jealousy and hatred.

RIGEL (16°50′, mag 1, Jupiter/Saturn), a glittering bluish white star on the left foot of Orion. It bestows benevolence, happiness, wealth and great, lasting success.

BELLATRIX (20°57′, mag 1, Mars/Mercury), a pale yellow star on the left shoulder of Orion, also known as Amazon or Female Warrior. It's associated with secular and military honors and it gives one energy, courage and a fighting spirit, but also verbal aggressiveness and danger to the eyes.

CAPELLA (21°51′, mag 1, Mercury/Moon), a white star on the body of the Goat in the arms of Auriga. It gives inquisitiveness, studiousness, honor, wealth, a public position of trust and eminent friends.

MINTAKA (22°24′, mag 2, Jupiter/Saturn), a white and purple double star in Orion's belt. It gives good fortune and is associated with grain crops.

BETELGEUSE (28°45′, mag 1, Mars/Mercury), an orange star on the right shoulder of Orion, associated with wealth, preferment and military honors.

STARS IN CANCER

ALHENA (9°06′, mag 1, Mercury/Venus), a brilliant white star on the left foot of Pollux. It bestows artistic gifts, inspiration and thirst for knowledge, but is also associated with foot injuries.

SIRIUS (14°05′, mag 1, Jupiter/Mars), a double star in the mouth of the Greater Dog. It's the brightest of all stars and has played an important role in the development of astronomy. It makes people passionate, faithful and dedicated; it gives recognition, honor and great success, but it can make one aggressive, and brings danger of dog bites.

CANOPUS (14°58′, mag 1, Saturn/Jupiter), a white star in the oars of the ship Argo. It gives devoutness, conservatism and studiousness. It brings wealth, honor and recognition, and is (today) also associated with worldliness, media success and travel.

CASTOR (20°15′, mag 1, Mercury), a white double star in the head of the Northern Twin, the "mortal twin", associated with the Greek god Apollo. It gives a keen intellect, success in law and publishing, and many travels. It can lead to glory and honor which is followed by loss of fortune and disgrace.

POLLUX (23°13′, mag 1, Mars), an orange star in the head of the Southern Twin, the "immortal twin", associated with the Greek good Hercules. It gives a subtle, crafty, brave, audacious and possibly vicious nature, and is associated with violence and tyranny. It sometimes shows cruel turns of destiny.

PROCYON (25°48′, mag 1, Mercury/Mars), a yellow and white double star in the Lesser Dog. It gives an acive, intelligent, determined and strong-willed nature, but can be hasty, impudent and easily angered. It also indicates wealth, fame and fortune.

STARS IN LEO

PRAESAEPE (7°20′, mag 5, Mars/Moon), a star in the head of the Crab, forming a cluster with the Aselli (North Asellus and South Asellus). It is dangerous to the eyes and gives rise to infectious diseases and addiction. It gives industriousness and fecundity, but also insolence and immorality.

ACUBENS (13°38′, mag 4, Saturn/Mercury), a white and red double star in the southern claw of the Crab. It is related to secrets and secret places, as well as to lies, toxins, poison and crime.

DUBHE (15°12′, mag 1, Mars), a yellow star in the Greater Bear, violent and dangerous.

ALGENUBI (20°42′, mag 3, Saturn/Mars), a yellow star in the Lion's mouth. Violent and disruptive, but also associated with artistic talents.

ALPHARD (27°17′, mag 2, Saturn/Venus), an orange star in the neck of Hydra, also called *Cor Hydrae* (Hydra's Heart). It gives wisdom and artistic gifts, but also strong passions and immorality. It can cause death by drowning or poisoning.

REGULUS (29°50′, mag 1, Jupiter/Mars), a triple white and blue star in the body of the Lion, known also as *Cor Leonis*, The Lion's heart. It was one of the four royal stars of the Persians, marking the summer solstice around 3000 BC. It stands for dignity, pride, generosity, independence, prominence and high office, but can also give rise to violence, destructiveness and ultimate failure.

STARS IN VIRGO

ALIOTH (8°56′, mag 1, Mars), a white star in the tail of the Great Bear, the largest in the constellation. It bestows self-confidence and patience, but also a tendency to anger and revenge.

ZOSMA (11°19′, mag 2, Saturn/Venus), a triple, pale yellow and purple star on the Lion's back. Associated with immorality, selfishness, melancholy, shamelessness and laziness.

MIZAR (15°42′, mag 2, Mars), a white double star on the tail of the Great Bear. It gives extraordinary courage, but also inclines to violence and bloodshed.

DENEBOLA (21°37′, mag 2, Saturn/Venus), a blue star in the Lion's tail. Its makes one noble, daring, intelligent, progressive and of swift judgment, but also quarrelsome. It causes regrets and public disgrace.

LABRUM (26°41′, mag 4, Venus/Mercury), the brightest star of the Crater, symbolically called Holy Grail. A fortunate star giving idealism, spirituality, intelligence, honor and riches.

ZAVIJAVA (27°09′, mag 3, Mercury/Mars), a pale yellow star on the left wing of Virgo. It gives personal power, persuasiveness, efficiency and competitiveness.

MARKEB (28°20′, mag 2, Saturn/Jupiter), a pale star in the sail of the Argo Navis ship. It gives religiousness, sophistication, educational work and voyages.

STARS IN LIBRA

ZANIAH (4°31′, mag 4, Mercury/Venus), a changeable star on the southern wing of Virgo. It gives a cordial, refined, friendly and orderly nature.

VINDEMIATRIX (9°57′, mag 2, Saturn/Mercury), a bright yellow star on the right wing of Virgo. An important star in ancient astronomy, but it's considered unfortunate. It's associated with lies, disgrace, gullibility and shame, and with widowship.

CAPHIR (10°09′, mag 2, Mercury/Venus), a slightly changeable, white double star on the left shoulder of Virgo. It shows a corteous, refined, loving nature, and is also associated with divination.

ALGORAB (13°27′, mag 3, Saturn/Mars), a double star, pale yellow and purple, on the right wing of the Raven. Makes people reckless, hypocritical, greedy, revengeful, manipulative, destructive and lying.

SEGINUS (17°40′, mag 3, Mercury/Saturn), a small star on the left shoulder of Bootes. It shows a sophisticated and reasonable person, but also losses through friends and business partners.

SPICA (23°50, mag 1, Venus/Mars), a brilliant white double star in the left hand of Virgo. Traditionally one of the most fortunate stars; it brings happiness, success and honors that go beyond expectations and personal abilities. It gives innate dignity, kindness and love of art and sicence.

ARCTURUS (24°14′, mag 1, Mars/Jupiter), a bright, golden yellow star on the left knee of Bootes. It is benevolent and gives riches, recognition and prosperity, and fortune by travels.

STARS IN SCORPIO

PRINCEPS (3°09′, mag 3, Mercury/Saturn), a pale yellow star in the spear of Bootes. It represents a serious, contemplative, deep mind and success in research. Generally happy, but draws attention to problems or defeat due to plainness and pessimism.

ACRUX (11°52′, mag 1, Jupiter), a triple star, the brightest in the Southern Cross, though never visible in the high northern latitudes. Unknown to Ptolemy it's now associated with Jupiter as a symbol of justice, spirituality and esotericism.

ALPHECCA (12°18′, mag 2, Mercury/Venus), a brilliant white star in the Northern Crown, bestowing dignity and success. It often comes up in the charts of artists and poets.

ZUBEN ELGENUBI (15°05′, mag 2, Mars/Saturn), a pale yellow and white double star, also known as South Scale. It is harmful, associated with shame, dishonesty, illness, betrayal and poisoning.

ZUBEN ELSCHEMALI (19°22′, mag 2, Mercury/Jupiter), a pale emerald star marking the north scale of Libra. Unlike the South Scale, it gives happiness, honor and success.

UNUKALHAI (22°04′, mag 2, Mars/Saturn), a pale yellow star in Scorpio's neck, also known as *Cor Serpentis*, the heart of the snake. It is unfortunate and harmful; it causes violence, accidents and disruptions, and is also connected with poisoning and infectious diseases.

AGENA (23°47′, mag 1, Venus/Jupiter), a bright star on the right front hoof of Centaur. It brings happiness, friendship, honor and good health, as well as nobility and high morale.

TOLIMAN (29°33′, mag 1, Venus/Jupiter), a white and yellow bright double star above the right front hoof of Centaur, also called Bungula. It is the closest visible star in our solar system and the third brightest star seen from Earth, although it is never visible in the northern latitudes. It brings friendship, happiness and honor. It is often associated with horses.

STARS IN SAGITTARIUS

ISIDIS (2°34′, mag 2, Saturn/Mars), a white star at the forehead of Scorpio. It is an evil star that shows immorality, cunning, malevolence and the danger of imprisonment or sudden violence.

ANTARES (9°46′, mag 1, Mars/Jupiter), a double star, fiery red and emerald green, in the constellation Scorpio. The name derives from anti-Ares, a rival of Mars. It is also known as *Cor Scorpionis*, the heart of the Scorpio. It was one of the royal stars of the Persians and is in an exact opposition to Aldebaran in Gemini. If it rises or culminates, it brings great honors and successes, but not of a permanent nature. In general, it is considered evil because its influence is warlike and as such it brings violence and conflicts.

RASTABAN (11°58′, mag 2, Saturn/Mars/Jupiter), a yellow double star in the head of the Dragon, also known as the "foggy star in the Dragon's Eye". An unlucky star related to crime, violence and disasters.

SABIK (17°58′, mag 2, Saturn/Venus), a pale yellow star in the right knee of Ophiuchus. It shows wastefulness and loss of energy, but it is supposed to give success to those who are evil and malicious.

RAS ALHAGUE (22°27′, mag 2, Saturn/Venus) a greenish blue star in the Ophiuchus' head. Generally evil, it shows misfortune from women, moral perversion and vice.

ETANIN (27°58′, mag 2, Saturn/Mars/Jupiter), a double star in the head of the Dragon. Some call it a zenith star, as it culminates over the Greenwich Observatory. It has an unpredictable and variable influence, but is also supposed to give an exceptional power of concentration and success in the esoteric field.

STARS IN CAPRICORN

POLIS (3°55′, mag 3, Jupiter/Mars), a triple star in the upper part of the bow of the Archer. It gives ambition, combativeness, physical skill and excellent perception.

FACIES (8°16′, mag 5, Sun/Mars), a nebula in the face of the Archer. It is associated with visual impairments, illnesses, accidents and violence.

ASCELLA (13°38′, mag 3, Mercury/Jupiter), a weak double star in the armpit of the Archer. It is good-natured, it brings happiness, friendship and protection.

VEGA (15°18′, mag 1, Mercury/Venus), a pale sapphire blue star in the lower part of the Lire. It is in opposition to Canopus (in Cancer). As one of the brightest stars in the sky it was very important in ancient astronomy. Usually, it is considered to be fortunate, as it gives sophistication, refinement, hope and idealism, but can also make one conceited and immoral.

DENEB (19°48′, mag 3, Mars/Jupiter), a green star in the tail of the Eagle. It gives an ability to command, coupled with success in war and martial arts, and a keen, penetrating mind.

TEREBELLUM (26°33′, mag 4, Venus/Saturn), the main star in the tail of the Archer. It brings luck which is later followed by frustration, disappointment and disgrace.

STARS IN AQUARIUS

ALTAIR (1°46′, mag 1, Mars/Jupiter), a pale yellow star in the neck of the Eagle. It gives a bold, ambitious and confident nature, strong will-power and position of command, but the honors it promises are often not long-lasting. It is also associated with bloodshed and danger from reptiles.

DABIH (4°03′, mag 3, Venus/Saturn), a double star, yellow and sky blue, in the left eye of the Goat. It gives a reserved, mistrustful, melanholic and conservative nature. It shows dignity, influence and success, but can also bring losses and scandals.

OCULUS (5°25′, mag 5, Saturn/Venus), a faint star in the right eye of the Goat. It gives one a clear, penetrating and witty mind.

CASTRA (20°12′, mag 4, Saturn/Jupiter), a small star in the tail of the Goat. Generally an unfortunate star, sometimes giving a fierce, violent and uncontrollable temper. It can bring disgrace.

DENEB ALGEDI (23°32′, mag 2, Saturn/Jupiter), a star in the tail of the Goat. Its nature is contradictory, as it brings happiness as well as misfortune. Only when it culminates, it is supposed to bring one great honor, wealth and fame by means of influential people.

STARS IN PISCES

FOMALHAUT (3°51′, mag 1, Mercury/Venus), a reddish star in the mouth of the Southern Fish. It was one of the royal stars to Persians. When rising or culminating, it gives power, fame and lasting honors, but it can also be malevolent. It is associated with magic, alchemy and occultism. It can lead to transition from material to spiritual life.

DENEB ADIGE (5°20′, mag 1, Mercury/Venus), a brilliant white star in the tail of the Swan. Natives under its influence are clever, imaginative and witty, often artistic with the ability to profit by their skills.

ACHERNAR (15°19′, mag 1, Jupiter), a white star in the mouth of the Eridanus River. It is beneficient and promises one success due to high moral standards. It is also associated with ecclasiastical dignity.

MARKAB (23°29′, mag 2, Mercury/Mars), a white star on the wing of Pegasus. It is of a variable nature and shows the possibility of success, mainly due to mental power, but also dangers of violence, fever, cuts, blows and fire.

SCHEAT (29°22′, mag 2, Mercury/Mars), a changeable dark yellow star on the left leg of Pegasus. It is evil and causes extreme misfortune, accidents, violence or suicide. It is particularly associated with accidents at sea (shipwrecks, drowning).

ARABIC PARTS

 first learned of the so-called **Arabic parts** (or lots) from the book THE ARABIC PARTS AND ASTROLOGY: A LOST KEY TO PREDICTION, written by the American mediaeval scholar and astrologer Robert Zoller. The technique is ancient; some speculate that the first astrologers who used parts were the Babylonians, but what is known is that after the collapse of the Roman Empire, Arab and Persian astrologers who built upon the ancient Greek and Roman heritage, began to use them extensively. The number of parts grew considerably during their time, hence their name.

The Arabic parts are mathematically ascertained relationships between three horoscopic factors, those usually being a pair of planets and the ascendant. Any part is calculated by first finding the distance between the pair of planets and then adding it to the ascendant. Instead of a planet, a house cusp or some other Arabic part can be used. The calculations were once done by hand, whereby the arithmetic lengths of the planets was ascertained according to their distance from 0° Aries (Taurus 30°, Gemini 60° and so on).

Parts, by the combined nature of the planets involved, or via their rule over a particular house, carry within them the energy of the matter they stand for. The degree of the part itself as well as the state of its dispositor, are important. But to what extent, it's difficult to say. I have decided to include them in this book because I know that many horary astrologers use them, but I do that rarely. The exception is part of fortune which I use in financial and missing objects charts, because in traditional astrology this part stands for the materialization of matter, or for the material (financial) sphere of life. Since *fortuna* is based on the three most important points in any chart (ascendent, Moon and Sun), it certainly belongs to those parts whose use is most meaningful. Although I have experimented with other parts quite a bit, in natal as well as in horary astrology, I have found that in most cases we can find a meaningful answer without them, so I gradually dropped them, similarly to other "extras" like asteroids, midpoints, antiscia, Chiron and Lilith, for example. All of those can be useful, but are not at all indispensable.

So how do we use them? We simply chose the one which best fits the context of our question, insert it into the chart and check its house, sign, aspects and dispositor. If most indications are good, the mater at hand is "strong" (good, positive etc.), and vice versa.

In line with the traditional distinction between the roles of the Sun, the Moon and the planets in diurnal and nocturnal charts, the old astrologers often used different formulas for day or night charts –and we still do that, of course. (But I must confess that it is a bit unsettling not to know their reasons for changing some formulas and not changing the others! This is one of the reasons why I am not comfortable with them.)

The two tables below list only the major parts – there are many more. Professsional astrology programs can calculate a huge number of parts, but the practitioners' problem usually is to decide for the best or most reliable ones. As already indicated, I must leave the choice to you. Practice makes perfect!

S = same formula for diurnal and nocturnal charts
C = change the last two with nocturnal charts
? = unknown

UNIVERSAL PARTS

ASC + THE SUN - THE MOON	C	SPIRIT
ASC + THE MOON - THE SUN	C	FORTUNE
ASC + VENUS - SPIRIT	C	LOVE
ASC + FORTUNE - MARS	C	COURAGE
ASC + JUPITER - SPIRIT	C	VICTORY

PARTS, RELATED TO INDIVIDUAL HOUSES

HOUSE	FORMULA		NAME
1	asc + Saturn - Jupiter	C	life
1	asc + Mars - The Moon	C	communication
2	asc + cusp H2 – ruler H2	S	wealth
2	asc + Mercury – The Moon	S	wealth
3	asc + Jupiter - Saturn	S	brothers and sisters
4	asc + Mars - Saturn	C	family
4	asc + Saturn – The Sun	C	father, parents
4	asc + The Moon - Saturn	S	inheritance
5	asc + Saturn - Jupiter	C	children
5	asc + Venus – The Moon	?	daughters
5	asc + The Moon - dispositor The Moon	S	sex of the child
5	asc + Jupiter – Mars	S	sons (Al-Biruni)
5	asc + Jupiter – The Moon	S	sons (Bonatti)
6	asc + The Moon - Mercury	S	servants
6	asc + Mars - Saturn	C	disease and accidents
7	asc + cusp H7 - Venus	S	marriage
7	asc + Venus – Saturn	S	marriage (men)
7	asc + Saturn - Venus	S	marriage (women)
7	Saturn + Mars - Mercury	C	theft
7	asc + Jupiter - Mars	C	litigation
8	Saturn + cusp H8 – The Moon	S	death
9	asc + Jupiter – The Sun	C	knowledge
9	asc + Mercury – The Moon	C	religion
9	asc + cusp H9 - RULER H9	S	travel
10	asc + The Moon – Venus	C	mother
10	asc + The Sun – Fortuna	C	reputation
10	asc + Saturn – The Sun	C	success
11	asc + Mercury – The Moon	S	friends
12	asc + cusp H12 - RULER H12	S	enemies

ANTISCIA

ntiscia (lat. sing. *antiscium*, pl. *antiscia*, "the opposing shadows") is an ancient technique of establishing a special kind of connection or "communication" between planets. The term **solstice points** has also been used, especially by some modern American astrologers. Numerous old astrologers mention antiscia in their books, notably Firmicus Maternus, a Roman astrologer from the 4th century. According to him, already Hipparchus, a Greek astrologer from the 2nd century BC, used and taught them, followed by other Hellenistic astrologers like Ptolemy, Paulus Alexandrinus, Dorotheus of Sidon and many others.

Antisica involves mirroring or reflecting. The starting point of measurements in this technique is the solstice axis - 0° Cancer/0° Capricorn. Every degree to the left and right of 0° Cancer has its mirroring degree on the other side of the circle. It is not only celestial geometry; the connection is deeply energetic, as it is established by the Sun's path (ecliptic). When the Sun is at any of those degrees, days and nights are of equal length. The Sun, for example, is at 5°Gemini each year on May 27, whereas on September 13 it is at 20° Virgo. Since both days are equally distant from 21 June (0° Cancer), the summer solstice when the day is at its longest and the night is at its shortest, on May 27 and September 15 (5°Gemini and 20° Virgo respectively), days and nights are of equal length. Thus, a relationship is established between the two dates/zodiacal degrees – the one is like a mirror to the other.

We say that the two zodiacal degrees which are equidistant from 0° Cancer and 0° Capricorn, are in an **antiscial relationship**, or that one degree casts an antiscion to the other. If two celestial bodies (the Sun, the Moon or any of the planets) are placed at those degrees, there is a connection between them, similar to an aspect. It is generally believed that the impact of antiscia is not as strong as that of a bodily aspect, but it is agreed that they are not to be overlooked. When two bodies are in an antiscial relationship, this can be viewed upon as a (weak) conjunction.

What about the orb? That's a delicate question. Generally, one degree orb is the safest option, but the orb should be decided by the planets involved. Any body can apply to the antiscia degree of another, and if that is the case in a horary chart, we count the number of degrees between the applying planet and the antiscia degree, and translate that into the number of time units.

The degree which is exactly opposite to the antiscion degree is called **contra-antiscion**. If, for example, a planet casts an antiscium to 5°10' Gemini, its contra-antiscion is 5°10' Sagittarius. The relation of the planet to the planet with which it is in a contra-antiscion, is considered less desirable, as it acts in the way of a disharmonious aspect.

Although antiscision is generally considered to have a harmonious nature ("coming together"), it is of course important to consider the general and individual characteristics of the participating planets - whether they are benefics or malefics, whether they are in fortunate or unfortunate houses, what houses they rule and are placed in, and so on. In case of Saturn and the Moon, for example, it would be very possible that Saturn would exert a negative impact on the Moon, acting as a frustrating influence.

Antiscia are not to be mistaken for declinations! Although the antiscion degrees of the Sun have the same declinations, this is not the case with the Moon and the planets, due to their varying speeds and latitudes.

HOW TO FIND ANTISCION DEGREES

We find the antiscion degree by counting the degrees from zero Cancer (or zero Capricorn) to the degree of a planet and then adding the same number of degrees to the opposite side of zero Cancer (or zero Capricorn). If there is a planet on this degree, both planets are in an antiscion relationship.

The following sign pairs are in an antiscision relationship:
- Cancer - Gemini
- Taurus - Leo
- Aries - Virgo
- Pisces - Libra
- Aquarius - Scorpio
- Capricorn - Sagittarius

If we want to calculate the exact degree and minute of an antiscion, we first look at the above table (sign pairs). If, for example, a planet is at 13°58' Libra, we can see that its antiscion is located in Pisces. To find the precise position of the antiscion, we subtract the degrees and minutes of the planet from 30°00' (or 29°60' - converted to make it easier for calculation). In our example, the calculation would be:

30°00' - 13°58' or 29°60' - 13°58' = 16°02'. The antiscion of a planet at 13°58' Libra is at 16°02' Pisces, and its contra-antiscion is exactly opposite, at 16°02' Virgo.

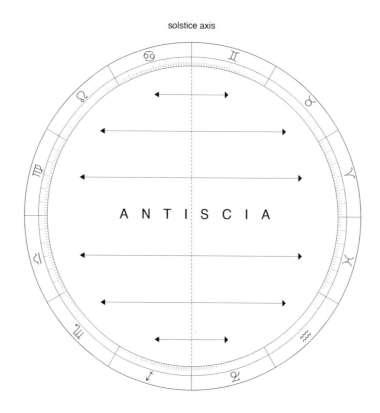

DECLINATION

spects in declination are legitimate aspects, but they are measured in the equatorial, not in the ecliptical system of measurements, like the usual aspects in longitude that we observe within a circle. The planets on the same degree of declination (or within a 1 degree orb) are in a **parallel** (of declination) – an aspect similar to a conjunction, whereas two planets at the opposite degrees of the equatorial plane are at a **contra-parallel** (of declination). Declination is measured from 0° (of the celestial equator) to the north or south. The Moon and the inner planets (including Mars) can reach up to 28.5°, N or S. The first astrologer (or one of the first, but the best known) who used declination in horary astrology was the American astrologer Ivy Goldstein-Jacobson who considered parallel of declination to be equivalent to a conjunction.

I must stress that I use declination a lot in my natal and predictive work. Without it, I can't even imagine doing either natal delineation or personal forecasting. But in horary astrology which is an ancient system based on planetary relationships that exist within a zodiacal/longitudinal circle, I have come to depend on longitudinal aspects alone. In spite of that, I strongly believe that declination could be extremely valuable in horary astrology too, and is therefore worth exploring.

Actually, I have been doing that lately. I remember a case when I found a correct answer to a horary question published in a traditional horary forum, by employing declination. But because the members of the forum abided rigorously by tradition (they even denied the influence of transsaturnians, on the grounds that our ancestors did not use them, so why should we), my interpretation caused a turbulent negative reaction. All my reasonable explanations of why a certain parallel of declination showed the correct result, were in vain – declination doesn't exist in horary, amen, they said. I could understand them because of our inclination to feel safe only within the limits of that which is known and has been thoroughly tested, but on the other hand, with astrology is like with any other discipline - without research there can be no progress.

I have also discovered that out-of-bound planets (those with declination greater than 23.5 degrees which is the maximum Sun's declination) can give valuable information regarding missing people and things (see Practice).

Recently, I received another, fascinating proof that declinations do work and that they indeed could become indispensable in horary astrology - if we only made an effort to really research and use them! The example is published in the Practice part of this book, on p. 312, in the section on missing objects. You will see how the Moon in that case showed correctly the number of time units that elapsed until the finding of a missing item.

I assume that the Moon, in fact, shows the time unit that will pass to the outcome of the matter, in many more cases as has so far been ascertained, but it should be used in ALL coordinate systems.

With this I conclude the first part of the book and invite you to explore the wealth of examples in the second part. I believe that each of them will teach you more than all the theory together. It is the same as with yoga; my first yoga teacher often said, five minutes of practice is worth more than ten hours of theory!

Happy "horarizing"!

152

PRACTICE

LOVE AND MARRIAGE

SIGNIFICATORS AND HOUSES

Love/marriage questions are relationship questions and as such they belong to the 1/7 axis. The querent is always ruled by the ascendant, its dispositor and the Moon while the person he/she is interested in (the quesited) is ruled by the descendant and its dispositor.

Planet/s in H1 and H7 can stand for other people who are involved in the situation, but they can also co-signify the querent (planet/s in H1) or the quesited (planet/s in H7), especially when they are in conjunction with the ascendant or the descendant. If the conjunction is very tight (up to three degrees), this planet can even act as the main significator (of the querent or the quesited) – especially if it is also the natural significator of the person it represents (the Sun for a man, for example).

In addition to planets in H1 and H7, other people (third parties) can also be shown by planets with which the significators of both parties are in aspects or in mutual receptions.

In cases of complex questions that involve several people, the choice of significators can be a difficult task. If the querent is married or in a permanent relationship and asks how his/her relationship with their lover (or potential lover) would develop, this person is signified by H7. But if the question also involves the spouse, H7 rules the spouse while the other person is shown by the planet that is strongly related to H1 or H7, either by being bodily placed in one of those houses, or by being in an aspect (or mutual reception) with H1 planet/s. There are no strictly defined rules in this respect - we must allow the chart to lead us! The chart sometimes shows clearly what is going on and which planets show whom (by describing their temperament, approximate age, occupation, general conditions at the time of asking etc.), but sometimes the process of "deciphering" is more difficult.

What about H5, you might ask? As we know, in modern astrology this house represents (among other things) fun, love and casual relationships. If in a horary chart this house is strong and fortunate (that is, occupied by benefics, ruled by them or by dignified planets etc.), this is certainly an encouraging indicator for the smooth development of the relationship we are asking about. When our questions relate to love affairs, we'll often find connections between H7 and H5. But H5 does not by itself rule lovers and extramarital partners. It is primarily the house of amusement and children – but those are often involved in such questions anyway.

All other houses are to be interpreted according to their meanings. If the significator (of the querent or of the quesited) is in H12, for example, they might be hiding or are helpless (oversensitive, shy), retreating into their private world, or they might be spying on the other party, or be unable to act due to some other circumstances – they might be literally in a hospital or in a prison! If in H9, they can be foreigners, currently traveling or, as this is a house of legal affairs, they might be filing for a divorce! If in H5, they are happy, hoping for love and fun, being motivated by a wish for an offspring, and so on. Still, we should always help ourselves by considering other indications. If, for example, the significator of the quesited is in H5 and in its detriment or fall, it could show someone who is cheating on the querent – having a love affair with another. And so on.

If H1 ruler is in H7, the querent shows more interest in the relationship, but if the ruler of H7 is in H1, it is the other way around – the quesited is "hotter". If the ruler of H7 is in H7, the quesited is probably not interested in the querent, but cares more for his/her own good. This is sometimes also the case if this planet is in H8.

If the significator of the quesited is linked with a third planet (by an aspect or a mutual reception), this planet often shows a person who plays an important role in the situation. To find out more about this person (whom the querent may or may not be aware of), we must study the house position of this planet and its house rulership/s – in both the radix and the turned chart, but we give priority to the turned chart. If this planet, for example, is the ruler of the radix H4 which is the derived H10, the wife of the querent might flirt with her boss, or with someone she knows through her job; if it rules the radix H5 (the derived H11), the wife may have a friend (lover) in the group in which she participates, and the like.

People often ask questions referring to their ex-partners; where do they "belong", which house rules them? The answer is simple: H7! Same if the querent is single and asking whether he/she will soon find a partner. Any person acting as a partner or lover, be it the present, past or future, real or potential, is ruled by H7.

We can get additional indications by means of **natural significators**, which are: the Moon for wives, Venus for female lovers, the Sun for husbands and Mars for male lovers. Generally, the Moon can stand for any woman (besides always co-signifying the querent which can of course complicate matters a bit) and the Sun for any man. William Lilly suggested that the co-significator for men in all questions relating to love, should be the Sun while for women it should be Venus. But John Frawley, a well known English horary astrologer, suggests we should take Saturn as the natural significator of the unwanted spouse. Use logic! Think what is the core meaning (substance) and the role of the person for whom you are trying to find the natural significator, and you will find it. If a woman is badly in love with her lover, cherishing and loving him endlessly, the symbolism of the Sun would certainly fit him best, but if he's just a casual lover whom she wants to hide from her respected husband, he'd be more properly described by Mars, and the husband by the Sun. But if she can't wait to get rid of her husband, or if he's suspicious of her and she's afraid of him, the symbolism of Saturn would surely fit him best.

Be careful though – do not make the mistake of giving the natural significators precedence over the "accidental" ones! I have seen many horaries flounder because astrologers used too many significators for a single person. Instead of gaining clarity, their charts thus became an unanswerable mess. The first and most potent significators are house rulers (or planets acting as house rulers by virtue of conjoining the ascendant or descendant), with the natural significators playing additional, much less important roles.

Natural significators are also used for other matters: Venus rules marriage, Uranus separation and divorce, Neptune cheating, deception and misunderstandings, Mars quarrels and aggression. Uranus in H1 or H7, especially when supported by the dynamic applying aspect of the Moon or one of the main significators, often indicates separation. Whenever any of the above-mentioned planets is found on an angle, conjuncting it within a 3 degree orb, it deserves our special attention.

A **retrograde significator** can show a return or a reunion – or a withdrawal. To grasp its meaning, we should always stick to the context of the question. It can mean that the querent/quesited will change their mind, or that they want to reunite (with the querent), or that they wish to abandon a certain process (the development of a relationship – or a divorce request!), and the like. The querent's retrograde significator can mean that they will change their mind about the relationship they desire, or it can suggest that it would be wise to give up on the pursuit of the quesited. *Will my ex come back to me?* The retrograde significator of my ex shows at least his intention or wish of getting back, although the re-establishment of the union is not guaranteed by this indication alone. *Does she love me?* Her retrograde significator says no, she doesn't, especially if it is linked with a planet other that the querent's significator.

ZODIACAL SIGNS

Zodiacal signs in which the significators are placed, help us evaluate the current state of the querent and the quesited. A significator in an earth sign would have different motives for making advances from a significator in a water sign, for example.

As in all horary charts, essentially dignified planets (those in their domicile, exaltation, triplicity or sect) show self-confident, powerful, capable, honest, good people, while peregrine or essentially weak significators show people who lack confidence and power to meet our expectations. Essentially debilitated significators can show people who are unworthy of our attention, – except when they are placed in H7 or H1. Remember that when H1 ruler is in H7, or vice versa, those planets are often in their detriment. The H1 ruler in H7 often suggests that the querent is extremely interested in the quesited, but feeling weak inside – the way we often feel when deeply in love but unsure of the opposite party's feelings toward us.

Planets in their detriment or fall, or OOB planets (those above the maximum Sun's declination of 23.5 degrees) sometimes refer to people who are of foreign nationality.

ASPECTS AND RECEPTIONS

The core situation and basic circumstances of the relationship issue we are concerned with, are partly discernable from the context and content of the question, as well as from the general condition of the significators (house placements, planetary strengths etc.), but the past, present and future developments of the situation is mainly revealed by the (eventual) aspects between the significators.

The most reliable indicator that a union is to be established (or renewed) is an applying conjunction or a harmonious aspect between the main significators. The closer the mutual aspect of the planets ruling the two people, the deeper their current bond. If the aspect is harmonious and applying, the relationship is evolving and getting stronger, but if the aspect (harmonious or disharmonious) is separating, the relationship might be cooling down or the couple might be virtually separating. *Are we going to be a couple?* A harmonious applying aspect points to a yes, a separating harmonious aspect points to a no. (All things considered, of course, because a careful consideration of the Moon's and co-significators' aspects is also necessary before the final conclusion can be reached.)

A disharmonious separating aspect between the significators usually shows a recent conflict or a serious disagreement between the two parties, or even their final (recent) parting.

If the aspect is an applying one and the orb is very loose, so that the planets have just entered the aspect, the two people might have known each other only briefly, or their relationship is at a beginning stage, but is evolving into a stronger and more binding one. The same applies to the separating aspects; a loose one suggests that the relationship has practically ceased to exist, and there is probably no chance of renewal.

In questions, asking for the possibility of a union, a mutual reception (even the strongest one which is by home) between the two significators does not warrant a positive answer. It does suggest that the two most probably like or even love each other, but a positive answer can only be given with the presence of at least one aspect of the Moon or co-significators – either with the main significators or even the ascendant and descendant degrees.

We must also be aware of the fact that in the case of the 1/7 rulers (except when judging by almuten rulers), mutual reception by home always occurs when the two planets are in the signs of their detriment (say Venus in Aries and Mars in Libra). Planets in detriment are like people who lack confidence and feel weak and helpless. Being in love often feels like this, because in such an emotional state we are completely dependent on the will of another - will they accept or reject us? A typical mutual reception of this kind would be reflected by a situation where the lovers are married (to other partners) and therefore cannot establish a partnership.

When speaking of aspects, I strongly feel that parallels and contraparallels of declinations should be given consideration too; whereas traditional horary astrology did not use them, research is still needed to confirm the possible validity of those aspects in establishing the outcome of questions. (And this goes for all horaries, not just the relationship ones!)

Below are the main rules for interpreting the outcome of the matter in horary charts relating to love, marriage and partnerships.

- An applying conjunction or a harmonious aspect (sextile or trine) between the significators (or between the Moon and the significator of the quesited) show a mutual willingness to form a relationship and the probability that it will be realized. The probability is greater if at least one significator receives the other (in its home or exaltation sign), if the application is supported by the Moon's translation of light between them, or if they are placed in strong and/or fortunate houses.
- The completion of the matter by means of mutual reception by home (without the mutual aspect of the significators) is possible if the indication is confirmed by the first (immediate) Moon's aspect with the Sun or a benefic (Venus, Jupiter or any other strongly placed planet), or if the chart shows any other similar positive indications (significators in fortunate houses or ruling them, a benefic conjunct an angle, etc.).
- If the significators do not mutually apply to an aspect, the union between them is still possible if they are getting linked by the third planet which translates or collects lights between them. The planet acting as "translator" or "collector" often represents a third person (a friend, relative, colleague etc. – judge by its house placement and rulership/s) who helps them in establishing their relationship.

- If the significators mutually apply to an opposition or a square, then a separation, conflict or any other negative outcome (depending on the nature of the question) is likely, but if they are linked in this fashion but also connected by a translation of light or a mutual reception, the positive outcome (coming together or staying together) is still possible, except that the situation in such cases is usually difficult: in the process of reaching their goal, the partners will have to overcome obstacles, and later they might even regret that they have initiated their tie, or that they got back together.

- If the main significators are not in aspect, but the Sun and the Moon – both strong and well-placed - apply to a harmonious aspect, there is hope; some kind of positive result is probable, although this chart feature alone does not suffice for a positive answer in charts, asking about the formation of a partnership. To get one, we must carefully examine the essential and accidental dignities of both significators, their dispositions and receptions, and the eventual involvement of third planets that can promote or inhibit their association.

- The partner ruled by the faster planet is usually more enthusiastic or eager to form a union, come to an agreement etc. He/she is also probably the one who gives the initiative or is more active in the process that is the subject matter of the question. If significators apply to a mutual conjunction or a harmonious aspect, the one ruled by the faster planet is more deserving of reaching the goal. *Will he call me?* Let us say that the significator of the querent is the Moon while the significator of the quesited is Saturn. The Moon applies to Saturn by a conjunction or a harmonious aspect. The correct answer would be: *No, he will not call you; instead, you will call him.* (Talk of free will, eh?!)

- The absence of an applying aspect, translation of light or collection of light suggests that the matter would not be completed, that is, the desired result would not be achieved. Same if the completion of an applying aspect is prevented by a frustration, prohibition or refranation. The "preventing" planet often indicates (describes) the person or situation that hinders (disables) the completion.

- The significator of the quesited in an aspect or mutual reception with a third planet which is unrelated to the significator/s of the querent, often shows that the quesited is in involved with someone else. Such person can also be shown by a planet in H7, especially if it is harmoniously linked with the main ruler of H7.

- If, in questions about a possible separation, the significators do not mutually apply to a disharmonious aspect, and if none of them is in a disharmonious (applying) aspect with a malefic, or if Uranus in H1, H7 or H10 is not linked to any of the significators and it doesn't "attack" the 1/7 axis by squaring the horizontal axis, or if the significators are applying to a mutual conjunction or a harmonious aspect, the separation is most likely not taking place.

I should add that in practice, when dealing with love/marriage and other partnership questions, I usually employ classical synastry (the branch of astrology dealing specifically with partnerships) beside horary, and, of course, various other predictive techniques. These are important questions and we should never make a mistake to treat them lightly.

1/1: WILL MY EX-WIFE RETURN TO ME?

7 August 1993 at 3:55 p.m. (15:55), Ljubljana, Slovenia
Hour ruler: Jupiter

The querent, a teacher in his middle age, said that his ex-wife whom he had recently divorced, was still occasionally visiting him, so he wondered whether their relationship would flourish again and if she would return to him? It seemed that his feelings for her had cooled and that he was asking more out of curiosity than because of the desire to make the relationship work, but he said that he would be willing to live together again, if she chose to. Will this happen, he asked?

His relaxed attitude to the problem is adequately described by his significator (ascendant ruler) Jupiter, planet of openness and good will, in Libra, the natural sign of partnerships. The lack of emotional involvement and his sober attitude is underlined by the fact that Jupiter is on a Saturn degree (by monomoiria). His co-significator is the Moon while his ex-wife is represented by Mercury as the dispositor of the Gemini descendant. Moon in H4 shows that he's thinking about home affairs. He admitted that he was basically interested in whether there would be a change in his domestic life, which was of course linked to the possible reunion with his ex-wife.

The harmonious planetary hour ruler (this being the same planet as the dispositor of the ascendant) shows that the chart is "radical", meaning that it can be reliably interpreted, so that it will help the querent.

The Moon which describes the course of events is separating from the opposition with Jupiter. Because the Moon is also the natural significator of wives, this aspect adequately describes their recent divorce. Its next aspect is a trine to the Sun, so the case will obviously evolve so that the querent will be pleased with the outcome - regardless of whether the answer is affirmative or negative. A closer look at the chart shows that the first aspect of the Moon will actually be a semi-square to Saturn. The semi-square is not among the traditional or "Ptolemaic" aspects which decide upon the outcome of horary questions, but is suggestive, under the circumstances, of their further separation - because it is a disharmonious aspect and because it involves Saturn, the planet of obstructions.

Of prime importance, of course, is the relationship between Mercury and Jupiter. They're not in aspect. Mercury is in Jupiter's exaltation sign (Cancer) but Jupiter is not in any of Mercury's dignities. The Sun to which the Moon applies does not indicate any of the two.

All this clearly shows that she will not return to him. Mercury in the exaltation of Jupiter nicely describes their current relationship: she occasionally comes to see him and is even his honored guest (exaltation); he receives her willingly and is open to their possible reunion, as is shown by Jupiter in Libra, the sign of relationships, and its dispositor, Venus, in Cancer. She apparently keeps visiting him due to nostalgia (Mercury in Cancer, the sign of home and family), but this cannot bring them back together because the chart doesn´t show any of the valid "perfections of the matter".

What about the other circumstances, related to the question? Mercury (she) is in a close applying sextile to Mars (in Virgo) which receives Mercury in its home and exaltation sign. It is obvious that this situation involves a third party, associated with her! She has indeed been visiting the querent but is already seeing someone else. Who? Mars rules the derived H6 (co-workers) and partly derived H10 (job). Since the aspect is an applying one, her relationship with this man will obviously continue.

All this prompted me to say: *No, your ex-wife will not come back to you; she's been visiting you out of nostalgia, but it seems that she is now with another man, and they have a happy relationship. It seems that she'll stay with him. He's probably her co-worker or connected to her job in some other way. The situation in the sphere of love and home life will, nevertheless, develop very well for you; it seems that you will soon meet another woman with whom you will be happy.*

As the continuation of the relationship between his ex-wife and her new friend (lover) is indicated by the application of Mercury to Mars, the querent's imminent encounter with another woman is suggested by the application of the Moon, his co-significator, to the Sun. The Sun in this context represents a person who will help him to enjoy life again and be happy in love.

But how do we know that he'll be happy? The Sun (his potential new partner) receives the Moon in the sign of its exaltation, which gives the trine aspect particular strength and promise of a good understanding between persons represented by the two lights. The dignified Sun (in its home sign) at the same time shows that this person will be good, honest and sincere.

1/1

7 Aug 1993
15:55 CEDT −2:00
Ljubljana, Slovenia
46°N03' 014°E31'

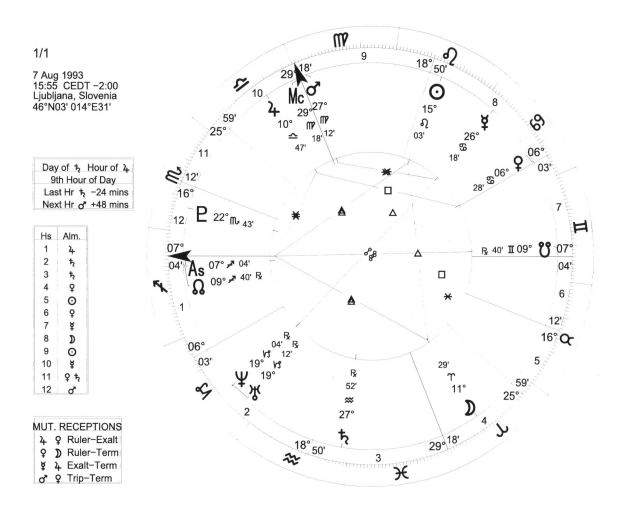

Day of ♄ Hour of ♃
9th Hour of Day
Last Hr ♄ −24 mins
Next Hr ♂ +48 mins

Hs	Alm.
1	♃
2	♄
3	♄
4	♀
5	☉
6	♀
7	☿
8	☽
9	☉
10	☿
11	♀ ♄
12	♂

MUT. RECEPTIONS
♃ ♀ Ruler−Exalt
♀ ☽ Ruler−Term
☿ ♃ Exalt−Term
♂ ♀ Trip−Term

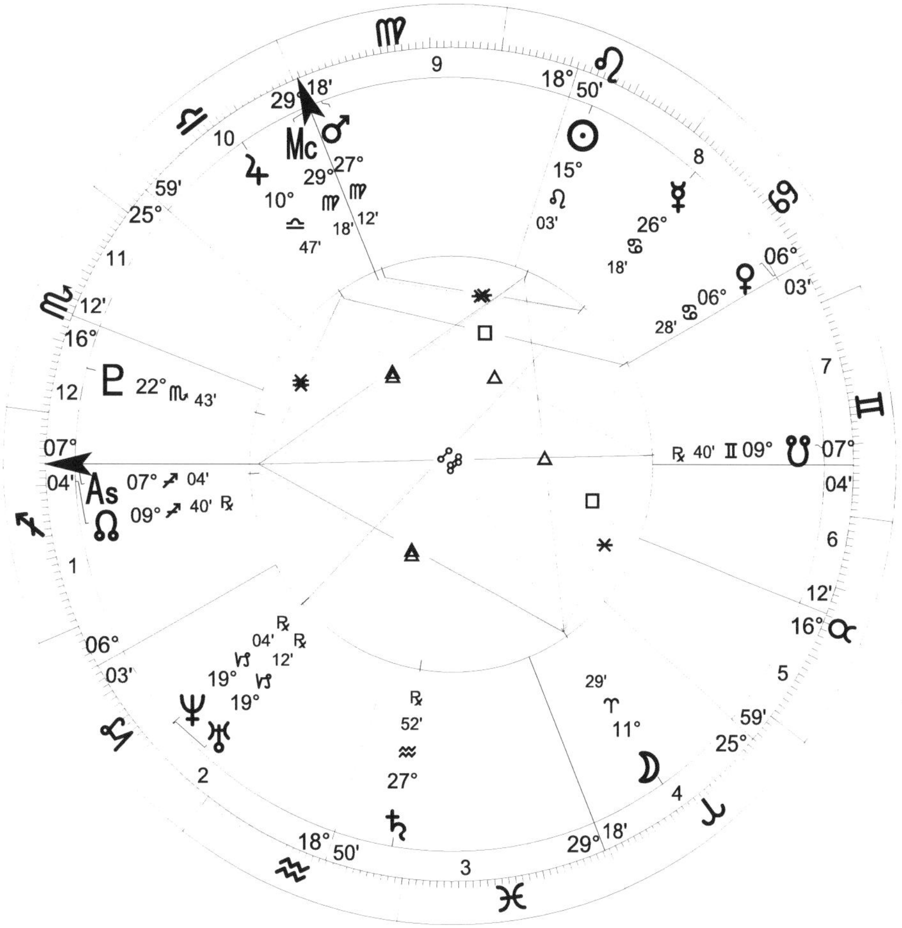

NEAREST ECLIPSES (NM/FM)					
☉ ●	21 May 1993	16:06	00°♊31	Partial	S118
☽ ●	4 Jun 1993	15:02	13°♐54	Total	S130
☉ ●	13 Nov 1993	23:34	21°♏31	Partial	S123
☽ ●	29 Nov 1993	08:30	07°♊03	Total	S135

traditionals.pts

Pt	Long.	Travel	Decl.	Last Stn	Next Stn	Last Stn	Next Stn	F/S	Antiscia	C.Ant.
☽	11°♈29'33"	+11°50'	+08°30'	–	–	–	–	Slow	18°♍30	18°♓30
☉	15°♌03'52"	+57'29"	+16°19'	–	–	–	–	Slow	14°♉56	14°♏56
☿	26°♋18	+01°16'	+20°06'	−12 days	+79 days	18°♋08'52"	22°♏30'41"	Fast	03°♊41	03°♐41
♀	06°♋28	+01°09'	+21°52'	−106 days	+431 days	03°♈44'27"	18°♏00'38"	Fast	23°♊31	23°♐31
♂	27°♍12	+37'27"	+01°40'	−173 days	+513 days	08°♋40'31"	02°♍40'08"	Fast	02°♈47	02°♎47
♃	10°♎47	+09'40"	−03°11'	−67 days	+204 days	04°♎45'27"	14°♏39'22"	Fast	19°♓12	19°♍12
♄	27°♒52 ℞	−04'20"	−13°37'	−58 days	+81 days	00°♓19'40"	23°♒38'00"	Retro	02°♏07	02°♉07

MOON ASPECTS
☽ ☌ ♈ 11°29' S
☽ ⚹ ☋ 1°48' S
☽ △ ☊ 1°48' S
☽ ☍ ♃ 0°42' S
☽ △ ☉ 3°34' A
☽ △ As 4°24' A

ESSENTIAL DIGNITIES

Pt	Ruler	Exalt	Trip	Term	Face	Detri	Fall	Score
☽	♂	☉	☉	♀	☉	♀	♄	−5 p
☉	☉ +	--	☉ +	♄	♃	♄	--	+8
☿	☽	♃	♀	♄	☽	♄	♂	−5 p
♀	☽	♃	♀ +	♂	♀ +	♄	♂	+4
♂	☿	☿	♀	♂ +	☿	♃	♀	+2
♃	♀	♄	♄	☿	♄	♂	☉	−5 p
♄	♄ +	--	♄ +	♄ +	☽	☉	--	+10

ASPECTS	
♅ ☌ ♆	0°07' A
☽ ☍ ♃	0°42' S
☿ ⚹ ♂	0°53' A
♃ ⚹ ☊	1°06' S
♃ △ ☋	1°06' S
☽ △ ☊	1°48' S
☽ ⚹ ☋	1°48' S
♂ ☌ Mc	2°06' S
☋ ☍ As	2°35' A
☊ ☌ As	2°35' A
☿ ⚹ Mc	2°59' S
☽ △ ☉	3°34' A

PLANETARY SECT

Planet		Cht	Plc	Sgn	Condition
☉	D	D	D	D	In Hayz
☽	N	D	N	D	
☿	D	D	D	N	
♀	N	D	D	N	
♂	N	D	D	N	
♃	D	D	D	D	In Hayz
♄	D	D	N	D	

D=Diurnal, N=Nocturnal

The querent later confirmed that his ex-wife had been having a relationship with a co-worker. He also told me that a few months after the question (between three and four, as shown by the number of degrees between the Moon and the Sun) he attended a conference abroad (the Sun rules H9 of foreign travel and education!) where he met a girl who at the time was in a steady relationship, but they fell in love and in about a year she moved to his house. He also confessed that they were very happy together.

1/2: IS SHE STAYING WITH ME?

13 September 1994 at 8:21 a.m., Ljubljana, Slovenia
Hour ruler: Sun

A young man asked what would happen in his love relationship. The girl he had been dating for several years asked him if they could stop seeing each other for a while because, emotionally, she needed a bit of peace and solitude. This worried him because he loved her and certainly did not like the idea of separation, even if for just a short period. They were also co-workers (waiters in a restaurant).

Helplessness and distress which he felt are shown by the unenviable placement of his two significators: Venus (the dispositor of the ascendant) is in detriment while the Moon (co-significator) is in fall. The Moon is also on a Saturn degree (by monomoiria) where it feels at its worst. The ascendant has two almutens, Venus and Saturn, therefore Saturn is the additional significator of the querent. This planet is also essentially weak because it is only in its face, while its retrograde state shows that the querent is averse to the change that his girlfriend had asked of him. Obviously, the young man felt completely helpless!

The main significator of the girl is Mars and her co-significator is the Sun, almuten of the descendant. Mars is accidentally strong in H10, a reflection of the fact that the reins, so to speak, are in her hands. Mars is also on its own degree which describes her as a strong, decisive, bold and independent woman. As the two main significators (Venus and Mars) of the partners are in water signs, we can assume their essential mutual understanding and harmony of character, but the planets are not in aspect and the co-significators also don't form any mutual aspects. Venus is in a Mars's sign confirming her "rulership" over him. Indeed, his fate is in her hands!

So, what's going on and what will happen? Let us examine the condition of Mars, the girl's main significator. It sextiles the Sun, and although the Sun is the girl's co-significator, it can, under the circumstances, show a third party – a man with whom she could have formed some kind of a bond. This would be a hidden or repressed (the Sun in H12) relationship and the man could have been older than she because Mars is east from the Sun which describes her as younger than him. That the girl might have a love affair with that man is confirmed by the fact that the Sun rules her derived H5 (love affairs), and because the Sun is in her derived H6, we can assume that she met him at work or that he is her co-worker. The querent should also know him because she was his co-worker. Their acquaintanceship is confirmed by the fact that the Sun in the triplicity of Venus.

OK, you might say, but the Sun is separating from the sextile of Mars, so their bond is already dissolving? Separative aspects of significators really indicate that two people are still together but their relationship weakens and will slowly fall apart, but in this case we have the situation of "collection of light" which, as we know, reconnects the parties involved. Planets functioning as collectors are even more than one: Neptune, Uranus and Pluto, to which both the Sun and Mars apply. As the two of them (Neptune and Uranus) are in the girl's H10, this is a further confirmation that they know each other through their job. We get the same answer if we take the Sun (almuten of the descendant) as the girl's significator, as it is applying by trine to Neptune (and to Uranus and Pluto, but Neptune receives the first aspect). In this case, another man is shown by Neptune. We can therefore conclude that their relationship will continue.

What about the querent? Venus applies by trine to a retrograde Saturn which is his co-significator and ruler of his H4 and H5. This reflects his nostalgia and a strong desire for further contacts with his girlfriend. Venus' next aspect is a conjunction with Jupiter and the north node, and only after that the trine to Mars (the girl) will be completed, but a look into the ephemeris tells us that Mars will leave Cancer before this happens. This is an example of frustration and refranation at the same time! There are numerous obstacles in front of him and their relationship - too numerous to be overcome. (You'll also notice that Jupiter is peregrine and that it rules the unfortunate H6, so it can't help the querent.)

1/2

13 Sep 1994
08:21 CEDT −2:00
Ljubljana, Slovenia
46°N03' 014°E31'

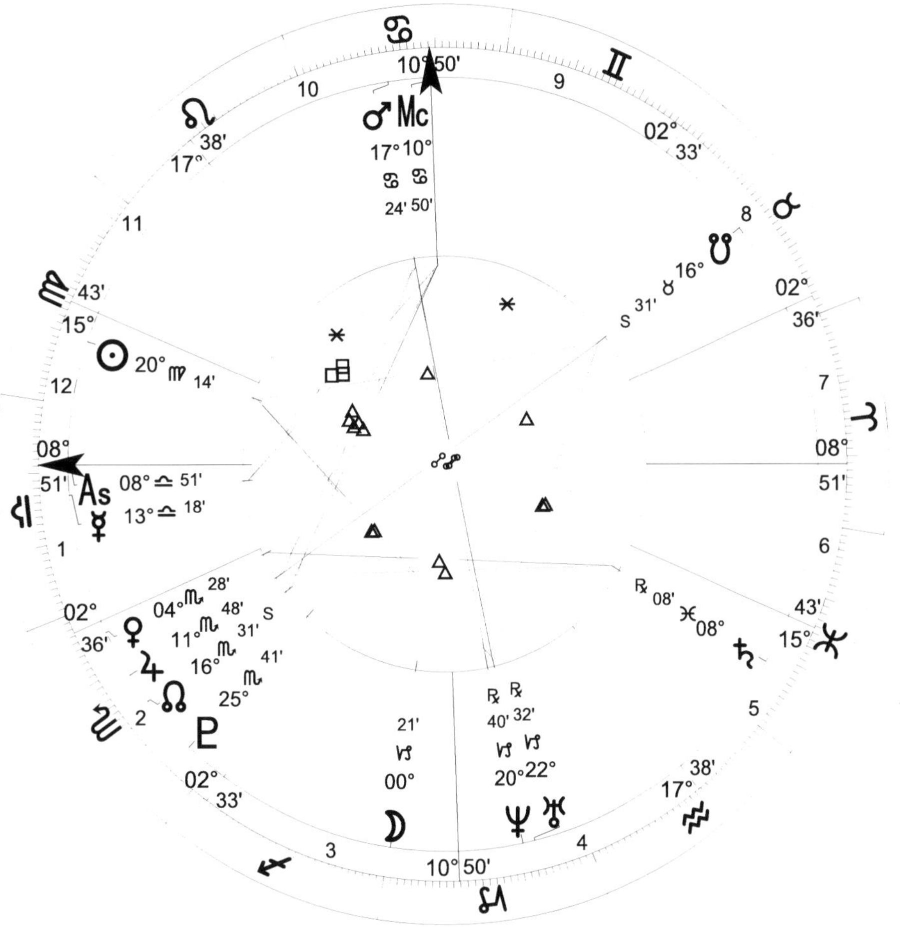

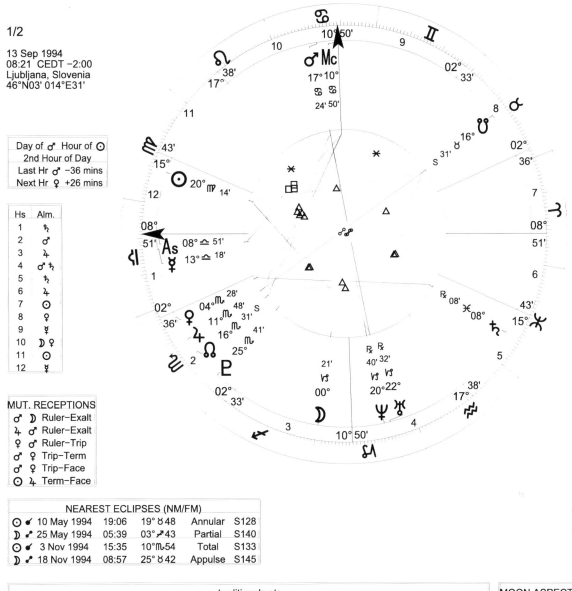

Day of ♂ Hour of ☉
2nd Hour of Day
Last Hr ♂ −36 mins
Next Hr ♀ +26 mins

Hs	Alm.
1	♄
2	♂
3	♃
4	♂ ♄
5	♄
6	♃
7	☉
8	♀
9	☿
10	☽ ♀
11	☉
12	☿

MUT. RECEPTIONS
♂ ☽ Ruler−Exalt
♃ ♂ Ruler−Exalt
♀ ♂ Ruler−Trip
♂ ♀ Trip−Term
♂ ♀ Trip−Face
☉ ♃ Term−Face

NEAREST ECLIPSES (NM/FM)					
☉ ●	10 May 1994	19:06	19° ♉ 48	Annular	S128
☽ ○	25 May 1994	05:39	03° ♐ 43	Partial	S140
☉ ●	3 Nov 1994	15:35	10° ♏ 54	Total	S133
☽ ○	18 Nov 1994	08:57	25° ♉ 42	Appulse	S145

traditionals.pts

Pt	Long.	Travel	Decl.	Last Stn	Next Stn	Last Stn	Next Stn	F/S	Antiscia	C.Ant.
☽	00°♑21'08"	+13°48'	−19°53'	–	–	–	–	Fast	29°♐38	29°♊38
☉	20°♍14'36"	+58'24"	+03°51'	–	–	–	–	Slow	09°♈45	09°♎45
☿	13°♎18	+01°22'	−06°15'	−68 days	+26 days	29°♊25'05"	06°♏28'57"	Fast	16°♓41	16°♍41
♀	04°♏28	+46'13"	−16°54'	−508 days	+29 days	03°♈44'27"	18°♏00'38"	Slow	25°♒31	25°♌31
♂	17°♋24	+36'36"	+22°55'	−574 days	+111 days	08°♋40'31"	02°♍40'08"	Fast	12°♊35	12°♐35
♃	11°♏48	+10'21"	−14°30'	−73 days	+200 days	04°♏46'04"	15°♐23'00"	Fast	18°♒11	18°♌11
♄	08°♓08 ℞	−04'24"	−10°21'	−82 days	+57 days	12°♓24'11"	05°♓40'45"	Retro	21°♎51	21°♈51

MOON ASPECTS
☽ ☌ ♑ 0°21' S
☽ ⚹ ♀ 3°38' A
☽ ⚹ ♄ 7°58' A

ESSENTIAL DIGNITIES

Pt	Ruler	Exalt	Trip	Term	Face	Detri	Fall	Score
☽	♄	♂	♀	☿	♃	☽ −	♃	−10 p
☉	☿	☿	♀	♃	☿	♃	♀	−5 p
☿	♀	♄	♄	☿ +	♄	♂	☉	+2
♀	♂	--	♀ +	♂	♂	♀ −	☽	−2
♂	☽	♃	♀	☿	☿	♄	♂ −	−9 p
♃	♂	--	♀	☿	☉	♀	☽	−5 p
♄	♃	♀	♀	♀	♄ +	☿	☿	+1

ASPECTS
☉ △ ♆ 0°25' A
♂ ⚹ ☋ 0°53' S
♂ △ ☊ 0°53' S
♃ △ Mc 0°57' S
♅ ⚹ ♇ 1°58' S
As □ Mc 1°58' S
♅ ☌ ♆ 2°10' A
☉ △ ♅ 2°17' A
☿ □ Mc 2°28' S
♄ △ Mc 2°40' S

PLANETARY SECT

Planet	Cht	Plc	Sgn	Condition
☉ D	D	D	N	
☽ N	D	N	N	
☿ N	D	N	D	
♀ N	D	N	N	
♂ N	D	D	N	
♃ D	D	N	N	
♄ D	D	N	N	

D=Diurnal, N=Nocturnal

The final answer is confirmed by yet another chart feature. Mercury, which can be considered as his additional co-significator due to its (albeit wide) conjunction with the ascendant, applies by square to Mars, while the Moon (via sextile with Venus, Saturn and Jupiter) applies to it by opposition. Since Mars signifies the girl and because the girl will apparently continue seeing the other man, it is clear that the querent has small chance of success.

Ethics requires that, in such cases, we are careful and considerate. If the querent is very worried or desperate (as in this case), it is best to say "let's give it some time" and not burden them with forecasts of doom and gloom. On the other hand, we must be honest; they have come to us in order to know the truth!

The comparison of both birth charts confirmed that the girl felt trapped, frustrated and unhappy in their relationship. In fact, it would be better for both of them to go their separate ways. I highlighted their relationship and tried to tell him to leave her alone until she so wishes. I mentioned that she might be emotionally attached to a co-worker. That is absolutely impossible, he said, adding that they had always been honest with each other and she claimed that no one else was involved.

A few months later he called me again with the same question. When would they be back together, he asked? He also said that I was right: she confessed that she was entangled in a relationship with one of their co-workers, a guy who was a few years older than her, and married. The querent was still convinced that nothing serious was going on, although she told him that this man had already filed for divorce. Could a hint be clearer than that? But love is always blind!

Let's throw another glance at the Sun's trine with Neptune. As already mentioned, the Sun as almuten of the descendant partially rules her, and you'll notice that the cusp of H6 (colleagues, work environment) is in Pisces. If we take Neptune as the modern ruler of Pisces, the connection is perfectly valid: the Sun is in her H6 in trine with Neptune, the modern ruler of the radix H6. Both H6 (radix and derived) are therefore linked - and this man was indeed her as well as his co-worker!

1/3: ARE WE STAYING TOGETHER?

29 June 1994 at 5:58 p.m. (17:58), Celje, Slovenia
Hour ruler: Saturn

Ascendant is in the early degrees of Sagittarius, the hour ruler is Saturn. Disharmonious planetary hour is a warning - chart may not be suitable for interpretation or the querent will not like the answer, or I won't be able to help her. Additional warning: Mercury is retrograde which can mean that the querent is hiding some fact which is important for the understanding of the situation and for the interpretation of the chart. This proved to be true, because she told me only after I gave my answer, that her boyfriend had actually already left her. It happened shortly before she called me, she said.

Let's see if this "risky" chart adequately describes the situation! Significators of the querent are Jupiter (ascendant ruler) and the Moon while her boyfriend is shown by Mercury. Both planets are in a harmonious trine, but separating, and Mercury's retrograde movement suggests that the boyfriend moves away from her – in other words, he is leaving her. Jupiter is retrograde too, but its movement towards Mercury shows that she "chases him". She wants him back! But Mercury is faster and will slip back into Gemini any minute, which indicates the imminent change in circumstances and the increasing distance between them. Her boyfriend is obviously on the brink of starting a new life – a life which will not involve her. All the more so because Mercury is now still in Jupiter's exaltation (she "receives" him and wants him back), but it is retreating from her "administrative area" and is approaching its own sign, indicating her lover's imminent independence and breaking of contacts with the querent. (Jupiter has no dignities in Gemini, contacts will be broken). The situation is all but encouraging, especially because Jupiter is peregrine and in conjunction with the cusp of H12 (failure, incompetence).

What about the Moon? It applies by sextile to Mars, her H5 ruler (amorous adventures, children) and the natural significator of young men and lovers. The aspect is two degrees short of being exact. This suggests a pleasant change in her love life, taking place in about two units of time. But Mars does not represent her current partner because it has no relation to H7 (her current boyfriend). This prompted me to say: *Unfortunately, it appears that you two will not stay together. It is quite obvious that he is leaving you. But heads up, there is a new lover on the horizon!*

1/3

29 Jun 1994
17:58 CEDT −2:00
Celje, Slovenia
46°N14' 015°E16'

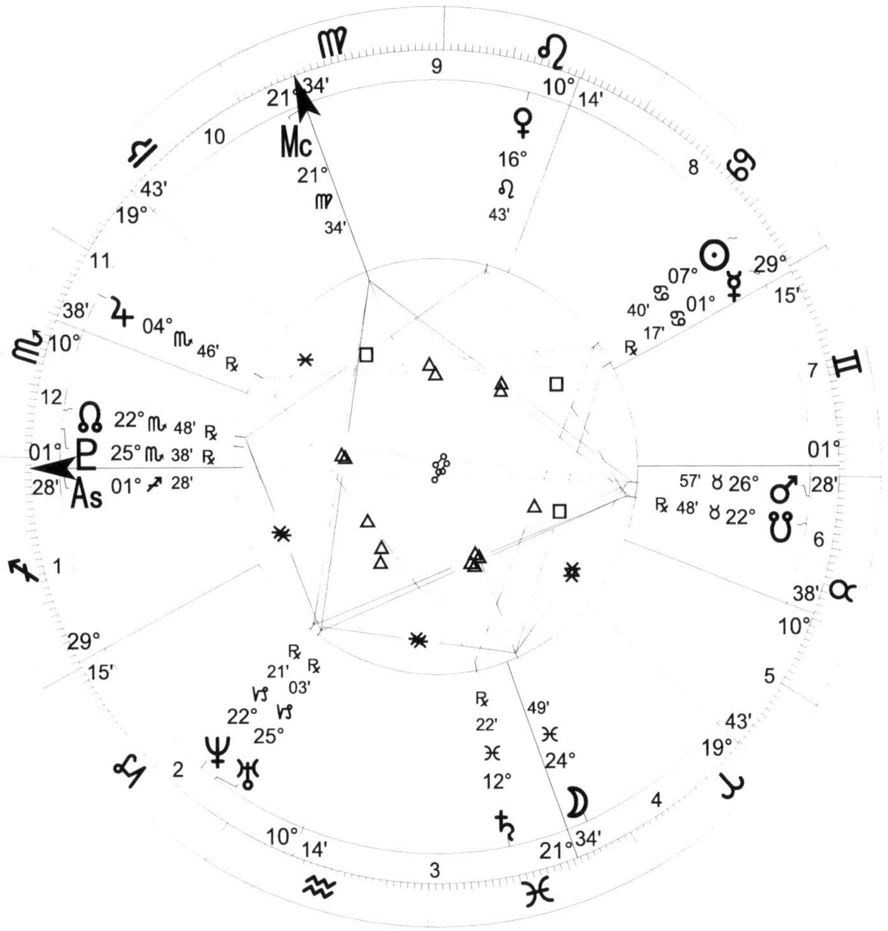

Day of ☿ Hour of ♄
10th Hour of Day
Last Hr ☽ −62 mins
Next Hr ♃ +15 mins

Hs	Alm.
1	♃
2	♃
3	♄
4	♀
5	☉
6	♀
7	☿
8	☿ ♄
9	☉
10	☿
11	♄
12	♂

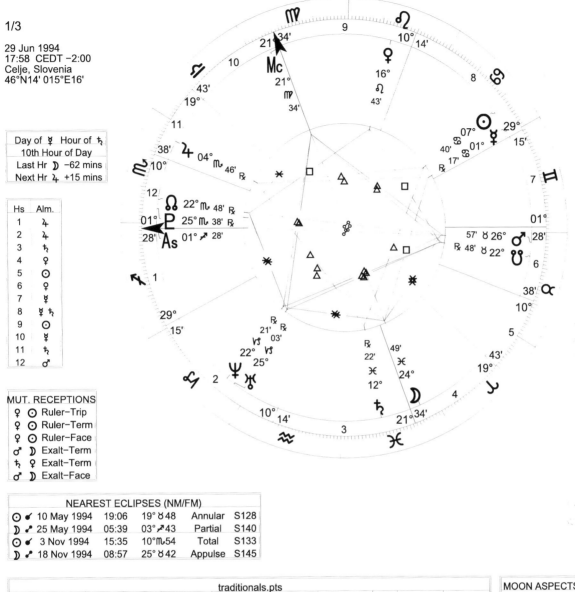

MUT. RECEPTIONS
♀ ☉ Ruler–Trip
♀ ☉ Ruler–Term
♀ ☉ Ruler–Face
♂ ☽ Exalt–Term
♄ ♀ Exalt–Term
♂ ☽ Exalt–Face

NEAREST ECLIPSES (NM/FM)					
☉	10 May 1994	19:06	19°♉48	Annular	S128
☽	25 May 1994	05:39	03°♐43	Partial	S140
☉	3 Nov 1994	15:35	10°♏54	Total	S133
☽	18 Nov 1994	08:57	25°♉42	Appulse	S145

traditionals.pts

Pt	Long.	Travel	Decl.	Last Stn	Next Stn	Last Stn	Next Stn	F/S	Antiscia	C.Ant.
☽	24°♓49'50"	+12°17'	+01°58'	–	–	–	–	Slow	05°♎10	05°♈10
☉	07°♋40'29"	+57'12"	+23°13'	–	–	–	–	Slow	22°♊19	22°♐19
☿	01°♋17 ℞	−28'47"	+18°47'	−16 days	+7,2 days	08°♋24'40"	29°♊25'05"	Retro	28°♊42	28°♐42
♀	16°♌43	+01°09'	+17°34'	−433 days	+105 days	03°♈44'27"	18°♏00'38"	Fast	13°♉16	13°♏16
♂	26°♉57	+42'55"	+19°02'	−499 days	+187 days	08°♋40'31"	02°♍40'08"	Fast	03°♌02	03°♒02
♃	04°♏46 ℞	−00'26"	−11°58'	−121 days	+2,5 days	14°♏39'22"	04°♏46'04"	Retro	25°♒13	25°♌13
♄	12°♓22 ℞	−00'38"	−08°34'	−6,5 days	+132 days	12°♓24'11"	05°♓40'45"	Retro	17°♎37	17°♈37

MOON ASPECTS
☽ ⚹ ♆ 2°30' S
☽ ⚹ ☋ 1°54' S
☽ △ ☊ 1°54' S
☽ ⚹ ♅ 0°04' S
☽ ⚹ ♂ 2°15' A
☽ △ ♇ 3°05' A
☽ ☌ ♈ 5°10' A
☽ □ ☿ 6°47' A

ESSENTIAL DIGNITIES

Pt	Ruler	Exalt	Trip	Term	Face	Detri	Fall	Score
☽	♃	♀	♀	♂	♂	☿	☿	−5 p
☉	☽	♃	♀ m	♀	♀	♄	♂	−5 p
☿	☽	♃	♀	♂	♀	♄	♂	−5 p
♀	☉	--	☉ m	♄	♃	♄	--	−5 p
♂	♀	☽	♀	♄	♄	♂ –	--	−10 p
♃	♂	--	♀	♂	♂	♀	☽	−5 p
♄	♃	♀	♀	♃	♃	☿	☿	−5 p

ASPECTS
☽ ⚹ ♅ 0°04' S
♆ △ ☋ 0°26' A
♆ ⚹ ☊ 0°26' A
♅ ⚹ ♇ 0°35' A
♆ △ Mc 0°46' S
☊ ⚹ Mc 1°13' S
☋ △ Mc 1°13' S
♂ △ ♅ 1°53' S
☽ △ ☊ 1°54' S
☽ ⚹ ☋ 1°54' S

PLANETARY SECT

Planet	Cht	Plc	Sgn	Condition
☉ D	D	D	N	
☽ N	D	N	N	
☿ D	D	D	N	
♀ N	D	D	D	Ex Cond
♂ N	D	N	N	
♃ D	D	D	N	
♄ D	D	N	N	

D=Diurnal, N=Nocturnal

The querent was not pleased by my answer, of course, because she still loved the man and wanted him back, but three months later I received her call, asking if she was pregnant?! She confirmed the break-up with her former boyfriend but she told me that she had met a new man in the beginning of September. That's two months after the first horary, which is shown by the two degrees between the Moon and Mars. She said that she was afraid she was pregnant, because she felt that the man was not good for her. He probably was not, indeed, because Mars is in its detriment - and in line with the negative function of a planet in its detriment, the adventure brought her more sadness than happiness.

1/4: IS THIS THE END OF OUR RELATIONSHIP?

17 July 2004 at 11:05 a.m., Paris, France
Hour ruler: Venus

A friend wrote me from Paris where she was staying for a multi-day study course. Her email sounded desperate. Her boyfriend, a jealous young man, was constantly calling her and on the phone, questioning and harassing her. He was checking on her even in the middle of the night, asking where and with whom she was. She described her disapproval of such behavior of her partner, saying that it can't go on like this. His jealousy had already been exhausting her for too long, she wrote, and she felt that she truly and finally had had enough. She decided to call it quits with him as soon as she arrived home. To confirm her decision, she wanted to hear my opinion, so she raised the above question.

I cast the chart for the time when her email arrived into my mailbox. She probably wrote it a minute to a few minutes earlier, but that would move the ascendant to a few minutes or one degree away at most. Location is of course Paris, where she was staying.

Ascendant is in Virgo. You will notice that Jupiter, the ruler of the descending sign and therefore the significator of her boyfriend, is conjunct the ascendant out of H12 in its fall (Virgo). This clearly reflects the boy's obsession with the querent and his indecent (fall) and manipulative (H12) harassment, but on the other hand, the querent obviously has power over him because Mercury, the ascendant ruler, receives Jupiter in its home and exaltation. This is confirmed by Venus, almuten of the descendant, which is also in a Mercury sign. Mercury itself is in Leo, on a degree where it has a weak dignity (term). It is also in conjunction with the cusp of H12 which reflects her sense of helplessness and "entrapment".

The Moon, her co-significator, is in an exact conjunction with the Sun. It has just reached the end of its monthly cycle and is therefore in its most helpless, vulnerable and sensitive stage. Horary charts with such a Moon placement usually describe a situation that is running out of vital energy and has weak chances of survival - but of what exactly, depends on the subject matter of the chart. In this case, the "exhausted" Moon describes her feelings of helplessness, apathy and the desire to end the relationship. But is the desire enough? We have the inclination, but without a confirmation of the main significators, no reliable assessment can be made. In addition, the Sun is the natural significator of men, the Moon of women. Seen from this perspective, she approaches him, she's not leaving.

Are there any aspects between the main significators? Mercury and Jupiter are not in aspect, while Venus (almuten of the descendant) is in a wide separating sextile with Mercury. You will notice that Mercury is void-of-course. The querent has no direction, no real objective or goal. She's lost and aimless. Their main significators don't apply into a dynamic aspect which would signify an imminent separation and there's also no aspect of Uranus, the natural ruler of divorce. He's after her, but lacks self-confidence (Jupiter in fall) while she doesn't have the courage and the will to act on her plan (to leave).

This moved me to write: *I understand how you feel but I don't see you leaving him. You simply do not have the energy to resist him and go your own way. You will continue to withdraw from him, but not in a decisive and effective enough way. You two are staying together. I'm not saying that it'll remain so forever, but the current crisis is not final.*

Upon her return, they made up and were a "happy" couple again. Much later, their ways parted, but this no longer falls within the domain of this horary chart. Still, if we look at Jupiter, H7 ruler (partnership as such), we can see that it first applies to sextile Saturn (stability, durability), but its next and final aspect is square Pluto (obstruction, termination).

Saturn, to which Jupiter is linked, plays another role in the chart. As she learnt later, her boyfriend went so far as to employ a friend who lived in Paris, to spy on her – and Saturn rules his (derived) H11!

1/4

17 Jul 2004
11:05 CEDT −2:00
Paris, France
48°N52' 002°E20'

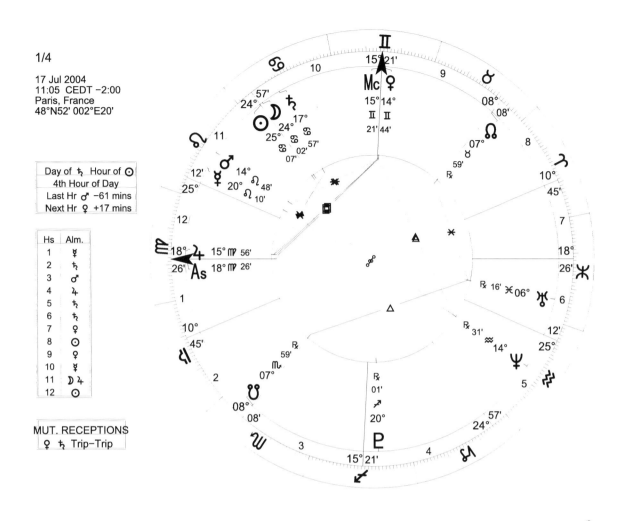

Day of ♄ Hour of ☉
4th Hour of Day
Last Hr ♂ −61 mins
Next Hr ♀ +17 mins

Hs	Alm.
1	☿
2	♄
3	♂
4	♃
5	♄
6	♄
7	♀
8	☉
9	♀
10	☿
11	☽ ♃
12	☉

MUT. RECEPTIONS
♀ ♄ Trip−Trip

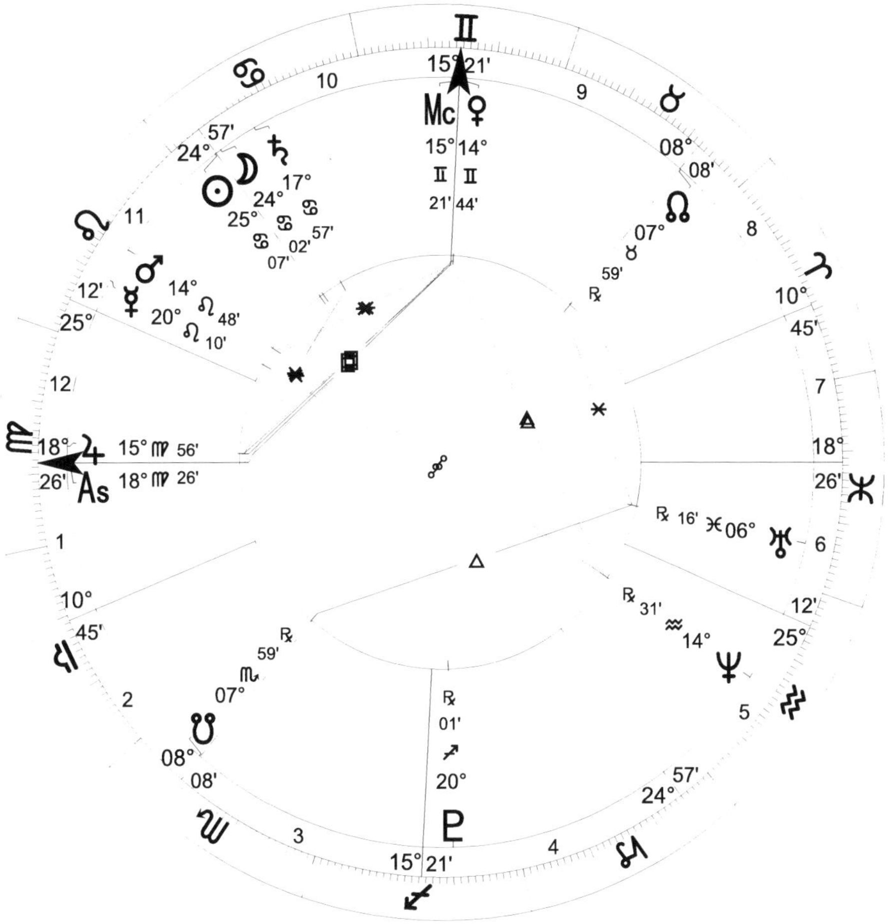

NEAREST ECLIPSES (NM/FM)					
☉	19 Apr 2004	15:21	29°♈49	Partial	S119
☽	4 May 2004	22:33	14°♏41	Total	S131
☉	14 Oct 2004	04:48	21°♎05	Partial	S124
☽	28 Oct 2004	05:07	05°♉02	Total	S136

traditionals.pts

Pt	Long.	Travel	Decl.	Last Stn	Next Stn	Last Stn	Next Stn	F/S	Antiscia	C.Ant.
☽	24°♋02'59"	+12°01'	+26°04'	–	–	–	–	Slow	05°♊57	05°♐57
☉	25°♋07'00"	+57'16"	+21°06'	–	–	–	–	Slow	04°♊52	04°♐52
☿	20°♌10	+01°21'	+15°16'	−77 days	+23 days	21°♈06'58"	08°♍46'28"	Fast	09°♉49	09°♏49
♀	14°♊44	+32'19"	+17°52'	−17 days	+525 days	09°♊37'32"	01°♒28'00"	Slow	15°♋15	15°♑15
♂	14°♌48	+37'50"	+17°31'	−294 days	+441 days	00°♓07'06"	23°♉22'20"	Fast	15°♉11	15°♏11
♃	15°♍56	+10'12"	+06°35'	−73 days	+199 days	08°♍54'52"	18°♎51'45"	Fast	14°♈03	14°♎03
♄	17°♋57	+07'45"	+21°58'	−131 days	+113 days	06°♋17'09"	27°♋20'35"	Fast	12°♊02	12°♐02

MOON ASPECTS
☽ ☌ ☉ 4°58' A
☽ ⚹ As 5°27' A
☽ ☌ ♌ 5°57' A

ESSENTIAL DIGNITIES

Pt	Ruler	Exalt	Trip	Term	Face	Detri	Fall	Score
☽	☽ +	♃	♀	♃	☽ +	♄	♂	+6
☉	☽	♃	♀	♃	☽	♄	♂	−5 p
☿	☉	--	☉	☿ +	♂	♄	--	+2
♀	☿	--	♄ m	♀ +	♂	♃	--	+2
♂	☉	--	☉	♄	♃	♄	--	−5 p
♃	☿	☿	♀	♀	♀	♃ −	♀	−10 p
♄	☽	♃	♀ m	☿	☿	♄ −	♂	−10 p

ASPECTS
♀ △ ♆ 0°06' S
♀ ⚹ ♂ 0°17' S
♄ ⚹ As 0°28' S
♂ ⚹ Mc 0°32' S
♃ □ Mc 0°34' S
☿ △ ♇ 0°38' S
♆ △ Mc 0°50' S
♂ ☍ ♆ 1°09' S
♀ □ ♃ 1°16' A
♇ □ As 1°34' S

PLANETARY SECT

Planet	Cht	Plc	Sgn	Condition
☉ D	D	D	N	
☽ N	D	D	N	
☿ N	D	D	D	Ex Cond
♀ N	D	D	D	Ex Cond
♂ N	D	D	D	Ex Cond
♃ D	D	D	N	
♄ D	D	D	N	

D=Diurnal, N=Nocturnal

1/5: WILL WE GO STEADY?

28 May, 2006 at 3:40 p.m. (15:40), Ljubljana, Slovenia
Hour ruler: Venus

The querent was besotted by a man she had been seeing for a few weeks. Their love affair was hot and it totally obsessed her, but things did not progress the way she would have wanted. He was not always available, he often didn't return her calls and she was having doubts as to whether anything serious would develop from it.

Planetary hour is harmonious, so we can confidently delineate the chart.

Her significators are Venus and partly Saturn (almuten of the ascendant), his are Mars and Sun (almuten of the descendant and also the natural significator of men).

The querent's condition is well described by the state of her main significator Venus which is in the partnership H7 and also in the sign of Mars, H7 ruler. This reflects her strong emotions and total power which he had upon her, but Venus is in detriment in Aries so her situation is all but enviable. The fact that Venus is at the end of the sign, reflecting her exhaustion, indicates that she's probably really approaching the end of this path. Since Venus is not only in the house and sign of her partner, but also on the degree of Mars and in the triplicity of the Sun, almuten of the descendant, it is obvious that the man has completely entranced her and that her happiness depends solely upon him. This is underlined by the accidental power of Mars which is placed in H10, showing that the decision is in his hands. Almuten of the ascendant is Saturn, placed in Leo, the sign of its fall. This shows that the querent feels really bad and that she hasn't got any big chances to succeed in the matter; she would like to have control over the situation, but her actions go against the objective which she seeks to achieve.

Is he at all interested in her? Mars is only in the triplicity of Venus while Venus is in many of Mars's dignities; therefore it is obvious that she was much more impressed by him than he by her. Venus and Mars are in a separating square, indicating their differences and illustrating the fact that they had been sleeping together but the situation is now dissolving (separation). This is confirmed by a separating aspect between the two almutens (the Sun separates from a sextile with Saturn).

The Moon, her co-significator, applies by sextile to Venus. This is a harmonious aspect and could give the querent some hope despite the fact that Venus does not show her partner but herself, but you will see that the first Moon's aspect is an opposition to Pluto, indicating an imminent obstruction – things are getting from bad to worse.

Because I felt sorry for her, I told her gently that there was clearly nothing that she could do, so it would be best to wait and just try to relax. But seeing that Venus, her main significator, is leaving the sign where she feels restricted and suppressed, and is entering a new sign (Taurus, her home), where she will find it easier to express herself, I told her that she will soon feel much better, stronger and more confident. Indications are actually encouraging, I said, just wait a little! The situation will soon change, and whatever happens, it'll be for the better! (I had no heart to tell her that her affair was obviously coming to an end soon.) I added that I would check their compatibility by synastry (comparison of two people's birth charts) as soon as I had time, which should be in a day or two.

The next evening I received her email, saying that I don't need to trouble myself with synastry because she had just left him. *I couldn't stand it any longer, it was too painful,* she said.

The horary chart reflects the course of events very nicely! Venus lacks a good degree to the end of the sign (a cardinal sign and angular house – a short time unit), corresponding to a day which passed until her decision – which was also a liberation. As she told me later, she suddenly really felt much better, as if a heavy burden had fallen from her shoulders. Although it took some time before she forgot him, the man did not make any attempt to get her back – in fact, he didn't even call and she never saw him again.

1/5

28 May 2006
15:40 CEDT −2:00
Ljubljana, Slovenia
46°N03' 014°E31'

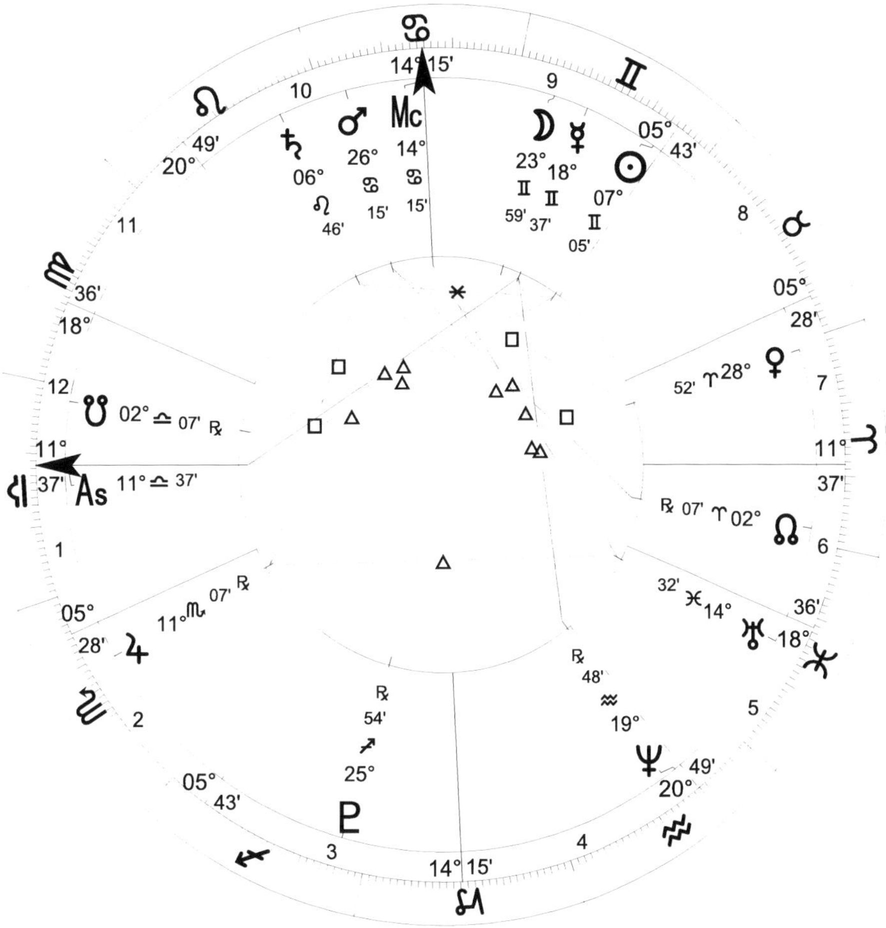

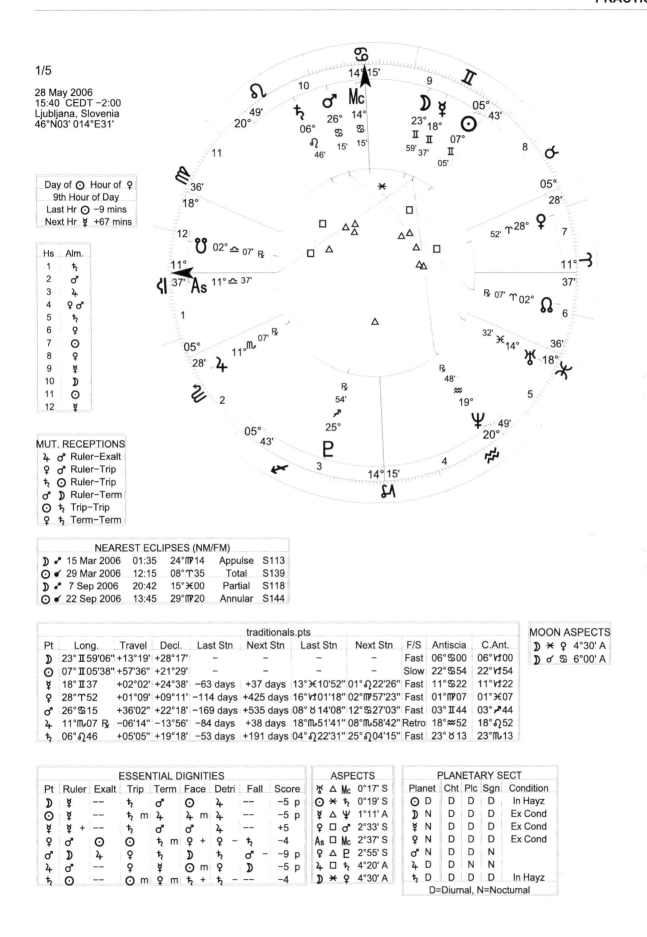

Day of ☉ Hour of ♀
9th Hour of Day
Last Hr ☉ −9 mins
Next Hr ☿ +67 mins

Hs	Alm.
1	♄
2	♂
3	♃
4	♀ ♂
5	♄
6	♀
7	☉
8	♀
9	☿
10	☽
11	☉
12	☿

MUT. RECEPTIONS		
♃	♂	Ruler−Exalt
♀	♂	Ruler−Trip
♄	☉	Ruler−Trip
♂	☽	Ruler−Term
☉	♄	Trip−Trip
♀	♄	Term−Term

NEAREST ECLIPSES (NM/FM)					
☽	15 Mar 2006	01:35	24°♍14	Appulse	S113
☉	29 Mar 2006	12:15	08°♈35	Total	S139
☽	7 Sep 2006	20:42	15°♓00	Partial	S118
☉	22 Sep 2006	13:45	29°♍20	Annular	S144

traditionals.pts

Pt	Long.	Travel	Decl.	Last Stn	Next Stn	Last Stn	Next Stn	F/S	Antiscia	C.Ant.
☽	23°♊59'06"	+13°19'	+28°17'	–	–	–	–	Fast	06°♋00	06°♑00
☉	07°♊05'38"	+57'36"	+21°29'	–	–	–	–	Slow	22°♋54	22°♑54
☿	18°♊37	+02°02'	+24°38'	−63 days	+37 days	13°♓10'52"	01°♌22'26"	Fast	11°♋22	11°♑22
♀	28°♈52	+01°09'	+09°11'	−114 days	+425 days	16°♑01'18"	02°♍57'23"	Fast	01°♍07	01°♓07
♂	26°♋15	+36'02"	+22°18'	−169 days	+535 days	08°♉14'08"	12°♋27'03"	Fast	03°♊44	03°♐44
♃	11°♏07 ℞	−06'14"	−13°56'	−84 days	+38 days	18°♏51'41"	08°♏58'42"	Retro	18°♒52	18°♌52
♄	06°♌46	+05'05"	+19°18'	−53 days	+191 days	04°♌22'31"	25°♌04'15"	Fast	23°♉13	23°♏13

MOON ASPECTS
☽ ⚹ ♀ 4°30' A
☽ ☌ ♋ 6°00' A

ESSENTIAL DIGNITIES

Pt	Ruler	Exalt	Trip	Term	Face	Detri	Fall	Score
☽	☿	--	♄	♂	☉	♃	--	−5 p
☉	☿	--	♄ m	♃	♃ m	♃	--	−5 p
☿	☿ +	--	♄	♂	♂	♃	--	+5
♀	♂	☉	☉	♄ m	♀ +	♀ −	♄	−4
♂	☽	♃	♀	♄	☽	♄	♂ −	−9 p
♃	♂	--	♀	☿	☉ m	♀	☽	−5 p
♄	☉	--	☉ m	♀ m	♄ +	♄ −	--	−4

ASPECTS
♅ △ Mc 0°17' S
☉ ⚹ ♄ 0°19' S
☿ △ ♆ 1°11' A
♀ □ ♂ 2°33' S
As □ Mc 2°37' S
♀ △ ♇ 2°55' S
♃ □ ♄ 4°20' A
☽ ⚹ ♀ 4°30' A

PLANETARY SECT

Planet		Cht	Plc	Sgn	Condition
☉	D	D	D	D	In Hayz
☽	N	D	D	D	Ex Cond
☿	N	D	D	D	Ex Cond
♀	N	D	D	D	Ex Cond
♂	N	D	D	N	
♃	D	D	N	N	
♄	D	D	D	D	In Hayz

D=Diurnal, N=Nocturnal

1/6: HOW LONG IS THIS RELATIONSHIP GOING TO LAST?

28 February 1994 at 12:50 p.m. (12:50), Ljubljana, Slovenia
Hour ruler: Mercury

The querent's significator is the Moon, Saturn signifies her partner. The Moon is also almuten of the ascendant while the descendant has no less than three almutens: Saturn, Venus and Mars. (Note: the table below the chart lists only Venus and Mars because it doesn't support more than two entries.)

The Moon in Libra is squaring the AS/DS axis, reflecting the querent's dissatisfaction and the desire to terminate the relationship. This is confirmed by Saturn and Venus (two almutens of the descendant) in Pisces, the sign inconjunct Libra, showing disharmony and stress. Neptune and Uranus in H7, without harmonious aspects, also don't bode well for her union because Neptune, so placed, indicates fraud, and Uranus separation. If we take Neptune as a modern ruler of Pisces, it would be in a mutual reception with Saturn which would suggest that her partner could be thinking of another woman or even have a secret liaison (Neptune). The possibility that he's hiding something from the querent is confirmed by the fact that Saturn is combust. This could also reflect some sort of weakness and/ or a degree of secrecy associated with her partnership as such. Retrograde Mercury, planetary hour ruler, suggests that the querent did not tell the whole truth or state all of the facts needed to understand the situation. As it turned out, this was true!

In any case, it seemed the chart showed that her partner was insincere to her, so I decided to go from there. Does she feel her partner is really being honest and fair to her? She remained silent (Mercury retrograde). Some seconds passed and then she said, please just tell me what you see. I proceeded to tell her that the chart quite clearly reflects her dissatisfaction as well as character incompatibility (which was confirmed by a quick look into their synastry), and I pointed to the possibility of their breakup because the Moon was not only in square with the descendant but also in an applying square with Neptune and Uranus in H7. I told the querent that it is clear from the chart that this partnership is suffering from confusion, probably also intrigue and dishonesty.

The woman then spoke and confirmed my suspicions. She said that her lover is a plain crook! He'd been seeing her for many years, whilst still married, and at the same time had been carrying on with yet another woman – for a year. A triple alliance, this is really too much, she said. (And I agreed, of course.) She said that she had actually decided to leave him, and now that she's heard my judgment she'd do that as soon as possible.

Although I never received additional feedback on how the matter actually resolved, and even though I basically just told her what she already knew, the chart is interesting because it clearly describes the situation which moved the woman to ask the question.

I also find it very interesting that the descendant has three almutens, which is nicely reflected in the number of women involved with her "partner".

1/6

28 Feb 1994
12:50 CET −1:00
Ljubljana, Slovenia
46°N03' 014°E31'

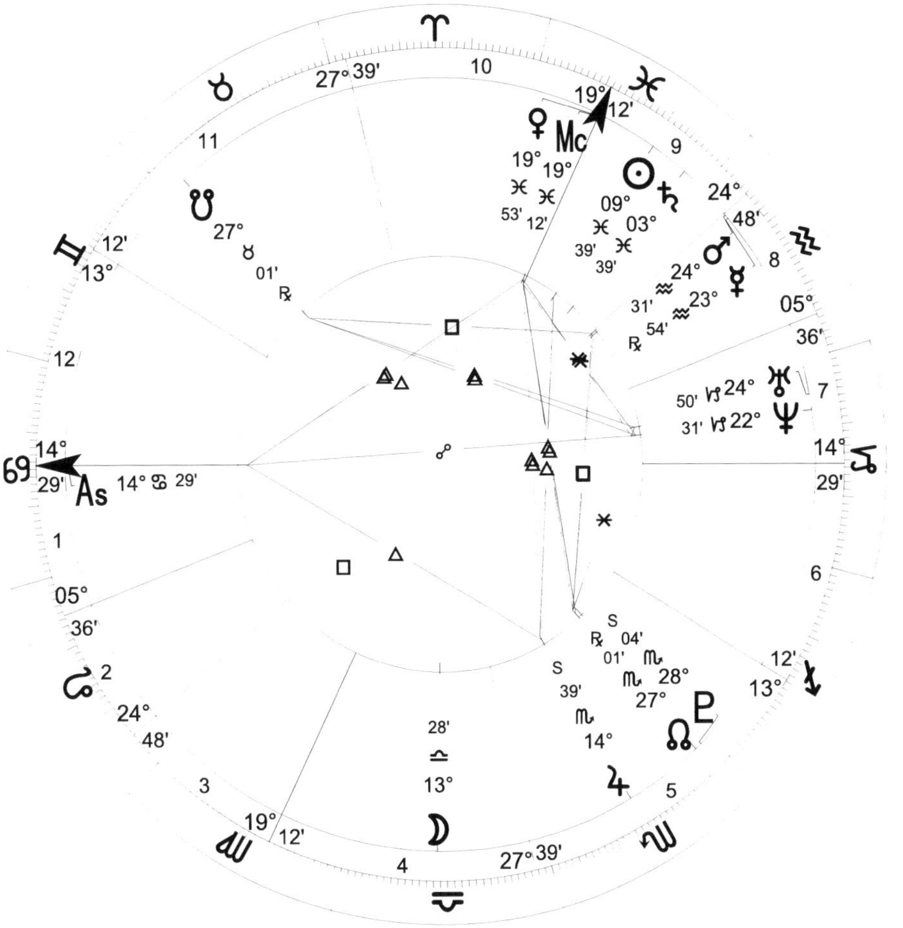

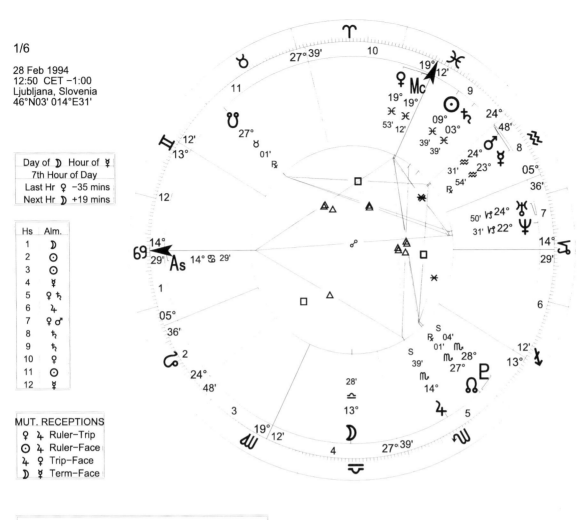

Day of ☽ Hour of ☿
7th Hour of Day
Last Hr ♀ −35 mins
Next Hr ☽ +19 mins

Hs	Alm.
1	☽
2	☉
3	☉
4	☿
5	♀ ♄
6	♃
7	♀ ♂
8	♄
9	♄
10	♀
11	☉
12	☿

MUT. RECEPTIONS	
♀ ♃	Ruler-Trip
☉ ♃	Ruler-Face
♃ ♀	Trip-Face
☽ ☿	Term-Face

NEAREST ECLIPSES (NM/FM)					
☉ ☌	13 Nov 1993	22:34	21°♏31	Partial	S123
☽ ☍	29 Nov 1993	07:30	07°♊03	Total	S135
☉ ☌	10 May 1994	18:06	19°♉48	Annular	S128
☽ ☍	25 May 1994	04:39	03°♐43	Partial	S140

traditionals.pts

Pt	Long.	Travel	Decl.	Last Stn	Next Stn	Last Stn	Next Stn	F/S	Antiscia	C.Ant.
☽	13°♎28'39"	+14°50'	−08°30'	–	–	–	–	Fast	16°♓31	16°♍31
☉	09°♓39'40"	+01°00'	−07°56'	–	–	–	–	Fast	20°♎20	20°♈20
☿	23°♒54 ℞	−32'54"	−10°55'	−17 days	+4,7 days	07°♓34'39"	22°♒37'32"	Retro	06°♏05	06°♉05
♀	19°♓53	+01°14'	−05°17'	−311 days	+226 days	03°♈44'27"	18°♏00'38"	Fast	10°♎06	10°♈06
♂	24°♒31	+47'09"	−14°23'	−378 days	+308 days	08°♋40'31"	02°♍40'08"	Fast	05°♏28	05°♉28
♃	14°♏39	+00'00"	−14°59'	−272 days	+2h 00m	04°♎45'27"	14°♏39'22"	Stat	15°♒20	15°♌20
♄	03°♓39	+07'16"	−11°30'	−123 days	+114 days	23°♒38'00"	12°♓24'11"	Fast	26°♎20	26°♈20

MOON ASPECTS
☽ ☌ ♎ 13°28' S
☽ □ As 1°00' S

ESSENTIAL DIGNITIES

Pt	Ruler	Exalt	Trip	Term	Face	Detri	Fall	Score
☽	♀	♄	♄	☿	♄	♂	☉	−5 p
☉	♃	♀	♀	♀	♄	☿	☿	−5 p
☿	♄	--	♄	♂	☽	☉	--	−5 p
♀	♃	♀ +	♀ +	♂	♃	☿	☿	+7
♂	♄	--	♄	♂ +	☽	☉	--	+2
♃	♂	--	♀	☿	☉	♀	☽	−5 p
♄	♃	♀	♀	♀	♄ +	☿	☿	+1

ASPECTS	
♃ △ As	0°09' S
☽ □ As	1°00' S
♀ ☌ Mc	1°33' S
♅ ⚹ ♇	1°58' A
♅ △ ☋	2°11' A
♅ ⚹ ☊	2°11' A
♂ □ ☋	2°30' A
♂ □ ☊	2°30' A
♀ ⚹ ♆	2°35' A
♂ □ ♇	3°10' A

PLANETARY SECT

Planet	Cht	Plc	Sgn	Condition
☉ D	D	D	N	
☽ N	D	N	D	
☿ D	D	D	D	In Hayz
♀ N	D	D	N	
♂ N	D	D	D	Ex Cond
♃ D	D	N	N	
♄ D	D	D	N	

D=Diurnal, N=Nocturnal

1/7: SHOULD I STAY OR SHOULD I GO?

16 June 1994 at 12:55 p.m. (12:55), Ljubljana, Slovenia
Hour ruler: The Moon

A woman in her early middle age asked me if it would be good to stay in a relationship with a man, and although they didn't live together, they had been going steady for quite some time. She explained that a couple of months ago she fell in love with a much younger man, which was also the reason for her uncertainty regarding the current partner.

Hour ruler is harmonious, giving me confidence that my answer will help the querent.

Her main significator is Mercury, co-significator is the Moon, and Jupiter shows her partner. To these, we could add Neptune as the modern ruler of Pisces, as well as Venus which is the almuten of the descendant.

Let us see if there are any links between the significators. Mercury is in Jupiter's exaltation as well as in the triplicity, term and face of Venus, the almuten of the descendant. All this shows that her partner loves her and probably has more power over her than she thinks or wants to believe. Mercury and Jupiter are in trine (mutual understanding and harmony), with Mercury retrograding back towards a trine with (also retrograde) Jupiter. As can be seen from the table below the chart, Mercury turned retrograde four days ago while Jupiter is very slow because it will turn direct 15 days later, so it is clear that the planets will shortly complete a trine. The answer is obvious – they are staying together! This is confirmed by the Moon's application by trine to Neptune, modern ruler of H7. The Moon's next application is to square the Sun (the natural significator of men), which draws attention to the possible problems which they might encounter some 5 weeks or months (the number of degrees separating the two lights) after the question, but due to other encouraging factors those problems will most likely be manageable.

What about the younger man? She said that they were not seeing each other; it was just a platonic affair but she felt strongly about him. Which planet in the chart represents him? We can see that the Moon is separating from a sextile of Mars, the natural significator of young men and lovers. Mars is in detriment (Taurus), showing that he could not perform as her true lover and could not make her really happy. This is supported by a separating opposition of the Moon from Saturn, her H5 ruler - an aspect, suggestive of the frustration and worry which resulted from an ill-fated platonic relationship.

A look into her progressions and transits revealed that at the time of her question, her progressed Venus was in sextile with Neptune while transiting Neptune opposed her Moon. Obviously, she wanted more than an "ordinary" affair can give! Neptune awakened in her a desire for magical, dream-like, boundless love, which she had hoped to find in the imaginary object of her affection. A skillful astrologer knows that Neptune always promises more than it delivers, especially when in disharmonious aspects to personal planets.

Don't be foolish, I said and explained to her the current Neptunian trends and assured her that she would soon feel solid ground under her feet again and realize that, in fact, she has a wonderful partner.

1/7

16 Jun 1994
12:55 CEDT −2:00
Ljubljana, Slovenia
46°N03' 014°E31'

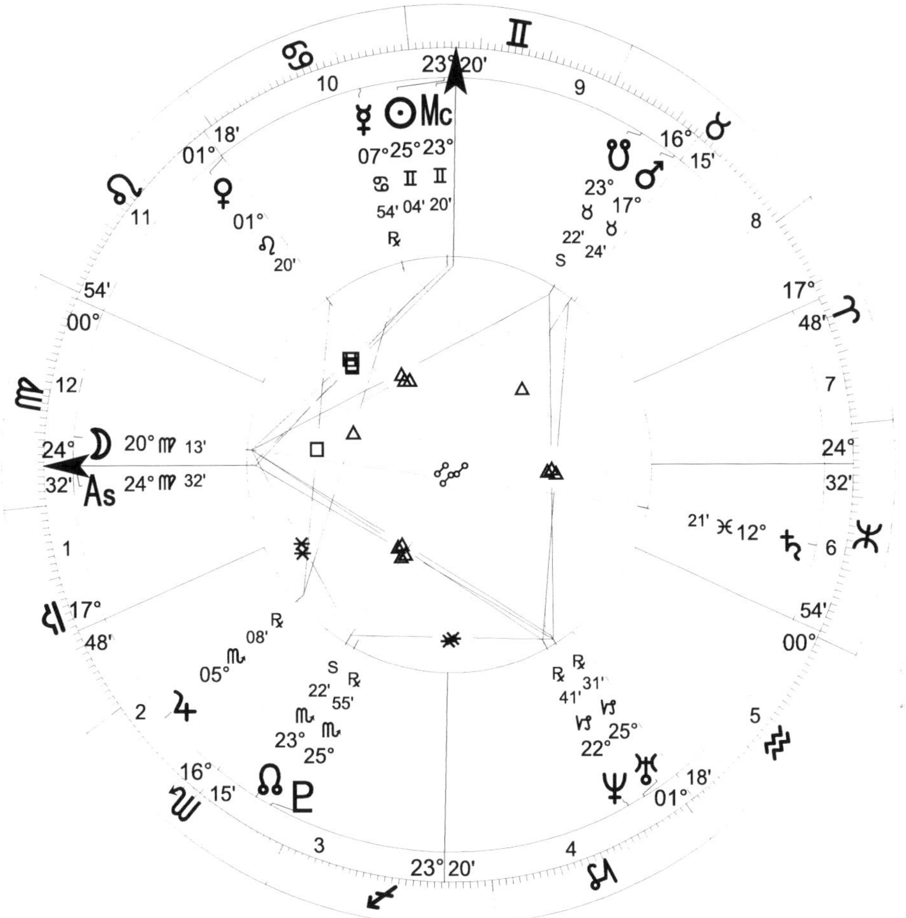

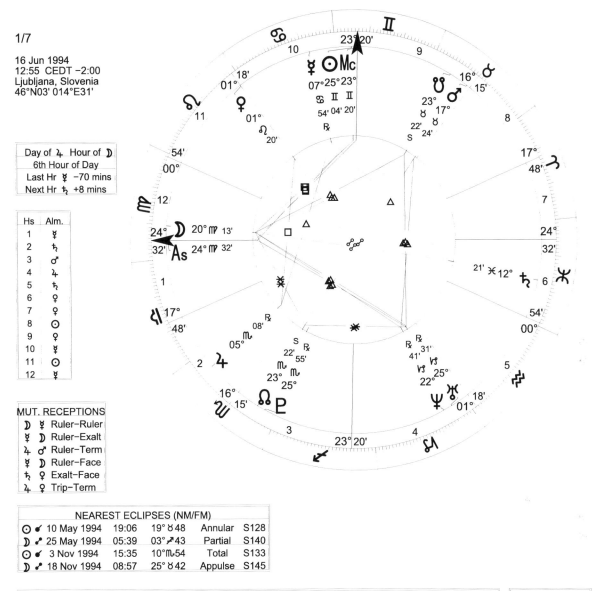

Day of ♃ Hour of ☽
6th Hour of Day
Last Hr ☿ −70 mins
Next Hr ♄ +8 mins

Hs	Alm.
1	☿
2	♄
3	♂
4	♃
5	♄
6	♀
7	♀
8	☉
9	♀
10	☿
11	☉
12	☿

MUT. RECEPTIONS		
☽	☿	Ruler–Ruler
☿	☽	Ruler–Exalt
♃	♂	Ruler–Term
☿	☽	Ruler–Face
♄	♀	Exalt–Face
♃	♀	Trip–Term

NEAREST ECLIPSES (NM/FM)					
☉ ●	10 May 1994	19:06	19° ♉48	Annular	S128
☽ ☍	25 May 1994	05:39	03°♐43	Partial	S140
☉ ●	3 Nov 1994	15:35	10°♏54	Total	S133
☽ ☍	18 Nov 1994	08:57	25° ♉42	Appulse	S145

traditionals.pts

Pt	Long.	Travel	Decl.	Last Stn	Next Stn	Last Stn	Next Stn	F/S	Antiscia	C.Ant.
☽	20°♍13'19"	+13°48'	−00°24'	–	–	–	–	Fast	09°♈46	09°♎46
☉	25°♊04'26"	+57'17"	+23°20'	–	–	–	–	Slow	04°♋55	04°♑55
☿	07°♋54 ℞	−15'54"	+21°14'	−3,7 days	+20 days	08°♋24'40"	29°♊25'05"	Retro	22°♊05	22°♐05
♀	01°♌20	+01°10'	+21°47'	−419 days	+118 days	03°♈44'27"	18°♏00'38"	Fast	28°♉39	28°♏39
♂	17°♉24	+43'44"	+16°27'	−486 days	+200 days	08°♋40'31"	02°♍40'08"	Fast	12°♌35	12°♒35
♃	05°♏08 ℞	−02'47"	−12°02'	−107 days	+15 days	14°♏39'22"	04°♏46'04"	Retro	24°♒51	24°♌51
♄	12°♓21	+00'39"	−08°31'	−231 days	+6,7 days	23°♒38'00"	12°♓24'11"	Slow	17°♎38	17°♈38

MOON ASPECTS			
☽	△	♂	2°37' S
☽	△	♆	2°24' A
☽	△	☋	3°14' A
☽	✶	☊	3°14' A
☽	□	☉	4°50' A
☽	△	♅	5°06' A
☽	✶	♇	7°49' A
☽	☌	♎	9°46' A

ESSENTIAL DIGNITIES

Pt	Ruler	Exalt	Trip	Term	Face	Detri	Fall	Score
☽	☿ m	☿	♀	♃	☿	♃	♀	+0 p
☉	☿	--	♄	♄	☉ +	♃	--	+1
☿	☽ m	♃	♀	♀	♀	♄	♂	+0 p
♀	☉	--	☉	♃	♄	♄	--	−5 p
♂	♀	☽	♀	♃ m	☽	♂ −	--	−10 p
♃	♂	--	♀	♂ m	♂	♀	☽	−5 p
♄	♃	♀	♀	♃	♃	☿	☿	−5 p

ASPECTS			
☉	□	As	0°31' S
♆	△	☋	0°40' S
♆	✶	☊	0°40' S
♅	✶	♇	0°47' A
♅	△	As	0°58' S
☋	△	As	1°10' S
☊	✶	As	1°10' S
As	□	Mc	1°12' S
☉	☌	Mc	1°44' S
♆	△	As	1°51' S

PLANETARY SECT

Planet		Cht	Plc	Sgn	Condition
☉	D	D	D	D	In Hayz
☽	N	D	D	N	
☿	N	D	D	N	
♀	N	D	D	D	Ex Cond
♂	N	D	D	N	
♃	D	D	N	N	
♄	D	D	N	N	

D=Diurnal, N=Nocturnal

1/8: WHEN WILL I FIND A BOYFRIEND?

27 December 2003 at 7:24 p.m. (19:24), Ljubljana, Slovenia
Hour ruler: Saturn

The querent was a friend to whom I sent a Christmas card, and a couple of days later I received her reply, saying that she was very lonely and she wondered if I could tell her, when she would find a boyfriend? I cast the chart for the moment it came into my mailbox, although I read it several hours later. She lives in the close vicinity of Ljubljana, so this is also the location of the horary chart.

Ascendant is in Leo, its ruler the Sun in Capricorn in H5 while her co-ruler Moon is in Pisces on cusp of H8. This Moon placement shows that she's going through some sort of crisis and that she suffers from loneliness and uncertainty, and that she was asking out of deep inner need for more security and a more grounded, stable life. Since she was not so young any more, there was also a fear that she'd stay alone (H8). The Moon's rulership over H12 of isolation and sacrifice tells a story of her passivity, helplessness and reluctance towards actively seeking a man. The conjunction of the Moon with the fixed star Fomalhaut describes her as "mystical" which she indeed is, since esotericism, astrology and related fields hold a great fascination for her.

Planetary hour ruler is Saturn which rules her H7, and this agrees with her concern (partnership). The hour ruler is inharmonious (Saturn has no affinity with Leo, the ascending sign), but as I wrote in the theoretical part of the book, I find that disharmonious hour rulers are not to be taken as a warning (for the chart not being "radical") when they have affinity with the subject matter of the chart. This is the case here, because Saturn rules H7 and the question refers to partnership. My answer was accurate and helped her, and this is one of the charts which prove my point – although I ask you to check out the rule for yourself, because it is not part of traditional teaching.

The Moon is in a close applying sextile with the Sun, her main significator, and this harmonious aspect is followed by a trine to Saturn, H7 ruler. Saturn is retrograde, placed in H11 of hope and desire, but in the sign of the "hidden" H12 and also in a wide conjunction with the cusp of this house. Its detriment is another weakening factor but because it's in the home of the Moon, co-significator of the querent, which applies to it by trine, it promises a partnership to the querent. Remember that aspects act stronger if at least one of the two planets receives the other! It is thus obvious that she'll find a boyfriend, but it's possible that this liaison will suffer some setback or that the couple will be faced with a necessity of concealment or renunciation (H12).

Does H7 tell us anything else? Descendant is in an exact conjunction with Neptune, which supports the weakening influence of Saturn on cusp of H12.

The next (and vital) question is, when will she meet him? From the Moon to Saturn are exactly 6 degrees, which are 6 units of time. The Moon is in a succedent house and cardinal sign, so the most appropriate time unit seemed to be month. Currently, the Moon is still in quick motion, but its pace is slowing down. All this moved me to say that she'd meet him in 6 months, which would be approximately at the end of June or start of July next year. I also mentioned that this partnership might require some hiding or denial, adding that the guy would probably be younger and of pleasing appearance, and that they would be very attracted to each other. This I concluded on the basis of the conjunction of Venus with the cusp of H7 (showing someone of lesser years and of handsome appearance), and the fact that Venus was in sextile with Mars (sex appeal). Although the aspect is a separative one, Neptune which is also in conjunction with the descendant, collects the light of the two planets. Due to the involvement of the "immaterial" Neptune I also mentioned that their relationship could be at least for some time only platonic.

I met the querent in the fall of the next year and she told me that she had met a nice guy pretty much the time I had predicted. He was much younger than her, but after many years they are still together, even though (for a few reasons) they are forced to hide their love - at least from some people.

An interesting additional fact is that this guy was initially her lodger, and you'll notice that Saturn, his significator, also rules H6 which stands for tenants. It is also true that initially they were just friends and that physical love between them developed later.

1/8

27 Dec 2003
19:24 CET −1:00
Ljubljana, Slovenia
46°N03' 014°E31'

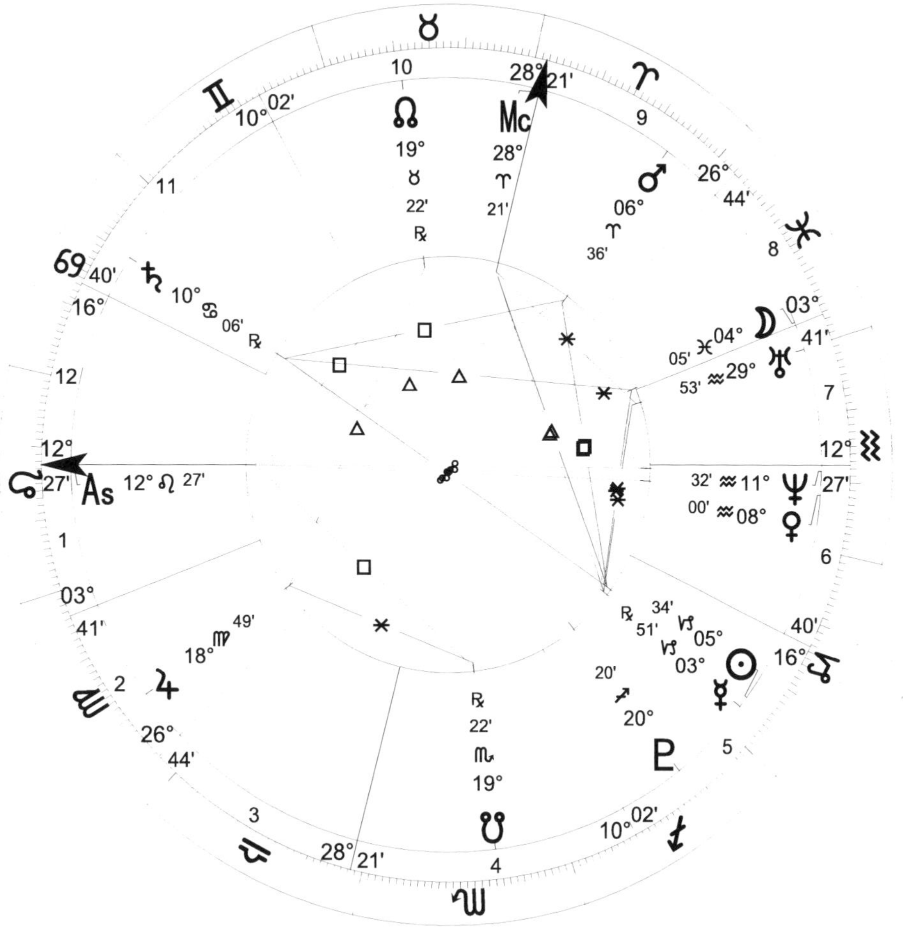

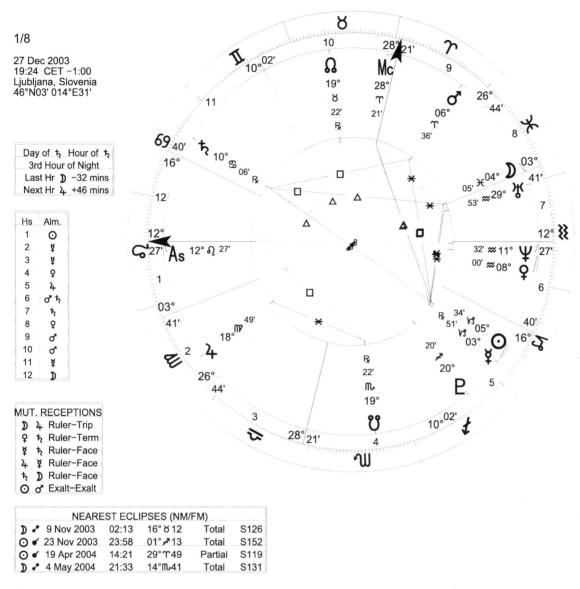

Day of ♄ Hour of ♄
3rd Hour of Night
Last Hr ☽ −32 mins
Next Hr ♃ +46 mins

Hs	Alm.
1	☉
2	☿
3	☿
4	♀
5	♃
6	♂ ♄
7	♄
8	♀
9	♂
10	♂
11	☿
12	☽

MUT. RECEPTIONS	
☽ ♃	Ruler–Trip
♀ ♄	Ruler–Term
☿ ♄	Ruler–Face
♃ ☿	Ruler–Face
♄ ☽	Ruler–Face
☉ ♂	Exalt–Exalt

NEAREST ECLIPSES (NM/FM)				
☽ ☍ 9 Nov 2003	02:13	16°♉12	Total	S126
☉ ☌ 23 Nov 2003	23:58	01°♐13	Total	S152
☉ ☌ 19 Apr 2004	14:21	29°♈49	Partial	S119
☽ ☍ 4 May 2004	21:33	14°♏41	Total	S131

traditionals.pts

Pt	Long.	Travel	Decl.	Last Stn	Next Stn	Last Stn	Next Stn	F/S	Antiscia	C.Ant.
☽	04°♓05'18"	+13°28'	−14°38'	–	–	–	–	Fast	25°♎54	25°♈54
☉	05°♑34'37"	+01°01'	−23°19'	–	–	–	–	Fast	24°♐25	24°♊25
☿	03°♑51 ℞	−01°21'	−20°52'	−10 days	+9,8 days	12°♑33'45"	26°♐16'10"	Retro	26°♐08	26°♊08
♀	08°♒00	+01°13'	−20°02'	−401 days	+142 days	00°♏03'12"	26°♊08'18"	Fast	21°♏59	21°♉59
♂	06°♈36	+36'01"	+02°35'	−91 days	+644 days	00°♓07'06"	23°♉22'20"	Fast	23°♍23	23°♓23
♃	18°♍49	+01'23"	+05°31'	−267 days	+7,2 days	08°♌03'38"	18°♍54'13"	Slow	11°♈10	11°♎10
♄	10°♋06 ℞	−04'56"	+22°22'	−62 days	+70 days	13°♋14'23"	06°♋17'09"	Retro	19°♊53	19°♐53

MOON ASPECTS
☽ ☌ ♓ 4°05' S
☽ ✶ ☿ 0°37' S
☽ ✶ ☉ 1°21' A
☽ △ ♄ 5°46' A

ESSENTIAL DIGNITIES

Pt	Ruler	Exalt	Trip	Term	Face	Detri	Fall	Score
☽	♃	♀	♂	♀	♄	☿	☿	−5 p
☉	♄	♂ m	☽	☿	♃	☽	♃	−1 p
☿	♄	♂	☽	☿ +	♃	☽	♃	+2
♀	♄	--	☿	♀ +	♀ +	☉	--	+3
♂	♂ +	☉ m	♃	♀	♂ +	♀	♄	+10
♃	☿	☿	☽	♃ +	♀	♃ −	♀	−3
♄	☽	♃	♂	♀	☿	♄ −	♂	−10 p

ASPECTS
♃ ✶ ☋ 0°33' A
♃ △ ☊ 0°33' A
☽ ✶ ☿ 0°37' S
♆ ☍ As 0°54' S
☉ □ ♂ 1°02' A
♃ □ ♇ 1°19' S
☽ ✶ ☉ 1°21' A
♀ ✶ ♂ 1°22' S
♅ ✶ Mc 1°32' S
☿ □ ♂ 2°44' S

PLANETARY SECT

Planet	Cht	Plc	Sgn	Condition
☉ D	N	N	N	Ex Cond
☽ N	N	N	N	In Hayz
☿ D	N	D	N	
♀ N	N	D	D	
♂ N	N	N	D	
♃ D	N	D	N	
♄ D	N	N	N	Ex Cond

D=Diurnal, N=Nocturnal

1/9: HOW WILL OUR RELATIONSHIP DEVELOP?

24 October 1994 at 8:26 p.m. (20:26), Ljubljana, Slovenia
Hour Ruler: Saturn

The question was asked by a man who wanted to know how the relationship with his then girlfriend would develop.

The Moon is void-of-course by classical definition which should be a warning: the matter may have "no future"; the answer is risky, the situation may soon change and the answer will no longer be needed, or there's nothing he can do about the situation.

But because the Moon is already within orb of two aspects, it's not really void! There will be a change, sure, because the Moon changes signs. But what exactly might be the nature of change, we can't know until we examine the whole chart. Only by taking into account all the factors we can find an answer.

Hour ruler is Saturn which rules H7 of partnerships - the subject of the question.

So what does this "tricky" chart tell us? The Moon, the querent's ruler, is in H12 and at the end of a sign. The question is obviously linked to a mystery or powerlessness which the querent feels about the matter, but on the other hand it seems that because the Moon is in the easy-going, intellectual sign of Gemini, his worry is probably not so severe; it is rather a superficial concern and may also show his own superficial emotions. This is confirmed by the fact that the Moon is not only in Mercury's sign, but also on a Mercury degree.

Significator of the girl is Saturn, who is also the hour ruler. Its retrograde state indicates that she may avoid him or that she has a secret which might be linked with another man, because Saturn is in a mutual reception with Neptune (provided we take Neptune for the modern ruler of Pisces), which is located in H7. An even stronger indication in this direction is the Sun in the applying trine with Saturn (Sun = another man). Neptune and Uranus in H7 point to a weak foundation upon which this relationship is built, and they suggest that this partnership might soon "dissolve" (Neptune) or break suddenly (Uranus). The Sun which points to the involvement of another man, is in H5 (derived H11 of friendship), and it rules H3 and the derived H9, which shows foreigners (amongst others). The Sun is on its own (Sun) degree so there's an even stronger stress on the involvement of H9.

So, will they stay together? There's only one chart feature speaking in favour of the continuation of the relationship, and this is the ascendant (the querent) in trine with Saturn (her). This aspect is within a one degree orb, therefore very strong, but interplanetary aspects are more important, so this slight affirmation can't outweigh the negative indications which point to the dissolution of their affair.

I replied: *It seems that you are asking this question because you have doubts regarding your girlfriend's fidelity. The chart shows that she may be avoiding you, perhaps because she's interested in someone else. This guy might be a foreigner or a friend who lives abroad. It's hard to say with certainty how your relationship will develop. I'm quite sure that your situation will soon change for the better (the Moon will soon enter its own sign which indicates an imminent improvement for the querent! - Author's Note), but there's a considerable chance that you'll not stay with this girl. I think you'll meet someone new with whom you can have a happier relationship. Your present girlfriend appears to be quite heavily involved with someone else.*

I saw the other woman who may come into his life, in the Sun with which the Moon will complete a trine before she reaches Saturn. Although the Sun in the chart indicates another man, because it is in aspect with Saturn (the girl), it may also represent another woman whom the querent will shortly meet, because the Moon, significator of the querent, applies to it too. (Remember that every planet in a horary chart can have several functions!)

When? The Moon will trine the Sun in 2.5 degrees which are equivalent to 2.5 units of time, but we can't judge the time unit with certainty because the Moon changes signs before the completion of the aspect.

In reply, the querent said that my judgment was perfectly valid in the sense that he knew that his girlfriend was being wooed by her ex-boyfriend who was living abroad, but had recently re-established contact with her. His worry was certainly connected with this man, which the chart so clearly revealed.

The final outcome of the question is not known because the querent never called back to confirm or negate my prediction, but I'm including this case because of several interesting features which make it a nice teaching example.

1/9

24 Oct 1994
20:26 CET −1:00
Ljubljana, Slovenia
46°N03' 014°E31'

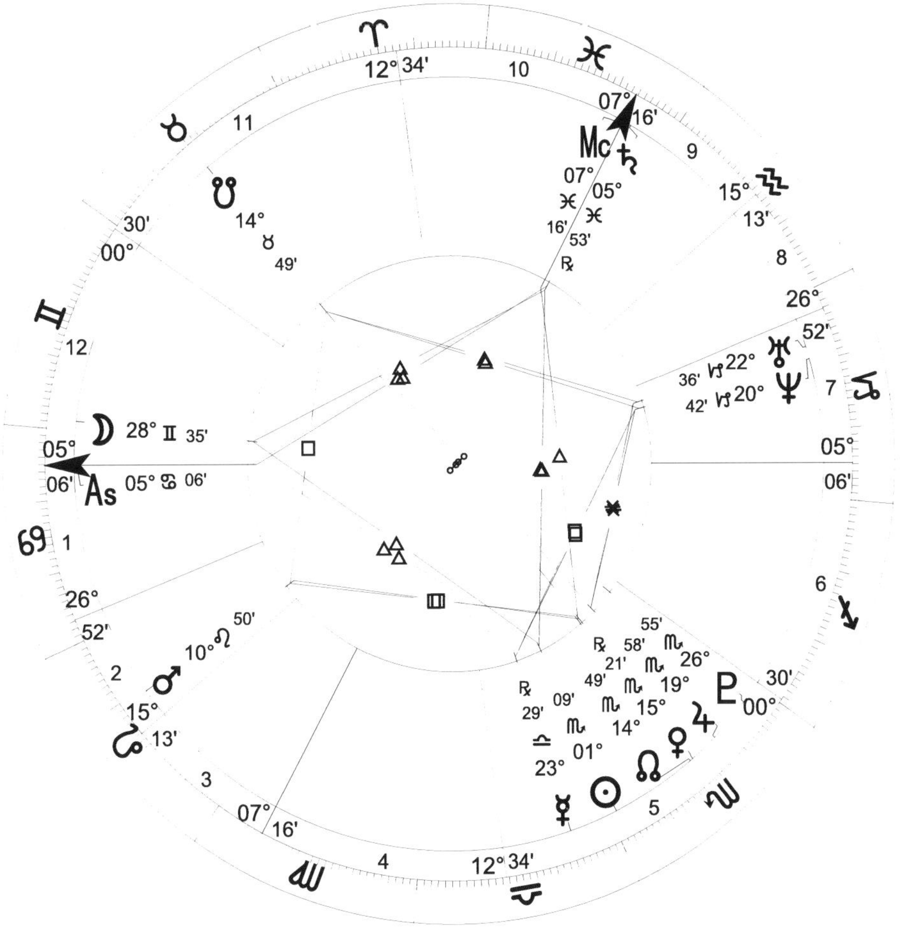

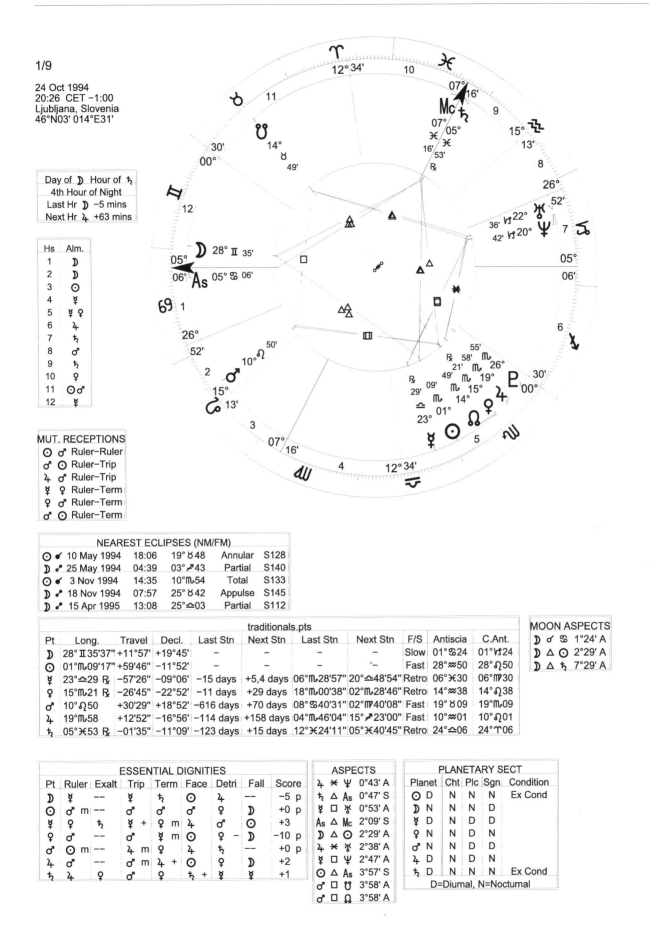

Day of ☽ Hour of ♄
4th Hour of Night
Last Hr ☽ −5 mins
Next Hr ♃ +63 mins

Hs	Alm.
1	☽
2	☽
3	☉
4	☿
5	☿ ♀
6	♃
7	♄
8	♂
9	♄
10	♀
11	☉♂
12	☿

MUT. RECEPTIONS
☉ ♂ Ruler–Ruler
♂ ☉ Ruler–Trip
♃ ♂ Ruler–Trip
☿ ♀ Ruler–Term
♀ ♂ Ruler–Term
♂ ☉ Ruler–Term

NEAREST ECLIPSES (NM/FM)					
☉ ●	10 May 1994	18:06	19°♉48	Annular	S128
☽ ☍	25 May 1994	04:39	03°♐43	Partial	S140
☉ ●	3 Nov 1994	14:35	10°♏54	Total	S133
☽ ☍	18 Nov 1994	07:57	25°♉42	Appulse	S145
☽ ☍	15 Apr 1995	13:08	25°♎03	Partial	S112

traditionals.pts										
Pt	Long.	Travel	Decl.	Last Stn	Next Stn	Last Stn	Next Stn	F/S	Antiscia	C.Ant.
☽	28°♊35'37"	+11°57'	+19°45'	–	–	–	–	Slow	01°♋24	01°♑24
☉	01°♏09'17"	+59'46"	−11°52'	–	–	–	–	Fast	28°♒50	28°♌50
☿	23°♎29 ℞	−57'26"	−09°06'	−15 days	+5,4 days	06°♏28'57"	20°♎48'54"	Retro	06°♓30	06°♍30
♀	15°♏21 ℞	−26'45"	−22°52'	−11 days	+29 days	18°♏00'38"	02°♏28'46"	Retro	14°♒38	14°♌38
♂	10°♌50	+30'29"	+18°52'	−616 days	+70 days	08°♋40'31"	02°♍40'08"	Fast	19°♉09	19°♏09
♃	19°♏58	+12'52"	−16°56'	−114 days	+158 days	04°♏46'04"	15°♐23'00"	Fast	10°♒01	10°♌01
♄	05°♓53 ℞	−01'35"	−11°09'	−123 days	+15 days	12°♓24'11"	05°♓40'45"	Retro	24°♎06	24°♈06

MOON ASPECTS
☽ ☌ ♋ 1°24' A
☽ △ ☉ 2°29' A
☽ △ ♄ 7°29' A

ESSENTIAL DIGNITIES								
Pt	Ruler	Exalt	Trip	Term	Face	Detri	Fall	Score
☽	☿	--	☿	♄	☉	♃	--	−5 p
☉	♂ m	--	♂	♂	♂	♀	☽	+0 p
☿	♀	♄	☿ +	♀ m	♃	♂	☉	+3
♀	♂	--	♂	☿ m	☉	♀ −	☽	−10 p
♂	☉ m	--	♃ m	♀	♃	♄	--	+0 p
♃	♂	--	♂ m	♃ +	☉	♀	☽	+2
♄	♃	♀	♂	♀	♄ +	☿	☿	+1

ASPECTS
♃ ⚹ ♆ 0°43' A
♄ △ As 0°47' S
☿ □ ♅ 0°53' A
As △ Mc 2°09' S
☽ △ ☉ 2°29' A
♃ ⚹ ♅ 2°38' A
☿ □ ♆ 2°47' A
☉ △ As 3°57' S
♂ □ ☋ 3°58' A
♂ □ ☊ 3°58' A

PLANETARY SECT				
Planet	Cht	Plc	Sgn	Condition
☉ D	N	N	N	Ex Cond
☽ N	N	N	D	
☿ D	N	D	D	
♀ N	N	D	N	
♂ N	N	D	D	
♃ D	N	D	N	
♄ D	N	N	N	Ex Cond
D=Diurnal, N=Nocturnal				

1/10: WHY IS MY HUSBAND JEALOUS?

31 March 1995 at 11:04 a.m., Murska Sobota, Slovenia
Hour ruler: Jupiter

A querent complained that her husband was very jealous. She said he had no reason for that and he was evil and tried to make life hard for her. She wondered why he was doing that and was it ever going to change?

She's shown by the Moon, H1 ruler, while her husband's significator is Saturn, ruler of H7. Hour ruler is Jupiter and planetary hour is harmonious because Jupiter has affinity with Cancer, the ascending sign.

The Moon is in Aries in H10, which describes her as courageous, impulsive, passionate and perhaps even commanding. The Moon is in a separating conjunction with the Sun and a separating trine with its dispositor Mars, and it applies by trine to Jupiter, placed in H6 and ruling both H6 and H10. As this planet is also the hour ruler, it thus becomes extremely important and relevant for the interpretation of the horary chart.

Her situation? It appears that she's currently very busy (Moon in H10) and in contact with several men with whom she's probably linked via her job or business-related issues. This is shown by Moon's aspects to "male" planets associated with H6 and H10. Are they connected in any other way? That's a bit hard to say. Venus, H5 (love affairs) ruler is not involved in the configuration but the Moon separates from Mars, ruler of the intercepted H5 sign (Scorpio) which might indicate that she's had an affair. As we know, intercepted signs often show hidden things which the querent doesn't want to confess or reveal. (Which is obviously true because she said that her husband had no reason for jealousy.) Combust Moon also points to secrecy and "hidden facts". This woman obviously has secrets, but whatever they are, she'll not say.

Her husband's ruler Saturn is placed in the suspicious sign of Pisces. Saturn is not in aspect with the Moon nor with its dispositor Mars, but it squares Jupiter, his own dispositor and significator of his wife's co-worker(s). Saturn has no essential dignity, suggesting that he lacks confidence, but nevertheless behaves in a domineering way (H10). His placement on cusp of H10 also shows that his thoughts are with her job and/or work. It seems that his jealousy is linked to her success, but also to a male who works with the querent, or to her male co-workers in general. Jupiter, to which the Moon applies, could in the context of the question, show a colleague who plays an important role in her life, and who is the reason for her husband's jealousy.

Your husband's jealousy is apparently related to your work. It seems that you invest a lot of time and energy into the achievement of your professional goals and that you are also in excellent relations with your male colleagues. There is one among them with whom you are on particularly good terms. It seems that this really bothers your husband! If you want to improve your marriage, you should discuss those issues with him and assure him of your fidelity!

She confirmed all that I said, but also stressed that her relations with colleagues were of a purely business nature. I don't know if she listened to my advice but the chart shows an alarming discord between her and her husband, based on differing interests and characters, therefore it's quite possible that their relationship worsened and that they were not able to bridge the gap.

1/10

31 Mar 1995
11:04 CEDT −2:00
Murska sobota, Slovenia
46°N40' 016°E10'

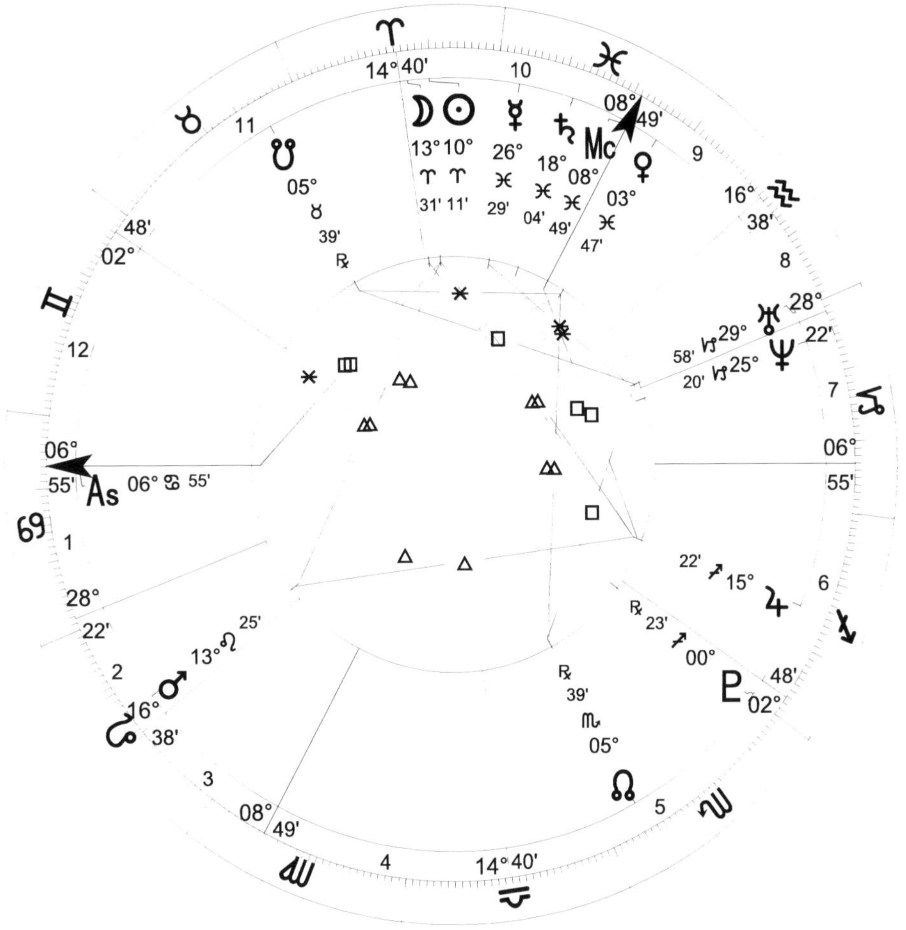

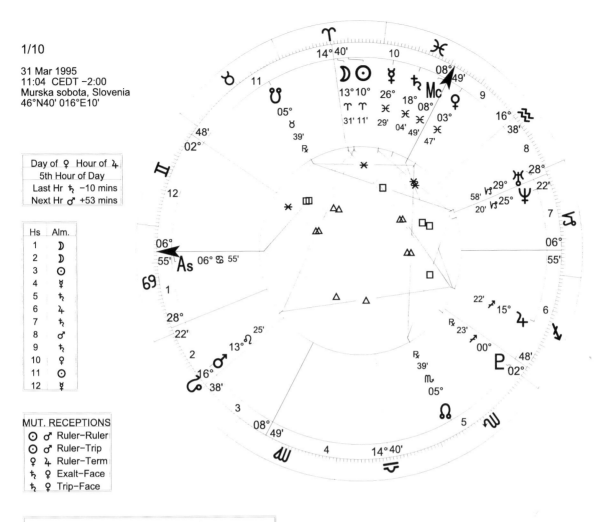

Day of ♀ Hour of ♃
5th Hour of Day
Last Hr ♄ −10 mins
Next Hr ♂ +53 mins

Hs	Alm.
1	☽
2	☽
3	☉
4	☿
5	♄
6	♃
7	♄
8	♂
9	♄
10	♀
11	☉
12	☿

MUT. RECEPTIONS
☉ ♂ Ruler–Ruler
☉ ♂ Ruler–Trip
♀ ♃ Ruler–Term
♄ ♀ Exalt–Face
♄ ♀ Trip–Face

NEAREST ECLIPSES (NM/FM)					
☉ ☌	3 Nov 1994	15:35	10°♏54	Total	S133
☽ ☍	18 Nov 1994	08:57	25°♉42	Appulse	S145
☽ ☍	15 Apr 1995	14:08	25°♎03	Partial	S112
☉ ☌	29 Apr 1995	19:36	08°♉56	Annular	S138

traditionals.pts

Pt	Long.	Travel	Decl.	Last Stn	Next Stn	Last Stn	Next Stn	F/S	Antiscia	C.Ant.
☽	13°♈31'45"	+12°32'	+07°09'	–	–	–	–	Slow	16°♍28	16°♓28
☉	10°♈11'17"	+59'16"	+04°02'	–	–	–	–	Fast	19°♍48	19°♓48
☿	26°♓29	+01°47'	−03°24'	−43 days	+53 days	05°♒37'16"	18°♊21'42"	Fast	03°♎30	03°♈30
♀	03°♓47	+01°11'	−10°50'	−127 days	+415 days	02°♏28'46"	28°♊17'52"	Fast	26°♎12	26°♈12
♂	13°♌25	+04'41"	+19°48'	−6,7 days	+677 days	13°♌09'54"	05°♎55'22"	Slow	16°♉34	16°♏34
♃	15°♐22	+00'12"	−21°49'	−272 days	+1,1 days	04°♏46'04"	15°♐23'00"	Slow	14°♑37	14°♋37
♄	18°♓04	+07'01"	−06°22'	−142 days	+96 days	05°♓40'45"	24°♓45'07"	Fast	11°♎55	11°♈55

MOON ASPECTS
☽ ☌ ♈ 13°31' S
☽ ☌ ☉ 3°52' S
☽ △ ♂ 0°17' S
☽ △ ♃ 1°54' A
☽ □ As 6°36' A

ESSENTIAL DIGNITIES

Pt	Ruler	Exalt	Trip	Term	Face	Detri	Fall	Score
☽	♂	☉	☉	☿	☉	♀	♄	−5 p
☉	♂ m	☉ +	☉ +	♀	☉ +	♀	♄	+13
☿	♃	♀	♀	♂	♂	☿ −	☿ −	−14 p
♀	♃	♀ +	♀ +	♀ +	♄	☿	☿	+9
♂	☉ m	--	☉	♄	♃	♄	--	+0 p
♃	♃ +	--	☉	♀	☽	☿	--	+5
♄	♃	♀	♀	☿	♃	☿	☿	−5 p

ASPECTS
☽ △ ♂ 0°17' S
♅ ⚹ ♇ 0°41' S
☿ ⚹ ♆ 1°11' S
☋ ⚹ As 1°16' S
☊ △ As 1°16' S
♂ △ ♃ 1°50' A
♀ △ ☊ 1°51' A
♀ ⚹ ☋ 1°51' A
As △ Mc 1°54' S
☽ △ ♃ 1°54' A

PLANETARY SECT

Planet	Cht	Plc	Sgn	Condition
☉ D	D	D	D	In Hayz
☽ N	D	D	D	Ex Cond
☿ D	D	D	N	
♀ N	D	D	N	
♂ N	D	N	D	
♃ D	D	N	D	
♄ D	D	D	N	

D=Diurnal, N=Nocturnal

1/11: WILL SHE DECIDE FOR ME OR FOR HIM?

28 May 1996 at 2:52 p.m (14:52) in Ljubljana, Slovenia
Hour ruler: Mars

The querent was in love with a girl who was already in a steady relationship, but had been seeing the querent also for the last few months. The day before he asked the question, the girl's boyfriend ditched her because he learnt that she was hiding something, and he suspected that she was cheating on him. She was shocked by her boyfriend's decision and told the querent that she must take some time to think things over, so she asked him to leave her alone until she made up her mind. Who would she choose, he wondered? Would she and her partner reconcile, or would she finally choose the querent?

Saturn in H7 is a traditional "caution against judgment", but not when the question refers to H7 (the partnership house), because in such cases Saturn refers to the person asked about, and partnership as such. Saturn in this house, however, is often a negative indication and can complicate matters and suppress harmonious development in this sphere.

Hour ruler is disharmonious but is related to the question because Mars rules H7.

The querent is shown by Venus, ruler of the ascending sign (Libra). Part rulers are the Moon (co-significator) and Saturn as almuten of the ascendant, while the girl is shown by Mars (which is also the hour ruler) and Saturn which is in conjunction with the descendant, but also by the Sun which is almuten of the descending sign. Can Saturn represent both parties? Yes! Such a planet has even more weight in the question, therefore it deserves utmost consideration!

Moon in the first house shows that the matter is of great importance to the querent who is very emotional about it. But his main significator Venus is retrograde, meaning it would be better if he withdrew. It warns him that if he proceeds, he risks a defeat, and advises him that it would be better, under the circumstances, to wait for her decision, without interfering. This is confirmed by his co-significator Saturn which is on cusp of H7 (she means a lot to him), but in its fall (weakness, insecurity). Since the same planet also shows her, it also reflects her own doubts and a sense of defeat.

What about the other significators? Mars (her) is in Taurus; Venus (he) accepts it in its home sign, confirming that she means a lot to him and that he wants her. But Mars is in conjunction with Mercury which represents another person - probably her boyfriend. Normally, the conjunction would be a separating one because Mercury is in a later degree than Mars, but at that time, Mercury was extremely slow because it was just changing course. It is marked by S – stationary – in the chart, but a closer look reveals that it has just turned its course from retrograde to direct. Its recent change of direction clearly shows the boyfriend's recent decision to leave the girl. But Mars will soon catch up with it, showing that she'll try to reconnect and be with him again. This is confirmed by the fact that the Moon (the querent) doesn't apply neither to Mars nor to Saturn (which due to its placement in H7 partly represents her) - from which it even separates by an opposition, reflecting the querent's recent painful experience with her.

I explained to him the situation as I saw it, telling him that the girl was obviously more closely connected with her steady boyfriend with whom she was trying to reconcile, and that I couldn't see their future together.

He later confirmed that the girl did not choose him, and that her need for some privacy was actually a "leave-me-alone-forever" note.

1/11

28 May 1996
14:52 CEDT −2:00
Ljubljana, Slovenia
46°N03' 014°E31'

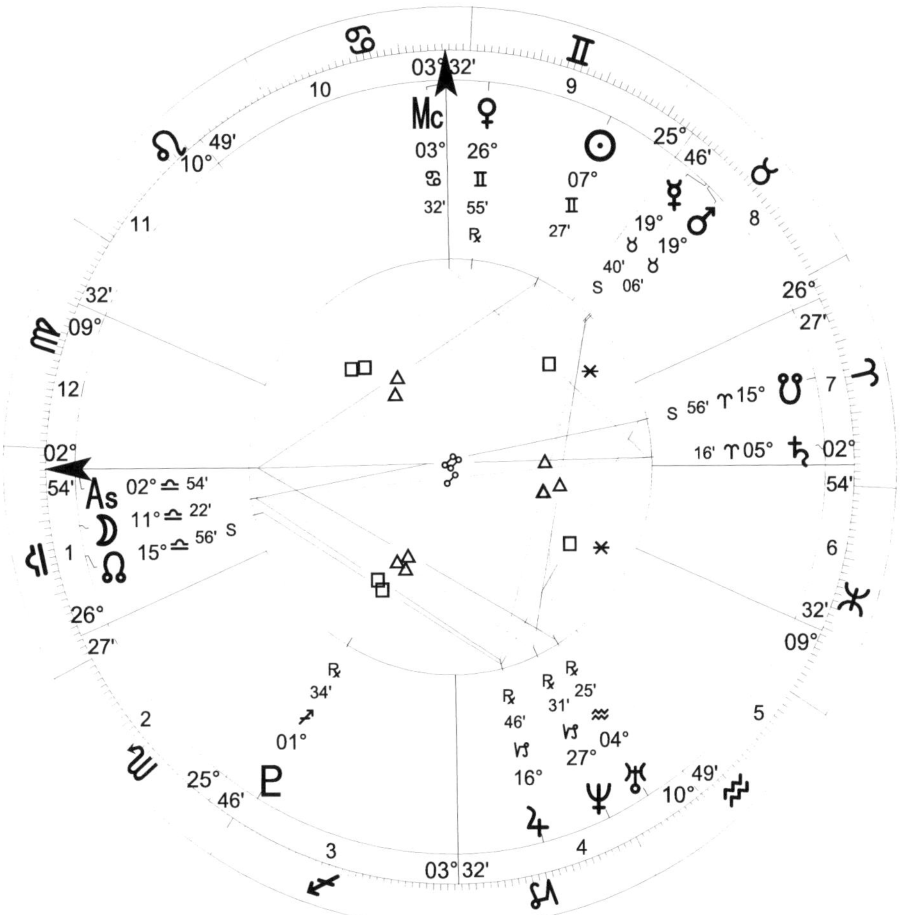

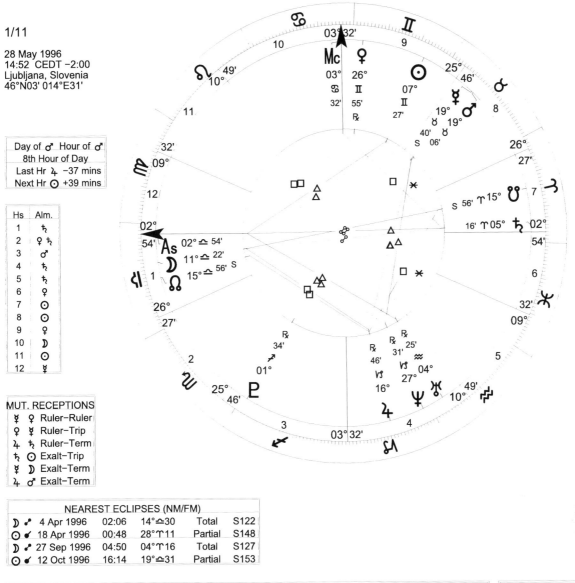

Day of ♂ Hour of ♂
8th Hour of Day
Last Hr ♃ −37 mins
Next Hr ☉ +39 mins

Hs	Alm.
1	♄
2	♀ ♄
3	♂
4	♄
5	♄
6	♀
7	☉
8	☉
9	♀
10	☽
11	☉
12	☿

MUT. RECEPTIONS
☿ ♀ Ruler–Ruler
♀ ☿ Ruler–Trip
♃ ♄ Ruler–Term
♄ ☉ Exalt–Trip
☿ ☽ Exalt–Term
♃ ♂ Exalt–Term

NEAREST ECLIPSES (NM/FM)				
☽ ☍ 4 Apr 1996	02:06	14°♎30	Total	S122
☉ ☌ 18 Apr 1996	00:48	28°♈11	Partial	S148
☽ ☍ 27 Sep 1996	04:50	04°♈16	Total	S127
☉ ☌ 12 Oct 1996	16:14	19°♎31	Partial	S153

traditionals.pts

Pt	Long.	Travel	Decl.	Last Stn	Next Stn	Last Stn	Next Stn	F/S	Antiscia	C.Ant.
☽	11°♎22'33"	+12°59'	−04°52'	–	–	–	–	Slow	18°♓37	18°♍37
☉	07°♊27'52"	+57'32"	+21°33'	–	–	–	–	Slow	22°♋32	22°♑32
☿	19°♉40	+03'19"	+14°11'	−17h 50m	+98 days	19°♉38'56"	03°♎29'20"	Stat	10°♌19	10°♒19
♀	26°♊55 ℞	−19'53"	+25°45'	−8,3 days	+34 days	28°♊17'52"	11°♊46'32"	Retro	03°♋04	03°♑04
♂	19°♉06	+43'46"	+17°15'	−430 days	+253 days	13°♌09'54"	05°♎55'22"	Fast	10°♌53	10°♒53
♃	16°♑46 ℞	−04'19"	−22°22'	−23 days	+98 days	17°♑39'18"	07°♑49'11"	Retro	13°♐13	13°♊13
♄	05°♈16	+04'42"	+00°05'	−188 days	+51 days	17°♓59'42"	07°♈24'02"	Fast	24°♍43	24°♓43

MOON ASPECTS
☽ ☌ ♎ 11°22' S
☽ △ ☉ 3°54' S
☽ ☌ ☊ 4°35' A
☽ ☍ ☋ 4°35' A
☽ □ ♃ 5°23' A
☽ □ Mc 7°50' A

ESSENTIAL DIGNITIES

Pt	Ruler	Exalt	Trip	Term	Face	Detri	Fall	Score
☽	♀	♄	♄	☿	♄	♂	☉	−5 p
☉	☿	--	♄ m	♃	♃	♃	--	−5 p
☿	♀ m	☽	♀	♃	☽	♂	--	+0 p
♀	☿ m	--	♄	♄	☉	♃	--	+0 p
♂	♀	☽	♀	♃	☽	♂ −	--	−10 p
♃	♄	♂	♀	♀	♂	☽	♃ −	−9 p
♄	♂	☉	☉ m	♃	♂	♀	♄ −	−9 p

ASPECTS
♇ ✶ As 0°22' S
As □ Mc 0°38' S
♃ □ ☊ 0°49' A
♃ □ ☋ 0°49' A
♄ ✶ ♅ 0°50' S
♅ △ As 1°31' S
♄ □ Mc 1°44' S
☉ ✶ ♄ 2°12' S
♂ △ ♃ 2°19' S
☿ △ ♃ 2°49' S

PLANETARY SECT

Planet	Cht	Plc	Sgn	Condition
☉ D	D	D	D	In Hayz
☽ N	D	N	D	
☿ D	D	D	N	
♀ N	D	D	D	Ex Cond
♂ N	D	D	N	
♃ D	D	N	N	
♄ D	D	D	D	In Hayz

D=Diurnal, N=Nocturnal

1/12: WILL WE BE TOGETHER AGAIN, AND WHEN?

February 12, 1999 at 8:42 p.m (20:42), Ljubljana, Slovenia
Hour ruler: Venus

I asked this question after my boyfriend left me. We were together for less than a year. It was an on-and-off relationship, but I grew very fond of him. Unfortunately, he often did not respond to my calls and we were also not seeing each other frequently because he lived a solitary life in a remote area. At the time of the question, I had not seen him nor heard of him for more than a month. Those were the times without mobile phones and internet, and because we had only one mutual friend, who was more of an acquaintance than a friend and I didn't even have his contacts, I didn't know who to ask about his whereabouts, or why he never picked up the phone. I hoped that he would change his mind with regard to our relationship because we spent some wonderful time together. I had no idea why he suddenly withdrew and where he was gone.

Hour ruler is Venus, and because the ascendant is in Libra, the sign of Venus, the chart is radical and suitable for judgment. Venus, my significator, is in Pisces, the romantic water sign which adequately describes my deep emotions and the desire for love. Venus is exalted in Pisces which was very good; I thought that my "essential dignity" surely meant that I was worthy of his love! But the unfortunate placement of Venus in H6 also shows my "accidental helplessness", a feeling of being lost, hopeless and also "pathless" - you will notice that Venus is also void-of-course!

This is confirmed by the Moon, my co-significator, which is in Capricorn (detriment). I was really very worried and sad, and this placement adequately describes my then emotional state. I'd like to point out that this is a night chart. In night charts it is particularly unfortunate if the Moon is below the horizon and essentially weak.

Let us now look at Saturn, almuten of the ascendant and my additional co-significator. This planet is also placed badly because it is in the unfortunate H8 (crisis, loss), in its fall and out of sect (a diurnal planet above the horizon in a night chart). The chart therefore clearly reflects the distress and worry that I felt.

He is represented by Mars, the H7 ruler. Mars is also almuten of the descendant and therefore his only significator. It is found in Scorpio, where it has its home, triplicity, term and face, giving him a maximum essential dignity score. In this context, the essential strength of the significator reflects the great value that he had for me, since I desperately wanted to see him and be with him again, besides showing his honesty and good intentions. But the planet is very slow, because it'll turn retrograde 33 days after the question. Recall what Ibn Ezra says about slow planets: *A planet slow in its course likens to an exhausted man who does not have the strength to carry on.* Mars is also in the derived H8 which could mean that he is going through some kind of crisis.

What is the relationship between the main significators? They are not in aspect, but are connected by the Moon which translates light from Mars to Venus. Mars receives the Moon in its exaltation and Venus in its triplicity, confirming the power he had over me, but it is in the detriment of Venus and in the fall of the Moon, which points to his inability to communicate with me, and to the inability of the Moon (which has some essential strength in Capricorn only by triplicity) to effectively translate light from Mars to Venus. Nevertheless, I hoped that the translation would work and indicate a positive result.

I checked the time by the distance from Moon to Venus which is nearly exactly seven degrees. This could ideally mean seven hours, but it could also be seven days or seven weeks. More time could certainly not elapse until our reconnection because the Moon is in an angular house and a cardinal sign.

Seven hours passed, seven days passed and seven weeks passed, but he didn't call. On April 14 I finally managed to find our joint acquaintance who was his good friend; he'll certainly be able to explain what is going on and why my (ex) boyfriend never answers the phone?

He told me that my love had committed suicide at the end of March. The funeral was almost exactly seven weeks from the time of my question.

When I came back to my senses and looked at the horary again, it struck me as immensely clear. The Moon (in the dark Capricorn) was in H4 which marks "the end of the matter" and is associated with graves. Its dispositor Saturn is in the H8 of death, while Mars (him) is "at the end of its path" (very slow) in the derived H8 (his death), while at the same time, due to its being in all of its essential dignities, also completely out-of-touch with the other planets. But there is one planet applying to Mars – Mercury, approaching it by a trine, but it is in its detriment and fall and it rules his derived H6 of diseases, and is located in Pisces and on cusp of his H12 (psychological problems, mental illness, hospitals). As I later learned, he spent some time before his death in a mental institution where he had often been treated in the years before we met. His illness was unknown to me because he skillfully concealed it.

Let us also have a look at Jupiter, which is in conjunction with the cusp of H7 and should therefore be considered as an additional significator of the querent. It is on the 29th degree of Pisces, the place of the fixed star Scheat – a portent of disasters and accidents, but also associated with suicide.

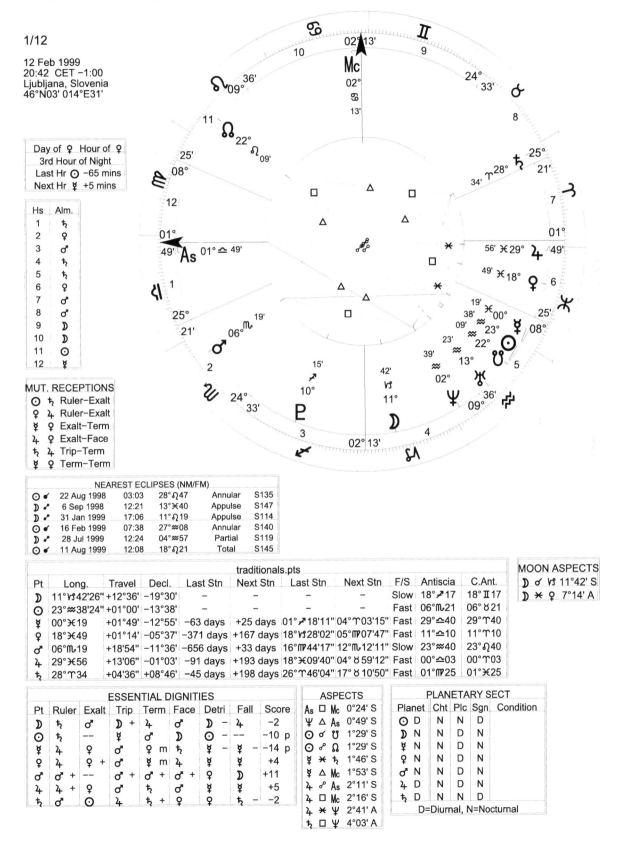

1/12

12 Feb 1999
20:42 CET −1:00
Ljubljana, Slovenia
46°N03' 014°E31'

Day of ♀ Hour of ♀
3rd Hour of Night
Last Hr ☉ −65 mins
Next Hr ☿ +5 mins

Hs	Alm.
1	♄
2	♀
3	♂
4	♄
5	♄
6	♀
7	♂
8	♂
9	☽
10	☽
11	☉
12	☿

MUT. RECEPTIONS	
☉ ♄	Ruler−Exalt
♀ ♃	Ruler−Exalt
☿ ♀	Exalt−Term
♃ ♀	Exalt−Face
♄ ♃	Trip−Term
☿ ♀	Term−Term

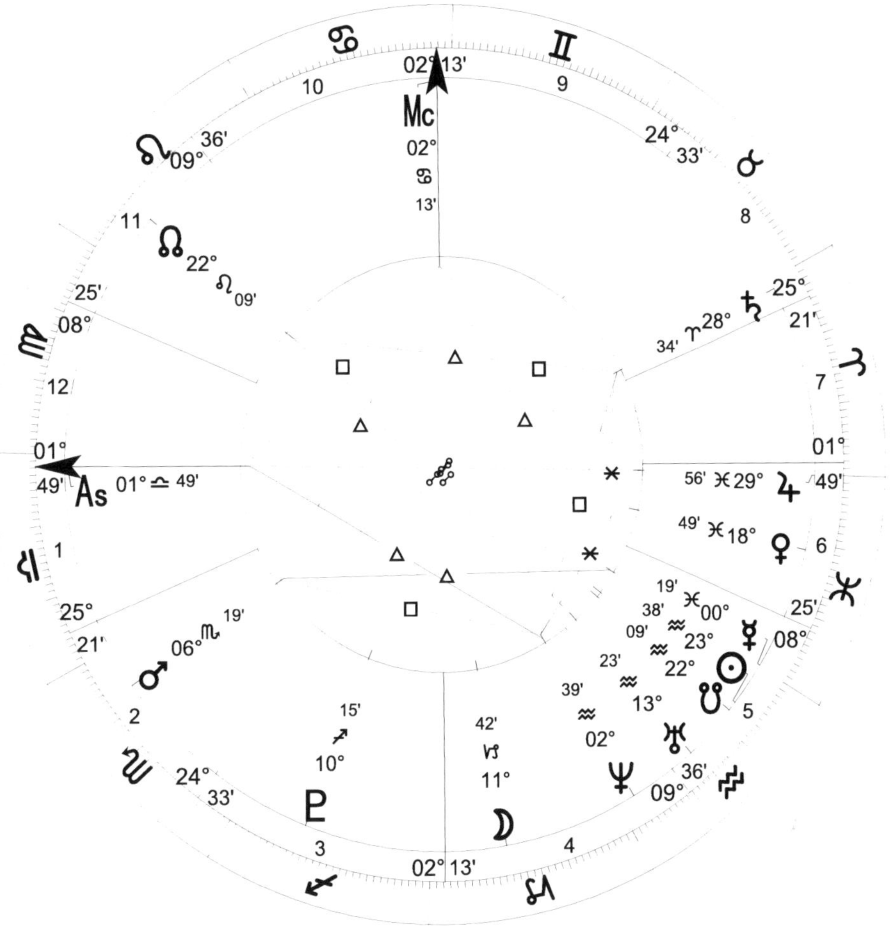

NEAREST ECLIPSES (NM/FM)					
☉ ☌	22 Aug 1998	03:03	28°♌47	Annular	S135
☽ ☍	6 Sep 1998	12:21	13°♓40	Appulse	S147
☽ ☍	31 Jan 1999	17:06	11°♌19	Appulse	S114
☉ ☌	16 Feb 1999	07:38	27°♒08	Annular	S140
☽ ☍	28 Jul 1999	12:24	04°♒57	Partial	S119
☉ ☌	11 Aug 1999	12:08	18°♌21	Total	S145

traditionals.pts

Pt	Long.	Travel	Decl.	Last Stn	Next Stn	Last Stn	Next Stn	F/S	Antiscia	C.Ant.
☽	11°♑42'26"	+12°36'	−19°30'	–	–	–	–	Slow	18°♐17	18°♊17
☉	23°♒38'24"	+01°00'	−13°38'	–	–	–	–	Fast	06°♏21	06°♉21
☿	00°♓19	+01°49'	−12°55'	−63 days	+25 days	01°♐18'11"	04°♈03'15"	Fast	29°♎40	29°♈40
♀	18°♓49	+01°14'	−05°37'	−371 days	+167 days	18°♑28'02"	05°♍07'47"	Fast	11°♎10	11°♈10
♂	06°♏19	+18'54"	−11°36'	−656 days	+33 days	16°♍44'17"	12°♏12'11"	Slow	23°♒40	23°♌40
♃	29°♓56	+13'06"	−01°03'	−91 days	+193 days	18°♓09'40"	04°♉59'12"	Fast	00°♎03	00°♈03
♄	28°♈34	+04'36"	+08°46'	−45 days	+198 days	26°♈46'04"	17°♉10'50"	Fast	01°♍25	01°♓25

MOON ASPECTS
☽ ☌ ♑ 11°42' S
☽ ⚹ ♀ 7°14' A

ESSENTIAL DIGNITIES

Pt	Ruler	Exalt	Trip	Term	Face	Detri	Fall	Score
☽	♄	♂	☽ +	♃	♂	☽ −	♃	−2
☉	♄	--	☿	♂	☽	☉ −	--	−10 p
☿	♃	♀	♂	♀ m	♄	☿ −	☿ −	−14 p
♀	♃	♀ +	♂	☿ m	♃	☿	☿	+4
♂	♂ +	--	♂ +	♂ +	♂ +	♀	☽	+11
♃	♃ +	♀	♂	♄	♂	☿	☿	+5
♄	♂	☉	♃	♄ +	♀	♀	♄ −	−2

ASPECTS
As □ Mc 0°24' S
♆ △ As 0°49' S
☉ ☌ ☋ 1°29' S
☉ ☍ ☊ 1°29' S
☿ ⚹ ♄ 1°46' S
☿ △ Mc 1°53' S
♃ ☍ As 2°11' S
♃ □ Mc 2°16' S
♃ ⚹ ♆ 2°41' A
♄ □ ♆ 4°03' A

PLANETARY SECT

Planet	Cht	Plc	Sgn	Condition
☉ D	N	N	D	
☽ N	N	D	N	
☿ N	N	D	N	
♀ N	N	D	N	
♂ N	N	D	N	
♃ D	N	D	N	
♄ D	N	N	D	
D=Diurnal, N=Nocturnal				

PREGNANCY

Am I pregnant?

This question used to be fairly frequent, but it is becoming increasingly rare today because we have ever more reliable medical tests for early detection of pregnancy. With a bit of humor, I can add that the advantage of the horary test is that it is even earlier! Theoretically, I think it perfectly acceptable and valid that a woman calls her astrologer immediately after the intercourse and asks her/him whether she has finally become pregnant.

Another advantage of the horary "test" over others is that it can also be used by women's partners, relatives and friends. *Is my girlfriend pregnant? When will my wife get pregnant?* You might say that pregnancy is a private matter for the woman and as such no business of others. I will not go into ethics in this place, as this would go beyond the purpose of this book. Ethics has been covered pretty thoroughly in the introductory passages of the Theory part of this book, so there is no need to repeat it here. The way I see it, there is just one question, specific to this chapter, which calls for a special ethical consideration, and this is *Should I keep my child, or should I abort*? I am covering it in Case 2/3.

Horary questions, belonging to this group, can also relate to the course of pregnancy, to the (approximate) date of birth and to the sex of the unborn child. It is true that some of these questions are a hard nut to crack, but if we follow the rules and sincerely want to help the querent, there is practically no limit to what we can do!

SIGNIFICATORS

- H1 (radix or derived) and the Moon – the querent
- H5 (radix or derived) – pregnancy, foetus
- Moon – the natural significator of pregnancy
- Jupiter – the natural significator of fertility

The Moon is particularly important in pregnancy charts. Although it acts as a co-significator in all kinds of horaries, its role in pregnancy charts is even more crucial, therefore we must give it absolute priority in interpretation. As the example cases will show, pregnancy cannot go well if the Moon is applying to difficult (disharmonious) aspects with planets, including the trans-Saturnians (Uranus, Neptune and Pluto).

ZODIACAL SIGNS

Pregnancy horaries make much use of the traditional distribution of signs into fruitful, partly fruitful and barren (fertile, partly fertile and infertile):
- fruitful signs: Cancer, Scorpio, Pisces
- partly fruitful signs: Aries, Taurus, Libra, Sagittarius, Capricorn, Aquarius
- barren signs: Gemini, Leo, Virgo

Although I don't want to oppose the tradition, I am a bit wary of including Taurus among the partly fruitful signs, as it seems very fruitful to me, whereas Capricorn, from the point of view of fertility, does have its place somewhere in the middle, but we must know that the Moon is in its detriment in Capricorn, therefore its placement in this sign is by no means desirable in pregnancy charts. It often shows a weakness, a pessimistic attitude or even a serious illness of the pregnant woman. In Scorpio where the Moon is in its fall, the situation is somewhat better, as Scorpio is a fruitful sign, but here too, the Moon cannot express itself completely unhindered - especially in the charts dealing with the course of pregnancy.

INDICATIONS OF PREGNANCY

An affirmative answer to questions concerning a confirmation of pregnancy or a happy delivery and birth, is indicated by:
- A harmonious applying aspect between the ascendant, the ascendant ruler or the Moon, the H5 ruler or the planet in H5;
- A disharmonious applying aspect of significators, but only with mutual reception, translation or collection of light;
- Emplacement (H1 ruler in H5 or H5 ruler in H1).

It is helpful, of course, if the planets are strong (dignified) and well placed; otherwise, complications may occur.

Attention: the last indication requires caution! Emplacement alone must be confirmed by other positive chart features, such as significators and the cusps of H1 and H5 in water (fertile) signs, the absence of disharmonious aspects, benefics on the angles, and such. A double emplacement (H1 ruler in H5 AND H5 ruler in H1) is a much stronger positive indicator, but even here, I would be extremely cautious.

Some charts have a strong "maternity" flavor, due to the dominance of fruitful signs or a number of harmonious aspects of the Moon, for example, but if the chart doesn't show any of the classic forms of "completion of the matter", there is no pregnancy.

Let us therefore list these encouraging chart features, but understand that they are only additional indications that can at most confirm the indications of the main significators, whereas in themselves they cannot promise a positive outcome.

These indications are taken from William Lilly's **Christian Astrology.**
- the ascendant or/and the cusp of H5 in fruitful signs (Cancer, Scorpio, Pisces);
- the Moon or H5 ruler in H1;
- the Moon or H1 ruler in H5;
- the Moon essentially strong, in a mutual reception with an angular planet;
- H1 ruler in H1, H5, H10 or H11, if in aspect with well placed benefics, provided Jupiter is strong in the chart;
- a benefic in H1 or in any other angular house, in a harmonious aspect with H1 ruler;
- the Moon, Jupiter, Venus and the Sun well placed, especially if in a harmonious applying aspect with the significators (Venus and Jupiter must be direct, not retrograde);
- Jupiter in H1, H5, H7 or H11, unafflicted;
- the ascendant in a fixed sign with a benefic in H1, or with the H5 ruler strong in H1 or H10;
- Venus in H5, unafflicted;
- the hour ruler angular, in a mutual reception with the ruler of an angle, or in H5 or H11 in a mutual reception with any of the significators;
- ruler of H1 or H5, or the Moon's dispositor, in an aspect or mutual reception with an essentially dignified angular planet;
- the ascendant ruler in a harmonious aspect with the ascendant;
- the Moon in a fortunate and strong house, in a harmonious aspect with an angular benefic;
- the Moon in a harmonious aspect with the cusp of H5, especially if the cusp of H5 is in Cancer or Taurus.

Additional indicators of non-pregnancy, infertility or risky pregnancy (beside the unconnectedness of the rulers of H1 and H5), according to Lilly, are:
- unfruitful signs on cusps of H1 and/or H5;
- malefics or essentially debilitated planets in H1, with a weak Jupiter and the H1 ruler;
- the Moon, the H1 in H5 rulers and the hours ruler unfortunately placed or afflicted;
- a malefic in H5 denies pregnancy, except if direct, quick, essentially dignified and otherwise strong;
- the H5 ruler retrograde, combust, peregrine or otherwise afflicted;
- an afflicted Jupiter or Venus in H5 (in disharmonious aspects with the malefics, combust or retrograde);
- Saturn, Mars or the south lunar node in H1 or H5 (indicate a possibility of abortion);
- Saturn or Mars in opposition or square with the cusp of H5 or with its ruler; know that an opposition tends to deny pregnancy whereas a square tends to only hinder or delay it;
- the H1 ruler in aspect with a retrograde or combust planet, or a planet in a cadent house.

According to Lilly, if the querent has been trying to get pregnant unsuccessfully for a long time, she may soon become pregnant if the horary charts shows one of these features:
- the ruler of H1 or H5 in H7;
- the ruler of H5 or H7 in H1;
- the Moon in aspect with the H7 ruler;
- the ruler of H1 in H4 or H7 shows that the woman will eventually get pregnant, but not so soon.

TWINS

The woman may be pregnant with twins (or triplets etc.) if the cusp of H1 or H5 is in a double-bodied sign (Gemini, Sagittarius or Pisces), but only on condition that this house contains a benefic. The probability is greater if the Sun, the Moon or H5 ruler are placed in any of these signs.

I should add that in my experience, Pisces is more associated with triplets than the rest of the double-bodied signs (which tend more to duality).

The possibility of twins is also increased if the north node is conjunct Jupiter or Venus in H5; same for an exact sextile or trine of Jupiter, Venus or the north node with the ascendant or the cusp of H5.

The embryo is single if the ascendant and/or the cusp of H5 are in fixed or cardinal signs, especially if H1 and/or H5 are occupied by the Sun or the Moon.

THE SEX OF THE UNBORN CHILD

Determining the sex of the unborn child (embryo) in a horary chart is a delicate matter; unfortunately, none of the techniques that are known, are completely reliable. According to Lilly, the child's gender is indicated by the placements of the rulers of H1 and H5, the hour ruler and the Moon. If most of these planets are in masculine signs (Aries, Gemini, Leo, Libra, Sagittarius, Aquarius) and/or in the masculine quarters of the sky (10, 11, 12 and 4, 5, 6), the child would be a boy, otherwise she'd be a girl.

Additional indicators are:
- Jupiter in H7 – a son;
- Pisces or Sagittarius on the cusp of H7 – a daughter;
- the Moon in H5, applying to Venus or Jupiter – a daughter;
- the masculine planets (the Sun, Mars, Jupiter and Saturn) give indications for boys, the feminine planets (the Moon and Venus) for girls; the sex of Mercury is determined by its aspects and position in relation to the Sun (east of the Sun masculine, west of the Sun feminine).

TIMING IN PREGNANCY CHARTS

We can be interested in several things: when a pregnant woman will give birth, when she would become pregnant, and the like. The timing procedure is the same as with other horary charts.

Lilly lists some odd (in my opinion, at least) rules in this regard, which I will not mention here because they do not seem to be meaningful; the curious student can find them in his **Christian Astrology**.

In addition to the Moon's guidelines, the nature of the signs involved is important; significators in cardinal signs tend to "earlier", in the fixed to "later". It is also very important if the H5 ruler is fast and/or direct (quickly, soon) or slow and/or retrograde (slowly, late).

An unafflicted benefic in H5 or conjunct the ascendant indicates "soon" or "sooner".

The time of birth or conception can also be judged by transits: such events often coincide with the transitting conjunction of the Sun or Mars with the H5 ruler, the Moon, the ascendant or the hour ruler, or with the entering of the querent's or the quesited's significator into a new sign.

Will the birth take place in the day or in the night time? The majority of the significators in diurnal (positive) signs speak for the day while their presence in nocturnal (negative) signs suggests the night.

2/1: AM I PREGNANT?

22 May 1994 at 9:46 p.m. (21:46), Ljubljana, Slovenia
Hour ruler: Mars

An acquaintance called me wanting to know whether she was pregnant. It was still early for a medical test, but she had a feeling that she had recently conceived.

Her significator is Jupiter (H1 ruler) and her (possible) pregnancy is shown by Venus (H5 ruler). Both planets are in fruitful signs (Venus is in Cancer, Jupiter in Scorpio) and are mutually applying by a trine aspect. The answer is obvious: yes, she's pregnant! This was good news, because Jupiter is in H11, the house of heart wishes, meaning that she wanted the child.

So far so good, but a closer look at the chart reveals that both significators have virtually no essential strength. Jupiter is peregrine (without any dignity) and is also retrograde, which describes the querent as physically weak or (maybe) unable to have a successful pregnancy. Venus (the foetus) is in the strong angular house, but has only a weak dignity by face. At the end of H5, already in conjunction with the cusp of H6, is the Moon's south node, which points to the possibility of abortion-related disease (the combined effect of H5 and H6).

But the strongest warning that there could be something going wrong, is the Moon's placement. The Moon shows the course of events (in this case, the course of pregnancy), but also the foetus itself, because it is the co-almuten of H5, so its condition is especially important. We can see that it is peregrine, at the end of its sign and in a close applying opposition with the destructive Mars placed in the angular H4. This house is also "terminal" - marks the end of the matter. To the exact opposition of the Moon to Mars is only 27' or half a degree. Since both planets were in cardinal signs and angular houses, I saw the danger of abortion (or inflammation, which may endanger the pregnancy) within 14 days or half a month, equivalent to half a degree. As already said, the situation was seen as critical because retrograde Jupiter shows the weakness of her body - as if it were in danger of soon being returned to its previous state (retrograde) of "non-pregnancy." You will also notice that Mars is the hour ruler, so it has an even more important role than it would have otherwise.

You might wonder why I decided for half a month, not for half a week or even half a day, since the Moon is in an angular house and a cardinal sign, suggesting a very short time unit. As mentioned in the theoretical part of the book, it is important that when choosing the appropriate time unit, we should use common sense, not just the table! At the time of the question, the querent felt very good, and miscarriages usually don't occur at such an early stage of pregnancy.

Yes, I'd say you're really pregnant, I told her, but because my voice was a little "strange", she asked, fearfully, if something might go wrong? I told her that she could really be in for some complications, but in case this really happens, it would be soon and would pass quickly (Moon was fast at the time of the question), therefore she should not be disturbed. I advised her to be calm and take good care of herself, but should there be the slightest suspicion that something was wrong, she should immediately see her doctor.

A few days later she called me and said that she had a medical test which confirmed her pregnancy. However, on 5 June, exactly 14 days after the question, she called me again. *Yesterday I started to bleed,* she said. *I went to the hospital. I had an early miscarriage – so, no child this time.*

2/1

22 May 1994
21:46 CEDT -2:00
Ljubljana, Slovenia
46°N03' 014°E31'

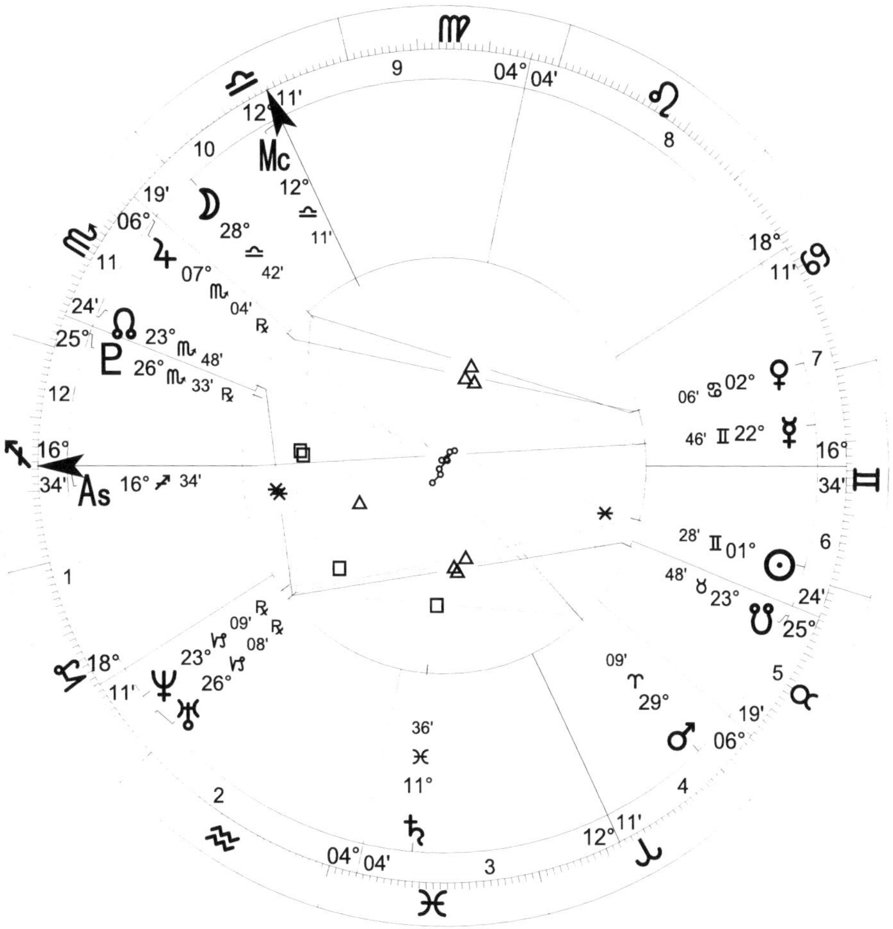

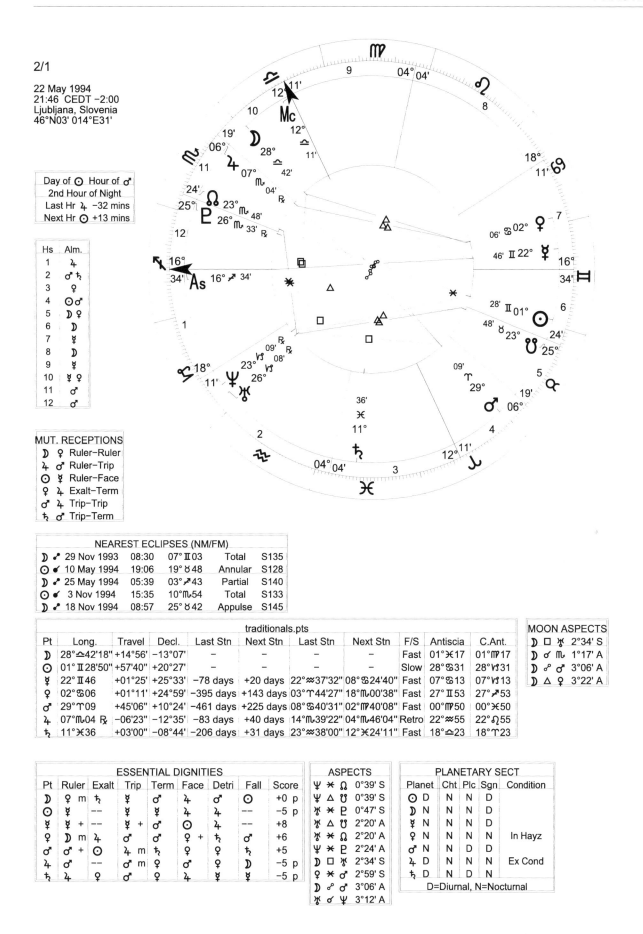

Day of ☉ Hour of ♂
2nd Hour of Night
Last Hr ♃ −32 mins
Next Hr ☉ +13 mins

Hs	Alm.
1	♃
2	♂ ♄
3	♀
4	☉♂
5	☽ ♀
6	☽
7	☿
8	☽
9	☿
10	☿ ♀
11	♂
12	♂

MUT. RECEPTIONS		
☽	♀	Ruler–Ruler
♃	♂	Ruler–Trip
☉	☿	Ruler–Face
♀	♃	Exalt–Term
♂	♃	Trip–Trip
♄	♂	Trip–Term

NEAREST ECLIPSES (NM/FM)					
☽	29 Nov 1993	08:30	07° ♊ 03	Total	S135
☉	10 May 1994	19:06	19° ♉ 48	Annular	S128
☽	25 May 1994	05:39	03° ♐ 43	Partial	S140
☉	3 Nov 1994	15:35	10° ♏ 54	Total	S133
☽	18 Nov 1994	08:57	25° ♉ 42	Appulse	S145

traditionals.pts

Pt	Long.	Travel	Decl.	Last Stn	Next Stn	Last Stn	Next Stn	F/S	Antiscia	C.Ant.
☽	28°♎42'18"	+14°56'	−13°07'	–	–	–	–	Fast	01°♓17	01°♍17
☉	01°♊28'50"	+57'40"	+20°27'	–	–	–	–	Slow	28°♋31	28°♑31
☿	22°♊46	+01°25'	+25°33'	−78 days	+20 days	22°♒37'32"	08°♋24'40"	Fast	07°♋13	07°♑13
♀	02°♋06	+01°11'	+24°59'	−395 days	+143 days	03°♈44'27"	18°♏00'38"	Fast	27°♊53	27°♐53
♂	29°♈09	+45'06"	+10°24'	−461 days	+225 days	08°♋40'31"	02°♍40'08"	Fast	00°♍50	00°♓50
♃	07°♏04 ℞	−06'23"	−12°35'	−83 days	+40 days	14°♏39'22"	04°♏46'04"	Retro	22°♒55	22°♌55
♄	11°♓36	+03'00"	−08°44'	−206 days	+31 days	23°♒38'00"	12°♓24'11"	Fast	18°♎23	18°♈23

MOON ASPECTS			
☽	□	♅	2°34' S
☽	☌	♏	1°17' A
☽	☍	♂	3°06' A
☽	△	♀	3°22' A

ESSENTIAL DIGNITIES

Pt	Ruler	Exalt	Trip	Term	Face	Detri	Fall	Score
☽	♀ m	♄	☿	♂	♃	♂	☉	+0 p
☉	☿	--	☿	☿	♃	♃	--	−5 p
☿	☿ +	--	☿ +	♂	☉	♃	--	+8
♀	☽ m	♃	♂	♂	♀ +	♄	♂	+6
♂	♂ +	☉	♃ m	♄	♀	♀	♄	+5
♃	♂	--	♂ m	♀	♂	♀	☽	−5 p
♄	♃	♀	♂	♀	♃	☿	☿	−5 p

ASPECTS			
♆	⚹	☊	0°39' S
♆	△	☋	0°39' S
♅	⚹	♇	0°47' S
♅	△	☋	2°20' A
♅	⚹	☊	2°20' A
♆	⚹	♇	2°24' A
☽	□	♅	2°34' S
♀	⚹	♂	2°59' S
☽	☍	♂	3°06' A
♅	☌	♆	3°12' A

PLANETARY SECT

Planet	Cht	Plc	Sgn	Condition
☉ D	N	N	D	
☽ N	N	N	D	
☿ N	N	N	D	
♀ N	N	N	N	In Hayz
♂ N	N	D	D	
♃ D	N	N	N	Ex Cond
♄ D	N	D	N	

D=Diurnal, N=Nocturnal

2/2: AM I PREGNANT?

11 July 1995 at 12:44 p.m. (12:44), Ljubljana, Slovenia
Hour ruler: Saturn

An acquaintance called me asking if she was pregnant. She is shown by Venus, the ascendant ruler, in the fruitful Cancer and in a (wide) conjunction with the cusp of H10, while her co-significator the Moon is in Capricorn, a partially fruitful sign. Almuten of the ascendant, Saturn, is also the hour ruler and the ruler of H5, therefore a crucially important planet. It is in a fruitful sign (Pisces) which is an additional indication of pregnancy.

A closer look at the state of the planets shows that Venus is quite strong since it's in its own triplicity, term and face, but Saturn is peregrine. The Moon, co-significator of the querent; is also peregrine, and what's more, it is also in detriment, which is particularly problematic in pregnancy charts. Moon applies by opposition to Venus, the main significator of the querent. The two planets are in a mixed mutual reception because Venus is in the Moon's domicile while the Moon is in Venus triplicity, which gives them some essential strength.

Saturn which plays a significant role in this chart, is very badly placed: peregrine, retrograde, located in H6 (of diseases) and at the same time in an exact applying opposition with the malefic Mars which "attacks" it from H12. If the querent really was pregnant, the foetus (Saturn) is obviously in a difficult situation. The physical condition of the querent is obviously bad, because Saturn is also almuten of the ascendant. If she is pregnant, there would be complications. This is highlighted by the square which Venus and Moon form with the ascendant. An additional warning is the fact that Venus is under the Sun's beams, which in this case adds to helplessness, fear or physical weakness of the querent.

So, is the querent pregnant or not? The chart shows one of the ways of completion. Let's recall: a disharmonious applying aspect of the significators can give a yes for an answer if the planets are in a mutual reception or if another body translates light between them, especially if at least one of them is in a fortunate and/or strong house. Here we have Venus (main significator of the querent) and the Moon (natural significator of pregnancy) in a disharmonious applying aspect involving mutual reception, with both planets in fairly fortunate houses (H3 and H9) and close to angles, so the answer could be yes. But I was puzzled by so much negativity and warnings in the chart, and I was also not sure whether the mixed reception involving triplicity was strong enough for an affirmative answer. But if we check monomoiria we can see that Venus and the Moon are in another MR because Venus is on the degree of the Moon while the Moon is on the degree of Venus! This also confirms pregnancy.

The unfortunate situation of Saturn nevertheless prompted me to reply that the chart shows a moderate chance of pregnancy but that I can't be entirely sure.

A few days passed and the querent called back to say that the medical test showed that she was indeed pregnant! The Sun, ruler of her H11 of heart wishes in trine with Saturn, significator of the embryo, shows that she desired it. I congratulated her and wished her good luck, but I did not mention the negative indications in the chart, because I did not want to make her worry. I only asked her if her boyfriend was displeased with her pregnancy. Mars, which afflicts Saturn, rules H7, so I thought that this might be the problematic part. Not at all, she said. He was only surprised, because the child was not planned, but was happy with the news. (This is actually adequately described by the Sun, almuten of H7 and the ruler of his H5, which is in an applying trine with Saturn.)

But time showed that her pregnancy was indeed critical. Moon wants 3°09' to an exact opposition (a critical aspect) with Venus. The two planets are in cardinal signs but in cadent houses which would translate into three weeks. Three weeks until what? Almost exactly that time (three weeks and one day) passed until the day when I received her message, saying that she was in hospital because the previous day she had to have an abortion due to an ectopic pregnancy.

Interestingly, the "sky" described this pregnancy as a kind of disease, since the ruler of H5 (strongly afflicted) was in H6. After all, it was a false pregnancy which could be considered a kind of a disease!

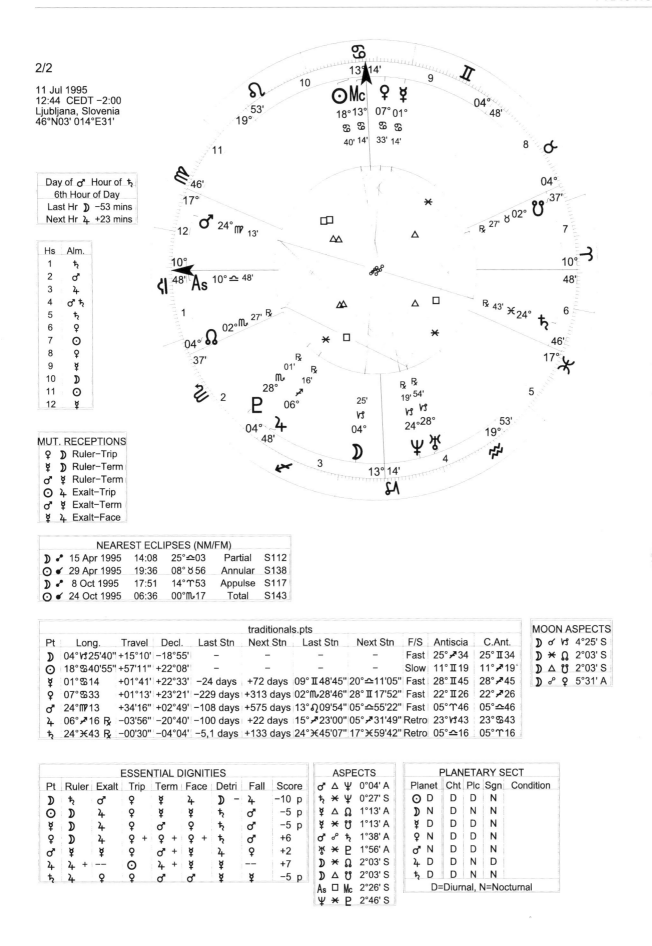

2/2

11 Jul 1995
12:44 CEDT −2:00
Ljubljana, Slovenia
46°N03' 014°E31'

Day of ♂ Hour of ♄
6th Hour of Day
Last Hr ☽ −53 mins
Next Hr ♃ +23 mins

Hs	Alm.
1	♄
2	♂
3	♃
4	♂ ♄
5	♄
6	♀
7	☉
8	♀
9	☿
10	☽
11	☉
12	☿

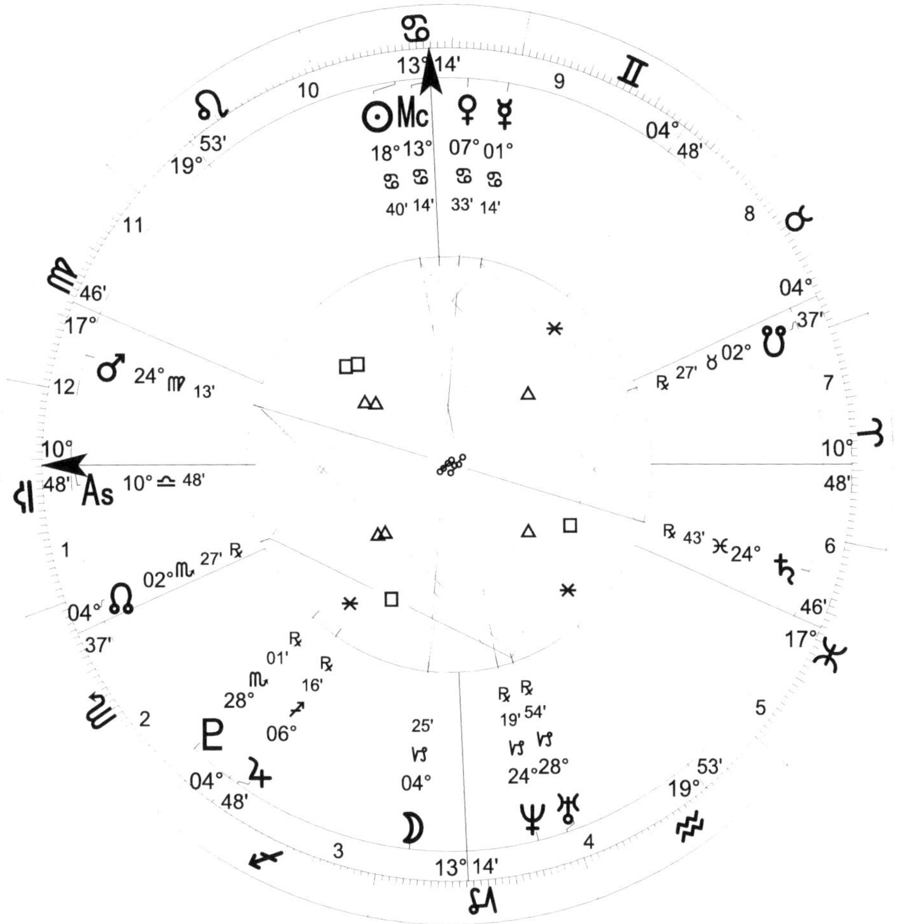

MUT. RECEPTIONS		
♀	☽	Ruler−Trip
☿	☽	Ruler−Term
♂	☿	Ruler−Term
☉	♃	Exalt−Trip
♂	☿	Exalt−Term
☿	♃	Exalt−Face

NEAREST ECLIPSES (NM/FM)					
☽ ☍	15 Apr 1995	14:08	25°♎03	Partial	S112
☉ ☌	29 Apr 1995	19:36	08°♉56	Annular	S138
☽ ☍	8 Oct 1995	17:51	14°♈53	Appulse	S117
☉ ☌	24 Oct 1995	06:36	00°♏17	Total	S143

traditionals.pts

Pt	Long.	Travel	Decl.	Last Stn	Next Stn	Last Stn	Next Stn	F/S	Antiscia	C.Ant.
☽	04°♑25'40"	+15°10'	−18°55'	–	–	–	–	Fast	25°♐34	25°♊34
☉	18°♋40'55"	+57'11"	+22°08'	–	–	–	–	Slow	11°♊19	11°♐19
☿	01°♋14	+01°41'	+22°33'	−24 days	+72 days	09°♊48'45"	20°♎11'05"	Fast	28°♊45	28°♐45
♀	07°♋33	+01°13'	+23°21'	−229 days	+313 days	02°♏28'46"	28°♊17'52"	Fast	22°♊26	22°♐26
♂	24°♍13	+34'16"	+02°49'	−108 days	+575 days	13°♌09'54"	05°♎55'22"	Fast	05°♈46	05°♎46
♃	06°♐16 ℞	−03'56"	−20°40'	−100 days	+22 days	15°♐23'00"	05°♐31'49"	Retro	23°♑43	23°♋43
♄	24°♓43 ℞	−00'30"	−04°04'	−5,1 days	+133 days	24°♓45'07"	17°♓59'42"	Retro	05°♎16	05°♈16

MOON ASPECTS			
☽	☌	♑	4°25' S
☽	⚹	☊	2°03' S
☽	△	☋	2°03' S
☽	☍	♀	5°31' A

ESSENTIAL DIGNITIES

Pt	Ruler	Exalt	Trip	Term	Face	Detri	Fall	Score
☽	♄	♂	♀	☿	♃	☽ −	♃	−10 p
☉	☽	♃	♀	☿	☿	♄	♂	−5 p
☿	☽	♃	♀	♂	☿	♄	♂	−5 p
♀	☽	♃	♀ +	♀ +	♀ +	♄	♂	+6
♂	☿	☿	♀	♂ +	☿	♃	♀	+2
♃	♃ +	--	☉	♃ +	☿	☿	--	+7
♄	♃	♀	♀	♂	♂	☿	☿	−5 p

ASPECTS			
♂	△	♆	0°04' A
♄	⚹	♆	0°27' S
☿	△	☊	1°13' A
☿	⚹	☋	1°13' A
♂	☍	♄	1°38' A
♅	⚹	♇	1°56' A
☽	⚹	☊	2°03' S
☽	△	☋	2°03' S
As	□	Mc	2°26' S
♆	⚹	♇	2°46' S

PLANETARY SECT

Planet		Cht	Plc	Sgn	Condition
☉	D	D	D	N	
☽	N	D	N	N	
☿	D	D	D	N	
♀	N	D	D	N	
♂	N	D	D	N	
♃	D	D	N	D	
♄	D	D	N	N	

D=Diurnal, N=Nocturnal

2/3: ARE WE STAYING TOGETHER IF I DECIDE TO ABORT?

12 July 1995 at 4:37 p.m. (16:37), Ljubljana, Slovenia
Hour ruler: Moon

Imagine that a pregnant woman asks you a question like this. How would you react? Wouldn't you feel embarrassed, like I did? Thinking whether to answer at all? The question includes a request for advice - to abort or not? But this is already a matter of ethics and personal attitude towards the matter. What if we, as astrologers, have a negative stance towards abortion? Wouldn't that suppress our ability to advise clients objectively? Wouldn't we be tempted to say: "Keep your child at any cost!" instead of stepping into their shoes and trying to advise them from their perspective?

I believe that astrologers whose ethical and moral values disagree with those of their clients, shouldn't moralize or even scold clients for their planned actions, because this is ultimately not our work, nor our right. If my client thinks (or feels) that abortion is morally acceptable, I don't try to persuade her to the contrary. I think that we astrologers shouldn't impose our views and beliefs upon our clients, be they political, religious, philosophical, ethical or whatever. This simply is not our job, but if we feel that our own stance might affect our judgment, I think it pays to be honest and let the client know how it might affect our answer.

I'm including this example also because it is a kind of proof that when clients ask for advice, their decisions are already known – as shown in the chart. Horary charts tell us stories about the future - about what will happen, because it is meant (fated) to happen! Although people often ask for advice, the chart usually shows how they will decide – no matter what we tell them. I even find this one of the greatest fascinations of horary astrology, although my clients are often surprised or sometimes even offended when I tell them what they will do – be it "wise" or not.

Mars (the ruler of H5 of pregnancy and the querent's main significator) is in an exact, although separating opposition with Saturn in H4 (end of the matter). This suggests that in her mind, the querent has already said goodbye to her child, because Saturn in opposition acts like a termination. Confirmation can be found in the fact that ascendant is in Scorpio, the sign of death and transformation, and in conjunction with Pluto - the planet with a similar meaning. The Moon in Capricorn (detriment) and in Saturn's term tells the same story. Pregnancy is not what the querent currently wants!

The sequence of events is shown by the Moon, which as the hour ruler has a particularly important role. It is strongly afflicted: peregrine, in detriment and opposed by the Sun, another "life-giver"). In addition, it co-rules H8 of death (Cancer is intercepted in that house) which is also the derived H4 - end of the matter for pregnancy (4/5). Moon's first aspect is conjunction with a retrograde Neptune, the modern ruler of H4 (end of the matter) and its second aspect is sextile to Saturn which is retrograde in the terminal H4. Because retrograde planets suggest a return to the previous state of affairs, all these factors confirm her desire to abort. Both aspects of the Moon will be reached before its trine with Mars (pregnancy, foetus), so the matter is clear: the querent will decide for an abortion.

And now to the core question – how would her partner react? Would they remain together? He is represented by Venus. Mars is in the fall of Venus, which throws a poor light on their relationship. Venus is under the Sun's beams which shows that her partner feels helpless or unable to influence the situation. Venus is also in the fall of Mars, so he probably doesn't care very much neither for her nor for the child (Mars rules both H1 and H5). But because the two planets are not in a disharmonious aspect and because there's no other firm indication of their imminent breakup, I said to her that abortion would probably not be the reason for the possible failure of their bond. (She actually wanted to abort because they had not been on the best of terms recently, and she was afraid that she'd be left alone with a child.) I tried to encourage her to keep the child because the Moon would finally apply to Mars by a fortunate trine, but I pointed out that the decision is in her hands. (And as already mentioned, the chart clearly shows what her decision would be.)

As I later learned, she had an abortion a few days after the question.

2/3

12 Jul 1995
16:37 CEDT −2:00
Ljubljana, Slovenia
46°N03' 014°E31'

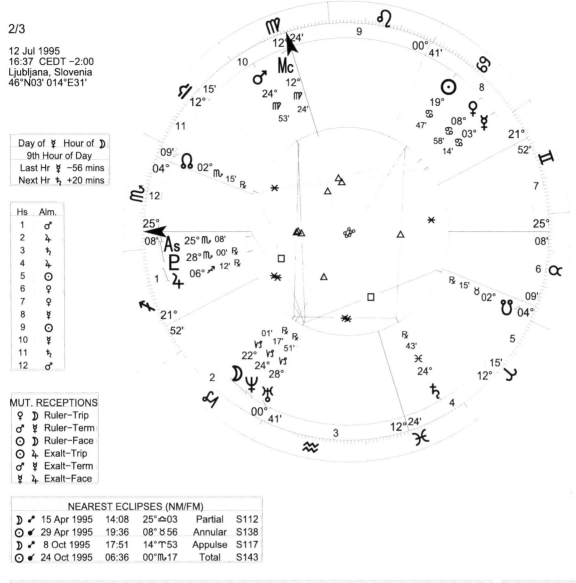

Day of ☿ Hour of ☽
9th Hour of Day
Last Hr ☿ −56 mins
Next Hr ♄ +20 mins

Hs	Alm.
1	♂
2	♃
3	♄
4	♃
5	☉
6	♀
7	♀
8	☿
9	☉
10	☿
11	♄
12	♂

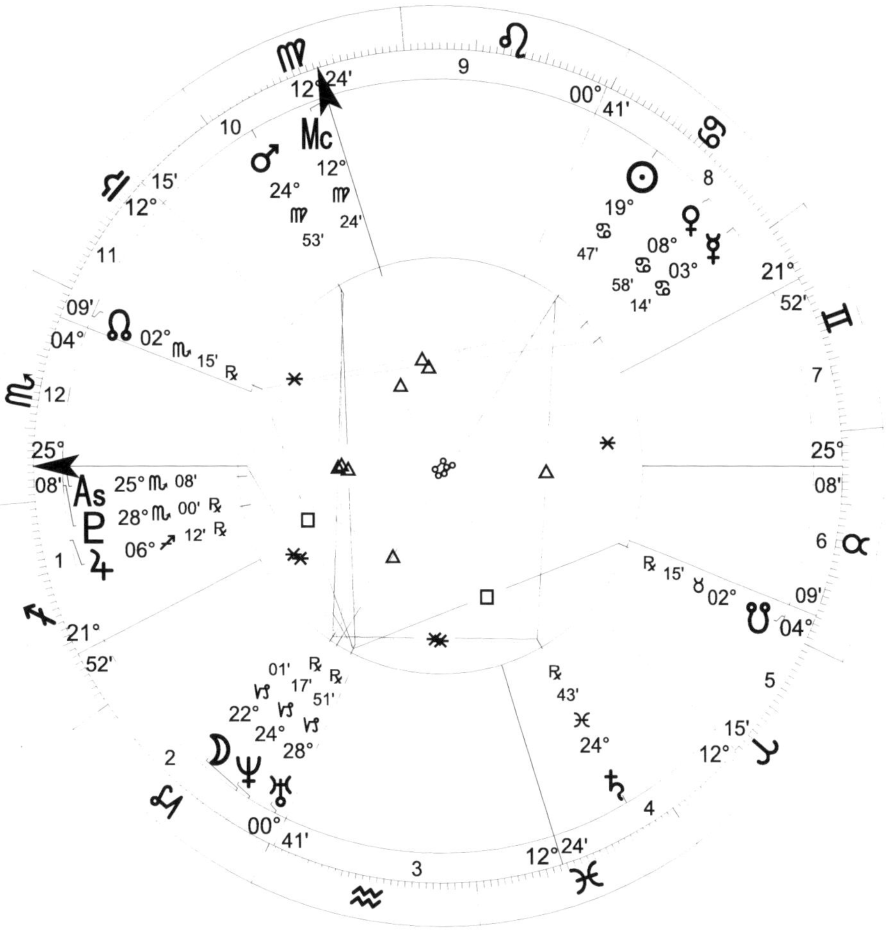

MUT. RECEPTIONS	
♀ ☽	Ruler–Trip
♂ ☿	Ruler–Term
☉ ☽	Ruler–Face
☉ ♃	Exalt–Trip
♂ ☿	Exalt–Term
☿ ♃	Exalt–Face

NEAREST ECLIPSES (NM/FM)					
☽ ☍	15 Apr 1995	14:08	25°♎03	Partial	S112
☉ ☌	29 Apr 1995	19:36	08°♉56	Annular	S138
☽ ☍	8 Oct 1995	17:51	14°♈53	Appulse	S117
☉ ☌	24 Oct 1995	06:36	00°♏17	Total	S143

traditionals.pts

Pt	Long.	Travel	Decl.	Last Stn	Next Stn	Last Stn	Next Stn	F/S	Antiscia	C.Ant.
☽	22°♑01'35"	+15°05'	−16°45'	–	–	–	–	Fast	07°♐58	07°♊58
☉	19°♋47'22"	+57'11"	+21°58'	–	–	–	–	Slow	10°♊12	10°♐12
☿	03°♋14	+01°45'	+22°46'	−25 days	+71 days	09°♊48'45"	20°♎11'05"	Fast	26°♊45	26°♐45
♀	08°♋58	+01°13'	+23°18'	−230 days	+312 days	02°♏28'46"	28°♊17'52"	Fast	21°♊01	21°♐01
♂	24°♍53	+34'24"	+02°32'	−109 days	+574 days	13°♌09'54"	05°♎55'22"	Fast	05°♈06	05°♎06
♃	06°♐12 ℞	−03'45"	−20°40'	−102 days	+21 days	15°♐23'00"	05°♐31'49"	Retro	23°♑47	23°♋47
♄	24°♓43 ℞	−00'37"	−04°04'	−6,3 days	+132 days	24°♓45'07"	17°♓59'42"	Retro	05°♎16	05°♈16

MOON ASPECTS	
☽ ⚹ As	2°58' S
☽ ⚹ ♄	3°01' A
☽ △ ♂	3°02' A
☽ ☌ ♆	4°56' A
☽ ⚹ ♇	6°05' A
☽ ☌ ♒	7°58' A

ESSENTIAL DIGNITIES

Pt	Ruler	Exalt	Trip	Term	Face	Detri	Fall	Score
☽	♄	♂	♀	♄	☉	☽ −	♃	−10 p
☉	☽	♃	♀	♃	☿	♄	♂	−5 p
☿	☽	♃	♀	♂	♀	♄	♂	−5 p
♀	☽	♃	♀ +	♀ +	♀ +	♄	♂	+6
♂	☿	☿	♀	♂ +	☿	♃	♀	+2
♃	♃ +	--	☉	♃ +	☿	☿	--	+7
♄	♃	♀	♀	♂	♂	☿	☿	−5 p

ASPECTS	
♂ ⚹ As	0°14' S
♄ △ As	0°26' S
♄ ⚹ ♆	0°28' S
♂ △ ♆	0°37' S
♆ ⚹ As	0°51' S
☿ ⚹ ☋	0°58' S
☿ △ ☊	0°58' S
♂ ☍ ♄	1°36' S
♅ ⚹ ♇	1°54' A
♆ ⚹ ♇	2°47' S

PLANETARY SECT

Planet		Cht	Plc	Sgn	Condition
☉	D	D	D	N	
☽	N	D	N	N	
☿	D	D	D	N	
♀	N	D	D	N	
♂	N	D	D	N	
♃	D	D	N	D	
♄	D	D	N	N	

D=Diurnal, N=Nocturnal

2/4: AM I PREGNANT?

6 April 1995 at 1:15 p.m. (13:15), Ljubljana, Slovenia
Hour ruler: Saturn

A student brought this chart to the class and asked if I could help, because she could not find the answer herself. I find it an interesting and instructive example, because it shows how important it is that we distinguish between separating and applying aspects, and because it teaches us that when looking for an answer, we must apply nearly "mathematical" precision.

Significator of the querent is the Sun which is also almuten of the ascendant, and the Moon is her co-significator. Mars also partly rules her because it is located in H1. Significator of her (possible) pregnancy is Jupiter, the H5 ruler and also placed there. Moon is void-of-course, which in itself gives a negative answer, but the rules teach us that the answer can be different if the main significators point to the contrary.

So what's going on there? We can see that all the three key planets (Sun, Jupiter and Mars) are connected by mutual trines. An eloquent and potent combination, by all means, but we must carefully consider the applications and separations. The Sun separates from a trine with Jupiter, confirming the likelihood of a negative answer. All the more so because Jupiter is retrograde! I'd opt for a negative answer right away, but was puzzled by the fact that Mars, her co-ruler, is in a fairly exact applying trine with Jupiter, which could mean, of course, that she indeed was pregnant! Especially because Mars is in a strong mutual reception with the Sun (by sign). We know that in such cases the two planets' positions can be exchanged. If we do this, we get a nice applying trine of the Sun (her) with Jupiter (pregnancy).

In cases where the chart shows conflicting factors, we must carefully consider the indications "for" and "against" to see which of them prevail. In this case, pregnancy is indicated only by the application of Mars to Jupiter, while all the other factors speak against it. Let's list them so as to gain a clear perspective:

- a separating trine between Sun and Jupiter;
- retrograde Jupiter;
- VOC Moon;
- Saturn as the hour ruler; not only that the planetary hour is inharmonious (which is one negative indication) - in matters of pregnancy, the barren nature of Saturn adds weight to that side of the scale which denies it;
- Jupiter square Saturn (the aspect is separating, therefore not crucial for our judgment, but nevertheless tends towards a negative answer);
- barren nature of Leo, the ascending sign;
- barren nature of Gemini, the Moon sign;
- Pluto which "sits" right on cusp of H5.

For the finishing touch, we can add that this is a day chart in which Mars as a night planet is weaker from the Sun and Jupiter, therefore the power of its trine to Jupiter is weakened, as well as its role of the co-significator of the querent. The Moon, the natural significator of pregnancy, is *ex-conditione*, meaning that as per sect it is completely without merit.

For all these reasons I replied: "No, you're not pregnant."

At our next class meeting she confirmed my judgment, adding that her doctor told her that nausea and weak menstruation were not caused by pregnancy but by a kidney disease. (Venus, the natural significator of kidneys, is in conjunction with Saturn, the H6 ruler!)

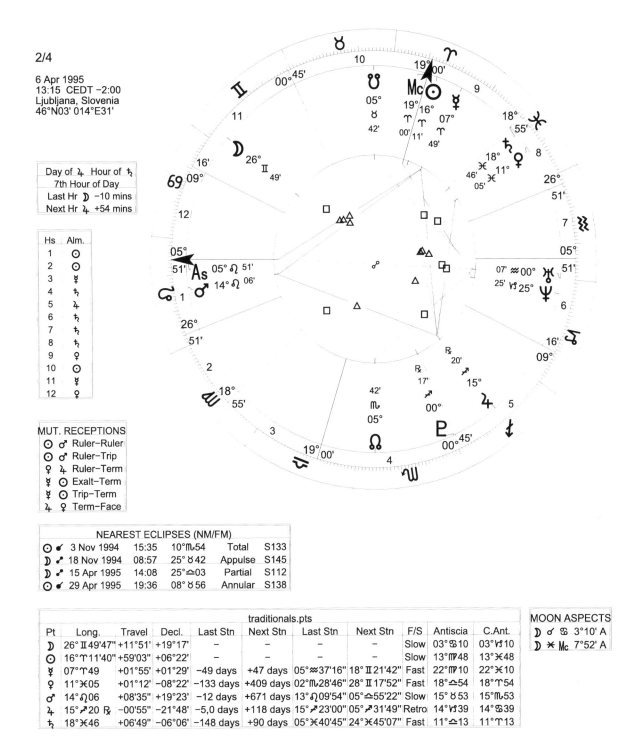

2/4

6 Apr 1995
13:15 CEDT −2:00
Ljubljana, Slovenia
46°N03' 014°E31'

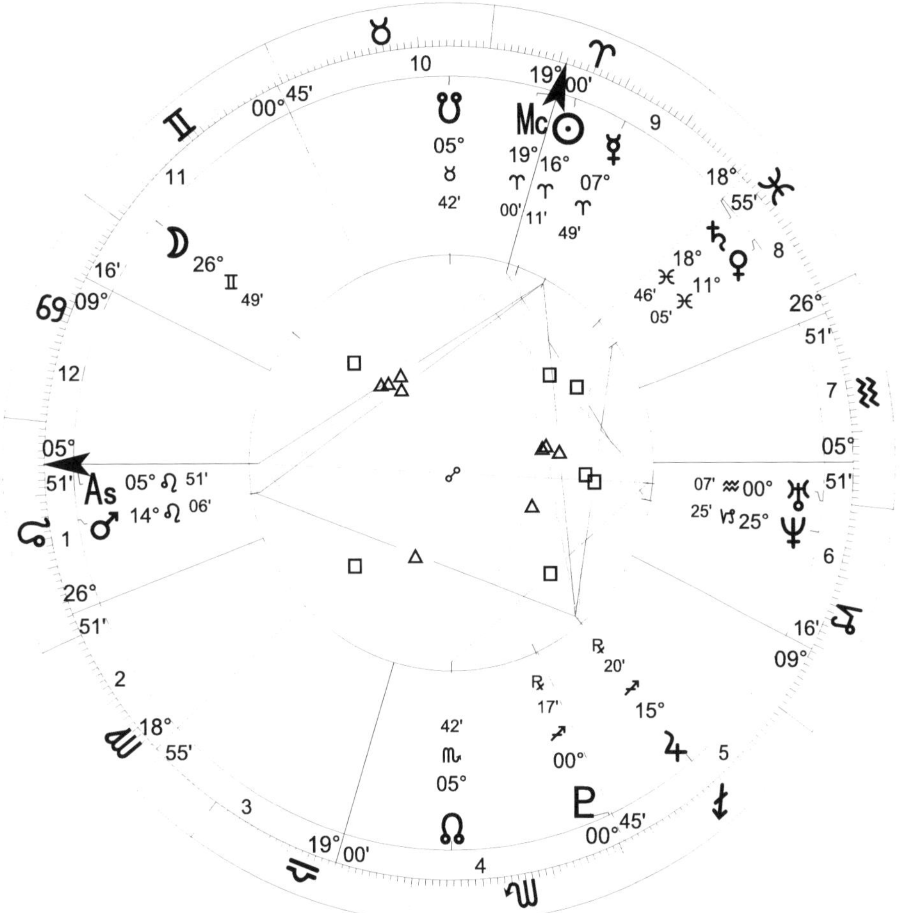

Day of ♃ Hour of ♄
7th Hour of Day
Last Hr ☽ −10 mins
Next Hr ♃ +54 mins

Hs	Alm.
1	☉
2	☉
3	☿
4	♄
5	♃
6	♄
7	♄
8	♄
9	♀
10	☉
11	☿
12	♀

MUT. RECEPTIONS
☉ ♂ Ruler–Ruler
☉ ♂ Ruler–Trip
♀ ♃ Ruler–Term
☿ ☉ Exalt–Term
☿ ☉ Trip–Term
♃ ♀ Term–Face

NEAREST ECLIPSES (NM/FM)					
☉ ☌	3 Nov 1994	15:35	10°♏54	Total	S133
☽ ☍	18 Nov 1994	08:57	25°♉42	Appulse	S145
☽ ☍	15 Apr 1995	14:08	25°♎03	Partial	S112
☉ ☌	29 Apr 1995	19:36	08°♉56	Annular	S138

traditionals.pts

Pt	Long.	Travel	Decl.	Last Stn	Next Stn	Last Stn	Next Stn	F/S	Antiscia	C.Ant.
☽	26°♊49'47"	+11°51'	+19°17'	–	–	–	–	Slow	03°♋10	03°♑10
☉	16°♈11'40"	+59'03"	+06°22'	–	–	–	–	Slow	13°♍48	13°♓48
☿	07°♈49	+01°55'	+01°29'	−49 days	+47 days	05°♒37'16"	18°♊21'42"	Fast	22°♍10	22°♓10
♀	11°♓05	+01°12'	−08°22'	−133 days	+409 days	02°♏28'46"	28°♊17'52"	Fast	18°♎54	18°♈54
♂	14°♌06	+08'35"	+19°23'	−12 days	+671 days	13°♌09'54"	05°♎55'22"	Slow	15°♉53	15°♏53
♃	15°♐20 ℞	−00'55"	−21°48'	−5,0 days	+118 days	15°♐23'00"	05°♐31'49"	Retro	14°♑39	14°♋39
♄	18°♓46	+06'49"	−06°06'	−148 days	+90 days	05°♓40'45"	24°♓45'07"	Fast	11°♎13	11°♈13

MOON ASPECTS
☽ ☌ ♋ 3°10' A
☽ ⚹ Mc 7°52' A

ESSENTIAL DIGNITIES

Pt	Ruler	Exalt	Trip	Term	Face	Detri	Fall	Score
☽	☿	--	♄	♄	☉	♃	--	−5 p
☉	♂ m	☉ +	☉ +	☿	☉ +	♀	♄	+13
☿	♂	☉	☉	♀	♂	♀	♄	−5 p
♀	♃	♀ +	♀ +	♀ +	♃	☿	☿	+9
♂	☉ m	--	☉	♄	♃	♄	--	+0 p
♃	♃ +	--	☉	♀	☽	☿	--	+5
♄	♃	♀	♀	☿	♃	☿	☿	−5 p

ASPECTS
☊ □ As 0°08' S
☋ □ As 0°08' S
☉ △ ♃ 0°50' S
♅ ⚹ ♇ 0°56' S
♂ △ ♃ 1°08' A
☿ △ As 1°59' S
☉ △ ♂ 2°07' S
☉ ☌ Mc 2°48' S
♆ ⚹ ♇ 3°52' A
♀ □ ♃ 4°14' A

PLANETARY SECT

Planet		Cht	Plc	Sgn	Condition
☉	D	D	D	D	In Hayz
☽	N	D	D	D	Ex Cond
☿	D	D	D	D	In Hayz
♀	N	D	D	N	
♂	N	D	N	D	
♃	D	D	N	D	
♄	D	D	D	N	

D=Diurnal, N=Nocturnal

2/5: AM I PREGNANT NOW?

5 March 1994 at 8:59 a.m., Ljubljana, Slovenia
Hour ruler: Mars

The question was raised by a client who came to me for her annual consultation. When I was evaluating the possibility of offspring which she heartily desired, using conventional prognostic techniques, and told her that obviously she'll not wait long for the baby, she set a concrete question: "Might I already be pregnant?" Although her progressions and eclipses indicated that she could indeed have already conceived, I decided to cast a horary, which is often the only way to get a concrete (yes or no) answer to a specific question.

The querent is shown by Venus (ruler of H1 and almuten of the ascendant) and the Moon, her (possible) pregnancy by the Sun (H5 ruler), but also by the Moon, of course, because it is the natural significator of pregnancy. Both main significators are in Pisces, a fruitful sign. They are in a wide conjunction, but Venus is faster and is separated from the Sun, which in itself would give a negative answer. What about the Moon? It is applying by square to Venus, without reception, but its last aspect was square the Sun (in Sagittarius, where the Sun has its day triplicity and therefore receives the Moon) which will be followed by a sextile with Mercury and a square with Venus. The Moon therefore translates light from the Sun (pregnancy) to Venus (the querent), whereby all the bodies are in Jupiter's domiciles (Sagittarius and Pisces), with their dispositor Jupiter in the fruitful Scorpio and in an exact applying trine with the Sun, significator of the (possible) embryo. The aspect is even stronger because the two bodies are in MR by face. All of this clearly speaks for pregnancy!

But let's get back to that translation of light. As already mentioned, the Moon first applies to Mercury (by sextile) and only later to Venus (by square). This could be a case of frustration, but because sextile is a mild and harmonious aspect and because the second part of H1 is in Gemini while the second part of H5 is in Virgo (Mercury signs), and also because Mercury sits happily in H11, I judged that this aspect could not "frustrate" the translation of light and thereby could not deny pregnancy.

Sun in H11 shows that pregnancy was the querent's heart's desire, especially because it is in conjunction with the "jupiterian" star Achernar.

My answer was, therefore, yes. As for the the course of pregnancy, I was a little worried about the fact that Venus was in H12 (weakness, hospitals etc.), especially since Venus is also co-ruler of H6 of disease. Although at the time of consultation the querent was healthy (Venus in exaltation and triplicity, and in sextile with the ascendant, which shows her current well-being and vitality), I advised her to take care of herself during pregnancy, because Venus will soon enter Aries where she's in detriment and therefore weak - particularly because it'll also be in H12. She told me that she feared complications because her first pregnancy was difficult. Her worry is reflected by the south node in H1, but because the Sun (H5 ruler) was in the fortunate H11 and nicely aspected, I comforted her that she doesn't need to worry for the wellbeing of the child. She could have some nausea and other pregnancy-related problems, but the foetus is obviously healthy and all will end well.

Is it going to be a boy or a girl, she wanted to know next. Let's see:
- ascendant in Taurus (female sign) = girl
- H1 ruler Venus in Pisces (female sign) = girl
- cusp H5 in Leo (male sign) = boy
- H5 ruler in Pisces (female sign) = girl

Most of the indicators speak for female gender, and this is confirmed by the application of the "female" Moon (which is in a male sign, but decreasing which is the "female" phase) to the both main significators, so I told her that it'll probably be a girl.

A couple of days later she called me and said that a medical test confirmed pregnancy. I heard from her again a few months after the birth of her daughter. She said that she was born on 21 October. Exact transits to the horary chart on that day were: the Moon's node conjunct Jupiter, Jupiter conjunct descendant, Sun and Mercury trine Mars.

She added that she had a difficult pregnancy and that both she and the baby were sickly after birth, but their health was now slowly improving.

2/5

5 Mar 1994
08:59 CET −1:00
Ljubljana, Slovenia
46°N03' 014°E31'

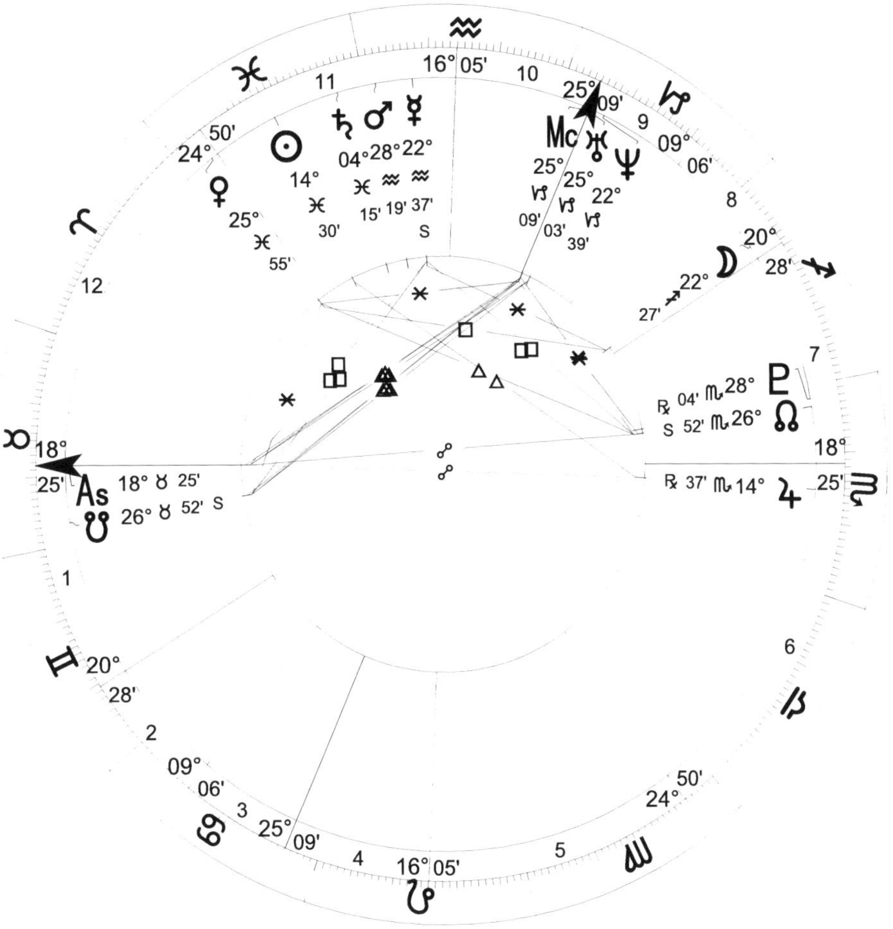

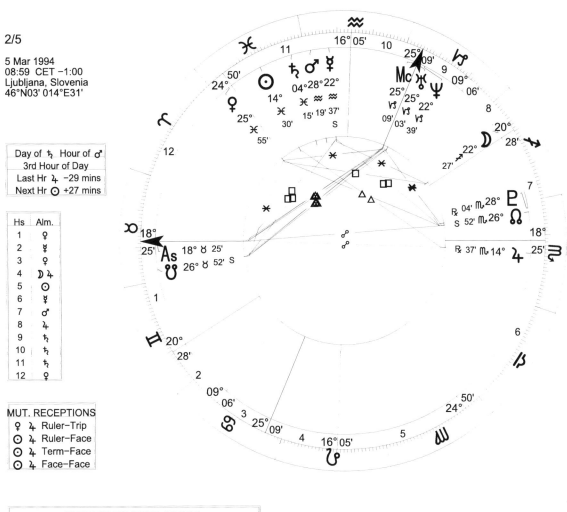

Day of ♄ Hour of ♂
3rd Hour of Day
Last Hr ♃ −29 mins
Next Hr ☉ +27 mins

Hs	Alm.
1	♀
2	☿
3	♀
4	☽ ♃
5	☉
6	☿
7	♂
8	♃
9	♄
10	♄
11	♄
12	♀

MUT. RECEPTIONS
♀ ♃ Ruler–Trip
☉ ♃ Ruler–Face
☉ ♃ Term–Face
☉ ♃ Face–Face

NEAREST ECLIPSES (NM/FM)					
☉ ☌	13 Nov 1993	22:34	21°♏31	Partial	S123
☽ ☍	29 Nov 1993	07:30	07°♊03	Total	S135
☉ ☌	10 May 1994	18:06	19°♉48	Annular	S128
☽ ☍	25 May 1994	04:39	03°♐43	Partial	S140

traditionals.pts

Pt	Long.	Travel	Decl.	Last Stn	Next Stn	Last Stn	Next Stn	F/S	Antiscia	C.Ant.
☽	22°♐27'54"	+13°33'	−21°02'	–	–	–	–	Fast	07°♑32	07°♋32
☉	14°♓30'50"	+01°00'	−06°05'	–	–	–	–	Fast	15°♎29	15°♈29
☿	22°♒37	+00'34"	−12°21'	−2h 10m	+99 days	22°♒37'32"	08°♋24'40"	Stat	07°♏22	07°♉22
♀	25°♓55	+01°14'	−02°50'	−316 days	+221 days	03°♈44'27"	18°♏00'38"	Fast	04°♎04	04°♈04
♂	28°♒19	+47'11"	−13°05'	−383 days	+303 days	08°♋40'31"	02°♍40'08"	Fast	01°♏40	01°♉40
♃	14°♏37 ℞	−00'53"	−14°57'	−4,8 days	+118 days	14°♏39'22"	04°♏46'04"	Retro	15°♒22	15°♌22
♄	04°♓15	+07'13"	−11°17'	−128 days	+109 days	23°♒38'00"	12°♓24'11"	Fast	25°♎44	25°♈44

MOON ASPECTS
☽ ⚹ ☿ 0°07' S
☽ □ ♀ 3°30' A
☽ ⚹ ♂ 5°55' A
☽ ☌ ♑ 7°32' A

ESSENTIAL DIGNITIES

Pt	Ruler	Exalt	Trip	Term	Face	Detri	Fall	Score
☽	♃	--	☉	♄	♄	☿	--	−5 p
☉	♃	♀	♀	♃	♃ m	☿	☿	−5 p
☿	♄	--	♄	♂	☽	☉	--	−5 p
♀	♃	♀ +	♀ +	♂	♂	☿	☿	+7
♂	♄	--	♄	♄	☽	☉	--	−5 p
♃	♂	--	♀	☿	☉ m	♀	☽	−5 p
♄	♃	♀	♀	♀	♄ +	☿	☿	+1

ASPECTS
☉ △ ♃ 0°06' A
☽ ⚹ ☿ 0°07' S
♅ ☌ Mc 0°28' S
♂ □ ♇ 0°31' S
♀ ⚹ Mc 0°46' S
♀ ⚹ ♅ 0°52' S
♀ ⚹ ☋ 0°57' A
♀ △ ☊ 0°57' A
♂ □ ☊ 1°26' S
♂ □ ☋ 1°26' S

PLANETARY SECT

Planet	Cht	Plc	Sgn	Condition
☉ D	D	D	N	
☽ N	D	D	D	Ex Cond
☿ D	D	D	D	In Hayz
♀ N	D	D	N	
♂ N	D	D	D	Ex Cond
♃ D	D	N	N	
♄ D	D	D	N	
D=Diurnal, N=Nocturnal				

2/6: AM I PREGNANT?

17 January 1995 at 4:14 p.m. (16:14), Ljubljana, Slovenia
Hour ruler: Moon

I asked this question soon after I met a friend who complimented me on my "extremely good looks" and hurried to ask if I was pregnant?! I didn't even think of pregnancy until that day, and I started to laugh. But then I remembered that lately I developed a taste for blood sausages - which I normally hate to see or smell, let alone eat – which was, actually, alarming. Am I really pregnant, I asked myself, and cast a chart.

Both the ascendant and cusp of H5 are in fruitful signs. My ruler is the Moon, strong in H1 and applying by trine to Jupiter in H5. The question was asked in the Moon hour with the ascendant in Cancer, the sign of the Moon, and Jupiter is not only a H5 planet but also the natural significator of fertility. All of this clearly speaks for pregnancy!

Both significators (the Moon as the dispositor of the ascendant and Jupiter as the fertility/pregnancy planet in H5) are not only connected (by aspect) but also strong: the Moon because of its placement in the angular H1 and as the hour ruler, and Jupiter because it's in its domicile, direct, quick and eastern in a day chart. All this gives it a fair number of points in both essential and accidental dignity. Besides, Jupiter is co-almuten of the ascendant, therefore my additional ruler, which makes for an even stronger connection between myself and pregnancy. What's more, it is accompanied by the Moon's north node and by Venus (also placed in H5), both associated with luck and good fortune.

What about the square of Jupiter to Saturn? At first sight, it looks like an applying square, but Saturn is accelerating while Jupiter reduces speed, and the ephemeris shows that the square will not be completed because Jupiter will turn retrograde at the beginning of April - before it could reach the aspect with Saturn.

There are two factors denying the possibility of pregnancy. Firstly, Mars as dispositor of Scorpio, on cusp of H5, is retrograde and applying by a square to Pluto in H5. Secondly, both Mars and the Moon are in traditionally "barren" signs (Virgo and Leo). The square with Pluto is not worrying because Pluto is not angular and therefore does not represent a serious threat. The indications speaking for pregnancy are by all means much stronger than those speaking against it, so the conclusion was clear: I was pregnant!

Having thus ascertained my pregnancy, I set myself another important question - is it a boy or a girl? Let's see:
- ascendant in Cancer (female sign) = girl
- H1 ruler Moon in Leo (male sign) = boy
- cusp H5 in Scorpio (female sign) = girl
- H5 ruler in Virgo (female sign) = girl

Indications for a girl are stronger than those for a boy, so it's a girl!

And so it was! In less than 8 months, I gave birth to a pretty, healthy baby girl. You will notice that the ascendant is 8 degrees before the next sign, which is an interesting "coincidence", as well as the fact that my daughter's ascendant is in Scorpio (at 0.5 degrees), the sign of the H5 in horary, and even in a very exact sextile with Mars, its dispositor!

2/6

17 Jan 1995
16:14 CET −1:00
Ljubljana, Slovenia
46°N03' 014°E31'

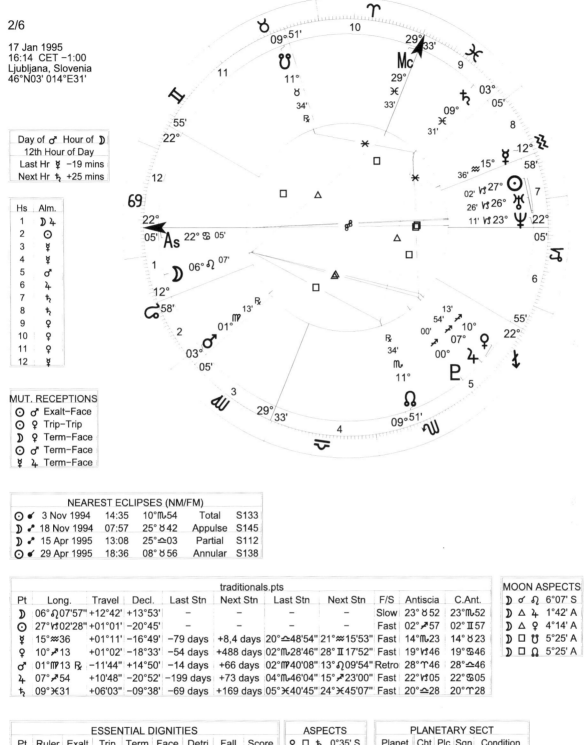

Day of ♂ Hour of ☽
12th Hour of Day
Last Hr ☿ −19 mins
Next Hr ♄ +25 mins

Hs	Alm.
1	☽ ♃
2	☉
3	☿
4	☿
5	♂
6	♃
7	♄
8	♄
9	♀
10	♀
11	♀
12	☿

MUT. RECEPTIONS
☉ ♂ Exalt-Face
☉ ♀ Trip-Trip
☽ ♀ Term-Face
☉ ♂ Term-Face
☿ ♃ Term-Face

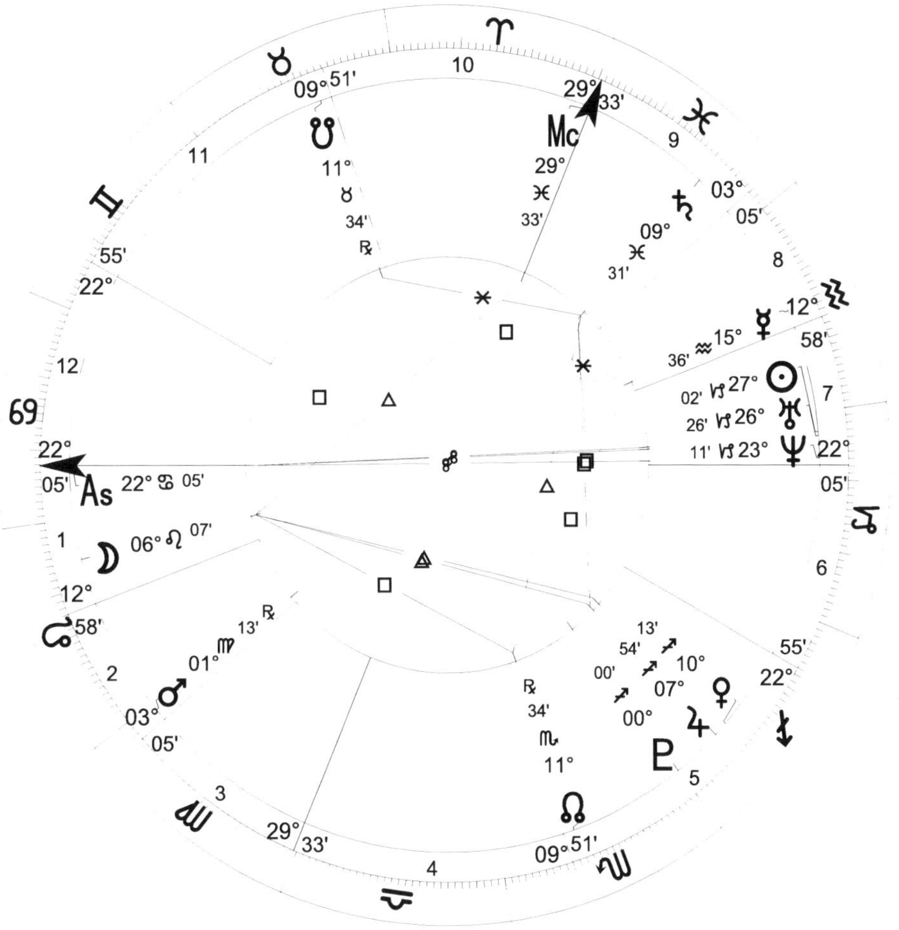

NEAREST ECLIPSES (NM/FM)					
☉ ☌	3 Nov 1994	14:35	10°♏54	Total	S133
☽ ☍	18 Nov 1994	07:57	25°♉42	Appulse	S145
☽ ☍	15 Apr 1995	13:08	25°♎03	Partial	S112
☉ ☌	29 Apr 1995	18:36	08°♉56	Annular	S138

traditionals.pts

Pt	Long.	Travel	Decl.	Last Stn	Next Stn	Last Stn	Next Stn	F/S	Antiscia	C.Ant.
☽	06°♌07'57"	+12°42'	+13°53'	–	–	–	–	Slow	23°♉52	23°♏52
☉	27°♑02'28"	+01°01'	−20°45'	–	–	–	–	Fast	02°♐57	02°♊57
☿	15°♒36	+01°11'	−16°49'	−79 days	+8,4 days	20°♎48'54"	21°♒15'53"	Fast	14°♏23	14°♉23
♀	10°♐13	+01°02'	−18°33'	−54 days	+488 days	02°♏28'46"	28°♊17'52"	Fast	19°♑46	19°♋46
♂	01°♍13 ℞	−11'44"	+14°50'	−14 days	+66 days	02°♍40'08"	13°♌09'54"	Retro	28°♈46	28°♎46
♃	07°♐54	+10'48"	−20°52'	−199 days	+73 days	04°♏46'04"	15°♐23'00"	Fast	22°♑05	22°♋05
♄	09°♓31	+06'03"	−09°38'	−69 days	+169 days	05°♓40'45"	24°♓45'07"	Fast	20°♎28	20°♈28

MOON ASPECTS
☽ ☌ ♌ 6°07' S
☽ △ ♃ 1°42' A
☽ △ ♀ 4°14' A
☽ □ ☋ 5°25' A
☽ □ ☊ 5°25' A

ESSENTIAL DIGNITIES

Pt	Ruler	Exalt	Trip	Term	Face	Detri	Fall	Score
☽	☉	--	☉	♀	♄	♄	--	−5 p
☉	♄	♂	♀ m	♂	☉ +	☽	♃	+1
☿	♄	--	♄	♃	☿ +	☉	--	+1
♀	♃	--	☉ m	♃	☽	☿	--	−5 p
♂	☿	☿	♀	☿	☉	♃	♀	−5 p
♃	♃ +	--	☉	♃ +	☿	☿	--	+7
♄	♃	♀	♀	♀	♄ +	☿	☿	+1

ASPECTS
♀ □ ♄ 0°35' S
☉ ☌ ♅ 0°46' S
♆ ☍ As 1°13' S
♇ △ Mc 1°20' S
♃ □ ♄ 1°38' A
☽ △ ♃ 1°42' A
☉ ⚹ ♇ 1°57' A
♄ ⚹ ☋ 2°03' A
♄ △ ☊ 2°03' A
♂ □ ♇ 2°08' A

PLANETARY SECT

Planet	Cht	Plc	Sgn	Condition
☉ D	D	D	N	
☽ N	D	N	D	
☿ N	D	D	D	Ex Cond
♀ N	D	N	D	
♂ N	D	N	N	
♃ D	D	N	D	
♄ D	D	D	N	
D=Diurnal, N=Nocturnal				

2/7: IS MY GIRLFRIEND PREGNANT?

30 August 2000 at 11:38 a.m., Ljubljana, Slovenia
Hour ruler: Mars

The question was asked by a male client, at the time when I was advising clients by way of a payable phone service. I opened that line primarily because I wanted to boost my practice of horary astrology, which is highly time-sensitive and asks for quick and short answers. And this is best done by phone!

The chart has a harmonious hour ruler which means "green light" or increases the possibility of meaningful indications which can give a correct answer.

Ascendant is in Scorpio, a fruitful sign. The querent's significator is Mars while his girlfriend is shown by Venus, H7 ruler. Venus is on the last degree of the Virgo, the sign of its fall, but in the fortunate H11 which indicates fulfilled hopes and wishes, but it is also the derived H5, the house of her pregnancy and children! The Moon, showing the querent's interest, is appropriately placed in H11 too.

So: is she pregnant? To confirm the "emplacement" (ruler of the derived H1 in the derived H5 - an indication that leans towards a positive answer) we need to see one of the classic, strong forms of completion. Mercury, the derived H5 ruler which indicates the girl's (possible) pregnancy, is in conjunction with the cusp of its own house (Mercury disposits H11 which has its cusp in Virgo). We can see that the Moon has separated from the conjunction with Mercury and is applying to a conjunction with Venus, so that it connects them. This is a classic and very nice example of translation of light. This is why I replied in the affirmative: *Yes, it's obvious that your girlfriend is really pregnant.*

Then he asked me how long she had been pregnant. Moon has separated from Mercury by 5°18' and because of her quick daily motion I said that around 5 weeks, a bit more perhaps, to which he replied that this is probably correct. I asked him why she hasn't done a medical test, and he replied that she has, and that the test confirmed pregnancy. (The question arises, of course, why he consulted me, then! It could be that he didn't believe her, or that he just wanted to test me.)

Then he asked me whether the pregnancy would proceed smoothly. He said that the expectant mother is a little unwell and that she worries how things would develop. Is everything going to be fine? A quick look into the chart moved me to say that there's no need to worry – she'll be fine! The reasons were three: Firstly, Venus is at the end of the sign of its detriment and will soon enter its domicile. This certainly indicates that the woman's condition is soon going to improve. Secondly, the Moon (the course of events/pregnancy) will reach Venus without frustration, and thirdly, the strong Mercury (embryo) shows that she'll deliver a healthy child.

2/7

30 Aug 2000
11:38 CEDT −2:00
Ljubljana, Slovenia
46°N03' 014°E31'

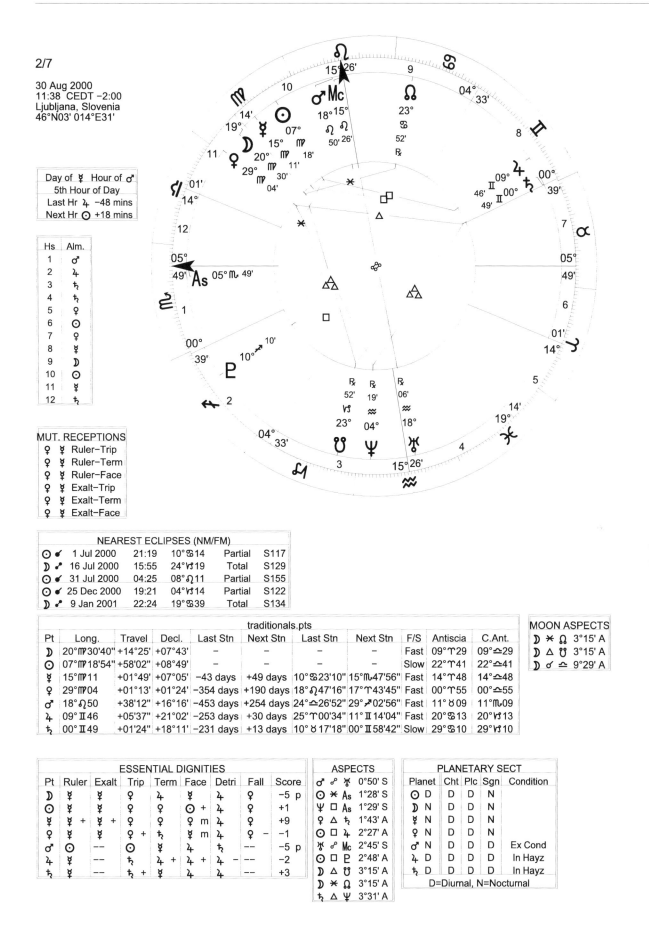

Day of ☿ Hour of ♂
5th Hour of Day
Last Hr ♃ −48 mins
Next Hr ☉ +18 mins

Hs	Alm.
1	♂
2	♃
3	♄
4	♄
5	♀
6	☉
7	♀
8	☿
9	☽
10	☉
11	☿
12	♄

MUT. RECEPTIONS
♀ ☿ Ruler−Trip
♀ ☿ Ruler−Term
♀ ☿ Ruler−Face
♀ ☿ Exalt−Trip
♀ ☿ Exalt−Term
♀ ☿ Exalt−Face

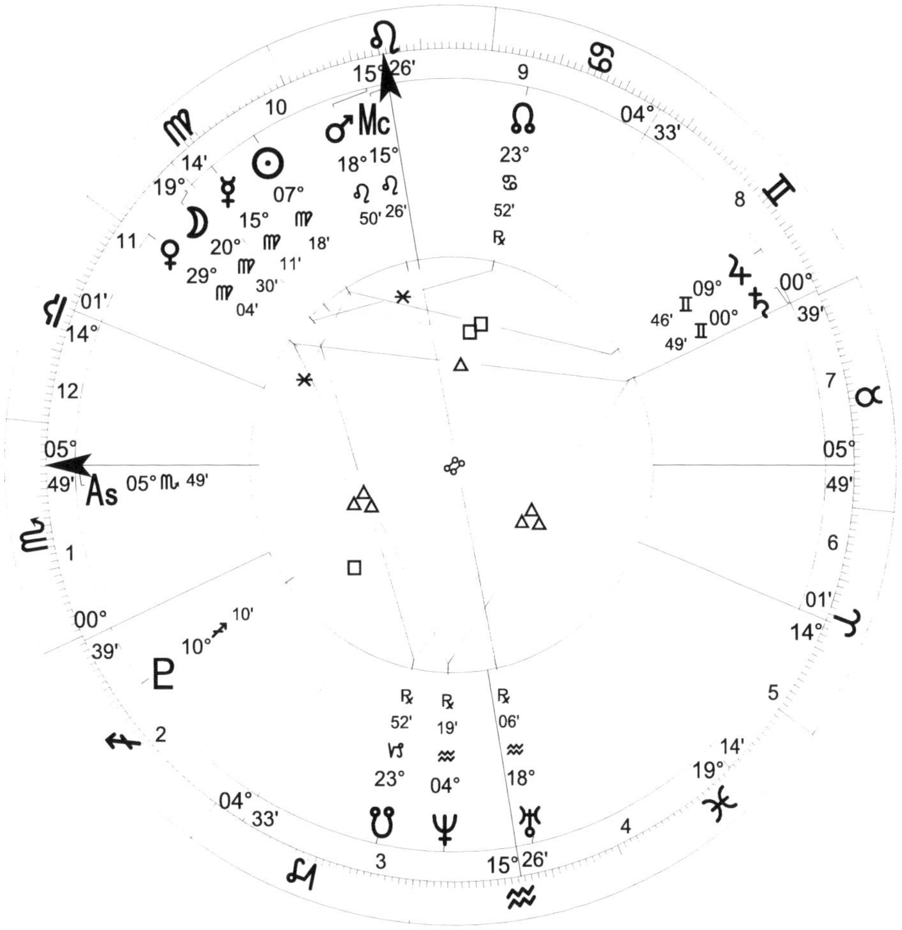

NEAREST ECLIPSES (NM/FM)					
☉ ☌	1 Jul 2000	21:19	10°♋14	Partial	S117
☽ ☍	16 Jul 2000	15:55	24°♑19	Total	S129
☉ ☌	31 Jul 2000	04:25	08°♌11	Partial	S155
☉ ☌	25 Dec 2000	19:21	04°♑14	Partial	S122
☽ ☍	9 Jan 2001	22:24	19°♋39	Total	S134

traditionals.pts

Pt	Long.	Travel	Decl.	Last Stn	Next Stn	Last Stn	Next Stn	F/S	Antiscia	C.Ant.
☽	20°♍30'40"	+14°25'	+07°43'	–	–	–	–	Fast	09°♈29	09°♎29
☉	07°♍18'54"	+58'02"	+08°49'	–	–	–	–	Slow	22°♈41	22°♎41
☿	15°♍11	+01°49'	+07°05'	−43 days	+49 days	10°♋23'10"	15°♏47'56"	Fast	14°♈48	14°♎48
♀	29°♍04	+01°13'	+01°24'	−354 days	+190 days	18°♌47'16"	17°♈43'45"	Fast	00°♈55	00°♎55
♂	18°♌50	+38'12"	+16°16'	−453 days	+254 days	24°♎26'52"	29°♐02'56"	Fast	11°♉09	11°♏09
♃	09°♊46	+05'37"	+21°02'	−253 days	+30 days	25°♈00'34"	11°♊14'04"	Fast	20°♋13	20°♑13
♄	00°♊49	+01'24"	+18°11'	−231 days	+13 days	10°♉17'18"	00°♊58'42"	Slow	29°♋10	29°♑10

MOON ASPECTS
☽ ⚹ ☊ 3°15' A
☽ △ ☋ 3°15' A
☽ ☌ ♎ 9°29' A

ESSENTIAL DIGNITIES

Pt	Ruler	Exalt	Trip	Term	Face	Detri	Fall	Score
☽	☿	☿	♀	♃	☿	♃	♀	−5 p
☉	☿	☿	♀	♀	☉ +	♃	♀	+1
☿	☿ +	☿ +	♀	♀	♀ m	♃	♀	+9
♀	☿	☿	♀ +	♄	☿ m	♃	♀ −	−1
♂	☉	--	☉	☿	♃	♄	--	−5 p
♃	☿	--	♄	♃ +	♃ +	♃ −	--	−2
♄	☿	--	♄ +	☿	♃	♃	--	+3

ASPECTS
♂ ☍ ♅ 0°50' S
☉ ⚹ As 1°28' S
♆ □ As 1°29' S
♀ △ ♄ 1°43' A
☉ □ ♃ 2°27' A
♅ ☍ Mc 2°45' S
☉ □ ♇ 2°48' A
☽ △ ☋ 3°15' A
☽ ⚹ ☊ 3°15' A
♄ △ ♆ 3°31' A

PLANETARY SECT

Planet		Cht	Plc	Sgn	Condition
☉	D	D	D	N	
☽	N	D	D	N	
☿	N	D	D	N	
♀	N	D	D	N	
♂	N	D	D	D	Ex Cond
♃	D	D	D	D	In Hayz
♄	D	D	D	D	In Hayz

D=Diurnal, N=Nocturnal

2/8: WILL MY SISTER EVER HAVE CHILDREN?

8 November 1998 at 7:37 a.m., Ljubljana, Slovenia
Hour ruler: Sun

This chart is different from the others because it doesn't ask about a current (possible) pregnancy but about the possibility of offspring – at anytime. As mentioned in the theoretical part of this section, it's "legitimate" and reasonable to answer such questions by means of horary astrology, although they don't refer to a current, on-going situation.

I asked on behalf of my sister, who had then been in a long-time harmonious partnership and already married, but they had no children. They were in the years when most of their peers already had offspring. We, their relatives, therefore secretly wondered whether they would ever have children.

A quick glance at the chart shows that the fruitful signs are heavily occupied. Ascendant is in Scorpio while the Moon, natural significator of pregnancy, is in Cancer, its domicile, and therefore very strong. It's applying firstly by trine to the Sun (in the fruitful Scorpio) which is important because it is the hour ruler and almuten of radix H5, and then to Venus, the derived ruler of H5 of children (5/3), which is also in Scorpio. Following its further course we can see that it'll also complete a trine to Jupiter (in the fruitful Pisces), the natural significator of fertility, and finally a sextile with Mars which is the ascendant ruler and the ruler of the sign on the cusp of radix H5. All these indicators clearly speak for pregnancy.

But Venus is combust, you might say, isn't that an affliction? Yes it is, but Venus is faster than the Sun so the combustion is a separating one. Let us remember that my question relates to the future, not to the current situation! Besides, Sun also represents pregnancy (almuten of radix H5).

So far so good, but I was really puzzled by the fact that H3 (my sister) in this chart is rather "poorly". H3 is occupied by Neptune and Uranus as well as the south node while its ruler Saturn is in its fall in Aries and retrograde. Does this reflect her worries and/or inability to conceive? Does she have problems? It's difficult to comment because we had never spoken about that. On second thought, however, the placement of Uranus is intriguing because it is a modern co-ruler of this house (Aquarius intercepted in H3) and applied to by a sextile of Mercury which also indicates children (though not babies). This is an encouraging indication, and given the fact that my sister gave birth to twins (Mercury is in Sagittarius, the double-bodied sign) nicely fits into the future developments regarding the question.

Despite the poor state of H3 I was optimistic about my sister's offspring, because the chart clearly indicates the dominance of positive factors – as described above.

And indeed, after some time, my sister gave birth to healthy twins, a boy and a girl. Judging by the date of their birth (9 March 2000) she became pregnant about 7 months after my question. The distance from the Moon to the exact trine with Venus, significator of my sister's pregnancy, is 6°07', and to Mars, the ascendant ruler, 7°12'. If we take into account the Moon's parallax, the Moon would be at 11°16' Cancer, making the distance between it and Venus 6°40'. Very accurate timing, don't you think?

A very interesting fact is that the twins have their ascendants at 15 and 16 degrees of Scorpio respectively –exactly conjunct the Sun (the ruler hour) and Venus! Again I have to say - in astrology there are no "coincidences"!

2/8

8 Nov 1998
07:37 CET −1:00
Ljubljana, Slovenia
46°N03' 014°E31'

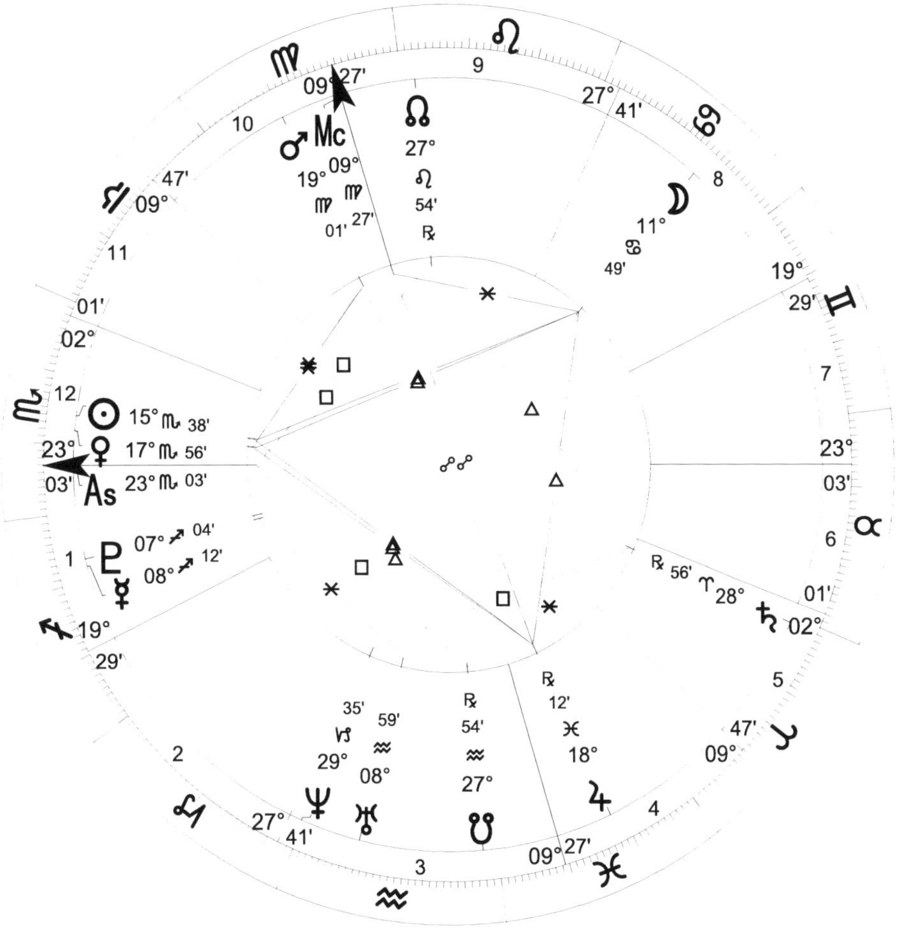

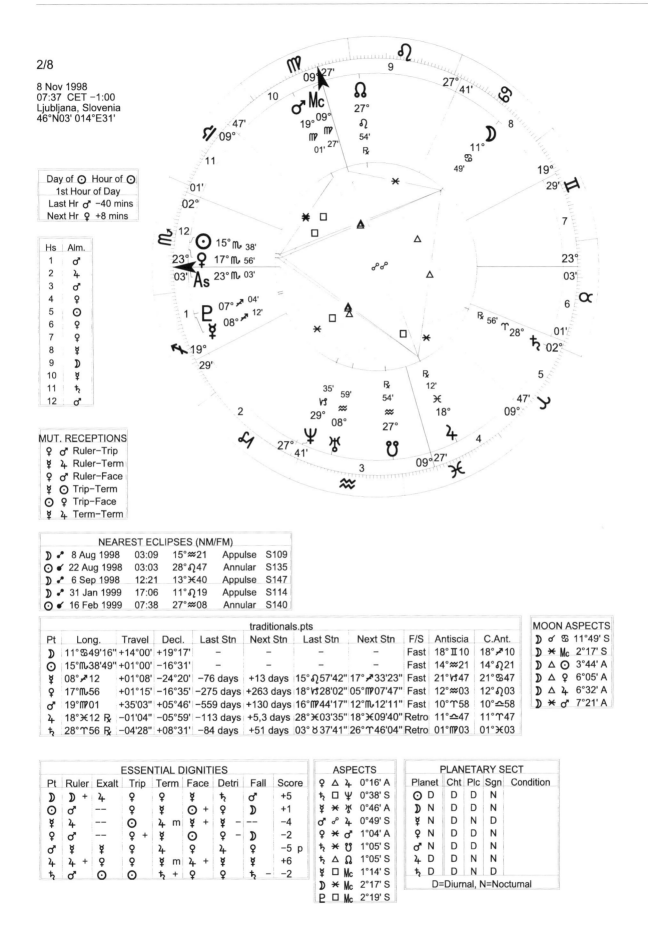

Day of ☉ Hour of ☉
1st Hour of Day
Last Hr ♂ −40 mins
Next Hr ♀ +8 mins

Hs	Alm.
1	♂
2	♃
3	♂
4	♀
5	☉
6	♀
7	♀
8	☿
9	☽
10	☿
11	♄
12	♂

MUT. RECEPTIONS
♀ ♂ Ruler–Trip
☿ ♃ Ruler–Term
♀ ♂ Ruler–Face
☿ ☉ Trip–Term
☉ ♀ Trip–Face
☿ ♃ Term–Face

NEAREST ECLIPSES (NM/FM)					
☽ ☍	8 Aug 1998	03:09	15°♒21	Appulse	S109
☉ ☌	22 Aug 1998	03:03	28°♌47	Annular	S135
☽ ☍	6 Sep 1998	12:21	13°♓40	Appulse	S147
☽ ☍	31 Jan 1999	17:06	11°♌19	Appulse	S114
☉ ☌	16 Feb 1999	07:38	27°♒08	Annular	S140

traditionals.pts

Pt	Long.	Travel	Decl.	Last Stn	Next Stn	Last Stn	Next Stn	F/S	Antiscia	C.Ant.
☽	11°♋49'16"	+14°00'	+19°17'	–	–	–	–	Fast	18°♊10	18°♐10
☉	15°♏38'49"	+01°00'	−16°31'	–	–	–	–	Fast	14°♒21	14°♌21
☿	08°♐12	+01°08'	−24°20'	−76 days	+13 days	15°♌57'42"	17°♐33'23"	Fast	21°♑47	21°♋47
♀	17°♏56	+01°15'	−16°35'	−275 days	+263 days	18°♑28'02"	05°♍07'47"	Fast	12°♒03	12°♌03
♂	19°♍01	+35'03"	+05°46'	−559 days	+130 days	16°♍44'17"	12°♏12'11"	Fast	10°♈58	10°♎58
♃	18°♓12 ℞	−01'04"	−05°59'	−113 days	+5,3 days	28°♓03'35"	18°♓09'40"	Retro	11°♎47	11°♈47
♄	28°♈56 ℞	−04'28"	+08°31'	−84 days	+51 days	03°♉37'41"	26°♈46'04"	Retro	01°♍03	01°♓03

MOON ASPECTS
☽ ☌ ♋ 11°49' S
☽ ⚹ Mc 2°17' S
☽ △ ☉ 3°44' A
☽ △ ♀ 6°05' A
☽ △ ♃ 6°32' A
☽ ⚹ ♂ 7°21' A

ESSENTIAL DIGNITIES

Pt	Ruler	Exalt	Trip	Term	Face	Detri	Fall	Score
☽	☽ +	♃	♀	♀	☿	♄	♂	+5
☉	♂	--	♀	☿	☉ +	♀	☽	+1
☿	♃	--	☉	♃ m	☿ +	☿ −	--	−4
♀	♂	--	♀ +	☿	☉	♀ −	☽	−2
♂	☿	☿	♀	♃	♀	♃	♀	−5 p
♃	♃ +	♀	♀	☿ m	♃ +	☿	☿	+6
♄	♂	☉	☉	♄ +	♀	♀	♄ −	−2

ASPECTS
♀ △ ♃ 0°16' A
♄ □ ♆ 0°38' S
☿ ⚹ ♅ 0°46' A
♂ ☍ ♃ 0°49' S
♀ ⚹ ♂ 1°04' A
♄ ⚹ ☋ 1°05' S
♄ △ ☊ 1°05' S
☿ □ Mc 1°14' S
☽ ⚹ Mc 2°17' S
♇ □ Mc 2°19' S

PLANETARY SECT

Planet		Cht	Plc	Sgn	Condition
☉	D	D	D	N	
☽	N	D	D	N	
☿	N	D	N	D	
♀	N	D	D	N	
♂	N	D	D	N	
♃	D	D	N	N	
♄	D	D	N	D	

D=Diurnal, N=Nocturnal

EMPLOYMENT AND CAREER

QUESTIONS

The most common questions of this type are:

Will I get this job?

Will I get a job soon?

Should I look for another job?

Should I accept this job offer?

Should I start a company?

Will the business project that I am planning, become a success?

Should I opt for a business partnership with this person?

The rules of interpretation are the same as for other types of questions: we must first find the links between the significators, check their essential and accidental strengths, applications and separations, and so on.

SIGNIFICATORS

The significator of the querent is always the ruler (almuten) of H1, the co-significator is the Moon; the significator of the job (aim, objective, goal) is MC with H10, business partners are in H7, the partner's funds are in H8, the profit from the business is in H11, the working environment and employees and subordinates are in H6. In the case of foreign activities (foreign business alliances, export/import trade etc.) we also examine the state of H9 which includes various legal issues related to career questions.

THE OUTCOME

The answer to the questions concerning getting a job, accomplishing a career objective, finalizing a project, etc., is almost sure to be positive, if:

- the significator of the querent or the Moon applies by a harmonious aspect to the ruler of H10 or to a planet in H10, or vice versa. The objective will be more easily achieved by the querent if the ruler of H10 applies to his significator (the job or success "comes" to him);in the opposite case, he will have to make more effort;
- the significators are connected by means of translation of light, collection of light, or by a strong mutual reception;
- the querent's significator or the Moon apply by a harmonious aspect to the Sun, or vice versa (shows help of superiors).

Additional positive indicators, which in themselves do not give a positive answer, are:
- the querent's significator or the Moon in H10, unafflicted;
- the ruler of H10 in H1, especially if this planet is faster than the ruler of H1, and if it is in aspect with a benefic;
- a benefic in H10 or H1, to which the Moon or the ruler of the ascendant applies.

Planets in a sextile or a trine with the rulers of H10 and/or H1 often show individuals who could help the querent get the job/reach the objective. Similarly, planets in a square or opposition with significators represent people who hinder them.

Significators in angular houses show a quick resolution of the matter (getting a job, finalizing a project and the like), in the succeddent houses a slower one and in cadent houses a slow progress and possible complications.

JOB CHANGES

Should I change my job? This question is fairly frequent. Students often ask if H10 shows the present job - or the future one? This depends on what exactly is on the querent's mind. If he's thinking of an actual new job that he's interested in or that is being offered to him, H10 would indicate this new job, but if his problem is that he can't decide whether to keep the current job or to rather look for a new one, H10 would show his current job. But where is that future job, then?

The late American astrologer Barbara Watters, the author of the book **HORARY ASTROLOGY AND THE JUDGMENT OF EVENTS,** used a technique whereby she gave the new job to H7 which is the derived H10 from H10 (10/10). She claimed that this technique originated from Arab astrology. In such cases, she says, we must first examine the essential and accidental dignities of the significator/s of the current job which is indicated by H10, and look for the harmony between them and the significator/s of the querent, and then examine the condition of H7 (the new job). If H10 is strong and in harmony with H1, the situation at the current job will probably improve and the change will not be desirable (necessary), but if H7 is better, the querent should go for the change.

I don't use these techniques. I prefer to follow Lilly who advises, in all questions of the desirability of a change, that we should check the Moon and/or the ruler of the ascendant – if they separate from aspects with malefics and apply to aspects with benefics, the change is desirable; otherwise, it is better to stay where we are, and not accept the new offer (or strive for a change). In case of positive indications for a change, there is an additional demand that the querent's significator and the Moon are not essentially weak or otherwise afflicted (weakened).

The Moon or H1 ruler in H10 (unafflicted) indicate that the current job suits the querent; same if both significators are in mutual reception.

I should add that we (as always) have to use our brains and common sense. Let's see what the chart tells us! We focus on the questioner and its signifiers. What's happening to him? Why is he asking this? What does he keep in mind when he asks?

The H1 ruler retrograde warns that the change is not desirable.

A retrograde ruler of H10 speaks for the job change only if the querent is returning to a position he once had, or is applying for a job in the company that he used to work for in the past. Normally, though, a retrograde significator of H10 speaks against the change.

3/1: WILL I GET THIS JOB?

21 January 1995 at 8:47 p.m. (20:47), Murska Sobota, Slovenia
Hour ruler: Jupiter

One evening, I was a guest astrologer at a radio station in another part of the country. With a view to introducing horary astrology, I decided to take some of the people's questions and answer them on air. I didn't yet have a laptop at that "ancient" time, so I prepared in advance some charts with the positions of the planets and the overview of the movement of cardinal points and house cusps, covering the interval of the 85 minutes that the broadcast lasted.

The above question was raised by a woman who called at 20:47. That was the first question after the five minutes music break. During that time, the Moon moved from a Venus' to a Mercury's degree, so I found it interesting that the voice sounded younger from those who called earlier (Mercury stands for young people). What's more, when I asked her what her Sun sign was, she said that she was a Gemini! A young "Mercurian", then - very appropriate!

She asked whether she'd get a job for which she had recently applied. After a quick glance at the current planetary and cuspal placements, I told her that she'd get a positive response within one week.

Whence my reasoning? Let's see! Significator of the querent is Mercury which also shows the job for which she had applied (H10 ruler). Co-significator of the querent is the Moon, and because it's in the first house, the sign which it occupies gets more significance. This sign is Libra and its ruler is Venus. To summarize, the chart's three most relevant planets are Mercury (main significator of the querent and the job), the Moon (co-significator of the querent), and Venus (Moon's dispositor).

The Moon is in an exact applying trine to the Sun - an excellent indication that her chances are good! As mentioned in the theoretical part of this chapter, a harmonious applying aspect of the Moon to the Sun is a strong indication of success in cases asking whether the querent would succeed in something which depends on the good-will of superiors or "authority".

What about the other chart features? Mercury is in H5, a fortunate house, with Venus, the Moon's dispositor, applying to it by a sextile. You might wonder why, since Mercury is on a later degree than Venus, so it's obviously separating. Normally, this would be the case, because Mercury is often faster than Venus, but looking at the table below the chart, we can see that Mercury was very slow on that day while Venus was fast. Mercury was slowing in its course to turn retrograde on January 26 and complete the sextile with Venus the day after (January 27). This is not a classic "completion of the matter" since Venus is only the dispositor of the Moon and therefore can't be regarded as the querent's significator, but like I said, it leans toward the affirmative answer because of Venus' connection to the Moon which isstrong in H1. In other words, this aspect facilitates the querent's and the job's "meeting". Another confirmation is shown by the fact that Mercury, the most important planet in the chart, is in its own triplicity and face and on its own degree, as well as being unafflicted, therefore quite strong.

More "help" is given by Jupiter, the hour ruler. It's in its own domicile, triplicity and term, with the Moon applying to it by a sextile. Jupiter is also the natural significator of luck and good fortune which the querent needs in this case.

I was quite surprised when the querent called me in some ten days. She reminded me of our conversation, thanked me again and said that that she had just started the new job!

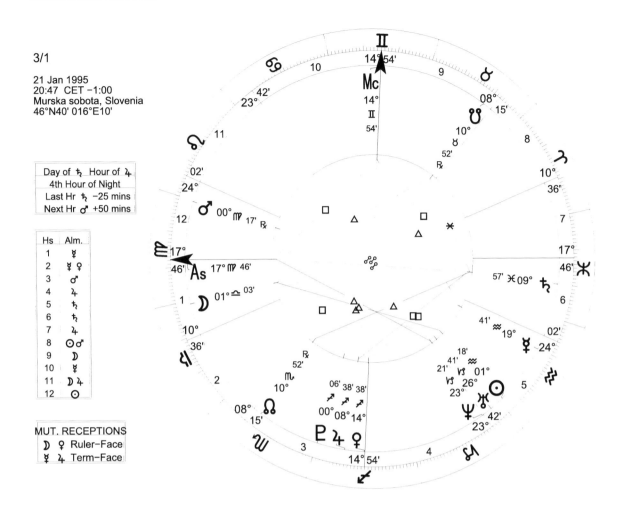

3/1

21 Jan 1995
20:47 CET −1:00
Murska sobota, Slovenia
46°N40' 016°E10'

Day of ♄ Hour of ♃
4th Hour of Night
Last Hr ♄ −25 mins
Next Hr ♂ +50 mins

Hs	Alm.
1	☿
2	☿ ♀
3	♂
4	♃
5	♄
6	♄
7	♃
8	☉♂
9	☽
10	☿
11	☽ ♃
12	☉

MUT. RECEPTIONS	
☽ ♀	Ruler–Face
☿ ♃	Term–Face

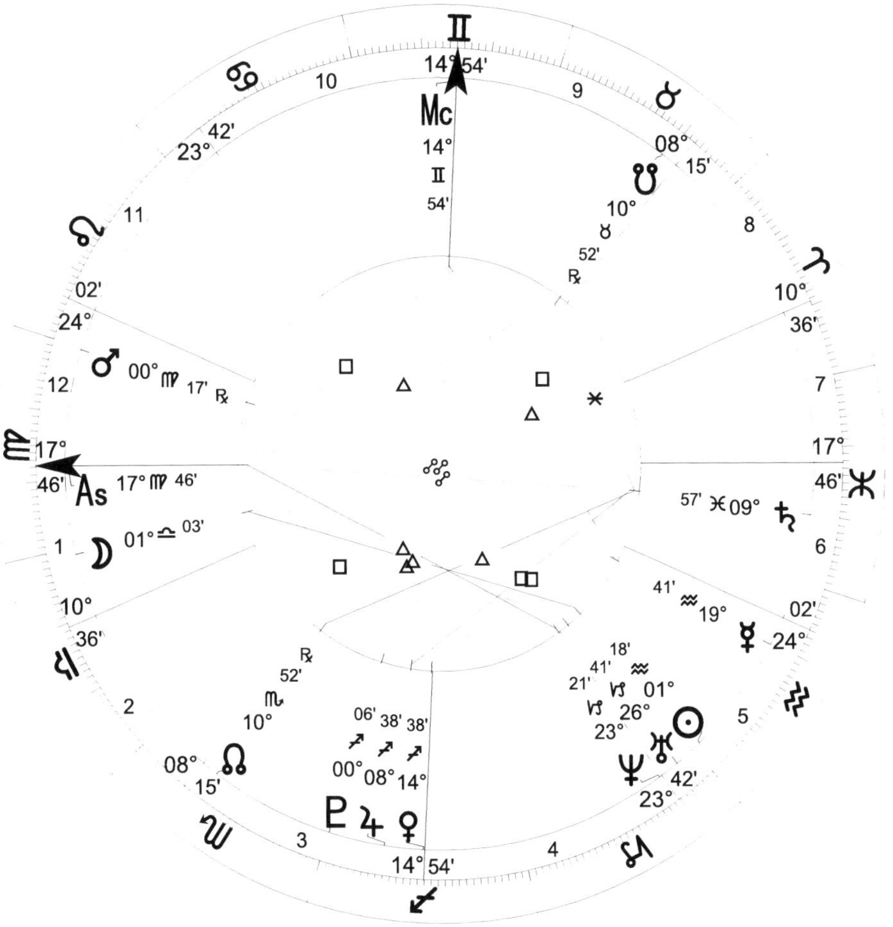

NEAREST ECLIPSES (NM/FM)					
☉ ☌	3 Nov 1994	14:35	10°♏54	Total	S133
☽ ☍	18 Nov 1994	07:57	25° ♉42	Appulse	S145
☽ ☍	15 Apr 1995	13:08	25°♎03	Partial	S112
☉ ☌	29 Apr 1995	18:36	08° ♉56	Annular	S138

traditionals.pts

Pt	Long.	Travel	Decl.	Last Stn	Next Stn	Last Stn	Next Stn	F/S	Antiscia	C.Ant.
☽	01°♎03'45"	+13°29'	−03°23'	–	–	–	–	Fast	28°♓56	28°♍56
☉	01°♒18'16"	+01°01'	−19°52'	–	–	–	–	Fast	28°♏41	28° ♉41
☿	19°♒41	+42'52"	−14°39'	−83 days	+4,2 days	20°♎48'54"	21°♒15'53"	Slow	10°♏18	10° ♉18
♀	14°♐38	+01°03'	−19°16'	−59 days	+484 days	02°♏28'46"	28° ♊17'52"	Fast	15°♑21	15°♋21
♂	00°♍17 ℞	−14'57"	+15°18'	−18 days	+61 days	02°♍40'08"	13°♌09'54"	Retro	29°♈42	29°♎42
♃	08°♐38	+10'25"	−20°59'	−203 days	+69 days	04°♏46'04"	15°♐23'00"	Fast	21°♑21	21°♋21
♄	09°♓57	+06'16"	−09°28'	−73 days	+165 days	05°♓40'45"	24°♓45'07"	Fast	20°♎02	20°♈02

MOON ASPECTS	
☽ ☌ ♎	1°03' S
☽ △ ☉	0°11' S
☽ ✶ ♇	0°53' A
☽ ✶ ♃	7°40' A

ESSENTIAL DIGNITIES

Pt	Ruler	Exalt	Trip	Term	Face	Detri	Fall	Score
☽	♀	♄	☿	♄	☽ +	♂	☉	+1
☉	♄	--	☿	☿	♀	☉ −	--	−10 p
☿	♄	--	☿ +	♃	☿ +	☉	--	+4
♀	♃	--	♃	♀ +	☽	☿	--	+2
♂	☿	☿	☽	☿	☉	♃	♀	−5 p
♃	♃ +	--	♃ +	♃ +	☿	☿	--	+10
♄	♃	♀	♂	♀	♄ +	☿	☿	+1

ASPECTS	
☽ △ ☉	0°11' S
☽ ✶ ♇	0°53' A
♄ ✶ ☋	0°55' A
♄ △ ☊	0°55' A
♂ □ ♇	1°09' A
♃ □ ♄	1°19' A
☉ ✶ ♇	2°03' S
♅ ✶ ♇	2°14' A
As □ Mc	2°52' A

PLANETARY SECT

Planet	Cht	Plc	Sgn	Condition
☉ D	N	N	D	
☽ N	N	D	D	
☿ N	N	D	D	
♀ N	N	D	D	
♂ N	N	N	N	In Hayz
♃ D	N	D	D	
♄ D	N	D	N	

D=Diurnal, N=Nocturnal

3/2: SHOULD I TAKE THIS JOB?

4 November 2002 at 5:39 p.m. (17:39), Ljubljana, Slovenia
Hour ruler: Venus

The querent, an acquaintance of mine, called me with the question of whether it would be good to accept a job that was offered to him. He said that he must decide quite soon but he was not quite sure whether the job would benefit him.

Venus as the hour ruler is not in harmony with Gemini, the ascending sign, and is also in a very poor state: in its detriment, peregrine, retrograde and in the unfortunate H6 which it also rules, beside H12 of helplessness and confinement. Such charts immediately get a few minus points because they suggest that things would not go as planned - usually in terms of the desired result.

Another indication that the question is "negatively loaded" is the applying conjunction of the Moon to the Sun. Moon's combustion is usually a bad omen for the vitality of the subject-matter of the question - unless the two celestial bodies are significators of two things or people "coming together". In this case, combustion only adds weight to other indications suggesting that this project has no future. The combust state of the Moon, co-significator of the querent, tells us that the querent was probably not aware of all the circumstances relating to the question, and that the decision regarding the job might not really be his. This is confirmed by the fact that Mercury, the main significator of the querent, is also combust. Combustion is even an approaching one because Mercury is faster than the Sun and will soon catch up with it. The querent's strength is getting consumed by the Sun, and besides, Mercury is peregrine (without essential dignity).

Neptune exerts a strong influence because it is conjunct MC. In career-related questions, the presence of Neptune in H10 shows that the querent might get disappointed or be in error, or that the question is raised so as to unintentionally mislead the astrologer. In this case, the indication is even stronger because Neptune is receiving an applying square from Mercury, the querent's significator.

Is there anything in the chart speaking for the job? Let's look at Saturn and Uranus, the traditional and modern H10 rulers. Saturn is in H1 (emplacement, a positive indication), but retrograde which could mean that the offer is unrealistic. Still, if the chart gave the feeling that the querent could really get the job, retrograde Saturn would whisper: *Don't accept it.*

The state of Uranus, modern ruler of Aquarius (MC), is very interesting. It is stationary and it occupies H10, meaning that it is a valid job significator (for those who use modern rulers, of course). Stationary planets usually show that our plans (or people and things – whatever they represent) are about to change. Often, it's of little consequence whether they are turning retrograde or direct – an immediate change of direction of a planet indicates an immediate change of direction of the affair which it represents.

Does the chart show any completion of the matter? Mercury receives Saturn in its domicile and triplicity, reflecting the fact that the querent is inclined to accept the job. Saturn's placement in Gemini, the ascending sign, also tells us that the job as such suits him. (He actually met all of the requirements regarding his qualification and such.) But Saturn doesn't receive Mercury in any of its dignities, meaning that the job "doesn't like him".

There is no aspect, neither translation of light nor mutual reception between Mercury and Saturn. What's more, the Moon and Mercury's direct application to the Sun (combustion) clearly show that nothing will come of the matter.

The querent asked for advice but as already stated, giving advice is practically impossible with the charts showing that the querent virtually has no choice.

It makes no sense to advise you whether to take this job or not, because the chart clearly shows that you're not getting it, I said, adding that I could nevertheless see his ability and suitability for the job at hand, and that he obviously also wants it. He was very surprised. He said that there were only two applicants and that during his last interview he had a very strong feeling that they already chose him.

A few days later he called me and confirmed my judgment. They chose the other candidate. His senses really cheated him, as is clearly shown by the Mercury's square to Neptune!

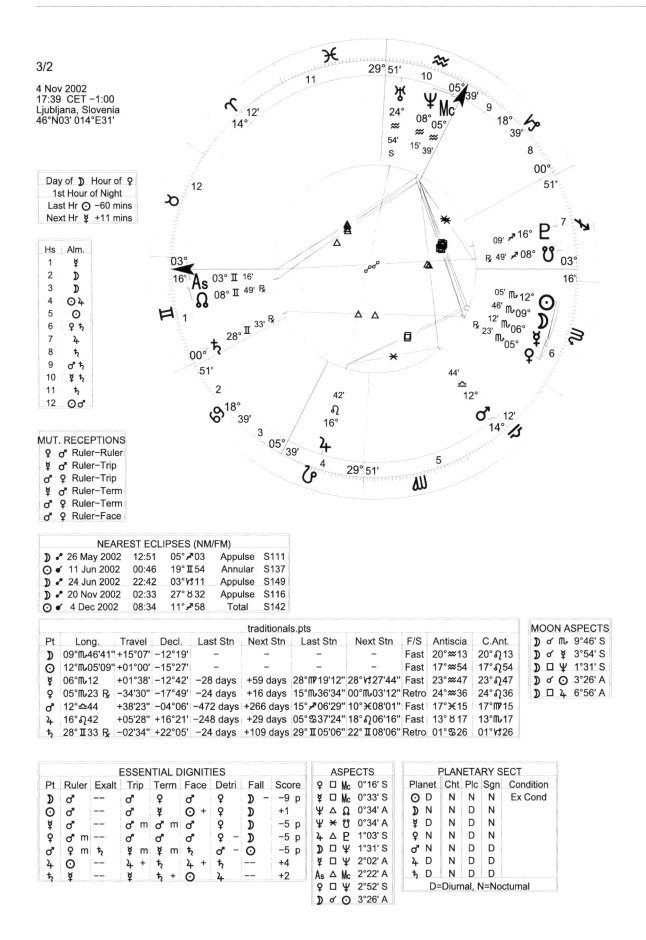

3/2

4 Nov 2002
17:39 CET −1:00
Ljubljana, Slovenia
46°N03' 014°E31'

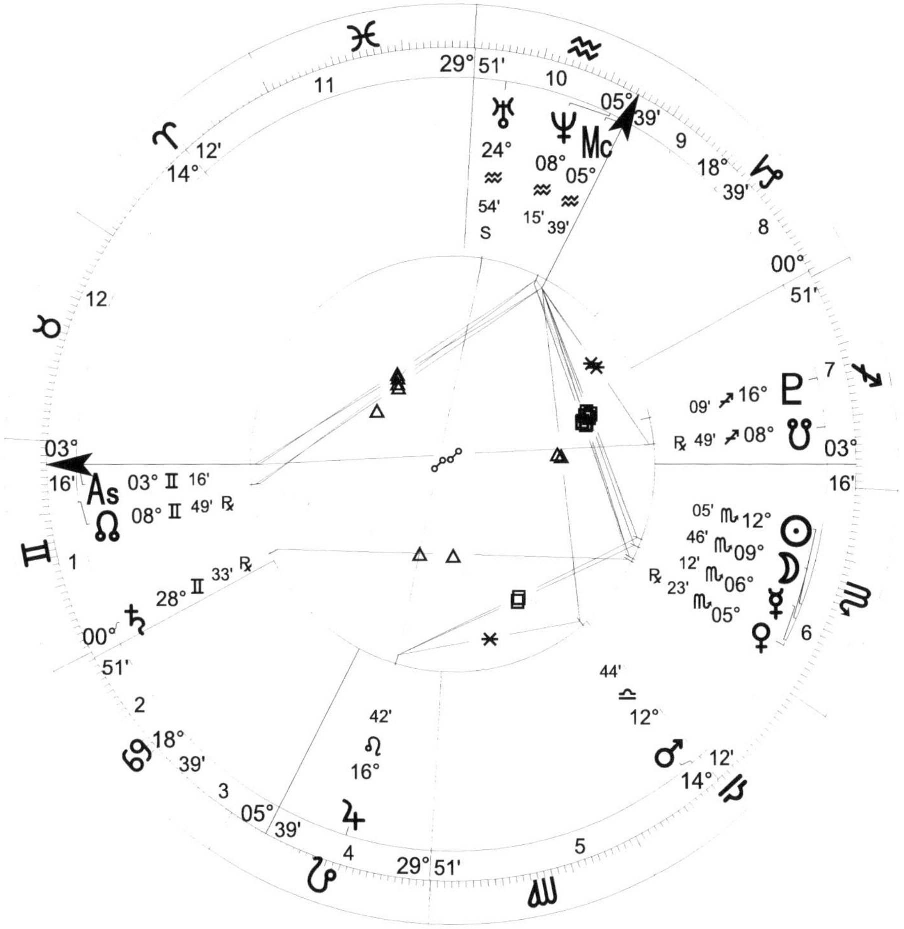

Day of ☽ Hour of ♀
1st Hour of Night
Last Hr ☉ −60 mins
Next Hr ☿ +11 mins

Hs	Alm.
1	☿
2	☽
3	☽
4	☉♃
5	☉
6	♀♄
7	♃
8	♄
9	♂♄
10	☿♄
11	♄
12	☉♂

MUT. RECEPTIONS	
♀ ♂	Ruler-Ruler
☿ ♂	Ruler-Trip
♂ ♀	Ruler-Trip
☿ ♂	Ruler-Term
♂ ♀	Ruler-Term
♂ ♀	Ruler-Face

NEAREST ECLIPSES (NM/FM)					
☽ ☍	26 May 2002	12:51	05°♐03	Appulse	S111
☉ ☌	11 Jun 2002	00:46	19°♊54	Annular	S137
☽ ☍	24 Jun 2002	22:42	03°♑11	Appulse	S149
☽ ☍	20 Nov 2002	02:33	27°♉32	Appulse	S116
☉ ☌	4 Dec 2002	08:34	11°♐58	Total	S142

traditionals.pts										
Pt	Long.	Travel	Decl.	Last Stn	Next Stn	Last Stn	Next Stn	F/S	Antiscia	C.Ant.
☽	09°♏46'41"	+15°07'	−12°19'	–	–	–	–	Fast	20°♒13	20°♌13
☉	12°♏05'09"	+01°00'	−15°27'	–	–	–	–	Fast	17°♒54	17°♌54
☿	06°♏12	+01°38'	−12°42'	−28 days	+59 days	28°♍19'12"	28°♑27'44"	Fast	23°♒47	23°♌47
♀	05°♏23 ℞	−34'30"	−17°49'	−24 days	+16 days	15°♏36'34"	00°♏03'12"	Retro	24°♒36	24°♌36
♂	12°♎44	+38'23"	−04°06'	−472 days	+266 days	15°♐06'29"	10°♓08'01"	Fast	17°♓15	17°♍15
♃	16°♌42	+05'28"	+16°21'	−248 days	+29 days	05°♋37'24"	18°♌06'16"	Fast	13°♉17	13°♏17
♄	28°♊33 ℞	−02'34"	+22°05'	−24 days	+109 days	29°♊05'06"	22°♊08'06"	Retro	01°♋26	01°♑26

MOON ASPECTS
☽ ☌ ♏ 9°46' S
☽ ☌ ☿ 3°54' S
☽ □ ♆ 1°31' S
☽ ☌ ☉ 3°26' A
☽ □ ♃ 6°56' A

ESSENTIAL DIGNITIES								
Pt	Ruler	Exalt	Trip	Term	Face	Detri	Fall	Score
☽	♂	--	♂	♀	♂	♀	☽ −	−9 p
☉	♂	--	♂	☿	☉ +	♀	☽	+1
☿	♂	--	♂ m	♂ m	♂	♀	☽	−5 p
♀	♂ m	--	♂	♂	♂	♀ −	☽	−5 p
♂	♀ m	♄	☿ m	☿ m	♄	♂ −	☉	−5 p
♃	☉	--	♃ +	♄	♃ +	♄	--	+4
♄	☿	--	☿	♄ +	☉	♃	--	+2

ASPECTS	
♀ □ Mc	0°16' S
☿ □ Mc	0°33' S
♆ △ ☊	0°34' A
♆ ✶ ☋	0°34' A
♃ △ ♇	1°03' S
☽ □ ♆	1°31' S
☿ □ ♆	2°02' A
As △ Mc	2°22' A
♀ □ ♆	2°52' S
☽ ☌ ☉	3°26' A

PLANETARY SECT					
Planet		Cht	Plc	Sgn	Condition
☉	D	N	N	N	Ex Cond
☽	N	N	D	N	
☿	D	N	D	N	
♀	N	N	D	N	
♂	N	N	D	D	
♃	D	N	D	D	
♄	D	N	D	D	
D=Diurnal, N=Nocturnal					

Let me add: if we know that two people compete (for a job or any other position), the other party is shown by H7. The winner is the one represented by the stronger planet. In this case, we see that Jupiter (H7 ruler, his rival) applies by sextile to Saturn (H10 ruler). The aspect is loose but Jupiter is in its own triplicity and face, therefore considerably stronger than the peregrine and accidentally weak Mercury. Besides, it's placed in the derived H10 (10/7). What an eloquent heavenly talk, don't you think so?

3/3: WILL I GET THIS JOB?

12 December 2003 at 5:08 p.m. (17:08), Liedekerke, Belgium
Hour ruler: Mars

The question was emailed to me by an acquaintance, a Slovenian woman married to a Belgian guy, with whom she had been living in his country for several years. It reached my mailbox at 17:10, from which I concluded that she probably wrote it a minute or two before, so I cast the chart for 17:08 – and for her location, of course.

She said that she was in the middle of negotiations for a new job. The (potential) employer's office was located in London, but she'd work for them from her home in Belgium. She had already had two interviews for the post and was looking forward to it, but wasn't sure if she would really get it.

The ascendant is on the last degree of Gemini while its ruler Mercury is in Capricorn, in an exact applying opposition to its dispositor Saturn, significator of the job (H10 ruler). Uranus, the modern H10 ruler, is in H10 in an exact trine with the ascendant. All this quite clearly shows her concern, especially because Saturn is in H1 (the querent). This is an example of emplacement – is the job "coming to her"?

There are, unfortunately, two strong reasons why the situation is all but rosy. The first is Mercury's applying opposition to Saturn - a pretty obvious sign that their agreement is not happening. The second is a poor condition of Saturn (in its detriment and retrograde) which substantially weakens its ability for a positive action. As already mentioned, Mercury is in Saturn's sign of domicile, Capricorn, meaning that she feels capable for the job and that it would suit her. But Mercury's opposition to its dispositor which is also the job ruler is really worrying - it suggests an obstruction.

There is yet another reason why she'd probably not get the job: a disharmonious planetary hour. While Mars, the hour ruler, is essentially and accidentally strong, it is not in any of Saturn's dignities - on the contrary, it's even in Mercury's detriment and fall!

What about the Moon? It's in Leo and void-of-course; although at the beginning of a sign, it's not in an orb of aspect with any visible planet, which defines it as void. Its applying opposition to Neptune can only make matters worse.

It's therefore clear that there's no completion of the matter in this chart! The Uranus/ascendant trine is not sufficient for a positive outcome, especially because the ascendant is at the very end of a sign, showing that the situation will soon change. And because Mercury is in a cardinal sign and an angular house, this change is obviously going to take place very soon.

Unfortunately, you are not getting this job, I wrote in reply. *It seems that something is going to complicate the arrangements which will soon crumble. The decision will be made shortly. Someone else is getting the job. I wish you more luck next time!*

On the same day at 21:21 (9:21 p.m.) I received her email: *Thank you very much for your reply. Half an hour ago they called me and told me that the position which interests me will not be available until July. I can't wait until then so I just turned it down. As you can see, you were not wrong.*

I find it fascinating how clearly the circumstances, described in her mail, are reflected in the chart! Namely, the delayed start of the (potential) job is nicely described by the retrograde state of Saturn, while her decision to terminate the negotiations is shown by the opposition of Mercury. Because this is the faster planet, it was she who decided to reject the offer. Besides, this was done on the same day, which is also very suitable (cardinality, angularity and the close proximity of the ascendant to the next sign). Less than one unit - less than a day!

I should add that I actually read her mail at 18:21 (6:21 p.m.). The chart, cast for that time, is not quite as revealing and impressive as the chart, cast for the time when she wrote down the question. But you can check it up and judge for yourself!

3/3

12 Dec 2003
17:08 CET −1:00
Liedekerke, Belgium
50°N52' 004°E05'

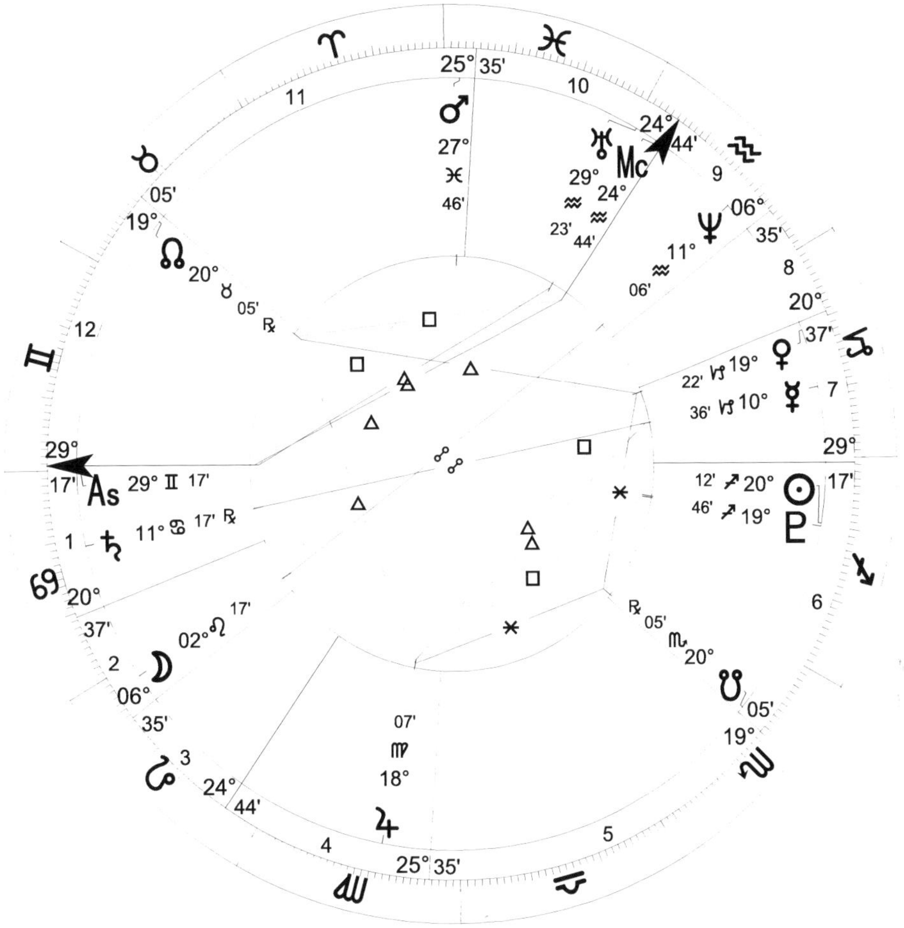

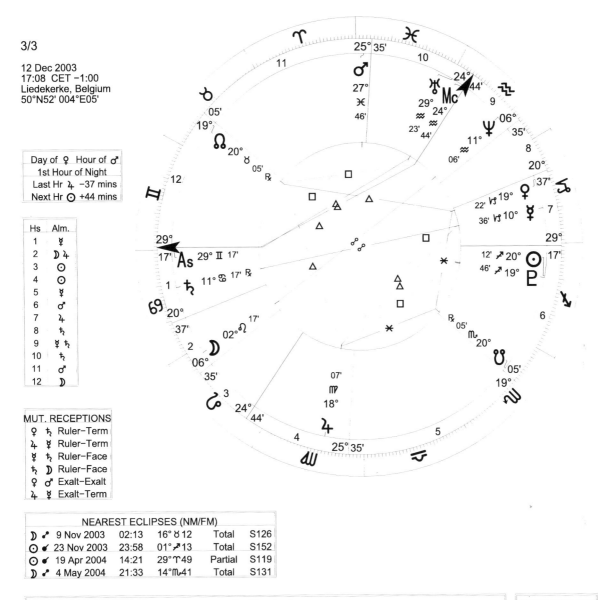

Day of ♀ Hour of ♂
1st Hour of Night
Last Hr ♃ −37 mins
Next Hr ☉ +44 mins

Hs	Alm.
1	☿
2	☽ ♃
3	☉
4	☉
5	☿
6	♂
7	♃
8	♄
9	☿ ♄
10	♄
11	♂
12	☽

MUT. RECEPTIONS	
♀ ♄	Ruler–Term
♃ ☿	Ruler–Term
☿ ♄	Ruler–Face
♄ ☽	Ruler–Face
♀ ♂	Exalt–Exalt
♃ ☿	Exalt–Term

NEAREST ECLIPSES (NM/FM)				
☽ 9 Nov 2003	02:13	16° ♉ 12	Total	S126
☉ 23 Nov 2003	23:58	01° ♐ 13	Total	S152
☉ 19 Apr 2004	14:21	29° ♈ 49	Partial	S119
☽ 4 May 2004	21:33	14° ♏ 41	Total	S131

traditionals.pts										
Pt	Long.	Travel	Decl.	Last Stn	Next Stn	Last Stn	Next Stn	F/S	Antiscia	C.Ant.
☽	02° ♌ 17'11"	+12°19'	+24°28'	–	–	–	–	Slow	27° ♉ 42	27° ♏ 42
☉	20° ♐ 12'27"	+01°00'	−23°04'	–	–	–	–	Fast	09° ♑ 47	09° ♋ 47
☿	10° ♑ 36	+43'24"	−24°38'	−83 days	+5,0 days	12° ♍ 12'13"	12° ♑ 33'45"	Slow	19° ♐ 23	19° ♊ 23
♀	19° ♑ 22	+01°14'	−23°42'	−386 days	+157 days	00° ♏ 03'12"	26° ♊ 08'18"	Fast	10° ♐ 37	10° ♊ 37
♂	27° ♓ 46	+34'09"	−01°19'	−76 days	+659 days	00° ♓ 07'06"	23° ♉ 22'20"	Slow	02° ♎ 13	02° ♈ 13
♃	18° ♍ 07	+04'09"	+05°43'	−252 days	+22 days	08° ♌ 03'38"	18° ♍ 54'13"	Slow	11° ♈ 52	11° ♎ 52
♄	11° ♋ 17 ℞	−04'25"	+22°15'	−47 days	+86 days	13° ♋ 14'23"	06° ♋ 17'09"	Retro	18° ♊ 42	18° ♐ 42

MOON ASPECTS
☽ ☌ ♌ 2°17' S

ESSENTIAL DIGNITIES								
Pt	Ruler	Exalt	Trip	Term	Face	Detri	Fall	Score
☽	☉	--	♃ m	♃	♄	♄	--	−5 p
☉	♃	--	♃	☿	♄	☿	--	−5 p
☿	♄	♂	☽	♃	♂	☽	♃	−5 p
♀	♄	♂ m	☽	♀ +	♂	☽	♃	+6
♂	♃	♀ m	♂ +	♂ +	♂ +	☿	☿	+10
♃	☿	☿	☽ m	♃ +	♀	♃ −	♀	−3
♄	☽	♃	♂	♀	☿	♄ −	♂	−10 p

ASPECTS			
♅	△	As	0°06' S
♀	⚹	☋	0°42' A
♀	△	☊	0°42' A
♀	△	♃	1°16' S
♃	□	♇	1°28' A
♂	□	As	1°31' S
♃	⚹	☋	1°59' A
♃	△	☊	1°59' A
☉	□	♃	2°05' S
☿	☍	♄	2°25' A

PLANETARY SECT				
Planet	Cht	Plc	Sgn	Condition
☉ D	N	N	D	
☽ N	N	D	D	
☿ N	N	N	N	In Hayz
♀ N	N	N	N	In Hayz
♂ N	N	N	N	In Hayz
♃ D	N	D	N	
♄ D	N	D	N	
D=Diurnal, N=Nocturnal				

3/4: POTATO CHIPS, CANDIES, BOTH, OR NONE?

21 November 1994 at 11:09 a.m., Ljubljana, Slovenia
Hour ruler: Venus

The querent was negotiating on business co-operation (co-investment) with two potential partners. The first business involved the production and selling of potato chips and the second the selling of candies, but he couldn't decide: should he choose the first or the second deal, or both of them? Or, perhaps, neither of them?

His main significator is Saturn, while the significators of potential business partners are the Moon and the Sun - the Moon as the main H7 ruler and the Sun as its co-ruler due to its rulership over Leo, the intercepted H7 sign. The planned business is signified by Mars, the H10 ruler. The Moon also functions as co-significator of the querent while at the same time describing the course of events.

The Sun and Mars are in a double mutual reception – by sign and by house. Mars in Leo and the Sun in Scorpio make for their MR by sign, while the Sun, the H7 co-ruler is in H10, and Mars, the H10 ruler, is in H7, making for a MR by house. As we know, mutual reception usually indicates a choice - and so it was because the querent was torn between two potential business deals / partnerships.

When deciding between two alternative options which belong to the same house or are under the domain of the same planet, we can make use of natural significators. Candies are clearly under Venus, the natural ruler of sweet taste, while the rulership over potato chips is a little more complicated, but due to its salinity I decided for the Moon which is the natural significator of salt. The choice of both natural significators looks quite logical and justified because Saturn (the querent) is in aspect with both Venus and the Moon.

The question is: which option should he choose? To get the answer we must examine the strengths and weaknesses of both significators. Venus is in detriment, peregrine and retrograde, but the Moon is in its domicile – essentially dignified. The decision looks easy! Chips have much advantage over candies also because the Moon (chips) applies by trine to Saturn (the querent) while the Moon separates from a trine with Venus. At the same time, Venus (candies) separates from a trine with Saturn (the querent), indicating a withdrawal – all the more so because it is retrograde.

Before I conveyed my opinion to the querent, I asked him whether he was first agreeing to a deal with "the chips partner". Namely, the Moon is the first H7 ruler and thus indicates the first partner while the Sun as the second H7 ruler indicates the second deal or the second partner. He replied in the affirmative, saying that his first talks related to the potato chips business. I also asked him whether the candies business was about importing/foreign trade. (Venus is in H9 which it also rules.) He confirmed this too.

Another confirmation is shown by the Sun's imminent crossing into the next sign, thus indicating the second partner's withdrawal.

I told him that it would no doubt be better to decide for the investment in the potato chips project, while the deal with candies would obviously be unsuccessful. I added that the chart clearly shows what he would decide to do.

He was very pleased with my answer. He said that I had dispelled his doubts and actually confirmed his wish, as he himself had been leaning towards the first option. Because the Moon is 2°55' away from an exact trine with Saturn, I told him that an important step towards the realization of his plans will take place in about three weeks. Yes, he said, the potato chips plant is actually due to start operating in three weeks' time!

In business decisions, financial matters are usually highly important, so I decided to check the condition of H2 and H8 (the finances of the querent and his business partner) as well as H11 (financial success or company's profit). Saturn on cusp of H2 shows the core of the querent's interest: earnings, while its ruler Jupiter in H10 clearly reflects his plan to invest in a business project. The rulers of both financial houses, Jupiter and Mercury, are applying to a conjunction in H10 of business (Mercury via square with Mars, but this planet rules H10), so the project will definitely bring profit to the investors. Financial success is also shown by Jupiter, H2 and H11 ruler, in H10, therefore accidentally strong.

The chart is very interesting also from the almutens' perspective: both ascendant and descendent have two almutens, which confirms and reflects the "duality" of the case. Almutens of the ascendant are Venus and Saturn - precisely those planets associated with the business options between which he was choosing, while also being connected with the Moon.

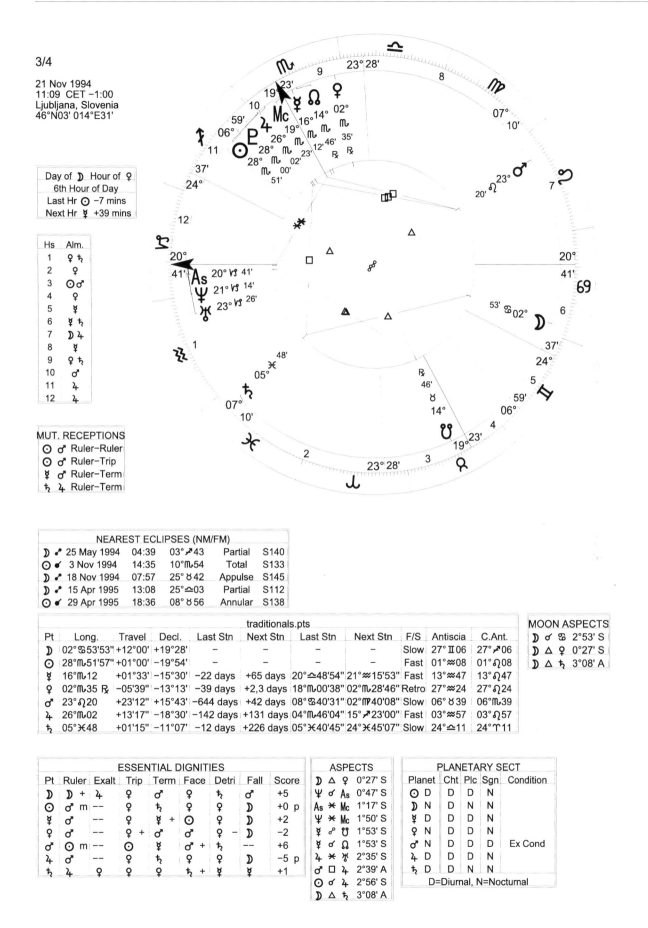

3/4

21 Nov 1994
11:09 CET −1:00
Ljubljana, Slovenia
46°N03' 014°E31'

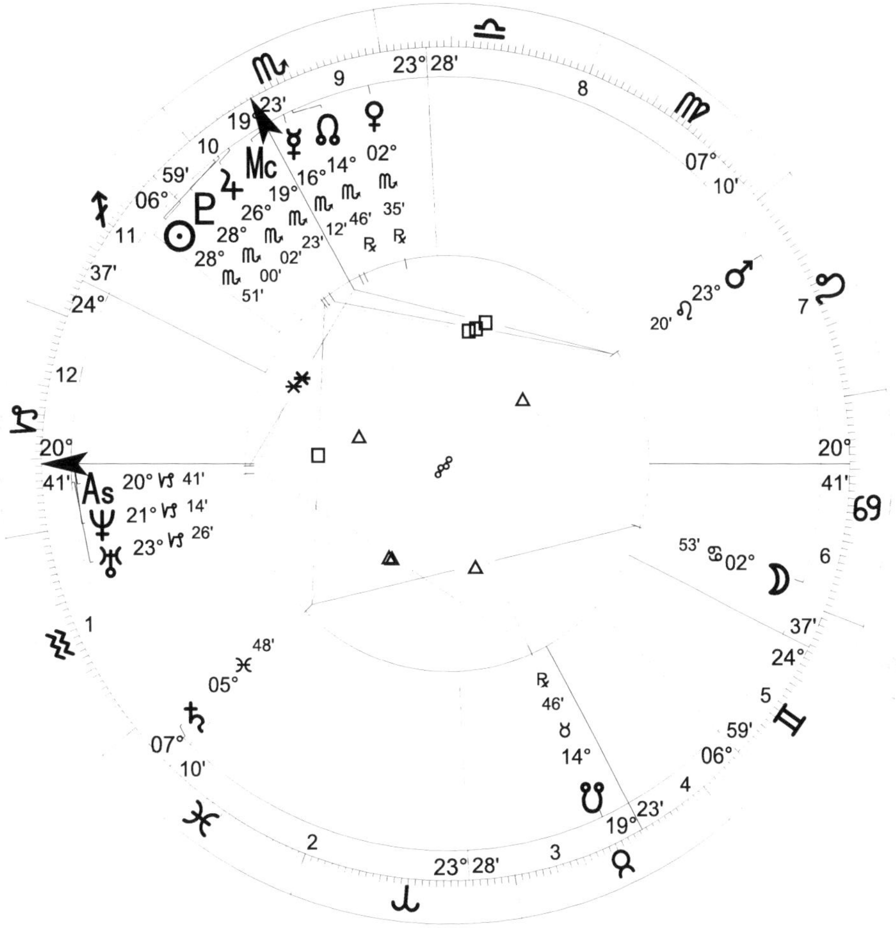

Day of ☽ Hour of ♀
6th Hour of Day
Last Hr ☉ −7 mins
Next Hr ☿ +39 mins

Hs	Alm.
1	♀ ♄
2	♀
3	☉ ♂
4	♀
5	☿
6	☿ ♄
7	☽ ♃
8	☿
9	♀ ♄
10	♂
11	♃
12	♃

MUT. RECEPTIONS
☉ ♂ Ruler-Ruler
☉ ♂ Ruler-Trip
☿ ♂ Ruler-Term
♄ ♃ Ruler-Term

NEAREST ECLIPSES (NM/FM)					
☽ ☍	25 May 1994	04:39	03°♐43	Partial	S140
☉ ☌	3 Nov 1994	14:35	10°♏54	Total	S133
☽ ☍	18 Nov 1994	07:57	25°♉42	Appulse	S145
☽ ☍	15 Apr 1995	13:08	25°♎03	Partial	S112
☉ ☌	29 Apr 1995	18:36	08°♉56	Annular	S138

traditionals.pts

Pt	Long.	Travel	Decl.	Last Stn	Next Stn	Last Stn	Next Stn	F/S	Antiscia	C.Ant.
☽	02°♋53'53"	+12°00'	+19°28'	–	–	–	–	Slow	27°♊06	27°♐06
☉	28°♏51'57"	+01°00'	−19°54'	–	–	–	–	Fast	01°♒08	01°♌08
☿	16°♏12	+01°33'	−15°30'	−22 days	+65 days	20°♎48'54"	21°♒15'53"	Fast	13°♒47	13°♌47
♀	02°♏35 ℞	−05'39"	−13°13'	−39 days	+2,3 days	18°♏00'38"	02°♏28'46"	Retro	27°♒24	27°♌24
♂	23°♌20	+23'12"	+15°43'	−644 days	+42 days	08°♋40'31"	02°♍40'08"	Slow	06°♉39	06°♏39
♃	26°♏02	+13'17"	−18°30'	−142 days	+131 days	04°♏46'04"	15°♐23'00"	Fast	03°♒57	03°♌57
♄	05°♓48	+01'15"	−11°07'	−12 days	+226 days	05°♓40'45"	24°♓45'07"	Slow	24°♎11	24°♈11

MOON ASPECTS
☽ ☌ ♋ 2°53' S
☽ △ ♀ 0°27' S
☽ △ ♄ 3°08' A

ESSENTIAL DIGNITIES

Pt	Ruler	Exalt	Trip	Term	Face	Detri	Fall	Score
☽	☽ +	♃	♀	♂	♀	♄	♂	+5
☉	♂ m	--	♀	♄	♀	♀	☽	+0 p
☿	♂	--	♀	☿ +	☉	♀	☽	+2
♀	♂	--	♀ +	♂	♂	♀ −	☽	−2
♂	☉ m	--	☉	☿	♂ +	♄	--	+6
♃	♂	--	♀	♄	♀	♀	☽	−5 p
♄	♃	♀	♀	♀	♄ +	☿	☿	+1

ASPECTS
☽ △ ♀ 0°27' S
♆ ☌ As 0°47' S
As ⚹ Mc 1°17' S
♆ ⚹ Mc 1°50' S
☿ ☍ ☋ 1°53' S
☿ ☌ ☊ 1°53' S
♃ ⚹ ♅ 2°35' S
♂ □ ♃ 2°39' A
☉ ☌ ♃ 2°56' S
☽ △ ♄ 3°08' A

PLANETARY SECT

Planet	Cht	Plc	Sgn	Condition
☉ D	D	D	N	
☽ N	D	N	N	
☿ D	D	D	N	
♀ N	D	D	N	
♂ N	D	D	D	Ex Cond
♃ D	D	D	N	
♄ D	D	N	N	

D=Diurnal, N=Nocturnal

3/5: WILL I SUCCEED IN ORGANIZING A COURSE AT OBALA?

25 October 1994 at 8:56 p.m. (20:56), Ljubljana, Slovenia
Hour ruler: Sun

A friend of mine said that she knew many people in the Slovenian coastal region (called simply Obala - The Coast) who were interested in astrology, and suggested that I organize a beginner's astrology course there. I liked the idea, so she found a classroom at the premises of the local community of Izola, a small coastal town, while I set myself to scheduling the program, and to advertising. The initial interest was significant, but with the approaching deadline for submission of applications, the situation was depressing: the applications were fewer than the numbers of fingers on one hand! I was thinking whether to invest in another (expensive) newspaper ad? Would that get me enough students by the planned time of the beginning of the course? I should have at least ten participants, or the project would not be profitable. I therefore posed the above question, wandering if the course would start without further investments/advertisements on my part.

My significator is the Moon, the ascendant ruler, and the course (my business venture) is shown by Jupiter, the H10 ruler. The group which I would teach is signified by Mars (H11 ruler) and Venus (the ruler of the intercepted Taurus in H11), the classroom by Mercury, H4 ruler. Peregrine Mars and retrograde Venus which is also in detriment, plus the south node in H11, reveal the scarcity of applications.

The Moon, my ruler, is very powerful: it's in its own domicile and conjunct the ascendant, therefore practically in H1. This in itself shows that I'm strong and have very good chances to succeed in this matter, but for the confirmation, there must be some kind of completion of the matter. The Moon applies by trine to Venus, H5 ruler and H11 co-ruler, which means that with a bit of luck (H5) I can get a sufficient number of students (H11). The Moon's next aspect is a trine to Jupiter, H10 ruler – the course will come to pass!

And so it was - even without another newspaper ad! I asked the friend who helped to organize the event, to try harder and remind her friends about the course again. She did, and more applications rolled in. A nice crowd was gathered by November 5 when the course started, as planned. This is 10 days from the time of the question. Moon and Jupiter are 9°19' apart, but since the Moon was slow on that day (its daily travel being 12°5'), which prolongs the time a bit, the date of the start actually exactly matched the indications in the horary chart.

In the meantime, I had to overcome another organizational problem. As shown by retrograde Mercury, H4 ruler, which separates from a square with Uranus and applies to a square with Neptune (both strong in the angular H7), there were some problems with the classroom that finally led me to decide to change it (Mercury retrograde!). A week before the start, I drove down to Izola to see the place, and found that the classroom was awkwardly built, the heating system didn't work, and there was no knowing what the rent would be. I therefore found a better classroom in the nearby Koper.

H5 in this chart is packed, and the course was indeed a lot of fun. The students were all very nice; during the breaks, we sat in a city cafe and chatted, and on completion of the course, one of the students invited us to a dinner in classy restaurant.

P.S. This example is one of those that my correspondence course students get for their homework. It is interesting that very few give the course to H10, which is the proper house for a business venture. Instead, they often go for H3. It is true that courses as such belong to H3, which also plays a minor role here, but not the major one, since the course was my business project! It's interesting that in this case, H3 ruler, the Sun, is also the hour ruler and that it applies by a harmonious trine to Saturn, placed in H9 which it also rules. Both "houses of knowledge" are thus harmoniously linked together to give an additional indication of a positive result.

3/5

25 Oct 1994
20:56 CET −1:00
Ljubljana, Slovenia
46°N03' 014°E31'

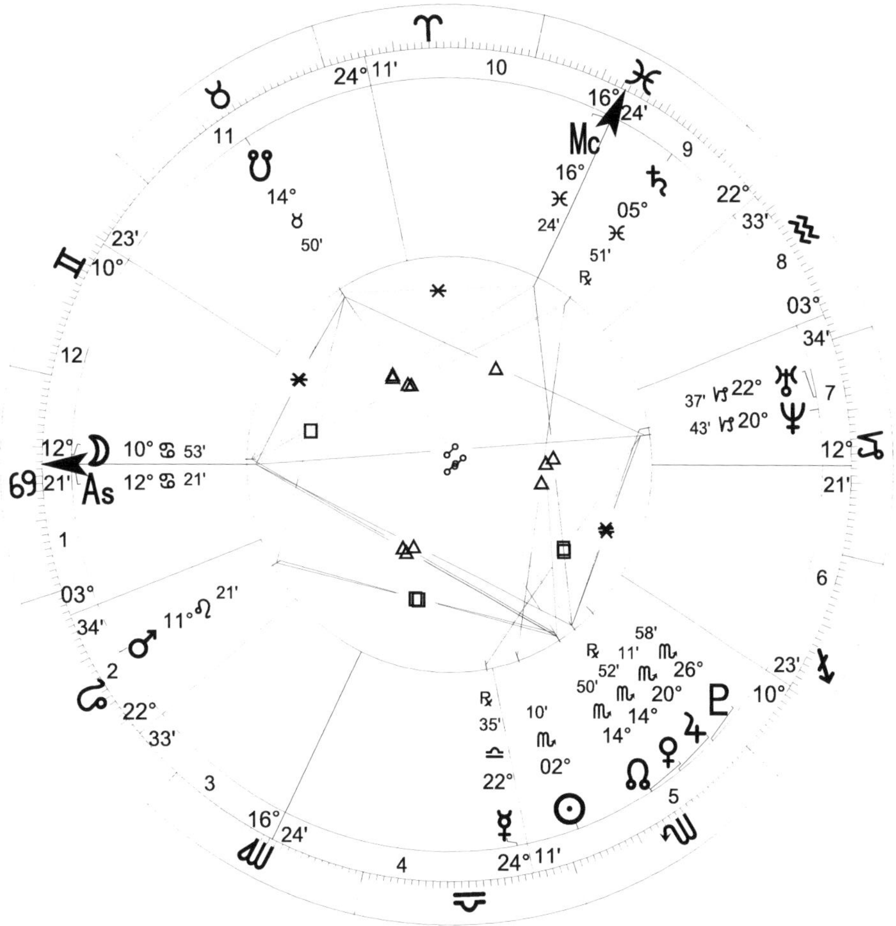

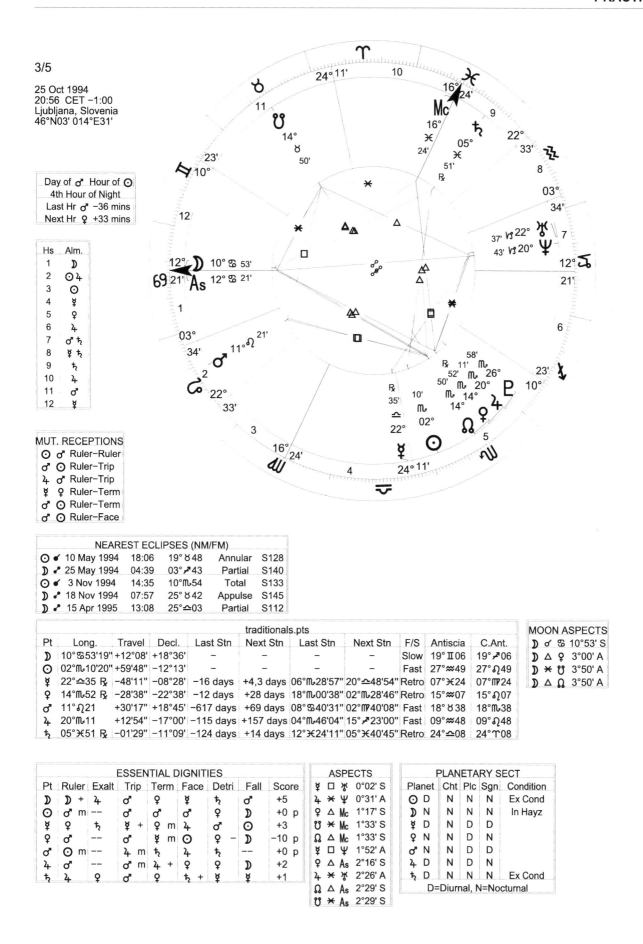

Day of ♂ Hour of ☉
4th Hour of Night
Last Hr ♂ −36 mins
Next Hr ♀ +33 mins

Hs	Alm.
1	☽
2	☉ ♃
3	☉
4	☿
5	♀
6	♃
7	♂ ♄
8	☿ ♄
9	♄
10	♃
11	♂
12	☿

MUT. RECEPTIONS
☉ ♂ Ruler-Ruler
♂ ☉ Ruler-Trip
♃ ♂ Ruler-Trip
☿ ♀ Ruler-Term
♂ ☉ Ruler-Term
♂ ☉ Ruler-Face

NEAREST ECLIPSES (NM/FM)					
☉ ●	10 May 1994	18:06	19°♉48	Annular	S128
☽ ●	25 May 1994	04:39	03°♐43	Partial	S140
☉ ●	3 Nov 1994	14:35	10°♏54	Total	S133
☽ ●	18 Nov 1994	07:57	25°♉42	Appulse	S145
☽ ●	15 Apr 1995	13:08	25°♎03	Partial	S112

traditionals.pts										
Pt	Long.	Travel	Decl.	Last Stn	Next Stn	Last Stn	Next Stn	F/S	Antiscia	C.Ant.
☽	10°♋53'19"	+12°08'	+18°36'	–	–	–	–	Slow	19°♊06	19°♐06
☉	02°♏10'20"	+59'48"	−12°13'	–	–	–	–	Fast	27°♒49	27°♌49
☿	22°♎35 ℞	−48'11"	−08°28'	−16 days	+4,3 days	06°♏28'57"	20°♎48'54"	Retro	07°♓24	07°♍24
♀	14°♏52 ℞	−28'38"	−22°38'	−12 days	+28 days	18°♏00'38"	02°♏28'46"	Retro	15°♒07	15°♌07
♂	11°♌21	+30'17"	+18°45'	−617 days	+69 days	08°♋40'31"	02°♍40'08"	Fast	18°♉38	18°♏38
♃	20°♏11	+12'54"	−17°00'	−115 days	+157 days	04°♏46'04"	15°♐23'00"	Fast	09°♒48	09°♌48
♄	05°♓51 ℞	−01'29"	−11°09'	−124 days	+14 days	12°♓24'11"	05°♓40'45"	Retro	24°♎08	24°♈08

MOON ASPECTS
☽ ☌ ♋ 10°53' S
☽ △ ♀ 3°00' A
☽ ✶ ☋ 3°50' A
☽ △ ☊ 3°50' A

ESSENTIAL DIGNITIES								
Pt	Ruler	Exalt	Trip	Term	Face	Detri	Fall	Score
☽	☽ +	♃	♂	♀	☿	♄	♂	+5
☉	♂ m	--	♂	♂	♂	♀	☽	+0 p
☿	♀	♄	☿ +	♀ m	♃	♂	☉	+3
♀	♂	--	♂	☿ m	☉	♀ −	☽	−10 p
♂	☉ m	--	♃ m	♄	♃	♄	--	+0 p
♃	♂	--	♂ m	♃ +	♀	♀	☽	+2
♄	♃	♀	♂	♀	♄ +	☿	☿	+1

ASPECTS
☿ □ ♅ 0°02' S
♃ ✶ ♆ 0°31' A
♀ △ Mc 1°17' S
☋ ✶ Mc 1°33' S
☊ △ Mc 1°33' S
☿ □ ♆ 1°52' A
♀ △ As 2°16' S
♃ ✶ ♅ 2°26' A
☊ △ As 2°29' S
☋ ✶ As 2°29' S

PLANETARY SECT					
Planet		Cht	Plc	Sgn	Condition
☉	D	N	N	N	Ex Cond
☽	N	N	N	N	In Hayz
☿	D	N	D	D	
♀	N	N	D	N	
♂	N	N	D	D	
♃	D	N	D	N	
♄	D	N	N	N	Ex Cond
D=Diurnal, N=Nocturnal					

3/6: WILL THE BOOK SERIES GET TRANSLATED?

17 February 1995 at 8:05 a.m., Ljubljana, Slovenia
Hour ruler: Mercury

The editor of the publishing house for which I occasionally translated astrological and related literature, sent me an astrology booklet in English, one of a series of twelve. He asked me if I would translate the books, adding that the whole project was still under consideration of the editor-in-chief who'd have the final word in confirming it.

I agreed. Time passed and there was no word from the editor, so I asked myself the above question. The sub-question was, of course, whether I would get the job, as this would only happen if the project received a green light.

My main significator is Jupiter which also rules H10 of professional activities, so it is very appropriate to find it in H9 of publishing, which it also rules. It's in its domicile and above the horizon in a day chart, eastern and fast, which gives it a high number of points and therefore much power of positive action. Its exact applying square to Saturn warns of possible obstacles or even a total obstruction, but a careful look into the ephemeris shows that the aspect will not perfect! Saturn's daily motion at the time of the question was a few arc seconds lower than that of Jupiter, but in the following days, Saturn accelerated and got ahead of Jupiter, so the square never came to pass. (See table – Jupiter's daily motion is 7'19" and Saturn's is 7'12", but to see whether the aspect would actually perfect, we need to check the ephemeris. I use graphic ephemeris for the check because it gives a clear presentation of planetary paths.)

My co-ruler is Mars (because it rules the intercepted Aries in H1). It's in the weak and unfortunate H6 but its role is significant because it applies (by retrograde motion) by trine to Jupiter, the all-important ruler of H1 and H10. It's like the job and I are coming together! The aspect will perfect without frustration, so this is a strong indication of success.

What about the Moon, which also co-rules me and shows the course of events? According to traditional criteria, it is void-of-course, but let us remember: if the main significators show a clear affirmative answer, a VOC Moon does not mean that the question has no future!

Let's go back to the core of the question. The books to be translated are ruled by Mercury which rules H3 and is also the natural significator of books. It's the hour ruler as well, meaning that it has something important to tell! We can see that it applies by sextile to Jupiter, and this is another confirmation that the series would get published. The books (Mercury) are going (applying sextile) to press (Jupiter in H9)!

We should, of course, check whether the sextile would really come to pass. You'll notice that Mercury was very slow on that day (daily travel 0°7'). If a planet's daily motion is much slower than its average, we must check whether it might station soon, which could prevent the completion of the aspect (refranation). A look into the ephemeris shows that Mercury moved direct (after a three-week retrograde motion) the previous day and that it'll soon accelerate and link up with Jupiter at 13° Aquarius. Everything is OK!

I might add that Mercury is on the cusp of H12, but it would be in the fortunate H11 in the system of whole sign houses, which is certainly a plus. Also, it is not afflicted and has some essential strength (term). It is also interesting that it's placed in Aquarius, the sign ruling astrology (according to some authors at least, including myself).

The editor called me exactly one month after the question (on 17 March) and said that the series was going to get translated and that I can start working on it, but that I didn't need to hurry because the deadline for submitting the translation has not yet been set. (This happened only towards the middle of April.)

You will see that the Moon is almost 4° away from an exact trine with Neptune. Four degrees correspond to four weeks or one month (the Moon in conjunction with the descendant can be considered cardinal, but it's in a movable sign which makes it slower), corresponding to the time which elapsed until the editor's call. We could say that Neptune was my co-significator as the modern ruler of Pisces, the ascending sign, while the Moon, due to its conjunction with the descendant, could also stand for the editor (the person I'm negotiating with).

On the other hand, the time unit of 4 weeks is also indicated by the Moon's distance to descendant. This is actually 5 degrees, but the Moon was fast and accelerating, which often shortens the time – especially when a quick-moving axis is involved.

3/6

17 Feb 1995
08:05 CET −1:00
Ljubljana, Slovenia
46°N03' 014°E31'

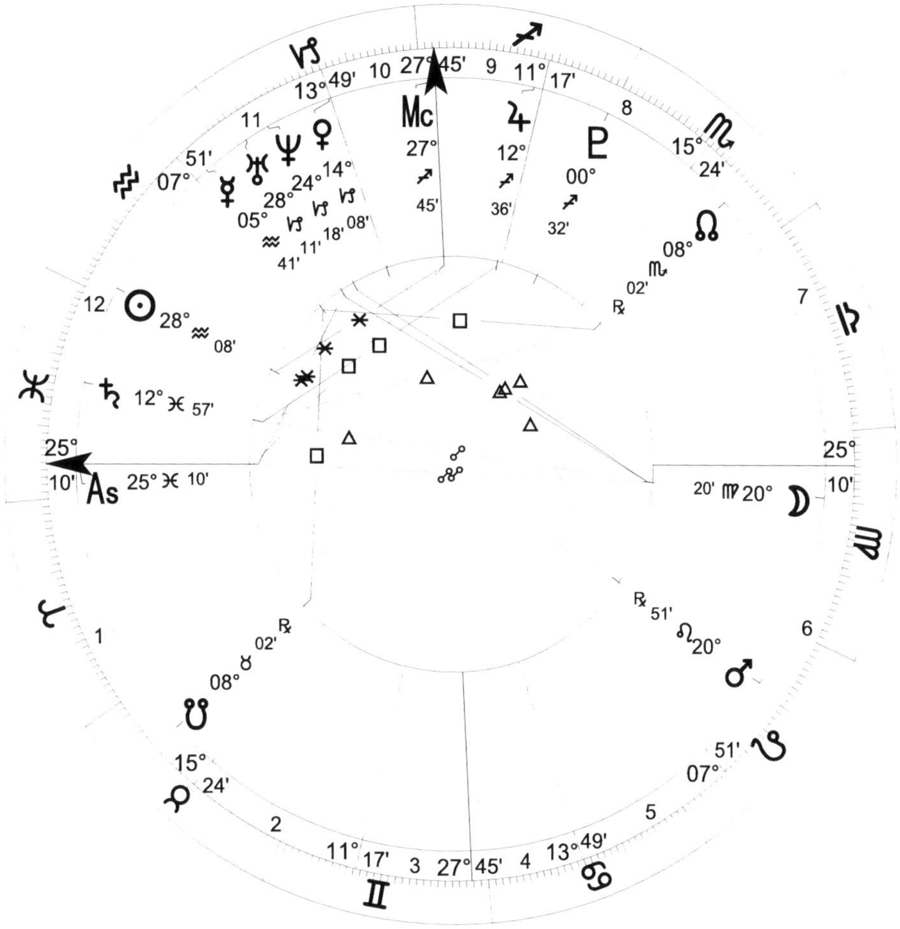

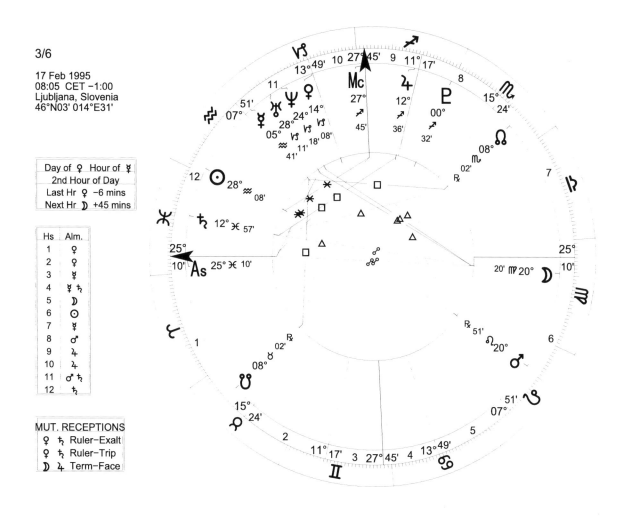

Day of ♀ Hour of ☿
2nd Hour of Day
Last Hr ♀ −6 mins
Next Hr ☽ +45 mins

Hs	Alm.
1	♀
2	♀
3	☿
4	☿ ♄
5	☽
6	☉
7	☿
8	♂
9	♃
10	♃
11	♂ ♄
12	♄

MUT. RECEPTIONS
♀ ♄ Ruler-Exalt
♀ ♄ Ruler-Trip
☽ ♃ Term-Face

NEAREST ECLIPSES (NM/FM)					
☉ ●	3 Nov 1994	14:35	10°♏54	Total	S133
☽ ●	18 Nov 1994	07:57	25°♉42	Appulse	S145
☽ ●	15 Apr 1995	13:08	25°♎03	Partial	S112
☉ ●	29 Apr 1995	18:36	08°♉56	Annular	S138

traditionals.pts

Pt	Long.	Travel	Decl.	Last Stn	Next Stn	Last Stn	Next Stn	F/S	Antiscia	C.Ant.
☽	20°♍20'54"	+13°37'	+00°23'	–	–	–	–	Fast	09°♈39	09°♎39
☉	28°♒08'48"	+01°00'	−12°07'	–	–	–	–	Fast	01°♏51	01°♉51
☿	05°♒41	+07'24"	−16°47'	−1,1 days	+96 days	05°♒37'16"	18°♊21'42"	Slow	24°♏18	24°♉18
♀	14°♑08	+01°09'	−20°51'	−85 days	+457 days	02°♏28'46"	28°♊17'52"	Fast	15°♐51	15°♊51
♂	20°♌51 ℞	−23'18"	+18°48'	−45 days	+35 days	02°♍40'08"	13°♌09'54"	Retro	09°♉08	09°♏08
♃	12°♐36	+07'19"	−21°32'	−230 days	+43 days	04°♏46'04"	15°♐23'00"	Fast	17°♑23	17°♋23
♄	12°♓57	+07'12"	−08°18'	−99 days	+139 days	05°♓40'45"	24°♓45'07"	Fast	17°♎02	17°♈02

MOON ASPECTS
☽ △ ♆ 3°54' A
☽ △ ♅ 7°42' A
☽ ☌ ♎ 9°39' A

ESSENTIAL DIGNITIES

Pt	Ruler	Exalt	Trip	Term	Face	Detri	Fall	Score
☽	☿	☿	♀	♃	☿	♃	♀	−5 p
☉	♄	--	♄	♄	☽	☉ −	--	−10 p
☿	♄	--	♄	☿ +	♀	☉	--	+2
♀	♄	♂	♀ +	♀ +	♂	☽	♃	+5
♂	☉	--	☉	☿	♂ +	♄	--	+1
♃	♃ +	--	☉	♀	☽	☿	--	+5
♄	♃	♀	♀	♃	♃	☿	☿	−5 p

ASPECTS
♃ □ ♄ 0°22' A
☉ ⚹ Mc 0°23' S
♆ ⚹ As 0°52' S
♀ ⚹ ♄ 1°04' S
♅ ⚹ ♇ 1°11' A
☉ □ ♇ 2°19' A
☿ □ ☋ 2°20' A
☿ □ ☊ 2°20' A
As □ Mc 2°35' S
☽ △ ♆ 3°54' A

PLANETARY SECT

Planet	Cht	Plc	Sgn	Condition
☉ D	D	D	D	In Hayz
☽ N	D	N	N	
☿ D	D	D	D	In Hayz
♀ N	D	D	N	
♂ N	D	N	D	
♃ D	D	D	D	In Hayz
♄ D	D	D	N	
D=Diurnal, N=Nocturnal				

There's another angle from which this chart can be viewed. If we take Neptune to rule Pisces, we can say that it's in mutual reception with Saturn (Neptune in Capricorn, Saturn in Pisces). As we know, planets in mutual reception can exchange places. In this case, Saturn takes the place of Neptune (and vice versa) and this is significant because Saturn could be considered a part ruler of H10 (the larger part of this house being in Capricorn) while also "serving" as the natural significator of jobs and business projects. The Moon's aspect to Saturn can also be regarded as completion of the matter: I (the Moon) am getting the job (Saturn).

I would like to stress that the chart indicates a positive answer even without these additional factors. But because this is a case where many different interpretative rules can be used (some of them questionable or downright unacceptable to traditional astrologers, I know), I have decided to mention them, as they may encourage traditional astrologers to research along modern lines. As mentioned in the Theory of the book, trans-Saturnians are often helpful, although they usually serve only as secondary or less important indicators.

3/7: WILL I GET THE PROMISED JOB DESPITE THE SICK LEAVE?

7 June 1995 at 9:26 a.m., Ljubljana, Slovenia
Hour ruler: Jupiter

The querent said that her employer promised her a new, better paid and generally more favourable position, but in the meantime, she fell ill and was on a sick leave for a couple of months. Now, back at work, she heard rumors that the position was going to one of her colleagues. Is this true or not, she wondered.

Her significators are the Sun (H1 ruler) and the Moon (co-ruler), significators of the job are Mars and Venus (Mars ruling MC and Venus the intercepted H10, plus being placed there). The Sun in H11 of heart wishes shows that she strongly desired the job, but the combust and retrograde Mercury (the planet describing her state of mind and the flow of information related to the question) reflects her distress and lack of proper information.

Will she get the promotion? The Sun is in the fortunate H11, but peregrine. Lack of essential dignity suggests that her "value" might have decreased in the eyes of her employer while she was away. Most important, however, is the fact that there're no links among the significators. They don't apply into an aspect, there's no mutual reception or translation of light. What's more - the Moon is void-of course and the hour ruler is retrograde. The answer is therefore negative.

But let us take a look at some other interesting chart features. The Moon separates from the opposition of Saturn, ruling her H6 of disease, by 2°46'; it's in a movable sign and a cadent house, therefore I asked her if she fell ill a bit over 2 and a half months before. She confirmed. The next Moon's aspect was trine Venus in H10, reflecting the promise of the new position, but because the aspect is a separating one, she's obviously not getting what had been promised to her.

I told her that, unfortunately, her senses were correct – she's not getting the promotion. At the same time I pointed out the possibility of a recurrence of her illness, because the Sun, her main significator, applies to a square of Saturn (illness), which is placed in a movable sign (a chronic, recurrent disease).

When the querent next called, she confirmed my reading and told me how very disappointed she was, because the post which had been promised to her, went to her colleague who was even her good friend! It's interesting that the friend is ruled not only by Saturn ruling her H6 of co-workers, but also by Mercury, ruling H11 of friends, the retrograde and combust state of which clearly reflects that her friend worked behind her back to achieve the promotion during the querent's absence.

3/7

7 Jun 1995
09:26 CEDT -2:00
Ljubljana, Slovenia
46°N03' 014°E31'

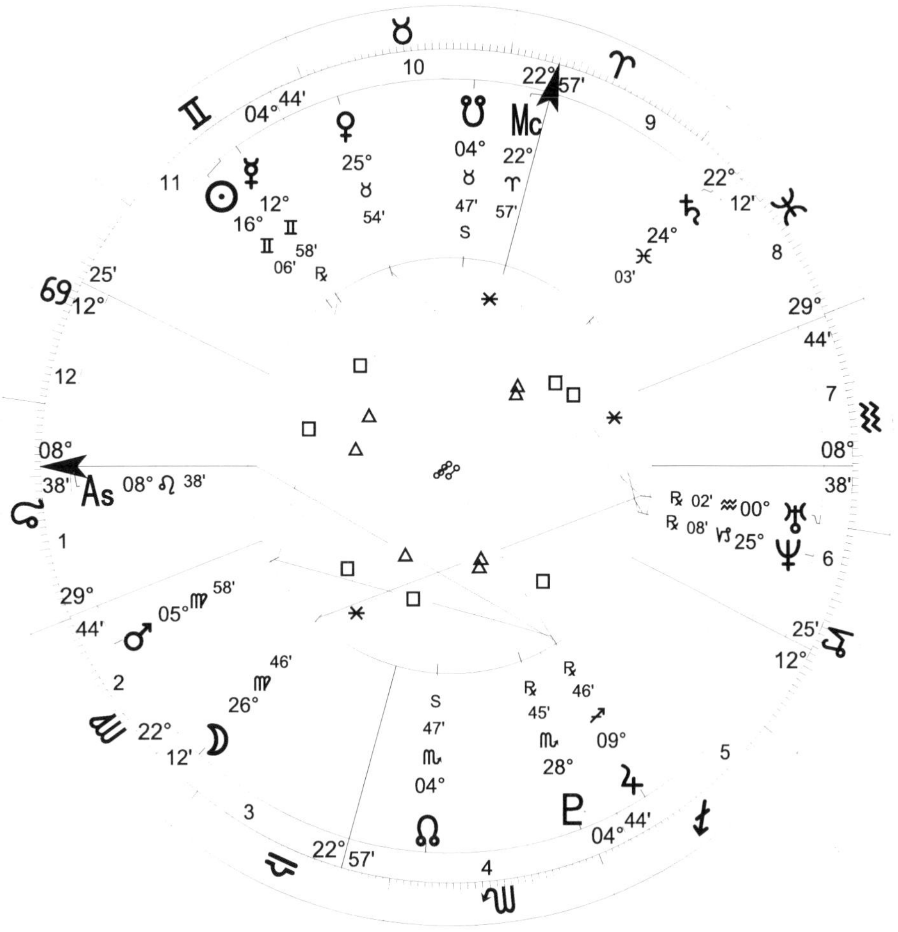

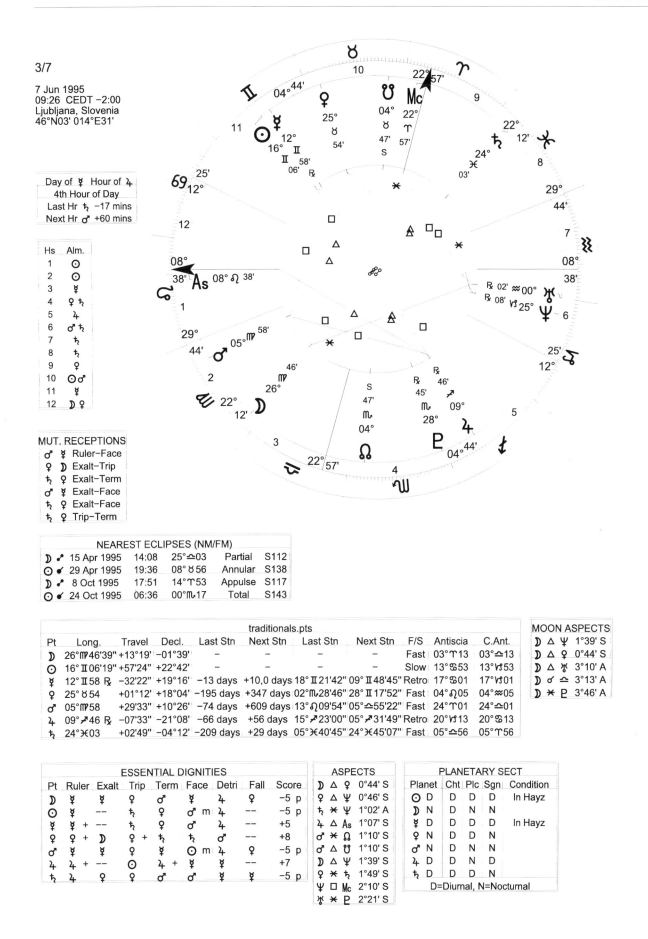

Day of ☿ Hour of ♃
4th Hour of Day
Last Hr ♄ -17 mins
Next Hr ♂ +60 mins

Hs	Alm.
1	☉
2	☉
3	☿
4	♀ ♄
5	♃
6	♂ ♄
7	♄
8	♄
9	♀
10	☉ ♂
11	☿
12	☽ ♀

MUT. RECEPTIONS
♂ ☿ Ruler-Face
♀ ☽ Exalt-Trip
♄ ♀ Exalt-Term
♂ ☿ Exalt-Face
♄ ♀ Exalt-Face
♄ ♀ Trip-Term

NEAREST ECLIPSES (NM/FM)				
☽ ☍ 15 Apr 1995	14:08	25°♎03	Partial	S112
☉ ☌ 29 Apr 1995	19:36	08°♉56	Annular	S138
☽ ☍ 8 Oct 1995	17:51	14°♈53	Appulse	S117
☉ ☌ 24 Oct 1995	06:36	00°♏17	Total	S143

traditionals.pts

Pt	Long.	Travel	Decl.	Last Stn	Next Stn	Last Stn	Next Stn	F/S	Antiscia	C.Ant.
☽	26°♍46'39"	+13°19'	-01°39'	–	–	–	–	Fast	03°♈13	03°♎13
☉	16°♊06'19"	+57'24"	+22°42'	–	–	–	–	Slow	13°♋53	13°♑53
☿	12°♊58 ℞	-32'22"	+19°16'	-13 days	+10,0 days	18°♊21'42"	09°♊48'45"	Retro	17°♋01	17°♑01
♀	25°♉54	+01°12'	+18°04'	-195 days	+347 days	02°♏28'46"	28°♊17'52"	Fast	04°♌05	04°♒05
♂	05°♍58	+29'33"	+10°26'	-74 days	+609 days	13°♌09'54"	05°♎55'22"	Fast	24°♈01	24°♎01
♃	09°♐46 ℞	-07'33"	-21°08'	-66 days	+56 days	15°♐23'00"	05°♐31'49"	Retro	20°♑13	20°♋13
♄	24°♓03	+02'49"	-04°12'	-209 days	+29 days	05°♓40'45"	24°♓45'07"	Fast	05°♎56	05°♈56

MOON ASPECTS
☽ △ ♆ 1°39' S
☽ △ ♀ 0°44' S
☽ △ ♅ 3°10' A
☽ ☌ ♎ 3°13' A
☽ ✶ ♇ 3°46' A

ESSENTIAL DIGNITIES

Pt	Ruler	Exalt	Trip	Term	Face	Detri	Fall	Score
☽	☿	☿	♀	♂	☿	♃	♀	-5 p
☉	☿	--	♄	♀	♂ m	♃	--	-5 p
☿	☿ +	--	♄	♀	♂	♃	--	+5
♀	♀ +	☽	♀ +	♄	♄	♂	--	+8
♂	☿	☿	♀	☿	☉ m	♃	♀	-5 p
♃	♃ +	--	☉	♃ +	☿	☿	--	+7
♄	♃	♀	♀	♂	♂	☿	☿	-5 p

ASPECTS
☽ △ ♀ 0°44' S
♀ △ ♆ 0°46' S
♄ ✶ ♆ 1°02' A
♃ △ As 1°07' S
♂ ✶ ☊ 1°10' S
♂ △ ☋ 1°10' S
☽ △ ♆ 1°39' S
♀ ✶ ♄ 1°49' S
♆ □ Mc 2°10' S
♅ ✶ ♇ 2°21' S

PLANETARY SECT

Planet	Cht	Plc	Sgn	Condition
☉ D	D	D	D	In Hayz
☽ N	D	N	N	
☿ D	D	D	D	In Hayz
♀ N	D	D	N	
♂ N	D	N	N	
♃ D	D	N	D	
♄ D	D	D	N	

D=Diurnal, N=Nocturnal

3/8: SHOULD I RETIRE?

12 July 1994 at 18:25 (6:25 p.m.), Ljubljana, Slovenia
Hour ruler: Mercury

The question was raised by a woman in her early fifties. She was considering early retirement, but could not decide, so she consulted me. I didn't ask her about the reasons for her dilemma because I thought that the question was expressed clearly enough and that her problems were described by the chart anyway.

She's shown by the ascendant in Sagittarius and by its ruler Jupiter, placed in Scorpio on cusp of H11, while the Moon, her co-significator, is in Virgo on cusp of H9. Jupiter's placement (H11 is 2/10) shows that her sub-question (albeit unexpressed) was that of the pension.

Significator of the job is Venus, H10 ruler. In order to be able to advise her, we must first evaluate the relationship between herself and her job: is it good or bad, favourable or unfavourable? Does her job basically suit her or not? Venus applies to Jupiter by sextile, with both planets in fortunate houses; despite the lack of essential dignities they are in a harmonious relationship with each other, therefore the answer is affirmative: her job suits her. It is true that both planets are in mutual detriments (Jupiter is the detriment of Venus while Venus is in the detriment of Jupiter and also in her own fall), which could mean that the job currently tires her, but the harmonious applying aspect of both significators suggests that the situation will improve in the near future.

Does the chart show yet another reason why she'd wish for an early retirement? We can see that Venus also rules her H6 of her co-workers and working environment, and that this house is occupied by Mars, Jupiter's dispositor. Mars looks anything but "friendly" because it is peregrine; the Moon has just completed the square with it and because separating aspects show what happened before the question and (often) what has led the querent to pose the question, we have a clear picture: there was a recent strife, or stressful relations with co-workers! Since the square is still within a one degree orb, these problems are obviously still ongoing but should eventually dissolve or at least diminish considerably.

I described the situation which I saw in the chart, and she confirmed it. You will notice that the Moon is separated from the aspects of the significators of herself and her job (Venus and Jupiter), reflecting her intention to leave the job. This confirms the previously mentioned fact that Jupiter is in Venus' detriment (she currently feels inadequate at work) while Venus is in Jupiter's detriment (her department is not happy with her or sees her as inefficient). In addition to these inconveniences it appears that she'd also like to retire so as to devote more time to education or travelling (ascendant Sagittarius, Moon in H9).

Jupiter in H11 also points to her financial concerns. Although a pension is usually ascribed to H8 (by modern authors), I'm kind of wary in this respect; I rather look at it as a combination of H11, H8 and H2. Jupiter is the natural significator of money, therefore its placement in H11 shows her hopes for a good pension which would allow for a reasonably comfortable life. But Jupiter is peregrine so she could be disappointed in this respect. This is confirmed by the Moon which applies to an opposition with a peregrine and retrograde Saturn, ruler of her H2 of personal income. Neptune and Uranus in H2, opposed by the Sun in H8, also suggest that her hopes for a comfortable pension might fail.

But this was not the main reason why I discouraged her from an early retirement. I did it mainly because I felt that due to the separating nature of the square between the Moon and Mars her relations with colleagues would gradually improve, and that the applying nature of the Venus/Jupiter sextile favoured her job, which - despite the current difficulties - essentially suits her. If she proceeded with her plans, she'd be disappointed (Moon applies to an opposition with Saturn).

Your job situation will soon improve, but if you retire, you'd find it difficult to live by your pension, so I think it would be better to not retire yet, I said to her.

She thanked me but did not listen. This is also indicated in the chart, because the Moon's opposition to retrograde Saturn – a difficult, depressing aspect – forced her to keep looking upon the matter from a negative perspective which finally led her to quitting (Saturn).

In the spring of 1995, she wrote me a letter, saying how much she regretted that, despite my advice, she had retired. She was lonely at home, she said, had no friends and missed the stimulating work environment.

3/8

12 Jul 1994
18:25 CEDT −2:00
Ljubljana, Slovenia
46°N03' 014°E31'

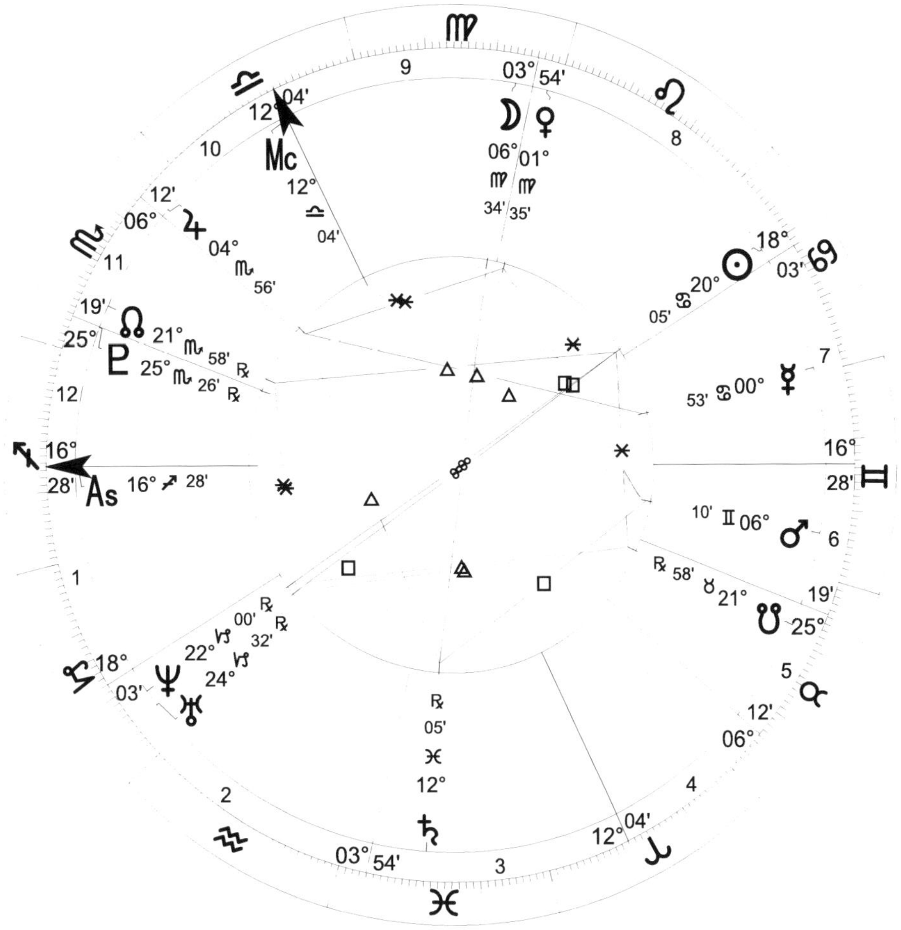

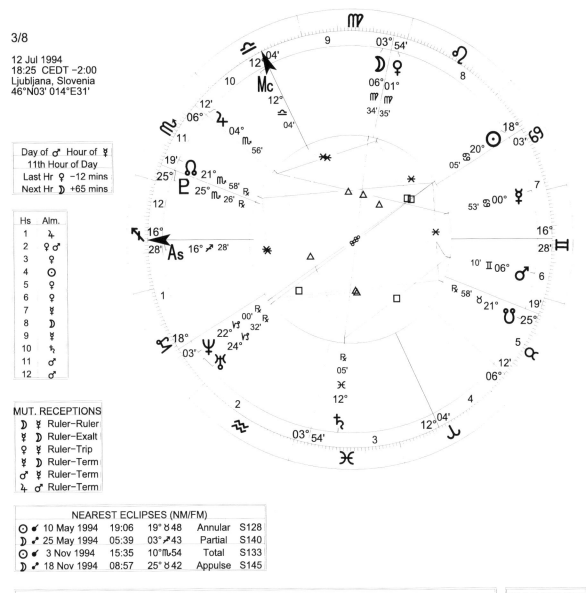

Day of ♂ Hour of ☿
11th Hour of Day
Last Hr ♀ −12 mins
Next Hr ☽ +65 mins

Hs	Alm.
1	♃
2	♀♂
3	♀
4	☉
5	♀
6	♀
7	☿
8	☽
9	☿
10	♄
11	♂
12	♂

MUT. RECEPTIONS		
☽	☿	Ruler-Ruler
☿	☽	Ruler-Exalt
♀	☿	Ruler-Trip
☿	☽	Ruler-Term
♂	☿	Ruler-Term
♃	♂	Ruler-Term

NEAREST ECLIPSES (NM/FM)					
☉ ☌	10 May 1994	19:06	19°♉48	Annular	S128
☽ ☍	25 May 1994	05:39	03°♐43	Partial	S140
☉ ☌	3 Nov 1994	15:35	10°♏54	Total	S133
☽ ☍	18 Nov 1994	08:57	25°♉42	Appulse	S145

traditionals.pts

Pt	Long.	Travel	Decl.	Last Stn	Next Stn	Last Stn	Next Stn	F/S	Antiscia	C.Ant.
☽	06°♍34'37"	+13°38'	+04°31'	–	–	–	–	Fast	23°♈25	23°♎25
☉	20°♋05'27"	+57'14"	+21°56'	–	–	–	–	Slow	09°♊54	09°♐54
☿	00°♋53	+30'17"	+19°49'	−5,9 days	+88 days	29°♊25'05"	06°♏28'57"	Slow	29°♊06	29°♐06
♀	01°♍35	+01°07'	+12°13'	−446 days	+92 days	03°♈44'27"	18°♏00'38"	Fast	28°♈24	28°♎24
♂	06°♊10	+42'01"	+21°03'	−512 days	+174 days	08°♋40'31"	02°♍40'08"	Fast	23°♋49	23°♑49
♃	04°♏56	+01'53"	−12°05'	−10 days	+262 days	04°♏46'04"	15°♐23'00"	Slow	25°♒03	25°♌03
♄	12°♓05 ℞	−01'53"	−08°43'	−19 days	+119 days	12°♓24'11"	05°♓40'45"	Retro	17°♎54	17°♈54

MOON ASPECTS			
☽	☌	♍	6°34' S
☽	⚹	♃	1°23' S
☽	□	♂	0°22' S

ESSENTIAL DIGNITIES

Pt	Ruler	Exalt	Trip	Term	Face	Detri	Fall	Score
☽	☿ m	☿	♀	☿	☉ m	♃	♀	+0 p
☉	☽	♃	♀	♃	☽ m	♄	♂	−5 p
☿	☽ m	♃	♀	♂	♀	♄	♂	+0 p
♀	☿	☿	♀ +	☿	☉	♃	♀ −	−1
♂	☿	--	♄	♃ m	♃ m	♃	--	−5 p
♃	♂	--	♀	♂ m	♂ m	♀	☽	−5 p
♄	♃	♀	♀	♃	♃	☿	☿	−5 p

ASPECTS			
♆	△	☋	0°02' S
♆	⚹	☊	0°02' S
♅	⚹	♇	0°17' A
☽	□	♂	0°22' S
☿	⚹	♀	0°53' S
☽	⚹	♃	1°23' S
☉	⚹	☋	1°53' A
☉	△	☊	1°53' A
☉	☍	♆	2°01' A
♆	⚹	♇	2°27' S

PLANETARY SECT

Planet		Cht	Plc	Sgn	Condition
☉	D	D	D	N	
☽	N	D	D	N	
☿	D	D	D	N	
♀	N	D	D	N	
♂	N	D	N	D	
♃	D	D	D	N	
♄	D	D	N	N	

D=Diurnal, N=Nocturnal

3/9: IS THIS A GOOD BUSINESS OPPORTUNITY?

13 January 2006 at 8:40 p.m. (20:40), Celje, Slovenia
Hour ruler: Mercury

The question was raised by an acquaintance who lived in Celje (Slovenia). After years of doing various jobs in catering and night clubs' management she was now seeking a new business opportunity. One night she called me with the above question, not saying what the opportunity was, but she mentioned that she was negotiating to rent business premises, and that the opportunity looked promising.

The ascendant is in Virgo, the sign of Mercury which is also the planetary hour ruler - and at the same time the job ruler because it rules MC in Gemini. Clearly, this is the most important planet in the chart, therefore it needs careful consideration. Firstly, we see that Mercury is in H5 which, among other things, rules catering business. This is very appropriate since she was renting – as she later disclosed – a pizzeria! As we can see, Mercury is just entering the orb of combustion. This is not good as it considerably weakens the planet. An applying combustion is much more debilitating than a separating one, indicating that she would soon start losing the power she now has. Mercury is further debilitated by being peregrine. An essentially weak planet in a fortunate house means that the person ruled by it has found "a lucky chance", but lacks the qualities needed to keep the chance going.

Next, we see that Mercury is in an exact but already separating sextile with Jupiter. This planet represents both the restaurant (by ruling H4) as well as the owner of the restaurant, since it rules H7 of business partners. The harmonious nature of the aspect suggests that their recent interview went smoothly and that the deal had practically been made. This is confirmed by the Moon, co-significator of the querent which can be found in H11 of hopes and desires, and in Cancer, its domicile, where it is also essentially strong. The Moon's placement in this sign is also appropriate because Cancer represents (among other things) food and drink. The Moon has just separated from the opposition with Mercury and trine with Jupiter, which nicely rounds off the picture. The agreement which promised a lot is behind her. But what's in front of her?

Sorry - nothing. All aspects are separating, so this deal has no future. Mercury is in Jupiter's fall which in this context can be understood as a further push towards separation. Saturn, Mercury's dispositor, is retrograde, confirming the decline of the matter. And this is what I had to tell her. Firstly, I said that this looks like another job in the hospitality industry (Mercury in H5). (I might add that this was an easy guess because I knew that she had been in this business for several years.) She confirmed, saying that she was renting a pizzeria. I proceeded to tell her that the situation for now indeed looked promising, but that, unfortunately, nothing would come out of it.

Why? You'll notice that Venus, ruler of H2, is combust, peregrine and retrograde. This suggests that she would not have enough money for the rent. I mentioned the possibility, but she said that this was not true; the rent had been agreed upon and she could afford it. Well, I said, I can't see you hiring this place, something will obviously go wrong.

A week later she called me with a question concerning another business. And what happened to the last one, I asked. *Oh*, she said. *The owner suddenly changed her mind and asked for the rent for half a year in advance, although at first we had settled for a monthly rent, but I don't have that much money and I also couldn't borrow it.*

That's an interesting twist which the chart nicely reflects. Mars, the H8 (2/7) ruler, showing the owner's financial assets, is in opposition with Jupiter, her significator. This reflects the owner's unethical stance and excessive financial demands towards the querent which she could not meet.

3/9

13 Jan 2006
20:40 CET −1:00
Celje, Slovenia
46°N14' 015°E16'

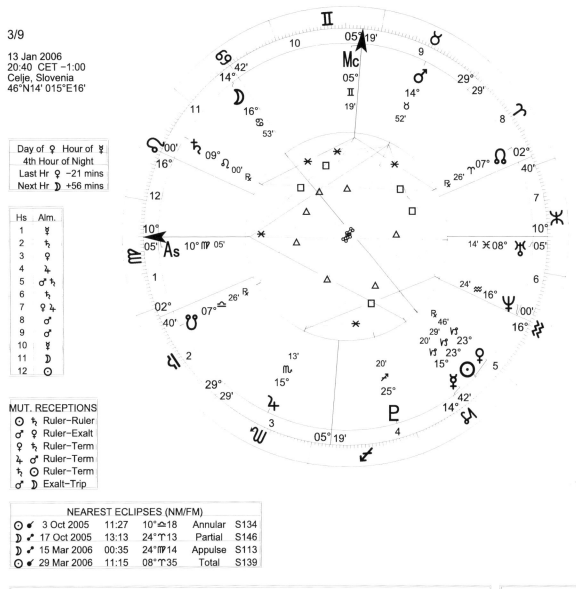

Day of ♀ Hour of ☿
4th Hour of Night
Last Hr ♀ −21 mins
Next Hr ☽ +56 mins

Hs	Alm.
1	☿
2	♄
3	♀
4	♃
5	♂ ♄
6	♄
7	♀ ♃
8	♂
9	♂
10	☿
11	☽
12	☉

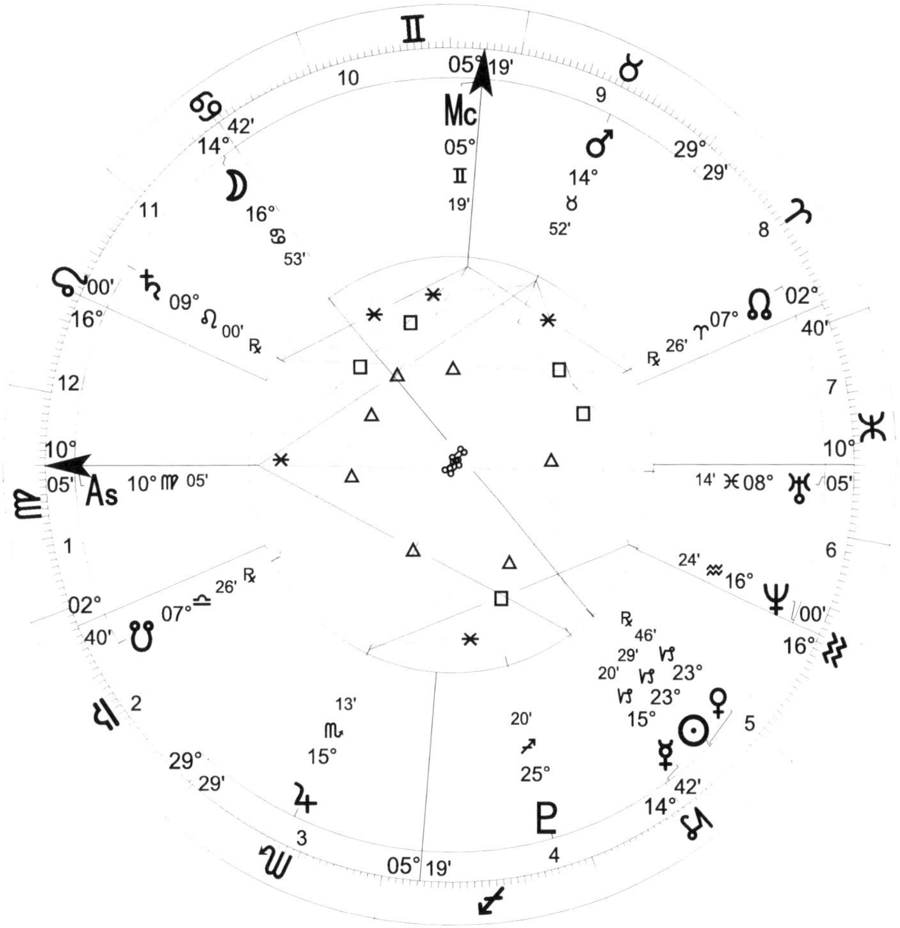

MUT. RECEPTIONS	
☉ ♄	Ruler−Ruler
♂ ♀	Ruler−Exalt
♀ ♄	Ruler−Term
♃ ♂	Ruler−Term
♄ ☉	Ruler−Term
♂ ☽	Exalt−Trip

NEAREST ECLIPSES (NM/FM)					
☉ ☌	3 Oct 2005	11:27	10°♎18	Annular	S134
☽ ☍	17 Oct 2005	13:13	24°♈13	Partial	S146
☽ ☍	15 Mar 2006	00:35	24°♍14	Appulse	S113
☉ ☌	29 Mar 2006	11:15	08°♈35	Total	S139

traditionals.pts

Pt	Long.	Travel	Decl.	Last Stn	Next Stn	Last Stn	Next Stn	F/S	Antiscia	C.Ant.
☽	16°♋53'54"	+12°14'	+27°16'	–	–	–	–	Slow	13°♊06	13°♐06
☉	23°♑29'07"	+01°01'	−21°23'	–	–	–	–	Fast	06°♐30	06°♊30
☿	15°♑20	+01°34'	−24°00'	−40 days	+48 days	24°♏44'16"	26°♓55'27"	Fast	14°♐39	14°♊39
♀	23°♑46 ℞	−36'58"	−15°56'	−20 days	+20 days	01°♒28'00"	16°♑01'18"	Retro	06°♐13	06°♊13
♂	14°♉52	+20'36"	+17°54'	−34 days	+670 days	08°♉14'08"	12°♋27'03"	Slow	15°♌07	15°♒07
♃	15°♏13	+08'12"	−15°19'	−222 days	+49 days	08°♎55'50"	18°♏51'41"	Fast	14°♒46	14°♌46
♄	09°♌00 ℞	−04'38"	+18°38'	−52 days	+81 days	11°♌18'40"	04°♌22'31"	Retro	20°♉59	20°♏59

MOON ASPECTS	
☽ ☍ ☿	3°48' S
☽ ⚹ ♂	1°58' S
☽ △ ♃	1°54' S
☽ ⚹ As	6°39' A
☽ ☌ ♌	13°06' A

ESSENTIAL DIGNITIES

Pt	Ruler	Exalt	Trip	Term	Face	Detri	Fall	Score
☽	☽ +	♃	♂ m	☿	☿	♄	♂	+5
☉	♄ m	♂	☽	♄	☉ +	☽	♃	+6
☿	♄	♂	☽	♀	♂	☽	♃	−5 p
♀	♄	♂	☽	♄ m	☉	☽	♃	−5 p
♂	♀	☽	☽ m	♃	☽	♂ −	−−	−10 p
♃	♂	−−	♂	☿	☉	♀	☽	−5 p
♄	☉ m	−−	♃	♀ m	♄ +	♄ −	−−	+1

ASPECTS	
☿ ⚹ ♃	0°10' S
☿ △ ♂	0°26' S
♃ □ ♆	1°12' A
♂ □ ♆	1°31' A
♄ ⚹ ☋	1°33' S
♄ △ ☊	1°33' S
☽ △ ♃	1°54' S
☽ ⚹ ♂	1°58' S
♅ ☍ As	1°59' S
☊ ⚹ Mc	2°06' S

PLANETARY SECT

Planet	Cht	Plc	Sgn	Condition
☉ D	N	N	N	Ex Cond
☽ N	N	N	N	In Hayz
☿ D	N	D	N	
♀ N	N	D	N	
♂ N	N	N	N	In Hayz
♃ D	N	D	N	
♄ D	N	N	D	

D=Diurnal, N=Nocturnal

3/10: WILL THE PLANNED WORKSHOP TAKE PLACE?

12 May 2006 at 10:53 a.m., Ljubljana, Slovenia
Hour ruler: Jupiter

I was organizing a workshop on financial and business astrology in Bovec, a small Slovenian town in the mountain region. It was scheduled for the summer in a hotel venue where the participants would also be accommodated. The initial interest was poor, so I cast the chart with the above question.

The chart is particularly interesting because the ascendant is in an exact conjunction with Saturn, the great malefic. This is a warning! "Negative forces" dominate, the project has no future. An exact conjunction of Saturn with any angle usually indicates that obstacles are too great to be overcome. Especially if Saturn is essentially debilitated, as here (in detriment).

Nevertheless, let's see the other features of the chart. I'm shown by the ascendant in Leo, the Sun (its ruler) and the Moon (my co-significator). The Sun is in the H10 of profession and business projects, which clearly shows my interest. The main significator of the workshop is Mars, the ruler of H10, and co-significators are Venus (ruler of the intercepted Taurus), Sun and Mercury (H10 planets). You will notice that Mercury rules H3 of study courses, so its placement in H10 is astro-logical.

The Sun is accidentally strong but without essential dignity. It would be peregrine if it weren't in mutual reception with Venus, but Venus is in detriment (Aries) and therefore weak; such reception is not very promising. The weak essential dignity of the Sun is understandable, considering that this would be my first course on business and financial astrology – I'd have to prepare really well! Did I lack self-confidence? Probably! The Sun is void-of-course which is not at all helpful.

The Moon, my co-significator, is in Scorpio (fall) in H4 – not a good house in this case due to its opposition to H10. It applies to conjunction with a retrograde Jupiter, ruler of H5 and H8. Jupiter is in a mixed reception (domicile/exaltation) with Mars, H10 ruler. H5, which Jupiter rules, indicates (among other things) hotels, and mutual reception indicates a choice. The application of a weak Moon to such a Jupiter reflects my dilemma which was in fact the choice between accommodating the students in the hotel or in private rooms. The hotel required prepayment for room reservations but because the number of participants was unknown and because I was uncertain whether the project would actually be carried out, I could not do this. On the other hand, if participants would be accommodated in private rooms, I had the same problem of how many guests to book, and where? Not to mention that the hotel offered a free lecture room but if we lived in private rooms I should hire a particularly expensive lecture room in the village Cultural Center. For the icing on the cake my candidates in turn communicated their various wishes: one wanted to stay with some friends in their holiday cottage, the other in a private room (because she found the hotel too expensive), the third would definitely want to sleep in a hotel, and so on. Oh my, the organization of a workshop is really too much for me, I thought, and finally decided to cancel the whole thing.

Looking at Mars, H10 ruler, in H12 (failure, weakness, sacrifice), the void-of-course and essentially weak Sun and the "drained" Moon, the outcome seems quite logical, but on the other hand, the chart nevertheless shows the possibility of the "completion of the matter". Namely, the Moon, after reaching the conjunction with Jupiter, goes on to trine Mars, H10 ruler. Technically speaking, the first aspect (conjunction of Jupiter) could also be considered a frustration, especially because Jupiter is retrograde (applications to retrograde planets often show a negative answer), but the two planets are in a strong mutual reception by domicile, which could allow for completion and an affirmative answer. Remember that with receptions, we can exchange the two planets' positions, so, in this case, the Moon would apply directly to Mars, the significator of the project. But mutual reception also means that we have a choice – which was very true in this case! As already said, I decided to opt out – due to too many obstacles which the chart clearly shows.

3/10

12 May 2006
10:53 CEDT −2:00
Ljubljana, Slovenia
46°N03' 014°E31'

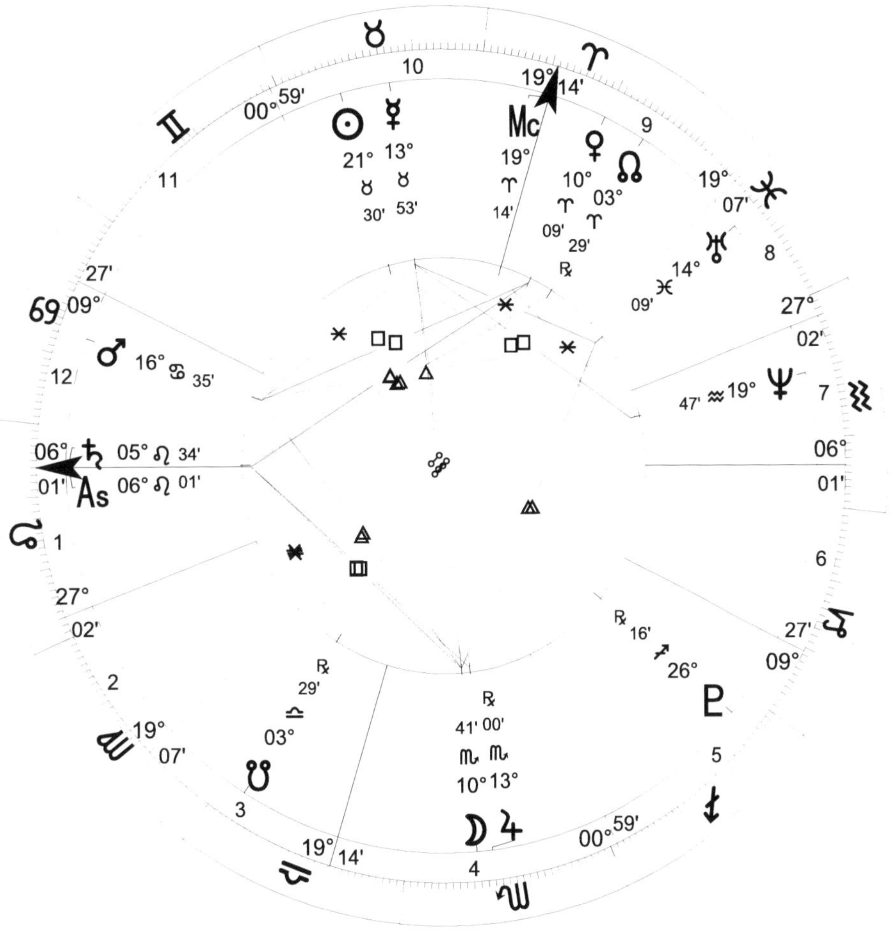

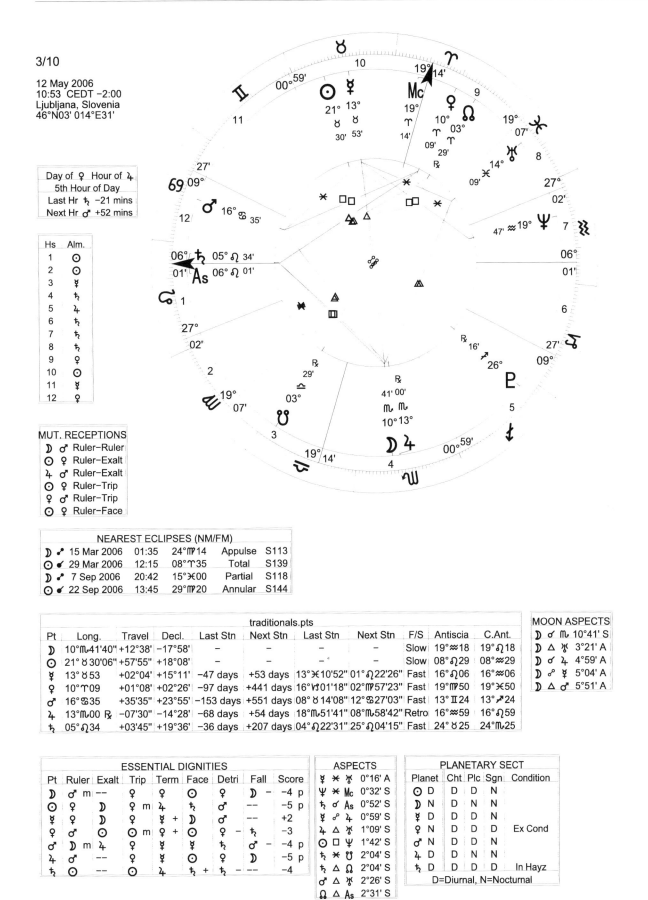

Day of ♀ Hour of ♃
5th Hour of Day
Last Hr ♄ −21 mins
Next Hr ♂ +52 mins

Hs	Alm.
1	☉
2	☉
3	☿
4	♄
5	♃
6	♄
7	♄
8	♄
9	♀
10	☉
11	☿
12	♀

MUT. RECEPTIONS	
☽ ♂	Ruler-Ruler
☉ ♀	Ruler-Exalt
♃ ♂	Ruler-Exalt
☉ ♀	Ruler-Trip
♀ ♂	Ruler-Trip
☉ ♀	Ruler-Face

NEAREST ECLIPSES (NM/FM)					
☽	15 Mar 2006	01:35	24°♍14	Appulse	S113
☉	29 Mar 2006	12:15	08°♈35	Total	S139
☽	7 Sep 2006	20:42	15°♓00	Partial	S118
☉	22 Sep 2006	13:45	29°♍20	Annular	S144

traditionals.pts										
Pt	Long.	Travel	Decl.	Last Stn	Next Stn	Last Stn	Next Stn	F/S	Antiscia	C.Ant.
☽	10°♏41'40"	+12°38'	−17°58'	–	–	–	–	Slow	19°♒18	19°♌18
☉	21°♉30'06"	+57'55"	+18°08'	–	–	–	–	Slow	08°♌29	08°♒29
☿	13°♉53	+02°04'	+15°11'	−47 days	+53 days	13°♓10'52"	01°♌22'26"	Fast	16°♌06	16°♒06
♀	10°♈09	+01°08'	+02°26'	−97 days	+441 days	16°♑01'18"	02°♍57'23"	Fast	19°♍50	19°♓50
♂	16°♋35	+35'35"	+23°55'	−153 days	+551 days	08°♉14'08"	12°♋27'03"	Fast	13°♊24	13°♐24
♃	13°♏00 ℞	−07'30"	−14°28'	−68 days	+54 days	18°♏51'41"	08°♏58'42"	Retro	16°♒59	16°♌59
♄	05°♌34	+03'45"	+19°36'	−36 days	+207 days	04°♌22'31"	25°♌04'15"	Fast	24°♉25	24°♏25

MOON ASPECTS
☽ ☌ ♏ 10°41' S
☽ △ ♅ 3°21' A
☽ ☌ ♃ 4°59' A
☽ ☍ ☿ 5°04' A
☽ △ ♂ 5°51' A

ESSENTIAL DIGNITIES								
Pt	Ruler	Exalt	Trip	Term	Face	Detri	Fall	Score
☽	♂ m	--	♀	♀	☉	♀	☽ −	−4 p
☉	♀	☽	♀ m	♃	♄	♂	--	−5 p
☿	♀	☽	♀	☿ +	☽	♂	--	+2
♀	♂	☉	☉ m	♀ +	☉	♀ −	♄	−3
♂	☽ m	♃	♀	☿	☿	♄	♂ −	−4 p
♃	♂	--	♀	☿	☉	♀	☽	−5 p
♄	☉	--	☉	♃	♄ +	♄ −	--	−4

ASPECTS
☿ ⚹ ♅ 0°16' A
♆ ⚹ Mc 0°32' S
♄ ☌ As 0°52' S
☿ ☍ ♃ 0°59' S
♃ △ ♅ 1°09' S
☉ □ ♆ 1°42' S
♄ ⚹ ☋ 2°04' S
♄ △ ☊ 2°04' S
♂ △ ♅ 2°26' S
☊ △ As 2°31' S

PLANETARY SECT					
Planet		Cht	Plc	Sgn	Condition
☉	D	D	D	N	
☽	N	D	N	N	
☿	D	D	D	N	
♀	N	D	D	D	Ex Cond
♂	N	D	D	N	
♃	D	D	N	N	
♄	D	D	D	D	In Hayz
D=Diurnal, N=Nocturnal					

3/11: WILL THE K CLUB PROJECT BRING ME SUCCESS?

28 January 2003 at 11:38 a.m., Ljubljana, Slovenia
Hour ruler: Saturn

I was offered a business opportunity - hosting astrological meetings at the K Club. Shortly before that I had a meeting with the organizer who laid out the business plan with which I agreed. The project would be launched in the autumn of the same year. But because I was pregnant at the time with the expected delivery in June, I was a little worried if I could handle it, with the baby and all. Nevertheless, I decided to accept the offer. (My progressed Moon was in the forward-looking and optimistic Sagittarius at that time which explains it, I guess!) We agreed that he'd call me again in a few months, or when the matter would be mature enough for a concrete agreement and a contract.

To make sure that I had made the right decision, I cast a horary chart. Would I be successful at this project? Will I find it pleasurable and satisfying, or, in other words, does it really make sense to go into this?

The chart surprised me. As mentioned above, the meeting seemed promising and I had basically accepted the offer, but the chart indications were all but promising. Let's see why.

The ascendant is in Taurus, so my significator is Venus which is found in Sagittarius, in the exact applying opposition with Saturn, significator of the project (H10 ruler). Moreover, my co-significator the Moon which also shows the course of events, applies to opposition with Saturn, too! Before that it conjuncts Pluto, the natural significator of "force majeure" or insurmountable obstacles. And to make things even worse, there is no reception between the Moon and Saturn. All this clearly shows that the project has no future.

It is interesting that the next aspect of Venus is a sextile to Uranus in H11 (clubs, groups). Uranus is the planet of astrology, but also the modern ruler of Aquarius, where we find the H11 cusp. This nicely reflects the nature of the planned project: hosting club nights on the subject of astrology. The entertaining nature of the (planned) meetings is shown by the Sun, ruler of H5, placed in H10 in conjunction with Neptune, the modern co-ruler of H11.

But, as the above indications show, it is obvious that nothing would come out of it. My question quickly lost its meaning. Why should I even wonder if I'd succeed, if the chart shows that I'm actually not in at all?! To make matters worse, the Sun in H10 separates from sextile Mars, the H10 almuten. It's like something is dissolving instead of building up.

The result was even worse than I had expected. The organizer never called again, despite his promise to do so in a couple of months. I later learned that the club had financial problems and had to be closed down that same summer.

3/11

28 Jan 2003
11:38 CET −1:00
Ljubljana, Slovenia
46°N03' 014°E31'

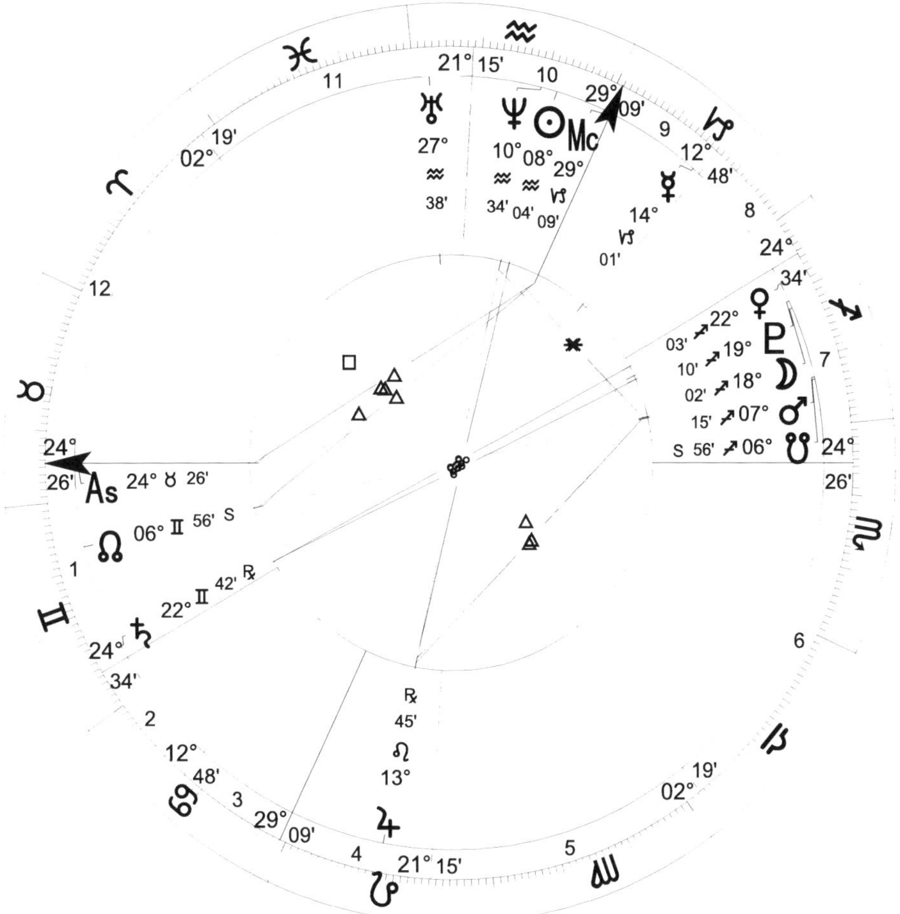

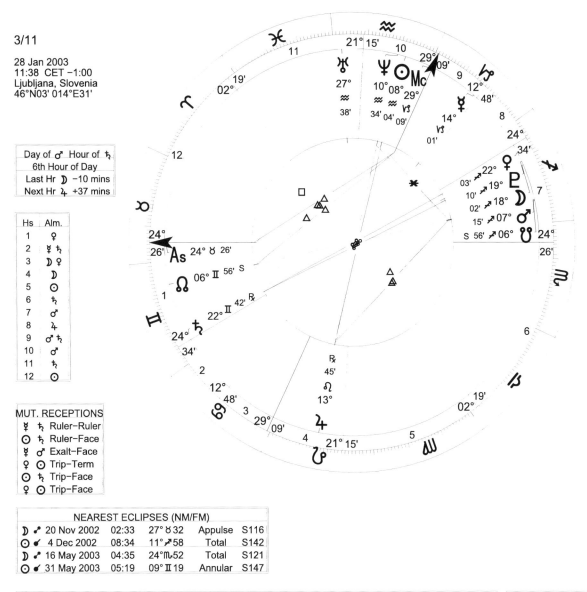

Day of ♂ Hour of ♄
6th Hour of Day
Last Hr ☽ −10 mins
Next Hr ♃ +37 mins

Hs	Alm.
1	♀
2	☿ ♄
3	☽ ♀
4	☽
5	☉
6	♄
7	♂
8	♃
9	♂ ♄
10	♂
11	♄
12	☉

MUT. RECEPTIONS
☿ ♄ Ruler-Ruler
☉ ♄ Ruler-Face
☿ ♂ Exalt-Face
♀ ☉ Trip-Term
☉ ♄ Trip-Face
♀ ☉ Trip-Face

NEAREST ECLIPSES (NM/FM)				
☽ 20 Nov 2002	02:33	27° ♉ 32	Appulse	S116
☉ 4 Dec 2002	08:34	11° ♐ 58	Total	S142
☽ 16 May 2003	04:35	24° ♏ 52	Total	S121
☉ 31 May 2003	05:19	09° ♊ 19	Annular	S147

traditionals.pts

Pt	Long.	Travel	Decl.	Last Stn	Next Stn	Last Stn	Next Stn	F/S	Antiscia	C.Ant.
☽	18°♐02'37"	+13°48'	−23°52'	–	–	–	–	Fast	11°♑57	11°♋57
☉	08°♒04'59"	+01°00'	−18°14'	–	–	–	–	Fast	21°♏55	21°♉55
☿	14°♑01	+35'33"	−20°44'	−5,4 days	+88 days	12°♑17'43"	20°♉33'12"	Slow	15°♐58	15°♊58
♀	22°♐03	+01°06'	−20°16'	−68 days	+475 days	00°♏03'12"	26°♊08'18"	Fast	07°♑56	07°♋56
♂	07°♐15	+38'39"	−21°06'	−557 days	+181 days	15°♐06'29"	10°♓08'01"	Fast	22°♑44	22°♋44
♃	13°♌45 ℞	−07'55"	+17°30'	−54 days	+65 days	18°♌06'16"	08°♌03'38"	Retro	16°♉14	16°♏14
♄	22°♊42 ℞	−02'41"	+22°02'	−108 days	+24 days	29°♊05'06"	22°♊08'06"	Retro	07°♋17	07°♑17

MOON ASPECTS
☽ ☍ ♄ 5°08' A
☽ ☌ ♀ 5°36' A
☽ ☌ ♑ 11°57' A

ESSENTIAL DIGNITIES

Pt	Ruler	Exalt	Trip	Term	Face	Detri	Fall	Score
☽	♃	--	☉	☿	☽ +	☿	--	+1
☉	♄	--	♄	♀	♀	☉ −	--	−10 p
☿	♄ m	♂	♀	♀	♂ m	☽	♃	+0 p
♀	♃	--	☉	♄	♄	☿	--	−5 p
♂	♃	--	☉	♃	☿ m	☿	--	−5 p
♃	☉	--	☉	♄	♃ +	♄	--	+1
♄	☿ m	--	♄ +	♂	☉	♃	--	+8

ASPECTS
♂ ☍ ☊ 0°31' S
♂ ☌ ☋ 0°31' S
☉ ⚹ ♂ 0°49' S
☉ ⚹ ☋ 1°08' S
☉ △ ☊ 1°08' S
♀ ☍ ♄ 1°50' A
☉ ☌ ♆ 2°29' A
♂ ⚹ ♆ 3°18' A
♃ ☍ ♆ 3°18' A
As △ Mc 4°42' A

PLANETARY SECT

Planet	Cht	Plc	Sgn	Condition
☉ D	D	D	D	In Hayz
☽ N	D	D	D	Ex Cond
☿ D	D	D	N	
♀ N	D	D	D	Ex Cond
♂ N	D	D	D	Ex Cond
♃ D	D	N	D	
♄ D	D	N	D	
D=Diurnal, N=Nocturnal				

3/12: WILL ROSALIE QUALIFY FOR THE NATIONAL CHAMPIONSHIP?

25 March 2008 at 9:27 a.m., Ljubljana, Slovenia
Hour ruler: Mercury

Qualifications for the national championship in hip-hop were rapidly nearing, and I asked whether my daughter Rosalie would get in. Although not explicitly expressed in the question, I had in mind her qualification in the category of solo dances, not pairs, which she was also taking with another dancer.

Rosie is my daughter, shown by Mercury, H5 ruler. Mercury is also the hour ruler. Her co-significator is Venus, ruler of Libra, the intercepted sign in H5. Both planets are exactly conjunct in H10 – a very nice placement in the house of success. The debilitated Mercury (in detriment and fall) separates from the exalted Venus but both are trined by the Moon - H2 ruler which is the derived H10 for the daughter and therefore stands for her success. The trine is exact and applying which made me think that she'll qualify.

Unfortunately, she didn't. Where did I miss?

The Moon (a very important factor in interpretation, since it shows my daughter's success and also the course of events) is in Scorpio (fall), in the unfortunate H6 and in an exact conjunction with the fixed star Zuben Elgenubi, which causes loss, defeat and disappointment. This is confirmed by Neptune in an exact conjunction with MC. Let us remember that planets in exact conjunctions with angles always contribute significantly important information relevant to the answer! The essentially and accidentally weak Moon, being only in two minor Venus's and Mercury's dignities (in Mercury's term and Venus's triplicity, but at the same time in Venus's detriment which nullifies the dignity by triplicity), cannot really "bring virtue" to Mercury and Venus who also don't receive the Moon in any of its dignities.

But there is a side-story to this case! Rosalie did qualify for the national championship in the category of pairs, which she performed with a friend. It's true that my question didn't refer to that particular part of her qualifications, but the issue shows in the chart itself, with a pair of planets closely conjunct in Pisces, the double-bodied sign. We have one debilitated planet (Mercury) and one exalted planet (Venus), with the second one alleviating the negativity of other indications and perhaps suggesting that she'd win in the other category? This should be a "hidden" one because Venus rules the intercepted H5 sign (Libra). And, as laid out in the Theory, intercepted signs often suggest a "question within a question", or a hidden situation of which at the time of the question we are not yet aware. Looking at it from this perspective, all becomes logical!

This chart warns that we should not blindly trust the constructive power of harmonious applying aspects in cases where the planets' essential (and/or accidental) dignity is very poor, lacking in mutual reception or being adversely affected by destructive fixed stars. At the same time it teaches us that we should be flexible in our approach - let's see what the chart is showing or suggesting or putting up on a plate for us, instead of sticking to our preconceived notions of what exactly it should reveal. Any additional information a chart provides can be a great help in finding the correct answer.

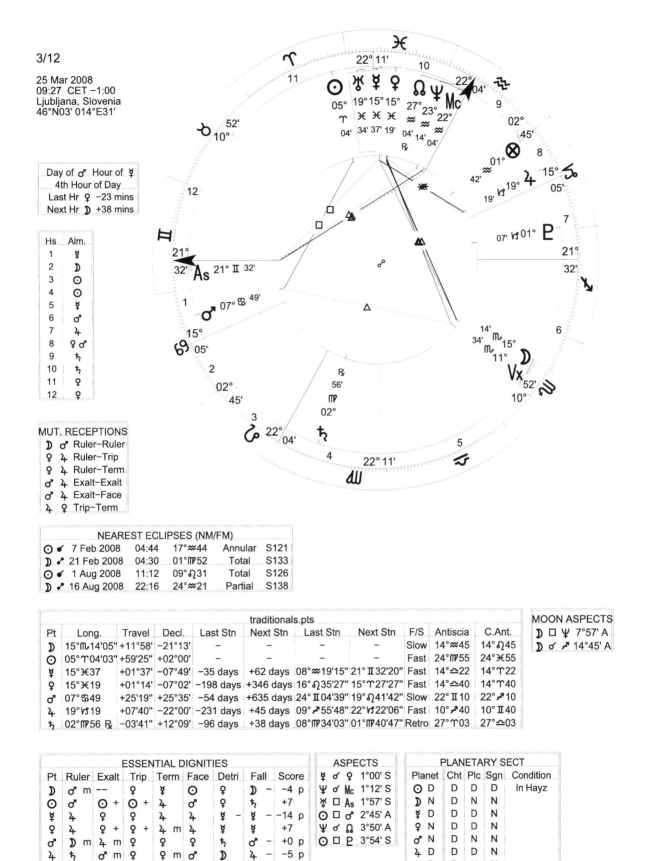

3/12

25 Mar 2008
09:27 CET −1:00
Ljubljana, Slovenia
46°N03' 014°E31'

Day of ♂ Hour of ☿
4th Hour of Day
Last Hr ♀ −23 mins
Next Hr ☽ +38 mins

Hs	Alm.
1	☿
2	☽
3	☉
4	☉
5	☿
6	♂
7	♃
8	♀ ♂
9	♄
10	♄
11	♀
12	♀

MUT. RECEPTIONS		
☽	♂	Ruler–Ruler
♀	♃	Ruler–Trip
♀	♃	Ruler–Term
♂	♃	Exalt–Exalt
♂	♃	Exalt–Face
♃	♀	Trip–Term

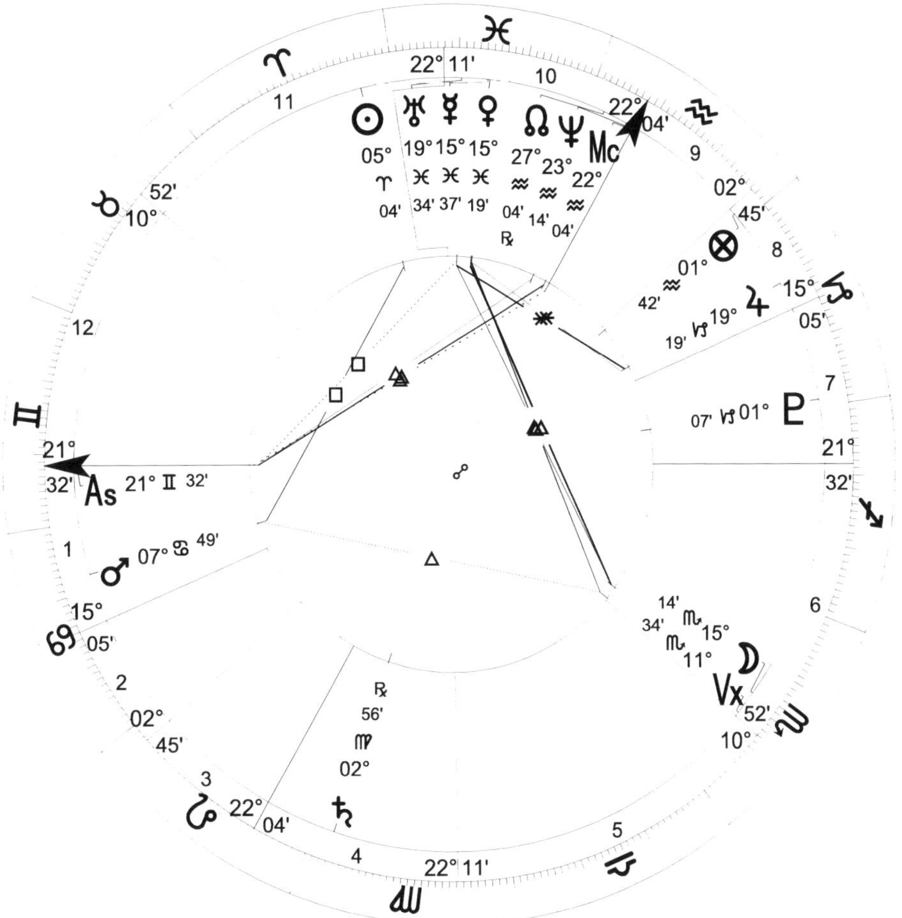

NEAREST ECLIPSES (NM/FM)					
☉ ☌	7 Feb 2008	04:44	17°♒44	Annular	S121
☽ ☍	21 Feb 2008	04:30	01°♍52	Total	S133
☉ ☌	1 Aug 2008	11:12	09°♌31	Total	S126
☽ ☍	16 Aug 2008	22:16	24°♒21	Partial	S138

traditionals.pts

Pt	Long.	Travel	Decl.	Last Stn	Next Stn	Last Stn	Next Stn	F/S	Antiscia	C.Ant.
☽	15°♏14'05"	+11°58'	−21°13'	–	–	–	–	Slow	14°♒45	14°♌45
☉	05°♈04'03"	+59'25"	+02°00'	–	–	–	–	Fast	24°♍55	24°♓55
☿	15°♓37	+01°37'	−07°49'	−35 days	+62 days	08°♒19'15"	21°♊32'20"	Fast	14°♎22	14°♈22
♀	15°♓19	+01°14'	−07°02'	−198 days	+346 days	16°♌35'27"	15°♈27'27"	Fast	14°♎40	14°♈40
♂	07°♋49	+25'19"	+25°35'	−54 days	+635 days	24°♊04'39"	19°♌41'42"	Slow	22°♊10	22°♐10
♃	19°♑19	+07'40"	−22°00'	−231 days	+45 days	09°♐55'48"	22°♑22'06"	Fast	10°♐40	10°♊40
♄	02°♍56 ℞	−03'41"	+12°09'	−96 days	+38 days	08°♍34'03"	01°♍40'47"	Retro	27°♈03	27°♎03

MOON ASPECTS			
☽	□	♆	7°57' A
☽	☌	♐	14°45' A

ESSENTIAL DIGNITIES							
Pt	Ruler	Exalt	Trip	Term	Face	Detri	Fall	Score
☽	♂ m	--	♀	☿	☉	♀	☽ −	−4 p
☉	♂	☉ +	☉ +	♃	♂	♀	♄	+7
☿	♃	♀	♀	♃	♃	☿ −	☿ −	−14 p
♀	♃	♀ +	♀ +	♃ m	♃	☿	☿	+7
♂	☽ m	♃ m	♀	♀	♀	♄	♂ −	+0 p
♃	♄	♂ m	♀	♀ m	♂	☽	♃ −	−5 p
♄	☿	☿	♀	☿	☉	♃	♀	−5 p

ASPECTS			
☿	☌	♀	1°00' S
♆	☌	Mc	1°12' S
♅	□	As	1°57' S
☉	□	♂	2°45' A
♆	☌	☊	3°50' A
☉	□	♇	3°54' S

PLANETARY SECT				
Planet	Cht	Plc	Sgn	Condition
☉ D	D	D	D	In Hayz
☽ N	D	N	N	
☿ D	D	D	N	
♀ N	D	D	N	
♂ N	D	N	N	
♃ D	D	D	N	
♄ D	D	N	N	

D=Diurnal, N=Nocturnal

REAL ESTATE

This group of horary questions includes those relating to buying, selling, renting or leasing of real estate (houses, apartments, shops, garages, business premises, land, etc.), and to relocations.

A sub-category are questions relating to buying and selling of movable property. The interpretation procedure is similar, and these charts are generally also easier to interpret.

SIGNIFICATORS

- the ascendant with H1 for the querent (seller, buyer, tenant, landlord etc.);
- the descendant with H7 for the other party/partners in business (seller, buyer, potential tenant, landlord etc.);
- IC with H4 for real estate (house, apartment, land plot, business premises etc.);
- MC with H10 for the price (of real estate);
- H2 for the financial ability of the querent;
- H8 for the financial ability of the buyer, seller or tenant;
- H9 for contracts and other related legal affairs/documents;
- H6 for (existing) tenants;
- H7 for relocation;
- H6 for real estate agents.

Agreement will be reached (or the sale/purchase/lease will take place), if:
- the rulers of H1 and H7, or the Moon and the ruler of H7, apply to a conjunction or a harmonious aspect;
- the rulers of H1 and H7, or Moon and the ruler of H7 are connected by translation or collection of light;
- the rulers of H1 and H7, or the Moon and the ruler of H7, apply to a disharmonious aspect, with the significators placed in strong and fortunate houses, or connected by translation or collection of light;
- the ruler of H1 or the Moon applies to the ruler of H4, or vice versa (the ruler of H4 to the ruler of H1), by conjunction or a harmonious aspect (or a disharmonious one, but helped by translation of light etc., as with H1 and H7);
- the Moon translates light from the ruler of H4 to the ruler of H1, or vice versa.

In case of translation of light, the deal might be concluded with the mediation of a third party, usually an agency or a land broker.

Additional indications, pointing to the affirmative answer, but not acting as independent confirmations, are:
- the ruler of H1 is in H7, or vice versa;
- the ruler of H1 or the Moon is in H4, or vice versa.

If the application is by a square, the business (purchase, sale, etc.) might come to pass, but with problems and after lengthy negotiations. Chances are better if the significators in a disharmonious aspect are connected by translation of light, collection of light or mutual reception.

Business is more desirable and takes less trouble if the significators are essentially and accidentally strong.

BUYING

With questions relating to the advisability of buying a certain property, we must look at whether the querent's significator (the ruler or almuten of H1) is in agreement with the nature of H4 that stands for the real estate. If such a connection doesn't exist or if both rulers are even in an opposition or a square, the purchase is not desirable; the property would sooner or later disappoint us.

If the H4 planets (the ruler and the eventual planet/s occupying H4) are very weak (in detriment, fall, peregrine, etc.), the property is in poor condition or not worth much – for any of the several reasons that can be inferred from the chart. We must, of course, use common sense: if the price is low and we are ready to invest in reconstruction, the purchase can nevertheless be desirable.

Malefics in H4 often show that repairs may be necessary, but sometimes they indicate problems that would arise after the purchase. To find out the nature of those problems, we must examine the nature of the malefic as well as of the sign in which it is located. I must point out, though, that the mere presence of a malefic in H4 is not in itself a sufficiently strong indication that something is wrong with the property. It is important to examine the planet's essential and accidental dignity and eventual aspects. If the malefic is afflicted and essentially and/or accidentally weak, or ruling an unfortunate house (H12, H8 or H6), this is a serious warning. Such a property should be avoided or at least thoroughly checked for possible shortcomings. The trans-Saturnians are considered malefics in this respect, but if in fortunate aspects with benefics, they can show some special benefits that can be gained by buying the property.

Individual malefics' meanings, associated with H4, are:
- Mars: heating devices, fireplaces, chimneys, stoves. An afflicted Mars (or afflicted planets in fire signs) often point to problems with the heating system.
- Uranus: electrical and telecommunication installation, electrical currents. Afflictions warn of the possibility of poor installations, or some sudden, unpleasant surprises related to the purchase, whereas good aspects with benefics suggest some special, unexpected gain.
- Neptune: gas installation, undercurrents. Afflictions suggest risk of moisture and decay, or misunderstandings related to the purchase.
- Pluto: the sewerage and drainage systems; can also stand for boilers and heaters;
- Saturn: a generally poor condition of the property due to decay and worn out installations.
- Any malefic in water signs warns of moisture or problems with plumbing or underground streams, or of the risk of flooding.

The purchase of such a property is, in short, undesirable.

The Moon in every horary chart shows where there is a change in sight; if in H10, the price is probably flexible. The H4 condition should be checked to see how much the price can be lowered: if it suggests that the real estate is highly valuable, we are advised to negotiate it a little bit (or as much as we can), but if H4 is poor, the property is probably not worth its estimated price, and should be lowered considerably.

SELLING

The interpretative rules are similar to those for purchases, but if we are selling something, we must check the state of H7 and H8, showing the buyers and their finances. If the ruler of H8 is strongly afflicted (in detriment, fall, peregrine, retrograde, combust or occupying an unfortunate house), the buyer may not be able to collect the purchase money. Similarly if H10 is very strong, as the price may be too high; we might need to lower it, especially if there's no buyer in sight as yet. A retrograde H7 ruler can show that the buyer we are negotiating with will change his mind, or that he hides some important information that could ultimately lead to the termination of the agreements.

RENTING

Tradition teaches that tenants "fall" into H6. This is true, but as long as we have not yet entered into an agreement with the potential tenant, or until we are still negotiating with them, they belong to H7 - just like any person with whom we are negotiating any other (potential) business. The sixth house rules only those people who are already in the tenant relationship with us.

When will our tenants leave? They are ruled by H6.

Should I accept this woman for my tenant? She is ruled by H7.

HIRING

The significators are the same as for buying. The premises we are hiring are ruled by H4, the landlord by H7, the rent by H10. When hiring business premises, it is also good to examine H9 (legal matters) to see whether the legal part of the business would proceed smoothly. Some landlords don't have the relevant documents which often disables an agreement – especially if it's a business one.

RELOCATION

If we are planning relocation, our current home is ruled by H4, the future one with H7. The significator that is better placed should decide whether it would be better to stay in the current home, or to move. If the relocation involves our income (a relocation of business premises, for example), we must also consider the state of H8 which reveals whether we would be financially successful in the new environment.

H3 is our present neighbourhood, H9 (3/7) the future one. It is important, of course, what kind of neighbours we will have, since they can make our life more pleasant – or cause us a lot of trouble!

Relocation is also recommended, if:
- the ruler of H7 is in the aspect with a benefic while the ruler of H4 is in aspect with a malefic;
- the ruler of H1 or the Moon is separating from a square or opposition with the rulers of H8, H6 or H12, or with malefics which rule H4 or H7.
- there is a malefic in H1 or H4, especially if it is peregrine or retrograde;
- the ruler of H1 or the Moon separates from an aspect with a malefic and applies to an aspect with a benefic.

Where would be best to move? To find out, we look at the directions of the sky where there are benefics or planets that are in a harmonious aspect with the ascendant and/or its ruler. See the Theory part of the book to find more about directions.

For this purpose, we can also use locational astrology. Additional knowledge is required for this technique, of course, but there are many programs around to facilitate our search. Local space lines and aspects in azimuth are especially revealing.

THE QUALITY OF THE LAND

When buying a building plot or a piece of land, the querent is often interested in the quality of the soil; he might be a hobby gardener, but even if he's not, the quality of the land that he's purchasing is an important consideration.

The rules for interpreting charts asking of selling/buying of land are the same as those for purchasing other kinds of real estate, but here we aim at specifically evaluating the quality of the soil.

The sign on the cusp of H4 (along with an eventual intercepted sign) describes the land as:

FIRE SIGNS: Dry and difficult to cultivate; the terrain can be undulating, steep or solitary. Saggitarius indicates a forested area, Aries a newer settlement, Leo dry and sun-lit land.

EARTH SIGNS: Fertile soil, very suitable for cultivation (especially Taurus nd Virgo).

AIR SIGNS: Slightly undulating terrain with a lot of shrubs or trees. Sometimes a densely populated area (Gemini especially).

WATER SIGNS: Proximity to water (springs, rivers, lakes, streams or the sea). There may be a fountain or pool on the plot. Low terrain, but with the presence of (afflicted) malefics, there is a danger of underground currents, or of floods.

OTHER PURCHASES AND SALES

The rules for the interpretation of horary charts relating to all types of purchases and sales (movables such as cars, furniture, clothing, technical equipment and similar, or domestic animals) are very similar to those for real estate charts, except that the significators are a bit different. Most of the items that are our personal property, are ruled by H2 – and so are those that are on sale and supposed to become our property. The exception are cars and other means of transport which are described by H3, and animals which belong to H6 – at least the small ones (dogs, cats, canary birds and the like) whereas the big ones (horses, cattle and the like) belong to H12. (But don't ask me about snakes – I think I'd have a bit of a trouble here.)

When faced with a choice, some astrologers use the method described by the (already mentioned) American astrologer Barbara Watters. In her book **HORARY ASTROLOGY AND THE JUDGMENT OF EVENTS,** she presents the technique with an example of buying a new car. Here's how:

Should I buy a new car or should I fix the old one? Cars belong to H3. The car that the querent owns is therefore ruled by H3, while the car to be purchased is ruled by the third house from the third, that is, by the fifth (H5). Which house is in better condition and in better relation with H1 (the querent)? If H3 is better, keep the old car, but if H5 is better, look for a new one.

The procedure with all kinds of choices is always the same: we take the house that rules the existing property/ situation/person, for the first choice, while for the second choice we calculate the same number of houses from the first one (3/3 for cars, for example). As already mentioned in the Employment and Career chapter, following this kind of analogy, some use H7 for the (potential) new job (because it is 10/10).

I must stress, though, that this technique is not traditional. In most cases, we will find the answer more quickly and reliably if we stick to traditional rules.

With regard to the purchase of movable property, some students have difficulty with understanding why H2 would be the property that we are buying. Doesn't it belong to H8, that is, the seller's property? The answer is no, it doesn't belong to H8. As soon as something is on the market and is the subject of our (planned) purchase, it belongs to "just" H2.

4/1: WILL I SELL THE HOUSE?

8 July 1993 at 2:46 p.m. (14:46), Ljubljana, Slovenia
Hour Ruler: Jupiter

This is one of my first horary charts. I cast it while I was studying horary astrology under the tutelage of Olivia Barclay (Horary Practitioner's Course) – and was very proud of myself because I managed to get it right!

An acquaintance asked me if he'd be able to sell the house which was a family heritage and had several owners. He had been unsuccessfully looking for a buyer for quite some time, and was losing hope to be ever able to sell it.

He's ruled by the ascendant and Mars, its ruler and almuten of the ascendant. The house is shown by Saturn, the H4 ruler, which it also occupies. Saturn is retrograde but in its own domicile, triplicity and term, therefore dignified. As the planet of time and old age, it shows by itself that the house is old but probably solidly built (Saturn dignified in Aquarius, a fixed sign); nonetheless, it seems to be neglected and in need of repair (Saturn retrograde). The querent confirmed all of this.

The potential buyer is shown by H7. Descendant is in Taurus, with its ruler Venus in Gemini where it applies by square to Mars in Virgo. The buyer (Venus) is therefore approaching the seller (Mars), but the planets are not receiving each other by any dignity, while their joint dispositor Mercury is weak due to its retrograde motion and an applying conjunction with the Sun (under the Sun's beams), therefore it can't help bring success or "completion of the matter". However, the Moon in Pisces (strongly affecting the situation due to its placement in H4) had separated from the square with Venus and had at the time of the question just reached an opposition with Mars, which can be considered as translation of light. This way, both planets are strongly connected and somehow "forced" to speak to each other, so to say. In other words, the querent would obviously be able to sell the house, but due to lack of receptions and the stressful aspectual relationship between significators, only with great difficulty. It is likely that negotiations would proceed slowly and with much trouble, and the querent might even regret the sale.

The buyer will obviously benefit more from the deal, because the first aspect of Venus is trine Jupiter; Venus receives Jupiter in its sign, and Jupiter is also the hour ruler, showing the buyer's profit. This is confirmed by the fact that Mars is in Venus' triplicity and term (albeit in its fall); this points to the existence of a potential buyer who'd be willing to strike a deal, while Venus is in none of Mars' dignities which could mean that the querent doesn't try very hard to sell the house.

I told the querent that the house would sell, but with difficulty. He said that the house really needed to get sold because he had agreed on that with his relatives (co-owners); if it belonged only to him, he probably would not want to sell it at all.

Several months later, he called to tell me that he had finally managed to sell the house, but with great effort and at a lower price than the one set initially. Due to the high costs of legal proceedings which he covered himself, his profit was close to nil, but he was happy because the deal was finally closed and the burden removed from his shoulders.

4/1

8 Jul 1993
14:46 CEDT −2:00
Ljubljana, Slovenia
46°N03' 014°E31'

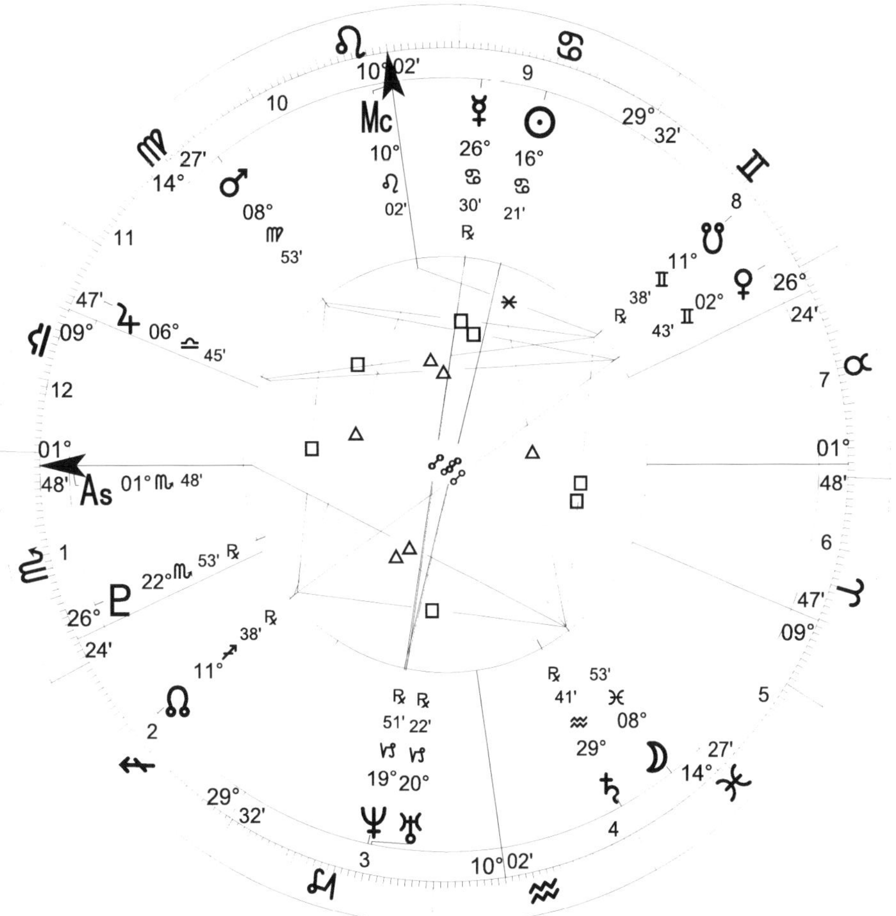

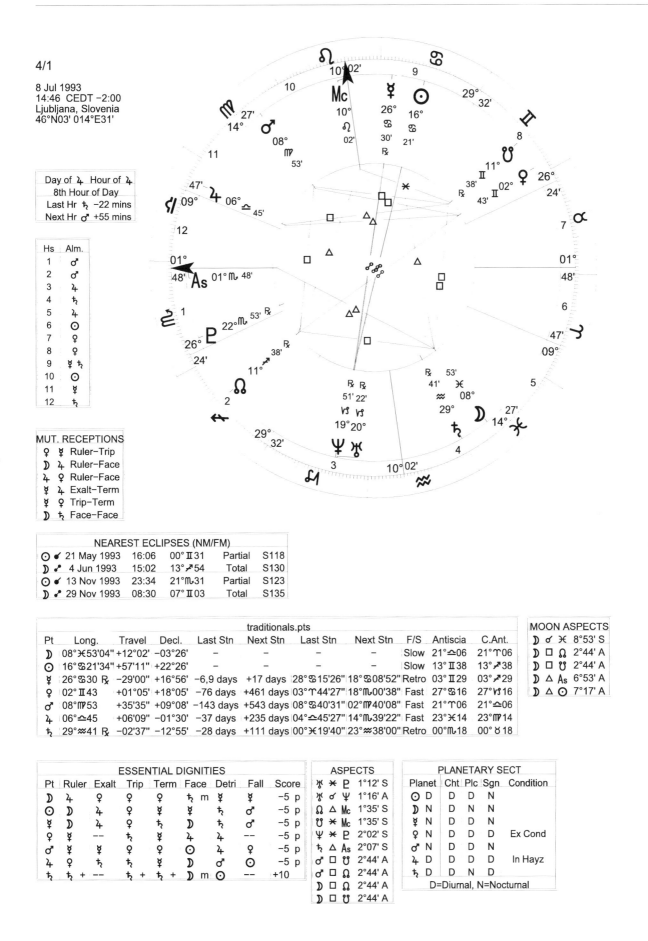

Day of ♃ Hour of ♃
8th Hour of Day
Last Hr ♄ −22 mins
Next Hr ♂ +55 mins

Hs	Alm.
1	♂
2	♂
3	♃
4	♄
5	♃
6	☉
7	♀
8	♀
9	☿ ♄
10	☉
11	☿
12	♄

MUT. RECEPTIONS	
♀ ☿	Ruler–Trip
☽ ♃	Ruler–Face
♃ ♀	Ruler–Face
☿ ♃	Exalt–Term
☿ ♀	Trip–Term
☽ ♄	Face–Face

NEAREST ECLIPSES (NM/FM)					
☉	21 May 1993	16:06	00°♊31	Partial	S118
☽	4 Jun 1993	15:02	13°♐54	Total	S130
☉	13 Nov 1993	23:34	21°♏31	Partial	S123
☽	29 Nov 1993	08:30	07°♊03	Total	S135

traditionals.pts

Pt	Long.	Travel	Decl.	Last Stn	Next Stn	Last Stn	Next Stn	F/S	Antiscia	C.Ant.
☽	08°♓53'04"	+12°02'	−03°26'	–	–	–	–	Slow	21°♎06	21°♈06
☉	16°♋21'34"	+57'11"	+22°26'	–	–	–	–	Slow	13°♊38	13°♐38
☿	26°♋30 ℞	−29'00"	+16°56'	−6,9 days	+17 days	28°♋15'26"	18°♋08'52"	Retro	03°♊29	03°♐29
♀	02°♊43	+01°05'	+18°05'	−76 days	+461 days	03°♈44'27"	18°♏00'38"	Fast	27°♋16	27°♑16
♂	08°♍53	+35'35"	+09°08'	−143 days	+543 days	08°♋40'31"	02°♍40'08"	Fast	21°♈06	21°♎06
♃	06°♎45	+06'09"	−01°30'	−37 days	+235 days	04°♎45'27"	14°♏39'22"	Fast	23°♓14	23°♍14
♄	29°♒41 ℞	−02'37"	−12°55'	−28 days	+111 days	00°♓19'40"	23°♒38'00"	Retro	00°♏18	00°♉18

MOON ASPECTS		
☽ ☌ ♓	8°53'	S
☽ □ ☊	2°44'	A
☽ □ ☋	2°44'	A
☽ △ As	6°53'	A
☽ △ ☉	7°17'	A

ESSENTIAL DIGNITIES

Pt	Ruler	Exalt	Trip	Term	Face	Detri	Fall	Score
☽	♃	♀	♀	♀	♄ m	☿	☿	−5 p
☉	☽	♃	♀	☿	☿	♄	♂	−5 p
☿	☽	♃	♀	♄	☽	♄	♂	−5 p
♀	☿	--	♄	☿	♃	♃	--	−5 p
♂	☿	☿	♀	♀	☉	♃	♀	−5 p
♃	♀	♄	♄	☿	☽	♂	☉	−5 p
♄	♄ +	--	♄ +	♄ +	☽ m	☉	--	+10

ASPECTS		
♅ ⚹ ♇	1°12'	S
♅ ☌ ♆	1°16'	A
☊ △ Mc	1°35'	S
☋ ⚹ Mc	1°35'	S
♆ ⚹ ♇	2°02'	S
♄ △ As	2°07'	S
♂ □ ☋	2°44'	A
♂ □ ☊	2°44'	A
☽ □ ☊	2°44'	A
☽ □ ☋	2°44'	A

PLANETARY SECT

Planet	Cht	Plc	Sgn	Condition
☉ D	D	D	N	
☽ N	D	N	N	
☿ N	D	D	N	
♀ N	D	D	D	Ex Cond
♂ N	D	D	N	
♃ D	D	D	D	In Hayz
♄ D	D	N	D	

D=Diurnal, N=Nocturnal

4/2: CAN I RENT THIS SURGERY?

21 October 2004 at 1:27 p.m. (13:17), Ljubljana, Slovenia
Hour ruler: Saturn

A dentist in a private practice was looking for new premises. The day before she raised the above question, she sent off an official request to rent a surgery which due to the recent death of the incumbent tenant became vacant. Now she wanted to know whether her application would be accepted.

Ascendant in Capricorn reflects the fact that the querent was interested in business and real estate matters, but as she was a dentist, it's interesting to note that teeth (like bones) fall under the dominion of Saturn, the ruler of the ascending sign – and planetary hour ruler. This being harmonious, the chances of a positive answer are slightly increased, and/or the chart can be interpreted with confidence.

But Saturn is in H7 in Cancer, its detriment. This indicates that the querent felt helpless and insecure. Of course, she had done what she could, and her "fate" was now in the hands of others (H7). Such placements (querent's significator essentially weak in H7) are frequent in cases when querents feel (or know) that the only thing they can do to reach their goal is to sit and wait (and, sometimes, suffer).

The ambulance is shown by H4 in Taurus and its ruler Venus in Virgo in H8. Interestingly, Venus in the "house of death" had just separated from a square to Pluto, the modern planet of death, which reflects the recent death of the incumbent tenant. A similar symbolism is shown by the Sun, the H8 ruler and the natural significator of men, in a close separating square of Saturn, significator of the querent.

Venus (the ambulance) is now "free", and it is going – to where, to whom? To a sextile with Saturn – the querent! The aspect would be completed without a frustration, albeit without a mutual reception; nevertheless, Saturn is in the triplicity of Venus, confirming that the querent can get hold of the ambulance.

But because the question is linked to her career, let us also check the H10 indications. This house is ruled by Mars (MC in Scorpio) and we have a H10 planet, Mercury. The Moon is at 5°40' Aquarius, having just completed a trine to Jupiter. This refers to her recent past – as already said, the querent submitted the application the day before. The Moon now applies to a square with Mercury (which due to its H10 placement is linked to her career, and is also Venus' dispositor) and then (via a conjunction with Neptune) to trine Mars, the significator of her job. All this led me to the conclusion that her wish would be granted – that is, the application for the ambulance would be approved.

When? The most reliable time indicator is the Moon, so let's see how many degrees separates it from the trine to Mars. Why Mars, you might ask, since the ambulance is ruled by Venus, not Mars? Well, simply because the Moon doesn't aspect Venus, so we must take what the chart offers, and see if the Moon applies to any other planet, involved with the issue at hand. In this case, this is Mars, the H10 ruler. There are 10°39' between the Moon and Mars which corresponds to 10.5 units of time. What units? The Moon in a cardinal house and a fixed sign = a mixed indication which could most logically be weeks. A look into the calendar showed that this would be the beginning of 2005 – the most probable time for starting the job in the new premises.

I therefore told the querent that her application would be approved and that she'd probably be able to start working there at the beginning of the next year, which she later confirmed.

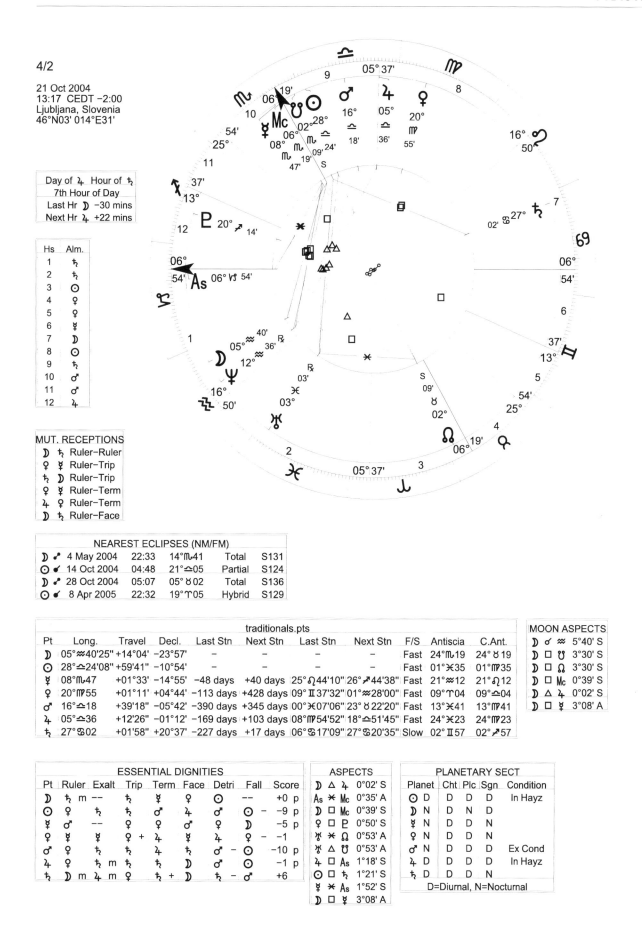

4/2

21 Oct 2004
13:17 CEDT −2:00
Ljubljana, Slovenia
46°N03' 014°E31'

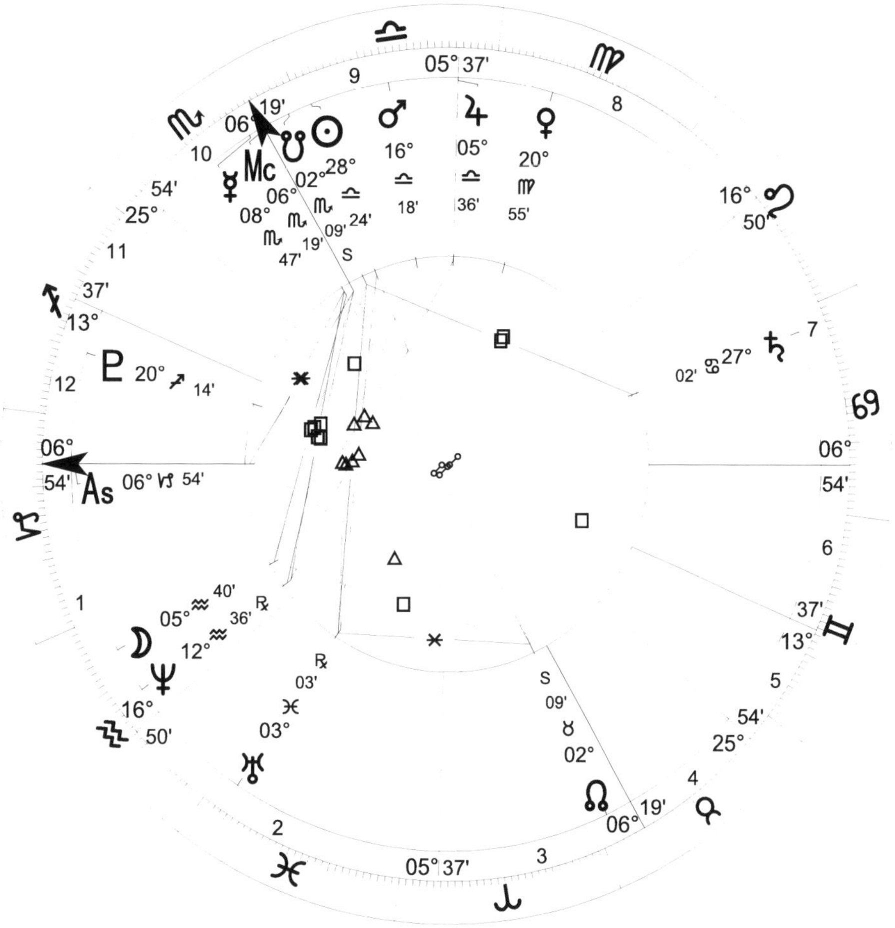

Day of ♃ Hour of ♄
7th Hour of Day
Last Hr ☽ −30 mins
Next Hr ♃ +22 mins

Hs	Alm.
1	♄
2	♄
3	☉
4	♀
5	♀
6	☿
7	☽
8	☉
9	♄
10	♂
11	♂
12	♃

MUT. RECEPTIONS		
☽	♄	Ruler−Ruler
♀	☿	Ruler−Trip
♄	☽	Ruler−Trip
♀	☿	Ruler−Term
♃	♀	Ruler−Term
☽	♄	Ruler−Face

NEAREST ECLIPSES (NM/FM)					
☽	4 May 2004	22:33	14°♏41	Total	S131
☉	14 Oct 2004	04:48	21°♎05	Partial	S124
☽	28 Oct 2004	05:07	05°♉02	Total	S136
☉	8 Apr 2005	22:32	19°♈05	Hybrid	S129

traditionals.pts

Pt	Long.	Travel	Decl.	Last Stn	Next Stn	Last Stn	Next Stn	F/S	Antiscia	C.Ant.
☽	05°♒40'25"	+14°04'	−23°57'	–	–	–	–	Fast	24°♏19	24°♉19
☉	28°♎24'08"	+59'41"	−10°54'	–	–	–	–	Fast	01°♓35	01°♍35
☿	08°♏47	+01°33'	−14°55'	−48 days	+40 days	25°♌44'10"	26°♐44'38"	Fast	21°♒12	21°♌12
♀	20°♍55	+01°11'	+04°44'	−113 days	+428 days	09°♊37'32"	01°♒28'00"	Fast	09°♈04	09°♎04
♂	16°♎18	+39'18"	−05°42'	−390 days	+345 days	00°♓07'06"	23°♉22'20"	Fast	13°♓41	13°♍41
♃	05°♎36	+12'26"	−01°12'	−169 days	+103 days	08°♍54'52"	18°♎51'45"	Fast	24°♓23	24°♍23
♄	27°♋02	+01'58"	+20°37'	−227 days	+17 days	06°♋17'09"	27°♋20'35"	Slow	02°♊57	02°♐57

MOON ASPECTS			
☽	☌	♒	5°40' S
☽	□	☋	3°30' S
☽	□	☊	3°30' S
☽	□	Mc	0°39' S
☽	△	♃	0°02' S
☽	□	☿	3°08' A

ESSENTIAL DIGNITIES

Pt	Ruler	Exalt	Trip	Term	Face	Detri	Fall	Score
☽	♄ m	--	♄	☿	♀	☉	--	+0 p
☉	♀	♄	♄	♂	♃	♂	☉ −	−9 p
☿	♂	--	♀	♀	♂	♀	☽	−5 p
♀	☿	☿	♀ +	♃	☿	♃	♀ −	−1
♂	♀	♄	♄	♃	♄	♂ −	☉	−10 p
♃	♀	♄ m	♄	♄	☽	♂	☉	−1 p
♄	☽ m	♃ m	♀	♄ +	☽	♄ −	♂	+6

ASPECTS			
☽	△	♃	0°02' S
As	⚹	Mc	0°35' A
☽	□	Mc	0°39' S
♀	□	♇	0°50' S
♅	⚹	☊	0°53' A
♅	△	☋	0°53' A
♃	□	As	1°18' S
☉	□	♄	1°21' S
☿	⚹	As	1°52' S
☽	□	☿	3°08' A

PLANETARY SECT

Planet		Cht	Plc	Sgn	Condition
☉	D	D	D	D	In Hayz
☽	N	D	N	D	
☿	N	D	D	N	
♀	N	D	D	N	
♂	N	D	D	D	Ex Cond
♃	D	D	D	D	In Hayz
♄	D	D	D	N	

D=Diurnal, N=Nocturnal

4/3: SHOULD WE BUY THIS HOUSE?

24 May 2006 at 4:13 p.m. (16:13), Ljubljana, Slovenia
Hour ruler: Moon

The question was raised by one of my students who was not skilled enough to trust his own judgement, so he asked me for help. He said that he and his girlfriend were planning to get married, and they had found a nice, newly built house in a beautiful area, but he was not quite sure whether the house would be really right for them. We agreed to delineate the chart in the classroom, as a "living" example of real estate horaries.

The querent is shown by the ascendant in Libra and its ruler Venus which we find in H7 in Aries. Venus' detriment indicates his uncertainty and a feeling of powerlessness, perhaps suggesting that the decision was not really in his hands – or not even in the hands of his fiancee. H7 is also occupied by the Moon, his co-significator and indicator of the course of events. In real estate transactions, this house shows "partners in business", in this case the sellers, but due to the specific nature of his question, it also (partly) describes his girlfriend. We know that in cases where a question is asked on behalf of a couple (or a group), both, or all are shown by H1, but H7 retains its signification of partners as independent persons, or of their own specific roles regarding the subject of the question. Although they were both the buyers, H7 relates specifically to her, maybe showing her attitude towards the planned purchase or the role she'd be playing in the negotiations.

We therefore have a situation where H7 shows three people: the querent, his girlfriend and the seller. This should not confuse us since such interconnectedness of the significators fits perfectly into the context of the question, and it adequately reflects the situation – negotiations between the querent/girlfriend/seller.

The house is shown by H4 which is in Capricorn, with its ruler Saturn in H10 in Leo. Saturn in detriment could mean that the property was not in the best condition, but the Sun, its dispositor and H11 ruler (the most fortunate house showing one's heart's desire), applies to it by sextile (from H8 but in the sign of the more fortunate H9), alleviating its malice and giving it more "virtue". Besides, both bodies are in mutual reception by triplicity. All this is encouraging and adequately describes the value of the property, which, as a new building, it certainly had. In view of the fact that the aspect was an applying one it is interesting to note that the house had only been finished up to the third phase – the construction would therefore continue.

I was intrigued by the fact that both Venus and the Moon are at the ending degrees and not completing any aspect until their entrance into the next signs. (Except for Venus trine Pluto, which is in itself a nice aspect, but Pluto is a trans-Saturnian and as such doesn't play the role of a significator.) This could indicate a nearby change of circumstances, but it could also show the outcome in the sense that the decision had already been made and/or that the querent practically had no power to influence the situation. This would nicely fit in with the detrimented Venus, placed in H7 (see above). Let us remember that in such cases, it helps to ask additional questions. Why is it that the querent feels so unconfident and helpless? Can he explain?

Did he pose the question just to make sure that he made the right decision? Hour ruler is, after all, disharmonious. (Let me remind you that I was delineating the chart along those lines in front of my students, therefore I didn't ask him about those additional circumstances. I wanted to see how far we could get, without questions.) Let's get back to the main significators. Venus (in H7, the house of the sellers) is separating from the square of Mars, its dispositor. This aspect in itself would show their disagreement and drifting away from each other, but because the Moon is separating from a square of Mars (the seller) and conjunction with Venus (the buyer), and is applying to a square with Saturn (the house), it translates light between them and thus enables the "completion of the matter". The Moon will soon change into its exaltation sign (Taurus) and "meet" Saturn in one of its strongest dignities. Besides, Venus and Mars are in a mutual reception (Venus in Mars' domicile and term, Mars in Venus' triplicity), suggesting that the sales agreement might have already been reached.

Not only the Moon, Venus too is soon to enter Taurus, its domicile where it has much more power than in Aries. The querent's situation would therefore soon be significantly improved.

When I was explaining to my students how the translation of light in this chart vividly described the purchase which might in fact already be decided upon, I pointed out the obvious connection between H7 (the seller) and H10, which could (besides showing the price) describe the girl's parents (H10 is 4/7). I came to think about them as playing a role here because the H4 ruler is in H10 (the girl's parents) while the H10 ruler the Moon is in H7

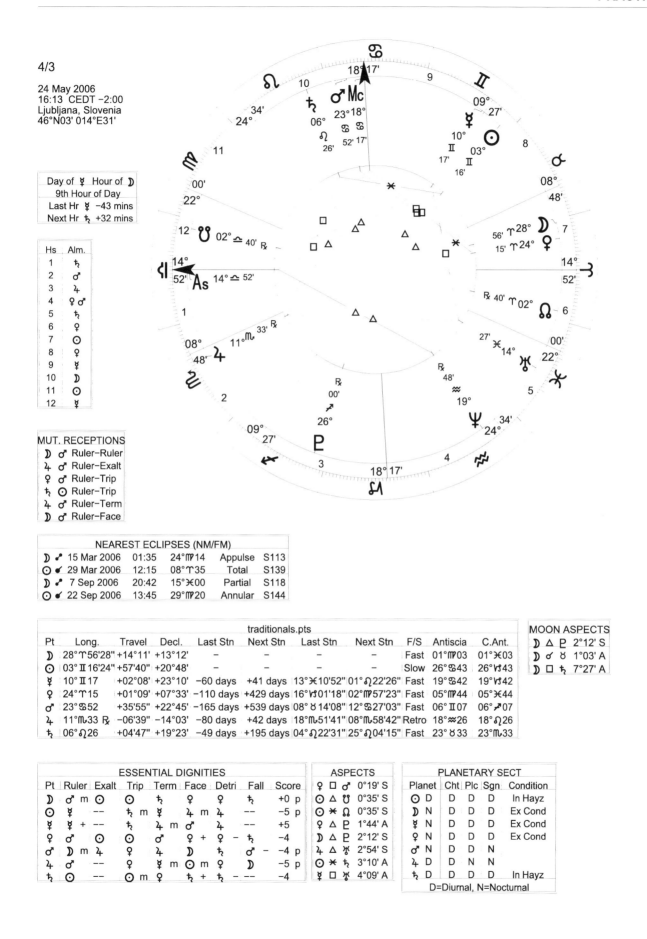

4/3

24 May 2006
16:13 CEDT −2:00
Ljubljana, Slovenia
46°N03' 014°E31'

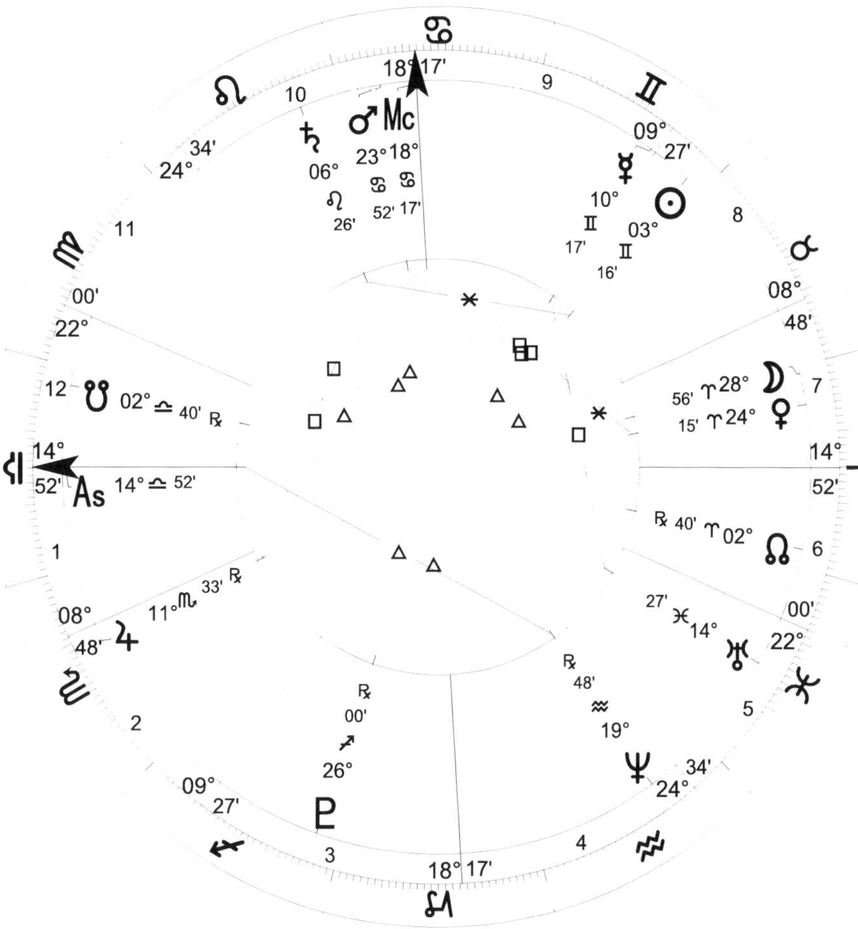

Day of ☿ Hour of ☽
9th Hour of Day
Last Hr ☿ −43 mins
Next Hr ♄ +32 mins

Hs	Alm.
1	♄
2	♂
3	♃
4	♀♂
5	♄
6	♀
7	☉
8	♀
9	☿
10	☽
11	☉
12	☿

MUT. RECEPTIONS
☽ ♂ Ruler–Ruler
♃ ♂ Ruler–Exalt
♀ ♂ Ruler–Trip
♄ ☉ Ruler–Trip
♃ ♂ Ruler–Term
☽ ♂ Ruler–Face

NEAREST ECLIPSES (NM/FM)					
☽ ☍	15 Mar 2006	01:35	24°♍14	Appulse	S113
☉ ☌	29 Mar 2006	12:15	08°♈35	Total	S139
☽ ☍	7 Sep 2006	20:42	15°♓00	Partial	S118
☉ ☌	22 Sep 2006	13:45	29°♍20	Annular	S144

traditionals.pts

Pt	Long.	Travel	Decl.	Last Stn	Next Stn	Last Stn	Next Stn	F/S	Antiscia	C.Ant.
☽	28°♈56'28"	+14°11'	+13°12'	–	–	–	–	Fast	01°♍03	01°♓03
☉	03°♊16'24"	+57'40"	+20°48'	–	–	–	–	Slow	26°♋43	26°♑43
☿	10°♊17	+02°08'	+23°10'	−60 days	+41 days	13°♓10'52"	01°♌22'26"	Fast	19°♋42	19°♑42
♀	24°♈15	+01°09'	+07°33'	−110 days	+429 days	16°♑01'18"	02°♍57'23"	Fast	05°♍44	05°♓44
♂	23°♋52	+35'55"	+22°45'	−165 days	+539 days	08°♉14'08"	12°♋27'03"	Fast	06°♊07	06°♐07
♃	11°♏33 ℞	−06'39"	−14°03'	−80 days	+42 days	18°♏51'41"	08°♏58'42"	Retro	18°♒26	18°♌26
♄	06°♌26	+04'47"	+19°23'	−49 days	+195 days	04°♌22'31"	25°♌04'15"	Fast	23°♉33	23°♏33

MOON ASPECTS
☽ △ ♇ 2°12' S
☽ ☌ ☋ 1°03' A
☽ □ ♄ 7°27' A

ESSENTIAL DIGNITIES

Pt	Ruler	Exalt	Trip	Term	Face	Detri	Fall	Score
☽	♂ m	☉	☉	♄	♀	♀	♄	+0 p
☉	☿	--	♄ m	☿	♃ m	♃	--	−5 p
☿	☿ +	--	♄	♃ m	♂	♃	--	+5
♀	♂	☉	☉	♂	♀ +	♀ −	♄	−4
♂	☽ m	♃	♀	♃	☽	♄	♂ −	−4 p
♃	♂	--	♀	☿ m	☉ m	♀	☽	−5 p
♄	☉	--	☉ m	♀	♄ +	♄ −	--	−4

ASPECTS
♀ □ ♂ 0°19' S
☉ △ ☋ 0°35' S
☉ ✶ ☊ 0°35' S
♀ △ ♇ 1°44' A
☽ △ ♇ 2°12' S
♃ △ ♅ 2°54' S
☉ ✶ ♄ 3°10' A
☿ □ ♅ 4°09' A

PLANETARY SECT

Planet		Cht	Plc	Sgn	Condition
☉	D	D	D	D	In Hayz
☽	N	D	D	D	Ex Cond
☿	N	D	D	D	Ex Cond
♀	N	D	D	D	Ex Cond
♂	N	D	D	N	
♃	D	D	N	N	
♄	D	D	D	D	In Hayz

D=Diurnal, N=Nocturnal

(their relationship with the seller), and the H7 ruler Mars is in H10, which is a case of mutual reception by house.

All this made me wonder whether the actual buyers were his girlfriend's parents? He confirmed this! He said that they had offered to buy the house in the present state (the third construction phase), while all the later expenses (the final construction phase, furniture etc.) would be the young couple's.

The Moon in an angular house and a cardinal sign, of quick motion, and at the end of a sign, synchronized with a rapid development: two days later, the girl's parents paid the deposit and the house was soon to become the couple's new home.

Obviously, the decision about the purchase was made before the querent asked the question, but the chart is no less interesting and descriptive for that matter.

They moved into the house on the day of the wedding (6 October 2007). This is extremely interesting from the timing perspective, because it confirms my theory about the advisability of using synodic rather than calendar months. Namely, exactly 18 synodic months and 8 days elapsed from the time of the question until their move, and there are exactly18 degrees and 10 minutes between the MC/IC axis and Saturn (the house). This is confirmed by the symbolic movement of the Moon: if we move it forward by 18 degrees, we get to the 17th degree of Taurus, where it's in a pretty exact trine with IC. Okay, one degree is missing, but this can be justified by the rapid daily motion of the Moon, which, as we know, "speeds up" action a bit so that less time – reflected in fewer degrees - elapses until the planned (foreseen, predicted) result.

4/4: SHOULD I LET MY APARTMENT TO THIS WOMAN?

3 April 1994 at 10:14 a.m., Ljubljana, Slovenia
Hour ruler: The Moon

The querent asked for advice, whether to let her apartment to a woman who expressed a wish to rent it. The querent had inherited the flat from her mother, and the potential tenant was a woman with a child who was then living in the same block of flats. Her current apartment was becoming too small for herself, her child and her mother who were sharing it, so she wanted to move into a bigger one. The querent was in doubt. She had basically consented, but was still undecided, therefore she wanted a confirmation that she would not regret her decision.

As with all questions relating to real estate, the querent is shown by the ascendant, its ruler and the Moon, the potential tenant by H7, the apartment by H4 and the price by H10. (Tenants belong to H6, sure, but because the querent was still at the negotiation stage with the woman who was therefore only her potential and not the actual tenant, she's shown by H7 of "any person out there").

The situation here is very illustrative, because Jupiter (the potential tenant) is in conjunction with the cusp of H6. The Moon's separating sextile to Jupiter nicely reflects their recent agreement, but Jupiter was retrograde, so I asked her whether she was sure that the woman would not change her mind? She said that it surely didn't seem so; on the contrary, she looked extremely interested!

The apartment is shown by the Sun which is in its exaltation, triplicity and face, and in the most fortunate H11. This shows a high quality property in an excellent condition. She confirmed that the flat had recently been renovated and that it was big and bright. But I became wary of the fact that H10, showing the price, was occupied by a "poor" Saturn which also ruled that house, so I asked her what was the rent that she required? Very low - as I expected. I told her that in view of the obvious value of her possession the rent seemed too low, and encouraged her to raise it.

The Moon has separated from the square with the Sun which also rules the querent's H3. I therefore wondered what was causing her distress, indicated by this tense aspect? She revealed to me that her uncertainty was linked to the fact that the potential tenant was a friend of her sister (H3!) with whom she was not on good terms. She worried that if this woman moved into her apartment, her sister would come to visit and turn the tenant against her or otherwise cause her harm.

Mercury, the querent's main significator, is essentially weak (in detriment and fall), showing her to be indecisive and not able to think clearly about the matter at hand, but its accidental dignitiy (H10) confirms that she nevertheless was "the boss"! Mercury applies to a conjunction with Mars, and the aspect is reinforced by the Moon's applying sextile to both planets. The aspect with Mars is strong because Mars receives the Moon in its exaltation sign. This

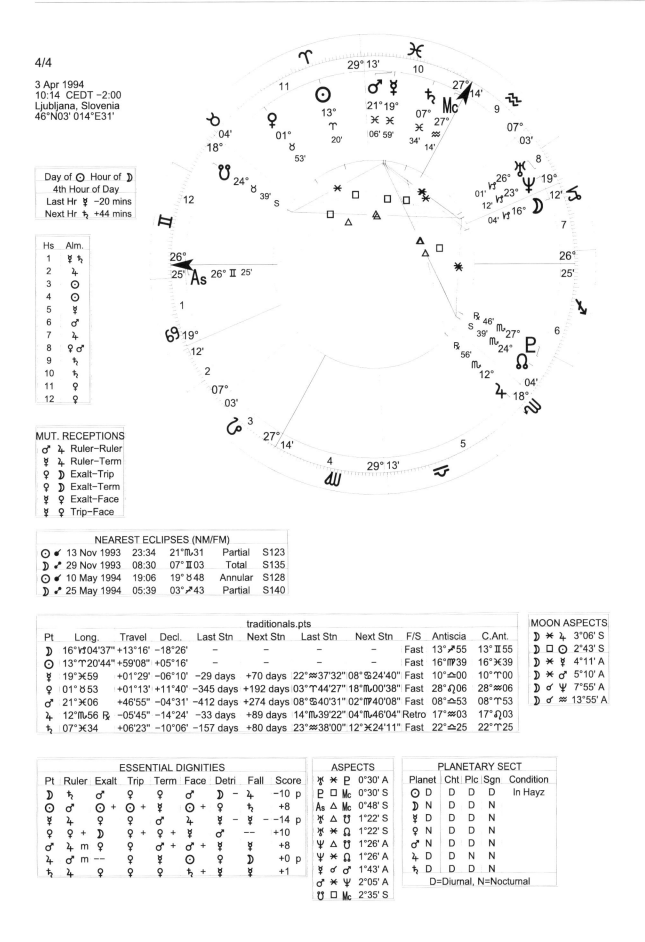

4/4

3 Apr 1994
10:14 CEDT −2:00
Ljubljana, Slovenia
46°N03' 014°E31'

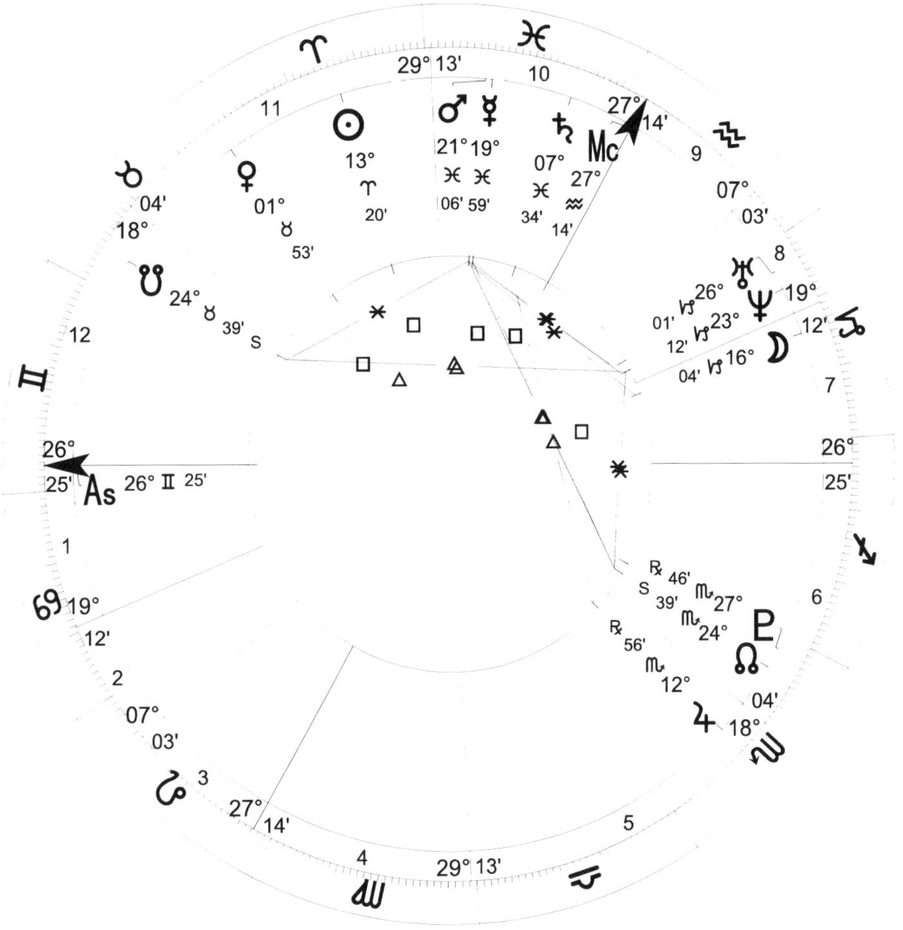

Day of ☉ Hour of ☽
4th Hour of Day
Last Hr ☿ −20 mins
Next Hr ♄ +44 mins

Hs	Alm.
1	☿ ♄
2	♃
3	☉
4	☉
5	☿
6	♂
7	♃
8	♀ ♂
9	♄
10	♄
11	♀
12	♀

MUT. RECEPTIONS
♂ ♃ Ruler–Ruler
☿ ♃ Ruler–Term
♀ ☽ Exalt–Trip
♀ ☽ Exalt–Term
☿ ♀ Exalt–Face
☿ ♀ Trip–Face

NEAREST ECLIPSES (NM/FM)					
☉ ●	13 Nov 1993	23:34	21°♏31	Partial	S123
☽ ☍	29 Nov 1993	08:30	07°♊03	Total	S135
☉ ●	10 May 1994	19:06	19°♉48	Annular	S128
☽ ☍	25 May 1994	05:39	03°♐43	Partial	S140

traditionals.pts

Pt	Long.	Travel	Decl.	Last Stn	Next Stn	Last Stn	Next Stn	F/S	Antiscia	C.Ant.
☽	16°♑04'37"	+13°16'	−18°26'	–	–	–	–	Fast	13°♐55	13°♊55
☉	13°♈20'44"	+59'08"	+05°16'	–	–	–	–	Fast	16°♍39	16°♓39
☿	19°♓59	+01°29'	−06°10'	−29 days	+70 days	22°♒37'32"	08°♋24'40"	Fast	10°♎00	10°♈00
♀	01°♉53	+01°13'	+11°40'	−345 days	+192 days	03°♈44'27"	18°♏00'38"	Fast	28°♌06	28°♒06
♂	21°♓06	+46'55"	−04°31'	−412 days	+274 days	08°♋40'31"	02°♍40'08"	Fast	08°♎53	08°♈53
♃	12°♏56 ℞	−05'45"	−14°24'	−33 days	+89 days	14°♏39'22"	04°♏46'04"	Retro	17°♒03	17°♌03
♄	07°♓34	+06'23"	−10°06'	−157 days	+80 days	23°♒38'00"	12°♓24'11"	Fast	22°♎25	22°♈25

MOON ASPECTS
☽ ⚹ ♃ 3°06' S
☽ □ ☉ 2°43' S
☽ ⚹ ☿ 4°11' A
☽ ⚹ ♂ 5°10' A
☽ ☌ ♆ 7°55' A
☽ ☌ ♒ 13°55' A

ESSENTIAL DIGNITIES

Pt	Ruler	Exalt	Trip	Term	Face	Detri	Fall	Score
☽	♄	♂	♀	♀	♂	☽ −	♃	−10 p
☉	♂	☉ +	☉ +	☿	☉ +	♀	♄	+8
☿	♃	♀	♀	♂	♃	☿ −	☿ −	−14 p
♀	♀ +	☽	♀ +	♀ +	☿	♂	--	+10
♂	♃ m	♀	♀	♂ +	♂ +	☿	☿	+8
♃	♂ m	--	♀	☿	☉	♀	☽	+0 p
♄	♃	♀	♀	♀	♄ +	☿	☿	+1

ASPECTS
♅ ⚹ ♇ 0°30' A
♇ □ Mc 0°30' S
As △ Mc 0°48' S
♅ △ ☋ 1°22' S
♅ ⚹ ☊ 1°22' S
♆ △ ☋ 1°26' A
♆ ⚹ ☊ 1°26' A
☿ ☌ ♂ 1°43' A
♂ ⚹ ♆ 2°05' A
☋ □ Mc 2°35' S

PLANETARY SECT

Planet		Cht	Plc	Sgn	Condition
☉	D	D	D	D	In Hayz
☽	N	D	D	N	
☿	D	D	D	N	
♀	N	D	D	N	
♂	N	D	D	N	
♃	D	D	N	N	
♄	D	D	D	N	

D=Diurnal, N=Nocturnal

planet clearly indicates another person, suggesting that the querent would soon find a better, more satisfactory arrangement. This cannot be doubted because Mars rules H6 of tenants! Besides, Mars is in a strong mutual reception with Jupiter, showing her current contender, and, as we know, mutual reception shows a choice. The future of this question obviously lies in the querent being able to choose between two applicants, but the chart clearly shows that she'd choose Mars, due to Mercury's applying conjunction to it.

But who is this person? Mars is the natural significator of young men, here especially so because of its eastern placement (rising before the Sun). It's in its term and face and in the strong H10, so I said to her: *Forget about this woman. You can let the apartment to her, sure, the choice is yours. I don't think that you'd have any problems with her, but I advise you to raise the rent and try to find someone new. It appears in fact that you'll rent the place to a young man who'll be able to afford it. He looks to be a business type with a good job (the Sun ruling the derived H10 – 10/6 – Author's Note), travelling or communicating a lot (Mars in conjunction with Mercury, the Moon in the derived H3– 3/6 – Author's Note).*

She said that she seriously doubted that because the apartment was, in her opinion, much too big for a single person, but said that she'd try. In a couple of months she called back to tell me that I was right: she had let the apartment to a young, single businessman who did a lot of travelling.

4/5: SHOULD I RENT MY FLAT TO THIS MAN?

28 January 2003 at 5:10 p.m. (17:10), Ljubljana, Slovenia
Hour ruler: Saturn

A friend who was about to rent her apartment called me to ask whether it would be wise to let it to a certain man who replied to her ad. She added that the man was a sportsman who was looking for a temporary accomodation in Ljubljana.

She is shown by the Sun (ascendant ruler) along with Jupiter, which sits right on the top of H1, and by the Moon (co-significator). The potential tenant's significator is Saturn, H7 ruler (the person with whom she's negotiating), but H7 is also strongly influenced by Neptune and the Sun which both conjunct the descendant.

Her interest is clearly shown by her ruler's (the Sun) placement in H7 as well as by the fact that Saturn rules both H6 (tenants) and H7 (the potential tenant).

After a quick glance at the chart I called her back to say that it makes no sense to decide whether to accept him or not, because it is obvious that he would not take the flat. *I think he'll soon change his mind,* I said.

Surprised, she said that this is hardly possible because he was very interested. She called me to help her decide. She wanted me to check if, as a tenant, he'd make any problems for her. She surely didn't expect me to say he'd back off!

But the chart clearly showed that the agreement would simply not take place. Firstly, Saturn is retrograde, suggesting his withdrawal. Secondly, Venus (H4 ruler and therefore the significator of her flat) exactly opposes it (applying), which doesn't lead to an agreement, but, on the contrary, to a separation. All of this is confirmed by the Moon which is very close to Venus and will therefore soon oppose Saturn too. On top of all these negative indications, there's Neptune (illusion, disappointment), acting as a co-significator of the potential tenant, showing that he might have some misconceptions regarding the lease or that he (probably unintentionally) misleads the querent. See that Neptune is combust, so the problem obviously has to do with some "blindness" or lack of information on the part of the quesited. He might be unaware of some crucial fact related to the potential deal.

The querent asked me, of course, why would he change his mind? Well, let's see! The rent is shown by Mars, the H10 ruler, and by Venus as the ruler of the intercepted sign of Taurus. (Note: as we know, a single planet in a horary chart can represent two or more things or people, involved in the situation!) Both planets are in H5 which is in opposition to H11, the place of Saturn – with Venus tightly opposing it. Therefore I said that he'd probably realize that he can't afford the rent. In reply, she said that this can't be true since a considerable part of the rent would be paid by his club; he'd only have to add a small amount.

Only a day passed before she called back, saying that the real estate agent confirmed the lease; the sportsman asked for the contract, so what do I suggest, when could they meet to sign it? I was, of course, quite unpleasantly surprised, but stayed firm in my opinion. She, however, called again in a couple of days, saying that the man suddenly changed his mind!

4/5

28 Jan 2003
17:10 CET −1:00
Ljubljana, Slovenia
46°N03' 014°E31'

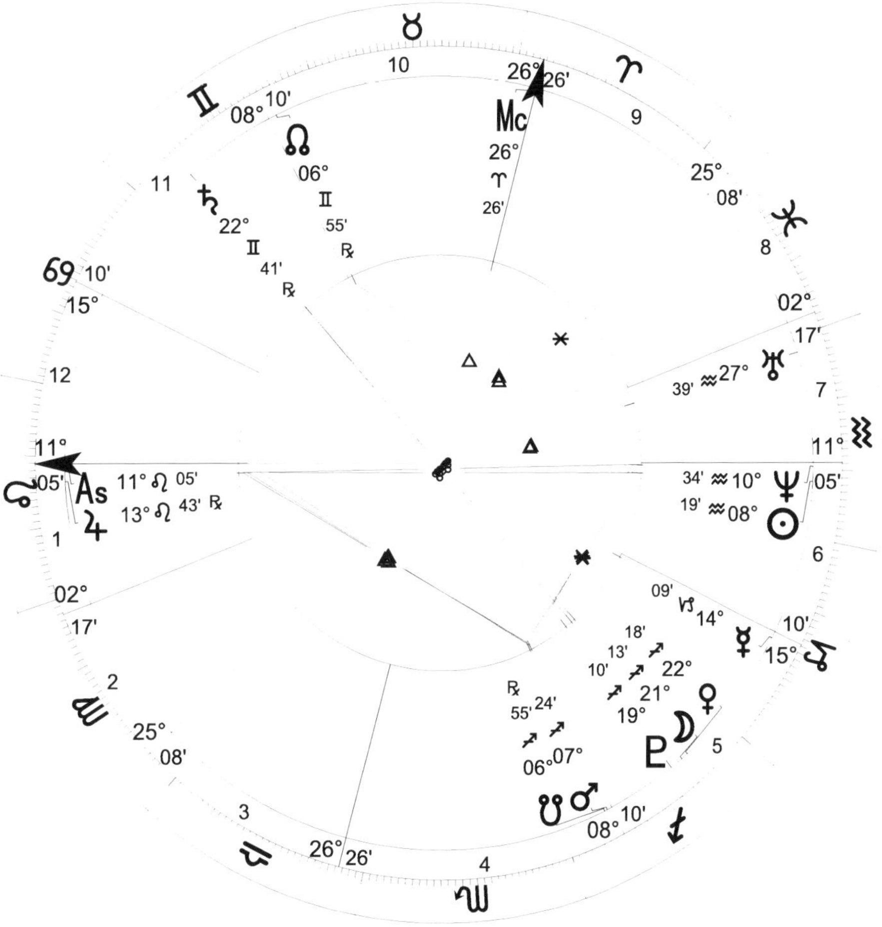

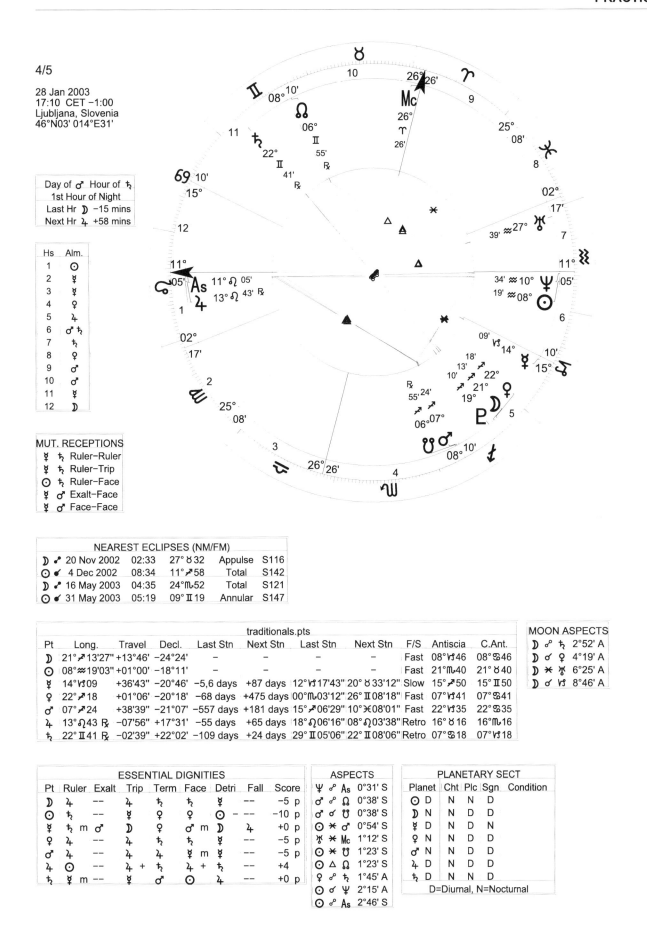

Day of ♂ Hour of ♄
1st Hour of Night
Last Hr ☽ −15 mins
Next Hr ♃ +58 mins

Hs	Alm.
1	☉
2	☿
3	☿
4	♀
5	♃
6	♂ ♄
7	♄
8	♀
9	♂
10	♂
11	☿
12	☽

MUT. RECEPTIONS
☿ ♄ Ruler-Ruler
☿ ♄ Ruler-Trip
☉ ♄ Ruler-Face
☿ ♂ Exalt-Face
☿ ♂ Face-Face

NEAREST ECLIPSES (NM/FM)					
☽	20 Nov 2002	02:33	27° ♉ 32	Appulse	S116
☉	4 Dec 2002	08:34	11° ♐ 58	Total	S142
☽	16 May 2003	04:35	24° ♏ 52	Total	S121
☉	31 May 2003	05:19	09° ♊ 19	Annular	S147

traditionals.pts

Pt	Long.	Travel	Decl.	Last Stn	Next Stn	Last Stn	Next Stn	F/S	Antiscia	C.Ant.
☽	21°♐13'27"	+13°46'	−24°24'	–	–	–	–	Fast	08°♑46	08°♋46
☉	08°♒19'03"	+01°00'	−18°11'	–	–	–	–	Fast	21°♏40	21°♉40
☿	14°♑09	+36'43"	−20°46'	−5,6 days	+87 days	12°♑17'43"	20°♉33'12"	Slow	15°♐50	15°♊50
♀	22°♐18	+01°06'	−20°18'	−68 days	+475 days	00°♏03'12"	26°♊08'18"	Fast	07°♑41	07°♋41
♂	07°♐24	+38'39"	−21°07'	−557 days	+181 days	15°♐06'29"	10°♓08'01"	Fast	22°♑35	22°♋35
♃	13°♌43 ℞	−07'56"	+17°31'	−55 days	+65 days	18°♌06'16"	08°♌03'38"	Retro	16°♉16	16°♏16
♄	22°♊41 ℞	−02'39"	+22°02'	−109 days	+24 days	29°♊05'06"	22°♊08'06"	Retro	07°♋18	07°♑18

MOON ASPECTS
☽ ☍ ♄ 2°52' A
☽ ☌ ♀ 4°19' A
☽ ⚹ ♅ 6°25' A
☽ ☌ ♑ 8°46' A

ESSENTIAL DIGNITIES

Pt	Ruler	Exalt	Trip	Term	Face	Detri	Fall	Score
☽	♃	--	♃	♄	♄	☿	--	−5 p
☉	♄	--	☿	♀	♀	☉ −	--	−10 p
☿	♄ m	♂	☽	♀	♂ m	☽	♃	+0 p
♀	♃	--	♃	♄	♄	☿	--	−5 p
♂	♃	--	♃	♃	☿ m	☿	--	−5 p
♃	☉	--	♃ +	♄	♃ +	♄	--	+4
♄	☿ m	--	☿	♂	☉	♃	--	+0 p

ASPECTS
♆ ☍ As 0°31' S
♂ ☍ ☊ 0°38' S
♂ ☌ ☋ 0°38' S
☉ ⚹ ♂ 0°54' S
♅ ⚹ Mc 1°12' S
☉ ⚹ ☋ 1°23' S
☉ △ ☊ 1°23' S
♀ ☍ ♄ 1°45' A
☉ ☌ ♆ 2°15' A
☉ ☍ As 2°46' S

PLANETARY SECT

Planet		Cht	Plc	Sgn	Condition
☉	D	N	N	D	
☽	N	N	D	N	
☿	D	N	D	N	
♀	N	N	D	D	
♂	N	N	D	D	
♃	D	N	D	D	
♄	D	N	N	D	

D=Diurnal, N=Nocturnal

I find it interesting that Saturn is in H11, standing for clubs and organizations, which might indicate that the contract would have to be signed by the club and not by the tenant himself! This is confirmed by the fact that H11 ruler Mercury occupies H6, while Mercury and Saturn are in a mutual reception, indicating a choice. I thought that the club probably found him another, cheaper apartment - especially because the Moon, the H12 ruler (the derived H2 of H11 – the club's financial assets) in opposition to Saturn suggested that the main problem was probably the amount of money asked for the rent.

4/6: WILL WE SELL THE HOUSE? WHEN?

9 May 2006 at 6:37 a.m., Ljubljana, Slovenia
Hour ruler: Mars

Like one of the previous real estate questions, this was contributed by one of my students who was interested in whether and when her family would sell the house with an attached large piece of land. The house had become too big for them, and the maintenance too costly. They had put it on the market only a short time before, but she hoped to sell it as soon as possible, so as to be freed of the burden that the house represented. I decided to discuss the chart in the class, making it a teaching example.

Ascendant is in Gemini and its ruler Mercury (significator of the querent) in Taurus in H12, while the property is shown by the Sun, H4 ruler, and by Saturn which conjuncts IC. The potential buyer is shown by Jupiter, H7 ruler, the price by Saturn, H10 ruler, and by Neptune which occupies H10. Since they employed a real estate agent, we must find his significator too – this is Venus, H6 ruler (in Aries) and partly Jupiter (H6 planet).

What immediately struck me was the "rigidity" of the main significators. The north angle (IC), Saturn and the Sun (the house) as well as Jupiter, H7 ruler – all were in fixed signs. Besides, Jupiter was retrograde. All these indications suggested that it would probably take a very long time before the house could be sold. This is confirmed by the weak state of the Sun and Mercury in the cadent H12, as well as that of Jupiter in the cadent H6. The chart gave a strong impression of the house going nowhere. What's more - the Moon (co-significator of the querent) was applying by sextile to Saturn (the house) indicating that the house stays with them. All the more so because the Moon, before the completion of the sextile with Saturn, makes a conjunction with its south node, suggesting a kind of barrier or bad luck.

In addition to all the said negative indications, there is the detrimented Venus (in Aries), ruling the real estate agents, suggesting that they were ineffective. There would be trouble with them, suggested by the Moon's application to it by an opposition. What's more, Venus was in no way related to the main significators.

At first glance (or at the first couple of glances) the chart therefore offered a negative answer, which should read as follows: No, the house would not be sold. But think what such an answer really means… Never, or what?! What could I say to the querent? What advice could I give?

Well, the truth is that in such cases, all one can say is that the chart doesn't show any "completion of the matter", meaning that the house obviously would probably not be sold in the foreseeable future.

This case is just a little bit different because there exists a weak kind of "completion", but really too weak to promise a positive answer. Namely, Mercury (the querent) separates from the square of Saturn (property) and applies to an opposition of Jupiter (the buyer). Technically, this is a case of translation of light, but without reception or essential strength of any of the significators, which together with other unpleasant indications suggests that the house might get sold "eventually", but only with great difficulty and at a significantly lowered price. The price seemed to be overblown anyway (Neptune in H10). In any event, it is a very weak and most probably an invalid completion.

(Note: when the light is being translated by any planet but the Moon or the Sun, we must check the ephemeris to make sure that this planet does not turn retrograde before getting its job done. In other words, see if the translation really gets accomplished! This was the case here but, as already said, it seemed to be "invalid" due to other reasons.)

Although I was eager to give my student an optimistic answer, I could not. The only advice I could give was to change the real estate agent. He was a "hideous, sweet-mouthed good-for-nothing", she complained, saying that he didn't show any interest in the sale, so she decided she'd find another. (This was such an adequate description of a detrimented Venus that my class and I all laughed!)

Still, the chart was very unpromising. Some day you might sell it, I said, but, obviously, in a distant and unforeseeable future.

The outcome? By December 2008 (two and a half years later) when I last heard from the querent, the house was still not sold. In the meantime, the querent's husband died, after a long and serious illness. (See Jupiter H7 ruler in H6 of disease! It doesn't fall within the context of the question, true, but it is nevertheless interesting.) They lowered the price a few times and changed a couple of real estate agencies, but finally realized that they could only sell it for very little money, so they took it off the market. She added that they had now decided to live in it for a couple more years.

4/6

9 May 2006
06:37 CEDT −2:00
Ljubljana, Slovenia
46°N03' 014°E31'

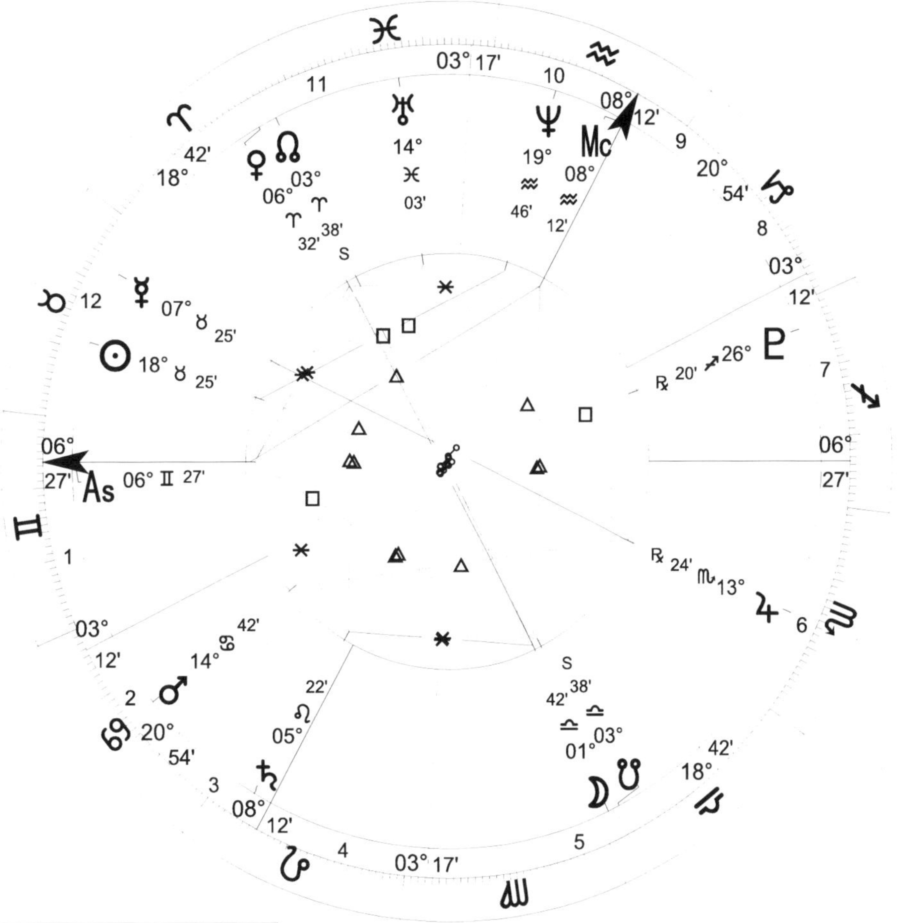

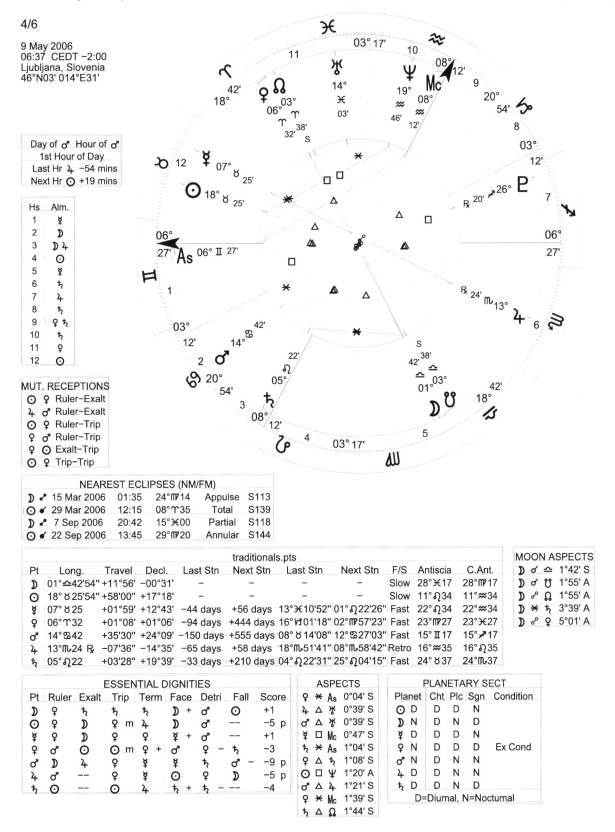

Day of ♂ Hour of ♂
1st Hour of Day
Last Hr ♃ −54 mins
Next Hr ☉ +19 mins

Hs	Alm.
1	☿
2	☽
3	☽ ♃
4	☉
5	☿
6	♄
7	♃
8	♄
9	♀ ♄
10	♄
11	♀
12	☉

MUT. RECEPTIONS
☉ ♀ Ruler–Exalt
♃ ♂ Ruler–Exalt
☉ ♀ Ruler–Trip
♀ ♂ Ruler–Trip
♀ ☉ Exalt–Trip
☉ ♀ Trip–Trip

NEAREST ECLIPSES (NM/FM)				
☽ ☍ 15 Mar 2006	01:35	24°♍14	Appulse	S113
☉ ☌ 29 Mar 2006	12:15	08°♈35	Total	S139
☽ ☍ 7 Sep 2006	20:42	15°♓00	Partial	S118
☉ ☌ 22 Sep 2006	13:45	29°♍20	Annular	S144

traditionals.pts

Pt	Long.	Travel	Decl.	Last Stn	Next Stn	Last Stn	Next Stn	F/S	Antiscia	C.Ant.
☽	01°♎42'54"	+11°56'	−00°31'	–	–	–	–	Slow	28°♓17	28°♍17
☉	18°♉25'54"	+58'00"	+17°18'	–	–	–	–	Slow	11°♌34	11°♒34
☿	07°♉25	+01°59'	+12°43'	−44 days	+56 days	13°♓10'52"	01°♌22'26"	Fast	22°♌34	22°♒34
♀	06°♈32	+01°08'	+01°06'	−94 days	+444 days	16°♑01'18"	02°♍57'23"	Fast	23°♍27	23°♓27
♂	14°♋42	+35'30"	+24°09'	−150 days	+555 days	08°♉14'08"	12°♋27'03"	Fast	15°♊17	15°♐17
♃	13°♏24 ℞	−07'36"	−14°35'	−65 days	+58 days	18°♏51'41"	08°♏58'42"	Retro	16°♒35	16°♌35
♄	05°♌22	+03'28"	+19°39'	−33 days	+210 days	04°♌22'31"	25°♌04'15"	Fast	24°♉37	24°♏37

MOON ASPECTS
☽ ☌ ♎ 1°42' S
☽ ☌ ☋ 1°55' A
☽ ☍ ☊ 1°55' A
☽ ✶ ♄ 3°39' A
☽ ☍ ♀ 5°01' A

ESSENTIAL DIGNITIES

Pt	Ruler	Exalt	Trip	Term	Face	Detri	Fall	Score
☽	♀	♄	♄	♄	☽ +	♂	☉	+1
☉	♀	☽	♀ m	♃	☽	♂	--	−5 p
☿	♀	☽	♀	♀	☿ +	♂	--	+1
♀	♂	☉	☉ m	♀ +	♂	♀ −	♄	−3
♂	☽	♃	♀	☿	☿	♄	♂ −	−9 p
♃	♂	--	♀	☿	☉	♀	☽	−5 p
♄	☉	--	☉	♃	♄ +	♄ −	--	−4

ASPECTS
♀ ✶ As 0°04' S
♃ △ ♅ 0°39' S
♂ △ ♅ 0°39' S
☿ □ Mc 0°47' S
♄ ✶ As 1°04' S
♀ △ ♄ 1°08' S
☉ □ ♆ 1°20' A
♂ △ ♃ 1°21' S
♀ ✶ Mc 1°39' S
♄ △ ☊ 1°44' S

PLANETARY SECT

Planet		Cht	Plc	Sgn	Condition
☉	D	D	D	N	
☽	N	D	N	D	
☿	D	D	D	N	
♀	N	D	D	D	Ex Cond
♂	N	D	N	N	
♃	D	D	N	N	
♄	D	D	N	D	

D=Diurnal, N=Nocturnal

4/7: SHOULD I SELL THE APARTMENT TO THIS BUYER?

10 November 2006 at 11:53 a.m., Ljubljana, Slovenia
Hour ruler: the Sun

This question was asked over the phone by a client who was selling her apartment and was currently negotiating the sale with a potential buyer. The agreement had practically been reached but since she valued my advice, she wanted me to confirm that she had made the right decision.

She's represented by Saturn which is placed in H7 (the buyer, showing her interest). Her co-significator, the Moon, is located in the same house, but due to its placement in the house of the buyers it partly rules them, besides showing the flow of events. The buyer is also partly shown by Saturn, the H7 planet. Complicated? Well, it depends. We know that a single planet can rule several people or things in a chart. And as we will shortly see, that doesn't need to cause concern.

For a positive answer we should see some connection between the Moon and Saturn, or between any of these bodies and Venus (H4 ruler and therefore the significator of the flat), but there is none. Let's see: The Moon separates from a trine with Venus, suggesting there's no coming together but rather drifting apart, while Venus applies to a square with Saturn, indicating an obstruction and an inability to bring negotiations to an end, as both planets are in detriment. There's also no mutual reception or translation of light between them, so the answer is a simple NO. The chart actually shows that the deal would simply not come to pass.

Why, she asked? *Well, it just seems so,* I said.

But the strong cardinality of the chart and the applying trine of the Moon to Jupiter in H10 encouraged me to say: *Don't worry, you'll soon find a better buyer! Raise the price and wait five days, because someone will show up by then who'll be willing to pay more.*

In disbelief, she replied that this was almost impossible because her apartment was already overpriced, at least in her opinion, and she thought how lucky she was to have found someone who'd buy it. Overpriced it is, I said, since Venus (the flat) was in detriment and therefore weak (although in its triplicity but this is a lesser dignity), suggesting that the flat was not in the best condition. But Venus' accidental dignity is very strong: she occupies the cardinal H10, is fast and conjuncts the great benefic Jupiter, showing that the price of the apartment is higher than its intrinsic value. But this is also the reason why I advised her to take advantage of the opportunity while it lasts! Especially because H10 (the price) also contains the "mighty" Jupiter, supported by the applying trine of the Moon. I therefore encouraged her to increase the purchase price.

My attention was next drawn to the intercepted signs in 1/7. Intercepted signs usually indicate "hidden" people and situations that are not yet known. The H7 intercepted sign is Leo which might indicate a new, yet unknown buyer. Leo is ruled by the Sun, and the Moon translates light from the Sun through Venus to Jupiter. This obviously supports indications for a new opportunity.

As for the timing, I calculated the number of degrees that separated the Moon from a trine to Jupiter: five. The Moon in an angular house and a cardinal sign spoke for the smallest time unit (hours), but this somehow didn't seem logical, therefore I decided for days.

She was not too happy with my reply; it embarrassed her and filled her with uncertainty. What does she do now, call off the deal which seemed more than she could hope for? That would be insane, she thought.

But a couple of days later she called me and said: *Listen, I can't believe it! You told me it would be five days, but only five hours passed from our conversation when another buyer called and offered as much as half a million SIT (about 7000 euros) more than the previous one! She has already put down the deposit and she'd pay the remainder in five weeks.*

They were hours, after all!

I'd like to add that if timing would always strictly conform to the rules, like here, I certainly wouldn't have made a mistake in the choice of the time unit, but time units usually depend not only on the nature of the houses and signs of the Moon and the significators, but also on the logic of the question, on the specific conditions of the case at hand and, ultimately, on several possible additional indications which tip the timing in this or that direction. In this case, the hours were the right choice also because the cardinal Moon was conjunct the descendant. The closer the angle, the faster the realization!

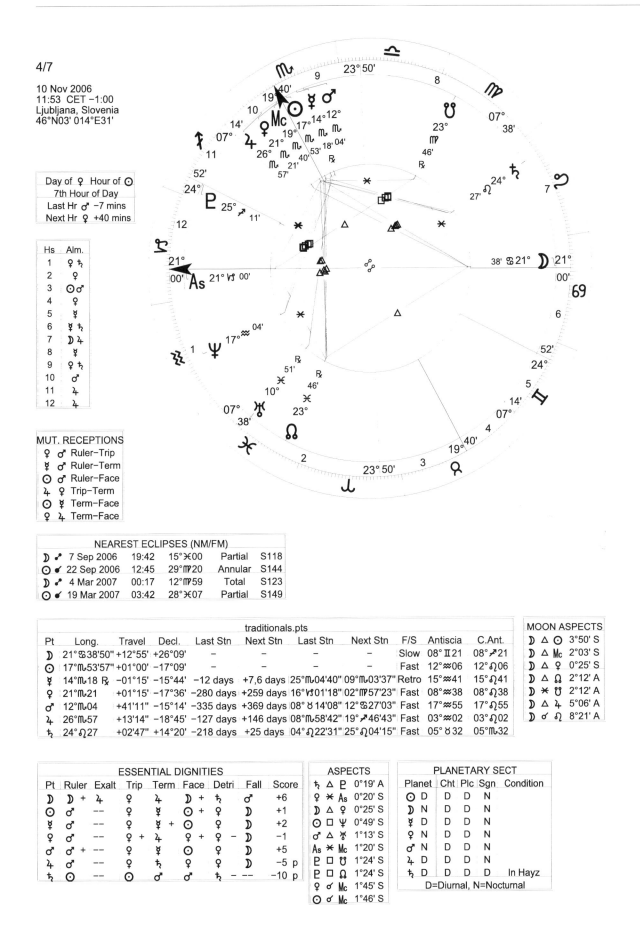

4/7

10 Nov 2006
11:53 CET −1:00
Ljubljana, Slovenia
46°N03' 014°E31'

Day of ♀ Hour of ☉
7th Hour of Day
Last Hr ♂ −7 mins
Next Hr ♀ +40 mins

Hs	Alm.
1	♀ ♄
2	♀
3	☉♂
4	♀
5	☿
6	☿ ♄
7	☽ ♃
8	☿
9	♀ ♄
10	♂
11	♃
12	♃

MUT. RECEPTIONS
♀ ♂ Ruler–Trip
☿ ♂ Ruler–Term
☉ ♂ Ruler–Face
♃ ♀ Trip–Term
☉ ☿ Term–Face
♀ ♃ Term–Face

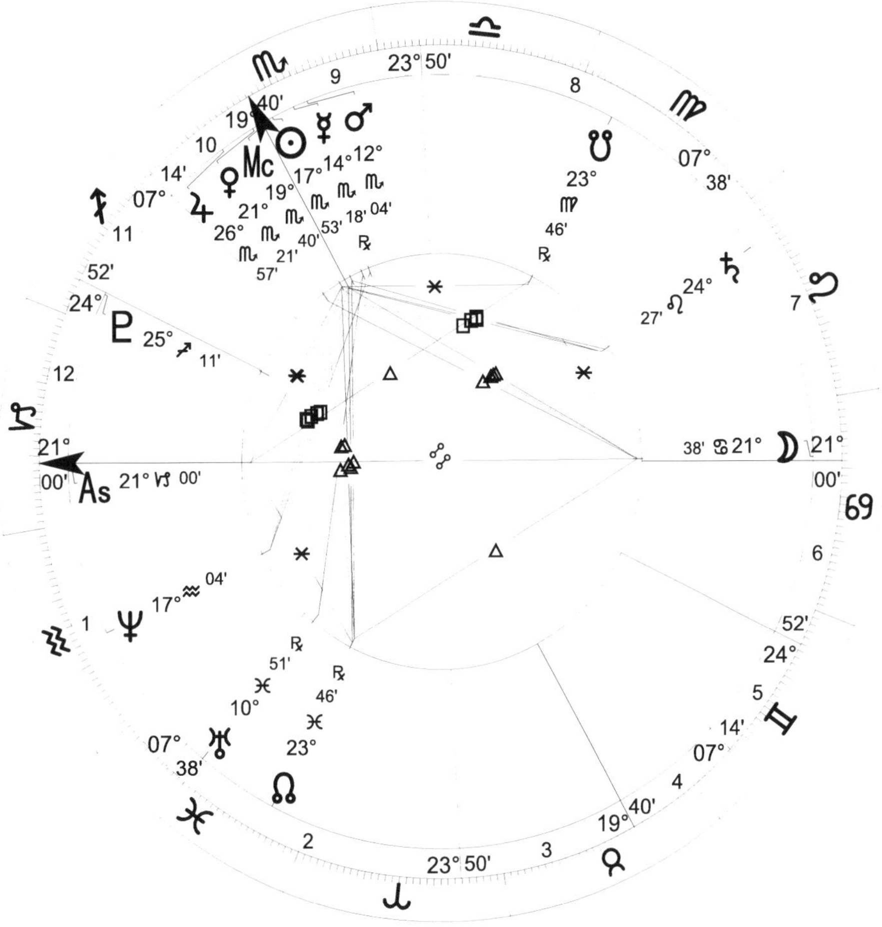

NEAREST ECLIPSES (NM/FM)					
☽ ☍	7 Sep 2006	19:42	15°♓00	Partial	S118
☉ ☌	22 Sep 2006	12:45	29°♍20	Annular	S144
☽ ☍	4 Mar 2007	00:17	12°♍59	Total	S123
☉ ☌	19 Mar 2007	03:42	28°♓07	Partial	S149

traditionals.pts

Pt	Long.	Travel	Decl.	Last Stn	Next Stn	Last Stn	Next Stn	F/S	Antiscia	C.Ant.
☽	21°♋38'50"	+12°55'	+26°09'	–	–	–	–	Slow	08°♊21	08°♐21
☉	17°♏53'57"	+01°00'	−17°09'	–	–	–	–	Fast	12°♒06	12°♌06
☿	14°♏18 ℞	−01°15'	−15°44'	−12 days	+7,6 days	25°♏04'40"	09°♏03'37"	Retro	15°♒41	15°♌41
♀	21°♏21	+01°15'	−17°36'	−280 days	+259 days	16°♑01'18"	02°♍57'23"	Fast	08°♒38	08°♌38
♂	12°♏04	+41'11"	−15°14'	−335 days	+369 days	08°♉14'08"	12°♋27'03"	Fast	17°♒55	17°♌55
♃	26°♏57	+13'14"	−18°45'	−127 days	+146 days	08°♏58'42"	19°♐46'43"	Fast	03°♒02	03°♌02
♄	24°♌27	+02'47"	+14°20'	−218 days	+25 days	04°♌22'31"	25°♌04'15"	Fast	05°♉32	05°♏32

MOON ASPECTS
☽ △ ☉ 3°50' S
☽ △ Mc 2°03' S
☽ △ ♀ 0°25' S
☽ △ ☊ 2°12' A
☽ ✶ ☋ 2°12' A
☽ △ ♃ 5°06' A
☽ ☌ ♌ 8°21' A

ESSENTIAL DIGNITIES

Pt	Ruler	Exalt	Trip	Term	Face	Detri	Fall	Score
☽	☽ +	♃	♀	♃	☽ +	♄	♂	+6
☉	♂	--	♀	☿	☉ +	♀	☽	+1
☿	♂	--	♀	☿ +	☉	♀	☽	+2
♀	♂	--	♀ +	♃	♀ +	♀ −	☽	−1
♂	♂ +	--	♀	☿	☉	♀	☽	+5
♃	♂	--	♀	♄	♀	♀	☽	−5 p
♄	☉	--	☉	♂	♂	♄ −	--	−10 p

ASPECTS
♄ △ ♇ 0°19' A
♀ ✶ As 0°20' S
☽ △ ♀ 0°25' S
☉ □ ♆ 0°49' S
♂ △ ♅ 1°13' S
As ✶ Mc 1°20' S
♇ □ ☋ 1°24' S
♇ □ ☊ 1°24' S
♀ ☌ Mc 1°45' S
☉ ☌ Mc 1°46' S

PLANETARY SECT

Planet		Cht	Plc	Sgn	Condition
☉	D	D	D	N	
☽	N	D	D	N	
☿	D	D	D	N	
♀	N	D	D	N	
♂	N	D	D	N	
♃	D	D	D	N	
♄	D	D	D	D	In Hayz

D=Diurnal, N=Nocturnal

4/8: SHOULD WE BUY THIS HOUSE?

13 April 2001 at 12:41 p.m. (12:41), Velenje, Slovenia
Hour ruler: Mars

The question was asked over the phone at the time when I worked at a commercial phone line. I had decided to try my hand at it just out of the desire to practise horary astrology. This is one of the few horary cases from that period that got feedback from the querent. The scarcity of feedback is understandable, of course. People usually don't want to spend even more money just to tell their astrologers whether their predictions came true!

The querent said that he and his wife were buying a certain house, and he wanted to know whether that was advisable or not. They both liked it, but was the house really suitable and would they be happy with it, he wondered?

He's shown by the Sun which is strong in H10 in Aries (exaltation). In the context of the question, this house shows the price of the property. The house itself is shown by Venus, H4 ruler, which is also in Aries, but it's essentially weak here (detriment) and retrograde, which makes its placement all the more precarious. It doesn't aspect the Sun, but the Moon (at 29 Sagittarius) is already in orb of a square with Venus. Let us recall: a square can indicate a "completion of the matter" if the planets are essentially strong, placed in the fortunate and/or angular houses, in mutual reception, or if they are connected by a third planet by means of translation of light. This, unfortunately, was not the case here! The Moon is in the unfortunate H6; both Venus and the Moon are in cadent houses; Venus is in detriment and the Moon will also be in detriment after it completes the square with Venus. The Moon as co-significator of the querent therefore clearly shows that the querent is somehow "approaching" the house, but he's obviously not coming to the possession of it. In other words, he and his wife are not going to buy it. The Moon at the end of a sign also shows that soon there will be a change of circumstances which would in the final run invalidate the question. In any event, I concluded that the querent really didn't need to decide about the purchase. It was obvious, from the chart, that the matter had no future!

But to be really sure I had to check the querent's relationship with the seller, shown by Saturn, the H7 ruler. Is there a connection of some kind? The Sun and Saturn are not in aspect, the Moon and Saturn likewise, but Venus moves back to sextile Saturn which vividly shows that the house is literally moving back to the owner!

Nothing comes of it, I said. *The house is apparently in worse shape than you think (weak Venus), but this really isn't the deciding factor. It simply seems that the house will soon move away from you, if I may say so, and the purchase will not happen.*

He was very surprised and only then told me that they had actually already decided to buy it and were about to sign the contract and pay the deposit already on that very day, but because it was Friday the thirteenth (Black Friday) and both were a little superstitious, as he put in, they asked the seller to postpone the signing of the contract till Monday. (In between, of course, they wanted to hear what the gypsy says.)

But on Monday, as he later told me, the problems began. The seller started to pull back, saying that he had not yet arranged the purchase of a new house at another location, but would nevertheless be willing to sell this one - for a higher price! (I can see your eyes jumping to the "fraudulent" Neptune in H7!) We can also see that the strong Sun in H10, indicating a price which was already high enough, applies by trine to Mars, its dispositor, which nicely reflects the further increase of the price.

The querent then, as he put it, got hot under the collar. The real estate agent tried to persuade the seller to stick with the original agreement, but to no avail, therefore the querent decided to drop the deal. He didn't have that kind of money and even if he did, he wasn't willing to go beyond the initial arrangement.

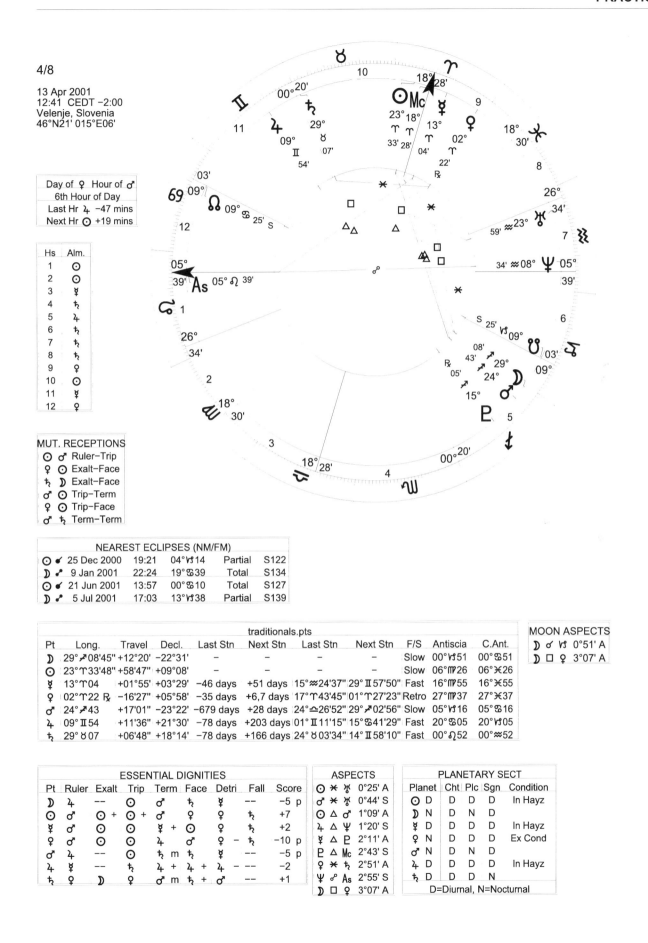

4/8

13 Apr 2001
12:41 CEDT −2:00
Velenje, Slovenia
46°N21' 015°E06'

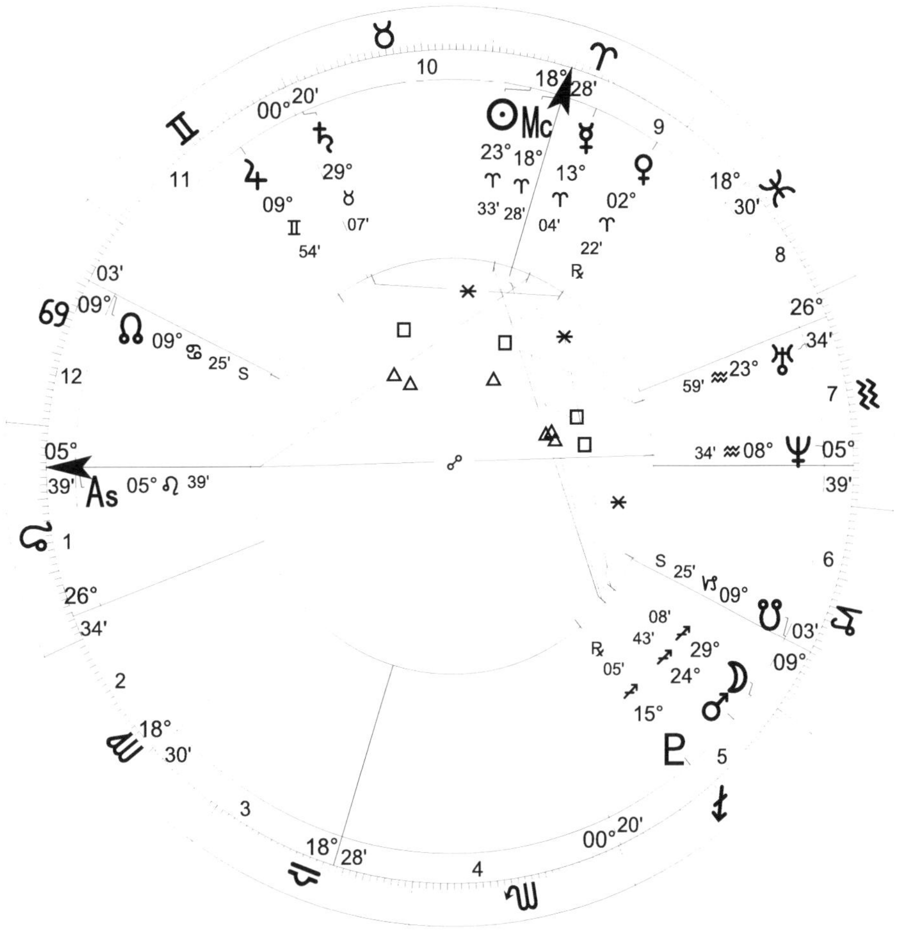

Day of ♀ Hour of ♂
6th Hour of Day
Last Hr ♃ −47 mins
Next Hr ☉ +19 mins

Hs	Alm.
1	☉
2	☉
3	☿
4	♄
5	♃
6	♄
7	♄
8	♄
9	♀
10	☉
11	☿
12	♀

MUT. RECEPTIONS		
☉	♂	Ruler–Trip
♀	☉	Exalt–Face
♄	☽	Exalt–Face
♂	☉	Trip–Term
♀	☉	Trip–Face
♂	♄	Term–Term

NEAREST ECLIPSES (NM/FM)					
☉ ●	25 Dec 2000	19:21	04°♑14	Partial	S122
☽ ☍	9 Jan 2001	22:24	19°♋39	Total	S134
☉ ●	21 Jun 2001	13:57	00°♋10	Total	S127
☽ ☍	5 Jul 2001	17:03	13°♑38	Partial	S139

traditionals.pts

Pt	Long.	Travel	Decl.	Last Stn	Next Stn	Last Stn	Next Stn	F/S	Antiscia	C.Ant.
☽	29°♐08'45"	+12°20'	−22°31'	–	–	–	–	Slow	00°♑51	00°♋51
☉	23°♈33'48"	+58'47"	+09°08'	–	–	–	–	Slow	06°♍26	06°♓26
☿	13°♈04	+01°55'	+03°29'	−46 days	+51 days	15°♒24'37"	29°♊57'50"	Fast	16°♍55	16°♓55
♀	02°♈22 ℞	−16'27"	+05°58'	−35 days	+6,7 days	17°♈43'45"	01°♈27'23"	Retro	27°♍37	27°♓37
♂	24°♐43	+17'01"	−23°22'	−679 days	+28 days	24°♎26'52"	29°♐02'56"	Slow	05°♑16	05°♋16
♃	09°♊54	+11'36"	+21°30'	−78 days	+203 days	01°♊11'15"	15°♋41'29"	Fast	20°♋05	20°♑05
♄	29°♉07	+06'48"	+18°14'	−78 days	+166 days	24°♉03'34"	14°♊58'10"	Fast	00°♌52	00°♒52

MOON ASPECTS			
☽	☌	♑	0°51' A
☽	□	♀	3°07' A

ESSENTIAL DIGNITIES

Pt	Ruler	Exalt	Trip	Term	Face	Detri	Fall	Score
☽	♃	--	☉	♂	♄	☿	--	−5 p
☉	♂	☉ +	☉ +	♂	♀	♀	♄	+7
☿	♂	☉	☉	☿ +	☉	♀	♄	+2
♀	♂	☉	☉	♃	♂	♀ −	♄	−10 p
♂	♃	--	☉	♄ m	♄	☿	--	−5 p
♃	☿	--	♄	♃ +	♃ +	♃ −	--	−2
♄	♀	☽	♀	♂ m	♄ +	♂	--	+1

ASPECTS			
☉	⚹	♅	0°25' A
♂	⚹	♅	0°44' S
☉	△	♂	1°09' A
♃	△	♆	1°20' S
☿	△	♇	2°11' A
♇	△	Mc	2°43' S
♀	⚹	♄	2°51' A
♆	☍	As	2°55' S
☽	□	♀	3°07' A

PLANETARY SECT

Planet		Cht	Plc	Sgn	Condition
☉	D	D	D	D	In Hayz
☽	N	D	N	D	
☿	D	D	D	D	In Hayz
♀	N	D	D	D	Ex Cond
♂	N	D	N	D	
♃	D	D	D	D	In Hayz
♄	D	D	D	N	

D=Diurnal, N=Nocturnal

4/9: WHEN WILL WE MOVE?

1 November, 1997 at 9:01 p.m. (21:01), Ljubljana, Slovenia
Hour ruler: Jupiter

I asked this question at the time when our new house was already built and there were only some internal works to be finished before we could move in. I was very keen for this to happen as soon as possible!

Hour ruler is harmonious therefore the chart is "radical" or "fit to be judged". Ascendant is in Cancer, the sign of the real estate, home and family. The Moon (my significator) is at 25°35' Scorpio. Moon has its fall in Scorpio, and since significators in signs which oppose their dignities often show people being away from where they belong (or feel safe etc.), this indicates that my family and I lived on premises which were not our own. We lived in my parents' house, and in spite of our good understanding I felt cramped there and I longed for independence which is shown by the following Moon sign, Sagittarius.

The question is explicit in that I was only interested in the time which would elapse until the event (the move). We know that the most dependable time indicator is the Moon, which is at the end of a sign, and we know that sign cusps are dividing lines, which in horary charts often indicate borders, transitions, changes, transfers, moves. We want to see how many degrees separate the Moon from the next sign (Sagittarius). Four and a half, which translated into time units could be 4.5 months – months being, under the circumstances, the most likely time unit, which is confirmed by the fact that a planet in a fixed sign and a succedent house (which is the case here) usually indicates a moderately long time unit. The number of time units is confirmed by the distance of IC (house) in Virgo to the next sign (Libra). Incidentally, this distance is the same (4.5 degrees)!

Four and a half months from the time of the question brings us to the middle of March 1998 - and this is exactly when I moved my office to the new house, where I have been working ever since. The family moved into the house in August 1998, which is 9 months after the question. Mercury, the H4 ruler, wants exactly 9 degrees to the next sign, Sagittarius! But even this time unit is confirmed by the Moon: as you can see, its distance to Pluto, the planet of "termination", also measures to almost exactly 9 degrees. I find it interesting that my natal ascendant is in early Sagittarius, therefore the indications of the horary chart match my own chart – a pretty common "coincidence" in our art.

But there is yet another time indication. Moves and relocations belong to H7, therefore we can also check Saturn, the H7 ruler, for the timing purposes. From the Moon to its trine with Saturn are a little less than 20 degrees. If we take these to be weeks and divide them by 4, we get 5 months. It is interesting to note that Saturn is placed in H10 of career, because after 5 months (actually 4.5, but that's quite close) my first move to the new house was related to my work (office).

4/9

1 Nov 1997
21:01 CET −1:00
Ljubljana, Slovenia
46°N03' 014°E31'

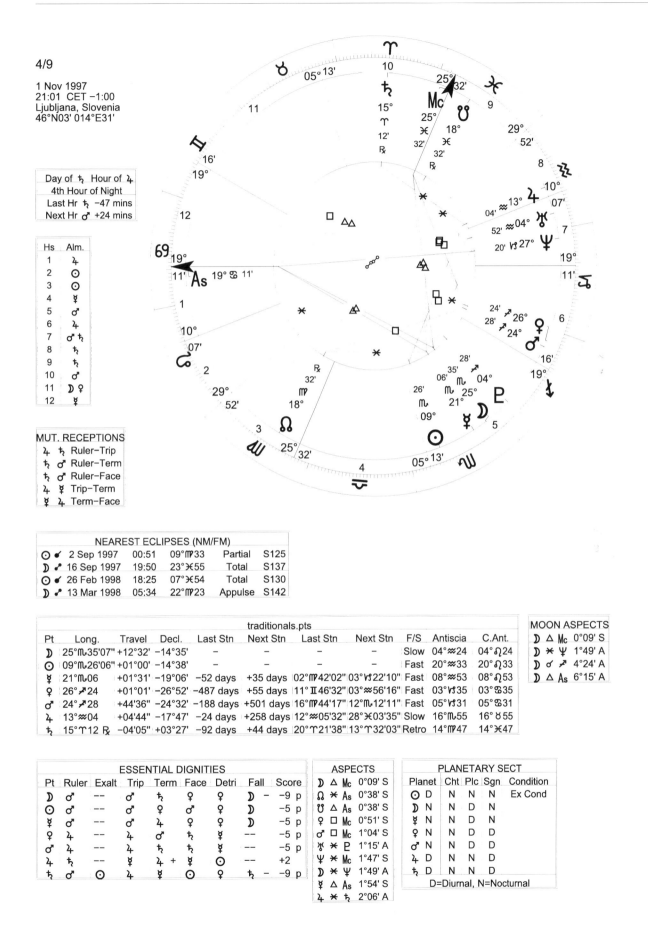

Day of ♄ Hour of ♃
4th Hour of Night
Last Hr ♄ −47 mins
Next Hr ♂ +24 mins

Hs	Alm.
1	♃
2	☉
3	☉
4	☿
5	♂
6	♃
7	♂ ♄
8	♄
9	♄
10	♂
11	☽ ♀
12	☿

MUT. RECEPTIONS
♃ ♄ Ruler−Trip
♄ ♂ Ruler−Term
♄ ♂ Ruler−Face
♃ ☿ Trip−Term
☿ ♃ Term−Face

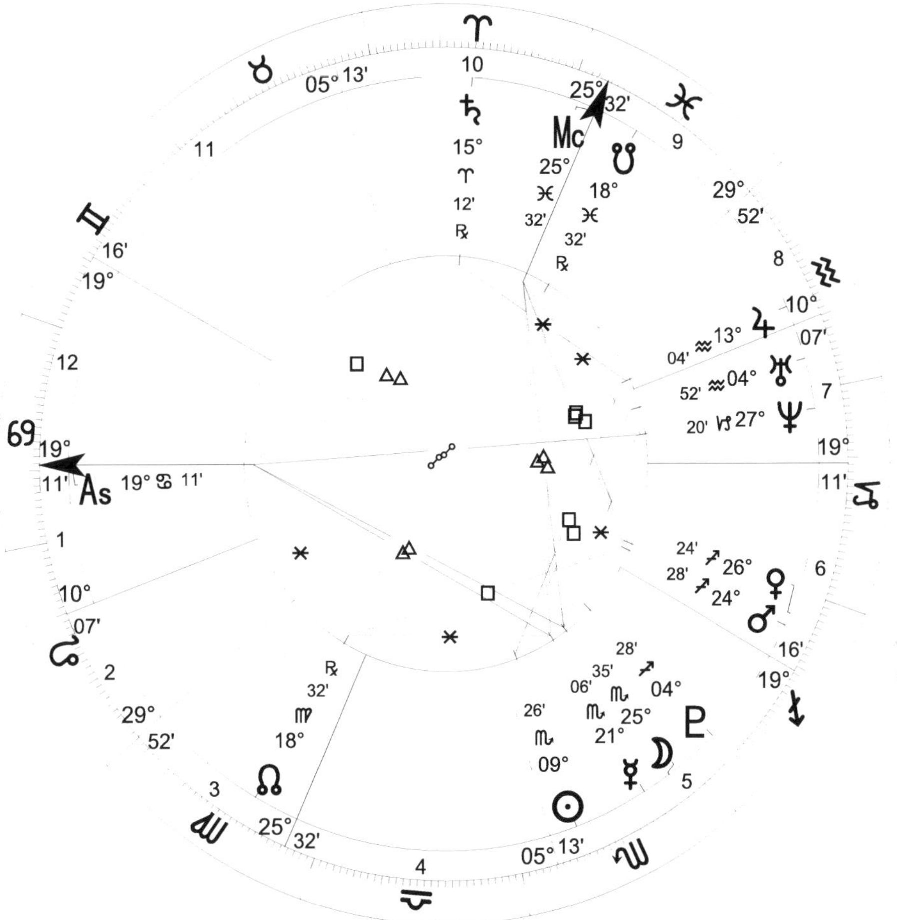

NEAREST ECLIPSES (NM/FM)					
☉ ☌	2 Sep 1997	00:51	09°♍33	Partial	S125
☽ ☍	16 Sep 1997	19:50	23°♓55	Total	S137
☉ ☌	26 Feb 1998	18:25	07°♓54	Total	S130
☽ ☍	13 Mar 1998	05:34	22°♍23	Appulse	S142

traditionals.pts

Pt	Long.	Travel	Decl.	Last Stn	Next Stn	Last Stn	Next Stn	F/S	Antiscia	C.Ant.
☽	25°♏35'07"	+12°32'	−14°35'	–	–	–	–	Slow	04°♒24	04°♌24
☉	09°♏26'06"	+01°00'	−14°38'	–	–	–	–	Fast	20°♒33	20°♌33
☿	21°♏06	+01°31'	−19°06'	−52 days	+35 days	02°♍42'02"	03°♑22'10"	Fast	08°♒53	08°♌53
♀	26°♐24	+01°01'	−26°52'	−487 days	+55 days	11°♊46'32"	03°♒56'16"	Fast	03°♑35	03°♋35
♂	24°♐28	+44'36"	−24°32'	−188 days	+501 days	16°♍44'17"	12°♏12'11"	Fast	05°♑31	05°♋31
♃	13°♒04	+04'44"	−17°47'	−24 days	+258 days	12°♒05'32"	28°♓03'35"	Slow	16°♏55	16°♉55
♄	15°♈12 ℞	−04'05"	+03°27'	−92 days	+44 days	20°♈21'38"	13°♈32'03"	Retro	14°♍47	14°♓47

MOON ASPECTS	
☽ △ Mc	0°09' S
☽ ⚹ ♆	1°49' A
☽ ☌ ♐	4°24' A
☽ △ As	6°15' A

ESSENTIAL DIGNITIES

Pt	Ruler	Exalt	Trip	Term	Face	Detri	Fall	Score
☽	♂	--	♂	♄	♀	♀	☽ −	−9 p
☉	♂	--	♂	♀	♂	♀	☽	−5 p
☿	♂	--	♂	♃	♀	♀	☽	−5 p
♀	♃	--	♃	♂	♄	☿	--	−5 p
♂	♃	--	♃	♄	♄	☿	--	−5 p
♃	♄	--	☿	♃ +	☿	☉	--	+2
♄	♂	☉	♃	☿	☉	♀	♄ −	−9 p

ASPECTS	
☽ △ Mc	0°09' S
☊ ⚹ As	0°38' S
☋ △ As	0°38' S
♀ □ Mc	0°51' S
♂ □ Mc	1°04' S
♅ ⚹ ♇	1°15' A
♆ ⚹ Mc	1°47' S
☽ ⚹ ♆	1°49' A
☿ △ As	1°54' S
♃ ⚹ ♄	2°06' A

PLANETARY SECT

Planet		Cht	Plc	Sgn	Condition
☉	D	N	N	N	Ex Cond
☽	N	N	D	N	
☿	N	N	D	N	
♀	N	N	D	D	
♂	N	N	D	D	
♃	D	N	N	D	
♄	D	N	N	D	

D=Diurnal, N=Nocturnal

4/10: WHEN WILL WE MOVE TO OUR APARTMENT?

3 August 2004 at 10:28 a.m. in Kranj, Slovenia
Hour ruler: Mercury

The question was asked by a friend. The works in the apartment which she and her partner had recently bought and were now renovating, had been dragging on. The deadline for the completion of the works was approaching but she was worrying that at that time the apartment would still not be ready. This is what she wrote me in an email that arrived into my mailbox at 10:28: *Ema, would you be so kind to look at my 'stars' and tell me, will we ever move into that apartment that we bought? The adaptation is going so slowly and things are getting ever more complicated. I'm at my wit's end. These people are all deceiving and double-crossing us...!*

I set up the chart for the time the question was sent to me. Ascendant is in Libra, which is also her natal ascendant. Its ruler Venus is in the last degrees of Gemini, indicating the proximity of their move. The cusp of the next sign (Cancer) is three degrees and a half (3°28', to be exact) away, which in view of the fact that Venus is in a mutable sign and in a cadent house (H9) could mean 3.5 months - or even 3.5 years, but years, in the context of the question, would be completely unrealistic, of course.

This was one timing indication, but the major "timer", as we know, is the Moon, so let's see what it does in the chart. It is in Pisces and in H6, and since it functions as the querent's co-significator, this clearly shows where her interest lies: in the workers (contractors) whose slowness frustrated her. They are signified by Jupiter, H6 ruler, which is placed in Virgo, the sign of its detriment, and in the weak H12, which eloquently describes their ineffectiveness. The Moon applies to it by an opposition; could this mean that the situation was getting worse?

The first applying aspect of the Moon is trine Saturn, the H4 ruler – significator of the flat. The aspect will be completed in 3°33' which is almost identical to the distance of Venus to 0° Cancer, and because the Moon is also in a mutable sign and a cadent house, this suggests the same time unit: month. So – in 3.5 months?

You will notice that Saturn is not only the significator of the flat but also almuten of the ascendant, therefore it partly rules the querent. Being in the sign of its detriment it describes her as unhappy, sad and frustrated.

I called her and said that they would be able to move to the renovated apartment in three and a half units of time, probably months. She said that this was impossible, because the deadline was the end of August, and this equals to three and a half weeks! Interesting, I said, maybe they would really be weeks and not months, but the chart suggested months. I was pretty sure about the number of time units elapsing until the predicted event, but suddenly not so sure about the true time unit.

It turned out that the chart described the time unit very precisely: they moved in mid-November 2004 which was exactly 3.5 months after the question!

It is also interesting that problems with the workers really went from bad to worse. They were very slow and when the querent and her partner finally moved into the renovated apartment, they soon found that the parquet was not laid properly because it started to lift. The poor state of Jupiter, the H6 ruler to which the Moon applies by an opposition (stress, conflict), shows this very clearly!

4/10

3 Aug 2004
10:28 CEDT −2:00
Kranj, Slovenia
46°N15' 014°E21'

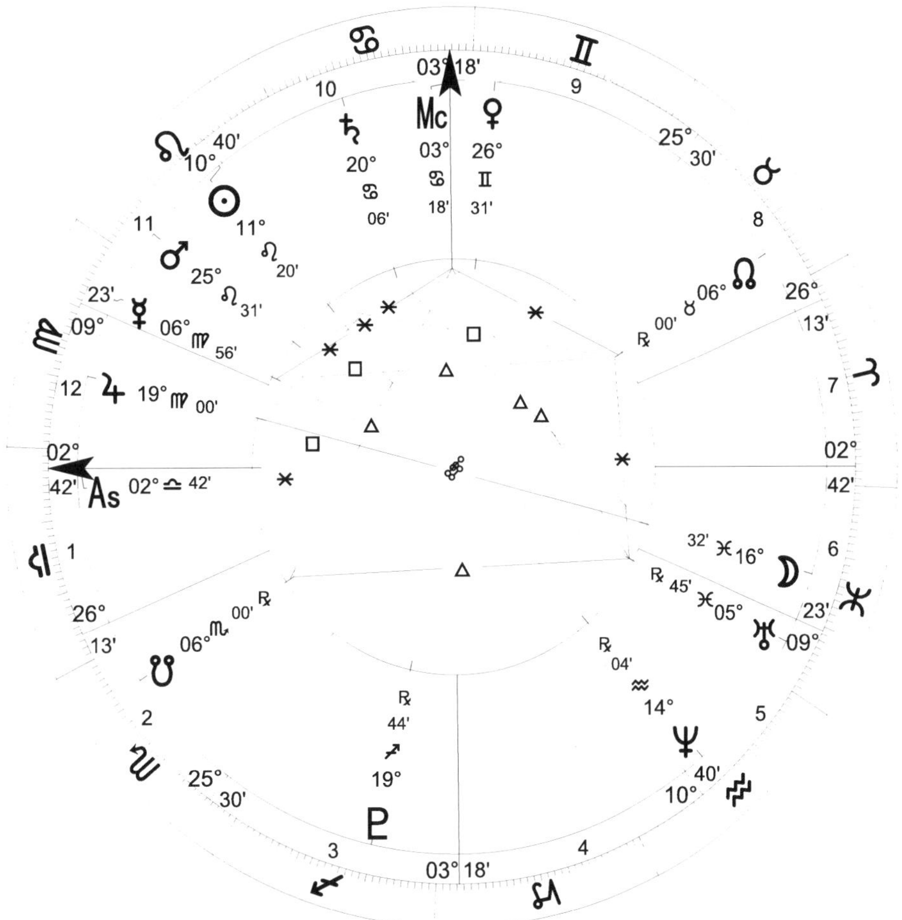

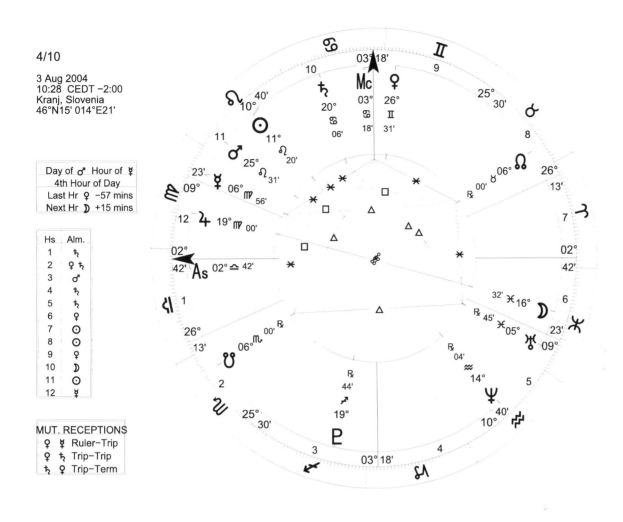

Day of ♂ Hour of ☿
4th Hour of Day
Last Hr ♀ −57 mins
Next Hr ☽ +15 mins

Hs	Alm.
1	♄
2	♀ ♄
3	♂
4	♄
5	♄
6	♀
7	☉
8	☉
9	♀
10	☽
11	☉
12	☿

MUT. RECEPTIONS		
♀	☿	Ruler−Trip
♀	♄	Trip−Trip
♄	♀	Trip−Term

NEAREST ECLIPSES (NM/FM)					
☉	19 Apr 2004	15:21	29°♈49	Partial	S119
☽	4 May 2004	22:33	14°♏41	Total	S131
☉	14 Oct 2004	04:48	21°♎05	Partial	S124
☽	28 Oct 2004	05:07	05°♉02	Total	S136

traditionals.pts

Pt	Long.	Travel	Decl.	Last Stn	Next Stn	Last Stn	Next Stn	F/S	Antiscia	C.Ant.
☽	16°♓32'15"	+13°58'	−08°49'	–	–	–	–	Fast	13°♎27	13°♈27
☉	11°♌20'05"	+57'24"	+17°22'	–	–	–	–	Slow	18°♉39	18°♏39
☿	06°♍56	+31'38"	+06°32'	−94 days	+6,7 days	21°♈06'58"	08°♍46'28"	Slow	23°♈03	23°♎03
♀	26°♊31	+49'16"	+19°14'	−34 days	+508 days	09°♊37'32"	01°♒28'00"	Slow	03°♋28	03°♑28
♂	25°♌31	+37'55"	+14°04'	−311 days	+424 days	00°♓07'06"	23°♉22'20"	Fast	04°♉28	04°♏28
♃	19°♍00	+11'26"	+05°21'	−90 days	+182 days	08°♍54'52"	18°♎51'45"	Fast	10°♈59	10°♎59
♄	20°♋06	+07'26"	+21°42'	−148 days	+96 days	06°♋17'09"	27°♋20'35"	Fast	09°♊53	09°♐53

MOON ASPECTS			
☽	□	♇	2°34' A
☽	△	♄	3°28' A
☽	☍	♃	3°40' A
☽	☌	♈	13°27' A

ESSENTIAL DIGNITIES

Pt	Ruler	Exalt	Trip	Term	Face	Detri	Fall	Score
☽	♃	♀	♀	☿	♃	☿	☿	−5 p
☉	☉ +	--	☉ +	♄	♃	♄	--	+8
☿	☿ +	☿ +	♀	☿ +	☉	♃	♀	+11
♀	☿	--	♄ m	♄	☉	♃	--	−5 p
♂	☉	--	☉	♂ +	♂ +	♄	--	+3
♃	☿	☿	♀	♃ +	♀	♃ −	♀	−3
♄	☽	♃	♀ m	♃	☽	♄ −	♂	−10 p

ASPECTS

♅	✶	☊	0°15' A
♅	△	☋	0°15' A
♃	□	♇	0°33' A
As	□	Mc	0°36' S
♀	✶	♂	0°48' S
☿	✶	☋	0°53' S
☿	△	☊	0°53' S
♃	✶	♄	1°05' A
♅	△	Mc	2°26' S
☽	□	♇	2°34' A

PLANETARY SECT

Planet		Cht	Plc	Sgn	Condition
☉	D	D	D	D	In Hayz
☽	N	D	N	N	
☿	N	D	D	N	
♀	N	D	D	D	Ex Cond
♂	N	D	D	D	Ex Cond
♃	D	D	D	N	
♄	D	D	D	N	

D=Diurnal, N=Nocturnal

4/11: WHEN WILL I SELL MY APARTMENT? SHOULD I LOWER THE PRICE?

1 September, 2008 at 5:01 a.m., Ljubljana, Slovenia
Hour ruler: Venus

A former student sent me an email with the chart data for the above question. He asked the question himself but was not sure how to go about it, so he asked me for help. It was a complicated chart, indeed, but at the same time a very interesting one!

Details and background? He and his wife had bought a new apartment into which they had not yet moved, whilst trying to sell the one in which they were still living. He wanted to sell it as soon as possible, because he had to borrow a lot of money to be able to buy the new apartment, and he was under pressure because he had to pay off the loan soon. His real estate broker was trying to convince him to lower the price. Should he do that, he asked? And, of course, when would his property sell?

Let's see! The angles are fixed, which in itself is not promising, because this usually shows a slow progression. The querent is shown by the Sun which is placed in Virgo in a close applying conjunction with Saturn, the H7 ruler (the potential buyer). The property is ruled by Mars which is right on the cusp of H3 in Libra, while the Moon (co-significator of the querent) is at the end of Virgo where it applies to a conjunction with Venus, Mercury and finally Mars (apartment). The real estate agent, whom he hired to negotiate the sale, is ruled by H6 and so her significator is the same planet as the H7 ruler - Saturn.

The Sun's application to Saturn inspired me to say to him, *You will sell the flat, that's for sure.* I added that the apartment probably needed some renovation (Mars in detriment) and that the sale price is relatively high (Venus, the ruler of H10 of the price of property, dignified) but that this really doesn't matter because the buyer will obviously be able to afford it.

Why did I say that? Well, the H8 ruler (the buyer's money) Jupiter applies by trine to the Sun (the querent, seller), indicating a smooth cash flow, like the potential buyer's agreeing with the price. Jupiter's retrograde motion facilitates this since the two bodies thus apply to each other.

I then asked him whether they planned to move to the new apartment in 5 weeks? This is shown by the Moon which needs 5 degrees to Libra, and this corresponds (based on the logic of the question) to 5 weeks. Yes, he said, they plan to move at the beginning of October. Okay, I said, if this is so, then I think you'll sell the flat in 13 weeks which would be the end of November. (This I judged in accordance with the number of degrees separating the Moon from Mars, the H4 ruler.)

I was a bit uneasy over the fact that the Moon would change signs in the process. This could complicate the matters, or it might mean that new, unforeseen circumstances would arise. I also noted that the Sun (the querent) would sooner complete the trine with Jupiter (the buyer's money) than Saturn (significator of the real estate agent) to which Jupiter also applied, so it seemed to me that the apartment would sell without the involvement of a third party. Could this be the change in the process that the Moon's sign change indicated?

Now to the result which I found quite fascinating! As the querent later told me, his cousin who lent him the money for the new flat, called him 11 days after the question and asked him if he'd be willing to sell the flat to her? The cousin is shown by H3 (brothers, sisters, cousins etc.) - on the cusp of which "sits" Mars, significator of the flat, while the Moon's first application is to Venus, the H3 ruler! Venus (cousin) receives Mars (the apartment) in its domicile, indicating that she liked the apartment. Venus is also the hour ruler which underlines its significance in the chart. The cousin wanted to buy the flat for her daughter who is ruled by H7 (5/3), so her rulers are Saturn and partly Neptune. The two women first came to see the apartment two weeks (or 14 days) after the question which almost exactly correspond to 13 degrees separating the Moon from Mars (13 days being almost exactly two weeks, of course). You will also notice that the Sun (the querent) is a good 2 degrees away from Saturn (signifying the cousin in the role of the buyer, and her daughter), which further confirms the timing.

They had to negotiate the price a bit, he said, but when all was said and done, the price was dropped by 10 (ten!) Euros - which practically means that he sold it for pretty exactly the money he initially wanted. The contract was signed in late November - 13 weeks after the question, as I predicted. No agent involved!

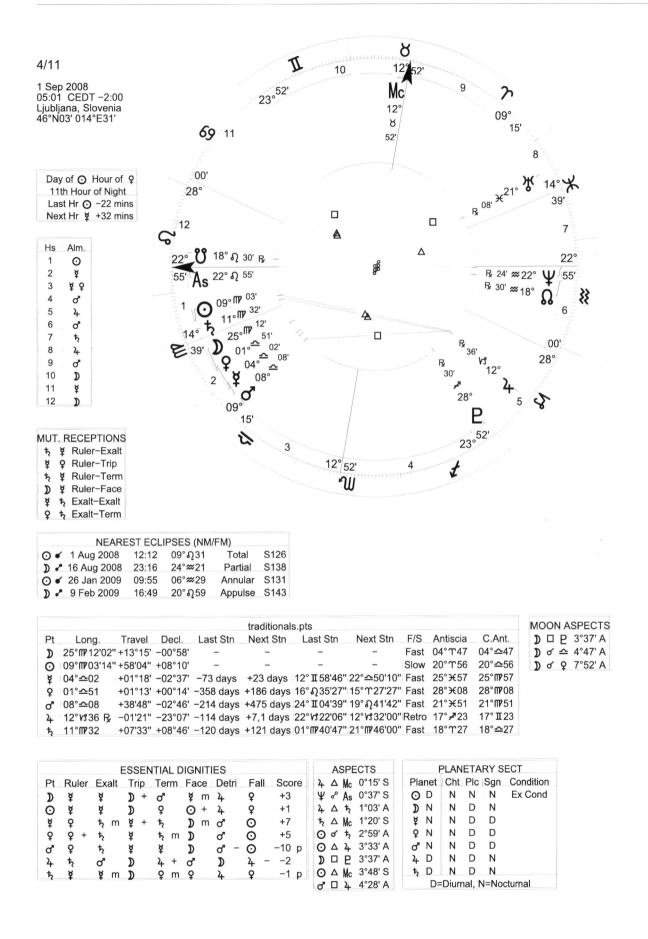

4/11

1 Sep 2008
05:01 CEDT −2:00
Ljubljana, Slovenia
46°N03' 014°E31'

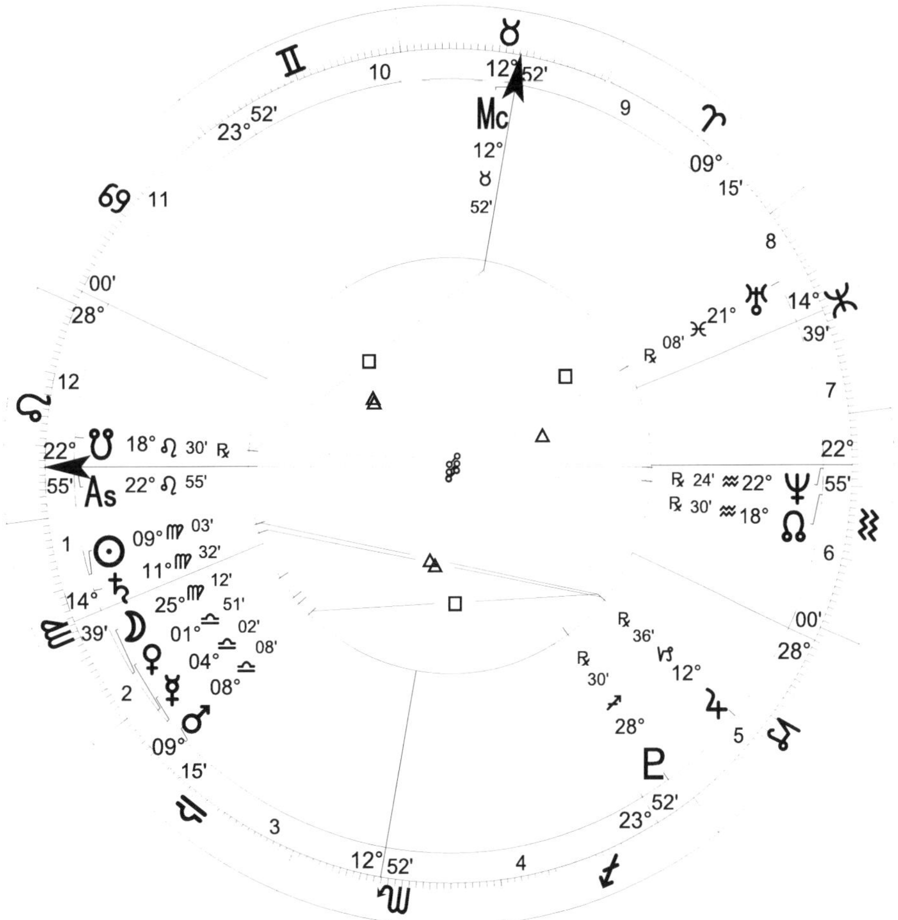

Day of ☉ Hour of ♀
11th Hour of Night
Last Hr ☉ −22 mins
Next Hr ☿ +32 mins

Hs	Alm.
1	☉
2	☿
3	☿ ♀
4	♂
5	♃
6	♂
7	♄
8	♃
9	♂
10	☽
11	☿
12	☽

MUT. RECEPTIONS		
♄	☿	Ruler–Exalt
☿	♀	Ruler–Trip
♄	☿	Ruler–Term
☽	☿	Ruler–Face
☿	♄	Exalt–Exalt
♀	♄	Exalt–Term

NEAREST ECLIPSES (NM/FM)					
☉ ☌	1 Aug 2008	12:12	09°♌31	Total	S126
☽ ☍	16 Aug 2008	23:16	24°♒21	Partial	S138
☉ ☌	26 Jan 2009	09:55	06°♒29	Annular	S131
☽ ☍	9 Feb 2009	16:49	20°♌59	Appulse	S143

traditionals.pts

Pt	Long.	Travel	Decl.	Last Stn	Next Stn	Last Stn	Next Stn	F/S	Antiscia	C.Ant.
☽	25°♍12'02"	+13°15'	−00°58'	–	–	–	–	Fast	04°♈47	04°♎47
☉	09°♍03'14"	+58'04"	+08°10'	–	–	–	–	Slow	20°♈56	20°♎56
☿	04°♎02	+01°18'	−02°37'	−73 days	+23 days	12°♊58'46"	22°♎50'10"	Fast	25°♓57	25°♍57
♀	01°♎51	+01°13'	+00°14'	−358 days	+186 days	16°♌35'27"	15°♈27'27"	Fast	28°♓08	28°♍08
♂	08°♎08	+38'48"	−02°46'	−214 days	+475 days	24°♊04'39"	19°♌41'42"	Fast	21°♓51	21°♍51
♃	12°♑36 ℞	−01'21"	−23°07'	−114 days	+7,1 days	22°♑22'06"	12°♑32'00"	Retro	17°♐23	17°♊23
♄	11°♍32	+07'33"	+08°46'	−120 days	+121 days	01°♍40'47"	21°♍46'00"	Fast	18°♈27	18°♎27

MOON ASPECTS			
☽	□	♇	3°37' A
☽	☌	♎	4°47' A
☽	☌	♀	7°52' A

ESSENTIAL DIGNITIES

Pt	Ruler	Exalt	Trip	Term	Face	Detri	Fall	Score
☽	☿	☿	☽ +	♂	☿ m	♃	♀	+3
☉	☿	☿	☽	♀	☉ +	♃	♀	+1
☿	♀	♄ m	☿ +	♄	☽ m	♂	☉	+7
♀	♀ +	♄	☿	♄ m	☽	♂	☉	+5
♂	♀	♄	☿	☿	☽	♂ −	☉	−10 p
♃	♄	♂	☽	♃ +	♂	☽	♃ −	−2
♄	☿	☿ m	☽	♀ m	♀	♃	♀	−1 p

ASPECTS			
♃	△	Mc	0°15' S
♆	☍	As	0°37' S
♃	△	♄	1°03' A
♄	△	Mc	1°20' S
☉	☌	♄	2°59' A
☉	△	♃	3°33' A
☽	□	♇	3°37' A
☉	△	Mc	3°48' S
♂	□	♃	4°28' A

PLANETARY SECT

Planet		Cht	Plc	Sgn	Condition
☉	D	N	N	N	Ex Cond
☽	N	N	D	N	
☿	N	N	D	D	
♀	N	N	D	D	
♂	N	N	D	D	
♃	D	N	D	N	
♄	D	N	D	N	

D=Diurnal, N=Nocturnal

4/12: WILL I BE ABLE TO RENT THESE PREMISES?

July 5, 2007 at 4:32 p.m. (16:32), Ljubljana, Slovenia
Hour ruler: Mars

A friend called me to ask whether she would be able to rent premises in the city centre where she planned to set up a small fashion store.

Her ruler is Mars, the ruler of the ascending sign Scorpio and also the hour ruler. The chart is therefore radical. The premises are shown by H4 where we find the Moon (the querent's interest) and Uranus, while the place itself is ruled by Jupiter (H4 in Pisces) and Venus (H4 almuten).

Mars is in detriment which doesn't bode well for her. It suggested that she felt helpless and stuck (Mars in the fixed Taurus). This is logical since all she could do at that stage, as we'll learn shortly, was to "sit and wait". Mars is also void-of-course - except for the sextile with the north node in H4. The node is not a planet, so this aspect cannot be taken as an indicator of completion – although it does add a bit of a positive flavor. Mars is placed in H6 which (among other things) indicates tenants, clearly showing that she's interested in the lease and not in the purchase of the property.

Jupiter (the premises) is in Sagittarius where it moves back from H2 to H1 by retrograde motion. This might be a case of "emplacement", but the two significators (Mars and Jupiter) are not in aspect neither connected by a mutual reception, translation of light or anything similar. Nor are they linked to the Moon which in H4 applies to a conjunction with retrograde Uranus, suggesting (in the context of the question) a sudden setback or an unpleasant surprise. All of this is confirmed by the fact that Venus, the H4 almuten, is void-of-course (except for its trine with the trans-Saturnian Pluto) and not connected to either Mars or the Moon.

I told her that, unfortunately, the chart doesn't show that her wish could be granted. She was surprised, because the lease, as she told me, had been granted to her by her ex-boyfriend who was a close relative of the city mayor, and she depended on his ability to help her. He is shown by Venus, the H7 and H11 ruler (partners, friends, helpers) and also functioning as the H4 almuten. With this new piece of information, I examined the chart anew. As already said, Venus applies to Pluto, the modern H1 ruler, by trine, but bears no relation to H4 and its dispositor Jupiter, therefore I told her that apparently he really wants to help, but would obviously not succeed in doing this.

Weeks went by, the querent's friend was avoiding her calls and she soon abandoned her plan to rent business premises, and found a regular job instead.

4/12

5 Jul 2007
16:32 CEDT −2:00
Ljubljana, Slovenia
46°N03' 014°E31'

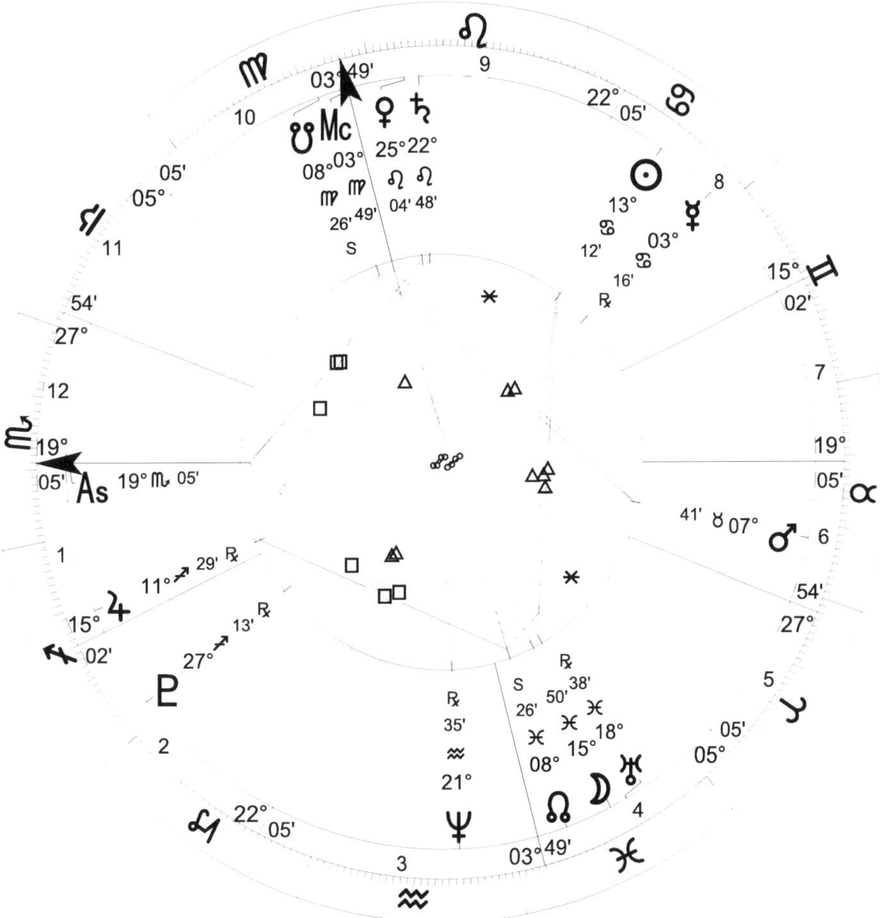

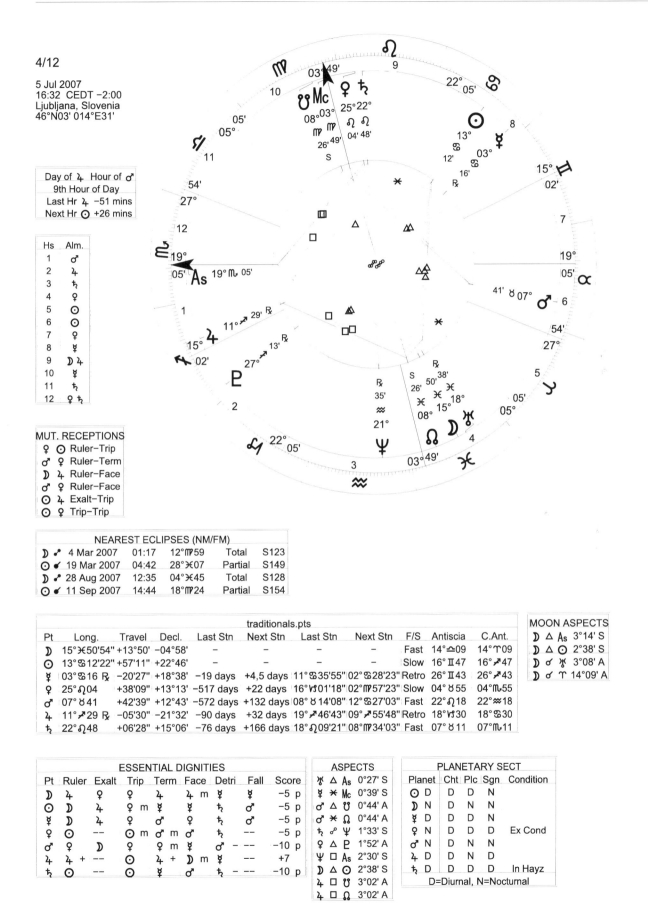

Day of ♃ Hour of ♂
9th Hour of Day
Last Hr ♃ −51 mins
Next Hr ⊙ +26 mins

Hs	Alm.
1	♂
2	♃
3	♄
4	♀
5	⊙
6	⊙
7	♀
8	☿
9	☽ ♃
10	☿
11	♄
12	♀ ♄

MUT. RECEPTIONS		
♀	⊙	Ruler−Trip
♂	♀	Ruler−Term
☽	♃	Ruler−Face
♂	♀	Ruler−Face
⊙	♃	Exalt−Trip
⊙	♀	Trip−Trip

NEAREST ECLIPSES (NM/FM)					
☽ ☍	4 Mar 2007	01:17	12°♍59	Total	S123
⊙ ☌	19 Mar 2007	04:42	28°♓07	Partial	S149
☽ ☍	28 Aug 2007	12:35	04°♓45	Total	S128
⊙ ☌	11 Sep 2007	14:44	18°♍24	Partial	S154

traditionals.pts

Pt	Long.	Travel	Decl.	Last Stn	Next Stn	Last Stn	Next Stn	F/S	Antiscia	C.Ant.
☽	15°♓50'54"	+13°50'	−04°58'	–	–	–	–	Fast	14°♎09	14°♈09
⊙	13°♋12'22"	+57'11"	+22°46'	–	–	–	–	Slow	16°♊47	16°♐47
☿	03°♋16 ℞	−20'27"	+18°38'	−19 days	+4,5 days	11°♋35'55"	02°♋28'23"	Retro	26°♊43	26°♐43
♀	25°♌04	+38'09"	+13°13'	−517 days	+22 days	16°♑01'18"	02°♍57'23"	Slow	04°♉55	04°♏55
♂	07°♉41	+42'39"	+12°43'	−572 days	+132 days	08°♉14'08"	12°♋27'03"	Fast	22°♌18	22°♒18
♃	11°♐29 ℞	−05'30"	−21°32'	−90 days	+32 days	19°♐46'43"	09°♐55'48"	Retro	18°♑30	18°♋30
♄	22°♌48	+06'28"	+15°06'	−76 days	+166 days	18°♌09'21"	08°♍34'03"	Fast	07°♉11	07°♏11

MOON ASPECTS			
☽	△	As	3°14' S
☽	△	⊙	2°38' S
☽	☌	♅	3°08' A
☽	☌	♈	14°09' A

ESSENTIAL DIGNITIES

Pt	Ruler	Exalt	Trip	Term	Face	Detri	Fall	Score
☽	♃	♀	♀	♃	♃ m	☿	☿	−5 p
⊙	☽	♃	♀ m	☿	☿	♄	♂	−5 p
☿	☽	♃	♀	♂	♀	♄	♂	−5 p
♀	⊙	−−	⊙ m	♂ m	♂	♄	−−	−5 p
♂	♀	☽	♀	♀ m	☿	♂ −	−−	−10 p
♃	♃ +	−−	⊙	♃ +	☽ m	☿	−−	+7
♄	⊙	−−	⊙	☿	♂	♄ −	−−	−10 p

ASPECTS			
♅	△	As	0°27' S
☿	⚹	Mc	0°39' S
♂	△	☋	0°44' A
♂	⚹	☊	0°44' A
♄	☍	♆	1°33' S
♀	△	♇	1°52' A
♆	□	As	2°30' S
☽	△	⊙	2°38' S
♃	□	☋	3°02' A
♃	□	☊	3°02' A

PLANETARY SECT

Planet		Cht	Plc	Sgn	Condition
⊙	D	D	D	N	
☽	N	D	N	N	
☿	D	D	D	N	
♀	N	D	D	D	Ex Cond
♂	N	D	N	N	
♃	D	D	N	D	
♄	D	D	D	D	In Hayz

D=Diurnal, N=Nocturnal

FINANCE

This chapter includes horaries relating to earnings, profits, speculation, investments, and the like. Who would not want to earn more money, make profit, or avoid financial failure due to unsuccessful speculation or a wrong investment? Obviously these are important questions, and although they are fairly common, they rarely occur as independent, autonomous questions. They are more often related to career charts, or they are so naïve that I don't even attempt to answer them. *What are my lucky numbers?* Yours are the same as mine, but if I knew them, I'd be now on one of the Fiji Islands, lying under a coconut palm and drinking cocktails. (You'd be surprised how many times I had to give this answer to people asking such questions.)

There is one more reason that I have relatively few financial charts among my horaries, this being that I rarely get feedback to my answers. I believe this is somehow related to the fact that H8 which plays such an important role in financial charts, is also the house of secrecy.

Will I ever be rich? I don't answer such questions with the horary technique, since they are very general and therefore more in the domain of natal than horary astrology. It is true that astrologers of past centuries answered them by means of the horary technique, but this was mainly due to the unavailability of their clients' birth data.

SIGNIFICATORS

The querent is ruled by the ascendant, its ruler, any planet/s in H1 and the Moon.

Finances are signified by the cusp of H2, the ruler of H2, any planet/s in H2, part of fortune (fortuna), fortuna's dispositor and Jupiter (as the natural significator of wealth).

An affirmative answer to the questions of the type *Will I get rich?* (earn some money, earn well etc.) is suggested by the following indications:

- the significators of finance placed in angular (possibly succedent) houses, especially if they are essentially and accidentally strong and free of afflictions;
- the querent's significators in conjunction or a harmonious aspect with the significators of finance, or connected with them by means of translation of light or mutual reception);
- a benefic in conjunction or a harmonious aspect with fortuna or ascendant;
- a benefic or fortuna in H2, unafflicted;
- the ruler of H2 in H1, or vice versa;
- a fixed star of the Venus or Jupiter nature in conjunction with the cusp of H2 or with fortuna;
- the rulers of H1 and H2 with Jupiter in H1, H2, H4, H7, H10 or H11.

How to make more money? From what sources can I expect a loan/earnings/profit? In this type of questions, we must study the houses associated with the significators of finance. If they are related to:

- H1, the querent will earn money without any special effort, or they will get it suddenly and unexpectedly, probably soon (H1 is "fast"!);
- H2, they will earn it by their own efforts, by being economical and by smartly allocating their resources;

- H3, they will earn it by writing, speaking, communicating, teaching, dealing in the transportation business, translating, proofreading, or through influential or generous kinship (brothers, sisters, cousins) or neighbours;
- H4, they will receive it from parents or grandparents, or through working for/with them, in the form of family heritage, through the sale of real estate, by gardening and land cultivation, and similar;
- H5, they will get it by speculation (betting, shares, stock exchange), sports competitions, performing (singing, dancing, entertaining), managing a restaurant or some kind of tourist or entertainment business, or they will be helped by their father (H5 is 2/4) or child;
- H6, they will earn it by being of service to others, by means of domestic animals (by breeding them, for example); by taking care of people's health, or from the aunts and uncles on their father's side;
- H7, they will be assisted by a marriage or business partner; money can also be earned by trading (buying and selling) or through a court (lawsuit);
- H8, they can receive it from an insurance company or their partner; and by all kinds of loans, inheritances and profits associated with relocation;
- H9, they will get it from abroad, through an import-export business, by marketing, publishing, working at an educational institution (by teaching, lecturing etc.) or in a media house (TV, press, radio etc), or through their partners' relatives;
- H10, they will earn it through regular work (as business owners, employers, employees or free-lancers), by a governmental office, public speaking, politics or by assuming some special high office. Profits from partners' real estate (4/7) or from grandchildren (2/9) also come under this house. Significators in this house generally promise good earnings;
- H11, they will come to the money with the help of their friends or mothers, or through clubs, organizations and political parties. Pensions, scholarships and companies' profits also come under this house.
- H12, they will receive it from charity institutions, from aunts and uncles on the mother's side, through trade in livestock, horse breeding, or from closed-type institutions (hospitals, asylums, prisons, monasteries and the like). This is generally the most unfortunate house and therefore suggests poor income.

There are several ways in which significators of money/income/profit can be associated with certain houses, standing for particular (kinds of) activities and people:
- the ruler of H2 in a house;
- the ruler of a house in H2;
- Jupiter in a house;
- a house ruler in aspect with the ruler of H2, a planet in H2, Jupiter or fortuna;
- the house of the ascendant ruler, Moon or Jupiter aspecting the planet ruling or occupying H2.

If the planet promising profit is the ascendant ruler, the querent will earn money by himself or through his own efforts, without the help of other people and institutions.

Often, indications will point to different directions. This should not confuse us. We should strive to find the planet that is the strongest because this will show us the main source of income, while the other, weaker planets will show us other, additional sources of income. Double-bodied signs on cusp of H2 often show more sources of income.

And what if the chart shows that someone has only a small chance of earning money, or will have little financial success? In such cases, we must carefully study the planets that afflicts (hinders) the significators of income. In what houses are those planets and what houses do they rule? If they are related to:
- H1, the fault is on the querent's side. Look at the afflicting planet: if it's Jupiter or Venus, they might be too lazy, wasteful or negligent; if it's Mars, too aggressive and uncooperative; if Saturn, sick, depressed, too old or anti-social; if Mercury, inconstant or uneducated; if Neptune, addicted (to drugs or alcohol) or unrealistic; if Uranus, too independent, rebellious or uncooperative; if Pluto, there's some *force majeure* working against them.
- H2, the querent may be lacking means or inner drive to start a business, or they may have too little self-confidence: they don't appreciate their own abilities, so they don't know how to earn money by them;

- H3, they can be held back by wicked neighbours, a brother or a sister, or be unable to drive or communicate properly;
- H4, they may be hindered by parents or grandparents, or by not living in the right place, and should therefore relocate;
- H5, their money may be spent wholly on their children, or be taken away from them by their children, or by unreasonable speculation, a demanding lover, or they may spend it on a regular basis on sports, entertainment and other free-time activities;
- H6, the problem may be with their subordinates, colleagues or accountants, or they need to spend a lot of money on treatments and medicals;
- H7, they are financially responsible for their partner, or the money is taken from them by their partners, opponents in business (competition), expensive lawsuits, and the like;
- H8, they spend a lot of money on high taxes, expensive loans and the like;
- H9, much money is spent on travel, education, legal matters, research, marketing, religious institutions, or similar;
- H10, their earnings are restrained by their superiors, government or a court decision, or they may have to take financial care of their mother;
- H11, their loss can be related to their friends, a child's partner or a partner's child, investments in clubs, associations or political organizations, and the like;
- H12, their money gets "lost" without an apparent reason, but this can also be negligence, forgetfulness, laziness, or a costly addiction.

LOANS

Loans are generally ruled by H8, the lenders by H7. In question asking of a possibility to get a loan, we need to look for connections between the planets associated with H1, H2, H7 and H8. Indications for an affirmative answer are:

- the application of the ascendant ruler or the Moon to the H8 planets;
- the H8 ruler in H1 or H2, but the H1 and H2 planets must receive this planet by any of their strong dignities (domicile or exaltation);
- the H1 ruler or the Moon in the applying aspect with a benefic (Venus, Jupiter or the Sun) that has dignities (domicile, exaltation or triplicity) in the ascending sign, or in a sign that is intercepted in H1;
- the H1 ruler or the Moon in an applying aspect with a benefic that is strong and well placed in H10 or H11; such a placement promises success even without a reception.

If we are borrowing money from a relative, we can use derived houses: for example, mothers are ruled by H10 and their money by H11, children by H5 and their money by H6, and so on.

SPECULATION AND STOCK MARKET TRADING

Will my lottery ticket win? If you have one in your pocket, we can try to find an answer. The rules are similar to other financial questions.

Lotteries, sports betting, stock trading and all other types of short-term investments, involving risk, belong to H5, while long-term investments belong to H2. As H2 is the main financial house, it must be taken into account in all types of speculation questions, though. It might show that we can't afford to speculate, for example!

The condition of H5 and the relations between the H5 planets and the H1 planets, benefics and fortuna will tell us whether a particular investment would be lucrative or not.

For stock market trading, the technique of "first trade charts" should be used, but as this is not the subject of horary astrology, the reader is advised to look for information elsewhere. Bill Meridian's books are an excellent source on this matter.

BETTING AND COMPETITION

Questions relating to betting and competition are a bit different from the rest of financial questions. If we have already placed a bet and are interested in whether we would win, then we proceed in the manner described above, that is, by studying H1 and H5. But if we want to know which party would win (a sports match, a bet or similar), we are actually asking which side is stronger. There are nearly always two opposing sides that compete for superiority, so we need to find out which of them is stronger, by calculating their significators' essential and accidental dignities. We use this technique with all competition charts such as sports competitions, horse races, games of chess, legal conflicts, wars and the like.

H1 always stands for the challenger, H7 for the challenged (the opposite side). But what if we don't know who the challenger is? Or if there is no challenger, because it's a "peaceful" competition? Well, there is usually one side that the querent identifies with, or wants it to win, and that side we give to H1 while the opposite side we give to H7. But if the querent is truly indifferent, not cheering for any side, we give H1 to the one that was first mentioned or bears more similarity to the ascending sign, its ruler and any planets in it. H1 can also be given to the home team – where applicable, of course.

To be able to evaluate the strength of part of fortune, Lilly advised the following procedure*:
* in Taurus or Pisces +5
* in Libra, Sagittarius, Leo or Cancer +4
* in Gemini +3
* in Virgo, in the term of Jupiter or Venus +2
* in conjunction with Jupiter or Venus +5
* in a trine with Jupiter or Venus +4
* in a sextile with Jupiter or Venus +4
* in conjunction with the north node +3
* in H1 or H10 +5
* in H7, H4 or H11 +4
* in H2 or H5 +3
* in H9 +2
* in H3 +1
* in conjunction with Regulus +6
* in conjunction with Spica +5
* not combust or under the Sun beams +5
* in Scorpio, Capricorn or Aquarius -5
* in Aries 0
* in conjunction with Saturn or Mars -5
* in conjunction with the south node -3
* in opposition to Saturn or Mars -4
* in a square to Saturn or Mars -3
* in a Saturn or Mars term -2
* in the 12th house -5
* in H8 or H6 -4
* in conjunction with Algol -4
* combust -5

* Formula for day charts: ascendant + Moon - Sun
 Formula for night charts: ascendant + Sun - Moon

5/1: SHOULD I INVEST IN GOLD OR IN CHINESE STOCKS?

12 December 1995 at 9:42 a.m., Ljubljana, Slovenia
Hour ruler: Venus

The querent was interested in how gold would fare on the world's stock markets in the near future. Would it rise or fall? And, of course - when? And how would the Chinese equity market fare? She was thinking of investing in it too, mentioning the WUHN stock.

Such questions are usually given the most reliable answers by practitioners who specialize in financial astrology. At the time of this question, I didn't have any such knowledge, and because I wanted to help her, I decided to use the horary method.

Looking at the chart, cast for the question, I was immediately caught by the Moon in Leo which was applying to a trine with the Sun, the natural significator of gold. Venus, ruling H9 of foreign countries, was right on the ascendant, with the H9 cusp in Libra - the sign traditionally ruling China! Venus was, interestingly, also one of the two almutens of the ascendant. The chart therefore aptly described the querent's interest. The said indications were confirmed by her main significator Saturn (ruler of Capricorn, the ascending sign) in H2 of finances. The chart looked "radical" also because the planetary hour was harmonious.

The applying trine of the Moon to its dispositor, the Sun, which "shone" in the fortunate H11, suggested an imminent rise of gold price. This was emphasized by the harmonious application of both lights to Jupiter, the natural significator of wealth, which was strong in its own sign of Sagittarius, although "hidden" in the weak H12, and combust. However, since this is a day chart, both the Sun and Jupiter above the horizon are more powerful than they would be if below the horizon. Because they are also in a diurnal sign, they are *in hayz*, therefore extremely strong.

But when can the rise be expected? The Moon (slow in motion) is 2 degrees and 18 minutes short of the trine of the Sun. It is in an angular house and in a fixed sign, corresponding to weeks or months. I said that the price of gold would start to rise in about two weeks, but if it wouldn't, she could expect it to rise in two months.

It turned out that the price of gold really started to rise in two weeks. After its completion of the trine with the Sun, Moon carries its light to Jupiter, within a 7°29' orb. Exactly that number of weeks (seven and a half) passed until the highest price of gold. This peaked to 415.10 dollars per ounce on 2nd February 1996 and then began to rapidly decline.

I must admit that I made a mistake here, because I based my timing on the distance between the Sun (gold) and Jupiter (the price rise) instead of relying on the Moon. But I was a beginner then and was not yet fully aware of the Moon's prime importance in timing. Because there were 5°10' from the Sun to Jupiter, I said that gold would peak in 5 weeks (or months). An important lesson to be repeated here: if a time unit is provided by the Moon's aspect with a significator, base your timing on the Moon – always!

Let me add that seven and a half weeks correspond approximately to two months – or to the 2°18' which are between the Moon and the Sun, but the distance between the Moon and Jupiter is much more indicative because it more accurately specifies the time elapsed till the peak gold price.

What about the Chinese shares? Venus is very strong (by adding her essential and accidental dignities it scores 21 points), so I told her that this investment also seems promising, but that in about five and a half weeks there seemed to be a change. I based my judgment on the fact that Venus (in a cardinal sign and an angular house) was applying to conjunct Neptune by a 5°37' orb. Neptune, as we know, is the planet of illusion and deception, but in financial astrology it often forecasts an unusually rapid and unreasonable growth (inflated value). But even if that kind of impact can be predicted, we are still dealing with the deceptive nature of Neptune, which calls for caution. I therefore told her that the most I can say about the Chinese market is that after 5.5 weeks it could start to behave "strangely". It could either rise or fall.

It turned out that the WUHN shares suddenly started to rise on 19 January 1996, exactly five and a half weeks after the question, whereas the composite index of Chinese shares started taking the bullish trend at the beginning of February 1996, and these shares in 1996 increased by about 300%. The soundness of this long-term investment is also suggested by an exact but still applying sextile of Venus to Saturn – significator of the querent which occupies H2 in the horary chart.

5/1

12 Dec 1995
09:42 CET −1:00
Ljubljana, Slovenia
46°N03' 014°E31'

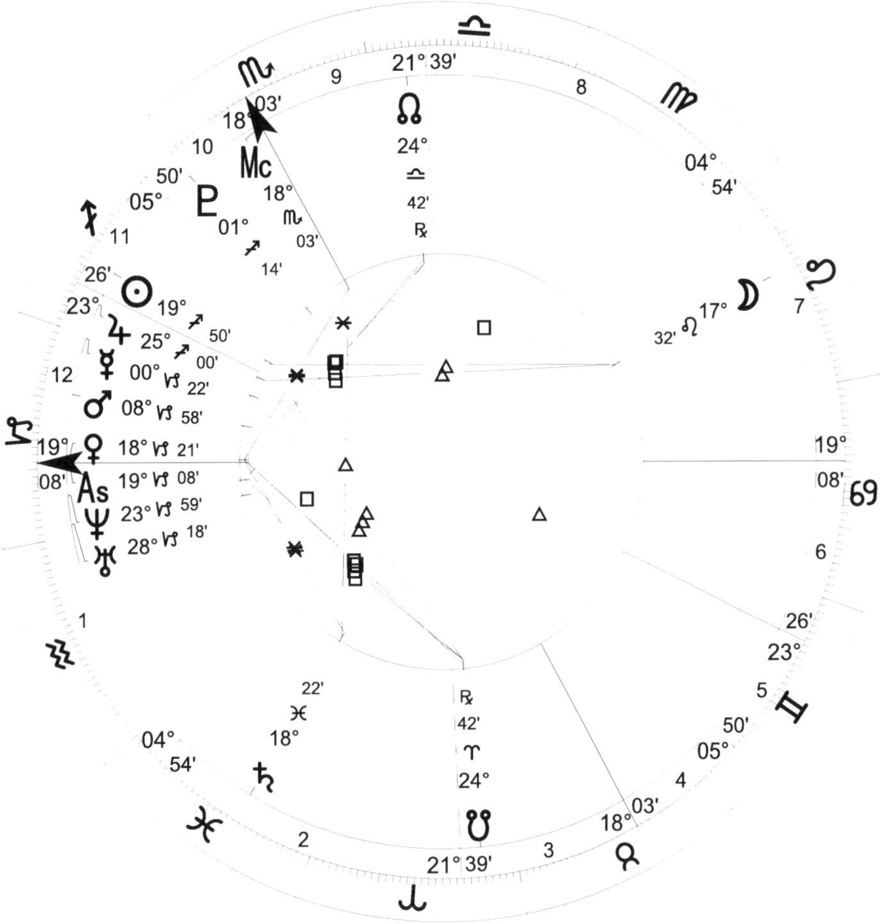

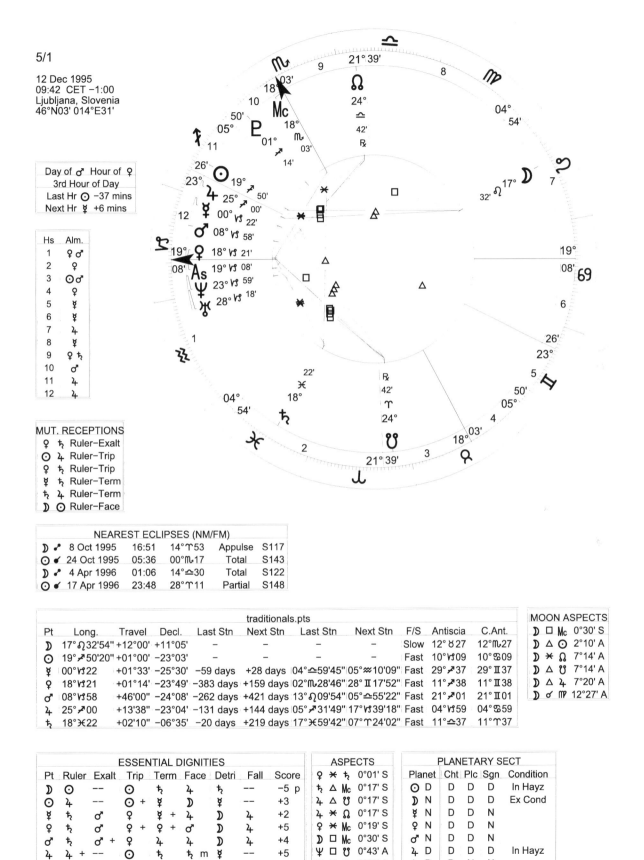

Day of ♂	Hour of ♀
3rd Hour of Day	
Last Hr ☉	−37 mins
Next Hr ☿	+6 mins

Hs	Alm.
1	♀♂
2	♀
3	☉♂
4	♀
5	☿
6	☿
7	♃
8	☿
9	♀♄
10	♂
11	♃
12	♃

MUT. RECEPTIONS	
♀ ♄	Ruler−Exalt
☉ ♃	Ruler−Trip
♀ ♄	Ruler−Trip
☿ ♄	Ruler−Term
♄ ♃	Ruler−Term
☽ ☉	Ruler−Face

NEAREST ECLIPSES (NM/FM)					
☽	8 Oct 1995	16:51	14°♈53	Appulse	S117
☉	24 Oct 1995	05:36	00°♏17	Total	S143
☽	4 Apr 1996	01:06	14°♎30	Total	S122
☉	17 Apr 1996	23:48	28°♈11	Partial	S148

traditionals.pts

Pt	Long.	Travel	Decl.	Last Stn	Next Stn	Last Stn	Next Stn	F/S	Antiscia	C.Ant.
☽	17°♌32'54"	+12°00'	+11°05'	–	–	–	–	Slow	12°♉27	12°♏27
☉	19°♐50'20"	+01°00'	−23°03'	–	–	–	–	Fast	10°♑09	10°♋09
☿	00°♑22	+01°33'	−25°30'	−59 days	+28 days	04°♎59'45"	05°♒10'09"	Fast	29°♐37	29°♊37
♀	18°♑21	+01°14'	−23°49'	−383 days	+159 days	02°♏28'46"	28°♊17'52"	Fast	11°♐38	11°♊38
♂	08°♑58	+46'00"	−24°08'	−262 days	+421 days	13°♌09'54"	05°♎55'22"	Fast	21°♐01	21°♊01
♃	25°♐00	+13'38"	−23°04'	−131 days	+144 days	05°♐31'49"	17°♑39'18"	Fast	04°♑59	04°♋59
♄	18°♓22	+02'10"	−06°35'	−20 days	+219 days	17°♓59'42"	07°♈24'02"	Fast	11°♎37	11°♈37

MOON ASPECTS	
☽ □ Mc	0°30' S
☽ △ ☉	2°10' A
☽ ⚹ ☊	7°14' A
☽ △ ☋	7°14' A
☽ △ ♃	7°20' A
☽ ☌ ♍	12°27' A

ESSENTIAL DIGNITIES

Pt	Ruler	Exalt	Trip	Term	Face	Detri	Fall	Score
☽	☉	--	☉	♄	♃	♄	--	−5 p
☉	♃	--	☉ +	☿	☽	☿	--	+3
☿	♄	♂	♀	☿ +	♃	☽	♃	+2
♀	♄	♂	♀ +	♀ +	♂	☽	♃	+5
♂	♄	♂ +	♀	♃	♃	☽	♃	+4
♃	♃ +	--	☉	♄	♄ m	☿	--	+5
♄	♃	♀	♀	☿	♃ m	☿	☿	−5 p

ASPECTS	
♀ ⚹ ♄	0°01' S
♄ △ Mc	0°17' S
♃ △ ☋	0°17' S
♃ ⚹ ☊	0°17' S
♀ ⚹ Mc	0°19' S
☽ □ Mc	0°30' S
♆ □ ☋	0°43' A
♆ □ ☊	0°43' A
♄ ⚹ As	0°44' S
As ⚹ Mc	1°04' S

PLANETARY SECT

Planet		Cht	Plc	Sgn	Condition
☉	D	D	D	D	In Hayz
☽	N	D	D	D	Ex Cond
☿	N	D	D	N	
♀	N	D	D	N	
♂	N	D	D	N	
♃	D	D	D	D	In Hayz
♄	D	D	N	N	

D=Diurnal, N=Nocturnal

5/2: AM I GOING TO WIN THIS SUNDAY'S LOTTERY?

29 June 1996 at 10:12 a.m., Ljubljana, Slovenia
Hour ruler: Sun

Although I was never fond of playing lottery (what with my poor natal H5!), I decided to try my luck one nice summer day. I bought a couple of lottery slips and eagerly awaited the outcome of the Sunday's draw. The huge amount of 35 million tolars (our then currency) was promised to the one who'd get all the seven numbers right.

To learn if I was to win some, I cast a horary chart for the above question, but after a quick glance at the chart my hope was gone. This is what I said to my husband whom I notified about my "investment" a couple of days before: *You know what, I'm not getting anything. But my horary chart also shows that nobody's getting the main prize this week.*

What chart indications made me come to this observation? My significators are Mercury, the ruler of H1, and the Moon (as my co-significator) while lottery winnings are signified by H5 which is ruled by Saturn. There are 3 planets in H5 (Jupiter, Neptune and Uranus), acting as co-significators of the winnings. Neither Mercury nor the Moon are in aspect with any of these planets. Mercury is even in Jupiter's detriment, therefore it's obvious that I can't hope to win a cent.

What about the second part of my assessment? Jupiter in H5 properly shows a high lottery stake to be won by someone who'd get all the seven numbers right, but because it is retrograde, the money "stays where it is". This is confirmed by the state of Saturn, ruler of H5, placed in H8 of loss, and essentially debilitated (fall).

Thus it was. The 35 million tolars stake was raised to 42 million after the next Sunday's draw, while I remained empty-handed.

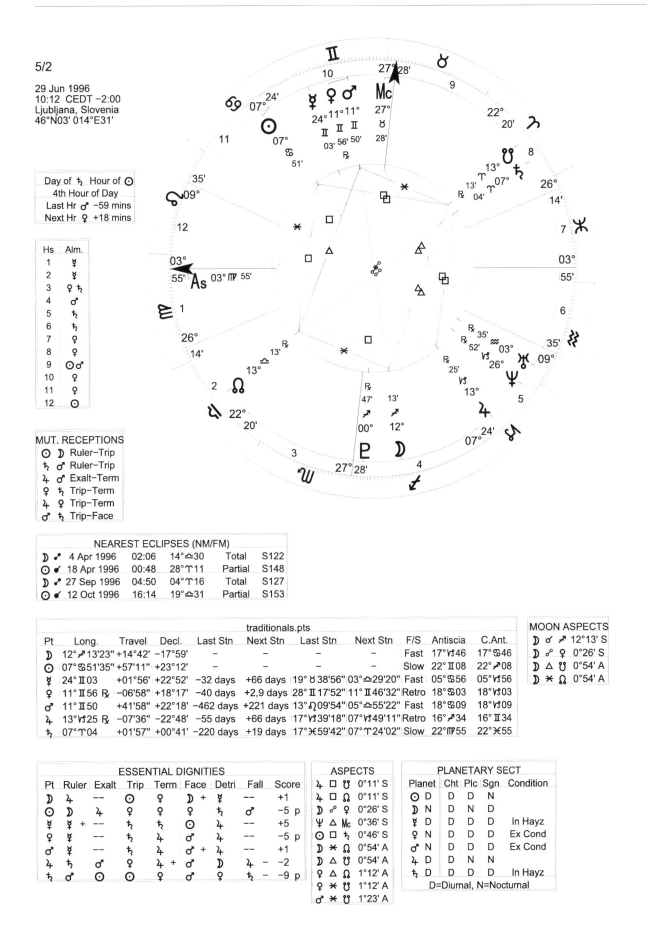

5/2

29 Jun 1996
10:12 CEDT −2:00
Ljubljana, Slovenia
46°N03' 014°E31'

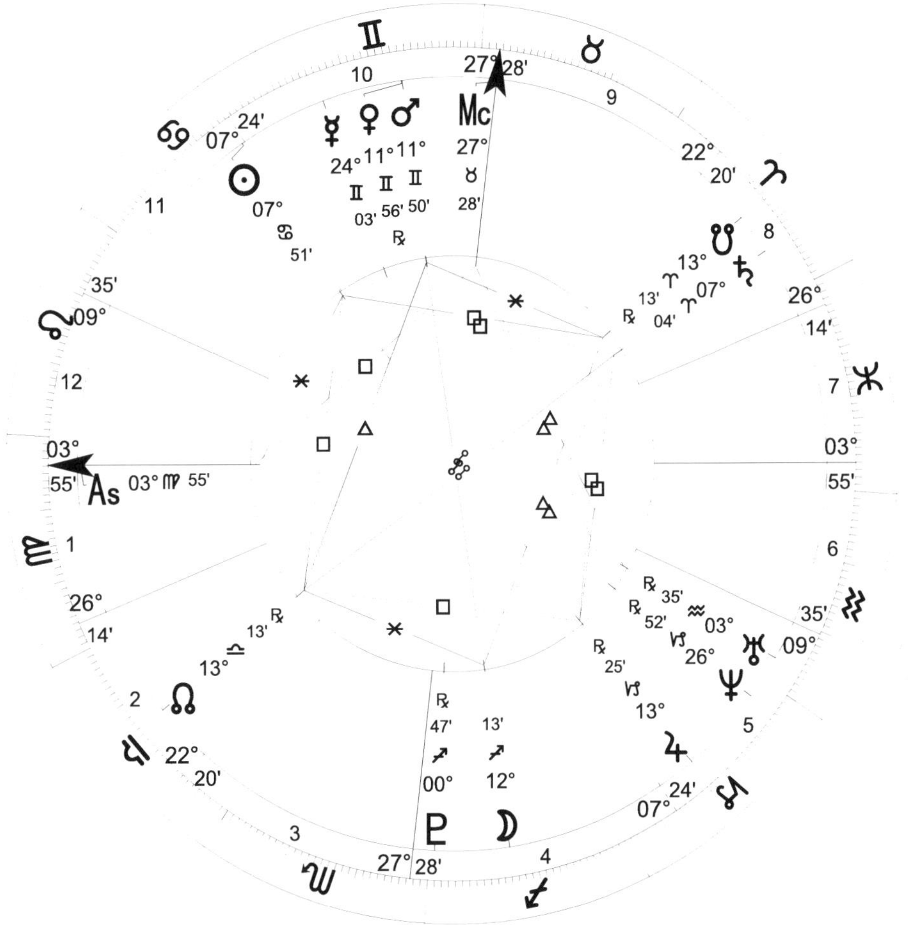

Day of ♄ Hour of ☉
4th Hour of Day
Last Hr ♂ −59 mins
Next Hr ♀ +18 mins

Hs	Alm.
1	☿
2	☿
3	♀ ♄
4	♂
5	♄
6	♄
7	♀
8	♀
9	☉♂
10	♀
11	♀
12	☉

MUT. RECEPTIONS		
☉	☽	Ruler−Trip
♄	♂	Ruler−Trip
♃	♂	Exalt−Term
♀	♄	Trip−Term
♃	♀	Trip−Term
♂	♄	Trip−Face

NEAREST ECLIPSES (NM/FM)					
☽	4 Apr 1996	02:06	14°♎30	Total	S122
☉	18 Apr 1996	00:48	28°♈11	Partial	S148
☽	27 Sep 1996	04:50	04°♈16	Total	S127
☉	12 Oct 1996	16:14	19°♎31	Partial	S153

traditionals.pts

Pt	Long.	Travel	Decl.	Last Stn	Next Stn	Last Stn	Next Stn	F/S	Antiscia	C.Ant.
☽	12°♐13'23"	+14°42'	−17°59'	–	–	–	–	Fast	17°♑46	17°♋46
☉	07°♋51'35"	+57'11"	+23°12'	–	–	–	–	Slow	22°♊08	22°♐08
☿	24°♊03	+01°56'	+22°52'	−32 days	+66 days	19°♉38'56"	03°♎29'20"	Fast	05°♋56	05°♑56
♀	11°♊56 ℞	−06'58"	+18°17'	−40 days	+2,9 days	28°♊17'52"	11°♊46'32"	Retro	18°♋03	18°♑03
♂	11°♊50	+41'58"	+22°18'	−462 days	+221 days	13°♌09'54"	05°♎55'22"	Fast	18°♋09	18°♑09
♃	13°♑25 ℞	−07'36"	−22°48'	−55 days	+66 days	17°♑39'18"	07°♑49'11"	Retro	16°♐34	16°♊34
♄	07°♈04	+01'57"	+00°41'	−220 days	+19 days	17°♓59'42"	07°♈24'02"	Slow	22°♍55	22°♓55

MOON ASPECTS			
☽	☌	♐	12°13' S
☽	☍	♀	0°26' S
☽	△	☋	0°54' A
☽	✶	☊	0°54' A

ESSENTIAL DIGNITIES

Pt	Ruler	Exalt	Trip	Term	Face	Detri	Fall	Score
☽	♃	--	☉	♀	☽ +	☿	--	+1
☉	☽	♃	♀	♀	♀	♄	♂	−5 p
☿	☿ +	--	♄	♄	☉	♃	--	+5
♀	☿	--	♄	♃	♂	♃	--	−5 p
♂	☿	--	♄	♃	♂ +	♃	--	+1
♃	♄	♂	♀	♃ +	♂	☽	♃ −	−2
♄	♂	☉	☉	♀	♂	♀	♄ −	−9 p

ASPECTS			
♃	□	☋	0°11' S
♃	□	☊	0°11' S
☽	☍	♀	0°26' S
Ψ	△	Mc	0°36' S
☉	□	♄	0°46' S
☽	✶	☊	0°54' A
☽	△	☋	0°54' A
♀	△	☊	1°12' A
♀	✶	☋	1°12' A
♂	✶	☋	1°23' A

PLANETARY SECT

Planet		Cht	Plc	Sgn	Condition
☉	D	D	D	N	
☽	N	D	N	D	
☿	D	D	D	D	In Hayz
♀	N	D	D	D	Ex Cond
♂	N	D	D	D	Ex Cond
♃	D	D	N	N	
♄	D	D	D	D	In Hayz

D=Diurnal, N=Nocturnal

5/3: SHOULD I ASK FOR A BANK LOAN, OR TRY TO GET IT FROM MY FATHER?

28 January, 1997 at 5:56 p.m. (17:56), Ljubljana, Slovenia
Hour ruler: Saturn

Our new house needed a facade, and I spent days thinking how to finance it. Circumstances were such that I had to provide for all such extra family expenses, and as the question suggests, I had two options. The more elegant (and less costly) option would be to borrow the money from my father, but he had already helped me a lot during the construction of the house, so I didn't want to mess with his money again. I was thinking if it wouldn't be better to take a bank loan.

I'm shown by the ascendant in Leo and its dispositor the Sun which is in Aquarius. The Sun's detriment shows my "poverty" (I was not really impoverished but I simply didn't have enough money for such a big expense) and a feeling of helplessness. The traditionally weak H6 where the Sun is located, confirms this and also shows the area of interest, related to the question: I needed the money to pay off the workers whom I had already asked to do the job. The tight separating opposition of my co-significator the Moon with Saturn aptly describes my emotional state at the time of the question: I was worried!

The main significator for the bank loan is Jupiter (as ruler of H8 with its cusp in Pisces) but we should also look at Neptune, the modern ruler of Pisces. My father is shown by H4 with the cusp in Scorpio, his significator being Mars, but also Pluto which is located in H4. His money is shown by H5 (2/4) which is ruled by Jupiter and occupied by the part of fortune and Mercury. (Venus is technically in H5 but on the cusp of H6 so it belongs to H6). Jupiter therefore has a dual role: it indicates both the bank loan as well as my father's money, besides being the natural significator of "big money".

Let's see then what is happening with Jupiter which is obviously the most important planet in this chart. It is in Aquarius in H6, with the Moon (my co-sigificator) separating from it by a trine. My main significator, the Sun, also separates from it (by conjunction) while not aspecting Neptune. There's obviously no connection between me and the bank loan – this part of the question therefore has no future.

We can see, however, that the first Moon's applying aspect is a conjunction with Mars which in the context of the question represents my father. In the process, the Moon translates light from Jupiter, from which it separates, to Mars to which it applies, so the answer is obvious: I should turn to my father! This is confirmed by the fact that my money (Mercury, H2 ruler) is in H5 which is 2/4 and therefore shows my father's money. My own funds are therefore closely linked to those of my father. It is true that his lending me his money would be more clearly shown by H5 ruler in H1 or H2 (like, father's money comes to me), but here you go, we can rarely have a "perfect" chart! The connection is still there and is confirmed by fortuna also occupying H5.

You'll also notice that the Moon, before conjuncting Mars, completes a sextile with Pluto, the modern ruler of Scorpio, which can be regarded as the co-significator of my father - especially since it occupies H4.

As the chart showed a strong inclination toward the possibility of getting a loan from my father, I plucked up the courage and asked him if he could lend me some money – much money, in fact. Of course, he said, he planned to give me the money anyway. Not lend, give. The funds were transferred to my account the next day and he, as promised, never asked me to give it back.

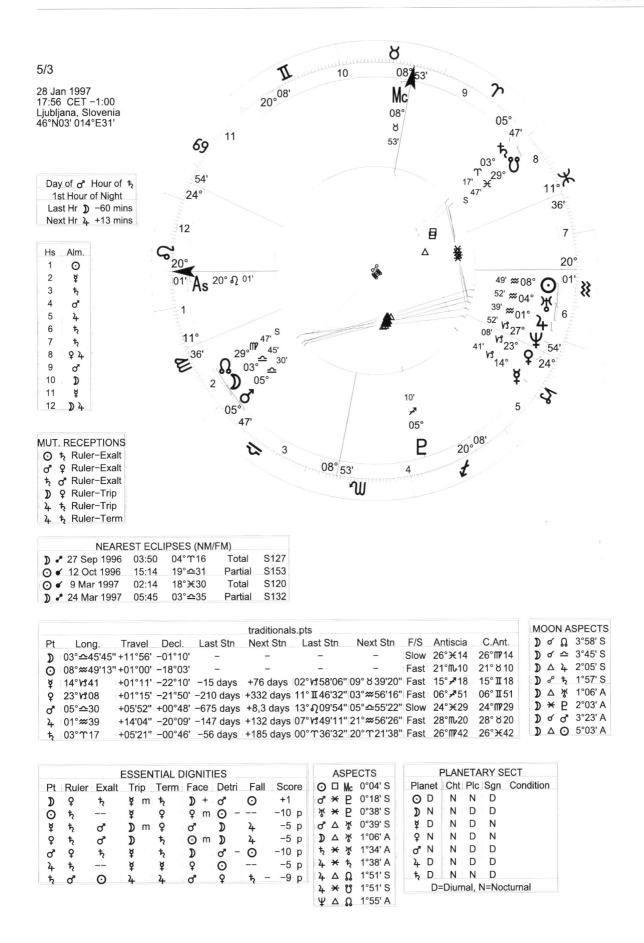

5/3

28 Jan 1997
17:56 CET −1:00
Ljubljana, Slovenia
46°N03' 014°E31'

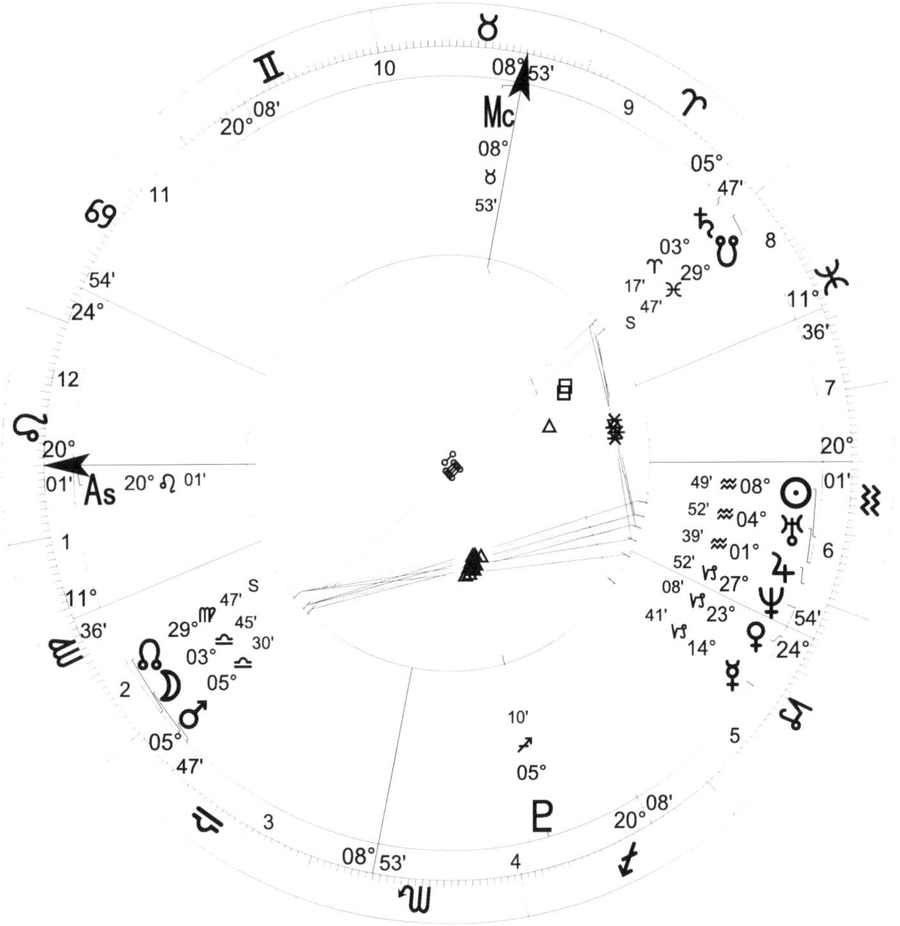

Day of ♂ Hour of ♄
1st Hour of Night
Last Hr ☽ −60 mins
Next Hr ♃ +13 mins

Hs	Alm.
1	☉
2	☿
3	♄
4	♂
5	♃
6	♄
7	♄
8	♀ ♃
9	♂
10	☽
11	☿
12	☽ ♃

MUT. RECEPTIONS		
☉	♄	Ruler-Exalt
♂	♀	Ruler-Exalt
♄	♂	Ruler-Exalt
☽	♀	Ruler-Trip
♃	♄	Ruler-Trip
♃	♄	Ruler-Term

NEAREST ECLIPSES (NM/FM)					
☽	27 Sep 1996	03:50	04°♈16	Total	S127
☉	12 Oct 1996	15:14	19°♎31	Partial	S153
☉	9 Mar 1997	02:14	18°♓30	Total	S120
☽	24 Mar 1997	05:45	03°♎35	Partial	S132

traditionals.pts

Pt	Long.	Travel	Decl.	Last Stn	Next Stn	Last Stn	Next Stn	F/S	Antiscia	C.Ant.
☽	03°♎45'45"	+11°56'	−01°10'	–	–	–	–	Slow	26°♓14	26°♍14
☉	08°♒49'13"	+01°00'	−18°03'	–	–	–	–	Fast	21°♏10	21°♉10
☿	14°♑41	+01°11'	−22°10'	−15 days	+76 days	02°♑58'06"	09°♉39'20"	Fast	15°♐18	15°♊18
♀	23°♑08	+01°15'	−21°50'	−210 days	+332 days	11°♊46'32"	03°♒56'16"	Fast	06°♐51	06°♊51
♂	05°♎30	+05'52"	+00°48'	−675 days	+8,3 days	13°♌09'54"	05°♎55'22"	Slow	24°♓29	24°♍29
♃	01°♒39	+14'04"	−20°09'	−147 days	+132 days	07°♑49'11"	21°♒56'26"	Fast	28°♏20	28°♉20
♄	03°♈17	+05'21"	−00°46'	−56 days	+185 days	00°♈36'32"	20°♈21'38"	Fast	26°♍42	26°♓42

MOON ASPECTS			
☽	☌	☊	3°58' S
☽	☌	♎	3°45' S
☽	△	♃	2°05' S
☽	☍	♄	1°57' S
☽	△	♅	1°06' A
☽	⚹	♇	2°03' A
☽	☌	♂	3°23' A
☽	△	☉	5°03' A

ESSENTIAL DIGNITIES

Pt	Ruler	Exalt	Trip	Term	Face	Detri	Fall	Score
☽	♀	♄	☿ m	♄	☽ +	♂	☉	+1
☉	♄	--	☿	♀	♀ m	☉ −	--	−10 p
☿	♄	♂	☽ m	♀	♂	☽	♃	−5 p
♀	♄	♂	☽	♄	☉ m	☽	♃	−5 p
♂	♀	♄	☿	♄	☽	♂ −	☉	−10 p
♃	♄	--	☿	☿	♀	☉	--	−5 p
♄	♂	☉	♃	♃	♂	♀	♄ −	−9 p

ASPECTS			
☉	□	Mc	0°04' S
♂	⚹	♇	0°18' S
♅	⚹	♇	0°38' S
♂	△	♅	0°39' S
☽	△	♅	1°06' A
♄	⚹	♅	1°34' A
♃	⚹	♄	1°38' A
♃	△	☊	1°51' S
♃	⚹	☋	1°51' S
♆	△	☊	1°55' A

PLANETARY SECT

Planet		Cht	Plc	Sgn	Condition
☉	D	N	N	D	
☽	N	N	D	D	
☿	D	N	D	N	
♀	N	N	D	N	
♂	N	N	D	D	
♃	D	N	D	D	
♄	D	N	N	D	

D=Diurnal, N=Nocturnal

5/4: WILL THE BANK GIVE US THE LOAN?

27 October, 2008 at 1:23 p.m. (13:23), Ljubljana, Slovenia
Hour ruler: Moon

The querent, an old client of mine, asked me whether he and his wife would get the bank loan for which they had recently applied.

The ascendant is in Aquarius and its ruler Saturn in Virgo in H7, but close to the cusp of H8 which shows his interest: a bank loan. This is confirmed by the Moon, his co-significator and at the same time hour ruler, located in H8. We can see that it is in an exact, although already separating conjunction with Mercury, the H8 ruler and therefore the significator of the loan. The Moon's next aspect is trine Neptune, the modern ruler of Pisces and thereby of H2, the cusp of which is in that sign. This is a good example of translation of light, although with the participation of a trans-Saturnian as a sign and house ruler. Let us remember: if the traditional sign rulers, acting as significators, do not indicate a completion of the matter (a positive result), but the modern sign rulers, placed in strong and fortunate houses, do, the completion of the matter is possible! In other words, trans-Saturnians as secondary sign rulers can, in certain circumstances, replace the traditional rulers, and this case certainly proves the point.

As so often, though, tradition has its say here too. Namely, the positive answer is also indicated by the strong mutual reception between Saturn (the querent) and Mercury (the loan): Saturn is in Mercury's domicile and exaltation while Mercury is in Saturn's exaltation, triplicity and face. There is, so to speak, a strong communication between the two planets, facilitating completion.

But let us explore this chart from yet another angle. Jupiter, the traditional ruler of H2 (the querent's finances), is in Capricorn in conjunction with the part of fortune, which is certainly promising, while the co-ruler of H2, Mars (which rules the intercepted sign of Aries) is in its own Scorpio in the fortunate H9, applying by sextile to Saturn, the querent's significator. The financial situation of the querent is thus clearly improving, although the said planets are not directly related to the subject matter, which is a loan. The acquisition of the loan is clearly shown by the already mentioned translation of light, combined with mutual receptions.

Given the fact that the Moon has just completed the conjunction with Mercury, from where it translates its light to Neptune, I said to the querent that the chart suggests a recent confirmation of their application.

It seems that you have already received the loan, I said.

That's actually true, he replied. *The bank has agreed to give us the loan, and now there's only the question of time, and I wonder when are we getting the contract and the money.*

Since there are only 21' between the Moon and Mercury, with the conjunction being in a cardinal sign and a succedent house, I asked him if the bank had approved of the loan a few days or less than half a week ago, which he confirmed. OK, we have the time unit, I thought, and told him that they would probably receive the loan in a little less than a month. Why? There are 3°41' from the Moon to the exact trine with Neptune, corresponding to a little less than four weeks.

And so it was, they received the loan after a little less than a month.

5/4

27 Oct 2008
13:23 CET −1:00
Ljubljana, Slovenia
46°N03' 014°E31'

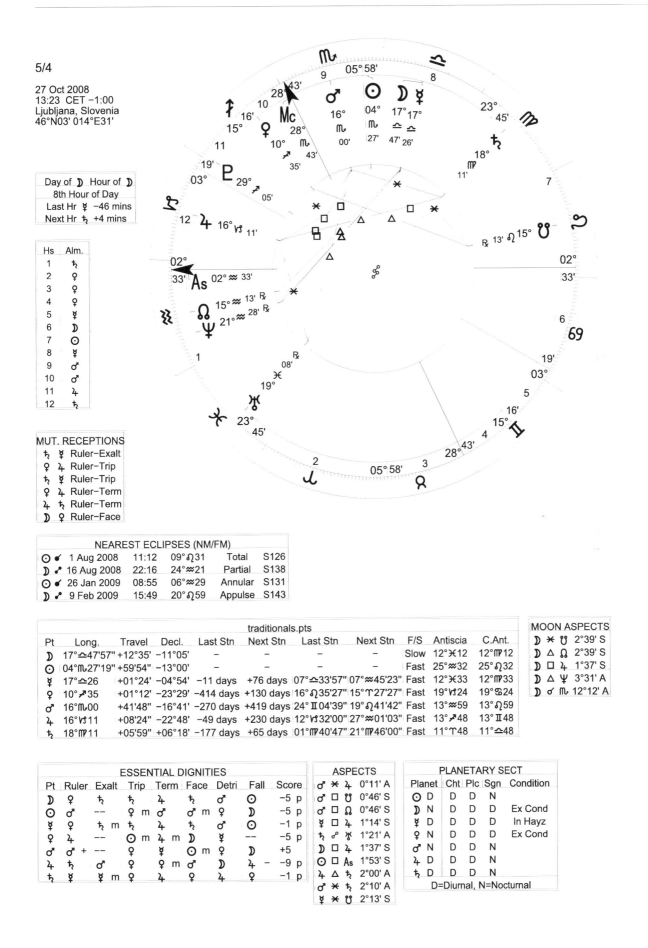

Day of ☽ Hour of ☽
8th Hour of Day
Last Hr ☿ −46 mins
Next Hr ♄ +4 mins

Hs	Alm.
1	♄
2	♀
3	♀
4	♀
5	☿
6	☽
7	☉
8	☿
9	♂
10	♂
11	♃
12	♄

MUT. RECEPTIONS		
♄	☿	Ruler-Exalt
♀	♃	Ruler-Trip
♄	☿	Ruler-Trip
♀	♃	Ruler-Term
♃	♄	Ruler-Term
☽	♀	Ruler-Face

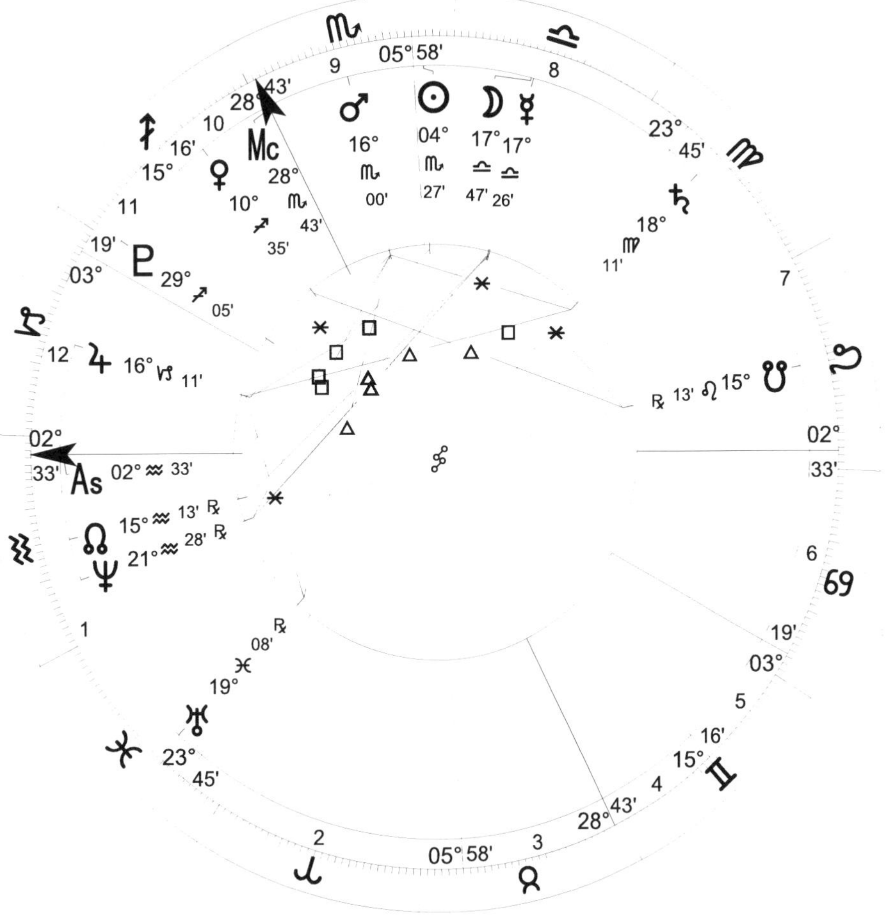

NEAREST ECLIPSES (NM/FM)					
☉ ☌	1 Aug 2008	11:12	09°♌31	Total	S126
☽ ☍	16 Aug 2008	22:16	24°♒21	Partial	S138
☉ ☌	26 Jan 2009	08:55	06°♒29	Annular	S131
☽ ☍	9 Feb 2009	15:49	20°♌59	Appulse	S143

traditionals.pts

Pt	Long.	Travel	Decl.	Last Stn	Next Stn	Last Stn	Next Stn	F/S	Antiscia	C.Ant.
☽	17°♎47'57"	+12°35'	−11°05'	–	–	–	–	Slow	12°♓12	12°♍12
☉	04°♏27'19"	+59'54"	−13°00'	–	–	–	–	Fast	25°♒32	25°♌32
☿	17°♎26	+01°24'	−04°54'	−11 days	+76 days	07°♎33'57"	07°♒45'23"	Fast	12°♓33	12°♍33
♀	10°♐35	+01°12'	−23°29'	−414 days	+130 days	16°♌35'27"	15°♈27'27"	Fast	19°♑24	19°♋24
♂	16°♏00	+41'48"	−16°41'	−270 days	+419 days	24°♊04'39"	19°♌41'42"	Fast	13°♒59	13°♌59
♃	16°♑11	+08'24"	−22°48'	−49 days	+230 days	12°♑32'00"	27°♒01'03"	Fast	13°♐48	13°♊48
♄	18°♍11	+05'59"	+06°18'	−177 days	+65 days	01°♍40'47"	21°♍46'00"	Fast	11°♈48	11°♎48

MOON ASPECTS			
☽	⚹	☋	2°39' S
☽	△	☊	2°39' S
☽	□	♃	1°37' S
☽	△	♆	3°31' A
☽	☌	♏	12°12' A

ESSENTIAL DIGNITIES

Pt	Ruler	Exalt	Trip	Term	Face	Detri	Fall	Score
☽	♀	♄	♄	♃	♄	♂	☉	−5 p
☉	♂	--	♀ m	♂	♂ m	♀	☽	−5 p
☿	♀	♄ m	♄	♃	♄	♂	☉	−1 p
♀	♃	--	☉ m	♃ m	☽	☿	--	−5 p
♂	♂ +	--	♀	☿	☉ m	♀	☽	+5
♃	♄	♂	♀	♀ m	♂	☽	♃ −	−9 p
♄	☿	☿ m	♀	♃	♀	♃	♀	−1 p

ASPECTS			
♂	⚹	♃	0°11' A
♂	□	☋	0°46' S
♂	□	☊	0°46' S
☿	□	♃	1°14' S
♄	☍	♅	1°21' A
☽	□	♃	1°37' S
☉	□	As	1°53' S
♃	△	♄	2°00' A
♂	⚹	♄	2°10' A
☿	⚹	☋	2°13' S

PLANETARY SECT

Planet		Cht	Plc	Sgn	Condition
☉	D	D	D	N	
☽	N	D	D	D	Ex Cond
☿	D	D	D	D	In Hayz
♀	N	D	D	D	Ex Cond
♂	N	D	D	N	
♃	D	D	D	N	
♄	D	D	D	N	

D=Diurnal, N=Nocturnal

MISSING ARTICLES

The greatest number of horary charts I do for myself refer to missing articles. These are usually keys or purses - things that I often mislay. But such questions are not easy, especially when answering people whose living environment we don't know well. If somebody asks us about the whereabouts of the glasses that he has mislaid somewhere in their house, a place we have never seen, our task is going to be more difficult than when searching for our own glasses that we misplaced in our house which we know well. In such cases, cooperation between the querent and the astrologer is essential.

In his **CHRISTIAN ASTROLOGY**, William Lilly gives elaborate rules for finding missing articles. He was so enthusiastic about this particular group of horaries that supposedly he used to entertain himself by ordering his servants to hide his things in the house (and around it) so that he could then search for them with horary astrology.

Lilly's most important instructions are given below. They are not literal transcriptions, as I have adjusted some of them so that they are more up-to-date, or have combined them with my own observations.

Since these rules are sometimes contradictory, they ask for a skillful approach. For example, if two indications in a chart suggest that the missing article is at home, whereas one shows it to be stolen, the article is probably at home.

These horaries ask for a lot of patience and for strict adherence to the interpretative rules, but they're also fun - and practice makes perfect!

SIGNIFICATORS

The querent is ruled by the ascendant, its ruler and the Moon, but the Moon is also the natural significator of missing articles and therefore plays a dual role in such questions. Generally, it is safe to give it priority as co-ruler of that which is missing, over co-ruling the querent.

Missing articles are ruled by H2 - by the ruler of that house and by any planets occupying it. If they belong to someone other than the querent, we make use of the derived houses: if, for example, the missing thing belongs to the querent's friend, it is ruled by H12 (2/11); if to his child, by H6 (2/5); if to his partner, by H8 (2/7), and so on.

In contemporary horary astrology, the belief that all missing (mislaid, stolen) objects are ruled by H2, is widely accepted. While the majority of stolen or missing articles have at least some value for us and as such they generally do belong to H2, some things that we own belong to different houses. Cars, bikes and other means of transport, for example, belong to H3. The stolen car is therefore described by H3, not by H2. H2 can reflect the value that the car has for us, and a good condition of H2 in a stolen car chart can help us get the car back, but H2 cannot play the role of the main significator of the car. This house also rules all kinds of documents and books, while learning material and study books fall into H9.

Missing animals are ruled by H6. This house also stands for work tools (plant, devices, machines).

H4 helps describe the environment of the lost or stolen thing. If we lose something in the house, we would look at the locations and directions of the sky suggested by the sign on H4 and its ruler - beside other indications, as will be shortly explained. Some astrologers use H4 to show the missing article, but this is erroneous. H4 is the house of real estate and all things "earthen", and as such it helps describe the place where the missing article hides, not its substance.

We must also examine the state of the natural significator of the lost thing. Mercury, for example, is the natural significator of keys, coins, books, documents; Venus of clothing, jewelry, ornamental items; Mars of knives, weapons, machines; Jupiter of money, high value items, religious objects and travel-related items (passports, for example); Saturn of leather or lead products, and of old, dark or heavy objects, agricultural tools, and the like; the Sun of gold (golden jewelry, for example), precious stones and other valuables; the Moon of glass, silver, pearls, or pale/white things – but the Moon stands for all missing things anyway!

Additional indications are given by the part of fortune and its dispositor.

But which significator is the strongest? We must let the chart guide us! If, for example, we have lost a document (an invoice, a contract or a magazine) and the cusp of H3 is in Gemini, the domicile of Mercury which is also the natural significator of all kinds of papers, this document is best described by H3. If, however, it is a valuable and important document (passport, for example) and there is Jupiter in H2, the strongest significator would be Jupiter, not the H2 ruler.

WHERE IS IT?

To find the missing article, we must skillfully combine the indications given by the H2 planet/s, the Moon, the part of fortune, H4, the ascendant and the eventual natural significators. The main criteria for finding the location are the quality of signs and directions of the sky, suggested by all of the above mentioned chart factors.

If we don't know whether the missing article is **at home or not**, we look at where the main significators (H2 planets, the Moon and the part of fortune) are. If at least one of them is in an angular house (particularly in H1, H4 and H10, whereas H7 can indicate theft), the thing is probably at home, not stolen or lost somewhere outside. Experience has taught me that the focus should be on the Moon and the planets, the part of fortune being less reliable in this respect. It is also possible that all significators are in succedent and cadent houses, but the missing thing is still at home; in such cases, the probability of finding that which has been lost, is indicated by other chart features: for example, the application of the H1 ruler to the ruler of the missing item, a retrograde significator (a very sure indication of return), or all the significators in the same sign or at least in the same quadrant.

As for the directions, tradition teaches that the Moon shows the direction by its position in the houses whereas the planets by their position in the signs – as listed below. But my experience has taught me that planets, in this sense, often act as the Moon; they show the direction according to the four cardinal points of the sky, depending on their house positions.

Due to a plethora of factors, the search for the missing is often difficult. Significators can point to the direction of a room (for example to the north, south, east or west of the house), or to the direction within a room (on the northern, southern, eastern or western wall, for example), or to the quality/characteristics of a location outside of home.

Understand that the basic and most dependable indicator of location is the Moon.

The **directions** of the sky shown by the position of the **Moon** (or planets, but mainly the Moon) in the houses, are:
- H1: east (E)
- H2: east-north-east (ENE)
- H3: north-north-east (NNE)
- H4: north (N)
- H5: north-north-west (NNW)
- H6: west-west-north (WWN)
- H7: west (W)
- H8: west-west-south (WWS)
- H9: south-south-west (SSW)
- H10: south (S)
- H11: south-south-east (SSE)
- H12: east-east-south (EES)

The **directions** of the sky, suggested by the **signs** (occupied by the planets, except for the Moon), are:
- Aries: east (E)
- Taurus: south-south-east (SSE)
- Gemini: west-west-south (WWS)
- Cancer: north (N)
- Leo: east-east-north (EEN)
- Virgo: south-south-west (SSW)
- Libra: west (W)
- Scorpio: north-north-east (NNE)
- Sagittarius: east-east-south (EES)
- Capricorn: south (S)
- Aquarius: west-west-north (WWN)
- Pisces: north-north-west (NNW)

As already mentioned, the above directions also apply when the missing is not at home, but somewhere outside. They are helpful in locating not only lost objects, but also runaway pets, missing people, stolen cars and similar.

Lilly examined directions according to where the majority of the following significators were:
- the ascending sign
- the ascendant's ruler sign
- the sign on the H4 cusp
- the sign of the H4 ruler
- Moon's sign
- the sign on the H2 cusp
- the sign of the H2 ruler
- the sign of the part of fortune

The problem with this system is that numerous indications usually give conflicting results. We will find the lost thing faster and easier if we rely on the main significators. I have found that the Moon and the main significator (the H2 ruler or the planet occupying it) are the most helpful.

As for the indications shown by H2 and H4, students often ask what is more relevant, as per location: the cusp of the house or the sign of its dispositor? My experience is that with H4, the sign on the cusp is more relevant, whereas with H2, ruling that which is missed, we must give priority to the sign occupied by the house ruler. Taking into account the two factors, of course, complicates the search, but it can also simplify it if both the sign and its ruler are in the same element or at least in related ones. Earth or water is lower, air or fire is higher, and similar.

Locations shown by houses

Significators in:
- **angular houses** show that the missing is in the vicinity of the owner - most probably at home - and that he will soon get it back. The exception is H7 which can indicate that the article has been stolen.
- **succedent houses** show that the missing is a little farther, but not too far. The exception is H2 which rules the missing thing itself, and this placement usually shows that the missing article is safe - sometimes even located where it should be, or where it is most often stored.
- **cadent houses** show that the thing is probably far away and might even never be found - if confirmed by other indications. The exception is H3 which shows immediate surroundings (garden, neighbourhood), or a car parked outside of the house or in a garage.

A word of caution: The houses are angular, succedent and cadent only in the radical (radix) chart! The derived angular, succedent and cadent houses do not exist. If, for example, that which is missing belongs to our child, its significator in the child's derived H10, H4, H7 or H1 is not angular.

Locations shown by individual houses:

- H1 – in close vicinity to the querent, or in that part of the house where he spends most of his time; same if the significator is in the same sign as the querent's ruler;
- H2 - where it should be, or where we often place (store) it;
- H3 - in the car, in the vicinity of the house (in the neighbourhood), at school, in the library, or with our brother, sister, cousin or neighbour;
- H4 - in the oldest part of the house (if such part exists), in the room of the elderly or in the dad's room (or suitcase, wardrobe etc.); could also be in the house of parents or some other ancestors.
- H5 - in a child's room, at a gym, in a casino, restaurant, club, shop, park, sports playground, etc.;
- H6 – in a workroom, in the utility room, in the pet's corner; at a clinic, etc.;
- H7 - in the partner's room or in their wardrobe, bag and the like (not applicable in cases of theft);
- H8 - in the garbage, or in a place where we keep useless, worn-out things;
- H9 – far away, abroad, in a travel bag, in a motorhome; at the faculty, in the church or at some other ceremonial place, etc.;
- H10 – if at home, it can be in a workroom or a home office, in the living room or in the room closest to the entrance of the house; if outside, it can be at one's place of work;
- H11 – if at home, it can be in the most social part of the house, say the reception or the living room; at a friend's place, at a community center, in a club;
- H12 – if at home, it can be in the bedroom; far away, usually well hidden.

Locations shown by planets (as H2 or H4 rulers, or as the Moon's dispositors):

- Saturn: cold and dark places (basements, cellars, garages, storage rooms, etc.);
- Jupiter: close to wood, wooden floors, or where we store valuables;
- Mars: places close to sources of heat (stoves, fireplaces, chimneys, boiler rooms, etc.); close to metal or iron;
- Sun: the living room, the reception area; places where we feel most creative;
- Venus: rooms inhabited or visited by women, bedrooms, wardrobes, dresses, cosmetics corners, women's handbags;
- Mercury: offices, bookshelves, school bags, places where small items are kept, etc.;
- Moon: kitchen, bathroom, laundry, places near water;
- Uranus: places near computers and TVs;
- Neptune: places where medicines or alcoholic beverages are stored;
- Pluto: toilets, dustbins, trash cans, drainage gutters, sewerage etc.

Locations shown by signs

For a detailed description of the locations shown by individual signs, see also Zodiacal Signs in the Theory part of this book (p. 42-48). Generally speaking, negative signs (earth and water) stand for lower places (ground floor, floor, lower shelves in cabinets and drawers, etc.) while positive signs (fire and air) indicate higher places (upper floors, higher areas in a room, upper shelves etc.).

- **Fire signs** – (close to) warm and hot places (furnaces, stoves, radiators, fireplaces, chimneys) and to walls, medium height in a room (house, wardrobe and the like); basic direction is East. **Aries**: newly developed areas, or wilderness / **Leo**: playgrounds, cinemas, theatres, clubs and all things or places central / **Sagittarius**: wooded areas, remote places.
- **Earth signs** – all kinds of storage places (shelves, cabinets, wardrobes, safes, wallets, bags etc.); close to the ground, low places, where there is soil, mud, etc.; basic direction is South. **Taurus**: garden, orchard, fields, pastures / **Virgo**: utility, drawers, small containers / **Capricorn**: low, dark, cold and old places.
- **Water signs** – places where water is used (bathrooms, toilets, kitchens), and damp places; close to some

water pipe or tube; near the ground; rivers, streams, ponds, wells; basic direction is North. **Cancer**: kitchen, nursery / **Scorpio**: toilets; marshy, swampy, uninhabited land; dustbins, dumping ground / **Pisces**: bathrooms, (home) pharmacy; seaside, coastline.

- **Air signs** - higher areas, upper floors; bright, airy rooms or rooms with views (with large windows, balconies, etc.); at some entrance or the beginning part of rooms etc.; places where people gather (classrooms, pubs, restaurants, libraries, shops, buses etc.). Basic direction is West. **Gemini**: bookshelves, schools, study rooms, shops, libraries / **Libra**: cinemas, theatres, pubs / **Aquarius**: close to electrical and telecommunications equipment (computers, TV's); hilly, airy, open areas.

Locations shown by modality

- **Cardinal signs** - higher areas, upper rooms, construction sites, new buildings, hilly landscapes. The significator of the missing thing in a cardinal sign can also show that it is close to the owner.
- **Fixed signs** - forests, parks, low places, on the grounds or close to the ground, hidden places.
- **Mutable signs** – covered (enclosed, sheltered) areas, cabinets, built-in cabinets, rooms within rooms, doorways, lobbies, drainage gutters and (sometimes) places near water.

The sign and house indications should be carefully combined. If, for example, a significator is in H8 in Virgo or Taurus, the earth signs showing drawers and storerooms, there is more chance that the thing will not end in garbage, as if it was in H8 in Scorpio, the sign standing for rubbish, drains, sewerage and similar.

The significator on the cusp of a house, or in the first or last degrees of a sign indicate that the thing is hidden behind or under some other thing, or that it is close to some boundary like a wall, a door, a window and the like. Similarly, a significator in the middle of a sign or a house shows that the missing thing is in the middle of something (like in the middle of a room, a shelf, a garden etc.).

WILL IT BE FOUND?

Note: With any reference to H2 know that this can also be replaced by other houses – with H3, for example, for missing cars or bicycles, or with any derived houses when using the turned chart.

The main indications of a find are:
- a harmonious applying aspect of the significator of the missing article with the significator of the owner (querent) or with the Moon;
- significator of the missing article retrograde;
- a retrograde planet in H2;
- significators of the querent and the missing thing in a strong mutual reception, or connected by means of translation or collection of light; the translating or collecting planet can show someone who finds the thing and returns it to the owner;
- the significator or the Moon in an angular house (especially close to the angles). *Caution*: H7 is the least reliable here, as it may indicate that the thing is in the hands of the thief - stolen!;
- H2 ruler in H1;
- H1 ruler in H2, but probably only after a long search;
- the Moon void-of-course. *Caution*: we must be careful in such cases, as this can sometimes show that nothing can be done to help in the case! But most often, this shows that the missing thing is where we left it, or that it did not go into foreign hands.
- If the significator of the missing article is in mutual reception with any planet, it is very possible that the thing has been moved somewhere and that we will not find it where we had lost it. If it's also retrograde, we will almost certainly find it – and probably when least expected.

Additional (less reliable) indications are:
- application of the Moon to any retrograde planet;
- any retrograde planet in conjunction with any angle - especially if this planet is also the hour ruler or the dispositor of the main significator or of the Moon;
- the application of the Moon or the H2 ruler to a planet in H2 or to the part of fortune;
- the application of the Moon to its dispositor;
- an applying sextile or trine of the Moon to the Sun;
- Sun in H1 (except in Libra and Aquarius);
- Moon in H1 or in a sextile or trine with the ascendant;
- Venus, Jupiter, the part of fortune or the north node well placed in H1, H2, H10 or H4;
- Moon in the terms of Venus or Jupiter;
- Venus or Jupiter in aspect with the ascendant;
- a harmonious application of the H1 ruler to the Sun, the H10 ruler or the Moon's dispositor;
- Sun and Moon above the horizon.

That the thing is "safe" (preserved in its entirety, undamaged and/or safely stored), is also shown by the overall well-being of its main significator, that is, by its essential and accidental strength or by its harmonious aspects with benefics. An afflicted significator suggests the opposite, of course: the thing is damaged, broken, stolen, and such. But sometimes, such a state of the significator simply shows that the lost thing is old, worn-out, or has little worth for some other reason.

The querent is **unlikely to find** the missing thing if:
- none of the above indications applies;
- both the Sun and the Moon are under the Earth (below the horizontal axis);
- the Moon and the H2 ruler are in cadent houses or far away from the owner's significator. Note, though: if we are sure that the missing thing has been lost somewhere in the house and that nobody could have stolen it, then we can find it even if its significator is in a cadent house, except that the search can take much longer;
- the Moon or the H2 ruler are in H7 or H8, or in an aspect with the H7 or H8 ruler (the thing might be stolen);
- Saturn, Mars or the south node in H2 (or the goods can be found, but are damaged), unless Saturn or Mars are retrograde or strongly fortified (in this case, the goods are not damaged);
- the cusp of H2, the H2 ruler and the Moon are afflicted - especially with the ascendant also afflicted;
- the Moon or the H2 ruler are combust (unless retrograde);
- the Moon or the H2 ruler separate from an aspect with their dispositor.

HOW DID IT GET LOST?

It s always helpful to learn how – in what circumstances – the missing thing got lost. Indicative are those planets from which either the Moon, the ascendant ruler or the significator of the missing thing separates (by conjunction or an aspect). If you're unsure of which planet to choose, give priority to the most recent separation – which is, in a large majority of cases, that of the Moon. If this planet is:
- **Saturn**: because of the owner's forgetfulness. If, in case of a runaway pet, its significator or the Moon separates from a square or opposition of Saturn, it may have escaped because the owner treated it badly or because something frightened it;
- **Jupiter**: due to absence of mind, carelessness, negligence, gullibility, or during some social gathering or festivity;
- **Mars**: due to haste or anger, or during a quarrel; the thing can be stolen or even burnt; a missing pet could have been hurt or even killed in an accident – especially in case of disharmonious aspects;

273

- **Sun**: the loss is associated with the father, husband or an authority;
- **Venus**: during partying, dancing, love-making, gambling or drinking, or the loss is associated with a woman;
- **Mercury**: while travelling, driving, shopping, negotiating or chatting; note that Mercury is also the natural significator of thieves!
- **Uranus**: because of a sudden unexpected event that shocked/ confused shocked/confused the owner, or make a missing pet run away.
- **Neptune**: due to forgetfulness, confusion, senility, drunkenness or indolence; the loss could also be related to medicines or drugs.
- **Pluto**: due to a threat, *force majeure* (a fatal obstacle or an accident), theft or robbery. But if the missing thing has been mislaid somewhere in the house, Pluto can indicate that we (or someone else) accidentally dumped it in the garbage or put it in a dark, solitary place.

If the missing thing was stolen, the planet from which the Moon last separated (by a conjunction or an aspect) describes the person who stole it. The thief is normally shown by an angular peregrine planet or by the ruler of H7, but logic tells us that the thing went away with the person represented by the planet with which the Moon was last in aspect. All indications should be carefully combined.

Recently, someone posted an example of a missing purse. She was referring to the question of her friend who had been searching for his deceased mother's purse. He had been living alone with his mother until her death several months ago. Venus, the significator of the purse, was in H8 while the Moon's last aspect was an opposition with Neptune, located in H4 (home). Seeing that the orb was 3.5 degrees and the Moon was very slow on that day, I asked her if there was someone in the house about four weeks ago who could be described by Neptune? She enquired at her friend and got back with the reply that yes, at about that time, her friend's drunken friend spent a night in the house. Alleluia, we found the answer! The combination of Neptune and H8 (thief's property) suggested that the purse was gone with that person. The case, unfortunately, never got an epilogue – Saturn was in H1, a warning about the inefficiency of the case - but the link nevertheless seemed fascinating.

WHEN WILL IT BE FOUND?

Horaries often indicate when the article, person or pet had gone missing, would be found or would return. Isn't this fascinating? If a horary chart can tell the location (of a missing thing, pet, person), why can't we find them immediately? We do only if it's "in the stars"! As laid out in the beginning chapters of the Theory part, horary astrology proves that our "free will" is nothing compared to the will of cosmos.

In addition to what you can learn about timing on p. 132 - 135, the following rules should be observed:
- significators in quick motion (fast) - soon;
- at least one significator angular - soon;
- if the application is by a retrograde motion, the find will be sudden and unexpected;
- significators in cardinal signs indicate the shortest time, in fixed signs the longest time and in movable signs something in between.

IS IT STOLEN?

How do we know that the missing thing has been stolen, not just misplaced or lost? If your car is not where you left it, nor was it dragged away by a tow truck, it is probably clear that it has been stolen. If a thief grabbed your handbag and ran away with it, the case is even clearer. In such cases, the questions usually asked by the querents, are: *Will I get it back? When? Where's the thief? Who's the thief?* And so on.

The significator of the thief is usually the H7 ruler (radix or derived), especially if peregrine and placed in one of the (radix!) angular houses (H1, H10, H4, H7), or in H2. If the H7 ruler is not peregrine, it can still signify the thief, but the thief in such cases will more probably be shown by any peregrine planet in an angle. If there're no peregrine angular planets, the thief can be shown by the planetary hour ruler - especially if this planet is also the ruler of H7. The natural significator of thieves is Mercury.

The stolen goods are signified by H2 – that is, by its ruler or a planet occupying the house, and by the Moon.

The place where the stolen thing is at the time of the question, is described by the H2 planets, by the Moon and by H4 and its ruler.

But often, of course, we do not know if the thing is stolen. A couple of days ago, my husband noticed that his wallet was not where it should be. The night before, he came back late from a concert. *Where is my wallet*, he asked me. *Is it stolen or have I just misplaced it?*

Main indications of theft:
- the significator of the missing thing, or the Moon, in H7 or H8;
- the significator of the thief (a peregrine planet or the H7 ruler) in H1 or H2;
- the Moon or the significator of the missing thing in the nearest aspect with the significator of the thief;
- the ascendant ruler in an aspect with the significator of the thief.

Note: A theft can be shown by an applying OR a separating aspect of the significator of the missing thing with the significator of the thief. If the aspect is separating, this of course means that the theft has already occurred, but if applying, it can mean either that the theft is yet to occur (for example, the wallet has fallen out of your pocket and waiting for someone to pick it up and take it with them), or that there is little chance of getting it back – because the thief is going to keep it, of course.

Additional indications of theft:
- the H2 ruler and Moon in H7, in a sextile or trine (although loose) with the H7 ruler;
- the Moon as the ascendant ruler in H1 or close to the ascendant, with the Sun as the H2 ruler in H10 in aspect with the H7 ruler, with the latter squaring or opposing the Moon;
- the Moon as the H7 ruler in an aspect with the ascendant ruler;
- the Moon separating from the H2 ruler with a square or an opposition;
- the Moon as H2 ruler separating from the ruler of the sign it occupies;
- a peregrine planet or the H7 ruler or Mercury applying to Jupiter or to the H2 ruler ("absolutely stolen and thief came with the intention to steal");
- the H2 ruler or Jupiter applying to a peregrine planet or to the H7 ruler or to Mercury (the thing offered itself to the thief, he stole it easily);
- the significator of the thief applying to the ascendant ruler with a square or an opposition;
- the significator of the thief in conjunction, square or opposition with the Moon or the ruler of its sign or term, or with the ruler of H2, the part of fortune or its dispositor;
- a planet in H1 in square or opposition with the significator of the thief;
- a peregrine planet in H1;
- a peregrine planet in aspect with the Moon, especially in conjunction, square or opposition;
- the ascendant ruler peregrine;
- the H7 ruler peregrine;
- the significator of the thief in conjunction, square or opposition with the ascendant ruler.
- the Moon in an aspect with Saturn, Mars, any planet in a cadent house, or the H8 ruler.

THE THIEF'S GENDER

The thief is **male** if the majority of the following planets are male:
- hour ruler;
- H7 ruler (or a planet therein);
- Moon's dispositor;
- the planet to which the Moon applies.

Also, if the thief's significator is in a male quadrant (in H10, H11, H12, H4, H5 or H6), or if it's an eastern planet (is ahead of the Sun).

The thief is **female** if the majority of the following planets are female:
- hour ruler;
- H7 ruler (or a planet therein);
- Moon's dispositor;
- the planet to which the Moon applies.

Also, if the thief's significator is in a female quadrant (in H9, H8, H7, H3, H2 or H1) or is western (behind the Sun).

THE THIEF'S AGE

The thief's age according to his significator:
- elderly: Saturn
- of late middle-age: Jupiter
- young to middle-aged: Mars or Sun
- young: Mercury or Venus
- a teenager or a child: Mercury or Moon

Although the Moon tends to signify younger people, the ages that it is associated with, depend on its phases: the first quarter indicates youth, the full moon middle age, the last quarter old age, and the intermediate stages intermediate periods.

Any significator as an eastern planet (that is, ahead of the Sun in the order of signs) reveals a younger thief whereas as a western planet (behind the Sun) an older one.

See also the corresponding chapters in the Theory part of this book.

6/1: WHERE ARE MY DAUGHTER'S SLIPPERS?

22 March 1994 at 8:43 a.m., Ljubljana, Slovenia
Hour ruler: Venus, POF 27 Vi

We had been missing my daughter's slippers for several days. She's shown by Virgo on H5 cusp (this sign ascended at her birth) and with Mercury in Pisces in H11. Her slippers are shown by the radix H6 (2/5 – the daughter's belongings). Since the cusp of H5 is in Libra, it is ruled by Venus which is placed in Aries on cusp of H12. As we can see, Venus is the hour ruler, so it well describes the subject of my interest. Slippers are also ruled by the Moon, the natural significator of missing things, and Jupiter, the planet occupying H6. Jupiter's color is blue, and slippers really were dark blue with white stripes. Their main significator Venus in detriment shows that they were not new; they were worn and a little torn on the sides.

Is there a clear indication in the chart that we'd find them? Yes, a retrograde planet in H6 (slippers). A retrograde ruler of the house ruling the missing item, or a retrograde planet in this house, are among the most reliable indicators for a finding or return. Adding to that, both Venus and the Moon accelerate in motion and are without afflictions while the Moon is also void-of-course and strong in its own sign. All of this points to the probability of the find.

But where to look for them? Venus is in a cadent house, which could indicate that the missing item is far from the owner, but I was convinced that no one took the slippers out. Moreover, Venus is in a cardinal sign which indicates proximity, and in the same quadrant as Mercury, ruling me and my daughter. These are additional testimonies that the slippers are not far from the owner. Both Venus and the Sun, the H4 ruler (which, as we know, helps describing the location) are in Aries, a fire sign. Fire signs indicate places near furnaces, chimneys and the like, or close to a wall, and central locations. The Sun as the H4 ruler suggests a living room or a reception room. There was no reception room in our house, so we're left with the living room. As my daughter was spending most of her time in the living room, slippers could well be hiding somewhere in there. Venus in H12 indicates that they are stuck away somewhere, or well hidden, but because the planet is right on the cusp, they must be at some edge or a border. The Moon in the watery Cancer, on the other hand, links it to a moist place or to a location close to a source of water or a water container. Venus, the Sun and the Moon all in cardinal signs clearly show a higher, above-the-ground position (middle height).

Equipped with the horary chart indications I undertook a thorough search of the living room, focusing on higher places close to the walls, and soon found them on one of the radiators. Radiators are hot and water runs through their pipes – a telltale combination of fire and water elements! They were well hidden behind the curtain (Venus on cusp of a house) which was just long enough to cover them, and exactly in the middle of the radiator – and Venus is right in the middle of Aries! As already said, I found them quite quickly, as indicated by the majority of the significators in cardinal signs (a quick recovery).

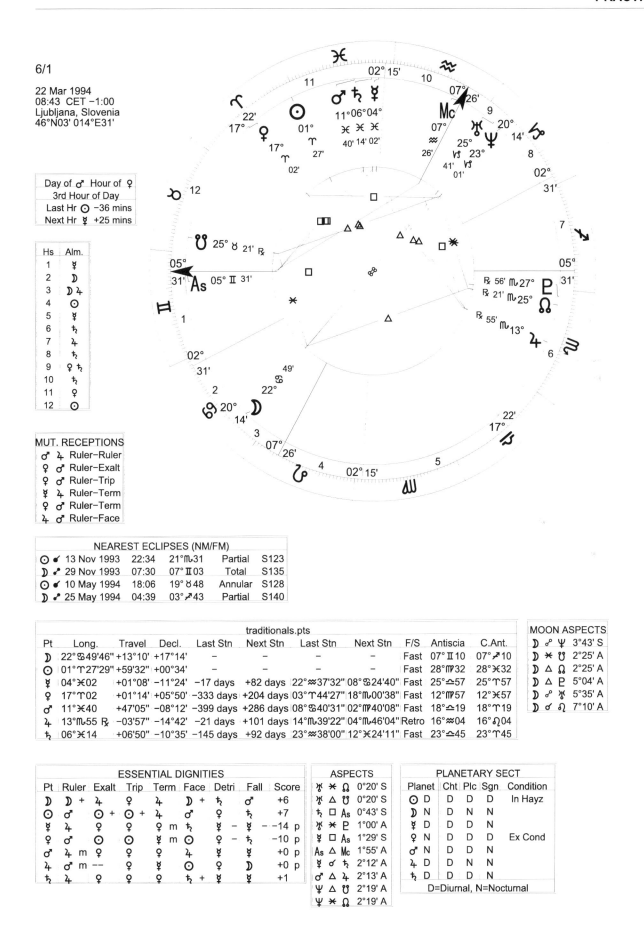

6/1

22 Mar 1994
08:43 CET −1:00
Ljubljana, Slovenia
46°N03' 014°E31'

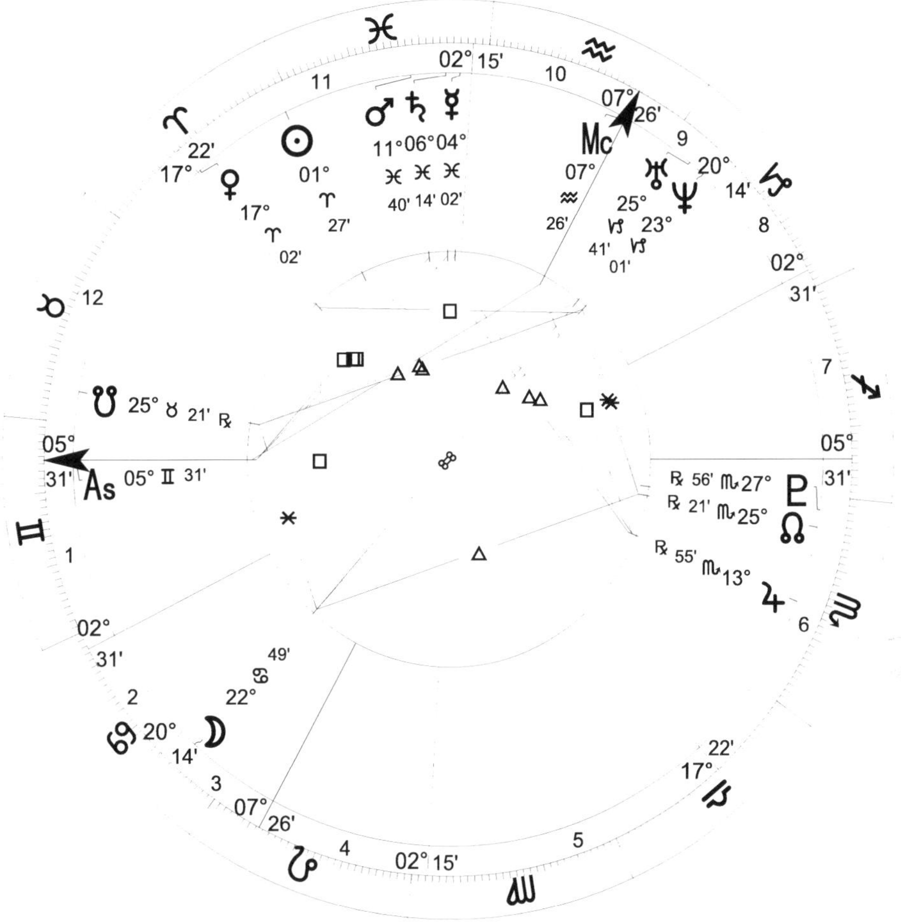

Day of ♂ Hour of ♀
3rd Hour of Day
Last Hr ☉ −36 mins
Next Hr ☿ +25 mins

Hs	Alm.
1	☿
2	☽
3	☽ ♃
4	☉
5	☿
6	♄
7	♃
8	♄
9	♀ ♄
10	♄
11	♀
12	☉

MUT. RECEPTIONS
♂ ♃ Ruler–Ruler
♀ ♂ Ruler–Exalt
♀ ♂ Ruler–Trip
☿ ♃ Ruler–Term
♀ ♂ Ruler–Term
♃ ♂ Ruler–Face

NEAREST ECLIPSES (NM/FM)					
☉ ☌	13 Nov 1993	22:34	21°♏31	Partial	S123
☽ ☍	29 Nov 1993	07:30	07°♊03	Total	S135
☉ ☌	10 May 1994	18:06	19°♉48	Annular	S128
☽ ☍	25 May 1994	04:39	03°♐43	Partial	S140

traditionals.pts

Pt	Long.	Travel	Decl.	Last Stn	Next Stn	Last Stn	Next Stn	F/S	Antiscia	C.Ant.
☽	22°♋49'46"	+13°10'	+17°14'	–	–	–	–	Fast	07°♊10	07°♐10
☉	01°♈27'29"	+59'32"	+00°34'	–	–	–	–	Fast	28°♍32	28°♓32
☿	04°♓02	+01°08'	−11°24'	−17 days	+82 days	22°♒37'32"	08°♋24'40"	Fast	25°♎57	25°♈57
♀	17°♈02	+01°14'	+05°50'	−333 days	+204 days	03°♈44'27"	18°♏00'38"	Fast	12°♍57	12°♓57
♂	11°♓40	+47'05"	−08°12'	−399 days	+286 days	08°♋40'31"	02°♍40'08"	Fast	18°♎19	18°♈19
♃	13°♏55 ℞	−03'57"	−14°42'	−21 days	+101 days	14°♏39'22"	04°♏46'04"	Retro	16°♒04	16°♌04
♄	06°♓14	+06'50"	−10°35'	−145 days	+92 days	23°♒38'00"	12°♓24'11"	Fast	23°♎45	23°♈45

MOON ASPECTS
☽ ☍ ♆ 3°43' S
☽ ⚹ ☋ 2°25' A
☽ △ ☊ 2°25' A
☽ △ ♇ 5°04' A
☽ ☍ ♅ 5°35' A
☽ ☌ ♌ 7°10' A

ESSENTIAL DIGNITIES

Pt	Ruler	Exalt	Trip	Term	Face	Detri	Fall	Score
☽	☽ +	♃	♀	♃	☽ +	♄	♂	+6
☉	♂	☉ +	☉ +	♃	♂	♀	♄	+7
☿	♃	♀	♀	♀ m	♄	☿ –	☿ –	−14 p
♀	♂	☉	☉	☿ m	☉	♀ –	♄	−10 p
♂	♃ m	♀	♀	♀	♃	☿	☿	+0 p
♃	♂ m	--	♀	☿	☉	♀	☽	+0 p
♄	♃	♀	♀	♀	♄ +	☿	☿	+1

ASPECTS
♅ ⚹ ☊ 0°20' S
♅ △ ☋ 0°20' S
♄ □ As 0°43' S
♅ ⚹ ♇ 1°00' A
☿ □ As 1°29' S
As △ Mc 1°55' A
☿ ☌ ♄ 2°12' A
♂ △ ♃ 2°13' A
♆ △ ☋ 2°19' A
♆ ⚹ ☊ 2°19' A

PLANETARY SECT

Planet	Cht	Plc	Sgn	Condition
☉ D	D	D	D	In Hayz
☽ N	D	N	N	
☿ D	D	D	N	
♀ N	D	D	D	Ex Cond
♂ N	D	D	N	
♃ D	D	N	N	
♄ D	D	D	N	
D=Diurnal, N=Nocturnal				

6/2: WHERE ARE THE APPLICATION FORMS?

12 November 1993 at 6:17 p.m. (18:17), Ljubljana, Slovenia
Hour ruler: Sun, POF 9 Ca

As head of the Astrological Society Merlin I had to circulate a letter to our members, but I couldn't find the folder with their application forms which hold their addresses. I knew it must be somewhere in the house, most likely in my bedroom, part of which served as my home office. But where exactly were they?

My ruler is Mercury, dispositor of the ascendant and also the natural ruler of papers and documents. Strictly speaking, the application forms belonged to the society and were therefore at least partially ruled by Venus, the H12 ruler (2/11), but they could also be signified by H2 because they were in my possession. (I never gave them to anybody.) H2 is ruled by the Moon which is also the natural ruler of missing things. The direct mutual application of both Venus and the Moon with a retrograde Mercury is a clear sign that I would find them.

But where are they? All significators (Venus, the Moon and the Sun as the ruler of H4 which helps locating missing things) are in Scorpio, a northeastern sign. In rooms, early degrees of signs usually indicate proximity of entrances (i.e. "beginnings" of rooms), while a fixed water sign (Scorpio) directs us to a lower position or to the ground.

And there it was: in my room which was located in the far northeastern part of the house. (Just a quick note here: this is not the same room as the office in Case 6/9, because I lived elsewhere then). On the floor, in close proximity to the entrance door, was a big pile of papers, and the folder with the application forms was hidden under a heap of other documents – as shown by Mercury, the natural significator of papers, books and documents.

The Moon which usually shows the direction of missing things, is in the southwestern part of the chart, and that pile really lay closest to the southern wall and to the entrance door leading to the room from the west side. In other words, the folder was in the southwestern part of the room, as suggested by the Moon's placement.

But I found them accidentally only two days after question. Why not sooner? Well, I didn't even begin to look for them because only a couple of minutes after the question it crossed my mind that I had all the addresses in my computer - so why loose time with the search?!

Now let me draw your attention to an important feature of this horary chart: the exact conjunction of Saturn with MC. As already mentioned in the theoretical part of the book, Saturn in an exact conjunction with any angle usually indicates that the question is "invalid", or that there are insurmountable difficulties associated with the question (or with the aim of the querent), and so it was, because the chart didn't help me find the forms - even if it accurately described their location. But since Saturn is strong in its own sign and because this sign is Aquarius - which among other things rules technology and computers, it kind of pointed at the result or at my "solution": the addresses I was looking for were in my computer!

Also interesting is the time of the find - 14 November at 15:46 (3_46 p.m.) when Venus was at 6°56' Scorpio in an exact conjunction with retrograde Mercury at 6°34' Scorpio, and both were exactly conjunct the descendant at 6°48' Scorpio!

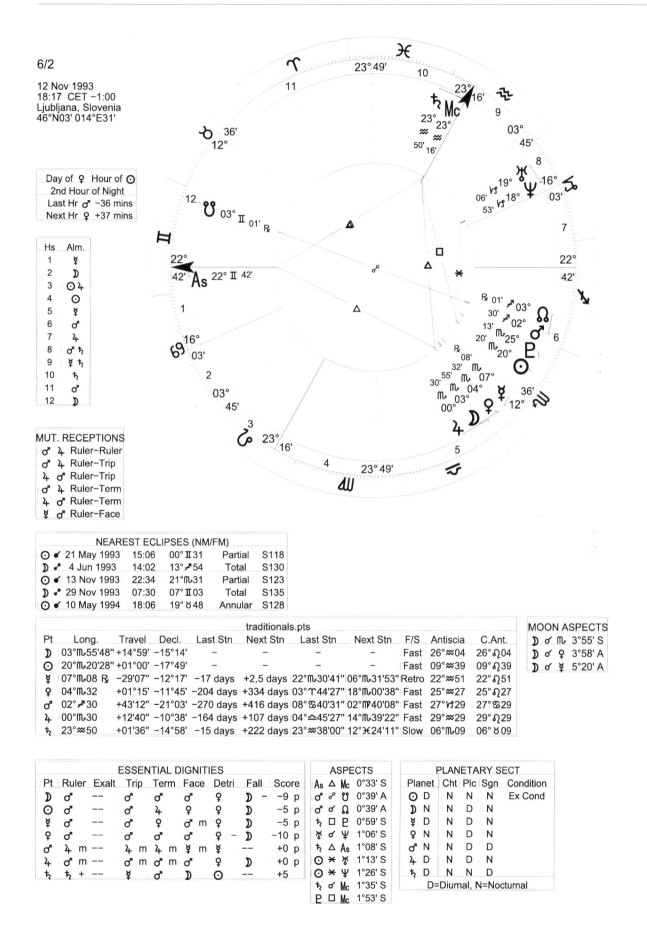

6/2

12 Nov 1993
18:17 CET −1:00
Ljubljana, Slovenia
46°N03' 014°E31'

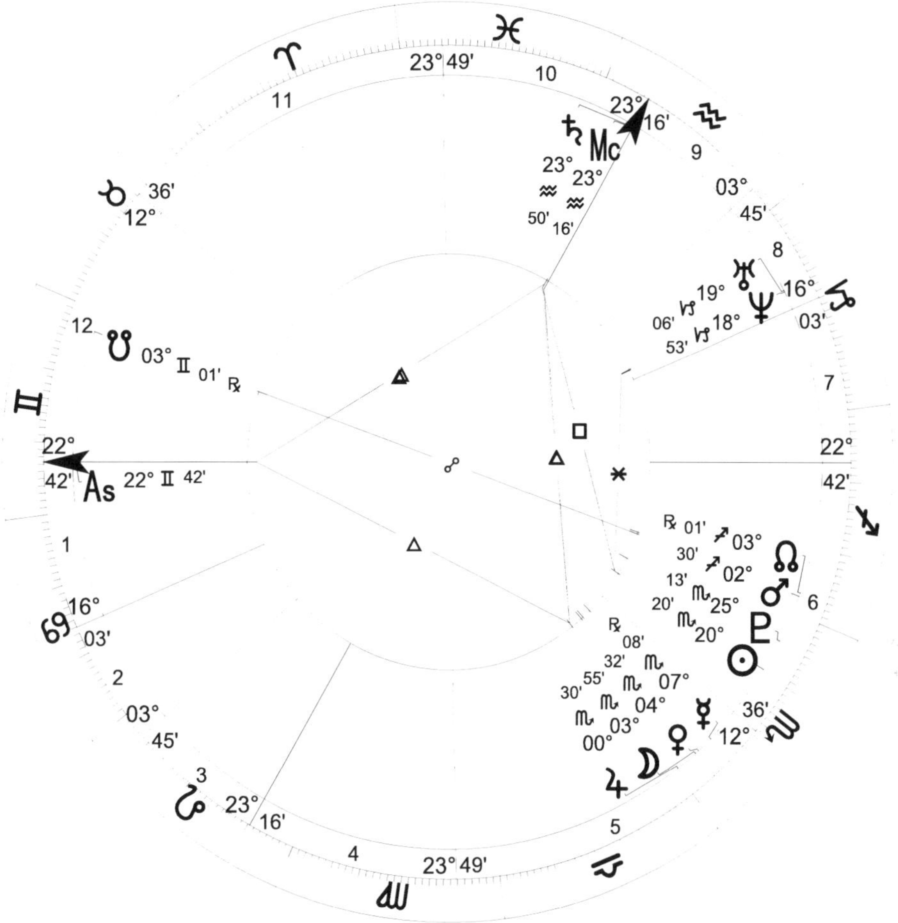

Day of ♀ Hour of ☉
2nd Hour of Night
Last Hr ♂ −36 mins
Next Hr ♀ +37 mins

Hs	Alm.
1	☿
2	☽
3	☉♃
4	☉
5	☿
6	♂
7	♃
8	♂ ♄
9	☿ ♄
10	♄
11	♂
12	☽

MUT. RECEPTIONS
♂ ♃ Ruler–Ruler
♂ ♃ Ruler–Trip
♃ ♂ Ruler–Trip
♂ ♃ Ruler–Term
♃ ♂ Ruler–Term
☿ ♂ Ruler–Face

NEAREST ECLIPSES (NM/FM)					
☉ ☌	21 May 1993	15:06	00° ♊ 31	Partial	S118
☽ ☍	4 Jun 1993	14:02	13° ♐ 54	Total	S130
☉ ☌	13 Nov 1993	22:34	21° ♏ 31	Partial	S123
☽ ☍	29 Nov 1993	07:30	07° ♊ 03	Total	S135
☉ ☌	10 May 1994	18:06	19° ♉ 48	Annular	S128

traditionals.pts

Pt	Long.	Travel	Decl.	Last Stn	Next Stn	Last Stn	Next Stn	F/S	Antiscia	C.Ant.
☽	03°♏55'48"	+14°59'	−15°14'	–	–	–	–	Fast	26°♒04	26°♌04
☉	20°♏20'28"	+01°00'	−17°49'	–	–	–	–	Fast	09°♒39	09°♌39
☿	07°♏08 ℞	−29'07"	−12°17'	−17 days	+2,5 days	22°♏30'41"	06°♏31'53"	Retro	22°♒51	22°♌51
♀	04°♏32	+01°15'	−11°45'	−204 days	+334 days	03°♈44'27"	18°♏00'38"	Fast	25°♒27	25°♌27
♂	02°♐30	+43'12"	−21°03'	−270 days	+416 days	08°♋40'31"	02°♍40'08"	Fast	27°♑29	27°♋29
♃	00°♏30	+12'40"	−10°38'	−164 days	+107 days	04°♎45'27"	14°♏39'22"	Fast	29°♒29	29°♌29
♄	23°♒50	+01'36"	−14°58'	−15 days	+222 days	23°♒38'00"	12°♓24'11"	Slow	06°♏09	06°♉09

MOON ASPECTS
☽ ☌ ♏ 3°55' S
☽ ☌ ♀ 3°58' A
☽ ☌ ☿ 5°20' A

ESSENTIAL DIGNITIES

Pt	Ruler	Exalt	Trip	Term	Face	Detri	Fall	Score
☽	♂	--	♂	♂	♂	♀	☽ −	−9 p
☉	♂	--	♂	♃	♀	♀	☽	−5 p
☿	♂	--	♂	♀	♂ m	♀	☽	−5 p
♀	♂	--	♂	♂	♂	♀ −	☽	−10 p
♂	♃ m	--	♃ m	♃ m	☿ m	☿	--	+0 p
♃	♂ m	--	♂ m	♂ m	♂	♀	☽	+0 p
♄	♄ +	--	☿	♂	☽	☉	--	+5

ASPECTS
As △ Mc 0°33' S
♂ ☍ ☋ 0°39' A
♂ ☌ ☊ 0°39' A
♄ □ ♇ 0°59' S
♅ ☌ ♆ 1°06' S
♄ △ As 1°08' S
☉ ⚹ ♅ 1°13' S
☉ ⚹ ♆ 1°26' S
♄ ☌ Mc 1°35' S
♇ □ Mc 1°53' S

PLANETARY SECT

Planet		Cht	Plc	Sgn	Condition
☉	D	N	N	N	Ex Cond
☽	N	N	D	N	
☿	D	N	D	N	
♀	N	N	D	N	
♂	N	N	D	D	
♃	D	N	D	N	
♄	D	N	N	D	

D=Diurnal, N=Nocturnal

6/3: WHERE ARE MY DAUGHTER'S SANDALS?

8 June 1995 at 5:02 p.m. (17:02), Ljubljana, Slovenia
Hour ruler: Sun, POF 2 Pi

I was looking for a pair of sandals which we bought for my daughter the previous summer. This year they should still fit her, I thought, but could not find them in any of the shoe closets, so I cast a horary chart.

My daughter is ruled by H5 and her sandals by H6 (2/5). Since the cusp of H6 is in Aries, sandals are ruled by Mars. This planet is in H10, an angular house, and because part of fortune is also in an angular house (H4), the sandals are obviously somewhere in the house. But where? Mars is in Virgo which usually shows cupboards, drawers and the like, so they should be somewhere packed and safe. Additional insight is provided by H4 which helps describe the location. The cusp is in Aquarius with its ruler Saturn in Pisces. Part of fortune is also in that sign, giving us an important clue as per location. In buildings, Pisces rules damp places on the ground floor or in the basement, and also bathrooms, while Saturn is associated with cold and dark places.

The Moon is in the east and a bit to the south, and since it's in an air sign, it directs us to a slightly higher position – or, in combination with Saturn in Pisces (low, dark) and Mars in Virgo (also low or at ground level), somewhere low to middle height, or at a higher position in the ground floor area.

Let us now take a look at the almuten of H6, the Sun: it's in Gemini and the Moon applies to it by trine – another confirmation that the sandals would be found.

Since all the significators (Mars as the main ruler, the Sun as almuten and Saturn as the H4 ruler) are in mutable signs, the next step is to ask ourselves what locations are common to those signs? They include various sheltered and covered places, cabinets, drawers, built-in wardrobes, lobbies and hallways.

Our final question is therefore: is there a dark, cold and possibly damp location to the east of the house where there's a wardrobe, a chest of drawers or a built-in cabinet? On the ground floor, in the northeastern part of the house, there were some steps leading towards the cellar, and down there by the door, in the dark, there was a small cupboard containing various small items which we seldom used. The whole place was like a little "room within a room", by the hallway leading to the cellar, which exactly fits the character of the movable signs. The cupboard stood on the eastern wall (the Moon in the eastern part of the chart), and there I found the sandals a little while later. They were on one of the middle shelves, as suggested by the Moon in an air sign. Unfortunately, though, we soon realized that they'd be of no use, because the damp had ruined them and my daughter had already overgrown them. No wonder - both Mars and the Sun are peregrine, indicating an item of little or no value.

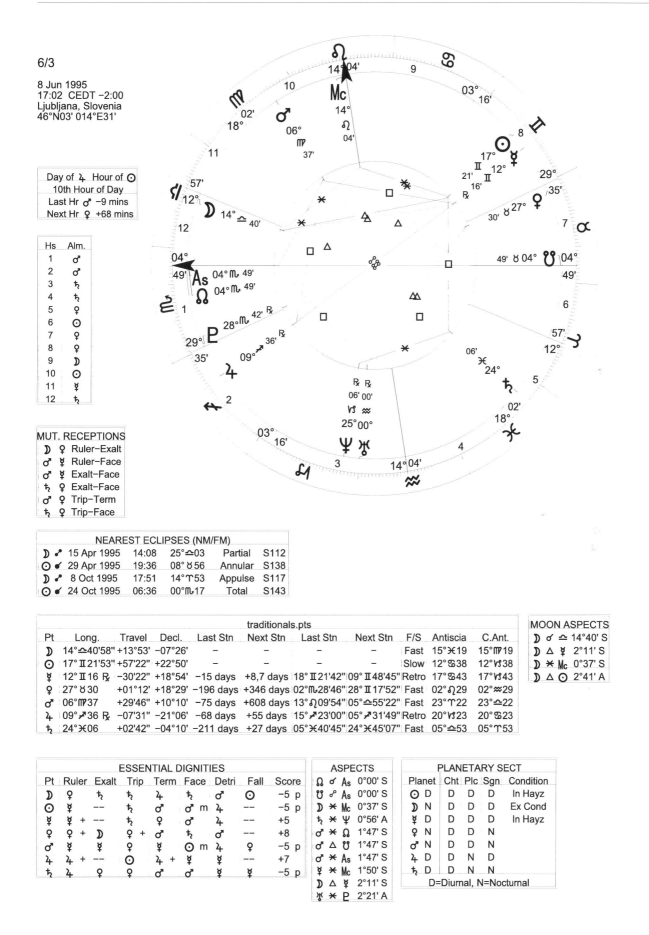

6/3

8 Jun 1995
17:02 CEDT −2:00
Ljubljana, Slovenia
46°N03' 014°E31'

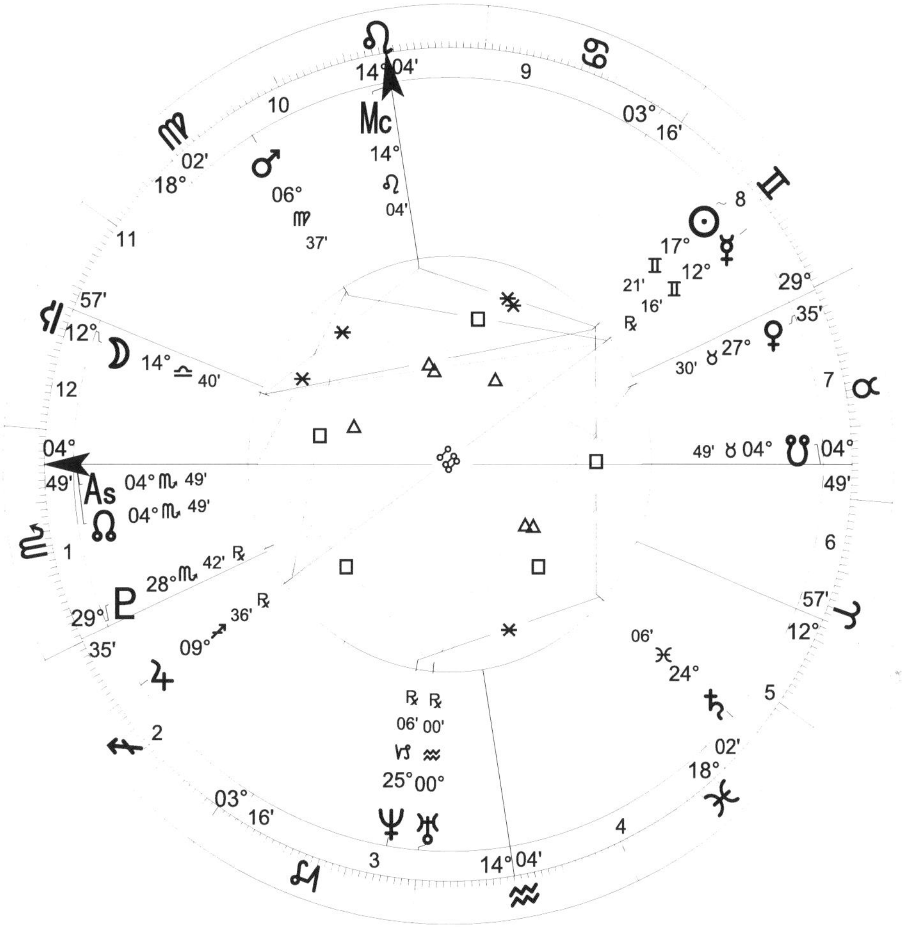

Day of ♃ Hour of ☉
10th Hour of Day
Last Hr ♂ −9 mins
Next Hr ♀ +68 mins

Hs	Alm.
1	♂
2	♂
3	♄
4	♄
5	♀
6	☉
7	♀
8	♀
9	☽
10	☉
11	☿
12	♄

MUT. RECEPTIONS		
☽	♀	Ruler–Exalt
♂	☿	Ruler–Face
♂	☿	Exalt–Face
♄	♀	Exalt–Face
♂	♀	Trip–Term
♄	♀	Trip–Face

NEAREST ECLIPSES (NM/FM)					
☽	15 Apr 1995	14:08	25°♎03	Partial	S112
☉	29 Apr 1995	19:36	08°♉56	Annular	S138
☽	8 Oct 1995	17:51	14°♈53	Appulse	S117
☉	24 Oct 1995	06:36	00°♏17	Total	S143

traditionals.pts

Pt	Long.	Travel	Decl.	Last Stn	Next Stn	Last Stn	Next Stn	F/S	Antiscia	C.Ant.
☽	14°♎40'58"	+13°53'	−07°26'	–	–	–	–	Fast	15°♓19	15°♍19
☉	17°♊21'53"	+57'22"	+22°50'	–	–	–	–	Slow	12°♋38	12°♑38
☿	12°♊16 ℞	−30'22"	+18°54'	−15 days	+8,7 days	18°♊21'42"	09°♊48'45"	Retro	17°♋43	17°♑43
♀	27°♉30	+01°12'	+18°29'	−196 days	+346 days	02°♏28'46"	28°♊17'52"	Fast	02°♌29	02°♒29
♂	06°♍37	+29'46"	+10°10'	−75 days	+608 days	13°♌09'54"	05°♎55'22"	Fast	23°♈22	23°♎22
♃	09°♐36 ℞	−07'31"	−21°06'	−68 days	+55 days	15°♐23'00"	05°♐31'49"	Retro	20°♑23	20°♋23
♄	24°♓06	+02'42"	−04°10'	−211 days	+27 days	05°♓40'45"	24°♓45'07"	Fast	05°♎53	05°♈53

MOON ASPECTS		
☽ ☌ ♎	14°40'	S
☽ △ ☿	2°11'	S
☽ ⚹ Mc	0°37'	S
☽ △ ☉	2°41'	A

ESSENTIAL DIGNITIES								
Pt	Ruler	Exalt	Trip	Term	Face	Detri	Fall	Score
☽	♀	♄	♄	♃	♄	♂	☉	−5 p
☉	☿	--	♄	♂	♂ m	♃	--	−5 p
☿	☿ +	--	♄	♀	♂	♃	--	+5
♀	♀ +	☽	♀ +	♂	♄	♂	--	+8
♂	☿	☿	♀	☿	☉ m	♃	♀	−5 p
♃	♃ +	--	☉	♃ +	☿	☿	--	+7
♄	♃	♀	♀	♂	♂	☿	☿	−5 p

ASPECTS		
☊ ☌ As	0°00'	S
☋ ☍ As	0°00'	S
☽ ⚹ Mc	0°37'	S
♄ ⚹ ♆	0°56'	A
♂ ⚹ ☊	1°47'	S
♂ △ ☋	1°47'	S
♂ ⚹ As	1°47'	S
☿ ⚹ Mc	1°50'	S
☽ △ ☿	2°11'	S
♅ ⚹ ♇	2°21'	A

PLANETARY SECT					
Planet		Cht	Plc	Sgn	Condition
☉	D	D	D	D	In Hayz
☽	N	D	D	D	Ex Cond
☿	D	D	D	D	In Hayz
♀	N	D	D	N	
♂	N	D	D	N	
♃	D	D	N	D	
♄	D	D	N	N	

D=Diurnal, N=Nocturnal

6/4: WHERE ARE MY HUSBAND'S KEYS?

8 September 2006 at 11:41 p.m. (23:41), Ljubljana, Slovenia
Hour ruler: The Moon, POF 8 Sa

My husband told me on that day that he missed his keys: all his keys (of home, car, office, mailbox etc.) were in the set he had lost, so it was important that he'd find them soon. I remembered that I had been using his keys a couple of days ago, but I couldn't remember when or where I last saw them. I searched around for a while and when by the end of the day none of us found them, I asked the above question and sat down to read the horary chart reading.

Ascendant in Gemini is in an exact trine with my natal Sun - the symbol of my husband. (I'm mentioning this link with my birth chart just as an interesting chart feature, although it has no bearing on the interpretation.) Mercury, my ruler, is in the analytical Virgo which is its home and exaltation sign, making it strong, but it's in conjunction with the south node and in square to Pluto (an obstruction, obstacle, powerlessness etc.) which reflects my helplessness in relation to this matter. Where on earth could I have put the keys - if it was really me who misplaced them?

The planetary hour ruler is the Moon, inharmonious with the Gemini ascendant, indicating that it's doubtful whether the chart can help me find the keys.

My husband is shown by Jupiter, the descendant sign ruler, in Scorpio on the cusp of the derived H12, but he's also signified by Pluto which is in an exact conjunction with the descendant. Both placements show him to be "stuck" and unable to act. He had tried everything – to no avail, so that's quite fitting. The significator of the keys is Saturn, the derived H2 (radix H8) ruler, placed in Leo in H3. Although Mars is co-almuten of H8, Saturn better describes the keys, because they are made of lead compounds.

So, where are they? The Moon (co-significator of the keys) is in H11, Saturn is in H3 and part of fortune is in H6. None of these houses is angular which worried me because the keys were obviously not in the house! But the Moon is void-of-course because it is not in an applying orb of aspect to any planet. This could well mean that the keys are not definitively lost, especially because the first next aspect of the Moon is trine Saturn which would be completed without any other intervening (frustrating) aspect. It is clear, therefore, that the keys would be found, but probably somewhere around the house, as H3 suggests.

How did they get lost? The last Moon's aspect was the opposition of Mars, so the keys might have been lost during some argument or in a rush, which could also be related to our children because of Mars' placement in H5. But my pondering over this possibility remained fruitless.

Both Saturn and Moon are in fire signs, so the keys could be close to a source of heat, and not on the ground but rather at middle height. Then it hit me: H3 rules cars – must be my car, of course! And Mars, from which the Moon separates, is the natural ruler of machines, so my firm conclusion was that I must have left the keys in my car. Off I went and carefully searched the car, but the keys I could not find. Disappointed and confused I returned to my office and looked helplessly at the horary chart. Where on earth are the damn keys?

The next chapter of this story follows in Case 6/5 which refers to the same key, only the querent was different.

6/4

8 Sep 2006
23:41 CEDT −2:00
Ljubljana, Slovenia
46°N03' 014°E31'

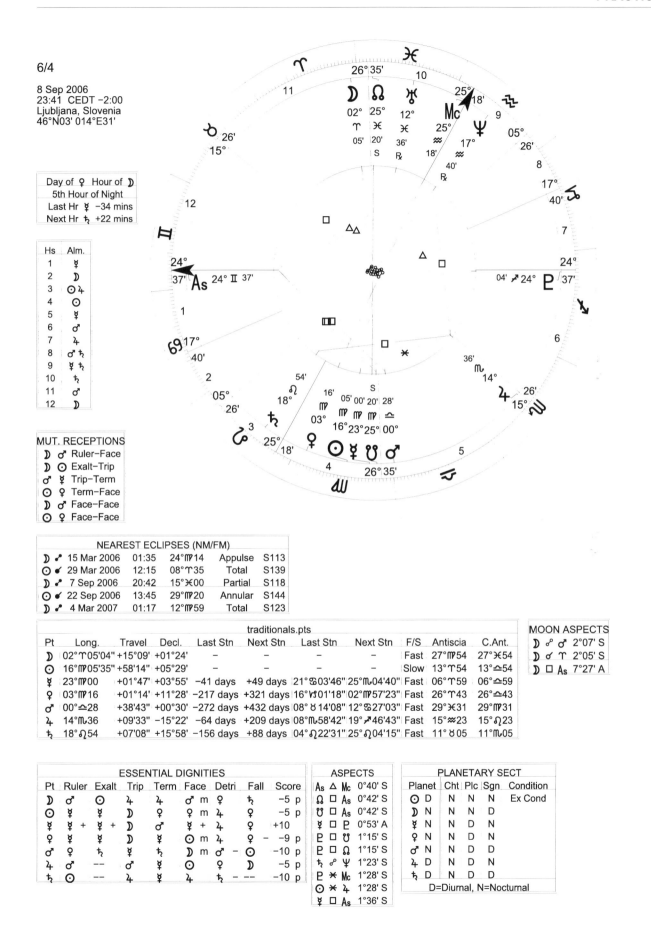

Day of ♀ Hour of ☽
5th Hour of Night
Last Hr ☿ −34 mins
Next Hr ♄ +22 mins

Hs	Alm.
1	☿
2	☽
3	☉♃
4	☉
5	☿
6	♂
7	♃
8	♂♄
9	☿♄
10	♄
11	♂
12	☽

MUT. RECEPTIONS
☽ ♂ Ruler–Face
☽ ☉ Exalt–Trip
♂ ☿ Trip–Term
☉ ♀ Term–Face
☽ ♂ Face–Face
☉ ♀ Face–Face

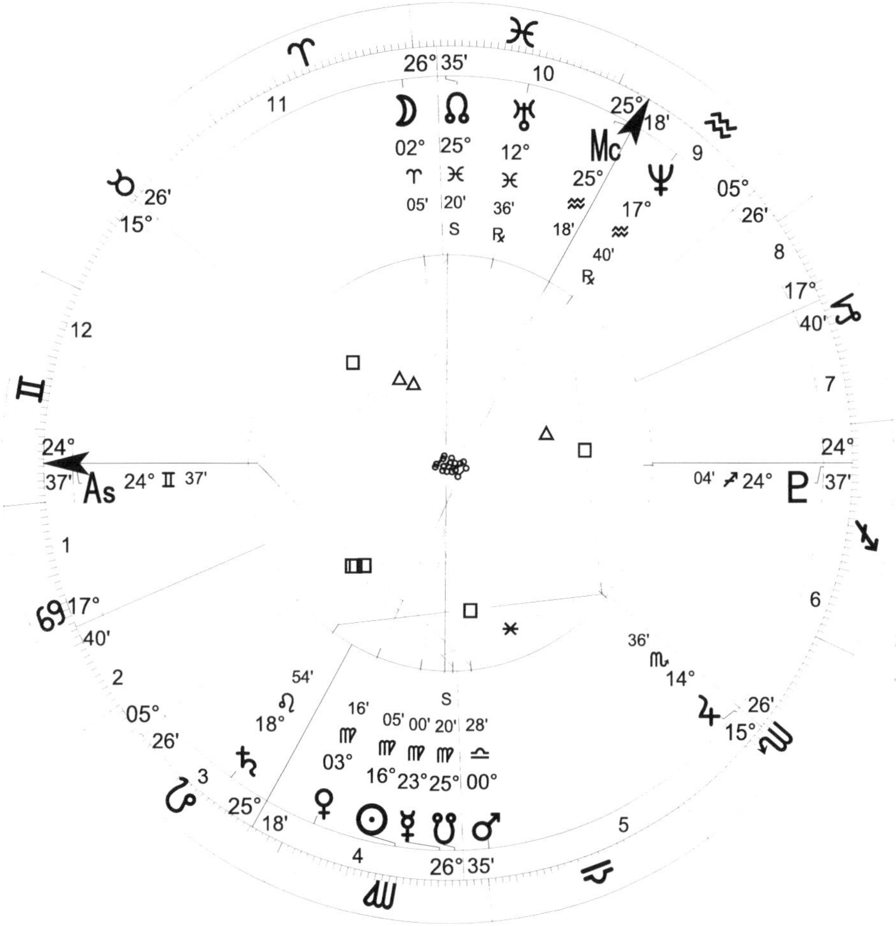

NEAREST ECLIPSES (NM/FM)					
☽	15 Mar 2006	01:35	24°♍14	Appulse	S113
☉	29 Mar 2006	12:15	08°♈35	Total	S139
☽	7 Sep 2006	20:42	15°♓00	Partial	S118
☉	22 Sep 2006	13:45	29°♍20	Annular	S144
☽	4 Mar 2007	01:17	12°♍59	Total	S123

traditionals.pts

Pt	Long.	Travel	Decl.	Last Stn	Next Stn	Last Stn	Next Stn	F/S	Antiscia	C.Ant.
☽	02°♈05'04"	+15°09'	+01°24'	–	–	–	–	Fast	27°♍54	27°♓54
☉	16°♍05'35"	+58'14"	+05°29'	–	–	–	–	Slow	13°♈54	13°♎54
☿	23°♍00	+01°47'	+03°55'	−41 days	+49 days	21°♋03'46"	25°♏04'40"	Fast	06°♈59	06°♎59
♀	03°♍16	+01°14'	+11°28'	−217 days	+321 days	16°♑01'18"	02°♍57'23"	Fast	26°♈43	26°♎43
♂	00°♎28	+38'43"	+00°30'	−272 days	+432 days	08°♉14'08"	12°♋27'03"	Fast	29°♓31	29°♍31
♃	14°♏36	+09'33"	−15°22'	−64 days	+209 days	08°♏58'42"	19°♐46'43"	Fast	15°♒23	15°♌23
♄	18°♌54	+07'08"	+15°58'	−156 days	+88 days	04°♌22'31"	25°♌04'15"	Fast	11°♉05	11°♏05

MOON ASPECTS
☽ ☍ ♂ 2°07' S
☽ ☌ ♈ 2°05' S
☽ □ As 7°27' A

ESSENTIAL DIGNITIES

Pt	Ruler	Exalt	Trip	Term	Face	Detri	Fall	Score
☽	♂	☉	♃	♃	♂ m	♀	♄	−5 p
☉	☿	☿	☽	♀	♀ m	♃	♀	−5 p
☿	☿ +	☿ +	☽	♂	☿ +	♃	♀	+10
♀	☿	☿	☽	☿	☉ m	♃	♀ −	−9 p
♂	♀	♄	☿	♄	☽ m	♂ −	☉	−10 p
♃	♂	--	♂	☿	☉	♀	☽	−5 p
♄	☉	--	♃	☿	♃	♄ −	--	−10 p

ASPECTS
As △ Mc 0°40' S
☊ □ As 0°42' S
☋ □ As 0°42' S
☿ □ ♇ 0°53' A
♇ □ ☋ 1°15' S
♇ □ ☊ 1°15' S
♄ ☍ ♆ 1°23' S
♇ ⚹ Mc 1°28' S
☉ ⚹ ♃ 1°28' S
☿ □ As 1°36' S

PLANETARY SECT

Planet	Cht	Plc	Sgn	Condition
☉ D	N	N	N	Ex Cond
☽ N	N	N	D	
☿ N	N	D	N	
♀ N	N	D	N	
♂ N	N	D	D	
♃ D	N	D	N	
♄ D	N	D	D	

D=Diurnal, N=Nocturnal

6/5: WHERE ARE MY KEYS?

10 September 2006 at 1:23 p.m. (13:23), Ljubljana, Slovenia
Hour ruler: Mars, POF 11 Ca

In terms of subject matter, this example is the continuation of Case 6/4.

A day and a half after my unsuccessful attempt to find my husband's keys, he came to me and said, *Listen, I've searched everywhere, it really seems that my keys are lost. But what does your astrology say? Can you do a chart to see if you can help?*

Sure, I said. *Wait a minute, I'll try.*

I immediately typed the data into my computer to get a new horary, asking for the same keys that I had searched for in vain in my own horary. Now that the question came from the lips of my husband, will I do better, I wondered?

The ascendant is in Sagittarius and the planetary hour ruler is Mars, making for a harmonious mixture because Mars has the same nature as the sign of Sagittarius - hot and dry. That's promising!

The Moon is in H5 and still in Aries, while the significator of the keys is the same planet as in the 6/4 case: Saturn, the ruler of Capricorn which is on the H2 cusp. But Saturn is in H9 this time – of course, the querent was my husband, not me, so the position of Saturn by house was now reversed. Then it clicked – his keys must be in my car, because H9 is the derived third of the seventh (3/7), ruling his wife's car! And the Moon was still in Aries, showing engines! The last Moon's aspect was trine Saturn, ruling H3 (car, travel). Indications were therefore quite similar to those of the previous chart, so there was little doubt that the keys must be in my car.

I immediately set myself to work again. I first opened the trunk and took out everything there was. The keys were not there. Then I embarked on the rear seats, front seats ... Nothing. Finally, I raised the rubbery mat which lay below the front passenger seat - and under its upper part, pressed against the front of the car, were my husband's keys. I find it quite interesting that they were in the part closest to the car's engine (significators in fire signs).

I triumphantly took the keys to my man who looked staggered because so little time passed since he had asked the question. *You asked me to cast a chart, didn't you?* I said innocently. *Why didn't you ask me sooner?!*

Another interesting feature of this chart is that my significator Mercury (the descendant's ruler) was now strong on cusp of H10, having just passed the conjunction with the restrictive south node and the square with Pluto which was inhibiting it before. Obviously, some time had to pass before the "sky" allowed me to be successful!

6/5

10 Sep 2006
13:23 CEDT −2:00
Ljubljana, Slovenia
46°N03' 014°E31'

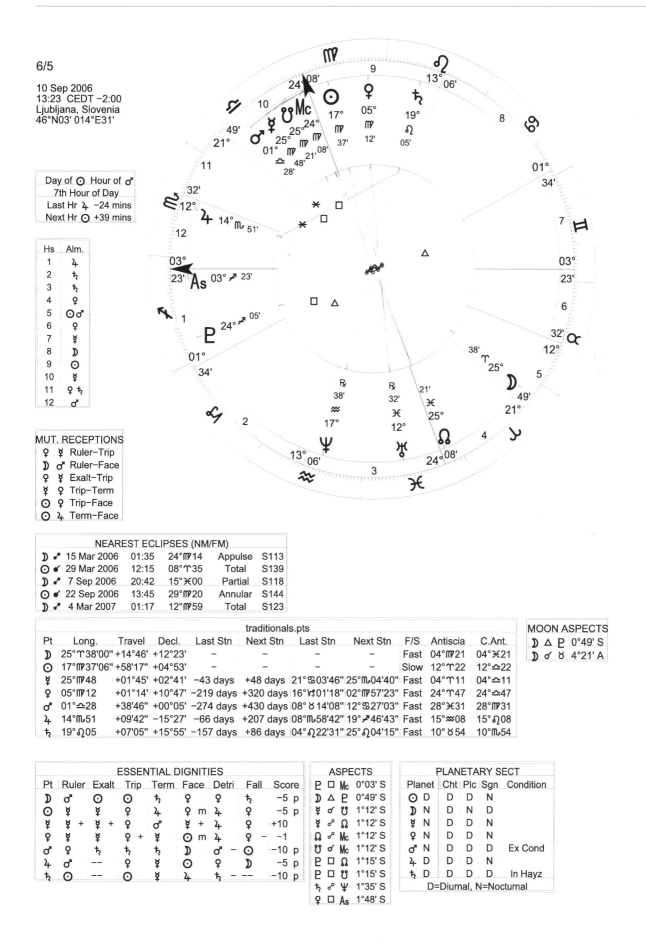

Day of ☉ Hour of ♂
7th Hour of Day
Last Hr ♃ −24 mins
Next Hr ☉ +39 mins

Hs	Alm.
1	♃
2	♄
3	♄
4	♀
5	☉♂
6	♀
7	☿
8	☽
9	☉
10	☿
11	♀ ♄
12	♂

MUT. RECEPTIONS		
♀	☿	Ruler–Trip
☽	♂	Ruler–Face
♀	☿	Exalt–Trip
☿	♀	Trip–Term
☉	♀	Trip–Face
☉	♃	Term–Face

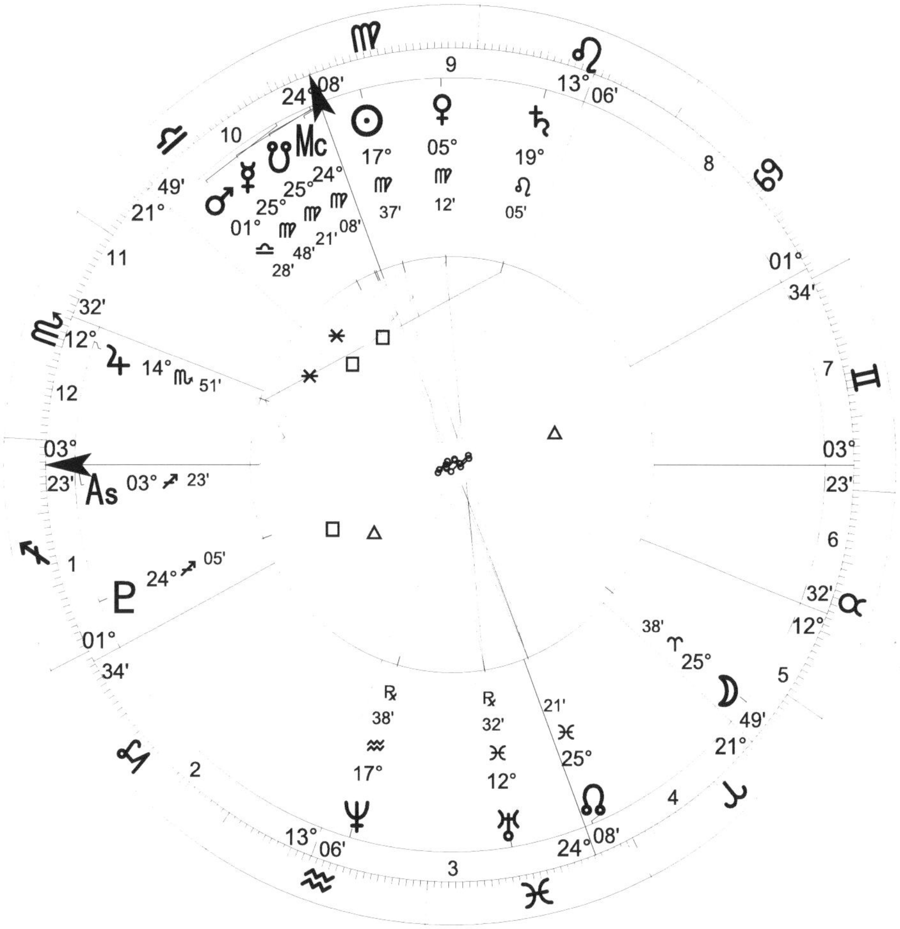

NEAREST ECLIPSES (NM/FM)					
☽ ☍	15 Mar 2006	01:35	24°♍14	Appulse	S113
☉ ☌	29 Mar 2006	12:15	08°♈35	Total	S139
☽ ☍	7 Sep 2006	20:42	15°♓00	Partial	S118
☉ ☌	22 Sep 2006	13:45	29°♍20	Annular	S144
☽ ☍	4 Mar 2007	01:17	12°♍59	Total	S123

traditionals.pts

Pt	Long.	Travel	Decl.	Last Stn	Next Stn	Last Stn	Next Stn	F/S	Antiscia	C.Ant.
☽	25°♈38'00"	+14°46'	+12°23'	–	–	–	–	Fast	04°♍21	04°♓21
☉	17°♍37'06"	+58'17"	+04°53'	–	–	–	–	Slow	12°♈22	12°♎22
☿	25°♍48	+01°45'	+02°41'	−43 days	+48 days	21°♋03'46"	25°♏04'40"	Fast	04°♈11	04°♎11
♀	05°♍12	+01°14'	+10°47'	−219 days	+320 days	16°♑01'18"	02°♍57'23"	Fast	24°♈47	24°♎47
♂	01°♎28	+38'46"	+00°05'	−274 days	+430 days	08°♉14'08"	12°♋27'03"	Fast	28°♓31	28°♍31
♃	14°♏51	+09'42"	−15°27'	−66 days	+207 days	08°♏58'42"	19°♐46'43"	Fast	15°♒08	15°♌08
♄	19°♌05	+07'05"	+15°55'	−157 days	+86 days	04°♌22'31"	25°♌04'15"	Fast	10°♉54	10°♏54

MOON ASPECTS			
☽	△	♇	0°49' S
☽	☌	☋	4°21' A

ESSENTIAL DIGNITIES

Pt	Ruler	Exalt	Trip	Term	Face	Detri	Fall	Score
☽	♂	☉	☉	♄	♀	♀	♄	−5 p
☉	☿	☿	♀	♃	♀ m	♃	♀	−5 p
☿	☿ +	☿ +	♀	♂	☿ +	♃	♀	+10
♀	☿	☿	♀ +	☿	☉ m	♃	♀ –	−1
♂	♀	♄	♄	♄	☽	♂ –	☉	−10 p
♃	♂	--	♀	☿	☉	♀	☽	−5 p
♄	☉	--	☉	☿	♃	♄ –	--	−10 p

ASPECTS			
♇	□	Mc	0°03' S
☽	△	♇	0°49' S
☿	☌	☋	1°12' S
☿	☍	☊	1°12' S
☊	☍	Mc	1°12' S
☋	☌	Mc	1°12' S
♇	□	☊	1°15' S
♇	□	☋	1°15' S
♄	☍	♆	1°35' S
♀	□	As	1°48' S

PLANETARY SECT

Planet	Cht	Plc	Sgn	Condition
☉ D	D	D	N	
☽ N	D	N	D	
☿ N	D	D	N	
♀ N	D	D	N	
♂ N	D	D	D	Ex Cond
♃ D	D	D	N	
♄ D	D	D	D	In Hayz

D=Diurnal, N=Nocturnal

6/6: WHERE IS MY WALLET?

1 March 2003 at 8:44 p.m. (20:44), Ljubljana, Slovenia
Hour ruler: Saturn, POF 29 Li

I am one of those people who often lose small items - including such valuables as wallets. Usually, upon noticing the loss, I thoroughly investigate all possible places where those things (wallet, keys, phone, etc.) could be, and only after I can't find them, I cast a horary.

This chart is one of those which almost immediately brought a deep sigh of relief. Let's see why. The planetary hour is harmonious, which increases the possibility that the chart would prove useful. I am ruled by Venus (the ascendant ruler) and my wallet by Mars (the ruler of Scorpio which holds the H2 cusp.). Mars is at 28°02' Sagittarius in H3, the Moon at 25°56' of Aquarius in H5. The Moon's direct application by sextile to Mars promises that I'd get my wallet back! This is confirmed by the retrograde state of Jupiter, Mars' (the wallet) dispositor and an important planet in every chart which asks about missing money (or other valuables).

All those positive indications related to the finding of the wallet, made me breathe easier, but there's the second part of the question: where is it? Only Jupiter and part of fortune are in angular houses. Although they belong to the group of significators, the most important ones (Mars and the Moon) are in other houses (cadent and succedent), therefore the wallet is probably not in our house.

But where could it be? Mars in H3 shows surrounding areas, while the combination of the Moon in the airy Aquarius and H5 where it is located, is indicative of places where people gather. This is confirmed by Saturn, the H4 ruler, in the airy Gemini, while the separating conjunction of Moon with Mercury suggests some kind of communication, exchange, transaction, trading... Hmmm, did I lose my wallet while paying for something? Yes, that would be logical! Then I remembered that I last saw the wallet earlier in the day when I was buying food at a nearby market store. I must have left it there, I thought, and because the chart showed that I'd get it back, I thought that the cashier (or someone who found it) kept it in a safe place.

Since the shop was already closed (I raised the question on a Saturday evening), I couldn't check for the wallet on that day and also not on Sunday, but on Monday morning I went to the store where a friendly saleswoman handed me my wallet. Need I add that nothing was missing?!

6/6

1 Mar 2003
20:44 CET −1:00
Ljubljana, Slovenia
46°N03' 014°E31'

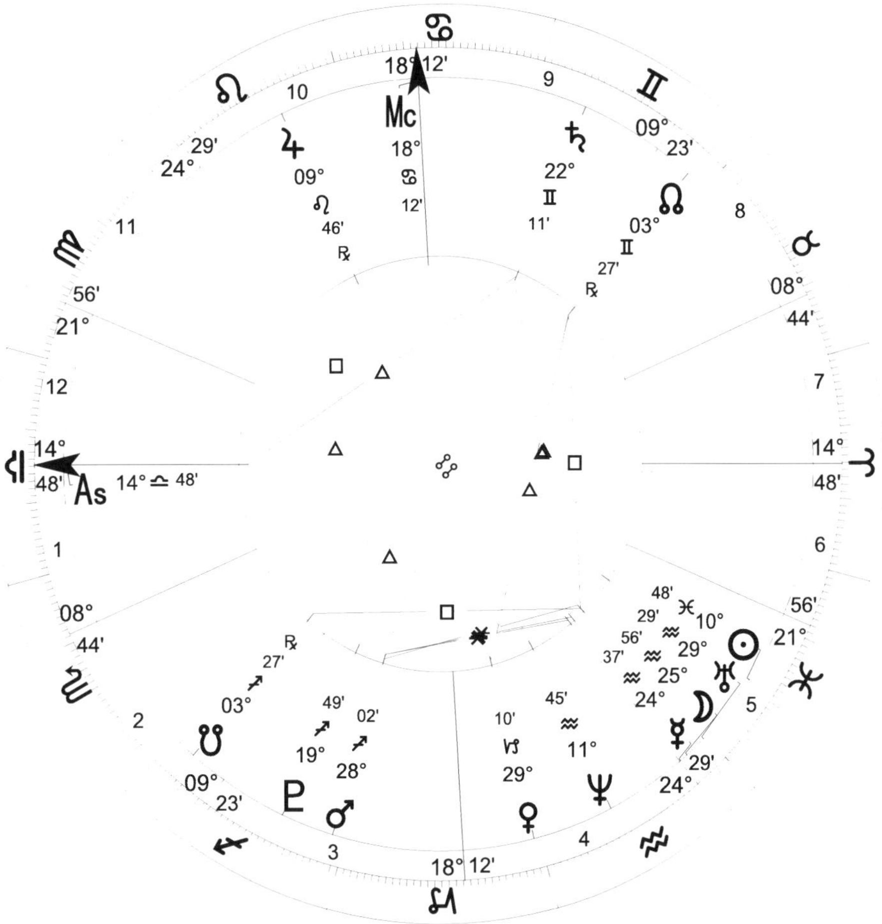

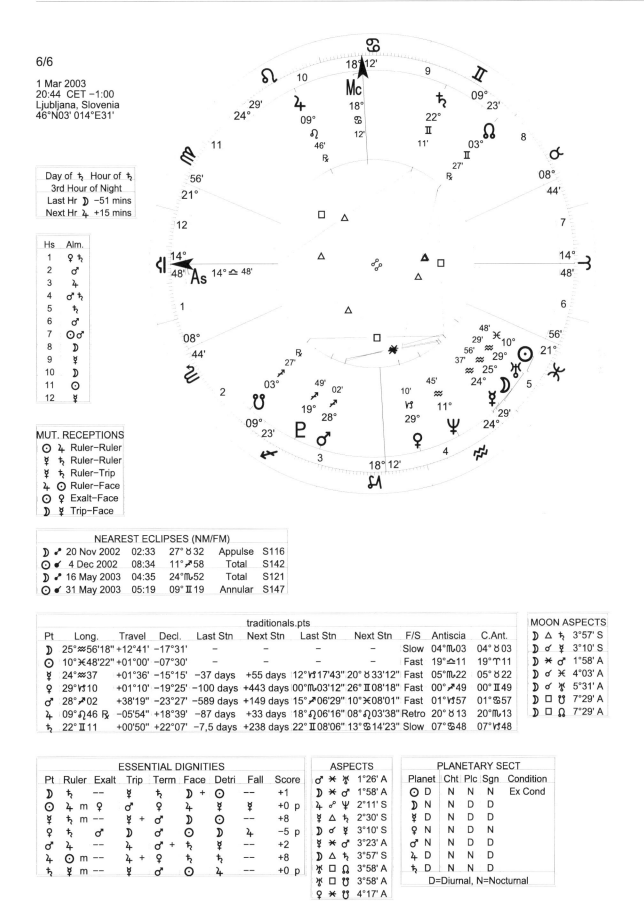

Day of ♄ Hour of ♄
3rd Hour of Night
Last Hr ☽ −51 mins
Next Hr ♃ +15 mins

Hs	Alm.
1	♀ ♄
2	♂
3	♃
4	♂ ♄
5	♄
6	♂
7	☉ ♂
8	☽
9	☿
10	☽
11	☉
12	☿

MUT. RECEPTIONS		
☉	♃	Ruler–Ruler
☿	♄	Ruler–Ruler
☿	♄	Ruler–Trip
♃	☉	Ruler–Face
☉	♀	Exalt–Face
☽	☿	Trip–Face

NEAREST ECLIPSES (NM/FM)					
☽ ●	20 Nov 2002	02:33	27°♉32	Appulse	S116
☉ ●	4 Dec 2002	08:34	11°♐58	Total	S142
☽ ●	16 May 2003	04:35	24°♏52	Total	S121
☉ ●	31 May 2003	05:19	09°♊19	Annular	S147

traditionals.pts

Pt	Long.	Travel	Decl.	Last Stn	Next Stn	Last Stn	Next Stn	F/S	Antiscia	C.Ant.
☽	25°♒56'18"	+12°41'	−17°31'	–	–	–	–	Slow	04°♏03	04°♉03
☉	10°♓48'22"	+01°00'	−07°30'	–	–	–	–	Fast	19°♎11	19°♈11
☿	24°♒37	+01°36'	−15°15'	−37 days	+55 days	12°♑17'43"	20°♉33'12"	Fast	05°♏22	05°♉22
♀	29°♑10	+01°10'	−19°25'	−100 days	+443 days	00°♏03'12"	26°♊08'18"	Fast	00°♐49	00°♊49
♂	28°♐02	+38'19"	−23°27'	−589 days	+149 days	15°♐06'29"	10°♓08'01"	Fast	01°♑57	01°♋57
♃	09°♌46 ℞	−05'54"	+18°39'	−87 days	+33 days	18°♌06'16"	08°♌03'38"	Retro	20°♉13	20°♏13
♄	22°♊11	+00'50"	+22°07'	−7,5 days	+238 days	22°♊08'06"	13°♋14'23"	Slow	07°♋48	07°♑48

MOON ASPECTS			
☽	△	♄	3°57' S
☽	☌	☿	3°10' S
☽	✶	♂	1°58' A
☽	☌	♓	4°03' A
☽	☌	♅	5°31' A
☽	□	☋	7°29' A
☽	□	☊	7°29' A

ESSENTIAL DIGNITIES

Pt	Ruler	Exalt	Trip	Term	Face	Detri	Fall	Score
☽	♄	--	☿	♄	☽ +	☉	--	+1
☉	♃ m	♀	♂	♀	♃	☿	☿	+0 p
☿	♄ m	--	☿ +	♂	☽	☉	--	+8
♀	♄	♂	☽	♂	☉	☽	♃	−5 p
♂	♃	--	♃	♂ +	♄	☿	--	+2
♃	☉ m	--	♃ +	♀	♄	♄	--	+8
♄	☿ m	--	☿	♂	☉	♃	--	+0 p

ASPECTS			
♂	✶	♅	1°26' A
☽	✶	♂	1°58' A
♃	☍	♆	2°11' S
☿	△	♄	2°30' S
☽	☌	☿	3°10' S
☿	✶	♂	3°23' A
☽	△	♄	3°57' S
♅	□	☊	3°58' A
♅	□	☋	3°58' A
♀	✶	☋	4°17' A

PLANETARY SECT

Planet		Cht	Plc	Sgn	Condition
☉	D	N	N	N	Ex Cond
☽	N	N	D	D	
☿	D	N	D	D	
♀	N	N	D	N	
♂	N	N	D	D	
♃	D	N	N	D	
♄	D	N	N	D	

D=Diurnal, N=Nocturnal

6/7: WHERE IS MY HUSBAND'S JACKET? WILL HE GET IT BACK?

26 August 2007 at 9:29 p.m. (21:29), Ljubljana, Slovenia
Hour ruler: Mars, POF 13 Sc

A couple of friends who were instructors in paragliding invited me and my husband for a ride in tandem. He excitedly accepted the invitation while I politely refused, saying that I love my life, if they can understand... (And added that I'd rather climb Krvavec - the mountain they were using as a starting point – three times in a single day than jump from it once.) When the big day arrived, my husband happily jumped and glided over the vast green fields below the Krvavec mountain while me and our children watched his fun from a safe distance close to the runway.

The adventure went well - which I partly attributed to the fact that on that Saturday morning, the Moon was in the airy Aquarius in sextile with Jupiter in Sagittarius, and the breeze was really just right. After the landing, my family and the instructors were hanging around for a while and then went for a meal in the nearby pizzeria. When we came home, it was already late evening, and my husband suddenly noticed that he missed his sports jacket which he wore during the glide.

It was a little late to go back to Krvavec, so we decided to go and search for the jacket the next day. If he left it on the landing ground (a large meadow where we spent some time after the glide, chatting), almost certainly no one would steal it, although it was possible, of course. But he could have left it it in the pizzeria. Anyway – I cast a horary chart as soon as the question arose in my mind.

Unfortunately, though, I made a mistake in calculation. In a hurry, I did not pay attention to the house system. Since my default house settings were Placidus which I use for natal chart calculation, my horary chart gave Placidean cusps. The chart which is published here has Regiomontanus cusps, because for the purpose of this exercise I cast the proper chart, but in the former one, the cusp of H8 (2/7 – partner's possessions) was at 28 ° Scorpio which would mean that his jacket would be ruled by Mars - and not by Jupiter, as shown in the valid chart where the cusp of H8 is at 3.5 degrees of Sagittarius.

It is understandable, then, that I came to the wrong conclusion - namely, that my husband would get his jacket back. Let's see, why! My husband's significator is Venus, the H7 ruler (and almuten) while his jacket would be shown by Mars, the H8 ruler and almuten. The Moon in Aquarius is applying directly to trine Mars, within less than half a degree orb, meaning that he should get the jacket back, and pretty soon! I guessed that would happen the very next day - which would be logical.

The next morning we headed to Krvavec and searched all the places where we were hanging the previous day. I even called our friends and asked them to look for the jacket in their car, because the Moon was in H11 and because Mars ruled H1 (3/11), but to no avail. Empty-handed and with a disgraced astrologer in our car we drove back home.

I went back to my horary to re-check for possible mistakes, and there I found it. As already said, in the Regiomontanus house system the H8 cusp is in Sagittarius, so my husband's jacket would be ruled by Jupiter. The Moon having just separated from the sextile of Jupiter clearly reflects his recent loss, as well as the probability that he was the last to handle it, before it was gone. The Moon's next aspect is trine Mars, ruling who? The ascendant represents me as the querent, true, but in the context of the question it is also the derived H7 (7/1) - "his" thief!

You might ask, why doesn't Mars co-rule my partner, since Scorpio is an intercepted sign in H7? It's because the role of Mars here is that of the (radix) ascendant ruler, so it can't be his co-significator; in the context of the question, Mars rules the (potential) thief. The trine also shows that the thief came to the jacket effortlessly. Most likely, he found it in the pizzeria - the Moon rules H5 of restaurants and is placed in H11 in Aquarius, a sign associated with places where people gather. I remembered that in the course of the evening, we once moved from one table to another. I thought it rather probable that my husband left the jacket at the first table, where someone found it and took it with him. This is quite clearly shown by the separating opposition of Mars (the thief) with Jupiter (the jacket), reinforced by the Moon's translation of light.

An interesting detail is added by the condition of my husband's significator, Venus. It's retrograde and in opposition to Neptune, reflecting his forgetfulness, which was probably also the result of a few beers that he'd had (Neptune). That the opposition lies across the 5/11 axis (pubs, society, entertainment) is no coincidence, of course!

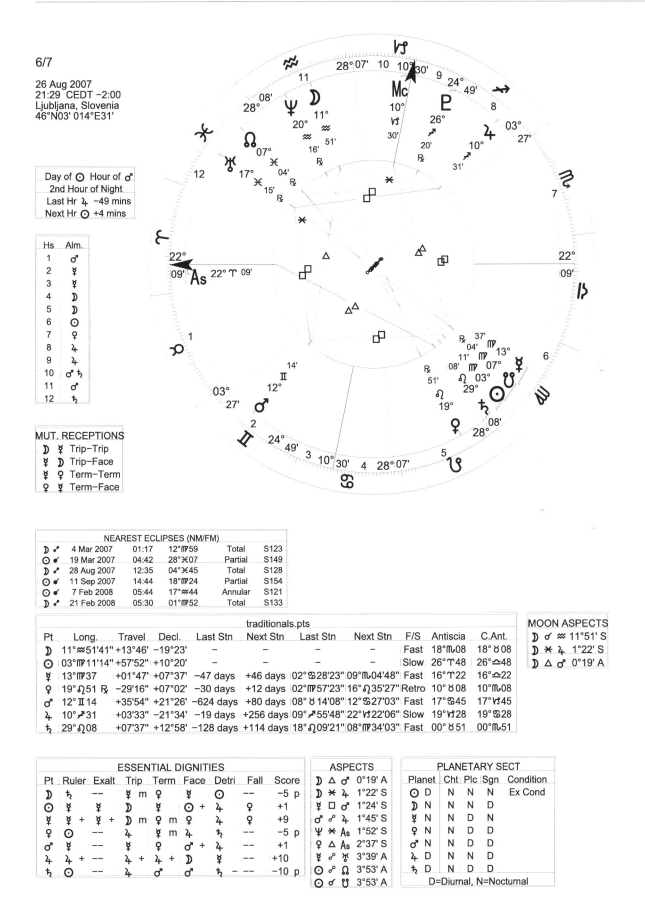

6/7

26 Aug 2007
21:29 CEDT −2:00
Ljubljana, Slovenia
46°N03' 014°E31'

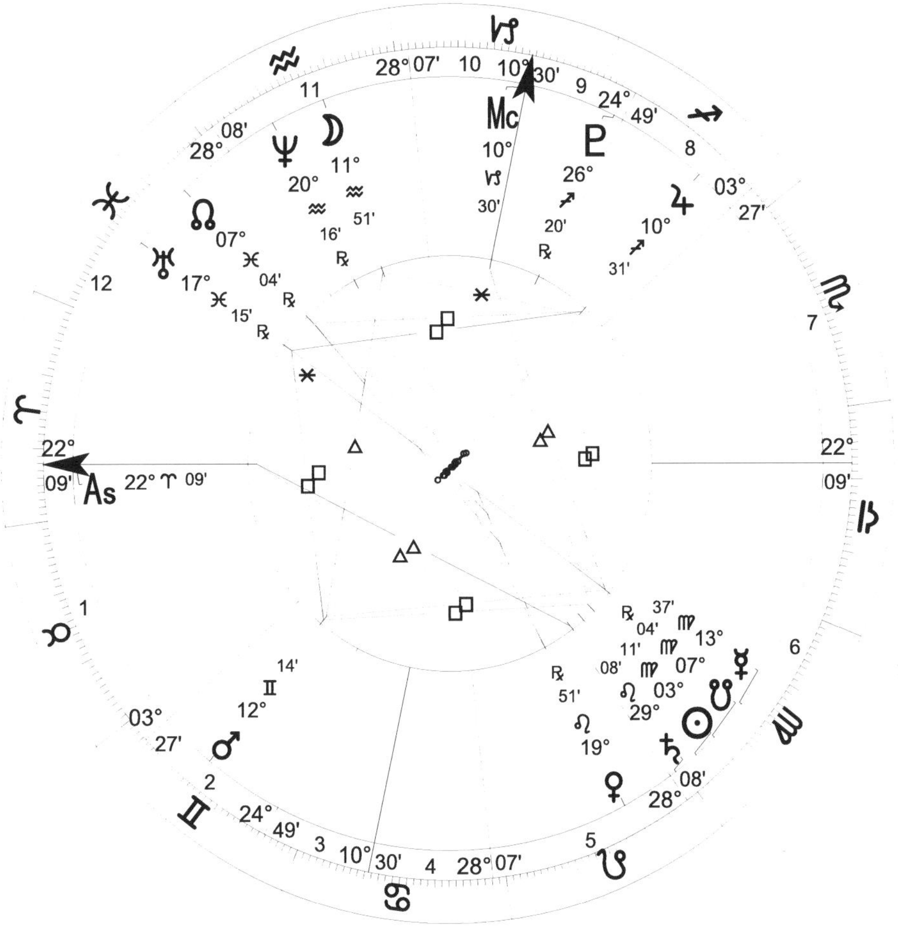

Day of ☉ Hour of ♂
2nd Hour of Night
Last Hr ♃ −49 mins
Next Hr ☉ +4 mins

Hs	Alm.
1	♂
2	☿
3	☿
4	☽
5	☽
6	☉
7	♀
8	♃
9	♃
10	♂ ♄
11	♂
12	♄

MUT. RECEPTIONS		
☽	☿	Trip−Trip
☿	☽	Trip−Face
☿	♀	Term−Term
♀	☿	Term−Face

NEAREST ECLIPSES (NM/FM)					
☽	4 Mar 2007	01:17	12°♍59	Total	S123
☉	19 Mar 2007	04:42	28°♓07	Partial	S149
☽	28 Aug 2007	12:35	04°♓45	Total	S128
☉	11 Sep 2007	14:44	18°♍24	Partial	S154
☉	7 Feb 2008	05:44	17°♒44	Annular	S121
☽	21 Feb 2008	05:30	01°♍52	Total	S133

traditionals.pts										
Pt	Long.	Travel	Decl.	Last Stn	Next Stn	Last Stn	Next Stn	F/S	Antiscia	C.Ant.
☽	11°♒51'41"	+13°46'	−19°23'	–	–	–	–	Fast	18°♏08	18°♉08
☉	03°♍11'14"	+57'52"	+10°20'	–	–	–	–	Slow	26°♈48	26°♎48
☿	13°♍37	+01°47'	+07°37'	−47 days	+46 days	02°♋28'23"	09°♏04'48"	Fast	16°♈22	16°♎22
♀	19°♌51 ℞	−29'16"	+07°02'	−30 days	+12 days	02°♍57'23"	16°♌35'27"	Retro	10°♉08	10°♏08
♂	12°♊14	+35'54"	+21°26'	−624 days	+80 days	08°♉14'08"	12°♋27'03"	Fast	17°♋45	17°♑45
♃	10°♐31	+03'33"	−21°34'	−19 days	+256 days	09°♐55'48"	22°♑22'06"	Slow	19°♑28	19°♋28
♄	29°♌08	+07'37"	+12°58'	−128 days	+114 days	18°♌09'21"	08°♍34'03"	Fast	00°♉51	00°♏51

MOON ASPECTS			
☽	☌	♒	11°51' S
☽	⚹	♃	1°22' S
☽	△	♂	0°19' A

ESSENTIAL DIGNITIES								
Pt	Ruler	Exalt	Trip	Term	Face	Detri	Fall	Score
☽	♄	--	☿ m	♀	☿	☉	--	−5 p
☉	☿	☿	☽	☿	☉ +	♃	♀	+1
☿	☿ +	☿ +	☽ m	♀ m	♀	♃	♀	+9
♀	☉	--	♃	☿ m	♃	♄	--	−5 p
♂	☿	--	☿	♀	♂ +	♃	--	+1
♃	♃ +	--	♃ +	♃ +	☽	☿	--	+10
♄	☉	--	♃	♂	♂	♄ −	--	−10 p

ASPECTS			
☽	△	♂	0°19' A
☽	⚹	♃	1°22' S
☿	□	♂	1°24' S
♂	☍	♃	1°45' S
♆	⚹	As	1°52' S
♀	△	As	2°37' S
☿	☍	♅	3°39' A
☉	☍	☊	3°53' A
☉	☌	☋	3°53' A

PLANETARY SECT					
Planet		Cht	Plc	Sgn	Condition
☉	D	N	N	N	Ex Cond
☽	N	N	N	D	
☿	N	N	D	N	
♀	N	N	D	D	
♂	N	N	D	D	
♃	D	N	N	D	
♄	D	N	D	D	
D=Diurnal, N=Nocturnal					

6/8: WHERE ARE MY SNEAKERS?

7 April 2004 at 9:20 p.m. (21:20), Ljubljana, Slovenia
Hour ruler: Venus, POF 6 Ar

I cast this chart after I had been missing my sneakers for a few days. I thought I might have left them at the fitness center where I mostly used them, but when I examined the chart, I soon realized that they must be at home.

Jupiter, the ruler of H2, standing for the sneakers, is in H10 while the Moon which co-rules them, is in H1. Both significators are therefore in angular houses, meaning that the missing item is at home. Because Jupiter is retrograde and the ascendant applies to it by sextile, and because there is a retrograde planet (Pluto) in H2, it was very clear that I'd find them. (Remember: any retrograde planet in H2, even if a trans-Saturnian, promises a return!)

But now to the core question: Where are they? Jupiter is in Virgo, suggesting that they were probably stashed into some closet, cupboard, a shelf or some other place where they were supposed to be kept safe. It was probably me who put them there, because the last aspect of Jupiter was square Mars, my ruler. The Moon is in the eastern part of the chart and slightly to the north, while Scorpio is a northern/northeastern sign. The closet, where I usually kept my sports bag, was in the lobby on the northern side of the house, meaning that they should be right in there. This seemed strange because I had already thoroughly investigated that closet.

Let's see what additional indications can be found in H4. The cusp is in Aquarius, with its dispositor Saturn in the water sign of Cancer. Could they be at a moist, damp place? Close to a water source? Well, that closet stood against the wall which it shared with the toilet, so underneath and next to it were water pipes. And Cancer is a northern sign! All of this led me to think that I might have just not investigated the closet as thoroughly as I should have. Because all the three significators (Jupiter, Moon and Saturn) were in water and earth signs which stand for low places, I went back and started to search the closet again at the floor level.

My search now proved successful - I found the sneakers very soon. They were at the very bottom of the closet, hidden under a large plastic bag.

It is interesting to note that Mercury was stationary on that day, as we often misplace and lose things on those days when Mercury changes direction.

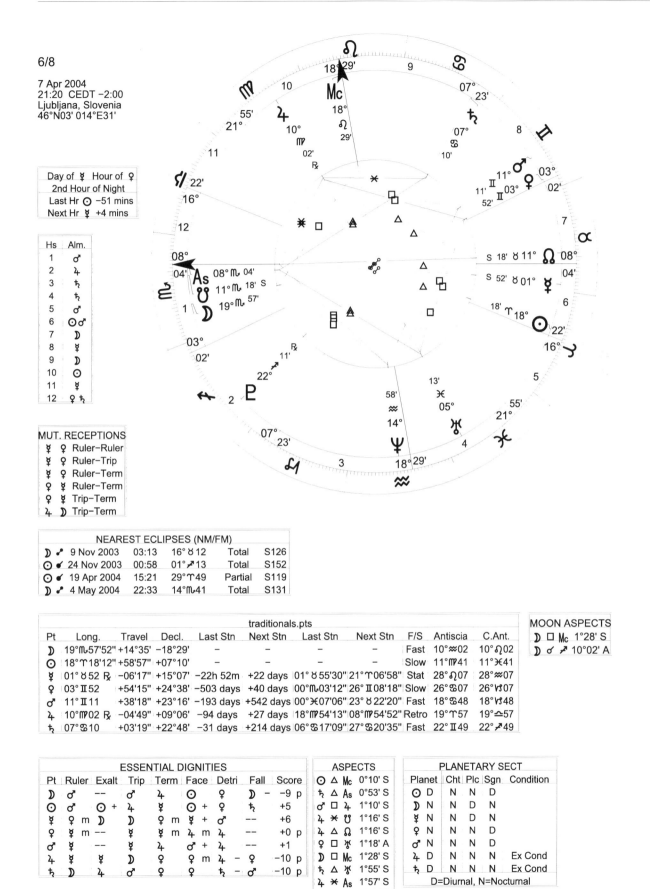

6/8

7 Apr 2004
21:20 CEDT −2:00
Ljubljana, Slovenia
46°N03' 014°E31'

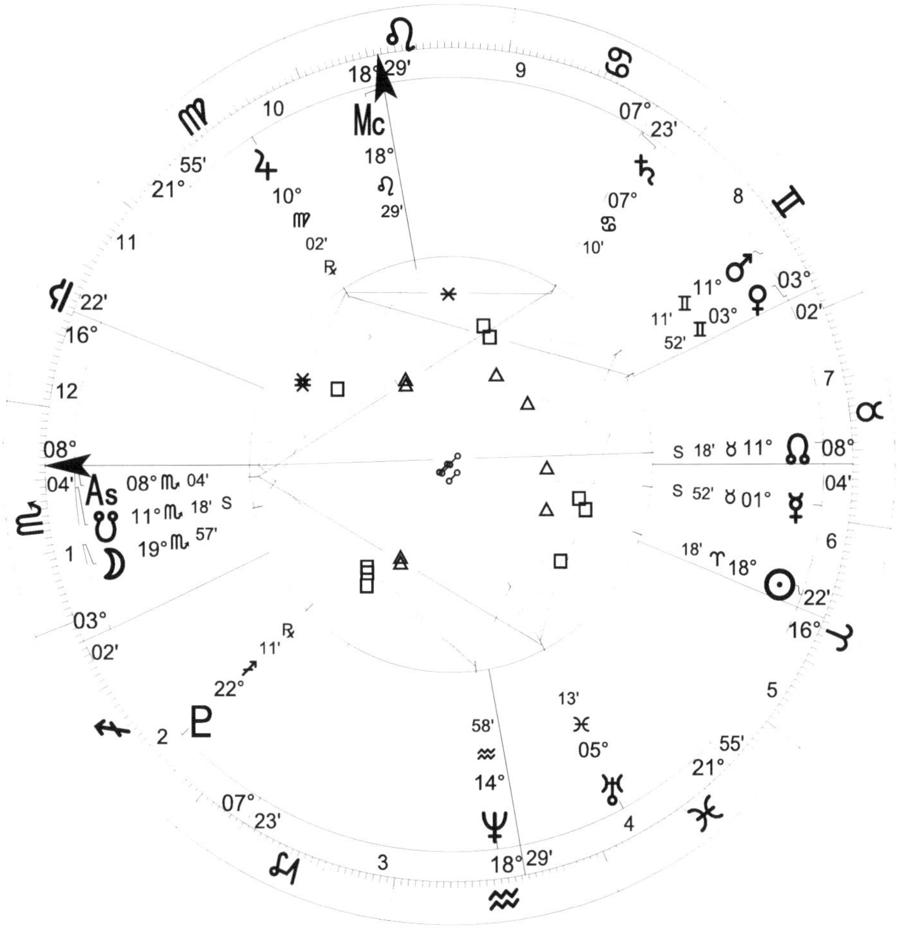

Day of ☿	Hour of ♀
2nd Hour of Night	
Last Hr ☉ −51 mins	
Next Hr ☿ +4 mins	

Hs	Alm.
1	♂
2	♃
3	♄
4	♄
5	♂
6	☉♂
7	☽
8	☿
9	☽
10	☉
11	☿
12	♀♄

MUT. RECEPTIONS		
☿	♀	Ruler–Ruler
☿	♀	Ruler–Trip
☿	♀	Ruler–Term
♀	☿	Ruler–Term
♀	☿	Trip–Term
♃	☽	Trip–Term

NEAREST ECLIPSES (NM/FM)					
☽ ☍	9 Nov 2003	03:13	16°♉12	Total	S126
☉ ☌	24 Nov 2003	00:58	01°♐13	Total	S152
☉ ☌	19 Apr 2004	15:21	29°♈49	Partial	S119
☽ ☍	4 May 2004	22:33	14°♏41	Total	S131

traditionals.pts

Pt	Long.	Travel	Decl.	Last Stn	Next Stn	Last Stn	Next Stn	F/S	Antiscia	C.Ant.
☽	19°♏57'52"	+14°35'	−18°29'	–	–	–	–	Fast	10°♒02	10°♌02
☉	18°♈18'12"	+58'57"	+07°10'	–	–	–	–	Slow	11°♍41	11°♓41
☿	01°♉52 ℞	−06'17"	+15°07'	−22h 52m	+22 days	01°♉55'30"	21°♈06'58"	Stat	28°♌07	28°♒07
♀	03°♊52	+54'15"	+24°38'	−503 days	+40 days	00°♏03'12"	26°♊08'18"	Slow	26°♋07	26°♑07
♂	11°♊11	+38'18"	+23°16'	−193 days	+542 days	00°♓07'06"	23°♉22'20"	Fast	18°♋48	18°♑48
♃	10°♍02 ℞	−04'49"	+09°06'	−94 days	+27 days	18°♍54'13"	08°♍54'52"	Retro	19°♈57	19°♎57
♄	07°♋10	+03'19"	+22°48'	−31 days	+214 days	06°♋17'09"	27°♋20'35"	Fast	22°♊49	22°♐49

MOON ASPECTS			
☽	□	Mc	1°28' S
☽	☌	♐	10°02' A

ESSENTIAL DIGNITIES

Pt	Ruler	Exalt	Trip	Term	Face	Detri	Fall	Score
☽	♂	--	♂	♃	☉	♀	☽ −	−9 p
☉	♂	☉ +	♃	☿	☉ +	♀	♄	+5
☿	♀ m	☽	☽	♀ m	☿ +	♂	--	+6
♀	☿ m	--	☽	☿ m	♃ m	♃	--	+0 p
♂	☿	--	☿	♃	♂ +	♃	--	+1
♃	☿	☿	☽	♀	♀ m	♃ −	♀	−10 p
♄	☽	♃	♂	♀	♀	♄ −	♂	−10 p

ASPECTS

☉	△	Mc	0°10' S
♄	△	As	0°53' S
♂	□	♃	1°10' S
♃	✶	☋	1°16' S
♃	△	☊	1°16' S
♀	□	♅	1°18' A
☽	□	Mc	1°28' S
♄	△	♅	1°55' S
♃	✶	As	1°57' S
♅	△	As	2°50' S

PLANETARY SECT

Planet		Cht	Plc	Sgn	Condition
☉	D	N	N	D	
☽	N	N	D	N	
☿	N	N	D	N	
♀	N	N	N	D	
♂	N	N	N	D	
♃	D	N	N	N	Ex Cond
♄	D	N	N	N	Ex Cond

D=Diurnal, N=Nocturnal

6/9: WHERE IS MY PURSE?

9 February 2003 at 11:13 p.m. (23:13), Ljubljana, Slovenia
Hour ruler: Moon, POF 23 Ca

I often cast lost purse charts because I often lose them. This loss I "declared to the heavens" one late evening, so I only had the time to search for it the next morning.

My ruler is Venus, placed in H3 in Capricorn, while the purse is signified by Mars, the ruler of H2. Mars also occupies that house. It's in Sagittarius and separating from its dispositor Jupiter by trine, while applying to conjunction with Pluto. Jupiter immediately attracted my attention as it is the highest planet in the chart, in the angular H10, and retrograde. Since Jupiter is also the natural ruler of valuables (which my wallet due to the money, bank cards and other documents held in it certainly was) and Mars' dispositor, its angular position and retrograde phase suggested that the wallet was obviously not lost, only misplaced, and that I would surely find it.

The Moon, co-significator of the wallet, is in Taurus on cusp of H8. This house is critical, as we know; it often shows a loss or a theft, but here the Moon is strong in Taurus, its exaltation sign, and not afflicted, which is certainly a positive indication that along with the promising position of the main significator shows that the wallet is most probably safe.

But where is it? The Moon is in the west and slightly to the south. Taurus indicates low places and storage items like drawers, boxes, bags, safes and the like, while Sagittarius and Leo which hold Mars and Jupiter, are fire signs, suggesting a slightly higher position.

Let us now turn to H4 which should help us find the location of the purse. IC is in the airy Aquarius and its ruler Saturn is also in an air sign, Gemini. Air signs indicate places where people gather and where there are books, computers and the like, and higher places. Mars in H2, which it also the rules, confirms that the wallet is in a safe place, and also that it's probably where it should be or where it is usually (or often) kept. Jupiter in H10 leads us to business premises (offices). The last Moon's separating aspect is a square with the Sun ruling H10, confirming indications of Jupiter in H10 and suggesting that the last time I had the wallet in my hands was probably when I worked in my home office. All this aligns with the indications of H4 (books, people, etc.), and the icing on the cake is offered by the direction of the Moon, as my office is right on the west side of the house, with a window facing south.

Most significators suggested middle ground, so the wallet was apparently not on the floor but probably stowed in some drawer (Moon in Taurus). As the rest of the significators suggested a higher position, I started my search at the uppermost office desk drawer. The purse was indeed in that drawer, hidden under several small items, as suggested by Mercury to which the Moon applies by a close trine.

6/9

9 Feb 2003
23:13 CET −1:00
Ljubljana, Slovenia
46°N03' 014°E31'

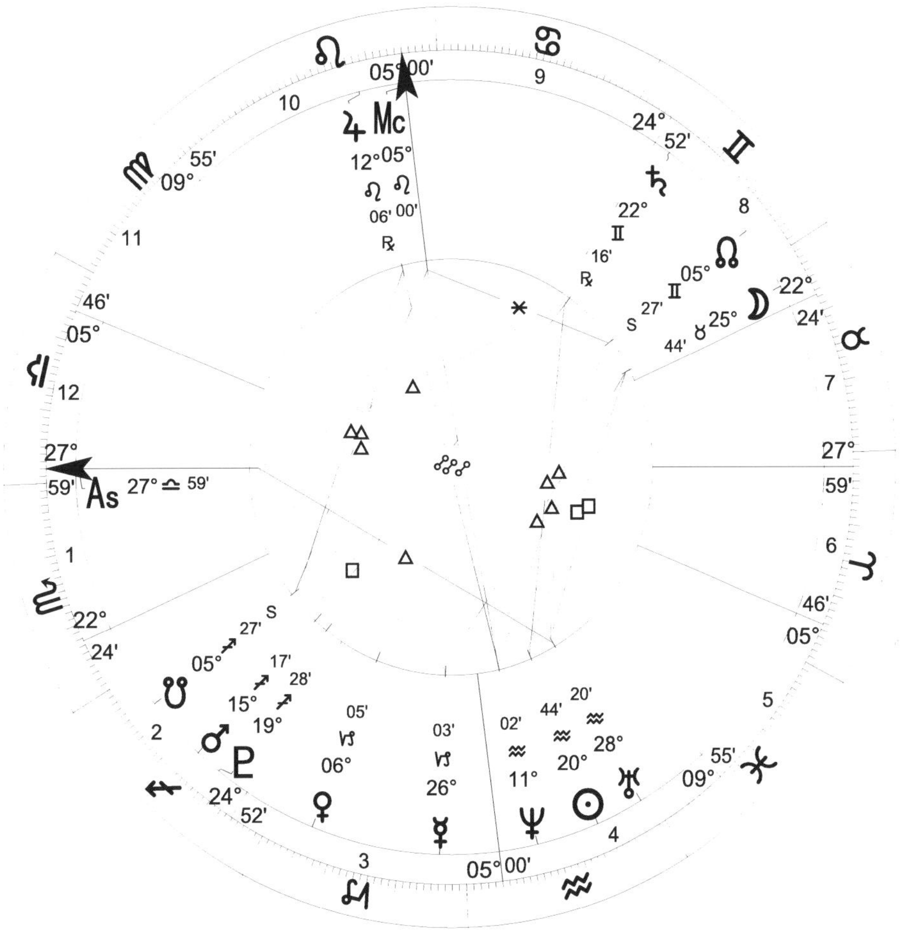

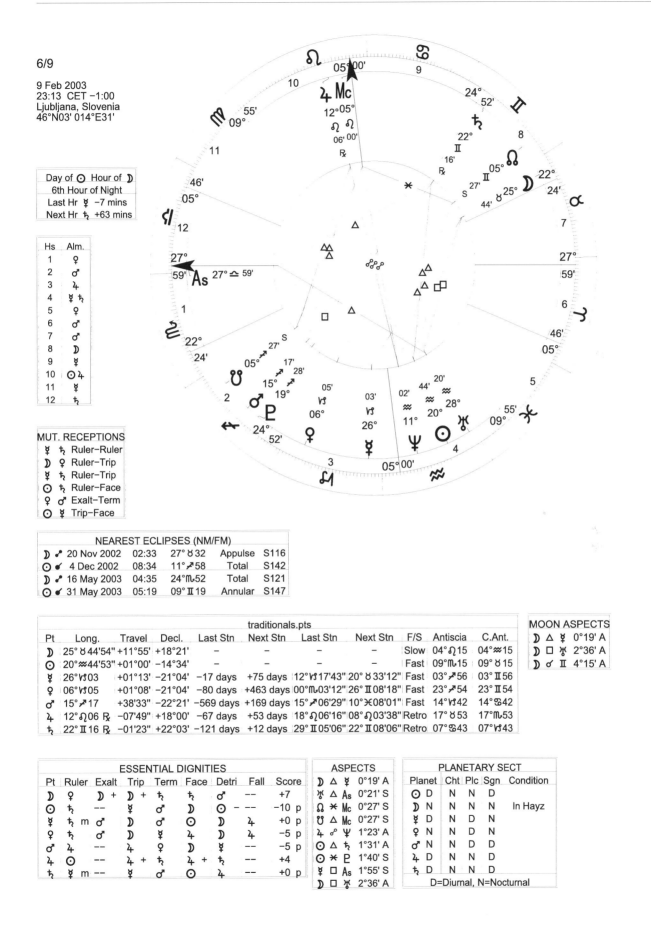

Day of ☉ Hour of ☽
6th Hour of Night
Last Hr ☿ −7 mins
Next Hr ♄ +63 mins

Hs	Alm.
1	♀
2	♂
3	♃
4	☿ ♄
5	♀
6	♂
7	♂
8	☽
9	☿
10	☉ ♃
11	☿
12	♄

MUT. RECEPTIONS		
☿	♄	Ruler−Ruler
☽	♀	Ruler−Trip
☿	♄	Ruler−Trip
☉	♄	Ruler−Face
♀	♂	Exalt−Term
☉	☿	Trip−Face

NEAREST ECLIPSES (NM/FM)					
☽ ☍	20 Nov 2002	02:33	27° ♉ 32	Appulse	S116
☉ ☌	4 Dec 2002	08:34	11° ♐ 58	Total	S142
☽ ☍	16 May 2003	04:35	24° ♏ 52	Total	S121
☉ ☌	31 May 2003	05:19	09° ♊ 19	Annular	S147

traditionals.pts

Pt	Long.	Travel	Decl.	Last Stn	Next Stn	Last Stn	Next Stn	F/S	Antiscia	C.Ant.
☽	25° ♉ 44'54"	+11°55'	+18°21'	–	–	–	–	Slow	04° ♌ 15	04° ♒ 15
☉	20° ♒ 44'53"	+01°00'	−14°34'	–	–	–	–	Fast	09° ♏ 15	09° ♉ 15
☿	26° ♑ 03	+01°13'	−21°04'	−17 days	+75 days	12° ♑ 17'43"	20° ♉ 33'12"	Fast	03° ♐ 56	03° ♊ 56
♀	06° ♑ 05	+01°08'	−21°04'	−80 days	+463 days	00° ♏ 03'12"	26° ♊ 08'18"	Fast	23° ♐ 54	23° ♊ 54
♂	15° ♐ 17	+38'33"	−22°21'	−569 days	+169 days	15° ♐ 06'29"	10° ♓ 08'01"	Fast	14° ♑ 42	14° ♋ 42
♃	12° ♌ 06 ℞	−07'49"	+18°00'	−67 days	+53 days	18° ♌ 06'16"	08° ♌ 03'38"	Retro	17° ♉ 53	17° ♏ 53
♄	22° ♊ 16 ℞	−01'23"	+22°03'	−121 days	+12 days	29° ♊ 05'06"	22° ♊ 08'06"	Retro	07° ♋ 43	07° ♑ 43

MOON ASPECTS			
☽	△	☿	0°19' A
☽	□	♅	2°36' A
☽	☌	♊	4°15' A

ESSENTIAL DIGNITIES

Pt	Ruler	Exalt	Trip	Term	Face	Detri	Fall	Score
☽	♀	☽ +	☽ +	♄	♄	♂	--	+7
☉	♄	--	☿	♂	☽	☉ −	--	−10 p
☿	♄ m	♂	☽	♂	☉	☽	♃	+0 p
♀	♄	♂	☽	☿	♃	☽	♃	−5 p
♂	♃	--	♃	♀	☽	☿	--	−5 p
♃	☉	--	♃ +	♄	♃ +	♄	--	+4
♄	☿ m	--	☿	♂	☉	♃	--	+0 p

ASPECTS			
☽	△	☿	0°19' A
♅	△	As	0°21' S
☊	⚹	Mc	0°27' S
☋	△	Mc	0°27' S
♃	☍	♆	1°23' A
☉	△	♄	1°31' A
☉	⚹	♇	1°40' S
☿	□	As	1°55' S
☽	□	♅	2°36' A

PLANETARY SECT

Planet		Cht	Plc	Sgn	Condition
☉	D	N	N	D	
☽	N	N	N	N	In Hayz
☿	D	N	D	N	
♀	N	N	D	N	
♂	N	N	D	D	
♃	D	N	N	D	
♄	D	N	N	D	

D=Diurnal, N=Nocturnal

6/10: WHERE IS MY WATCH?

4 June 1996 at 6:32 a.m., Ljubljana, Slovenia
Hour ruler: Mars, POF 4 Aq

I had been missing my hand watch for several days. Before going to bed I used to place it somewhere near my computer, bathtub, bed and the like, and never had any trouble finding it when I needed it, but this time, the watch was nowhere in sight. Although I raised the question early in the morning, I only committed myself to the chart close to the noon when I had to leave for some errands in town and therefore urgently needed it. (If you wonder why, let me remind you of the year in question - 1996! Cell phones were still a rarity at the time, and wearing a hand watch was almost a must.)

The Moon rules me and the watch, since it is the dispositor of the ascendant as well as of H2 with the cusp in Cancer. But because the co-almuten of H2 is Jupiter, this planet co-rules the watch. Both bodies are in H7, an angular house, which could well mean that the watch is at home – except if it was stolen. But since I was almost convinced that I didn't take it out of the house before it went missing, and since the Moon was in an exact applying conjunction with a retrograde planet, this even being Jupiter, the co-ruler of the watch, it became clear that the watch must be at home and that I would find it soon.

But where is it? The Moon is in Capricorn – an earth sign, indicating the floor and the lower areas. Because IC and its dispositor Mercury are also in earth signs (Virgo and Taurus), there's no doubt that the watch is somewhere low.

As already mentioned, the Moon is in a very exact applying conjunction with a retrograde Jupiter. This made me think that the watch must be very close to where I was and that I'd find it any moment. Then I remembered that Jupiter symbolizes wood. What's made of wood in my immediate surroundings, and low down to the grounds? The parquet, of course! Virgo on the H4 cusp indicates drawers and other storage places, so the watch must be on the floor close to some drawers.

I immediately rose from my chair, moved it away, knelt down and looked at the floor under the desk. There was my watch, lying on the parquet under the desk, actually under the chest of drawers which stood on the left side of the desk. The location was pretty much in the middle of the room – as the conjunction of the Moon and Jupiter in the middle of the sign suggests.

6/10

4 Jun 1996
06:32 CEDT −2:00
Ljubljana, Slovenia
46°N03' 014°E31'

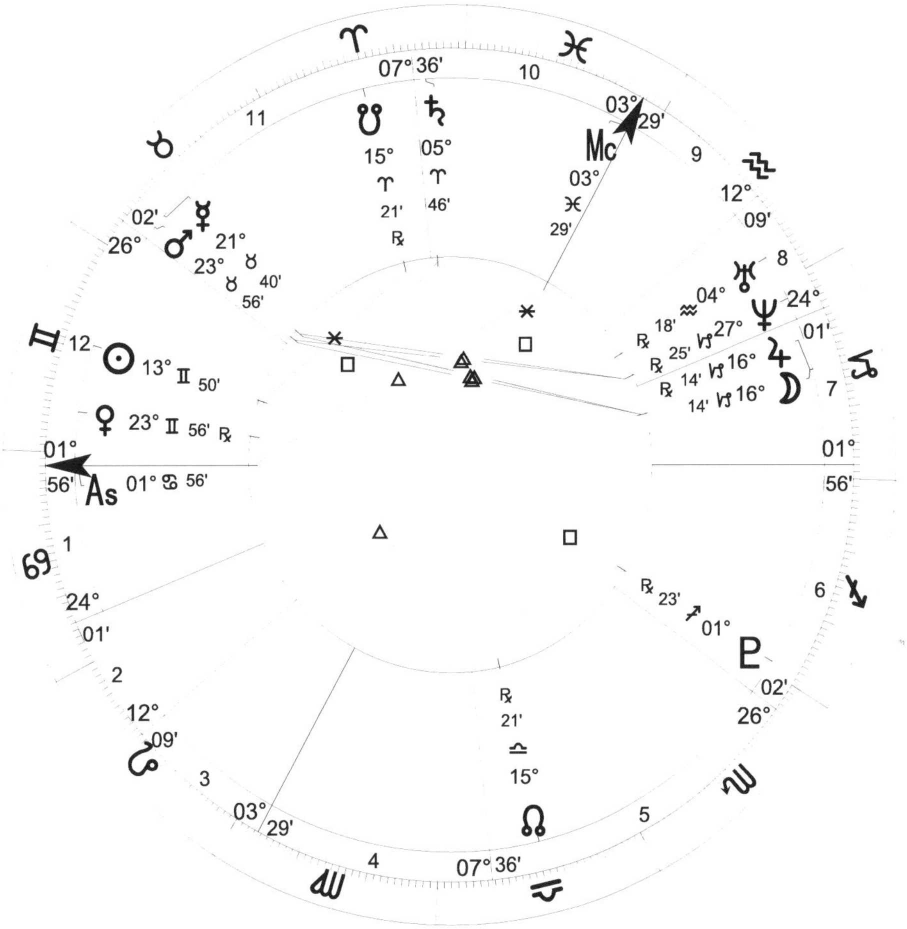

Day of ♂ Hour of ♂
1st Hour of Day
Last Hr ♃ −73 mins
Next Hr ☉ +4 mins

Hs	Alm.
1	☽
2	☽ ♃
3	☉
4	☿
5	♄
6	♂
7	♄
8	♄
9	♄
10	♀
11	☉
12	♀

MUT. RECEPTIONS		
☿	♀	Ruler-Ruler
♀	☿	Ruler-Trip
♂	♀	Ruler-Term
♃	♄	Ruler-Term
♄	♂	Ruler-Term
♄	♂	Ruler-Face

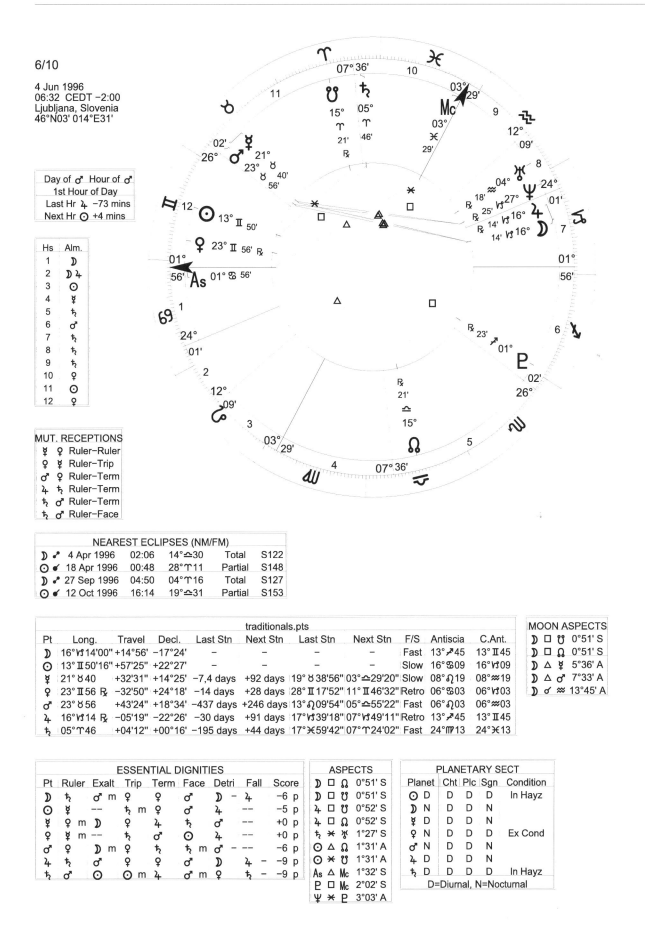

NEAREST ECLIPSES (NM/FM)					
☽ ☍	4 Apr 1996	02:06	14°♎30	Total	S122
☉ ☌	18 Apr 1996	00:48	28°♈11	Partial	S148
☽ ☍	27 Sep 1996	04:50	04°♈16	Total	S127
☉ ☌	12 Oct 1996	16:14	19°♎31	Partial	S153

traditionals.pts

Pt	Long.	Travel	Decl.	Last Stn	Next Stn	Last Stn	Next Stn	F/S	Antiscia	C.Ant.
☽	16°♑14'00"	+14°56'	−17°24'	–	–	–	–	Fast	13°♐45	13°♊45
☉	13°♊50'16"	+57'25"	+22°27'	–	–	–	–	Slow	16°♋09	16°♑09
☿	21°♉40	+32'31"	+14°25'	−7,4 days	+92 days	19°♉38'56"	03°♎29'20"	Slow	08°♌19	08°♒19
♀	23°♊56 ℞	−32'50"	+24°18'	−14 days	+28 days	28°♊17'52"	11°♊46'32"	Retro	06°♋03	06°♑03
♂	23°♉56	+43'24"	+18°34'	−437 days	+246 days	13°♌09'54"	05°♎55'22"	Fast	06°♌03	06°♒03
♃	16°♑14 ℞	−05'19"	−22°26'	−30 days	+91 days	17°♑39'18"	07°♑49'11"	Retro	13°♐45	13°♊45
♄	05°♈46	+04'12"	+00°16'	−195 days	+44 days	17°♓59'42"	07°♈24'02"	Fast	24°♍13	24°♓13

MOON ASPECTS			
☽	□	☋	0°51' S
☽	□	☊	0°51' S
☽	△	☿	5°36' A
☽	△	♂	7°33' A
☽	☌	♒	13°45' A

ESSENTIAL DIGNITIES

Pt	Ruler	Exalt	Trip	Term	Face	Detri	Fall	Score
☽	♄	♂ m	♀	♀	♂	☽ −	♃	−6 p
☉	☿	--	♄ m	♀	♂	♃	--	−5 p
☿	♀ m	☽	♀	♃	♄	♂	--	+0 p
♀	☿ m	--	♄	♂	☉	♃	--	+0 p
♂	♀	☽ m	♀	♄	♄ m	♂ −	--	−6 p
♃	♄	♂	♀	♀	♂	☽	♃ −	−9 p
♄	♂	☉	☉ m	♃	♂ m	♀	♄ −	−9 p

ASPECTS			
☽	□	☊	0°51' S
☽	□	☋	0°51' S
♃	□	☋	0°52' S
♃	□	☊	0°52' S
♄	⚹	♅	1°27' S
☉	△	☊	1°31' A
☉	⚹	☋	1°31' A
As	△	Mc	1°32' S
♇	□	Mc	2°02' S
♆	⚹	♇	3°03' A

PLANETARY SECT

Planet	Cht	Plc	Sgn	Condition
☉ D	D	D	D	In Hayz
☽ N	D	D	N	
☿ D	D	D	N	
♀ N	D	D	D	Ex Cond
♂ N	D	D	N	
♃ D	D	D	N	
♄ D	D	D	D	In Hayz

D=Diurnal, N=Nocturnal

6/11: WHERE IS MASHA'S PENCIL CASE?

2 November 2008 at 7:06 p.m. (19:06), Ljubljana, Slovenia
Hour ruler: Sun, POF 2 Ta

The autumn holidays were over and kids had to go back to school. But when on a Sunday afternoon I and my first-grade pupil Masha were getting her school bag ready, we found that her pencil case was missing. As she was absent from school the whole week before the start of the holidays, due to an illness, she wasn't using the pencil case for schoolwork all that time. We thought, though, that she would have probably used it at home because she was often drawing, writing or creating something. On the other hand, there were crayons and pencils elsewhere in the house, and they also had them in the hospital where Masha spent a week before the holidays. We brought her the school bag there so that she could do her homework, but we couldn't remember whether she really had the pencil case in her hands. It could also be at her school where the children were leaving bags during schooldays, and only brought them home for the weekends. But because Masha brought her schoolbag home the last Friday she was at school, the pencil case was probably not there. Could she forget it in the hospital? I doubted that because the nurses would certainly let us know.

As the pencil case was nowhere to be found, I cast a horary chart. Masha is ruled by Mercury, the H5 ruler, the pencil case with Mars which rules H6 (2/5). Conjunct the cusp of H6 is the Sun, the hour ruler, and as we know, the hour ruler (or the Moon or the ascendant ruler) is often located in a house that is the subject matter of a horary question.

We can see that Mars is located right there on the cusp of the derived H2, and is also in its own sign, Scorpio. This suggests two things: firstly, the pencil case is not damaged (Mars essentially strong), and secondly, the pencil is right where it should be! The only such place is the school bag, I thought, but when I searched it over for another three times, it became clear that something was wrong with my deductions.

Are there any other indications that Masha would get her pencil case back? Between Mercury, her ruler, and Mars, the significator of the missing item, are less than 30 degrees, which confirms the probability of finding it. In the light of these indications, we can assume that the Moon in H7 does not mean that is was stolen – not to mention the fact that it would be utterly strange that someone would steal it, of course. It must be somewhere close, in a safe place, and coming to sight.

Mars is in a water sign, the Moon in an earth sign and the Sun, the H4 ruler (describing the place of the missing item) also in a water sign (Cancer). All this points to lower locations. Scorpio as a fixed sign gives the impression that the pencil case was firmly "anchored" somewhere and that nobody had moved it anywhere, ever since it went missing. The last aspect of the Moon was a conjunction with Pluto, the modern dispositor of Mars in Scorpio, so this planet can be considered as a co-significator of the pencil case, while the second to last aspect was a sextile with Mercury, Masha's ruler. It is evident that she was the last to have it in her hands!

Given the fact that the Moon was in the western part of the chart and that Scorpio is a northern sign, while the children's room is in the attic which is to the east of the house, I searched her room again with little hope that I would find the missing item there. And, of course, I didn't.

The next day, Masha went to school without the pencil case. But when I came to pick her up in the afternoon, she told me: *Mom, the pencil case was in my school drawer!* She added that she did not find it herself, but her classmate Jaka who helped her look for it, did, after he uncovered a pile of papers in her drawer.

A re-examination of the chart revealed a fascinatingly clear picture which I could not have "decoded" myself (hour ruler inharmonious!), but in retrospect, it all became very logical.

The Moon is in H7 which is 3/5 – Masha's school. In Capricorn, an earth sign: securely stored in a drawer. And also, of course, this is "where it should be" (H2 ruler in H2), since this was the usual place where Masha kept her stuff in the school. Mars separates from Jupiter, the H7 ruler which is 3/5 (my kid's school), reflecting the fact that the pencil case was in a school drawer, not at home. (You will notice though that Mars' last separating aspect with a traditional planet was a sextile to Saturn which disposes Jupiter, and, moreover, the sextile to Jupiter is stronger because Mars receives Jupiter in its exaltation sign.) This is confirmed by the Sun, ruler of the radix H3 (schools) on the cusp of H6. Mars, the main significator, in a fixed sign: the pencil case lay there untouched for two weeks. Hidden under some papers: of course, Mars is under the Sun's beams, indicating that the item was not immediately

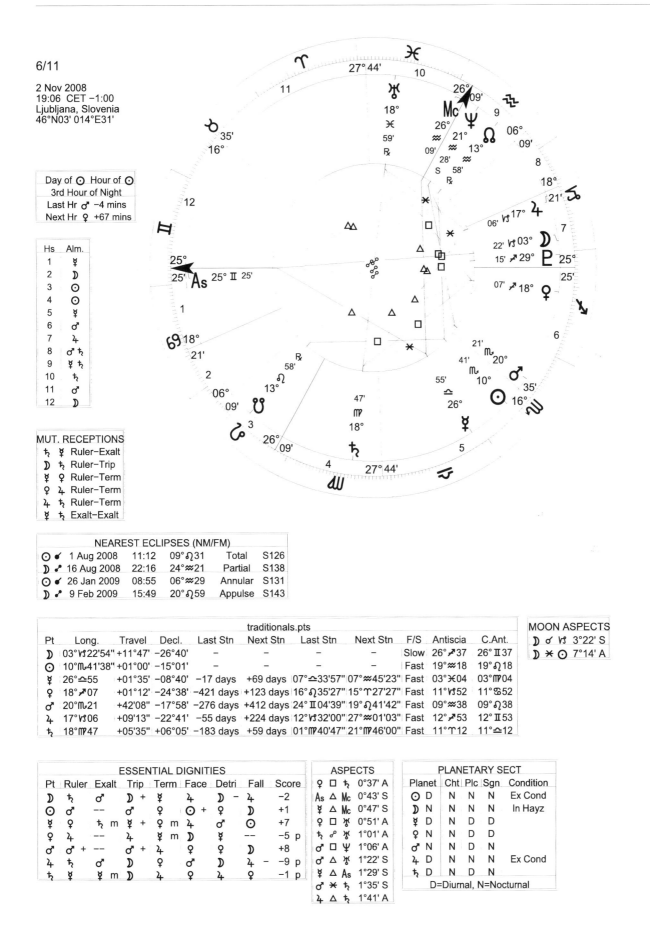

6/11

2 Nov 2008
19:06 CET −1:00
Ljubljana, Slovenia
46°N03' 014°E31'

Day of ☉ Hour of ☉
3rd Hour of Night
Last Hr ♂ −4 mins
Next Hr ♀ +67 mins

Hs	Alm.
1	☿
2	☽
3	☉
4	☉
5	☿
6	♂
7	♃
8	♂ ♄
9	☿ ♄
10	♄
11	♂
12	☽

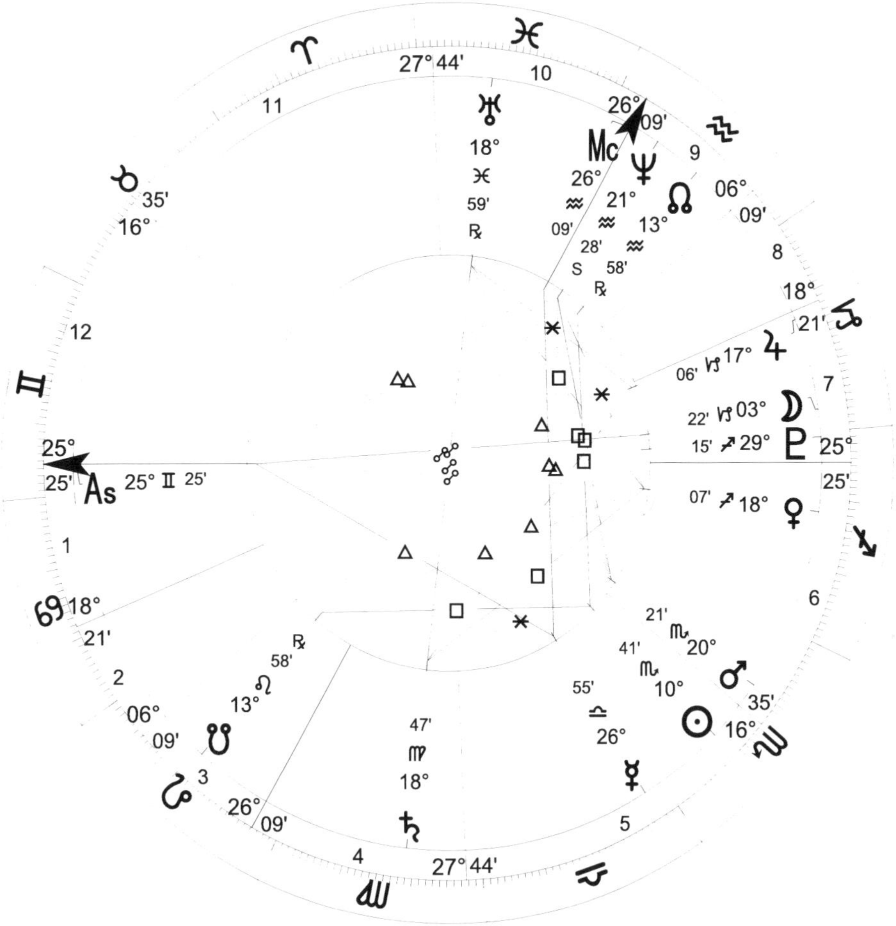

MUT. RECEPTIONS		
♄	☿	Ruler–Exalt
☽	♄	Ruler–Trip
☿	♀	Ruler–Term
♀	♃	Ruler–Term
♃	♄	Ruler–Term
☿	♄	Exalt–Exalt

NEAREST ECLIPSES (NM/FM)					
☉ ☌	1 Aug 2008	11:12	09°♌31	Total	S126
☽ ☍	16 Aug 2008	22:16	24°♒21	Partial	S138
☉ ☌	26 Jan 2009	08:55	06°♒29	Annular	S131
☽ ☍	9 Feb 2009	15:49	20°♌59	Appulse	S143

traditionals.pts

Pt	Long.	Travel	Decl.	Last Stn	Next Stn	Last Stn	Next Stn	F/S	Antiscia	C.Ant.
☽	03°♑22'54"	+11°47'	−26°40'	–	–	–	–	Slow	26°♐37	26°♊37
☉	10°♏41'38"	+01°00'	−15°01'	–	–	–	–	Fast	19°♒18	19°♌18
☿	26°♎55	+01°35'	−08°40'	−17 days	+69 days	07°♎33'57"	07°♒45'23"	Fast	03°♓04	03°♍04
♀	18°♐07	+01°12'	−24°38'	−421 days	+123 days	16°♌35'27"	15°♈27'27"	Fast	11°♑52	11°♋52
♂	20°♏21	+42'08"	−17°58'	−276 days	+412 days	24°♊04'39"	19°♌41'42"	Fast	09°♒38	09°♌38
♃	17°♑06	+09'13"	−22°41'	−55 days	+224 days	12°♑32'00"	27°♒01'03"	Fast	12°♐53	12°♊53
♄	18°♍47	+05'35"	+06°05'	−183 days	+59 days	01°♍40'47"	21°♍46'00"	Fast	11°♈12	11°♎12

MOON ASPECTS			
☽	☌	♑	3°22' S
☽	✶	☉	7°14' A

ESSENTIAL DIGNITIES

Pt	Ruler	Exalt	Trip	Term	Face	Detri	Fall	Score
☽	♄	♂	☽ +	☿	♃	☽ −	♃	−2
☉	♂	--	♂	♀	☉ +	♀	☽	+1
☿	♀	♄ m	☿ +	♀ m	♃	♂	☉	+7
♀	♃	--	♃	☿ m	☽	☿	--	−5 p
♂	♂ +	--	♂ +	♃	♀	♀	☽	+8
♃	♄	♂	☽	♀	♂	☽	♃ −	−9 p
♄	☿	☿ m	☽	♃	♀	♃	♀	−1 p

ASPECTS			
♀	□	♄	0°37' A
As	△	Mc	0°43' S
☿	△	Mc	0°47' S
♀	□	♅	0°51' A
♄	☍	♅	1°01' A
♂	□	♆	1°06' A
♂	△	♅	1°22' S
☿	△	As	1°29' S
♂	✶	♄	1°35' S
♃	△	♄	1°41' A

PLANETARY SECT

Planet		Cht	Plc	Sgn	Condition
☉	D	N	N	N	Ex Cond
☽	N	N	N	N	In Hayz
☿	D	N	D	D	
♀	N	N	D	D	
♂	N	N	D	N	
♃	D	N	N	N	Ex Cond
♄	D	N	D	N	

D=Diurnal, N=Nocturnal

visible. Found by Masha's classmate (who was also her best friend): this too is reflected in the chart since Mars (the pencil case) and Mercury (Masha) are not connected, while Mars is being applied to by the Sun, ruler of the radix H3 which is the derived H11 (11/5) of her friends.

6/12: WHERE IS THE MISSING BOOK?

24 March 2002 at 11:10 a.m., Ljubljana, Slovenia
Hour ruler: Jupiter, POF 13 Sc

I raised this question when I realized that my book **Declination: The Other Dimension** by Kt Bohrer went missing. The planetary hour ruler is harmonious (Jupiter in Cancer, the ascending sign), making the chart radical.

Generally, all moveable property belongs to H2, but William Lilly clearly stated that books belong to H9 while various letters and documents to H3. Personally, I'm inclined to think that fiction and other stuff that we read for fun, could be ruled by H3, while study materials and books related to the field of "higher knowledge", should belong to H9. But most modern horary books and teachers claim that all movable stuff that we own, belongs to H2. Even my teacher Olivia Barclay, who followed dutifully in the steps of Lilly, never mentioned books in connection with H9.

So let us assume, for the start, that the book is ruled by H2. The ruler of H2 is the Sun, placed in the angular H10, in its exaltation sign (Aries), and the Moon, my co-significator (as the ruler and almuten of the ascending degree) which the Sun receives in its domicile sign Leo, applies to it by a tight trine. The Moon also acts as co-significator of the book as it "sits" on the cusp of H2. We therefore have a close applying aspect of both significators, with one receiving the other, and with one planet angular and the other on cusp of the house showing the missing item. What stronger indication of an affirmative answer could you have? If the book was ruled by H2, I would have found it very soon. The powerful, unafflicted Sun also suggests that the book would be intact.

Mercury, the natural ruler of books, in H10, is another indication that the book is somewhere close – except that it's in Pisces, in its detriment and fall, therefore ineffective.

Driven by a strong need to find the book, and because I thought that such a nice chart indicated that the book would soon be back in my hands, I thoroughly searched all the places to which the indications of H2 led me, as well as all the other places in the house, to no avail.

I got back to my chart, remembering Lilly's rules, and turned to H9. The cusp of this house is in Aquarius and its modern ruler Uranus is right on its cusp. Incidentally, this is also the planet of astrology. Yes, this seemed very appropriate! The traditional ruler of Aquarius, Saturn, is in Gemini - the sign associated with learning and books, but on cusp of the cadent H12. This could mean two things: either the book was lost, or it was safe, but somewhere far away. The first option was hardly possible because Saturn was essentially strong (in its triplicity) and also because the Moon applied to it by a sextile. It is true that before this aspect would be completed, the Moon would reach a trine with the Sun, but because the Sun was so powerful and disposing of the Moon ruling H2, this couldn't be regarded as a frustration. It became clear that the book was far from me but that one day I'd get it back. The Moon in a fixed sign needs 7 degrees to reach Saturn in a mutable sign and a cadent house. In 7 months?

The outcome? Sometime between 2011 and 2013 (I can't remember the exact year and date) a distant friend who was once my student, asked me out for a drink. While we chatted, she said, listen, I still have that book of yours, I must give it back to you. Which book, I asked. Oh, that one about declinations, she said.

In the chart, my friend is shown by Mars, the H11 ruler, occupying its own house, but in Taurus, the intercepted sign of H11. As we know, intercepted signs usually show things and people of whom we are unaware, or those who are "hidden". And so it was because lending the book to her had long escaped my memory! Mars in detriment could describe her as unfair - but we know how it is with the books that we lend. People seldom return them unless they are asked to. It's interesting to note that Mars disposits (by sign) the Sun – the ruler of H2 of my possessions. Yes, she was in the possession of my possession, but as this possession was a book, its fate was ruled by H9!

Now to another fascinating part of this case. You will see that both Saturn (the main significator of the missing book) and Mercury (the natural significator of books) are in double-bodied signs (Gemini and Pisces respectively). Mercury is even angular and very close to MC, so this duality must somehow affect the outcome. And it did! Even

6/12

24 Mar 2002
11:10 CET −1:00
Ljubljana, Slovenia
46°N03' 014°E31'

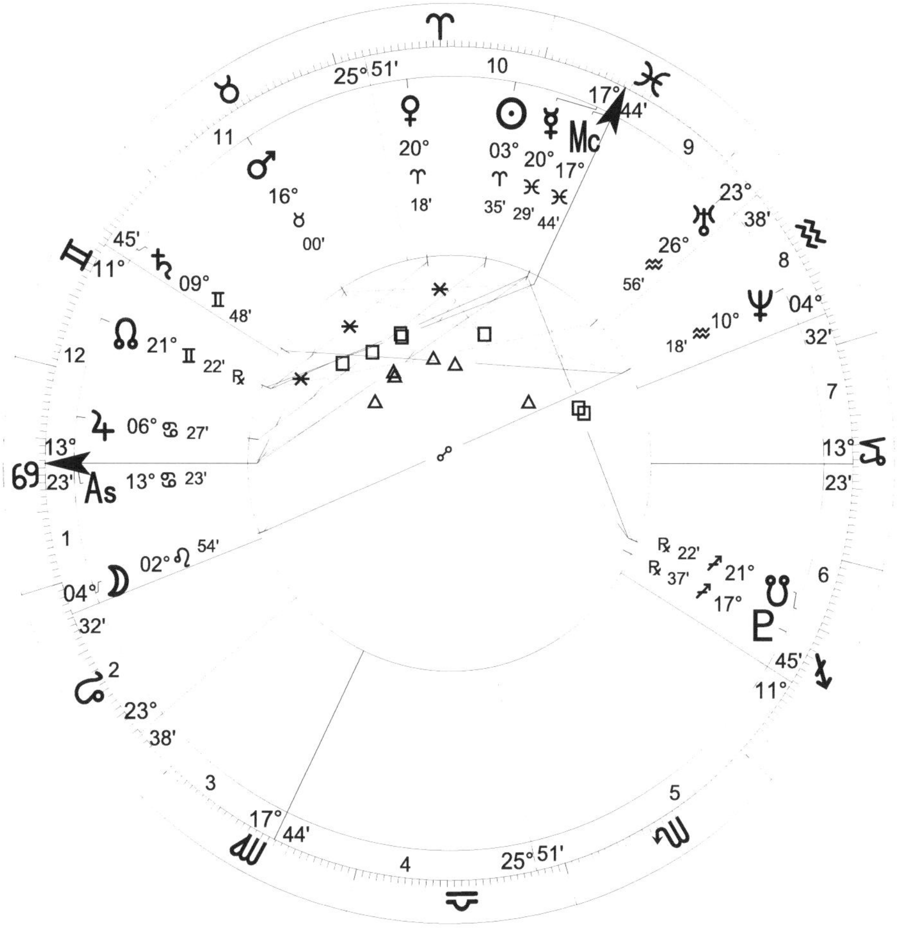

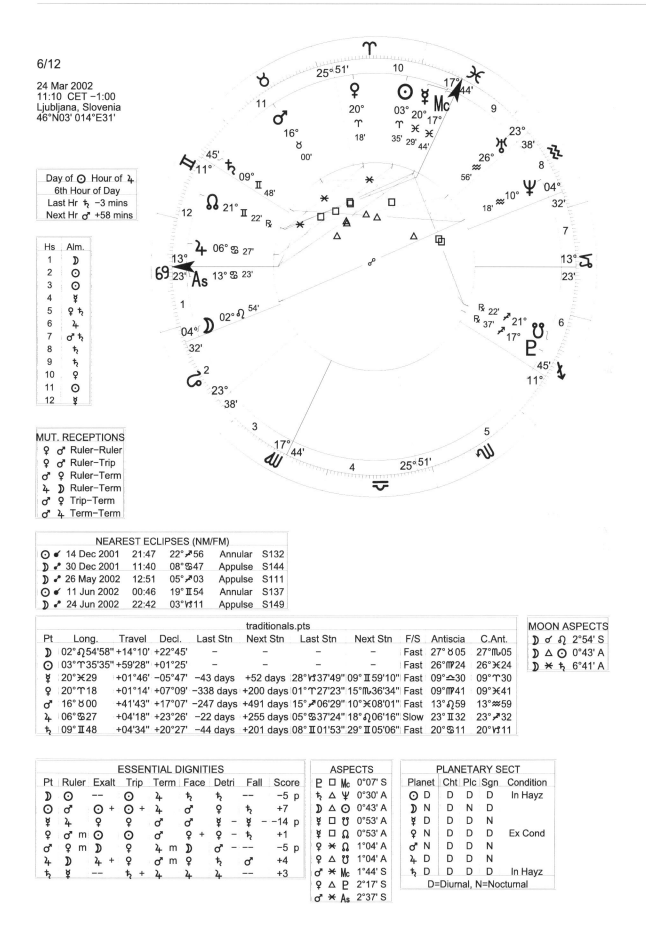

Day of ☉ Hour of ♃
6th Hour of Day
Last Hr ♄ −3 mins
Next Hr ♂ +58 mins

Hs	Alm.
1	☽
2	☉
3	☉
4	☿
5	♀ ♄
6	♃
7	♂ ♄
8	♄
9	♄
10	♀
11	☉
12	☿

MUT. RECEPTIONS	
♀ ♂	Ruler–Ruler
♀ ♂	Ruler–Trip
♂ ♀	Ruler–Term
♃ ☽	Ruler–Term
♂ ♀	Trip–Term
♂ ♃	Term–Term

NEAREST ECLIPSES (NM/FM)					
☉	14 Dec 2001	21:47	22°♐56	Annular	S132
☽	30 Dec 2001	11:40	08°♋47	Appulse	S144
☽	26 May 2002	12:51	05°♐03	Appulse	S111
☉	11 Jun 2002	00:46	19°♊54	Annular	S137
☽	24 Jun 2002	22:42	03°♑11	Appulse	S149

traditionals.pts

Pt	Long.	Travel	Decl.	Last Stn	Next Stn	Last Stn	Next Stn	F/S	Antiscia	C.Ant.
☽	02°♌54'58"	+14°10'	+22°45'	–	–	–	–	Fast	27°♉05	27°♏05
☉	03°♈35'35"	+59'28"	+01°25'	–	–	–	–	Fast	26°♍24	26°♓24
☿	20°♓29	+01°46'	−05°47'	−43 days	+52 days	28°♑37'49"	09°♊59'10"	Fast	09°♎30	09°♈30
♀	20°♈18	+01°14'	+07°09'	−338 days	+200 days	01°♈27'23"	15°♏36'34"	Fast	09°♍41	09°♓41
♂	16°♉00	+41'43"	+17°07'	−247 days	+491 days	15°♐06'29"	10°♓08'01"	Fast	13°♌59	13°♒59
♃	06°♋27	+04'18"	+23°26'	−22 days	+255 days	05°♋37'24"	18°♌06'16"	Slow	23°♊32	23°♐32
♄	09°♊48	+04'34"	+20°27'	−44 days	+201 days	08°♊01'53"	29°♊05'06"	Fast	20°♋11	20°♑11

MOON ASPECTS
☽ ☌ ☊ 2°54' S
☽ △ ☉ 0°43' A
☽ ⚹ ♄ 6°41' A

ESSENTIAL DIGNITIES

Pt	Ruler	Exalt	Trip	Term	Face	Detri	Fall	Score
☽	☉	--	☉	♃	♄	♄	--	−5 p
☉	♂	☉ +	☉ +	♃	♂	♀	♄	+7
☿	♃	♀	♀	♂	♂	☿ −	☿ −	−14 p
♀	♂ m	☉	☉	♂	♀ +	♀ −	♄	+1
♂	♀ m	☽	♀	♃ m	☽	♂ −	--	−5 p
♃	☽	♃ +	♀	♂ m	♀	♄	♂	+4
♄	☿	--	♄ +	♃	♃	♃	--	+3

ASPECTS			
♇	□	Mc	0°07' S
♄	△	♆	0°30' A
☽	△	☉	0°43' A
☿	□	☋	0°53' A
☿	□	☊	0°53' A
♀	⚹	☊	1°04' A
♀	△	☋	1°04' A
♂	⚹	Mc	1°44' S
♀	△	♇	2°17' S
♂	⚹	As	2°37' S

PLANETARY SECT

Planet	Cht	Plc	Sgn	Condition
☉ D	D	D	D	In Hayz
☽ N	D	N	D	
☿ D	D	D	N	
♀ N	D	D	D	Ex Cond
♂ N	D	D	N	
♃ D	D	D	N	
♄ D	D	D	D	In Hayz

D=Diurnal, N=Nocturnal

before my friend gave me back the book, I received - in the beginning of July 2006 - its duplicate. The book was a rarity; I could not buy another copy because it was out of print, so I asked my friends on an astrology forum if they could help. An American friend sent me a photocopied version which looked exactly like the original – a spiral-bound version which looked exactly the same as my original. This happened when transiting Saturn was in a very exact (to the minute) sextile to Saturn in the horary chart! Another timing peculiarity: exactly 224 weeks passed until the day I received the copy. If we move the horary Moon 224 degrees forward, we get to the exact degree of the horary MC! Yet another timing is shown by the distance of Mercury (the co-significator of the book) to Mars, significator of my circle of friends. Between them there are 57 degrees, and the book was sent to me in 57 synodic lunar months. Moreover, there are exactly 57 degrees between the ascendant and Mars! (To which I just must add: isn't astrology fascinating?)

This is one of the several charts in my book proving that horary charts are not necessarily short-lived. Every horary chart is active (operating) until the matter is finally resolved - in one way or another.

6/13: WHERE IS THE MISSING REMOTE KEY?

23 March 2015 at 11:03 a.m., Ljubljana, Slovenia
Hour ruler: Sun, POF 6 Aq

At 10:30 on that day, I had a dentist appointment. At about ten, I walked out of my home office with a client and closed the gate after her with a remote key, so that I could let the dog out for a few minutes before leaving. That's what I did, but when the dog was back in the house, I couldn't find the key to reopen the gate. Without it, I couldn't leave because my car was in the driveway. The unfortunate coincidence was that our fixed gate control was out of order. We had another spare key somewhere in the house, but that one I had misplaced already several days before.

As it was getting late for my appointment, I started to frantically search all the places that I visited, or could have visited, during those five minutes: bathroom, office, kitchen... But when after a quarter of an hour I could still not find it, and knowing that it was too late to call a cab, I called the dental assistant and told her that I was unfortunately unable to come due to *force majeure*.

I was angry and confused. My renewed search was in vain, so I sat down by my computer and typed in the question: *Where is the d**n gate key?!*

The key is shown by the Sun, the ruler of H2, and by the Moon, the co-significator of missing items. There is a retrograde planet in H2 (Jupiter, co-ruling the key) - a sure sign that the lost item would be found. This is confirmed by the Sun in H10, an angular house. The Moon in Taurus applies by a sextile to Mercury, while its last separating aspect was a square with Jupiter. This shows that I lost the key due to distraction - which is logical, because I was in a hurry when it went missing. Both the Sun and the Moon are exalted, a sure indication that the key is not damaged. Both are also in fortunate houses and above the horizon, which is encouraging.

But where is it? This was, as always, a difficult question, especially since the key is partly ruled by Mercury, the natural significator of small things, playing a particularly important role here due to its aspect with the Moon. Applications show what will happen, so, something was definitely going to happen soon, because Mercury is in an angular house, suggesting a quick, immediate action. The Moon, before completing the sextile with Mercury, makes a trine to Pluto, which is good because it confirms the "regenerative" indications given elsewhere. Mercury is in a double-bodied sign (Pisces) showing some kind of duality. In missing items horaries this often indicates a duplicate. As already mentioned, I had been missing the duplicate of this key for several days. And because the Moon shows the flow of events and will soon (a good two degrees orb) activate Mercury, it is kind of astro-logical that I first found the duplicate!

Seeing that the Moon first applied to Mercury, I focused my attention on this planet. Mercury is in Pisces, a northern sign. Above the horizon – upstairs, on the top floor? In a water sign - in the bathroom? I examined the bathroom on the top floor which lies to the north, but the key was not there. Then I remembered that Mercury ruled H12 in the chart, this house symbolizing bedrooms, so I went to the bedroom which is adjacent to the bathroom and also in the northern part of the house. I searched the pockets of a few sweaters that were hanging in the closet - and in one of them I found the duplicate. This key differed slightly from the one that I lost that morning

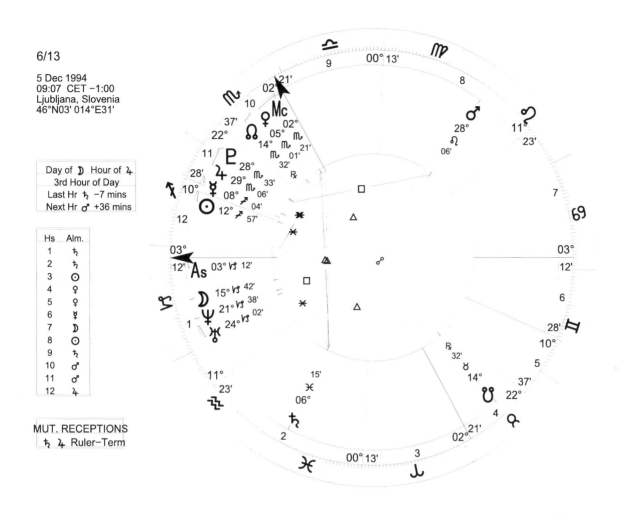

6/13

5 Dec 1994
09:07 CET −1:00
Ljubljana, Slovenia
46°N03' 014°E31'

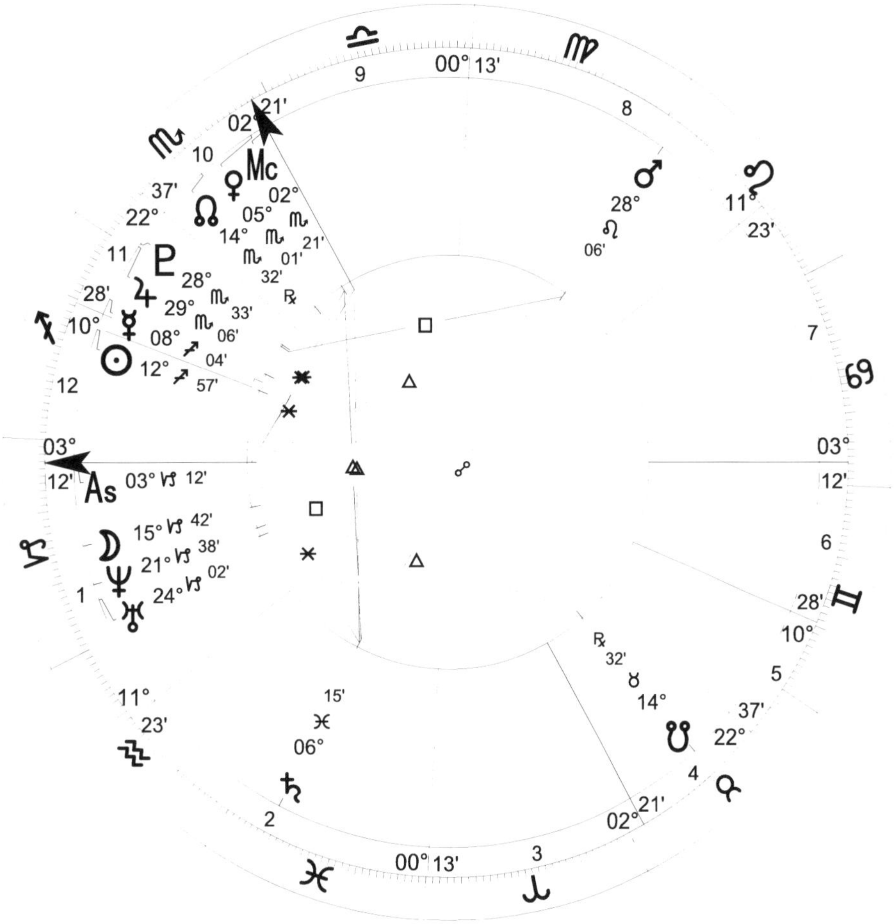

Day of ☽ Hour of ♃
3rd Hour of Day
Last Hr ♄ −7 mins
Next Hr ♂ +36 mins

Hs	Alm.
1	♄
2	♄
3	☉
4	♀
5	♀
6	☿
7	☽
8	☉
9	♄
10	♂
11	♂
12	♃

MUT. RECEPTIONS
♄ ♃ Ruler−Term

NEAREST ECLIPSES (NM/FM)					
☉ ☌	3 Nov 1994	14:35	10°♏54	Total	S133
☽ ☍	18 Nov 1994	07:57	25°♉42	Appulse	S145
☽ ☍	15 Apr 1995	13:08	25°♎03	Partial	S112
☉ ☌	29 Apr 1995	18:36	08°♉56	Annular	S138

traditionals.pts

Pt	Long.	Travel	Decl.	Last Stn	Next Stn	Last Stn	Next Stn	F/S	Antiscia	C.Ant.
☽	15°♑42'41"	+14°39'	−17°57'	–	–	–	–	Fast	14°♐17	14°♊17
☉	12°♐57'28"	+01°00'	−22°21'	–	–	–	–	Fast	17°♑02	17°♋02
☿	08°♐04	+01°34'	−22°01'	−36 days	+51 days	20°♎48'54"	21°♒15'53"	Fast	21°♑55	21°♋55
♀	05°♏01	+24'54"	−11°35'	−11 days	+531 days	02°♏28'46"	28°♊17'52"	Slow	24°♒58	24°♌58
♂	28°♌06	+17'36"	+14°29'	−658 days	+28 days	08°♋40'31"	02°♍40'08"	Slow	01°♉53	01°♏53
♃	29°♏06	+13'07"	−19°12'	−156 days	+117 days	04°♏46'04"	15°♐23'00"	Fast	00°♒53	00°♌53
♄	06°♓15	+02'40"	−10°55'	−25 days	+212 days	05°♓40'45"	24°♓45'07"	Fast	23°♎44	23°♈44

MOON ASPECTS	
☽ △ ☋	1°15' S
☽ ⚹ ☊	1°15' S
☽ ☌ ♆	7°09' A
☽ ☌ ♒	14°17' A

ESSENTIAL DIGNITIES

Pt	Ruler	Exalt	Trip	Term	Face	Detri	Fall	Score
☽	♄	♂	♀	♀	♂	☽ −	♃	−10 p
☉	♃	--	☉ +	♀	☽	☿	--	+3
☿	♃	--	☉	♃	☿ +	☿ −	--	−4
♀	♂	--	♀ +	♂	♂	♀ −	☽	−2
♂	☉	--	☉	♂ +	♂ +	♄	--	+3
♃	♂	--	♀	♄	♀	♀	☽	−5 p
♄	♃	♀	♀	♀	♄ +	☿	☿	+1

ASPECTS	
♂ □ ♇	0°08' S
As ⚹ Mc	0°51' A
♂ □ ♃	0°57' A
☽ ⚹ ☊	1°15' S
☽ △ ☋	1°15' S
♀ △ ♄	1°16' A
♀ ⚹ As	1°48' S
☿ □ ♄	1°49' S
♅ ⚹ ♇	3°19' A
☉ ☌ ☿	4°53' A

PLANETARY SECT

Planet	Cht	Plc	Sgn	Condition
☉ D	D	D	D	In Hayz
☽ N	D	N	N	
☿ D	D	D	D	In Hayz
♀ N	D	D	N	
♂ N	D	D	D	Ex Cond
♃ D	D	D	N	
♄ D	D	N	N	

D=Diurnal, N=Nocturnal

(it was a bit scratched on one side), but it served the same purpose, so that, hallelujah, I could now at least open the gate!

Since my main problem was now essentially solved, I stopped looking for the other key, but I found it incidentally on 28 March at 20:46. It was in the kitchen, in the top cutlery drawer, squeezed to the edge of the front side. The kitchen is in the northeastern part of the house, on the ground floor. The chest-of-drawers lies on the northern kitchen wall, next to the stove. In retrospect, the chart describes the location really well, but I didn't take trouble to analyze it before I incidentally spotted the key when looking for some cutlery. Let us check the directions:

- the ascending sign Cancer - N
- the ascendant ruler Moon in H11 - SE
- H4 cusp in Virgo (drawers, cupboards, cabinets etc.) - SSW
- H4 dispositor Mercury (and the natural significator of keys) in Pisces (near water, kitchen) - NNW
- Moon sign Taurus – SSE
- H2 cusp Leo - EEN
- H2 ruler Sun in Aries – close to a source of heat (stove) - E
- Part of fortune in Leo - EEN

The majority of significators point to northeast - the actual location of the key. There is some inclination to the south too, which I ascribe to the fact that the little thing was pressed to the southern side of the drawer.

The timing is indicated, too. The key was found five days after the question – exactly matching the number of degrees separating the ascendant from the trine with Mercury.

6/14: WHERE IS MY DAUGHTER'S PURSE? WILL SHE GET IT BACK?

16 November 2014 at 12:16 p.m. (12:16), Ljubljana, Slovenia
Hour ruler: Mars, POF 13 Pi

One Sunday morning my daughter found that she was missing her purse. The last time she saw it was on Friday night when she was partying with her friends in a nightclub. She came home by cab in the early morning hours on Saturday. She told me that she paid the cab with the money she had in her pocket, and on Saturday she didn't use the purse so it was not until Sunday that she realized it was gone. She remembered, however, that the purse was still in her handbag when she left the club.

This was the information I received from her, and I immediately cast a horary to see how the matter would resolve.

My daughter's significator is Mercury, the H5 ruler while her purse is shown by the Moon, the ruler and almuten of H6 (2/5), and also the general significator of missing things. The Moon is separating from a sextile with Mercury – as if the purse had "left" her. This is confirmed by Mercury's placement in Scorpio, the sign of the Moon's fall. The last planet the Moon had bodily passed over was Jupiter, sitting in H7. This house is the third from the fifth (3/5) standing for my daughter's transportation. Has she forgotten the purse in the cab?

Mercury is in H9 which is 5/5, standing for the club where she was partying on that night. This house is ruled by Mars and (modern) Pluto. Both the Moon and Mercury are applying by harmonious aspects to both of them, with Mars receiving Mercury in its domicile. Mars and Pluto collect the lights of both significators, and the Moon translates light from Mercury (my daughter) to Mars and Pluto (the club). Mercury receives the Moon in its domicile and exaltation sign and Mars is dignified (in its exaltation), showing that the purse is in safe hands, and that she'd get it back.

As soon as I found the answer, I published my prediction on my Facebook Horary Astrology Group: *I believe that my daughter will get her purse back in two days (the number of degrees separating the Moon from Mars). Because H9 (the derived H5) in this chart plays such a vital role, it seems that she'll receive it at the club. I asked her to immediately call the club because the purse was obviously there, but she was just leaving for a dance audition where she'd stay until the evening, so I guess she'll call them tomorrow. I think that the taxi driver might have found the purse in the cab and took it to the club in front of which he picked her up.*

6/14

4 Feb 2007
16:14 CET −1:00
Celje, Slovenia
46°N14' 015°E16'

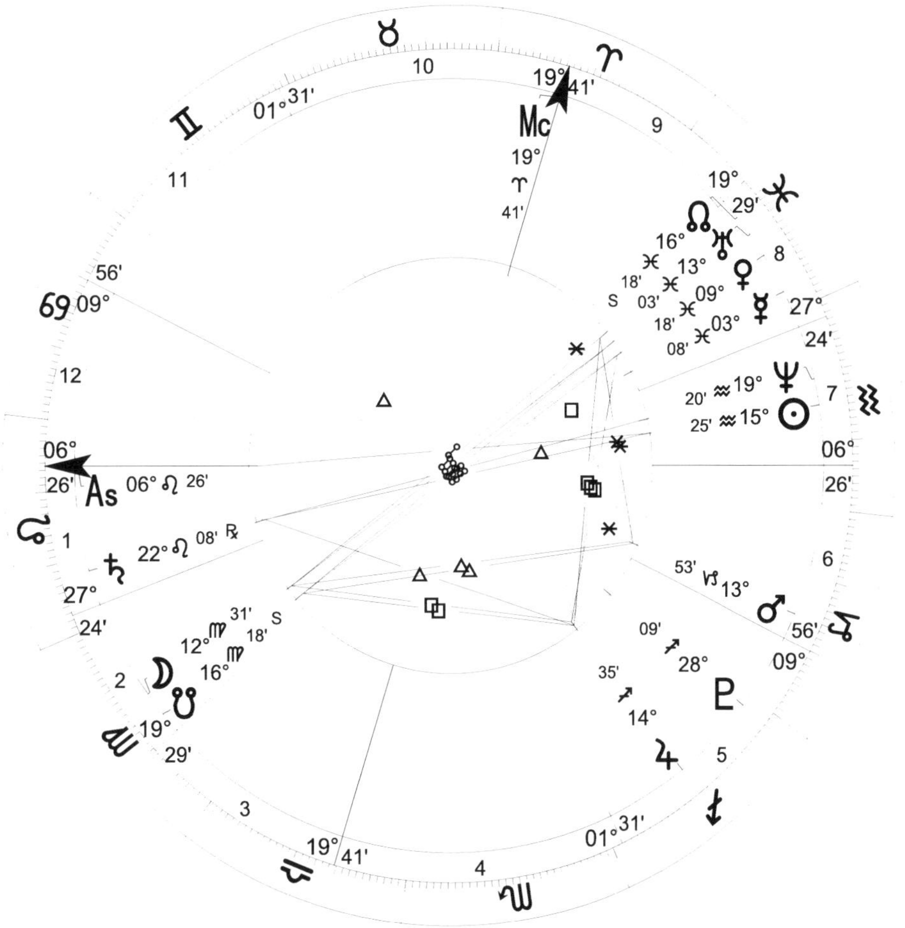

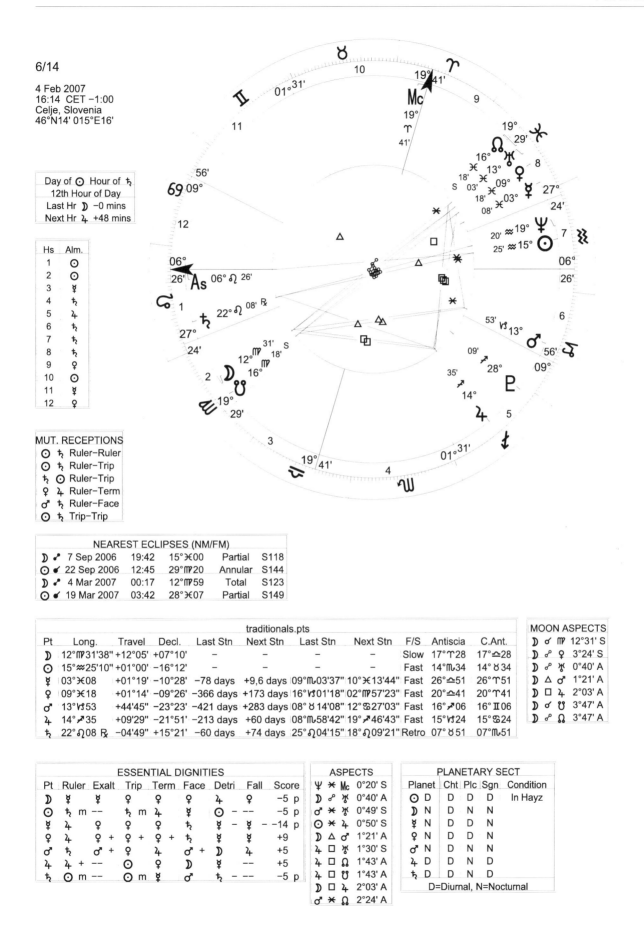

Day of ☉ Hour of ♄
12th Hour of Day
Last Hr ☽ −0 mins
Next Hr ♃ +48 mins

Hs	Alm.
1	☉
2	☉
3	☿
4	♄
5	♃
6	♄
7	♄
8	♄
9	♀
10	☉
11	☿
12	♀

MUT. RECEPTIONS
☉ ♄ Ruler−Ruler
☉ ♄ Ruler−Trip
♄ ☉ Ruler−Trip
♀ ♃ Ruler−Term
♂ ♄ Ruler−Face
☉ ♄ Trip−Trip

NEAREST ECLIPSES (NM/FM)				
☽ 7 Sep 2006	19:42	15°♓00	Partial	S118
☉ 22 Sep 2006	12:45	29°♍20	Annular	S144
☽ 4 Mar 2007	00:17	12°♍59	Total	S123
☉ 19 Mar 2007	03:42	28°♓07	Partial	S149

traditionals.pts

Pt	Long.	Travel	Decl.	Last Stn	Next Stn	Last Stn	Next Stn	F/S	Antiscia	C.Ant.
☽	12°♍31'38"	+12°05'	+07°10'	–	–	–	–	Slow	17°♈28	17°♎28
☉	15°♒25'10"	+01°00'	−16°12'	–	–	–	–	Fast	14°♏34	14°♉34
☿	03°♓08	+01°19'	−10°28'	−78 days	+9,6 days	09°♏03'37"	10°♓13'44"	Fast	26°♎51	26°♈51
♀	09°♓18	+01°14'	−09°26'	−366 days	+173 days	16°♑01'18"	02°♍57'23"	Fast	20°♎41	20°♈41
♂	13°♑53	+44'45"	−23°23'	−421 days	+283 days	08°♉14'08"	12°♋27'03"	Fast	16°♐06	16°♊06
♃	14°♐35	+09'29"	−21°51'	−213 days	+60 days	08°♏58'42"	19°♐46'43"	Fast	15°♑24	15°♋24
♄	22°♌08 ℞	−04'49"	+15°21'	−60 days	+74 days	25°♌04'15"	18°♌09'21"	Retro	07°♉51	07°♏51

MOON ASPECTS
☽ ☌ ♍ 12°31' S
☽ ☍ ♀ 3°24' S
☽ ☍ ♅ 0°40' A
☽ △ ♂ 1°21' A
☽ □ ♃ 2°03' A
☽ ☌ ☋ 3°47' A
☽ ☍ ☊ 3°47' A

ESSENTIAL DIGNITIES

Pt	Ruler	Exalt	Trip	Term	Face	Detri	Fall	Score
☽	☿	☿	♀	♀	♀	♃	♀	−5 p
☉	♄ m	−−	♄ m	♃	☿	☉ −	−−	−5 p
☿	♃	♀	♀	♀	♄	☿ −	☿ −	−14 p
♀	♃	♀ +	♀ +	♀ +	♄	☿	☿	+9
♂	♄	♂ +	♀	♃	♂ +	☽	♃	+5
♃	♃ +	−−	☉	♀	☽	☿	−−	+5
♄	☉ m	−−	☉ m	☿	♂	♄ −	−−	−5 p

ASPECTS
♆ ✶ Mc 0°20' S
☽ ☍ ♅ 0°40' A
♂ ✶ ♅ 0°49' S
☉ ✶ ♃ 0°50' S
☽ △ ♂ 1°21' A
♃ □ ♅ 1°30' S
♃ □ ☊ 1°43' A
♃ □ ☋ 1°43' A
☽ □ ♃ 2°03' A
♂ ✶ ☊ 2°24' A

PLANETARY SECT

Planet	Cht	Plc	Sgn	Condition
☉ D	D	D	D	In Hayz
☽ N	D	N	N	
☿ N	D	D	N	
♀ N	D	D	N	
♂ N	D	N	N	
♃ D	D	N	D	
♄ D	D	N	D	

D=Diurnal, N=Nocturnal

Two days later, on Tuesday, I was able to confirm the prediction: *Here is the result: my daughter got her purse back today - it was in the club! When she was leaving, she checked for the purse in her bag, and saw it there; then she pulled her sweater out of the bag and walked down the street towards the cab. It appears that while she was taking out her sweater, the purse came with it and fell to the ground, and then someone found it and took it to the club's reception desk.*

6/15: MY FRIEND'S CAR GOT STOLEN, WILL HE GET IT BACK?

5 December 1994 at 9:07 a.m., Ljubljana, Slovenia
Hour ruler: Jupiter, POF 26 Sc

My husband called me while at work, saying that his good friend's car was stolen a couple of days ago. He's very worried, he said, can I look it up? Will he get it back?

H1 stands for my husband, H11 shows his friend while H1 (3/11) shows the stolen car.

The Moon in H1 reflects the subject of the query – the car. Saturn, its ruler, points to an old car (especially as it is peregrine in the chart), and this was an 8-year old black Opel Kadett (a Germanmake). As for the color, let's take a look at Lilly's CA, p. 86: *Saturn giveth black colour. Capricorn: blacke or russet, or a swart browne.* We can see that the car is adequately described by the sign and its ruler.

Beside the Moon, there are the "electric" Uranus and "musical" Neptune in H1 which is very much in accord with the fact that there were two electric and one classic guitars in the car.

That the querent's friend is very much concerned with his loss is shown by Jupiter, ruler of his H2 (radix H12) in H11 (derived H1), while his own significator Mars, placed in the radix H8 of loss, applies to it by a tight square. This is very suggestive of his worry and loss, but since Mars receives Jupiter by domicile, this gives some hope of recovering his possession.

Have I just moved the car from H3 into H2? No! The car remains in H3, but the value it has for the owner is indeed shown by H2. This is confirmed by the fact that there's Mercury, the derived H8 ruler (of insurance money, in this case) on cusp of the derived H2, but it is combust and in detriment, showing that the car was not insured, so he was not likely to get any refund in case it was stolen or damaged. His H2 is all about money and (possible) loss, implied in the question, whereas the car as such is more properly described by the derived H3.

Will he get it back? Mars (the car's owner) is not in aspect neither with Saturn nor with the Moon, but the Moon's first application (apart from the trans-Saturnians in H1) is a sextile to the conjunction of Jupiter and Pluto, co-ruling the owner on account of being placed in his H1, while Pluto is also the modern ruler of Scorpio – a sure sign that he'll get it back. This is confirmed by the interaction of the owner's H1 and H2, reinforcing the probability of re-possession.

Who is the thief? According to Lilly, the thief is shown by the peregrine planet which is closest to an angle, but thieves can be several if there're more peregrine planets on angles; in this case, the most angular peregrine planet is Venus, but since the Moon, which is also the H7 ruler (the house of thieves), practically "sits" in the car, it also shows the thief/thieves, so that we obviously have more than one thief. That Venus shows at least one thief, is confirmed by this planet's trine with Saturn (the car). Because the Moon was in her first quarter and Venus was oriental, I told my husband that the thieves were obviously very young people.

Where is the car? I hated this part, you see. Stolen cars are often moving around, so locating them is very difficult. The Moon was angular and in a movable sign – this could mean that the car was not far from where it was stolen. The Moon was in an eastern part of the map and in a southern sign (Capricorn), while Saturn (the car) and Venus (H4 ruler) were in water signs, so I judged the car to be somewhere southeast of where it was stolen, and this part of our town is incidentally bordering on swampland. This much I could say, but not more.

Two and a half days after the question (and four days after the theft) the policemen - while on their regular duty - stopped a car in the centre of Ljubljana; the car seemed suspicious because it was damaged and inhabited by a gang of merry teenagers, so they stopped it. It was our man's car, yes! One guitar was missing, and the owner of the car later told us that he heard that the third guitar was in a southeastern part (!) of Ljubljana, though I don't know whether he ever got it back.

6/15

16 Nov 2014
12:16 CET −1:00
Ljubljana, Slovenia
46°N03' 014°E31'

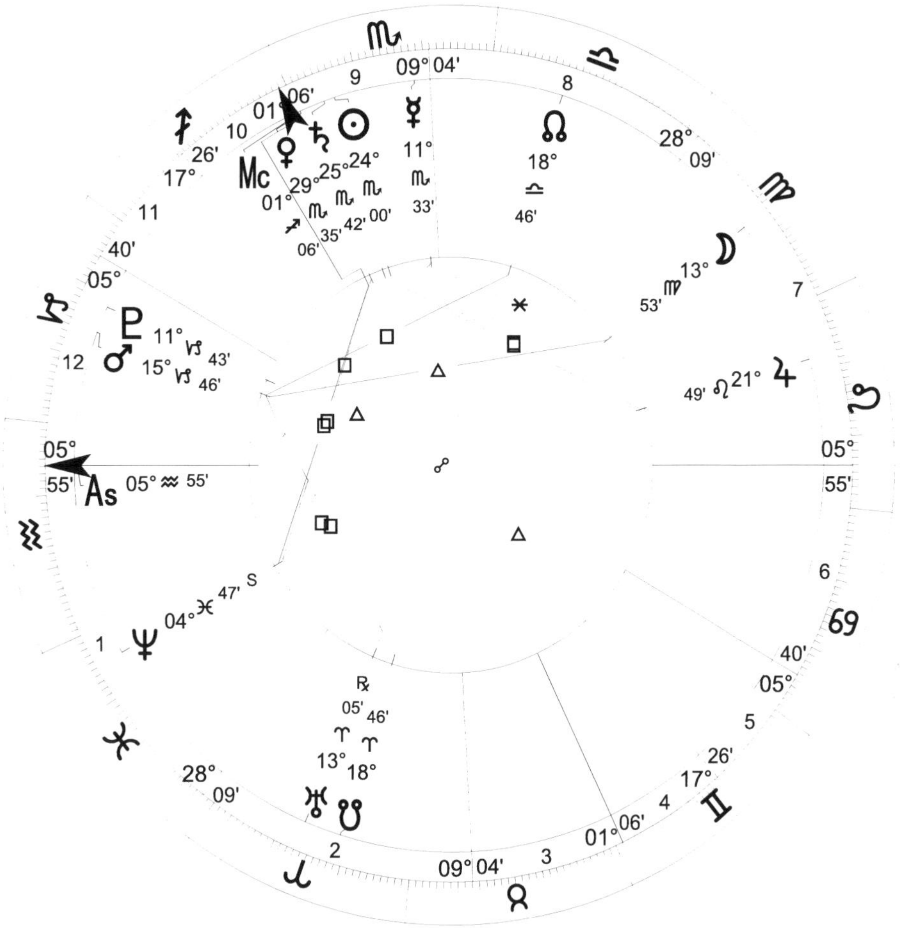

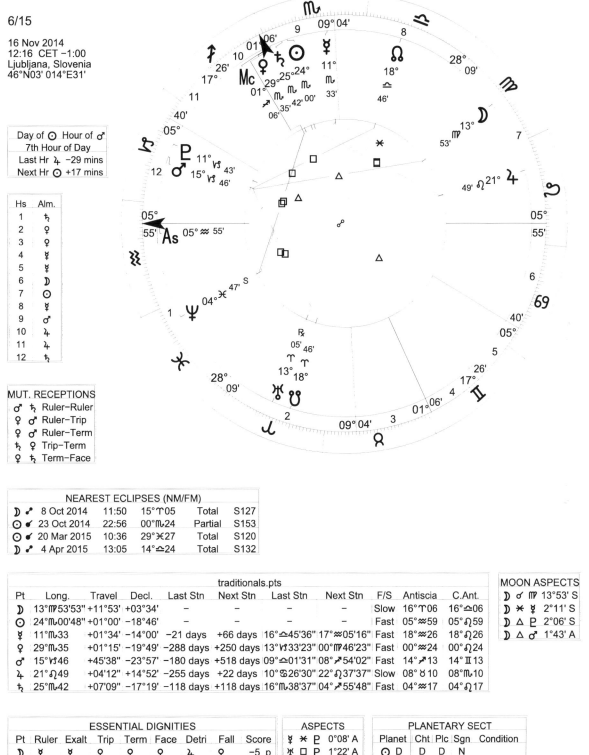

Day of ☉ Hour of ♂
7th Hour of Day
Last Hr ♃ −29 mins
Next Hr ☉ +17 mins

Hs	Alm.
1	♄
2	♀
3	♀
4	☿
5	☿
6	☽
7	☉
8	☿
9	♂
10	♃
11	♃
12	♄

MUT. RECEPTIONS		
♂	♄	Ruler−Ruler
♀	♂	Ruler−Trip
♀	♂	Ruler−Term
♄	♀	Trip−Term
♀	♄	Term−Face

NEAREST ECLIPSES (NM/FM)					
☽ ☍	8 Oct 2014	11:50	15°♈05	Total	S127
☉ ☌	23 Oct 2014	22:56	00°♏24	Partial	S153
☉ ☌	20 Mar 2015	10:36	29°♓27	Total	S120
☽ ☍	4 Apr 2015	13:05	14°♎24	Total	S132

traditionals.pts

Pt	Long.	Travel	Decl.	Last Stn	Next Stn	Last Stn	Next Stn	F/S	Antiscia	C.Ant.
☽	13°♍53'53"	+11°53'	+03°34'	–	–	–	–	Slow	16°♈06	16°♎06
☉	24°♏00'48"	+01°00'	−18°46'	–	–	–	–	Fast	05°♒59	05°♌59
☿	11°♏33	+01°34'	−14°00'	−21 days	+66 days	16°♎45'36"	17°♒05'16"	Fast	18°♒26	18°♌26
♀	29°♏35	+01°15'	−19°49'	−288 days	+250 days	13°♑33'23"	00°♍46'23"	Fast	00°♒24	00°♌24
♂	15°♑46	+45'38"	−23°57'	−180 days	+518 days	09°♎01'31"	08°♐54'02"	Fast	14°♐13	14°♊13
♃	21°♌49	+04'12"	+14°52'	−255 days	+22 days	10°♋26'30"	22°♌37'37"	Slow	08°♉10	08°♏10
♄	25°♏42	+07'09"	−17°19'	−118 days	+118 days	16°♏38'37"	04°♐55'48"	Fast	04°♒17	04°♌17

MOON ASPECTS			
☽	☌	♍ 13°53'	S
☽	✶	☿ 2°11'	S
☽	△	♇ 2°06'	S
☽	△	♂ 1°43'	A

ESSENTIAL DIGNITIES

Pt	Ruler	Exalt	Trip	Term	Face	Detri	Fall	Score
☽	☿	☿	♀	♀	♀	♃	♀	−5 p
☉	♂	--	♀	♄	♀	♀	☽	−5 p
☿	♂	--	♀	☿ +	☉	♀	☽	+2
♀	♂	--	♀ +	♄	♀ +	♀ −	☽	−1
♂	♄ m	♂ +	♀	♀	♂ +	☽	♃	+10
♃	☉	--	☉	☿	♂	♄	--	−5 p
♄	♂ m	--	♀	♄ +	♀	♀	☽	+7

ASPECTS			
☿	✶	♇	0°08' A
♅	□	♇	1°22' A
♀	☌	Mc	1°31' S
☽	△	♂	1°43' A
☽	△	♇	2°06' S
☉	□	♃	2°11' S
☽	✶	☿	2°11' S
☉	☌	♄	2°33' A
♂	□	♅	2°42' S
♂	□	☊	3°00' A

PLANETARY SECT

Planet		Cht	Plc	Sgn	Condition
☉	D	D	D	N	
☽	N	D	D	N	
☿	D	D	D	N	
♀	N	D	D	N	
♂	N	D	D	N	
♃	D	D	D	D	In Hayz
♄	D	D	D	N	

D=Diurnal, N=Nocturnal

As for the timing – since the car was found 2.5 days after the question it seems quite interesting that MC is 2.5 degrees from conjuncting Venus (bringing the thieves into focus), while the ascendant is roughly the same (3 degrees) before it sextiles Saturn (the car).

Since Saturn is the natural ruler of police, its trine with Venus (the youngsters) shows that the policemen were lucky, with the thieves practically falling into their hands (an applying trine of Venus to Saturn). But the car was not insured, so the owner didn't get any insurance money for the damages done to it – as the chart also suggests.

6/16: WILL I GET BACK THE STOLEN PURSE?

4 February 2007 at 4:14 p.m. (16:14), Celje, Slovenia
Hour ruler: Saturn, POF 3 Pi

My husband's aunt invited us to dinner, celebrating her 60th birthday. We met in a restaurant in Celje, a town in the eastern part of Slovenia, but I was only enjoying myself until I found that my purse was missing. I immediately searched all the places where it could get lost – the restaurant hall, the car, the toilets and the garden in front of the inn where our children played. Incidentally, I had a lot of money in my purse on that day, much more than usually. Then I remembered that I last saw the purse a few hours earlier at a gas station where we stopped after turning from the highway. I remembered that I took the purse out of my handbag, and my memory sharply stopped at the picture of me putting the purse on the toilet shelf.

I instantly sat in the car and drove to the gas station, but the purse was not in the toilet, not in the shop, not anywhere. Nobody had seen it. Except, of course, the one who obviously stole it! He got a small fortune, but for me, it was not just the money, there were all my credit cards, my driving license and several other cards - not only mine, but also those of my children. Devastated, I drove back to the restaurant.

I had to leave earlier than the rest of the family because I was a guest at a Sunday TV show. As I was driving back home, the above question arose in my mind at exactly 16:14.

The ascendant is in Leo, so my ruler is the Sun which also rules H2 of my belongings. Where is the Sun? In H7 of the thief, of course! The H7 ruler is Saturn which is also the planetary hour ruler, peregrine and placed in the angular H1, so there's no doubt that Saturn is the significator of the thief.

Will I get my purse back? The Sun is in detriment and so is Saturn. Of course, Saturn is the villain! But it's also appropriate for my significator to be in detriment, the fool that I was, having left the purse on a toilet shelf! But the Sun is in Saturn's domicile while Saturn is in the Sun's domicile, so the two bodies are in a strong mutual reception. Mutual reception usually gives hope of recovery, but because both planets are also in their detriment, the hope is much less.

And what information can we get from the Moon? It is a co-significator of the purse because it is placed in H2 and is also the natural significator of missing items. It's applying by trine to Mars, but this planet is in the unfortunate H6 and it doesn't rule me, so that's not really helpful. Moreover, the Moon is exactly at the place of the nearest lunar eclipse (of March 4, 2007) which was even a total one, and this clearly shows that the purse was gone.

But due to the mutual reception between the Sun and Saturn I didn't entirely give up. I waited patiently, thinking that the reception might mean that I'd get back at least the documents. From the Moon to its aspect with the "honest" (exalted) Mars is a little more than a degree, so I waited a month and a half, but nothing happened, and towards the end of March I set myself on the strenuous task of renewing my and the children's documents.

On 31 March, that is less than 2 months after the question, the postman brought me a thick envelope. I opened it, and there was my purse! Without the money, unfortunately (but logically, eh?), but there were all the documents that I had just canceled, along with the credit cards - which I had canceled immediately after the loss, of course. Mutual reception by domicile, with both planets in detriment, was therefore totally astro-logical: it gave an empty purse, deprived of anything that would still have any value for me.

The application of the Moon to an exalted Mars suggests that the emptied purse came into the hands of a honest person who sent it to my address, written on my personal ID card. Other people's mail is H9 (3/7) which has its cusp in Pisces, so its ruler is Jupiter. The Moon applies to a square with Jupiter by almost exactly 2 degrees, corresponding to 2 months which passed until my receiving of the parcel. Had I been smart enough, I'd wait just a little longer!

6/16

4 Feb 2007
16:14 CET −1:00
Celje, Slovenia
46°N14' 015°E16'

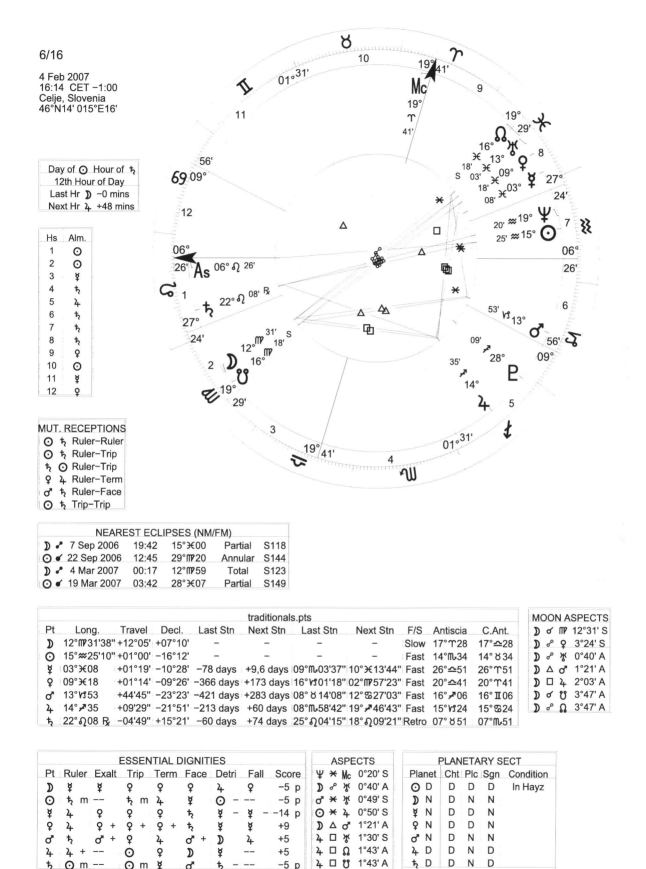

Day of ☉ Hour of ♄
12th Hour of Day
Last Hr ☽ −0 mins
Next Hr ♃ +48 mins

Hs	Alm.
1	☉
2	☉
3	☿
4	♄
5	♃
6	♄
7	♄
8	♄
9	♀
10	☉
11	☿
12	♀

MUT. RECEPTIONS		
☉	♄	Ruler−Ruler
☉	♄	Ruler−Trip
♄	☉	Ruler−Trip
♀	♃	Ruler−Term
♂	♄	Ruler−Face
☉	♄	Trip−Trip

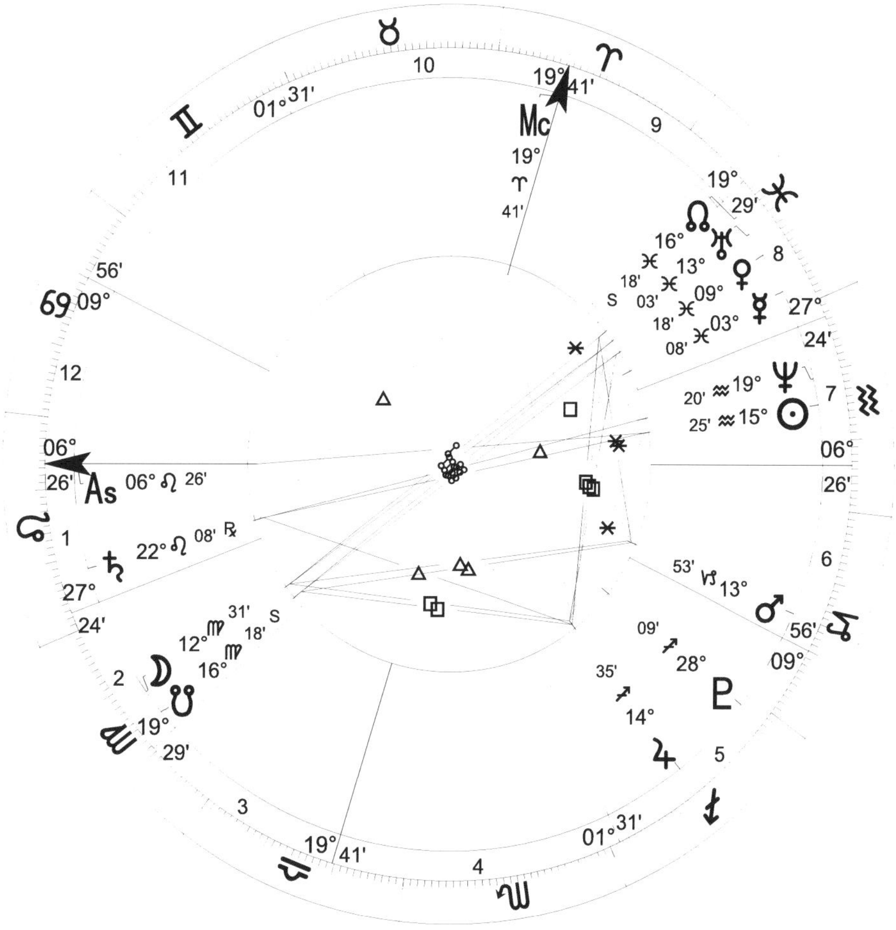

NEAREST ECLIPSES (NM/FM)						
☽	☍	7 Sep 2006	19:42	15°♓00	Partial	S118
☉	☌	22 Sep 2006	12:45	29°♍20	Annular	S144
☽	☍	4 Mar 2007	00:17	12°♍59	Total	S123
☉	☌	19 Mar 2007	03:42	28°♓07	Partial	S149

traditionals.pts

Pt	Long.	Travel	Decl.	Last Stn	Next Stn	Last Stn	Next Stn	F/S	Antiscia	C.Ant.
☽	12°♍31'38"	+12°05'	+07°10'	–	–	–	–	Slow	17°♈28	17°♎28
☉	15°♒25'10"	+01°00'	−16°12'	–	–	–	–	Fast	14°♏34	14°♉34
☿	03°♓08	+01°19'	−10°28'	−78 days	+9,6 days	09°♏03'37"	10°♓13'44"	Fast	26°♎51	26°♈51
♀	09°♓18	+01°14'	−09°26'	−366 days	+173 days	16°♑01'18"	02°♍57'23"	Fast	20°♎41	20°♈41
♂	13°♑53	+44'45"	−23°23'	−421 days	+283 days	08°♉14'08"	12°♋27'03"	Fast	16°♐06	16°♊06
♃	14°♐35	+09'29"	−21°51'	−213 days	+60 days	08°♏58'42"	19°♐46'43"	Fast	15°♑24	15°♋24
♄	22°♌08 ℞	−04'49"	+15°21'	−60 days	+74 days	25°♌04'15"	18°♌09'21"	Retro	07°♉51	07°♏51

MOON ASPECTS			
☽	☌	♍	12°31' S
☽	☍	♀	3°24' S
☽	☍	♅	0°40' A
☽	△	♂	1°21' A
☽	□	♃	2°03' A
☽	☌	☋	3°47' A
☽	☍	☊	3°47' A

ESSENTIAL DIGNITIES

Pt	Ruler	Exalt	Trip	Term	Face	Detri	Fall	Score
☽	☿	☿	♀	♀	♀	♃	♀	−5 p
☉	♄ m	−−	♄ m	♃	☿	☉ −	−−	−5 p
☿	♃	♀	♀	♀	♄	☿ −	☿ −	−14 p
♀	♃	♀ +	♀ +	♀ +	♄	☿	☿	+9
♂	♄	♂ +	♀	♃	♂ +	☽	♃	+5
♃	♃ +	−−	☉	♀	☽	☿	−−	+5
♄	☉ m	−−	☉ m	☿	♂	♄ −	−−	−5 p

ASPECTS			
♆	⚹	Mc	0°20' S
☽	☍	♅	0°40' A
♂	⚹	♅	0°49' S
☉	⚹	♃	0°50' S
☽	△	♂	1°21' A
♃	□	♅	1°30' S
♃	□	☊	1°43' A
♃	□	☋	1°43' A
☽	□	♃	2°03' A
♂	⚹	☊	2°24' A

PLANETARY SECT

Planet		Cht	Plc	Sgn	Condition
☉	D	D	D	D	In Hayz
☽	N	D	N	N	
☿	N	D	D	N	
♀	N	D	D	N	
♂	N	D	N	N	
♃	D	D	N	D	
♄	D	D	N	D	

D=Diurnal, N=Nocturnal

Soon after the loss I posted this case on a horary forum, and one of my ex-students observed that my ruler the Sun was separating from a sextile with Jupiter, suggesting that the querent (according to Lilly) *"left the missing thing somewhere and forgot about it"*. All the more so, he added, because the Sun also ruled my purse. There was a slight possibility of the return of the documents, added he, because Mercury, the H3 ruler, was conjunct the part of fortune on a benevolent fixed star Fomalhaut. Incidentally, my natal chart ruler Jupiter is at 3° Pisces, in H3!

6/17: WHERE IS MY MISSING GAUS?

5 March 2015 at 4:54 a.m., Gainesville, Florida
Hour ruler: Moon, POF 9 Le

An astrology friend of mine posted the above question on a Facebook horary group where a small group of established horary astrologers offered free readings. Horary is not her specialty so she didn't cast her own chart, but she hoped that those (supposedly) experienced horary astrologers would help. I noticed her post and because she is my friend and I wanted to help her, I recorded the exact time when the question was posted, and cast a horary chart for her locality.

Fiona (a fictitious name) was missing a gaus (part of a Tibetan amulet). The little thing, containing particles of soil from various places in Tibet, meant a lot to her because it was a gift from Tibetan lamas. She remembered that about half a year ago her dog playfully jumped on her and tore the chain on which the gaus was hanging. She then placed the amulet and the gaus on a table in the living room, and since then she hadn't seen it again. In between, there were workers in the house, renovating the apartment, and she was afraid that the amulet was gone with one of them.

The astrologer who took over her case, cast a horary chart for the time and place when and where he read and understood the question, and came up with the answer that she'd probably never see the gaus again. He mentioned the dog who could have dragged the gaus to the garden where it got lost.

My chart was different, of course, because I used the original time and place of the question. After having scrutinized the chart, I sent her a private message, saying: *Fiona, it seems obvious to me that your gaus is not lost; it's only misplaced. You'll get it back. Just look at the chart. The gaus is shown by H2 which is ruled by Jupiter and Neptune, and also by the Sun, sitting on cusp of H2 - very appropriate for a religious object which has great value for you. Jupiter is retrograde and in a mutual reception with the Sun, suggesting that you misplaced it, but also that it will get back to where it belongs - to you. If it's not with your husband (I would surely check him first, ask him if he can take a thorough look among his things), then maybe someone took it by accident and will return it. Could be a friend because Jupiter rules H11. Did you take the gaus with you when visiting a group? Was there a friend visiting whom you showed it? I think it's in the house! Even one of the workers could misplace it. I think you should be able to find it in approximately 4 weeks after the question - that would be around that lunar eclipse on April 4th. The location? Mixed indications here but most probably in the western part of the house and a bit to the north. In a drawer, somewhere safe, and the item is not damaged. In the middle part of (a cupboard, a drawer), not on the floor but I think on a higher level. Could be close to a source of heat. If your house has more than one floor, it could be the upper floor. Does anything ring a bell with you? And, yes, the item seems to be kept among other small valuable items. But it can't be immediately seen, you will have to remove something before you can discover it.*

My logic? The Moon in Virgo and IC in Taurus - chests of drawers, cupboards, safely kept. Jupiter and Venus, the H4 ruler, in fire signs – close to a heat source. Moon and Jupiter indicate west, the Sun and H2 in Pisces north.

Fiona thanked me, saying that she'd start searching as soon as possible, but I warned her that the gaus would probably not be found soon. *A retrograde significator of the lost thing indicates that you'll probably find it when least expected! As already said, I see four units of time - if not weeks, could even be months.*

Four weeks passed without a word from Fiona. After five weeks I started to feel a little embarrassed —was I wrong? But on May 2nd, I received her message: *Hey you! Just wanted you to know that I found my gaus and the amulet in a drawer in the office about five feet from the fireplace. Tried to give you a shout out on the horary group, but it would tag you so then I thought that might be a sign not to post it there, as you reached out to me privately. I was looking for something else and thought, 'Ema said after the eclipse...Let me look one more time in this cabinet...' And there they were! It was at 6:25 pm EDT, Gainesville FL on May 1st that I found them. Thanks for encouraging me not to lose hope. Hugs!*

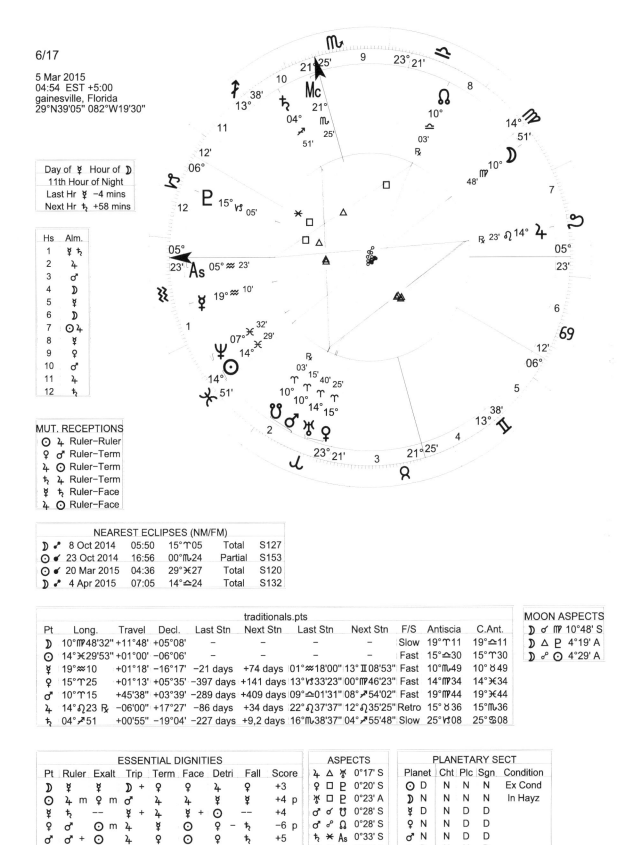

6/17

5 Mar 2015
04:54 EST +5:00
gainesville, Florida
29°N39'05" 082°W19'30"

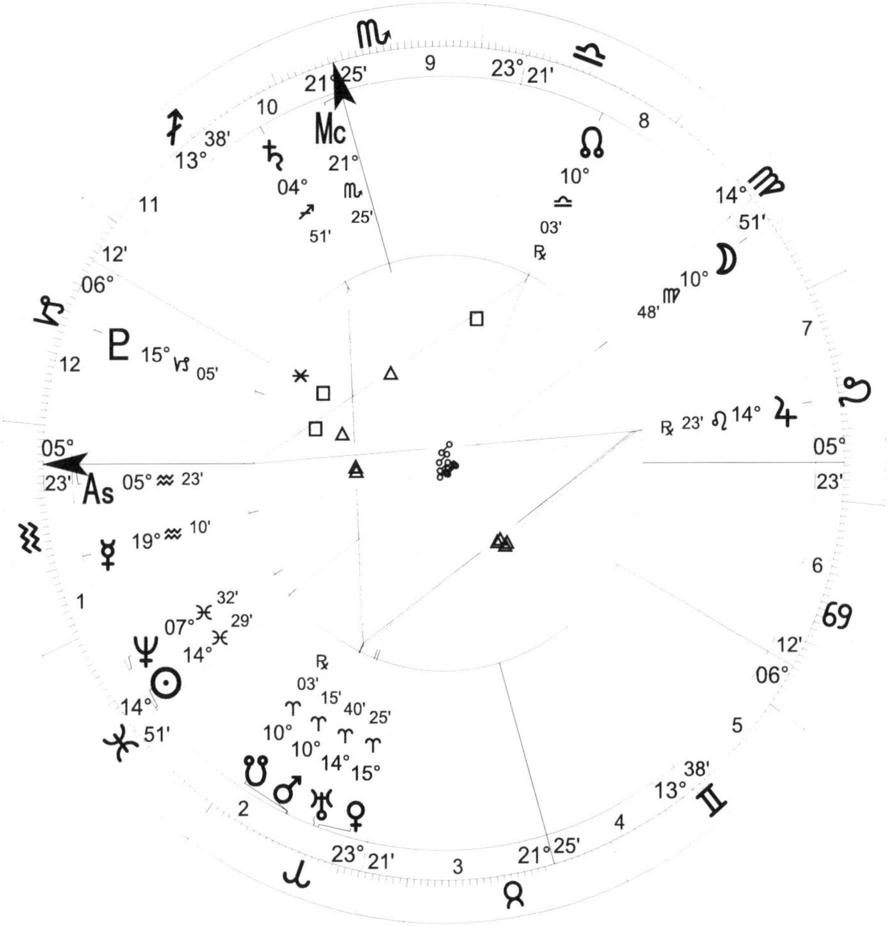

Day of ☿	Hour of ☽
11th Hour of Night	
Last Hr ☿	−4 mins
Next Hr ♄	+58 mins

Hs	Alm.
1	☿ ♄
2	♃
3	♂
4	☽
5	☿
6	☽
7	☉ ♃
8	☿
9	♀
10	♂
11	♃
12	♄

MUT. RECEPTIONS		
☉	♃	Ruler-Ruler
♀	♂	Ruler-Term
♃	☉	Ruler-Term
♄	♃	Ruler-Term
☿	♄	Ruler-Face
♃	☉	Ruler-Face

NEAREST ECLIPSES (NM/FM)				
☽ 8 Oct 2014	05:50	15°♈05	Total	S127
☉ 23 Oct 2014	16:56	00°♏24	Partial	S153
☉ 20 Mar 2015	04:36	29°♓27	Total	S120
☽ 4 Apr 2015	07:05	14°♎24	Total	S132

traditionals.pts

Pt	Long.	Travel	Decl.	Last Stn	Next Stn	Last Stn	Next Stn	F/S	Antiscia	C.Ant.
☽	10°♍48'32"	+11°48'	+05°08'	–	–	–	–	Slow	19°♈11	19°♎11
☉	14°♓29'53"	+01°00'	−06°06'	–	–	–	–	Fast	15°♎30	15°♈30
☿	19°♒10	+01°18'	−16°17'	−21 days	+74 days	01°♒18'00"	13°♊08'53"	Fast	10°♏49	10°♉49
♀	15°♈25	+01°13'	+05°35'	−397 days	+141 days	13°♑33'23"	00°♍46'23"	Fast	14°♍34	14°♓34
♂	10°♈15	+45'38"	+03°39'	−289 days	+409 days	09°♎01'31"	08°♐54'02"	Fast	19°♍44	19°♓44
♃	14°♌23 ℞	−06'00"	+17°27'	−86 days	+34 days	22°♌37'37"	12°♌35'25"	Retro	15°♉36	15°♏36
♄	04°♐51	+00'55"	−19°04'	−227 days	+9,2 days	16°♏38'37"	04°♐55'48"	Slow	25°♑08	25°♋08

MOON ASPECTS			
☽	☌	♍	10°48' S
☽	△	♇	4°19' A
☽	☍	☉	4°29' A

ESSENTIAL DIGNITIES

Pt	Ruler	Exalt	Trip	Term	Face	Detri	Fall	Score
☽	☿	☿	☽ +	♀	♀	♃	♀	+3
☉	♃ m	♀ m	♂	♃	♃	☿	☿	+4 p
☿	♄	--	☿ +	♃	☿ +	☉	--	+4
♀	♂	☉ m	♃	☿	☉	♀ −	♄	−6 p
♂	♂ +	☉	♃	♀	☉	♀	♄	+5
♃	☉ m	--	♃ +	♄ m	♃ +	♄	--	+9
♄	♃	--	♃	♃ m	☿	☿	--	−5 p

ASPECTS			
♃	△	♅	0°17' S
♀	□	♇	0°20' S
♅	□	♇	0°23' A
♂	☌	☋	0°28' S
♂	☍	☊	0°28' S
♄	⚹	As	0°33' S
☉	⚹	♇	0°33' A
♀	☌	♅	0°44' S
♀	△	♃	1°01' S
☿	□	Mc	2°15' S

PLANETARY SECT

Planet		Cht	Plc	Sgn	Condition
☉	D	N	N	N	Ex Cond
☽	N	N	N	N	In Hayz
☿	D	N	D	D	
♀	N	N	D	D	
♂	N	N	D	D	
♃	D	N	N	D	
♄	D	N	N	D	

D=Diurnal, N=Nocturnal

And is her office in the north-west of the house, I wondered again – because that was the direction the chart showed? *Yes the room is in the NW corner of the house. So spot on about that…. And it was in a drawer of a cabinet that I had scoured multiple times in search of it. (I had laid the gaus and amulet on top of that cabinet when the dog broke my chain, so it seemed the most natural place.)*

So, everything worked except for the timing! Eight weeks had passed, but I thought that it would be only 4 weeks (or months) because so many degrees separated the Moon from an aspect with the Sun. (Judging by an opposition was not the best choice, I agree, but that was the only timing indicator that seemed to be there in the chart.)

After having checked all the possible indications again, and none fitted, I thought of declination. I drew a declination graph (see below) which shows that the Moon would reach its lowest point (the turning point) in eight days. Hallelujah! This is a very unusual and almost completely unexplored way of searching for a time unit, but it works, as has been confirmed by a few examples that I have done. Eight days could have passed until the find, of course, but in this case, those were weeks because the Moon was in a mutable sign and conjuncting a succedent house (H8).

It is also interesting to note that the Moon then reached a contraparallel with Jupiter, significator of the gaus, and a parallel with MC, an important angular point.

The graph below shows the 14-day movement of the Moon and planets by declination. The graph begins at midnight on 5 March, so the days count starts somewhere in the first third of that date (the question was asked at 4:45 in the morning.). As you can see, the Moon reaches its lowest point almost exactly eight days later.

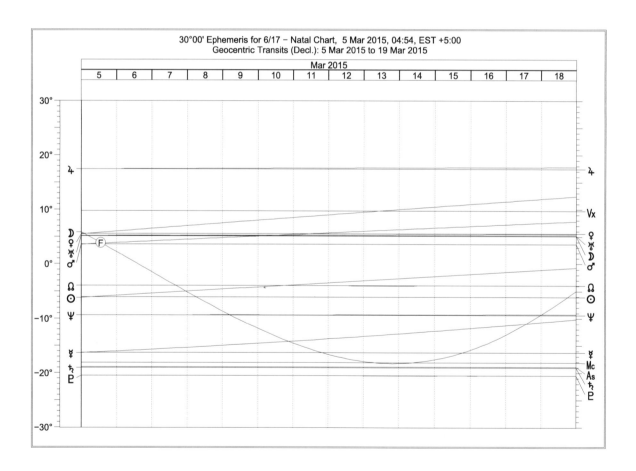

313

MISSING PEOPLE AND PETS

SIGNIFICATORS AND HOUSES

Horary astrologers often receive questions about missing people. *Where is he? Is he alive and well?* This is how it usually begins when people inquire after someone (a relative, lover, friend…) who has gone missing. Obviously, the main question referes to their whereabouts, safety and (possible) time of reconnection.

Questions about missing pets are also common. *Our kitty's gone missing. Is she okay, coming back, and when?*

The missing person's significator is the ruler of the house that represents them (eg, the H5 ruler if it is the son or the daughter of the querent, and the eventual planet/s occupying that house), but if the question refers to someone with whom the querent is not in a specific relationship, or to someone whose disappearance has been announced by the media, that person is ruled by H1 and the Moon. Very occasionally, though, this person can be ruled by H7, but only when H7 truly and without any doubt describes the missing person better than H1, or when the querent is somehow involved in the matter – in which case H1 rules him, of course.

A missing child, personally unknown to the querent, is also described by H1, only in exceptional cases by H5.

I well remember a case of a much publicised disappearance of a missing captain of a ship. Someone posted a horary chart, related to his whereabouts, on a forum, and all the members »voted« for H7 as ruling the man. But I chose H1 (based on my logic and experience), and I was the only one who gave a correct answer - namely, that the captain was alive and well, and would be found. All the others judged that he was dead, based on the (existing) links between H7 and H8.

Missing pets are ruled by H6 – except for the big ones like horses, for example.

Similarly as with missing things, the Moon is always the co-significator of missing people and pets.

THE OUTCOME

In order to find the answer to a missing person/pet question, we must first check the condition of the significator(s) and of the Moon – that is, ascertain their essential and accidental dignities, their house placements and their connections to other planets (by aspects and receptions).

The locality, direction and surroundings of the missing, as well as their (approximate) distance from the querent, are ascertained in the same way as for lost and stolen objects.

DEAD OR ALIVE?

Death of the missing person is usually shown by the links between H1 and H8 - that is, between the missing person's significator (or the Moon) and the ruler of the radix or the derived H8, or a planet therein. Planets can be mutually related by aspects (especially conjunctions and oppositions), by translation or collection of light, or by emplacement (for example, H1 ruler in H8 or vice versa). A critical condition of the missing can also be shown by besiegement (placement of the significator between Mars and Saturn) or by inharmonious aspects of the missing's significator with the natural malefics (Mars and Saturn in particular, but also with Neptune, Uranus or Pluto). A misfortune is suggested when houses 1, 8, 4, 6 and 12 are involved. A disease or a physical mishap is shown by links to H6 (radix or derived), whereas H8 stands specifically for death. H4 traditionally stands for graves, therefore the placement of the significator of the missing person or pet in this house can also alert us to the possibility of death.

But even if the astrologer is very certain of the death of the missing person, such a prediction is risky and unwise, and is also considered unethical today, therefore I urge you to be vary of making it, especially publicly. If we can't help the querent with any information that would facilitate the search, it's better not to say anything at all. We can always revert to our »strictures and cautions« - which will probably be there in such charts anyway.

ECLIPSES, LOCAL SPACE LINES AND OOB PLANETS

In the recent years, I have been successfully experimenting with non-traditional approaches to horary, such as declinations, eclipses and local space lines. (See the corresponding chapters in the Theory part of the book).

Although **eclipses** are an age-old technique, I was not taught to use them in horary astrology and I have also not seen other astrologers use it, except for Barbara Watters, but she applied them in a different manner, relying more on the nodes which partake in the formation of eclipses. I have started to apply eclipses to this kind of horaries after becoming aware of their enormous use in personal forecasting.

If the missing person's or pet's significator, the Moon or any of the angles is on the degree of one of the nearest (the previous or the next) solar or lunar eclipse, or forms an exact dynamic aspect with this degree, this is a serious warning that the missing is probably in a critical state (dead, forever gone, or seriously afflicted). This applies especially in cases where the corresponding eclipse is a total one. The time orb with total eclipses can be extended to up to two years, but the orb should not exceed 1 degree – except for the angles where we can apply a 2 degrees orb. In other words, if the significator of the missing is within a 1 degree orb of a total eclipse which took place (or will take place) within a 1-2 year time span, this will have a strong bearing on the outcome.

This technique can also be used in charts of missing objects, as well as in charts asking about the well-being of sick people. If the significator of the querent (i.e. of the sick) or the significator of the illness or the Moon is associated with an accompanying eclipse in the manner described above, the illness could be critical (deadly.)

Several example cases in my book confirm the validity of this approach.

Local space lines help us find the direction in which the missing person/pet has gone. Local space lines are essentially a more sophisticated form of the ancient technique of dividing the sky into directions. Starting in the centre (the chart's location), those lines extend around the celestial globe. With missing people, their main significators' and the Moon's lines are to be traced for their possible location – or direction, at least, since in horary astrology we do not have a dependable technique ascertaining the distance of the missing.

Locational astrology requires the application of computer software. I use *Solar Maps* which is part of the *Solar Fire* program, while the best source on the general meaning and application of local space lines are books by Martin Davis.

An **OOB (out-of-bound) Moon** (See DECLINATION, p. 151)or the missing person's/pet's **significator** is found in an above-average number of cases, especially in those with an unfortunate outcome. In line with the meaning of an OOB planet (*beyond* the maximum Sun's declination), such a person/pet is often found *beyond* or *outside* his/her/its realm or territory, in unusual (unsafe, dangerous) environments or circumstances, and such.

7/1: WHERE IS PETER? IS HE ALIVE AND WELL?

26 May 1993 at 12:45 p.m. (12:45), Ljubljana, Slovenia
Hour ruler: Sun

The question was asked by Ana, Peter's friend and neighbour. She and Peter's wife were worried because Peter had left home two days ago, saying that he was going on a business trip and to visit his parents who lived in another town, but he had still not returned, nor phoned. (At that time we didn't have cell phones yet, so they couldn't call him.) Several hours earlier, his parents said that he didn't come to see them, nor did he call. Ana and Peter's wife worried that might have suffered an asthma attack (a chronic condition of his) while driving, which could be followed by a car accident. Was he hurt or even killed, they wondered?

Because Peter is Ana's friend, his significator is the Moon, the H11 ruler. The Moon is unafflicted as it separates from a sextile with Jupiter and applies to a sextile with the Sun, its dispositor - a clear indication that Peter is alive and well. Moon in the south-eastern part of the chart shows that at the time of question Peter was southeast of Ljubljana, his home town, therefore I assumed that he was somewhere close to his parents who lived in that part of Slovenia. An almost to the minute exact separating sextile to Jupiter, the ruler of his H9 and occupant of his H4 of parental home, suggested that he might have just left his parents' home and set on a trip abroad or to a coastal town (the cusp of the H9 in Pisces, the sign of the sea). The Moon's immediate application to the Sun in H10 of the radix chart gives much hope that his family will soon see him again.

When? Seeing that there are a mere 12' until the completion of a sextile with the Sun ("bringing to light"), that would probably be the same day. The Moon is 12°24 ' distant from Mercury, the significator of the querent, which in this context could mean hours; adding the given number of hours to the time of the question, we arrive at 1:09 of the next day, but since the Moon will sooner aspect the Sun and Mars (there are 9°30 between the Moon and Mars), I said that he'd probably come home sometime between 10 p.m. and midnight of that day.

But if nothing happened to him, why didn't he come back the same day, or at least give a call to his wife, Ana wondered? A logical question! The Moon is in a harmonious applying sextile with the Sun which also receives it, as it is placed in Leo, so I asked her if he left home on his own, or in somebody's company? Namely, the said aspect suggested that Peter was not alone! Could there be a woman involved, I asked Ana carefully. As we know, an aspect of a significator with any planet not directly related to the question, can point to a third party with whom the quesited is (secretly) involved - provided the nature of the question allows for that possibility, of course.

My suspicion was supported by the fact that the Moon was separated from an inconjunction with Saturn, ruler of H5 which is the derived H7 and therefore rules Peter's wife. This aspect, I thought, draws attention to the potential stress in their marriage. This is confirmed by Neptune and Uranus in his H7, to which Venus, the natural significator of marriage, applies by a square, indicating a risk of fraud and divorce.

Ana replied: *Yes, that's very possible!* She said that Peter left home in the company of their neighbour, a young woman whom he was supposed to give a lift to some place along the route, but she agreed that there could be more between them than just friendship.

The outcome? Peter called his parents just after 10 pm on the same day, and they immediately called his wife to tell her that he was OK. He arrived home safely the next day. You will notice that Mars rules H8 (the cusp of this house is technically still in Pisces but only a few minutes separated from Aries, so we can safely judge H8 as being ruled by Mars), the derived H10 (10/11 - his mother), therefore the application of the Moon to Mars explains his first contact with the mother. The first lunar aspect is indeed a sextile to the Sun, but the Sun disposits of both the Moon and Mars and it is bodily placed in H10, the house of mothers, so this also fits. It turned out that he spent those three days with the neighbouring girl, and soon thereafter he also divorced his wife.

Let us now turn to the locational aspect of the case. As mentioned before, Peter first called his mother who lives in Krško, a small town in the southeast of Slovenia. As seen in the graph on p. 342, the local space Moon line (Peter) runs straight through that town!

7/1

26 May 1993
12:45 CEDT −2:00
Ljubljana, Slovenia
46°N03' 014°E31'

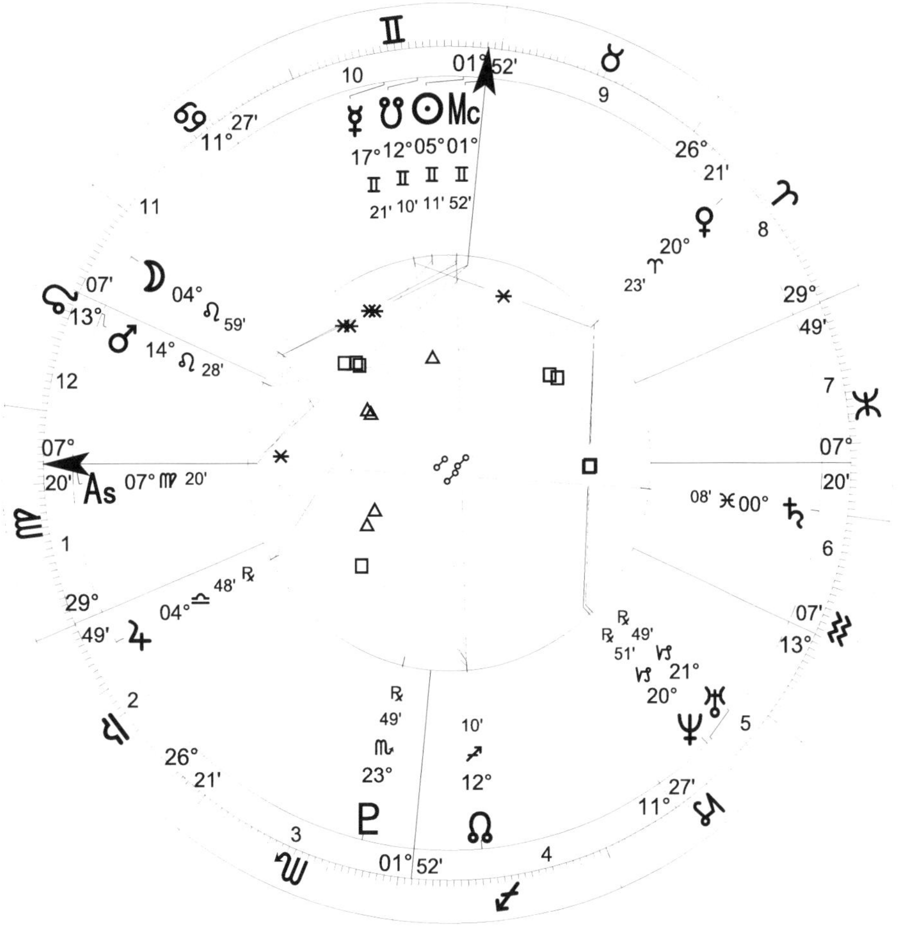

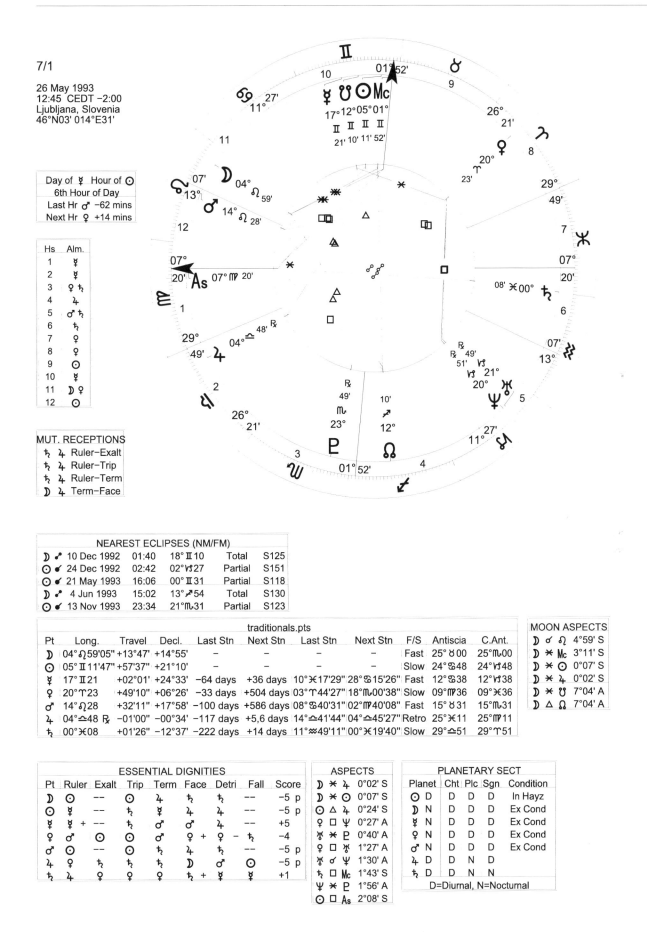

Day of ☿	Hour of ☉
6th Hour of Day	
Last Hr ♂	−62 mins
Next Hr ♀	+14 mins

Hs	Alm.
1	☿
2	☿
3	♀ ♄
4	♃
5	♂ ♄
6	♄
7	♀
8	♀
9	☉
10	☿
11	☽ ♀
12	☉

MUT. RECEPTIONS		
♄	♃	Ruler-Exalt
♄	♃	Ruler-Trip
♄	♃	Ruler-Term
☽	♃	Term-Face

NEAREST ECLIPSES (NM/FM)					
☽	10 Dec 1992	01:40	18°♊10	Total	S125
☉	24 Dec 1992	02:42	02°♑27	Partial	S151
☉	21 May 1993	16:06	00°♊31	Partial	S118
☽	4 Jun 1993	15:02	13°♐54	Total	S130
☉	13 Nov 1993	23:34	21°♏31	Partial	S123

traditionals.pts

Pt	Long.	Travel	Decl.	Last Stn	Next Stn	Last Stn	Next Stn	F/S	Antiscia	C.Ant.
☽	04°♌59'05"	+13°47'	+14°55'	–	–	–	–	Fast	25°♉00	25°♏00
☉	05°♊11'47"	+57'37"	+21°10'	–	–	–	–	Slow	24°♋48	24°♑48
☿	17°♊21	+02°01'	+24°33'	−64 days	+36 days	10°♓17'29"	28°♋15'26"	Fast	12°♋38	12°♑38
♀	20°♈23	+49'10"	+06°26'	−33 days	+504 days	03°♈44'27"	18°♏00'38"	Slow	09°♍36	09°♓36
♂	14°♌28	+32'11"	+17°58'	−100 days	+586 days	08°♋40'31"	02°♍40'08"	Fast	15°♉31	15°♏31
♃	04°♎48 ℞	−01'00"	−00°34'	−117 days	+5,6 days	14°♎41'44"	04°♎45'27"	Retro	25°♓11	25°♍11
♄	00°♓08	+01'26"	−12°37'	−222 days	+14 days	11°♒49'11"	00°♓19'40"	Slow	29°♎51	29°♈51

MOON ASPECTS			
☽	☌	♌	4°59' S
☽	⚹	Mc	3°11' S
☽	⚹	☉	0°07' S
☽	⚹	♃	0°02' S
☽	⚹	☋	7°04' A
☽	△	☊	7°04' A

ESSENTIAL DIGNITIES

Pt	Ruler	Exalt	Trip	Term	Face	Detri	Fall	Score
☽	☉	--	☉	♃	♄	♄	--	−5 p
☉	☿	--	♄	☿	♃	♃	--	−5 p
☿	☿ +	--	♄	♂	♂	♃	--	+5
♀	♂	☉	☉	♂	♀ +	♀ −	♄	−4
♂	☉	--	☉	♄	♃	♄	--	−5 p
♃	♀	♄	♄	♄	☽	♂	☉	−5 p
♄	♃	♀	♀	♀	♄ +	☿	☿	+1

ASPECTS			
☽	⚹	♃	0°02' S
☽	⚹	☉	0°07' S
☉	△	♃	0°24' S
♀	□	♆	0°27' A
♅	⚹	♇	0°40' A
♀	□	♅	1°27' A
♅	☌	♆	1°30' A
♄	□	Mc	1°43' S
♆	⚹	♇	1°56' A
☉	□	As	2°08' S

PLANETARY SECT

Planet		Cht	Plc	Sgn	Condition
☉	D	D	D	D	In Hayz
☽	N	D	D	D	Ex Cond
♀	N	D	D	D	Ex Cond
☿	N	D	D	D	Ex Cond
♂	N	D	D	D	Ex Cond
♃	D	D	N	D	
♄	D	D	N	N	

D=Diurnal, N=Nocturnal

7/2: WHERE IS MY DAUGHTER?

31 March 1994 at 9:12 a.m., Ljubljana, Slovenia
Hour ruler: Sun

This is one of the most unfortunate charts that I have ever studied. It refers to the then infamous disappearance of a young woman who had been missing for several days. Her mother called me, in distress, and asked if I could help find her.

The chart is easy from an astrologer's point of view, as it clearly shows that the missing girl was dead. But how to disclose such devastating news to her mother? As so many years have passed since the case, I don't remember what exactly I said to her, but I know that I only tried to describe the location of her whereabouts. Fortunately, she didn't even ask whether the daughter was alive or dead, so I couldn't be blamed for hiding the dire truth which the chart revealed.

The querent is shown by the ascendant in Gemini and its ruler Mercury which due to its rulership of H5 of children also signifies her missing daughter. As the question relates to her daughter, Mercury primarily rules her, of course. A look at the chart reveals that Mercury is besieged – bodily placed between Saturn and Mars. A besieged planet, by virtue of being caught between two destructive forces, shows a person (or a thing) to be trapped or otherwise endangered, so this obviously shows a very difficult situation for the quesited. It actually looks like things are going from bad to worse for her. Her circumstances seem even more difficult because Mercury is weak in Pisces - the sign of its detriment and fall. Its placement in H11, which is otherwise a fortunate house, can in this context only reflect her mother's heart's desire and hope to find the daughter alive. Because, obviously, H11 is the derived H7 for the daughter – which is the house of open enemies. (Of marriage, too, of course, but such a precarious state of Mercury could hardly point to her escape with a view to get married.) It seemed obvious that she was in the hands of the abductor or attacker, in short, of an opponent.

Mercury separates from a conjunction with Saturn, the H8 ruler, pointing to the possibility of death, while Mars, to which Mercury applies, co-rules the unfortunate H6 and rules the unfortunate H12, but it is also (more importantly) the ruler of the daughter's derived H8 (8/5). In this chart, H8 (crisis, loss, death) comes strongly to the fore.

Does the Moon give more hope? Its role is that of the co-significator of the missing girl and it also shows the course of events. Its first applying aspect is a square with Saturn. This is always a bad indication, confirming here the dire indications of the rest of the chart.

Yet another indication of the girl's ill fate is provided by the fact that Mercury's dispositor Jupiter is in Scorpio, the sign of death, and in the unfortunate H6. Its retrograde state might in the context of the question only be interpreted as the probability of finding her dead body.

How about eclipses? Back then, I did not yet use this technique in horary, but a glance at the eclipse table (see chart) shows that the previous total lunar eclipse was at 7 ° Gemini, exactly on the ascendant of the horary chart, and at the same time in an exact square of Saturn!

The unfortunate young woman was soon thereafter found dead in the bushes of the city park. In the light of the fact that IC which helps describing the location of missing things (people, animals etc.) is in Leo, showing (among others) city parks, the chart is shockingly revealing from this perspective, too.

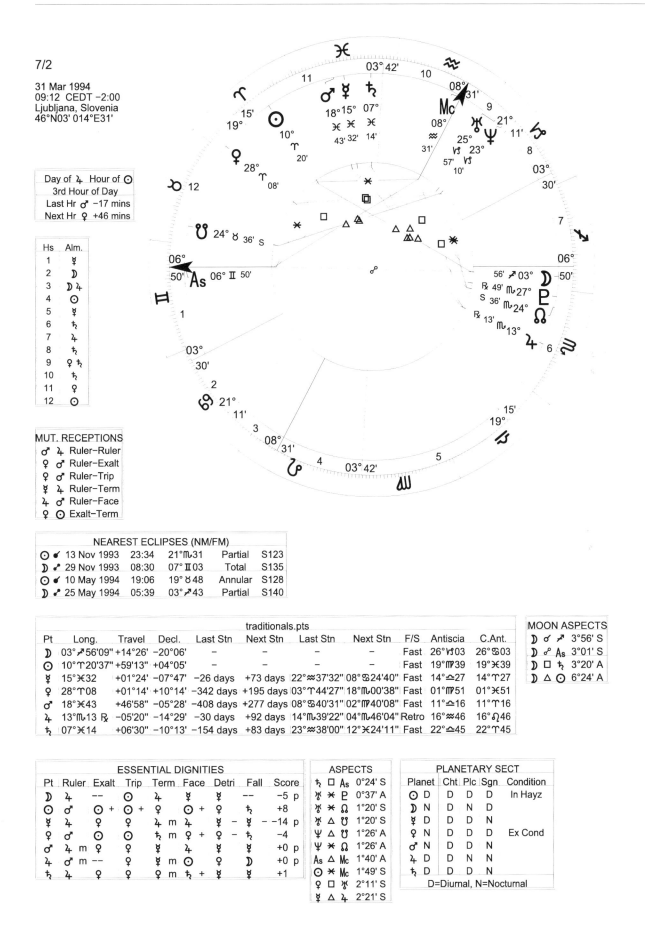

7/2

31 Mar 1994
09:12 CEDT −2:00
Ljubljana, Slovenia
46°N03' 014°E31'

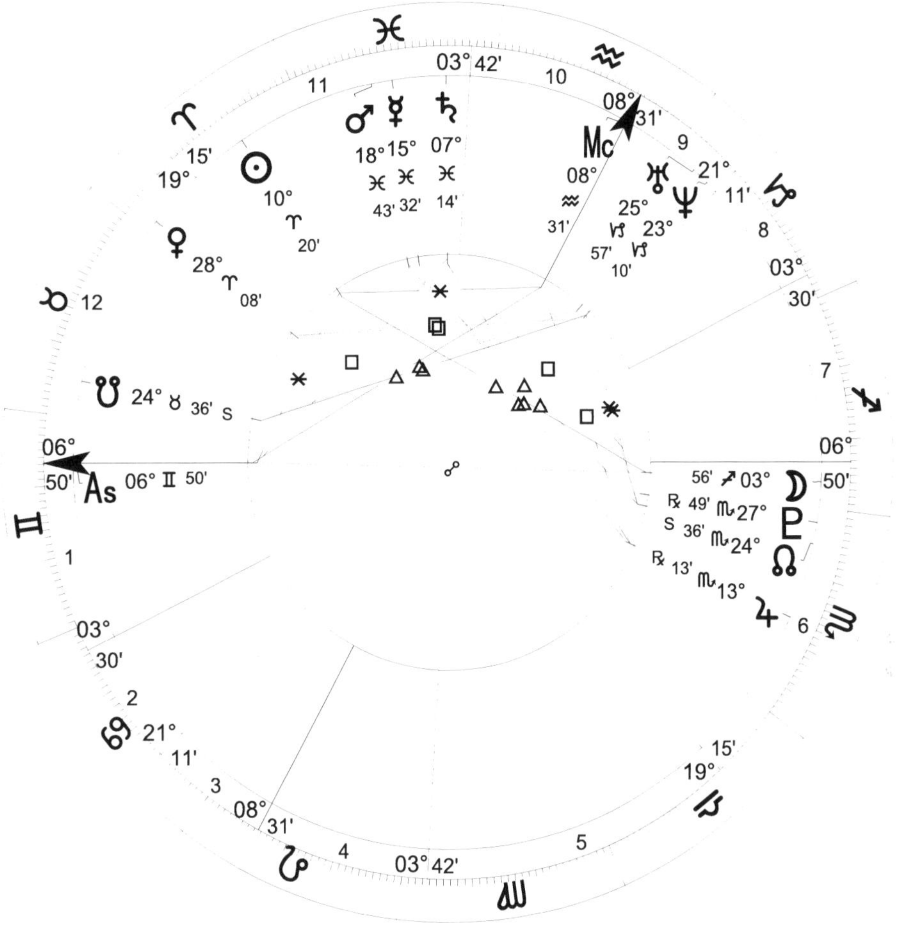

Day of ♃ Hour of ☉
3rd Hour of Day
Last Hr ♂ −17 mins
Next Hr ♀ +46 mins

Hs	Alm.
1	☿
2	☽
3	☽♃
4	☉
5	☿
6	♄
7	♃
8	♄
9	♀♄
10	♄
11	♀
12	☉

MUT. RECEPTIONS	
♂ ♃	Ruler–Ruler
♀ ♂	Ruler–Exalt
♀ ♂	Ruler–Trip
☿ ♃	Ruler–Term
♃ ♂	Ruler–Face
♀ ☉	Exalt–Term

NEAREST ECLIPSES (NM/FM)					
☉ ☌	13 Nov 1993	23:34	21°♏31	Partial	S123
☽ ☍	29 Nov 1993	08:30	07°♊03	Total	S135
☉ ☌	10 May 1994	19:06	19°♉48	Annular	S128
☽ ☍	25 May 1994	05:39	03°♐43	Partial	S140

traditionals.pts

Pt	Long.	Travel	Decl.	Last Stn	Next Stn	Last Stn	Next Stn	F/S	Antiscia	C.Ant.
☽	03°♐56'09"	+14°26'	−20°06'	–	–	–	–	Fast	26°♑03	26°♋03
☉	10°♈20'37"	+59'13"	+04°05'	–	–	–	–	Fast	19°♍39	19°♓39
☿	15°♓32	+01°24'	−07°47'	−26 days	+73 days	22°♒37'32"	08°♋24'40"	Fast	14°♎27	14°♈27
♀	28°♈08	+01°14'	+10°14'	−342 days	+195 days	03°♈44'27"	18°♏00'38"	Fast	01°♍51	01°♓51
♂	18°♓43	+46'58"	−05°28'	−408 days	+277 days	08°♋40'31"	02°♍40'08"	Fast	11°♎16	11°♈16
♃	13°♏13 ℞	−05'20"	−14°29'	−30 days	+92 days	14°♏39'22"	04°♏46'04"	Retro	16°♒46	16°♌46
♄	07°♓14	+06'30"	−10°13'	−154 days	+83 days	23°♒38'00"	12°♓24'11"	Fast	22°♎45	22°♈45

MOON ASPECTS		
☽ ☌ ♐	3°56'	S
☽ ☍ As	3°01'	S
☽ □ ♄	3°20'	A
☽ △ ☉	6°24'	A

ESSENTIAL DIGNITIES

Pt	Ruler	Exalt	Trip	Term	Face	Detri	Fall	Score
☽	♃	--	☉	♃	☿	☿	--	−5 p
☉	♂	☉ +	☉ +	♀	☉ +	♀	♄	+8
☿	♃	♀	♀	♃ m	♃	☿ −	☿ −	−14 p
♀	♂	☉	☉	♄ m	♀ +	♀ −	♄	−4
♂	♃ m	♀	♀	☿	♃	☿	☿	+0 p
♃	♂ m	--	♀	☿ m	☉	♀	☽	+0 p
♄	♃	♀	♀	♀ m	♄ +	☿	☿	+1

ASPECTS		
♄ □ As	0°24'	S
♅ ⚹ ♇	0°37'	A
♅ ⚹ ☊	1°20'	S
♅ △ ☋	1°20'	S
♆ △ ☋	1°26'	A
♆ ⚹ ☊	1°26'	A
As △ Mc	1°40'	A
☉ ⚹ Mc	1°49'	S
♀ □ ♅	2°11'	S
☿ △ ♃	2°21'	S

PLANETARY SECT

Planet		Cht	Plc	Sgn	Condition
☉	D	D	D	D	In Hayz
☽	N	D	N	D	
☿	D	D	D	N	
♀	N	D	D	D	Ex Cond
♂	N	D	D	N	
♃	D	D	N	N	
♄	D	D	D	N	

D=Diurnal, N=Nocturnal

7/3: WHERE IS MY FATHER? IS HE HURT, WILL THEY FIND HIM?

28 April 2005 at 7:18 a.m., Ljubljana, Slovenia
Hour ruler: Mars

A former student sent me an email asking if I could help locate her father who went missing. He was last seen the previous afternoon when he walked past a sports field, close to a nursing home where he resided. He was an elderly dementia patient, so it was obvious that he probably got lost. The police searched for him from around 8 p.m. on that day till about half past one in the morning, and the search would continue the next morning. *I guess they should find him, if he is alive, because they're looking for him with special cameras which detect warmth – except if he fell into some hole,* she wrote.

I first cast a horary chart for 8:20 a.m., the time when I read the question (on the same day) - unfortunately, because, as I shall explain later, my answer would be more accurate from the timing point of view if I had cast the chart for the time when the letter arrived in my mailbox – that is, when the querent sent it to me. That was the original time of the question which held the best information as per the outcome. I'm posting that chart (cast for 7:18 a.m.) here while the one upon which I based my judgment (cast for 8:20 a.m.) had the following positions of quickly moving points: ascendant 23 Gemini, IC 23°31' Leo, the Moon 28°05' Sagittarius, while the Sun was in H11 instead of in H12 – although in a wide conjunction with the cusp of H12, which makes it practically a H12 body. Fortunately, the angles in that chart were in the same signs as in the "true" chart, therefore the significators were the same. The difference between the two charts refers mainly to the timing which I judged by the Moon.

Mercury stands for the querent while the Sun, ruler of H4, represents her father. The Sun is in Taurus in H12, together with its dispositor Venus.

Our first question is, of course, is the old man alive and well? The Sun has no essential dignity in Taurus, and H12 is an unfortunate house, but since he was obviously lost and "out of sight", this placement of his main significator is quite fitting. In missing persons horaries it's more important to see if their significator is bodily afflicted by a discordant aspect to a (natural or accidental) malefic, as this could mean that they had an accident or are in a difficult situation. But in this case, the Sun is completely safe! Its only aspects are a wide conjunction with Venus (which also protects it because it's the Sun's dispositor and strong in its own sign) and a tight applying sextile to Uranus, which is good, as it indicates some sort of a liberation.

What about the Moon, which is always a co-significator of missing people? It's (in the "true" chart) at the end of Sagittarius and in a close applying sextile with Mars which co-rules his (derived) H3 and rules his H9. None of these aspects is bad and both suggest movement and communication. It seemed that the old man had just lost his way and was wandering around. (As already said, I judged this on the basis of the Moon at 28°05' Sagittarius, which would mean that it was void-of-course, but the meaning would be the same.) His state of being lost is also in line with an OOB Moon.

Where could he be? The Sun is in Taurus which indicates fields, meadows, plains, pastures and the like. Given the fact that the old people's home was in the village, surrounded by fields and vineyards, this was pretty logical. In any event, it is certain that he did not fall into a hole. The direction? The Moon is in the western part of the chart, so I felt that he went in that direction. Because Sagittarius indicates higher grounds, he might have been wandering through a hilly area, but since the Moon would soon change signs I judged that he would shortly come down from some high (Sagittarius) to lower grounds (Capricorn, the next Moon's sign, is an earth sign showing lower areas). I thought that he'd not be found before the Moon's crossing (by a symbolic movement, of course) into Capricorn, where it would start to "give light to" the man's significator, the Sun. Based on the distance between the Moon and the cusp of Capricorn (2 degrees), I judged that they would find him two days later.

I wrote: *I'm quite sure that your father is alive and unhurt. He's OK, as much as he can be in that uncomfortable situation, of course, but I don't see him injured. They'll find him in two units of time (probably two days, but could be two hours). I believe that he went to the west and is currently on some lower grounds, close to a farm, a pasture or a field.*

According to the message that the querent sent me later, they found him on Saturday afternoon, which is two and a half days from the time of the question, not two days. Where did I miss? Of course, I cast the chart for a wrong time! In the "true" chart, the Moon wants 2.5 degrees to the end of its sign (instead of the two degrees in the "untrue" chart) which exactly correspond to the time of the find!

7/3

28 Apr 2005
07:18 CEDT −2:00
Ljubljana, Slovenia
46°N03' 014°E31'

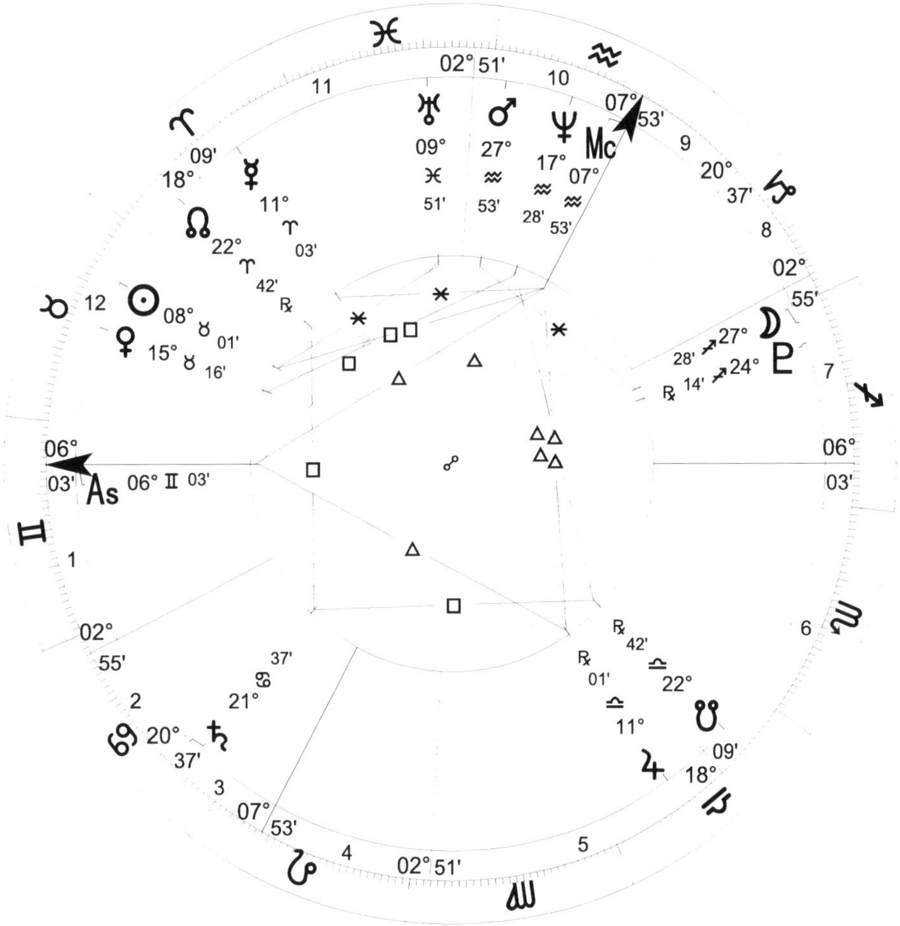

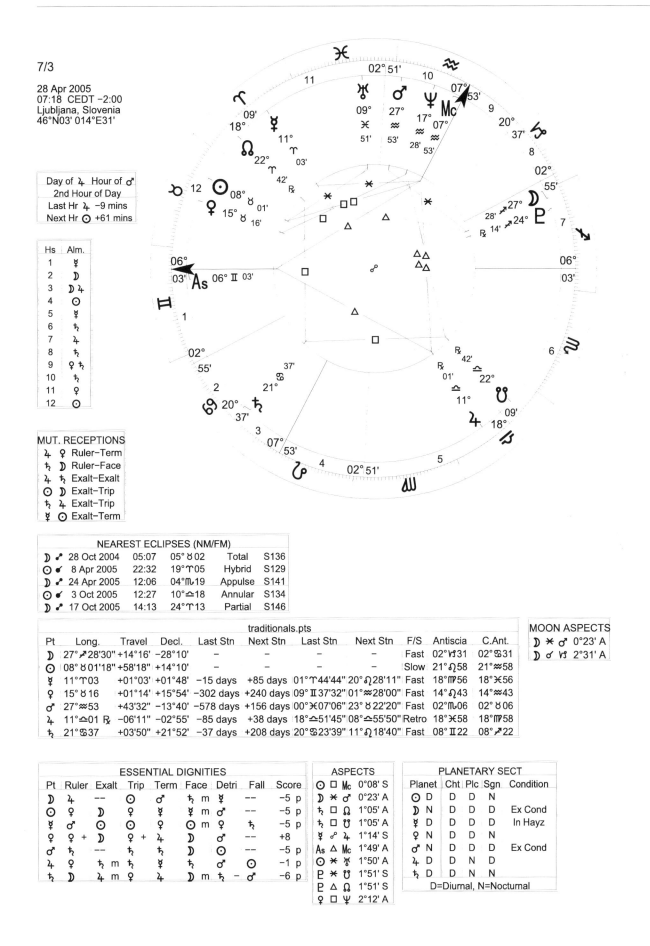

Day of ♃ Hour of ♂
2nd Hour of Day
Last Hr ♃ −9 mins
Next Hr ☉ +61 mins

Hs	Alm.
1	☿
2	☽
3	☽ ♃
4	☉
5	☿
6	♄
7	♃
8	♄
9	♀ ♄
10	♄
11	♀
12	☉

MUT. RECEPTIONS	
♃ ♀	Ruler–Term
♄ ☽	Ruler–Face
♃ ♄	Exalt–Exalt
☉ ☽	Exalt–Trip
♄ ♃	Exalt–Trip
☿ ☉	Exalt–Term

NEAREST ECLIPSES (NM/FM)					
☽ ☍	28 Oct 2004	05:07	05°♉02	Total	S136
☉ ☌	8 Apr 2005	22:32	19°♈05	Hybrid	S129
☽ ☍	24 Apr 2005	12:06	04°♏19	Appulse	S141
☉ ☌	3 Oct 2005	12:27	10°♎18	Annular	S134
☽ ☍	17 Oct 2005	14:13	24°♈13	Partial	S146

traditionals.pts

Pt	Long.	Travel	Decl.	Last Stn	Next Stn	Last Stn	Next Stn	F/S	Antiscia	C.Ant.
☽	27°♐28'30"	+14°16'	−28°10'	–	–	–	–	Fast	02°♑31	02°♋31
☉	08°♉01'18"	+58'18"	+14°10'	–	–	–	–	Slow	21°♌58	21°♒58
☿	11°♈03	+01°03'	+01°48'	−15 days	+85 days	01°♈44'44"	20°♌28'11"	Fast	18°♍56	18°♓56
♀	15°♉16	+01°14'	+15°54'	−302 days	+240 days	09°♊37'32"	01°♒28'00"	Fast	14°♌43	14°♒43
♂	27°♒53	+43'32"	−13°40'	−578 days	+156 days	00°♓07'06"	23°♉22'20"	Fast	02°♏06	02°♉06
♃	11°♎01 ℞	−06'11"	−02°55'	−85 days	+38 days	18°♎51'45"	08°♎55'50"	Retro	18°♓58	18°♍58
♄	21°♋37	+03'50"	+21°52'	−37 days	+208 days	20°♋23'39"	11°♌18'40"	Fast	08°♊22	08°♐22

MOON ASPECTS
☽ ⚹ ♂ 0°23' A
☽ ☌ ♑ 2°31' A

ESSENTIAL DIGNITIES

Pt	Ruler	Exalt	Trip	Term	Face	Detri	Fall	Score
☽	♃	--	☉	♂	♄ m	☿	--	−5 p
☉	♀	☽	♀	☿	☿ m	♂	--	−5 p
☿	♂	☉	☉	♀	☉ m	♀	♄	−5 p
♀	♀ +	☽	♀ +	♃	☽	♂	--	+8
♂	♄	--	♄	♄	☽	☉	--	−5 p
♃	♀	♄ m	♄	☿	♄	♂	☉	−1 p
♄	☽	♃ m	♀	♃	☽ m	♄ −	♂	−6 p

ASPECTS	
☉ □ Mc	0°08' S
☽ ⚹ ♂	0°23' A
♄ □ ☊	1°05' A
♄ □ ☋	1°05' A
☿ ☍ ♃	1°14' S
As △ Mc	1°49' A
☉ ⚹ ♅	1°50' A
♇ ⚹ ☋	1°51' S
♇ △ ☊	1°51' S
♀ □ ♆	2°12' A

PLANETARY SECT

Planet		Cht	Plc	Sgn	Condition
☉	D	D	D	N	
☽	N	D	D	D	Ex Cond
☿	D	D	D	D	In Hayz
♀	N	D	D	N	
♂	N	D	D	D	Ex Cond
♃	D	D	N	D	
♄	D	D	N	N	

D=Diurnal, N=Nocturnal

As the chart showed, the man was indeed rumbling around, and they found him in a vineyard, close to a field and a beehive that he was once renting. She also said, upon my inquiry, that he obviously came down there from a hill. The direction of his stroll? West and slightly north.

Always cast horary charts for the time when questions are born (thought of, written down and sent to you), not for the time when you read and understand them!

7/4: WHERE IS TONI R.? WILL HE RETURN HOME SAFELY?

2 September 2002 at 9:16 a.m., Ljubljana, Slovenia
Hour ruler: Jupiter

At the end of August 2002, Slovenian news media reported that the parents of 28-year Toni R. had long been in the dark about the whereabouts of their son who had been travelling the Asian continent for a couple of years. The last news they had of him was in his email of 14 April 2002 which he wrote from Pakistan. On 3 July 2002 his parents heard from a police officer in Maribor who informed them that their son might be held in one of the Pakistani's prisons. The news was supposed to come from Interpol who received an anonymous email notice, but with no further data, so that nobody actually knew where Toni was imprisoned, and on what charges. On the same day the parents contacted the Slovenian Foreign Ministry who established a connection with the Slovenian Embassy in Tehran, to begin the search for the missing man.

The question came to my mind when I read a piece of news in a daily newspaper, saying that Toni was probably still in prison because despite extensive media campaign there was no news of him. My question was, what happened to him, where was he and would he return home safely?

As always in cases when we do not personally know the missing person, or their relationship with us is not defined, Toni is shown by the ascendant and H1. Ascendant is in Libra, together with its dispositor Venus which occupies H1. This in itself gives plenty of hope, because H1 is an angular and powerful house, while Libra is Venus' home sign. The young man is obviously alive and well! Venus applies to a retrograde Uranus by a close trine, which predicts a sudden happy turn or literally the liberation of the captive. The next Venus' aspect is a trine with Saturn, ruler of H4 of homeland. Obviously, Toni will be back home soon!

And what does the Moon, his co-significator, say? It's also in its own sign (Cancer), confirming the indications that the missing person is alive and well. The Moon's placement in H9 is very appropriate, since Toni was abroad. Interestingly, the Moon is also OOB – often the case when the missing person is abroad (beyond his country's borders). It applies to a square with Mercury, which rules H9 and H12. The combined signature of both houses could be encapsulated by "a prison in a foreign country". Since the Moon has not yet reached the square with Mercury, he was probably still in prison at the moment of the question, but this aspect could also point to his close encounter with a lawyer, as H9 also stands for advocacy.

But I was sure that Toni would be freed soon. The aforementioned positive indications are supported by the fact that the next Moon's aspect (after a square with Mercury) would be a sextile with the Sun which is placed in H11 and rules it. As this is the most fortunate house, it's obvious that his desire would be fulfilled. Another positive indicator is Jupiter (the hour ruler) in conjunction with fortuna in H10. The chart therefore clearly indicates that all is well with Toni and that he would be happily back home soon.

When? The Moon is in a cardinal sign and in an (albeit loose) conjunction with MC, so those could be days? There are 4 degrees separating the Moon and the Sun, so maybe 4 days? That's quite possible, as Venus' trine to a retrograde Uranus promises a quick and unexpected return, especially since Uranus is placed in a fortunate H5. Obviously, that'll be a pleasant surprise!

Thus it was. News came soon that Toni sent an email to his family "over the weekend" - which could be 6, 7 or 8 September – four or five days after the question. "Fortunate news" is properly described by the aforementioned conjunction of Jupiter, the ruler of H3 of communication, with fortuna in H10. He wrote that he had been imprisoned in Pakistan for the last four months, because his visa expired and he forgot to prolong it, but now that was settled and he was finally coming back home.

The locational chart for this example is shown on p. 342. I have included only the Venus (Toni's significator) local space line which runs exactly across Pakistan. An interesting "coincidence", don't you agree?

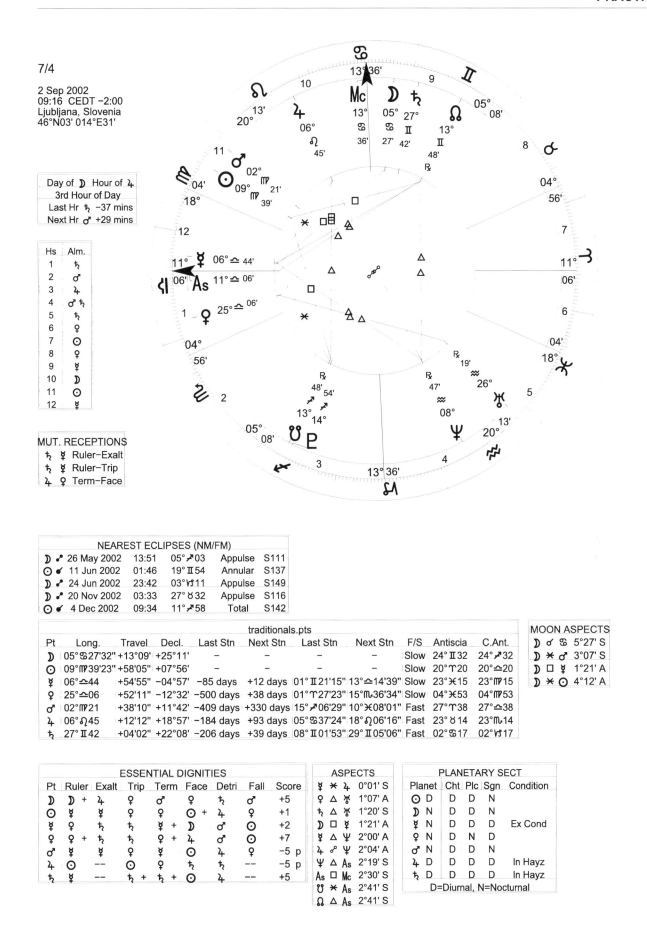

7/4

2 Sep 2002
09:16 CEDT −2:00
Ljubljana, Slovenia
46°N03' 014°E31'

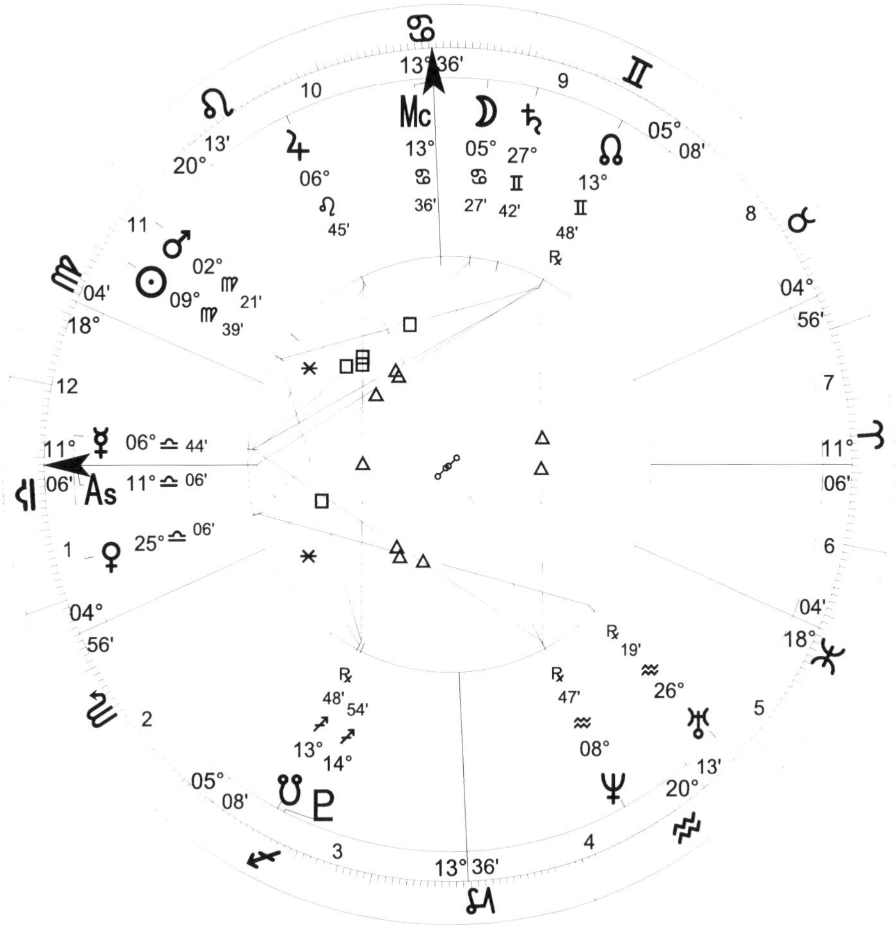

Day of ☽	Hour of ♃
3rd Hour of Day	
Last Hr ♄	−37 mins
Next Hr ♂	+29 mins

Hs	Alm.
1	♄
2	♂
3	♃
4	♂ ♄
5	♄
6	♀
7	☉
8	♀
9	☿
10	☽
11	☉
12	☿

MUT. RECEPTIONS		
♄	☿	Ruler−Exalt
♄	☿	Ruler−Trip
♃	♀	Term−Face

NEAREST ECLIPSES (NM/FM)					
☽ ☍	26 May 2002	13:51	05°♐03	Appulse	S111
☉ ☌	11 Jun 2002	01:46	19°♊54	Annular	S137
☽ ☍	24 Jun 2002	23:42	03°♑11	Appulse	S149
☽ ☍	20 Nov 2002	03:33	27°♉32	Appulse	S116
☉ ☌	4 Dec 2002	09:34	11°♐58	Total	S142

traditionals.pts

Pt	Long.	Travel	Decl.	Last Stn	Next Stn	Last Stn	Next Stn	F/S	Antiscia	C.Ant.
☽	05°♋27'32"	+13°09'	+25°11'	–	–	–	–	Slow	24°♊32	24°♐32
☉	09°♍39'23"	+58'05"	+07°56'	–	–	–	–	Slow	20°♈20	20°♎20
☿	06°♎44	+54'55"	−04°57'	−85 days	+12 days	01°♊21'15"	13°♎14'39"	Slow	23°♓15	23°♍15
♀	25°♎06	+52'11"	−12°32'	−500 days	+38 days	01°♈27'23"	15°♏36'34"	Slow	04°♓53	04°♍53
♂	02°♍21	+38'10"	+11°42'	−409 days	+330 days	15°♐06'29"	10°♓08'01"	Fast	27°♈38	27°♎38
♃	06°♌45	+12'12"	+18°57'	−184 days	+93 days	05°♋37'24"	18°♌06'16"	Fast	23°♉14	23°♏14
♄	27°♊42	+04'02"	+22°08'	−206 days	+39 days	08°♊01'53"	29°♊05'06"	Fast	02°♋17	02°♑17

MOON ASPECTS			
☽	☌	♋	5°27' S
☽	⚹	♂	3°07' S
☽	□	☿	1°21' A
☽	⚹	☉	4°12' A

ESSENTIAL DIGNITIES

Pt	Ruler	Exalt	Trip	Term	Face	Detri	Fall	Score
☽	☽ +	♃	♀	♂	♀	♄	♂	+5
☉	☿	☿	♀	♀	☉ +	♃	♀	+1
☿	♀	♄	♄	☿ +	☽	♂	☉	+2
♀	♀ +	♄	♄	♀ +	♃	♂	☉	+7
♂	☿	☿	♀	☿	☉	♃	♀	−5 p
♃	☉	--	☉	♀	♄	♄	--	−5 p
♄	☿	--	♄ +	♄ +	☉	♃	--	+5

ASPECTS			
☿	⚹	♃	0°01' S
♀	△	♅	1°07' A
♄	△	♅	1°20' S
☽	□	☿	1°21' A
☿	△	♆	2°00' A
♃	☍	♆	2°04' A
♆	△	As	2°19' S
As	□	Mc	2°30' S
☋	⚹	As	2°41' S
☊	△	As	2°41' S

PLANETARY SECT					
Planet		Cht	Plc	Sgn	Condition
☉	D	D	D	N	
☽	N	D	D	N	
☿	N	D	D	D	Ex Cond
♀	N	D	N	D	
♂	N	D	D	N	
♃	D	D	D	D	In Hayz
♄	D	D	D	D	In Hayz

D=Diurnal, N=Nocturnal

7/5: WHAT HAS HAPPENED TO KT BOEHRER?

27 December 2003 at 7:52 a.m., Ljubljana, Slovenia
Hour ruler: Jupiter

Kt Boehrer – an American astrologer who wrote a book on little explored area of astrology, **DECLINATION - THE OTHER DIMENSION**, was, like myself, a member of an international astrological forum. Towards the end of December 2003, as we were exchanging holiday greetings, one of the members alerted us to the fact that we had long not heard from Kt. This was really strange because she was a very communicative lady and an active member of the group who she posted regularly, although was well advanced in age. Since I knew her exact birth data, I immediately checked her transits and progressions, which were quite difficult, so I sent a message to the forum in which I expressed my concern that Kt could be sick. I also made a horary chart for the above question, and this strongly reinforced my concerns.

Her significator? Kt was neither my relative nor a personal friend, neither my boss nor my enemy or anything that could be placed in a particular, person-related house; she was only my internet acquaintance, so it seemed appropriate that she'd be shown by the ascendant and H1. This proved to be quite fitting since the ascendant was in Capricorn, standing for old people. The rising degree is in an exact conjunction with the Sun, fitting to well-known and successful people, and with Mercury, standing for writers and intellectuals - traditionally also for astrologers. Her co-significator the Moon is at the end of Aquarius.

So, what is Kt's situation? Saturn, the ascendant ruler, almuten and dispositor of the planets in Capricorn, is in Cancer, the sign of its detriment, and retrograde. This shows her to be in an unenviable situation. Detriment could mean that she was literally "away from home", but is at the same time drawing attention to her possible weakness or/and inability to act. True, retrogradation could also indicate an imminent return, but since Saturn is in H7, opposing her own house, and in an applying opposition to the Sun, the natural significator of vitality, acting also as her own co-significator, such a state of her main significator rather points to her helplessness which could be a result of sickness.

So – is she really sick? Mercury, the ruler of H6 of disease, conjuncts the ascendant - yes! The disease is apparently "within her". Mercury is peregrine, retrograde and combust, so the illness is probably serious. The Sun which also exactly conjuncts the ascendant, rules the critical H8 which adds to the worrying indications and gives little hope of recovery. (Remember that any planet exactly on an angle plays a crucially important role!). Mercury is actually moving away from the Sun but Saturn (Kt) and the Sun (H8 ruler) mutually apply into an opposition, essentially meaning that she could be fighting a losing battle.

Let us now turn to the Moon. We can see that its first next aspect is a conjunction with Uranus. This could indicate a sudden change in the near future. But because Uranus is a trans-Saturnian and not angular, this aspect cannot act as a dependable indicator of the outcome, so let us take the Moon forward to see its next aspect which will be completed only in Pisces. That'll be a sextile with Mercury (illness), followed immediately by a sextile to the unfortunately aspected Sun (possibility of death).

Conclusion: Kt is obviously seriously ill, and according to all the negative indications her illness could be fatal. I did not publish my judgment in the group. This would be contrary to ethics and, finally, no one posed a specific question except me, therefore I decided that the answer should remain with me.

Outcome: on 4 January 2004, 8 days after my question, Kt's daughter announced the sad news that Kt made her passing on that day, "in the morning hours". She said that her health deteriorated drastically in the course of the previous week, and that she was too weak to be able to overcome her illness.

See that the Moon's distance from the Sun, ruling H8 of death, is almost exactly 8 degrees - and Kt actually passed away 8 days after the question.

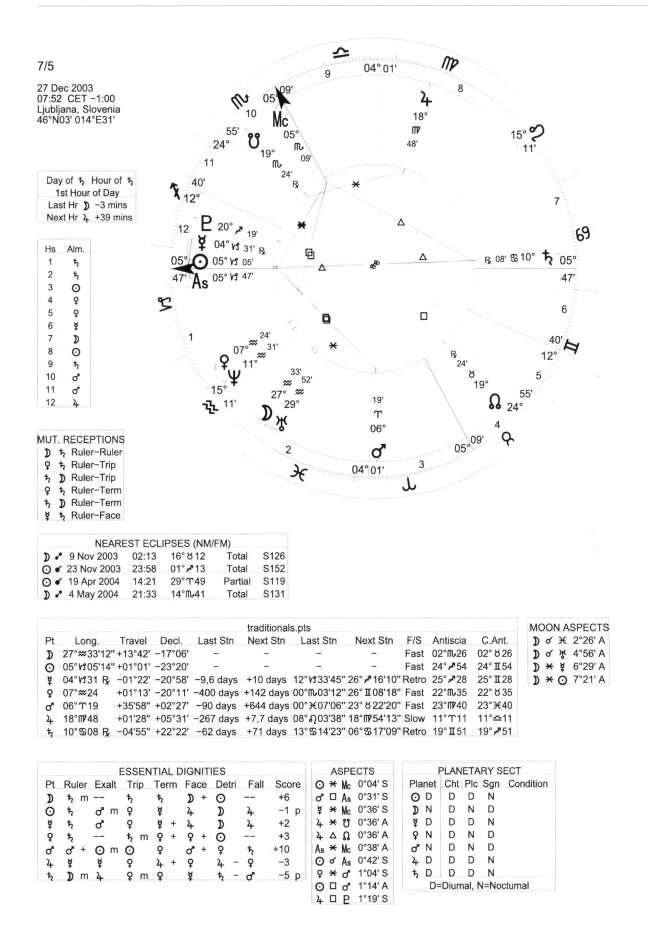

7/5

27 Dec 2003
07:52 CET −1:00
Ljubljana, Slovenia
46°N03' 014°E31'

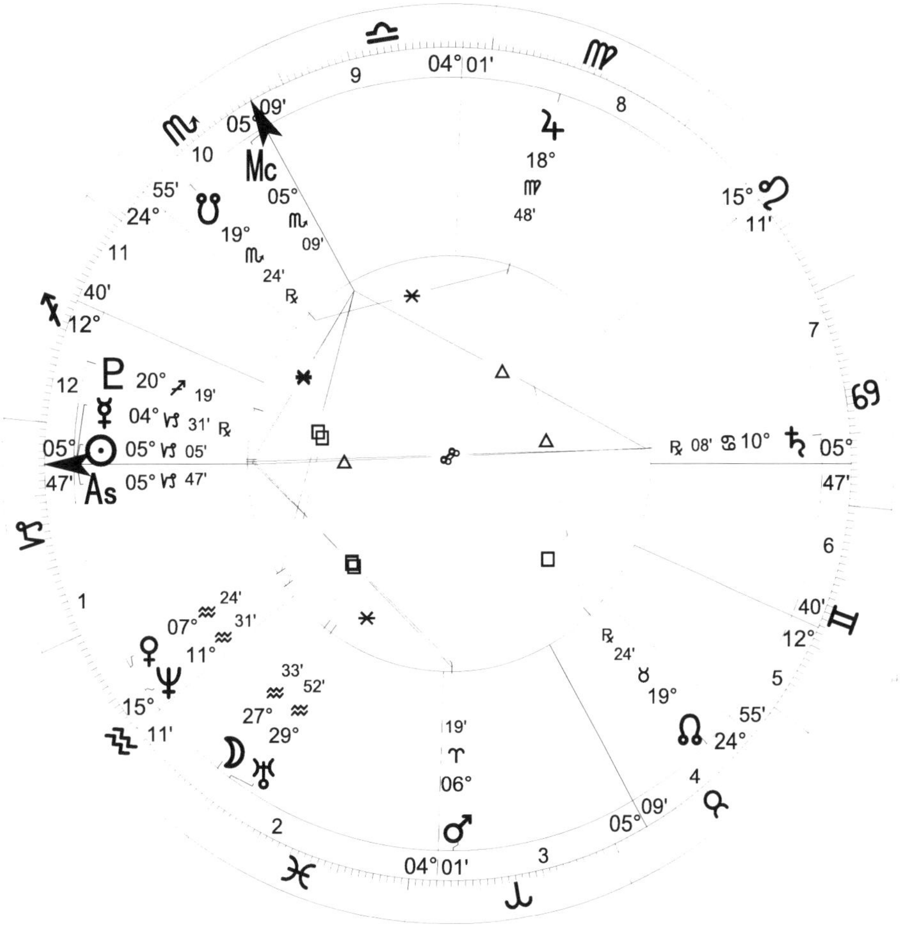

Day of ♄ Hour of ♄
1st Hour of Day
Last Hr ☽ −3 mins
Next Hr ♃ +39 mins

Hs	Alm.
1	♄
2	♄
3	☉
4	♀
5	♀
6	☿
7	☽
8	☉
9	♄
10	♂
11	♂
12	♃

MUT. RECEPTIONS		
☽	♄	Ruler-Ruler
♀	♄	Ruler-Trip
♄	☽	Ruler-Trip
♀	♄	Ruler-Term
♄	☽	Ruler-Term
☿	♄	Ruler-Face

NEAREST ECLIPSES (NM/FM)					
☽ ☍	9 Nov 2003	02:13	16° ♉ 12	Total	S126
☉ ☌	23 Nov 2003	23:58	01° ♐ 13	Total	S152
☉ ☌	19 Apr 2004	14:21	29° ♈ 49	Partial	S119
☽ ☍	4 May 2004	21:33	14° ♏ 41	Total	S131

traditionals.pts

Pt	Long.	Travel	Decl.	Last Stn	Next Stn	Last Stn	Next Stn	F/S	Antiscia	C.Ant.
☽	27°♒33'12"	+13°42'	−17°06'	–	–	–	–	Fast	02°♏26	02° ♉ 26
☉	05°♑05'14"	+01°01'	−23°20'	–	–	–	–	Fast	24°♐54	24° ♊ 54
☿	04°♑31 ℞	−01°22'	−20°58'	−9,6 days	+10 days	12°♑33'45"	26°♐16'10"	Retro	25°♐28	25° ♊ 28
♀	07°♒24	+01°13'	−20°11'	−400 days	+142 days	00°♏03'12"	26°♊08'18"	Fast	22°♏35	22° ♉ 35
♂	06°♈19	+35'58"	+02°27'	−90 days	+644 days	00°♓07'06"	23°♉22'20"	Fast	23°♍40	23°♓40
♃	18°♍48	+01'28"	+05°31'	−267 days	+7,7 days	08°♌03'38"	18°♍54'13"	Slow	11°♈11	11°♎11
♄	10°♋08 ℞	−04'55"	+22°22'	−62 days	+71 days	13°♋14'23"	06°♋17'09"	Retro	19° ♊ 51	19°♐51

MOON ASPECTS		
☽ ☌ ♓	2°26' A	
☽ ☌ ♅	4°56' A	
☽ ✶ ☿	6°29' A	
☽ ✶ ☉	7°21' A	

ESSENTIAL DIGNITIES

Pt	Ruler	Exalt	Trip	Term	Face	Detri	Fall	Score
☽	♄ m	--	♄	♄	☽ +	☉	--	+6
☉	♄	♂ m	♀	☿	♃	☽	♃	−1 p
☿	♄	♂	♀	☿ +	♃	☽	♃	+2
♀	♄	--	♄ m	☿ +	♀ +	☉	--	+3
♂	♂ +	☉ m	☉	♀	♂ +	♀	♄	+10
♃	☿	☿	♀	♃ +	♀	♃ −	♀	−3
♄	☽ m	♃	♀ m	♀	☿	♄ −	♂	−5 p

ASPECTS	
☉ ✶ Mc	0°04' S
♂ □ As	0°31' S
☿ ✶ Mc	0°36' S
♃ ✶ ☋	0°36' A
♃ △ ☊	0°36' A
As ✶ Mc	0°38' A
☉ ☌ As	0°42' S
♀ ✶ ♂	1°04' S
☉ □ ♂	1°14' A
♃ □ ♇	1°19' S

PLANETARY SECT

Planet	Cht	Plc	Sgn	Condition
☉ D	D	D	N	
☽ N	D	N	D	
☿ D	D	D	N	
♀ N	D	N	D	
♂ N	D	N	D	
♃ D	D	D	N	
♄ D	D	D	N	

D=Diurnal, N=Nocturnal

7/6: WHERE IS THE MISSING R.H.? WILL HE RETURN SAFELY?

12 May 12 2007 at 1:26 p.m. (13:26), Ljubljana, Slovenia
Hour ruler: Moon

On that day (it was Saturday) I read in the news that R.H., a well-known Slovenian businessman and playboy who often filled tabloid pages, had gone missing. His relatives and friends had not seen him or heard of him since Wednesday. His disappearance was reported to the police by his friend and business partner with whom he had agreed a meeting, but didn't show up and was unreachable on phone for several days. The police had no idea where to look for him, but his friends were afraid that something bad had happened to him because he seemed worried for the last two weeks before his disappearance. A month before that, someone broke into his car, so they came to a conclusion that he had enemies who might have hurt him.

I immediately raised the above question and cast the chart which I delineated publicly on two astrology forums.

The missing person in shown by H1. Ascendant is in Virgo, with Mercury the ascendant ruler in Gemini in H10. The rising degree is in an exact sextile with Venus and fortuna in H11, which I took as an indication of his safety. I suggested that he might be spending some leisure time in the company of a beauty! Mercury is strong essentially and accidentally, since it's in its own sign and in the strong, angular H10, and also above the horizon without any bad aspects with malefics. This clearly shows that he's not endangered. Due to the nature of Gemini, a mutable sign, it seemed likely that he's on the road, moving about, travelling and communicating. Most importantly: it is obvious that he is free! You will see that Mercury is separated from the conjunction with the Sun, and while it's still under the Sun's beams, reflecting his "concealment" (he was missing, after all), it will soon become wholly visible due to its quick motion. In other words: his whereabouts will soon be known and he will soon be "seen" again!

For confirmation we must look to the Moon which always gives insight into the state of missing people. It's in Pisces, in H7, close to the cusp of H8. Its last aspect was conjunction with Uranus combined with a square with Jupiter; the separation by a little over 3 degrees exactly corresponds to the number of days he was missing. Uranus points to an unexpected turn of events while Jupiter co-rules his H4 (of home), reflecting his recent leaving of the home – and possibly his home country. Jupiter also rules his H7 and H8. This may not be good, because H7 represents his opponents (the house of "open enemies"), but it could also stand for his business partners. That's logical because on the day he went missing, he didn't show up for a business meeting. What about H8? This is related to his financial affairs. Could they be the reason for his absence? Well, we'll soon know, obviously, because the next Moon's aspect is a sextile to the Sun, so things will come to light shortly – and the aspect is a very close one, meaning very soon! This is a wonderful indication of a fortunate outcome, especially because the two lights are above the horizon, with the Moon receiving the Sun in its dignity (exaltation).

But where is he? Mercury is at the beginning of its sign, with its last aspect (when it was still in Taurus) being a sextile with Mars, the H9 ruler, so I reckoned that he was abroad. (Slovenia is a very small country, bordering on several neighbouring countries, so driving anywhere out of the state is a matter of a an hour, really.) Mars is on cusp of H8, confirming the indications speaking for the possibility that he was settling business finances.

But H8 is associated with death, how about that, you may ask? Is this not a bad indication? Well, his main significators show that he is alive and well and will soon be back, so H8 in this context obviously means something else!

The direction of his whereabouts? The Moon is in H7 which indicates west, while Gemini (Mercury's sign) is a south-western sign, meaning that he probably traveled to the southwest. To the south of Slovenia is Croatia and its coastal part lies to the southwest, so that's where he must be, I thought.

Two days later, on 14 May, we learnt that R.H. came back home - alive and healthy. According to media reports, he was "already in Slovenia", clearly suggesting that he was indeed abroad. On 15 May came the confirmation: yes, he was in Croatia! He resolutely denied the suspicions of his abduction or any similar detention by force. He said that for the first couple of days he was busy with some business meetings and that he took a few days off after that. (Spending some "quality" time with a beauty, I guess, but that was never confirmed, of course.)

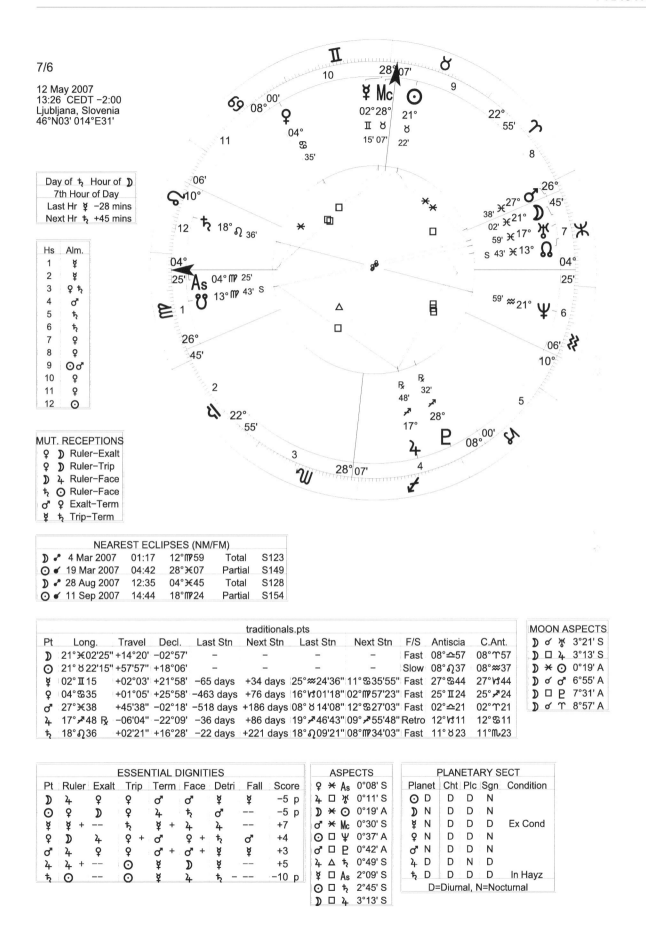

7/6

12 May 2007
13:26 CEDT −2:00
Ljubljana, Slovenia
46°N03' 014°E31'

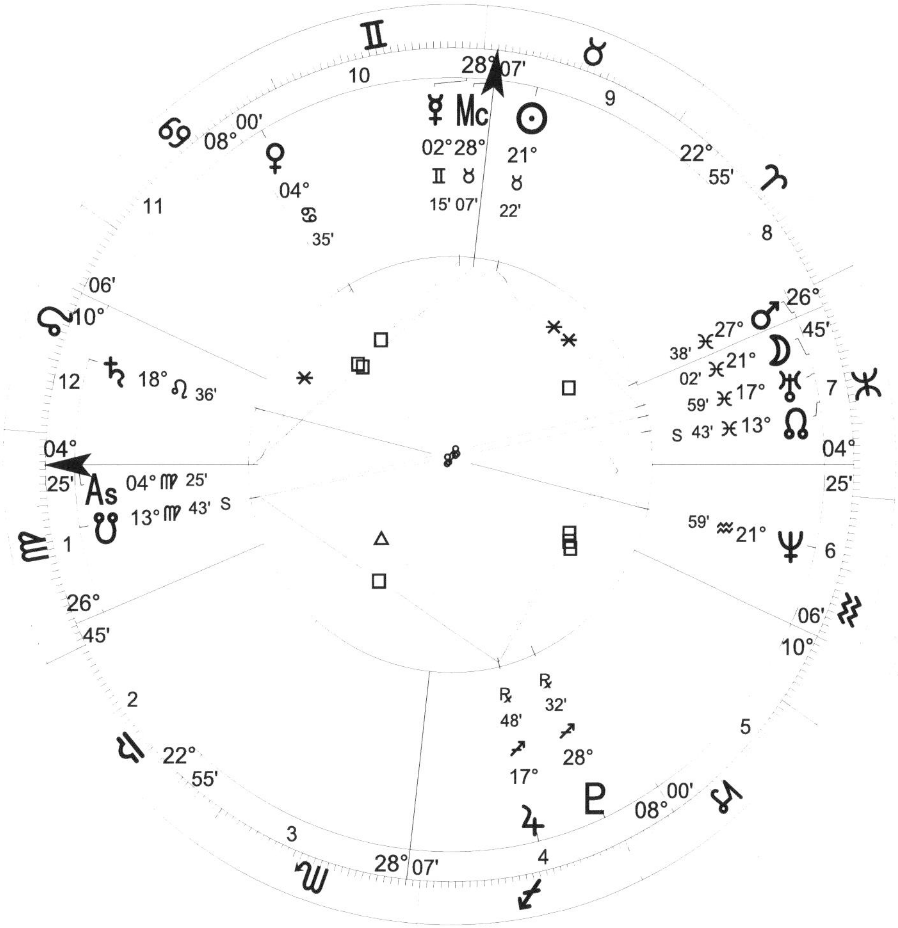

Day of ♄ Hour of ☽
7th Hour of Day
Last Hr ☿ −28 mins
Next Hr ♄ +45 mins

Hs	Alm.
1	☿
2	☿
3	♀ ♄
4	♂
5	♄
6	♄
7	♀
8	♀
9	☉♂
10	♀
11	♀
12	☉

MUT. RECEPTIONS	
♀ ☽	Ruler-Exalt
♀ ☽	Ruler-Trip
☽ ♃	Ruler-Face
♄ ☉	Ruler-Face
♂ ♀	Exalt-Term
☿ ♄	Trip-Term

NEAREST ECLIPSES (NM/FM)					
☽ ☍	4 Mar 2007	01:17	12°♍59	Total	S123
☉ ☌	19 Mar 2007	04:42	28°♓07	Partial	S149
☽ ☍	28 Aug 2007	12:35	04°♓45	Total	S128
☉ ☌	11 Sep 2007	14:44	18°♍24	Partial	S154

traditionals.pts

Pt	Long.	Travel	Decl.	Last Stn	Next Stn	Last Stn	Next Stn	F/S	Antiscia	C.Ant.
☽	21°♓02'25"	+14°20'	−02°57'	–	–	–	–	Fast	08°♎57	08°♈57
☉	21°♉22'15"	+57'57"	+18°06'	–	–	–	–	Slow	08°♌37	08°♒37
☿	02°♊15	+02°03'	+21°58'	−65 days	+34 days	25°♒24'36"	11°♋35'55"	Fast	27°♋44	27°♑44
♀	04°♋35	+01°05'	+25°58'	−463 days	+76 days	16°♑01'18"	02°♍57'23"	Fast	25°♊24	25°♐24
♂	27°♓38	+45'38"	−02°18'	−518 days	+186 days	08°♉14'08"	12°♋27'03"	Fast	02°♎21	02°♈21
♃	17°♐48 ℞	−06'04"	−22°09'	−36 days	+86 days	19°♐46'43"	09°♐55'48"	Retro	12°♑11	12°♋11
♄	18°♌36	+02'21"	+16°28'	−22 days	+221 days	18°♌09'21"	08°♍34'03"	Fast	11°♉23	11°♏23

MOON ASPECTS		
☽ ☌ ♅	3°21' S	
☽ □ ♃	3°13' S	
☽ ✶ ☉	0°19' A	
☽ ☌ ♂	6°55' A	
☽ □ ♇	7°31' A	
☽ ☌ ♈	8°57' A	

ESSENTIAL DIGNITIES

Pt	Ruler	Exalt	Trip	Term	Face	Detri	Fall	Score
☽	♃	♀	♀	♂	♂	☿	☿	−5 p
☉	♀	☽	♀	♃	♄	♂	−−	−5 p
☿	☿ +	−−	♄	☿ +	♃	♃	−−	+7
♀	☽	♃	♀ +	♂	♀ +	♄	♂	+4
♂	♃	♀	♀	♂ +	♂ +	☿	☿	+3
♃	♃ +	−−	☉	☿	☽	☿	−−	+5
♄	☉	−−	☉	☿	♃	♄ −	−−	−10 p

ASPECTS	
♀ ✶ As	0°08' S
♃ □ ♅	0°11' S
☽ ✶ ☉	0°19' A
♂ ✶ Mc	0°30' S
☉ □ ♆	0°37' A
♂ □ ♇	0°42' A
♃ △ ♄	0°49' S
☿ □ As	2°09' S
☉ □ ♄	2°45' S
☽ □ ♃	3°13' S

PLANETARY SECT

Planet	Cht	Plc	Sgn	Condition
☉ D	D	D	N	
☽ N	D	D	N	
☿ N	D	D	D	Ex Cond
♀ N	D	D	N	
♂ N	D	D	N	
♃ D	D	N	D	
♄ D	D	D	D	In Hayz

D=Diurnal, N=Nocturnal

7/7: WHERE IS THE MISSING NATASHA? IS SHE ALIVE?

24 September 2001 at 9:53 a.m., Ljubljana, Slovenia
Hour ruler: Jupiter

I received this question by phone from a dowser who was investigating the case of Natasha – a young woman who had been missing for about 10 days. She had left home in the middle of September, for an unknown destination. The police launched a search campaign which was until the day of the question still fruitless. The woman disappeared without a trace. The dowser asked me whether I, as an astrologer, could help with some clue as for her whereabouts.

Natasha is shown by the ascendant in Scorpio. This is not a good indication in a chart of a missing person since Scorpio, as we know, is a sign associated with crises, trials and death. Her ruler Mars is in Capricorn, the sign of its exaltation which in itself gives hope, although, on the other hand, this is a sign of loneliness, isolation and coldness. The fact that Mars is OOB adds to the possibility that she has gone to some unusual, distant, uninhabited place. All of this is not encouraging, considering she was 10 days missing.

The Moon, her co-significator, is also in Capricorn. That's another worrisome fact as the Moon is in detriment here, indicating – in the context of the question – the probability of the woman's distress and helplessness. The preponderance of Scorpio and Capricorn, Martian and Saturnian signs, led me to ask whether she was a brunette or black-haired, of pale complexion and taciturn, introverted nature? Yes, he said, this description fitted perfectly. (I should add here that I had not learnt of this case from the media before he consulted me.)

The Moon's placement in this chart is alarming because it's not only in detriment but is also afflicted by a tense applying square to the Sun and by an exact applying conjunction with the south node. A square is a disharmonious aspect and the south node has a Saturnian connotation – all of this inclines towards the possibility of a loss of life. Especially since the Sun is in its fall (Libra), so both lights – showing vitality and life - are considerably weakened.

The sign of Capricorn where both significators are placed, is ruled by Saturn, therefore the condition of this planet is crucial. It is in the critical H8 where it separates from an opposition with Pluto, the natural ruler of death and at the same time the modern ruler of Scorpio, the ascending sign. The Moon's last aspect (in the previous sign) was a sextile with Mercury, placed in the unfortunate H12 (isolation) and co-ruling H8 while also dispositing Saturn, located in that house in Gemini. All of this led me to a conclusion that the quesited was in a miserable condition. I expressed the fear that probably something very dire happened to her. The dowser said that he felt the same. We agreed that there's little hope for Natasha to be found alive.

But where is she? Mars and the Moon are in H3, indicating the surrounding area. Capricorn stands for lonely, deserted, hilly and rocky areas, so I asked the querent if there was such a site in the vicinity of her home? He confirmed that the woman lived in a village which was surrounded by hills.

Which direction was she likely to have taken? Capricorn is a southern sign but the most likely direction would be northeast because the Moon as well as Mars, her main significator, were in that part of the chart.

In the beginning of March 2002, close to half a year after the question, newspapers published the news that a decomposing corpse was found in a deserted part of a quarry (Capricorn!) which was located on the outskirts of the mountainous village where the missing woman lived. This explains the significators in H3 – the surrounding area! The corpse was found by geodesists who were carrying out some terrain measuring there. The site was not easily accessible as it was hidden behind a huge rock. Although the body was unrecognizable, the identity of the ill-fated Natasha was revealed by the clothes which were sufficiently preserved.

Although I did not yet use eclipses in horary astrology at that time, it's interesting to note that the previous solar eclipse – a total one at that! – was at 0°10' Cancer, in an exact opposition of the horary Moon, and aligned with the "fateful" nodal axis. This is yet another case which confirms the value of using eclipses in horary work.

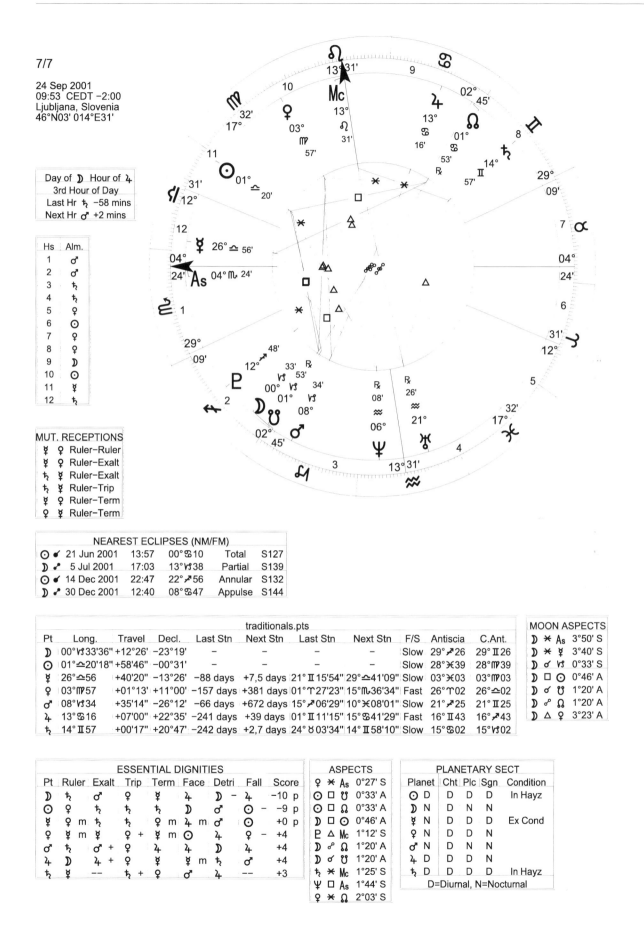

7/7

24 Sep 2001
09:53 CEDT -2:00
Ljubljana, Slovenia
46°N03' 014°E31'

Day of ☽ Hour of ♃
3rd Hour of Day
Last Hr ♄ -58 mins
Next Hr ♂ +2 mins

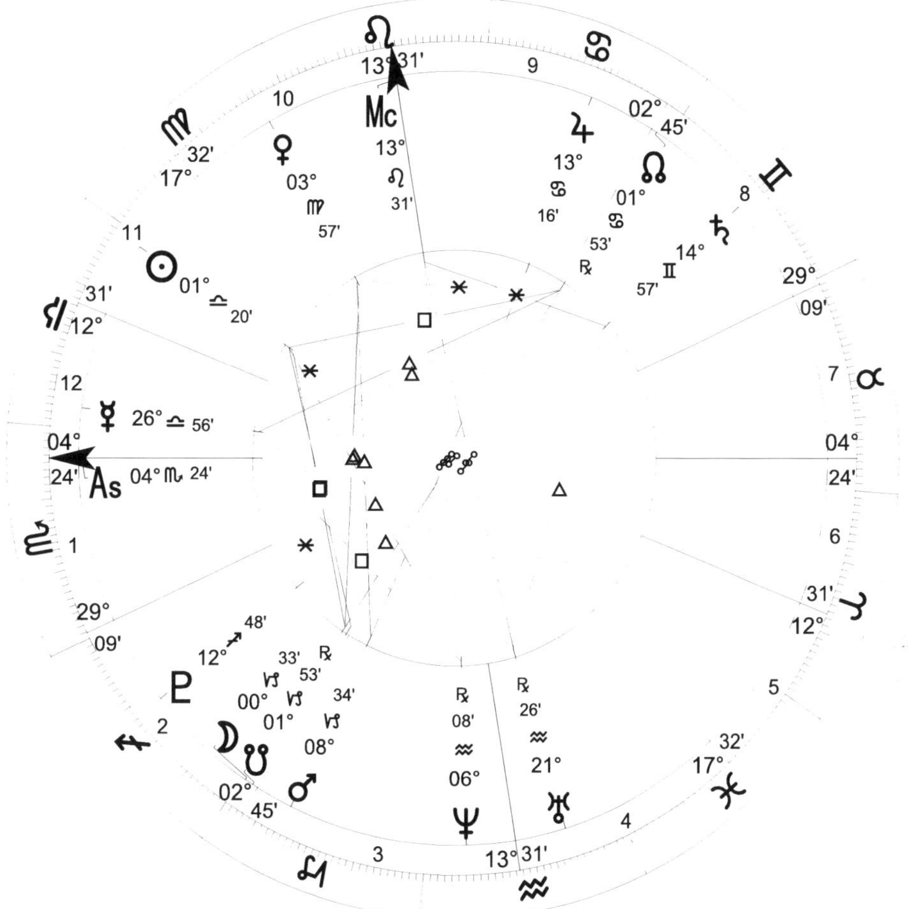

Hs	Alm.
1	♂
2	♂
3	♄
4	♄
5	♀
6	☉
7	♀
8	♀
9	☽
10	☉
11	☿
12	♄

MUT. RECEPTIONS		
☿	♀	Ruler-Ruler
☿	♀	Ruler-Exalt
♄	☿	Ruler-Exalt
♄	☿	Ruler-Trip
☿	♀	Ruler-Term
♀	☿	Ruler-Term

NEAREST ECLIPSES (NM/FM)					
☉ ●	21 Jun 2001	13:57	00°♋10	Total	S127
☽ ●	5 Jul 2001	17:03	13°♑38	Partial	S139
☉ ●	14 Dec 2001	22:47	22°♐56	Annular	S132
☽ ●	30 Dec 2001	12:40	08°♋47	Appulse	S144

traditionals.pts

Pt	Long.	Travel	Decl.	Last Stn	Next Stn	Last Stn	Next Stn	F/S	Antiscia	C.Ant.
☽	00°♑33'36"	+12°26'	-23°19'	–	–	–	–	Slow	29°♐26	29°♊26
☉	01°♎20'18"	+58'46"	-00°31'	–	–	–	–	Slow	28°♓39	28°♍39
☿	26°♎56	+40'20"	-13°26'	-88 days	+7,5 days	21°♊15'54"	29°♎41'09"	Slow	03°♓03	03°♍03
♀	03°♍57	+01°13'	+11°00'	-157 days	+381 days	01°♈27'23"	15°♏36'34"	Fast	26°♈02	26°♎02
♂	08°♑34	+35'14"	-26°12'	-66 days	+672 days	15°♐06'29"	10°♓08'01"	Slow	21°♐25	21°♊25
♃	13°♋16	+07'00"	+22°35'	-241 days	+39 days	01°♊11'15"	15°♋41'29"	Fast	16°♊43	16°♐43
♄	14°♊57	+00'17"	+20°47'	-242 days	+2,7 days	24°♉03'34"	14°♊58'10"	Slow	15°♋02	15°♑02

MOON ASPECTS			
☽	⚹	As	3°50' S
☽	⚹	☿	3°40' S
☽	☌	♑	0°33' S
☽	□	☉	0°46' A
☽	☌	☋	1°20' A
☽	☍	☊	1°20' A
☽	△	♀	3°23' A

ESSENTIAL DIGNITIES

Pt	Ruler	Exalt	Trip	Term	Face	Detri	Fall	Score
☽	♄	♂	♀	☿	♃	☽ -	♃	-10 p
☉	♀	♄	♄	♄	☽	♂	☉ -	-9 p
☿	♀ m	♄	♄	♀ m	♃ m	♂	☉	+0 p
♀	☿ m	☿	♀ +	☿ m	☉	♃	♀ -	+4
♂	♄	♂ +	♀	♃	♃	☽	♃	+4
♃	☽	♃ +	♀	☿	☿ m	♄	♂	+4
♄	☿	--	♄ +	♀	♂	♃	--	+3

ASPECTS			
♀	⚹	As	0°27' S
☉	□	☋	0°33' A
☉	□	☊	0°33' A
☽	□	☉	0°46' A
♇	△	Mc	1°12' S
☽	☍	☊	1°20' A
☽	☌	☋	1°20' A
♄	⚹	Mc	1°25' S
♆	□	As	1°44' S
♀	⚹	☊	2°03' S

PLANETARY SECT

Planet		Cht	Plc	Sgn	Condition
☉	D	D	D	D	In Hayz
☽	N	D	N	N	
☿	N	D	D	D	Ex Cond
♀	N	D	D	N	
♂	N	D	N	N	
♃	D	D	D	N	
♄	D	D	D	D	In Hayz

D=Diurnal, N=Nocturnal

7/8: WHAT HAPPENED TO MADDIE? WILL THEY FIND HER?

8 May 2007 at 8:57 p.m. (20:57), Ljubljana, Slovenia
Hour ruler: Saturn

In May 2007, astrological forums were flooded with charts related to Maddie – a four-year old English girl who on 3 May disappeared from a holiday apartment in the Portuguese resort of Praia da Luz. At about half past eight that evening, her parents went to a nearby restaurant for dinner, leaving the sleeping child in her bed, but when they returned about an hour and a half later, the child was gone. After several days of unsuccessful search it became clear that something was very wrong. Horary charts relating to the whereabouts of Maddie, created by some of my colleagues, were quite pessimistic. I also asked the question because I strongly sympathized with the unfortunate parents.

Maddie is shown by the ascendant in Scorpio - the sign that was also rising at the alleged time of her abduction. Mars, its dispositor, is in Pisces in H4. Pisces is the sign of the sea, H4 (among other things) of the grave. Mercury, the H8 ruler, is in an exact applying sextile with Mars, and in conjunction with the descendant, showing a possible kidnapper, while Mars itself applies to a square with Pluto, the natural significator of crimes, tragedies and death.

The Moon separates from an exact inconjunction with Venus (H7 ruler, placed in H8), but it doesn't apply anywhere; in other words, the Moon is void-of-course. It's true that later in her course she'd be applying to a square with the Sun and to an opposition with Saturn, but the aspects are not yet within orbs. A void-of-course Moon can mean that "there is nothing to do about the matter". The Moon's future motion in this case clearly does not inspire any more hope than that of Mars, the main significator – quite to the contrary.

To date (mid-2015) Maddie has still not been found. After a year of fruitless search the case was temporarily closed, but in 2013, Scotland Yard posted an e-fit picture of a man who on that evening, at around 10 pm, was taking a child in his lap toward the beach. Unfortunately, they didn't find out anything else.

My colleagues who also attempted this case, dealt with different charts, of course – based on the time and place of their own questions - but it's interesting to note that in nearly all of those charts Mars featured strongly as well. As already mentioned, Mars applies to square Pluto at 28.5 Sagittarius, this planet being in an exact square with the previous solar eclipse at 28° Pisces. This is also the degree of the fixed star Scheat (29° Pisces, to be exact) - one of the most destructive stars, associated with maritime accidents, drowning and floods. (It played an important role in the sinking of Titanic, for example). The "fatality" of this chart is also shown by the MC at 13° Virgo - this being the exact degree of the previous total lunar eclipse.

I should add that, according to some, missing children are shown by H5. I can't see why a missing child would be shown by another house than a missing adult, although it is true that children generally "belong" to H5. In this case, the significator is the same (Mars), so there's no dilemma, but if it was, I'd proceed as usually in cases of doubt – I'd choose that significator which would better describe the kid.

The locational chart (see p. 343) is extremely interesting again. See the horary Moon (co-significator of the missing girl) going exactly over the area where the girl disappeared!

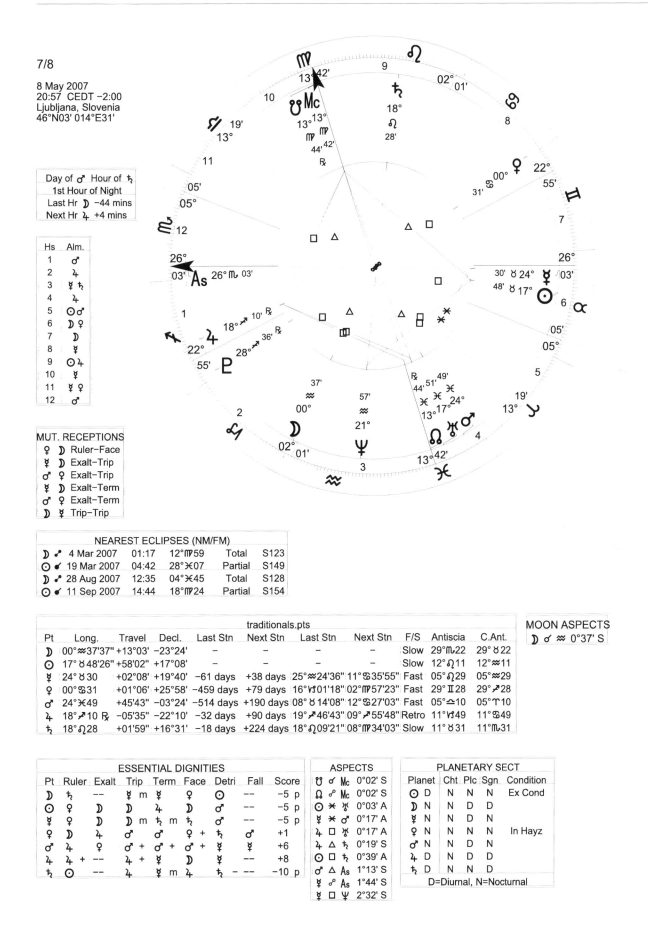

7/8

8 May 2007
20:57 CEDT −2:00
Ljubljana, Slovenia
46°N03' 014°E31'

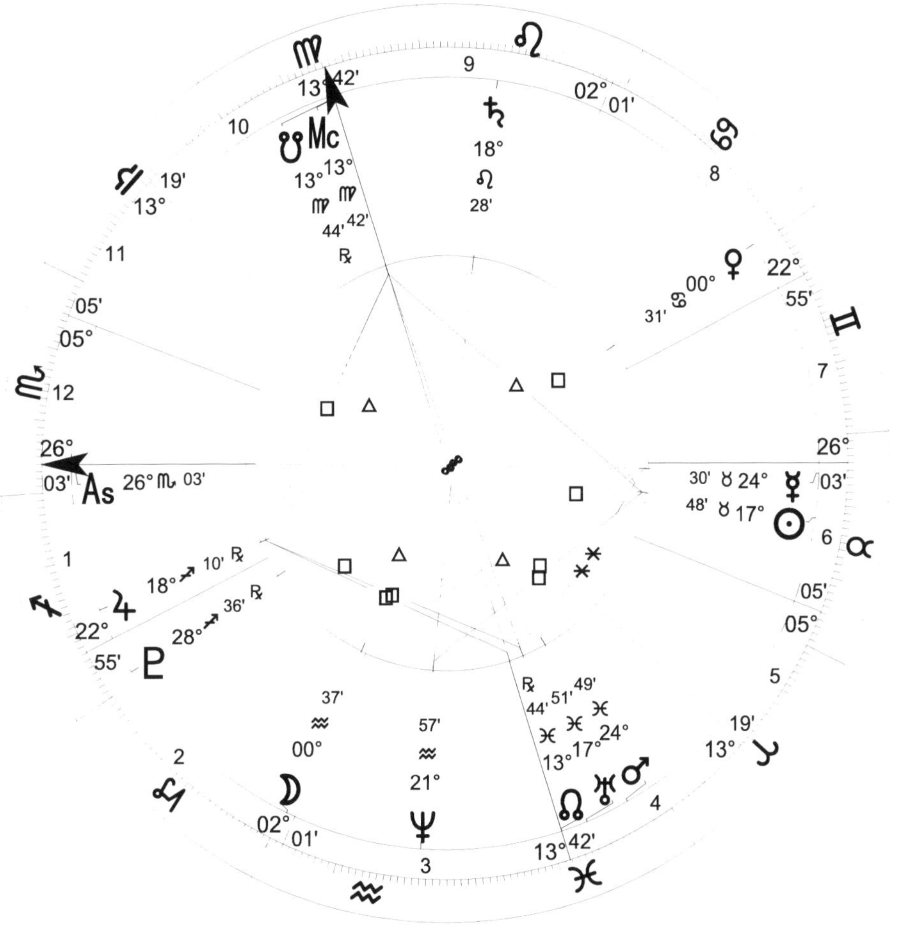

Day of ♂ Hour of ♄
1st Hour of Night
Last Hr ☽ −44 mins
Next Hr ♃ +4 mins

Hs	Alm.
1	♂
2	♃
3	☿ ♄
4	♃
5	☉♂
6	☽ ♀
7	☽
8	☿
9	☉♃
10	☿
11	☿ ♀
12	♂

MUT. RECEPTIONS
♀ ☽ Ruler−Face
☿ ☽ Exalt−Trip
♂ ♀ Exalt−Trip
☿ ☽ Exalt−Term
♂ ♀ Exalt−Term
☽ ☿ Trip−Trip

NEAREST ECLIPSES (NM/FM)					
☽ ●	4 Mar 2007	01:17	12°♍59	Total	S123
☉ ●	19 Mar 2007	04:42	28°♓07	Partial	S149
☽ ●	28 Aug 2007	12:35	04°♓45	Total	S128
☉ ●	11 Sep 2007	14:44	18°♍24	Partial	S154

traditionals.pts

Pt	Long.	Travel	Decl.	Last Stn	Next Stn	Last Stn	Next Stn	F/S	Antiscia	C.Ant.
☽	00°♒37'37"	+13°03'	−23°24'	–	–	–	–	Slow	29°♏22	29°♉22
☉	17°♉48'26"	+58'02"	+17°08'	–	–	–	–	Slow	12°♌11	12°♒11
☿	24°♉30	+02°08'	+19°40'	−61 days	+38 days	25°♒24'36"	11°♋35'55"	Fast	05°♌29	05°♒29
♀	00°♋31	+01°06'	+25°58'	−459 days	+79 days	16°♑01'18"	02°♍57'23"	Fast	29°♊28	29°♐28
♂	24°♓49	+45'43"	−03°24'	−514 days	+190 days	08°♉14'08"	12°♋27'03"	Fast	05°♎10	05°♈10
♃	18°♐10 ℞	−05'35"	−22°10'	−32 days	+90 days	19°♐46'43"	09°♐55'48"	Retro	11°♑49	11°♋49
♄	18°♌28	+01'59"	+16°31'	−18 days	+224 days	18°♌09'21"	08°♍34'03"	Slow	11°♉31	11°♏31

MOON ASPECTS
☽ ☌ ♒ 0°37' S

ESSENTIAL DIGNITIES

Pt	Ruler	Exalt	Trip	Term	Face	Detri	Fall	Score
☽	♄	--	☿ m	☿	♀	☉	--	−5 p
☉	♀	☽	☽	♃	☽	♂	--	−5 p
☿	♀	☽	☽ m	♄ m	♄	♂	--	−5 p
♀	☽	♃	♂	♂	♀ +	♄	♂	+1
♂	♃	♀	♂ +	♂ +	♂ +	☿	☿	+6
♃	♃ +	--	♃ +	☿	☽	☿	--	+8
♄	☉	--	♃	☿ m	♃	♄ −	--	−10 p

ASPECTS
☋ ☌ Mc 0°02' S
☊ ☍ Mc 0°02' S
☉ ✶ ♅ 0°03' A
☿ ✶ ♂ 0°17' A
♃ □ ♅ 0°17' A
♃ △ ♄ 0°19' S
☉ □ ♄ 0°39' A
♂ △ As 1°13' S
☿ ☍ As 1°44' S
☿ □ ♆ 2°32' S

PLANETARY SECT

Planet		Cht	Plc	Sgn	Condition
☉	D	N	N	N	Ex Cond
☽	N	N	D	D	
☿	N	N	D	N	
♀	N	N	N	N	In Hayz
♂	N	N	D	N	
♃	D	N	D	D	
♄	D	N	N	D	

D=Diurnal, N=Nocturnal

7/9: WHERE IS TOMAŽ HUMAR? WILL THEY FIND HIM ALIVE?

11 November 2009 at 10:05 p.m. (22:05), Ljubljana, Slovenia
Hour ruler: Saturn

I believe there isn't a single adult Slovenian who wouldn't know Tomaž Humar. He was one of our best mountain climbers. In his long and distinguished career he completed over 1500 ascents and won several domestic and international awards. He wrote a book titled NO IMPOSSIBLE WAYS. He became widely recognized in 1999 after his famous solo ascent of the south face of Dhaulagiri, considered one of the deadliest routes in the Himalayas. During a solo attempt to climb Nanga Parbat in August 2005, Humar became trapped by avalanches and melting snow at an altitude of nearly 6000 meters. After six days in a snow cave he was rescued by a Pakistan army helicopter crew. Back then I cast a horary chart (which unfortunately I did not save) which showed that he'd be rescued in two days. Since we were personal friends, I sent the message with this information to his base camp, and when we met several months later he told me that he received the message and that it gave him extra strength and courage. Admittedly he was rescued two days later.

Tomaž often narrowly escaped death. In early November 2009, he embarked on a solo climb of the Himalayan mountain Langtang Lirung. The last time he called his Sherpa was on 9 November, saying that he was injured (a broken leg, ribs and spine) and that he needed immediate help. He was then at an altitude of about 6300 m. After that he no longer responded to calls. The rescue team set off on 10 November, but weather conditions forced them to turn back that day. Rescuing became impossible until 14 November when Tomaž was finally found, but, unfortunately, dead. His body lay about 600 m below the place from where he called for help. It is believed that he died on the night of November 10.

When I cast the horary chart for the above question, I quickly realized that for Tomaž there was no more hope. I wrote on my astro facebook page that I see him "motionless". To say anything bolder than that would be risky and maybe even unethical, from the layman's point of view, because Tomaž was a national hero and people were very emotional about him and full of hope that he'd be found alive. (Me too, of course, but indications in my horary chart simply spoke against this.)

Let's look at the chart. Tomaž is shown by the Sun, ruling the Leo ascendant. It's in H4 in Scorpio, the sign of losses, crises and death. Its dispositor Mars in H1 is in a close conjunction with the ascendant, so it acts as his co-significator. Both bodies are in a mutual reception – indicative of the fact that he was not found in the place from where he called for help, but elsewhere (much lower). As we know, planets in a mutual reception often show some kind of exchange or replacement.

The likelihood of his recent death is quite clearly shown by the separating square of the Sun with Jupiter, the ruler of H8, as well as by the Sun in Scorpio in H4, the house of the endings and graves. Among other things, of course, but in this case, a grave certainly fits best, also because the Sun's dispositor Mars, a natural malefic, conjuncts the ascendant. Besides, all significators in fixed signs suggest an "immobility" of his body.

What about the applying sextile of the Moon to the Sun? Usually, this is a fortunate aspect, but not in this case, for several reasons. Firstly, both lights are below the horizon, suggesting a loss (of life); secondly, the Moon rules the unfortunate H12 (entrapment, exile, powerlessness); and thirdly, the lights don't receive each other, with the Sun even being in the Moon's fall. In such circumstances, a harmonious aspect can't bring the desired effect.

7/9

11 Nov 2009
22:05 CET −1:00
Ljubljana, Slovenia
46°N03' 014°E31'

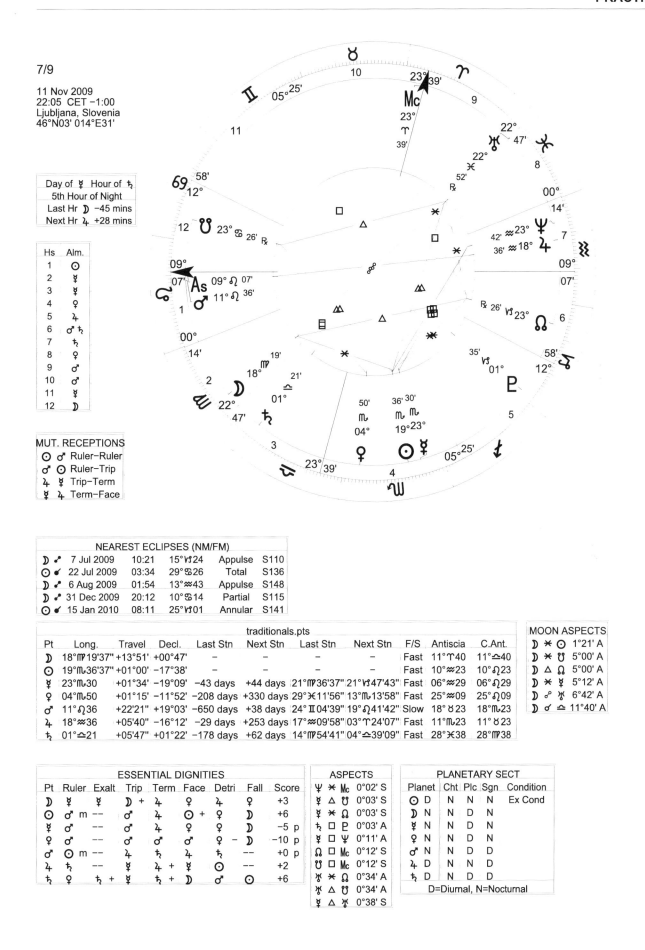

Day of ☿ Hour of ♄
5th Hour of Night
Last Hr ☽ −45 mins
Next Hr ♃ +28 mins

Hs	Alm.
1	☉
2	☿
3	☿
4	♀
5	♃
6	♂ ♄
7	♄
8	♀
9	♂
10	♂
11	☿
12	☽

MUT. RECEPTIONS	
☉ ♂	Ruler–Ruler
♂ ☉	Ruler–Trip
♃ ☿	Trip–Term
☿ ♃	Term–Face

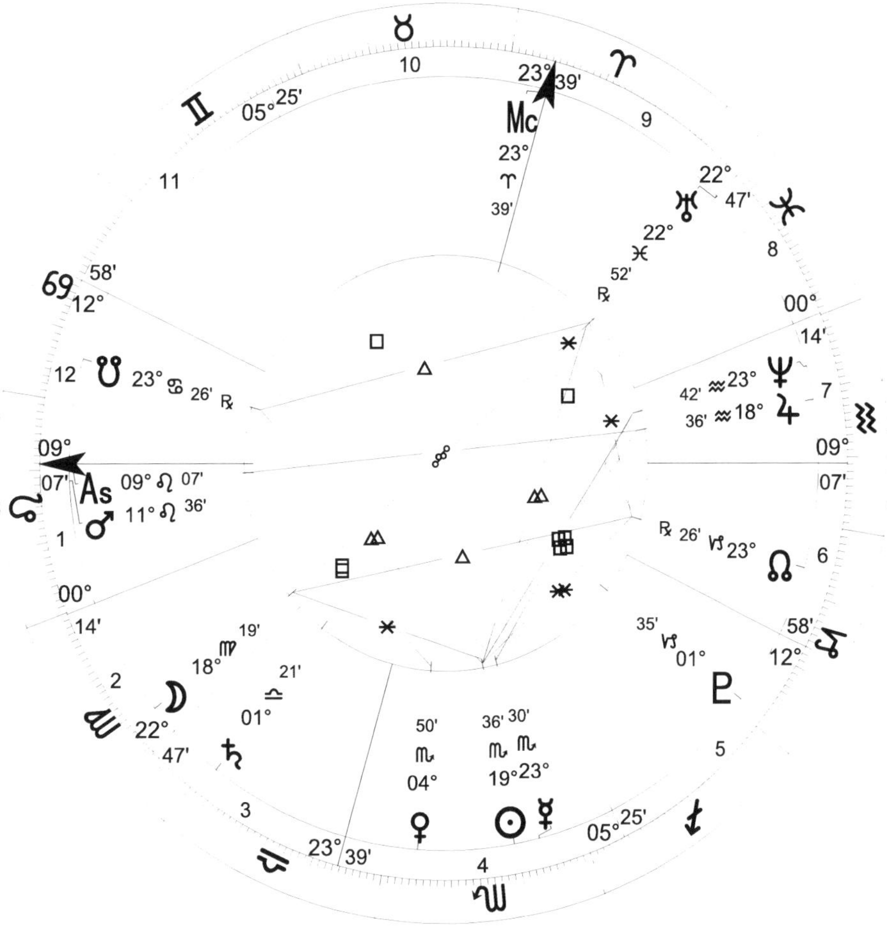

NEAREST ECLIPSES (NM/FM)					
☽	7 Jul 2009	10:21	15°♑24	Appulse	S110
☉	22 Jul 2009	03:34	29°♋26	Total	S136
☽	6 Aug 2009	01:54	13°♒43	Appulse	S148
☽	31 Dec 2009	20:12	10°♋14	Partial	S115
☉	15 Jan 2010	08:11	25°♑01	Annular	S141

traditionals.pts

Pt	Long.	Travel	Decl.	Last Stn	Next Stn	Last Stn	Next Stn	F/S	Antiscia	C.Ant.
☽	18°♍19'37"	+13°51'	+00°47'	–	–	–	–	Fast	11°♈40	11°♎40
☉	19°♏36'37"	+01°00'	−17°38'	–	–	–	–	Fast	10°♒23	10°♌23
☿	23°♏30	+01°34'	−19°09'	−43 days	+44 days	21°♍36'37"	21°♑47'43"	Fast	06°♒29	06°♌29
♀	04°♏50	+01°15'	−11°52'	−208 days	+330 days	29°♓11'56"	13°♏13'58"	Fast	25°♒09	25°♌09
♂	11°♌36	+22'21"	+19°03'	−650 days	+38 days	24°♊04'39"	19°♌41'42"	Slow	18°♉23	18°♏23
♃	18°♒36	+05'40"	−16°12'	−29 days	+253 days	17°♒09'58"	03°♈24'07"	Fast	11°♏23	11°♉23
♄	01°♎21	+05'47"	+01°22'	−178 days	+62 days	14°♍54'41"	04°♎39'09"	Fast	28°♓38	28°♍38

MOON ASPECTS	
☽ ✶ ☉	1°21' A
☽ ✶ ☋	5°00' A
☽ △ ☊	5°00' A
☽ ✶ ☿	5°12' A
☽ ☍ ♅	6°42' A
☽ ☌ ♎	11°40' A

ESSENTIAL DIGNITIES

Pt	Ruler	Exalt	Trip	Term	Face	Detri	Fall	Score
☽	☿	☿	☽ +	♃	♀	♃	♀	+3
☉	♂ m	--	♂	♃	☉ +	♀	☽	+6
☿	♂	--	♂	♃	♀	♀	☽	−5 p
♀	♂	--	♂	♂	♂	♀ −	☽	−10 p
♂	☉ m	--	♃	♄	♃	♄	--	+0 p
♃	♄	--	☿	♃ +	☿	☉	--	+2
♄	♀	♄ +	☿	♄ +	☽	♂	☉	+6

ASPECTS	
♆ ✶ Mc	0°02' S
☿ △ ☋	0°03' S
☿ ✶ ☊	0°03' S
♄ □ ♇	0°03' A
☿ □ ♆	0°11' A
☊ □ Mc	0°12' S
☋ □ Mc	0°12' S
♅ ✶ ☊	0°34' A
♅ △ ☋	0°34' A
☿ △ ♅	0°38' S

PLANETARY SECT

Planet	Cht	Plc	Sgn	Condition
☉ D	N	N	N	Ex Cond
☽ N	N	D	N	
☿ N	N	D	N	
♀ N	N	D	N	
♂ N	N	D	D	
♃ D	N	N	D	
♄ D	N	D	D	

D=Diurnal, N=Nocturnal

7/10: WHEN WILL GIGI RETURN?

26 January 2003 at 1:45 p.m. (13:45), Ljubljana, Slovenia
Hour ruler: Sun

My husband's cat disappeared. Gigi was our cat, in fact, because he moved into our house together with my husband who brought him along when he moved in. But because one of my daughters was allergic to cats, we couldn't keep Gigi in the house. He dwelled in the garden until it was warm, and at the time of his disappearance (in the beginning of January) my husband was just working on making a hole in the window so that Gigi could freely enter one of the rooms where he could spend cold winter nights. Obviously, though, Gigi couldn't wait and set off to find a warm place elsewhere. Because Mercury was retrograde when Gigi left, I said to my husband, don't worry, he'll come back.

But days went by and Gigi wasn't back. One Sunday we had lunch at my husband's parental house and when he started talking about Gigi, again I said, don't worry, he'll be back! If that is so, he replied, tell me, when? Okay, I said, I'll try. I wrote down the time of his question and when we were back home, I cast a horary chart.

Mercury, the querent's significator (ruler of Gemini, the ascending sign), is in H7 in Capricorn. Gigi is shown by the Moon in H6, the house of pets, and since the Moon also co-rules the querent, this placement nicely reflects my husband's interest. The main ruler of the missing pet is Mars, the ruler of Scorpio which is on cusp of H6, and Mars also occupies this house. The chart is very clear about the subject of the question!

Let us first see if the chart confirms my belief that Gigi will be back? Mars (Gigi) receives Mercury (my husband) in its exaltation, signaling the cat's affection for his master, but Mars is in the sign of Mercury's detriment, which in the context of the question shows that the cat is away from home, or separated from his owner. The planets are not in aspect but they are in a mixed reception by exaltation and face. This alone does not suffice for an affirmative answer, despite indicating a bond between the two. I found hope in the fact that Jupiter, the dispositor of Mars and H6 stellium, was retrograde (signifying return) and that it was located in H3 of the surrounding area. Considering the fact that both Mars and Jupiter were in Leo – a fire sign, I assumed that Gigi had found a refuge somewhere warm. That the cat is not far from the owner is confirmed by the fact that Mars is exactly sextiled by the Sun, H3 ruler, and that Mercury and Mars are in the neighbouring signs. The Sun in a harmonious aspect gives vitality to Mars, and because neither Mars nor the Moon aspect neither the ruler of the radix H8 (Saturn) nor the ruler of the derived H8 (Mercury), Gigi is obviously alive and well! He's should be somewhere in the neighbourhood, and because the first aspect of the Moon will be a conjunction with Mars (albeit in the next sign), there is a great deal of hope that Gigi would be back.

But the main question was: when? Let's see! From the Moon to Mars there are 14°35' which correspond to 14.5 days or 2 weeks. The Moon is in a fixed sign and the aspect will be completed in a cadent house and a mutable sign; all of this, strictly speaking, should mean a much longer time unit, but let us use logic! It would be pretty unusual for the cat to return in 14 months or even years, right?! Even 14 weeks seemed odd. But 2 units of time are confirmed by the distance of the ascendant (28° Gemini) to the next sign, Cancer; 2 degrees, translated into the most logical time unit, arrived at by the other timing indication, would again mean 2 weeks.

Fourteen days (2 weeks) after the question was 9 February 2003. In order to confirm the timing indication, I checked transits on that date, to see if they coincided with the indications in the horary chart. (I really wanted to be sure, as I didn't want to disappoint my husband!) A look into the ephemeris showed that Mars would trine Jupiter, its dispositor, a day or two earlier - actually in the night from 7 to 8 February. But on 8 February another important aspect would complete: the Sun sextile to Pluto. This in itself is an aspect of regeneration, but since Pluto is also the modern ruler of Scorpio – the sign on cusp of H6, I had to include this aspect into my "arsenal" of factors in the search for the most probable time of Gigi's return.

Gigi will be back in two weeks, around 8 February, maybe on that day, but might be a day earlier or a day later, I said to my husband.

On 8 February my daughter and I strolled down our street past the elementary school (some 500 meters from our home), when she suddenly exclaimed: *Look, Gigi!* Then it struck me, today is 8 February! Where is he, I quickly asked. There he was, I saw him by the school wall, she said. And how do you know it was him, I asked? Well, I saw his broken tail, and he was gray like our Gigi, she said. Of course, I remembered, Gigi had a broken tail, his

7/10

26 Jan 2003
13:45 CET −1:00
Ljubljana, Slovenia
46°N03' 014°E31'

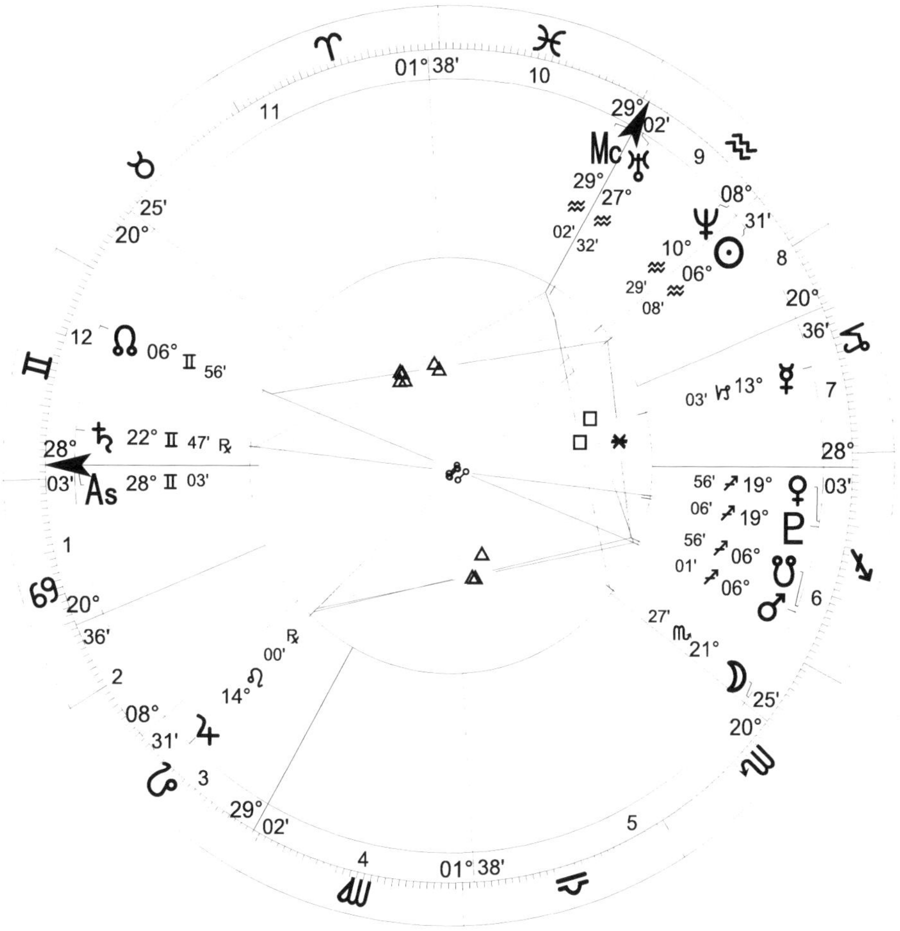

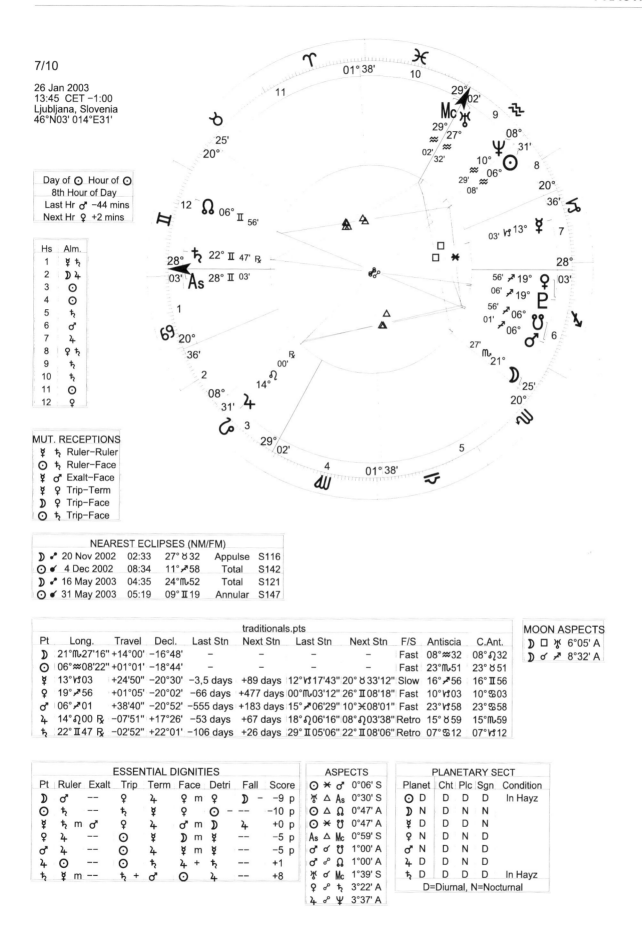

Day of ☉ Hour of ☉
8th Hour of Day
Last Hr ♂ −44 mins
Next Hr ♀ +2 mins

Hs	Alm.
1	☿ ♄
2	☽ ♃
3	☉
4	☉
5	♄
6	♂
7	♃
8	♀ ♄
9	♄
10	♄
11	☉
12	♀

MUT. RECEPTIONS	
☿ ♄	Ruler−Ruler
☉ ♄	Ruler−Face
☿ ♂	Exalt−Face
☿ ♀	Trip−Term
☽ ♀	Trip−Face
☉ ♄	Trip−Face

NEAREST ECLIPSES (NM/FM)					
☽ ☍	20 Nov 2002	02:33	27°♉32	Appulse	S116
☉ ☌	4 Dec 2002	08:34	11°♐58	Total	S142
☽ ☍	16 May 2003	04:35	24°♏52	Total	S121
☉ ☌	31 May 2003	05:19	09°♊19	Annular	S147

traditionals.pts

Pt	Long.	Travel	Decl.	Last Stn	Next Stn	Last Stn	Next Stn	F/S	Antiscia	C.Ant.
☽	21°♏27'16"	+14°00'	−16°48'	–	–	–	–	Fast	08°♒32	08°♌32
☉	06°♒08'22"	+01°01'	−18°44'	–	–	–	–	Fast	23°♏51	23°♉51
☿	13°♑03	+24'50"	−20°30'	−3,5 days	+89 days	12°♑17'43"	20°♉33'12"	Slow	16°♐56	16°♊56
♀	19°♐56	+01°05'	−20°02'	−66 days	+477 days	00°♏03'12"	26°♊08'18"	Fast	10°♑03	10°♋03
♂	06°♐01	+38'40"	−20°52'	−555 days	+183 days	15°♐06'29"	10°♓08'01"	Fast	23°♑58	23°♋58
♃	14°♌00 ℞	−07'51"	+17°26'	−53 days	+67 days	18°♌06'16"	08°♌03'38"	Retro	15°♉59	15°♏59
♄	22°♊47 ℞	−02'52"	+22°01'	−106 days	+26 days	29°♊05'06"	22°♊08'06"	Retro	07°♋12	07°♑12

MOON ASPECTS
☽ □ ♅ 6°05' A
☽ ☌ ♐ 8°32' A

ESSENTIAL DIGNITIES

Pt	Ruler	Exalt	Trip	Term	Face	Detri	Fall	Score
☽	♂	--	♀	♃	♀ m	♀	☽ –	−9 p
☉	♄	--	♄	☿	♀	☉ –	--	−10 p
☿	♄ m	♂	♀	♃	♂ m	☽	♃	+0 p
♀	♃	--	☉	☿	☽ m	☿	--	−5 p
♂	♃	--	☉	♃	☿ m	☿	--	−5 p
♃	☉	--	☉	♄	♃ +	♄	--	+1
♄	☿ m	--	♄ +	♂	☉	♃	--	+8

ASPECTS	
☉ ⚹ ♂	0°06' S
♅ △ As	0°30' S
☉ △ ☊	0°47' A
☉ ⚹ ☋	0°47' A
As △ Mc	0°59' S
♂ ☌ ☋	1°00' A
♂ ☍ ☊	1°00' A
♅ ☌ Mc	1°39' S
♀ ☍ ♄	3°22' A
♃ ☍ ♆	3°37' A

PLANETARY SECT

Planet		Cht	Plc	Sgn	Condition
☉	D	D	D	D	In Hayz
☽	N	D	D	N	
☿	D	D	D	N	
♀	N	D	N	D	
♂	N	D	N	D	
♃	D	D	N	D	
♄	D	D	D	D	In Hayz

D=Diurnal, N=Nocturnal

characteristic by which it was possible to identify him even from a distance. We tried to locate him again, but he disappeared and we couldn't pass behind the school fence to come closer, so we phoned my husband who arrived in a couple of minutes, went behind the fence and made that whistle by which he always called Gigi. Soon he came back with Gigi in his arms. We took him home, gave him food and cuddled him, but his heart was obviously elsewhere because after a day or two of hanging around the house he disappeared again, this time forever, and we never saw him again.

7/11: WILL THE MISSING KITTEN BE BACK?

25 October 2006 at 9:10 p.m. (21:10), Ptuj, Slovenia
Hour ruler: Mercury

During an online chat which was part of my horary course, I was just explaining the use of significators to my students when one of them said, on the spur of the moment, that she had been missing her kitten for several days and that she was worried, wondering if she'd come back? Could we do the chart for this question and learn from it, she asked?

Of course, I said, let us write down the time and place of her question, and let everybody cast the chart.

The querent is ruled by the Moon, the ascendant ruler. This "light of the time" (it's a night chart) is quite fittingly placed in H6 of pets, reflecting her interest or concern which currently bothers her. The Moon, of course, also plays the role of a co-significator of the cat. Notice that it is below the horizon in a night chart, and that it's out-of-bounds – suggesting the kitten to be beyond the territory she usually occupies.

Which planet is the main significator of the cat? The cusp of H6 is at the penultimate degree of Scorpio, but we have an intercepted sign of Sagittarius in H6 which the Moon occupies, so it seemed more appropriate that the cat be ruled by Jupiter, co-ruling H6 and dispositing the Moon, than Mars. But Mars should be taken into account as well, of course, especially because it's the natural significator of animals.

So what's the condition of Jupiter? It is in Scorpio, essentially undignified (except for a weak term) and in a totally exact square with Saturn. Saturn rules radix H8 of death while the Moon rules the derived H8. Its last aspect, showing recent past, was a stressful square with an angular Uranus (sudden shock, an unpleasant surprise) while her first next aspect will be (except for a sextile with Neptune which plays a less important role here because it's not angular) a square with the aforementioned Saturn.

Looking at Mars, we can see that it's also in Scorpio, and combust, showing the kitten to be out of sight, weakened and (probably) unable to act. Venus, ruling the derived H12 of imprisonment, had recently separated from it. The answer is therefore obvious: the missing cat is apparently already dead, it will not be back.

As sad as the answer was, it was also accurate: the cat was never seen again.

7/11

25 Oct 2006
21:10 CEDT −2:00
Ptuj, Slovenia
46°N25' 015°E52'

Day of ☿ Hour of ☿
3rd Hour of Night
Last Hr ♀ −65 mins
Next Hr ☽ +4 mins

Hs	Alm.
1	☽
2	☽ ♃
3	☉
4	☿
5	☿ ♀
6	♂
7	♄
8	♄
9	♄
10	♀
11	☉♂
12	☽

MUT. RECEPTIONS
☿ ♄ Term−Term

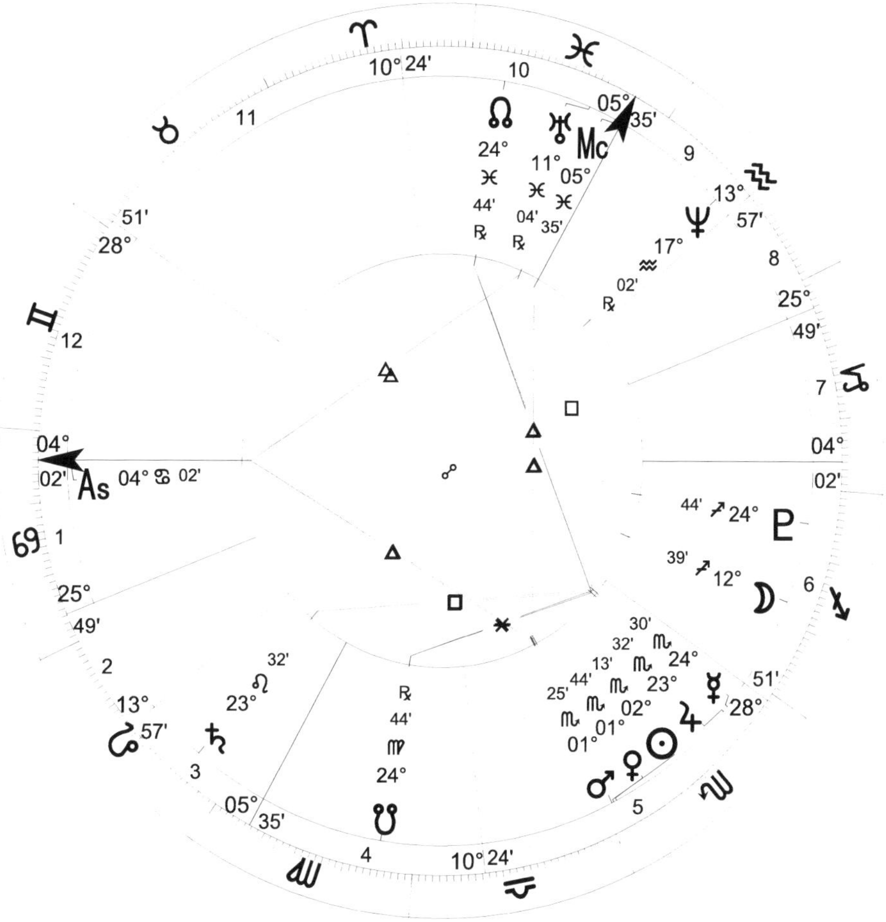

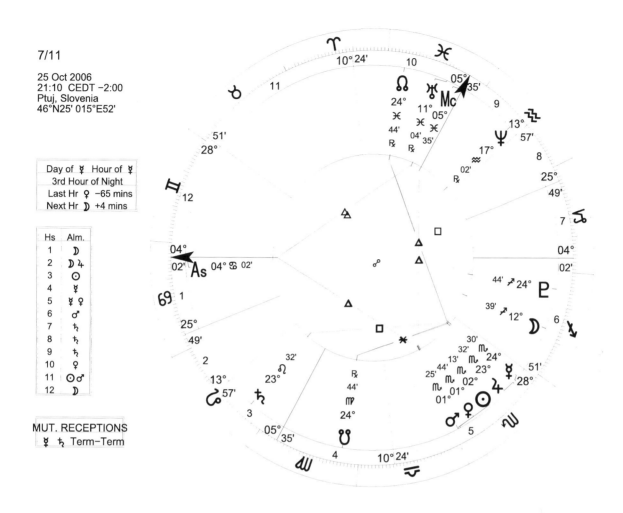

NEAREST ECLIPSES (NM/FM)					
☽ ☍	7 Sep 2006	20:42	15°♓00	Partial	S118
☉ ☌	22 Sep 2006	13:45	29°♍20	Annular	S144
☽ ☍	4 Mar 2007	01:17	12°♍59	Total	S123
☉ ☌	19 Mar 2007	04:42	28°♓07	Partial	S149

traditionals.pts

Pt	Long.	Travel	Decl.	Last Stn	Next Stn	Last Stn	Next Stn	F/S	Antiscia	C.Ant.
☽	12°♐39'27"	+12°36'	−27°19'	–	–	–	–	Slow	17°♑20	17°♋20
☉	02°♏13'51"	+59'49"	−12°14'	–	–	–	–	Fast	27°♒46	27°♌46
☿	24°♏30	+21'52"	−21°51'	−88 days	+3,0 days	21°♋03'46"	25°♏04'40"	Slow	05°♒29	05°♌29
♀	01°♏44	+01°15'	−11°06'	−264 days	+274 days	16°♑01'18"	02°♍57'23"	Fast	28°♒15	28°♌15
♂	01°♏25	+40'32"	−11°37'	−319 days	+385 days	08°♉14'08"	12°♋27'03"	Fast	28°♒34	28°♌34
♃	23°♏32	+12'48"	−17°55'	−111 days	+162 days	08°♏58'42"	19°♐46'43"	Fast	06°♒27	06°♌27
♄	23°♌32	+04'16"	+14°35'	−203 days	+41 days	04°♌22'31"	25°♌04'15"	Fast	06°♉27	06°♏27

MOON ASPECTS
☽ ☌ ♐ 12°39' S
☽ □ ♅ 1°38' S
☽ ⚹ ♆ 4°27' A

ESSENTIAL DIGNITIES

Pt	Ruler	Exalt	Trip	Term	Face	Detri	Fall	Score
☽	♃	--	♃	♀	☽ +	☿	--	+1
☉	♂	--	♂	♂	♂	♀	☽	−5 p
☿	♂	--	♂	♄ m	♀	♀	☽	−5 p
♀	♂	--	♂	♂	♂	♀ −	☽	−10 p
♂	♂ +	--	♂ +	♂ +	♂ +	♀	☽	+11
♃	♂	--	♂	♃ +	♀	♀	☽	+2
♄	☉	--	♃	☿ m	♂	♄ −	--	−10 p

ASPECTS
♃ □ ♄ 0°00' S
♇ □ ☊ 0°00' S
♇ □ ☋ 0°00' S
☿ △ ☊ 0°11' A
☿ ⚹ ☋ 0°11' A
♀ ☌ ♂ 0°43' S
♄ △ ♇ 0°48' A
☉ ☌ ♂ 0°53' S
☿ □ ♄ 1°01' S
☉ ☌ ♀ 1°08' A

PLANETARY SECT

Planet		Cht	Plc	Sgn	Condition
☉	D	N	N	N	Ex Cond
☽	N	N	D	D	
☿	N	N	D	N	
♀	N	N	D	N	
♂	N	N	D	N	
♃	D	N	D	N	
♄	D	N	D	D	

D=Diurnal, N=Nocturnal

7/12: WILL OUR KITTEN BE BACK?

8 April 2008 at 9:50 a.m., Bled, Slovenia
Hour ruler: Mercury

My friend, an astrology student, sent me an email with the data for a horary chart she made for the above question which she asked herself after their cat had been missing for a few days. Her daughter was very attached to it and very worried. She asked me if I can help delineate her chart as she didn't feel up to it.

She is shown by Mercury, ruler of Gemini, the ascending sign, while the kitten is ruled by Mars, the H6 ruler. Mars is in H1 in Cancer. Its condition? It is peregrine and even in its fall, but because it is in a strong house (H1 but bordering on H2), this gives some hope. Mercury, the querent's ruler, applies to it by a square. This is a tense and stressful aspect, but it does connect the querent to the kitten, so that the question does have a sort of a "future" – that's the least that can be said. But it's worrying that Mercury rules the derived H8, and that Mars is placed in the derived H8 (H1 being 8/6). You will notice that Mars is also out-of-bounds, another negative indication.

The Moon, co-significator of the cat, is in an unfortunate H12, indicating helplessness, entrapment and disorientation. But because the Moon was in Taurus, exalted and in a close applying trine with Jupiter, I felt that the matter could still have a happy ending and that the cat could be found. Since there are close to 2 degrees between Moon and Jupiter, I thought that this would happen in two days.

Encouraged by what I told her, my friend set off to inquire about the kitten with their neighbours. Two days later she learnt from one of them that the poor kitten was found trampled on the road, and because it didn't show any signs of life, he called the municipal service to take it away.

Poor kitten! I was a bit ashamed too because I didn't see that it was dead. In my eagerness to help I turned a blind eye to all the H8 indications, hoping that the cat was only trapped somewhere, and not dead. I depended on the Moon's trine to the fortunate Jupiter, but the Moon (in the unfortunate H12) was applying to Jupiter which is in the H8 of death!

But as the timing showed, the outcome was indeed known two days later, and the querent was at least happy to know what had happened to the kitten, so that the family could stop searching.

This example illustrates how very important it is to take into account the nature of the houses occupied by significators! Even a harmonious aspect with a fortunate planet can show a negative answer, if planets rule (or occupy) unfortunate houses - or rather such a form of "completion of the matter" as bringing sadness to the querent.

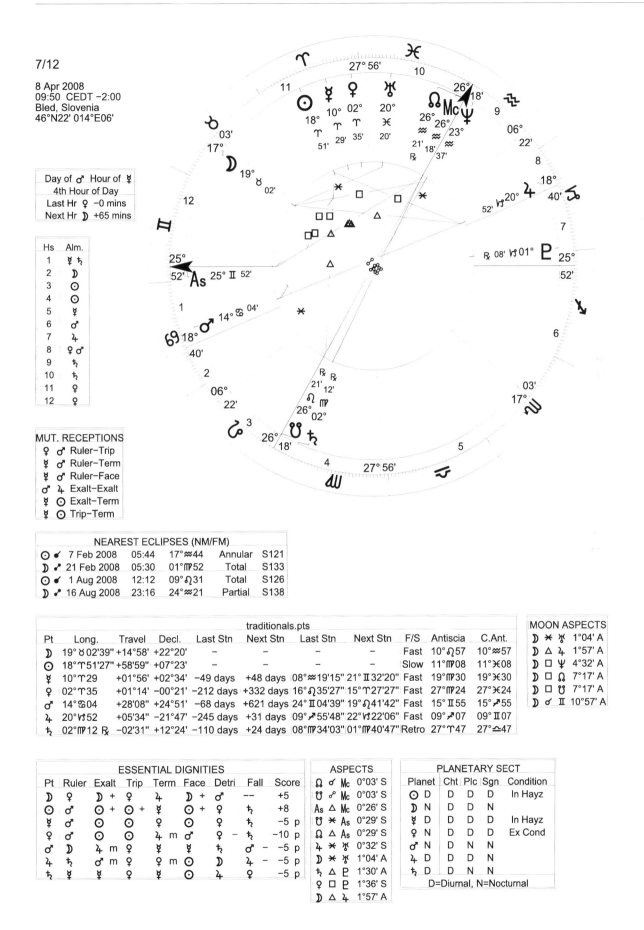

7/12

8 Apr 2008
09:50 CEDT −2:00
Bled, Slovenia
46°N22' 014°E06'

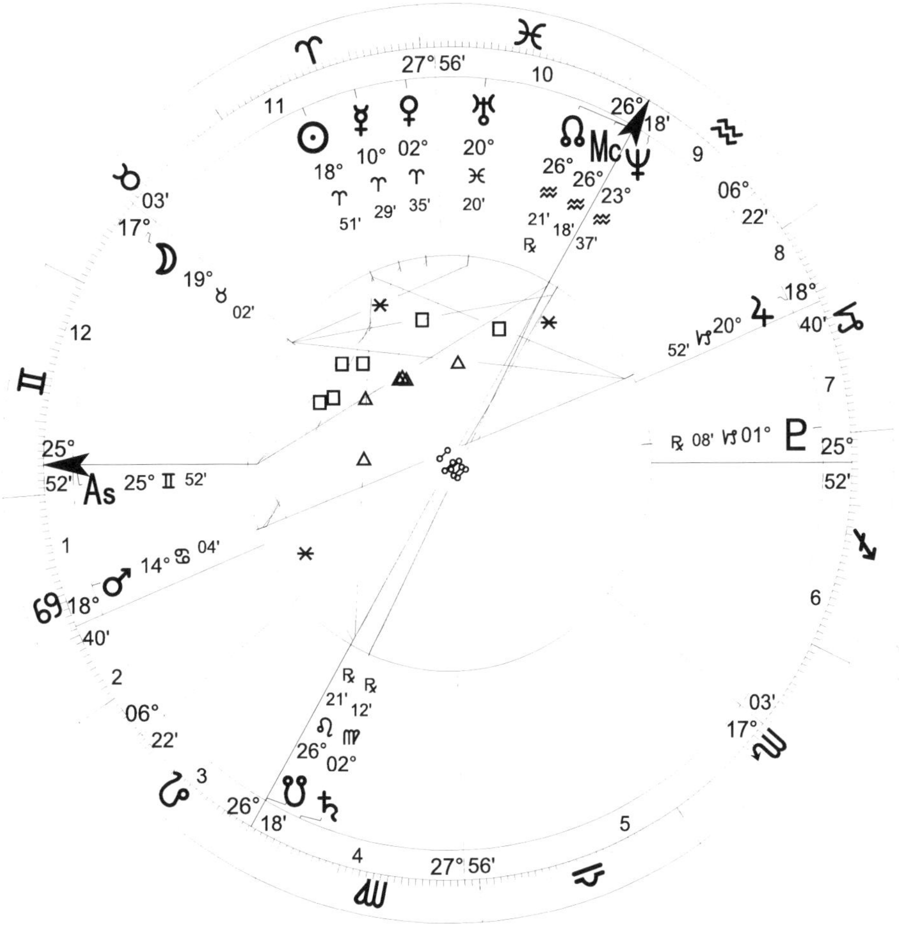

Day of ♂ Hour of ☿
4th Hour of Day
Last Hr ♀ −0 mins
Next Hr ☽ +65 mins

Hs	Alm.
1	☿ ♄
2	☽
3	☉
4	☉
5	☿
6	♂
7	♃
8	♀ ♂
9	♄
10	♄
11	♀
12	♀

MUT. RECEPTIONS		
♀	♂	Ruler−Trip
☿	♂	Ruler−Term
☿	♂	Ruler−Face
♂	♃	Exalt−Exalt
☿	☉	Exalt−Term
☿	☉	Trip−Term

NEAREST ECLIPSES (NM/FM)					
☉ ●	7 Feb 2008	05:44	17°♒44	Annular	S121
☽ ●	21 Feb 2008	05:30	01°♍52	Total	S133
☉ ●	1 Aug 2008	12:12	09°♌31	Total	S126
☽ ●	16 Aug 2008	23:16	24°♒21	Partial	S138

traditionals.pts

Pt	Long.	Travel	Decl.	Last Stn	Next Stn	Last Stn	Next Stn	F/S	Antiscia	C.Ant.
☽	19°♉02'39"	+14°58'	+22°20'	–	–	–	–	Fast	10°♌57	10°♒57
☉	18°♈51'27"	+58'59"	+07°23'	–	–	–	–	Slow	11°♍08	11°♓08
☿	10°♈29	+01°56'	+02°34'	−49 days	+48 days	08°♒19'15"	21°♊32'20"	Fast	19°♍30	19°♓30
♀	02°♈35	+01°14'	−00°21'	−212 days	+332 days	16°♌35'27"	15°♈27'27"	Fast	27°♍24	27°♓24
♂	14°♋04	+28'08"	+24°51'	−68 days	+621 days	24°♊04'39"	19°♌41'42"	Fast	15°♊55	15°♐55
♃	20°♑52	+05'34"	−21°47'	−245 days	+31 days	09°♐55'48"	22°♑22'06"	Fast	09°♐07	09°♊07
♄	02°♍12 ℞	−02'31"	+12°24'	−110 days	+24 days	08°♍34'03"	01°♍40'47"	Retro	27°♈47	27°♎47

MOON ASPECTS			
☽	⚹	♅	1°04' A
☽	△	♃	1°57' A
☽	□	♆	4°32' A
☽	□	☊	7°17' A
☽	□	☋	7°17' A
☽	☌	♊	10°57' A

ESSENTIAL DIGNITIES

Pt	Ruler	Exalt	Trip	Term	Face	Detri	Fall	Score
☽	♀	☽ +	♀	♃	☽ +	♂	--	+5
☉	♂	☉ +	☉ +	☿	☉ +	♀	♄	+8
☿	♂	☉	☉	♀	☉	♀	♄	−5 p
♀	♂	☉	☉	♃ m	♂	♀ −	♄	−10 p
♂	☽	♃ m	♀	☿	☿	♄	♂ −	−5 p
♃	♄	♂ m	♀	♀ m	☉	☽	♃ −	−5 p
♄	☿	☿	♀	☿	☉	♃	♀	−5 p

ASPECTS			
☊	☌	Mc	0°03' S
☋	☍	Mc	0°03' S
As	△	Mc	0°26' S
☋	⚹	As	0°29' S
☊	△	As	0°29' S
♃	⚹	♅	0°32' S
☽	⚹	♅	1°04' A
♄	△	♇	1°30' A
♀	□	♇	1°36' S
☽	△	♃	1°57' A

PLANETARY SECT

Planet		Cht	Plc	Sgn	Condition
☉	D	D	D	D	In Hayz
☽	N	D	D	N	
☿	D	D	D	D	In Hayz
♀	N	D	D	D	Ex Cond
♂	N	D	N	N	
♃	D	D	D	N	
♄	D	D	N	N	

D=Diurnal, N=Nocturnal

7/13: WHERE IS MY DOG? WILL WE FIND HIM?

8 January 2008 at 5:24 p.m. (17:24) in Ljubljana, Slovenia
Hour ruler: Saturn

One of my former students asked me for help with her own horary chart which she cast for a missing dog. On 1 January he strayed from her home and went into an unknown direction. She gave me the data of her own chart so that I could calculate it.

Ascendant is at the last degrees of a sign which could indicate that it is too late for help. It is ruled by the Moon which is (again!) located in H6 of house pets. (You will notice that the Moon is in H6 in three out of four of our missing pets' cases!) The main significator of the dog is Saturn, placed in Virgo where it retrogrades from the cusp of H3 back into H2. A retrograde significator promises a return, or at least the finding of that which is missing. Additional significators of the dog are the H6 planets: Jupiter, the Moon and the Sun. Jupiter is closest to the cusp of the house, showing the dog as big, beautiful and "valuable" – as it indeed was, and the querent really loved him. But Jupiter is in its fall, the Sun is peregrine and the Moon is in detriment, combust and out-of-bounds, while also ruling the derived H8 (radix H1, 8/6) which in the context of the question could obviously mean that the dog was dead. Besides, the planet last separated from Saturn is Venus, ruling the radix H4 (of grave) and being placed in the derived H12 of loss and entrapment. That should be a clear enough indication that the querent will not find her dog alive, but unfortunately I made a technical mistake while calculating the chart, and therefore made a wrong judgment.

What happened? In my computer settings, I had Placidean houses (which I use for natal astrology) which I forgot to switch to Regiomontanus, so "my" chart had the cusp of H6 in Sagittarius instead of in Capricorn. (There's another similar case among the examples in this book - a reminder that we need to be very careful with the settings!) The ruler of Sagittarius is Jupiter which is placed in H6 and acts as a co-ruler of the dog, but not as the main ruler! Jupiter looks quite safe because even if it's in its fall, it's not afflicted by bad aspects, therefore I considered the dog alive. But I did stress that as the Moon was void-of-course and out-of-bounds, the dog was obviously lost and couldn't find its way back home. The Moon is already in an orb of aspect (conjunction) with Mercury, but this planet is in the next sign and as the H3 ruler indicates the surrounding area, so even this aspect can't help bring the strayed dog back home.

It turned out that the chart which I later created by using Regiomontanus houses, was totally "right" in that it described the whole situation much more accurately than the previous one. On 15 March, an acquaintance from the village approached the querent and told her that she saw a dead dog by the railway tracks some 2 kilometres down the road. The querent later identified the dog as hers.

It is interesting to note that Saturn in this chart is in a mutual reception with Mercury which rules H3 of traffic and transport, and that Saturn itself is in conjunction with the cusp of this house - even though, as already mentioned, it separates from it. But because the dog was apparently hit by a train, the symbolism of H3 (traffic) is completely appropriate. In the light of retrogradation (coming back, returning) of the main significator it is also fitting that the dog was eventually found – although dead (ruler of the radix H8).

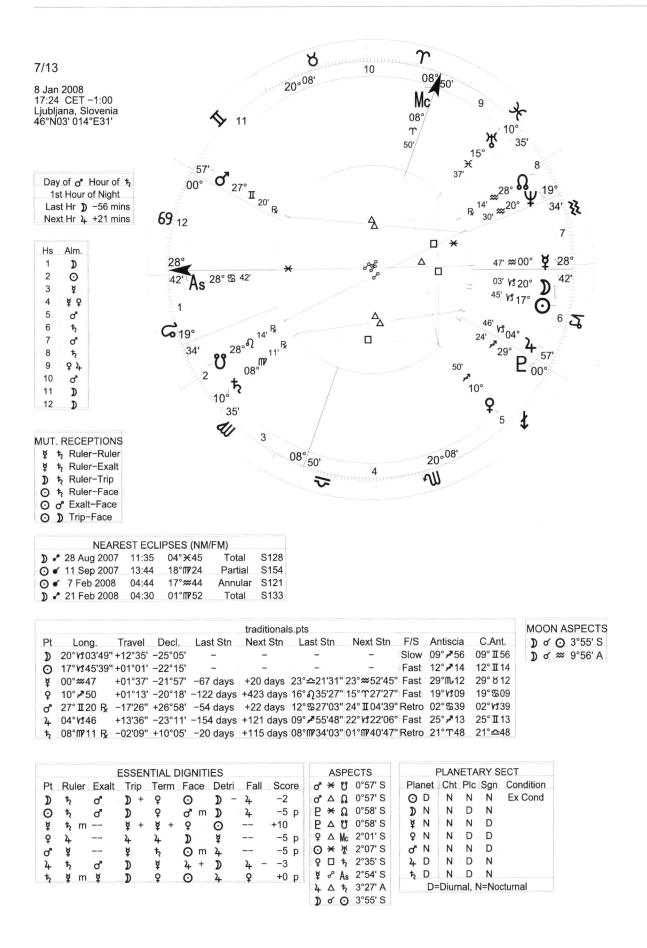

7/13

8 Jan 2008
17:24 CET −1:00
Ljubljana, Slovenia
46°N03' 014°E31'

Day of ♂ Hour of ♄
1st Hour of Night
Last Hr ☽ −56 mins
Next Hr ♃ +21 mins

Hs	Alm.
1	☽
2	☉
3	☿
4	☿ ♀
5	♂
6	♄
7	♂
8	♄
9	♀ ♃
10	♂
11	☽
12	☽

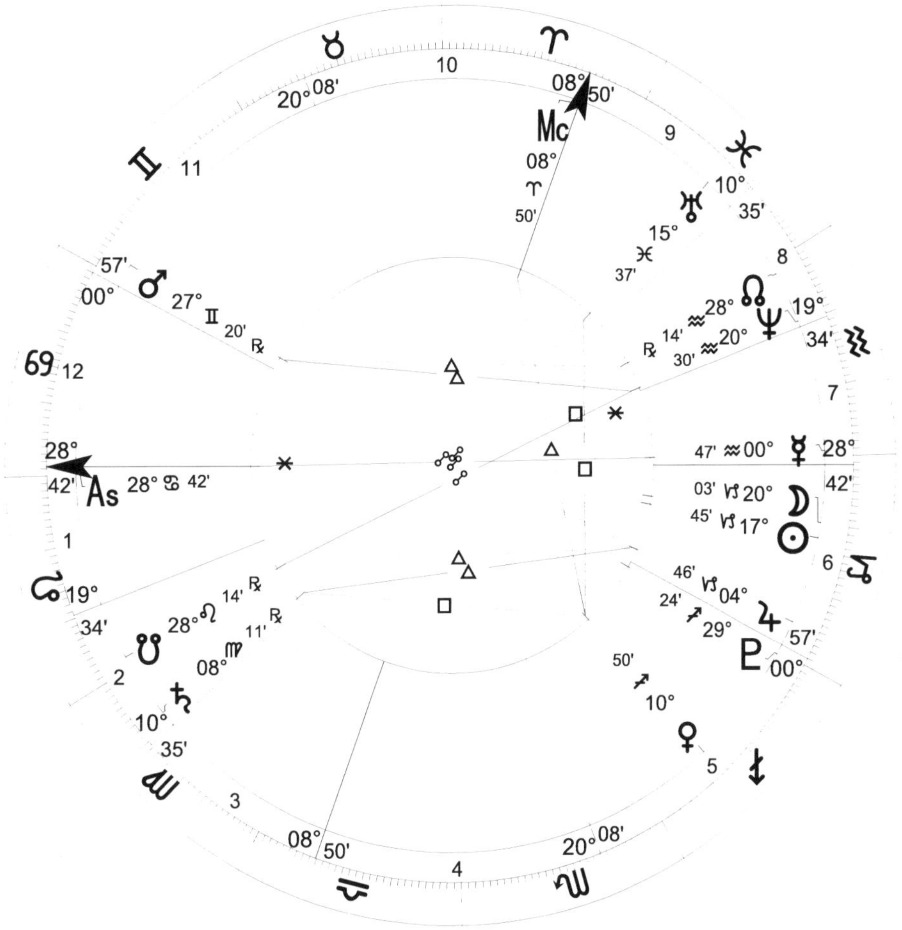

MUT. RECEPTIONS		
☿	♄	Ruler–Ruler
☿	♄	Ruler–Exalt
☽	♄	Ruler–Trip
☉	♄	Ruler–Face
☉	♂	Exalt–Face
☉	☽	Trip–Face

NEAREST ECLIPSES (NM/FM)					
☽ ☍	28 Aug 2007	11:35	04°♓45	Total	S128
☉ ☌	11 Sep 2007	13:44	18°♍24	Partial	S154
☉ ☌	7 Feb 2008	04:44	17°♒44	Annular	S121
☽ ☍	21 Feb 2008	04:30	01°♍52	Total	S133

traditionals.pts

Pt	Long.	Travel	Decl.	Last Stn	Next Stn	Last Stn	Next Stn	F/S	Antiscia	C.Ant.
☽	20°♑03'49"	+12°35'	−25°05'	–	–	–	–	Slow	09°♐56	09°♊56
☉	17°♑45'39"	+01°01'	−22°15'	–	–	–	–	Fast	12°♐14	12°♊14
☿	00°♒47	+01°37'	−21°57'	−67 days	+20 days	23°♎21'31"	23°♒52'45"	Fast	29°♏12	29°♉12
♀	10°♐50	+01°13'	−20°18'	−122 days	+423 days	16°♌35'27"	15°♈27'27"	Fast	19°♑09	19°♋09
♂	27°♊20 ℞	−17'26"	+26°58'	−54 days	+22 days	12°♋27'03"	24°♊04'39"	Retro	02°♋39	02°♑39
♃	04°♑46	+13'36"	−23°11'	−154 days	+121 days	09°♐55'48"	22°♑22'06"	Fast	25°♐13	25°♊13
♄	08°♍11 ℞	−02'09"	+10°05'	−20 days	+115 days	08°♍34'03"	01°♍40'47"	Retro	21°♈48	21°♎48

MOON ASPECTS	
☽ ☌ ☉	3°55' S
☽ ☌ ♒	9°56' A

ESSENTIAL DIGNITIES

Pt	Ruler	Exalt	Trip	Term	Face	Detri	Fall	Score
☽	♄	♂	☽ +	♀	☉	☽ −	♃	−2
☉	♄	♂	☽	♀	♂ m	☽	♃	−5 p
☿	♄ m	--	☿ +	☿ +	♀	☉	--	+10
♀	♃	--	♃	♃	☽	☿	--	−5 p
♂	☿	--	☿	♄	☉ m	♃	--	−5 p
♃	♄	♂	☽	☿	♃ +	☽	♃ −	−3
♄	☿ m	☿	☽	♀	☉	♃	♀	+0 p

ASPECTS	
♂ ⚹ ☋	0°57' S
♂ △ ☊	0°57' S
♇ ⚹ ☊	0°58' S
♇ △ ☋	0°58' S
♀ △ Mc	2°01' S
☉ ⚹ ♅	2°07' S
♀ □ ♄	2°35' S
☿ ☍ As	2°54' S
♃ △ ♄	3°27' A
☽ ☌ ☉	3°55' S

PLANETARY SECT

Planet	Cht	Plc	Sgn	Condition
☉ D	N	N	N	Ex Cond
☽ N	N	D	N	
☿ N	N	N	D	
♀ N	N	D	D	
♂ N	N	N	D	
♃ D	N	D	N	
♄ D	N	D	N	
D=Diurnal, N=Nocturnal				

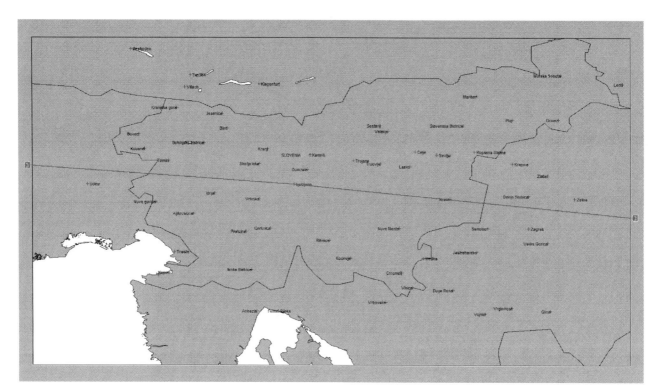

Case 7/1: Moon's local space line

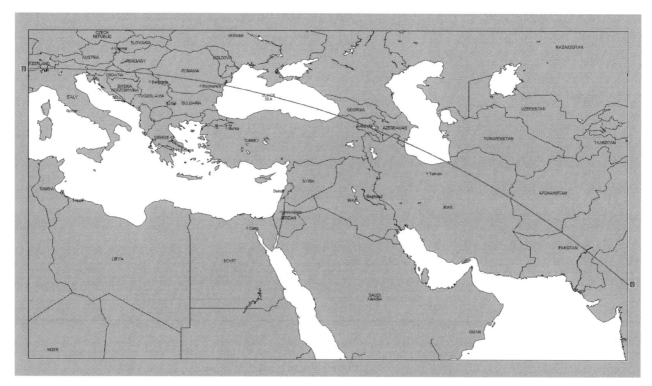

Case 7/4: Venus' local space line

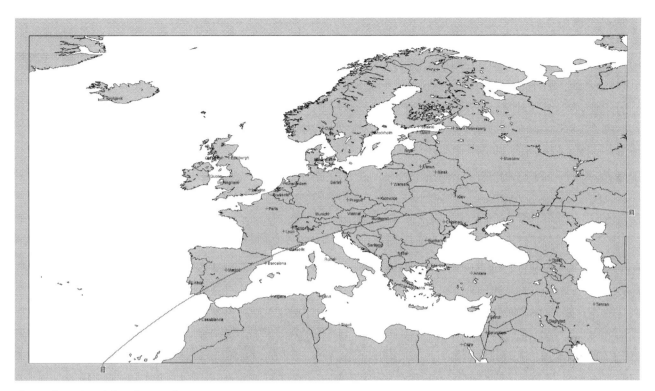

Case 7/8: Moon's local space line

PHYSICAL WELL-BEING

Disease-related questions are among the most sensitive, and also among the most difficult. Horary astrology can help us find out a lot about ailments which concern our clients. They often say to me that their doctors cannot figure out why they feel bad, or that they even tell them that nothing is wrong with them, although they feel sick. Then they turn to me to find out what causes their indisposition.

What is wrong with me? Am I really ill? When will I feel better? Is my husband's health good or should he consult a doctor? What causes my kid's headaches? Horary astrology helps us determine the cause of the disease, its origin and its consequences, sometimes even the appropriate treatment. Alternatively (if the chart shows no disease), we can calm the client and tell them that everything is fine and that they will soon be better. It's wonderful if we can soothe a frightened person, but it's very difficult to see someone's health deteriorating and not being able to help. If the chart clearly shows that someone's condition is getting worse and we astrologers know that there is no hope, it pays to be discreet and not say the dire truth.

There is also the fact that when people ask about their (or their beloved's) health, they are usually worried and in fear. When asking our own questions, we must pay particular attention to the possibility of our emotions blurring our mind.

In his Christian Astrology, the famous English Renaissance astrologer William Lilly has devoted more than 50 pages to health questions, but in the recent centuries, medicine has progressed so much that without a thorough knowledge of current medical practice, some of his rules and instructions have become obsolete. On the other hand, much of the practice of old astrologers is interesting and useful. In addition to Lilly's book, I especially recommend the book ASTROLOGICAL JUDGMENT OF DISEASES by Nicholas Culpeper, the famous English physician and astrologer from the 17th century.

But because much astrological literature relating to medical horary dates from the Middle Ages and the Renaissance, we should realise that back then, diagnostic astrological charts were often cast for the time when the patient brought his urine to the doctor, or for the time when he took to bed. The last ones are called decumbiture charts. Horary questions, as we know them today, were in a minority, but, fortunately, the rules of interpretation are practically the same.

The development of modern astromedicine (the branch of astrology examining the connection between astrology, health and treatment) goes much in the direction of connecting signs, planets and aspects with vitamins, minerals and other elements necessary for physical and mental health. Incorporating this kind of knowledge into horary astrology is certainly a challenge for every modern astrologer who is interested in both medicine and astrological tradition.

SIGNIFICATORS IN HEALTH QUESTIONS

- H1: the querent and his vitality, health
- H6: the disease or malfunction;
- H7: the doctor
- H8: surgery, death
- H10: the medicine
- H12: hospitals and other health facilities; chronic diseases

I emphasize that in all traditional and horary astrology **H6 does not show health** (as we can read in modern astrological textbooks) but **disease**, that is, its nature and all that is related to it. **H1**, on the contrary, is the place of **life, vitality and health**, as it represents the physical body of the querent. Despite the need to differentiate between the significance of both houses, H1 can help us determine the nature of the disease, because if the ruler (or almuten or any planet in H1 close to ASC) is afflicted, this planet (or the afflicting planet) points to the endangered part of the body or the deteriorating body function.

Regarding the severity of the disease, the **power ratio between H1 and H6** should be examined: if H1 is stronger than H6, the patient is vital enough to overcome the disease; otherwise, the disease is severe and can only be healed by long-term treatment, or even not at all. We should be aware, though, that shis is not the only criterion in determining the severity of the disease or the degree of the patient's vitality. Other factors must be considered.

But hold on, things are not easy. When calculating planetary dignities (strengths and weaknesses), we must to be careful, because **an essentially and accidentally weak significator of the disease does not show a weak** (feeble, non-dangerous) **illness** - on the contrary! Such a disease can be menacing and life-threatening, therefore we should be very careful in the examination of the significators of the patient and his disease.

In order to determine the **nature of the disease**, the following are to be considered:
- H1 and planets in it;
- H6 and planets in it;
- the sign and the house of the Moon (the development of the condition);
- the planet/s afflicting the Moon and the ascendant (see their houses, signs and house rulerships)

ZODIACAL SIGNS AND DISEASES

In Lilly's times (17th century) physicians considered that any disease was caused by an imbalance between the four body humours: blood, phlegm, yellow bile and black bile. They were also at the base of the four classical temperaments: sanguine, phlegmatic, choleric and melancholic.

Air signs (Gemini, Libra, Aquarius) are **sanguine**. They are warm and moist and related to blood.

Water signs (Cancer, Scorpio, Pisces) are **phlegmatic**. They are cold and moist, associated with the mucous membrane (phlegm) lining by the respiratory tract and stomach.

Fire signs (Aries, Leo, Sagittarius) are **choleric**. They are hot and dry, associated with the yellow bile and liver.

Earth signs (Taurus, Virgo, Capricorn) are **melancholic.** They are cold and dry, associated with the black bile.

See the table below for more associations.

ELEMENT	HUMOUR	SEAT	RULER	NATURE
Earth	Melancholic (black bile)	Spleen	Saturn	Cold & dry
Water	Phlegmatic (phlegm)	Lungs	Moon and Venus	Cold & moist
Ether	-	Heart	Mercury	-
Fire	Choleric (yellow bile)	Gall	Sun and Mars	Hot & dry
Air	Sanguine (blood)	Liver	Jupiter	Hot & moist

As the table shows, in addition to the classic four elements there was once the fifth element called **ether** which had its seat in the heart and was ruled by Mercury. Ether was considered a connecting principle and the source of the invisible **vital force**.

The dominance of this or that humour helped the astrologer determine the temperament of his client, as well as identify (potential) diseases associated with a too big or too small amount of a particular humour. A healthy person has all the four humours harmoniously distributed in the body, while a sick persons's balance is destroyed. For example, if someone has an overdose of phlegm which is cold and moist, he is prone to colds, water retention and similar. But for a disease to really take place, there are usually afflictions (disharmonious aspects) of malefics to planets in certain triplicities, associated with certain humours. In short, it's not easy.

THE NATURE AND CAUSE OF DISEASE

According to Lilly (CHRISTIAN ASTROLOGY, pages 244-245), significators or the cusps of H1 and H6 in:
- **FIRE SIGNS** point to feverish conditions. In this type of disease, the choleric humour is predominant.
- **EARTH SIGNS** show long and severe diseases, or those originating from melancholy (e.g. tuberculosis);
- **AIR SIGNS** suggest blood irregularities/diseases, leprosy or gout;
- **WATER SIGNS** show diseases originating from coldness and humidity (colds, coughs), and abdominal disease.

SIGNS, BODY PARTS AND ASSOCIATED DISEASES

This section includes modern sources, added by Lilly's suggestions. In CHRISTIAN ASTROLOGY (p. 119) Lilly published a table in which he associated various parts of the body with each planet in each sign, but I don't use it because it seems rather illogical and brings confusion into the existing knowledge. (For example, he attributes the Sun in Aries to thighs and the Sun in Taurus to knees; the Sun in Virgo to throat and the Moon in Aries to knees and the head; Saturn in Gemini to stomach and heart, etc.).

ARIES
Body parts: head, face, brain
Diseases: inflammation, rashes, acne, boils, scabies, lichens, smallpox, scarlet fever, epilepsy, insomnia, neuralgia of the facial muscles, brain haemorrhage, stroke, headache, migraine, baldness, tooth disorders, cuts, wounds, severe bleeding, fractures
Lilly: all kinds of diseases affecting the head and face, and those originating in choleric humour; smallpox, pimples, rash.

TAURUS
Body parts: neck, throat
Diseases: diseases of/in the neck and throat, goitre, tonsilitis, laryngitis, swollen lymph glands, suffocation, thyroid disease
Lilly: neck and throat diseases, and those originating in melancholy

GEMINI
Body parts: hands, shoulders, lungs, respiratory organs
Diseases: diseases of the lungs, bronchi and respiratory system; pneumonia, tuberculosis, asthma, nervous diseases; damage to the hands and shoulders
Lilly: diseases and injuries of shoulders and arms; blood disorders

CANCER
Body parts: chest, abdomen, uterus
Diseases: gastrointestinal diseases; gastric ulcer, edema, cancer, tumors, cysts, women's diseases, chest diseases
Lilly: chest pain, breast cancer, poor digestion, pulmonary disease, melancholy (as a result of spleen disorder), diseases of the upper abdomen and those that originate in phlegmatic humour

LEO
Body parts: heart, arteries, backbone, upper back, ribs
Diseases: heart disease, coronary thrombosis, spinal cord injury, fever
Lilly: diseases of the back, hip, ribs, heart and lower part of breast; diseases that originate in choleric humour

VIRGO
Body parts: gastrointestinal tract, intestines (small intestine in particular)
Diseases: gastrointestinal and intestinal diseases; gastroenteritis, diarrhea, constipation, inflammation of the appendix, duodenal ulcer, inflammation of the pancreas, hernia
Lilly: gastrointestinal disorders, dysentery

LIBRA
Body parts: kidney, lower back
Diseases: diseases of kidneys or ovaries, diabetes, skin problems, loin pain
Lilly: kidney stones, venereal diseases; diseases due to overindulgence in food, drink and sex; pain in buttocks, hips and thighs

SCORPIO
Body parts: bladder, male and female seual organs, prostate, groin, buttocks
Diseases: diseases of excretory and sexual organs, and of bladder and urethra , hemorrhoids, hernia, rectum and colon problems; various infectious diseases
Lilly: diseases of the sexual organs and bladder; groin pain, hemorrhoids, inflammation of the bladder, difficulty in urinating

SAGITTARIUS
Body parts: hips, thighs, blood
Diseases: liver and blood diseases; problems with blood sugar and hips; sciatica, gout
Lilly: pain in the hips and thighs; fistula, itching, sciatica

CAPRICORN
Body parts: knees, teeth, skin, bones
Diseases: colds, rheumatism, arthritis, gout, skin diseases (dermatitis, psoriasis, eczema), knee problems and various chronic diseases
Lilly: knees, the back of the thighs; knee problems, diseases as a result of melancholia

AQUARIUS
Body parts: ankles; bloodstream
Diseases: circulatory diseases, ankle damage, cramps, nervous problems; diseases transmitted by the blood (inflammation of the bone marrow, malaria, leukemia)
Lilly: legs, shins, ankles

PISCES
Body parts: feet, liver, psyche
Diseases: diseases of the lymphatic glands, allergies, alcohol and drug problems, pulmonary tuberculosis, diseases of the fluid system, poisoning, mental illness
Lilly: feet, gout

PLANETS AND RELATED DISEASES (ACCORDING TO W. LILLY)

- SATURN: headache, deafness, bone and tooth pain, gout, scabies (infectious skin disease), leprosy, paralysis, tuberculosis, black jaundice, recurrent chills, constipation, diarrhea, cough, nausea, cold
- JUPITER: lungs, ribs, cartilage, liver, heartbeat, sperm, arteries; pleurisy, heart pain, cramps, inflammation of the liver, headache, a shooting pain in the spine or near it, flatulence, blood poisoning
- MARS: left ear, gall bladder, kidneys, sexul organs; stones, plague, facial injuries, exhaustion, fever, yellow jaundice, epilepsy, boils, cysts, fistulae, inflammatory skin diseases
- SUN: brain, heart, vision, the right eye of a man, the left eye of a woman; cramps, irrgular heart pulse, heartburn, eye irritation, catarrh
- VENUS: uterus, female sexual organs, breast nipples, throat, liver, sperm, ovaries; uterine diseases, urinary tract disorders, gonorrhea, impotence, abdominal and liver conditions, syphilis, nausea (vomiting)
- MERCURY: brain, speech, tongue, fingers, hands, senses; numbness, stutter, hoarseness, epilepsy
- MOON: the left eye of a man, the right eye of a woman, brain, small intestine, bladder, taste; epilepsy, paralysis, colic (intestinal cramps), menstruation, discharge and any hardened, indigested bodily juices.

THE HOUSES AND RELATED BODY PARTS (ACCORDING TO W. LILLY)

- H1: head, eyes, face, ears
- H2: throat, neck, lymphatic glands
- H3: shoulders, arms, hands
- H4: belly, chest, lungs
- H5: back, the back of the shoulders, abdomen, liver, heart, hips
- H6: lower abdomen, gut, liver, kidneys
- H7: thighs, hips, small intestine, bladder, uterus, genital organs
- H8: spine, buttocks, groin
- H9: hips
- H10: knees
- H11: ankles, thighs
- H12: feet

LILLY'S RULES OF INTERPRETATION

As for the duration and severity of diseases, Lilly starts by saying that those occurring in winter are usually more severe and prolonged than those occurring in the summer. Spring ailments are supposed to be of a healing (purifying) nature and as such even somehow desirable, whereas the ones occuring in the autumn are destructive or even lethal.

Prolonged (or chronic) are also the so-called "cold and dry" diseases that are caused by Saturn, but can be healed by the Sun. "Hot and dry" diseases, attributed to the influence of Mars and the Sun, are usually short-lived, similarly Jupiter's diseases. Martian disorders are short, intense and feverish. Venusian and Mercurian ailments are somewhere in between, whereas the Moon points to chronic diseases (epilepsy, dizziness, vertigo, gout, etc.). The sign on the cusp of H6 suggests:

- FIXED: a long illness;
- CARDINAL: a short illness;
- MUTABLE: a medium-long or chronic, recurrent disease, but usually not severe.

Below are some of William Lilly's interpretive guidelines. See his **CHRISTIAN ASTROLOGY** for more.

If the H6 cusp is in the last degrees of a sign, the disease is almost healed, or the patient's condition will soon change (for better or for worse, depending on the nature of the next sign). Fixed signs point to the necessity of a longer and more complicated healing.

If the H6 ruler is a malefic and placed in H6 warns of a long, severe illness.

If the H6 ruler is stronger than the H1 ruler, the disease is stronger than the patient and can't be treated lightly, but if the H6 ruler is weaker than the H1 ruler, the patient's vitality is strong and he will soon be healed.

Saturn in H6 or the ruler of H6 in a fixed sign warns of a long and difficult illness, especially if it is retrograde and slow, but if this planet is cardinal and quick, it is less dangerous.

A cardinal sign on the cusp of H6, or the Moon in a cardinal sign (without affliction) indicates an imminent recovery.

If the Moon or the H6 ruler applies by a square or an opposition to the ruler of the ascendant, the patient's condition is worsening. Similarly, if the ruler of H6 is in H8 or H12. If there is a malefic in H6 at the end of a sign, the patient's condition will soon change. Count the number of degrees that separate the planet from the next sign, to see when the change would take place, and choose the most fitting time unit according to the nature of the sign.

If the ruler of H6 is retrograde or combust in H8 or H12, and applies by a square, opposition or conjunction to Mars, Saturn or the ruler of H8 or H4, the disease is dangerous and could be fatal. Similarly, if the ruler of H6 is in H8 while the ruler of H8 is in H6, especially if they apply to each other by a difficult aspect.

If the patient's significator applies to a conjunction with the Sun (is combust), his condition will deteriorate.

Saturn or Mars in H6 indicate worsening except if they are essentially dignified.

If the ruler of H6 is in H1, the disease will continue, but if in H3 or H9, there's not much to worry about. The disease is also dangerous if the ruler of H6 is in H6, H8 or H12.

If both lights are in cadent houses and their dispositors are badly placed and afflicted, this is a bad sign.

If the ruler of H6 is combust, retrograde, in detriment or fall, and in H8 in a conjunction, square or opposition with Saturn or Mars, the disease is very severe - especially if the Moon and the ascendant ruler are weak. The Moon and/or the ascendant ruler in disharmonious aspects with benefics promise a recovery, but one that will not happen soon.

If the Moon is squared by Venus, the patient is to be responsible for his illness (poor nutrition, bad habits etc.); if Venus is in Scorpio, the disease is probably a venereal (sexual) one.

The patient will get well soon if the significator of the patient and the Moon are not in a conjunction or a disharmonious aspect with Mars or Saturn, and are direct, fast, not combust, not in detriment, fall or peregrine, nor in H8, H6 or H12, nor in aspect with the rulers of these houses.

If the ascendant ruler is in H4 or H8, but unafflicted, the patient will recover.

If H6 is in a fixed sign, but there is a benefic in this house, the patient's condition will soon improve.

If the Moon decreases in light and motion, and comes to a conjunction, square or opposition of Saturn, the patient's illness is dangerous.

If the Moon is in a conjunction with an oriental, direct and swift planet, the sickness will be short, but if she is joined to a retrograde or occidental planet, judge to the contrary.

WHERE IN THE BODY?

The H6 ruler above the horizon shows that the disease is on the right side or in the upper part of the body (or an organ), but if below the horizon, it is on the left side or in the lower part of the body (or an organ). Positive signs indicate the front, negative the back side of the body.

The significator of the disease in a female (negative) sign and in an aspect with a female planet - the disease is on the left side of the body, but if it is in a male (positive) sign and in an aspect with a male planet, it is on the right side of the body.

A significator in the initial degrees of a sign represents the upper part of the body, in the central part of a sign the middle part of the body, and in the last degrees of a sign the lower part of the body.

A complicated mixture of rules, right? But practice makes perfect!

ARABIC PARTS IN HEALTH QUESTIONS

Arabic parts should be used with caution. Generally speaking, if any of them is strongly emphasized in the chart (on the ascendant, for example), this contributes to the general "negativity" of the chart.

Some of the more often used medical parts are:

illness:	ASC + Mars - Saturn
operation:	ASC + Saturn - Mars
death:	Saturn + cusp of H8 – Moon
PD (Part of Death)	ASC + cusp of H8 – Moon
DP (Death Point)	Mars + Saturn - MC

As we can see, there are (at least) three "points of death". Death Point, abbreviated as DP, has been introduced by Barbara Watters in her book HORARY ASTROLOGY AND THE JUDGMENT OF EVENTS. She claims that it's more reliable than the other two parts dealing with death.

It would seem logical that the parts associated with death should be emphasized in horary charts dealing with the possibility of death. On the basis of the rare "fatal" medical cases that I have dealt with in my practice, I tend to agree with Barbara Watters that the Death Point is the most reliable.

Arabic parts should not take precedence over the main interpretive technique. They should serve only as additional, side indications. Personally, I'm not a big fan of them, and use them only in difficult cases when all the other indications don't give me a dependable clue. In cases of fatality (death, incurable disease) I find eclipses to be a more powerful tool.

8/1: HOW WILL MY HUSBAND'S SURGERY GO? WILL HE RECOVER?

18 July 2006 at 4:59 p.m. (16:59), Ljubljana, Slovenia
Hour ruler: Venus

The querent was deeply concerned about her husband who on that day was diagnosed with a brain tumor - after an epileptic seizure on the previous day. She sent me the question by email on 18 July 2006 at 16:59, but I was on holiday then, so I only read her post when I was back home, on 21 July at 18:00. I cast the chart for the original time of the question, and am citing the other set of data for comparison purposes only.

The querent's ruler Jupiter is suitably placed in the "dark" Scorpio; technically it is in H11 (hope), but on cusp of H12 (renunciation, loss). H12 is the derived H6 (the husband's disease). This is very appropriate! She is hopeful but at the same fears loss. The Moon, showing the course of events, i.e. of illness, acting also as H8 ruler, applies by opposition to Jupiter, co-ruling the illness, while Jupiter itself applies to a square of Saturn in H8. These indications are worrying.

The subject of the question is also adequately shown by Venus, the hour ruler, ruling H6 of illness and occupying H7 – the house representing her sick husband. Venus therefore co-rules the quesited, and its placement in the last degree of a sign suggests an imminent change of situation. Venus is on a Moon monomoiria degree, and as the Moon rules H8 of crisis and death, but also of operations, this clearly indicates the pending operation of the patient.

It is interesting that the descending degree is ruled by Mars (by monomoiria) which in turn rules H12 or derived H6 (illness), while the radix H6 is ruled by Venus which occupies H7 – visually describing that the disease is "in" her partner. We will get back to Venus when we'll look further into the course of the disease. The cusp of the derived H6 is in Scorpio, traditionally ruled by Mars. This planet occupies a "fatal" degree – the degree of the Moon's nodes (27). Barbara Watters, a famous late American horary astrologer, has found that such a placement of a significator shows a special kind of negative fatality. A fatal disease? That the disease is serious, grave and persistent, is confirmed by the fact that both the cusp of H6 is and its ruler Mars are in fixed signs (Scorpio and Leo), with Mars being doubly strong due to its placement on its own degree (by monomoiria).

But most significant, however, is the husband's ruler, Mercury. It's in the critical H8 (!), retrograde, heavily combust (in a 1 degree orb of conjunction with the Sun), and slow. Its dispositor Moon is exalted in Taurus, but afflicted by an applying square to Saturn which rules the derived H8 (radix H2 with the cusp in Capricorn). Mercury's first applying aspect is an inconjunction with Pluto. Inconjunctions are very important in health-related questions! Here, all the more so because Pluto is the modern ruler of Scorpio which holds the cusp of the derived H6.

The development of the disease is also shown by Venus, the radix H6 ruler. As already mentioned, it's at the end of a sign, about to enter the sign (and cusp) of H8, showing the pending operation. But due to all the negative indications (the very weak Mercury and the afflicted Moon in particular), the surgery was unsuccessful, as metastases were already spread to several other organs.

I couldn't give much hope to the querent, of course. The strongest indicator that matters would go from bad to worse, is certainly the applying square of the Moon to Saturn, which is especially malevolent here due to its essential debility (detriment), an absence of mutual receptions and the rulership of the critical and deadly H8.

The patient died on 8 January 2007. In horary, the principal means of timing is the Moon. The time that elapsed until his death is shown by the number of degrees separating the Moon from the square with Saturn: there are 5 degrees and 51 minutes between them, and because the Moon is in a fixed sign and a succedent house, this corresponds to months. Translated into time, that would be exactly 5 months and 25 days. This is stunningly correct, as 5 months and 21 days elapsed since the date of question to the patient's death.

This case is definitely one of those which have greatly strengthened my belief that the true time of a horary question is the moment when it arises in the consciousness of the querent and gets expressed (either verbally or in a written form), and not the time when the astrologer reads and understands it. We astrologers are just "translators", not creators!

8/1

18 Jul 2006
16:59 CEDT −2:00
Ljubljana, Slovenia
46°N03' 014°E31'

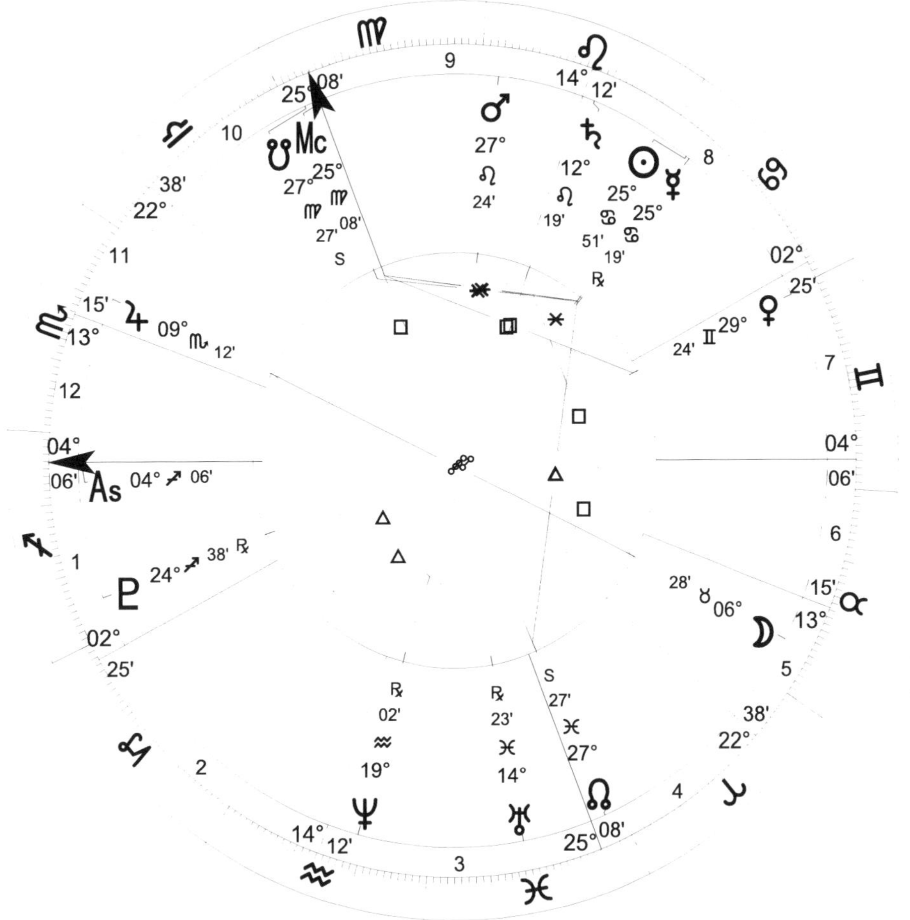

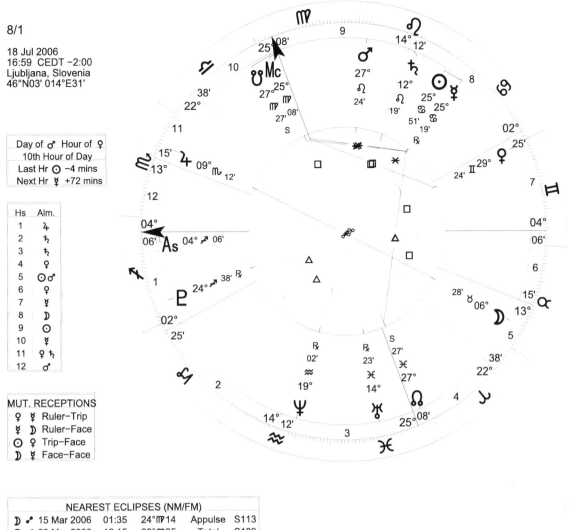

Day of ♂ Hour of ♀
10th Hour of Day
Last Hr ☉ −4 mins
Next Hr ☿ +72 mins

Hs	Alm.
1	♃
2	♄
3	♄
4	♀
5	☉♂
6	♀
7	☿
8	☽
9	☉
10	☿
11	♀ ♄
12	♂

MUT. RECEPTIONS	
♀ ☿	Ruler−Trip
☿ ☽	Ruler−Face
☉ ♀	Trip−Face
☽ ☿	Face−Face

NEAREST ECLIPSES (NM/FM)					
☽ ☍	15 Mar 2006	01:35	24°♍14	Appulse	S113
☉ ☌	29 Mar 2006	12:15	08°♈35	Total	S139
☽ ☍	7 Sep 2006	20:42	15°♓00	Partial	S118
☉ ☌	22 Sep 2006	13:45	29°♍20	Annular	S144

traditionals.pts

Pt	Long.	Travel	Decl.	Last Stn	Next Stn	Last Stn	Next Stn	F/S	Antiscia	C.Ant.
☽	06°♉28'10"	+13°44'	+16°42'	–	–	–	–	Fast	23°♌31	23°♒31
☉	25°♋51'01"	+57'15"	+20°58'	–	–	–	–	Slow	04°♊08	04°♐08
☿	25°♋19 ℞	−39'54"	+16°12'	−13 days	+10 days	01°♌22'26"	21°♋03'46"	Retro	04°♊40	04°♐40
♀	29°♊24	+01°12'	+22°42'	−165 days	+374 days	16°♑01'18"	02°♍57'23"	Fast	00°♋35	00°♑35
♂	27°♌24	+37'12"	+13°25'	−220 days	+484 days	08°♉14'08"	12°♋27'03"	Fast	02°♉35	02°♏35
♃	09°♏12	+02'11"	−13°32'	−12 days	+261 days	08°♏58'42"	19°♐46'43"	Slow	20°♒47	20°♌47
♄	12°♌19	+07'29"	+17°51'	−104 days	+140 days	04°♌22'31"	25°♌04'15"	Fast	17°♉40	17°♏40

MOON ASPECTS	
☽ ☌ ♉	6°28' S
☽ ☍ ♃	5°04' A
☽ □ ♄	5°47' A
☽ ⚹ ♅	7°47' A

ESSENTIAL DIGNITIES

Pt	Ruler	Exalt	Trip	Term	Face	Detri	Fall	Score
☽	♀	☽ +	♀	♀	☿ m	♂	--	+4
☉	☽	♃	♀	♃	☽	♄	♂	−5 p
☿	☽	♃	♀	♃	☽ m	♄	♂	−5 p
♀	☿	--	♄	♄	☉	♃	--	−5 p
♂	☉	--	☉	♂ +	♂ +	♄	--	+3
♃	♂	--	♀	♀	♂	♀	☽	−5 p
♄	☉	--	☉	♄ +	♃	♄ −	--	−3

ASPECTS	
☿ ⚹ Mc	0°02' S
♇ □ Mc	0°30' S
☉ ⚹ Mc	0°42' S
☉ △ ☊	1°36' A
☉ ⚹ ☋	1°36' A
♀ □ ☋	1°56' S
♀ □ ☊	1°56' S
♀ ⚹ ♂	1°58' S
☿ △ ☊	2°15' S
☿ ⚹ ☋	2°15' S

PLANETARY SECT

Planet		Cht	Plc	Sgn	Condition
☉	D	D	D	N	
☽	N	D	N	N	
☿	D	D	D	N	
♀	N	D	D	D	Ex Cond
♂	N	D	D	D	Ex Cond
♃	D	D	D	N	
♄	D	D	D	D	In Hayz

D=Diurnal, N=Nocturnal

8/2: AM I SICK? WHAT WILL THE LABORATORY TESTS SHOW?

15 October 2008 at 6:22 p.m. (18:22), Harrington, Delaware (USA)
Hour ruler: Sun

This chart was posted on one of the astrology forums by a woman who wrote that she had been feeling unwell for quite some time, so she went in for laboratory tests. Was she really sick, she wondered? She was of the opinion that the chart "didn't look good", and one other astrologer agreed. But my own understanding of the chart differed from theirs, and I wrote:

Your ruler Mars is in Scorpio, essentially strong, which indicates your physical strength, endurance and resistance to disease. This in itself indicates that you're not really sick. The Moon opposes Mars from Taurus, its exaltation sign. You should know that mutual reception by detriment doesn't exist! (Note: The querent commented that the Moon and Mars were in mutual reception by detriment, and interpreted this as a "bad sign".) *Here we are simply dealing with an opposition of two dignified planets, and because they both rule you (the Moon as co-significator), this reflects the fact that you don't feel well, but nothing more than that. A disease would be shown by a link between your significators and significators of the disease. These are Mercury (H6 ruler) and Saturn (the planet occupying H6). Mars is not in aspect with any of these planets while the Moon is in a wide applying trine to Saturn, but it will trine Jupiter before that and thereby annihilate the possibility of a disease. I therefore believe that you are not ill - at least not seriously. Your problem may be related to poor digestion or to bowel movement (involvement of Scorpio and Virgo). I would advise to cleanse your bowels (by fasting, for example), as this is a good therapeutic treatment for all "scorpionic" ailments. I should add that you have another ruler, Venus, ruling the intercepted H1 sign, Taurus. But Venus is also not linked to H6, which confirms the above indications. It's true that Venus is in detriment, showing your momentary weakness, but it will soon cross over to Sagittarius, indicating an imminent improvement of your well-being.*

The querent in response noted that she may be anaemic, to which I replied: *I very much doubt that you are anaemic. Mars (red blood cells) is strong in this chart and it even applies by sextile to Jupiter, and the combination of Mars and Jupiter in medical astrology shows healthy blood.*

Some two weeks later, the querent came back with the news that lab tests showed no illness. The blood tests also confirmed that she had healthy blood.

A closer look at the chart reveals that Mercury is stationary and that it would turn direct in only two hours. The question was therefore asked in a "heavenly" state of uncertainty, with the querent's mind on the point of change. In accordance with the nature of stationary planets turning direct, the change would be positive and the querent more forward-looking. It's quite possible that she had been also a bit depressed, which is fairly common in Mercury retrograde periods. People often find it difficult to view their life situations in a positive light when this planet moves backwards.

Let me also point out that Mars (the querent's main significator) is not only in its own sign, but also on its own degree by monomoiria, adding to its strength. Besides, it's interesting to note that ascendant is on a Mercury degree, this planet acting as H6 ruler – and she was interested in her (potential) disease. Monomoiria are fascinating!

8/2

15 Oct 2008
18:22 EDT +4:00
Harrington, Delaware
38°N55'25" 075°W34'41"

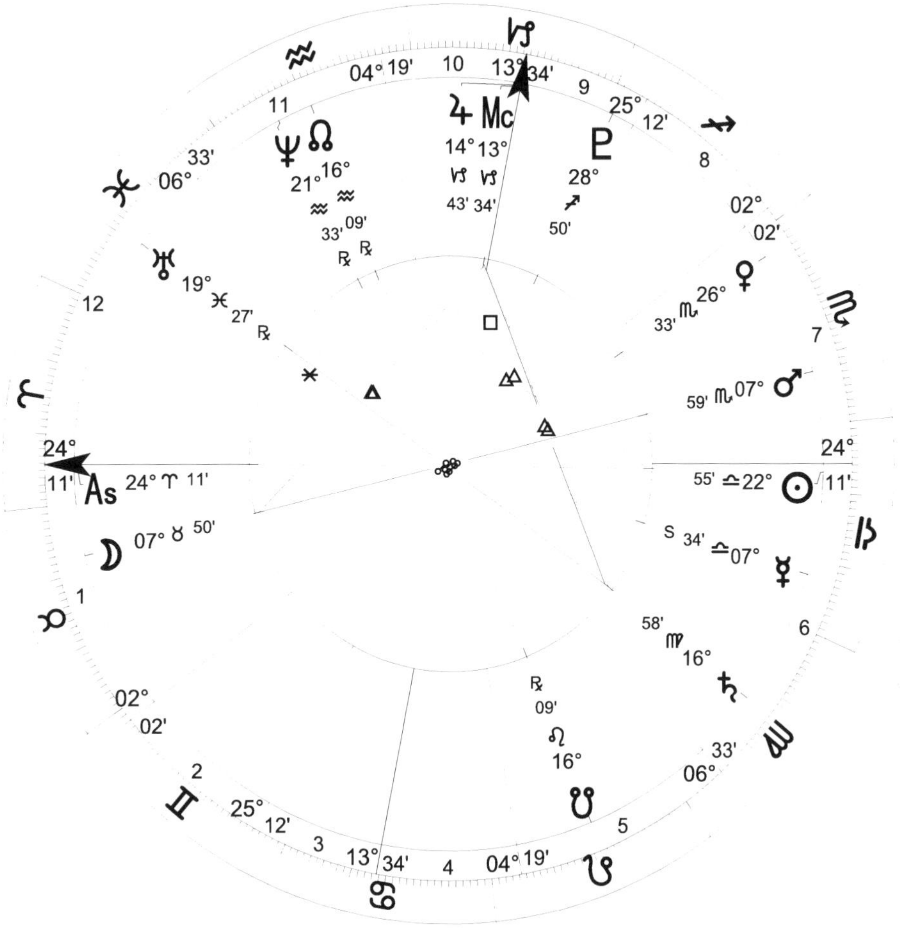

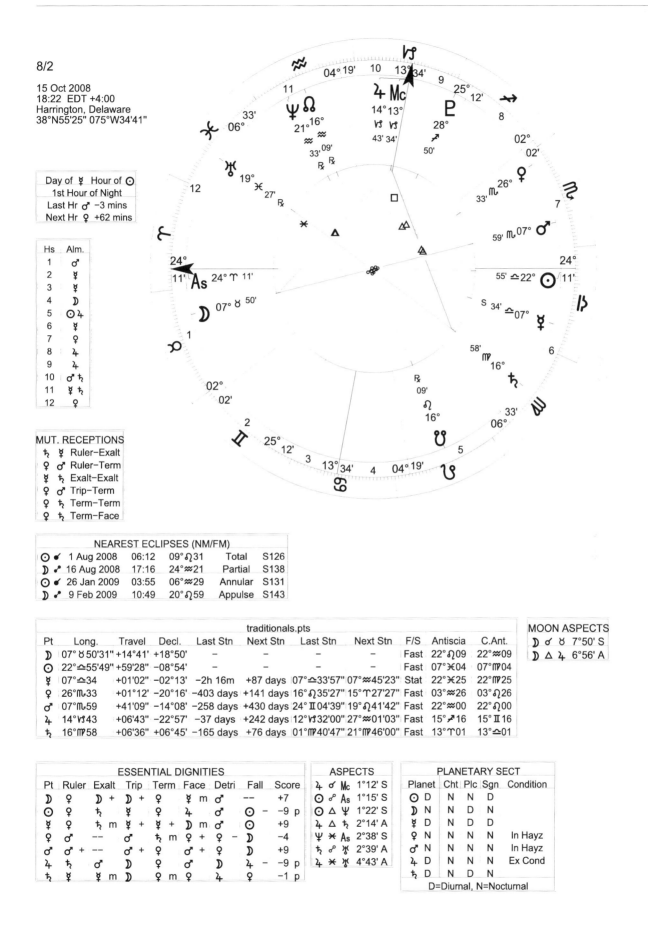

Day of ☿ Hour of ☉
1st Hour of Night
Last Hr ♂ −3 mins
Next Hr ♀ +62 mins

Hs	Alm.
1	♂
2	☿
3	☿
4	☽
5	☉ ♃
6	☿
7	♀
8	♃
9	♃
10	♂ ♄
11	☿ ♄
12	♀

MUT. RECEPTIONS		
♄	☿	Ruler−Exalt
♀	♂	Ruler−Term
☿	♄	Exalt−Exalt
♀	♂	Trip−Term
♀	♄	Term−Term
♀	♄	Term−Face

NEAREST ECLIPSES (NM/FM)					
☉ ●	1 Aug 2008	06:12	09°♌31	Total	S126
☽ ☍	16 Aug 2008	17:16	24°♒21	Partial	S138
☉ ●	26 Jan 2009	03:55	06°♒29	Annular	S131
☽ ☍	9 Feb 2009	10:49	20°♌59	Appulse	S143

traditionals.pts										
Pt	Long.	Travel	Decl.	Last Stn	Next Stn	Last Stn	Next Stn	F/S	Antiscia	C.Ant.
☽	07°♉50'31"	+14°41'	+18°50'	–	–	–	–	Fast	22°♌09	22°♒09
☉	22°♎55'49"	+59'28"	−08°54'	–	–	–	–	Fast	07°♓04	07°♍04
☿	07°♎34	+01'02"	−02°13'	−2h 16m	+87 days	07°♎33'57"	07°♒45'23"	Stat	22°♓25	22°♍25
♀	26°♏33	+01°12'	−20°16'	−403 days	+141 days	16°♌35'27"	15°♈27'27"	Fast	03°♒26	03°♌26
♂	07°♏59	+41'09"	−14°08'	−258 days	+430 days	24°♊04'39"	19°♌41'42"	Fast	22°♒00	22°♌00
♃	14°♑43	+06'43"	−22°57'	−37 days	+242 days	12°♑32'00"	27°♒01'03"	Fast	15°♐16	15°♊16
♄	16°♍58	+06'36"	+06°45'	−165 days	+76 days	01°♍40'47"	21°♍46'00"	Fast	13°♈01	13°♎01

MOON ASPECTS
☽ ☌ ♉ 7°50' S
☽ △ ♃ 6°56' A

ESSENTIAL DIGNITIES								
Pt	Ruler	Exalt	Trip	Term	Face	Detri	Fall	Score
☽	♀	☽ +	☽ +	♀	☿ m	♂	--	+7
☉	♀	♄	☿	♀	♃	♂	☉ −	−9 p
☿	♀	♄ m	☿ +	☿ +	☽ m	♂	☉	+9
♀	♂	--	♂	♄ m	♀ +	♀ −	☽	−4
♂	♂ +	--	♂ +	♀	♂ +	♀	☽	+9
♃	♄	♂	☽	♀	♂	☽	♃ −	−9 p
♄	☿	☿ m	☽	♀ m	♀	♃	♀	−1 p

ASPECTS
♃ ☌ Mc 1°12' S
☉ ☍ As 1°15' S
☉ △ ♆ 1°22' S
♃ △ ♄ 2°14' A
♆ ⚹ As 2°38' S
♄ ☍ ♅ 2°39' A
♃ ⚹ ♅ 4°43' A

PLANETARY SECT					
Planet		Cht	Plc	Sgn	Condition
☉	D	N	N	D	
☽	N	N	D	N	
☿	D	N	D	D	
♀	N	N	N	N	In Hayz
♂	N	N	N	N	In Hayz
♃	D	N	N	N	Ex Cond
♄	D	N	D	N	
D=Diurnal, N=Nocturnal					

8/3: WILL MY HUSBAND'S UNCLE GET WELL?

22 November 2003 at 8:55 a.m., Ljubljana, Slovenia
Hour ruler: Mars

A striking feature of this chart is that Pluto is in a very exact conjunction with the ascendant. As we know, planets so placed have a special power - even if they are trans-Saturnians! Several examples in this book demonstrate the value of trans-Saturnians, and it often makes sense to even give them co-rulership of signs. It is true that our ancestors could do without them - but why would we do this when it is obvious that they can contribute significantly to the understanding and delineating of our horary charts?!

My husband's uncle fell ill with cancer. As his mother's brother, he is ruled by H6 (3/4, with H4 ruling his mother). The cusp of this house is in Taurus, so he's ruled by Venus, but Mercury could be given co-rulership since the major part of H6 is in Gemini. His character (friendly, sociable and hospitable) was indeed very "venusian" – although this might be just a coincidence. (As said earlier in the book, I don't think that people's significators describe their characters.) Venus is a natural benefic but here it is peregrine in H1, void-of-course and out-of-bound. (OOB - due to its declination beyond the Sun's maximum declination of 23.5 degrees.) Mercury is in detriment and in an applying square with Mars, the radix H11 (or derived H6) ruler. The cusp of H11 is in Scorpio – conjunct the Moon, which clearly demonstrates my interest (the husband uncle's illness), while Mars, H11 ruler, is also the hour ruler. This is yet another example – out of many – where the hour ruler points to the subject matter of the question.

The "poor" (undignified) Venus - the patient – is in H1 which is the derived H8 (8/6). This places him in the house of death. The negative indication is supported by Pluto, the modern ruler of Scorpio and H11 and therefore co-significator of his illness, in an exact conjunction with ascendant (8/6), suggesting a deadly disease. Pluto is also the natural significator of crisis, death and transformation, so his disease is obviously fatal.

Jupiter, the dispositor of the Sagittarius stellium, is on a Saturn degree (by monomoiria). Saturn is the natural significator of disease and death. In the chart, Saturn is strongly debilitated, being in detriment, retrograde and in the sign of H8. Jupiter is exactly opposed by Mars, which is on a Sun's monomoiria degree – with the Sun ruling Leo, the intercepted H8 sign.

Where is the disease? Scorpio points to colon, prostate or rectum. The original cancer was in this area, but the patient developed another one in the throat - part of the body which is attributed to Taurus, and this sign is at the cusp of H6!

Both Mars and Pluto (significators of the disease) are in double-bodied signs (Pisces and Sagittarius), and he indeed had two cancers. I find it interesting that the cusp of H6 is conjunct Algol (throat cancer), while Mercury, which could be considered the uncle's co-ruler, is in a mutable sign, related to digestive system (as the ruler of Virgo).

You will notice that Mercury and Jupiter (8/6) are in a strong mutual reception. This could mean that the square might not prove fatal and the patient could be healed, but Mercury also applies closely to Mars, H6 ruler, strongly suggesting the continuation of the disease. And with all the other negative indications!

As it turned out, the uncle's condition did not improve; he slowly withered and in the beginning of October 2006 he died. The time of his death (and funeral) is exactly indicated by the symbolic movement of the Moon (radix H8 ruler): there are 38°31' separating it from Mercury (ruler of H9 which is 4/6, showing his grave). Moon in a fixed sign and succedent house would be months: 38 synodic lunar months and 10 days elapsed until his funeral.

8/3

22 Nov 2003
08:55 CET −1:00
Ljubljana, Slovenia
46°N03' 014°E31'

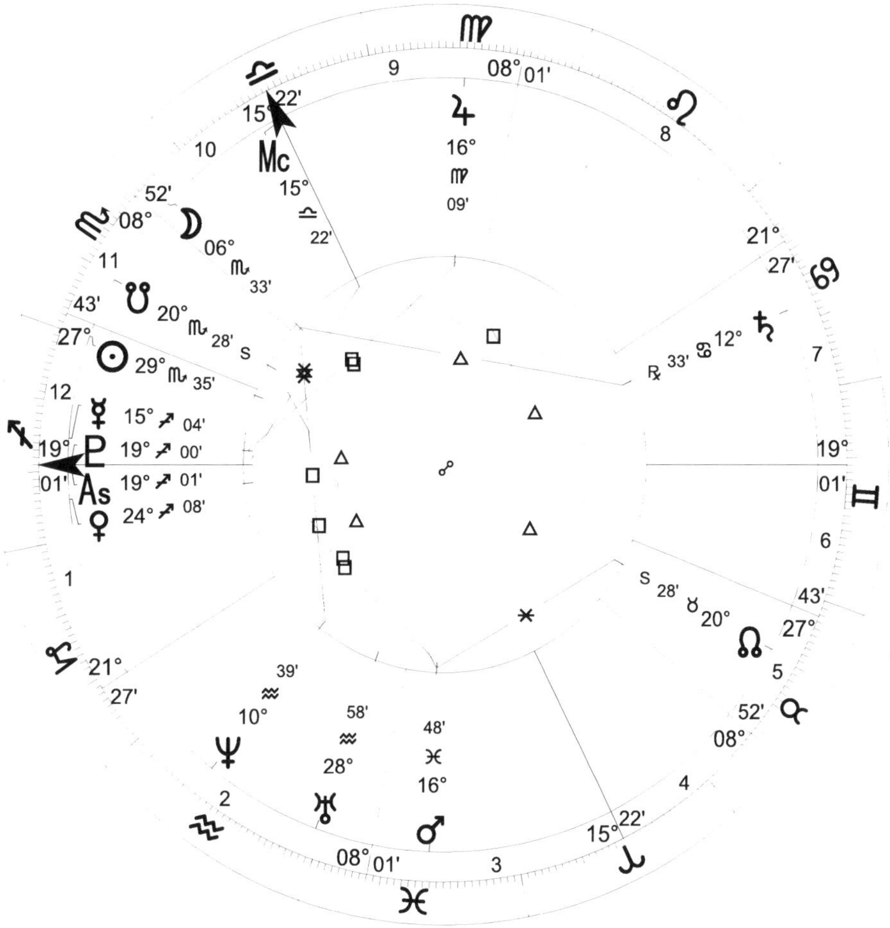

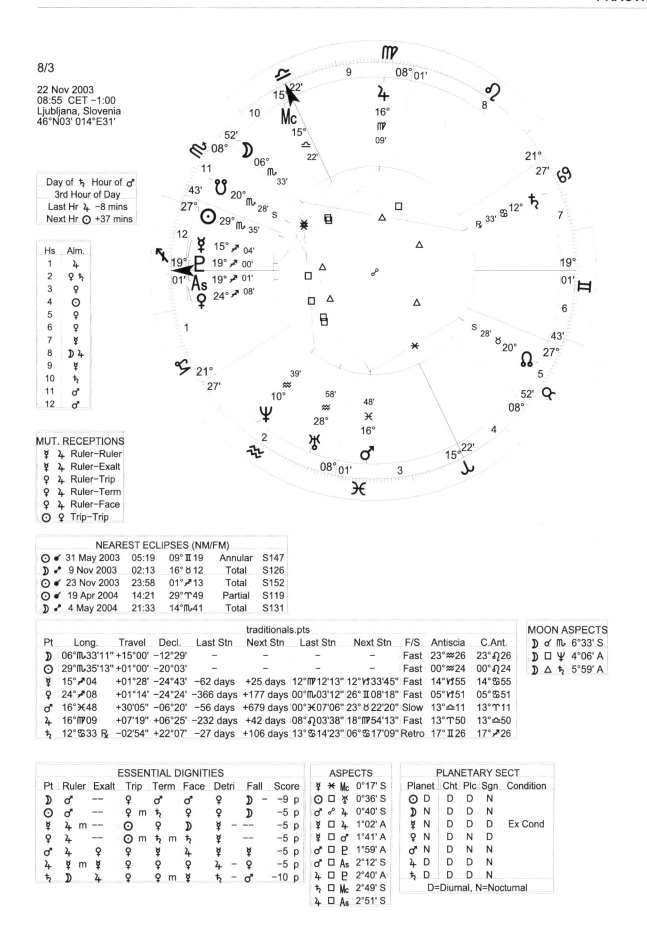

Day of ♄ Hour of ♂
3rd Hour of Day
Last Hr ♃ −8 mins
Next Hr ☉ +37 mins

Hs	Alm.
1	♃
2	♀ ♄
3	♀
4	☉
5	♀
6	♀
7	☿
8	☽ ♃
9	☿
10	♄
11	♂
12	♂

MUT. RECEPTIONS		
☿	♃	Ruler–Ruler
☿	♃	Ruler–Exalt
♀	♃	Ruler–Trip
♀	♃	Ruler–Term
♀	♃	Ruler–Face
☉	♀	Trip–Trip

NEAREST ECLIPSES (NM/FM)					
☉ ☌	31 May 2003	05:19	09° ♊ 19	Annular	S147
☽ ☍	9 Nov 2003	02:13	16° ♉ 12	Total	S126
☉ ☌	23 Nov 2003	23:58	01° ♐ 13	Total	S152
☉ ☌	19 Apr 2004	14:21	29° ♈ 49	Partial	S119
☽ ☍	4 May 2004	21:33	14° ♏ 41	Total	S131

traditionals.pts

Pt	Long.	Travel	Decl.	Last Stn	Next Stn	Last Stn	Next Stn	F/S	Antiscia	C.Ant.
☽	06°♏33'11"	+15°00'	−12°29'	–	–	–	–	Fast	23°♒26	23°♌26
☉	29°♏35'13"	+01°00'	−20°03'	–	–	–	–	Fast	00°♒24	00°♌24
☿	15°♐04	+01°28'	−24°43'	−62 days	+25 days	12°♍12'13"	12°♑33'45"	Fast	14°♑55	14°♋55
♀	24°♐08	+01°14'	−24°24'	−366 days	+177 days	00°♏03'12"	26°♊08'18"	Fast	05°♑51	05°♋51
♂	16°♓48	+30'05"	−06°20'	−56 days	+679 days	00°♓07'06"	23°♉22'20"	Slow	13°♎11	13°♈11
♃	16°♍09	+07'19"	+06°25'	−232 days	+42 days	08°♌03'38"	18°♍54'13"	Fast	13°♈50	13°♎50
♄	12°♋33 ℞	−02'54"	+22°07'	−27 days	+106 days	13°♋14'23"	06°♋17'09"	Retro	17°♊26	17°♐26

MOON ASPECTS		
☽ ☌	♏ 6°33'	S
☽ □ ♆	4°06'	A
☽ △ ♄	5°59'	A

ESSENTIAL DIGNITIES

Pt	Ruler	Exalt	Trip	Term	Face	Detri	Fall	Score
☽	♂	--	♀	♂	♂	♀	☽ –	−9 p
☉	♂	--	♀ m	♄	♀	♀	☽	−5 p
☿	♃ m	--	☉	♀	☽	☿ –	--	−5 p
♀	♃	--	☉ m	♄ m	♄	☿	--	−5 p
♂	♃	♀	♀	☿	♃	☿	☿	−5 p
♃	☿ m	☿	♀	♀	♀	♃ –	♀	−5 p
♄	☽	♃	♀	♀ m	☿	♄ –	♂	−10 p

ASPECTS		
☿ ⚹ Mc	0°17'	S
☉ □ ♅	0°36'	S
♂ ☍ ♃	0°40'	S
☿ □ ♃	1°02'	A
☿ □ ♂	1°41'	A
♂ □ ♇	1°59'	A
♂ □ As	2°12'	S
♃ □ ♇	2°40'	A
♄ □ Mc	2°49'	S
♃ □ As	2°51'	S

PLANETARY SECT

Planet		Cht	Plc	Sgn	Condition
☉	D	D	D	N	
☽	N	D	D	N	
☿	N	D	D	D	Ex Cond
♀	N	D	N	D	
♂	N	D	N	N	
♃	D	D	D	N	
♄	D	D	D	N	

D=Diurnal, N=Nocturnal

8/4: IS MASHA GOING TO BE OK?

21 April 2006 at 6:49 p.m. (18:49), Ljubljana, Slovenia
Hour ruler: Jupiter

Upon arrival from kindergarten, Masha, my (then) four year old daughter, complained of a pain in her heart. It had never happened before and I wondered, is it real and how does a child know that the pain is really in her heart? She couldn't explain, but whatever it was, it was soon over and I stopped worrying.

However, a couple of hours later when we were driving to my mother's home, she started complaining again. She even cried, saying that it really hurts! My husband immediately took her to hospital.

Back home, I cast a horary chart. Will Masha be OK? What's wrong with her heart?

Hour ruler is Jupiter, which also rules H5 of children and radix H6 of disease. My ruler Venus is located in H5 – both placements clearly indicate my interest. Venus also rules my daughter, as it is a H5 planet and also the almuten of that house. (It's interesting to note that my daughter's natal ascendant is Pisces, with Venus exactly conjuncting it.) But since I'm concerned about my daughter's (possible) illness, we must look at H10 (6/5) which is ruled by the Moon. The Moon is in Aquarius, an air sign, therefore I wondered if her pain might be related to some complications with breathing or air flow? Saturn in H10 in Leo adequately describes the pain that she felt in the heart area.

But was it just a momentary disorder, or something more serious? To find the answer to this question, we must see how all the significators are linked in the chart. We have Jupiter and Venus for Masha and the Moon and Saturn for her illness. Jupiter is retrograde and peregrine in Scorpio, but without bad aspects and also in the monomoiria degree of the Sun, the natural significator of vitality and health. Venus is separating from Jupiter by a trine while Jupiter is applying by retrograde motion to trine Uranus, which is also placed in H5. Neptune, the modern ruler of Pisces and therefore another co-significator of my daughter, is in her (derived) H12, together with the Moon, reflecting the fact that at the time of my question she was in hospital. The Moon is applying by a wide square to Jupiter, which could mean that the disease will continue, but Saturn, as the most malevolent planet, is connected neither with the Moon nor with Venus or Jupiter. I took this as a very good sign. The Moon was even separating from Saturn, suggesting that the worst was behind her. I was also comforted by the fact that Venus, the natural benefic, was strong (exalted) in my daughter's H1 and that Jupiter was retrograding to trine Uranus in H5, showing the probability of a sudden improvement. I judged that if she was seriously ill, the chart indications would have to be much more "threatening".

So it was. A couple of hours later they returned home and Masha no longer complained of a pain in her heart. The cause was not discovered, but the ailment never returned.

I should add that in the Placidus house system, the H5 cusp would be in Aquarius, making Saturn, not Jupiter, her main ruler. Saturn would thus take a more prominent role, and because it is detrimented in Leo, with the Sun, the natural significator of the heart, applying to it by a square, the situation would be much more alarming. Although the Sun receives Saturn in its domicile, making the aspect a bit easier, the applying nature of the aspect would obviously suggest a continuation of her ill-being. This is yet another example that clearly speaks in favour of the Regiomontanus house system.

8/4

21 Apr 2006
18:49 CEDT −2:00
Ljubljana, Slovenia
46°N03' 014°E31'

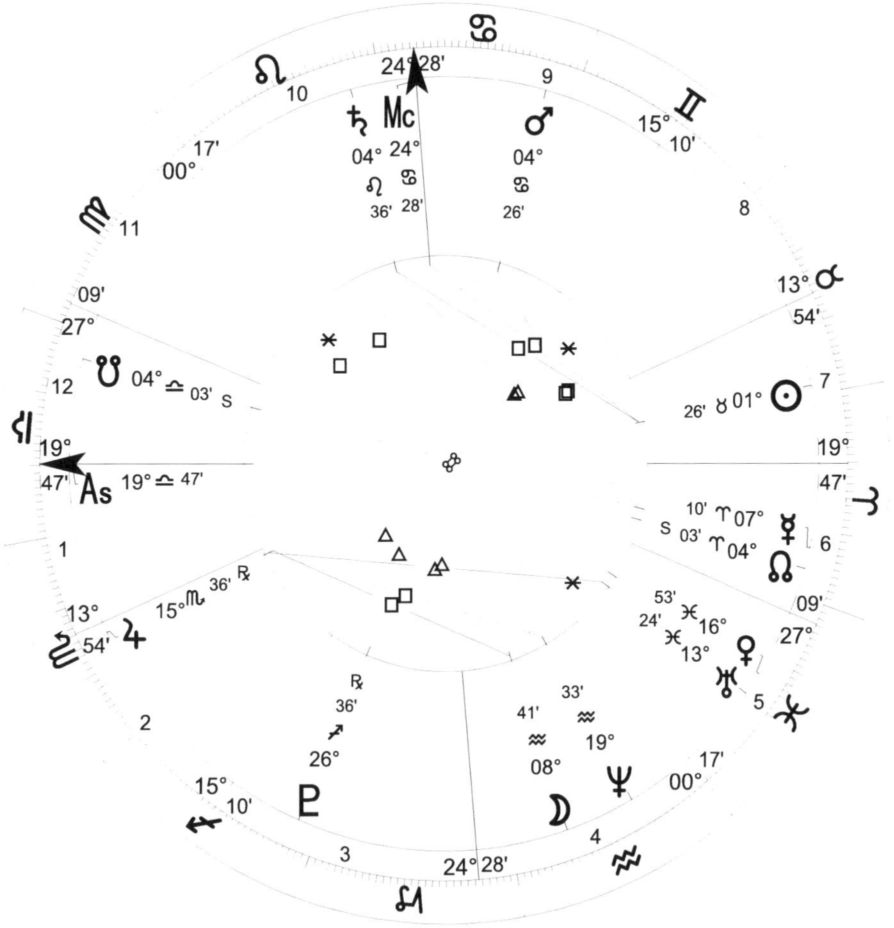

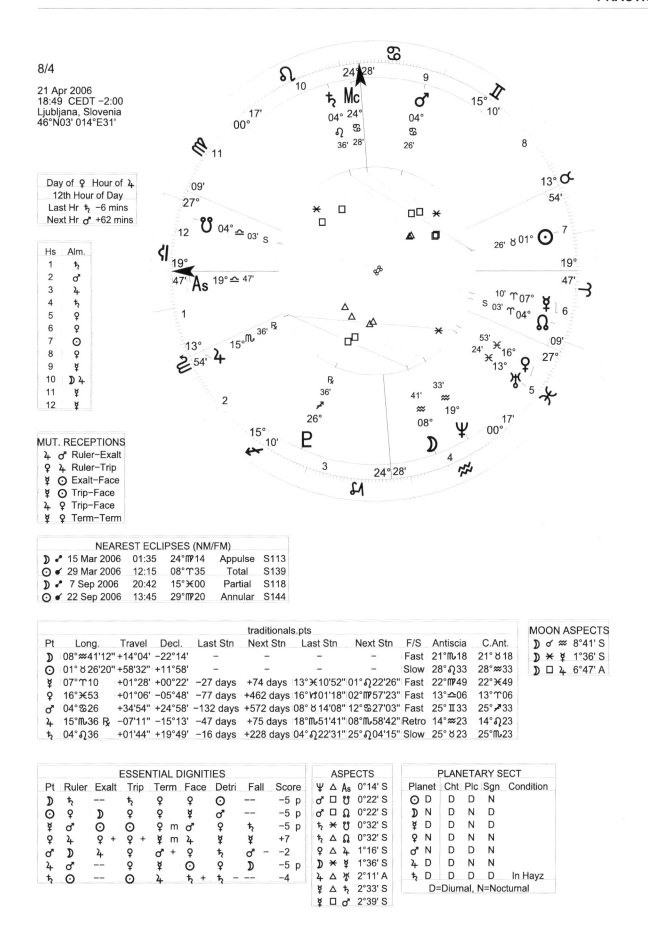

Day of ♀ Hour of ♃
12th Hour of Day
Last Hr ♄ −6 mins
Next Hr ♂ +62 mins

Hs	Alm.
1	♄
2	♂
3	♃
4	♄
5	♀
6	♀
7	☉
8	♀
9	☿
10	☽ ♃
11	☿
12	☿

MUT. RECEPTIONS		
♃	♂	Ruler–Exalt
♀	♃	Ruler–Trip
☿	☉	Exalt–Face
☿	☉	Trip–Face
♃	♀	Trip–Face
☿	♀	Term–Term

NEAREST ECLIPSES (NM/FM)					
☽ ☍	15 Mar 2006	01:35	24°♍14	Appulse	S113
☉ ☌	29 Mar 2006	12:15	08°♈35	Total	S139
☽ ☍	7 Sep 2006	20:42	15°♓00	Partial	S118
☉ ☌	22 Sep 2006	13:45	29°♍20	Annular	S144

traditionals.pts

Pt	Long.	Travel	Decl.	Last Stn	Next Stn	Last Stn	Next Stn	F/S	Antiscia	C.Ant.
☽	08°♒41'12"	+14°04'	−22°14'	–	–	–	–	Fast	21°♏18	21°♉18
☉	01°♉26'20"	+58'32"	+11°58'	–	–	–	–	Slow	28°♌33	28°♒33
☿	07°♈10	+01°28'	+00°22'	−27 days	+74 days	13°♓10'52"	01°♌22'26"	Fast	22°♍49	22°♓49
♀	16°♓53	+01°06'	−05°48'	−77 days	+462 days	16°♑01'18"	02°♍57'23"	Fast	13°♎06	13°♈06
♂	04°♋26	+34'54"	+24°58'	−132 days	+572 days	08°♉14'08"	12°♋27'03"	Fast	25°♊33	25°♐33
♃	15°♏36 ℞	−07'11"	−15°13'	−47 days	+75 days	18°♏51'41"	08°♏58'42"	Retro	14°♒23	14°♌23
♄	04°♌36	+01'44"	+19°49'	−16 days	+228 days	04°♌22'31"	25°♌04'15"	Slow	25°♉23	25°♏23

MOON ASPECTS			
☽	☌	♒	8°41' S
☽	✶	☿	1°36' S
☽	□	♃	6°47' A

ESSENTIAL DIGNITIES

Pt	Ruler	Exalt	Trip	Term	Face	Detri	Fall	Score
☽	♄	--	♄	♀	♀	☉	--	−5 p
☉	♀	☽	♀	♀	☿	♂	--	−5 p
☿	♂	☉	☉	♀ m	♂	♀	♄	−5 p
♀	♃	♀ +	♀ +	☿ m	♃	☿	☿	+7
♂	☽	♃	♀	♂ +	♀	♄	♂ −	−2
♃	♂	--	♀	☿	☉	♀	☽	−5 p
♄	☉	--	☉	♃	♄ +	♄ −	--	−4

ASPECTS

♆	△	As	0°14' S
♂	□	☋	0°22' S
♂	□	☊	0°22' S
♄	✶	☋	0°32' S
♄	△	☊	0°32' S
♀	△	♃	1°16' S
☽	✶	☿	1°36' S
♃	△	♅	2°11' A
☿	△	♄	2°33' S
☿	□	♂	2°39' S

PLANETARY SECT

Planet		Cht	Plc	Sgn	Condition
☉	D	D	D	N	
☽	N	D	N	D	
☿	D	D	N	D	
♀	N	D	N	N	
♂	N	D	D	N	
♃	D	D	N	N	
♄	D	D	D	D	In Hayz

D=Diurnal, N=Nocturnal

8/5: HAS RUBY GOT GRANULOMA?

25 December 2006 at 8:25 p.m. (20:25), Ljubljana, Slovenia
Hour ruler: Saturn

Just before setting off on a vacation, my (then) 14 year old daughter Ruby complained of an ache on the right side of her head, in an area extending from upper teeth to the top of the head. It had started in the afternoon as a slight pain which got worse in the evening. My husband asked her some strategic questions and concluded that Ruby most probably had a granuloma. Such pain comes from a bad tooth, he said.

Ouch… Dentists don't work on holidays (it was Christmas day), so we'd obviously have to take her to an emergency centre, and if it was really a granuloma, the healing would take several days. But our holiday started in two days!

Then I remembered that I was a horary astrologer, after all, and that I have my own way of finding the truth. I immediately cast the chart with the question: *Has Ruby got a granuloma?*

I'm shown by the Leo ascendant and the "heavy" Saturn sitting on top of it, retrograde and in detriment, with Saturn also acting as the hour ruler. Since it also rules H6 of diseases – my concern - this clearly demonstrates my worry and sense of helplessness due to the suddenly emerging situation in which we found ourselves. Since I'm interested in my daughter's matters, it's quite logical that the Sun, my ruler, is in H5 of children.

My daughter is ruled by Jupiter, H5 ruler, and by several planets in H5. There is a conjunction of Mercury and Pluto right on cusp of the house, the Sun (also showing me – her worried mother), and Venus – very appropriately placed here since it rules H10, the derived H6 (6/5).

I noticed immediately that Jupiter was very strong in the chart: in its domicile, triplicity and term, direct, east of the Sun, not combust or under the Sun's beams, and unafflicted. Does this mean that Ruby is not really sick? By all means, I thought, such a strong and fortunate planet can't indicate a sick person! What about Venus, her H6 ruler, in her H1? This is "emplacement", but for the illness to be real and harmful, Venus would have to be linked with any of my daughter's significators, which was not the case. Besides, Venus is a natural benefic and has a weak dignity by term in the chart. The Moon, describing the course of events and co-ruling my daughter's illness by virtue of being almuten of H10 (6/5), applies to Venus by a wide sextile, which is a fortunate aspect and could only show a continuation of a mild pain, but its first application to another planet (Mars, separating from Jupiter) "disconnects" it from an illness.

So – it looks like Ruby doesn't have a granuloma! I found a further confirmation in the fact that Saturn, the natural significator of teeth, was not in any aspect with her significators, nor with the Moon.

But where does her pain come from? Mercury in conjunction with Pluto in her H1 gave me the clue. It made me think that it was probably some small nerve disorder, as Mercury rules nerves and Pluto all kinds of obstructions. But whatever it was, it couldn't be serious.

Ruby doesn't have a granuloma! I exclaimed upon entering the living room.

And so it was. She took an aspirin, the pain eased away and the next day she was completely well again.

8/5

25 Dec 2006
20:25 CET −1:00
Ljubljana, Slovenia
46°N03' 014°E31'

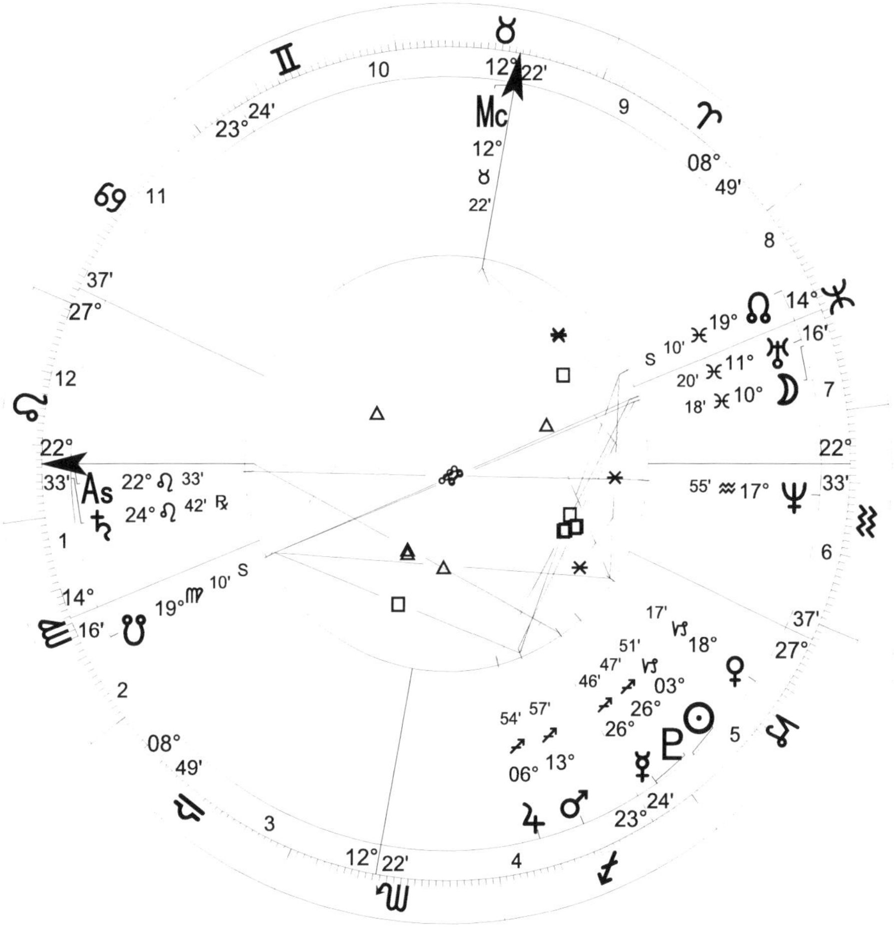

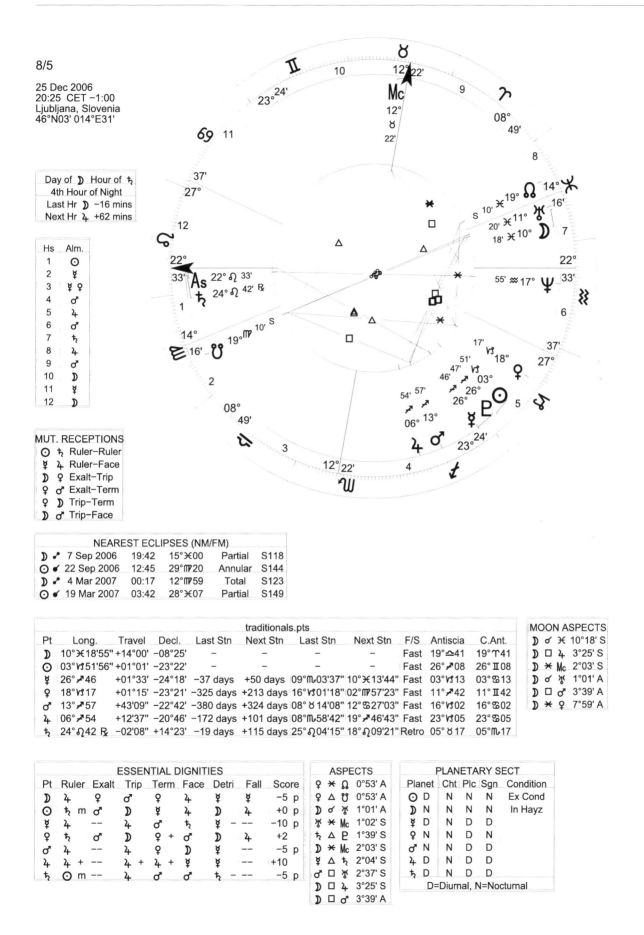

Day of ☽ Hour of ♄
4th Hour of Night
Last Hr ☽ −16 mins
Next Hr ♃ +62 mins

Hs	Alm.
1	☉
2	☿
3	☿ ♀
4	♂
5	♃
6	♂
7	♄
8	♃
9	♂
10	☽
11	☿
12	☽

MUT. RECEPTIONS
☉ ♄ Ruler−Ruler
☿ ♃ Ruler−Face
☽ ♀ Exalt−Trip
♀ ♂ Exalt−Term
♀ ☽ Trip−Term
☽ ♂ Trip−Face

NEAREST ECLIPSES (NM/FM)				
☽ ☍ 7 Sep 2006	19:42	15°♓00	Partial	S118
☉ ☌ 22 Sep 2006	12:45	29°♍20	Annular	S144
☽ ☍ 4 Mar 2007	00:17	12°♍59	Total	S123
☉ ☌ 19 Mar 2007	03:42	28°♓07	Partial	S149

traditionals.pts

Pt	Long.	Travel	Decl.	Last Stn	Next Stn	Last Stn	Next Stn	F/S	Antiscia	C.Ant.
☽	10°♓18'55"	+14°00'	−08°25'	–	–	–	–	Fast	19°♎41	19°♈41
☉	03°♑51'56"	+01°01'	−23°22'	–	–	–	–	Fast	26°♐08	26°♊08
☿	26°♐46	+01°33'	−24°18'	−37 days	+50 days	09°♏03'37"	10°♓13'44"	Fast	03°♑13	03°♋13
♀	18°♑17	+01°15'	−23°21'	−325 days	+213 days	16°♑01'18"	02°♍57'23"	Fast	11°♐42	11°♊42
♂	13°♐57	+43'09"	−22°42'	−380 days	+324 days	08°♉14'08"	12°♋27'03"	Fast	16°♑02	16°♋02
♃	06°♐54	+12'37"	−20°46'	−172 days	+101 days	08°♏58'42"	19°♐46'43"	Fast	23°♑05	23°♋05
♄	24°♌42 ℞	−02'08"	+14°23'	−19 days	+115 days	25°♌04'15"	18°♌09'21"	Retro	05°♉17	05°♏17

MOON ASPECTS
☽ ☌ ♓ 10°18' S
☽ □ ♃ 3°25' S
☽ ⚹ Mc 2°03' S
☽ ☌ ♅ 1°01' A
☽ □ ♂ 3°39' A
☽ ⚹ ♀ 7°59' A

ESSENTIAL DIGNITIES

Pt	Ruler	Exalt	Trip	Term	Face	Detri	Fall	Score
☽	♃	♀	♂	♀	♃	☿	☿	−5 p
☉	♄ m	♂	☽	☿	♃	☽	♃	+0 p
☿	♃	--	♃	♂	♄	☿ −	--	−10 p
♀	♄	♂	☽	♀ +	♂	☽	♃	+2
♂	♃	--	♃	♀	☽	☿	--	−5 p
♃	♃ +	--	♃ +	♃ +	☿	☿	--	+10
♄	☉ m	--	♃	♂	♂	♄ −	--	−5 p

ASPECTS
♀ ⚹ ☊ 0°53' A
♀ △ ☋ 0°53' A
☽ ☌ ♅ 1°01' A
♅ ⚹ Mc 1°02' S
♄ △ ♇ 1°39' S
☽ ⚹ Mc 2°03' S
☿ △ ♄ 2°04' S
♂ □ ♅ 2°37' S
☽ □ ♃ 3°25' S
☽ □ ♂ 3°39' A

PLANETARY SECT

Planet	Cht	Plc	Sgn	Condition
☉ D	N	N	N	Ex Cond
☽ N	N	N	N	In Hayz
☿ D	N	D	D	
♀ N	N	D	N	
♂ N	N	D	D	
♃ D	N	D	D	
♄ D	N	D	D	
D=Diurnal, N=Nocturnal				

8/6: WILL ADAM FALL ILL WITH SCARLET FEVER?

19 September 2008 at 3:11 p.m. (15:11), Ljubljana, Slovenia
Hour ruler: Mercury

In our local kindergarten, several kids fell ill with scarlet fever. There were a few cases of this infectious diseases registered in my son's group, and parents were alerted of the danger by a huge panel notice. Statistics says that if a child spends time in a group where someone is infected with scarlet fever, there is a 25% chance of getting the disease himself. This freaked me out. The disease itself is not dangerous, but it would be upsetting if my son got sick, of course!

The H5 cusp of the chart which I cast for the above question, is at 23°24' Taurus, in conjunction with the Moon, my co-significator. This nicely reflects my interest - my child's condition. Its ruler Venus (which also rules my son's ascending sign, Libra), placed in Libra in H9, adequately describes him as an attractive and friendly boy. The significator of the potential disease is Mercury, ruling radix H6 with the cusp in Gemini. Too see if my child would fall ill with scarlet fever, we should find some connections between H5, H6 and H10 (6/5).

Mercury, signifying the disease, is also the hour ruler, agreeing with the subject of the question. It's placed next to Venus and Mars in Libra in H9. At first glance it seems that Mercury is catching up with Venus, but a look into the ephemeris (see tables) shows that it was very slow on this day, about to become stationary retrograde. If Mercury would catch Venus, that would mean that Adam would fall ill (because illness would "catch" him), but this is obviously not going to happen. It's vice versa – Mercury and Mars which are seemingly distancing themselves from each other, are actually mutually applying into a conjunction. Mars rules the derived H6 (radix H10 or 6/5 – my child's potential disease), but since Venus is the fastest of the two, it will "escape" – meaning Adam will not get sick.

The chart has a couple of other indications supporting this conclusion: Venus is in its domicile and therefore strong, reflecting my son's good health and resilience, while the Moon which co-rules him due to its placement on cusp of H5, in exaltation, meaning practically the same. The Moon also applies by trine to the Sun which is a general indication of good health.

I published this chart, together with the above assessment, on an online horary forum, and was just too glad to be able to post an update several weeks later: *I must confirm that my son did not fall ill with scarlet fever! There was just one more case of the disease in his group, but since more than two weeks (the incubation period) have passed since then, I'm verifying that my judgment was correct.*

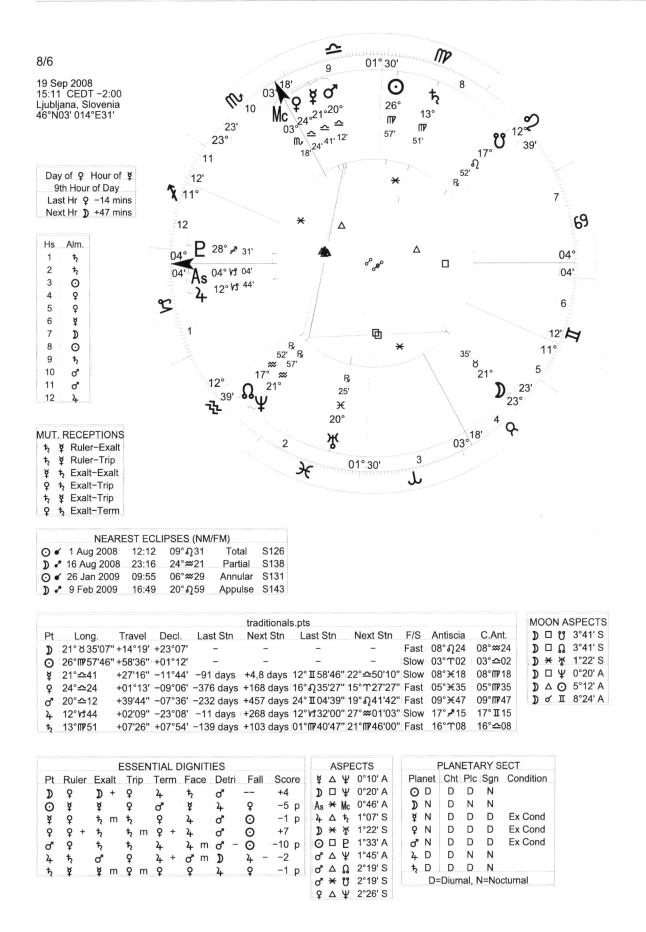

8/6

19 Sep 2008
15:11 CEDT −2:00
Ljubljana, Slovenia
46°N03' 014°E31'

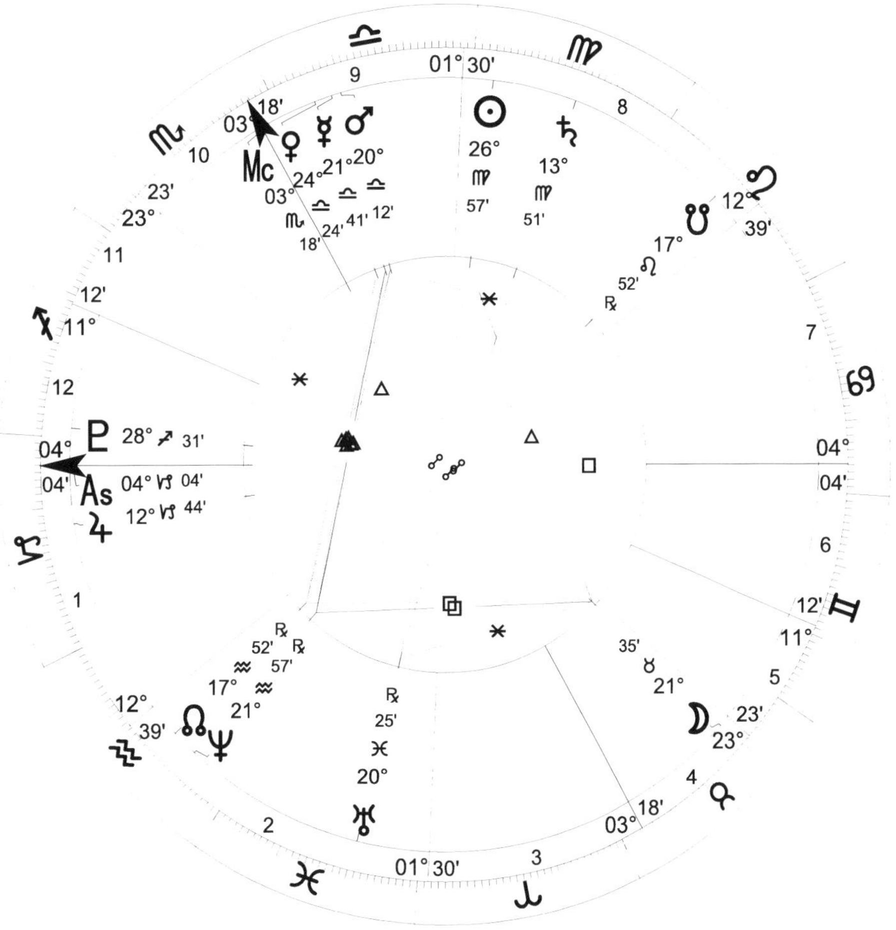

Day of ♀ Hour of ☿
9th Hour of Day
Last Hr ♀ −14 mins
Next Hr ☽ +47 mins

Hs	Alm.
1	♄
2	♄
3	☉
4	♀
5	♀
6	☿
7	☽
8	☉
9	♄
10	♂
11	♂
12	♃

MUT. RECEPTIONS		
♄	☿	Ruler–Exalt
♄	☿	Ruler–Trip
☿	♄	Exalt–Exalt
♀	♄	Exalt–Trip
♄	☿	Exalt–Trip
♀	♄	Exalt–Term

NEAREST ECLIPSES (NM/FM)					
☉	1 Aug 2008	12:12	09°♌31	Total	S126
☽	16 Aug 2008	23:16	24°♒21	Partial	S138
☉	26 Jan 2009	09:55	06°♒29	Annular	S131
☽	9 Feb 2009	16:49	20°♌59	Appulse	S143

traditionals.pts

Pt	Long.	Travel	Decl.	Last Stn	Next Stn	Last Stn	Next Stn	F/S	Antiscia	C.Ant.
☽	21°♉35'07"	+14°19'	+23°07'	–	–	–	–	Fast	08°♌24	08°♒24
☉	26°♍57'46"	+58'36"	+01°12'	–	–	–	–	Slow	03°♈02	03°♎02
☿	21°♎41	+27'16"	−11°44'	−91 days	+4,8 days	12°♊58'46"	22°♎50'10"	Slow	08°♓18	08°♍18
♀	24°♎24	+01°13'	−09°06'	−376 days	+168 days	16°♌35'27"	15°♈27'27"	Fast	05°♓35	05°♍35
♂	20°♎12	+39'44"	−07°36'	−232 days	+457 days	24°♊04'39"	19°♌41'42"	Fast	09°♓47	09°♍47
♃	12°♑44	+02'09"	−23°08'	−11 days	+268 days	12°♑32'00"	27°♒01'03"	Slow	17°♐15	17°♊15
♄	13°♍51	+07'26"	+07°54'	−139 days	+103 days	01°♍40'47"	21°♍46'00"	Fast	16°♈08	16°♎08

MOON ASPECTS			
☽	□	☋	3°41' S
☽	□	☊	3°41' S
☽	⚹	♅	1°22' S
☽	□	♆	0°20' A
☽	△	☉	5°12' A
☽	☌	♊	8°24' A

ESSENTIAL DIGNITIES

Pt	Ruler	Exalt	Trip	Term	Face	Detri	Fall	Score
☽	♀	☽ +	♀	♃	♄	♂	--	+4
☉	☿	☿	♀	♂	☿	♃	♀	−5 p
☿	♀	♄ m	♄	♀	♃	♂	☉	−1 p
♀	♀ +	♄	♄ m	♀ +	♃	♂	☉	+7
♂	♀	♄	♄	♃	♃ m	♂ −	☉	−10 p
♃	♄	♂	♀	♃ +	♂ m	☽	♃ −	−2
♄	☿	☿ m	♀ m	♀	♀	♃	♀	−1 p

ASPECTS			
☿	△	♆	0°10' A
☽	□	♆	0°20' A
As	⚹	Mc	0°46' A
♃	△	♄	1°07' S
☽	⚹	♅	1°22' S
☉	□	♇	1°33' A
♂	△	♆	1°45' A
♂	△	☊	2°19' S
♂	⚹	☋	2°19' S
♀	△	♆	2°26' S

PLANETARY SECT

Planet		Cht	Plc	Sgn	Condition
☉	D	D	D	N	
☽	N	D	N	N	
☿	N	D	D	D	Ex Cond
♀	N	D	D	D	Ex Cond
♂	N	D	D	D	Ex Cond
♃	D	D	N	N	
♄	D	D	D	N	

D=Diurnal, N=Nocturnal

8/7: WILL MY COUSIN'S HUSBAND GET WELL AGAIN?

23 January 2007 at 6:53 p.m. (18:53), Ljubljana, Slovenia
Hour ruler: Jupiter

My mother told me that my cousin's husband was seriously ill. Heavy headaches, combined with a general feeling of being unwell, had been warning him that his health was failing. Medical tests revealed that he had a brain tumor. It was not yet known whether the tumor was cancerous or not, but due to a sudden severe deterioration of his health the doctors kept him in the hospital.

My cousin is shown by Venus, ruler of H3, which stands for brothers, sisters and cousins. Venus is in conjunction with the descendant, peregrine (insecure, helpless) and in a close separating opposition with the heavy, burdensome Saturn (doubly harmful by being in detriment and retrograde), indicating her serious concern and sadness.

Hour ruler (Jupiter) is harmonious, showing the chart to be radical. In view of the imminent operation of the patient it's interesting to note that Jupiter rules H8, the house of surgery.

Her husband is shown by H9 with its cusp in Aries, making Mars his main significator. This planet is in the fortunate H5 and essentially strong (exalted). His co-significator is the Sun which is co-almuten of the H9 cusp. So suitable to find it in the radix H6 of disease!

Mercury, the significator of his illness (due to its rulership of the radix H2 which is 6/9), is also placed in H6, but is not in aspect with either Mars or the Sun. Saturn, the radix H6 ruler, doesn't aspect them either, which bodes well for the patient. Saturn and the Sun are in mutual reception by domicile – a helpful indication since MR strengthens the participating planets and shows a relief or an "escape" from a difficult situation. All indicators are therefore very encouraging – the patient's life is clearly not in danger!

It is interesting to note that by monomoiria, Mars is on a Mercury degree, with this planet ruling H2 or the derived H6 (6/9), which confirms the nature of the problem and connects my cousin's husband with the disease. Still, this is a minor dignity which only shows the connection – it can't affect the patient in a negative way.

The fact is, however, that his condition is currently precarious. The Moon in H8 is in a close applying square with Mars, his main significator, indicating that an operation is imminent – especially because the Moon is in a cardinal sign, showing a need to act quickly. Less than a degree separates it from an exact aspect, meaning that the operation was due in less than a week. (This seemed to be the most logical time unit also according to circumstances.) So it was – the surgery took place on January 29, 6 days after the question.

Mars being strong, with the help of a mutual reception of the two bodies (Mars receives the Moon in its domicile while the Moon receives Mars in its triplicity), the square can't be destructive - to the opposite! Although Mars is in the Moon's detriment, it is nevertheless in its exaltation and in the fortunate H5, so the combination of factors speaks for a successful surgery. This is confirmed by a mutual reception between the Sun and Saturn; the Sun (the patient) can exchange places with Saturn (H6 ruler) and get into Leo, its domicile.

Thus it was. The doctors found that the tumour was neither cancerous nor life-threatening, so that after the surgery, the patient gradually fully recovered.

You might ask, what about the application of the Moon to Jupiter (its next aspect after the square with Mars) which rules H8 of death? Besides, Jupiter is placed in the derived H8! True, H8 is prominent in this chart but we have already found that the patient was basically strong and that the chart did not show the continuation of the disease. Besides, Mars and the Sun (his significators) are not linked with either the radix H8 nor the derived H8, so there's no worry! Jupiter is also the natural benefic, especially here since it's placed in its own sign, Sagittarius, and therefore acts more like a healing force. There's also a mutual reception between Jupiter and the Moon (triplicity/face) which stresses the benevolent nature of the aspect.

Again, this chart clearly demonstrates how important it is to consider all the indications and combine them into a meaningful whole.

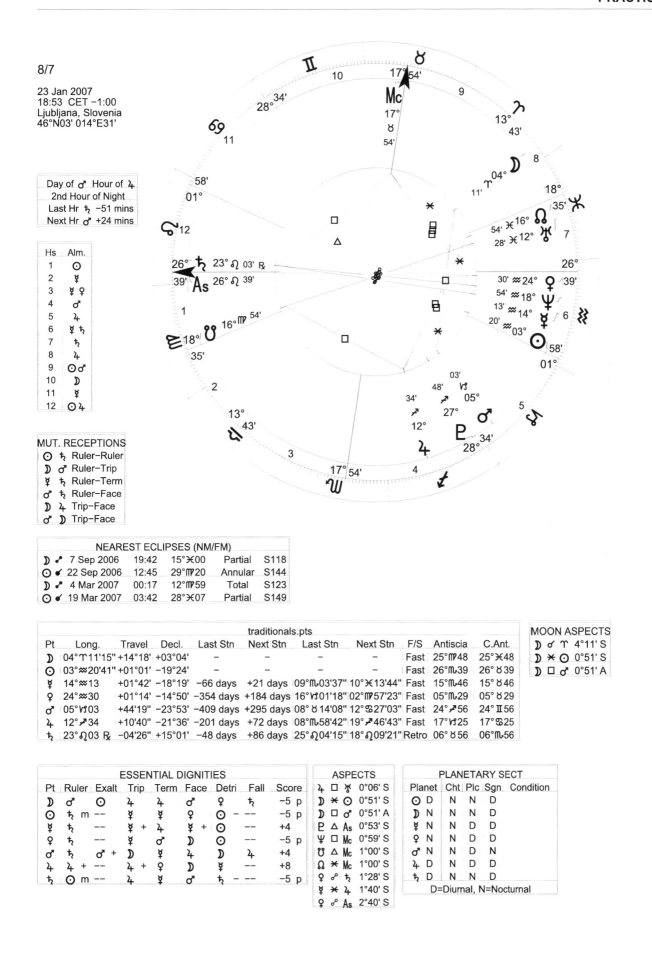

8/7

23 Jan 2007
18:53 CET −1:00
Ljubljana, Slovenia
46°N03' 014°E31'

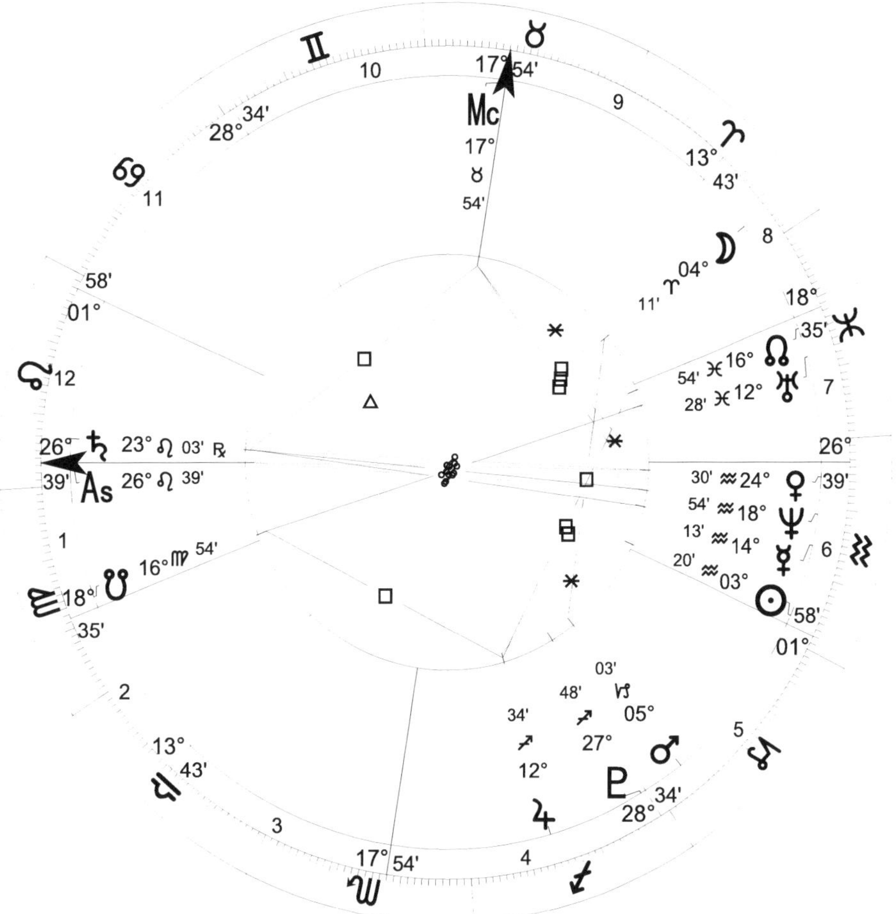

Day of ♂ Hour of ♃
2nd Hour of Night
Last Hr ♄ −51 mins
Next Hr ♂ +24 mins

Hs	Alm.
1	☉
2	☿
3	☿ ♀
4	♂
5	♃
6	☿ ♄
7	♄
8	♃
9	☉♂
10	☽
11	☿
12	☉♃

MUT. RECEPTIONS		
☉	♄	Ruler-Ruler
☽	♂	Ruler-Trip
☿	♄	Ruler-Term
♂	♄	Ruler-Face
☽	♃	Trip-Face
♂	☽	Trip-Face

NEAREST ECLIPSES (NM/FM)					
☽ ☍	7 Sep 2006	19:42	15°♓00	Partial	S118
☉ ☌	22 Sep 2006	12:45	29°♍20	Annular	S144
☽ ☍	4 Mar 2007	00:17	12°♍59	Total	S123
☉ ☌	19 Mar 2007	03:42	28°♓07	Partial	S149

traditionals.pts

Pt	Long.	Travel	Decl.	Last Stn	Next Stn	Last Stn	Next Stn	F/S	Antiscia	C.Ant.
☽	04°♈11'15"	+14°18'	+03°04'	–	–	–	–	Fast	25°♍48	25°♓48
☉	03°♒20'41"	+01°01'	−19°24'	–	–	–	–	Fast	26°♏39	26°♉39
☿	14°♒13	+01°42'	−18°19'	−66 days	+21 days	09°♏03'37"	10°♓13'44"	Fast	15°♏46	15°♉46
♀	24°♒30	+01°14'	−14°50'	−354 days	+184 days	16°♑01'18"	02°♍57'23"	Fast	05°♏29	05°♉29
♂	05°♑03	+44'19"	−23°53'	−409 days	+295 days	08°♉14'08"	12°♋27'03"	Fast	24°♐56	24°♊56
♃	12°♐34	+10'40"	−21°36'	−201 days	+72 days	08°♏58'42"	19°♐46'43"	Fast	17°♑25	17°♋25
♄	23°♌03 ℞	−04'26"	+15°01'	−48 days	+86 days	25°♌04'15"	18°♌09'21"	Retro	06°♉56	06°♏56

MOON ASPECTS			
☽	☌	♈	4°11' S
☽	⚹	☉	0°51' S
☽	□	♂	0°51' A

ESSENTIAL DIGNITIES

Pt	Ruler	Exalt	Trip	Term	Face	Detri	Fall	Score
☽	♂	☉	♃	♃	♂	♀	♄	−5 p
☉	♄ m	--	☿	☿	♀	☉ −	--	−5 p
☿	♄	--	☿ +	♃	☿ +	☉	--	+4
♀	♄	--	☿	♂	☽	☉	--	−5 p
♂	♄	♂ +	☽	☿	♃	☽	♃	+4
♃	♃ +	--	♃ +	♀	☽	☿	--	+8
♄	☉ m	--	♃	☿	♂	♄ −	--	−5 p

ASPECTS			
♃	□	♅	0°06' S
☽	⚹	☉	0°51' S
☽	□	♂	0°51' A
♇	△	As	0°53' S
♆	□	Mc	0°59' S
☋	△	Mc	1°00' S
☊	⚹	Mc	1°00' S
♀	☍	♄	1°28' S
☿	⚹	♃	1°40' S
♀	☍	As	2°40' S

PLANETARY SECT

Planet		Cht	Plc	Sgn	Condition
☉	D	N	N	D	
☽	N	N	N	D	
☿	N	N	D	D	
♀	N	N	D	D	
♂	N	N	D	N	
♃	D	N	D	D	
♄	D	N	N	D	

D=Diurnal, N=Nocturnal

8/8: HAS STEVEN REALLY GOT CANCER?

27 October 2008 at 4:10 p.m. (16:10) in Ljubljana, Slovenia
Hour ruler: Sun

A friend of mine told me that her ex-husband Steven (the name is fictitious) who is also the father of her child, had health problems. As she said in our phone conversation, he had testicular lumps and skin blemishes which were specific to a particular type of cancer. Besides, he suffered frequent headaches and felt unwell. Samples of tissue had just been sent to a clinic abroad, asking to confirm or refute the suspicion.

You know that I'm an astrologer and you can ask me a question, I said to her. *I dare not*, she said, *I'm too scared*.

Days went by and the matter didn't go out of my head. Steven was also my own friend, after all, so I was concerned. Has he really got cancer? The thought was scary. He was so young! Having asked the above question, I placed Steven in H11. Hour ruler, the Sun, is quite fitting, since the cusp of H6 (disease) is in Leo.

In order to determine whether someone is really ill, we must check whether the planets representing him and his potential illness are in any way connected. Steven's significator Saturn (ruler of Capricorn which holds the cusp of H11) is found in H6 of disease – very appropriately. Still, it would be worse if the H6 ruler were in his H1, showing an illness to be "in his body". This way, we only have some sort of connection which in itself needn't be fatal.

The derived H6 cusp is in Gemini, with Mercury becoming the main significator of his potential disease. It's placed in Libra in H7 (together with the Moon and the Sun, the ruler of the radix H6) which is the derived H9 (9/11). This is interesting due to the fact that the tissues were sent abroad. The Sun is in Scorpio, the sign of sexual organs.

But to confirm the existence of a disease, the main significators should be strongly linked, or they would have to be severely afflicted. There would have to be an aspect between Saturn and Mercury, or between Saturn and the Sun (ruler of the radix H6), or between the Moon and any of the significators of the disease. But there is no aspect between Saturn and Mercury; they are in a mixed MR (domicile/exaltation), showing a connection between the two but also a way out of a difficult situation. The Moon doesn't aspect Mercury or the Sun either. It is true that it's is in a wide applying conjunction with the Sun, actually under its beams - which is an affliction - but the first Moon's aspect is a soothing trine with Neptune, followed by a regenerative sextile with Pluto, and the malefic conjunction with the Sun will only be completed after the Moon's sign change. All these indications speak in favour of Steven's health.

By strictly following traditional rules - that is, without taking into account the Moon's aspect with the trans-Saturnians, and by observing the Moon's sign change before its conjunction with the Sun, the Moon is actually void-of-course. The answer, in such cases, is usually "no". No, he hasn't got cancer. But if we take into account the said Moon's aspects with the trans-Saturnians, the situation also bodes well. The Moon's harmonious aspect with a retrograde Neptune suggests a return of the body into its previous condition, and Pluto suggests regeneration. Either way, the Moon doesn't seem to really afflict the patient.

Crucial is the fact that Saturn (Steven) is not afflicted. It's opposed by Uranus, true, but it is getting a much stronger support from Mars which applies to it by sextile from Scorpio, its domicile sign. Well-aspected planets in Scorpio stand for resilience and recuperative powers. Saturn is also applied to by the "healing" great benefic Jupiter which Saturn receives in its domicile. This aspect (a harmonious trine) adds substantially to Steven's well-being. It is obvious that his body is getting stronger and healthier, therefore we can expect that he'll soon feel better.

I think that Steven hasn't got cancer, I said to my friend when we next met. *He does feel unwell presently, and there is some kind of weakness in his body, but he's going through a regenerative process which will get him well again.*

She soon confirmed my judgment, saying that the medical tests were negative. His problems were apparently related to stress which he was going through at that time, but the headaches and general weakness slowly passed and also testicular lumps were soon gone.

8/8

29 Oct 2008
16:10 CET −1:00
Ljubljana, Slovenia
46°N03' 014°E31'

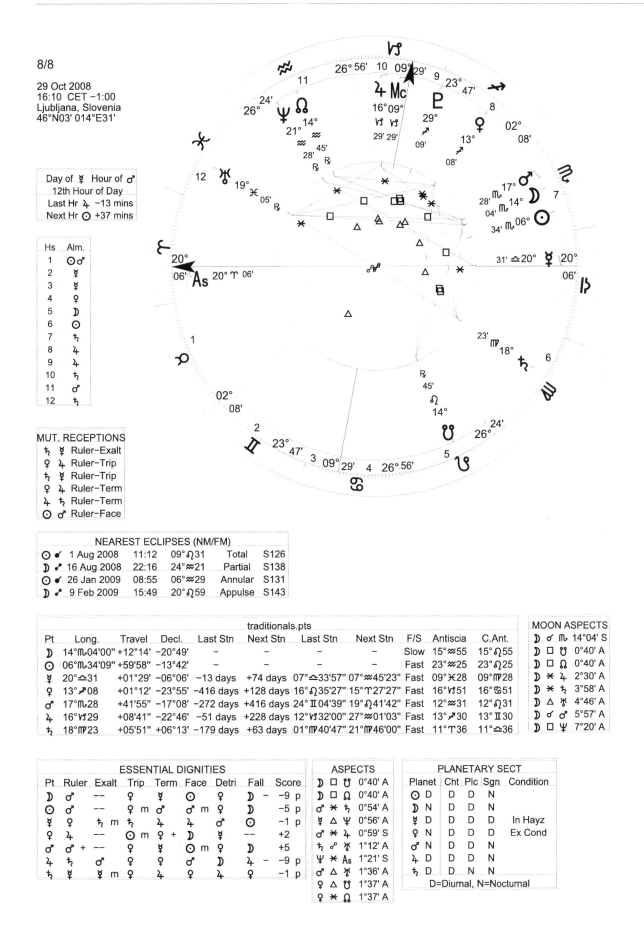

Day of ☿ Hour of ♂
12th Hour of Day
Last Hr ♃ −13 mins
Next Hr ☉ +37 mins

Hs	Alm.
1	☉ ♂
2	☿
3	☿
4	♀
5	☽
6	☉
7	♄
8	♃
9	♃
10	♄
11	♂
12	♄

MUT. RECEPTIONS

♄	☿	Ruler−Exalt
♀	♃	Ruler−Trip
♄	☿	Ruler−Trip
♀	♃	Ruler−Term
♃	♄	Ruler−Term
☉	♂	Ruler−Face

NEAREST ECLIPSES (NM/FM)					
☉ ☌	1 Aug 2008	11:12	09°♌31	Total	S126
☽ ☍	16 Aug 2008	22:16	24°♒21	Partial	S138
☉ ☌	26 Jan 2009	08:55	06°♒29	Annular	S131
☽ ☍	9 Feb 2009	15:49	20°♌59	Appulse	S143

traditionals.pts											MOON ASPECTS		
Pt	Long.	Travel	Decl.	Last Stn	Next Stn	Last Stn	Next Stn	F/S	Antiscia	C.Ant.			
☽	14°♏04'00"	+12°14'	−20°49'	–	–	–	–	Slow	15°♒55	15°♌55	☽ ☌ ♏	14°04' S	
☉	06°♏34'09"	+59'58"	−13°42'	–	–	–	–	Fast	23°♒25	23°♌25	☽ □ ☋	0°40' A	
☿	20°♎31	+01°29'	−06°06'	−13 days	+74 days	07°♎33'57"	07°♒45'23"	Fast	09°♓28	09°♏28	☽ □ ☊	0°40' A	
♀	13°♐08	+01°12'	−23°55'	−416 days	+128 days	16°♌35'27"	15°♈27'27"	Fast	16°♑51	16°♋51	☽ ✳ ♃	2°30' A	
♂	17°♏28	+41'55"	−17°08'	−272 days	+416 days	24°♊04'39"	19°♌41'42"	Fast	12°♒31	12°♌31	☽ ✳ ♄	3°58' A	
♃	16°♑29	+08'41"	−22°46'	−51 days	+228 days	12°♑32'00"	27°♒01'03"	Fast	13°♐30	13°♊30	☽ △ ⛢	4°46' A	
♄	18°♍23	+05'51"	+06°13'	−179 days	+63 days	01°♍40'47"	21°♍46'00"	Fast	11°♈36	11°♎36	☽ ☌ ♂	5°57' A	
											☽ □ ♆	7°20' A	

ESSENTIAL DIGNITIES									ASPECTS			PLANETARY SECT				
Pt	Ruler	Exalt	Trip	Term	Face	Detri	Fall	Score				Planet	Cht	Plc	Sgn	Condition
☽	♂	––	♀	☿	☉	♀	☽ −	−9 p	☽ □ ☋	0°40' A		☉	D	D	N	
☉	♂	––	♀ m	♂	♂ m	♀	☽	−5 p	☽ □ ☊	0°40' A		☽	N	D	N	
☿	♀	♄ m	♄	♃	♃	♂	☉	−1 p	♂ ✳ ♄	0°54' A		☿	D	D	D	In Hayz
♀	♃	––	☉ m	♀ +	☽	☿	––	+2	☿ △ ♆	0°56' A		♀	N	D	D	Ex Cond
♂	♂ +	––	♀	☿	☉ m	♀	☽	+5	♂ ✳ ♃	0°59' S		♂	N	D	N	
♃	♄	♂	♀	♀	♂	☽	♃ −	−9 p	♄ ☍ ⛢	1°12' A		♃	D	D	N	
♄	☿	♂ m	♀	♃	♀	♃	♀	−1 p	♆ ✳ As	1°21' S		♄	D	D	N	
									♂ △ ⛢	1°36' A			D=Diurnal, N=Nocturnal			
									♀ △ ☋	1°37' A						
									♀ ✳ ☊	1°37' A						

8/9: WILL MY FATHER GET WELL AND BE ABLE TO WALK AGAIN?

12 October 2008 at 12:58 p.m. (12:58), Kranj, Slovenia
Hour ruler: Mars

A former student sent me an email saying that a couple of days ago, on October 9, her father who was nearly 90 years old, suffered a stroke. She cast a horary chart for the above question herself, but since she wasn't sure how to go about it, she sent me the horary data and asked if I could delineate the chart for her. She wrote that her father was now in hospital, at an intensive care unit in the vascular department, holding onto life by means of life-saving devices. She had not yet received the doctors' opinion.

Let's see the chart! Her father is shown by H4 with its cusp in Aries, making Mars his ruler. This planet is also the hour ruler – a nice "parallel" with the subject matter of the horary chart! Mars is placed in Scorpio in H10 which is the derived H7 of doctors, reflecting the fact that he was then in his doctors' hands. But even so, Mars is the most dignified planet in the chart. Angular and in its own sign - this alone shows the father to be strong and resilient, and because Mars is not afflicted and is even fortified by an applying sextile to Jupiter in H1, I judged that he'd soon be back on his own two feet. H1 is the derived H10 for the father (10/4), and since H10 rules medication, this will obviously do him good and help him recover.

But his derived H6 (radix H9, 6/4) has Saturn on its cusp, and this made me think that his illness is not to be taken lightly. Besides, Mercury, its dispositor and H9 ruler, is retrograde, suggesting the possibility of a recurring medical condition. (You'll notice that the Moon is on a Mercury degree by monomoiria, making this planet even more important.) The Moon separates from Saturn (by opposition), but it applies directly to Uranus, the natural ruler of strokes. This points to a possibility of another stroke, especially because Uranus is retrograde, suggesting a recurring condition. On top of these worrying indications, the Moon applies to inconjunct the Sun which in turn applies to inconjunct Uranus. These aspects are all the more important because the Sun co-rules the father by virtue of being co-almuten of H4. The Sun is specifically related to the heart, indicating his fragile heart which is obviously at risk of being hit by another stroke. The Sun is also essentially weak (in its fall) which is certainly not helpful.

We therefore have a mixture of a strong, resilient and muscular body (dignified Mars) and a weak, failing heart (afflicted Sun).

In my reply, I wrote that her father was obviously in a very good physical condition, fit and strong enough to be able to walk again soon. Unfortunately, though, his heart is weak and there is even a possibility of another stroke which could happen in about a month - possibly a year. (I judged this by a 1-degree orb, the Moon being in a cadent house and a mutable sign. Obviously, the most probable unit would be a year, but as the aspect is a conjunction with a retrograde planet involved, I though a month more probable.)

On 2 December my student called to say that her father suffered another stroke on 28 November. It was not as severe as the previous one, she said, but he tumbled down and hurt his hip. While walking, I asked? Yes, she said. Soon after the first stroke, he was back on his own two feet! He occasionally used a crutch, but generally he was able to walk without any help.

Calculation shows that a month and a half elapsed from 12 October to 28 November. My timing was therefore not totally accurate, but looking at the transits on the day of the stroke, we can see that Mars, the father's significator, reached an exact sextile with Mercury in the horary chart, and thus activated the indicated relapse. What's more, if we move MC forward by 46/47 degrees, the number of days that elapsed till the stroke, we get to the 8th degree of Sagittarius, the degree of Mars on the day of the stroke.

There is another timing indication, involving the Moon. As we know, Moon is the primary "timer"! Move it 47 degrees (the exact number of days elapsing until the second stroke) from 18.5 Pisces and we get to 5.5 Taurus where it forms an exact opposition with Mars, the father's ruler. The Moon's role in timing never ceases to fascinate me!

8/9

12 Oct 2008
12:58 CEDT −2:00
Kranj, Slovenia
46°N15' 014°E21'

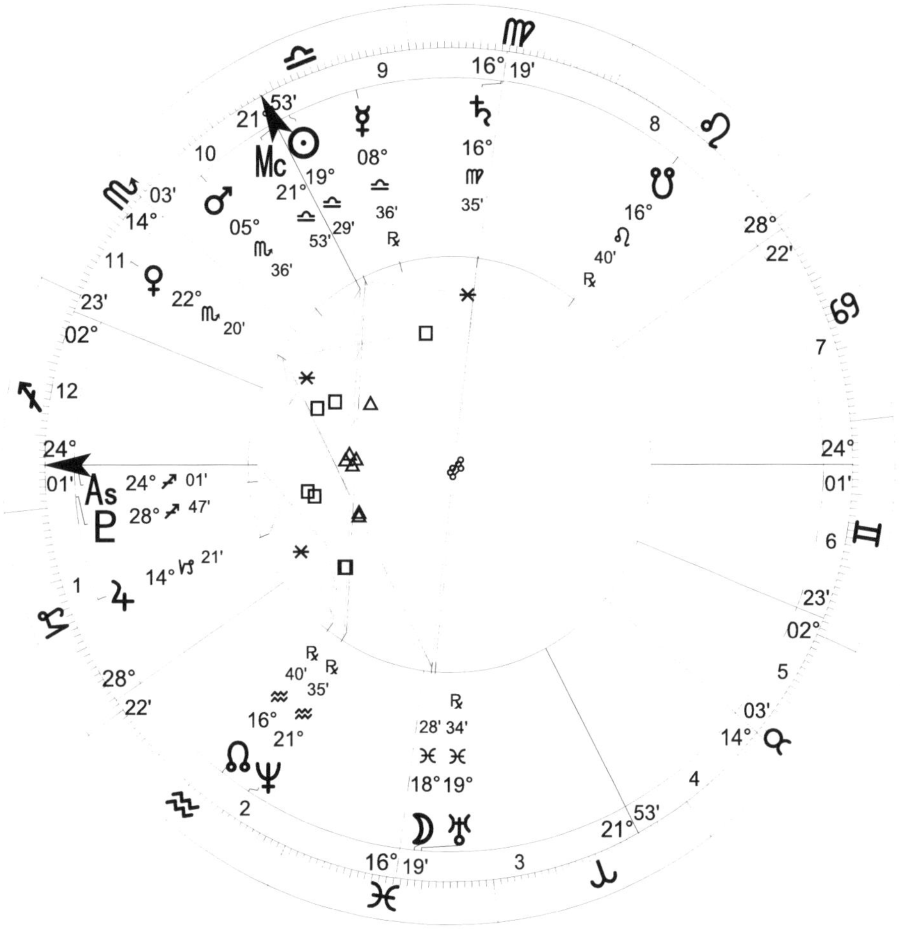

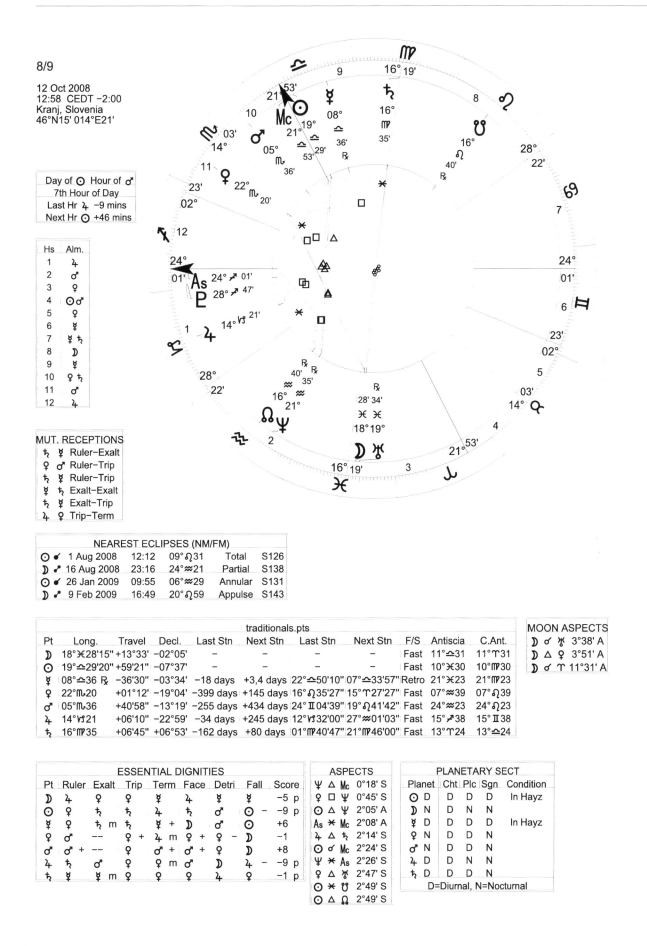

Day of ☉ Hour of ♂
7th Hour of Day
Last Hr ♃ −9 mins
Next Hr ☉ +46 mins

Hs	Alm.
1	♃
2	♂
3	♀
4	☉♂
5	♀
6	☿
7	☿ ♄
8	☽
9	☿
10	♀ ♄
11	♂
12	♃

MUT. RECEPTIONS		
♄	☿	Ruler–Exalt
♀	♂	Ruler–Trip
♄	☿	Ruler–Trip
☿	♄	Exalt–Exalt
♄	☿	Exalt–Trip
♃	♀	Trip–Term

NEAREST ECLIPSES (NM/FM)					
☉ ☌	1 Aug 2008	12:12	09°♌31	Total	S126
☽ ☍	16 Aug 2008	23:16	24°♒21	Partial	S138
☉ ☌	26 Jan 2009	09:55	06°♒29	Annular	S131
☽ ☍	9 Feb 2009	16:49	20°♌59	Appulse	S143

traditionals.pts

Pt	Long.	Travel	Decl.	Last Stn	Next Stn	Last Stn	Next Stn	F/S	Antiscia	C.Ant.
☽	18°♓28'15"	+13°33'	−02°05'	–	–	–	–	Fast	11°♎31	11°♈31
☉	19°♎29'20"	+59'21"	−07°37'	–	–	–	–	Fast	10°♓30	10°♍30
☿	08°♎36 ℞	−36'30"	−03°34'	−18 days	+3,4 days	22°♎50'10"	07°♎33'57"	Retro	21°♓23	21°♍23
♀	22°♏20	+01°12'	−19°04'	−399 days	+145 days	16°♌35'27"	15°♈27'27"	Fast	07°♒39	07°♌39
♂	05°♏36	+40'58"	−13°19'	−255 days	+434 days	24°♊04'39"	19°♌41'42"	Fast	24°♒23	24°♌23
♃	14°♑21	+06'10"	−22°59'	−34 days	+245 days	12°♑32'00"	27°♒01'03"	Fast	15°♐38	15°♊38
♄	16°♍35	+06'45"	+06°53'	−162 days	+80 days	01°♍40'47"	21°♍46'00"	Fast	13°♈24	13°♎24

MOON ASPECTS			
☽	☌	♅	3°38' A
☽	△	♀	3°51' A
☽	☌	♈	11°31' A

ESSENTIAL DIGNITIES

Pt	Ruler	Exalt	Trip	Term	Face	Detri	Fall	Score
☽	♃	♀	♀	☿	♃	☿	☿	−5 p
☉	♀	♄	♄	♃	♄	♂	☉ −	−9 p
☿	♀	♄ m	♄	☿ +	☽	♂	☉	+6
♀	♂	--	♀ +	♃ m	♀ +	♀ −	☽	−1
♂	♂ +	--	♀	♂ +	♂ +	♀	☽	+8
♃	♄	♂	♀	♀ m	♂	☽	♃ −	−9 p
♄	☿	☿ m	♀	♀	♀	♃	♀	−1 p

ASPECTS			
♆	△	Mc	0°18' S
♀	□	♆	0°45' S
☉	△	♆	2°05' A
As	⚹	Mc	2°08' A
♃	△	♄	2°14' S
☉	☌	Mc	2°24' S
♆	⚹	As	2°26' S
♀	△	♅	2°47' S
☉	⚹	☋	2°49' S
☉	△	☊	2°49' S

PLANETARY SECT

Planet	Cht	Plc	Sgn	Condition
☉ D	D	D	D	In Hayz
☽ N	D	N	N	
☿ D	D	D	D	In Hayz
♀ N	D	D	N	
♂ N	D	D	N	
♃ D	D	N	N	
♄ D	D	D	N	

D=Diurnal, N=Nocturnal

8/10: WILL SONIA GET WELL?

4 September 2008 at 9:44 p.m. (21:44), Ljubljana, Slovenia
Hour ruler: Jupiter

Sonia (a fictitious name) was a good friend (and neighbour) of my parents-in-law. I asked the question because she had an ovarian cancer. Because we were not in any specific relationship, it seemed appropriate that I place her in H1 which represents any (undefined) third party in cases when the querent's own situation is not the subject matter of the question. I could employ derived houses, but this could get too complicated. When undecided about the choice of a significator, it always pays to take the simple route – especially if the chosen significator fits the description of the quesited.

The ascendant is in Taurus, Sonia's Sun sign, so she's ruled by Venus which adequately describes her as friendly, charming and artistically inclined. Venus is in H6 of illness which also fits. The Moon is her co-significator and is even more important in this chart by virtue of conjuncting an angle. The sign involved is Scorpio, associated with the genital organs, and this placement of the Moon (essentially debilitated and angular) well describes a woman suffering from an ovarian cancer.

At the time of the question, Sonja had long been ill, so the chances of her recovery were slim. The chart confirmed my fear that the disease would prove fatal. Let's see why!

Added to the poor condition of the Moon is the precarious placement of Venus, her significator. Although in Libra, its domicile and therefore essentially strong, it's in the unfortunate H6 (of disease) and applies by conjunction to the malevolent Mars. In the context of the question, this planet shows her doctors (Mars rules H7), but it's in detriment and peregrine, suggesting that they were not able to cure her. But Mars also co-rules her disease, by virtue of being placed in H6. The conjunction of her significator with such a debilitated malefic indicates that her condition is getting worse. (Remember that an essentially weak planet in a horary chart shows a dangerous and serious disease!)

Mercury, the main ruler of her disease (H6), reaches Mars before Venus, so that Mars actually collects their lights. All the three planets apply to square Jupiter, the ruler of H8 of death, along with the Moon which applies to it by a sextile. Both Sonja's significators applying to H8 ruler show that, unfortunately, for her there's no hope.

You will notice that the result would be the same if I took H7 to represent her. In this case, her ruler would be Mars, conjunct Mercury, the derived H8 ruler, and the illness would be Jupiter to which Mars applies by a square, showing that the illness persists – and actually ends with her death. As suggested by the Moon's sextile to Jupiter, her transition was calm and peaceful. If you wonder why this sextile of the Moon with the benefic Jupiter doesn't make for her recovery, know that Jupiter is an accidental malefic (by ruling the unfortunate H8 and H12); besides, the Moon applies to it from its fall, while Jupiter is in its own fall and in the Moon's detriment, so that they meet in a weak or "lifeless" situation.

Sonja died on 27 December 2008. This is 114 days or 16 weeks and two days after the question. Does the chart show that? We can see that between Venus and Mars, the malefic to which Venus bodily applies, there are exactly 4 degrees and 9 minutes which, translated into time units (4 months or 16 weeks) nearly exactly corresponds to the time that elapsed until her death. This is another proof that the patient was properly placed in H1! By forwarding the Moon 114 degrees, we get to 6 Pisces – an exact inconjunct with Venus.

It is also interesting to note that on the day of her death Venus reached the 22nd degree of Aquarius which is the degree of Neptune in the chart, and that Neptune on that day was at exactly the same degree and minute as in the horary chart! This planet of physical weakness but enhanced spirituality had in the meantime moved forward for a good degree, then turned retrograde, and on 27 December (the day of her transition) moved back to 22°18' of Aquarius. The Sun (the natural significator of life and vitality), on the other hand, reached an exact square with horary Venus, which further confirms the loss of power that had befallen Sonia on that day.

8/10

4 Sep 2008
21:44 CEDT −2:00
Ljubljana, Slovenia
46°N03' 014°E31'

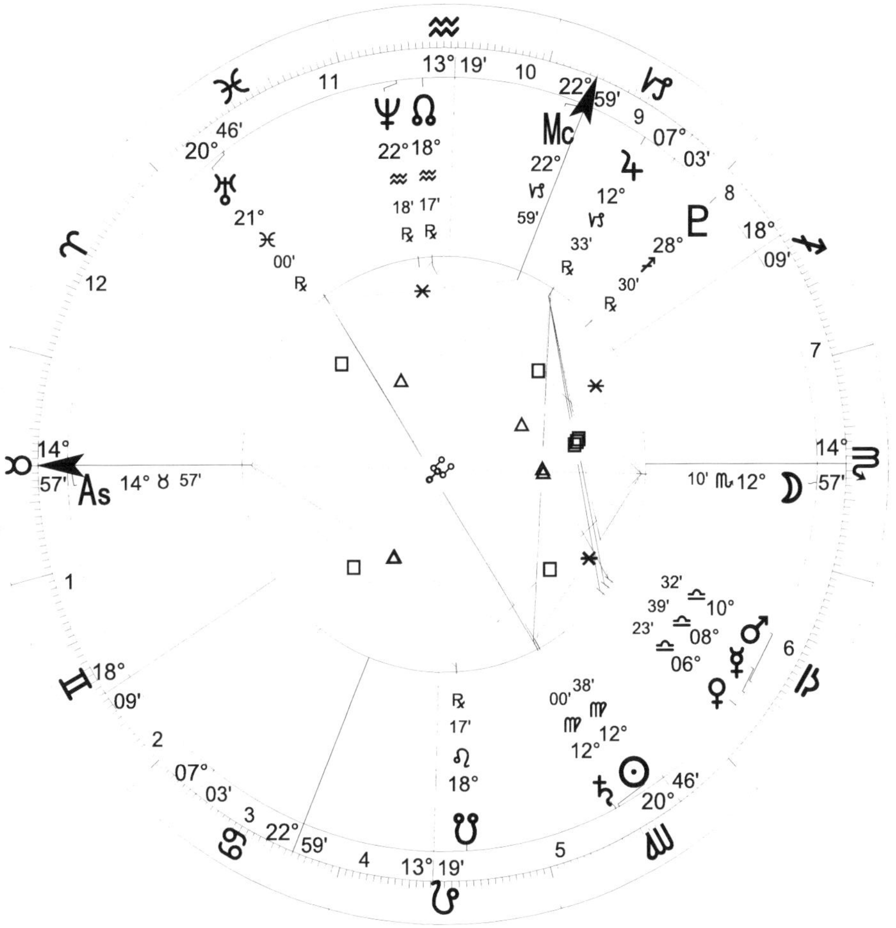

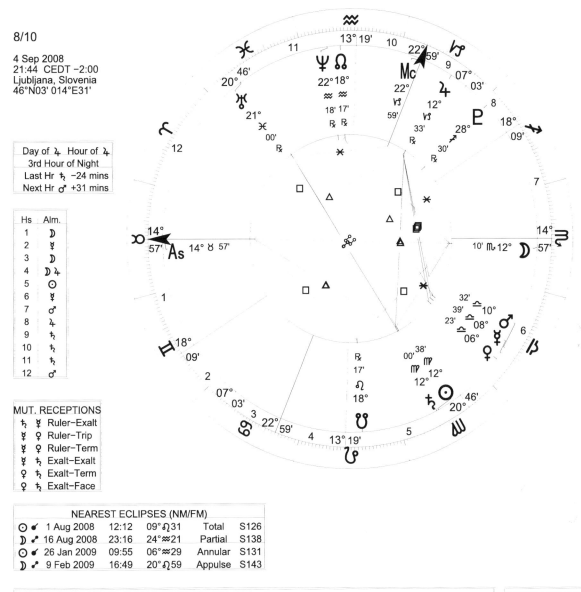

Day of ♃ Hour of ♃
3rd Hour of Night
Last Hr ♄ −24 mins
Next Hr ♂ +31 mins

Hs	Alm.
1	☽
2	☿
3	☽
4	☽ ♃
5	☉
6	☿
7	♂
8	♃
9	♄
10	♄
11	♄
12	♂

MUT. RECEPTIONS		
♄	☿	Ruler–Exalt
☿	♀	Ruler–Trip
☿	♀	Ruler–Term
☿	♄	Exalt–Exalt
♀	♄	Exalt–Term
♀	♄	Exalt–Face

NEAREST ECLIPSES (NM/FM)					
☉ ☌	1 Aug 2008	12:12	09°♌31	Total	S126
☽ ☍	16 Aug 2008	23:16	24°♒21	Partial	S138
☉ ☌	26 Jan 2009	09:55	06°♒29	Annular	S131
☽ ☍	9 Feb 2009	16:49	20°♌59	Appulse	S143

traditionals.pts

Pt	Long.	Travel	Decl.	Last Stn	Next Stn	Last Stn	Next Stn	F/S	Antiscia	C.Ant.
☽	12°♏10'24"	+12°12'	−20°25'	–	–	–	–	Slow	17°♒49	17°♌49
☉	12°♍38'07"	+58'10"	+06°49'	–	–	–	–	Slow	17°♈21	17°♎21
☿	08°♎39	+01°11'	−04°57'	−77 days	+19 days	12°♊58'46"	22°♎50'10"	Fast	21°♓20	21°♍20
♀	06°♎23	+01°13'	−01°39'	−362 days	+182 days	16°♌35'27"	15°♈27'27"	Fast	23°♓36	23°♍36
♂	10°♎32	+38'59"	−03°45'	−217 days	+471 days	24°♊04'39"	19°♌41'42"	Fast	19°♓27	19°♍27
♃	12°♑33 ℞	−00'38"	−23°08'	−118 days	+3,4 days	22°♑22'06"	12°♑32'00"	Retro	17°♐26	17°♊26
♄	12°♍00	+07'33"	+08°36'	−124 days	+117 days	01°♍40'47"	21°♍46'00"	Fast	17°♈59	17°♎59

MOON ASPECTS			
☽	☌	♏	12°10' S
☽	⚹	♄	0°29' S
☽	⚹	☉	0°19' A
☽	⚹	♃	0°28' A
☽	□	☋	6°06' A
☽	□	☊	6°06' A

ESSENTIAL DIGNITIES

Pt	Ruler	Exalt	Trip	Term	Face	Detri	Fall	Score
☽	♂	--	♂	☿	☉	♀	☽ −	−9 p
☉	☿	☿	☽	♀	♀	♃	♀	−5 p
☿	♀	♄ m	☿ +	☿ +	☽	♂	☉	+9
♀	♀ +	♄	☿	☿	☽	♂	☉	+5
♂	♀	♄	☿	☿	♄	♂ −	☉	−10 p
♃	♄	♂	☽	♃ +	♂	☽	♃ −	−2
♄	☿	☿ m	☽	♀	♀	♃	♀	−1 p

ASPECTS			
☉	△	♃	0°05' S
☽	⚹	☉	0°19' A
☽	⚹	♃	0°28' A
☽	⚹	♄	0°29' S
♃	△	♄	0°32' A
☉	☌	♄	1°47' S
♅	⚹	Mc	1°58' S
♂	□	♃	2°00' A
☉	△	As	2°19' S
♃	△	As	2°24' S

PLANETARY SECT

Planet		Cht	Plc	Sgn	Condition
☉	D	N	N	N	Ex Cond
☽	N	N	D	N	
☿	N	N	D	D	
♀	N	N	D	D	
♂	N	N	D	D	
♃	D	N	N	N	Ex Cond
♄	D	N	D	N	

D=Diurnal, N=Nocturnal

LEGAL QUESTIONS

SIGNIFICATORS

The querent (the plaintiff or the defendant) is ruled by the ascendant, its ruler, the Moon and any planet(s) in H1, while the opposing party is shown by the descendant, its ruler and any planet/s in H7.

However, if the querent is someone who plays merely the role of an observer and is not personally involved in the case, we give the plaintiff H1 and the defendant H7.

The meanings of houses in legal questions:
- H1 = the querent
- H2 = the querent's witnesses/supporters
- H3 = the lawyer of the opposing party
- H7 = the opponent
- H8 = the opponent's witnesses/supporters
- H9 = the querent's lawyer
- H10 = the judge
- H11 = jury
- H12 = prison

Natural significators in legal disputes:
- Moon = the jury
- Mercury = lawyers (Lilly) or evidence (B.Watters)
- Jupiter = the judge

Mars also plays an important role as it is the natural significator of competitiveness, fighting spirit and conquest. *Should I sue this person?* If Mars is strong in the chart, go for it! A weak Mars, on the other hand, lowers the possibility of winning. Filing a lawsuit (or attacking others in other ways) in a Mars retrograde period doesn't bode well for the plaintiff.

It's always good to check what kind of links Mars (as a natural significator) has with the significators of both parties involved in a dispute.

In charts relating to court procedures dealing with violence, Mars can also represent the bully or the act of cruelty/aggression that he is supposed to have committed. In certain cases, this this role can also be played by Pluto.

THE PROCEDURE

In a very general sense, the winner of a legal dispute is found by calculating the essential and accidental dignities of both parties. The winner is that party whose significator/s is/are stronger. The conclusion/result/answer can sometimes be easily achieved, but when in doubt, other interpretative rules must be applied.

Below is the summary of Lilly's rules for interpretation of legal disputes charts. (CA, pages 369 and 372-376). They are a little old-fashioned but can be easily adapted to modern cimrcumstances. I must stress that no rule is 100% reliable in itself! For the final judgment, a thorough examination of all the factors is needed.

WHO WILL WIN A LEGAL DISPUTE?

If the rulers of H1 and H7 are both angular, there will be no winner.

See if a significator is in an aspect with a malefic planet in a cadent house – that party will lose.

If both significators are aspected by malefics, both parties will lose more than gain by the dispute; in other words, none will achieve justice.

If one significator is strong and the other weak, and if the strong one is not in a cadent house and in an aspect with malefic, and if the weak one is not essentially dignified and in an aspect with a benefic, the party ruled by the stronger significator will win.

If the ruler of H1 is in conjunction with the ruler of the H7, or in a sextile or trine with a mutual reception, the two sides will make up or reach an agreement without the mediation of the court. However, if only one significator receives another, the two parties will agree without a lawsuit, but not without the intervention of a third party. These intermediaries will be friends or acquaintances of the one whose significator receives the significator of the other party.

If the rulers of H1 and H7 are in a square or opposition with mutual reception, or in a sextile or trine without reception, they will reach an agreement, but not without an initial legal dispute. An acceptable solution will be proposed by the one whose significator is quicker and/or is located in the domicile of the opponent's significator. The agreement will be more solid if the planets receive each other (in any of their dignities). If a quicker/lighter planet applies to the slower/heavier and does not receive it, while the heavier planet receives the lighter one, then this heavier planet represents the person who will propose the agreement.

Next we look at whether the H10 ruler (the judge) is in the aspect with the ruler of H1 or H7. If the H1 ruler "hurries" into a conjunction with the H7 ruler, or vice versa (that is, the H7 ruler to conjunction with the H1 ruler) and the H10 ruler disables their meeting by means of a frustration, they will probably not agree earlier than in the court.

We must also see if the Moon or any planet translates light between both significators; if so, then a third party will mediate between them, even if the court proceedings are already pending.

Then we look at which of the two significators is stronger (by calculating their essential and accidental strengths), and judge the stronger party to win. The stronger is usually the one placed in an angular house and essentially dignified. If such a planet receives another planet, this shows that the person represented by it has friends who will help him.

If we find that the two parties will be reconciled, the proposal will come from the one that is signified by a lighter planet.

If the H7 ruler is in H1, the querent will definitely win, and the opponent will be defeated. Similarly, if the H1 ruler is in H7, the opponent will win. This applies not only to legal disputes, but also to sport matches, quarrels and wars.

A retrograde significator shows that the person represented by this planet is weak and hesitant; he will deny the truth and argue that the opponent is wrong.

If the H1 ruler separates from the H7 ruler or vice versa, the court proceedings will be long and time consuming.

If the H1 ruler applies to an aspect with the Sun or the Moon, without prohibition or frustration, this is a good sign for the querent. Care is needed only in case of a conjunction with the Sun, because this is an affliction (combustion) - unless the planet is in the heart of the Sun (cazimi), as it is then strengthened. If, therefore, the H1 ruler aspects the Sun or the Moon, or is placed in Cancer or Leo, or if the Sun or the Moon are in H1, this gives power to the querent, but if the H7 ruler is so placed, the opponent is stronger.

THE JUDGE (CA, P. 374)

Is the H10 ruler direct and in any aspect with the significators? If so, the judge will act in accordance with the law and try to resolve the matter as soon as possible. However, if the ruler H10 is retrograde, he will delay or act inappropriately in some other way.

If the H1 ruler applies to an aspect with the H10 ruler, the querent will approach the judge with the matter and may even bribe him to judge in his favour.

If the H10 ruler receives the H2 ruler, the judge will be well paid, or he may even accept a bribe.

If the H10 ruler receives the H1 ruler, the judge will grant the querent's wish.

If the H10 ruler is a lighter planet than the H1 ruler and is in aspect with this planet, the judge will favour the querent, even if there will be no personal contact between them.

If the H7 ruler aspects the H10 ruler, the opponent will approach the judge; if the H10 ruler receives it, the judge will help him, but if this planet receives the H8 ruler, he will accept his bribe.

If the H10 ruler receives both significators, the judge will decide on the matter even before the actual court proceedings.

If the H10 ruler is in H10 and in its domicile, the judge will be fair, unless this planet is Saturn. However, if the H10 ruler is only in its triplicity or term, he will judge justly but will not really care for either side.

If a planet in H10 is not essentially dignified and is not in reception with the H10 ruler, neither party will be happy with the judge; they might fear him or want to replace him with another.

If the judge is ruled by Saturn, his decision will not be fair. If, in such a case, Jupiter, Venus, Sun, Mercury or the Moon are in any aspect with Saturn, except for an opposition, there will be rumors and allegations of his unfairness which will soon be refuted, but if the aspect be an opposition, the accusations will be more severe and it could be proven that the judge's decision was not correct. The scandal will be even greater if the planet opposing Saturn is Mars, unless Mars is in Capricorn.

If there are several planets in H1 and H2, the querent has more friends (supporters, witnesses), but if more planets are in H7 and H8, the support is more on the opponent's side.

If both significators are in an aspect with a third planet, this planet represents someone who mediates between them.

If the cusps of H1 and H7 are fixed, both sides are determined to win. In case of cardinal signs, the procedure will be short, but if those signs are mutable, the court case will drag on for a long time and possibly be taken from one court to another.

That side of the chart (east/west) which has more malefics in it will generally suffer more damage, prejudice and sorrow in the conflict.

9/1: WILL PK BE FOUND GUILTY OF MURDERING HIS WIFE?

12 April 1995 at 8:34 p.m. (20:34), Ljubljana, Slovenia
Hour ruler: Venus

I raised this question after having read the news of the forthcoming trial against PK, a young man who was accused of murdering his wife. He was supposed to have drowned her one August evening in 1994 while they were swimming in Lake Bled. Interrogations were held for two months and they attracted much public attention. The accused defended himself by claiming that the bruises which were found on the head of the deceased, were caused by involuntary movements of his foot while swimming by her side. Her head injuries were the only evidence as there were no witnesses. But some unpleasant facts spoke strongly against him: she was rich, he had a mistress (allegedly) and he purchased life insurance on her just a few days before her death. Besides, he wanted her body to be cremated only a day after her death, but her relatives prevented that. They requested an autopsy which revealed the head injuries.

I cast the chart for the above question and brought it to my regular horary class. It was only a day before the trial, and I used the chart to introduce principles behind the legal questions charts.

I am the querent, but since I'm asking as an independent and indifferent third party, the plaintiff is ruled by H1 while H7 stands for the accused. The descendant is in Taurus, ruled by Venus, but there are two almutens of the descendant, Venus and the Moon. Venus should be regarded as his main significator because it's also the hour ruler, while the Moon also stands for the jury – by virtue of being placed in H11, besides being the natural ruler of juries.

Venus as an eastern planet and in the terms and degree of Mercury (by monomoiria) describes him as a younger man of pleasant appearance and likeable manners, of pale complexion (Venus in Pisces) and dark hair (Venus conjunct Saturn). Venus is in the derived H11 (11/7), reflecting his strong hope for an acquittal. But its close applying conjunction with Saturn gives little hope that his wish could be granted. The two planets are in a separating square with Jupiter (Venus' dispositor!) which is placed in the derived H8 of death, while the Moon's last aspect, showing the past, was also a square with Jupiter. Moreover, Mars which could also stand for his dead wife (7/1), has just separated from a trine with Jupiter. Because Mars is also the natural significator of crime and murder and rules the derived H7, H8 and H12, the connection of his deceased wife with murder, death and secrets is clearly emphasized.

Mercury, the natural significator of evidence, is combust, peregrine and placed in the weak, cadent and unfortunate H6. This fully agrees with the purported lack of evidence which could help clarify the case.

The south node in his H1 indicates bad luck and potential loss. H10 (the judge) is occupied by Mars, ruling H1 and therefore standing for the prosecutors; this shows the judge to agree with the prosecution and suggests that (according to the hot nature of Mars) he/she probably hopes to promptly wind up the case. In favour of the prosecutors, of course, because Mars is in a strong mutual reception with the Sun (in Aries, Mars' sign), the main significator of the judge, showing their agreement, while none of these planets receives Venus, the significator of the defendant. The Sun is even in the detriment of Venus - a clear sign that the judge strongly disapproves of the defendant.

The jury is shown by the Moon which applies to oppose Venus, without reception, suggesting that the jurors are also against him. Venus applies to conjunct the restrictive, malignant Saturn, which together with the rest of indications suggests the obvious answer – PK would be found guilty. But for the final confirmation we can simply calculate the strengths of both significators. Mars (prosecution) scores (according to Lilly's system) 19 points while Venus (the accused) scores 9. This is another argument that the accused will be convicted. Finally, we can see that the Sun, the ruler of the derived H4 (end of the matter) is in the derived H12 of imprisonment, clearly showing the defendant's "destiny".

Having explained all of this to my students, one of them said that her intuition told her that the defendant would be acquitted. Many astrologers – beginners especially - like to praise themselves for strong intuition which supposedly helps them read charts. But the fact is that we astrologers can use intuition only after we have wholly mastered the theory! If an answer, arrived to by an astrologer's intuition, can't be justified by firm theoretical principles, what's all the theory worth? On the other hand, what's intuition worth if it doesn't bring consistent results? Only after many years of persistent hard work can astrologers develop that specific type of intuition which also distinguishes experts on other fields of knowledge - this is when you "feel" the truth simply because you get used

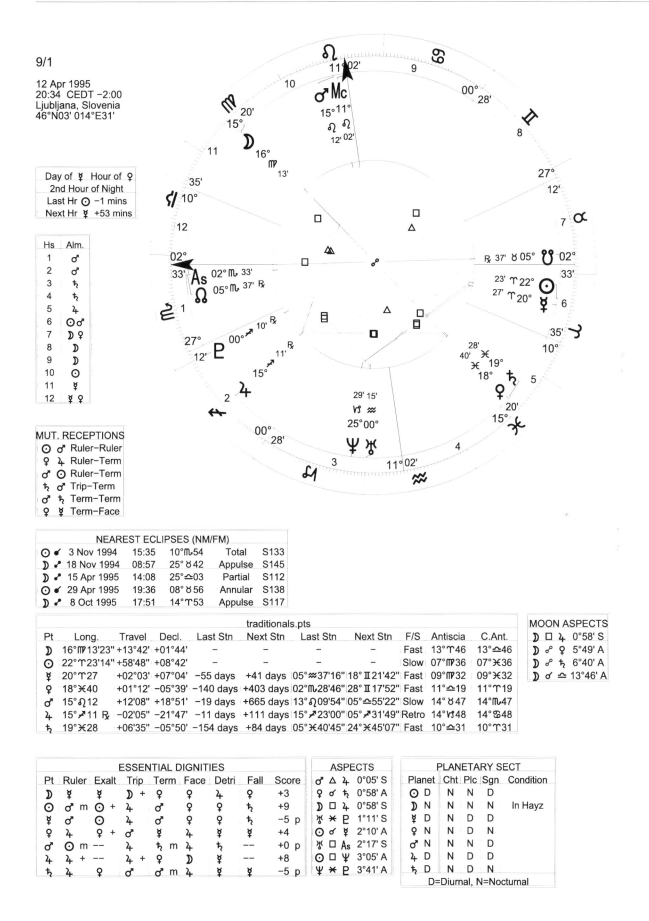

9/1

12 Apr 1995
20:34 CEDT −2:00
Ljubljana, Slovenia
46°N03' 014°E31'

Day of ☿	Hour of ♀
2nd Hour of Night	
Last Hr ☉ −1 mins	
Next Hr ☿ +53 mins	

Hs	Alm.
1	♂
2	♂
3	♄
4	♄
5	♃
6	☉♂
7	☽♀
8	☽
9	☽
10	☉
11	☿
12	☿♀

MUT. RECEPTIONS	
☉ ♂	Ruler−Ruler
♀ ♃	Ruler−Term
♂ ☉	Ruler−Term
♄ ♂	Trip−Term
♂ ♄	Term−Term
♀ ☿	Term−Face

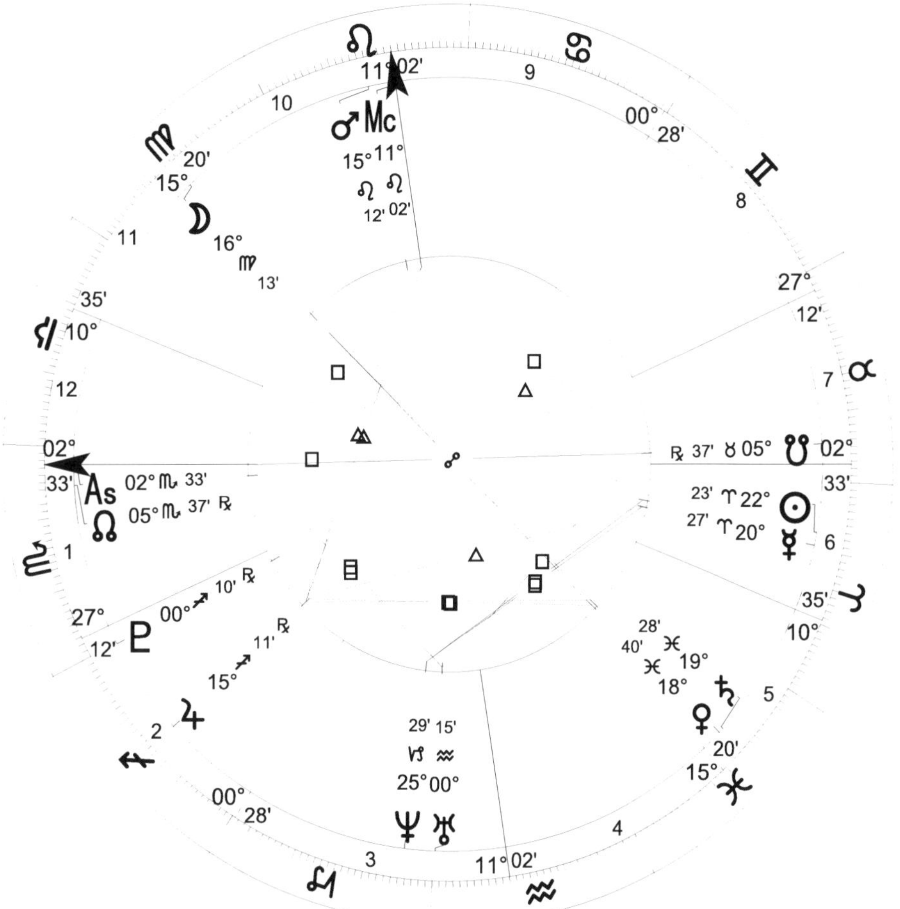

NEAREST ECLIPSES (NM/FM)					
☉ ☌	3 Nov 1994	15:35	10°♏54	Total	S133
☽ ☍	18 Nov 1994	08:57	25°♉42	Appulse	S145
☽ ☍	15 Apr 1995	14:08	25°♎03	Partial	S112
☉ ☌	29 Apr 1995	19:36	08°♉56	Annular	S138
☽ ☍	8 Oct 1995	17:51	14°♈53	Appulse	S117

traditionals.pts

Pt	Long.	Travel	Decl.	Last Stn	Next Stn	Last Stn	Next Stn	F/S	Antiscia	C.Ant.
☽	16°♍13'23"	+13°42'	+01°44'	–	–	–	–	Fast	13°♈46	13°♎46
☉	22°♈23'14"	+58'48"	+08°42'	–	–	–	–	Slow	07°♍36	07°♓36
☿	20°♈27	+02°03'	+07°04'	−55 days	+41 days	05°♒37'16"	18°♊21'42"	Fast	09°♍32	09°♓32
♀	18°♓40	+01°12'	−05°39'	−140 days	+403 days	02°♏28'46"	28°♊17'52"	Fast	11°♎19	11°♈19
♂	15°♌12	+12'08"	+18°51'	−19 days	+665 days	13°♌09'54"	05°♎55'22"	Slow	14°♉47	14°♏47
♃	15°♐11 ℞	−02'05"	−21°47'	−11 days	+111 days	15°♐23'00"	05°♐31'49"	Retro	14°♑48	14°♋48
♄	19°♓28	+06'35"	−05°50'	−154 days	+84 days	05°♓40'45"	24°♓45'07"	Fast	10°♎31	10°♈31

MOON ASPECTS	
☽ □ ♃	0°58' S
☽ ☍ ♀	5°49' A
☽ ☍ ♄	6°40' A
☽ ☌ ♎	13°46' A

ESSENTIAL DIGNITIES

Pt	Ruler	Exalt	Trip	Term	Face	Detri	Fall	Score
☽	☿	☿	☽ +	♀	♀	♃	♀	+3
☉	♂ m	☉ +	♃	♂	♀	♀	♄	+9
☿	♂	☉	♃	♂	♀	♀	♄	−5 p
♀	♃	♀ +	♂	☿	♃	☿	☿	+4
♂	☉ m	--	♃	♄ m	♃	♄	--	+0 p
♃	♃ +	--	♃ +	♀	☽	☿	--	+8
♄	♃	♀	♂	♂ m	♃	☿	☿	−5 p

ASPECTS	
♂ △ ♃	0°05' S
♀ ☌ ♄	0°58' A
☽ □ ♃	0°58' S
♅ ✶ ♇	1°11' S
☉ ☌ ☿	2°10' A
♅ □ As	2°17' S
☉ □ ♆	3°05' A
♆ ✶ ♇	3°41' A

PLANETARY SECT

Planet		Cht	Plc	Sgn	Condition
☉	D	N	N	D	
☽	N	N	N	N	In Hayz
☿	D	N	D	D	
♀	N	N	D	N	
♂	N	N	N	D	
♃	D	N	D	D	
♄	D	N	D	N	

D=Diurnal, N=Nocturnal

to quickly scan all the data so that you feel like it was intuition which brought you the answer, when it was in fact conscious reasoning. This is the only type of intuition that is dependable and that I personally acknowledge in astrology. My strong advice to astrologers, especially to beginners, is: do not rely on intuition because it can do you more harm than good!

Anyway. On 14 April 1995, PK was found guilty of murdering his wife, and was sentenced to nine years in prison.

9/2: WILL JOHN APPEAL AGAINST THE COURT RULING?

15 September 2006 at 5:37 p.m. (17:37), Ljubljana, Slovenia
Hour ruler: Saturn

I raised this question after having received the court decision that John (a fictitious name) who had taken me to court on the charge that I owed him a large sum of money, was not justified in his claim. John was a construction worker who - contrary to our contract agreement - raised the price of his service to me in the middle of the construction process. He now had to pay all the litigation costs too, of course, which were substantial. Would he appeal against the court ruling, I wondered?

I'm shown by Saturn, the H1 ruler, which looks "helpless" in the house of my opponent (H7) and in the sign of its detriment (Leo). This is quite appropriate since I was not in control of this situation; all I could do was to sit and wait! This placement gives the power of acting to my opponent, but that's logical according to the nature of the question. Saturn is also the hour ruler, and being a malefic by nature, the question is obviously about some kind of a power struggle.

John is shown by the Sun, the H7 ruler, placed in his own H1. The fact that the Sun applies by a square to Pluto and by a conjunction to the south node, shows him to be worried and very much concerned about his safety and "survival". The Sun is also peregrine so his path is clearly insecure. The debilitated Saturn in H7, although ruling me, also acts as his own co-significator (by virtue of being placed in his H1). This combination of planetary indications predicts his potential loss, exhaustion and bad luck. He would be advised against an appeal! But the question is – what will he do?

His H1 is packed, and, theoretically, all the planets in this house can be considered his co-significators. Mercury in particular because it disposits the Sun, his main significator. Mercury is on the cusp of H8 (the derived H2, his money), in a very exact applying conjunction with Mars, the natural significator of anger and conflict – and also the ruler of the radical H2, my money. It is clear, therefore, that John is very angry and definitely set on getting my money - or in other words, to fight on. He's also fearful of losing more money since he had to pay the litigation costs for the first trial, but the intention of his appeal is evident. This is confirmed by the rigidity of the AS/DS axis which shows perseverance, stubbornness and resistance to change – in this case, the resistance to accept one's lot.

Although the answer is quite obvious (yes, he would appeal), let us observe the chart in a little bit more detail. There's one more planet in H7 - Venus, the radix H3 ruler which is the derived H9 (9/7) and therefore stands for his lawyer while also ruling his H2. Its opposition to Uranus in my H1 shows the threat of losing more money, or/ and the necessity to repay the court costs – the problem with which he was currently faced. But the Moon which shows the course of events, applies directly to sextile Venus, confirming that he'd contact his lawyer and take the case further. This is confirmed by the application of Jupiter (in H9 of legal matters) to square Saturn (me and him), showing the litigation to be continued.

And so it was. I soon received my lawyer's letter that John had appealed to the court decision.

But was this a wise decision? Although my question did not in itself relate to the (possible) new trial, as I was only interested if he'd take the case further, there are indications in the chart as per advisability of such action. Beside the already mentioned precarious condition of his rulers, see that his lawyer (Venus) is in its fall (Virgo), under the Sun's beams and in a close applying opposition with Uranus. This suggests that my opponent's lawyer did not advise his client wisely. More on p. ... which discusses my new question related to the new process.

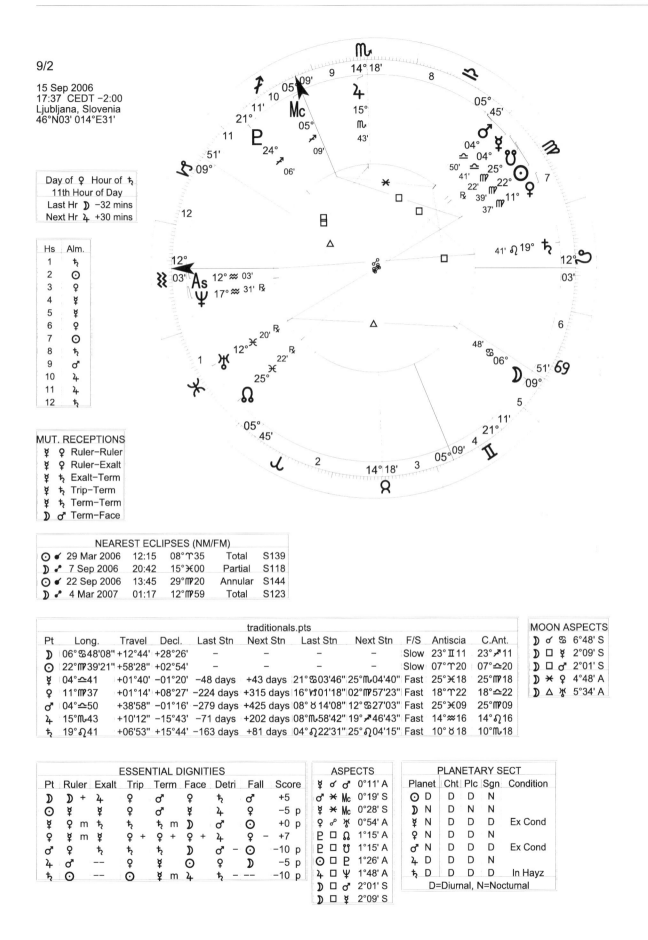

9/2

15 Sep 2006
17:37 CEDT −2:00
Ljubljana, Slovenia
46°N03' 014°E31'

Day of ♀ Hour of ♄
11th Hour of Day
Last Hr ☽ −32 mins
Next Hr ♃ +30 mins

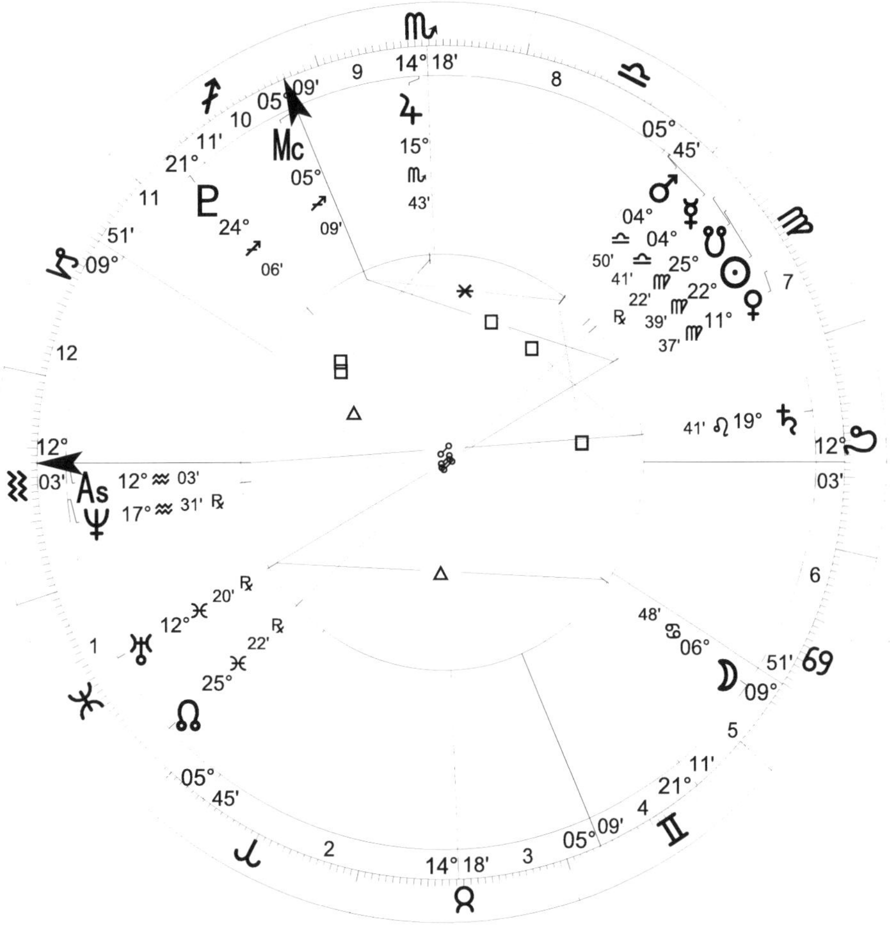

Hs	Alm.
1	♄
2	☉
3	♀
4	☿
5	☿
6	♀
7	☉
8	♄
9	♂
10	♃
11	♃
12	♄

MUT. RECEPTIONS	
☿ ♀	Ruler-Ruler
☿ ♀	Ruler-Exalt
☿ ♄	Exalt-Term
☿ ♄	Trip-Term
☿ ♄	Term-Term
☽ ♂	Term-Face

NEAREST ECLIPSES (NM/FM)					
☉ ●	29 Mar 2006	12:15	08°♈35	Total	S139
☽ ☍	7 Sep 2006	20:42	15°♓00	Partial	S118
☉ ●	22 Sep 2006	13:45	29°♍20	Annular	S144
☽ ☍	4 Mar 2007	01:17	12°♍59	Total	S123

traditionals.pts

Pt	Long.	Travel	Decl.	Last Stn	Next Stn	Last Stn	Next Stn	F/S	Antiscia	C.Ant.
☽	06°♋48'08"	+12°44'	+28°26'	–	–	–	–	Slow	23°♊11	23°♐11
☉	22°♍39'21"	+58'28"	+02°54'	–	–	–	–	Slow	07°♈20	07°♎20
☿	04°♎41	+01°40'	−01°20'	−48 days	+43 days	21°♋03'46"	25°♏04'40"	Fast	25°♓18	25°♍18
♀	11°♍37	+01°14'	+08°27'	−224 days	+315 days	16°♑01'18"	02°♍57'23"	Fast	18°♈22	18°♎22
♂	04°♎50	+38'58"	−01°16'	−279 days	+425 days	08°♉14'08"	12°♋27'03"	Fast	25°♓09	25°♍09
♃	15°♏43	+10'12"	−15°43'	−71 days	+202 days	08°♏58'42"	19°♐46'43"	Fast	14°♒16	14°♌16
♄	19°♌41	+06'53"	+15°44'	−163 days	+81 days	04°♌22'31"	25°♌04'15"	Fast	10°♉18	10°♏18

MOON ASPECTS			
☽ ☌	♋	6°48'	S
☽ □	☿	2°09'	S
☽ □	♂	2°01'	S
☽ ✶	♀	4°48'	A
☽ △	♅	5°34'	A

ESSENTIAL DIGNITIES

Pt	Ruler	Exalt	Trip	Term	Face	Detri	Fall	Score
☽	☽ +	♃	♀	♂	♀	♄	♂	+5
☉	☿	☿	♀	♂	☿	♃	♀	−5 p
☿	♀ m	♄	♄	♄ m	☽	♂	☉	+0 p
♀	☿ m	☿	♀ +	♀ +	♀ +	♃	♀ −	+7
♂	♀	♄	♄	♄	☽	♂ −	☉	−10 p
♃	♂	--	♀	☿	☉	♀	☽	−5 p
♄	☉	--	☉	☿ m	♃	♄ −	--	−10 p

ASPECTS		
☿ ☌ ♂	0°11'	A
♂ ✶ Mc	0°19'	S
☿ ✶ Mc	0°28'	S
♀ ☍ ♅	0°54'	A
♇ □ ☊	1°15'	A
♇ □ ☋	1°15'	A
☉ □ ♇	1°26'	A
♃ □ ♆	1°48'	A
☽ □ ♂	2°01'	S
☽ □ ☿	2°09'	S

PLANETARY SECT

Planet		Cht	Plc	Sgn	Condition
☉	D	D	D	N	
☽	N	D	N	N	
☿	N	D	D	D	Ex Cond
♀	N	D	D	N	
♂	N	D	D	D	Ex Cond
♃	D	D	D	N	
♄	D	D	D	D	In Hayz

D=Diurnal, N=Nocturnal

9/3: WILL JOHN SUCCEED WITH HIS COURT APPEAL?

4 October 2006 at 8:26 a.m., Ljubljana, Slovenia
Hour ruler: Moon

As for the subject matter, this case is the continuation of the previous one (9/2). When I received my lawyer's letter that John requested a retrial, I immediately raised a new question: Will John's appeal succeed?

A quick glance into the chart reassured me, since it clearly showed that this was not going to happen.

Hour ruler is the Moon which co-rules H9 (legal affairs). It doesn't agree with the ascendant, but the fact that the Moon is closely related to the subject matter of the question, adds to the validity of the chart.

I am shown by Venus, ruler of H1, and Saturn, which is co-almuten of the ascending degree, while John is ruled by Mars and the Sun, co-almuten of the descending degree. The judge has two significators: the Sun, ruler of H10, and Saturn which occupies H10. To these, Jupiter can be added as the natural ruler of judges.

We therefore have an interesting mix of significators which must be carefully studied as to the various roles they play in the chart. The connection of our almutens with the main rulers of the judge is fascinating, but to avoid confusion, I decided to give the main say to Venus for me and to Mars for John.

Both Venus and Mars are in conjunction with the Sun – the judge. Their combust state clearly reflects the fact that we were both powerless or at the mercy of the judge. Saturn in H10 and in the fixed sign of Leo also rules H4 (end of the matter) which led me to think that the judge might consider the original verdict final or, in other words, that he'd be averse to another trial. This is confirmed by the position of all the three main significators in H12 which is the derived H4 (4/9, end of the matter for legal proceedings).

See that Saturn (the judge) is in detriment, but in direct motion, suggesting that there'll be no delays in the proceedings. A debilitated Saturn in H10 might be perceived as a judge who is unfair, but its several mutual receptions with the Sun (domicile/exaltation, domicile/triplicity, domicile/face and exaltation/triplicity) add to his dignity (honesty, integrity). The Sun is in detriment, but according to the criteria of sect it's very powerful - in *hayz*.

Venus, my main ruler, is essentially strong in Libra – much stronger than Mars which is essentially weak by being placed in the sign of its detriment. Besides, my co-significator Saturn (almuten of the ascendant) is accidentally strong in H10 while the Sun, his co-significator (almuten of H7) is accidentally weak in H12.

On 29 January 2007, a few days short of 4 months after the question, I received my lawyer's letter informing me of the court's decision that another trial would not take place as the judge decided that the original court ruling was final.

Transits to the horary chart on that day are very interesting: Venus, my significator, came to 1° Pisces where it conjuncts the Moon and trines Mercury which as the H9 ruler shows my lawyer. Its conjunction with my ascendant and trine with the Moon (applying) describes him as fluent of speech and acting in my favour, while my opponent's lawyer, shown by Jupiter on cusp of my H2 (trying to get hold of my money) applies to square Saturn - denial. What a fabulous mixture of eloquent horary indications!

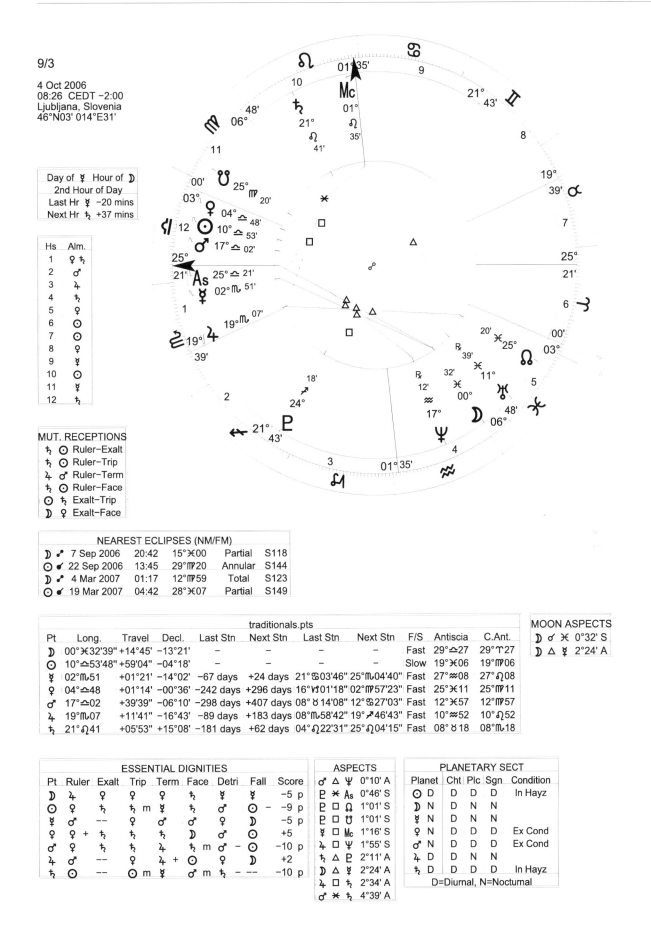

9/3

4 Oct 2006
08:26 CEDT −2:00
Ljubljana, Slovenia
46°N03' 014°E31'

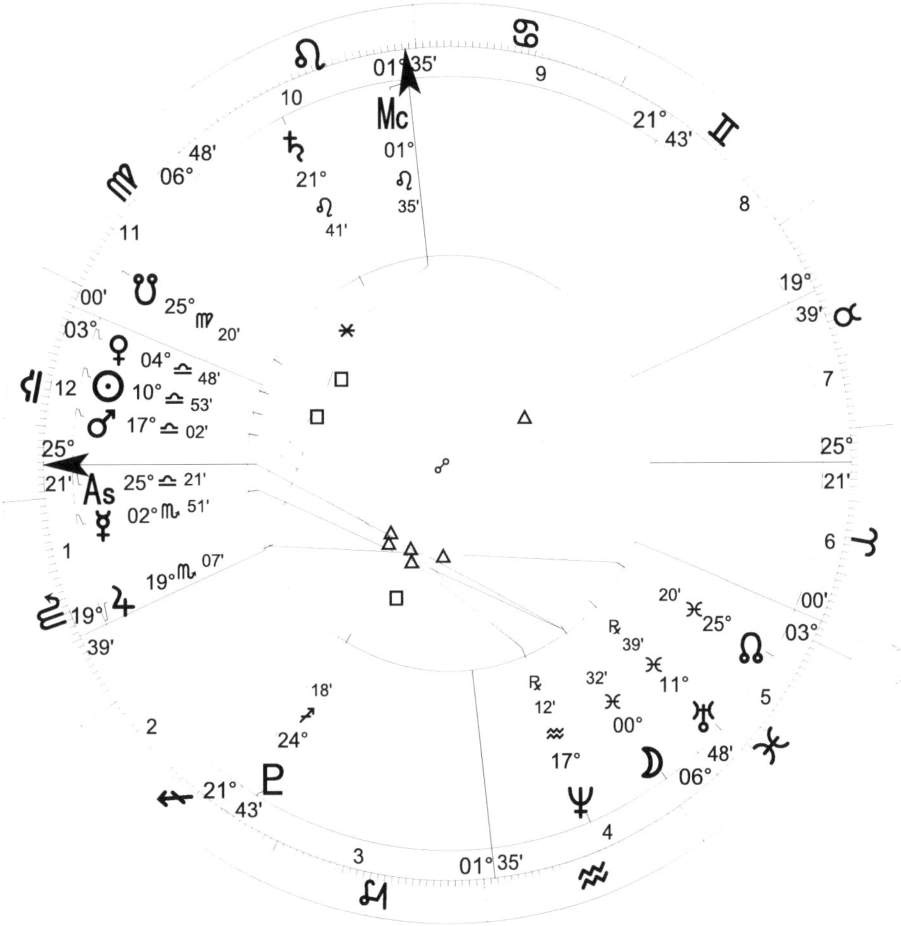

Day of ☿ Hour of ☽
2nd Hour of Day
Last Hr ☿ −20 mins
Next Hr ♄ +37 mins

Hs	Alm.
1	♀ ♄
2	♂
3	♃
4	♄
5	♀
6	☉
7	☉
8	♀
9	☿
10	☉
11	☿
12	♄

MUT. RECEPTIONS		
♄	☉	Ruler-Exalt
♄	☉	Ruler-Trip
♃	♂	Ruler-Term
♄	☉	Ruler-Face
☉	♄	Exalt-Trip
☽	♀	Exalt-Face

NEAREST ECLIPSES (NM/FM)					
☽ ☍	7 Sep 2006	20:42	15°♓00	Partial	S118
☉ ☌	22 Sep 2006	13:45	29°♍20	Annular	S144
☽ ☍	4 Mar 2007	01:17	12°♍59	Total	S123
☉ ☌	19 Mar 2007	04:42	28°♓07	Partial	S149

traditionals.pts

Pt	Long.	Travel	Decl.	Last Stn	Next Stn	Last Stn	Next Stn	F/S	Antiscia	C.Ant.
☽	00°♓32'39"	+14°45'	−13°21'	–	–	–	–	Fast	29°♎27	29°♈27
☉	10°♎53'48"	+59'04"	−04°18'	–	–	–	–	Slow	19°♓06	19°♍06
☿	02°♏51	+01°21'	−14°02'	−67 days	+24 days	21°♋03'46"	25°♏04'40"	Fast	27°♒08	27°♌08
♀	04°♎48	+01°14'	−00°36'	−242 days	+296 days	16°♑01'18"	02°♍57'23"	Fast	25°♓11	25°♍11
♂	17°♎02	+39'39"	−06°10'	−298 days	+407 days	08°♉14'08"	12°♋27'03"	Fast	12°♓57	12°♍57
♃	19°♏07	+11'41"	−16°43'	−89 days	+183 days	08°♏58'42"	19°♐46'43"	Fast	10°♒52	10°♌52
♄	21°♌41	+05'53"	+15°08'	−181 days	+62 days	04°♌22'31"	25°♌04'15"	Fast	08°♉18	08°♏18

MOON ASPECTS			
☽	☌	♓	0°32' S
☽	△	☿	2°24' A

ESSENTIAL DIGNITIES

Pt	Ruler	Exalt	Trip	Term	Face	Detri	Fall	Score
☽	♃	♀	♀	♀	♄	☿	☿	−5 p
☉	♀	♄	♄ m	☿	♄	♂	☉ −	−9 p
☿	♂	--	♀	♂	♂	♀	☽	−5 p
♀	♀ +	♄	♄	♄	☽	♂	☉	+5
♂	♀	♄	♄	♃	♄ m	♂ −	☉	−10 p
♃	♂	--	♀	♃ +	☉	♀	☽	+2
♄	☉	--	☉ m	☿	♂ m	♄ −	--	−10 p

ASPECTS			
♂	△	♆	0°10' A
♇	⚹	As	0°46' S
♇	□	☊	1°01' S
♇	□	☋	1°01' S
☿	□	Mc	1°16' S
♃	□	♆	1°55' S
♄	△	♇	2°11' A
☽	△	☿	2°24' A
♃	□	♄	2°34' A
♂	⚹	♄	4°39' A

PLANETARY SECT

Planet	Cht	Plc	Sgn	Condition
☉ D	D	D	D	In Hayz
☽ N	D	N	N	
☿ N	D	N	N	
♀ N	D	D	D	Ex Cond
♂ N	D	D	D	Ex Cond
♃ D	D	N	N	
♄ D	D	D	D	In Hayz

D=Diurnal, N=Nocturnal

9/4: WILL MY HUSBAND GET CONVICTED?

16 May 2000 at 11:17 a.m. in Ljubljana, Slovenia
Hour ruler: Moon

The querent wanted to know if her husband who was held in custody, would be convicted, or acquitted and released from jail? She was convinced of his innocence.

The man is shown by Saturn, ruler of H7, and partly by Uranus which is located in H7 and is also the modern ruler of Aquarius which holds the cusp of H7. The ascendant with H1 stands for the querent but it also relates to the plaintiff who in this case was the public prosecutor. The Moon shows the course of events and acts as the natural significator of the jury.

So, how do we find the answer? One way to go is to look for any links between the radix H7 and H12 and H6, as H12 rules prison and H6 is the derived H12 (12/7). A mutual application or even a reception between the significators (or the Moon and significators) would give an affirmative answer (conviction and imprisonment). In this case, Saturn rules both the accused and his imprisonment (since it rules H7 and the derived H12) while the radix H12 (jail) is ruled by the Moon. The Moon receives Saturn in its exaltation but Saturn doesn't receive the Moon; this suggests that the Moon (prison) has power over Saturn (the accused).

Another indication that he would remain in prison is the predominance of fixed signs which are occupied by all the significators (AS/DS axis, Saturn, the Moon and Uranus). This simply suggests that things would stay as they are, there would be no change.

But let us consider the chart in more detail.

Saturn is in Taurus in H10, surrounded by several other planets. This reflects the fact that there were several people involved in the alleged criminal offense. Saturn is combust, and although its conjunction with the Sun is a separating one, it's still detrimental for him. Saturn has more essential dignity (face) than the Sun which is peregrine, but we essentially want to know if there is any indication that the accused could be set free. As already said, the vast majority of the planets, along with the Moon and the angles of the chart, are fixed, and the least we can conclude from this is that he doesn't appear to be out of the prison soon. Saturn's conjunction with Venus and Jupiter, both natural benefics applying to Saturn, may seem promising at first sight, but the two planets are in the exaltation and face of the Moon (the jury), while Saturn is in its own face, so the support that Saturn could receive form them, is lessened. What's more, Both Jupiter and Venus are hindered from reaching Saturn by squaring the angular Uranus (co-ruler of the accused) first. This is a case of frustration, also showing the judge's aversion to the accused.

The jury is shown by Mercury, the H11 ruler, and by the Moon. Mercury is strong in its own sign, describing the jury as fair, but still inclined to follow in the prosecutor's steps because Mercury is combust (by the Sun which rules the prosecution). Saturn is in the Moon's exaltation sign, showing the jury's power over the accused, but it is in its fall and peregrine, describing it as "malevolent" or disinclined to help the defendant. The decision might not be an easy one (the Moon applying to inconjunct Mercury) but the final impression is that of the jury sticking with the prosecution. This is further confirmed by the Moon's applying square to Neptune, indicating lies, deception and mistakes, so it is obvious that the jury can't act fairly. Mercury (evidence) is combust, showing lack of evidence, but the jury would obviously turn a blind eye to this fact.

Unfortunately, I said to the querent, *it looks like your husband will stay in prison. There's not enough evidence to sentence him rightfully but, obviously, the prosecutors are strong and unbending, and they'll have the support of the judge and the jury.*

So it was. In spite of lack of evidence, the accused was convicted and sentenced to prison.

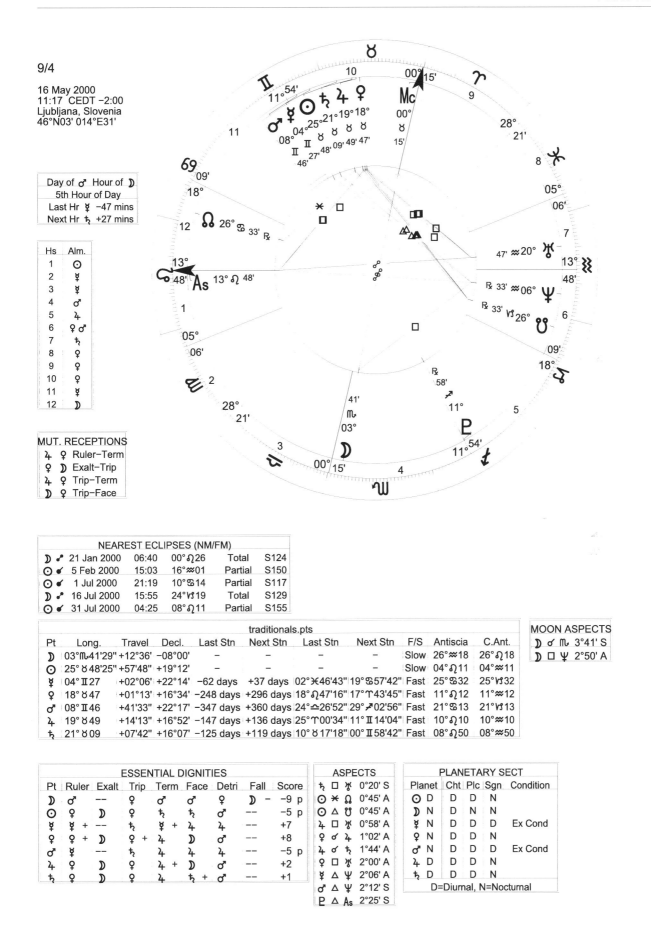

9/4

16 May 2000
11:17 CEDT −2:00
Ljubljana, Slovenia
46°N03' 014°E31'

Day of ♂ Hour of ☽
5th Hour of Day
Last Hr ☿ −47 mins
Next Hr ♄ +27 mins

Hs	Alm.
1	☉
2	☿
3	☿
4	♂
5	♃
6	♀ ♂
7	♄
8	♀
9	♀
10	♀
11	☿
12	☽

MUT. RECEPTIONS
♃ ♀ Ruler–Term
♀ ☽ Exalt–Trip
♃ ♀ Trip–Term
☽ ♀ Trip–Face

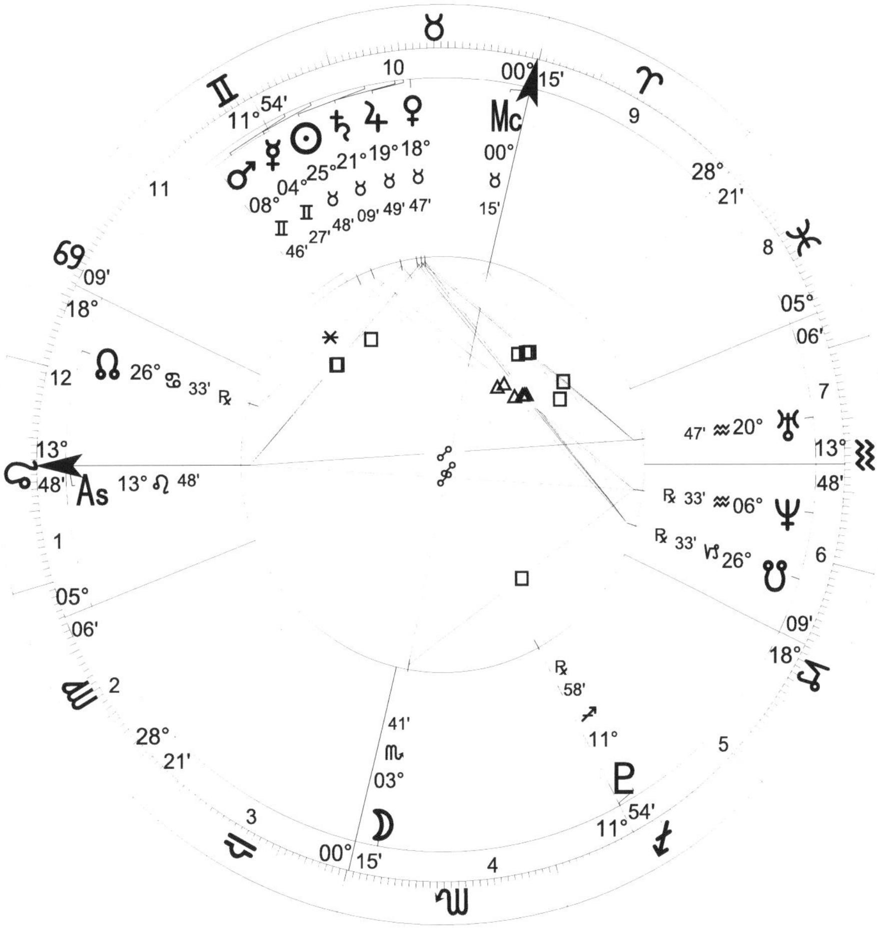

NEAREST ECLIPSES (NM/FM)					
☽ ☍	21 Jan 2000	06:40	00°♌26	Total	S124
☉ ☌	5 Feb 2000	15:03	16°♒01	Partial	S150
☉ ☌	1 Jul 2000	21:19	10°♋14	Partial	S117
☽ ☍	16 Jul 2000	15:55	24°♑19	Total	S129
☉ ☌	31 Jul 2000	04:25	08°♌11	Partial	S155

traditionals.pts

Pt	Long.	Travel	Decl.	Last Stn	Next Stn	Last Stn	Next Stn	F/S	Antiscia	C.Ant.
☽	03°♏41'29"	+12°36'	−08°00'	–	–	–	–	Slow	26°♒18	26°♌18
☉	25°♉48'25"	+57'48"	+19°12'	–	–	–	–	Slow	04°♌11	04°♒11
☿	04°♊27	+02°06'	+22°14'	−62 days	+37 days	02°♓46'43"	19°♋57'42"	Fast	25°♋32	25°♑32
♀	18°♉47	+01°13'	+16°34'	−248 days	+296 days	18°♌47'16"	17°♈43'45"	Fast	11°♌12	11°♒12
♂	08°♊46	+41'33"	+22°17'	−347 days	+360 days	24°♎26'52"	29°♐02'56"	Fast	21°♋13	21°♑13
♃	19°♉49	+14'13"	+16°52'	−147 days	+136 days	25°♈00'34"	11°♊14'04"	Fast	10°♌10	10°♒10
♄	21°♉09	+07'42"	+16°07'	−125 days	+119 days	10°♉17'18"	00°♊58'42"	Fast	08°♌50	08°♒50

MOON ASPECTS
☽ ☌ ♏ 3°41' S
☽ □ ♆ 2°50' A

ESSENTIAL DIGNITIES

Pt	Ruler	Exalt	Trip	Term	Face	Detri	Fall	Score
☽	♂	--	♀	♂	♂	♀	☽ −	−9 p
☉	♀	☽	♀	♄	♄	♂	--	−5 p
☿	☿ +	--	♄	☿ +	♃	♃	--	+7
♀	♀ +	☽	♀ +	♃	☽	♂	--	+8
♂	☿	--	♄	♃	♃	♃	--	−5 p
♃	♀	☽	♀	♃ +	☽	♂	--	+2
♄	♀	☽	♀	♃	♄ +	♂	--	+1

ASPECTS
♄ □ ♅ 0°20' S
☉ ✶ ☊ 0°45' A
☉ △ ☋ 0°45' A
♃ □ ♅ 0°58' A
♀ ☌ ♃ 1°02' A
♃ ☌ ♄ 1°44' A
♀ □ ♅ 2°00' A
☿ △ ♆ 2°06' A
♂ △ ♆ 2°12' S
♇ △ As 2°25' S

PLANETARY SECT

Planet		Cht	Plc	Sgn	Condition
☉	D	D	D	N	
☽	N	D	N	N	
☿	N	D	D	D	Ex Cond
♀	N	D	D	N	
♂	N	D	D	D	Ex Cond
♃	D	D	D	N	
♄	D	D	D	N	

D=Diurnal, N=Nocturnal

TRAVEL

SIGNIFICATORS

The querent is shown by the ascendant, its ruler, the Moon and any planets in H1.

The direction or destination of the journey is traditionally indicated by the descendant, its ruler and any planet in H7 – but I confess to not observing this rule in cases when questions relate to travel. H7 is to be observed, though, in relocation questions. *Should I relocate to New York?* If H7 is better (stronger, more fortunate) than H1, go. If it's vice versa, stay.

The other significators associated with travel, are:
- H3 = short journeys
- H9 = long journeys
- any other houses related to the purpose of travel
- Moon = change, the journey as such
- natural significators associated with the purpose of travel

Travel horaries can be broadly divided into two types: those that are long and involve foreign travel, and those that are shorter and don't involve crossing of state (country) borders. As shown in the bullet points, the first are generally ruled by H9 while the second are more appropriately signified by H3.

But the choice is often difficult. How to decide which journeys are long and which are short? And do all trips to foreign countries necessarily belong to H9 (as H9 traditionally rules long-distance travel), or maybe not?

Centuries ago, when the theory of horary astrology was in its developing stages, there was no such dilemma, because every long-distance journey was an accomplishment. People travelled to foreign countries by ships (overseas trips) or land-based journeys were made, but each trip was longer than today, as the means of transport were much slower, and travel was also more risky (increased possibility of damage to vehicles, the risk of robbery and similar). Today, we board a plane in the morning, conduct a business meeting in another state/country, and fly back in the afternoon. I live in a very small country which can be travelled by a car in less than 2 hours in any direction. Residents of Ljubljana (the capital), for example, can take an afternoon shopping trip to Trieste in Italy or a day trip to the Austrian Carinthia or the Croatian coast, but although all those trips involve foreign countries, they are not considered (nor experienced) as long-distance travel - they are just short trips really. In Lilly's time, a short journey was a trip which took one less than a day, but today we can get to another continent in just a couple of hours – and we wouldn't consider flying from Europe to New York or South Africa a "short journey", would we?

This dilemma is a frequent subject of polemics in astrological forums. I personally feel that H9 can only be given to those journeys that last at least a couple of days and involve the crossing of a state/country border. If it is a day trip (setting off and returning within the same day), even if to a foreign country or another state, the journey can be safely allocated to H3.

We should also consider the purpose of the travel. If it is a tourist/holiday trip, we look for additional indications in H5; if it's a business trip, in H10; travel for educational purposes involves H3, etc. In addition, natural significators relating to the purpose of the trip are to be examined: for education (conferences, seminars etc.) take Mercury and Jupiter, for a business trip Saturn, the Sun and Mercury, for a holiday Jupiter or Venus, for a sports competition Mars, and so on. (You will notice, for example, the importance of Venus in one of the practice cases, asking about the possibility of travelling to a distant country with the aim to attending a wedding.)

Tradition associates certain countries and cities with individual zodiacal signs; if you want to apply this technique, please see Lilly's **CHRISTIAN ASTROLOGY** or any other traditional source. You will find plenty of such information on the internet too, but I have not found great value in those designations and have therefore omitted them from my book. I find much more value in locational astrology which I always employ when advising clients on best travel or relocation destinations. For the directions of the sky which also play a role in this type of questions, see the chapter dealing with missing items, people and pets.

LILLY'S INTERPRETIVE GUIDELINES

To what part of heaven it's best the querent direct his affairs, or wherein he may live most happily. (A summary of Lilly's notes in CA, pp. 132-133.)

In this chapter, Lilly first lays out the directions of the sky. As we already know, the ascendant points to the east, the descendant to the west, the MC to the south, the IC to the north, and the intermediate houses, of course, mark the intermediate areas.

The querent should be directed to where the planet which promises him most good, is located. It is advisable to travel in the directions of Jupiter, Venus, Moon and the part of fortune. The more benefics pointing to one direction, the easier the choice! If the part of fortune and the Moon are free from affliction, he should travel in the direction indicated by the Moon. We must be aware, though, that although Venus and Jupiter are benefics, they can become accidental malefics if they rule the unfortunate H8, H6 or H12. In such cases, we should avoid the directions that these planets indicate, and give priority to the Moon, the part of fortune and the H1 ruler. If possible, avoid the directions of the malefics Mars and Saturn, especially if those planets are also accidental malefics. They can promise good, though, if they are placed in H1, H2, H10 or H11, and if they are also essentially dignified.

If the querent wants to know where to relocate in order to improve his health, we should choose the directions of the H1 ruler or the Moon. The priority is given to the planet that is stronger (more dignified) and in a better aspect with the ascendant. If he wants to know where he would earn more money, we look into the planets connected with H2, the part of fortune and its dispositor.

Of short journeys (CA, p. 195-196)

"By a short journey I intend twenty, thirty or forty miles, or so farre from one's home, as he may goe and come in a day."

The querent's (or quesited's) short journey will be successful, if the ruler of H1 and/or the Moon are:
- fast;
- in any of the dignities of the H3 ruler (i.e. in its domicile, exaltation, triplicity etc.);
- placed in H3;
- in a conjunction or a harmonious aspect with the H3 ruler or with a benefic in H3;
- in a harmonious aspect with the ascendant.

If the querent wants to know in which direction he should travel, consider the sign on the cusp of H3, the sign holding the H3 ruler, and the sign holding the Moon. We give priority to that significator which has most essential dignity. If, for example, this planet is in a northern sign, he should go north, if it is in the west, he should go west, and so on.

10/1: WILL RUBY RECEIVE HER PASSPORT IN TIME?

26 September 2006 at 12:54 p.m. (12:54), Ljubljana, Slovenia
Hour ruler: Jupiter

My then 14-years old daughter Ruby's dance group was setting out on a tour to Novi Sad (Serbia). They would leave in two days. Preparations were underway and her bags were already packed when she says, innocently: *Mom, where's my passport? What passport*, I said. *Can't you enter that country by a personal identity card?* Then it struck me; of course not! Serbia was not part of the EU so we couldn't travel there as easily as to Croatia, for example. But the unfortunate fact was that Ruby didn't have a passport! I immediately called the registry office, only to learn that it would take about 10 days to get it. Then I called her dance teacher who told me that she wouldn't take her on the bus without a passport. It was too risky. The custom officers sometimes checked the passengers' documents and sometimes they didn't, she said. But how was she to know? She suggested that I drive behind the bus to the Serbian border to be able to take Ruby back in case the custom officers refused her crossing the border.

Ouch ... That was bad. I was coming to terms with the unfortunate possibility that I'd follow my daughter's bus for those 500 km when Ruby came and told me that she had just spoken to her friend who was once in a similar situation and got a new passport in just two days. How is that, I wondered? Ah, she told them that it was urgent, she said. I promptly called the registry office again, and the official who was apparently in a better mood than the one with which I spoke before, said that it's possible to get the document quickly if we have a recommendation or a proof of urgency.

I wasted no time, but before we set off, I cast a horary chart with the above question. Is there any hope? A cursory look at the chart soothed my nerves quickly.

So, what did I see? The hour ruler was harmonious with the ascending sign of Sagittarius (naturally associated with travel) which was good, but not enough for an affirmative answer, of course.

The H5 cusp is at 29 Aries, but as mentioned in the theoretical part of the book, in cases where the cusp of a house is at the very last degree of a sign (especially if it's a sign of short ascension, like here), I tend to make the ruler of the next sign the significator of the quesited. In this case, that's Venus, the ruler of Taurus. It really fits better because Venus is a female planet (Ruby was a girl), it rules dancing and is here placed in Virgo, my daughter's natal ascending sign. What's more, it's in H9 of travel. I should add that a cusp of the quesited at the end of a sign can also suggest that person's changing circumstances or even (if applicable) an imminent change of location – and this is what was desired!

I was a little worried by the fact that Venus was in its fall and in a tight applying conjunction with the south node which indicated an obstacle, obstruction or frustration. Is that final, or is there a way out? My eyes wandered to the Moon which applies tightly to Jupiter in the fortunate H11. Jupiter rules H1 which is the derived H9 (9/5) and co-rules H3, the house signifying documents, and is also the natural significator of passports. It surely looks like we're getting one! What's more, Venus is in a strong mutual reception with Mercury, the natural ruler of papers and documents, and the ruler of H7 which is the derived H3 (3/5). Mercury is in H10, representing the registry office. This vividly shows that my daughter and her passport "attract" each other; Venus can "escape" from her captivity and get (via the document) where she wants: abroad.

We promptly left house, stopped by a photographer, then rushed to her dance studio where we got the letter of recommendation, and soon we were at the home office where a friendly official quickly arranged matters. Ruby's passport arrived in the mail the next day.

10/1

Natal Chart
26 Sep 2006
12:54 CEDT −2:00
Ljubljana, Slovenia
46°N03' 014°E31'

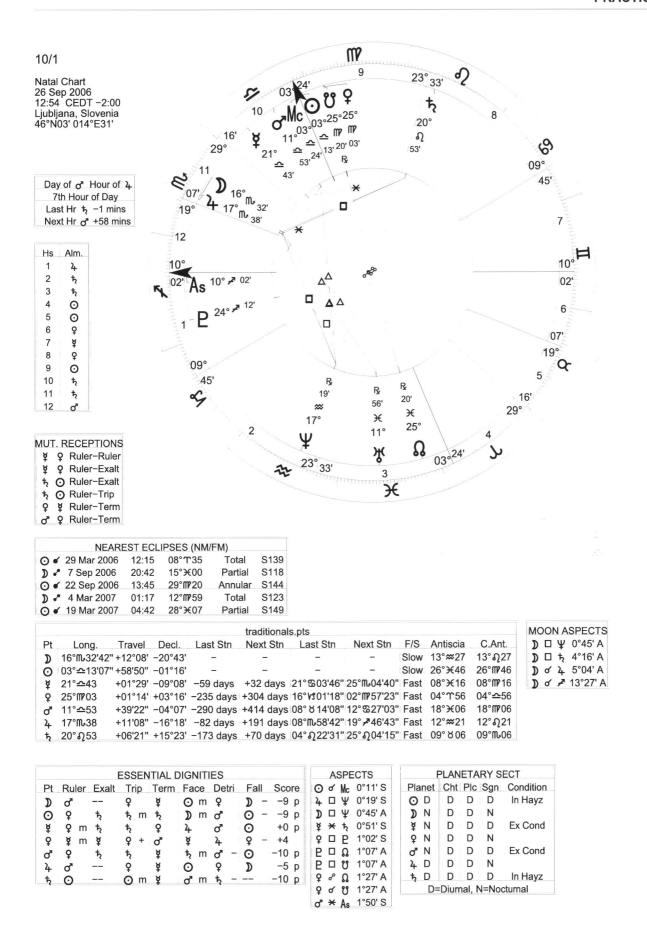

Day of ♂ Hour of ♃
7th Hour of Day
Last Hr ♄ −1 mins
Next Hr ♂ +58 mins

Hs	Alm.
1	♃
2	♄
3	♄
4	☉
5	☉
6	♀
7	☿
8	♀
9	☉
10	♄
11	♄
12	♂

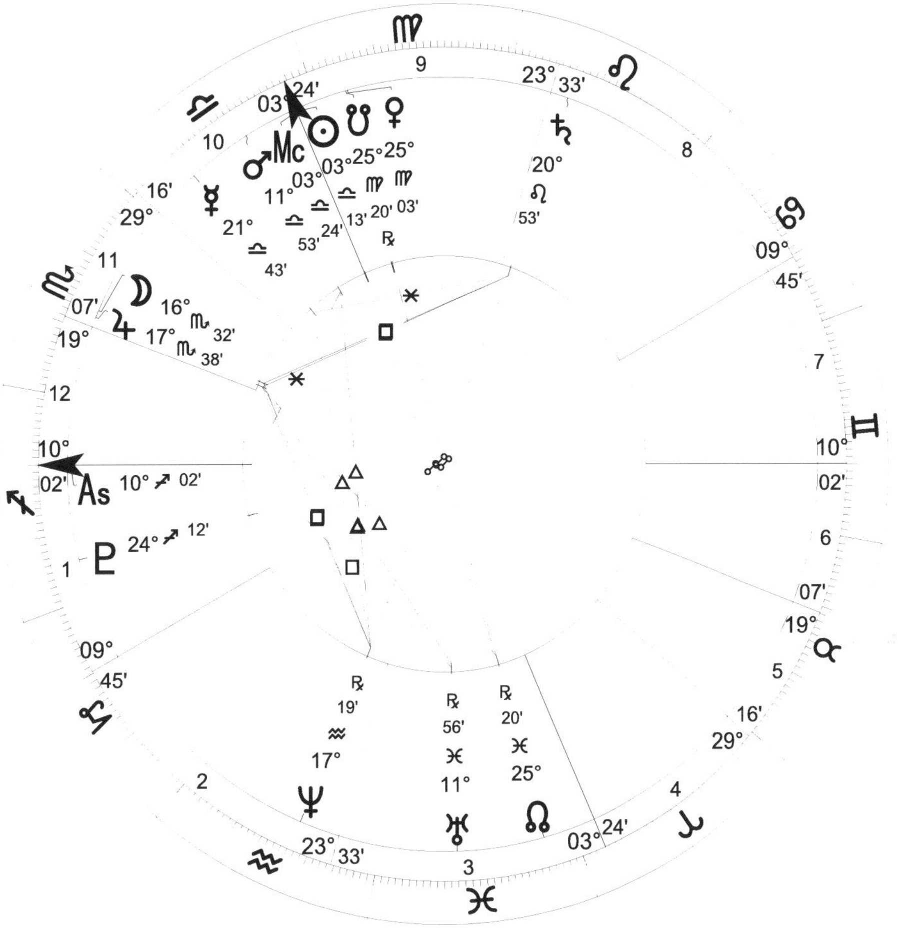

MUT. RECEPTIONS		
☿	♀	Ruler-Ruler
☿	♀	Ruler-Exalt
♄	☉	Ruler-Exalt
♄	☉	Ruler-Trip
♀	☿	Ruler-Term
♂	♀	Ruler-Term

NEAREST ECLIPSES (NM/FM)					
☉	29 Mar 2006	12:15	08°♈35	Total	S139
☽	7 Sep 2006	20:42	15°♓00	Partial	S118
☉	22 Sep 2006	13:45	29°♍20	Annular	S144
☽	4 Mar 2007	01:17	12°♍59	Total	S123
☉	19 Mar 2007	04:42	28°♓07	Partial	S149

traditionals.pts

Pt	Long.	Travel	Decl.	Last Stn	Next Stn	Last Stn	Next Stn	F/S	Antiscia	C.Ant.
☽	16°♏32'42"	+12°08'	−20°43'	–	–	–	–	Slow	13°♒27	13°♌27
☉	03°♎13'07"	+58'50"	−01°16'	–	–	–	–	Slow	26°♓46	26°♍46
☿	21°♎43	+01°29'	−09°08'	−59 days	+32 days	21°♋03'46"	25°♏04'40"	Fast	08°♓16	08°♍16
♀	25°♍03	+01°14'	+03°16'	−235 days	+304 days	16°♑01'18"	02°♍57'23"	Fast	04°♈56	04°♎56
♂	11°♎53	+39'22"	−04°07'	−290 days	+414 days	08°♉14'08"	12°♋27'03"	Fast	18°♓06	18°♍06
♃	17°♏38	+11'08"	−16°18'	−82 days	+191 days	08°♏58'42"	19°♐46'43"	Fast	12°♒21	12°♌21
♄	20°♌53	+06'21"	+15°23'	−173 days	+70 days	04°♌22'31"	25°♌04'15"	Fast	09°♉06	09°♏06

MOON ASPECTS			
☽	□	♆	0°45' A
☽	□	♄	4°16' A
☽	☌	♃	5°04' A
☽	☌	♐	13°27' A

ESSENTIAL DIGNITIES

Pt	Ruler	Exalt	Trip	Term	Face	Detri	Fall	Score
☽	♂	--	♀	☿	☉ m	♀	☽ −	−9 p
☉	♀	♄	♄ m	♄	☽ m	♂	☉ −	−9 p
☿	♀ m	♄	♄	♀	♃	♂	☉	+0 p
♀	☿ m	☿	♀ +	♂	☿	♃	♀ −	+4
♂	♀	♄	♄	☿	♄ m	♂ −	☉	−10 p
♃	♂	--	♀	☿	☉	♀	☽	−5 p
♄	☉	--	☉ m	☿	♂ m	♄ −	--	−10 p

ASPECTS			
☉	☌	Mc	0°11' S
♃	□	♆	0°19' S
☽	□	♆	0°45' A
☿	⚹	♄	0°51' S
♀	□	♇	1°02' S
♇	□	☊	1°07' A
♇	□	☋	1°07' A
♀	☍	☊	1°27' A
♀	☌	☋	1°27' A
♂	⚹	As	1°50' S

PLANETARY SECT

Planet		Cht	Plc	Sgn	Condition
☉	D	D	D	D	In Hayz
☽	N	D	D	N	
☿	N	D	D	D	Ex Cond
♀	N	D	D	N	
♂	N	D	D	D	Ex Cond
♃	D	D	D	N	
♄	D	D	D	D	In Hayz

D=Diurnal, N=Nocturnal

10/2: WILL P AND V TRAVEL TO GREECE THIS SUMMER?

22 February 2001 at 12:12 p.m. (12:12), Ljubljana, Slovenia
Hour ruler: Moon

My partner and I had been in a serious relationship for less than a year, and I was all but delighted to hear that he and his best friend were planning a "solo" trip to Greece. They would travel in late spring or summer. They had been planning this vacation for years but always something came up to prevent it. During our time together, I once also went on a solo travel (to an astrology conference in the USA), so I wasn't really justified to complain. But, clearly, I wasn't very happy about it, so I asked the above question.

The ascendant is in Cancer so I'm ruled by the Moon; P (my partner) is Saturn, ruler of H7 while his friend V is Venus, the ruler of radix H5 or the derived H11. But because they'd travel together (my question refers to them as a team), both can be ruled by H7. Besides, I was primarily interested if my partner would go, not his friend. And what's more, Saturn is almuten of H5, so the chart itself shows that Saturn rules P as well as V I could take Venus only as a co-significator of V, maybe showing some particular conditions referring to him.

Their destination is shown by the Sun which rules the derived H9 (very fitting for Greece which is a sunny and warm country), but we must also check the radix H9 which is also ruled by Saturn (H9 cusp in Aquarius), and partly by Mercury, Uranus and the Moon, the H9 planets.

The Moon in H9 adequately reflects my interest. Since it is also the hour ruler, it becomes a most significant body in the chart – showing myself (unimportant, as I am not the subject of the question), the trip and the general course of events (very important).

The Moon is in an exact applying square with Saturn (P and V), therefore the answer is clear: no, they will not go to Greece this summer. It's true that the Moon and Saturn are in a strong mixed reception by domicile and exaltation, and in a weaker mutual reception by exaltation and triplicity, which could, in a general theoretical frame of reference, give a way out or provide a positive answer. But in this case, such resolution is not possible due to several factors: firstly, Saturn is the natural ruler of obstructions; secondly, Saturn is right on the cusp of the unfortunate H12, showing denial and loss; thirdly, the Moon is cadent and under the Sun's beams, therefore weak; and, finally, any aspect between a pair of significators is more potent than their mutual reception – and the aspect in this case is a frustrating square.

Furthermore, neither Saturn nor the Moon are in any way related to the Sun, the derived H9 ruler. The Sun is conjunct MC (aim, ambition); the Moon actually applies to conjunct it, but the completion of the aspect is prevented by the Moon's square to Saturn, which is a case of frustration. By contrast, the Sun is in a strong mutual reception with Venus (by exaltation), and the two bodies also mutually receive each other by exaltation/triplicity, but this only shows that V (my partner's friend) was more eager to travel and probably also the one who gave the initiative.

I didn't say anything, of course, but I was relieved. As time passed, there was no more mentioning of Greece, and by the end of the summer it was clear that my judgment was correct (to my utter delight, of course).

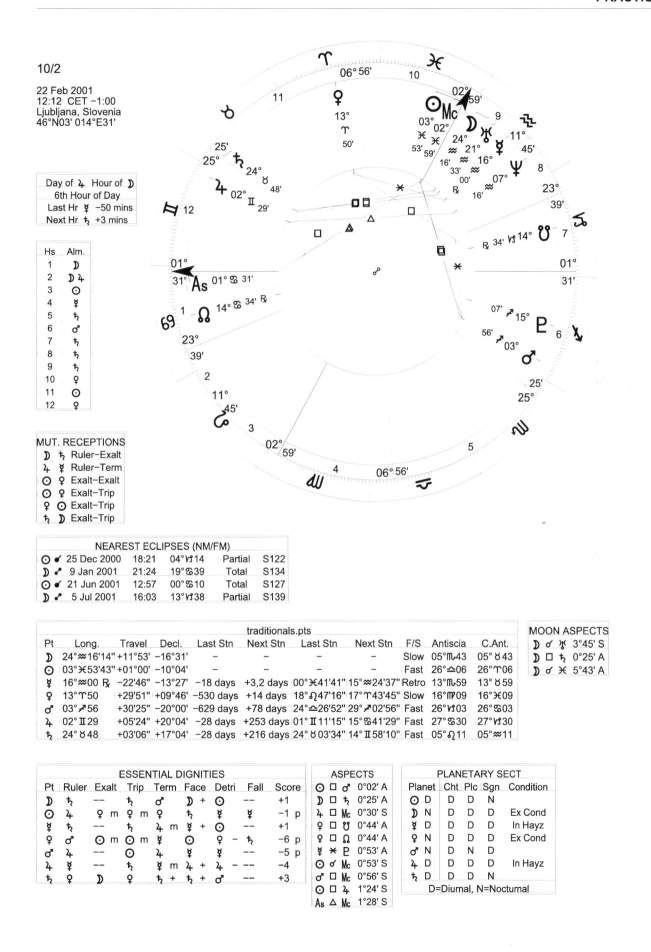

10/2

22 Feb 2001
12:12 CET −1:00
Ljubljana, Slovenia
46°N03' 014°E31'

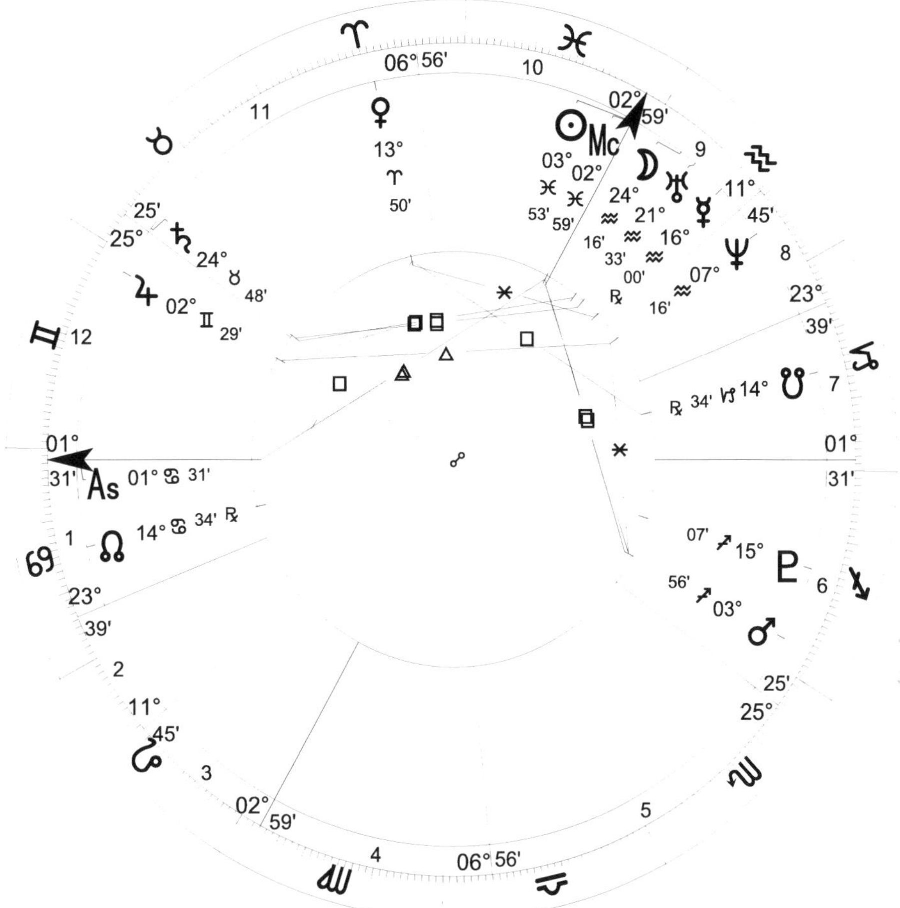

Day of ♃ Hour of ☽
6th Hour of Day
Last Hr ☿ −50 mins
Next Hr ♄ +3 mins

Hs	Alm.
1	☽
2	☽ ♃
3	☉
4	☿
5	♄
6	♂
7	♄
8	♄
9	♄
10	♀
11	☉
12	♀

MUT. RECEPTIONS		
☽	♄	Ruler−Exalt
♃	☿	Ruler−Term
☉	♀	Exalt−Exalt
☉	♀	Exalt−Trip
♀	☉	Exalt−Trip
♄	☽	Exalt−Trip

NEAREST ECLIPSES (NM/FM)					
☉ ☌	25 Dec 2000	18:21	04°♑14	Partial	S122
☽ ☍	9 Jan 2001	21:24	19°♋39	Total	S134
☉ ☌	21 Jun 2001	12:57	00°♋10	Total	S127
☽ ☍	5 Jul 2001	16:03	13°♑38	Partial	S139

traditionals.pts

Pt	Long.	Travel	Decl.	Last Stn	Next Stn	Last Stn	Next Stn	F/S	Antiscia	C.Ant.
☽	24°♒16'14"	+11°53'	−16°31'	–	–	–	–	Slow	05°♏43	05°♉43
☉	03°♓53'43"	+01°00'	−10°04'	–	–	–	–	Fast	26°♎06	26°♈06
☿	16°♒00 ℞	−22'46"	−13°27'	−18 days	+3,2 days	00°♓41'41"	15°♒24'37"	Retro	13°♏59	13°♉59
♀	13°♈50	+29'51"	+09°46'	−530 days	+14 days	18°♌47'16"	17°♈43'45"	Slow	16°♍09	16°♓09
♂	03°♐56	+30'25"	−20°00'	−629 days	+78 days	24°♎26'52"	29°♐02'56"	Fast	26°♑03	26°♋03
♃	02°♊29	+05'24"	+20°04'	−28 days	+253 days	01°♊11'15"	15°♋41'29"	Fast	27°♋30	27°♑30
♄	24°♉48	+03'06"	+17°04'	−28 days	+216 days	24°♉03'34"	14°♊58'10"	Fast	05°♌11	05°♒11

MOON ASPECTS			
☽	☌	♅	3°45' S
☽	□	♄	0°25' A
☽	☌	♓	5°43' A

ESSENTIAL DIGNITIES

Pt	Ruler	Exalt	Trip	Term	Face	Detri	Fall	Score
☽	♄	--	♄	♂	☽ +	☉	--	+1
☉	♃	♀ m	♀ m	♀	♄	☿	☿	−1 p
☿	♄	--	♄	♃ m	☿ +	☉	--	+1
♀	♂	☉ m	☉ m	☿	☉	♀ −	♄	−6 p
♂	♃	--	☉	♃	☿	☿	--	−5 p
♃	☿	--	♄	☿ m	♃ +	♃ −	--	−4
♄	♀	☽	♀	♄ +	♄ +	♂	--	+3

ASPECTS			
☉	□	♂	0°02' A
☽	□	♄	0°25' A
♃	□	Mc	0°30' S
♀	□	☋	0°44' A
♀	□	☊	0°44' A
☿	⚹	♇	0°53' A
☉	☌	Mc	0°53' S
♂	□	Mc	0°56' S
☉	□	♃	1°24' S
As	△	Mc	1°28' S

PLANETARY SECT

Planet		Cht	Plc	Sgn	Condition
☉	D	D	D	N	
☽	N	D	D	D	Ex Cond
☿	D	D	D	D	In Hayz
♀	N	D	D	D	Ex Cond
♂	N	D	N	D	
♃	D	D	D	D	In Hayz
♄	D	D	D	N	

D=Diurnal, N=Nocturnal

10/3: WILL I BE ABLE TO JOIN THE EXCURSION TO IRELAND?

16 May 2005 at 10:48 a.m., Ljubljana, Slovenia
Hour ruler: Sun

My sister emailed me with this question. She wrote that the company for which she worked was organizing an excursion to Ireland (on May 26). She wanted to take part but there were no more vacancies and she learnt that she could only go if someone would cancel. Would that happen, she asked?

I cast the chart for the time I read her letter which was 11:08. At that time I still believed that such an approach was correct. That chart's ascendant was at 11°58' Leo, Moon at 25°41' Leo and the Sun at 25°36' Taurus while the positions in the chart cast for the true time of her question (the time when her mail was sent and arrived in my mailbox) were only slightly different, but the difference was significant in two respects. Namely, in the first chart, the Moon was void-of-course (at least according to the "old" definition which does not take into account the Moon's aspects in the next sign) and the ascendant separated from a sextile with Jupiter, significator of the trip, whereas in the second chart (published here) the ascendant applied to sextile it – a major difference.

The chart cast for the time when I read the question didn't give much hope: the Sun - significator of the querent - was not in aspect with Jupiter, H9 ruler (placed in H3), nor in any reception with it, while the Moon (the action, the course of events) was separated from a square to the Sun, which suggested there'd be no more action.

But as this was a business excursion, involving some learning besides sightseeing, I also took notice of H10 and H3. The chart clearly reflects this, because the Sun (the querent) is in H10, together with Mercury, the ruler of H3. Besides, the ruler of H9 (a foreign country) is in H3, connecting a trip abroad with learning and communicating.

The question is: could the Moon give a positive answer, because it'll perfect a trine with Mercury, co-significator of the excursion, in the next sign? The aspect is already in orb, so the answer is yes! All the more so because the Moon in Virgo will be in mixed mutual reception (domicile/exaltation) with Mercury, enabling a powerful exchange of energies. What's more - the two bodies are separated by 10°58', which almost exactly corresponds to the ten days which elapsed till the trip!

This should give me a clue, but I admit that due to my then conception of the void-of-course Moon I expressed doubt that my sister's wish could be granted. I told her that her progressions and transits (predictive techniques which I used to help me find the answer) indicate that the trip was possible, but that the horary chart denied it.

Two days later, my sister told me that someone cancelled the trip and that she could now take his place. Ouch… I was glad for her but seriously disappointed in myself. Where did I go wrong?

I took another look at the chart and realized that I should've considered the Moon's aspect with Mercury. But then again, the chart still didn't seem totally OK. The Sun was void-of course and something was missing. Then I decided to cast another chart – that for the time of my sister asking the question. I cast another chart for the time when her email arrived in my mailbox.

As mentioned before, this chart's ascendant applies to sextile Jupiter, significator of the trip. 1.5 degrees separates it from exactness, but I reckoned that my sister wrote her question a couple of minutes before she sent the mail, which would move the ascendant at least half a degree back, so that it would apply by 2 degrees – which is exactly the number of days that elapsed until the confirmation of the trip. Besides, in the "new" chart the Moon applies to square the Sun. Although the aspect is disharmonious, it suggests further activity because there's a strong mutual reception between the lights (the Moon is in the domicile of the Sun while the Sun is in the Moon's exaltation) which are also powerfully placed in angular houses. This aspect indicates completion - through an exchange, shown by mutual reception, which literally indicates that my sister exchanged places with someone else. This action was followed by her actually taking the trip 10 days later, as shown by the Moon's next aspect to Mercury.

I can't know, of course, whether I'd give her a correct answer if I had judged this chart form the start, but in retrospect I certainly believe that it's much clearer and that it reflects the reality of the situation and its development much better than the chart which I cast for the time when I read and understood her question. This is one of those charts that convinced me to always use the "original" chart!

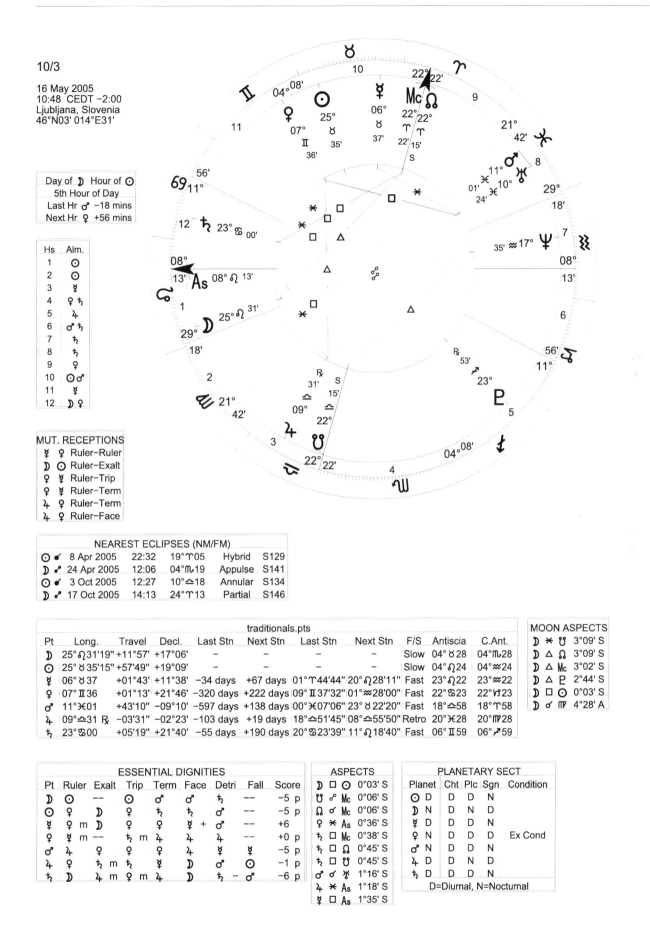

10/3

16 May 2005
10:48 CEDT −2:00
Ljubljana, Slovenia
46°N03' 014°E31'

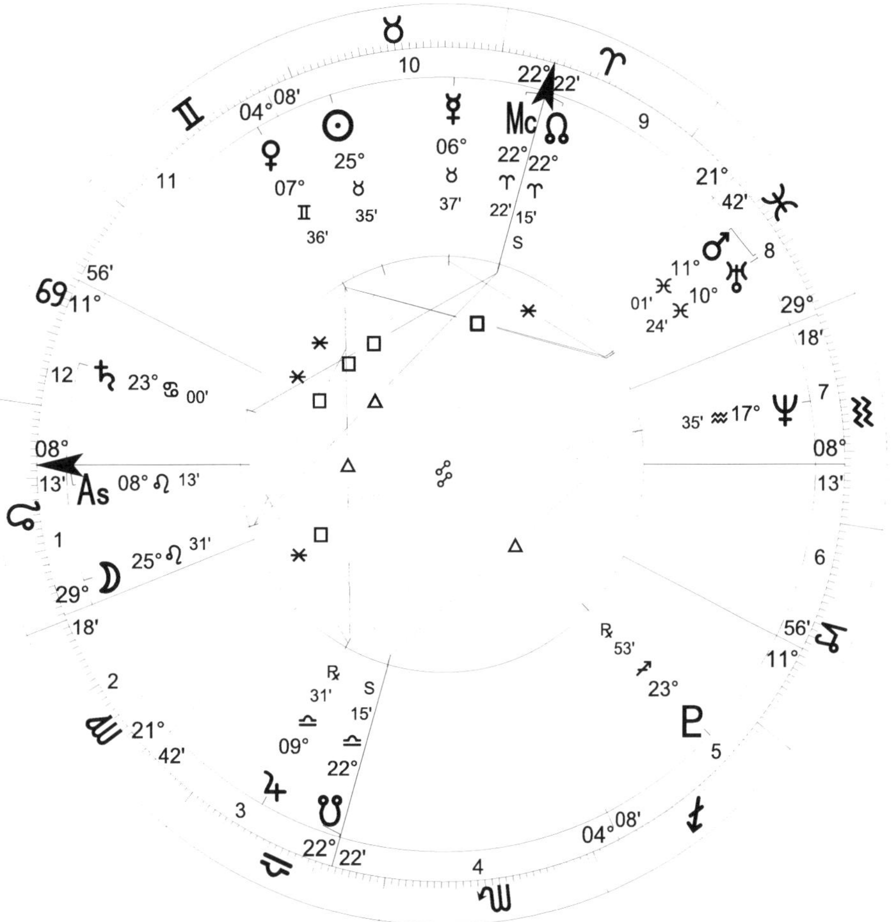

Day of ☽ Hour of ☉
5th Hour of Day
Last Hr ♂ −18 mins
Next Hr ♀ +56 mins

Hs	Alm.
1	☉
2	☉
3	☿
4	♀ ♄
5	♃
6	♂ ♄
7	♄
8	♄
9	♀
10	☉♂
11	☿
12	☽ ♀

MUT. RECEPTIONS		
☿	♀	Ruler–Ruler
☽	☉	Ruler–Exalt
♀	☿	Ruler–Trip
♀	☿	Ruler–Term
♃	♀	Ruler–Term
♃	♀	Ruler–Face

NEAREST ECLIPSES (NM/FM)					
☉ ●	8 Apr 2005	22:32	19°♈05	Hybrid	S129
☽ ☍	24 Apr 2005	12:06	04°♏19	Appulse	S141
☉ ●	3 Oct 2005	12:27	10°♎18	Annular	S134
☽ ☍	17 Oct 2005	14:13	24°♈13	Partial	S146

traditionals.pts

Pt	Long.	Travel	Decl.	Last Stn	Next Stn	Last Stn	Next Stn	F/S	Antiscia	C.Ant.
☽	25°♌31'19"	+11°57'	+17°06'	–	–	–	–	Slow	04°♉28	04°♏28
☉	25°♉35'15"	+57'49"	+19°09'	–	–	–	–	Slow	04°♌24	04°♒24
☿	06°♉37	+01°43'	+11°38'	−34 days	+67 days	01°♈44'44"	20°♌28'11"	Fast	23°♌22	23°♒22
♀	07°♊36	+01°13'	+21°46'	−320 days	+222 days	09°♊37'32"	01°♒28'00"	Fast	22°♋23	22°♑23
♂	11°♓01	+43'10"	−09°10'	−597 days	+138 days	00°♓07'06"	23°♉22'20"	Fast	18°♎58	18°♈58
♃	09°♎31 ℞	−03'31"	−02°23'	−103 days	+19 days	18°♎51'45"	08°♎55'50"	Retro	20°♓28	20°♍28
♄	23°♋00	+05'19"	+21°40'	−55 days	+190 days	20°♋23'39"	11°♌18'40"	Fast	06°♊59	06°♐59

MOON ASPECTS			
☽	⚹	☋	3°09' S
☽	△	☊	3°09' S
☽	△	Mc	3°02' S
☽	△	♇	2°44' S
☽	□	☉	0°03' S
☽	☌	♍	4°28' A

ESSENTIAL DIGNITIES

Pt	Ruler	Exalt	Trip	Term	Face	Detri	Fall	Score
☽	☉	--	☉	♂	♂	♄	--	−5 p
☉	♀	☽	♀	♄	♄	♂	--	−5 p
☿	♀ m	☽	♀	♀	☿ +	♂	--	+6
♀	☿ m	--	♄ m	♃	♃	♃	--	+0 p
♂	♃	♀	♀	♀	♃	☿	☿	−5 p
♃	♀	♄ m	♄	☿	☽	♂	☉	−1 p
♄	☽	♃ m	♀ m	♃	☽	♄ −	♂	−6 p

ASPECTS			
☽	□	☉	0°03' S
☋	☍	Mc	0°06' S
☊	☌	Mc	0°06' S
♀	⚹	As	0°36' S
♄	□	Mc	0°38' S
♄	□	☊	0°45' S
♄	□	☋	0°45' S
♂	☌	♅	1°16' S
♃	⚹	As	1°18' S
☿	□	As	1°35' S

PLANETARY SECT

Planet		Cht	Plc	Sgn	Condition
☉	D	D	D	N	
☽	N	D	N	D	
☿	D	D	D	N	
♀	N	D	D	D	Ex Cond
♂	N	D	D	N	
♃	D	D	N	D	
♄	D	D	D	N	

D=Diurnal, N=Nocturnal

10/4: WILL WE VISIT SARAJEVO FOR THE NEW YEAR HOLIDAYS?

21 November 2005 at 3:09 p.m. (15:09) in Ljubljana, Slovenia
Hour ruler: Mars

The New Year holidays were just a month away and my husband and I were thinking of a short getaway. We hoped that his parents could babysit for a few days so that we could go without the kids. I hadn't been to Sarajevo in a long time, so I suggested a trip to this Bosnian city, and my hubby agreed. The kids were too small to go with us, and we desperately needed rest. But it all depended on his parents, so I asked the above question.

The ascendant in Taurus stands for the two of us, and our ruler Venus is in H9 of travel, but conjunct MC or the cusp of H10 which is the derived H4 – my husband's parents. Yes, they were my main concern! The Moon conjuncts the cusp of H5 which signifies entertainment, vacation and leisure, and the sign of Leo is also indicative of my desire which gave birth to the question: to relax and have fun!

Our travel destination is shown by Saturn, the H9 ruler which is placed in H5, confirming the purpose of the planned trip – a holiday. The Moon applies to conjunct Saturn which at first sight gives an affirmative answer. But, alas, before this happens, the Moon squares Jupiter and then squares Mars! Both planets are angular so this is a clear case of frustration. Jupiter is peregrine and rules H8, the derived H2 – could my husband find that we can't afford it financially? (Note: as a couple, we are ruled by H1, of course, but in H1 and H7 we can find additional indications for each of us, influencing the course of events, therefore H7 also represents him.)

Mars is the planetary hour ruler and because the ascendant is in Taurus, it's inharmonious, leaning towards a negative answer. Mars is also more harmful than Jupiter, since it's a natural malefic, and because it is in detriment and retrograde, while accidentally strong in H1, which increases its malice. This is a double frustration! Incidentally, Mars is co-almuten of H10, my husband's parents. There are insurmountable obstacles in front of us, obviously, connected with my husband and his parents.

Thus it was. We soon abandoned our travel plans because my husband's parents had other arrangements for the New Year's celebrations, and couldn't babysit. We therefore spent the holidays at home.

It is interesting to note that Saturn in this chart is stationary, and since it's a retrograde station and Saturn rules my husband's parents (the ruler of H10 or 4/7), this quite appropriately reflects their withdrawal and inability to help.

10/4

21 Nov 2005
15:09 CET −1:00
Ljubljana, Slovenia
46°N03' 014°E31'

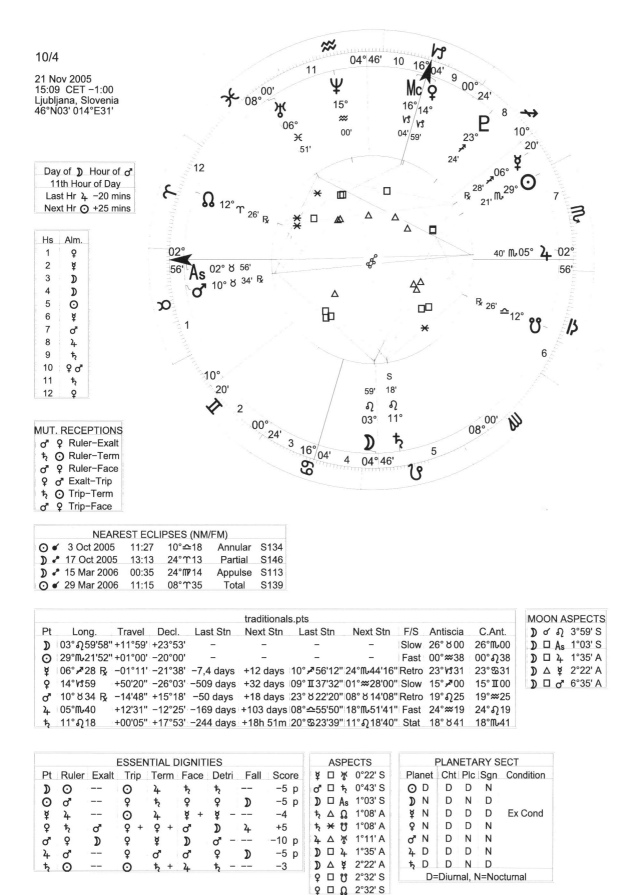

Day of ☽ Hour of ♂
11th Hour of Day
Last Hr ♃ −20 mins
Next Hr ☉ +25 mins

Hs	Alm.
1	♀
2	☿
3	☽
4	☽
5	☉
6	☿
7	♂
8	♃
9	♄
10	♀♂
11	♄
12	♀

MUT. RECEPTIONS
♂ ♀ Ruler–Exalt
♄ ☉ Ruler–Term
♂ ♀ Ruler–Face
♀ ♂ Exalt–Trip
♄ ☉ Trip–Term
♂ ♀ Trip–Face

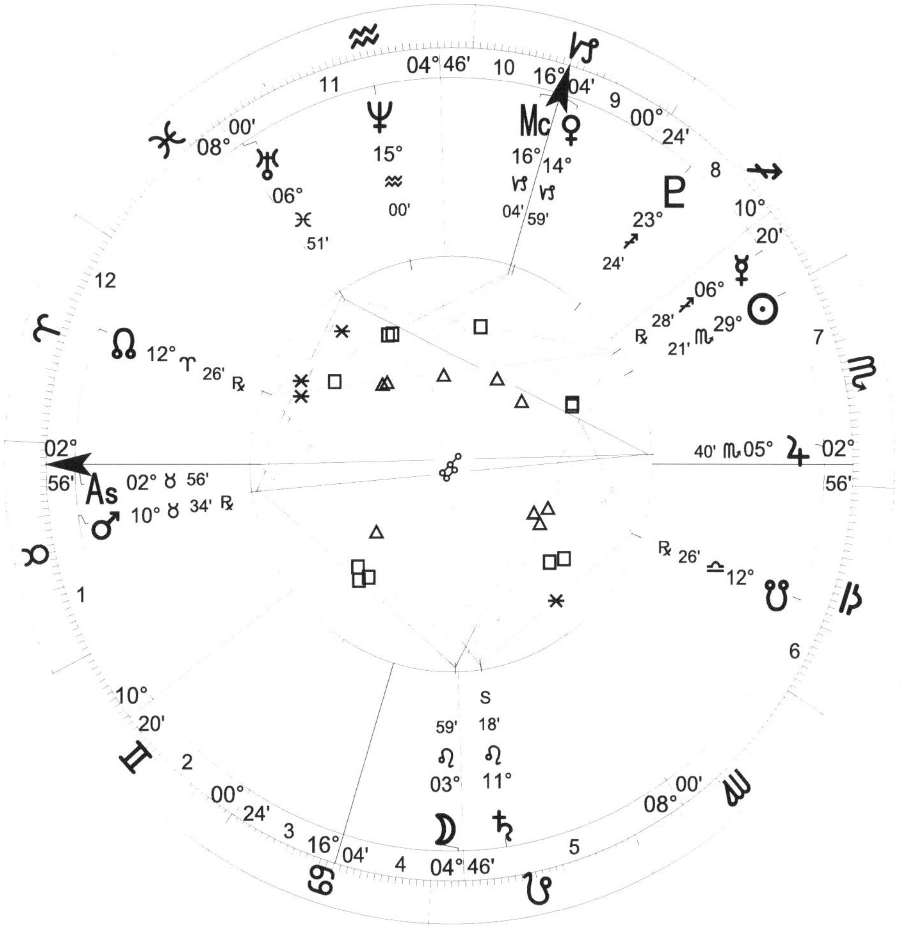

NEAREST ECLIPSES (NM/FM)					
☉ ☌	3 Oct 2005	11:27	10°♎18	Annular	S134
☽ ☍	17 Oct 2005	13:13	24°♈13	Partial	S146
☽ ☍	15 Mar 2006	00:35	24°♍14	Appulse	S113
☉ ☌	29 Mar 2006	11:15	08°♈35	Total	S139

traditionals.pts

Pt	Long.	Travel	Decl.	Last Stn	Next Stn	Last Stn	Next Stn	F/S	Antiscia	C.Ant.
☽	03°♌59'58"	+11°59'	+23°53'	–	–	–	–	Slow	26°♉00	26°♏00
☉	29°♏21'52"	+01°00'	−20°00'	–	–	–	–	Fast	00°♒38	00°♌38
☿	06°♐28 ℞	−01°11'	−21°38'	−7,4 days	+12 days	10°♐56'12"	24°♏44'16"	Retro	23°♑31	23°♋31
♀	14°♑59	+50'20"	−26°03'	−509 days	+32 days	09°♊37'32"	01°♒28'00"	Slow	15°♐00	15°♊00
♂	10°♉34 ℞	−14'48"	+15°18'	−50 days	+18 days	23°♉22'20"	08°♉14'08"	Retro	19°♌25	19°♒25
♃	05°♏40	+12'31"	−12°25'	−169 days	+103 days	08°♎55'50"	18°♏51'41"	Fast	24°♒19	24°♌19
♄	11°♌18	+00'05"	+17°53'	−244 days	+18h 51m	20°♋23'39"	11°♌18'40"	Stat	18°♉41	18°♏41

MOON ASPECTS
☽ ☌ ♌ 3°59' S
☽ □ As 1°03' S
☽ □ ♃ 1°35' A
☽ △ ☿ 2°22' A
☽ □ ♂ 6°35' A

ESSENTIAL DIGNITIES

Pt	Ruler	Exalt	Trip	Term	Face	Detri	Fall	Score
☽	☉	--	☉	♃	♄	♄	--	−5 p
☉	♂	--	♀	♄	♀	♀	☽	−5 p
☿	♃	--	☉	♃	☿ +	☿ −	--	−4
♀	♄	♂	♀ +	♀ +	♂	☽	♃	+5
♂	♀	☽	♀	☿	☽	♂ −	--	−10 p
♃	♂	--	♀	♂	♂	♀	☽	−5 p
♄	☉	--	☉	♄ +	♃	♄ −	--	−3

ASPECTS
☿ □ ♅ 0°22' S
♂ □ ♄ 0°43' S
☽ □ As 1°03' S
♄ △ ☊ 1°08' A
♄ ✶ ☋ 1°08' A
♃ △ ♅ 1°11' A
☽ □ ♃ 1°35' A
☽ △ ☿ 2°22' A
♀ □ ☋ 2°32' S
♀ □ ☊ 2°32' S

PLANETARY SECT

Planet		Cht	Plc	Sgn	Condition
☉	D	D	D	N	
☽	N	D	N	D	
☿	N	D	D	D	Ex Cond
♀	N	D	D	N	
♂	N	D	N	N	
♃	D	D	D	N	
♄	D	D	N	D	

D=Diurnal, N=Nocturnal

10/5: WILL WE COMPETE AT THE EUROPEAN CHAMPIONSHIP?

11 September 2008 at 8:06 a.m., Ljubljana, Slovenia
Hour ruler: Mars

My dance group "hip-hop mothers" won first place at the national championship which took place in the spring of that year. Back then we were planning to attend the June world championship in Bremen, Germany, but nothing came of it because several dancers had other obligations. But there was another chance for competing - the European Championship in Denmark in October. At the time of my asking the above question we were discussing the possibility but had not yet arrived at a decision. Denmark is several thousand kilometers away from my country, so it would be a time- and money-consuming trip, but on the other hand, many of us strongly wished to go.

The first question was, what houses (and planets) rule our group? Let's remember: when someone asks a question on behalf of a group to which he/she belongs, this group is represented by the ascendant with H1, of course. We'd go all together, or none of us! It would be different if there was a possibility that the group travels without the querent. In such a case, the group would be assigned to H11 (teams, groups of people), but in my case it was clear that we could only attend as a group, therefore the whole group gets H1.

The ascendant is in Libra - the sign associated with arts. Its ruler Venus is strong in its own sign and in H1, properly describing us as a capable, strong group - clearly, as we were the winning group of the national championship! Co-significator is Mars, by virtue of being placed in H1, while our destination (Denmark, a foreign country) is also ruled by Venus, the main ruler of H9, and Mercury, the ruler of the intercepted H9 sign (Gemini). As we know, one planet can have multiple functions in a horary chart. The fact that Venus has a double meaning in this chart only makes the planet more important. Venus therefore plays a crucial role, as well as the Moon, showing the course of events. Saturn, as almuten of the ascendant, is also to be considered, but is second in importance to Venus and other significators.

Let us check the Moon first. It's at the last degree of a sign, in detriment and not in orb of an aspect with any planet, therefore void-of-course. This points to a negative answer. The hour ruler is inharmonious as well, supporting the indication. But as we know, the answer could still be a yes if there'd be a strong completion between the main significators. Venus and Mercury, the H9 rulers, are in H1 - emplacement? Yes, but as we know, emplacement alone does not suffice for an affirmative answer. There must be a strong support from other chart indications, otherwise the answer remains negative.

The outcome, reflected by the conjunction of the three planets in H1, is very interesting. Mercury is often faster than Venus, so at first glance it appears to be moving away from Venus, but a look into the table reveals that it was slower on this day, because it stationed retrograde on September 24. Venus will soon "catch" it and this could indicate completion: the group (Venus) traveling abroad (Mercury). But because Venus meets Mars before meeting Mercury, Mars acts as a frustrating influence. Especially because it's also the hour ruler, therefore doubly important in the chart. Mars as the ruler of H7 stands for the "opponents", and its placement in H1 of the group clearly reflects the fact: the group was not uniform! Some of us (Venus) voted for the travel (as Venus rules both H1 and H9) while the others (Mars, ruler of H7, in H1) voted against it. The split within the group actually prevented the positive outcome.

The negative result is confirmed by Saturn in H12 (denial, loss, failed hopes) and combust (inability to act), and by the south node in H11 of hopes, with its dispositor the Sun also in H12 in an applying opposition to Uranus (discontinuation, stress.)

10/5

11 Sep 2008
08:06 CEDT −2:00
Ljubljana, Slovenia
46°N03' 014°E31'

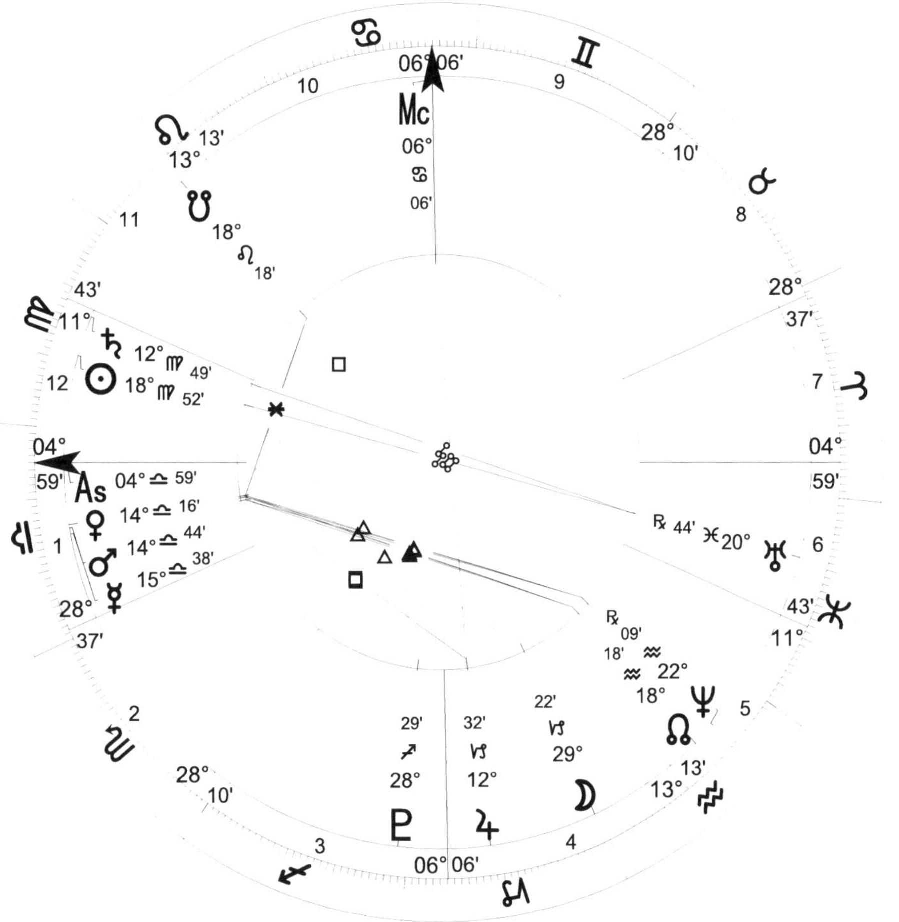

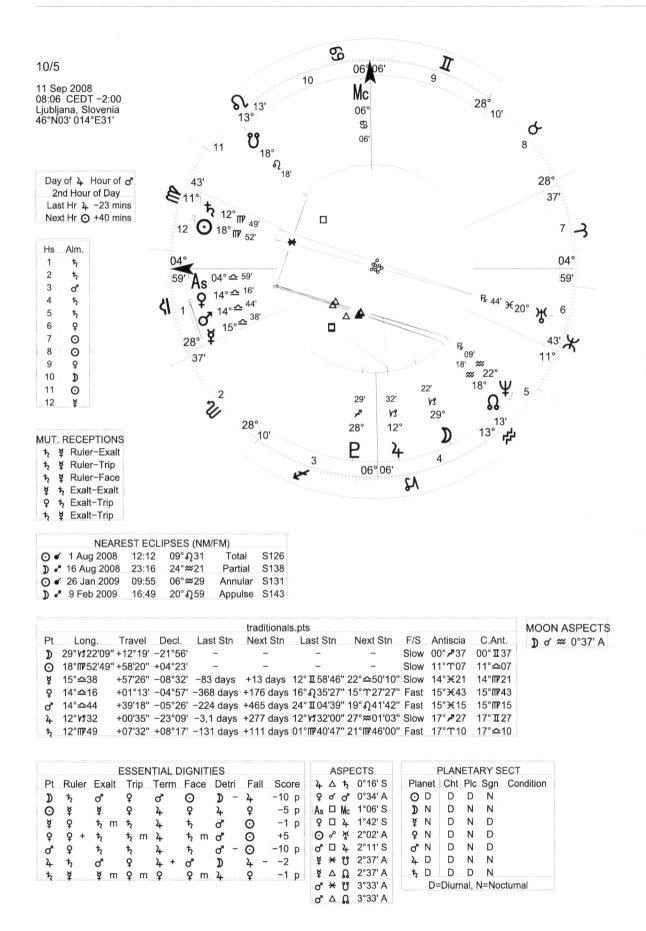

Day of ♃ Hour of ♂
2nd Hour of Day
Last Hr ♃ −23 mins
Next Hr ☉ +40 mins

Hs	Alm.
1	♄
2	♄
3	♂
4	♄
5	♄
6	♀
7	☉
8	☉
9	♀
10	☽
11	☉
12	☿

MUT. RECEPTIONS		
♄	☿	Ruler−Exalt
♄	☿	Ruler−Trip
♄	☿	Ruler−Face
☿	♄	Exalt−Exalt
♀	♄	Exalt−Trip
♄	☿	Exalt−Trip

NEAREST ECLIPSES (NM/FM)					
☉ ☌	1 Aug 2008	12:12	09°♌31	Total	S126
☽ ☍	16 Aug 2008	23:16	24°♒21	Partial	S138
☉ ☌	26 Jan 2009	09:55	06°♒29	Annular	S131
☽ ☍	9 Feb 2009	16:49	20°♌59	Appulse	S143

traditionals.pts

Pt	Long.	Travel	Decl.	Last Stn	Next Stn	Last Stn	Next Stn	F/S	Antiscia	C.Ant.
☽	29°♑22'09"	+12°19'	−21°56'	–	–	–	–	Slow	00°♐37	00°♊37
☉	18°♍52'49"	+58'20"	+04°23'	–	–	–	–	Slow	11°♈07	11°♎07
☿	15°♎38	+57'26"	−08°32'	−83 days	+13 days	12°♊58'46"	22°♎50'10"	Slow	14°♓21	14°♍21
♀	14°♎16	+01°13'	−04°57'	−368 days	+176 days	16°♌35'27"	15°♈27'27"	Fast	15°♓43	15°♍43
♂	14°♎44	+39'18"	−05°26'	−224 days	+465 days	24°♊04'39"	19°♌41'42"	Fast	15°♓15	15°♍15
♃	12°♑32	+00'35"	−23°09'	−3,1 days	+277 days	12°♑32'00"	27°♒01'03"	Slow	17°♐27	17°♊27
♄	12°♍49	+07'32"	+08°17'	−131 days	+111 days	01°♍40'47"	21°♍46'00"	Fast	17°♈10	17°♎10

MOON ASPECTS
☽ ☌ ♒ 0°37' A

ESSENTIAL DIGNITIES								
Pt	Ruler	Exalt	Trip	Term	Face	Detri	Fall	Score
☽	♄	♂	♀	♂	☉	☽ −	♃	−10 p
☉	☿	☿	♀	♃	♀	♃	♀	−5 p
☿	♀	♄ m	♄	♃	♄	♂	☉	−1 p
♀	♀ +	♄	♄ m	♃	♄ m	♂	☉	+5
♂	♀	♄	♄	♃	♄	♂ −	☉	−10 p
♃	♄	♂	♀	♃ +	♂	☽	♃ −	−2
♄	☿	☿ m	♀ m	♀	♀ m	♃	♀	−1 p

ASPECTS			
♃	△	♄	0°16' S
♀	☌	♂	0°34' A
As	□	Mc	1°06' S
♀	□	♃	1°42' S
☉	☍	♅	2°02' A
♂	□	♃	2°11' S
☿	⚹	☋	2°37' A
☿	△	☊	2°37' A
♂	⚹	☋	3°33' A
♂	△	☊	3°33' A

PLANETARY SECT					
Planet		Cht	Plc	Sgn	Condition
☉	D	D	D	N	
☽	N	D	N	N	
☿	N	D	N	D	
♀	N	D	N	D	
♂	N	D	N	D	
♃	D	D	N	N	
♄	D	D	D	N	

D=Diurnal, N=Nocturnal

10/6: WILL I TRAVEL TO INDIA TO RAJEEV'S MARRIAGE?

1 September 2007 at 1:43 p.m. (13:43), Ljubljana, Slovenia
Hour ruler: The Moon

In the morning of the first day of September 2007, I opened an email which came from my internet acquaintance Rajeev whom I had met a couple of years before through an online astrological forum. Back then, I helped him with astrological advice and encouragement when he was going through an emotional crisis. Now he wrote that he had finally found the woman of his dreams and that he'd be very happy if I, his good friend, would come to their wedding which would take place on October 8, 2007 in Kerala, India. The mail was accompanied by an official invitation addressed to the whole family.

I took a deep breath. To Kerala for the wedding? Oh, I'd love to! Kerala, a south-western Indian state with its long sandy beaches, lush vegetation and beautiful scenery, had long been one of my dream destinations. But if I travelled that far, I would have liked to spend more than just a few days in India. Besides, I would have to travel alone. We had four children, two of them school-age, meaning that my husband would have to stay with them, but even in that case, I couldn't leave them alone for so long. Not to mention the costs which were considerable. My husband said that the decision was all mine, but after a few days of contemplating and not being able to decide, I finally cast a horary chart. Will I go or not?

The Ascendant is at zero Sagittarius, with its ruler Jupiter essentially and accidentally strong (in its domicile sign and in H1). Many astrologers would say that an early ascendant means it's too early to ask, but the fact was that it was rather too late than too early, as the wedding date was fast approaching. Ascendant at the beginning of a sign seemed very appropriate to me, because it suggested that this was something entirely new in my life (I'd never been to India before), and new beginnings are often shown by the ascendant (or a significator) at an early degree. In this case, with the ascendant in Sagittarius, the sign of travel, it seemed as if "heavens" were waiting with my question to come into my mind at the time when the ascendant moved to Sagittarius, the sing of travel.

I thought that the dignified Jupiter represented my honourable role in the matter, since Rajeev wrote that he sent the first invitation to me! Such was his thankfulness and respect for the help he had received from me.

The hour ruler is inharmonious – not good. The journey is ruled by the Sun, the H9 ruler, also placed in H9 in Virgo. The Sun applies to Jupiter by a square. This aspect could bring the matters to completion if the planets received each other, but that was not the case. The Sun is even in the detriment of Jupiter, which I perceived as a sign that Kerala somehow "didn't like" me.

My co-significator the Moon, in Taurus in H5, applies by trine to the Sun, which at first glance looks promising, but before the completion of this aspect, the Moon makes a sextile to the north node and a trine to the south node. Should this be considered a frustration? South node often signifies barriers and losses, and since it's in H9, this could indicate a loss in relation to my travel plans. The north node is in the sign of H4 (home, family) which certainly favours this area, while its placement in H3 is indicative of the work that awaited me shortly: writing texts for my yearly publication Moon Guide. It seemed like the chart was saying that I should give priority to plans, related to my home and work issues. There's no reception between the Moon and the Sun; such aspects, even if harmonious, do not have much power for constructive action. The Moon in a fixed sign, and even in the beginning of it, also doesn't seem to indicate a travel. Fixed signs are averse to change.

We must also check the condition of Venus, the natural significator of marriage. Interestingly, it's in H9, suitably placed for the purpose of my travel. All the more so because it's in an exact parallel of declination with the Sun, ruler of H9, while Jupiter, my ruler, is on a Venus degree by monomoiria. But Venus is in a poor condition: retrograde, peregrine and in a very exact applying inconjunction with an angular Uranus. (Note that Uranus is exactly on the northern angle which makes it very powerful). Venus is not in aspect with Jupiter neither with the Moon. Its precarious placement is all the more unfortunate because it disposits the Moon. The Moon is on a Saturn degree (by monomoiria) while this malefic exactly squares the ascendant - from H9!

There's another strong indication that nothing will come of the matter: MC in an exact conjunction with the degree of the approaching solar eclipse. Charts closely linked to nearby eclipses indicate strong barriers!

The result? Due to a number of inhibiting factors I soon decided against the travel.

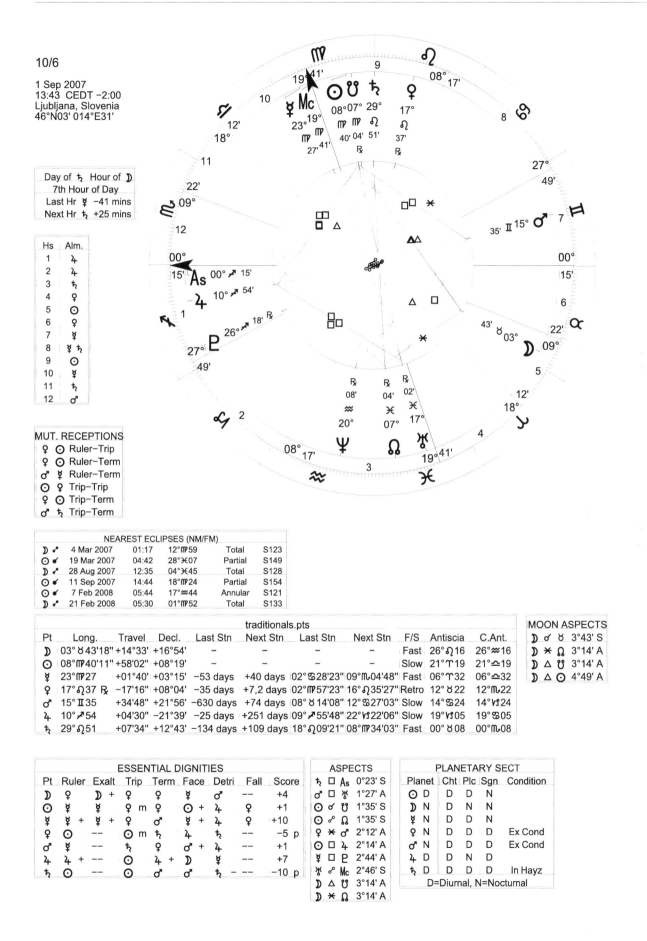

10/7: WILL I GO TO THE ISAR CONFERENCE IN LA?

19 March 2000 at 4:09 p.m. (16:09), Ljubljana, Slovenia
Hour ruler: Moon

This question "found me" when I was thinking of attending the ISAR (International Society of Astrological Research) conference in Annaheim, LA. The conference was scheduled for October 5 - 10, so I had plenty of time to decide. But would I really go, I wondered? I strongly wished I could go, as it would also be my first visit to the USA.

My significator Mercury, the H1 ruler, is in H7 in Pisces. That's its fall and detriment, indicating that I felt insecure due to setbacks. My younger daughter would turn 5 on 5th of October, so I'd miss her birthday. I really didn't want that, beside the fact that I lived alone with my two daughters at the time which meant that I'd need ample support of my relatives.

Overseas is represented by H9 which has its cusp in Aries and is occupied by three planets: Mars (H9 ruler and placed right on cusp of the house), Jupiter and Saturn. Jupiter is the natural significator of travel and conferences, so it plays a particularly important role here. Mercury applies to it by sextile and because Jupiter also receives it by domicile, this is a powerful aspect, suggesting an affirmative answer.

And there is another, although less obvious clue: Venus, co-ruler of H9 (since it rules the intercepted sign of Taurus) conjuncts Mercury. Mercury is usually faster, so at first sight it looks like it applies to Venus, which would be another positive indication. But since Mercury was very slow on that day, having just turned direct a few days earlier, it's slower than Venus and will not catch it. Although - theoretically - this would lessen my prospects, Venus is in a strong mutual reception with Jupiter (by domicile), so we can exchange both planets' placements and imagine Jupiter at 7°36' Pisces and Venus at 6°27' Taurus. Mercury's direct application to the slower Jupiter would also give an affirmative.

As for Mercury's essential debility due to its detriment and fall: such planets can literally show one to be "away from home", and because the question refers to a possibility of travel, the debility in this case is not necessarily an obstruction. It rather confirms the other indications that travel is a real possibility for me. We must always view planetary afflictions through the lenses of the context of the question, as this sheds additional light on the matter and can even turn a weakness to a virtue (from the interpretation point of view).

The result? My plane took off on October 3rd. 6.5 months or 28.5 weeks elapsed from the time of my question. An exact sextile between Mercury and Jupiter was formed on 25 March, in the afternoon, so exactly 6 days passed since then, which translated into months would be 6 months. Approximately correct, but off by half a month. As always, timing is best judged by the Moon, so let us check its course. (Because the main significators clearly indicate the completion of the matter, I haven't mentioned the Moon so far, although it should never be neglected in a horary chart.) It's at 22°09' Virgo and applying to an opposition of the Sun, co-ruler of H9 (almuten of the house), offering a clear timing clue. There are 7°10' between the Moon and the Sun - exactly the number of synodic months that elapsed until my journey: 7 months (7 degrees) and 6 days (10 minutes).

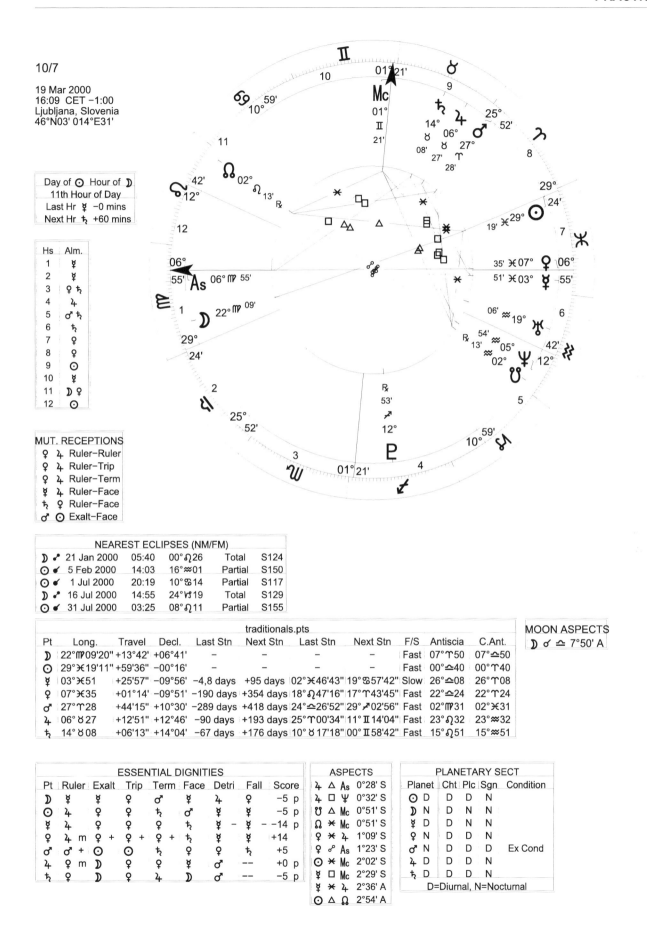

10/7

19 Mar 2000
16:09 CET −1:00
Ljubljana, Slovenia
46°N03' 014°E31'

Day of ☉ Hour of ☽
11th Hour of Day
Last Hr ☿ −0 mins
Next Hr ♄ +60 mins

Hs	Alm.
1	☿
2	☿
3	♀ ♄
4	♃
5	♂ ♄
6	♄
7	♀
8	♀
9	☉
10	☿
11	☽ ♀
12	☉

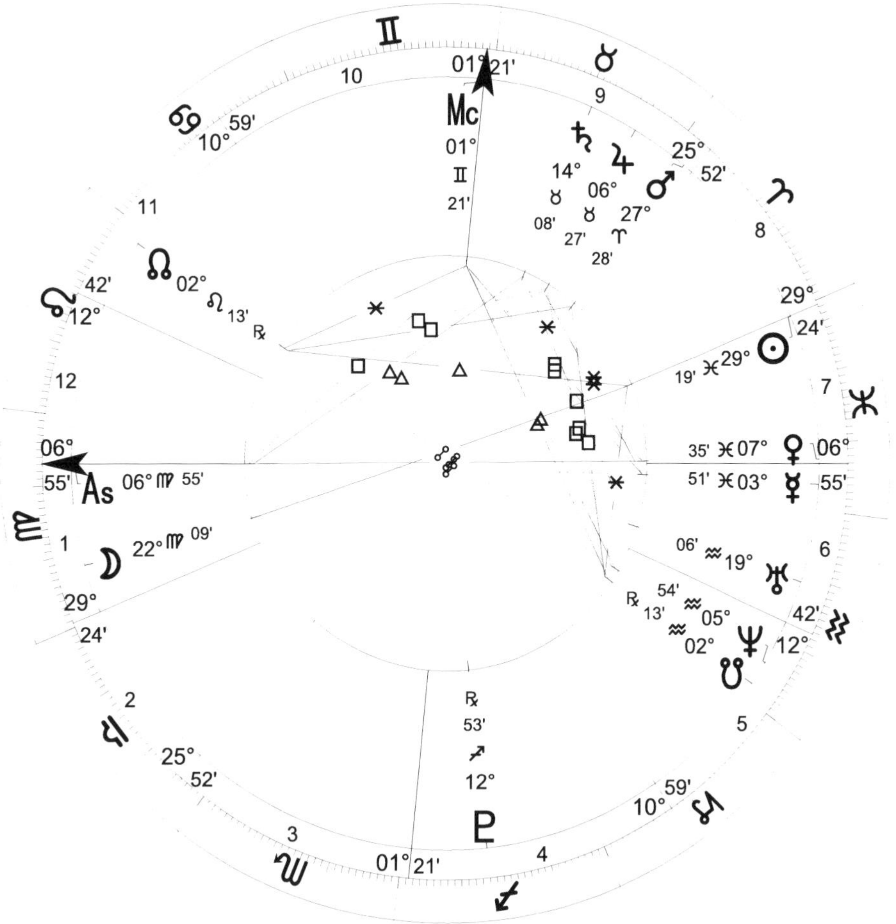

MUT. RECEPTIONS		
♀	♃	Ruler−Ruler
♀	♃	Ruler−Trip
♀	♃	Ruler−Term
☿	♃	Ruler−Face
♄	♀	Ruler−Face
♂	☉	Exalt−Face

NEAREST ECLIPSES (NM/FM)					
☽	21 Jan 2000	05:40	00°♌26	Total	S124
☉	5 Feb 2000	14:03	16°♒01	Partial	S150
☉	1 Jul 2000	20:19	10°♋14	Partial	S117
☽	16 Jul 2000	14:55	24°♑19	Total	S129
☉	31 Jul 2000	03:25	08°♌11	Partial	S155

traditionals.pts

Pt	Long.	Travel	Decl.	Last Stn	Next Stn	Last Stn	Next Stn	F/S	Antiscia	C.Ant.
☽	22°♍09'20"	+13°42'	+06°41'	−	−	−	−	Fast	07°♈50	07°♎50
☉	29°♓19'11"	+59'36"	−00°16'	−	−	−	−	Fast	00°♎40	00°♈40
☿	03°♓51	+25'57"	−09°56'	−4,8 days	+95 days	02°♓46'43"	19°♋57'42"	Slow	26°♎08	26°♈08
♀	07°♓35	+01°14'	−09°51'	−190 days	+354 days	18°♌47'16"	17°♈43'45"	Fast	22°♎24	22°♈24
♂	27°♈28	+44'15"	+10°30'	−289 days	+418 days	24°♎26'52"	29°♐02'56"	Fast	02°♍31	02°♓31
♃	06°♉27	+12'51"	+12°46'	−90 days	+193 days	25°♈00'34"	11°♊14'04"	Fast	23°♌32	23°♒32
♄	14°♉08	+06'13"	+14°04'	−67 days	+176 days	10°♉17'18"	00°♊58'42"	Fast	15°♌51	15°♒51

MOON ASPECTS
☽ ☌ ♎ 7°50' A

ESSENTIAL DIGNITIES

Pt	Ruler	Exalt	Trip	Term	Face	Detri	Fall	Score
☽	☿	☿	♀	♂	☿	♃	♀	−5 p
☉	♃	♀	♀	♄	♂	☿	☿	−5 p
☿	♃	♀	♀	♀	♄	☿ −	☿ −	−14 p
♀	♃ m	♀ +	♀ +	♀ +	♄	☿	☿	+14
♂	♂ +	☉	☉	♄	♀	♀	♄	+5
♃	♀ m	☽	♀	♀	☿	♂	−−	+0 p
♄	♀	☽	♀	♃	☽	♂	−−	−5 p

ASPECTS	
♃ △ As	0°28' S
♃ □ ♆	0°32' S
☋ △ Mc	0°51' S
☊ ⚹ Mc	0°51' S
♀ ⚹ ♃	1°09' S
♀ ☍ As	1°23' S
☉ ⚹ Mc	2°02' S
☿ □ Mc	2°29' S
☿ ⚹ ♃	2°36' A
☉ △ ☊	2°54' A

PLANETARY SECT

Planet		Cht	Plc	Sgn	Condition
☉	D	D	D	N	
☽	N	D	N	N	
☿	D	D	N	N	
♀	N	D	D	N	
♂	N	D	D	D	Ex Cond
♃	D	D	D	N	
♄	D	D	D	N	

D=Diurnal, N=Nocturnal

10/8: WILL MY HUSBAND GO TO HUNGARY?

28 October 2008 at 11:34 a.m., Ljubljana, Slovenia
Hour ruler: Saturn

My husband told me that he might soon go on a one-week business trip to Hungary, to assist the local business partners in web programming. He could perform the job from home, by network connection, but they'd rather have him there in person. He was not particularly fond of the trip, and said that all depends on the agreement.

I immediately raised the question: Will he really go?

The chart for the question shows a weak Moon, combust and at the end of a sign, about to enter Scorpio, the sign of its fall. It's also in the *via combusta* - the area of the zodiac which is considered to be problematic due to a cluster of violent, unpredictable stars there. (As explained in the theoretical part of the book, I don't take those clusters seriously, but am mentioning it here for the sake of accuracy). Since the Moon is the significator of my husband (H7 ruler), its imminent entering of the next sign would, under normal circumstances, predict his travel (crossing of the border), but the Moon in Scorpio doesn't feel well, so the trip is not recommended, or is not viable. Combustion is also an obstacle, of course, possibly indicating hidden facts which have not yet been revealed. All of this describes the situation and its possible future development quite well: my husband thinking of the trip, but not really wanting it, beside the possibility that some facts may turn up which would prevent him from going.

What could be the nature of the obstacle? The job to be performed abroad is shown by Venus, H4 ruler (10/7). It's in Sagittarius and applies by a square to Saturn. What or who is Saturn? His business partners, of course, shown by the ascendant in Capricorn (7/7), but also their resources, as Saturn rules their H2 with the cusp in Aquarius. This could indicate financial problems, insolvency of his business partners, or their unwillingness to comply with my husband's financial requirements. The Moon (husband) and Venus (his job and also the significator of travel in the radix chart, as it rules H9) are not connected, and none of these bodies is associated with Mars, the ruler of the derived H9. All of this denies the possibility of his business trip.

And so it was. After a few days' negotiations, the Hungarians decided that my husband's hourly rate was too high, and as he didn't want to lower it, they decided he would rather work for them online.

It's interesting to note that Saturn is the hour ruler, and as we have seen, its connection with the financial houses had a decisive impact on the outcome of the question.

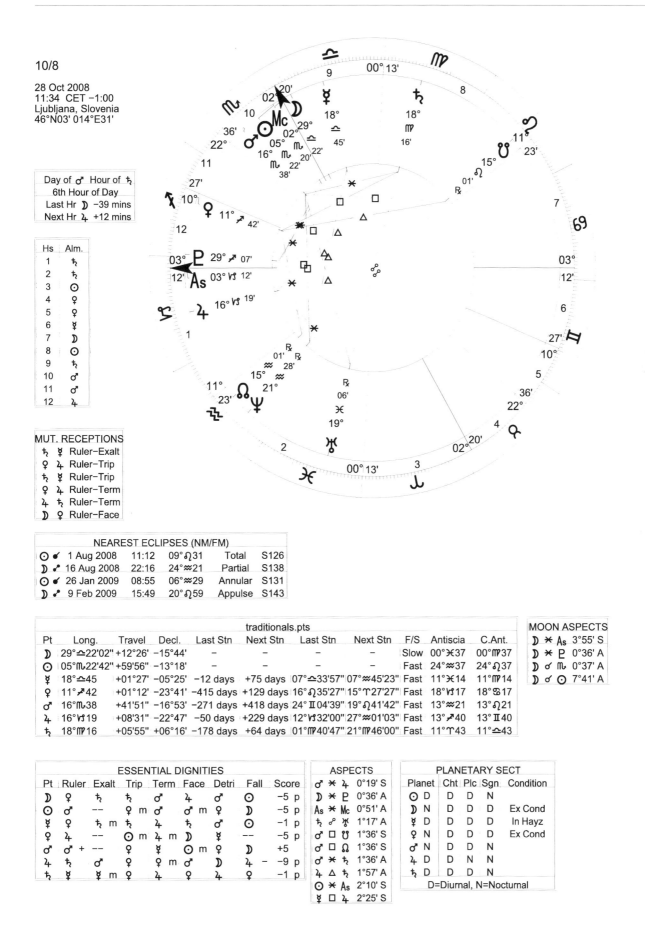

10/8

28 Oct 2008
11:34 CET −1:00
Ljubljana, Slovenia
46°N03' 014°E31'

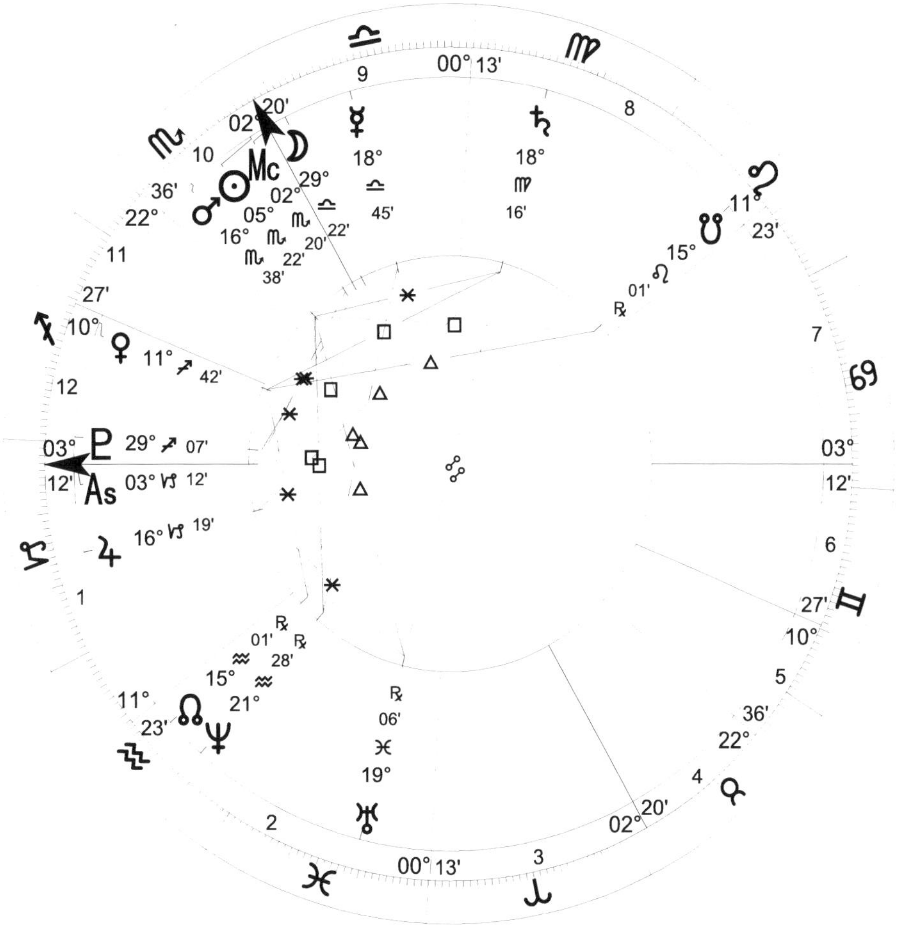

Day of ♂ Hour of ♄
6th Hour of Day
Last Hr ☽ −39 mins
Next Hr ♃ +12 mins

Hs	Alm.
1	♄
2	♄
3	☉
4	♀
5	♀
6	☿
7	☽
8	☉
9	♄
10	♂
11	♂
12	♃

MUT. RECEPTIONS	
♄ ☿	Ruler−Exalt
♀ ♃	Ruler−Trip
♄ ☿	Ruler−Trip
♀ ♃	Ruler−Term
♃ ♄	Ruler−Term
☽ ♀	Ruler−Face

NEAREST ECLIPSES (NM/FM)					
☉ ●	1 Aug 2008	11:12	09°♌31	Total	S126
☽ ●	16 Aug 2008	22:16	24°♒21	Partial	S138
☉ ●	26 Jan 2009	08:55	06°♒29	Annular	S131
☽ ●	9 Feb 2009	15:49	20°♌59	Appulse	S143

traditionals.pts

Pt	Long.	Travel	Decl.	Last Stn	Next Stn	Last Stn	Next Stn	F/S	Antiscia	C.Ant.
☽	29°♎22'02"	+12°26'	−15°44'	−	−	−	−	Slow	00°♓37	00°♍37
☉	05°♏22'42"	+59'56"	−13°18'	−	−	−	−	Fast	24°♒37	24°♌37
☿	18°♎45	+01°27'	−05°25'	−12 days	+75 days	07°♎33'57"	07°♒45'23"	Fast	11°♓14	11°♍14
♀	11°♐42	+01°12'	−23°41'	−415 days	+129 days	16°♌35'27"	15°♈27'27"	Fast	18°♑17	18°♋17
♂	16°♏38	+41'51"	−16°53'	−271 days	+418 days	24°♊04'39"	19°♌41'42"	Fast	13°♒21	13°♌21
♃	16°♑19	+08'31"	−22°47'	−50 days	+229 days	12°♑32'00"	27°♒01'03"	Fast	13°♐40	13°♊40
♄	18°♍16	+05'55"	+06°16'	−178 days	+64 days	01°♍40'47"	21°♍46'00"	Fast	11°♈43	11°♎43

MOON ASPECTS		
☽ ⚹ As	3°55' S	
☽ ⚹ ♇	0°36' A	
☽ ☌ ♏	0°37' A	
☽ ☌ ☉	7°41' A	

ESSENTIAL DIGNITIES

Pt	Ruler	Exalt	Trip	Term	Face	Detri	Fall	Score
☽	♀	♄	♄	♂	♃	♂	☉	−5 p
☉	♂	--	♀ m	♂	♂ m	♀	☽	−5 p
☿	♀	♄ m	♄	♃	♄	♂	☉	−1 p
♀	♃	--	☉ m	♃ m	☽	☿	--	−5 p
♂	♂ +	--	♀	☿	☉ m	♀	☽	+5
♃	♄	♂	♀	♀ m	♂	☽	♃ −	−9 p
♄	☿	☿ m	♀	♃	♀	♃	♀	−1 p

ASPECTS	
♂ ⚹ ♃	0°19' S
☽ ⚹ ♇	0°36' A
As ⚹ Mc	0°51' A
♄ ☍ ♅	1°17' A
♂ □ ☋	1°36' S
♂ □ ☊	1°36' S
♂ ⚹ ♄	1°36' A
♃ △ ♄	1°57' A
☉ ⚹ As	2°10' S
☿ □ ♃	2°25' S

PLANETARY SECT

Planet	Cht	Plc	Sgn	Condition
☉ D	D	D	N	
☽ N	D	D	D	Ex Cond
☿ D	D	D	D	In Hayz
♀ N	D	D	D	Ex Cond
♂ N	D	D	N	
♃ D	D	N	N	
♄ D	D	D	N	

D=Diurnal, N=Nocturnal

SERVICES

Questions on services are so common that they deserve a special chapter.

Is this worker suitable for carrying out the works?
Will the company with which I have been negotiating the kitchen renovation, do the job well?
When will the plumber come to replace the broken sink?
Can I trust my neighbour with the baby-sitting job?

You probably agree that we often ask such questions. Horary astrology is an excellent tool to resolve them.

SIGNIFICATORS

The ascendant with H1 stands for the querent while H6 is for all kinds of service workers. This house also stands for tenants, but only for the actual ones, whereas potential tenants are shown by H7. *Would this person be a good tenant, should I accept him*? He is shown by H7. *When will my tenant leave?* In this case, the tenant is ruled by H6.

In contrast, all service workers belong to H6 from the start, that is, even before we negotiate business with them. The reason is simply that they are service workers by profession, and this role doesn't change whether we employ them or not. Companies performing such tasks also fall under H6, although we know that companies generally belong to H10. In real estate matters, H6 stands for the agents.

But if you ask whether your neighbor Shirley would be a suitable person to watch your children, Shirley would be shown by H3 - or H11, if she is more of a friend to you.

The exceptions among service workers are doctors and other therapists who deal with our bodies (and souls). These traditionally fall under H7.

The condition of service workers is judged by the state of H6. Is the worker capable, suitable, well-trained, skilled? This is shown by the essential strength of his significator(s). Will he have time to do what we ask of him and is it "destined" that he perform his task well and to our mutual satisfaction? This will be easier to assess by means of accidental strength of the planets. Will he work for us at all? This question is tackled by the conventional ways of the completion of the matter.

If the (planned) job/s relate to home, office or any kind of building, we must of course also take into account H4 which represents homes and parts of buildings (kitchens, bathrooms, gardens, etc.).

11/1: SHOULD WE DEMAND A RE-LAYING OF PARQUET FLOORING?

10 November 2004 at 7:47 a.m., Ljubljana, Slovenia
Hour ruler: Mercury

A friend asked me the above question by email, after she and her partner had realized that the recently laid parquet flooring in their renovated apartment was undulating. They were planning a move to the renovated premises shortly, and were seriously concerned about the newly arisen situation.

I read the question at 8:04, but it was asked a little earlier, because the email arrived in my inbox at 7:47. If I would cast the chart for 8:04, the ascendant would be in Sagittarius, with its ruler Jupiter without afflictions in H10, while the chart cast for 7:47 had the ascendant in Scorpio. This sign itself much better describes the "critical" emotional state of the querent who was worried because of the damage and the threat of a financial loss. This is confirmed by Scorpio's ruler Mars, weak in its detriment and placed in the last degree of a sign, as if the querent was exhausted from the long struggle. She really felt like that! Not only that she and her partner waited much too long for the works to get carried out; many other problems arose during the adaptation, and now - for the icing on the cake - the undulating parquet!

Her co-significator is the Moon which is also in Libra, peregrine. It is separating from the conjunction with Venus, the H6 ruler, signifying the parquetry floor layer, which properly describes their recent cooperation. Venus is strong in its own sign and in the fortunate H11, meaning that the worker was obviously qualified and efficient, so I concluded that the fault did not appear to be on his part, and that the reason for the problem probably lay elsewhere.

The sequence of events? The Moon applies by a square to Saturn, weak and "evil" by being retrograde, in detriment and in H8. This, along with the unenviable situation of Mars (which had recently separated by square from the same planet), suggests that the querent doesn't have much chance to settle the matter according to her wish. I told her that she apparently doesn't have the power to persuade him to do the re-laying, and that she should look for other options to the solution to the problem. I added that I also find it strange that the guilt should be on the part of the worker, as the chart showed that he had probably done his job well. Could there be another reason for the problem?

She agreed, saying that the floor layer warned her, before starting the works, that the screed (the concrete foundation) was poorly laid and that he feared that it would cause the undulation of the parquet. On the second thought, however, he decided to lay the parquet on the existing screed which he had previously coated with a protective layer. Alas, it didn't help.

It turned out that I was right. In spite of my advice, the querent requested the re-laying of the parquet, but the worker refused to do that, saying that the blame was entirely on the side of those who laid the screed.

A lawsuit followed, and there was a mediation which attempted to reconcile both sides by negotiating how they could jointly repair the damage. The screed worker insisted that the parquetry worker was to be blamed, and vice versa. The parquetry guy finally agreed to re-laying the parquet at his own costs, but the customers (the querent and her partner) should cover the costs of buying the new parquet. They disagreed, but on the recommendation of their lawyer they stopped the legal action. They received some compensation for damages from the insurance company and bought the new parquet by adding some of their own funds, but this took several years so that the parquet was finally re-laid only in the summer of 2008.

A little less than 4 years passed until the summer of 2008 – nearly so many time units as there are degrees from the Ascendant to the end of its sign (a little less than 4), showing a transition into a new phase (repair, modification).

Although horary charts are usually limited to the core question, they often reveal additional aspects of the "story", not directly related to the question. In this case, the querent's lawyer is shown by the Sun, the ruler of H9 which is in Scorpio, the ascending sign, showing that he really wanted to help and that, in the given situation, he did the most he could. The compensation which they received from the insurance company is shown by a harmonious applying sextile of Mercury, the ruler of H8 (insurance), to Jupiter, the ruler of H2 (their money).

I hope we can see that this chart describes the situation and the unraveling of the events much better than the chart cast for the time when I read and understood the question. You have the data - check it out!

11/1

10 Nov 2004
07:47 CET −1:00
Ljubljana, Slovenia
46°N03' 014°E31'

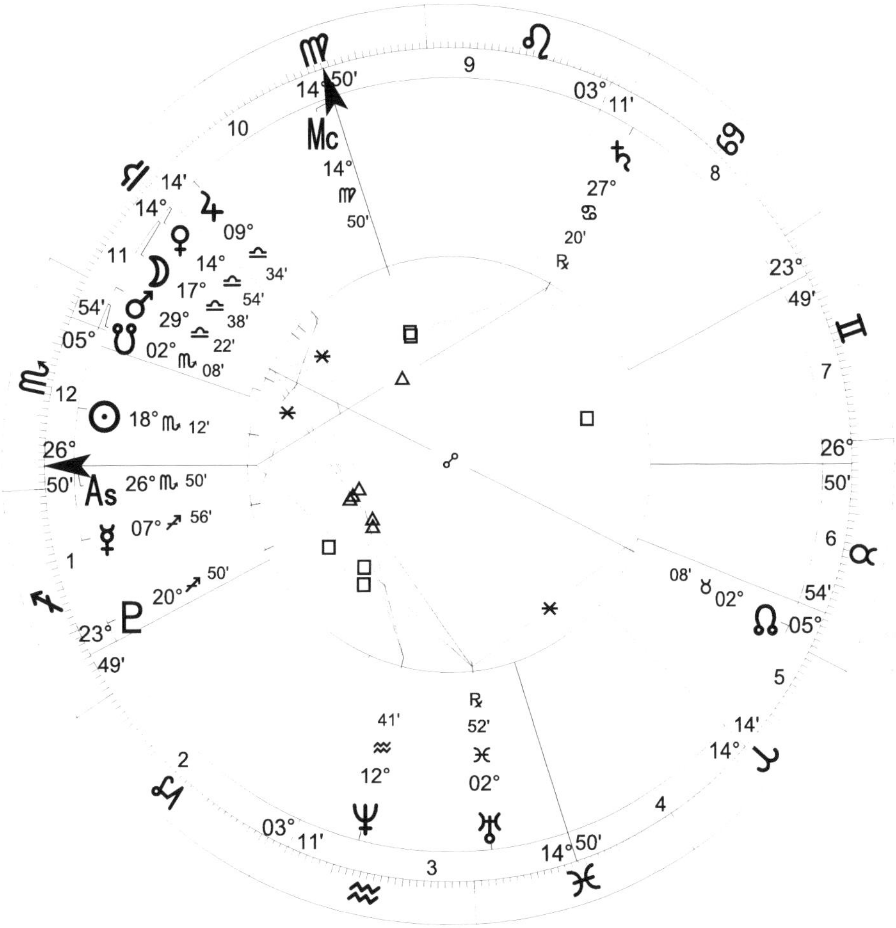

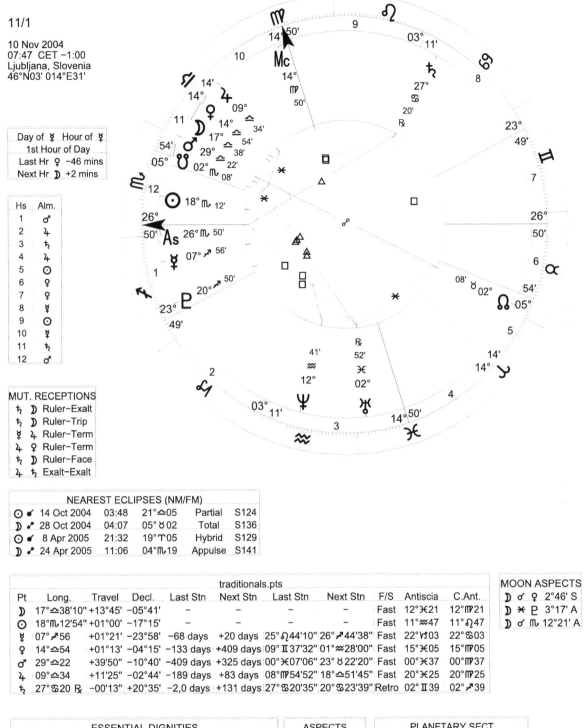

Day of ☿	Hour of ☿
1st Hour of Day	
Last Hr ♀	−46 mins
Next Hr ☽	+2 mins

Hs	Alm.
1	♂
2	♃
3	♄
4	♃
5	☉
6	♀
7	♀
8	☿
9	☉
10	☿
11	♄
12	♂

MUT. RECEPTIONS		
♄	☽	Ruler–Exalt
♄	☽	Ruler–Trip
☿	♃	Ruler–Term
♃	♀	Ruler–Term
♄	☽	Ruler–Face
♃	♄	Exalt–Exalt

NEAREST ECLIPSES (NM/FM)						
☉	●	14 Oct 2004	03:48	21°♎05	Partial	S124
☽	☍	28 Oct 2004	04:07	05°♉02	Total	S136
☉	●	8 Apr 2005	21:32	19°♈05	Hybrid	S129
☽	☍	24 Apr 2005	11:06	04°♏19	Appulse	S141

traditionals.pts

Pt	Long.	Travel	Decl.	Last Stn	Next Stn	Last Stn	Next Stn	F/S	Antiscia	C.Ant.
☽	17°♎38'10"	+13°45'	−05°41'	–	–	–	–	Fast	12°♓21	12°♍21
☉	18°♏12'54"	+01°00'	−17°15'	–	–	–	–	Fast	11°♒47	11°♌47
☿	07°♐56	+01°21'	−23°58'	−68 days	+20 days	25°♌44'10"	26°♐44'38"	Fast	22°♑03	22°♋03
♀	14°♎54	+01°13'	−04°15'	−133 days	+409 days	09°♊37'32"	01°♒28'00"	Fast	15°♓05	15°♍05
♂	29°♎22	+39'50"	−10°40'	−409 days	+325 days	00°♓07'06"	23°♉22'20"	Fast	00°♓37	00°♍37
♃	09°♎34	+11'25"	−02°44'	−189 days	+83 days	08°♍54'52"	18°♎51'45"	Fast	20°♓25	20°♍25
♄	27°♋20 ℞	−00'13"	+20°35'	−2,0 days	+131 days	27°♋20'35"	20°♋23'39"	Retro	02°♊39	02°♐39

MOON ASPECTS			
☽	☌	♀	2°46' S
☽	⚹	♇	3°17' A
☽	☌	♏	12°21' A

ESSENTIAL DIGNITIES

Pt	Ruler	Exalt	Trip	Term	Face	Detri	Fall	Score
☽	♀	♄	♄	♃	♄ m	♂	☉	−5 p
☉	♂	--	♀	☿	☉ +	♀	☽	+1
☿	♃	--	☉	♃ m	☿ +	☿ −	--	−4
♀	♀ +	♄	♄ m	♃	♄	♂	☉	+5
♂	♀	♄	♄	♂ +	♃	♂ −	☉	−3
♃	♀	♄ m	♄	☿ m	☽	♂	☉	−1 p
♄	☽	♃ m	♀ m	♄ +	☽ m	♄ −	♂	+1

ASPECTS			
♄	△	As	0°29' S
♅	⚹	☊	0°43' A
♅	△	☋	0°43' A
☿	⚹	♃	1°32' A
♂	□	♄	2°02' S
♀	△	♆	2°13' S
☽	☌	♀	2°46' S
♂	☍	☊	2°49' A
♂	☌	☋	2°49' A
♃	△	♆	3°06' A

PLANETARY SECT

Planet		Cht	Plc	Sgn	Condition
☉	D	D	D	N	
☽	N	D	D	D	Ex Cond
☿	N	D	N	D	
♀	N	D	D	D	Ex Cond
♂	N	D	D	D	Ex Cond
♃	D	D	D	D	In Hayz
♄	D	D	D	N	

D=Diurnal, N=Nocturnal

11/2: CAN THIS CARPENTER DO HIS JOB WELL AND WILL HE BUILD THE ROOF?

11 December 1994 at 5:26 p.m. (17:26), Ljubljana, Slovenia
Hour ruler: Jupiter

I had long been looking for a suitable carpenter to do the roofing in the new house, but to no avail. Some were too expensive, the others were constantly busy, and the third ones were not interested because they thought the roofing design was too complicated. I finally found someone who was ready to accept the challenge. But due to so many failed tries I wanted to make sure that this carpenter would do his job well, and I also wondered, of course, if our initial agreement would come into force at all.

The Ascendant is in Cancer - the sign which often rises in questions related to home, family and property. My significator is therefore the Moon, also showing the flow of events. In Aries, close to the cusp of H11, it clearly reflects my eagerness, hope and heart's desire to finally reach my goal.

The carpenter's significator is Jupiter, the ruler of H6 and also the planetary hour ruler. Since the ascendant is in Cancer, Jupiter's exaltation sign, the hour ruler is harmonious, and the planet puts additional weight on the subject matter (carpenter). Jupiter is in its own sign of Sagittarius, essentially dignified (domicile), so I assumed that the carpenter was a capable and honest man who would do his job well. (As you can see, Jupiter is by far the most essentially dignified planet in the chart, because it is also in its triplicity, term and monomoiria degree.)

But will he really do the job and not turn his back on me, as the others had done? He was honest, it seemed, but what about "fate" or forces beyond our control? In other words, will everything go as planned? For an affirmative answer, we need some kind of "completion of the matter". Do we have it? The Moon is separating from a trine with Jupiter, which in itself tends towards a negative answer, but you'll notice that its next aspect is a trine with Mercury – this being the significator of our house, as the cusp of H4 is in Virgo. We are dealing, therefore, with a beautiful example of translation of light, with the Moon separating from one significator and applying to another, enabling completion and giving an affirmative answer.

Another confirmation can be found in the fact that Mercury rules H4 and is placed in H6 – as if our house would be "in the hands" of the carpenter. Technically, this situation is called emplacement and contributes to a positive answer.

But we can see that Mercury is conjunct the Sun - combust. What could this mean, in the context of the question? As we know, combustion shows some kind of concealment, entrapment or powerlessness. It can literally mean "invisibility". And so it was: shortly thereafter, the house got covered with snow, so that we had to postpone the works for a few months. But the carpenter kept his promise and began working in the spring. We never had any problems either with him or with the beautifully designed roofing which he masterfully constructed.

11/2

11 Dec 1994
17:26 CET −1:00
Ljubljana, Slovenia
46°N03' 014°E31'

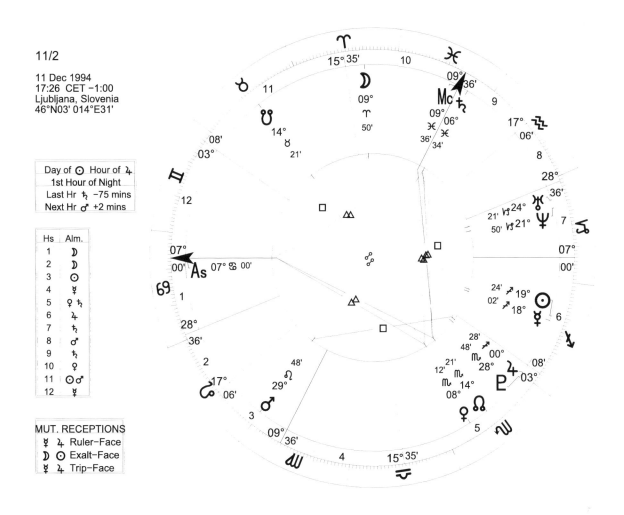

Day of ☉ Hour of ♃
1st Hour of Night
Last Hr ♄ −75 mins
Next Hr ♂ +2 mins

Hs	Alm.
1	☽
2	☽
3	☉
4	☿
5	♀ ♄
6	♃
7	♄
8	♂
9	♄
10	♀
11	☉♂
12	☿

MUT. RECEPTIONS
☿ ♃ Ruler–Face
☽ ☉ Exalt–Face
☿ ♃ Trip–Face

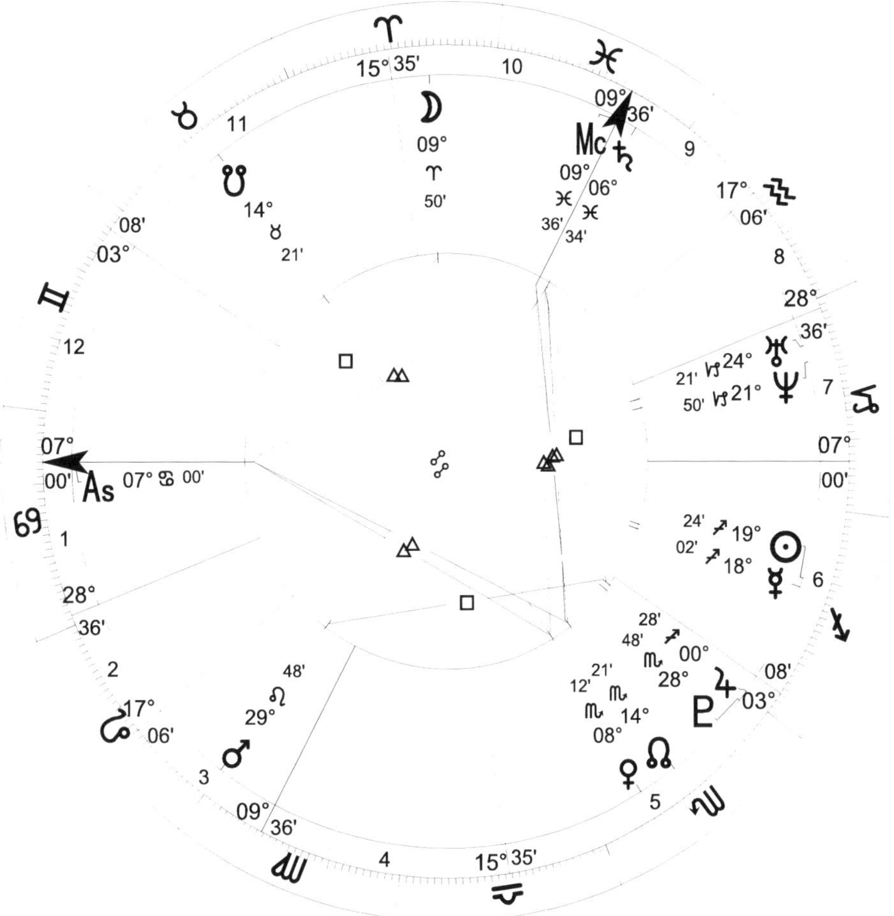

NEAREST ECLIPSES (NM/FM)					
☉ ●	3 Nov 1994	14:35	10°♏54	Total	S133
☽ ○	18 Nov 1994	07:57	25°♉42	Appulse	S145
☽ ○	15 Apr 1995	13:08	25°♎03	Partial	S112
☉ ●	29 Apr 1995	18:36	08°♉56	Annular	S138

traditionals.pts

Pt	Long.	Travel	Decl.	Last Stn	Next Stn	Last Stn	Next Stn	F/S	Antiscia	C.Ant.
☽	09°♈50'35"	+12°05'	+06°37'	–	–	–	–	Slow	20°♍09	20°♓09
☉	19°♐24'18"	+01°00'	−23°01'	–	–	–	–	Fast	10°♑35	10°♋35
☿	18°♐02	+01°34'	−23°55'	−42 days	+45 days	20°♎48'54"	21°♒15'53"	Fast	11°♑57	11°♋57
♀	08°♏12	+34'58"	−11°53'	−17 days	+525 days	02°♏28'46"	28°♊17'52"	Slow	21°♒47	21°♌47
♂	29°♌48	+14'28"	+14°05'	−664 days	+22 days	08°♋40'31"	02°♍40'08"	Slow	00°♉11	00°♏11
♃	00°♐28	+12'57"	−19°30'	−162 days	+110 days	04°♏46'04"	15°♐23'00"	Fast	29°♑31	29°♋31
♄	06°♓34	+03'16"	−10°48'	−32 days	+206 days	05°♓40'45"	24°♓45'07"	Fast	23°♎25	23°♈25

MOON ASPECTS
☽ ☌ ♈ 9°50' S
☽ □ As 2°49' S

ESSENTIAL DIGNITIES

Pt	Ruler	Exalt	Trip	Term	Face	Detri	Fall	Score
☽	♂	☉	♃	♀	♂	♀	♄	−5 p
☉	♃	--	♃	☿	☽	☿	--	−5 p
☿	♃	--	♃	☿ +	☽	☿ −	--	−3
♀	♂	--	♂	♀ +	♂	♀ −	☽	−3
♂	☉	--	♃	♂ +	♂ +	♄	--	+3
♃	♃ +	--	♃ +	♃ +	☿	☿	--	+10
♄	♃	♀	♂	♀	♄ +	☿	☿	+1

ASPECTS
♄ △ As 0°25' S
♂ □ ♃ 0°38' A
♀ △ As 1°09' S
♀ △ Mc 1°21' S
♀ △ ♄ 1°35' S
♂ □ ♇ 1°36' S
☉ ☌ ☿ 1°42' A
As △ Mc 2°35' S
☽ □ As 2°49' S
♅ ✶ ♇ 3°15' A

PLANETARY SECT

Planet		Cht	Plc	Sgn	Condition
☉	D	N	N	D	
☽	N	N	N	D	
☿	D	N	D	D	
♀	N	N	D	N	
♂	N	N	D	D	
♃	D	N	D	D	
♄	D	N	N	N	Ex Cond

D=Diurnal, N=Nocturnal

11/3: WILL MY DESIGNER GET HIS WORK DONE BY MONDAY?

16 December 2006 at 741 p.m. (19:41), Ljubljana, Slovenia
Hour ruler: Saturn

For a week I had been trying in vain to reach my designer who had to make some adjustments on the cover of my forthcoming book. He should have finished the cover a while ago, as I was already late in getting the book to print. I called him on the cellphone, I sent him several emails and even showed up in his office, where I found only his colleagues who said they did not know where he was, but that as far as they know, he had been very busy lately. Back home, I wrote yet another desperate email, saying that Monday morning was the very last deadline and that I trust I'd have his cover by then. Shortly after that I posed the above question.

The designer is shown by H6 with the cusp in Capricorn. His significator is Saturn (also the hour ruler, stressing the subject matter and thus giving validity to the chart, considering the fact that the planetary hour is disharmonious), placed in H1, retrograde and in detriment (Leo). Is he tired and/or not feeling well? He might be, but the planet's retrograde movement shows that he's coming back - to me (H1)! Very good! The Sun, my ruler, is in Sagittarius and in the fortunate H5, in an exact applying trine with Saturn which it also receives in its domicile. (OK, I was angry, but of course I was "receiving" him as I desperately wanted the job to be done!)

This is definitely a very good indication, I thought. But what about the Moon? It's in Scorpio, as my co-significator nicely describing my helplessness, frustration and anger (besides being the Moon's fall, Scorpio is a Martian sign!). But the Moon is closely applying by trine to Uranus, promising a sudden fortunate turn. It's a clear hint that my problems were coming to an end!

However, despite the good prospects in the chart it would not be appropriate to stop "pushing" him. On Monday morning I called him twice on a cell phone but he cut off the ring tone both times, making me feel like a complete fool. OK, maybe he's in a meeting, I thought. Then - surprise! His majesty called me himself, politely apologizing and saying that he had to focus on a "major project" for the whole past week. (Like my project was trash - or...?). He saw my emails, he said, but he had so little time that he couldn't even open and read them. Today, however, he'd do what he had promised, he said.

I said that I believed him, and indeed: by the evening all his files were in my email.

Case closed, but let me turn your attention to the co-almuten of H6, Mars. I didn't take that into account when initially judging the chart, and it also wasn't necessary, as the main H6 ruler is also the hour ruler and should be given priority. Nevertheless, it's interesting that Mars is in an exact trine with the ascendant, in H5 of creativity, and in the derived H12 (12/6). The man was actually "hiding" from me and others, so as to be able to dedicate himself to other creative jobs that were pressing on him.

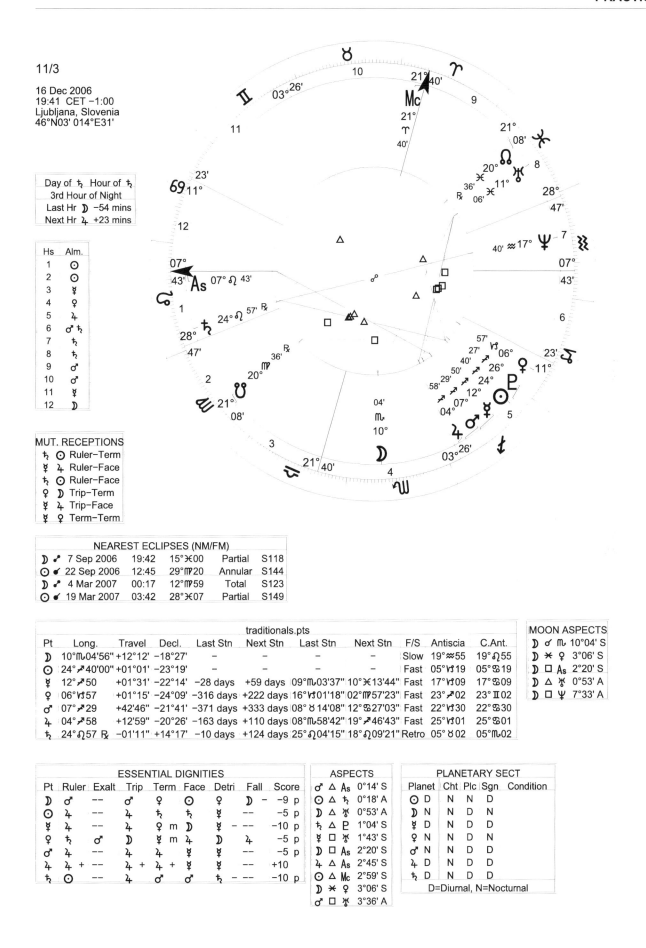

11/3

16 Dec 2006
19:41 CET −1:00
Ljubljana, Slovenia
46°N03' 014°E31'

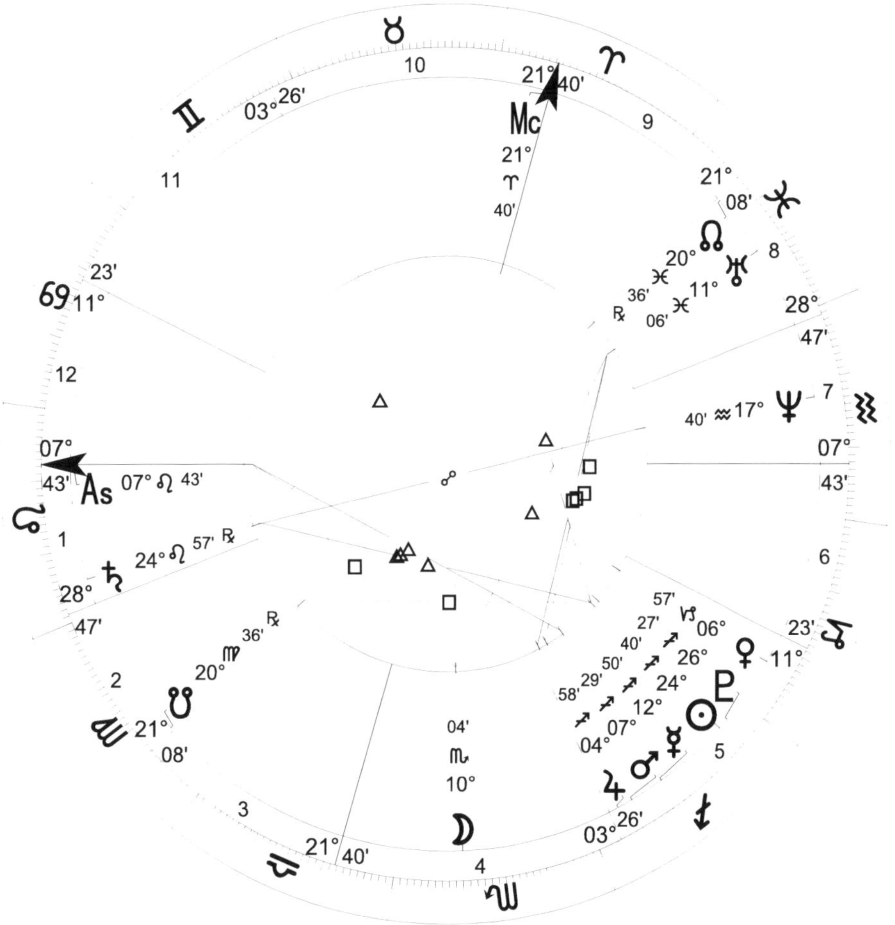

Day of ♄ Hour of ♄
3rd Hour of Night
Last Hr ☽ −54 mins
Next Hr ♃ +23 mins

Hs	Alm.
1	☉
2	☉
3	☿
4	♀
5	♃
6	♂ ♄
7	♄
8	♄
9	♂
10	♂
11	☿
12	☽

MUT. RECEPTIONS		
♄	☉	Ruler−Term
☿	♃	Ruler−Face
♄	☉	Ruler−Face
♀	☽	Trip−Term
☿	♃	Trip−Face
☿	♀	Term−Term

NEAREST ECLIPSES (NM/FM)					
☽ ☍	7 Sep 2006	19:42	15°♓00	Partial	S118
☉ ☌	22 Sep 2006	12:45	29°♍20	Annular	S144
☽ ☍	4 Mar 2007	00:17	12°♍59	Total	S123
☉ ☌	19 Mar 2007	03:42	28°♓07	Partial	S149

traditionals.pts

Pt	Long.	Travel	Decl.	Last Stn	Next Stn	Last Stn	Next Stn	F/S	Antiscia	C.Ant.
☽	10°♏04'56"	+12°12'	−18°27'	–	–	–	–	Slow	19°♒55	19°♌55
☉	24°♐40'00"	+01°01'	−23°19'	–	–	–	–	Fast	05°♑19	05°♋19
☿	12°♐50	+01°31'	−22°14'	−28 days	+59 days	09°♏03'37"	10°♓13'44"	Fast	17°♑09	17°♋09
♀	06°♑57	+01°15'	−24°09'	−316 days	+222 days	16°♑01'18"	02°♍57'23"	Fast	23°♐02	23°♊02
♂	07°♐29	+42'46"	−21°41'	−371 days	+333 days	08°♉14'08"	12°♋27'03"	Fast	22°♑30	22°♋30
♃	04°♐58	+12'59"	−20°26'	−163 days	+110 days	08°♏58'42"	19°♐46'43"	Fast	25°♑01	25°♋01
♄	24°♌57 ℞	−01'11"	+14°17'	−10 days	+124 days	25°♌04'15"	18°♌09'21"	Retro	05°♉02	05°♏02

MOON ASPECTS			
☽ ☌	♏	10°04'	S
☽ ⚹	♀	3°06'	S
☽ □	As	2°20'	S
☽ △	♅	0°53'	A
☽ □	♆	7°33'	A

ESSENTIAL DIGNITIES

Pt	Ruler	Exalt	Trip	Term	Face	Detri	Fall	Score
☽	♂	--	♂	♀	☉	♀	☽ −	−9 p
☉	♃	--	♃	♄	♄	☿	--	−5 p
☿	♃	--	♃	♀ m	☽	☿ −	--	−10 p
♀	♄	♂	☽	☿ m	♃	☽	♃	−5 p
♂	♃	--	♃	♃	☿	☿	--	−5 p
♃	♃ +	--	♃ +	♃ +	☿	☿	--	+10
♄	☉	--	♃	♂	♂	♄ −	--	−10 p

ASPECTS		
♂ △ As	0°14'	S
☉ △ ♄	0°18'	A
☽ △ ♅	0°53'	A
♄ △ ♇	1°04'	S
☿ □ ♅	1°43'	S
☽ □ As	2°20'	S
♃ △ As	2°45'	S
☉ △ Mc	2°59'	S
☽ ⚹ ♀	3°06'	S
♂ □ ♅	3°36'	A

PLANETARY SECT

Planet		Cht	Plc	Sgn	Condition
☉	D	N	N	D	
☽	N	N	D	N	
☿	D	N	D	D	
♀	N	N	D	N	
♂	N	N	D	D	
♃	D	N	D	D	
♄	D	N	D	D	

D=Diurnal, N=Nocturnal

11/4: WILL TONY CONSTRUCT OUR FIREPLACE?

2 October 2008 at 10:34 a.m., Ljubljana, Slovenia
Hour ruler: Venus

In the autumn of 2007, I made a mistake: I bought a fireplace stove on a Mercury retrograde day. That was a big, heavy and awkward thing which only four strong men could lift and carry for a few inches at a time. Because we planned to construct the fireplace in the winter, we let it stay on the trailer, parked in the front yard, until the workers arrived and could carry it into the house. It turned out that the fireplace was not constructed during that winter because we couldn't find a suitable craftsman, so the stove remained stuck on the trailer. We diligently avoided it all year long, until the autumn of 2008 when the new heating season started. We had been negotiating the works with a certain craftsman, let's call him Tony, since the previous season. He promised he'd start working in the summer, but when summer arrived he had all kinds of excuses: once he was on leave, then he was sick, or too busy, or his coworker fell ill, or he was off on another leave, until (already late in the autumn) he was supposed to be confined to bed with severe pneumonia. I'll call you in 2 weeks, he said. He didn't, but I did, only to hear a new excuse. OK, I said, if he can't say directly that he won't do the job, let's give him the opportunity to apologize through a friend - the one who recommended him. So I called this guy and said, can you please check whether Tony is really ill, or is he just fooling us? He did and assured me that Tony would soon come to work for us – it's been settled, he said. But I somehow no longer believed his promises and therefore raised the above question.

Tony is shown by Mars, the ruler of H6, placed in H12 (secrecy, resignation, powerlessness), in detriment and void-of-course, suggesting that "nothing comes of the matter". Checking the Sun, almuten of H6, we find it in Libra, again in detriment and in an applying square with Jupiter, the ruler of H4 (our home), without reception. Since Mars also rules myself, we should find some connection between the Moon (course of events), Mars and Jupiter (or the Sun) for a positive answer, but there is none. The answer is therefore a clear NO, and this is confirmed by an inharmonious planetary hour ruler (Venus).

And so it was: Tony never called again.

The poor state of Mars also reflects my own worry and hopelessness, of course, but you'll notice that Mars is in a strong mutual reception with Venus (by domicile) which indicates that I have a choice, and actually shows a way out. If we mutually exchange Mars' and Venus' placements, we can imagine Mars at 10 degrees Scorpio applying by sextile to Jupiter (our home) and Saturn (natural significator of construction). It is clear that we'll find another worker! This is confirmed by the Moon translating light from Jupiter to Saturn.

And we did find him, in about a month. He was a capable craftsman who carried out the works to our utmost satisfaction. The time which had passed until our meeting is reflected by two chart factors: the Moon needs one degree (one month) to a sextile with Saturn, and 4 degrees (4 weeks or one month) to reach the ascendant. Saturn is in the detriment of Jupiter, but it receives Jupiter in its domicile, while Jupiter applies to it by trine, with the aspect being supported by the translation of light, so there's a good and strong connection between the planets which clearly reflects the harmonious development of the situation.

It is also interesting that the hour ruler is Venus – exactly the planet which represents the second craftsman, for the reasons already stated (mutual reception with Mars). The hour ruler is disharmonious which in this case contributed to a negative answer, but it also helps to understand the final result.

11/4

2 Oct 2008
10:34 CEDT −2:00
Ljubljana, Slovenia
46°N03' 014°E31'

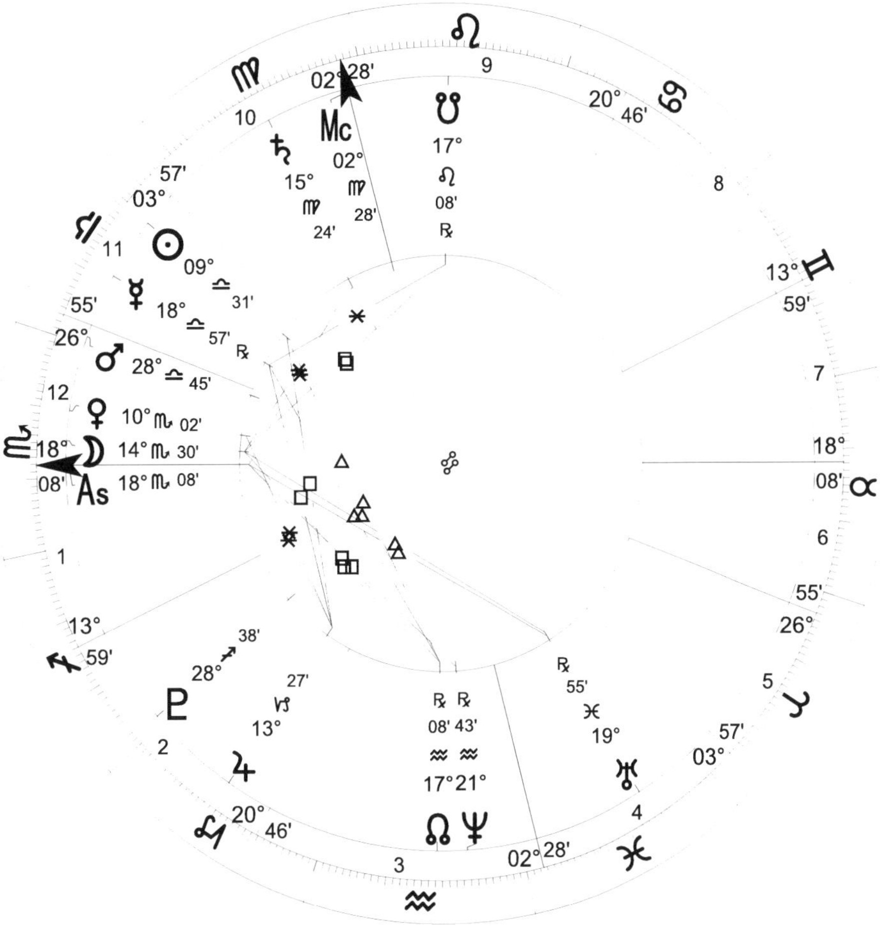

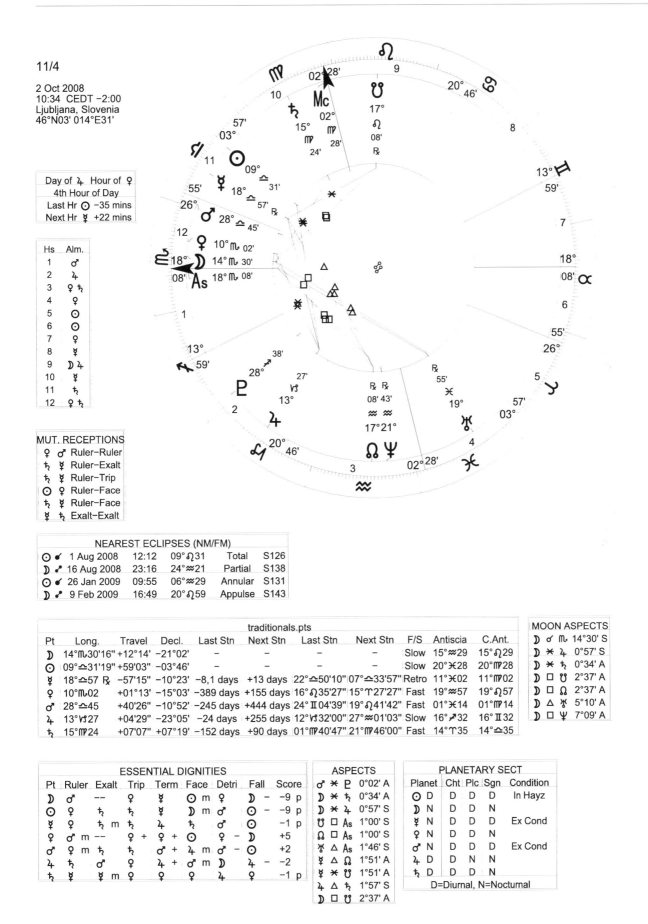

Day of ♃ Hour of ♀
4th Hour of Day
Last Hr ☉ −35 mins
Next Hr ☿ +22 mins

Hs	Alm.
1	♂
2	♃
3	♀ ♄
4	♀
5	☉
6	☉
7	♀
8	☿
9	☽ ♃
10	☿
11	♄
12	♀ ♄

MUT. RECEPTIONS	
♀ ♂	Ruler–Ruler
♄ ☿	Ruler–Exalt
♄ ☿	Ruler–Trip
☉ ♀	Ruler–Face
♄ ☿	Ruler–Face
☿ ♄	Exalt–Exalt

NEAREST ECLIPSES (NM/FM)					
☉ ●	1 Aug 2008	12:12	09°♌31	Total	S126
☽ ☍	16 Aug 2008	23:16	24°♒21	Partial	S138
☉ ●	26 Jan 2009	09:55	06°♒29	Annular	S131
☽ ☍	9 Feb 2009	16:49	20°♌59	Appulse	S143

traditionals.pts

Pt	Long.	Travel	Decl.	Last Stn	Next Stn	Last Stn	Next Stn	F/S	Antiscia	C.Ant.
☽	14°♏30'16"	+12°14'	−21°02'	–	–	–	–	Slow	15°♒29	15°♌29
☉	09°♎31'19"	+59'03"	−03°46'	–	–	–	–	Slow	20°♓28	20°♍28
☿	18°♎57 ℞	−57'15"	−10°23'	−8,1 days	+13 days	22°♎50'10"	07°♎33'57"	Retro	11°♓02	11°♍02
♀	10°♏02	+01°13'	−15°03'	−389 days	+155 days	16°♌35'27"	15°♈27'27"	Fast	19°♒57	19°♌57
♂	28°♎45	+40'26"	−10°52'	−245 days	+444 days	24°♊04'39"	19°♌41'42"	Fast	01°♓14	01°♍14
♃	13°♑27	+04'29"	−23°05'	−24 days	+255 days	12°♑32'00"	27°♒01'03"	Slow	16°♐32	16°♊32
♄	15°♍24	+07'07"	+07°19'	−152 days	+90 days	01°♍40'47"	21°♍46'00"	Fast	14°♈35	14°♎35

MOON ASPECTS			
☽	☌	♏	14°30' S
☽	⚹	♃	0°57' S
☽	⚹	♄	0°34' A
☽	□	☋	2°37' A
☽	□	☊	2°37' A
☽	△	♅	5°10' A
☽	□	♆	7°09' A

ESSENTIAL DIGNITIES

Pt	Ruler	Exalt	Trip	Term	Face	Detri	Fall	Score
☽	♂	--	♀	☿	☉ m	♀	☽ −	−9 p
☉	♀	♄	♄	☿	☽ m	♂	☉ −	−9 p
☿	♀	♄ m	♄	♃	♄	♂	☉	−1 p
♀	♂ m	--	♀ +	♀ +	☉	♀ −	☽	+5
♂	♀ m	♄	♄	♂ +	♃ m	♂ −	☉	+2
♃	♄	♂	♀	♃ +	♂ m	☽	♃ −	−2
♄	☿	☿ m	♀	♀	♀	♃	♀	−1 p

ASPECTS			
♂	⚹	♇	0°02' A
☽	⚹	♄	0°34' A
☽	⚹	♃	0°57' S
☋	□	As	1°00' S
☊	□	As	1°00' S
♅	△	As	1°46' S
☿	△	☊	1°51' A
☿	⚹	☋	1°51' A
♃	△	♄	1°57' S
☽	□	☋	2°37' A

PLANETARY SECT

Planet		Cht	Plc	Sgn	Condition
☉	D	D	D	D	In Hayz
☽	N	D	D	N	
☿	N	D	D	D	Ex Cond
♀	N	D	D	N	
♂	N	D	D	D	Ex Cond
♃	D	D	N	N	
♄	D	D	D	N	

D=Diurnal, N=Nocturnal

11/5: WHEN WILL THE WORKERS ARRIVE?

17 November 2008 at 6:36 p.m. (18:36), Droitwich (UK)
Hour ruler: Mercury

This question was raised on one of the horary forums. The querent had an appointment with the workers who were to replace an old window with a new one. They said that they would come sometime during the next day, but they didn't say exactly when. Now, since the querent had a busy day ahead, with some task to accomplish outside the house, she was eager to know when exactly they would knock at her door. Being an astrologer, she cast a horary chart and posted it in the group, asking fellow astrologers for help her read the chart.

The querent is shown by the Moon, ruler of H1, at 28°30' Cancer. The workers are shown by Jupiter, ruling H6, and Jupiter is in Capricorn at 19°38'. Now, because the Moon, our querent, is in a wide separating opposition with Jupiter, she thought that the answer could be no, they wouldn't come at all. But, as she told us in another post dated 19th November, they did come, at exactly 10 minutes past midday. How does the chart show that, she wondered?

To begin with, there is a planet in H6 which should be regarded as a co-significator of the workers: Mars. Moon's application to Mars by trine is certainly a favorable indication, but the orb is 3°31'. Could that mean that they'd be 3 days late? Not necessarily, because, as I have outlined in the timing chapter, the timing can be arrived at by means of the angles, that is, by their distance to/from significators.

Knowing that, I found the corresponding time unit in a few minutes. I wrote: *The question was not whether the workers would come but when would that happen. Ten minutes past midday are 17.5 hours after the question which was asked at 18:36 (6:36 p.m.) on the previous day. If we move the MC/IC axis which runs along 2° Pisces/Virgo, by 17.5 degrees, we arrive at 19.5 Pisces/Virgo which is in an exact trine/sextile to Jupiter (the workers), while at the same time the IC (home matters) comes to the conjunction with Saturn which is placed in the 4th house, showing the job at hand. You will notice that Saturn also disposits Jupiter so that the two planets reinforce each other.*

The responses to my post showed that astrologers who participated in the discussion were completely unaware of this timing method; someone wondered if it's "legal", and one other group member even mocked me, saying that my imagination has run wild. To me, it was just another proof that horary charts speak to us in more ways than we are used to consider. "My" method is perfectly consistent with astro-logic and also with the tradition which mentions it, albeit rarely. But this is another example of how extremely useful and reliable are the angles when looking for the timing.

I should add that taking into account the parallax, the Moon moves from 28°29' to 29°00' Cancer, which makes it exactly 1 degree distant from the next sign. Translated into time units, that would make it one day. The precise timing, however, can only be obtained by the above mentioned technique!

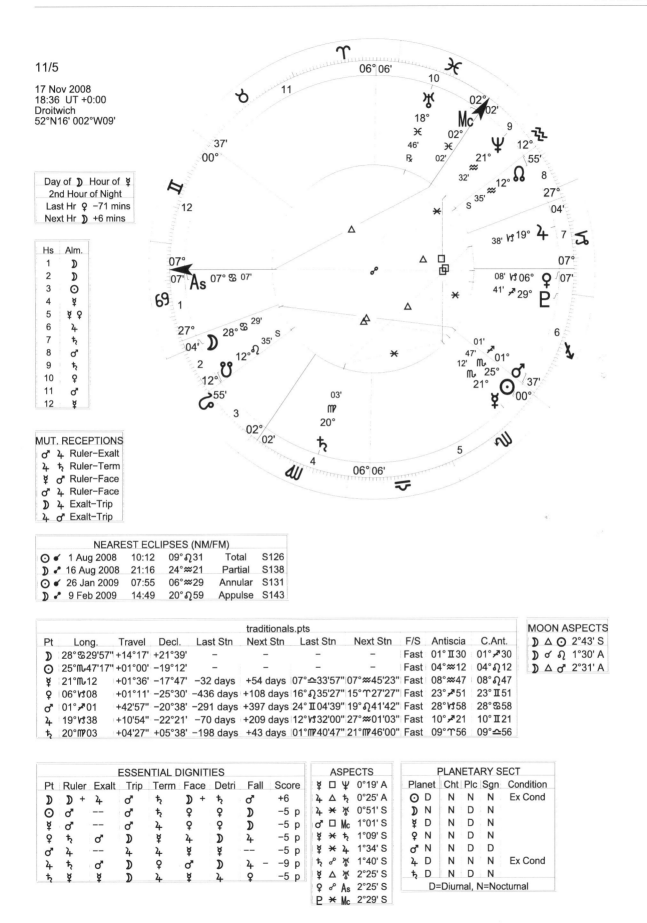

11/5

17 Nov 2008
18:36 UT +0:00
Droitwich
52°N16' 002°W09'

Day of ☽ Hour of ☿
2nd Hour of Night
Last Hr ♀ −71 mins
Next Hr ☽ +6 mins

Hs	Alm.
1	☽
2	☽
3	☉
4	☿
5	☿ ♀
6	♃
7	♄
8	♂
9	♄
10	♀
11	♂
12	☿

MUT. RECEPTIONS
♂ ♃ Ruler–Exalt
♃ ♄ Ruler–Term
☿ ♂ Ruler–Face
♂ ♃ Ruler–Face
☽ ♃ Exalt–Trip
♃ ♂ Exalt–Trip

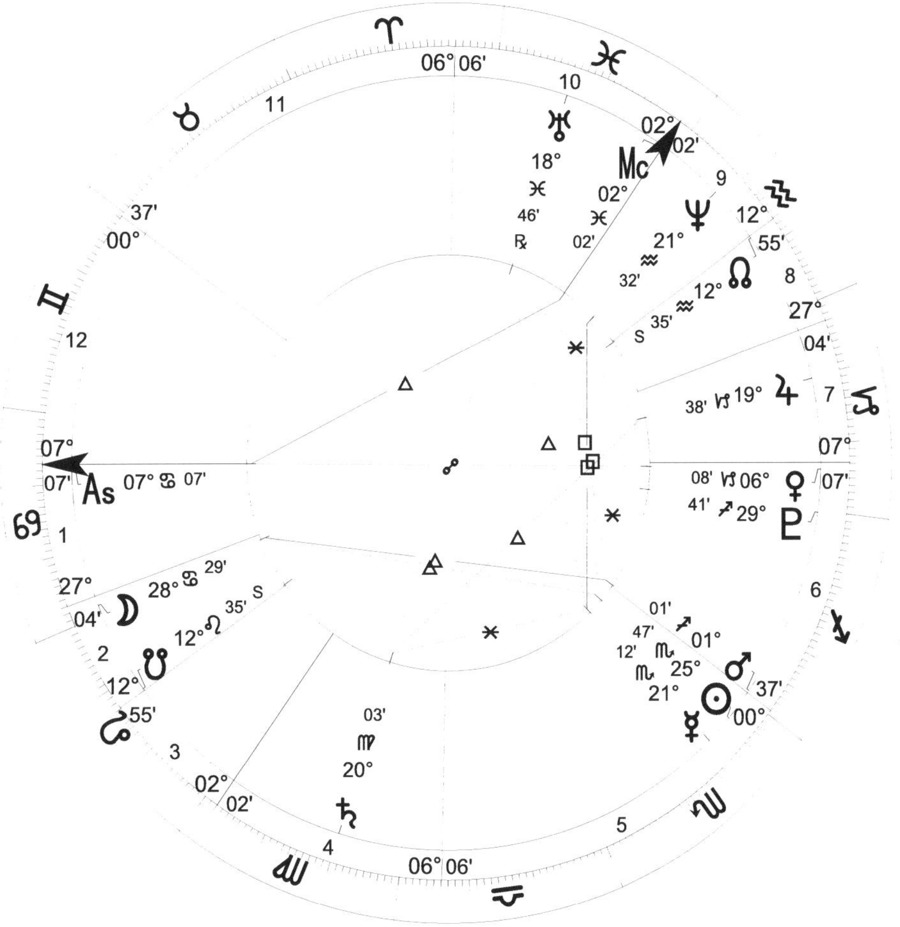

NEAREST ECLIPSES (NM/FM)					
☉ ●	1 Aug 2008	10:12	09°♌31	Total	S126
☽ ☍	16 Aug 2008	21:16	24°♒21	Partial	S138
☉ ●	26 Jan 2009	07:55	06°♒29	Annular	S131
☽ ☍	9 Feb 2009	14:49	20°♌59	Appulse	S143

traditionals.pts

Pt	Long.	Travel	Decl.	Last Stn	Next Stn	Last Stn	Next Stn	F/S	Antiscia	C.Ant.
☽	28°♋29'57"	+14°17'	+21°39'	–	–	–	–	Fast	01°♊30	01°♐30
☉	25°♏47'17"	+01°00'	−19°12'	–	–	–	–	Fast	04°♒12	04°♌12
☿	21°♏12	+01°36'	−17°47'	−32 days	+54 days	07°♎33'57"	07°♒45'23"	Fast	08°♒47	08°♌47
♀	06°♑08	+01°11'	−25°30'	−436 days	+108 days	16°♌35'27"	15°♈27'27"	Fast	23°♐51	23°♊51
♂	01°♐01	+42'57"	−20°38'	−291 days	+397 days	24°♊04'39"	19°♌41'42"	Fast	28°♑58	28°♋58
♃	19°♑38	+10'54"	−22°21'	−70 days	+209 days	12°♑32'00"	27°♒01'03"	Fast	10°♐21	10°♊21
♄	20°♍03	+04'27"	+05°38'	−198 days	+43 days	01°♍40'47"	21°♍46'00"	Fast	09°♈56	09°♎56

MOON ASPECTS
☽ △ ☉ 2°43' S
☽ ☌ ♌ 1°30' A
☽ △ ♂ 2°31' A

ESSENTIAL DIGNITIES

Pt	Ruler	Exalt	Trip	Term	Face	Detri	Fall	Score
☽	☽ +	♃	♂	♄	☽ +	♄	♂	+6
☉	♂	--	♂	♄	♀	♀	☽	−5 p
☿	♂	--	♂	♃	♀	♀	☽	−5 p
♀	♄	♂	☽	☿	♃	☽	♃	−5 p
♂	♃	--	♃	♃	☿	☿	--	−5 p
♃	♄	♂	☽	♀	♂	☽	♃ −	−9 p
♄	☿	☿	☽	♃	☿	♃	♀	−5 p

ASPECTS
☿ □ ♆ 0°19' A
♃ △ ♄ 0°25' A
♃ ⚹ ♅ 0°51' S
♂ □ Mc 1°01' S
☿ ⚹ ♄ 1°09' S
☿ ⚹ ♃ 1°34' S
♄ ☍ ♅ 1°40' S
☿ △ ♅ 2°25' S
♀ ☍ As 2°25' S
♇ ⚹ Mc 2°29' S

PLANETARY SECT

Planet		Cht	Plc	Sgn	Condition
☉	D	N	N	N	Ex Cond
☽	N	N	D	N	
☿	D	N	D	N	
♀	N	N	D	N	
♂	N	N	D	D	
♃	D	N	N	N	Ex Cond
♄	D	N	D	N	

D=Diurnal, N=Nocturnal

11/6: WHOM SHOULD I HIRE, ARIF OR STEPHEN?

23 March 1994 at 6:52 a.m., Ljubljana, Slovenia
Hour ruler: Mercury

I raised this question when I was in a big dilemma. I planned building a house sometime in May, and I was choosing between two construction workers: Arif and Stephen. Arif's group had built a house of my parents' neighbours two years ago, while Stephen was currently building the house of my (future) neighbours. I already had a loose agreement with Arif, since the previous year; his fee was accessible and the man seemed honest and capable. But I hesitated because my future neighbor highly praised Stephen, saying that he was a master-builder, diligent and reliable, although a bit more expensive than Arif. He told me that he had already spoken to Stephen and that he agreed to work for me.

So, what to do? I already had a deal with Arif; I'd have to wait for Stephen a bit longer, and he was more expensive, but on the other hand, I heard rumors that Arif was a bit clumsy. But rumors can't be trusted, I thought, so I decided to consult the "heavens". Whom should I hire?

The significators are: the ascendant, Mars and the Moon for me (partly Venus, ruling the intercepted H1 sign of Taurus, and the Sun, the almuten of the ascendant), Saturn for Arif and Jupiter for Stephen. Why? Significators of both parties are found by using the derived houses: H1 represents me, H3 my neighbor, and H8 (6/3) his worker; because the cusp of H8 is in Sagittarius, ruled by Jupiter, this planet stands for Stephen. Similarly H4 represents my parents, H6 (3/4) their neighbor and H11 (6/6) their worker; as H11 is ruled by Saturn, this planet stands for Arif. (I could add that the H11 almuten is Mars, but this planet already rules me, so we leave it out.)

The next step is to examine the essential dignities of the two workers' significators. The planet which is more powerful by this criteria should point to the more skillful and reliable candidate. Saturn (Arif) is in its face, while Jupiter has no essential dignity (is peregrine), but it's in a strong mutual reception with Mars, ruling me. As for accidental dignity, Saturn (8 points) leads Jupiter (4 points), possibly reflecting the fact that I was at that time favoring Arif. (I hadn't even met Stephen.)

The next step is to examine the contacts between all the significators. Mars separates from a conjunction with Saturn (Arif), showing our recent agreement, but due to the separating nature of the aspect we are obviously getting apart. Since the separation has not been completed, with both planets still in an orb of aspect, we'll probably meet again, but since neither the Moon nor Venus and not even the Sun have any contacts with Saturn, it is clear that our agreement will not come to fruition.

What about Jupiter and Mars? Mars and the retrograde Jupiter mutually apply to each other by a trine, and since they're also in a mutual reception by domicile (plus in a couple of weaker receptions), it is clear that I'll hire Stefan. The Moon applies to Jupiter by a wide square, which is not so good, but it can't spoil the promise of the main significators. I was a bit worried about Jupiter's retrograde state, as this could show a delay or at least a slow progress, but it could also describe Stephen as a reserved and quiet man. All of this proved to be true!

I phoned Arif again, but when I told him that it would be necessary to build the house completely according to the construction plan and that his team would be monitored by a supervisor, his enthusiasm quickly vanished; although he said that he'd call me to confirm our deal, he never did.

I soon arranged a meeting with Stefan and his team, but due to his work overload the meeting got delayed (retrograde Jupiter!). I first met him on 16 April when the transiting Sun was at 26° Aries - exactly conjunct the horary ascendant - while the Moon was at 24° Gemini, on the cusp of H3 of the horary chart, so of course it was no coincidence that we met at my neighbor's place!

Stefan proved to be a competent and diligent worker, although quiet and reserved by nature. The works on the house went well and the only problem I had with him was his occasional unavailability due to another job he did simultaneously. But all in all, I was sure that "the heavens" made the right decision.

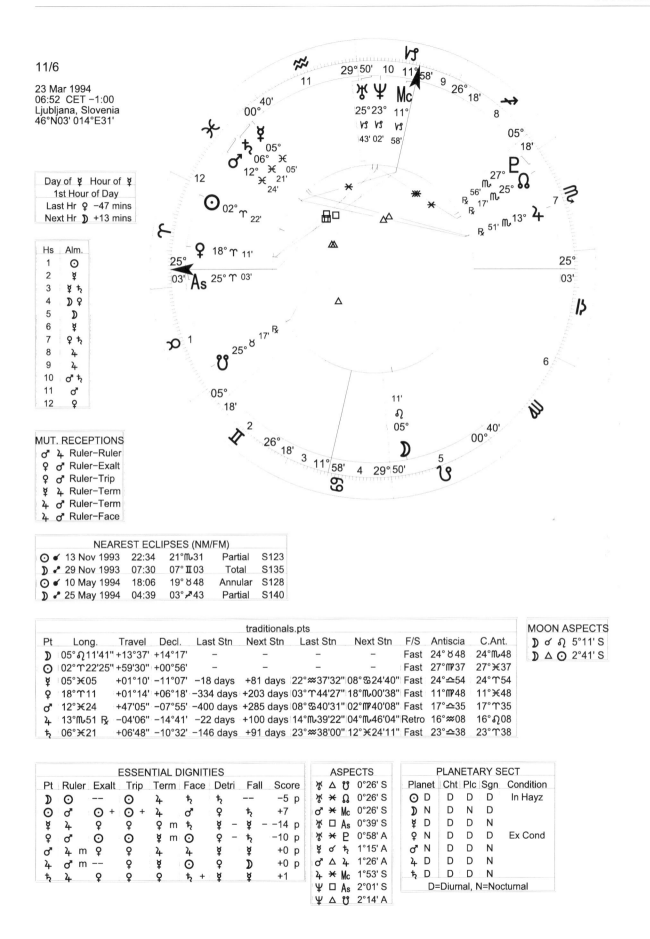

11/6

23 Mar 1994
06:52 CET −1:00
Ljubljana, Slovenia
46°N03' 014°E31'

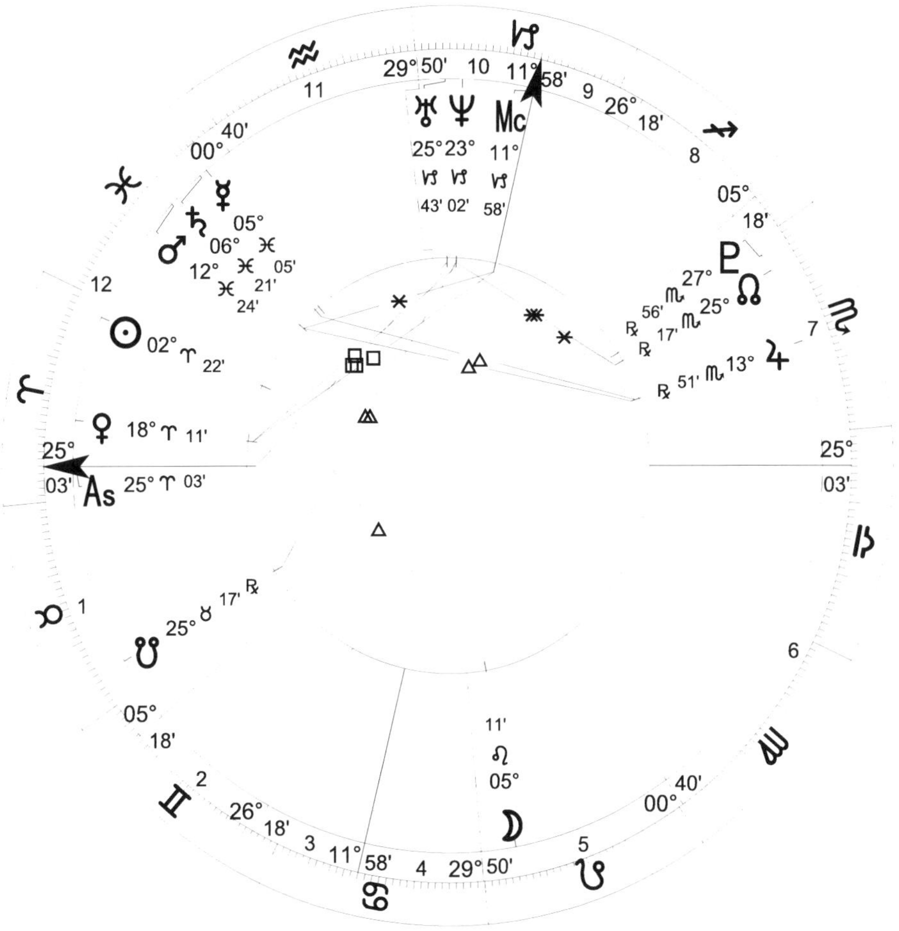

Day of ☿	Hour of ☿
1st Hour of Day	
Last Hr	♀ −47 mins
Next Hr	☽ +13 mins

Hs	Alm.
1	☉
2	☿
3	☿ ♄
4	☽ ♀
5	☽
6	☿
7	♀ ♄
8	♃
9	♃
10	♂ ♄
11	♂
12	♀

MUT. RECEPTIONS		
♂	♃	Ruler-Ruler
♀	♂	Ruler-Exalt
♀	♂	Ruler-Trip
☿	♃	Ruler-Term
♃	♂	Ruler-Term
♃	♂	Ruler-Face

NEAREST ECLIPSES (NM/FM)					
☉ ☌	13 Nov 1993	22:34	21°♏31	Partial	S123
☽ ☍	29 Nov 1993	07:30	07°♊03	Total	S135
☉ ☌	10 May 1994	18:06	19°♉48	Annular	S128
☽ ☍	25 May 1994	04:39	03°♐43	Partial	S140

traditionals.pts

Pt	Long.	Travel	Decl.	Last Stn	Next Stn	Last Stn	Next Stn	F/S	Antiscia	C.Ant.
☽	05°♌11'41"	+13°37'	+14°17'	–	–	–	–	Fast	24°♉48	24°♏48
☉	02°♈22'25"	+59'30"	+00°56'	–	–	–	–	Fast	27°♍37	27°♓37
☿	05°♓05	+01°10'	−11°07'	−18 days	+81 days	22°♒37'32"	08°♋24'40"	Fast	24°♎54	24°♈54
♀	18°♈11	+01°14'	+06°18'	−334 days	+203 days	03°♈44'27"	18°♏00'38"	Fast	11°♍48	11°♓48
♂	12°♓24	+47'05"	−07°55'	−400 days	+285 days	08°♋40'31"	02°♍40'08"	Fast	17°♎35	17°♈35
♃	13°♏51 ℞	−04'06"	−14°41'	−22 days	+100 days	14°♏39'22"	04°♏46'04"	Retro	16°♒08	16°♌08
♄	06°♓21	+06'48"	−10°32'	−146 days	+91 days	23°♒38'00"	12°♓24'11"	Fast	23°♎38	23°♈38

MOON ASPECTS			
☽	☌	☊	5°11' S
☽	△	☉	2°41' S

ESSENTIAL DIGNITIES

Pt	Ruler	Exalt	Trip	Term	Face	Detri	Fall	Score
☽	☉	--	☉	♃	♄	♄	--	−5 p
☉	♂	☉ +	☉ +	♃	♂	♀	♄	+7
☿	♃	♀	♀	♀ m	♄	☿ −	☿ −	−14 p
♀	♂	☉	☉	☿ m	☉	♀ −	♄	−10 p
♂	♃ m	♀	♀	♃	♃	☿	☿	+0 p
♃	♂ m	--	♀	☿	☉	♀	☽	+0 p
♄	♃	♀	♀	♀	♄ +	☿	☿	+1

ASPECTS			
♅	△	☋	0°26' S
♅	⚹	☊	0°26' S
♂	⚹	Mc	0°26' S
♅	□	As	0°39' S
♅	⚹	♇	0°58' A
☿	☌	♄	1°15' A
♂	△	♃	1°26' A
♃	⚹	Mc	1°53' S
♆	□	As	2°01' S
♆	△	☋	2°14' A

PLANETARY SECT

Planet		Cht	Plc	Sgn	Condition
☉	D	D	D	D	In Hayz
☽	N	D	N	D	
☿	D	D	D	N	
♀	N	D	D	D	Ex Cond
♂	N	D	D	N	
♃	D	D	D	N	
♄	D	D	D	N	

D=Diurnal, N=Nocturnal

MISCELLANEOUS CASES

12/1: WILL MILAN KUČAN BE RE-ELECTED?

3 October 1997 at 11:10 a.m., Ljubljana, Slovenia
Hour ruler: Jupiter

I asked this question out of sheer curiosity. Milan Kučan, our then President of the state, was re-nominated for this position. The elections were announced for 23 November 1997. Will he be re-elected, I wondered?

The president is ruled by H10 whereas the natural significator of presidents is the Sun. His rivals (other canidates running for the office) are shown by the opposite house, H4. All we have to do now is find out who is stronger.

Placed in H10 are the north node, Mercury and the Sun. Mercury rules H10 and is therefore the president's main significator while the Sun, the natural significator of presidents, is in conjunction with the cusp of the most fortunate H11. All of this bodes well for his re-election. It seems obvious that he is safe in his position! The north node in his (derived) H1 also gives him advantage over his rivals, because the south node occupies their house, of course.

Mercury is accidentally strong but does not have much essential dignity. It is in a weak, mixed mutual reception with Saturn (exaltation/term) but it is still stronger than Jupiter, ruling the opposing party, as this is completely peregrine. The applying sextile with an accidentally powerful Mars in H1 further favors it. Mercury's only weaknesses are under the Sun's beams condition and the eastern placement (a debility in Lilly's system), but on the other hand, it is in its sect and *in hayz*.

The condition of the Sun is very interesting. It is in its fall (essential debility) but it applies by a trine to a retrograde planet, and although this planet is Jupiter, standing for his opponents, this configuration could be interpreted as a return to the previous state. In other words: no change for the president! In addition, Jupiter is the great benefic and the trine that it forms with the Sun is a harmonious aspect, but the power is thus given to the Sun, whereas the retrograde phase of Jupiter shows the underperformance of the rivals whom it represents; they are retreating instead of progressing.

The Sun is in several mutual receptions with Saturn which is also in its fall, but the mutual receptions strenghten both bodies. In the context of the question, Saturn shows the many president's supporters. Interestingly, Saturn represents old, traditional or conservative political forces, and Kučan indeed belonged to the "old-timers", as far as politics go.

The chart clearly suggests that Milan Kucan would remain the president of our country – and so he did, as he won the elections and received another mandate.

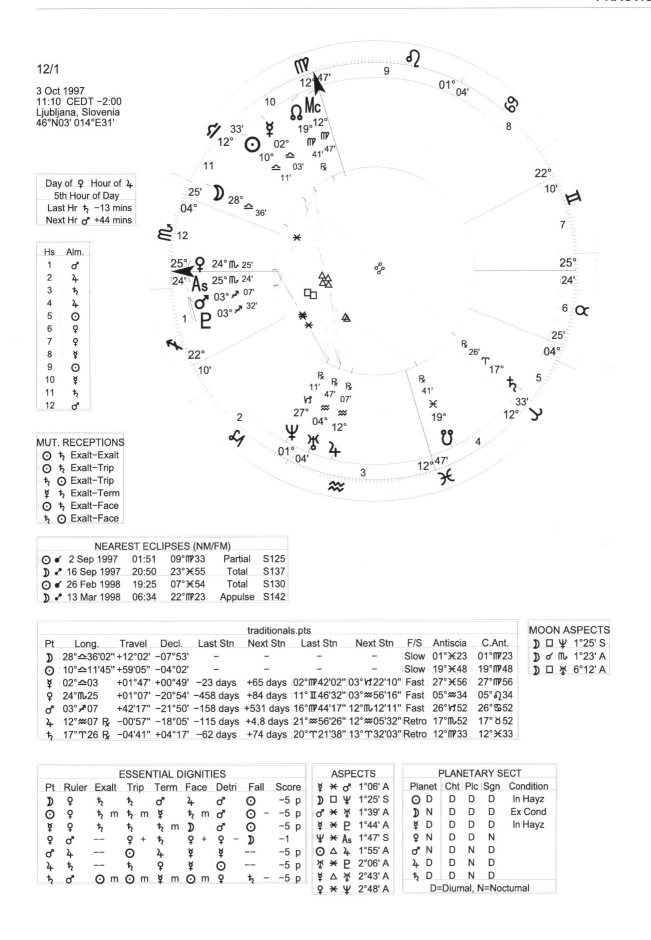

12/1

3 Oct 1997
11:10 CEDT −2:00
Ljubljana, Slovenia
46°N03' 014°E31'

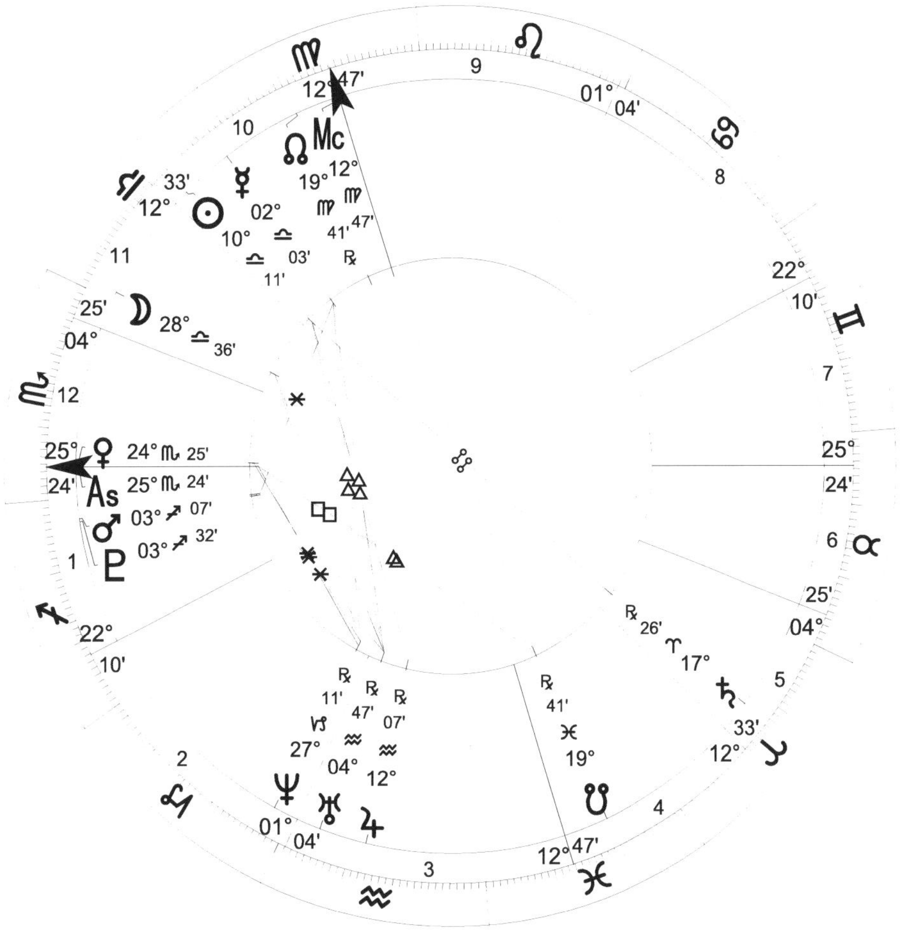

Day of ♀ Hour of ♃
5th Hour of Day
Last Hr ♄ −13 mins
Next Hr ♂ +44 mins

Hs	Alm.
1	♂
2	♃
3	♄
4	♃
5	☉
6	♀
7	♀
8	☿
9	☉
10	☿
11	♄
12	♂

MUT. RECEPTIONS		
☉	♄	Exalt–Exalt
☉	♄	Exalt–Trip
♄	☉	Exalt–Trip
☿	♄	Exalt–Term
☉	♄	Exalt–Face
♄	☉	Exalt–Face

NEAREST ECLIPSES (NM/FM)					
☉ ☌	2 Sep 1997	01:51	09°♍33	Partial	S125
☽ ☍	16 Sep 1997	20:50	23°♓55	Total	S137
☉ ☌	26 Feb 1998	19:25	07°♓54	Total	S130
☽ ☍	13 Mar 1998	06:34	22°♍23	Appulse	S142

traditionals.pts

Pt	Long.	Travel	Decl.	Last Stn	Next Stn	Last Stn	Next Stn	F/S	Antiscia	C.Ant.
☽	28°♎36'02"	+12°02'	−07°53'	–	–	–	–	Slow	01°♓23	01°♍23
☉	10°♎11'45"	+59'05"	−04°02'	–	–	–	–	Slow	19°♓48	19°♍48
☿	02°♎03	+01°47'	+00°49'	−23 days	+65 days	02°♍42'02"	03°♑22'10"	Fast	27°♓56	27°♍56
♀	24°♏25	+01°07'	−20°54'	−458 days	+84 days	11°♊46'32"	03°♒56'16"	Fast	05°♒34	05°♌34
♂	03°♐07	+42'17"	−21°50'	−158 days	+531 days	16°♍44'17"	12°♏12'11"	Fast	26°♑52	26°♋52
♃	12°♒07 ℞	−00'57"	−18°05'	−115 days	+4,8 days	21°♒56'26"	12°♒05'32"	Retro	17°♏52	17°♉52
♄	17°♈26 ℞	−04'41"	+04°17'	−62 days	+74 days	20°♈21'38"	13°♈32'03"	Retro	12°♍33	12°♓33

MOON ASPECTS			
☽	□	♆	1°25' S
☽	☌	♏	1°23' A
☽	□	♅	6°12' A

ESSENTIAL DIGNITIES

Pt	Ruler	Exalt	Trip	Term	Face	Detri	Fall	Score
☽	♀	♄	♄	♂	♃	♂	☉	−5 p
☉	♀	♄ m	♄ m	☿	♄ m	♂	☉ −	−5 p
☿	♀	♄		♄ m	☽	♂	☉	−5 p
♀	♂	--	♀ +	♄	♀ +	♀ −	☽	−1
♂	♃	--	☉	♃	☿	☿	--	−5 p
♃	♄	--	♄	♀	☿	☉	--	−5 p
♄	♂	☉ m	☉ m	☿ m	☉ m	♀	♄ −	−5 p

ASPECTS

☿	✶	♂	1°06' A
☽	□	♆	1°25' S
♂	✶	♅	1°39' A
☿	✶	♇	1°44' A
♆	✶	As	1°47' S
☉	△	♃	1°55' A
♅	✶	♇	2°06' A
☿	△	♅	2°43' A
♀	✶	♆	2°48' A

PLANETARY SECT

Planet		Cht	Plc	Sgn	Condition
☉	D	D	D	D	In Hayz
☽	N	D	D	D	Ex Cond
☿	D	D	D	D	In Hayz
♀	N	D	D	N	
♂	N	D	N	D	
♃	D	D	N	D	
♄	D	D	N	D	

D=Diurnal, N=Nocturnal

12/2: WILL MY PARENTS-IN-LAW WATCH OUR KIDS TODAY?

5 February 2005 at 7:56 a.m., Ljubljana, Slovenia
Hour ruler: Saturn

It was Saturday and I was eager to do some writing and tend to some papers that had been piling up on my office desk. On Saturdays or Sundays, our two toddlers were often taken care of by my parents-in-law, so that my husband and I could have some time for ourselves. Sometimes, their babysitting was settled a day or two in advance, but sometimes they just called in the morning and asked if they can come to take the kids to their home.

I asked this question early in the morning, as I was wondering whether they would call, although we didn't have any prior arrangements.

Some charts are so simple, and this is one of them. I can hear you asking – but what about the ascendant at the end of a sign? It is true that such charts indicate uncertainty, especially if the ascendant is in any of the signs of short ascension where it moves very fast, as in this case. But every chart feature must be brought into the context of the question! If we focus on the essence of the question, such special features give additional indications and help us instead of confusing us. In this case, the chart suggested an imminent change of circumstances, as it is in the very last degree of a sign. Something about the situation is about to change very soon. Do I want that change? Well, the momentary situation was that the children were supposed to stay at home; a change would mean that they would go elsewhere. Very simple. I wanted that, of course!

The chart is radical because the hour ruler Saturn is harmonious with the ascendant in Aquarius (the sign ruler) – an additional indication of a positive answer.

In what condition am I, as the querent? Saturn, my ruler, is retrograde in its detriment, showing that I felt uncertain and helpless. Clearly, I wouldn't dare to call and ask my parents-in-law about their plans – all I could do was sit and wait. Also, as Cancer is the sign of motherhood and Saturn doesn't feel well there, this was an indication that I wasn't crazy about spending the day with my kids. Work (Saturn) was waiting!

Let us now turn to the kids. The Moon, the ruler of H5, the house of children, is in H10, and this is the derived H4 from H7, showing the home of my partner's parents, that is, the home of my parents-in-law. Children will obviously go to them! This is why I wrote in the beginning that some charts are so simple. The chart visually shows the transfer of our kids to another place; the change is »in the air«, the case is almost decided, only that we (perhaps) do not know it yet.

But looking at the chart, I was certain that they would call. And indeed - at 8:02, just six minutes after the question, my mother-in-law called if she can come take the kids for the day.

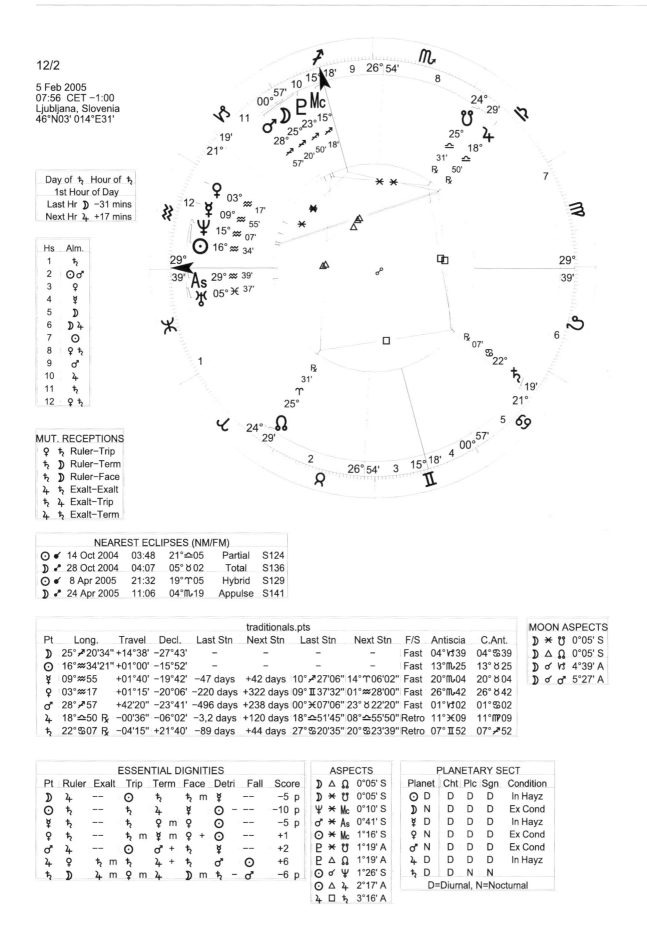

12/2

5 Feb 2005
07:56 CET -1:00
Ljubljana, Slovenia
46°N03' 014°E31'

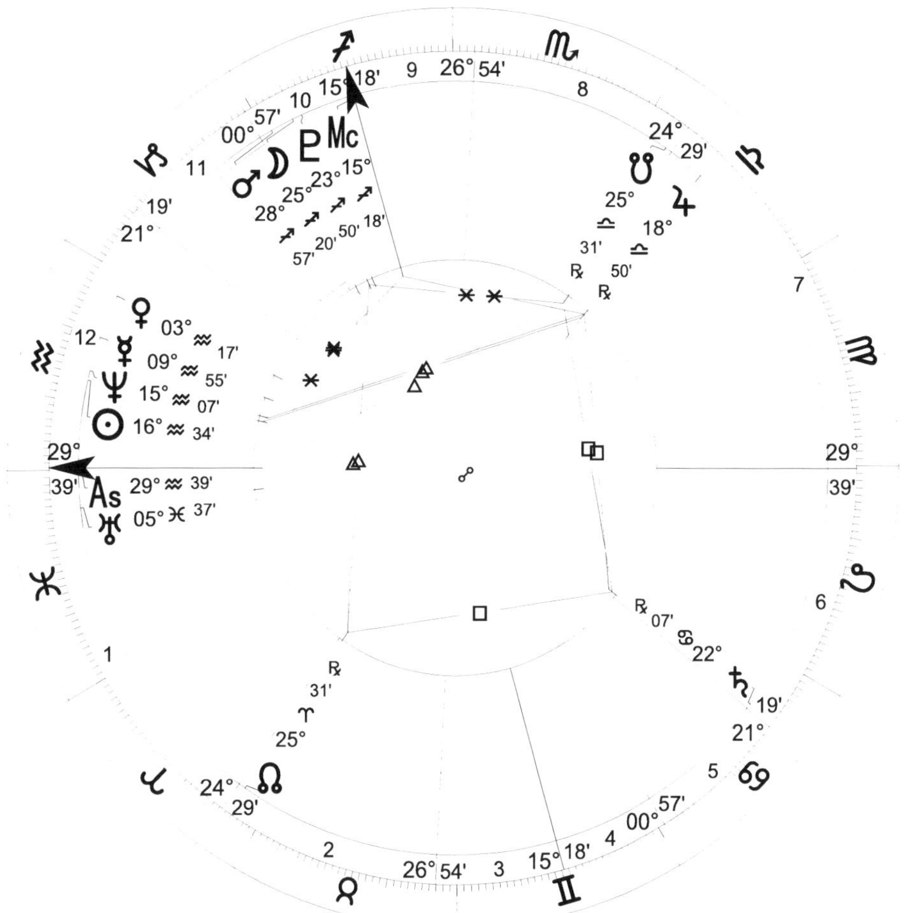

Day of ♄	Hour of ♄
1st Hour of Day	
Last Hr ☽	-31 mins
Next Hr ♃	+17 mins

Hs	Alm.
1	♄
2	☉♂
3	♀
4	☿
5	☽
6	☽♃
7	☉
8	♀♄
9	♂
10	♃
11	♄
12	♀♄

MUT. RECEPTIONS		
♀	♄	Ruler-Trip
♄	☽	Ruler-Term
♄	☽	Ruler-Face
♃	♄	Exalt-Exalt
♄	♃	Exalt-Trip
♃	♄	Exalt-Term

NEAREST ECLIPSES (NM/FM)					
☉ ☌	14 Oct 2004	03:48	21°♎05	Partial	S124
☽ ☍	28 Oct 2004	04:07	05°♉02	Total	S136
☉ ☌	8 Apr 2005	21:32	19°♈05	Hybrid	S129
☽ ☍	24 Apr 2005	11:06	04°♏19	Appulse	S141

traditionals.pts

Pt	Long.	Travel	Decl.	Last Stn	Next Stn	Last Stn	Next Stn	F/S	Antiscia	C.Ant.
☽	25°♐20'34"	+14°38'	-27°43'	-	-	-	-	Fast	04°♑39	04°♋39
☉	16°♒34'21"	+01°00'	-15°52'	-	-	-	-	Fast	13°♏25	13°♉25
☿	09°♒55	+01°40'	-19°42'	-47 days	+42 days	10°♐27'06"	14°♈06'02"	Fast	20°♏04	20°♉04
♀	03°♒17	+01°15'	-20°06'	-220 days	+322 days	09°♊37'32"	01°♒28'00"	Fast	26°♏42	26°♉42
♂	28°♐57	+42'20"	-23°41'	-496 days	+238 days	00°♓07'06"	23°♉22'20"	Fast	01°♑02	01°♋02
♃	18°♎50 ℞	-00'36"	-06°02'	-3,2 days	+120 days	18°♎51'45"	08°♎55'50"	Retro	11°♓09	11°♍09
♄	22°♋07 ℞	-04'15"	+21°40'	-89 days	+44 days	27°♋20'35"	20°♋23'39"	Retro	07°♊52	07°♐52

MOON ASPECTS			
☽	⚹	☋	0°05' S
☽	△	☊	0°05' S
☽	☌	♑	4°39' A
☽	☌	♂	5°27' A

ESSENTIAL DIGNITIES

Pt	Ruler	Exalt	Trip	Term	Face	Detri	Fall	Score
☽	♃	--	☉	♄	♄ m	☿	--	-5 p
☉	♄	--	♄	♃	☿	☉ -	--	-10 p
☿	♄	--	♄	♀ m	♀	☉	--	-5 p
♀	♄	--	♄ m	☿ m	♀ +	☉	--	+1
♂	♃	--	☉	♂ +	♄	☿	--	+2
♃	♀	♄ m	♄	♃ +	♄	♂	☉	+6
♄	☽	♃ m	♀ m	♃	☽ m	♄ -	♂	-6 p

ASPECTS			
☽	△	☊	0°05' S
☽	⚹	☋	0°05' S
♆	⚹	Mc	0°10' S
♂	⚹	As	0°41' S
☉	⚹	Mc	1°16' S
♇	⚹	☋	1°19' A
♇	△	☊	1°19' A
☉	☌	♆	1°26' S
☉	△	♃	2°17' A
♃	□	♄	3°16' A

PLANETARY SECT

Planet		Cht	Plc	Sgn	Condition
☉	D	D	D	D	In Hayz
☽	N	D	D	D	Ex Cond
☿	D	D	D	D	In Hayz
♀	N	D	D	D	Ex Cond
♂	N	D	D	D	Ex Cond
♃	D	D	D	D	In Hayz
♄	D	D	N	N	

D=Diurnal, N=Nocturnal

12/3: WILL I HAVE MY B-DAY PARTY IN THE GROMKA CLUB?

14 November 2004 at 5:18 p.m. (17:18), Ljubljana, Slovenia
Hour ruler: Jupiter

Although I usually celebrate my birthday in October, I couldn't do it this time. There was too much work, because my first Moon Guide – a yearly publication which was to become periodical – was due for release at the end of the month, so I was very busy with the marketing and other tasks that come with it. Free weekends were out of the question, so I decided that I would celebrate my birthday in November. A friend told me that he could organize a venue – a club called Gromka. It might be a bit difficult, he said, as the club was normally not open to private parties, but he would try because the owners were his personal friends. I liked the idea and asked the above question while eagerly anticipating his confirmation.

But a look at the chart disappointed me because the indications seemed quite clear: there will be no party in Gromka! I'm ruled by Mercury which seems helpless in H7 in the sign of its detriment – but of course, I thought, there's nothing I can do but sit and wait. This chart feature alone would not suffice for a negative answer, but my (potential) party is represented by H5 with the cusp in Virgo, so Mercury also signifies the object of my question. The fact that it separates from a sextile with Neptune in H10 (my wish, my goal) and a sextile with Jupiter (ruling H11 or my friend and showing our recent conversation) is not helpful either. Things are dissolving, not advancing.

But there is more. The Moon in Sagittarius has just separated from a sextile with Venus, reflecting my recent hope and opportunity which I thought was unique (Venus dignified in its domicile) - but the Moon is now not going anywhere! In other words, it is void-of-course, making no aspects with any planet while in its present sign. It would trine the south node and sextile Mars and Uranus in the next sign, but the orb is too wide, and circumstances would change by then; besides, Mars (which doesn't rule the club), is in the unfortunate H6 and ruling the unfortunate H12 and H6, so nothing will come of the matter.

And so it was. My friend soon called to say that the club owners decided not to let the club to "outsiders" - meaning me, in this case.

This is a simple but clear example of a negative answer given by a void-of-course Moon, backed by a weak essential dignity of the main significators, and the inharmonious hour ruler.

12/3

14 Nov 2004
17:18 CET −1:00
Ljubljana, Slovenia
46°N03' 014°E31'

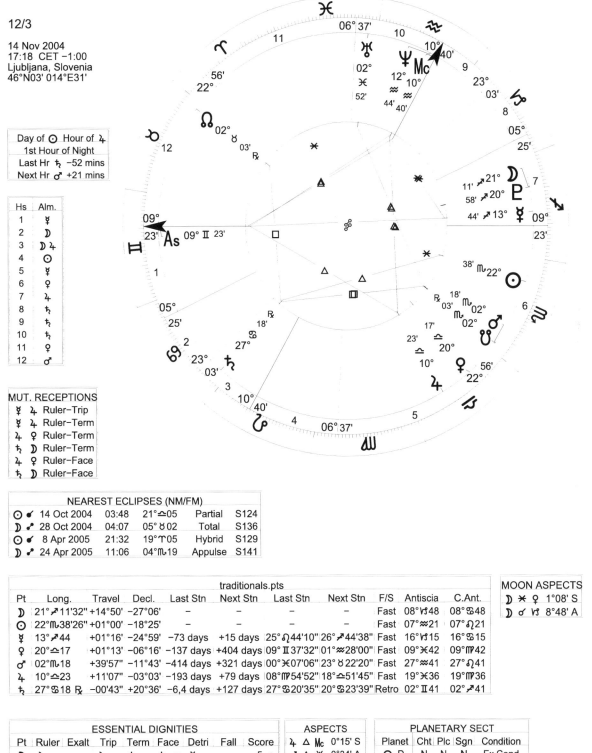

Day of ☉ Hour of ♃
1st Hour of Night
Last Hr ♄ −52 mins
Next Hr ♂ +21 mins

Hs	Alm.
1	☿
2	☽
3	☽ ♃
4	☉
5	☿
6	♀
7	♃
8	♄
9	♄
10	♄
11	♀
12	♂

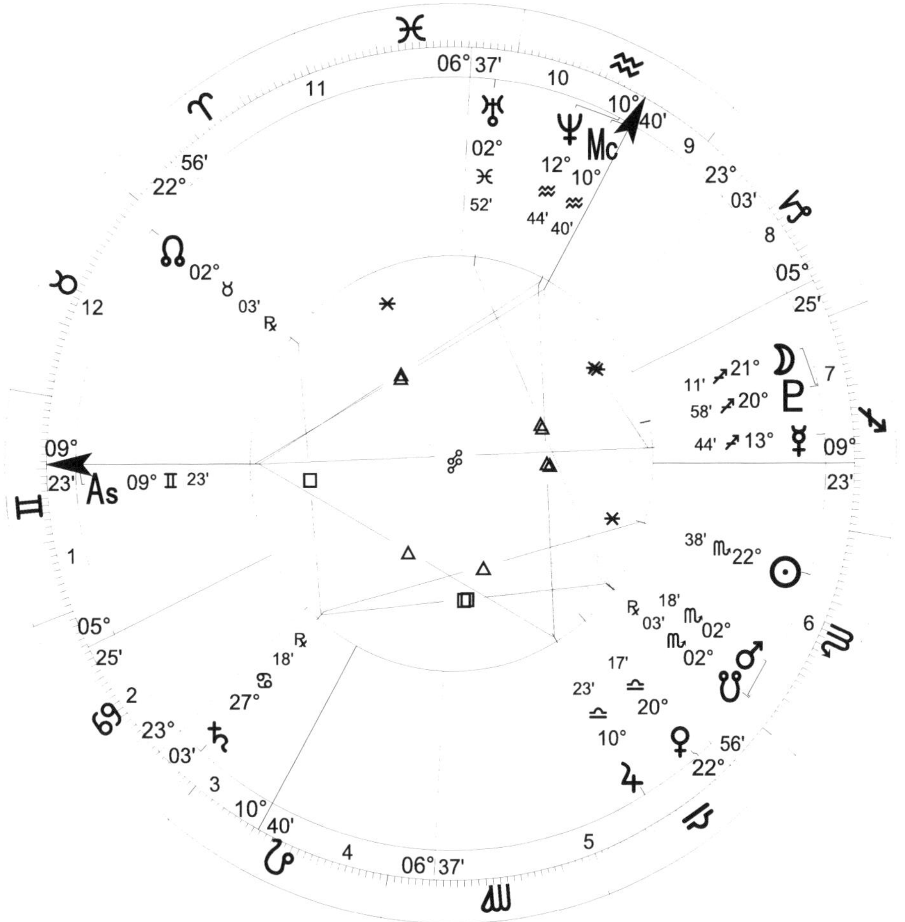

MUT. RECEPTIONS		
☿	♃	Ruler-Trip
☿	♃	Ruler-Term
♃	♀	Ruler-Term
♄	☽	Ruler-Term
♃	♀	Ruler-Face
♄	☽	Ruler-Face

NEAREST ECLIPSES (NM/FM)					
☉	14 Oct 2004	03:48	21°♎05	Partial	S124
☽	28 Oct 2004	04:07	05°♉02	Total	S136
☉	8 Apr 2005	21:32	19°♈05	Hybrid	S129
☽	24 Apr 2005	11:06	04°♏19	Appulse	S141

traditionals.pts

Pt	Long.	Travel	Decl.	Last Stn	Next Stn	Last Stn	Next Stn	F/S	Antiscia	C.Ant.
☽	21°♐11'32"	+14°50'	−27°06'	–	–	–	–	Fast	08°♑48	08°♋48
☉	22°♏38'26"	+01°00'	−18°25'	–	–	–	–	Fast	07°♒21	07°♌21
☿	13°♐44	+01°16'	−24°59'	−73 days	+15 days	25°♌44'10"	26°♐44'38"	Fast	16°♑15	16°♋15
♀	20°♎17	+01°13'	−06°16'	−137 days	+404 days	09°♊37'32"	01°♒28'00"	Fast	09°♓42	09°♍42
♂	02°♏18	+39'57"	−11°43'	−414 days	+321 days	00°♓07'06"	23°♉22'20"	Fast	27°♒41	27°♌41
♃	10°♎23	+11'07"	−03°03'	−193 days	+79 days	08°♍54'52"	18°♎51'45"	Fast	19°♓36	19°♍36
♄	27°♋18 ℞	−00'43"	+20°36'	−6,4 days	+127 days	27°♋20'35"	20°♋23'39"	Retro	02°♊41	02°♐41

MOON ASPECTS	
☽ ⚹ ♀	1°08' S
☽ ☌ ♑	8°48' A

ESSENTIAL DIGNITIES

Pt	Ruler	Exalt	Trip	Term	Face	Detri	Fall	Score
☽	♃	--	♃	♄	♄ m	☿	--	−5 p
☉	♂	--	♂	♃	♀	♀	☽	−5 p
☿	♃	--	♃ m	♀	☽	☿ −	--	−10 p
♀	♀ +	♄	☿	♃	♃	♂	☉	+5
♂	♂ +	--	♂ +	♂ +	♂ +	♀	☽	+11
♃	♀	♄ m	☿ m	☿	♄	♂	☉	−1 p
♄	☽	♃ m	♂	♄ +	☽ m	♄ −	♂	+1

ASPECTS	
♃ △ Mc	0°15' S
♂ △ ♅	0°34' A
♂ ☍ ☊	0°38' S
♂ ☌ ☋	0°38' S
♀ ⚹ ♇	0°44' A
♅ ⚹ ☊	0°48' S
♅ △ ☋	0°48' S
☿ ⚹ ♆	0°58' S
♃ △ As	0°59' S
☽ ⚹ ♀	1°08' S

PLANETARY SECT

Planet		Cht	Plc	Sgn	Condition
☉	D	N	N	N	Ex Cond
☽	N	N	N	D	
☿	N	N	N	D	
♀	N	N	D	D	
♂	N	N	D	N	
♃	D	N	D	D	
♄	D	N	D	N	

D=Diurnal, N=Nocturnal

12/4: IS MY DANCING PARTNER QUITTING THE AGREEMENT?

19 January 2007 at 7:17 p.m. (19:17), Ljubljana, Slovenia
Hour ruler: Venus

A day or two after my progressed Moon entered Aquarius, a well-known TV host called me to ask if I would participate in the Dancing with the Stars show. I agreed, as it seemed a nice opportunity to foster my career and keep up the public profile that I had been building over the years by promoting astrology in my country. The project promised much fun too, of course - something that I badly needed after the long, exhausting Capricorn period. My dancing partner/teacher was supposed to be a former professional dancer who was hesitant at first, as the lady from the organizing committee told me, due to too many obligations, but finally agreed, and it was decided that we meet at the earliest opportunity. He would call me the next day, she said. Several days passed, but nothing happened, so I wrote him an e-mail, saying that I had been waiting for his call. Was there a misunderstanding, I wondered? But he didn't answer, so I thought that he might have changed his mind and quietly dropped the deal. Is this true, I asked myself.

It was apparent, from the chart, that my assumption was correct. The ascendant is at the end of a sign - the situation is changing. My ruler Sun is in Capricorn and at the last degree of this sign, and its ruler Saturn (dispositor of the descendant) is retrograde – a clear sign that he is reneging. All the more so because Saturn is in its detriment and in H12 of concealment, denial and loss. Both planets are in mutual reception, though, which is a kind of connection, but in this context it should be interpreted rather as a possibility of some kind of exchange. He's obviously going to be substituted with someone else!

There are two degrees separating the ascendant from the next sign, suggesting two days until a change. (There couldn't be two weeks as the other couples' workouts were already in progress.) And so it was: two days later, on January 21, the lady in charge called me again, saying that my candidate had resigned, but that she had already found another dancer who would substitute him. He would call me shortly, she said, and he did - on the same day.

By moving the ascendant two degrees ahead we come to Virgo, with the descendant in Pisces. The rulers of both signs, Mercury and Jupiter, are in an applying sextile, and the connection between them is even stronger because it is supported by a partile applying conjunction of the Moon to Mercury, with the next Moon's aspect being a sextile with Jupiter. This is a sub-form of translation of light, and the whole configuration clearly indicates a new dancing partnership.

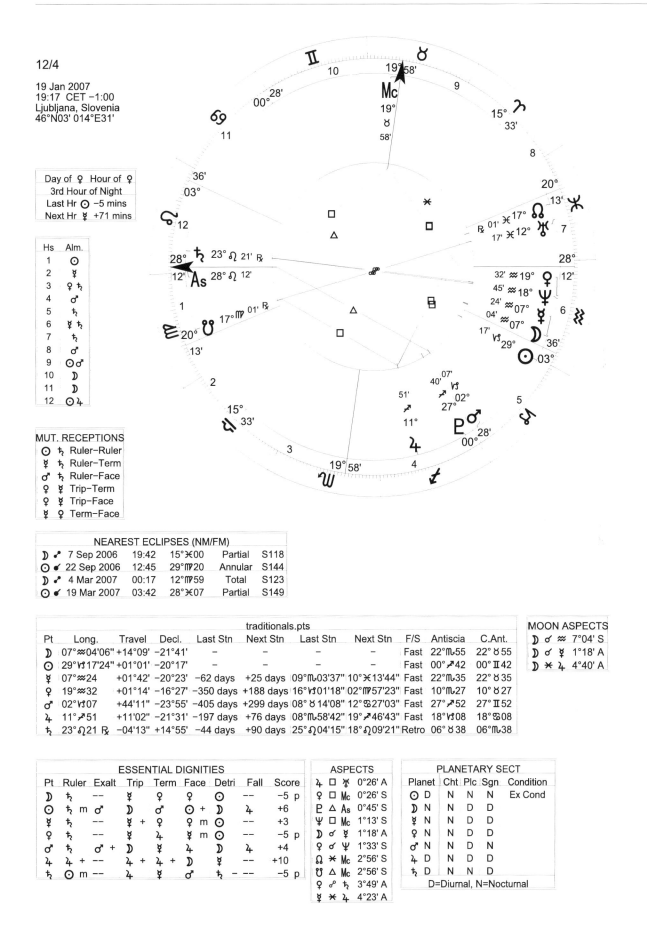

12/4

19 Jan 2007
19:17 CET −1:00
Ljubljana, Slovenia
46°N03' 014°E31'

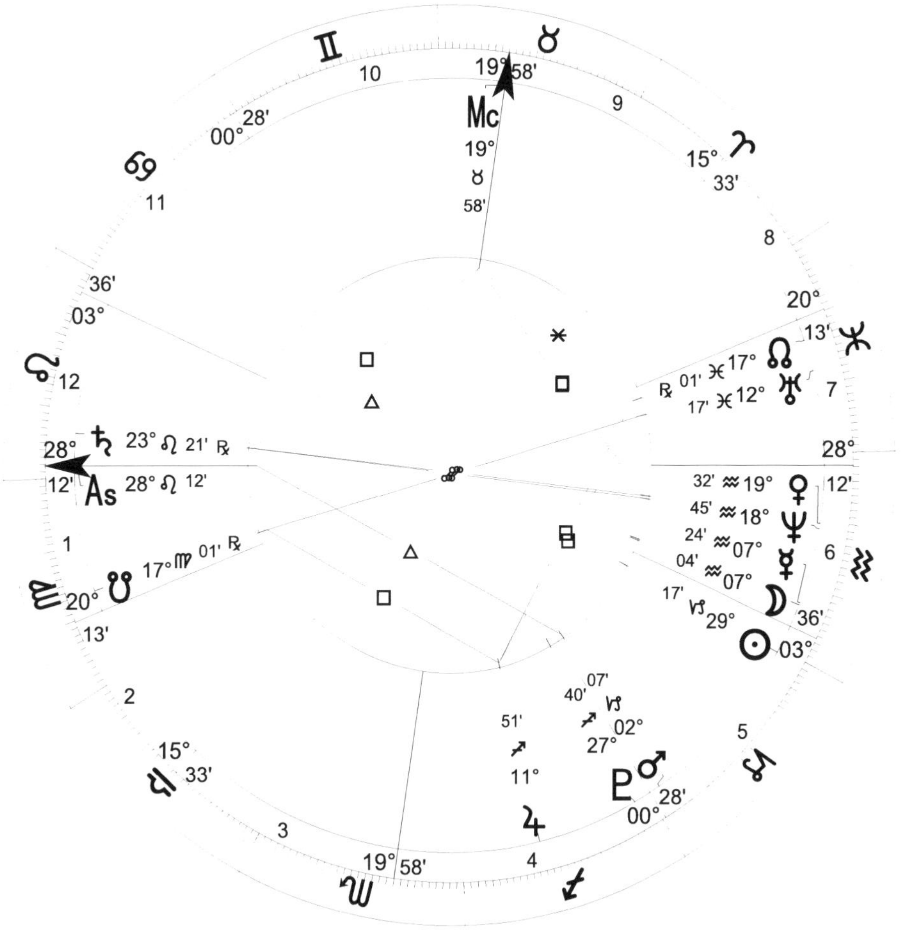

Day of ♀ Hour of ♀
3rd Hour of Night
Last Hr ☉ −5 mins
Next Hr ☿ +71 mins

Hs	Alm.
1	☉
2	☿
3	♀ ♄
4	♂
5	♄
6	☿ ♄
7	♄
8	♂
9	☉ ♂
10	☽
11	☽
12	☉ ♃

MUT. RECEPTIONS		
☉	♄	Ruler−Ruler
☿	♄	Ruler−Term
♂	♄	Ruler−Face
♀	☿	Trip−Term
♀	☿	Trip−Face
☿	♀	Term−Face

NEAREST ECLIPSES (NM/FM)					
☽ ☍	7 Sep 2006	19:42	15°♓00	Partial	S118
☉ ☌	22 Sep 2006	12:45	29°♍20	Annular	S144
☽ ☍	4 Mar 2007	00:17	12°♍59	Total	S123
☉ ☌	19 Mar 2007	03:42	28°♓07	Partial	S149

traditionals.pts

Pt	Long.	Travel	Decl.	Last Stn	Next Stn	Last Stn	Next Stn	F/S	Antiscia	C.Ant.
☽	07°♒04'06"	+14°09'	−21°41'	–	–	–	–	Fast	22°♏55	22°♉55
☉	29°♑17'24"	+01°01'	−20°17'	–	–	–	–	Fast	00°♐42	00°♊42
☿	07°♒24	+01°42'	−20°23'	−62 days	+25 days	09°♏03'37"	10°♓13'44"	Fast	22°♏35	22°♉35
♀	19°♒32	+01°14'	−16°27'	−350 days	+188 days	16°♑01'18"	02°♍57'23"	Fast	10°♏27	10°♉27
♂	02°♑07	+44'11"	−23°55'	−405 days	+299 days	08°♉14'08"	12°♋27'03"	Fast	27°♐52	27°♊52
♃	11°♐51	+11'02"	−21°31'	−197 days	+76 days	08°♏58'42"	19°♐46'43"	Fast	18°♑08	18°♋08
♄	23°♌21 ℞	−04'13"	+14°55'	−44 days	+90 days	25°♌04'15"	18°♌09'21"	Retro	06°♉38	06°♏38

MOON ASPECTS			
☽	☌	♒	7°04' S
☽	☌	☿	1°18' A
☽	⚹	♃	4°40' A

ESSENTIAL DIGNITIES

Pt	Ruler	Exalt	Trip	Term	Face	Detri	Fall	Score
☽	♄	--	☿	♀	♀	☉	--	−5 p
☉	♄ m	♂	☽	♂	☉ +	☽	♃	+6
☿	♄	--	☿ +	♀	♀ m	☉	--	+3
♀	♄	--	☿	♃	☿ m	☉	--	−5 p
♂	♄	♂ +	☽	☿	♃	☽	♃	+4
♃	♃ +	--	♃ +	♃ +	☽	☿	--	+10
♄	☉ m	--	♃	☿	♂	♄ −	--	−5 p

ASPECTS			
♃	□	♅	0°26' A
♀	□	Mc	0°26' S
♇	△	As	0°45' S
♆	□	Mc	1°13' S
☽	☌	☿	1°18' A
♀	☌	♆	1°33' S
☊	⚹	Mc	2°56' S
☋	△	Mc	2°56' S
♀	☍	♄	3°49' A
☿	⚹	♃	4°23' A

PLANETARY SECT

Planet		Cht	Plc	Sgn	Condition
☉	D	N	N	N	Ex Cond
☽	N	N	D	D	
☿	N	N	D	D	
♀	N	N	D	D	
♂	N	N	D	N	
♃	D	N	D	D	
♄	D	N	N	D	

D=Diurnal, N=Nocturnal

12/5: WHO HAS BEEN HARASSING ME OVER THE PHONE ?

15 September 2008 at 2:04 p.m. (14:04), Brežice, Slovenia
Hour ruler: Moon

A client called me with the question of who had been harassing her over the phone. She had been receiving anonymous calls for several months, but she had no idea who was calling her, and why. She was also not sure whether it was a man or a woman, as the person never said anything.

The ascendant is in Sagittarius, so her ruler is Jupiter, in Capricorn in H1 in an applying trine with Saturn. She is co-ruled by the Moon, also showing the course of events, at 24°31' Pisces and void-of-course - unless we consider its square with Pluto. It is interesting (and quite appropriate) that the Moon occupies H3 of communications, including phone calls. Besides, the Moon is the hour ruler!

A void-of-course Moon is a caution, of course, but also suggesting that "nothing comes of the matter", therefore I told her that the situation was not likely to get worse, the harassment would slowly die away, and that she would probably never find out and get evidence of who the person was.

Okay, she said, but can I tell her more, because my description of the possible perpetrator could nevertheless help her identify him (or her).

So – how to identify such a person? The procedure is the same as when searching for a thief: they are shown by a peregrine planet on an angle. If there is none such planet, we should look into H7 which is the house of the querent's adversaries. In this case, a peregrine planet on an angle is Mars, conjuncting MC. This is very appropriate as Mars also rules H12, the house of secrecy and people acting behind our backs. Since Mercury, the ruler of H7, is also peregrine and in the same sign and house as Mars, I took it for the co-ruler of the harasser. Additional indications could be given by the Moon which in such cases is closely linked with the subject of the question.

I described the person as a man (as Mars is a male planet, and both Mars and Mercury were in a positive sign) of early middle age or about the same age as the querent (in late 30s), because the Moon in opposition of the Sun shows middle age whereas Mercury generally describes younger people and Mars, younger men. Accordingly I decided that the person should be between 30 and 40 years old, of thin or slender stature (a strong body would be rather signified by the Sun or Jupiter), of blonde or light brown hair (because Venus conjuncts Mercury which usually indicates brighter colours), sociable, flirty and never or rarely alone (stellium in the airy Libra). The querent knows him through her job; she might be meeting him at her working place, as both significators are in her H10 of the office. What kind of job does she do, I asked? She said that she was a waitress, and she confirmed that she could well be meeting such a person at the local pub where she works. (This is confirmed by Mercury's conjunction with Venus which rules H5, standing for pubs and restaurants.)

She told me that my description fitted a certain man that she suspected, and added if I could tell her, does the chart show that she ever had sexual intercourse with this person, or not? Let's see! Mars and Mercury are separating from a square with Jupiter, her significator. Any aspect between significators shows some kind of a contact; this was a past contact because the aspect is already separating, but since a square is a tense, disharmonious aspect, and because there is no mutual reception between Mars/Mercury and Jupiter, it was an unsatisfactory contact, showing lack of mutual understanding. It seemed, therefore, that the querent was not involved with this person in any intimate or enjoyable way, but he might have pursued her, albeit without success. No, you didn't sleep with him, I said, although it seems that he was after you.

She was very pleased with my answer, saying that it gave her the final clue for identifying the harasser.

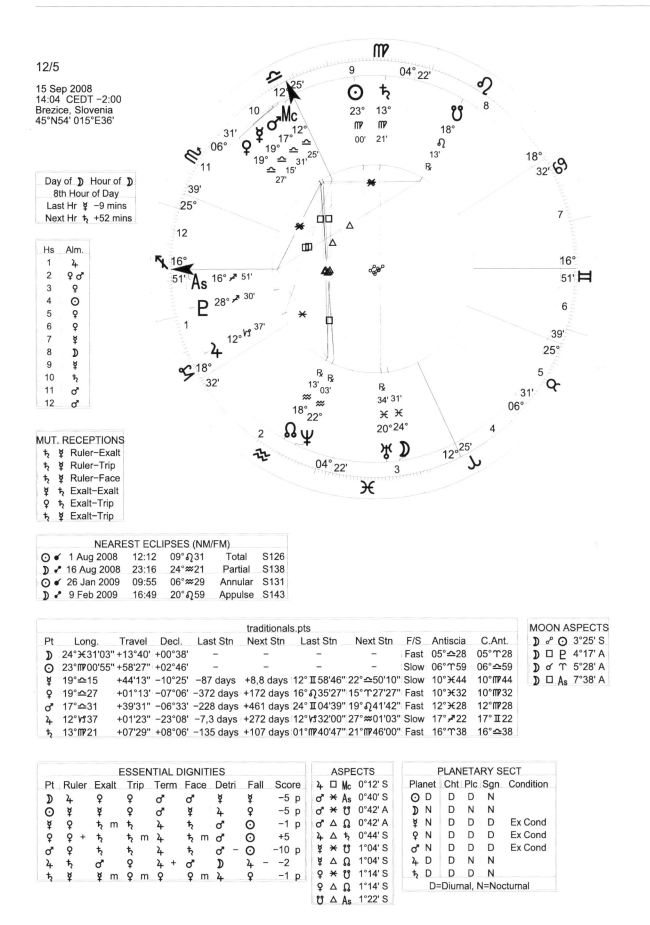

12/5

15 Sep 2008
14:04 CEDT −2:00
Brezice, Slovenia
45°N54' 015°E36'

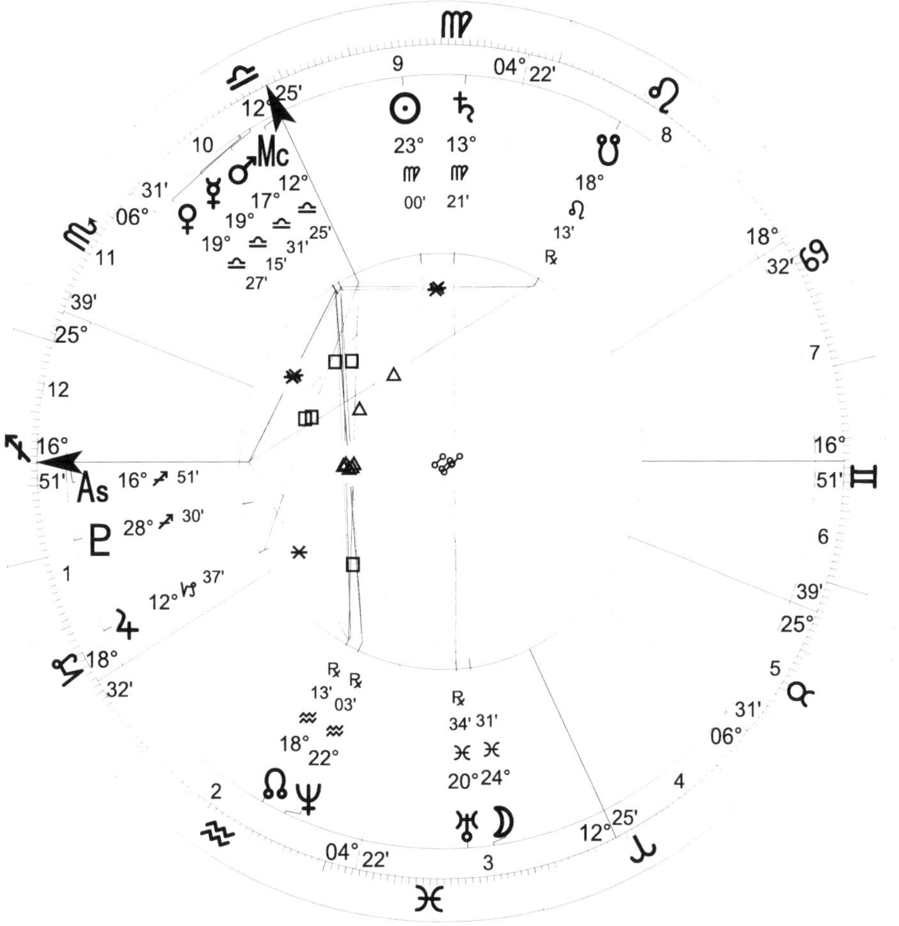

Day of ☽ Hour of ☽
8th Hour of Day
Last Hr ☿ −9 mins
Next Hr ♄ +52 mins

Hs	Alm.
1	♃
2	♀♂
3	♀
4	☉
5	♀
6	♀
7	☿
8	☽
9	☿
10	♄
11	♂
12	♂

MUT. RECEPTIONS		
♄	☿	Ruler–Exalt
♄	☿	Ruler–Trip
♄	☿	Ruler–Face
☿	♄	Exalt–Exalt
♀	♄	Exalt–Trip
♄	☿	Exalt–Trip

NEAREST ECLIPSES (NM/FM)					
☉ ☌	1 Aug 2008	12:12	09°♌31	Total	S126
☽ ☍	16 Aug 2008	23:16	24°♒21	Partial	S138
☉ ☌	26 Jan 2009	09:55	06°♒29	Annular	S131
☽ ☍	9 Feb 2009	16:49	20°♌59	Appulse	S143

traditionals.pts

Pt	Long.	Travel	Decl.	Last Stn	Next Stn	Last Stn	Next Stn	F/S	Antiscia	C.Ant.
☽	24°♓31'03"	+13°40'	+00°38'	–	–	–	–	Fast	05°♎28	05°♈28
☉	23°♍00'55"	+58'27"	+02°46'	–	–	–	–	Slow	06°♈59	06°♎59
☿	19°♎15	+44'13"	−10°25'	−87 days	+8,8 days	12°♊58'46"	22°♎50'10"	Slow	10°♓44	10°♍44
♀	19°♎27	+01°13'	−07°06'	−372 days	+172 days	16°♌35'27"	15°♈27'27"	Fast	10°♓32	10°♍32
♂	17°♎31	+39'31"	−06°33'	−228 days	+461 days	24°♊04'39"	19°♌41'42"	Fast	12°♓28	12°♍28
♃	12°♑37	+01'23"	−23°08'	−7,3 days	+272 days	12°♑32'00"	27°♒01'03"	Slow	17°♐22	17°♊22
♄	13°♍21	+07'29"	+08°06'	−135 days	+107 days	01°♍40'47"	21°♍46'00"	Fast	16°♈38	16°♎38

MOON ASPECTS			
☽	☍	☉	3°25' S
☽	□	♇	4°17' A
☽	☌	♈	5°28' A
☽	□	As	7°38' A

ESSENTIAL DIGNITIES

Pt	Ruler	Exalt	Trip	Term	Face	Detri	Fall	Score
☽	♃	♀	♀	♂	♂	☿	☿	−5 p
☉	☿	☿	♀	♂	☿	♃	♀	−5 p
☿	♀	♄ m	♄	♃	♄	♂	☉	−1 p
♀	♀ +	♄	♄ m	♃	♄ m	♂	☉	+5
♂	♀	♄	♄	♃	♄	♂ −	☉	−10 p
♃	♄	♂	♀	♃ +	♂	☽	♃ −	−2
♄	☿	☿ m	♀ m	♀	♀ m	♃	♀	−1 p

ASPECTS			
♃	□	Mc	0°12' S
♂	✶	As	0°40' S
♂	✶	☋	0°42' A
♂	△	☊	0°42' A
♃	△	♄	0°44' S
☿	✶	☋	1°04' S
☿	△	☊	1°04' S
♀	✶	☋	1°14' S
♀	△	☊	1°14' S
☋	△	As	1°22' S

PLANETARY SECT

Planet		Cht	Plc	Sgn	Condition
☉	D	D	D	N	
☽	N	D	N	N	
☿	N	D	D	D	Ex Cond
♀	N	D	D	D	Ex Cond
♂	N	D	D	D	Ex Cond
♃	D	D	N	N	
♄	D	D	D	N	

D=Diurnal, N=Nocturnal

12/6: WILL CHRIS COME TO ME BEFORE THE MEETING?

11 September 2008 at 7:39 p.m. (19:39), Los Angeles, CA, USA
Hour ruler: Moon

The question was put forward on one of the astrological forums. The querent was dealing with some legal matters and was assisted by Chris who was more versed in dealing with such stuff than she, even though he was not a lawyer. Since she had an important meeting scheduled in a day or two, requiring the papers to be settled, she hoped that Chris would come to her before the meeting, so as to examine the documents and correct any possible errors.

The querent is ruled by Mars, the ascendant ruler, Chris with Venus, the ruler of H7. Why H7, you might ask? Simply because Chris' relationship with the querent was not defined, so he could be considered as "any person out there", belonging to H7. (This was also the choice of the querent who was a hobby astrologer.) Mars is placed in H7 - very appropriate, as she is asking about that other person. Mars is in a very tight conjunction with Venus. The querent wondered, does this exact conjunction still shows completion, or should we consider it as a separating aspect? Her reasoning was inspired by Lilly's view that an aspect becomes a separating one when the significators are separated by more than 6 minutes (of arc). But my experience was different, so I wrote back:

I think that the answer is NO. Venus is much quicker so it can be seen as already separating from Mars. Also, Venus is on the quesited's side of the chart, in his own H1, meaning that he is currently busy with his own affairs and does not have time to see you. In other words, I think that Chris will not come to you before the meeting. This is confirmed by your ruler, Mars, which is in detriment and therefore reflects your powerlessness. You two will meet, but only after your own business meeting. When? At the quickest it would be in 5 days, but I think it more likely 5 weeks while possibly communicating via email in between, as Venus and Mars are applying to Mercury ruling your H3. P.S. I also wonder if Chris is younger than you?

My evaluation of the time that would pass until their meeting was based on the Moon's applying trine to both planets, with an orb of 5°17'. Given that the Moon is in a fixed sign and a succedent house, that would mean a bit over 5 weeks.

You might also wonder why I wrote that Venus and Mars are applying to Mercury, when this planet is at a later degree? This it is but it's much slower than Venus, and would soon also reach Mars, because, as a look into the ephemerides shows, Mercury will turn retrograde on 24 September, meaning that it would soon catch up with both planets. This example teaches us how important it is to know the current velocity of the planets.

It turned out that I was right - Chris did not have time to turn up at the querent's house before her meeting.

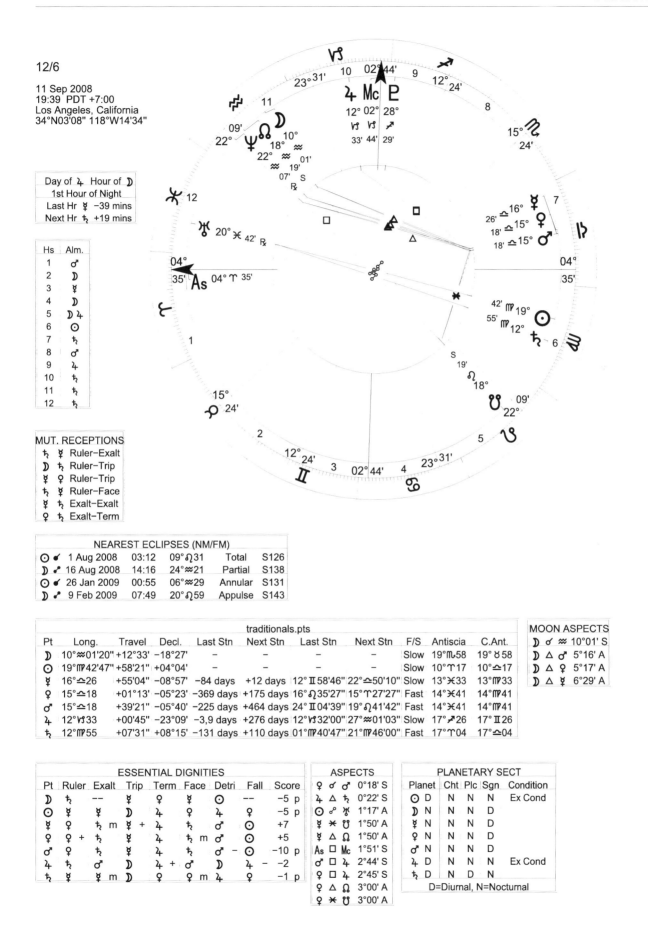

12/6

11 Sep 2008
19:39 PDT +7:00
Los Angeles, California
34°N03'08" 118°W14'34"

Day of ♃ Hour of ☽
1st Hour of Night
Last Hr ☿ −39 mins
Next Hr ♄ +19 mins

Hs	Alm.
1	♂
2	☽
3	☿
4	☽
5	☽ ♃
6	☉
7	♄
8	♂
9	♃
10	♄
11	♄
12	♄

MUT. RECEPTIONS
♄	☿	Ruler–Exalt
☽	♄	Ruler–Trip
☿	♀	Ruler–Trip
♄	☿	Ruler–Face
☿	♄	Exalt–Exalt
♀	♄	Exalt–Term

NEAREST ECLIPSES (NM/FM)
☉ ☌	1 Aug 2008	03:12	09°♌31	Total	S126
☽ ☍	16 Aug 2008	14:16	24°♒21	Partial	S138
☉ ☌	26 Jan 2009	00:55	06°♒29	Annular	S131
☽ ☍	9 Feb 2009	07:49	20°♌59	Appulse	S143

traditionals.pts
Pt	Long.	Travel	Decl.	Last Stn	Next Stn	Last Stn	Next Stn	F/S	Antiscia	C.Ant.
☽	10°♒01'20"	+12°33'	−18°27'	–	–	–	–	Slow	19°♏58	19°♉58
☉	19°♍42'47"	+58'21"	+04°04'	–	–	–	–	Slow	10°♈17	10°♎17
☿	16°♎26	+55'04"	−08°57'	−84 days	+12 days	12°♊58'46"	22°♎50'10"	Slow	13°♓33	13°♍33
♀	15°♎18	+01°13'	−05°23'	−369 days	+175 days	16°♌35'27"	15°♈27'27"	Fast	14°♓41	14°♍41
♂	15°♎18	+39'21"	−05°40'	−225 days	+464 days	24°♊04'39"	19°♌41'42"	Fast	14°♓41	14°♍41
♃	12°♑33	+00'45"	−23°09'	−3,9 days	+276 days	12°♑32'00"	27°♒01'03"	Slow	17°♐26	17°♊26
♄	12°♍55	+07'31"	+08°15'	−131 days	+110 days	01°♍40'47"	21°♍46'00"	Fast	17°♈04	17°♎04

MOON ASPECTS
☽ ☌ ♒	10°01' S	
☽ △ ♂	5°16' A	
☽ △ ♀	5°17' A	
☽ △ ☿	6°29' A	

ESSENTIAL DIGNITIES
Pt	Ruler	Exalt	Trip	Term	Face	Detri	Fall	Score
☽	♄	--	☿	♀	☿	☉	--	−5 p
☉	☿	☿	☽	♃	♀	♃	♀	−5 p
☿	♀	♄ m	☿ +	♃	♄	♂	☉	+7
♀	♀ +	♄	☿	♃	♄ m	♂	☉	+5
♂	♀	♄	☿	♃	♄	♂ −	☉	−10 p
♃	♄	♂	☽	♃ +	♂	☽	♃ −	−2
♄	☿	☿ m	☽	♀	♀ m	♃	♀	−1 p

ASPECTS
♀ ☌ ♂	0°18' S	
♃ △ ♄	0°22' S	
☉ ☍ ♅	1°17' A	
☿ ✶ ☋	1°50' A	
☿ △ ☊	1°50' A	
As □ Mc	1°51' S	
♂ □ ♃	2°44' S	
♀ □ ♃	2°45' S	
♀ △ ☊	3°00' A	
♀ ✶ ☋	3°00' A	

PLANETARY SECT
Planet	Cht	Plc	Sgn	Condition
☉ D	N	N	N	Ex Cond
☽ N	N	N	D	
☿ N	N	N	D	
♀ N	N	N	D	
♂ N	N	N	D	
♃ D	N	N	N	Ex Cond
♄ D	N	D	N	
D=Diurnal, N=Nocturnal				

12/7: WHEN WILL MY HUSBAND BE RELEASED FROM PRISON?

6 May 2001 at 3:57 p.m. (15:57), Ljubljana, Slovenia
Hour ruler: Venus

The querent is shown by ascendant in Virgo, exactly squared by Mars, while her ruler, Mercury, is in its domicile of Gemini in an exact conjunction with Saturn. This shows her to be angry (Mars) and frustrated (Saturn) by the long waiting for the trial; she was thinking of the law while at the same time turning to the Divinity (H9) to find the answer to her burning question. She loved her husband and waited eagerly for his return.

The Moon, in its many roles of her co-significator, timer and indicator of the flow of events, is at 3°25' Scorpio, in its fall, confirming the bad state she was in. Her imprisoned husband is shown by Venus, the occupant of H7, and by Jupiter, the planet ruling H7. In cases where there's a planet close to the cusp of the house showing the person inquired after, I'm inclined to put some more weight upon that planet, and since Venus was also the hour ruler and the husband was her "beloved one", I thought Venus should rightfully have more say in the matter. But as it's in its detriment, it shows him to be unhappy and virtually "away from home".

As for the prison: both houses 12, the radical and the turned one, are ruled by Mercury and Jupiter too, like the querent and the quesited – somewhat logically. But Jupiter also rules H4 of their home; this could complicate matters a bit, but since Venus is his main significator, let's rather take a closer look at what this planet is doing in the chart.

Venus is in a mixed mutual reception with the Sun (domicile/exaltation), ruling the fortunate H11. That's good, especially because Venus is approaching Jupiter by sextile, with Jupiter ruling the H4 of their home, so this obviously shows him to be coming home – eventually, that is, because the orb is quite wide, suggesting "not so soon". There're 8.5 degrees separating them in the chart and 14 degrees separating them in terms of their actual sextile which perfects on May 24, but since I don't measure time by taking the distance between planets, this only told me "not soon", especially because Venus was slow, her daily motion being only 0°31'. The Moon in a fixed sign and cadent house confirms a loooong time. Its first application is opposition to the Sun, being somehow applicable on account of its mutual reception with Venus. There are 12°41' separating them which could show 12.5 months, but I didn't feel that this was a reliable timing indication because the Sun doesn't rule his imprisonment; if it did, that could show the time of his being released from prison, but since it didn't this could only show the time passing until some decision was made in his favour.

There was no immediate application of the Moon to either Mercury nor Jupiter nor Venus. Its further aspects in the sign are a trine with the lunar node, a square with Neptune, an opposition with the Sun and, finally, a square with Uranus. Numerous Moon's aspects with the planets, with none of them specifically pointing to the husband's release from prison, confused me, therefore I said to her that, unfortunately, I can't find any reliable time indicator that would allow for a concrete answer, but, generally speaking, it would obviously not happen anytime soon.

Time passed and the husband was released on 19 December 2001, which is exactly 227 days or 7.5 months or 32.5 weeks after the question. Now how on earth does the chart show this?

There is one obvious indication, shown by the distance of the ascendant/descendant axis to Venus, which is exactly 7°24'. Translated into months that gives us 7.5 months. But I wasn't completely satisfied. There must be more, I thought.

Since the Moon is the querent's co-ruler plus the most reliable timing indicator, and Venus is the husband, the most logical thing would be to see when the two of them become re-united, and to this purpose we must count the number of degrees separating the Moon from the degree of her first aspect with Venus. Let's count. The Moon needs 26°35' till the end of Scorpio and another 6°05' to trine Venus, the husband, 32°40' in all. This is the number of time units elapsing till her husband's return.

Another crucial question: which time units? Strictly speaking, the Moon in a fixed sign and cadent house would give the longest time unit which is years, but since he didn't kill anybody, that seems out of question. Months? Hardly because he didn't even try to kill somebody, neither did he rob a bank nor did something similarly offensive. The querent actually told me that she expected him home soon because he was taken in under a false accusation and the court lacked proof against him. The most logical time unit would be weeks, then. 32.5 weeks brings us to the 19 (or 20) December 2001 – and as already said, he was released and back home on December 19. Incidentally, the Sun on that day reached the 28th degree of Sagittarius – the IC (home) of the horary chart.

12/7

6 May 2001
15:57 CEDT −2:00
Ljubljana, Slovenia
46°N03' 014°E31'

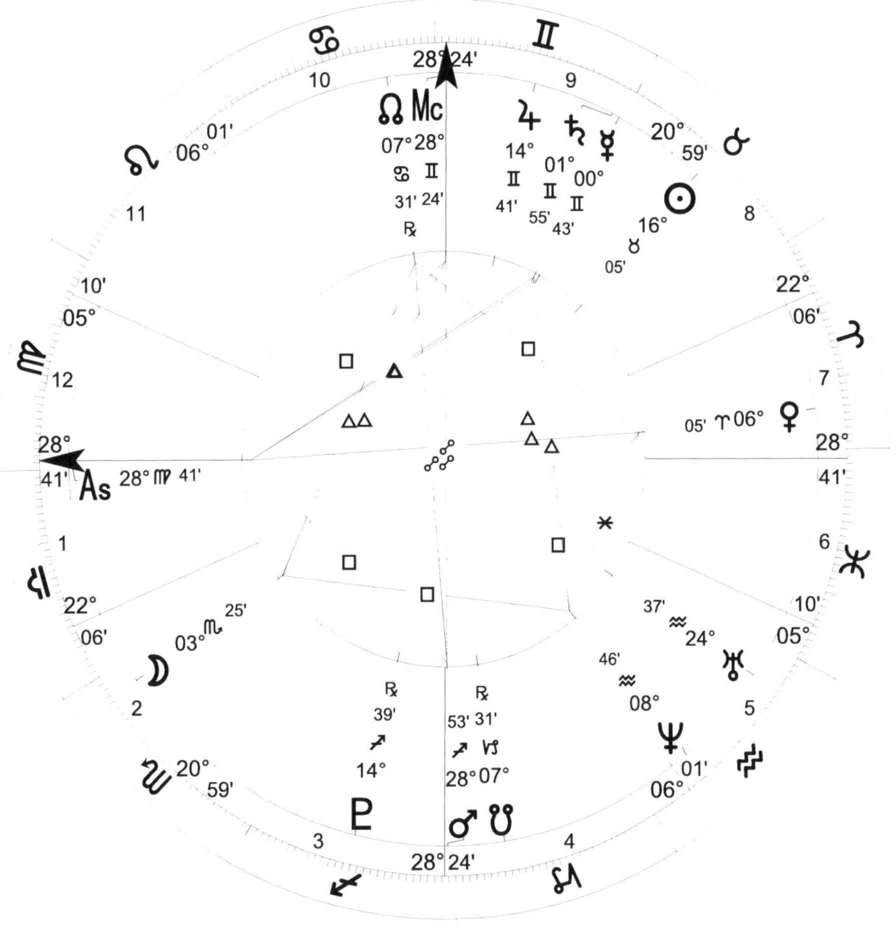

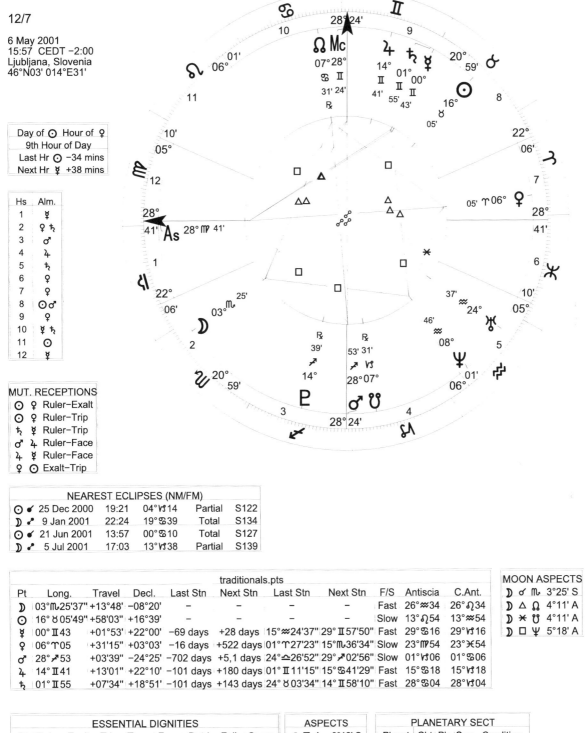

Day of ☉ Hour of ♀
9th Hour of Day
Last Hr ☉ −34 mins
Next Hr ☿ +38 mins

Hs	Alm.
1	☿
2	♀ ♄
3	♂
4	♃
5	♄
6	♀
7	♀
8	☉ ♂
9	♀
10	☿ ♄
11	☉
12	☿

MUT. RECEPTIONS		
☉	♀	Ruler–Exalt
☉	♀	Ruler–Trip
♄	☿	Ruler–Trip
♂	♃	Ruler–Face
♃	☿	Ruler–Face
♀	☉	Exalt–Trip

NEAREST ECLIPSES (NM/FM)					
☉ ☌	25 Dec 2000	19:21	04°♑14	Partial	S122
☽ ☍	9 Jan 2001	22:24	19°♋39	Total	S134
☉ ☌	21 Jun 2001	13:57	00°♋10	Total	S127
☽ ☍	5 Jul 2001	17:03	13°♑38	Partial	S139

traditionals.pts

Pt	Long.	Travel	Decl.	Last Stn	Next Stn	Last Stn	Next Stn	F/S	Antiscia	C.Ant.
☽	03°♏25'37"	+13°48'	−08°20'	–	–	–	–	Fast	26°♒34	26°♌34
☉	16°♉05'49"	+58'03"	+16°39'	–	–	–	–	Slow	13°♌54	13°♒54
☿	00°♊43	+01°53'	+22°00'	−69 days	+28 days	15°♒24'37"	29°♊57'50"	Fast	29°♋16	29°♑16
♀	06°♈05	+31'15"	+03°03'	−16 days	+522 days	01°♈27'23"	15°♏36'34"	Slow	23°♍54	23°♓54
♂	28°♐53	+03'39"	−24°25'	−702 days	+5,1 days	24°♎26'52"	29°♐02'56"	Slow	01°♑06	01°♋06
♃	14°♊41	+13'01"	+22°10'	−101 days	+180 days	01°♊11'15"	15°♋41'29"	Fast	15°♋18	15°♑18
♄	01°♊55	+07'34"	+18°51'	−101 days	+143 days	24°♉03'34"	14°♊58'10"	Fast	28°♋04	28°♑04

MOON ASPECTS			
☽ ☌	♏	3°25'	S
☽ △	☊	4°11'	A
☽ ⚹	☋	4°11'	A
☽ □	♆	5°18'	A

ESSENTIAL DIGNITIES

Pt	Ruler	Exalt	Trip	Term	Face	Detri	Fall	Score
☽	♂	--	♀	♂	♂	♀	☽ –	−9 p
☉	♀	☽	♀ m	♃	☽	♂	--	−5 p
☿	☿ +	--	♄	☿ +	♃	♃	--	+7
♀	♂	☉	☉ m	♀ +	♂	♀ –	♄	−3
♂	♃	--	☉	♂ +	♄	☿	--	+2
♃	☿	--	♄	♀	♂	♃ –	--	−10 p
♄	☿	--	♄ +	☿	♃	♃	--	+3

ASPECTS		
♂ □ As	0°12'	S
As □ Mc	0°17'	S
♂ ☍ Mc	1°06'	S
♀ □ ☋	1°26'	A
♀ □ ☊	1°26'	A
☿ △ As	2°02'	S
♀ ⚹ ♆	2°40'	A
☿ ☌ ♄	3°40'	A
☽ △ ☊	4°11'	A
☽ ⚹ ☋	4°11'	A

PLANETARY SECT

Planet		Cht	Plc	Sgn	Condition
☉	D	D	D	N	
☽	N	D	N	N	
☿	N	D	D	D	Ex Cond
♀	N	D	D	D	Ex Cond
♂	N	D	N	D	
♃	D	D	D	D	In Hayz
♄	D	D	D	D	In Hayz

D=Diurnal, N=Nocturnal

So what is the lesson of this horary chart? In timing, disregard sign boundaries. Disregard the so-called "frustrations". If something is bound to happen and the only question is »when«, just take the Moon (or an angle) and bring it to the nearest angle or the aspect with a significator. That's the simplest and most reliable timing procedure. So simple, but so difficult because our ancient (nor modern) textbooks do not encourage us to be bold.

12/8: WILL I BUY A MINIVAN THIS YEAR?

4 January 2005 at 11:28 a.m., Ljubljana, Slovenia
Hour ruler: Saturn

My husband and I each had our own car, but as our family grew to six, I felt increasingly uncomfortable with the family splitting in two whenever we travelled somewhere together. While I felt strongly that we need a minivan, my husband seemed quite happy with travelling in two cars, so I decided to make a purchase myself. But I was not sure if I could make it, so I asked the question.

The ascendant is in Aries (of course, I am interested in a "machine"!), my ruler Mars in Sagittarius in H8. Cars belong to H3, therefore I had to examine Mercury, the H3 ruler, as well as the Moon showing the flow of events. The Moon is in H7 which always plays an important role in sales. It is in an exact, but already separating (by 3 minutes of arc) sextile with Mercury, located in Sagittarius in H9. There is no connection between Mars and Mercury, therefore it doesn't seem like I am getting a new car. The answer is negative, and even confirmed by the unfortunate state of the hour ruler Saturn which is retrograde and in its detriment. Such charts incline towards a negative answer, or that things would not develop according to the querent's wish.

But there was something curious about this chart. My attention was drawn to the fact that H7 and H9 were strongly emphasized. H7 stands for partners while H9 as 3/7 (the third from the seventh) form my partner's partner car. Hmmm, is it possible that my husband would buy a new car? The Moon in H7 definitely points to a change in my partner's affairs, so let's see what exactly is going on! The Moon's last separating aspect was a sextile with Mercury, ruling the radix H3 of cars, and the one before last was a conjunction with Jupiter, ruling the derived H3 or my partner's car. The next Moon's aspect is a sextile with Venus, the ruler of H7, ruling him, and at the same time his car, as it is located in the derived H3 and therefore also shows where his own interest might be! (It seems that we were thinking about the same thing, except that his plans were not yet known to me!) We are dealing with a classic example of the translation of light: The Moon connects Mercury and Jupiter, both car significators, with Venus, the significator of my husband. So – there is a change in sight, but not involving me; something's changing on the side of my partner!

Indeed, it was my husband who bought a new car in that year. The contract was signed on 1 June 2005 which is 5 months after the question, but since the car was not new and needed some repairs before he could drive it safely, he started to use it only in the middle of summer. From the descendant to Jupiter, the ruler of H3 and dispositor of key planets in Sagittarius, is 6 degrees and a half, which (translated into months) brings us to mid-August of that year.

I bought the minivan only in the beginning of April 2007. It is interesting how the chart shows this, although it should theoretically "expire" by the end of year. (The question was whether I would buy a new car by the end of the year.) The answer was indeed correct – I didn't buy a new car in that period – but at the time of my purchase, transiting Jupiter was at 19.5 Sagittarius - in a very exact conjunction with the cusp of H9, opposing the cusp of H3 and therefore showing a change (selling the old car and buying a minivan).

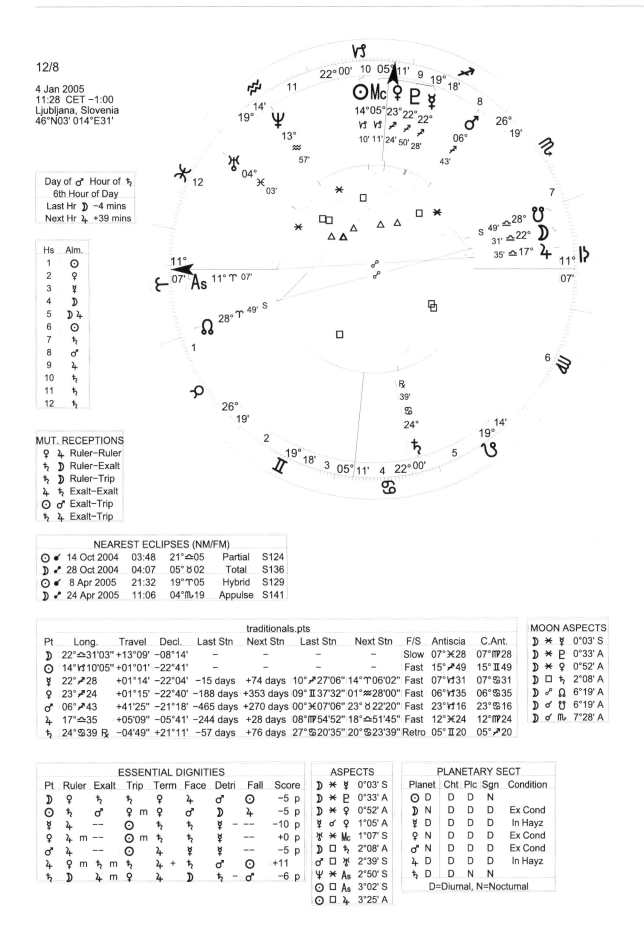

12/8

4 Jan 2005
11:28 CET −1:00
Ljubljana, Slovenia
46°N03' 014°E31'

Day of ♂ Hour of ♄
6th Hour of Day
Last Hr ☽ −4 mins
Next Hr ♃ +39 mins

Hs	Alm.
1	☉
2	♀
3	☿
4	☽
5	☽ ♃
6	☉
7	♄
8	♂
9	♃
10	♄
11	♄
12	♄

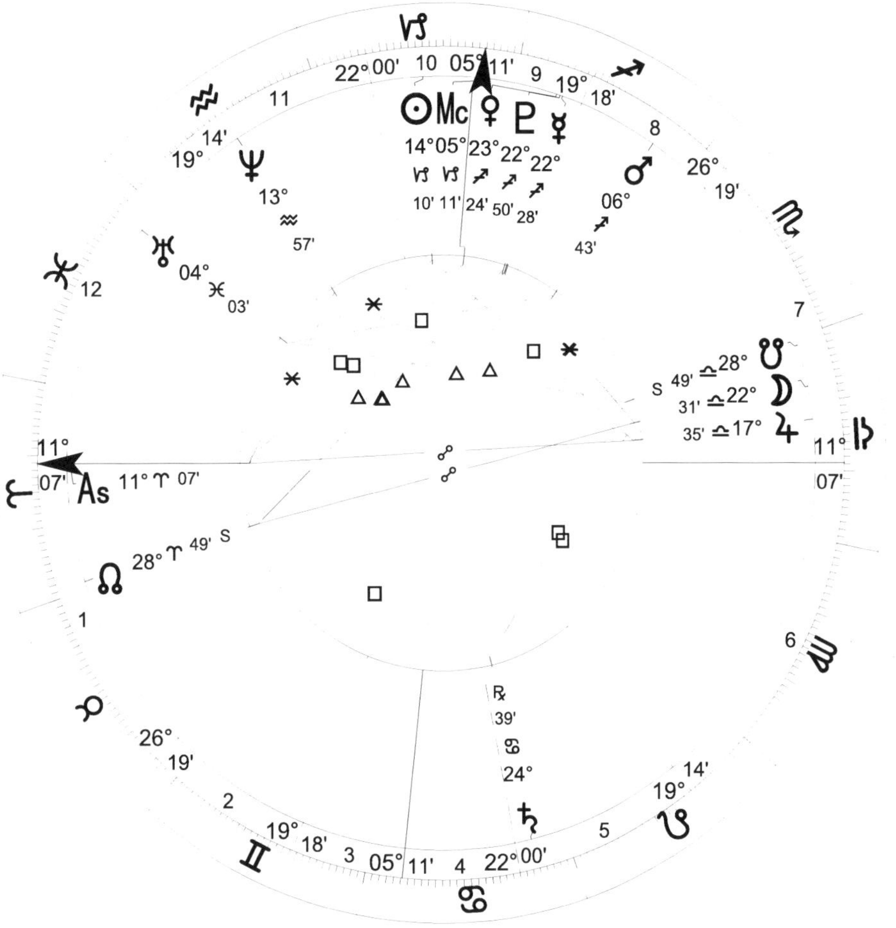

MUT. RECEPTIONS	
♀ ♃	Ruler–Ruler
♄ ☽	Ruler–Exalt
♄ ☽	Ruler–Trip
♃ ♄	Exalt–Exalt
☉ ♂	Exalt–Trip
♄ ♃	Exalt–Trip

NEAREST ECLIPSES (NM/FM)					
☉ ☌	14 Oct 2004	03:48	21°♎05	Partial	S124
☽ ☍	28 Oct 2004	04:07	05°♉02	Total	S136
☉ ☌	8 Apr 2005	21:32	19°♈05	Hybrid	S129
☽ ☍	24 Apr 2005	11:06	04°♏19	Appulse	S141

traditionals.pts

Pt	Long.	Travel	Decl.	Last Stn	Next Stn	Last Stn	Next Stn	F/S	Antiscia	C.Ant.
☽	22°♎31'03"	+13°09'	−08°14'	–	–	–	–	Slow	07°♓28	07°♍28
☉	14°♑10'05"	+01°01'	−22°41'	–	–	–	–	Fast	15°♐49	15°♊49
☿	22°♐28	+01°14'	−22°04'	−15 days	+74 days	10°♐27'06"	14°♈06'02"	Fast	07°♑31	07°♋31
♀	23°♐24	+01°15'	−22°40'	−188 days	+353 days	09°♊37'32"	01°♒28'00"	Fast	06°♑35	06°♋35
♂	06°♐43	+41'25"	−21°18'	−465 days	+270 days	00°♓07'06"	23°♉22'20"	Fast	23°♑16	23°♋16
♃	17°♎35	+05'09"	−05°41'	−244 days	+28 days	08°♍54'52"	18°♎51'45"	Fast	12°♓24	12°♍24
♄	24°♋39 ℞	−04'49"	+21°11'	−57 days	+76 days	27°♋20'35"	20°♋23'39"	Retro	05°♊20	05°♐20

MOON ASPECTS	
☽ ⚹ ☿	0°03' S
☽ ⚹ ♇	0°33' A
☽ ⚹ ♀	0°52' A
☽ □ ♄	2°08' A
☽ ☍ ☊	6°19' A
☽ ☌ ☋	6°19' A
☽ ☌ ♏	7°28' A

ESSENTIAL DIGNITIES								
Pt	Ruler	Exalt	Trip	Term	Face	Detri	Fall	Score
☽	♀	♄	♄	♀	♃	♂	☉	−5 p
☉	♄	♂	♀ m	♀	♂	☽	♃	−5 p
☿	♃	--	☉	♄	♄	☿ −	--	−10 p
♀	♃ m	--	☉ m	♄	♄	☿	--	+0 p
♂	♃	--	☉	♃	☿	☿	--	−5 p
♃	♀ m	♄ m	♄	♃ +	♄	♂	☉	+11
♄	☽	♃ m	♀	♃	☽	♄ −	♂	−6 p

ASPECTS	
☽ ⚹ ☿	0°03' S
☽ ⚹ ♇	0°33' A
☽ ⚹ ♀	0°52' A
☿ ☌ ♀	1°05' A
♅ ⚹ Mc	1°07' S
☽ □ ♄	2°08' A
♂ □ ♅	2°39' S
♆ ⚹ As	2°50' S
☉ □ As	3°02' S
☉ □ ♃	3°25' A

PLANETARY SECT				
Planet	Cht	Plc	Sgn	Condition
☉ D	D	D	N	
☽ N	D	D	D	Ex Cond
☿ D	D	D	D	In Hayz
♀ N	D	D	D	Ex Cond
♂ N	D	D	D	Ex Cond
♃ D	D	D	D	In Hayz
♄ D	D	N	N	
D=Diurnal, N=Nocturnal				

12/9: WILL OLIMPIJA HERTZ BECOME NATIONAL CHAMPS THIS YEAR?

7 April 1995 at 11:10 a.m., Ljubljana, Slovenia
Hour ruler: Jupiter

A friend who was a fan of the hockey team Olimpija Hertz asked me the above question before the start of the national championship which took place between the finalists Acroni Jesenice and Olimpija Hertz. Acroni had been national champions for ten seasons in a row, so she posed the question with anxious expectation. Will her team finally succeed?

Such questions belong to the 1/7 axis, similarly to charts of legal disputes and various competition charts. Since the querent was the Olimpija fan, I gave H1 to Olimpija and H7 to Acroni. ("We" against "them".) The procedure is then simple: we calculate the power/dignity of both sides and see which is stronger. The winner will be the one which leads in the sum of the essential and accidental dignities, of course!

Olimpija Hertz is ruled by the Moon (the H1), so let us first calculate its points: it is in Cancer its domicile sign (+5), in H1 – by virtue of conjuncting the ascendant (+5), waxing (+2), not combust or under the Sun's beams (+5) but slow (-2), getting a total of 15 points.

The descendant is in Capricorn, so the Acroni Jesenice is ruled by Saturn. This planet is in H10 (+5), direct (+4), eastern (+2), fast (+2), not combust or under the Sun's beams (+5), but peregrine (-5). The total number of points is 13.

The score therefore slightly favours Olimpija which is clearly a more capable team due to its superior essential dignity, than Acroni whose main significator is peregrine.

We could stop here and proclaim Olimpija the winner, but for accuracy sake, let us also check the respective 5th and 10th houses because in questions of this kind, luck (H5) is of prime importance, while success (H10) of each party should also be somehow seen in the chart.

The Moon is applying by a trine to two planets in H10: first to Venus, the ruler of their fortunate H5 – a wonderful confirmation of success. The second planet to which the Moon applies is Saturn, their opponent (Acroni). Saturn is in its own (derived) H4 which opposes their H10 of success, and this house is also occupied by Mercury, the ruler of their H10. Could this suggest the Acroni's "fall from power"? Still, H10 is a strong house, so the presence of crucial planets here should not be underestimated. Mercury is combust, though, which is another debility, whereas the chances of Olimpija are improved by the fact that their H10 ruler Jupiter is in its domicile where it applies (by retrograde movement) to trine Mars, the co-ruler of their H5 of luck.

The result? I told the querent that both teams seem pretty equal; the fight will probably be long and tough, but the power ratio shows that Olimpija Hertz will finally become the national champions –"her" team. *But because both teams are so even, I think that Olimpija will take the lead only in the last match*, I added.

And so it was. In the sixth, final match of the national championship, the Olimpija players took a lead of 5:1 and beat Acroni by the final result 4:2.

12/9

7 Apr 1995
11:10 CEDT −2:00
Ljubljana, Slovenia
46°N03' 014°E31'

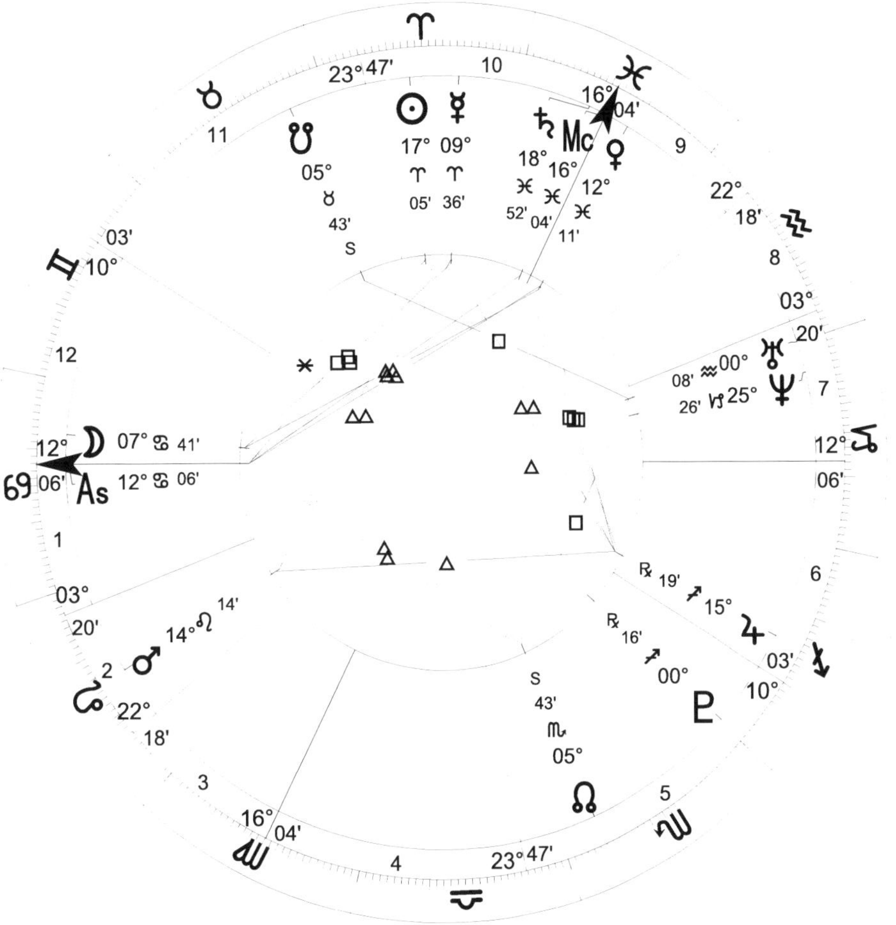

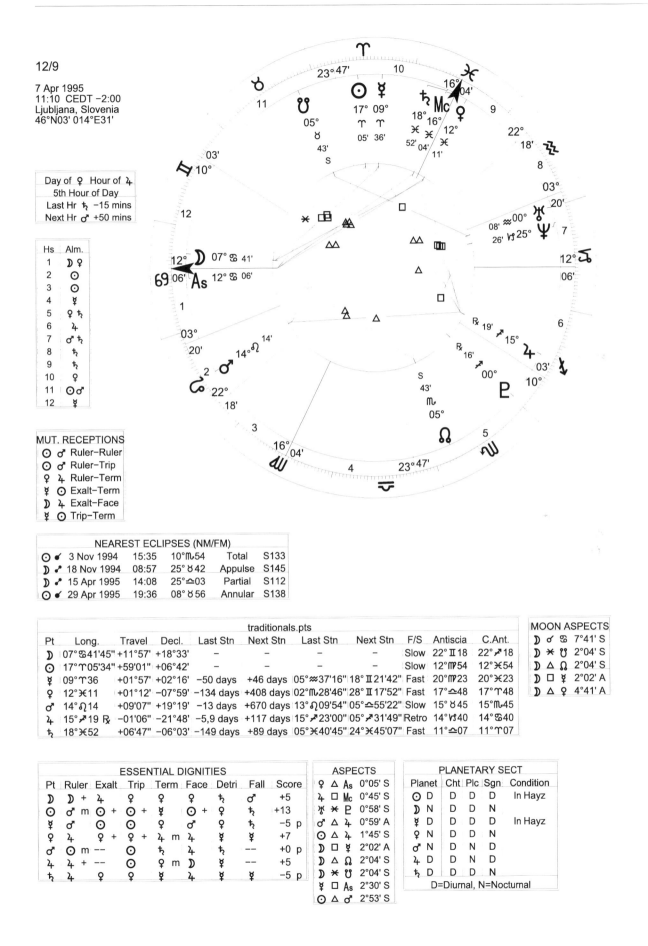

Day of ♀ Hour of ♃
5th Hour of Day
Last Hr ♄ −15 mins
Next Hr ♂ +50 mins

Hs	Alm.
1	☽ ♀
2	☉
3	☉
4	☿
5	♀ ♄
6	♃
7	♂ ♄
8	♄
9	♄
10	♀
11	☉ ♂
12	☿

MUT. RECEPTIONS		
☉	♂	Ruler–Ruler
☉	♂	Ruler–Trip
♀	♃	Ruler–Term
☿	☉	Exalt–Term
☽	♃	Exalt–Face
☿	☉	Trip–Term

NEAREST ECLIPSES (NM/FM)					
☉ ☌	3 Nov 1994	15:35	10°♏54	Total	S133
☽ ☍	18 Nov 1994	08:57	25°♉42	Appulse	S145
☽ ☍	15 Apr 1995	14:08	25°♎03	Partial	S112
☉ ☌	29 Apr 1995	19:36	08°♉56	Annular	S138

traditionals.pts

Pt	Long.	Travel	Decl.	Last Stn	Next Stn	Last Stn	Next Stn	F/S	Antiscia	C.Ant.
☽	07°♋41'45"	+11°57'	+18°33'	–	–	–	–	Slow	22°♊18	22°♐18
☉	17°♈05'34"	+59'01"	+06°42'	–	–	–	–	Slow	12°♍54	12°♓54
☿	09°♈36	+01°57'	+02°16'	−50 days	+46 days	05°♒37'16"	18°♊21'42"	Fast	20°♍23	20°♓23
♀	12°♓11	+01°12'	−07°59'	−134 days	+408 days	02°♏28'46"	28°♊17'52"	Fast	17°♎48	17°♈48
♂	14°♌14	+09'07"	+19°19'	−13 days	+670 days	13°♌09'54"	05°♎55'22"	Slow	15°♉45	15°♏45
♃	15°♐19 ℞	−01'06"	−21°48'	−5,9 days	+117 days	15°♐23'00"	05°♐31'49"	Retro	14°♑40	14°♋40
♄	18°♓52	+06'47"	−06°03'	−149 days	+89 days	05°♓40'45"	24°♓45'07"	Fast	11°♎07	11°♈07

MOON ASPECTS			
☽ ☌	♋	7°41'	S
☽ ⚹	☋	2°04'	S
☽ △	☊	2°04'	S
☽ □	☿	2°02'	A
☽ △	♀	4°41'	A

ESSENTIAL DIGNITIES

Pt	Ruler	Exalt	Trip	Term	Face	Detri	Fall	Score
☽	☽ +	♃	♀	♀	♀	♄	♂	+5
☉	♂ m	☉ +	☉ +	☿	☉ +	♀	♄	+13
☿	♂	☉	☉	♀	♂	♀	♄	−5 p
♀	♃	♀ +	♀ +	♃ m	♃	☿	☿	+7
♂	☉ m	--	☉	♄	♃	♄	--	+0 p
♃	♃ +	--	☉	♀ m	☽	☿	--	+5
♄	♃	♀	♀	☿	♃	☿	☿	−5 p

ASPECTS		
♀ △ As	0°05'	S
♃ □ Mc	0°45'	S
♅ ⚹ ♇	0°58'	S
♂ △ ♃	0°59'	A
☉ △ ♃	1°45'	S
☽ □ ☿	2°02'	A
☽ △ ☊	2°04'	S
☽ ⚹ ☋	2°04'	S
☿ □ As	2°30'	S
☉ △ ♂	2°53'	S

PLANETARY SECT

Planet		Cht	Plc	Sgn	Condition
☉	D	D	D	D	In Hayz
☽	N	D	D	N	
☿	D	D	D	D	In Hayz
♀	N	D	D	N	
♂	N	D	N	D	
♃	D	D	N	D	
♄	D	D	D	N	

D=Diurnal, N=Nocturnal

12/10: WHAT WILL BE THE RESULT OF THE MARKET INSPECTION?

24 September 2008 at 1:33 p.m. (13:33), Ljubljana, Slovenia
Hour ruler: Venus

The morning of that day I received a phone call from a lady who introduced herself as the market inspector. She told me that my company was selected for a routine investigation which the inspectorate was performing on various kinds of businesses. We agreed that I come to her office with all my company's documents: contracts, bills, bank statements and so on. She stressed that the inspection was not the consequence of anybody's expressing dissatisfaction with my company's performance – it was really just a routine examination.

Who is crazy about visiting an inspector when we are the subject of an investigation? They can always find inconsistency and mistakes, potentially causing us a lot of trouble. With this on my mind, I asked the above question a couple of hours after her call, and immediately cast the chart.

Venus, the hour ruler, is inharmonious but it rules H10 (official affairs, inspectorate) where it is also located, therefore the chart seemed radical.

My first concern was, was she telling the truth when she said that nobody reported me? The H7 ruler (my potential opponent or enemy) is Mercury, placed in H10 in conjunction with Mars, the ruler of H12 of hidden enemies, but since none of those planets was in an aspect with Jupiter, my ruler, I concluded that this link indeed didn't exist. That was a good sign!

What planet rules the inspector? The natural significator of inspectors is Saturn, the planet of order and discipline, but the house associated with authority is H10. This is ruled by Venus (appropriately, since the inspector was a woman) and co-ruled by Mercury and Mars, the occupants of H10. The Sun should be considered too, as it rules all kinds of influential people and authorities.

So many significators could complicate the matter, of course, but we must see which of them describe the situation best, and which are most active in the chart. In case of contradictory indications we will look at the Moon which shows the consequence of events and also acts as my co-significator.

Jupiter is in Capricorn in H1, close to the cusp of H2, showing my focus on organizing my business/financial affairs. Its applying trine to Saturn, its dispositor, standing for the inspector, is a strong suggestion of a harmonious flow of events. What's more, the Moon's first aspect is a sextile with the Sun, and this completely calmed me down - the outcome will obviously be favourable!

Our meeting was scheduled for six days after the question. A careful look at the chart shows that this is exactly the number of degrees separating the ascendant from sextile with Mercury, a H10 planet. Mercury rules H9 which stands for the Ministry of Economy, as the market inspectorate is one of its departments. All ministries belong to H9, and, incidentally (or not so, of course) this house is occupied by the two natural significators of inspectors and authority!

I came well prepared, and it turned out that the inspector was a very kind lady. After about three hours of a detailed examination of my documentation and website, she came to the conclusion that I had been violating the law in one single instance, this being related to my website contents. She ordered that I correct the information within a week. Ironically, the irregularity was potentially harming myself, not my clients, so I was really happy that she pointed it out, and took care that it was settled in less than a week.

How very agreeable our meeting was can be inferred from the fact that it concluded with our discussion of the best recipe for a tarragon cake.

12/10

24 Sep 2008
13:33 CEDT −2:00
Ljubljana, Slovenia
46°N03' 014°E31'

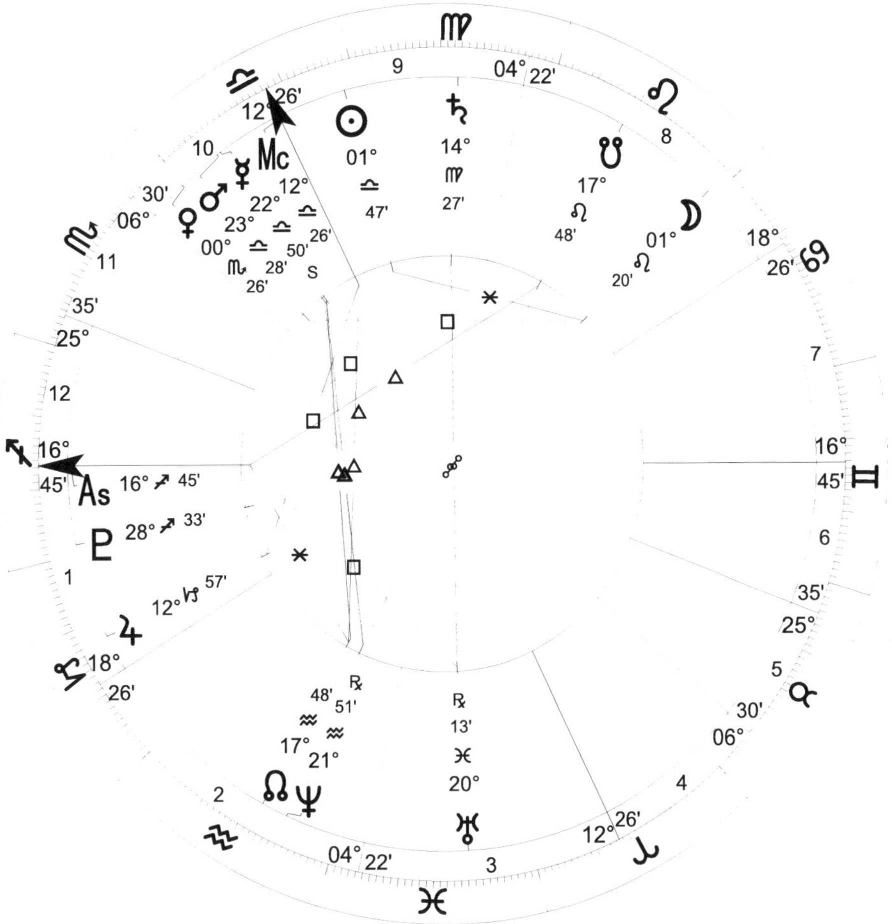

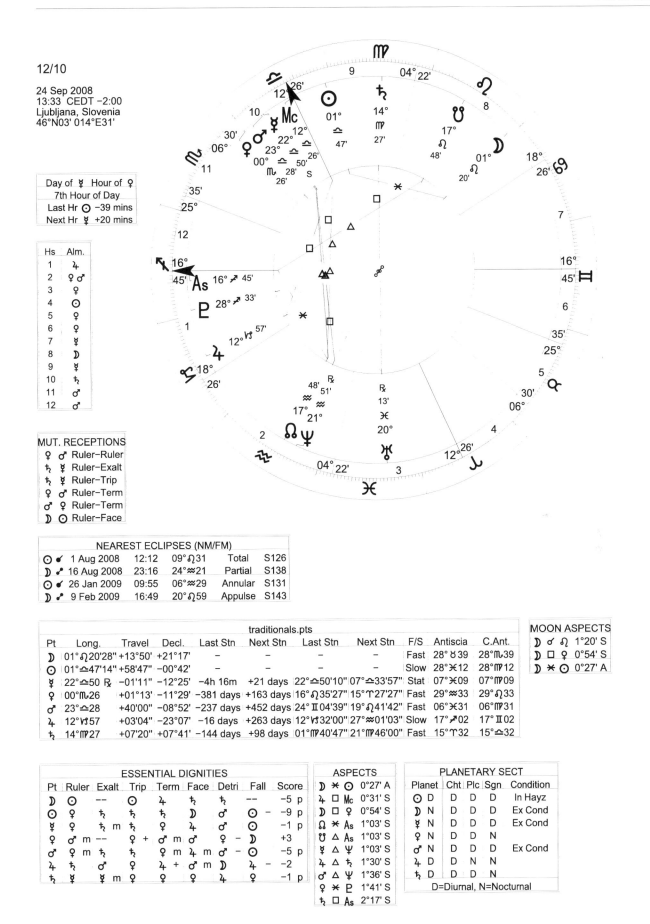

Day of ☿ Hour of ♀
7th Hour of Day
Last Hr ☉ −39 mins
Next Hr ☿ +20 mins

Hs	Alm.
1	♃
2	♀ ♂
3	♀
4	☉
5	♀
6	♀
7	☿
8	☽
9	☿
10	♄
11	♂
12	♂

MUT. RECEPTIONS		
♀	♂	Ruler−Ruler
♄	☿	Ruler−Exalt
♄	☿	Ruler−Trip
♀	♂	Ruler−Term
♂	♀	Ruler−Term
☽	☉	Ruler−Face

NEAREST ECLIPSES (NM/FM)					
☉ ●	1 Aug 2008	12:12	09°♌31	Total	S126
☽ ☍	16 Aug 2008	23:16	24°♒21	Partial	S138
☉ ●	26 Jan 2009	09:55	06°♒29	Annular	S131
☽ ☍	9 Feb 2009	16:49	20°♌59	Appulse	S143

traditionals.pts

Pt	Long.	Travel	Decl.	Last Stn	Next Stn	Last Stn	Next Stn	F/S	Antiscia	C.Ant.
☽	01°♌20'28"	+13°50'	+21°17'	–	–	–	–	Fast	28°♉39	28°♏39
☉	01°♎47'14"	+58'47"	−00°42'	–	–	–	–	Slow	28°♓12	28°♍12
☿	22°♎50 ℞	−01'11"	−12°25'	−4h 16m	+21 days	22°♎50'10"	07°♎33'57"	Stat	07°♓09	07°♍09
♀	00°♏26	+01°13'	−11°29'	−381 days	+163 days	16°♌35'27"	15°♈27'27"	Fast	29°♒33	29°♌33
♂	23°♎28	+40'00"	−08°52'	−237 days	+452 days	24°♊04'39"	19°♌41'42"	Fast	06°♓31	06°♍31
♃	12°♑57	+03'04"	−23°07'	−16 days	+263 days	12°♑32'00"	27°♒01'03"	Slow	17°♐02	17°♊02
♄	14°♍27	+07'20"	+07°41'	−144 days	+98 days	01°♍40'47"	21°♍46'00"	Fast	15°♈32	15°♎32

MOON ASPECTS			
☽	☌	♌	1°20' S
☽	□	♀	0°54' S
☽	⚹	☉	0°27' A

ESSENTIAL DIGNITIES

Pt	Ruler	Exalt	Trip	Term	Face	Detri	Fall	Score
☽	☉	--	☉	♃	♄	♄	--	−5 p
☉	♀	♄	♄	♄	☽	♂	☉ −	−9 p
☿	♀	♄ m	♄	♀	♃	♂	☉	−1 p
♀	♂ m	--	♀ +	♂ m	♂	♀ −	☽	+3
♂	♀ m	♄	♄	♀ m	♃ m	♂ −	☉	−5 p
♃	♄	♂	♀	♃ +	♂ m	☽	♃ −	−2
♄	☿	☿ m	♀	♀	♀	♃	♀	−1 p

ASPECTS			
☽	⚹	☉	0°27' A
♃	□	Mc	0°31' S
☽	□	♀	0°54' S
☊	⚹	As	1°03' S
☋	△	As	1°03' S
☿	△	♆	1°03' S
♃	△	♄	1°30' S
♂	△	♆	1°36' S
♀	⚹	♇	1°41' S
♄	□	As	2°17' S

PLANETARY SECT

Planet		Cht	Plc	Sgn	Condition
☉	D	D	D	D	In Hayz
☽	N	D	D	D	Ex Cond
☿	N	D	D	D	Ex Cond
♀	N	D	D	N	
♂	N	D	D	D	Ex Cond
♃	D	D	N	N	
♄	D	D	D	N	

D=Diurnal, N=Nocturnal

12/11: WILL I THROW A PARTY NEXT SATURDAY?

8 October 2008 at 8:56 p.m. (20:56), Ljubljana, Slovenia
Hour ruler: Mercury

This year, my birthday (October 18) fell on a Saturday. I thought that we should celebrate it in a big way, as Saturdays are the best days for parties. Unfortunately, I remembered a little late that a lot of fun asks for a lot of space. I started to look for a venue, but all the places that seemed suitable were already booked, or too expensive. Ten days before my birthday, as nothing was coming up, I started to feel a little anxious, so I asked myself the above question.

I am shown by the ascendant in Gemini, ruled by Mercury which is quite suitably placed in H5 of parties (my focus and intention), but is retrograde and combust. Not good! True, I was worried and uncertain, and Mercury's condition adequately describes me. But sitting on the cusp of H5 there is Saturn – we don't need the old grump at a party, do we? Mercury conjuncts the Sun, ruling H4. My home? Mercury moves away from the Sun, actually coming out of combustion, and both are in a harmonious trine with the ascendant, so I thought – why not organize the party in our house? This is how we did it last year and everyone was happy. I actually wanted to invite more people this year, but we could give them pillows to sit on the floor if the place got too crowded and the chairs were too few.

No sooner said than done. I immediately set myself on sending out the invites and started to plan the drinks and snacks.

But let us go back to the chart. The Moon, my co-significator, applies by a trine to Mercury, the ruler of H5, by a 10 degrees orb – but of course, the party was planned for exactly 10 days later! (You might ask how come because the Moon is in a fixed sign and in a cadent house which should indicate longer time units; true, but let us remember that the real circumstances should always take priority when deciding on the time unit.) Anyway, I saw this "coincidence" as the final proof that the party would indeed take place.

Still, there are indications in the chart that the situation would not proceed smoothly. Beside the old grump sitting in H5, the Moon is frustrated by squaring Mars in H6. Certainly, this frustration seems annoying; it could be overcome, I thought, but what kind of trouble could it bring? H6 is the house of illness, and Mars is the planet of fever. Then it struck me – is it possible that I would get sick? Mercury, my main significator, seemed weak, confirming my hunch. Two of my kids were already affected by a cold, so it seemed kind of logical that the virus could spread on me. There are 1°39' separating the Moon from the exact square of Mars, which translated into weeks would give a good week and a half – exactly 10 days, actually. Ooops, would I be sick on my birthday?

Unfortunately, this is exactly what happened. In the beginning of the next week, I started to feel a little feverish, so I got to sipping sage tea and swallowing propolis pills. In spite of that, my temperature rose and on Thursday evening my throat was so sore and painful that on Friday morning I had to start treating myself with antibiotics. They helped me to stay on my feet on Saturday night when my grand party was taking place, but I dropped to bed soon after midnight whereas my friends went on celebrating my birthday right until the morning hours.

There are three additional interesting features in the chart; firstly, the Moon is in a mixed mutual reception with Saturn (domicile/triplicity), indicating my choice between either to drop the party (Saturn in H5) or exchange places with Saturn by moving myself (the Moon) into H5; secondly, both Mercury and the Moon are on Jupiter degrees by monomoiria (party, joy, fun, an optimistic attitude) whereas (thirdly) Mars in H6 is on the Mercury monomoiria degree - a respiratory disease.

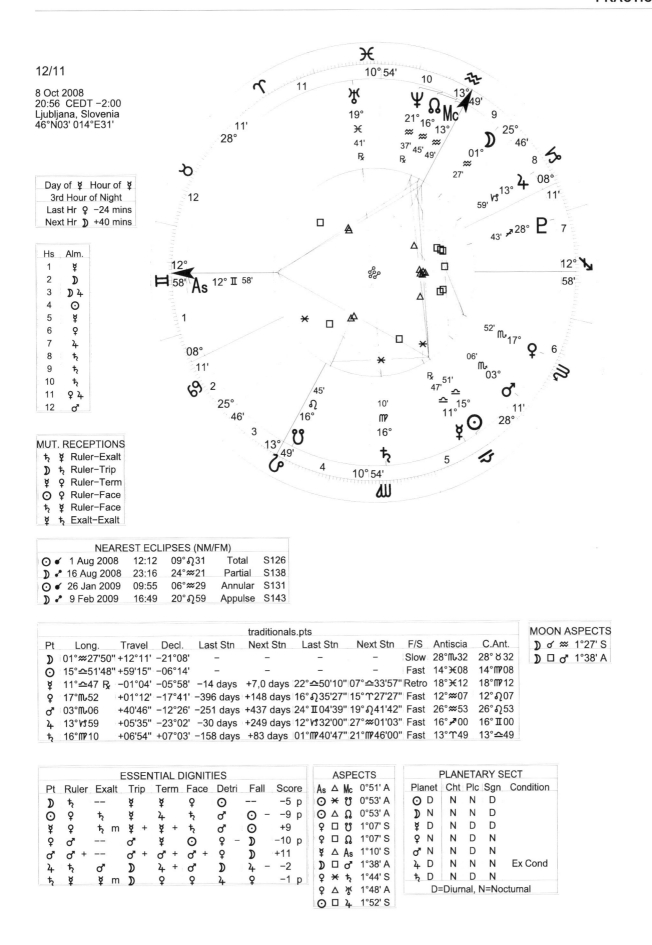

12/11

8 Oct 2008
20:56 CEDT −2:00
Ljubljana, Slovenia
46°N03' 014°E31'

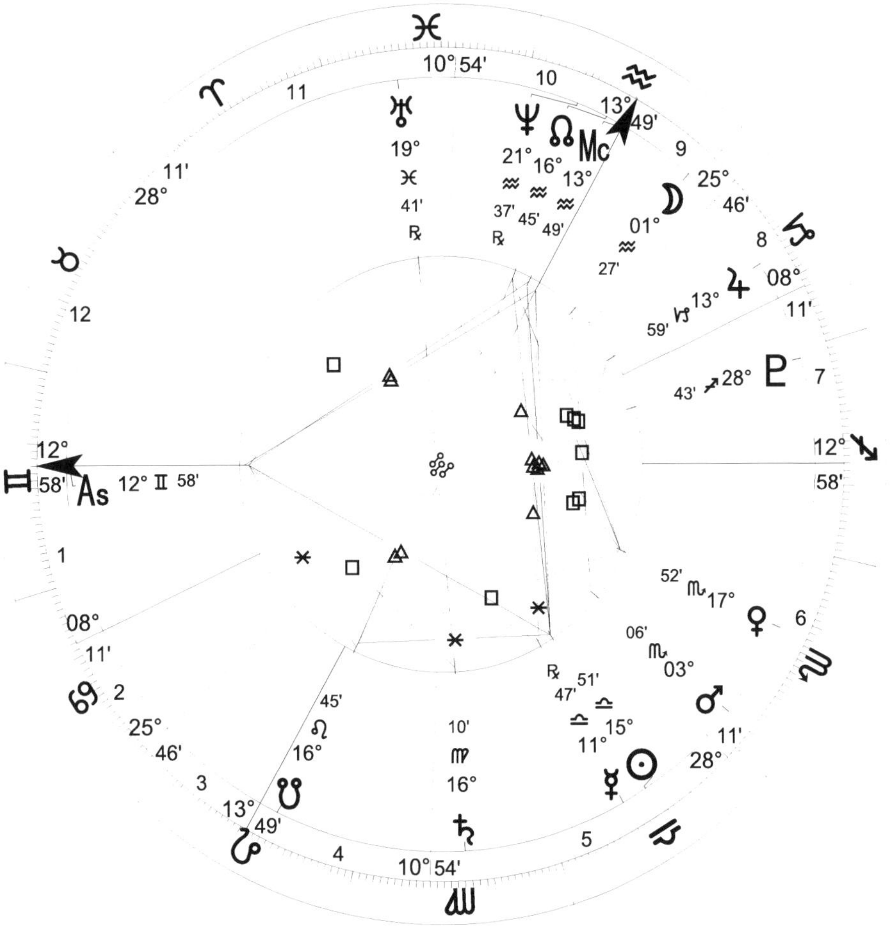

Day of ☿	Hour of ☿
3rd Hour of Night	
Last Hr ♀	−24 mins
Next Hr ☽	+40 mins

Hs	Alm.
1	☿
2	☽
3	☽ ♃
4	☉
5	☿
6	♀
7	♃
8	♄
9	♄
10	♄
11	♀ ♃
12	♂

MUT. RECEPTIONS		
♄	☿	Ruler-Exalt
☽	♄	Ruler-Trip
☿	♀	Ruler-Term
☉	♀	Ruler-Face
♄	☿	Ruler-Face
☿	♄	Exalt-Exalt

NEAREST ECLIPSES (NM/FM)					
☉ ☌	1 Aug 2008	12:12	09°♌31	Total	S126
☽ ☍	16 Aug 2008	23:16	24°♒21	Partial	S138
☉ ☌	26 Jan 2009	09:55	06°♒29	Annular	S131
☽ ☍	9 Feb 2009	16:49	20°♌59	Appulse	S143

traditionals.pts

Pt	Long.	Travel	Decl.	Last Stn	Next Stn	Last Stn	Next Stn	F/S	Antiscia	C.Ant.
☽	01°♒27'50"	+12°11'	−21°08'	–	–	–	–	Slow	28°♏32	28°♉32
☉	15°♎51'48"	+59'15"	−06°14'	–	–	–	–	Fast	14°♓08	14°♍08
☿	11°♎47 ℞	−01°04'	−05°58'	−14 days	+7,0 days	22°♎50'10"	07°♎33'57"	Retro	18°♓12	18°♍12
♀	17°♏52	+01°12'	−17°41'	−396 days	+148 days	16°♌35'27"	15°♈27'27"	Fast	12°♒07	12°♌07
♂	03°♏06	+40'46"	−12°26'	−251 days	+437 days	24°♊04'39"	19°♌41'42"	Fast	26°♒53	26°♌53
♃	13°♑59	+05'35"	−23°02'	−30 days	+249 days	12°♑32'00"	27°♒01'03"	Fast	16°♐00	16°♊00
♄	16°♍10	+06'54"	+07°03'	−158 days	+83 days	01°♍40'47"	21°♍46'00"	Fast	13°♈49	13°♎49

MOON ASPECTS			
☽	☌	♒	1°27' S
☽	□	♂	1°38' A

ESSENTIAL DIGNITIES

Pt	Ruler	Exalt	Trip	Term	Face	Detri	Fall	Score
☽	♄	--	☿	☿	♀	☉	--	−5 p
☉	♀	♄	☿	♃	♄	♂	☉ –	−9 p
☿	♀	♄ m	☿ +	☿ +	♄	♂	☉	+9
♀	♂	--	♂	☿	☉	♀ –	☽	−10 p
♂	♂ +	--	♂ +	♂ +	♂ +	♀	☽	+11
♃	♄	♂	☽	♃ +	♂	☽	♃ –	−2
♄	☿	☿ m	☽	♀	♀	♃	♀	−1 p

ASPECTS			
As	△	Mc	0°51' A
☉	✶	☋	0°53' A
☉	△	☊	0°53' A
♀	□	☋	1°07' S
♀	□	☊	1°07' S
☿	△	As	1°10' S
☽	□	♂	1°38' A
♀	✶	♄	1°44' S
♀	△	♅	1°48' A
☉	□	♃	1°52' S

PLANETARY SECT

Planet		Cht	Plc	Sgn	Condition
☉	D	N	N	D	
☽	N	N	N	D	
☿	D	N	D	D	
♀	N	N	D	N	
♂	N	N	D	N	
♃	D	N	N	N	Ex Cond
♄	D	N	D	N	

D=Diurnal, N=Nocturnal

12/12: WHEN WILL MY DAUGHTER BE BACK FROM HOSPITAL?

21 October 2008 at 8:10 p.m. (20:10), Ljubljana, Slovenia
Hour ruler: Jupiter

My 6-year old daughter Masha fell ill with pneumonia and was taken to hospital due to high fever and breathing difficulty. Her doctor said that she would have to stay there at least until Friday. A day after they took her in, I asked the above question.

Masha is shown by Mercury, ruling H5, and co-ruled by the Moon. Saturn on the cusp of H5, ruling the turned H6 in the airy Aquarius shows her breathing-related disease: inflammation of the lungs. Mercury in square of Jupiter, ruling lungs, confirms those indications. Her (that is, our) home is ruled by the Sun (IC in Leo). The Moon is in a tight applying trine with Venus, ruling the radical H12 of hospitals.

To find the answer we must focus on the core question: when is she (Mercury, Moon) coming home (Sun). The Moon, also showing the course of events, is separating from a square with the Sun and applying (via Venus, the hospital) to sextile Mercury, thereby connecting her (Mercury) with our home (Sun), in 8°28'. Eight and a half days? I thought this improbable; she was ill but not THAT ill! The Sun needs 1°17' until the next sign. A bit over one day? Not probable because they said she would have to stay there at least until Friday. I was scratching my head long before I gave up.

My daughter was released from hospital on Saturday, at just about midday. As soon as we came home I started to scratch my head again because I'm always adamant to find the answer in a chart. I'm convinced that if a question about timing is sincere the answer must be somewhere in the chart! And it surely was, but in a most unusual kind of ways.

Eight hours less than 4 days elapsed until Masha's return. How does the chart show this? I couldn't find days, so I thought, let us count the hours. The question was asked on Tuesday at 20:10. There are roughly 3 hours until midnight. Wednesday, Thursday and Friday add up to 72 hours (3 times 24). There are 12 hours left until midday on Saturday. Adding it all up we come to 87 hours. Following the logic of taking 1 hour per 1 degree, add 87 degrees to 2 Leo, the degree of the Moon, and we come to 28°43' of Libra – the degree of the Sun, standing for our (Masha's) home. Fascinating, isn't it?

This case teaches us that we should be very flexible when doing the timing. Horary astrologers are generally not used to employ hours in their timing procedures, but those small units of time are reasonable and viable, and should come handy especially in cases when we expect something to happen within a day, as opposed to larger units of time (weeks, months or years).

12/12

21 Oct 2008
20:10 CEDT −2:00
Ljubljana, Slovenia
46°N03' 014°E31'

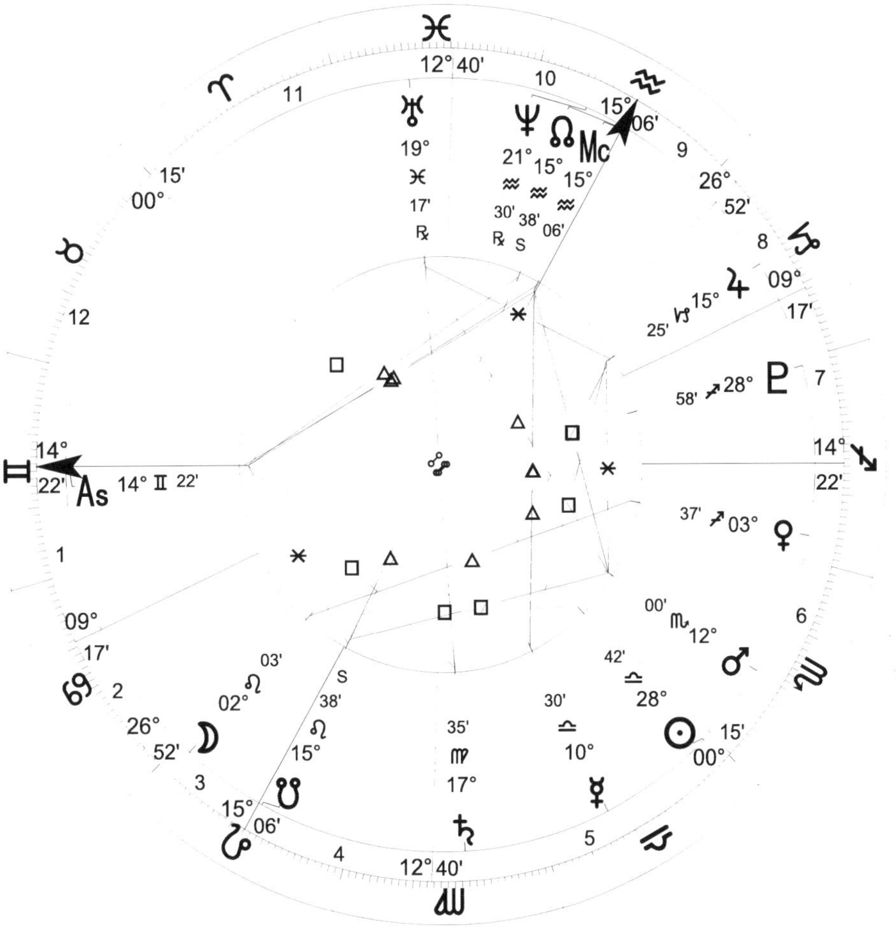

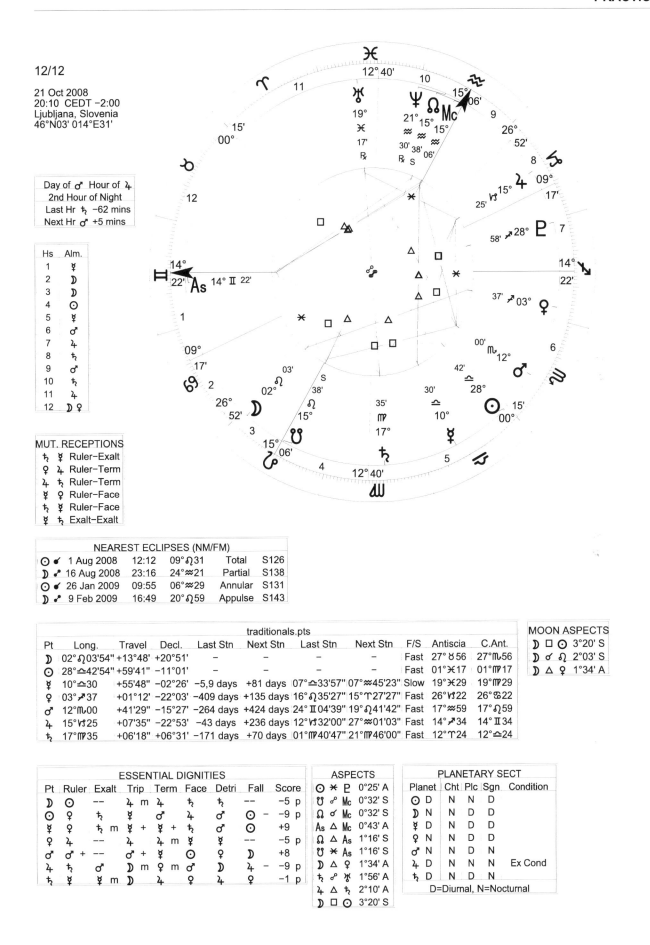

Day of ♂ Hour of ♃
2nd Hour of Night
Last Hr ♄ −62 mins
Next Hr ♂ +5 mins

Hs	Alm.
1	☿
2	☽
3	☽
4	☉
5	☿
6	♂
7	♃
8	♄
9	♂
10	♄
11	♃
12	☽ ♀

MUT. RECEPTIONS	
♄ ☿	Ruler–Exalt
♀ ♃	Ruler–Term
♃ ♄	Ruler–Term
☿ ♀	Ruler–Face
♄ ☿	Ruler–Face
☿ ♄	Exalt–Exalt

NEAREST ECLIPSES (NM/FM)					
☉ ☌	1 Aug 2008	12:12	09°♌31	Total	S126
☽ ☍	16 Aug 2008	23:16	24°♒21	Partial	S138
☉ ☌	26 Jan 2009	09:55	06°♒29	Annular	S131
☽ ☍	9 Feb 2009	16:49	20°♌59	Appulse	S143

traditionals.pts

Pt	Long.	Travel	Decl.	Last Stn	Next Stn	Last Stn	Next Stn	F/S	Antiscia	C.Ant.
☽	02°♌03'54"	+13°48'	+20°51'	–	–	–	–	Fast	27°♉56	27°♏56
☉	28°♎42'54"	+59'41"	−11°01'	–	–	–	–	Fast	01°♓17	01°♍17
☿	10°♎30	+55'48"	−02°26'	−5,9 days	+81 days	07°♎33'57"	07°♒45'23"	Slow	19°♓29	19°♍29
♀	03°♐37	+01°12'	−22°03'	−409 days	+135 days	16°♌35'27"	15°♈27'27"	Fast	26°♑22	26°♋22
♂	12°♏00	+41'29"	−15°27'	−264 days	+424 days	24°♊04'39"	19°♌41'42"	Fast	17°♒59	17°♌59
♃	15°♑25	+07'35"	−22°53'	−43 days	+236 days	12°♑32'00"	27°♒01'03"	Fast	14°♐34	14°♊34
♄	17°♍35	+06'18"	+06°31'	−171 days	+70 days	01°♍40'47"	21°♍46'00"	Fast	12°♈24	12°♎24

MOON ASPECTS	
☽ □ ☉	3°20' S
☽ ☌ ♌	2°03' S
☽ △ ♀	1°34' A

ESSENTIAL DIGNITIES

Pt	Ruler	Exalt	Trip	Term	Face	Detri	Fall	Score
☽	☉	--	♃ m	♃	♄	♄	--	−5 p
☉	♀	♄	☿	♂	♃	♂	☉ −	−9 p
☿	♀	♄ m	☿ +	☿ +	♄	♂	☉	+9
♀	♃	--	♃	♃ m	☿	☿	--	−5 p
♂	♂ +	--	♂ +	☿	☉	♀	☽	+8
♃	♄	♂	☽ m	♀ m	♂	☽	♃ −	−9 p
♄	☿	☿ m	☽	♃	♀	♃	♀	−1 p

ASPECTS	
☉ ⚹ ♇	0°25' A
☋ ☍ Mc	0°32' S
☊ ☌ Mc	0°32' S
As △ Mc	0°43' A
☊ △ As	1°16' S
☋ ⚹ As	1°16' S
☽ △ ♀	1°34' A
♄ ☍ ♅	1°56' A
♃ △ ♄	2°10' A
☽ □ ☉	3°20' S

PLANETARY SECT

Planet		Cht	Plc	Sgn	Condition
☉	D	N	N	D	
☽	N	N	D	D	
☿	D	N	D	D	
♀	N	N	D	D	
♂	N	N	D	N	
♃	D	N	N	N	Ex Cond
♄	D	N	D	N	

D=Diurnal, N=Nocturnal

12/13: ARE WE GETTING ANY SNOW THIS WINTER?

14 January 2007 at 1:16 p.m. (13:16), Ljubljana, Slovenia
Hour ruler: Sun

It was Sunday 14 January 2007 when I was looking nostalgically through the window, wondering if there'd be any snow at all this winter. We hadn't seen any in that season yet, which was pretty unusual. But I really missed snow. Sledding on the freshly fallen snow was so much fun, especially for our children!

Which planet rules snow? Wouldn't it be Saturn - the coldest planet that presides over winter weather and low temperatures? True, but in my inner vision of what snow would bring to us, this wasn't anything cold and gloomy, but something bright and beautiful! It was actually my heart desire, hope and longing which would be more appropriately ruled by Jupiter and H11. Incidentally (or rather not so!), H11 in this chart is ruled by Jupiter! And where is this planet located? At 10°52' of Sagittarius, 2°40' from the descendant.

The Moon should also be examined, as all precipitation is ruled by it, being a cold and moist body and the natural significator of everything wet; besides, the Moon is most important in weather prediction generally. It is in Scorpio, a water sign, and applying to Mercury (me) by 1°36'. Since Scorpio is a fixed sign and the Moon here in a cadent house, that could be 1.5 months before it snows, I thought. Or would it be a bit over 2.5 months, as the distance from the descendant to Jupiter suggests?

It turned out we did have some snow that winter – at least in the lowlands where we live. A few centimetres fell on March 20 and even that bit melted in a couple of days (Jupiter in Sagittarius, a fire sign, showing warmth), but we finally experienced some real winter joy.

Anyway – March 20 is nine weeks after the question. This is a week less than 2.5 months, as Jupiter suggested, but more than 1.5 months, as indicated by the Moon.

I then calculated the Moon parallax, to see if the new position would give a more correct result. The Moon is at 26°55' in the "normal" chart, but allowing for the parallax it would be moved to 26°27'. The orb of the applying sextile of the Moon to Mercury would then be 2°04', giving a more correct result. The Moon was also slow on that day, so the time could be a bit "stretched", getting us a pretty exact timing. (Nine weeks would exactly correspond to 2 degrees and 15 minutes whereas the difference here was 2 degrees and 4 minutes.)

Another interesting fact is that if we add 65 degrees (the number of days that elapsed until the snowfall) to the Moon, we get to 22 Capricorn, the degree of the H9 cusp, where it closely conjuncts the Sun, ruling H4 and also acting as the hour ruler. In weather astrology, H4 is associated with weather formation, so there could be a link there.

I should add that I was unsure of the result when I first looked at the chart, but the hour ruler (the Sun) was inharmonious, and such charts often don't get the correct answer. Except in retrospect, of course.

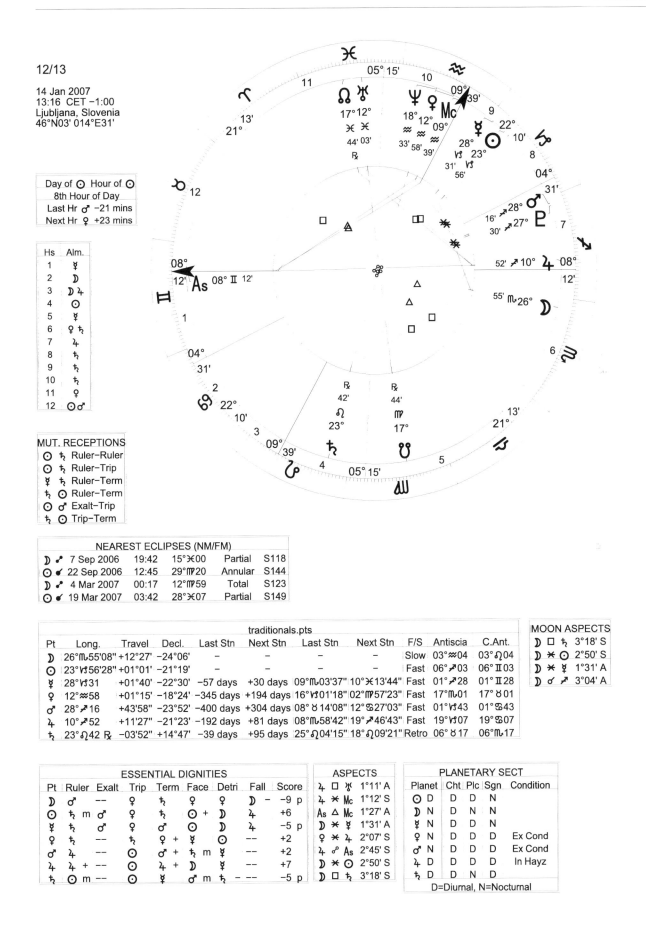

12/13

14 Jan 2007
13:16 CET −1:00
Ljubljana, Slovenia
46°N03' 014°E31'

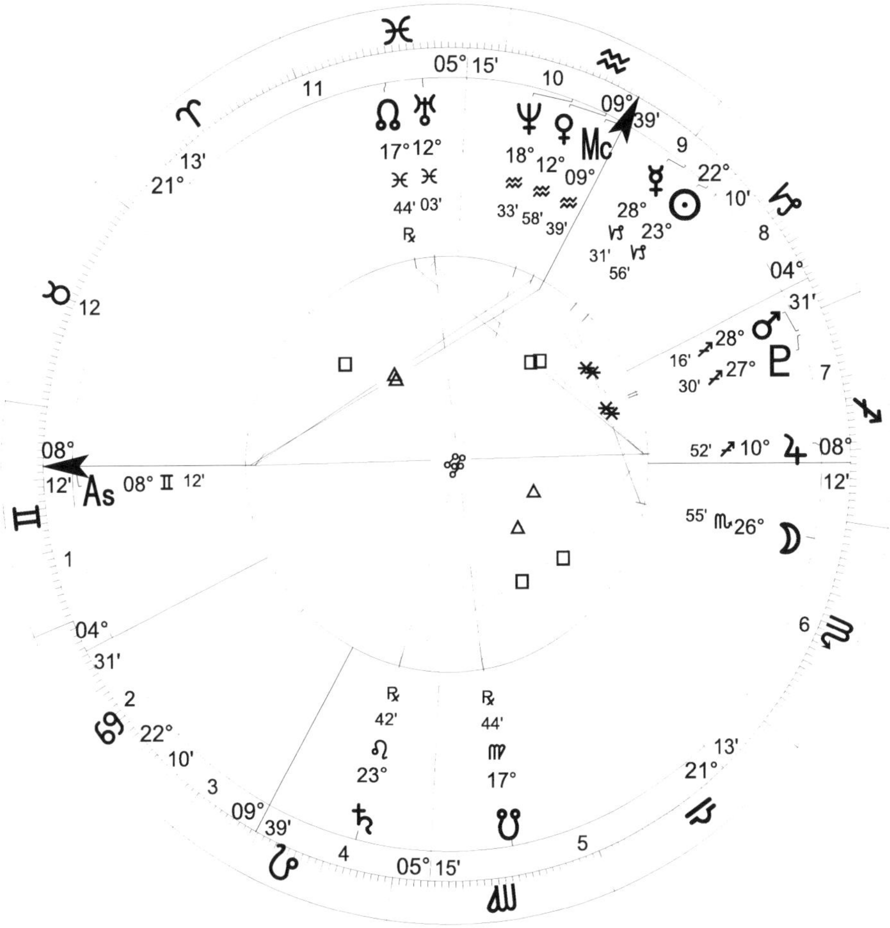

Day of ☉ Hour of ☉
8th Hour of Day
Last Hr ♂ −21 mins
Next Hr ♀ +23 mins

Hs	Alm.
1	☿
2	☽
3	☽ ♃
4	☉
5	☿
6	♀ ♄
7	♃
8	♄
9	♄
10	♄
11	♀
12	☉ ♂

MUT. RECEPTIONS
☉ ♄ Ruler–Ruler
☉ ♄ Ruler–Trip
☿ ♄ Ruler–Term
♄ ☉ Ruler–Term
☉ ♂ Exalt–Trip
♄ ☉ Trip–Term

NEAREST ECLIPSES (NM/FM)					
☽	7 Sep 2006	19:42	15°♓00	Partial	S118
☉	22 Sep 2006	12:45	29°♍20	Annular	S144
☽	4 Mar 2007	00:17	12°♍59	Total	S123
☉	19 Mar 2007	03:42	28°♓07	Partial	S149

traditionals.pts

Pt	Long.	Travel	Decl.	Last Stn	Next Stn	Last Stn	Next Stn	F/S	Antiscia	C.Ant.
☽	26°♏55'08"	+12°27'	−24°06'	–	–	–	–	Slow	03°♒04	03°♌04
☉	23°♑56'28"	+01°01'	−21°19'	–	–	–	–	Fast	06°♐03	06°♊03
☿	28°♑31	+01°40'	−22°30'	−57 days	+30 days	09°♏03'37"	10°♓13'44"	Fast	01°♐28	01°♊28
♀	12°♒58	+01°15'	−18°24'	−345 days	+194 days	16°♑01'18"	02°♍57'23"	Fast	17°♏01	17°♉01
♂	28°♐16	+43'58"	−23°52'	−400 days	+304 days	08°♉14'08"	12°♋27'03"	Fast	01°♑43	01°♋43
♃	10°♐52	+11'27"	−21°23'	−192 days	+81 days	08°♏58'42"	19°♐46'43"	Fast	19°♑07	19°♋07
♄	23°♌42 ℞	−03'52"	+14°47'	−39 days	+95 days	25°♌04'15"	18°♌09'21"	Retro	06°♉17	06°♏17

MOON ASPECTS
☽ □ ♄ 3°18' S
☽ ⚹ ☉ 2°50' S
☽ ⚹ ☿ 1°31' A
☽ ☌ ♐ 3°04' A

ESSENTIAL DIGNITIES

Pt	Ruler	Exalt	Trip	Term	Face	Detri	Fall	Score
☽	♂	--	♀	♄	♀	♀	☽ −	-9 p
☉	♄ m	♂	♀	♄	☉ +	☽	♃	+6
☿	♄	♂	♀	♂	☉	☽	♃	-5 p
♀	♄	--	♄	♀ +	☿	☉	--	+2
♂	♃	--	☉	♂ +	♄ m	☿	--	+2
♃	♃ +	--	☉	♃ +	☽	☿	--	+7
♄	☉ m	--	☉	☿	♂ m	♄ −	--	-5 p

ASPECTS
♃ □ ♅ 1°11' A
♃ ⚹ Mc 1°12' S
As △ Mc 1°27' A
☽ ⚹ ☿ 1°31' A
♀ ⚹ ♃ 2°07' S
♃ ☍ As 2°45' S
☽ ⚹ ☉ 2°50' S
☽ □ ♄ 3°18' S

PLANETARY SECT

Planet		Cht	Plc	Sgn	Condition
☉	D	D	D	N	
☽	N	D	N	N	
☿	N	D	D	N	
♀	N	D	D	D	Ex Cond
♂	N	D	D	D	Ex Cond
♃	D	D	D	D	In Hayz
♄	D	D	N	D	

D=Diurnal, N=Nocturnal

12/14: WILL I BUY THE DOG?

6 April 2007 at 3:39 p.m. (15:39), Ljubljana, Slovenia
Hour ruler: Mercury

The question was asked by one of my former students. He published it on a forum that was part of my astrology school's website. He wondered whether he would buy a dog that his wife desired. He wasn't keen on having a pet in the house as he was aware of the responsibility and hard work involved, and he was also anxious about lack of space, as they lived in a small apartment.

The chart shows the Moon at the end of a sign and void-of-course, according to traditional criteria. Would that be a no? Not necessarily, because the Moon is already within orbit of a square with Mars, which it also receives in its domicile; besides, the Moon is on a Mars monomoiria degree. Because Mars is technically still in H6 of pets (although in conjunction with the cusp of H7) and is also the natural significator of animals, whereas the Moon is in a strong angular H4, this applying square even suggests an affirmative answer. All the more so because of the harmonious hour ruler.

But the Moon (co-significator of the querent) is in its fall, reflecting the querent's concern, uncertainty and vulnerability. This is confirmed by Mercury, his main significator, in Pisces (detriment and fall). Since Mercury also rules H2 and conjuncts the cusp of H8, we can assume that he also worries of the costs that he and his wife would have with the dog. The querent is clearly in an unenviable position!

The condition of his wife, ruled by Jupiter (H7 in Pisces), is quite different. We find it in Sagittarius, its domicile sign, showing her to be strong and self-confident; yes, she wants that dog badly, and it surely looks she's full of faith, having no doubts! But a closer look shows that Jupiter is stationary - it actually turned retrograde already 12 hours earlier (see the table). From here, it applies by trine to Saturn, the ruler of the radix H6, located in H12 or the derived H6 (his wife's pets); Saturn itself is being applied to by the Sun (by trine) which rules the turned H6 and is also Saturn's dispositor. Such a powerful and harmonious connection of significators confirms the purchase of the dog who is obviously going to be the pet of the querent's wife. It is interesting to note that Mars, the natural significator of animals, is on the Jupiter monomoiria degree.

The peculiar state of the Moon which will complete the aspect with Mars only when in the next sign, shows something else: something crucial to the question will change before the purchase is made. But what could that be, I wondered?

As it turned out later, the puppy who the querent and his wife bought, was at the time of the question not yet delivered! This happened only three weeks after the question, and they received it towards the end of June. Unfortunately, the querent couldn't remember when they first saw it and chose it among the several puppies born of the same mother dog. We can only assume that this happened a month and a half after the question, corresponding to a degree and a half that are separating the Moon from Mars.

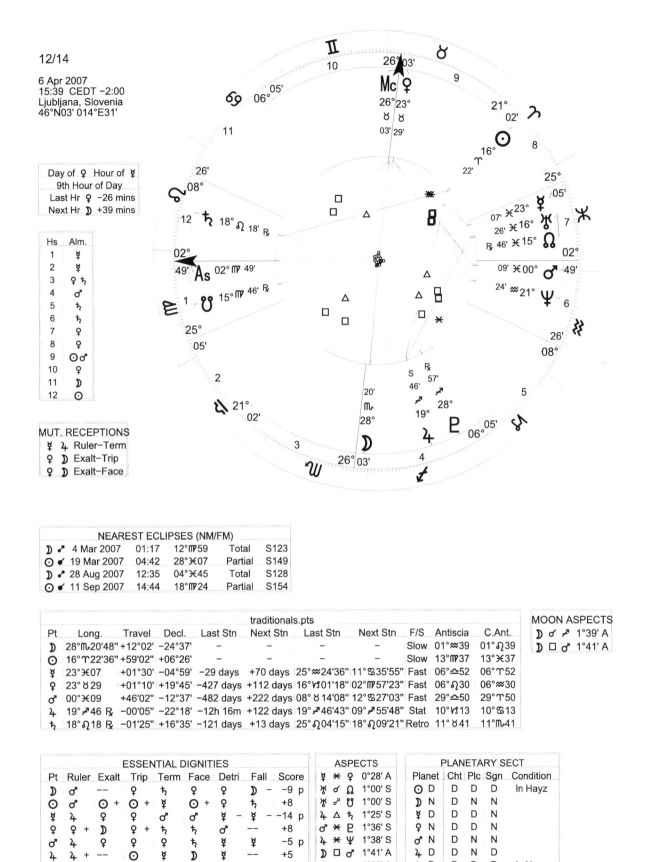

12/14

6 Apr 2007
15:39 CEDT −2:00
Ljubljana, Slovenia
46°N03' 014°E31'

Day of ♀ Hour of ☿
9th Hour of Day
Last Hr ♀ −26 mins
Next Hr ☽ +39 mins

Hs	Alm.
1	☿
2	☿
3	♀ ♄
4	♂
5	♄
6	♄
7	♀
8	♀
9	☉ ♂
10	♀
11	☽
12	☉

MUT. RECEPTIONS
☿ ♃ Ruler−Term
♀ ☽ Exalt−Trip
♀ ☽ Exalt−Face

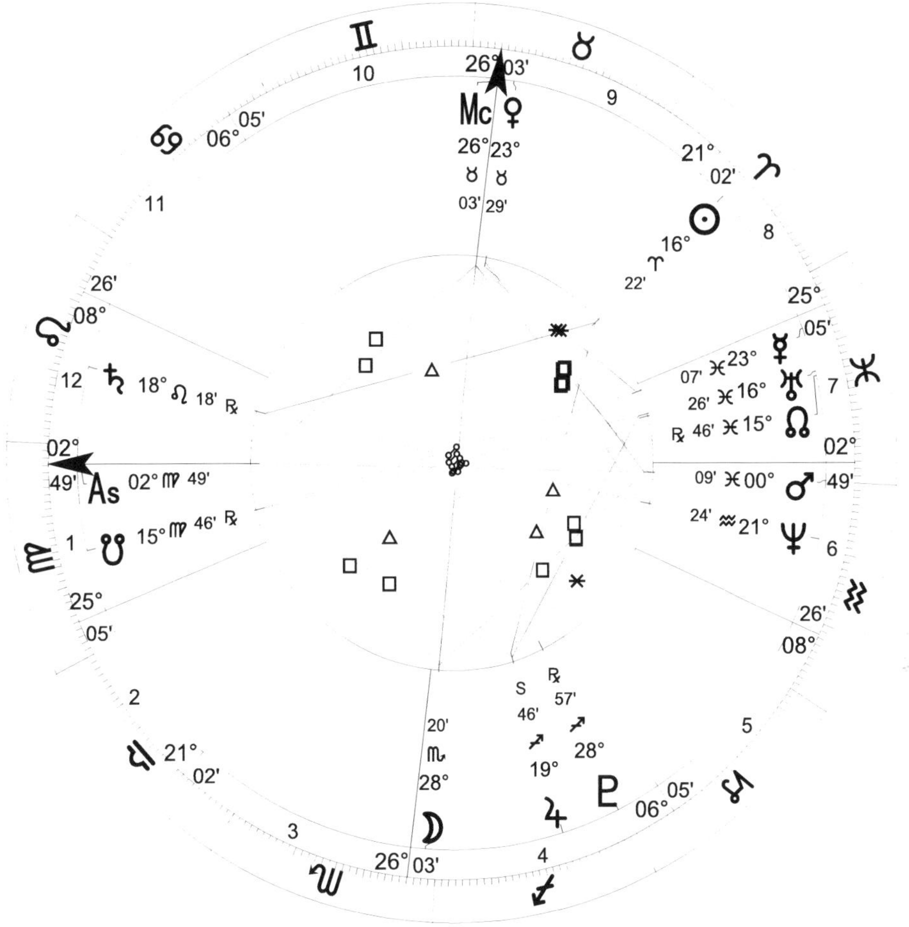

NEAREST ECLIPSES (NM/FM)				
☽ ☍ 4 Mar 2007	01:17	12°♍59	Total	S123
☉ ☌ 19 Mar 2007	04:42	28°♓07	Partial	S149
☽ ☍ 28 Aug 2007	12:35	04°♓45	Total	S128
☉ ☌ 11 Sep 2007	14:44	18°♍24	Partial	S154

traditionals.pts

Pt	Long.	Travel	Decl.	Last Stn	Next Stn	Last Stn	Next Stn	F/S	Antiscia	C.Ant.
☽	28°♏20'48"	+12°02'	−24°37'	–	–	–	–	Slow	01°♒39	01°♌39
☉	16°♈22'36"	+59'02"	+06°26'	–	–	–	–	Slow	13°♍37	13°♓37
☿	23°♓07	+01°30'	−04°59'	−29 days	+70 days	25°♒24'36"	11°♋35'55"	Fast	06°♎52	06°♈52
♀	23°♉29	+01°10'	+19°45'	−427 days	+112 days	16°♑01'18"	02°♍57'23"	Fast	06°♌30	06°♒30
♂	00°♓09	+46'02"	−12°37'	−482 days	+222 days	08°♉14'08"	12°♋27'03"	Fast	29°♎50	29°♈50
♃	19°♐46 ℞	−00'05"	−22°18'	−12h 16m	+122 days	19°♐46'43"	09°♐55'48"	Stat	10°♑13	10°♋13
♄	18°♌18 ℞	−01'25"	+16°35'	−121 days	+13 days	25°♌04'15"	18°♌09'21"	Retro	11°♉41	11°♏41

MOON ASPECTS
☽ ☌ ♐ 1°39' A
☽ □ ♂ 1°41' A

ESSENTIAL DIGNITIES

Pt	Ruler	Exalt	Trip	Term	Face	Detri	Fall	Score
☽	♂	--	♀	♄	♀	♀	☽ −	−9 p
☉	♂	☉ +	☉ +	☿	☉ +	♀	♄	+8
☿	♃	♀	♀	♂	♂	☿ −	☿ −	−14 p
♀	♀ +	☽	♀ +	♄	♄	♂	--	+8
♂	♃	♀	♀	♀	♄	☿	☿	−5 p
♃	♃ +	--	☉	☿	☽	☿	--	+5
♄	☉	--	☉	☿	♃	♄ −	--	−10 p

ASPECTS
☿ ⚹ ♀ 0°28' A
♅ ☌ ☊ 1°00' S
♅ ☍ ☋ 1°00' S
♃ △ ♄ 1°25' S
♂ ⚹ ♇ 1°36' S
♃ ⚹ ♆ 1°38' S
☽ □ ♂ 1°41' A
☉ △ ♄ 1°55' A
♀ □ ♆ 2°05' S
☿ ⚹ Mc 2°57' S

PLANETARY SECT

Planet	Cht	Plc	Sgn	Condition
☉ D	D	D	D	In Hayz
☽ N	D	N	N	
☿ D	D	D	N	
♀ N	D	D	N	
♂ N	D	N	N	
♃ D	D	N	D	
♄ D	D	D	D	In Hayz

D=Diurnal, N=Nocturnal

12/15: WILL THE UAC COMMITTEE CHANGE THE SCHEDULE?

23 March 2012 at 10:13 p.m. (22:13), Ljubljana, Slovenia
Hour ruler: Moon

The full question was: Will the UAC committee revise and change the schedule for free lunch-time lectures?

The 2012 UAC (United Astrology Conference) in New Orleans was drawing near when I asked the above question. I was to speak as a "lunchtime lecturer" - meaning that I was among the group of lectureres who would deliver free talks during lunchtime.

A couple of days earlier, someone from the group emailed the rest of the speakers that the UAC Free Lecture committee was considering the possibility of moving the time of midday lectures to morning hours, that is, before the start of regular lectures, or to the late afternoon or evening hours. By doing that, they wanted to ensure that more people could attend those lectures, because, obviously, what people want to do at lunch break is - eat lunch. I was excited about the possibility of the schedule change, so I asked the above question, and also emailed the answer that I received from the chart, to the group.

What houses and planets rule the schedule, or the decision of the committee? That could be a hard nut if I didn't let common sense and the chart guide me. I was interested in something that was not directly related to me - although it would, of course, influence me. But the decision was entirely in the hands of other people and I was looking at it from the distance, as an uninvolved third person, therefore it seemed logical that I place the subject matter into H1. The logic is similar to placing missing people whom we do not know personally, into H1, the house of the querent but also of anything or anyone that doesn't have a definite place in any other house.

So, the "fate" of the schedule revision is shown by the ascendant in Scorpio and its ruler Mars. The ascendant is in a fixed sign, and fixed signs resist change. Scorpio's ruler Mars is in H10, ruling the committee (the authorities taking decisions and being in charge of the schedule) - a very suitable placement, nicely reflecting the fact that the decision was in the hands of the committee.

Mars is in Virgo, peregrine and not supported by any harmonious aspect, therefore the prospects of a schedule change are poor. What's more, Mars is retrograde; this visually shows the revising or re-examining of the schedule, but due to the lack of support from other parts of the chart, the revision doesn't seem to lead to any kind of change.

We must then check Mercury, the ruler of H10 (the committee) and Mars' dispositor. This planet is in an even worse state than Mars - in detriment and fall, combust, retrograde and exactly conjunct the malefic fixed star Scheat. This shows that the committee's advancement with its plan (proposal for a change) is very stressed and probably doomed to fail.

And what is the relationship between Mars (the schedule) and Mercury (the committee)? Mercury receives Mars in its domicile, exaltation and term whereas Mars receives Mercury in its triplicity. The many receptions between the planets show that the matter is being discussed, but on top of the before mentioned negative indications, the next Moon's aspect is opposition with Saturn, definitely showing that the answer is no - the schedule will remain unchanged.

And so it was. Still, the purported unsuitable schedule didn't seem to cause problems – my lecture room, at least, filled to the last corner.

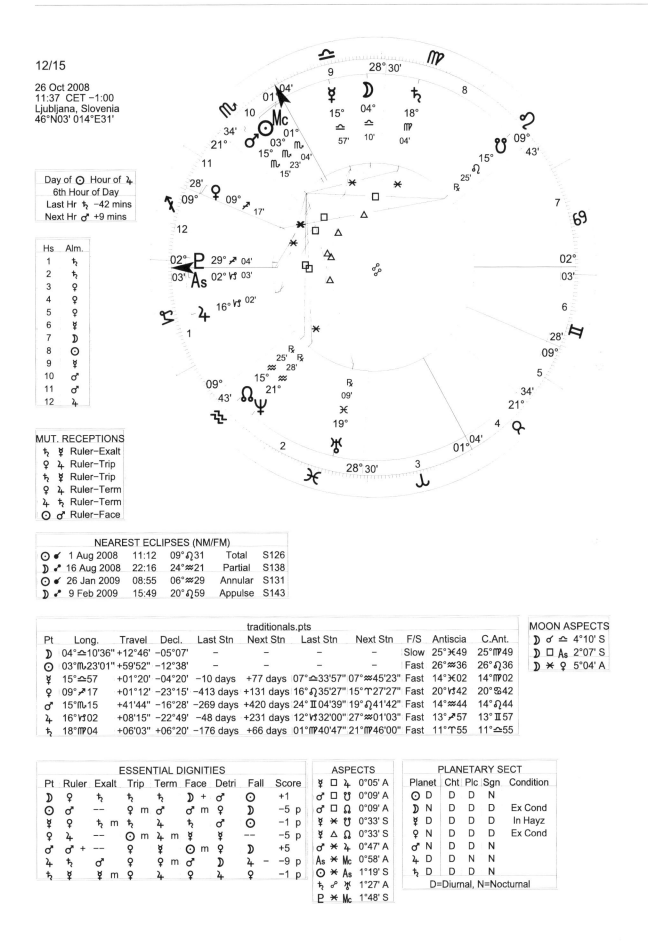

12/15

26 Oct 2008
11:37 CET −1:00
Ljubljana, Slovenia
46°N03' 014°E31'

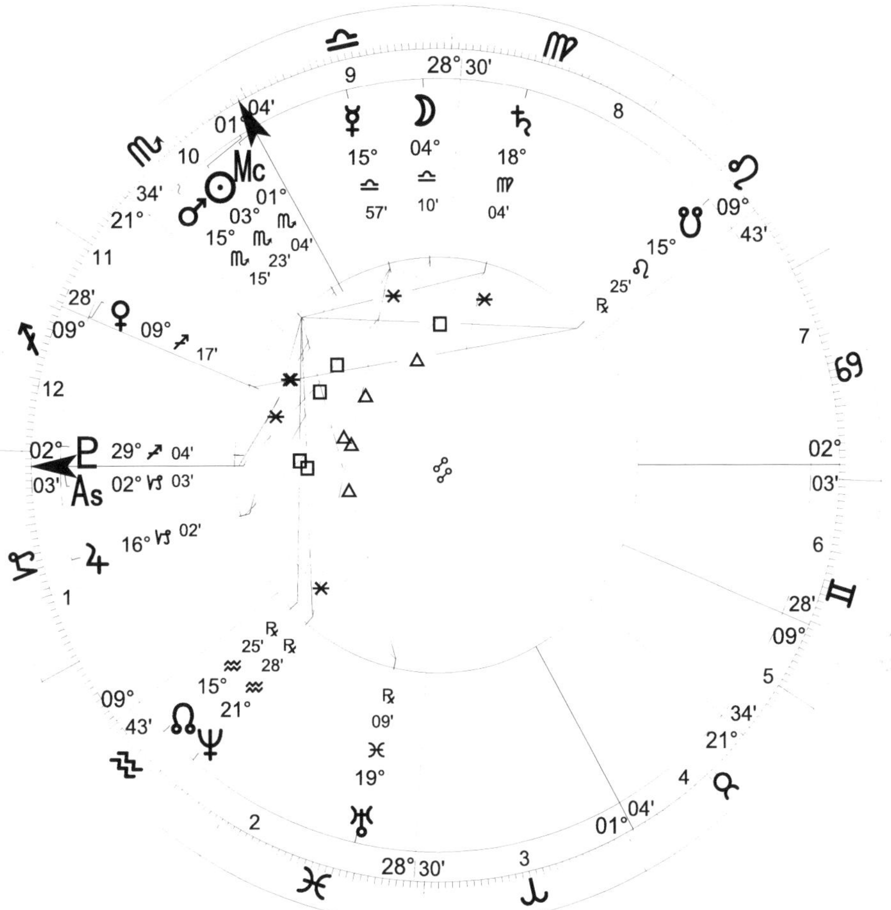

Day of ☉ Hour of ♃
6th Hour of Day
Last Hr ♄ −42 mins
Next Hr ♂ +9 mins

Hs	Alm.
1	♄
2	♄
3	♀
4	♀
5	♀
6	☿
7	☽
8	☉
9	☿
10	♂
11	♂
12	♃

MUT. RECEPTIONS		
♄	☿	Ruler−Exalt
♀	♃	Ruler−Trip
♄	☿	Ruler−Trip
♀	♃	Ruler−Term
♃	♄	Ruler−Term
☉	♂	Ruler−Face

NEAREST ECLIPSES (NM/FM)					
☉	1 Aug 2008	11:12	09°♌31	Total	S126
☽	16 Aug 2008	22:16	24°♒21	Partial	S138
☉	26 Jan 2009	08:55	06°♒29	Annular	S131
☽	9 Feb 2009	15:49	20°♌59	Appulse	S143

traditionals.pts

Pt	Long.	Travel	Decl.	Last Stn	Next Stn	Last Stn	Next Stn	F/S	Antiscia	C.Ant.
☽	04°♎10'36"	+12°46'	−05°07'	–	–	–	–	Slow	25°♓49	25°♍49
☉	03°♏23'01"	+59'52"	−12°38'	–	–	–	–	Fast	26°♒36	26°♌36
☿	15°♎57	+01°20'	−04°20'	−10 days	+77 days	07°♎33'57"	07°♒45'23"	Fast	14°♓02	14°♍02
♀	09°♐17	+01°12'	−23°15'	−413 days	+131 days	16°♌35'27"	15°♈27'27"	Fast	20°♑42	20°♋42
♂	15°♏15	+41'44"	−16°28'	−269 days	+420 days	24°♊04'39"	19°♌41'42"	Fast	14°♒44	14°♌44
♃	16°♑02	+08'15"	−22°49'	−48 days	+231 days	12°♑32'00"	27°♒01'03"	Fast	13°♐57	13°♊57
♄	18°♍04	+06'03"	+06°20'	−176 days	+66 days	01°♍40'47"	21°♍46'00"	Fast	11°♈55	11°♎55

MOON ASPECTS			
☽	☌	♎	4°10' S
☽	□	As	2°07' S
☽	⚹	♀	5°04' A

ESSENTIAL DIGNITIES

Pt	Ruler	Exalt	Trip	Term	Face	Detri	Fall	Score
☽	♀	♄	♄	♄	☽ +	♂	☉	+1
☉	♂	--	♀ m	♂	♂ m	♀	☽	−5 p
☿	♀	♄ m	♄	♃	♄	♂	☉	−1 p
♀	♃	--	☉ m	♃ m	☿	☿	--	−5 p
♂	♂ +	--	♀	☿	☉ m	♀	☽	+5
♃	♄	♂	♀	♀ m	♂	☽	♃ −	−9 p
♄	☿	☿ m	♀	♃	♀	♃	♀	−1 p

ASPECTS			
☿	□	♃	0°05' A
♂	□	☋	0°09' A
♂	□	☊	0°09' A
☿	⚹	☋	0°33' S
☿	△	☊	0°33' S
♂	⚹	♃	0°47' A
As	⚹	Mc	0°58' A
☉	⚹	As	1°19' S
♄	☍	♅	1°27' A
♇	⚹	Mc	1°48' S

PLANETARY SECT

Planet		Cht	Plc	Sgn	Condition
☉	D	D	D	N	
☽	N	D	D	D	Ex Cond
☿	D	D	D	D	In Hayz
♀	N	D	D	D	Ex Cond
♂	N	D	D	N	
♃	D	D	N	N	
♄	D	D	D	N	

D=Diurnal, N=Nocturnal

12/16: WILL WE GET A MEDAL?

10 June 2015 at 3:46 p.m. (15:46), Ljubljana, Slovenia
Hour ruler: Moon

I am including this case because I find it a convincing example of the importance of almutens. The chart was discussed at length in my Horary Astrology Group where I posted it immediately after casting it.

My hip-hop adult dancing group was setting off to the European Championship in Kielce, Poland. I was wondering whether we could hope to win any of the first three places (which come with a medal, of course), although I knew that our chances were slim because the competition was very tough. But my first impression after casting the chart was good. Hmmm, it's quite possible that we get the third place, I thought.

I noticed, namely, that the ascendant ruler (signifying our group) was Venus, placed in H10, to which the Moon applied by a trine, with Moon ruling Cancer, the sign holding MC. The orb was 3.5 degrees - exactly the number of days that were separating us from the competition which was scheduled for the evening of 13th of June. It is true that the Moon, before completing the trine, would sextile Mercury, but this planet rules H9 (our travel abroad), so I thought that Mercury couldn't be considered a "frustrator" but more like some kind of a "conductor", pointing to our forthcoming trip (13 hours by bus). But because Venus was peregrine, I thought we couldn't hope for the 1st or 2nd place. Anyway - 3rd place would do, too!

I also thought that we'd win at least the 3rd place because Mars, ruling H7 (our competitors) seemed weak by having only one weak essential dignity (term) and was combust and in a weak H9. (We were lording over the cardinal H10!)

It turned out that I was wrong. We ended at the 9th out of twelve possible places, which was actually not surprising to all involved. As already said, the competition was really tough. We competed in the Adult 2 category (dancers over 31 years of age), but none of us had ever danced professionally, whereas our competitors who came from all over Europe, had many members who only a couple of years ago were still competing as regular adults (below 31 years of age).

Still – the horary chart seemed so promising. Where did I make a mistake? A closer look at the chart told it all. Firstly, Mars was applied to by the Sun, the H10 ruler – a strong indication of the others being more powerful than ourselves, especially because the Sun also applies by sextile to Uranus, conjuncting H7. Next, I found that I forgot to consider almutens. The co-almuten of H1 is Saturn, retrograde and peregrine (weak, unable, losing strength) while the co-almuten of H7 is the Sun which sextiles Jupiter in H10. It is true that the sextile is already separating, but the Sun translates light from Jupiter to Mars - the ruler of Aries, standing for our competition. Besides, both the Sun and Jupiter could be considered natural significators of medals - especially Jupiter which is placed in H10. All The medals go to others! What is more - the Moon, applying to trine Venus in H10, is in the sign of H7, albeit in H6. As for the sect, the Sun, co-almuten of H7, is *in hayz* and as such extremely powerful – additional indication that many other groups are stronger than ours.

You will notice that Mercury, the hour ruler, is retrograde in this chart. This is a warning – the querent might be misled or not aware of all the facts needed to accurately assess the situation and give a correct answer. This indeed was the case, as I was driven by too much ambition which blurred my vision. Besides, I was unaware of the number of groups that would compete – I thought, mistakenly, that there'd be only a few. Still – we enjoyed the competition and had much fun (Venus)!

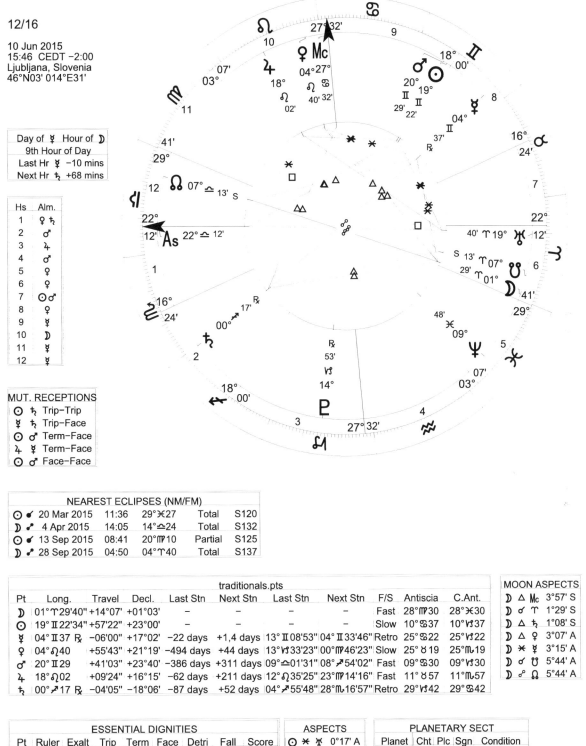

12/16

10 Jun 2015
15:46 CEDT −2:00
Ljubljana, Slovenia
46°N03' 014°E31'

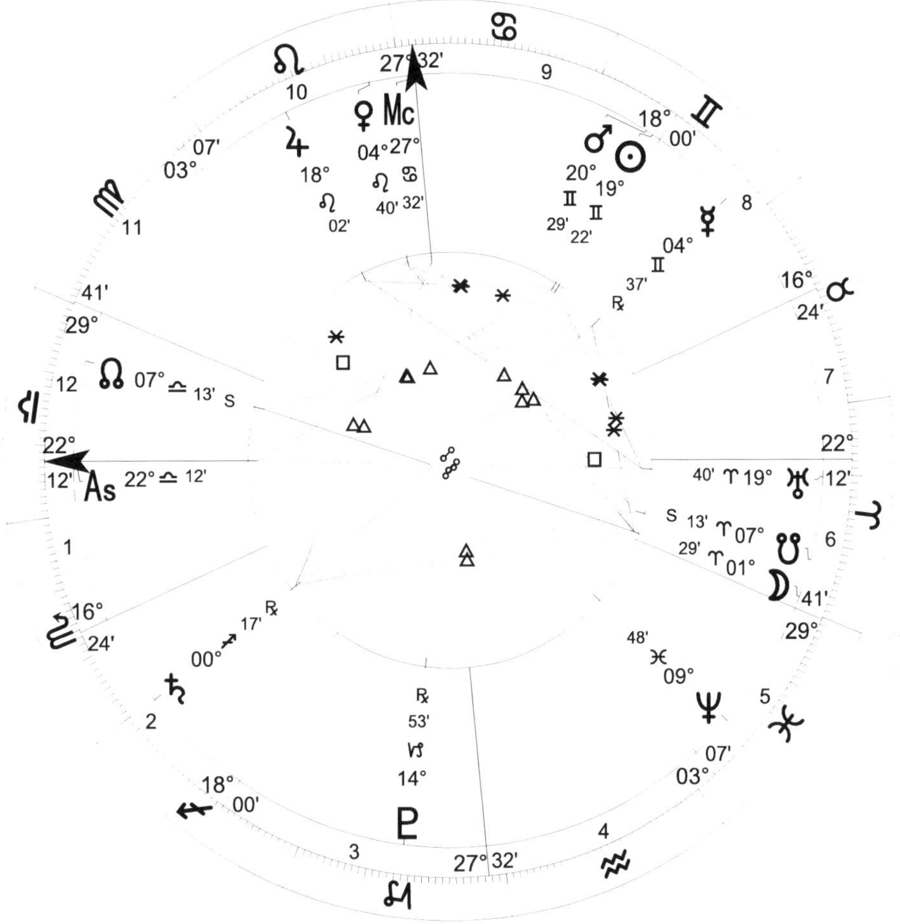

Day of ☿ Hour of ☽
9th Hour of Day
Last Hr ☿ −10 mins
Next Hr ♄ +68 mins

Hs	Alm.
1	♀ ♄
2	♂
3	♃
4	♂
5	♀
6	♀
7	☉ ♂
8	♀
9	☿
10	☽
11	☿
12	☿

MUT. RECEPTIONS		
☉	♄	Trip–Trip
☿	♄	Trip–Face
☉	♂	Term–Face
♃	☿	Term–Face
☉	♂	Face–Face

NEAREST ECLIPSES (NM/FM)					
☉ ●	20 Mar 2015	11:36	29°♓27	Total	S120
☽ ☍	4 Apr 2015	14:05	14°♎24	Total	S132
☉ ●	13 Sep 2015	08:41	20°♍10	Partial	S125
☽ ☍	28 Sep 2015	04:50	04°♈40	Total	S137

traditionals.pts

Pt	Long.	Travel	Decl.	Last Stn	Next Stn	Last Stn	Next Stn	F/S	Antiscia	C.Ant.
☽	01°♈29'40"	+14°07'	+01°03'	–	–	–	–	Fast	28°♍30	28°♓30
☉	19°♊22'34"	+57'22"	+23°00'	–	–	–	–	Slow	10°♋37	10°♑37
☿	04°♊37 ℞	−06'00"	+17°02'	−22 days	+1,4 days	13°♊08'53"	04°♊33'46"	Retro	25°♋22	25°♑22
♀	04°♌40	+55'43"	+21°19'	−494 days	+44 days	13°♑33'23"	00°♍46'23"	Slow	25°♉19	25°♏19
♂	20°♊29	+41'03"	+23°40'	−386 days	+311 days	09°♎01'31"	08°♐54'02"	Fast	09°♋30	09°♑30
♃	18°♌02	+09'24"	+16°15'	−62 days	+211 days	12°♌35'25"	23°♍14'16"	Fast	11°♉57	11°♏57
♄	00°♐17 ℞	−04'05"	−18°06'	−87 days	+52 days	04°♐55'48"	28°♏16'57"	Retro	29°♑42	29°♋42

MOON ASPECTS			
☽	△	Mc	3°57' S
☽	☌	♈	1°29' S
☽	△	♄	1°08' S
☽	△	♀	3°07' A
☽	✶	☿	3°15' A
☽	☌	☋	5°44' A
☽	☍	☊	5°44' A

ESSENTIAL DIGNITIES

Pt	Ruler	Exalt	Trip	Term	Face	Detri	Fall	Score
☽	♂	☉	☉	♃	♂	♀	♄	−5 p
☉	☿	--	♄ m	♂	♂ m	♃	--	−5 p
☿	☿ +	--	♄	☿ +	♃	♃	--	+7
♀	☉	--	☉	♃	♄	♄	--	−5 p
♂	☿	--	♄	♂ +	☉ m	♃	--	+2
♃	☉	--	☉	☿	♃ +	♄	--	+1
♄	♃	--	☉ m	♃	☿	☿	--	−5 p

ASPECTS			
☉	✶	♅	0°17' A
☿	✶	♀	0°20' S
♂	✶	♅	0°49' S
☽	△	♄	1°08' S
☉	☌	♂	1°15' A
☉	✶	♃	1°19' S
♃	△	♅	1°37' A
♂	△	As	1°43' S
♂	✶	♃	2°27' S
☿	△	☊	2°29' S

PLANETARY SECT

Planet		Cht	Plc	Sgn	Condition
☉	D	D	D	D	In Hayz
☽	N	D	N	D	
☿	D	D	D	D	In Hayz
♀	N	D	D	D	Ex Cond
♂	N	D	D	D	Ex Cond
♃	D	D	D	D	In Hayz
♄	D	D	N	D	

D=Diurnal, N=Nocturnal

12/17: WHEN WILL THIS BOOK BE FINISHED?

26 October 2008 at 11:37 a.m., Ljubljana, Slovenia
Hour ruler: Jupiter

The date of the question tells you that I started to write this book a long time ago. I actually wrote its first sentences in 2008, although I had been collecting the material (example cases, notes etc.) already since much earlier.

My question was born out of curiosity, of course, mixed with hope and expectation – as can be inferred from Jupiter, the hour ruler. Jupiter is not harmonious with the ascending sign (Capricorn), but it rules H3, representing my book, and is placed in H1 (me), so the chart seems to describe the situation well. This is confirmed by the Moon in H9 of publishing and books with educational content.

My significator is Saturn (the ruler of Capricorn, the ascending sign) while co-significators are Jupiter (the H1 planet) and the Moon, also describing the course of events.

H3 is ruled by Jupiter and Mars, the ruler of the intercepted sign Aries, but also by Venus, the H3 almuten. Mars is in H10 – very appropriate because it shows my goal and ambition – the book! This planet is doubly important in the chart because it also rules H10 – my aim and (career) ambition. My ruler Saturn is in Virgo in H8, but in the sign of H9, again linking me with the book/publishing. So – when do I get there?

I was hopeful and my vision was blurred by unreasonable expectation, so I thought that the book could be finished and in print in 5 months, according to the number of degrees that separate the Moon from Venus, its dispositor and almuten of H3. But I overlooked the fact that both Moon and Venus were in cadent houses, showing "a long time", and that the Moon was slow. I also overlooked the fact that Mars, the main significator of the project (co-ruler of H3, main ruler of H10 and occupant of H10), was under the Sun's beams - applying! This actually means that soon, Mars will be combust. Since the Sun rules the unfortunate H8 (crisis, loss) which also holds my own significator, things are obviously not going to proceed according to plan. Besides, the sign of Scorpio where Mars is located, is fixed, again pointing to »a long time«.

Five months later, the book was not even close to being written; due to my very busy schedule, family obligations and my astrological research going in all sorts of other directions, I soon put it aside and came back to it several years later, so that it was completed only in June 2015, and it came out in early November 2015. (I am speaking of the Slovenian version – this book is my own translation of it.)

The fact is, six years and eight months passed until the book was finished, and seven years until it was published. Timing is shown by three unusual factors:
- lunar declination
- solar eclipse
- Pluto and Saturn transits

In the declination graph, we can see that the Moon will change direction in 6.5 days after the question, which translated into years is just about the time that passed until the book was finished. (Note: the chart drawing starts at midnight but the question was raised in the middle of the day, so we must start counting the days from the middle of the section indicating the date of the horary chart). This is the same astro-logic as in the case of the missing amulet (see Case 6/17) where we got the appropriate time unit in exactly the same way. This brings us to an unusual, but totally viable timing technique – count the number of days that will pass until the lunar change of direction (which can be compared to a sign change in longitude), and equate it with the number of appropriate time units. They were years in this case – on account of several indications previously mentioned.

This example is also very interesting from the eclipses' point of view. The last solar eclipse before the completion of the book was that of 20 March 2015 (a total solar eclipse) on the 29th degree Pisces, exactly on the cusp of H3 in the chart. This degree is in an exact square with Pluto, the modern ruler of Scorpio and therefore the modern dispositor of MC, Mars and the Sun. Pluto is definitely an important planet in the chart due to its rather close conjunction with the ascendant. Eclipses predict beginnings and endings. I also find it particularly interesting that the main eclipse of 2008 when I started to write the book, was at 9.5 Leo, in an exact midpoint between the Sun and Mars in H10 (in this chart), whereas the total lunar eclipse of February of the same year was at 2 Virgo, in a very exact trine with the chart's ascendant.

12/17

26 Oct 2008
11:37 CET −1:00
Ljubljana, Slovenia
46°N03' 014°E31'

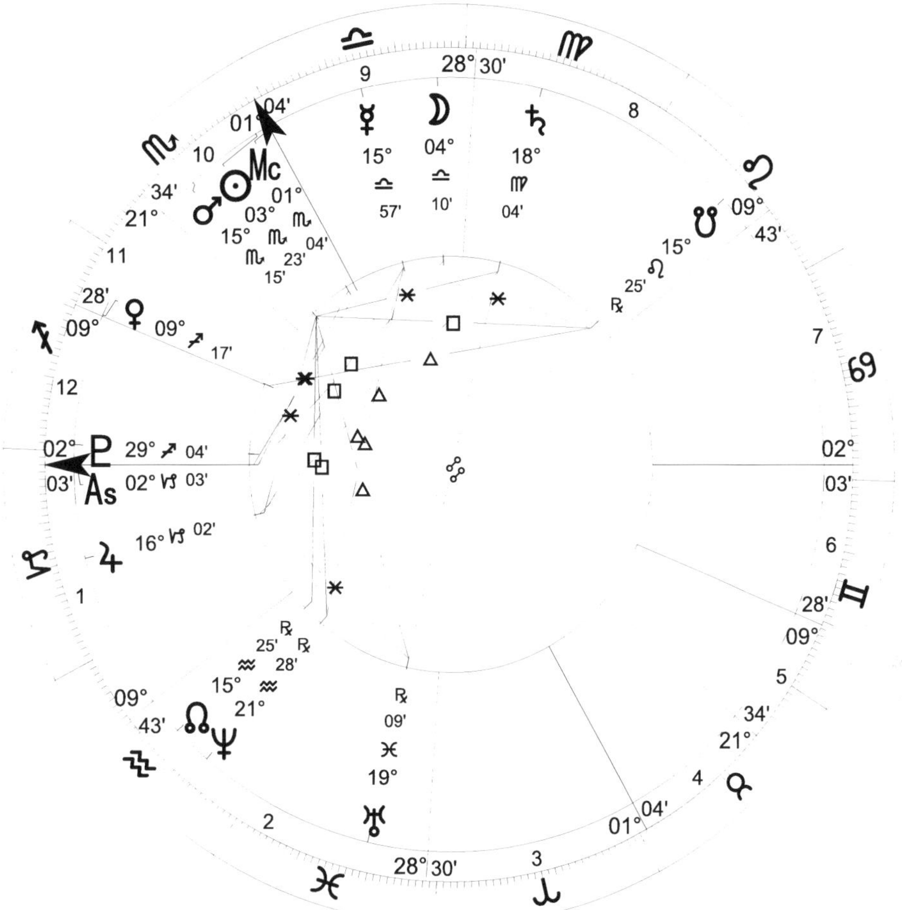

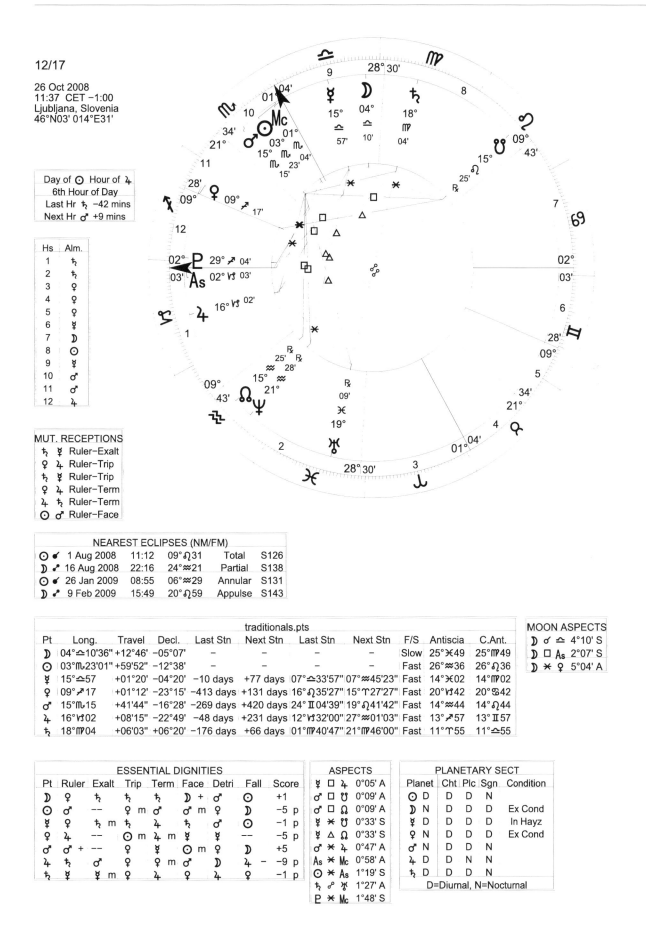

Day of ☉ Hour of ♃
6th Hour of Day
Last Hr ♄ −42 mins
Next Hr ♂ +9 mins

Hs	Alm.
1	♄
2	♄
3	♀
4	♀
5	♀
6	☿
7	☽
8	☉
9	☿
10	♂
11	♂
12	♃

MUT. RECEPTIONS		
♄	☿	Ruler−Exalt
♀	♃	Ruler−Trip
♄	☿	Ruler−Trip
♀	♃	Ruler−Term
♃	♄	Ruler−Term
☉	♂	Ruler−Face

NEAREST ECLIPSES (NM/FM)					
☉	1 Aug 2008	11:12	09°♌31	Total	S126
☽	16 Aug 2008	22:16	24°♒21	Partial	S138
☉	26 Jan 2009	08:55	06°♒29	Annular	S131
☽	9 Feb 2009	15:49	20°♌59	Appulse	S143

traditionals.pts

Pt	Long.	Travel	Decl.	Last Stn	Next Stn	Last Stn	Next Stn	F/S	Antiscia	C.Ant.
☽	04°♎10'36"	+12°46'	−05°07'	–	–	–	–	Slow	25°♓49	25°♍49
☉	03°♏23'01"	+59'52"	−12°38'	–	–	–	–	Fast	26°♒36	26°♌36
☿	15°♎57	+01°20'	−04°20'	−10 days	+77 days	07°♎33'57"	07°♒45'23"	Fast	14°♓02	14°♍02
♀	09°♐17	+01°12'	−23°15'	−413 days	+131 days	16°♌35'27"	15°♈27'27"	Fast	20°♑42	20°♋42
♂	15°♏15	+41'44"	−16°28'	−269 days	+420 days	24°♊04'39"	19°♌41'42"	Fast	14°♒44	14°♌44
♃	16°♑02	+08'15"	−22°49'	−48 days	+231 days	12°♑32'00"	27°♒01'03"	Fast	13°♐57	13°♊57
♄	18°♍04	+06'03"	+06°20'	−176 days	+66 days	01°♍40'47"	21°♍46'00"	Fast	11°♈55	11°♎55

MOON ASPECTS			
☽	☌	♎	4°10' S
☽	□	As	2°07' S
☽	⚹	♀	5°04' A

ESSENTIAL DIGNITIES

Pt	Ruler	Exalt	Trip	Term	Face	Detri	Fall	Score
☽	♀	♄	♄	♄	☽ +	♂	☉	+1
☉	♂	--	♀ m	♂	♂ m	♀	☽	−5 p
☿	♀	♄ m	♄	♃	♄	♂	☉	−1 p
♀	♃	--	☉ m	♃ m	☿	☿	--	−5 p
♂	♂ +	--	♀	☿	☉ m	♀	☽	+5
♃	♄	♂	♀	♀ m	♂	☽	♃ −	−9 p
♄	☿	☿ m	♀	♃	♀	♃	♀	−1 p

ASPECTS			
☿	□	♃	0°05' A
♂	□	☋	0°09' A
♂	□	☊	0°09' A
☿	⚹	☋	0°33' S
☿	△	☊	0°33' S
♂	⚹	♃	0°47' A
As	⚹	Mc	0°58' A
☉	⚹	As	1°19' S
♄	☍	♅	1°27' A
♇	⚹	Mc	1°48' S

PLANETARY SECT

Planet		Cht	Plc	Sgn	Condition
☉	D	D	D	N	
☽	N	D	D	D	Ex Cond
☿	D	D	D	D	In Hayz
♀	N	D	D	D	Ex Cond
♂	N	D	D	N	
♃	D	D	N	N	
♄	D	D	D	N	

D=Diurnal, N=Nocturnal

As for the transits – at the finishing stage (March-June 2015), transiting Pluto was stationing at 15 Capricorn, in a very exact sextile to horary Mars, whereas in the first days of November when the book was officially released, Saturn was in a very exact sextile with the Moon.

Lastly – the Moon, the queen of timing, just has to have her say! The number of degrees that separate it from Pluto, are 85, and the book was released in a bit over 84 calendar months (7 x 12). But if we take synodic months – which provide more exact timing, as pointed out in the relevant chapter in the theoretical part of the book – we get 87, bringing the Moon to 1 Capricorn, just 1 degree short of the horary ascendant (end of "journey", release).

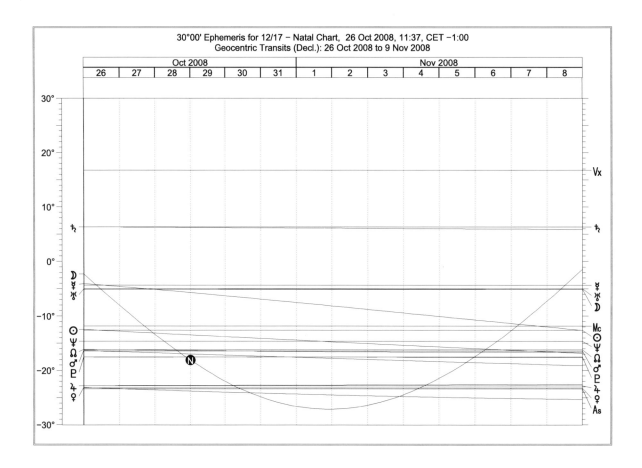

CONSULTATION CHARTS

So far, we have been dealing with classical horary charts, that is, with charts created for particular questions that a client (the querent) asks the astrologer. Those charts have (hopefully) convinced you that planetary positions at the time of the question reflect the querent's frame of mind or the cosmic reality of the situation, and show the resolution to the question (the answer that the querent seeks). We have learnt how to find significators and examine the chart so that it can lead us to finding the answer.

Unlike a horary chart, the consultation chart is cast for the time and place of the meeting between the astrologer and his client. In practising this technique, the client doesn't need to verbalize the question, because the technique is based on the assumption that the quality of the moment when the client seeks divination, holds the answer/s to the querent's future question(s). The astrologer looks into the chart and tries to find the answer to his own questions: who is the person sitting in front of him? What issues is he/she dealing with? What is their past and what will the (foreseeable) future bring them?

In the consultation chart technique, we employ the same rules as when reading the "normal" horary charts. Based on the indications in the consultation chart, the astrologer can immediately gain the client's trust by divining his present conditions, and maybe even guess what has brought the client into the consultation room. Obviously, this is a good start to the meeting! To some astrologers, the consultation chart serves even as some kind of a substitute for their natal chart. But whereas the birth chart shows the innate potential of our clients, it rarely points to the current issues with which our client are dealing. In determining future trends, astrologers also help themselves by other techniques, of course, such as eclipses, transits, progressions, solar and lunar returns, and so on, but the consultation chart is a more immediate and all-encompassing technique, and can be invaluable in terms of getting to the core issues that brought the client to us.

Finally, even the birth chart can be read as a kind of a horary or even a consultation chart. Who is the person sitting in front of us? What is their mission in life? What their destiny in various fields of life, shown by the energy flow, related to specific houses?

Experience shows that the consultation chart is an interesting and useful technique. Ideally, we can tell the client just why he/she has come to us, even before they open their mouth! But it is important that the astrologer is experienced and well versed in the basic horary technique before attempting the consultation chart. Because – as easy it can be to get the client to our side, it is also easy that we drive them away by "guessing" all the wrong things. Technique and experience, again, are essential.

So – how is it done? Basically, we proceed in the same way as when delineating a horary chart. The ascendant, its ruler and the Moon are the most important factors to consider, since their placements (especially in the houses) show the areas of the client's interest or the core question/problem that he is currently dealing with. (Beware, though – derived houses are important, so make every effort to ask questions, when appropriate.)

The planets that aspect the ascendant, its ruler and the Moon, describe the additional circumstances that affect the client - the separating aspects show the past while the applying show the future. Planets in H1 (if there are any) are also important; we must examine their nature and house rulership because all the topics associated with those houses might play a role in the client's present or near future.

The next step is to apply the so-called adjusted consultation chart whereby we place the radix positions of the client's chart onto the consultation chart. This is similar to looking at the transits, but it helps us to orientate ourselves by seeing the larger picture.

CONSULTATION CHART: EXAMPLE CASE

21 April 2006 at 2:05 p.m. (14:05), Ljubljana, Slovenia
Hour ruler: Sun

Simone was a young woman with light hair, and she wore eye-glasses. She is ruled by the ascendant at 26° Leo and the Sun at 1° Taurus. The Sun is in H9 and on the Mercury monomoiria degree: this seemed reasonable, as she gave the impression of being learned and bright. She was also more slender as we'd expect from the signs of Leo and Taurus which usually give larger and broader frames.

The harmonious chart ruler suggested that the consultation chart would serve me well, therefore I proceeded with confidence.

The ascendant is in the last degrees of its sign, indicating that she was close to some kind of a change. What change? The Moon, so often showing where our thoughts are, was in H6, the house of illness, worry and work environment (among other things), whereas the Sun in H9 pointed to education, foreign affairs and legal matters. Any of those issues could be in play here, so I asked her what was the main reason for her visit.

"My job" said she. She wanted to know how to resolve the strained relationships that she had with her boss. Would they improve?

MC (the boss, superiors) is in Taurus, in sextile with its dispositor Venus. Since Venus is in the soft, sensitive Pisces, dignified by exaltation, I said that her boss doesn't seem like a bad man. To the contrary – he seems to be kind and compassionate, but maybe too weak or indecisive for a person in his position. I continued to say that his attitude towards her seemed better than she thought it was, because Venus receives the Sun its domicile. Whereas this in itself doesn't show any kind of sympathy, only the fact that Venus "presides over" the Sun (which was logical, in the context), but my opinion was based on the fact that Venus didn't seriously afflict the Sun, nor the Moon, the client's co-significator. Venus was in a semisquare to the Sun which shows a mild tension, but the aspect is already separating.

She confirmed, saying that my description fitted him perfectly. But what was causing the strain, then? I said that he was probably under the influence of some other person, which she confirmed too, saying that he was a gentle, soft guy but easily fell under the influence of others. She then told me that she was currently working with a woman who was hostile to her. This is confirmed by the opposition of the Moon (Simone's co-significator but also describing the circumstances in her work environment) to Saturn, the ruler of H6, of a decidedly malicious character because in detriment, therefore I judged that her colleague indeed had bad intentions. But because the opposition was already separating, I concluded that the animosity would soon be over and the tension eased. This is confirmed by the separating nature of the semisquare between Venus and the Sun, showing that her relationship with her boss would soon get back to normal.

She was happy with my insight and then asked me if she would change her job anytime soon. Let us see! MC is in a fixed sign (permanence, stability) and close to the middle of the sign, whereas Venus (the H10 ruler) was also is in the middle of a sign, without any applying aspects. What's more, the fixity of the Sun and Moon confirmed me in the belief that a change of job was not an option in the near future.

But the ascendant was at the end of the sign, suggesting that there was some kind of a change in sight; I told her that and asked her if she was thinking of making some change in her real-estate matters, even a place of living, perhaps? I thought of that because the Sun applied to Mars, ruling her H4. Yes, she said. She told me that she had just put down a deposit for a new apartment and that she would move there shortly.

Her next question related to partnership. The Sun (she) applies to square Saturn, the H7 ruler while the Moon separates from an opposition with Saturn. This clearly shows that her partnership was on the rocks; if she had a partner, they were probably going through some turbulent times, so I said that this aspect of her life seemed pretty more problematic. I asked her about her current condition in this sphere and she told me that her partner had left her just lately. The separating opposition of the Moon with Saturn shows this clearly! Will he come back to her, she wondered? My answer was negative because the Sun applied to Saturn by a square. Since Saturn was in the Sun's domicile, she obviously still had some power over him, but due to Saturn's detriment I told her that it's better to leave things as they were. Better be alone than go through another struggle.

This said, I must add that I always combine indications in the consultation chart with other (above mentioned) predictive techniques. When clients pay, they want good service – or you will never see them again. Therefore, it pays to learn, and I am happy if by this book I have helped you to do just this.

CONSULTATION

21 Apr 2006
14:05 CEDT −2:00
Ljubljana, Slovenia
46°N03' 014°E31'

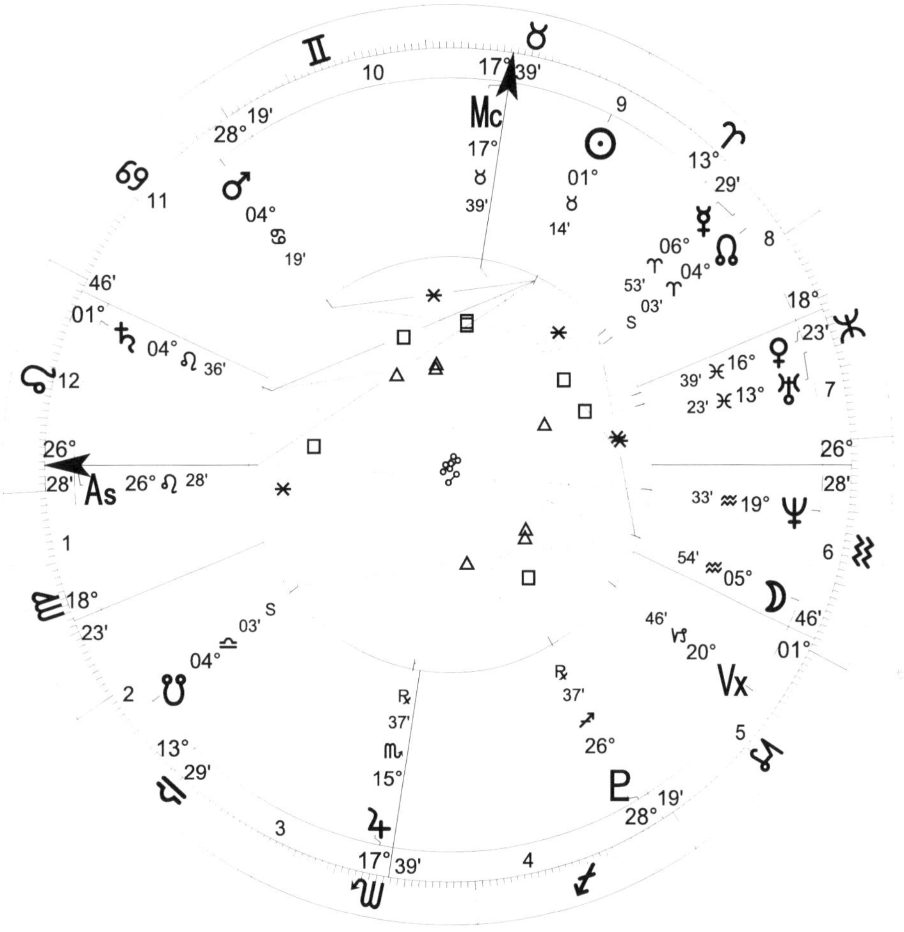

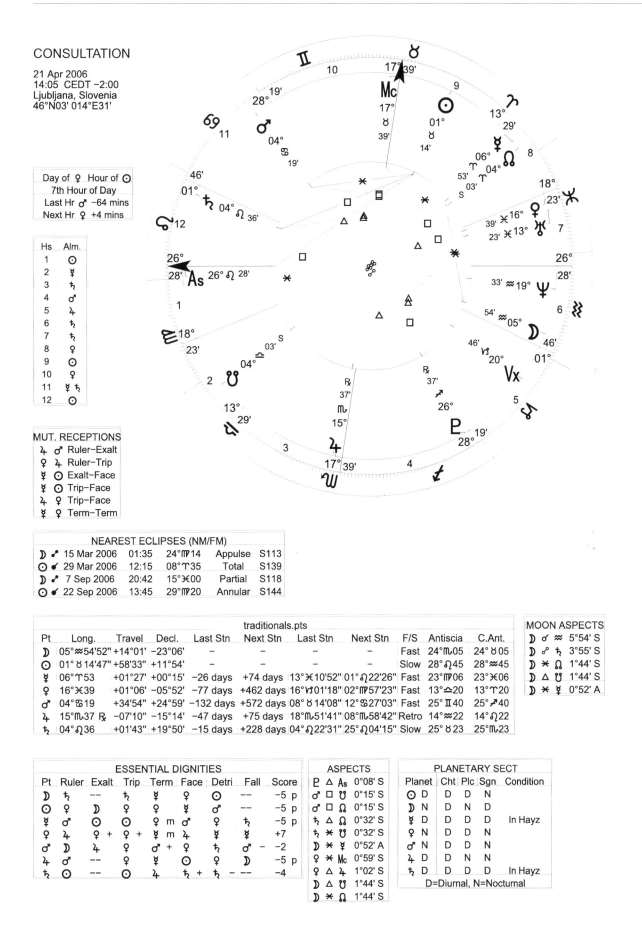

Day of ♀ Hour of ☉
7th Hour of Day
Last Hr ♂ −64 mins
Next Hr ♀ +4 mins

Hs	Alm.
1	☉
2	☿
3	♄
4	♂
5	♃
6	♄
7	♄
8	♀
9	☉
10	♀
11	☿ ♄
12	☉

MUT. RECEPTIONS	
♃ ♂	Ruler−Exalt
♀ ♃	Ruler−Trip
☿ ☉	Exalt−Face
☿ ☉	Trip−Face
♃ ♀	Trip−Face
☿ ♀	Term−Term

NEAREST ECLIPSES (NM/FM)					
☽ ☍	15 Mar 2006	01:35	24°♍14	Appulse	S113
☉ ☌	29 Mar 2006	12:15	08°♈35	Total	S139
☽ ☍	7 Sep 2006	20:42	15°♓00	Partial	S118
☉ ☌	22 Sep 2006	13:45	29°♍20	Annular	S144

traditionals.pts

Pt	Long.	Travel	Decl.	Last Stn	Next Stn	Last Stn	Next Stn	F/S	Antiscia	C.Ant.
☽	05°♒54'52"	+14°01'	−23°06'	–	–	–	–	Fast	24°♏05	24°♉05
☉	01°♉14'47"	+58'33"	+11°54'	–	–	–	–	Slow	28°♌45	28°♒45
☿	06°♈53	+01°27'	+00°15'	−26 days	+74 days	13°♓10'52"	01°♌22'26"	Fast	23°♍06	23°♓06
♀	16°♓39	+01°06'	−05°52'	−77 days	+462 days	16°♑01'18"	02°♍57'23"	Fast	13°♎20	13°♈20
♂	04°♋19	+34'54"	+24°59'	−132 days	+572 days	08°♉14'08"	12°♋27'03"	Fast	25°♊40	25°♐40
♃	15°♏37 ℞	−07'10"	−15°14'	−47 days	+75 days	18°♏51'41"	08°♏58'42"	Retro	14°♒22	14°♌22
♄	04°♌36	+01'43"	+19°50'	−15 days	+228 days	04°♌22'31"	25°♌04'15"	Slow	25°♉23	25°♏23

MOON ASPECTS		
☽ ☌ ♒	5°54' S
☽ ☍ ♄	3°55' S
☽ ✶ ☊	1°44' S
☽ △ ☋	1°44' S
☽ ✶ ☿	0°52' A

ESSENTIAL DIGNITIES

Pt	Ruler	Exalt	Trip	Term	Face	Detri	Fall	Score
☽	♄	--	♄	☿	♀	☉	--	−5 p
☉	♀	☽	♀	☿	☿	♂	--	−5 p
☿	♂	☉	☉	♀ m	♂	♀	♄	−5 p
♀	♃	♀ +	♀ +	☿ m	♃	☿	☿	+7
♂	☽	♃	♀	♂ +	♀	♄	♂ −	−2
♃	♂	--	♀	☿	☉	♀	☽	−5 p
♄	☉	--	☉	♃	♄ +	♄ −	--	−4

ASPECTS	
♇ △ As	0°08' S
♂ □ ☋	0°15' S
♂ □ ☊	0°15' S
♄ △ ☊	0°32' S
♄ ✶ ☋	0°32' S
☽ ✶ ☿	0°52' A
♀ ✶ Mc	0°59' S
♀ △ ♃	1°02' S
☽ △ ☋	1°44' S
☽ ✶ ☊	1°44' S

PLANETARY SECT

Planet	Cht	Plc	Sgn	Condition
☉ D	D	D	N	
☽ N	D	N	D	
☿ D	D	D	D	In Hayz
♀ N	D	D	N	
♂ N	D	D	N	
♃ D	D	N	N	
♄ D	D	D	D	In Hayz

D=Diurnal, N=Nocturnal

PLANETS, SIGNS AND ASPECTS

PLANET	SYMBOL	SIGN	SYMBOL	ASPECT	SYMBOL
Sun	☉	Aries	♈	Conjunction	☌
Moon	☽	Taurus	♉	Opposition	☍
Mercury	☿	Gemini	♊	Trine	△
Venus	♀	Cancer	♋	Square	□
Mars	♂	Leo	♌	Sextile	△
Jupiter	♃	Virgo	♍		
Saturn	♄	Libra	♎		
Uranus	♅	Scorpio	♏		
Neptune	♆	Sagittarius	♐		
Pluto	♇	Capricorn	♑		
North Node	☊	Aquarius	♒		
South Node	☋	Pisces	♓		

SIGNS AND THEIR RULING PLANETS

♈	♉	♊	♋	♌	♍	♎	♏	♐	♑	♒	♓
♂	♀	☿	☽	☉	☿	♀	♂ ♇	♃	♄	♄ ♅	♃ ♆

ALMUTENS: DAY

	♈	♉	♊	♋	♌	♍	♎	♏	♐	♑	♒	♓
0	☉	♀	☿	☽	☉	☿	♄	♂	♃	♄	♄	♀
1	☉	♀	☿	☽	☉	☿	♄	♂	♃	♄	♄	♀
2	☉	♀	☿	☽	☉	☿	♄	♂	♃	♄	♄	♀
3	☉	♀	☿	☽	☉	☿	♄	♂	♃	♄	♄	♀
4	☉	♀	☿	☽	☉	☿	♄	♂	♃	♄	♄	♀
5	☉	♀	☿	☽	☉	☿	♄	♂	♃	♄	♄	♀
6	☉	♀	☿	☽	☉	☿	♄	♂	♃	♄	♄	♀
7	☉	♀	☿	☽	☉	☿	♄	♂	♃	♄	♄	♀
8	☉	♀	☿	☽	☉	☿	♄	♂	♃	♄	♄	♀
9	☉	♀	☿	☽	☉	☿	♄	♂	♃	♄	♄	♀
10	☉	♀	☿	☽	☉	☿	♄	♂	♃	♄ ♂	♄	♀
11	☉	♀	☿	☽	☉	☿	♄	♂	♃	♄ ♂	♄	♀
12	☉	♀	☿	☽	☉	☿	♄	♂	♃	♄ ♂	♄	♃
13	☉	♀	☿	☽	☉	☿	♄	♂	♃	♄ ♂	♄	♃
14	☉	♀	☿	☽	☉	☿	♄	♂	♃	♄ ♂ ♀	♄	♃
15	☉	♀	☿	☽	☉	☿	♄	♂	♃	♄ ♂ ♀	♄	♃
16	☉	♀	☿	☽	☉	☿	♄	♂	♃	♄ ♂ ♀	♄	♀
17	☉	♀	☿	☽	☉	☿	♄	♂	♃	♄ ♂ ♀	♄	♀
18	☉	♀	☿	☽	☉	☿	♄	♂	♃	♄ ♂ ♀	♄	♀
19	☉	♀	☿	♃	☉	☿	♄	♂	♃	♄ ♂ ♀	♄	♀
20	☉ ♂	♀	☿	☽ ♃	☉	☿	♄	♂	♃	♄ ♀	♄	♀
21	☉ ♂	♀	☿	☽ ♃	☉	☿	♄ ♀	♂	♃	♄ ♀	♄	♀
22	☉ ♂	♀	☿	☽ ♃	☉	☿	♄ ♀	♂	♃	♄	♄	♀
23	☉ ♂	♀	☿	☽ ♃	☉	☿	♄ ♀	♂	♃	♄	♄	♀
24	☉ ♂	♀	☿ ♄	☽ ♃	☉	☿	♄ ♀	♂	♃	♄	♄	♀
25	☉	♀	☿ ♄	☽ ♃	☉	☿	♄ ♀	♂	♃	♄	♄	♀
26	☉	♀	☿ ♄	☽	☉	☿	♄ ♀	♂	♃	♂	♄	♀
27	☉	♀	☿ ♄	☽	☉	☿	♄ ♀	♂	♃	♂	♄	♀
28	☉	♀	☿ ♄	☽	☉	☿	♄	♂	♃	♂	♄	♀
29	☉	♀	☿ ♄	☽	☉	☿	♄	♂	♃	♂	♄	♀

ALMUTENS: NIGHT

	♈	♉	♊	♋	♌	♍	☊	♏	♐	♑	♒	♓
0	♂	♀ ☽	☿	☽	☉ ♃	☿	♄	♂	♃	♄	♄ ☿	♀
1	♂	♀ ☽	☿	☽	☉ ♃	☿	♄	♂	♃	♄	♄ ☿	♀
2	♂	♀ ☽	☿	☽	☉ ♃	☿	♄	♂	♃	♄	♄ ☿	♀
3	♂	♀ ☽	☿	☽	☉ ♃	☿	♄	♂	♃	♄	♄ ☿	♀
4	♂	♀ ☽	☿	☽	☉ ♃	☿	♄	♂	♃	♄	♄ ☿	♀
5	♂	♀ ☽	☿	☽	☉ ♃	☿	♄	♂	♃	♄	♄ ☿	♀
6	♂	♀ ☽	☿	☽	☉	☿	♀ ☿	♂	♃	♄	♄ ☿	♀
7	♂	♀ ☽	☿	☽	☉	☿	♀ ☿	♂	♃	♄	♄	♀
8	♂	☽	☿	☽	☉	☿	♀ ☿	♂	♃	♄	♄	♀
9	♂	☽	☿	☽	☉	☿	♀ ☿	♂	♃	♄	♄	♀
10	♂ ☉	☽	☿	☽	☉	☿	♀ ♄ ☿	♂	♃	♄ ♂	♄	♀ ♃
11	♂ ☉	☽	☿	☽	☉	☿	♀ ♄ ☿	♂	♃	♄ ♂	♄	♀ ♃
12	♂ ☉	☽	☿	☽	☉	☿	♀ ♄ ☿	♂	♃	♄ ♂	♄	♃
13	♂ ☉	☽	☿	☽	☉	☿	♀ ♄ ☿	♂	♃	♄ ♂	♄	♃
14	♂ ☉	☽	☿	☽	☉	☿	♀ ♄	♂	♃	♄ ♂	♄	♃
15	♂ ☉	☽	☿	☽	☉	☿	♀ ♄	♂	♃	♄ ♂	♄	♃
16	♂ ☉	☽	☿	☽	☉	☿	♀ ♄	♂	♃	♄ ♂	♄	♃
17	♂ ☉	☽	☿	☽	☉	☿	♀ ♄	♂	♃	♄ ♂	♄	♃
18	♂ ☉	☽	☿	☽	☉	☿	♀ ♄	♂	♃	♄ ♂	♄	♃
19	♂ ☉	☽	☿	♃	☉	☿	♀ ♄	♂	♃	♄ ♂	♄	♃
20	♂	☽	☿	☽ ♃	☉	☿	♀	♂	♃	♄	♄	♂
21	♂	☽	☿	☽ ♃	☉	☿	♀	♂	♃	♄	♄	♂
22	♂	☽	☿	☽ ♃	☉	☿	♀	♂	♃	♄	♄	♂
23	♂	☽	☿	☽ ♃	☉	☿	♀	♂	♃	♄	♄	♂
24	♂	☽	☿	☽ ♃	☉	☿	♀	♂	♃	♄	♄	♂
25	♂	☽	☿	☽ ♃	☉	☿	♀	♂	♃	♄	♄	♂
26	♂	☽	☿	☽	☉	☿	♀	♂	♃	♂	♄	♂
27	♂	☽	☿	☽	☉	☿	♀	♂	♃	♂	♄	♂
28	♂	☽	☿	☽	☉	☿	♀	♂	♃	♂	♄	♃
29	♂	☽	☿	☽	☉	☿	♀	♂	♃	♂	♄	♃

MONOMOIRIA

SIGN/S						♑♒	♐♓	♈♏	♌	♉♎	♊♍	♋
DEGREES	0	7	14	21	28	♄	♃	♂	☉	♀	☿	☽
	1	8	15	22	29	♃	♂	☉	♀	☿	☽	♄
	2	9	16	23		♂	☉	♀	☿	☽	♄	♃
	3	10	17	24		☉	♀	☿	☽	♄	♃	♂
	4	11	18	25		♀	☿	☽	♄	♃	♂	☉
	5	12	19	26		☿	☽	♄	♃	♂	☉	♀
	6	13	20	27		☽	♄	♃	♂	☉	♀	☿

TABLE OF ESSENTIAL DIGNITIES OF PLANETS

SIGN	DOMIC. (5)	EXALT. (4)	TRIPLICITY (3)		TERM (2)					FACE (1)			DETR. (-5)	FALL (-4)
			DAY	NIGHT						1	2	3		
♈ Aries	♂	☉	☉	♃	0♃5	6♀11	12☿19	20♂24	25♄29	♂	☉	♀	♀	♄
♉ Taurus	♀	☽	♀	☽	0♀7	8☿13	14♃21	22♄26	27♂29	☿	☽	♄	♂	
♊ Gemini	☿	(☊)	♄	☿	0☿5	6♃11	12♀16	17♂23	24♄29	♃	♂	☉	♃	(☋)
♋ Cancer	☽	♃	♀	♂	0♂6	7♀12	13☿18	19♃25	26♄29	♀	☿	☽	♄	♂
♌ Leo	☉		☉	♃	0♃5	6♀11	12♄17	18☿23	24♂29	♄	♃	♂	♄	
♍ Virgo	☿	☿	♀	☽	0☿6	7♀16	17♃20	21♂27	28♄29	☉	♀	☿	♃	♀
♎ Libra	♀	♄	♄	☿	0♄5	6☿13	14♃20	21♀27	28♂29	☽	♄	♃	♂	☉
♏ Scorpio	♂		♀	♂	0♂6	7♀10	11☿18	19♃23	24♄29	♂	☉	♀	♀	☽
♐ Sagittar.	♃	(☋)	☉	♃	0♃11	12♀16	17☿20	21♄26	27♂29	☿	☽	♄	☿	(☊)
♑ Capric.	♄	♂	♀	☽	0☿6	7♃13	14♀21	22♄25	26♂29	♃	♂	☉	☽	♃
♒ Aquairus	♄		♄	☿	0☿6	7♀12	13♃19	20♂24	25♄29	♀	☿	☽	☉	
♓ Pisces	♃	♀	♀	♂	0♀11	12♃15	16☿18	19♂27	28♄29	♄	♃	♂	☿	☿

Numbers in brackets (below the names of the dignities) stand for the numbers of plus or minus points that the planets receive when they are in their dignities (plus points) or opposite them (minus points).

The degrees are numbered 0-29 (0° to 0°59' is 0, 1° to 1°59' is 1, 5° to 5°59' is 5, and so on).
Triplicities are Hellenistic (according to Dorotheus of Sidon), **terms** are Egyptian.
By **term**, planets rule degrees between the first and second number, listed on the left and right of the planetary symbol. (Ex: The first six degrees of Aries - 0, 1, 2, 3, 4, 5 – are ruled by Jupiter, the next six - 6, 7, 8, 9, 10, 11 – by Venus, the next eight - 12, 13, 14, 15, 16, 17, 18, 19 – by Mercury, and so on).
By **face**, planets always rule degrees between 0-9, 10-19 and 20-29.

Index

This is a short index listing mainly references to technical terms. Most frequently used words like planet, sign, Moon, aspect, house, significator, dispositor etc. have been left out due to shortage of space.

A

Accidental dignity 41, 101, 105, 107, 109, 110, 196, 229, 244, 414
Al-Biruni 115, 148
Almuten 56, 74, 76, 89, 98, 99, 138, 156, 160, 162, 164, 166, 168, 170, 178, 180, 186, 188, 192, 194, 196, 200, 202, 224, 229, 232, 250, 254, 282, 284, 290, 296, 300, 304, 324, 345, 358, 360, 364, 368, 380, 388, 392, 394, 398, 408, 410, 414, 446, 448
Antiscion 149, 150
Arabic parts 5, 147

B

Barclay 2, 9, 10, 25, 95, 112, 113, 114, 115, 133, 138, 232, 300, 462
Besiegement, Besieged 122, 131, 314

C

Collection of light 122, 124, 128, 157, 160, 183, 202, 228, 272, 314
Combust 75, 80, 81, 100, 104, 105, 107, 108, 109, 110, 112, 115, 124, 168, 184, 200, 206, 216, 220, 230, 240, 259, 260, 273, 306, 324, 336, 340, 349, 352, 360, 376, 380, 382, 394, 400, 406, 432, 436, 444, 446, 448
Completion 53, 58, 67, 105, 115, 124, 127, 128, 130, 131, 132, 156, 157, 174, 183, 188, 198, 204, 206, 208, 212, 214, 216, 222, 232, 236, 242, 246, 250, 254, 260, 266, 316, 338, 388, 390, 394, 396, 398, 402, 406, 426, 448

D

Declination 32, 33, 40, 122, 135, 136, 151, 155, 312, 315, 356, 396, 448

E

Eclipse 138, 139, 308, 310, 315, 318, 328, 330, 396, 448
Emplacement 67, 183, 198, 206, 208, 254, 314, 360, 394, 406
Essential dignity 4, 35, 38, 41, 42, 43, 44, 45, 46, 47, 48, 86, 89, 108

F

Frustration 4, 124, 129

I

Intercepted 66, 67, 76, 176, 190, 200, 210, 212, 214, 216, 222, 226, 231, 240, 244, 258, 266, 290, 300, 336, 354, 356, 394, 398, 414, 448

L

Lilly 4, 10, 14, 20, 25, 27, 41, 42, 56, 64, 73, 91, 93, 94, 95, 99, 101, 105, 106, 107, 109, 111, 113, 133, 137, 155, 183, 184, 185, 203, 259, 268, 270, 300, 306, 310, 344, 345, 346, 347, 348, 349, 372, 376, 384, 385, 416, 426
Local space 315, 316, 322, 342, 343

M

Monomoiria 89, 95, 96, 158, 160, 188, 352, 354, 356, 358, 364, 368, 376, 396, 406, 436, 442, 452
Mutual reception 89, 96, 97, 98, 99, 109, 122, 124, 127, 154, 156, 157, 168, 174, 183, 188, 192, 202, 203, 206, 210, 216, 222, 226, 228, 234, 236, 238, 240, 242, 244, 246, 254, 256, 266, 272, 308, 310, 332, 340, 354, 356, 364, 373, 376, 386, 388, 390, 398, 410, 414, 416, 422, 424, 428, 436

N

Nodes 5, 86, 92, 114, 136, 137, 138, 315, 352

O

Outcome 14, 18, 21, 53, 57, 59, 70, 77, 78, 87, 95, 96, 99, 114, 122, 124, 125, 126, 127, 128, 131, 137, 151, 156, 157, 158, 174, 183, 202, 208, 222, 236, 243, 262, 300, 314, 315, 316, 320, 324, 326, 338, 394, 400, 434

P

Peregrine 89, 98, 100, 108, 110, 112, 155, 160, 162, 184, 186, 188, 190, 206, 208, 210, 216, 218, 220, 222, 229, 230, 274, 275, 276, 282, 306, 308, 324, 338, 340, 349, 356, 358, 364, 370, 376, 378, 382, 392, 396, 404, 414, 416, 424, 432, 444, 446
Placidus, Placidean 290, 358
Planetary hour 116, 117, 118, 119, 158, 162, 168, 176, 192, 208, 220, 234, 260, 275, 284, 286, 288, 300, 308, 392, 406, 408, 410

R

Refranation 4, 124, 130
Regiomontanus 27, 49, 133, 290, 340, 358

S

Sect 4, 51, 73, 77, 80, 91, 93, 94, 95, 100, 107, 109, 110, 155, 180, 192, 380, 416, 446

T

Timing 4, 14, 17, 31, 39, 53, 70, 78, 79, 104, 125, 132, 133, 134, 135, 185, 200, 238, 244, 248, 250, 252, 260, 275, 302, 304, 308, 312, 320, 334, 338, 352, 368, 398, 412, 428, 430, 438, 440, 448, 450
Translation of light 122, 124, 127, 128, 129, 156, 157, 194, 198, 202, 206, 216, 228, 232, 236, 242, 244, 246, 254, 256, 266, 290, 406, 410, 422, 430

74263858R00252

Made in the USA
Columbia, SC
11 September 2019